Mastering **Management**

FINANCIAL TIMES

Mastering
Management

Mastering Management

The product of a merger in 1990 of IMI-Geneva and IMEDE, IMD International in Lausanne, Switzerland is best known for its executive education programs. Its small (80-student) MBA program is also highly regarded.

IMD bases its teaching material on the experience of its 43-member international faculty and the relationship it maintains with the 125 Partner and Business Associate companies, many of whom are involved in major research projects with the school. In addition, IMD produces the annual World Competitiveness Yearbook.

Founded in 1965, London Business School has firmly established itself as a leading international business school.

London Business School offers a 21-month MBA program as well as a one-year Masters in Finance course. Additionally, London Business School offers a range of general management and specialist senior executive courses.

Wharton
The Wharton School
University of Pennsylvania

The Wharton School of the University of Pennsylvania, founded in 1881, as the first collegiate school of management in the United States, is recognized around the world for its innovative leadership and broad academic strengths across every major discipline and at every level of business education. With 182 faculty, 11 academic departments, 19 research centers and leading programs at undergraduate, MBA, doctoral and executive education levels, the Wharton School is committed to creating the highest value and impact on the practice of business and management worldwide.

Currently, Wharton has 4,695 students from more than 50 countries enrolled in its degree programs, nearly 10,000 participants in its executive education programs each year and a network of 70,000 alumni in more than 100 countries.

Mastering **Management**

PETER LORANGE
Dean,
IMD International

Mastering Management brings together three of the world's leading business schools, including the highly international executive development program portfolio of IMD. These three distinctive teaching perspectives complement each other, and add an extra dimension to a truly balanced and exciting book for executives.

Creative life-long learning is key for today's executives, and organizations which recognize this are increasingly willing to invest in their people. This state-of-the-art book aids this investment process by offering busy executives a chance to study cutting-edge issues, presented by top-calibre professors from an international blend of faculty members. It gives leading executives an ideal operational vehicle with which to invest in themselves.

The benefits are manifold, but perhaps the most compelling advantage is the ease with which each reader may develop their own learning menu based on their particular interests and needs. Given the busy schedules of today's leading executives, *Mastering Management* offers a time-efficient way to stay on top of recent management development trends.

PROFESSOR
GEORGE BAIN
Principal,
London Business
School

Management has long been a profession, requiring experience to be underpinned by systematic knowledge. Business schools have developed because of this, but today's particular need is for knowledge to be widely diffused. Managers with different specialist skills have to understand one another and require a wide range of knowledge if the implementation of their skills is to be effective within the broader context in which they have to be applied. Both aspects have become essential in a world which, as we all know, is changing rapidly in practically all aspects of business.

Mastering Management helps to meet these varied needs and enables managers in all fields to acquaint themselves with the issues which are arising; it will therefore stimulate as well as inform. We at London Business School, nearly fifty of whose faculty have contributed to the series, are proud to join our partners in this enterprise.

THOMAS P.
GERRITY
Dean,
The Wharton
School of the
University of
Pennsylvania

The challenges for today's managers have never been greater. Today's corporations are undergoing a period of unprecedented transformation in response to rapid changes in the competitive global environment. Vertical structures of the past are tilting into more horizontal organizations. Hierarchies are being interlaced with teams. Business process re-engineering has moved across functions to remold the organization.

Mastering Management draws together the insights of leading faculty in diverse disciplines from among the world's leading business schools to provide insights and perspectives into how managers can effectively meet these challenges.

As the world's first school of management, the Wharton School is dedicated to providing the highest value and impact in the understanding of business and the practice of management worldwide. We are pleased to join our colleagues from IMD and the London Business School to offer the intellectual leadership that will advance business practice and education into the 21st century.

Executive Editor	Tim Dickson
Editor	George Bickerstaffe
School Co-ordinators	Jean-Pierre Salzmann, IMD International
	Emeritus Professor Harold Rose, London Business School
	Professor Janice Bellace, The Wharton School of the University of Pennsylvania

PITMAN PUBLISHING
128 Long Acre, London WC2E 9AN
Tel: +44 (0)171 447 2000
Fax: +44 (0)171 240 5771

A Division of Pearson Professional Limited

First published in Great Britain in 1997

ISBN 0 273 63076 8

British Library Cataloguing in Publication Data
A CIP catalogue record for this book can be obtained from the British Library

10 9 8 7 6 5 4 3 2 1

Typeset by Land and Unwin (Data Sciences) Limited, Bugbrooke
Charts and figures designed by Michela Magas and Cleve Jones
Printed and bound in Great Britain by William Clowes Ltd

The Publishers' policy is to use paper manufactured from sustainable forests.

Contents

Preface		viii
Mastering *Mastering Management*		x
Module 1	**Introduction to General Management**	1
Module 2	**Accounting**	15
Module 3	**Finance**	57
Module 4	**Applied Statistics and Decision Support**	123
Module 5	**Marketing**	161
Module 6	**Organizational Behavior**	213
Module 7	**Human Resource Management**	247
Module 8	**Managing People in Organizations**	275
Module 9	**Production and Operations Management**	293
Module 10	**Information Management**	343
Module 11	**Business Ethics**	365
Module 12	**International Financial Markets**	383
Module 13	**Managing Across Cultures**	405
Module 14	**Applied Microeconomics and Industry Analysis**	447
Module 15	**International Macroeconomy and Competitiveness**	479
Module 16	**Leadership Skills**	503
Module 17	**Managing Change**	535
Module 18	**Strategic Management and Implementation**	557
Module 19	**Socio-political Context and the Business Environment**	613
Module 20	**The Future of General Management**	627
Subject index		657
Name index		670
Organization index		674

Preface

When our sister paper, *Financial Times* of London, approached three international business schools to co-operate in the production of a 20-part series on management, none of those involved had any inkling of how successful this collaboration would be.

Given that the series ultimately included at least one memorable half page footnote explaining the mathematical underpinnings of stratified sampling in an early discussion of applied statistics, it might well have been judged worthy but dull. Certainly mixing journalists, with a bias to readability, and academics, favoring depth and detail, was unpredictable at best.

By every yardstick, however, *FT Mastering Management* has proved to be an outstanding success. The series has been translated in Spanish, German, French, Danish, Portuguese and Korean and published in more than a dozen countries.

Canadian readers responded enthusiastically, collecting the series, ordering back issues and spending an average of 75 minutes with each edition.

Perhaps the series' reception should not have been such a surprise. In a post-industrial economy of knowledge workers and global competitiveness, management excellence has been increasingly recognized as vital to success; as much by individuals, who have taken on the responsibility of developing their own careers, as by companies, struggling to thrive in a fast and changing world.

Not all the answers lie in business schools – not

by any means – but anyone who has obtained a master's degree in business administration or attended a short executive course will appreciate the sheer weight of ideas and collective wisdom in many of these institutions. No longer seen as leafy idylls for the education of the young and the pursuit of esoteric research, business schools have become integral players in developing global competitiveness and management excellence.

Unfortunately only the privileged few have the time or the money to take advantage of what schools have to offer, which is why the edition of *FT Mastering Management* represents a significant publishing milestone. Here in a fully updated and re-edited version of the newspaper series; readers can access the knowledge and ideas of top professors at three of the leading business schools of the world. We hope it is also the ideal companion to, or refresher after an MBA.

FT Mastering Management is a remarkable tour of modern management thinking and our thanks must go to our partners at *Financial Times* of London who conceived and nurtured the project and to the academics of IMD, London Business School and Wharton who created it.

The most important acknowledgement for this book must obviously go to the more than 90 academic contributors who gave generously of their time and cheerfully met strict and sometimes painful deadlines.

Thanks are also due to a number of backroom individuals without whom *Mastering Management* would have been impossible. These include most notably the school co-ordinators who marshalled enthusiastic but occasionally wayward academics to deliver highly readable articles. These were Harold Rose of LBS, Janice Bellace, Chris Hardwick and Michael Baltes at the Wharton School of the University of Pennsylvania, and Jean-Pierre Salzmann and Lucie Arm at IMD. Special thanks also go to Financial Post AME Clive Frampton and his team who worked painstakingly with *FT Mastering Management* to ensure its relevance to Canadian readers.

Douglas W. Knight
Publisher & Chief Executive Officer,
The Financial Post

Mastering Mastering Management

Mastering Management originally appeared as a weekly supplement to the UK edition of the *Financial Times*. This book contains the complete updated text of the whole 20-week series. However, the arrangement is somewhat different to the newspaper series and some guidelines as to how to get the best from the contents may be useful.

Mastering Management is loosely modeled on the 'core' curriculum of a typical MBA degree. That is, it covers the main functional disciplines of management. The theory behind the structure of an MBA is that, as an academic qualification for general management, students need to be conversant with, though not expert in, all aspects of management. In many MBA programs, this 'core' is often followed by a series of 'elective', or optional, courses, which do allow some specialization.

Mastering Management groups the core management disciplines into 18 main modules plus a general introductory module that deals with the history and philosophy of general management and a concluding module that examines the future of management.

It should be noted, though, that although structured in this way *Mastering Management* was never designed as, nor intended to be, a replacement for an MBA. Rather it is an introduction to and 'sampler' of the latest thinking on modern management.

The newspaper series also attempted to mimic the integrated nature of a typical MBA program. Most MBA programs progress from the basics of business, such as accounting and finance, to the more rarefied aspects of management, such as strategy in a logical sequence. But they also attempt to display the way various functions fit together and depend on each other by teaching several subjects at the same time, rather than progressing though the accounting course, then on to finance and so on. For this reason the newspaper series ran sections from four or five modules each week.

In this book the modules are grouped *together*, making it possible to read the book from beginning to end since the modules progress in the accepted logical sequence, starting with accounting and finance and ending with strategy formulation and implementation and the socio-political context of business.

To achieve an integrated approach, it is possible to read articles from several modules to gain an idea of the integrated nature of modern management. However, ideally groups of early modules should be completed before moving on to later ones since the concepts introduced are often used or developed later.

It is also, of course, possible to read the modules in any order according to interest.

The plan of the whole 20 modules is set out in the *Contents* on page vii and there are three indices to help readers navigate. Each module also has its own list of contents and a short introduction to set it in context as well as photographs and biographies of the contributing academics.

In whichever way the book is used, once the reader has completed the whole text he or she should have a full and rounded grasp of all the major concepts of modern management, considerable knowledge of the issues involved and some useful techniques for applying them.

The important thing is to start now! *Mastering Management* has already attracted thousands of readers who have found it stimulating and readily applicable to their working lives.

And don't forget to try your hand at the quiz at the end of the book, which will let you know how far you have succeeded in mastering *Mastering Management*.

George Bickerstaffe

Editor, *FT Mastering Management*

Introduction to General Management

Contents

Modern imperatives 4
Ross A. Webber, The Wharton School of the
University of Pennsylvania
*The functions and knowledge that form the basis of
general management.*

Contributors

 **Ross A. Webber** is Professor of
Management at the The Wharton School
of the University of Pennsylvania, and
formerly Vice-President for Development
and University Relations at the University
of Pennsylvania, Chairperson of the
Management Department, and Academic
Director of the Wharton Executive
Development Program: 'The transition
from functional to general management'.

Introduction

Mastering Management is about general management but that subject itself is not covered as such since general management is the synthesis of many management functions, such as accounting and marketing, which are covered in their own right in other modules of *Mastering Management*.

However, it is appropriate to begin with an in-depth look at what general management actually is. This introductory module looks at how general management has developed over time, what a general manager actually does and the changes that are affecting his or her role, what makes a successful general manager and techniques of management development and examines some of the stresses on general managers.

Modern imperatives

■ **This introduction to general management serves as a launch pad for the whole *Mastering Management* series, which will explore the functions and knowledge that form the basis of general management. The section deals with the historical development of general management, the changes that are affecting the role of the general manager, the attributes of a successful general manager and the ways they can be developed. It finally looks at some of the pressures general managers face.**

by **Ross A. Webber**

As with everything else today, the notion of general management is in a state of transition.

The concept of the generalist executive who could utilize his or her general management principles effectively in any country, company or industry is dying. Conglomerate diversification is out; disciplined focus on core competencies within an industry is in.

Also going is the assumption that a lifetime of geographic and functional moves will prepare a manager for general executive responsibilities. New educational and organizational design models that facilitate functional synthesis are being sought. Emerging are models of the 'generalizing specialist' and the 'specializing generalist'. To understand these concepts, however, we need to examine an older view of how generalists were developed.

The former path upwards

The Horatio Alger myth, that a determined young person could enter via the mail room and by dint of hard work and pluck move upward to the executive suite, died in the virtually universal requirement that one have at least a college education to get one's foot on the lower rung of the professional and managerial ladder.

In all industrialized companies the hierarchical pyramid was replaced by a two-class structure comprised of a larger, truncated lower pyramid of operating employees topped by a smaller pyramid of specialist managers and executives. From 1900 to the late 1980s in the industrialising countries, this administrative pyramid grew from roughly 5 to 25 per cent of total employees. Increasingly, one had to have the appropriate higher education to get access to the lower rungs of the upper pyramid which was entered directly, usually right out of college.

Those operating white-collar, blue-collar and white-coverall personnel in the lower pyramid have been increasingly restricted. The boundary between the two pyramids has become less permeable. Today, a three-class system may be emerging with post-college education (MBAs, LLDs and PhDs) becoming essential for a chance of making it to general management levels. For example, the budding stars nominated by their firms to attend the Wharton Advanced Management Program possess the following degrees or equivalents: bachelors degrees (both US and non-US), 100 per cent; masters degrees, US 22 per cent, non-US 44 per cent; doctorates, US 29 per cent, non-US 22 per cent.

The upper managerial pyramid could be visualized as divided into three bands, each defined by the skills most relevant to effective performance. Thus, the lower portion into which a new graduate entered was primarily defined by technical or knowledge-based skills.

If a young person did well, then in five years or so he or she might begin the transition upward into the middle skill band, which would draw on interpersonal aptitudes or people skills. Here one would have to supplement technical ability with skill in communicating, directing and leading others. For many engineers and technocrats, of course, this could be a difficult transition, but if successfully navigated, it would set the stage for a second, more difficult, transition some 10 to 15 years later.

The skills at the upper levels were described a bit more ambiguously, but generally were seen as conceptual or integrating skills that is, the ability to see the big picture, particularly in integrating the company's various functions.

Assumed in this model was that the 15 to 20-year climb upward would be characterized by diagonal moves that would expose the future general manager to the organization's relevant activities so that in time there would emerge a happy congruence of level, skill and authority. Unfortunately, this assumption has collapsed.

Size and complexity have sharply undermined the time = level = knowledge assumption. The pace of technical innovation and environmental change means that beyond the smaller firm no individual's career can embrace all the relevant dimensions. Indeed, complexity has forced increased focus in a career so that a manager's upward movement became increasingly restricted within a specialized silo. As a result, the transition into the synthesizing duties of senior general management became increasingly difficult with a consequent loss of visionary leadership at the top.

The managerial pyramid

The concept of technical, human relations and conceptual skills is still relevant. But, increasingly, organizations are demanding that young specialists and managers possess all three skills sooner in their careers.

This desire was clearly expressed by both managers and corporations when the Wharton School began revising its curricula five years ago. In executive education, it canvassed mid-career managers to see what they desired in a mid-career executive program.

Overwhelmingly they wanted a program that would assist them in making the transition from functional to general management. Up to around 35 years of age, everything in their education and careers had rewarded them for specializing in narrowing areas. But they recognized that they were bumping against the tops of their various functional silos or, if they had already been promoted to cross-functional responsibilities, that they were lacking in the integrating skills.

Accordingly, Wharton has developed an intense program that emphasizes participant heterogeneity and functional interdependence, coupled with encouraging thinking about the ambiguous and even paradoxical duties that confront senior executives.

Wharton's MBA program revision included some similar ideas. In response to its questioning, the corporate world told Wharton that it needed to strengthen its students' skills in teamwork, interpersonal relations, negotiations and communications while also encouraging greater 'depth' in their 'breadth'.

Given today's common matrix-like structures that demand cross-functional, multi-product/service, inter-regional teams, young professionals no longer have time to work alone while developing their interpersonal skills. These skills are increasingly required from the beginning. Accordingly, the most dramatic innovations in Wharton's program are the required team-oriented experiential courses in foundations of leadership and a cross-functional immersion in a real company.

In addition, given the sophistication of the specialities brought to bear on problems today, organizations want their young managers to be stronger in multiple areas. Wharton was told to maintain its tradition of an MBA major and to explore requiring all students to have multiple majors. (Although this latter suggestion was not formally implemented, students themselves have made it a *de facto* reality, since 85 per cent of strategic management majors also have a second major, often finance.)

Trends in power axis functions

The years since the Second World War have seen significant changes in the power of the various functional specialities to control senior general management. National culture and tradition have affected these trends differently, but competition is forcing convergence.

The US, for example, came out of the war with an emphasis on manufacturing. Strong production managers tended to be those selected for the post of chief executive officer. Hence, the production function was closest to an imaginary power axis up through the center of the managerial pyramid. Other functions were distant from the axis, with some, such as personnel, on the pyramid's surface. Even today, of chief executives of the 1,000 most valuable US companies, only one has a functional background primarily in human resource management.

The prominence of engineering and manufacturing made sense in the immediate post-war era because it reflected the central challenge then confronting North American companies: the conversion from wartime to peacetime products, which had mostly been designed years before in the 1930s. Given pent-up civilian demands, selling was easy.

In a short time, however, immediate demand was met, competition for discretionary dollars intensified and an increased need to differentiate products and services emerged. With this need the modern marketing function began to move toward the power axis so that by the early 1960s it became the number-one supplier of US chief executives.

As recently as the 1960s, financial specialists were generally not seen as candidates for senior general management. The 'bean counter', 'green eye-shade' stereotype was still strong and they were judged as lacking the synthesizing big-picture skills necessary for the top. It was not until the rampant inflation of the 1970s and the dramatic increase in competition for equity and debt, along with the escalating sophistication of financial instruments, that the finance function moved to the power axis.

Today, among the chief executives of the 1,000 most valuable US companies, 264 are from finance backgrounds, 217 from marketing, 193 from engineering/technical, 144 were company founders, 110 from production/manufacturing, 73 from law, and seven from corporate planning.

However understandable the recent dominance of the marketing and financial functions in the US, it did create problems. Interest in manufacturing and production declined. Academic programs stagnated or disappeared, and the brightest American students focussed elsewhere. In Europe and Japan, of course,

operations management never went out of style, which gave them an advantage in the 1970s and 1980s.

In recent years, US companies have rediscovered the centrality of these functional skills, and the latest generation of chief executives in many companies are drawn from the production function (and, as at General Motors and Ford, often developed while heading European operations). During Wharton's curriculum reform, students demanded that the core component on operations management be expanded.

Of course, too narrow a production orientation also has its drawbacks. In my past consulting with some European industrial companies, I was frequently struck by the gap between their managers' impressive engineering expertise and their naivety about marketing to customer desires. And not a few Japanese observers have commented on American and European inadequacies in human resource management. In a typical Japanese company, the senior human resource executive may be second in influence only to the chief executive officer.

The point is not what function should be dominant nor what country has the greatest relevant functional strength. What is called for are people and processes that effectively synthesize the specialist functions into general management.

Specializing generalists
The post-1987 stock market crash environment, particularly in the US, led to an era of unprecedented downsizing. The strengthening of shareholder demands for emphasis on total return from dividends and share price appreciation led to the emergence of a general manager who was a turnaround specialist.

Experience in the industry was deemed less important than the will to impose a cost-cutting vision that would rapidly improve corporate profits and make the company more attractive to a prospective acquirer.

Scott Paper offers a dramatic illustration of this skill and its transferability. After earning some $100m (£64.5m) for resuscitating Scott and selling it to Kimberly-Clark, Albert Dunlop advertised himself as available to do it again for another group of owners 'anywhere'. The directors of the SunBeam company have now asked him to repeat his tough magic there.

Whatever the merits of such turnaround specializing generalist executives, they do not offer a model for general executives because the challenge they face is relatively simple at least in comparison with the long-run building of a viable business strategy.

Such a specializing generalist focuses on the functional areas having the quickest payback (on closing plants, dismissing staff and reducing costs in the case of Scott) to the detriment of relations with surviving employees, customers and communities.

Another version of the specializing generalist is the 'habitual' entrepreneur who creates multiple new business ventures. Such creators are the ultimate generalists, since in the early days of a new firm the entrepreneur must play many roles because staff tends to be very thin. Entrepreneurship, therefore, is the most 'on-the-job' training for general management that exists because it demands daily action in multiple functional areas.

Nonetheless, even the most courageous entrepreneur will probably be more successful if he or she has had significant work experience as an employee in the industry and market in which they expect to lead a new company (seven years or so appears to be the optimal time. Less means inadequate knowledge of the business, and more may mean excessive conservatism).

Entrepreneurs seldom provide models of general management in large corporations, however. They tend to be loners, primarily interested in personal achievement and un-comfortable with exercising power over a large organization. Their personal career anchors tend toward 'autonomy/independence' or 'functional/technical' rather than aspiring personally to lead a large company. They are uneasy with the 'interdependence' that management requires.

Often, once the company is successfully launched and has grown beyond a size that he or she can control personally, the entrepreneur becomes frustrated with the emergence of big-company-like bureaucracy and sells and/or departs the company.

Seymour Cray and Gene Amdahl both left large computer firms (Control Data and IBM) to found their own firms because of dissatisfaction with senior management's lack of adventur-ousness. But in time, with the success and perceived bureaucratization of their own creations, they left once again to found new firms they could more personally control.

Edward Moldt, who played an important role in the early teaching in the Wharton School's Snider Entrepreneurial Center, has started more than 25 successful companies.

Even when the entrepreneurial founding general executive stays and is effective, the chronic problem is often succession. Personal technical knowledge and leadership charisma, coupled with a disinclination to delegate significant authority, blocks the development of subordinate managers. The unhappy experience of Wang Laboratories after the death of its namesake founder is all too common.

The generalizing specialist

A happier (to this writer) general executive model is offered by Louis Gerstner, chief executive at IBM, who represents a specialist able to generalize his expertise so that it reinvigorates an overly narrow company.

The core consumer marketing function orientation he brought to IBM seems to be exercising a beneficial influence on the company's technical culture to help it better define its product and service strategy in a way that prospective customers can understand. By taking a marketing orientation approach and inte-grating it into a strong but complementary organizational culture, longer-run possibilities emerge.

Of course, even this approach is not without pain of staff reduction, as old products and hoped-for innovations are jettisoned when no viable market can be developed. Nonetheless, the survivors will be less traumatized, to the extent that the senior executives are able to conceptualize and articulate how a new core emphasis is energising all of the company's functional activities.

Percy Barnevik of ABB presents another example of the generalizing specialist who takes a critical skill and generalizes it for the total organization's benefit. At ABB this is an organizational design philosophy that emphasizes every manager's responsibility to network within the family of companies. Developing informal relationships and looking for synergistic opportunities is every manager's responsibility, not just the top's. Thus the intent is to disperse a synthesizing perspective throughout the organization.

General management attributes

When Wharton Executive Program participants were asked what attribute they most admired in their personal heroes, the most common response was the ability to communicate a 'vision'.

Unfortunately, what former President George Bush once described as 'the vision thing' has become something of a cliché in recent years, as the expectation grew that effective leaders had to be able to commune with higher authority on some mist-covered mountain, returning with the magical words that would give everyone a sense of direction and mission.

So we heard that firms were 'over-managed' and 'underled'; leading to an unfortunate distinction between management and leadership with the pernicious implication that good management is somehow inferior and less important than leadership.

The distinction can cause great mischief when embodied in the belief that a senior executive need only be a good leader rather than an effective manager. Influential leaders who did not know how to manage have done much damage in human affairs as they raised expectations without the ability to deliver on them. And no effective number-two executive officer/chief operating officer/executive vice-president type can totally compensate for the destructive effects of a charismatic leader who has no aptitude for the nitty-gritty of actual management.

Of course, the good manager/non-leader can be boringly bureaucratic. In the long run such narrow people can also reduce human liberties and spirit, as adherence to rules becomes an end instead of a means. The worldwide scepticism about government-run business reflects this unhappy experience.

The effective general executive does not need to be an improbable philosopher-king, but does need an ability to uncover vision and convert it into action. Gerstner at IBM probably exaggerated when he exclaimed that his company did not need a new vision, just more effective execution. But he was correct in implying that the chief executive alone does not have to be the creator of the unifying vision. The vision may be more collective in origin than one individual, but clearly it must be shared and converted into management practice.

Proactive communication skills are important and the ability and willingness to initiate communications to stakeholders is critical. Verbal articulation is increasingly important to general managers. Some studies suggest that public speaking is our most feared activity, which may explain why the most common training requested by newly appointed senior executives is speech-making. Because of the worldwide competition for capital and the increased activism of corporate owners as represented by financial analysts, pension holdings, mutual funds and potential raiders speaking to stockholders, individually or in groups, is one of the most rapidly expanding time demands on senior executives.

Fostering approachability

Even more important than initiating communications, however, is the ability to receive them: that is, willingness to create an environment of approachability. My own research on how managers spend their time suggests that the most effective general executives spend less time on communications they initiate and more time talking to others who start the conversations. (Those rated more effective spent 16 hours per week communicating in response to others, and only 9.5 hours on conversations they initiated; less effective executives spent 11.3 hours per week on self-initiated conversations and only 6.5 hours responding to others).

The more effective executives control less by self-initiated interrogation and more by availability and receptivity to subordinates and colleagues. The best create an atmosphere of tranquillity and focus that communicates to their visitors that their presence is enjoyable and is at the moment the most important activity that the executive could be doing. Colleagues of as diverse a set of leader-managers as Winston Churchill and Reginald Jones, former chief executive of General Electric, have commented admiringly on this skill.

Some dramaturgy is involved in creating this environment, of course: not talking across a crowded desk but rising to move to another chair when a visitor enters; silent buzzers that prompt a secretary 'accidentally' to interrupt a meeting to remind the executive of some real or imaginary pressing matter.

More fundamentally, however, effective general executives intrinsically enjoy conversation when people come to them and this enjoyment reinforces the willingness, especially of subordinates, to approach them. It is not that the subordinates habitually come to the executive with a request for permission to do something. Rather they come for advice: 'Boss, I'm thinking of doing this; my analysis suggests it will work, but I know you've been down this road before; am I missing anything?'

Most such conversations do not end with the general executive's directive, but they do offer a mutual learning experience (and of course the opportunity for a veto if the subordinate's intended action promises disaster).

The greatest advantage of general executive receptivity is the encouragement of an upward flow of communications that helps top managers to understand better the operating and environmental realities. It counters the kind of 'velvet cocoon' (a term coined by President Lyndon Johnson's press secretary to describe the isolation that surrounded Johnson in the later days of his administration) in which a senior executive can become enveloped when he implies that it is dangerous to communicate truthfully when such truth conveys other than success – a chronic problem for tyrants from Hitler and Stalin back down the ages. As an ancient Persian saying puts it: 'The messenger who conveys ambiguous news should have one foot in the stirrup.'

When Gert Tagge became chairman of Siemens of Germany some years ago, he commented that he needed to 'Americanise' the company by encouraging a more spontaneous flow of upward communications. While describing this as 'Americanisation' was perhaps ill-advised in a German company , the notion is valid. In working with companies in Thailand, for example, I have seen how reluctant managers are to approach senior executives physically. It is not that they are afraid of the boss, but that their sense of his power is just so great that they fear making some social gaffe.

Tolerance for error

Encouraging candid upward communication requires substantial tolerance for error and even foolishness, of course. Churchill reportedly never criticised a subordinate's proposal at first hearing. He recognized that a creative idea is most vulnerable shortly after birth. Rather, he expressed boyish enthusiasm about the most unrealistic ideas (some of which like the First World War's ill-fated Dardinelles invasion got implemented with less than desirable results).

But more importantly, his subordinates were not afraid to voice new ideas so the organization was rich with creativity. Such a leader-manager, of course, cannot accept all proposals, but necessary vetoes can be issued on a somewhat delayed and more private basis so that the future floating of ideas is not discouraged.

A variant of this encouragement of honest upward communication was expressed by Harold Geneen when he headed ITT. He warned his managers that the worst of ITT sins was not to communicate bad news in the misguided hope they could turn the situation around before Geneen found out about it.

Finally, senior general executives require great behavioral flexibility. Among all kinds of specialist and manager positions, general management allows the incumbent the greatest discretionary control of personal behavior and requires the greatest behavioral flexibility.

Unlike functional control managers, service managers and other specialized positions, general managers have the potential for personality to be reflected in how they spend their time. The time horizons and decision demands, for example, are much longer than those for an operating supervisor. But this means that general managers must have a wider repertoire of behaviors:

enduring periods of uncertainty about what subordinates are doing; withstanding the temptation to intervene prematurely after they have supposedly delegated authority; accepting results inferior to those they could have achieved by doing the task themselves; listening through a subordinate's proposal when they could simply tell him or her what to do in a fraction of the time (a patience associated with Dwight Eisenhower that earned him great dedication from his people).

And, of course, general executives must know when their leadership style should be participative and when authoritarian. Being authoritarian all the time is the easiest style. It will work in lower management levels, with entrepreneurial start-ups and in many corporate turnaround situations where the objectives are clearly defined and the problem relatively simple intellectually if not behaviorally.

But such a constant authoritarianism will be disastrous in a competitive and changing environment where the company's success depends on the ability to utilize all the divergent skills present among its key players. Even here, however, talk must eventually come to an end and action commence. In those circumstances when consensus cannot be reached, the senior general executive must issue the decisive word.

The Japanese have a most descriptive term for the person who can do this. He is the one who listens with an 'inner ear' to the implicit consensus of which the management team is not yet aware, and then articulates it at the propitious moment.

Developing generalized skills

Since specialized skills and education will remain critical to a viable organizational career, the challenge seems to be how to help the specialist gain himself or herself a generalised expertise as rapidly as possible. As we have seen, in general management the ability to conceptualize how parts and functions fit together is critical. This is an integrating, or synthesizing, skill (in contrast to the specialist's analysing, or breaking-apart, approach).

This synthesizing ability is related to creativity, most of which consists not of conjuring up totally new ideas but in putting common elements together in novel ways, often by borrowing from a separate context. For example, a professional architect/amateur fisherman who was designing a roof for a tropical building wondered how the flounder changes its colour depending on the sea bottom. The technology of small bubbles, which expand or contract among fish scales, was adopted to the building of the roof, white balloons expanding to reflect heat; contracting to absorb it.

Such creative synthesizing ability is not totally understood, but there are some instructive lessons for developing general executives. People who are more creative tend to expose themselves to a more heterogeneous mix of incoming stimuli for example, more varied reading, odder hobbies and a wider diversity of people with whom they talk.

This curiosity may be reinforced by a more liberal education since there is some evidence at a leading US university that liberal arts students during their undergraduate years tend to increase their synthesizing skill, while this skill stagnates for engineering students (but engineering students increase their analytical skills which, equally, appear to stagnate among liberal arts students).

It is not clear what the impact is of under-graduate business education, but the intention at most such institutions is to combine the analytical development of a technical education with the integration of liberal arts development. Thus, variety of experience provides the potential cues for borrowing synthesizing ideas.

One of the paradoxes of management development is that one must sometimes throw away specialized knowledge, so painfully gained, by periodically changing functional respon-sibilities. Short-term individual and corporate performance must be harmed in the interest of building stronger integrating forces.

Research on conflict resolution strongly supports the conclusion that homogeneous groups composed of people with no personal experience of an opposed group are much less likely to resolve their differences with that group than when at least some members in each group have had experience in the other. As a native American saying puts it: 'Walking a mile in the moccasins of your opponent enables you to understand his grievance'.

In addition, the rhetorical gap between senior executives and recruiting managers should be bridged. Many general executives offer vocal support for the hiring of humanities and liberal arts students for managerial careers. But the operating departments doing the actual hiring mainly look for more narrowly educated technocrats.

Finally, the dramatic pruning of corporate staff and middle managers in recent years has led to new concerns about the elimination of general management positions crucial to developing people for top executive jobs.

General Electric's Jack Welch has been cited as endeavouring to reduce the number of hier-archical levels by half in order to promote more rapid decision making. But this objective might backfire if it fosters increased centralization of integrating-type decisions so that lower managers are excluded until they have climbed higher.

Whether reducing bureaucratic levels aids or hinders development of future general managers appears to depend on the causes of the pruning. If the drive is to reduce expenses and quickly improve profits, power flows upward rapidly and lower-level discretion is squeezed out. Morale declines and personal development slows down even among the survivors.

If, however, the pruning is accompanied by viable product and service innovation that draws on close-to-the market multi-functional teams, the opportunities for general management training increase.

The threat of success

Personal career success can be a grave threat to those who have climbed to the general management ranks. Unhappily, such success often leads to inflexibility as one loses the motivation and courage to change. With time we tend to lose the ability to distinguish the new from the old, the unique from the regular. We interpret cues as warranting previously successful responses inappropriate to the changed situation. It is the very 'busy-ness' of managerial life that contributes to the problem.

The reality of most executives' days is not like that implied in management textbooks, neatly divided into periods of planning, controlling, structuring, staffing and directing. Rather, it is a seeming chaos of time, talking in many short conversations covering multiple topics, broken by five or so previously scheduled meetings per day.

On an average day, the managers whom I have observed each talk with more than 25 different people, which takes over 60 per cent of their time (perhaps 13 hours per week on the telephone!). And the day is jumpy: the average interval of quiet time without interruption is less than 10 minutes; the average incident, such as talking to someone, lasts about two minutes.

Under such conditions, an executive's day is extremely fractionated, devoted mainly to responding to various telephone calls, visitors and meetings. His or her life is dominated by the present and by fighting immediate fires. The future shrinks in apparent importance because there is no time to deal with it.

Now making transitions from short-run emergencies to longer-run challenges is tough; ten minutes alone are helpful only for work on small, immediate issues. They are unsuitable for longer-range, less-structured projects. Many executives simply do not believe they have up to 90 minutes alone each day; they feel that they scarcely have time to start a new task, drink a cup of coffee or even take a deep breath before being interrupted by a ringing telephone, an unexpected fax, an uninvited visitor or a clanging bell on the computer announcing another incoming e-mail message.

Continual dominance by immediate demands means inadequate time for future-oriented reading and thinking. As a result, many executives tend to be narrow in their interests, concentrating on technical and business reading. Time-harried people take insufficient time for exploration of the different. Dominated by response behavior for long periods, they can lose track of who they are and what they believe. Losing touch with their own values and aspirations, they find it impossible to initiate fundamental changes. The future is never confronted.

Short-term performance measures also

encourage executives to concentrate on the now. They feel that they are rewarded or punished for this year, based on annual measures of costs, earnings and growth. In the long run, they will be dead or transferred.

Every competitive business system requires short-term performance results; only a monopoly can ignore them. Nonetheless, even given world-wide competition, performance tends to be measured over too limited a time span. Concentrating on the present is often rewarded, while sacrificing for the future is ignored (or punished).

Short-term busy-ness contributes to habits and preoccupations that are the ultimate threats of success. As we master our jobs and grow older, we tend to behave without thinking, a sort of sleepwalking through our lives allowing our perceptive skills to atrophy. Men over 50 particularly demonstrate a propensity to insulate themselves, to draw back from the competitive fray, to lose touch with customers and markets.

One study of 2,000 executives concluded that the single most important attribute of those who handled success well (and were able to maintain it) was their ability to embrace change. To stay so vital requires maintaining the ability to perceive uniquely, to see differences.

Experience can be a great source of learning, of course. It can certainly save a lot of time as we fit current problems into the learned categories of the past. Unfortunately it can also waste time and cause disaster if we categorize issues prematurely and erroneously.

Confronting the unknown

You have heard of people who have worked for 20 years, but do not have 20 years experience; they merely repeated the first year 20 times. Such people may treat a new problem as if it were like past ones, when in fact it is new and unique. Keeping alive this ability to perceive deeply requires frequent exercise. This means building into our daily lives regular repetition of the process of letting go of the known and confronting the unknown change for the sake of change.

Every three to six months senior executives might define an innovation objective by focussing on a major aspect of their job and putting it on trial. Could it be eliminated? Could it be ignored until someone complains? Or could they experiment with changing it?

I once asked a group of managers at Johnson & Johnson what activity they found most difficult, so much so that it was the number-one task at which they procrastinated. Their most common reply was giving a negative performance evaluation, particularly to a subordinate older in age than the evaluating manager. They wanted to avoid an unpleasant confrontation; they did not believe the older person would change anyway; or they were not confident of their performance criteria.

The answer to this problem could be to focus on one unsatisfactory more senior subordinate for a few months, experimenting with changing the mode of performance feedback. Perhaps the managers could write a note to themselves every time they observe the subordinate in action; then they could schedule time every week to discuss these observations while they are fresh, rather than letting unrecorded impressions pile up until a fruitless annual interview ritual. The new approach may or may not work, but the very action of confronting a difficult new behavior will help preserve executive vitality.

Similarly, off the job, executives can define personal growth objectives that encourage focusing on a new activity: learning to play the piano at age 35; studying a foreign language at age 40; starting to paint at 50. All of these can be vehicles for keeping alive the ability to perceive uniquely because they involve modest but repeated confrontations with the unknown.

In these encounters it is less important that the new be actually mastered than that a good effort be made. Humans can 'deny' death (psychologically if not physically) by exercising the capacity to give up the well-known task and confronting the new.

Numerous senior executives have said to me that they never really felt comfortable in their careers until they 'transcended' their ambitions. It is not that they give up the race, but they become less concerned with winning and happier with merely running. The key to this turning point lies in accepting oneself and giving up the tyranny of external evaluations. Paradoxically, this very lessening of career centrality can promote personal success as we become less fearful of making mistakes and more willing to act on intuition.

No one of course can truly 'transcend' time, but ultimately, the most effective general executives seem to lift their time horizons.

Most achievement-oriented managers are dominated by a Newtonian view of time as constant, unvarying motion in which each interval is unique but equal. The activist ethic, associated with this perspective, encourages constant, short-range activity. It discourages speculation and fosters guilt feelings when one is not busy.

The paradox for general executives is that they need to relax a little in order to work more effectively relax the intensity of their work on present problems and address themselves more to future possibilities. They need to value today less and tomorrow more.

Executives tend to avoid thought about the future because it is ambiguous. Clear-cut, short-run problems may be difficult but they are satisfying to solve. In contrast, formulating wishes about the future, conceiving what we want the future to be and perceiving the future as history is difficult and threatening.

We tend to fear the kind of time necessary for such thought. It must be open, unstructured and seemingly non-directed, attributes counter to time-haunted, efficiency-minded people. Wide-open time, like space, can be frightening.

Defining fundamental values

In addition, incorporating concern about the future into the present necessitates clarifying what we really want. And this means defining fundamental values of management, organizations and society. As we wrestle with problems of international competitiveness, chronic unemployment, government debt and global environmental pollution, such clarification is critical for all of our futures.

An old native American proverb states: 'All that is seen is temporary.' The present is not unimportant nor is the world an illusion, but future-oriented, time-transcending general executives should have the detachment of people who accomplish great things while refusing to be devoured by current events.

One of the chief executive officers whom I most admire is Franz Luttmer, Chairman of Heidemij, N.V., a Netherlands-based international environmental consulting and engineering company. He holds a Ph.D. degree in science but is a talented classical pianist. He has lived for many years in underdeveloped countries as a land development consultant but is a cosmopolitan man, at home in Amsterdam, Denver and Jakarta (helped by being able to speak four languages).

A business meeting will include references to both the Dutch championship soccer team as well as a visiting Tokyo string quartet. Most importantly, he will repeatedly raise a vision of where the company should be competitively in the 21st century – global and vertically integrated but focussed on what customers see as the core services they need.

Few of us will be able to match this diversity, but it does represent a prototypical general executive for a multinational business.

Summary

The old certainties in general management are breaking down. Size and complexity have undermined the traditional three-tier upward climb, which starts with technical knowledge and qualifications, continues as broader interpersonal aptitudes are developed, and ends with mastery of the big picture and an ability to integrate all the company's functions. Increasingly organizations want young managers to acquire all these skills at an earlier stage.

The power axis of management has also changed over the last 50 years. In the US, at least, the prominence of engineering/manufacturing made sense after the Second World War. Marketing people became more assertive in the 1960s, while finance gained more importance as competition for debt and equity increased in the inflationary 1970s. The point, though, is not what function should be dominant today: the current environment calls for people and processes that effectively synthesize specialist functions into general management.

One broad type is the specializing generalist, such as the 'turnaround' executives of the late-1980s or the 'habitual' entrepreneur who creates multiple new business ventures. A happier model

is the generalizing specialist able to reinvigorate an overly narrow company. Vision and leadership, though, are no substitute for the nitty gritty. Effective general management includes the ability to communicate, to be approachable, to encourage and respond to the upward flow of ideas, and to adopt great behavioral flexibility.

Creative, synthesizing skills are vital, as is a preparedness sometimes to discard painfully gained specialist knowledge.

Accounting

Contents

The problem with accounting 19
Chris Higson and Jochen Zimmermann, London
Business School
*Accounting appears straightforward, but in fact it is
fraught with difficulties.*

The different centers of control 21
Chris Higson, London Business School
*How and why 'responsibility centers' are set up and
their advantages and drawbacks.*

Budget foundations 24
Jochen Zimmermann, London Business School
*The two functions of budgeting – planning and control
– are closely interlinked. But behind that simple
statement lies a wealth of detail.*

Measuring return on quality 26
Christopher D. Ittner, Wharton School of the
University of Pennsylvania
*Accounting is coming up with a way of putting
financial figures on quality.*

Counting the cost 29
Jochen Zimmermann, London Business School
*Knowing how much a product costs to produce is an
essential element in profitability.*

Return on capital employed (ROCE) 32
Chris Higson, London Business School
*ROCE is one of the central accounting measures but
there are some problem areas in employing it as a
measure of company performance.*

Accounting for changing prices 34
Ronnie Barnes, London Business School
*The historic cost approach to accounting poses
difficulties for interpreting company information.
Different techniques can be used to allow for the
effects of changing prices.*

What is a bank worth? 38
Paul A. Griffin, University of California at Davis,
visiting London Business School
*The financial valuation of commercial banks is not just
a matter a looking at a few simple ratios. A new
model that combines conventional ratio analysis with
an analysis of the discounted future free cash flows of
the bank.*

Harmonizing accounts worldwide 41
Sir Bryan Carsberg, London Business School
*How can a company make a profit when it reports in
one country and a loss when it reports in another?
The case for a worldwide system of accounting.*

Bottom-line discord 44
Andy Simmonds, Touche Ross visiting London
Business School
*An exploration of some of the causes of differences in
national accounting systems and the obstacles to a
truly transferable accounting regime.*

Regulating the regulators 47
Paul Bircher, Ernst & Young visiting London Business
School
*Have regulators gone too far in devising conceptual
frameworks and lost sight of their role of codifying
best practice?*

**Asset valuation: case studies from the
oil and gas industry** 50
Mimi Alciatore, London Business School
*The oil and gas industry provides examples of some
of the issues and problems in valuing and reporting
assets.*

Accounting for takeovers 53
Chris Higson, London Business School
*Takeovers represent probably the most complex of
accounting problems – not least because of differing
approaches in different countries.*

 **Dr Chris Higson** is Chairman of the Accounting group at London Business School. He is a chartered accountant and author of *Business Finance* (1995) Butterworths, London, and publishes widely in the areas of mergers and acquisitions, taxation, and shareholder value.

 **Sir Bryan Carsberg** is visiting Professor of Accounting at London Business School and Secretary General of the International Accounting Standards Committee. Formerly he was Director General of Fair Trading in the UK and Director General of Telecommunications, also in the UK.

 **Dr Jochen Zimmermann** is a member of the accounting group at London Business School and publishes in the field of financial reporting and control, especially for financial intermediaries.

 **Andy Simmonds** is a principal with Deloitte & Touche and a visiting lecturer at London Business School.

 **Professor Christopher D. Ittner** is KPMG Peat Marwick Term Assistant Professor of Accounting at the Wharton School of the University of Pennsylvania. His research interests are in the areas of production economics and cost management.

 **Dr Paul Bircher** is a senior manager in Ernst & Young's Technical Services Department and a visiting assistant professor at the London Business School. He writes in a personal capacity.

 **Ronnie Barnes** is Teaching Fellow at London Business School. His research interests include applications of models of asymmetric information to accounting issues, and accounting for derivative products.

 **Mimi Alciatore** is visiting Assistant Professor of Accounting at London Business School. Her research interests include capital markets research with a focus on accounting and financial reporting issues for the oil and gas industry.

 **Paul A. Griffin** is Professor of Management at the Graduate School of Management, University of California at Davis and a regular visiting Professor at London Business School. His research interests include financial valuation and securities analysis.

Introduction

Accounting is concerned with the measurement, recording and control of the central facet of business life – money. Its importance can therefore hardly be overstated. The development of accounting predated and to a large extent made possible the evolution of banking and commerce.

In some societies, notably the UK and notably among accountants, many have in the past viewed an accounting background as the only training necessary for general management. That may now be old-fashioned but there is little doubt that a grasp of accounting fundamentals is an essential prerequisite for assuming the role of a general manager.

There are 13 separate sections within the Accounting module. These include an intro-duction to the subject and explanation of the role of accounting in control systems, budgeting and costing, including the important new area of accounting for quality costs, return on capital employed, accounting under inflation, financial analysis of banks, accounting standards and regulations, asset valuation and takeover accounting.

The problem with accounting

■ **Accounting appears straightforward, but in fact it is fraught with difficulties. Here, some of the issues and problems are discussed.**

by **Chris Higson and Jochen Zimmermann**

Accounting is a central activity in economic life. Even in the simplest economies we need to keep a record of the assets we have and what we owe, and of our transactions with others. The role of accounting becomes even more important in complex modern economies. Since resources are scarce we have to choose between alternatives, and accounting data is needed to identify the best alternatives.

In broad terms, accounting is about the collection, presentation and interpretation of economic data. We use the term 'managerial accounting' to describe this activity within the organization, and 'financial accounting' when the organization is reporting to outsiders.

Described this way, accounting sounds like a simple business: worthy and necessary; probably costly, requiring the time of many clerks and many computers; but basically straightforward. In fact, accounting is fraught with difficulty. In this article we discuss some of the challenges in designing systems of accounting.

Accounting is not neutral

Individuals respond to the way in which they are measured. Sometimes the response can be unforeseen and dysfunctional. Accounting can bring about dysfunctionalities in a number of ways. Broadly speaking, they can be classified as follows:

Qualitative responses to financial measures. Managers can respond to budgets and targets set in purely financial terms by lowering quality and effort. This response may not show in their own financial results but in someone else's. An example is a purchasing department that lowers the quality of purchases to stay inside a budget. Poorer supplies will lead to more waste in production departments, and the organization as a whole will usually be worse off since the trade-off between scrap and quality of input has not been made rationally.

Shifting management focus for relative measures. Some accounting measures are relative, for example ROCE (return on capital employed). Managers might find it easier to improve ROCE by lowering the asset base. This can leave firms overly slim and unable to respond to future challenges in the corporate environment.

Abusing reports. Accountants often produce profit and variance measures. These variances are only meaningful when they are interpreted over a period, so that blips for which managers may not be responsible can be smoothed. Overusing variance analyses can lead managers to become overly risk-averse.

Finding loopholes. As accounting measures tend to focus on the key problem areas of a company they can be incomplete. For example, their design can have left out the cost of asset utilisation. Subsequently, these uncharged assets get overused: computer systems might run for too long or their support be requested too often; phone lines can be blocked because they are not costed adequately; or machines congested.

Creative accounting. There is scope for presenting the same events in different ways. There are good reasons for this. Much of accounting requires judgments about the future which inevitably bring subjectivity into play. Moreover, as we note below, society enacts accounting standards that must cope with a great variety of companies. As a result, some companies are able to exploit the flexibility of accounting by presenting their results in ways that flatter.

Not everything that is important can be easily quantified

It is plain that not everything can readily be quantified, and accounting data needs to be used with common-sense. In many important decisions it is the qualitative factors that dominate – a new investment may have negative forecast cash flows, but gives the company a valuable strategic position from which to exploit future developments in the marketplace; a new motorway is costly but will reduce the level of road traffic accidents. In both cases enthusiasts might set about putting a value on the benefits, but they are probably better left to the judgment of the decision-maker.

In the same way, accounting is often accused of being an interested party in the ideological debate about the role of the market economy. So we hear 'the accountants are running the hospitals'. In fact, accounting serves all masters. It is hard to imagine any society whose resources are limited relative to its needs that will not wish to make the best use of accounting data.

There are many prices

Even when an activity is quantifiable the prices that we should use to do this may be hard to ascertain. Accounting numbers are the products of quantities and prices. The quantities of inputs and outputs, and of assets in place, are usually fairly easy to determine. But it can be very hard to know which prices to use, and users of accounting data need to be very careful to understand which prices they are getting. There are two sources of difficulty.

First, there are different prices for different purposes. For example, the balance sheet is a list of the assets a company has and the claims outstanding against those assets. We want companies to earn a fair return on the assets they use. So it would be useful if the balance sheet recorded assets at their 'opportunity cost', i.e. their value in terms of the best alternative use which is sacrificed by using them here. Normally, this is the cost of replacing the asset.

But if the business is failing, or break-up is likely, then what we want is the realisable value of the assets, i.e. what they could be sold for.

Replacement cost is, in any case, not always easy to determine. What, for example, is the replacement cost of a unique intangible asset such as a patent? And what is the replacement cost of the stock of assets inherited by a privatised water company?

The second problem is that prices change, both relative to each other, and because of general inflation. Internationally, the norm is for accounts to be prepared at historic cost, that is, what was actually paid. This can be seriously misleading where there is inflation. For example, a brewery company may have purchased its town-center brewery site 100 years ago. Under historic cost accounting it could continue to carry that real estate at the price paid, which is likely to bear little resemblance to its current value. Some countries, such as the US, enforce historic cost accounting rather strictly. Others, including the UK, offer scope for companies to revalue their fixed assets in the balance sheet.

The problem of changing prices arises potently in reporting and interpreting the financial performance of a multinational group. If exchange rates are changing, when we produce a financial report for the whole group we will have to combine the costs, revenues, assets and liabilities of the various subsidiary companies at prices that are different.

Complex and changing world

Because information gathering and processing is costly, we always need to be sure that the benefits of extra accounting exceed the costs.

The world is a complex and changing place. It may be hard to find simple and robust approaches to accounting that meet all needs.

The regulations that govern the financial reporting of companies are constantly evolving, but how these data should be interpreted, and whether they meet the needs of the disparate group of stakeholders including society, employees, shareholders and creditors, is a constant source of debate.

Internal reporting systems may not always provide up-to-date information about the internal financial performance. If there is a change in a company's activities, a change in the markets served, the resources employed, the strategies pursued, then the information system needs updating.

The assumptions that underlie the design of information systems must be checked regularly, to see whether they still fit with company reality.

Summary
Accounting is about the collection, presentation and interpretation of economic data. 'Managerial accounting' describes the activity inside an organization, 'financial accounting' is used when reporting to outsiders. Users need to allow for the human dimension, the fact that some measures are relative, variances, loopholes and creative accounting. Not everything can be measured; the distinction between replacement and realisable cost and the impact on assets of inflation must be understood.

The different centers of control

■ **Accounting is a key element in measuring output and ensuring managers are performing. Jochen Zimmermann explains how and why 'responsibility centers' are set up and their advantages and drawbacks.**

An organization without control is impossible. Every organization has control systems that co-ordinate the exercise of decision rights that are dispersed among individuals. Control systems also serve another important function in the organization. They measure how effectively decisions have been translated into results. This second feature of control systems relates to the goal achievement of the company. In this perspective, control systems are about influencing the behavior of individuals in the interest of the corporation. Both functions are closely interlinked.

Control systems consist of formal and informal elements. Formal elements are laid down guidelines and procedures; informal guidelines include 'tradition', handed-down practice, office or corporate culture. The design of control systems is primarily concerned with the formal elements. Whereas an intuitive approach would identify only the physical controls in a company (such as passwords or guards) and instructions in either written or oral form, sometimes even non-verbal communication, too, belong in the realm of control systems. One of the most abstract and powerful types of control system is the accounting system that operates in an organization. This includes the way in which numbers within this system are arranged and interpreted.

There are several reasons for the vital role of accounting within the set of control systems. First, accounting language is the common language of every business organization. It is difficult to aggregate and compare physical performance measures such as delivery speed, customer satisfaction and the like. Accounting figures easily fit the organizational requirement of quick aggregability and comparability. Furthermore, accounting numbers are primarily designed for what is at the heart of the business process: output control. Accounting systems measure managerial effectiveness, not the nature of behavior, effort or diligence. Their strong bias towards results instead of inputs make them a tool to monitor financial performance, and it is financial performance that is of ultimate interest to the shareholders of the company.

This orientation towards results creates certain prerequisites for the successful implementation of an accounting system. First, one has to ascertain the form in which output is measured and ensure that the technology that translates action into results is stable and regular. Only if the ability to measure output is high, can an accounting control system be used successfully. A typical example of highly measurable outputs are sales results; a typical example to the contrary is the output of a research laboratory.

The external environment may also complicate measurement by imposing random fluctuations on results. The observed outputs might then be garbled as a result of external noise. In this event, a successful implementation of an accounting system needs to be able to identify ways of distilling the true results from preliminary 'noisy' figures.

Control is always exercised from the top; it is essentially hierarchical. This does not imply, however, that all control rights have to be vested into a single decision maker. Usually a set of accounting controls is implemented through 'responsibility centers'. In responsibility centers, managers decide certain business problems based on their own judgments without interference from the top of the organization. They are only judged by the results that they produce. This autonomy requires a company to establish criteria as to how to measure performance and how to co-ordinate action if areas of responsibility are not totally disconnected, which is a common case. One can distinguish three types of responsibility center: cost centers, profit centers, and investment centers.

Cost centers

Cost centers can operate in two different ways. According to the efficiency principle, an optimal decision either maximizes output with a certain given output; or input is minimized to achieve a certain given output. It depends on the business situation as to which design is preferable.

If one considers, for example, a marketing department, it is often given a fixed budget (a fixed amount of resources or input) and with these given resources its task is to maximize its 'output'. By contrast, other service departments of an organization often operate as input-minimizing cost centers. For example, a cleaning department has the task of maintaining a given number of offices and has to use the minimum resources possible. Personnel or production departments also follow this rationale and are set up as cost centers.

In both cases, the control system allows managers to make autonomous decisions about how to combine inputs to achieve a certain given task and be responsible for meeting the set targets. In both cases, managers are not allowed to decide on the scale of the operations or the prices charged. In the above example, marketing is not allowed to increase sales by lowering prices, and the cleaning department cannot reduce inputs by scaling down the number of offices cleaned.

However, if both types of cost center have the same decision right about input choice, they also have the same type of incentive from an accounting system that merely relies on financial figures: the incentive to lower quality to save costs. This clearly indicates the need for an additional check on quality if a cost center structure is chosen. As a performance measure, a comparison of either budgeted vs actual output or budgeted vs actual cost is suggestive. One should be wary of the performance measure of minimized average costs because this measure creates an incentive to increase output and to build up inventories in conjunction with certain accounting systems.

Profit centers

Unlike cost center managers, profit center managers have decision rights about inputs and outputs. The goal of a profit center is to maximize profits by adjusting the parameters of input mix, output quantity and price. Since the managers have all current decision-making elements under their direct control, they do not benefit from lowering quality. Lower quality does not help them to achieve their financial performance target, which is measured by the difference between actual and budgeted profits.

While the implementation of profit centers does away with the incentive to reduce quality to lower cost, it can introduce difficulties in the cases of mutual dependency or upstream fixed costs. In the first case, the installation of two profit centers can lead to suboptimization when the choices of input-output mixes collide.

An illustrative example is the creation of two 'profit' centers: production and sales departments for which interdivisional sales constitute the respective positive or negative transactions.

Production might respond to the profit maximization task by choosing a level production strategy; sales uses heavy promotions to push products. The promotions generate demand that can only be met if production changes the level of manufacturing processes, which is costly and reduces the results in the production profit center. It is advisable in these cases to treat departments as separate cost centers, and to ensure there is a further hierarchy of decision making that combines cost centers in a profit center.

Investment centers

Although profit centers eliminate the incentive to reduce quality, they do not touch the problem of the capital base. This can lead to the squandering of resources by departments. It is therefore useful to give responsibility centers the right to make their own investment decisions, i.e. to allocate given funds to projects.

These so-called investment centers are assessed on performance measures that include the use of capital. A popular method uses ROI (return on investment) to establish the relative profitability of an investment center. ROI is the profit achieved within the decision-making unit relative to its (nominal) asset base. This relative measure allows easy comparisons between units. To provide comparable results, the rules of how to value assets have to be uniform throughout all centers. However, the relative nature disguises the importance of a unit to the company. It can also lead to 'denominator management', when managers choose to run down the denominator, asset base, in an attempt to maintain or increase

short-term profits instead of concentrating on the numerator, profits.

Multiple decision making within the company requires co-ordination between responsibility centers. Two control systems take care of these tasks: budgeting and transfer pricing. Transfer prices are administrative procedures that mimic the functions of market prices within an organization. Services between the semi-autonomous responsibility centers are charged according to some previously agreed mechanism. Obvious transfer pricing occurs when divisions exchange products. A less obvious transfer price is the charge attached to services rendered by cost centers to other parts of the organization.

The correct transfer price is a charge that will induce everyone within the organization to make the right, i.e. profit-maximizing decisions. A standard rule to arrive at such a transfer price is to charge the market price for transactions and to give the divisions the right to buy from outside. This arrangement sustains competitive momentum.

Another suggestion is to charge at full costs, assuming that full costs are a lower boundary of the market price. While this suggestion is acceptable in standard cases, it can lead to suboptimal decisions in off-standard situations. When market prices are depressed, decision makers might buy from outside, leaving the fixed costs of the internal supplier uncovered. When market prices are high, the reverse can occur. The supplying division sells to the outside, leaving the capacity in the internal production chain idle. Additional administrative procedures are needed to control these situations.

Summary

Control is always exercised from the top but a set of accounting controls is usually implemented through 'responsibility centers'. There are three types of responsibility center: cost centers, where managers make choices about how to combine inputs to achieve their targets but where there is often an incentive to lower quality; profit centers, where input mix, output quantity and prices can all be adjusted; and investment centers where performance measures include the use of capital.

Suggested further reading

Elliott, B. and Jamie Elliott *Financial Accounting and Reporting*, 2nd edn (forthcoming), Prentice Hall.

Schroeder, Richard G. and Myrtle Clark *Accounting Theory: Text and Readings*, 5th edn, John Wiley & Sons.

Zimmerman, Jerold L. *Accounting for Decision Making and Control*, Irwin.

Emmanuel C., Otley D. and Merchant, K. *Accounting for Management Control*, Chapman & Hall.

Budget foundations

■ **The two functions of budgeting planning and control are closely interlinked. But behind that simple statement lies a wealth of detail, says** Jochen Zimmerman

Budgeting is one step in implementing a company's strategy. It translates loose key planning assumptions about corporate strategy into numerical representations about markets and resources. Sales targets embody the company's strategy about markets; the capital allocated to decision makers in the various responsibility centers reflects the choice about resources that the company will use.

In that perspective, budgeting is a part of the planning process. However, budgeting also establishes benchmarks for control by setting standards. This is often referred to as the dual role of budgeting. A budget has the function of co-ordinating the company's activities and the function of serving as a base for control by comparing estimated (budgeted) figures and actual performance.

A so-called master budget forms the consolidated picture of the company's activities. Typically, this master budget is a forecast of the organization's financial reports, i.e. a combination of income statement, balance sheet and cash flow statement. To arrive at these highly aggregate figures, the budgeting process considers all the activities of the company that will finally be accounted for in the master budget.

A logical starting point is the sales budget prepared by the marketing department. Given the sales figures, the production strategy and the resource procurement (including the asset base) have to be determined. From the overall production strategy and procurement, one can then derive the budgets for single responsibility centers. Production will be reflected in budgets for inventory, overheads, labour and materials. These are benchmarks for which the production managers can be held responsible. Usually, the budgeting process requires several loops to be completed, as figures must be reconciled.

Depending on originating and final decision-making powers, one can distinguish between 'top-down' and 'bottom-up' budgeting. In a bottom-up process, the starting figures are submitted by lower-level managers and reconciled by those at the top. This type of process has several advantages. It increases the 'ownership' of the budget and therefore employee commitment to achieve the targets. It also brings to bear the more specific knowledge that decision makers have at lower levels.

On the downside, bottom-up budgeting is a lengthy process and needs a great amount of reconciliation. This means that the submitted figures have to be altered by top management, which can lead to employee disillusionment. Additionally, bottom-up figures are typically 'skewed'. The submitted figures may have some slack built in so that achievement of the target does not become a problem. Given these disadvantages, organizations rarely use bottom-up budgeting. It is usually only found where top management cannot make meaningful forecasts. A top-down budget fulfills the communication and co-ordination needs of the organization, and because of the absence of slack it also forms a yardstick for performance measurement. Only top-down budgets can cope with the dual role of budgeting. Within the overall framework there are a number of specific types of budgets and routines.

Line-item budgets

Line-item budgets refer to budgets that allow decision makers to spend only a fixed maximum amount on specified items. This prevents managers from making too bold decisions about substituting between budgeted inputs. This safeguard is useful because the agreed mix of input factors in the budget has to be closely maintained for co-ordination reasons. While often attributed to government organizations, a high percentage of for-profit organizations also use line item budgets to curtail the decision-making power of managers in responsibility centers.

Lapsing budgets

Lapsing budgets do not allow the carry-over of unused funds into the next budgeting period. There are several advantages to budget lapsing. Lapsing budgets allow tighter controls on managers, and the amount of resources in the company can be controlled easily since there are no hidden or saved resources, which simplifies the planning process. However, this simpli-fication comes at a cost. At the end of a budgeting period, managers might spend a lot of their time inventing ways to spend remaining funds, and resources are thus wasted. It seems, though, that the benefits of lapsing budgets outweigh their costs for they are common in nearly every organization.

Forecasting and zero-based budgeting

Forecasting the resources that are needed to achieve the production and sales targets correctly is critical for the success and credibility of the budgeting process. Most companies use an incremental method to derive their budgets. This method takes last period's figures and increases or decreases them by a set percentage. Changes reflect inflation, learning or other increases in productivity. Although the changes are some-times reviewed, the base, or core, budget, remains unrevised.

Zero-based budgeting (ZBB) questions this very core. ZBB develops budgets without using the guidance of last year's figures. Every activity is built from scratch (zero base). This helps managers to think creatively about their activities and thus reduces slack within the organization. The obvious disadvantage of ZBB is the long and intricate process that is required.

In most organizations, therefore, ZBB is used infrequently. If it is implemented as a regular budgeting technique, managers will often resort to the same explanation as the previous year, tacitly turning ZBB into incremental budgeting.

Flexible budgets

Planning budgets communicate planned volumes and planned prices. Control budgets need some modification. This is due to the fact that some managers do not have volumes under their direct control and cannot be held responsible for budget deviations that stem from volume changes. For a performance analysis, budget allowances for these managers have to vary with volume. One calls these varying budgets flexible budgets in contrast to static budgets. Flexible budgets are functions of a volume measure.

An example illustrates this easily. If a production manager has a set budget for producing 100 units, but marketing (being responsible for the sales numbers) requires the procurement of 120, then the production managers cannot automatically be held res-ponsible for a cost overrun. A deviation from the budget might be solely attributable to the fact that sales figures are higher, which is totally beyond his or her control. Flexible budgets adjust for these volume changes. The budget against which the production manager will be compared is the flexed budget that indicates how much cost should have been incurred for the procurement of 120 units. If managers are responsible for volumes and costs per unit, however, this flexing is not helpful. In these cases a static budget that compares planned to actual performance without volume adjustments is more appropriate.

Budgets are an important mechanism for co-ordination and control in an organization. The number of separate budgets that have to be drawn up depends on the design of responsibility centers and the decision rights within them. The budget cycle and the number of loops depend on the complexity of the reconciliation, the budgeting techniques and the corporate environment. For control purposes, budgets link closely with the costing systems of the company, as flexible budgets rely on the cost figures and cost drivers of the organization's internal accounting system.

Summary

Budgeting translates loose planning assumptions about corporate strategy into numerical representations about markets and resources. By setting standards, it also establishes benchmarks for control. Only top down budgeting can cope with this dual role.

Line-item budgets allow decision makers to spend only a fixed maximum on specified items. Lapsing budgets do not allow the carrying over of unused funds. Zero-based budgeting develops budgets without the guidance of last year's figures.

Suggested further reading:

Merchant, Kenneth A. (1989) *Rewarding Results, Motivating Profit Center Managers*, Harvard Business School.

Measuring return on quality

■ **Everyone knows that improved quality is the only way to stay in the competitive game. Now accounting is coming up with a way of putting financial figures on quality.**

by Christopher D. Ittner

Over the past decade, nearly every firm has implemented some form of quality improvement program, ranging from simple inspection and customer complaint processing to extensive efforts to develop a 'customer-focussed' organization. Yet despite years of effort, most firms find it difficult to demonstrate an association between quality improvement activities and financial performance. Many companies have begun to question the relationship between quality and financial performance, and quality departments are under considerable pressure to demonstrate that their efforts and expenditures are producing substantial economic returns.

One reason firms have such difficulty assessing the financial benefits from quality improvement is the methods used to evaluate the financial return on quality. Nearly every firm makes some attempt to quantify losses due to scrap, rework, and warranty claims, costs that are relatively easy to extract from existing accounting systems. Others have implemented more elaborate cost of quality systems to capture a wider variety of quality costs.

The 'cost of quality' represents the difference between the actual cost of a product or service and what that cost would be if everyone performed 100 per cent to standard, that is defect-free or error-free performance.

The four categories of quality costs relate to: prevention of defects; inspection and appraisal – to monitor ongoing quality; internal failure – correction of defective products or services before delivery to the customer; external failure – repairs, replacement, discounts, or refunds for defective products or services caught after delivery to the customer. (Examples of quality cost elements are shown below in Table 1.)

Table 1: Examples of Quality Costs

Prevention Costs: Quality engineering. Quality training. Quality systems development. Quality circles. Statistical process control activities. Quality data gathering and analysis. Quality improvement projects.

Appraisal Costs: Receiving inspection. In-process product inspection. Final inspection and testing. Laboratory tests. Field tests at customer sites. Quality audits. Supervision and supplies for inspection and test activities.

Internal Failure Costs: Scrap. Rework and repair. Spoilage. Rescheduling due to quality problems. Expediting due to quality problems. Downtime due to quality problems. Excess inventory held to buffer operations from quality problems. Defect analysis.

External Failure Costs: Warranty charges. Liability claims. Complaint handling and investigation. Product recalls. Penalties. Returns and allowances for defective products. Opportunity costs of lost sales due to quality problems.

Studies indicate that quality costs consume between 20 per cent and 30 per cent of sales revenue in manufacturing companies and 30 per cent to 50 per cent in service firms. Many companies have developed quality cost reporting systems to assist in the identification and minimization of these costs. The information provided by a quality cost system serves several purposes.

First, quality cost information helps managers see the financial implications of poor quality. Managers are frequently unaware of the magnitude of their quality costs because these costs cut across departmental boundaries and are not normally tracked and accumulated by the cost accounting system. When first presented with a quality cost report, managers are often surprised when they see the amount of cost involved. By computing and reporting quality costs, organizations can highlight the potentially significant returns from investing in quality improvements.

Second, quality cost information helps managers to prioritize improvement efforts. For example, the quality cost report may indicate that the firm is incurring excessive scrap or warranty costs for a specific product line. Based on this information, quality improvement efforts can be specifically directed at the problems causing the greatest financial losses.

Third, quality cost information helps managers to see whether their quality costs are optimally distributed among the four categories. In the early stages of a quality program, companies can typically achieve significant reductions in internal and external failure costs by investing more in prevention and inspection activities. As the quality program becomes more refined and failure costs begin to fall, efforts for further reductions in these costs should focus more on prevention activities and less on inspection, thereby eliminating the defects rather than merely detecting them before delivery to the customer. By understanding where quality costs are being incurred, managers can redistribute quality expenditures when appropriate.

Fourth, quality cost information provides a basis for establishing budgets for quality improvement as management seeks to reduce the total cost of quality. These budgets can then be used to evaluate the performance of the quality program.

Although quality costs systems can undoubtedly provide useful information for managing a quality program, they suffer from a number of limitations.

First, simply measuring and reporting quality costs does not solve quality problems. Without organizational mechanisms in place for identifying and eliminating the root causes of quality problems, reporting quality cost information provides little benefit. Second, quality costs may not provide accurate short-term feedback on current operations. Compared with non-financial quality measures such as statistical process control charts, defect rates and product throughput, quality cost reports are issued typically in a more aggregated form and are less timely, making them less useful for identifying the exact sources of problems.

Third, quality efforts and accomplishments are typically not matched in a single reporting period. Investments in prevention may take months or even years to pay off, causing potential problems if performance is evaluated mainly on short-term reductions in total quality costs. Fourth, many quality costs are typically omitted from reported quality costs. These include the indirect productivity losses from quality-related congestion and schedule delays, and the opportunity costs of lost sales due to poor product design or loss of customer goodwill. In fact, studies indicate that cost of quality systems generally capture less than a third of internal failure costs, and an even smaller percentage of external failure costs.

Finally, quality cost reports focus on the costs of poor quality but ignore the revenue benefits from improved customer satisfaction and loyalty, which are potentially the greatest sources of economic value from quality improvement.

Instead, non-financial customer satisfaction indices are used to assess the quality program's impact on customer attitudes, under the assumption that higher customer satisfaction automatically translates into improved financial performance. However, the traditional customer satisfaction surveys used by most companies suffer from a number of limitations that make it difficult, if not impossible, to directly link increases in these indices to increases in financial performance.

First, single 'top-box' measures that are based on the percent of respondents rating the product or service in the top one or two rating categories or boxes on a survey are frequently used to evaluate and track customer satisfaction, often using only a small number of scale points. Unfortunately, this approach yields considerable measurement error in the indices, making it difficult to detect customer satisfaction improvements or to demonstrate their relation to financial performance.

Second, most customer satisfaction measures are constructed in isolation of their ultimate use. That is, the measures are not specifically designed so that higher scores exhibit an ability to predict higher customer loyalty and improved economic performance, the ultimate goals of the quality program. Since most firms cannot quantitatively link their customer satisfaction measures to firm performance, they experience considerable difficulty identifying the quality improvement projects offering the highest economic returns.

More sophisticated customer satisfaction measures can overcome many of the problems linking changes in customer satisfaction to financial performance. In particular, recent company experience and academic research indicates that the methodology used to compute the American Customer Satisfaction Index (ACSI) provides customer satisfaction measures that are economically relevant to the stock market and predictive of future financial performance. The ACSI methodology offers a number of advantages over the customer satisfaction measures calculated by most companies. First, the use of multiple questionnaire items increases the precision of the customer satisfaction estimate relative to the more typical single 'top box' measure. Second, the individual questionnaire items are measured on a ten-point scale as opposed to more typical three to five point scales in order to enhance statistical reliability. More importantly, the customer satisfaction measure is constructed using a statistical technique known as Partial Least Squares that weight individual customer satisfaction questions such as overall satisfaction, confirmation of expectations, and comparison to ideal such that the resulting index has the maximum correlation with economic performance.

Customer satisfaction measures constructed using the ACSI methodology have been found to be positively related to accounting performance and stock market measures. In addition, the ACSI measures are predictive of future customer purchase behavior, providing a method for estimating the revenue-enhancing benefits from improved quality and customer satisfaction. By employing more sophisticated customer satis-faction measures such as the ACSI and linking these measures to financial performance, firms can overcome many of the difficulties currently plaguing efforts to estimate the financial return on quality.

Summary

Quality information allows managers to see the financial implications of poor quality, prioritise improvement efforts, balance prevention and inspection, and set budgets. Quality cost systems, though, do have their limitations. Measuring and reporting quality does not solve the problem and the short-term feedback on current operations may not be accurate. Quality cost reports often omit certain items and ignore the revenue benefits of stronger customer loyalty which flow from quality improvement.

Suggested further reading

Atkinson, Hawley, Hamburg, J., and Ittner, C., *Linking Quality to Profits: Quality-Based Cost Management*, Milwaukee, WI: ASQC Press, 1994.

Ittner, Christopher D. and Larcker, David F. 'Measuring the impact of quality initiatives on firm financial performance', *Advances in the Management of Organizational Quality*, Vol. 1, 1996, pp. 1–37.

Counting the cost

■ **Knowing how much a product costs to produce is an essential element in profitability, writes** Jochen Zimmermann

Besides control and budgeting (covered respectively in the accompanying section and in Part 2 of Mastering Management), costing forms an essential element of the managerial accounting activities in a company. Costing concerns itself with establishing how many expenses were used up by a product, a product group, a particular activity or a set of business activities.

The ultimate goal of a company is the creation of shareholder value, but measuring this goal is a difficult task. One often relies on approximate measures, on more or less aggregate levels. Profits that are disclosed in financial statements are of the most aggregate nature. While segmental profits can provide detailed infor-mation for the external analyst, management often wants to identify the factors contributing to company profits with much greater accuracy. Deriving product cost and comparing it with the prices charged is such a detailed analysis. The difference of these two, called contribution, gives insights into the profitability of the company's various activities.

Deriving costs

Costing is a three-step process. First, one has to separate product cost from period cost. Second, direct product costs are allocated to the individual products, whereas indirect costs are allocated to cost pools. Third, indirect costs are attributed from the pool to the products according to their usage. The sum of direct and allocated indirect cost forms the product cost.

Costing has a strong tradition in manu-facturing. For this reason, costing procedures typically recognise selling and general ad-ministrative expenses (SG&A) as period costs that are not attributable to individual products or product groups. Product costs are principally:

expenses for material, labor and machinery (in the form of depreciation). Other product costs might include expenses as various as light, heating, insurance, waste and so on.

Having separated product from period cost, one can perform the second step of costing, allocating direct cost to a product or any other cost object that is the subject of managerial analysis. Direct costs are expenses that are incurred uniquely for a particular product. The direct nature of the cost is quite obvious for material bills, but international differences already exist in the treatment of labor. While Anglo-American systems treat labor other than supervisory as a direct cost, continental European practice often regards all labor cost as indirect. This is due to the different regulatory practices, reflecting the lower flexibility that continental labor law permits. Remaining are now only the indirect costs, which will in some industries make for the lion's share of the cost.

The third step of costing – attribution of indirect cost – is the most important for achieving accuracy. All indirect costs, which are sometimes also referred to as overheads, are first allocated to cost pools. Cost pools can be areas of decision making (responsibility centers), service departments or simple accounting entities. A cost pool absorbs all those costs that vary with a certain cost driver (activity measure); and it is this cost driver that reflects the services rendered to a product.

Assume, for example, a machine that is used for the manufacturing of various products. The depreciation for the machine is first registered as indirect cost. This indirect cost must now be accurately attributed to the various products. This is done by (1) measuring how many services were rendered to all products at what total cost (2) how individual products used these services and (3) multiplying the activity measure for one product by the cost of one activity measure.

In our example, the cost for the services rendered is the depreciation charge. In the next step, one would find that the machine ran 60 per cent of the time for product A and 40 per cent of the time for product B. Usually, activity studies or engineering estimates provide these figures. Given a daily (or weekly, monthly or whatever)

output of X for product A and Y for product B, one can find the attribution rate per minute per product, for example, that the machine runs for 5 minutes when one unit of product A is produced; and for 3 minutes for one unit of product B. This is the activity measure (minutes per product unit), which is then multiplied with the cost per activity measure (depreciation per day divided by total machine hours a day). Then the attributable cost is charged to the product; the sum of all indirect charges sum up to the total product cost.

Controversy usually arises over the question of what kind of activity measure is to be used and by implication how many cost pools are to be formed. In the most straightforward case, one would use only one cost pool and attribute the pool's indirect cost with a unitary activity measure such as direct labor cost. Obviously, this method suffers from deficiencies. For one thing, direct labor costs are a product of hours spent and hourly pay. If products differ in these components – one using a lot of cheap labor and the other a small amount of expensive labor – then the representation of services rendered from the cost pool might not be correct. Additionally, since all charges are derived from a cost pool that includes expenses as diverse as depreciation, supervision, insurance and so on, then no matter what activity measure one uses, it will not reflect the true nature of usage. More cost pools will be needed.

The choice of how many cost pools to form and the cost drivers must strike a balance between accuracy and expediency. The choice of too few cost drivers will leave undetected major differences in product demand for services. This is especially true when a company changes its product portfolio or when one follows a strategy of differentiation. Also, different customer demand patterns and their cost implications might be disguised. Only a regular scrutiny of the organization's activities and the cost drivers will ensure that the overhead allocation still reflects the demand for services.

Revealing true profitability

Having implemented a more differentiated system of cost drivers to allocate from cost pools to products, a number of companies have found that seemingly profitable products were making losses because of their overhead requirements. Activity-based costing gives guidelines on how to implement a sufficient number of cost drivers to reveal true product profitability.

More attention has also been given recently to SG&A expenses. The rationale for treating them as period costs stems from financial regulation. Management accounting techniques have simply followed the procedure prescribed for financial reporting. From the viewpoint of profitability analysis, there might be scope for reintroducing some SG&A expenses into the category of product cost. This is especially true when some products require different administrative handling or marketing. Again, the true profitability of a product will be disguised if no allocation of these period costs takes place.

Historic, normal or standard cost can all be the basis for the costing process. For control and pricing, the use of standard costs is essential. Standard costs can be estimated by statistical analyses. These analyses establish prospective prices for the goods and services used and the cost behavior as a function of the activity measure. A different technique is engineering analysis. In this case, technical estimates serve as the basis for forecasting cost behavior. This is more time-consuming but also more accurate and less prone to statistical errors. Standard costs then serve as a benchmark for comparison with historic or actual cost.

While these comparisons are informative for product pricing because they serve as indicators of the accuracy of future forecasts, they are essential for variance analysis within the responsibility centers. Costing and a meaningful variance analysis depend on one another. The cost drivers serve as volume adjustments for flexible budgets, and with these adjustments, the efficiency or inefficiency of decisions taken in responsibility centers can be assessed.

If the activity measures of the accounting system do not reflect the true nature of the services performed, however, then this not only reports wrong product costs but also wrong variances. Efficiencies or inefficiencies will be overstated or understated. This effect of averaging out will affect the credibility of the entire system, making it unusable for both costing and control.

Summary

Costing is a three-step process. First, one has to separate product costs from period costs; next, one allocates direct product costs to individual products and individual costs to 'cost pools', finally, indirect costs are attributed from these pools to the products according to usage. The last is the most important when it comes to achieving accuracy. Historic, normal, or standard cost can all be the basis of the costing process but the use of standard costs is essential for control and pricing.

Suggested further reading

Johnson, Thomas H. and Kaplan, Robert S. *Relevance Lost: the Rise and Fall of Management Accounting*, Harvard Business School

Kaplan, Robert S. *Measures for Manufacturing Excellence*, Harvard Business School

Return on capital employed (ROCE)

■ ROCE is one of the central accounting measures but, as Chris Higson explains, there are some problems in employing it as a measure of company performance.

Most business activity involves committing resources in the present to yield income in the future. Because resources are scarce we need to allocate finance to those investments that we expect to give the most valuable stream of income in the future. How to make these choices is a central concern in corporate finance.

But it is equally important to monitor the return from existing investments. Outsiders such as regulators, investors and potential competitors, as well as a company's own management, want to know which areas of activity are profitable. Equally, they need to identify activities that do not yield an adequate return; this can signal mismanagement, or may indicate disinvestment, liquidation or contraction. Return on capital employed (ROCE) is the measure most frequently used for this purpose.

How ROCE is measured

The two primary accounting statements, the balance sheet and the profit and loss account, appear to provide just the information we need to measure ROCE. As a simple example consider the balance sheet and profit and loss account of the Widget Co. (*see* Figure 1).

The balance sheet lists the assets of the company and the claims of shareholders and the other liabilities at December 31 1995. Though the company uses £90m of assets, these are partly financed by credit received from the tax authorities, suppliers and others. We will define the *capital employed* of Widget, as the sum of its *equity* finance (shareholders funds, £40m) and its *debt* (borrowings, £10m + £20m). This is the finance that investors have provided for the business.

The profit and loss account shows how much profit Widget made by employing this capital and how it was distributed as interest and tax, and how much was available to shareholders. On sales of £150m, Widget made gross profit, after direct manufacturing costs, of £90m. After the

Figure 1: Widget & Co

Profit and Loss Account for the year ended 31 December 1995 (£m)

Sales	150
Cost of Goods Sold	60
Gross Profit	**90**
Sales and Administration Expense	75
Operating Profit	**15**
Interest Paid	3
Profit before tax	**12**
Taxation	4
Profit after tax, available to Shareholders	**8**

Balance Sheet at 31 December 1995 (£m)

Assets

Fixed Assets	Land and Buildings	20
	Plant and Machinery	30
		50
Current Assets	Inventory	15
	Receivables	20
	Cash	5
		40
		90

Claims

Shareholders Funds	Share Capital	15
	Retained Earnings	25
		40
Long-Term Liabilities	Borrowings	10
	Other Payables	5
		15
Current Liabilities	Borrowings	20
	Trade Payables	10
	Corporation Tax	5
		35
		90

indirect costs of running the business, operating profit was £15m. This is the key number, since it is the profit generated from the capital employed before paying interest and tax. The return on capital employed is thus £15m against £70m = 21 per cent, the profit before interest and tax as a percentage of capital employed.

ROCE may sometimes be defined in slightly different ways. For example, average capital employed through the year may be used in the denominator; some users prefer to measure ROCE net of cash and net of the interest received on cash; and there is some disagreement as to whether capital employed should include deferred tax provisions or exclude intangible assets. It can go under different names (including return on net assets and accounting rate of return). But in some form, return on capital employed is almost universally used in performance measurement.

Some difficulties in using ROCE

Some difficulties in using and interpreting ROCE are caused by the limitations of accounting data, by using accounting data out of context and sometimes by setting ROCE as a target.

Is the balance sheet complete?   Though the balance sheet lists the assets and claims of a company, for various reasons this may not be a complete list. Under the *historic* cost convention of accounting, assets will only be recorded if they were acquired in a transaction, for value, but not if they were acquired as windfalls. Moreover the *conservatism* convention dictates writing-off the costs of building assets such as brands, intellectual property and R&D as they are incurred, rather than carrying them in the balance sheet. The balance sheet may understate the capital employed of the business in these circumstances.

Managers can render the balance sheet still more incomplete by using 'off-balance-sheet' accounting techniques. Moreover, there are 'completeness' worries in the profit and loss account also. The prime focus of the P&L is to describe the profit the company makes by its operations. For example, part of the return that a company delivers to its investors may be in the form of unrealised holding gains on assets such as real estate. As noted below, these may or may not be recognised, and even when they are, they may rarely be passed through the P&L.

How is the balance sheet valued?   Related, and even more troublesome, is the problem of valuation. Widget, in our example, had £20*m* of land and buildings in its balance sheet. But under historic cost accounting this may be the price the company founder paid for the assets 100 years ago. There is no compulsion to revalue fixed assets, and in countries such as the US, a company is not permitted to revalue. Clearly, when the balance sheet is incomplete, or assets are valued at out-of-date prices, comparisons of ROCE between companies or through time can be hazardous.

Often, regulators or investors will want to compare ROCE with an external benchmark such as a capital market required return. Again, this will be a flawed comparison unless capital employed measures the *opportunity* cost of the capital stock, which will generally be the cost of replacing the income-generating capacity of the company in full at current prices, and unless the P&L measures the cost of consuming these assets. Economists have analysed quite closely the biases that arise when using accounting rates of return to proxy economic returns. (For a thorough review, *see* Edwards, Kay and Mayer 'Suggested further reading'.)

ROCE and disinvestment. As a signal for disinvestment, accounting returns have to be treated with care. Activity that is unprofitable in terms of the replacement cost of the needed assets is not worth undertaking. But if the investment has *already been made* it does not follow that we should disinvest. Now the question becomes what the assets can be sold for. The opportunity cost of the capital stock is its realisable value. Particularly for assets with few alternative uses there can be a big gap between realisable value and replacement cost.

The importance of thinking in opportunity cost terms is particularly relevant for governments making social investment or disinvestment decisions. In this case profitability measures such as ROCE that use company accounting data can be quite inappropriate, since the private costs and benefits that are reflected in company accounting statements may not measure social costs and benefits.

As an example, take the cost of labor in an economy with unemployment. To the company, the cost of labor includes wages, social security, taxes and pension provisions; saving these costs might be a good reason for closing some activities. But from the point of view of the economy as a whole these payments are transfers; the cost is the foregone output from the labor, which could be zero if there is no alternative employment for the labor.

Summary

Return on capital employed is the measure most frequently used for identifying areas of business which are profitable and ones which are underperforming. ROCE is typically calculated by taking profit before interest and tax as a percentage of the sum of a company's equity finance and its debt. Difficulties can be caused by the limitations of accounting data, the use of accounting data out of context (e.g. when assets have been valued at out of date prices), and the setting of ROCE as a target.

Suggested further reading

Edwards, J.S.S., Kay, J.A. and Mayer, C.P. (1987) *The Economic Analysis of Accounting Profitability*, Oxford University Press.

Higson, C. (1995) *Business Finance*, 2nd edn, Butterworths.

Accounting for changing prices

■ **The historic cost approach to accounting poses difficulties for interpreting information. Ronnie Barnes explains the techniques used to allow the effects of changing prices to be incorporated into accounting.**

Traditionally, financial accounting has been closely linked to the stewardship function that arises from the separation of ownership and control characteristic of the corporation. The owners (shareholders) of a corporation provide the business with economic resources and entrust the management (board of directors) with the utilisation of these resources.

In this context, accounting information may be thought of as a report from the management to the owners describing how they have discharged their responsibility and, for this purpose, a statement of the transactions undertaken recorded in historic cost terms is perfectly adequate.

In recent years, however, the uses (and users) of accounting information have expanded considerably beyond this traditional role. A wide range of economic agents including regulatory bodies, investment analysts and taxation authorities now routinely use accounts to assist in their decision-making processes. However, the informational needs of these different constituencies vary widely and in many cases (and particularly when prices are changing rapidly) the standard historic cost approach is inappropriate.

This section considers the weaknesses of historic cost accounts that make them an unsuitable basis on which to make economic decisions. It then goes on to describe various alternative approaches to accounting that explicitly take account of the effect of changing prices (and which are collectively known as current value accounting) and indicate the principal strengths and deficiencies of each approach.

Weaknesses of historic cost accounting

A balance sheet is a summary of the assets used by a business and of the various claims on those assets. Consequently, the economic relevance of balance sheet information is obviously enhanced if it is expressed in value, rather than cost, terms.

Under historic cost accounting, any asset is included on the balance sheet at the cost at which it was originally acquired and this is often vastly different from its value (however defined).

Similarly, if we consider the profit for a period to be the maximum amount that could be distributed to shareholders while maintaining their capital, then in an environment where prices are increasing, profits will generally be overstated. This is because the costs incurred in generating revenues (for example, the cost of goods sold and the depreciation of fixed assets) are stated at historic cost. If profits calculated on this basis are distributed, the purchasing power of shareholders' capital interest will be diminished.

In addition to this incorrect measurement of profits, historic cost accounts also suffer from the fact that certain other gains and losses are not recognised. Specifically, holding gains (those that arise from the fact that the value of the specific assets held for continuing use in the business is increasing) and monetary gains and losses (when general price levels are increasing, the value of monetary assets and liabilities will decline), which form an important element of the economic concept of income, are excluded from historic cost profits.

Finally, and of particular importance in investment analysis, trends of historic cost results can offer a misleading impression of the development of a business over time. As price levels increase, any particular transaction will contribute a correspondingly greater historic cost profit although its economic impact is actually unchanged.

Current value accounting

As the above discussion would indicate, the two principal questions to be answered in developing an alternative system of accounting are the appropriate form of asset valuation basis and what concept of capital maintenance should be used.

Asset valuation. Perhaps the conceptually most 'pure' approach to asset valuation is one in which any individual asset or liability is stated at an amount that reflects the discounted value of the future cash flows expected to be generated by the item.

However, the value of a business as a whole will in many cases depend on other factors in addition to the assets already in place. Hence a balance sheet prepared using such a valuation basis can only represent a valuation statement of the entire business if assets and liabilities are defined in such a way as to include various items (principally intangible in nature) that are excluded under all conventional accounting rules.

Because this type of approach would inevitably lead to a significant increase in the level of subjectivity involved in the preparation of financial statements, it seems unlikely that the balance sheet will ever be used as a genuine valuation statement. This does not, however, detract from the theoretical soundness of the discounted cash flow approach to valuing individual assets and liabilities, although in practice attempts to introduce systems of current value accounting have typically rejected this approach.

Alternatives to this value-based approach may be broadly split into current purchasing power (CPP) systems (where assets and liabilities are included on the balance sheet at amounts based on historic cost adjusted in some way to take account of general price level changes) and current cost accounting (CCA) systems.

Under the latter approach, assets are valued at what is generally described as either value to the business or deprival value. This is defined as the lower of net current replacement cost and recoverable amount, which in turn is defined as the higher of net realisable value and the amount recoverable from future use (i.e., economic value). The idea here is that to value an asset, the first step is to assess whether it is better to retain the asset in use or to dispose of it – this determines the recoverable amount. The asset is then included on the balance sheet at the amount of loss the business would suffer if it were deprived of the asset. For example, if replacement cost exceeds recoverable amount, it would not be worthwhile replacing the asset and the loss to the business would equate to recoverable amount.

Similarly, liabilities should be valued at what is termed relief value and which is defined analogously. However, previous attempts at current cost accounting have generally focussed much more on the asset side of the balance sheet and have typically ignored the appropriate valuation of liabilities.

In most circumstances, the value of an asset to a business will be found to be equal to its appropriately depreciated replacement cost and is therefore relatively straightforward to compute. (The principal exception is where technological change makes it difficult to identify the replacement cost of a particular asset. In this case, the most appropriate valuation is probably the current cost of an equivalent service potential). Additionally, it is less subjective than the value based system when considering assets, the cash flows generated by which are not readily identifiable.

For example, tangible fixed assets such as land and buildings and computer systems (although of obvious crucial importance to the future prospects of the business) do not in general independently generate any cash flows and so assigning a value to such assets is inherently problematic.

Further, there is little correlation between movements in general price levels and price changes of relevance to a specific business; consequently, a CCA system produces information that is intrinsically more relevant from an economic viewpoint than the output of a CPP system. Hence it is generally accepted that any meaningful approach to current value accounting will include a balance sheet based on values determined under some form of CCA system.

Capital maintenance. The second key element of a system of current value accounting is the capital maintenance concept. As discussed above, the basic idea is that financial statements should only record a profit after sufficient funds have been set aside to ensure that shareholder capital is maintained.

Essentially, there are two main variations of capital maintenance. First, there is what is usually termed operating capital maintenance (OCM) under which the amount set aside is sufficient to maintain the ability of the business to produce a given volume of goods and services. To achieve this, revenues are charged with the current cost (at the point of consumption) of the inputs that have been used to generate these revenues.

Many inputs, such as wages and distribution expenses, are booked at that cost even in a historic cost system. The only exceptions are items that are acquired and then used at some later date, principally stocks and fixed assets. Therefore, in order to arrive at the profit for a period under the OCM concept, the historic cost profit is adjusted so that cost of sales and depreciation are based on current, rather than historic, costs.

Two other adjustments are also made under OCM, namely the monetary working capital adjustment (MWCA) and the gearing adjustment. Both attempt to recognize that in a period where general price levels are increasing, a business benefits from holding monetary liabilities but suffers from holding monetary assets. The MWCA reflects the net gain/loss from holding such assets and liabilities as part of working capital and (since under CCA, monetary assets and liabilities are not revalued) takes the form of a transfer from the profit and loss account to what is called the current cost reserve.

This is also true of the gearing adjustment that essentially represents the element of the cost of sales, depreciation and monetary working capital adjustments accruing to the debtholders of the business rather than the shareholders.

In addition to the cost of sales adjustment, the MWCA and the gearing adjustment (the depreciation adjustment is set against the balance sheet value of the fixed assets) the current cost reserve also includes any unrealized gains arising on the restatement of asset values to current costs. By the very definition of OCM, such gains cannot be distributed and are not therefore a part of profit.

The second form of capital maintenance is called financial capital maintenance (FCM). Here, the amount set aside for capital maintenance is calculated so as to maintain the general purchasing power of shareholders' funds (which is essentially the historic cost amount uplifted by increases in the general price level index since the date at which the funds were committed).

Under FCM, any appreciation in asset value in excess of this capital maintenance adjustment is profit. The profit for a particular period is therefore calculated by adding unrealised holding gains to the historic cost profit (which already includes realised holding gains) and then deducting the capital maintenance adjustment that is transferred to a reserve account.

Whereas there are several strong arguments for the use of CCA, the case for OCM versus FCM is far less clear-cut and depends to a large extent on the nature of the particular business. For example, a business that consists of purchasing and reselling goods is particularly amenable to OCM, whereas for a financial services organization (which does not have an easily defined operating capital), FCM is more appropriate.

Unit of measurement. A final question that also needs to be answered is the unit of measurement – is the nominal unit of currency (under which no effect is taken of the variability in the purchasing power of the currency) or the unit of constant purchasing power (UCPP) (under which all amounts, including comparative information, are restated to remove the effects of such variability, usually in terms of the year end unit of currency) more appropriate?

Generally, it is acknowledged that the UCPP is more theoretically valid but the additional complexity that it introduces may be difficult to justify, except perhaps in the context of trend information. Hence, most proposals for current value accounting will be based on the nominal unit of currency.

Summary

Users (and uses) of accounting information have expanded, and the standard historic cost approach is not always appropriate. In an environment of rising prices, profits can be overstated and values distorted. Holding gains and monetary gains and losses, for example, are excluded from historic cost profits.

The two key questions in developing an alternative system are finding the appropriate basis for asset valuations and what concept of capital maintenance should be used. Any meaningful approach to current value accounting is likely to include a balance sheet based on values determined under some form of current cost accounting (CCA) system, rather than a current purchasing power (CPP) system. The two main variations of capital maintenance are OCM and FCM. The choice here is less clear cut and will depend on the nature of the business.

Another issue is the best unit of measurement. The unit of constant purchasing power is more theoretically valid, but for practical reasons most proposals for current value accounting will be based on the nominal unit of currency.

Suggested further reading

Whittington, G. (1993) *Inflation Accounting: An Introduction to the Debate*, Cambridge University Press.

Accounting Standards Committee (1986) *Accounting for the Effects of Changing Prices, A Handbook*.

What is a bank worth?

■ **The valuation of commercial banks is not a matter of looking at a few simple ratios.**
Paul Griffin outlines a model that combines conventional ratio analysis with an analysis of the discounted future free cash flows of the bank.

When analysts and investment bankers first broach the subject of the financial valuation of a commercial bank, one often hears just two questions: 'What's the bank's market-to-book ratio?' and 'What's the bank's price-to-earnings ratio?'

What is needed is an approach to bank financial valuation analysis that goes further than one or two simple ratios. Here we summarize a new approach for assessing bank shareholder value that combines conventional ratio analysis with an analysis of the discounted future free cash flows of the bank based on modern financial theory.

As a tool for analysts looking at a bank from the outside, the approach has several benefits. First, it recognises that many financial statement values are biassed, incomplete and subject to artificial rules in the form of generally accepted accounting principles. Loan loss provisions are a case in point for which there is wide latitude in the accounting measurement and recognition practices.

Second, because the approach relies on future cash flows it naturally incorporates much non-accounting data such as future lending and borrowing rates, company information about the policies and strategies of the bank, and known events after balance sheet date, for example, debt and asset transactions. Third, the approach incorporates off-balance sheet data, which appears to be on the increase, especially regarding the value of financial instruments and derivatives.

Cash flow valuation approach

The approach first requires an assessment of the future cash flows from the bank's value-creating operations. These would normally include cash used in lending, received from depositors, applied to trading and investing, and used in offering banking products and fee-based services such as investment banking, foreign exchange, credit cards, and information services.

We assume that these operating activities are financed by long-term debt, other interest-bearing liabilities, subordinated capital and stockholders' equity.

This enables us to define 'free cash flow' as the net cash available to the debt and equity holders after providing for operations and any net additional investment required to sustain the expected level of growth of operations (for example, increases in loans outstanding, increases in investment securities and trading assets, decreases in deposits).

For a given category of operations, investment or financial activity, an appropriate ratio of recent and past performance (for example, trend in loan or deposit growth, return on average loans outstanding) is often the best point for future performance and balance sheet values. Ratios and growth rates are used as inputs at all stages of model development.

The first stage is an analysis and forecast of a bank's net interest margin (interest revenues less interest expenses). This requires the development of year-by-year interest rates for all interest-bearing loans and deposits classified by major group (for example, consumer versus commercial and domestic versus foreign), where for each group the most recent interest rate based on financial statements is assumed to drift to a long-term rate reflecting both the policies of the bank and economic trends more broadly. These interest rate profiles are then applied to the forecasted levels of each of the loan and deposit categories based on expected growth rates to develop a cash flow forecast.

At the second stage, the cash flow approach requires an analysis of the bank's loan loss provisions, loan write-downs and transfers of loans to other asset accounts such as 'other real estate owned'. Loan reserves (a balance sheet allowance) and loan provisions (an expense) and the cash flow implications thereof are quantified using assumptions about the accounting relationships. These include assumptions about future amounts of performing and non-performing loans and financial policies regarding the determination of the loan loss allowance, loan write-offs, recoveries and other transactions.

Third, the cash flow approach requires an assessment of the bank's value-creating operations other than the lending and deposit aspects of the business.

The fourth stage entails the calculation of the bank's cost of capital. Conceptually, a bank's cost of capital is a single rate used to discount the forecasted free cash flows that collectively represent the individual after-tax returns required by all suppliers of capital to the business.

Cost of capital for a bank can be even more nettlesome in that bank financing comes from sources well beyond simple common equity and straight dollar-denominated debt.

The cash flow model also views the determination of a bank's cost of capital as part of an iterative process that acknowledges that bank valuation and the cost of capital are but two sides of the same coin.

Hence, after developing an initial estimate of the bank's weighted average cost of capital, based on fair market value weights wherever possible, as a reality check the market value of equity implied by the cost of capital estimates is compared with the traded stock market value of equity. Significant differences, while they may suggest a mispricing opportunity, can also signal a need to reassess some of the inputs, including another look at the calculation of the bank's cost of capital.

Application

As an example, take Citicorp, which was, until recently, the largest US bank. Citicorp has also been an interesting stock for investors; its stock price has swung from a low of $8.625 per share (December 1991) to recent highs in the $60s and $70s.

How does this estimate of shareholder value

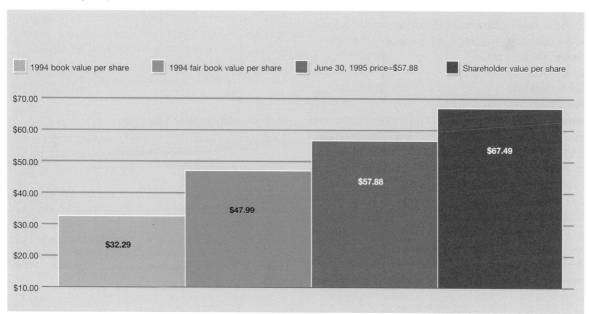

Figure 1: Citicorp. Book value per share vs. shareholder value per share

compare with the book value of Citicorp as of December 31, 1994? Figure 1 above compares the estimated shareholder value per share from the cash flow model with the December 31, 1994 accounting book value per share and adjusted book value per share, where the adjustments are based on the fair book value disclosures now required under US accounting standards.

The fair value disclosures increase the accounting book value by $15.70 ($47.99 less $32.29) per share. However, consistent with recent research on the relevance of fair value disclosure information, this increase accounts for substantially less than the difference between shareholder value and book value per share of $35.20 ($67.49 less $32.29).

We would normally check the responsibility of the estimate of shareholder value from the cash flow valuation model in a number of ways but most important is to compare it with the market price. Because Citicorp is a large, well researched company, shareholder value and stock market value should reflect common public information and thus shareholder value and share value should not be too divergent.

Based on the June 30, 1995 stock price, estimated shareholder value exceeded stock market value by $9.61 ($67.49 less $57.88) and by substantially more if an earlier 1995 share price is used. The model therefore would appear to be broadly consistent with the stock market's assessment of value.

Conclusion

We have outlined a cash flow shareholder valuation model for a commercial bank and applied that model to Citicorp using its 1994 and prior years' annual financial statements. The model relies solely on public information and thus simplifies the analysis well beyond what one would do if valuing the bank with complete access to management.

This approach has merit, however, because it systematically and comprehensively captures relevant financial and economic information from bank financial statements and elsewhere and converts this information into key value drivers to derive an estimate of shareholder value.

These key value drivers include current levels and long-term trends in asset and liability interest rates, estimated growth rates in specific areas of bank activity such as lending and investing, the expected policies regarding loan provisions and write-offs, and estimates of non interest revenues and expenses.

The cash flow approach also has the advantage that it is relatively free of the effects of accrual accounting, which can bias and possibly render incomplete extant valuation methods based on multiples of reported earnings or book value of shareholders' equity. It certainly goes a lot further than just the use of two accounting ratios.

Summary

Many financial statements are biassed or incomplete. The cash flow approach to valuation recognises this and reflects much non-accounting data such as future lending and borrowing rates, information about strategy, and post year end debt and asset transactions. It also incorporates off balance sheet data. The cash flow analysis involves calculating the bank's cost of capital and comparing the implied market value with the traded stock market value. The model can be shown in Citicorp's case, for example, to be broadly consistent with the stock market's assessment of value.

Suggested further reading

Barth, M. E., Beaver, W. H., and Landsman, W. R., Value-relevance of banks' fair value disclosures under SFAS 107, Research paper, Graduate School of Business, Stanford University, August 1995.

Copeland, T., Koller, T., and Murrin, J. (1994) *Valuation: Measuring and Managing the Value of Companies*, McKinsey and Company Inc., New York.

Eisen, K. S., and Griffin, P. A., 'Bank financial statements and shareholder value: a forecasted cash flow approach', *Journal of Financial Statement Analysis*, forthcoming, Winter 1996.

Harmonizing accounts worldwide

■ **How can a company make a profit when it reports in one country and a loss when it reports in another? The answer is national accounting standards.** Sir Bryan Carsberg **argues for a worldwide system of accounting.**

There can be few who have not thought how good it would be to have one accounting language throughout the world. At present, accounting is far from that objective. Accountants inhabit a kind of Tower of Babel where we not only speak different languages but also give different interpretations of the same events and transactions.

The desirability of uniform accounting has become compelling in the last 20 years or so, and more recently the pressures for uniformity have become irresistible.

One factor has been the increasing globalization of business. Economic trends are bringing more and more incentives to encourage genuinely international operation.

The successful completion of the Uruguay round of GATT, leading to the establishment of the World Trade Organization, will at least maintain the pace of change. Developments in the European Union are another important factor, as new countries join the union and as companies adapt their businesses to become European companies.

If businesses are multinational in scope, it is likely that they will wish and need to raise their capital in many different countries. They are assisted in this by increasing competition among the capital markets, each anxious to increase its share of world business.

The privatisation movement has also played a role. The transfer of utilities from state ownership to private ownership in many countries over the last ten years or so has created new demands for private-sector capital.

The motivations for companies seeking a uniform accounting system are strong. If companies have to prepare their accounts according to several different sets of rules, they incur a considerable cost penalty. Managers also want to achieve as much congruence as possible between internal reporting and external reporting: only then can the incentives for good performance internally be linked faithfully to the measure by which the company will be judged in the outside world.

However, the issue is fundamentally about the credibility of accounting. If a company reports dramatically different results for its operations, for a given year, because it has to publish results according to the rules in different countries, confidence in accounting will suffer.

The well-known case of the results of Daimler-Benz provides a dramatic example. In 1994, its reported profit under German rules was DM895m, whereas its profit under US accounting rules was DM1,052m. However, in 1983, accounting under German rules showed a profit of DM615m; but US accounting led to reporting a loss of DM1,839m.

Daimler-Benz does not provide the only example. The Norwegian company Norsk Hydro reported a profit of NKR167m under Norwegian rules in 1992 but a profit of NKR1,763m under US rules. News Corporation, an Australian company, reported a profit of A$502m under Australian rules against a profit of A$241m under US rules, also for 1992.

The case of News Corporation, showing a difference of over 100 per cent from US accounting to Australian accounting, is especially telling because people have tended to assume that differences of this kind arise only in contrasts between the rules of English-speaking countries and the rules of others.

National differences in accounting

When it comes to systems of accounting rules countries tend to be grouped into two categories.

On the one hand, there are countries where business finance is provided more by loans than by equity capital, where accounting rules are dominated by taxation considerations and where legal systems customarily incorporate codes with detailed rules for matters such as accounting.

The effect of the taxation systems can be particularly pervasive. Often, the taxation systems effectively offer tax breaks for business by allowing a generous measurement of expenses and modest measurements of revenues but use these measurements for general reporting purposes. Companies have strong incentives to take advantage of these taxation concessions. But the penalty is a lack of full transparency for investors. Major countries in this category include France, Germany and Japan.

The other group of countries is one in which equity sources of finance are more important, accounting measurements are not dominated by taxation considerations because tax breaks can be enjoyed independently of the way results are reported to shareholders and common law systems prevail.

These countries generally have some private-sector system for setting accounting standards, often within a general statutory framework. The role of equity finance is important because capital market pressures are then brought to bear most strongly to improve the quality of information available to investors: the absence of detailed codes, crystallised in the law, leaves flexibility to respond to pressures. The US, the UK, Australia and the Netherlands are examples of countries in this category.

No one nation has a set of accounting rules that appear to have such clear merits that they deserve adoption by the whole world. The US has the longest history of standards-setting; it has the largest standards-setting organization, which is characterized by high levels of professionalism. But even the rules of the US exhibit compromises between different interests of a kind that could reasonably have been decided differently.

A great deal more work is needed by accountants from different countries before we can reach the point of having a well-founded basis for uniformity. This work can take place, effectively, only at the international level.

The International Accounting Standard Committee

The board of the International Accounting Standard Committee (IASC) has existed for 22 years. Originally, the objective of the board was to produce 'basic standards'. This, no doubt, reflected the view that it would be easier to reach agreement on basic standards than on highly detailed standards. It also addressed the wish to have standards that would be readily usable in developing countries as well as improving the level of harmonization among the richer countries of the world. Early standards often allowed alternative treatments to accommodate the different approaches adopted by national standards-setters.

Today IASC continues to give importance to providing standards that will bring greater uniformity to accounting reports of multinational companies, particularly those with stock market quotations. But we continue also to wish to have our standards used in developing countries.

A number of countries, some relatively wealthy and others relatively poor, take international standards as the basis for local standards, issuing them locally with little or no amendment. However, the idea that we could restrict our standards to basic matters has long since been abandoned. As the world develops more and more complex contractual arrangements – including financial instruments – genuine uniformity in global accounting calls for more extensive and sophisticated standards.

IASC has also recognised the need to reduce alternatives wherever possible. Allowing alternatives can work against real harmonization. Their elimination can cause pain to businesses that have become accustomed to the flexibility provided by alternative treatments but the IASC has been able to make a good deal of progress in eliminating alternatives, particularly in its omnibus project on Improvements and Comparability, completed in 1993.

IASC has just issued its 32nd statement of International Accounting Standards. It also has a framework document that deals with the objectives of financial reporting and definitions of the qualities required in financial reporting and the elements of financial statements. Its framework document is similar to corresponding statements of the national standards-setters.

The Iosco Agreement

Acceptance of the international standards for financial reporting connected with stock exchange listings is another important way for IASC to make progress. Our standards are already accepted by several stock exchanges, the London Stock Exchange having led the way soon after the foundation of IASC.

However, the regulatory arrangements in some key countries still do not permit the use of international standards for stock exchange purposes – North America and Japan are prominent among these. IASC has therefore been holding discussions with the International Organization of Securities Commissions (Iosco) to explore the possibility that Iosco would endorse our standards and thereby give some additional impetus to movements towards acceptance in stock exchanges.

Some members of Iosco took the view that endorsement should be withheld until IASC had completed a core set of standards, a set that dealt comprehensively with the main financial reporting issues of the day.

In 1995 IASC decided to accept the need to complete a core set of standards before endorsement could be expected. Completion of this core set is a desirable objective for IASC in any event and acceptance of this objective enabled us to make a good agreement with Iosco in which we both undertook to co-operate in seeking to complete the core set of standards as effectively and quickly as possible and in which Iosco expressed warm support for our objectives.

IASC and Iosco published this agreement in July 1995. It focussed on a work program that would be completed in mid-1999 and which

covered all the areas that Iosco saw as needing attention for IASC to have completed its core set of standards.

Conclusion

The objective of one uniform system of accounting throughout the world is clear. No doubt it will take a good deal of time to get there. But what is the implication of this plan for the present structure of standards-setting ?

Will there be room for several national standards-setters in the world of the future or will the world have just one standards-setter and will that one be IASC? This is an understandable question although asking it is a bit like asking whether we shall have world government one day.

I do not think anyone at IASC is looking to a time when there will be only one standards-setter. The extent to which individual countries use our standards as national standards, or maintain their own procedures, is a matter for decision at the national level. As far as IASC is concerned, a co-operative relationship with national standards-setters provides the best prospect for progress.

We need the contribution of people who are well versed in local views about accounting and we need the help of the expertise of national standards-setters more generally. Setting accounting standards is strangely complex and controversial. Good solutions are likely to come from the maintenance of several standards-setting bodies that can contribute to the debate but which agree on the importance of international harmonization.

Summary

Accountants inhabit a kind of Tower of Babel – but the pressures for uniformity have become irresistible. They include the need for efficiency and the desirability of congruence between internal and external reporting, as well as a growing recognition that accounting's credibility is at stake.

There are two categories of country: one where finance is provided more by loan than equity, where detailed codes are laid down, and where taxation considerations are pervasive

(e.g. France, Germany and Japan); the other in which equity is more important and tax breaks are enjoyed independently of the way results are reported (e.g. the US and UK).

The International Accounting Standard Committee, which used to restrict its focus to basic matters, has long recognised that uniformity requires more extensive and sophisticated standards. A co-operative relationship with national standards-setters provides the best prospect for progress.

Bottom-line discord

■ **Andy Simmonds explores some of the causes of differences in national accounting systems and the obstacles to a truly transferable accounting regime.**

Free movement of capital, the evaluation of cross-border mergers and joint ventures, and international credit assessment all depend on information being prepared in one country and understood in others. One of the most frequent needs for cross-border information – non-US groups raising capital in the US – always ends with the same outcome: preparation of information under US rules.

Despite its claim to be the most comprehensive system of rules in the world, many people do not see US rules as the right basis of international consensus. The plain fact is that US accounting rules are more affected by the US tax system than is often admitted.

Within the European Union, the program of harmonization has not resulted in comparable bottom-line profits. In addition to differences caused by tax regimes, a company reports different profits in different countries due to accounting choices. Four inter-related factors lie behind these differences: legal systems; business structures and raising capital; tax systems; and the strength of the accounting profession.

Historical basis of differences

Legal systems can be traced back to historical events – often conquest or revolution. The UK common law system has its roots in the Norman conquest, with judicial decisions gradually laying down a foundation of rules based on precedent. The ability of the courts to evolve UK law through new decisions remains. One consequence is that rules set down by parliament tend to be a framework only. Similar systems are found in countries of the Commonwealth.

The legal systems of France and Germany, and consequently many of the countries they have ruled over the years, have their roots in Justinian's 6th Century Roman legal system. This tends towards more rules written in legal commercial codes, with the courts looking back to the original meaning of the law. In France, the system is overlaid with Napolean's centralization of information, frequent state intervention and detailed mandatory charts of accounts adopted from the Germans during times of occupation this century.

In Germany itself, the federal constitution is a model of detail and precision. The experience of economic collapse between the two world wars has left a legacy of super-prudence.

The models for business structures and capital raising are linked to the scale of historical international trade. It is not surprising that modern accounting traces its roots to renaissance Italy, where international trade (and the need to account for it) were booming.

As British and Dutch trade grew, capital was raised directly from investors. The result was the establishing of large joint-stock companies, the development of the Amsterdam and London stock exchanges as the largest in Europe and the need for managers to account to the owners. Naturally, the same ideas went with British and Dutch settlers to the new world.

By comparison, France and Germany exhibit a much greater number and variety of small businesses that look to large banks for their main finance. While UK banks generally limit their involvement to lending, German banks, such as Deutsche and Commerzbank, often invest through strategic shareholdings, with a consequent greater degree of involvement at a managerial level than their UK counterparts.

The stock exchanges of Paris, Frankfurt, Milan and Madrid have, to date, listed a far smaller number of companies than London. While London investors have a tendency to short-termism, German investors take a longer-term view. Where stock exchanges developed, there was a consequence both for tax collection and the accounting profession. It is a fact that in the UK not a single company set up under the 1844 Joint Stock Act remains in existence today.

The high failure rate of the first companies meant that a large proportion of Victorian accountants were involved in insolvency. As companies began to be taxed, such accounts as were produced were for absentee investors. Tax collectors therefore based their assessment on separate statements of taxable profit. This led to the development of separate disciplines in large accounting professions of audit and taxation.

Taken together with law containing only a basic framework of rules, it also encouraged the profession to develop and evolve detailed mandatory accounting rules based on commercial logic.

In contrast, countries where there is a more direct involvement of owners in management and a more detailed system of written law have developed annual accounts for the purpose of taxation and central statistics. Accounting professions have been much smaller, tax and audit are a single discipline and there are few mandatory accounting rules outside the law. Rules are more difficult to change and consequently change very little.

European attempts at harmonization

Against this historic and commercial diversity come those who would narrow the differences. The European Union attempted the feat through a program of legal harmonization starting in the mid-1970s to the late-1980s.

A common directive begins: 'Whereas annual accounts must give a true and fair view . . . whereas to this end a mandatory layout must be prescribed.' The directive, which was approved by the Commission in 1978 in nine official languages, gives directions to each member state to pass national laws. There are a series of problems with this process.

First, the directive is a melting pot of concepts. For example, 'true and fair view' was a UK idea which means different things to different countries. Second, options were negotiated to gain agreement that inevitably allow some countries to avoid change. Third, translation from the original German draft to nine official languages may not preserve original meanings. Fourth, progress through national parliaments is subject to national processes by the government of the day, which colors the law that emerges. And finally, once the law is enacted, it is read and interpreted in a national context in response to national custom and practice.

To its credit, the European experience can be counted a success in terms of formats of accounts and their availability to the public. When it comes to comparing bottom-line profit, the procedure has not worked at all.

A project conducted by Touche Ross in 1989 showed that when the same set of transactions was given to accountants in different countries, application of 'rules most likely to be used' produced very different profit numbers. A further exercise showed that, by flexing accounting rules within available boundaries, there was a range of possible profits. It was not

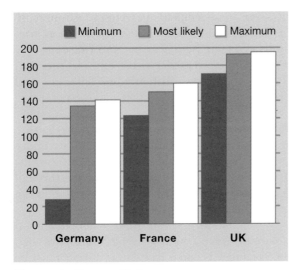

Figure 1: Net profit the same company

surprising that the UK could generate the highest profit and Germany the lowest. (*see* Figure 1).

While the conclusions of this study confirmed many suppositions, there have been some surprises in recent years. When Daimler-Benz agreed to reconcile its 1993 profit to US rules, it was naturally assumed that it would be higher than profit under German rules. In fact the reverse was true. Profit of DM615m under German rules became a loss of DM1,839m under US rules.

The major factor that had not been appreciated until then was the extent to which Daimler-Benz had squirreled away profit into hidden reserves in the good years and used it to mask losses in bad years.

Other causes of bottom-line differences are numerous: depreciation can be avoided (UK) or accelerated (Germany); goodwill can be charged to profit (most countries) or eliminated without touching profits (UK); profit on contracts can be spread over the contract (UK) or deferred until completion (Germany); and so the list goes on.

The lesson of the European experience is clear: legal harmonization does not make profits comparable.

Do we need to be all the same?

But before we put any great effort into trying to make them the same, we might ask whether they should be the same or even need to be the same. A group may well be happy with the status quo, arranging for management accounts that avoid differences, national statutory accounts that exploit the most advantageous tax strategy and consolidated accounts prepared in the most lenient environment (probably the UK).

The prime limiting factor for Europe is that companies in different countries respond primarily to economic and fiscal pressures that occur on a national basis and not a Europe-wide basis.

Investment analysts have developed tools that enable them to do their job. They are perhaps more concerned with comparisons of companies within a country than across boundaries. Cross-border mergers and joint ventures, although needing information, do not occur with sufficient regularity to drive harmonization.

Some users of information are very happy with the competitive advantage that comes both from accounting differences and financial culture. German banks are an example. Their presence on many of their customers' management boards gives access to management information without worrying about the limited information available to outsiders. This makes it more difficult for foreign banks to break into the German corporate lending market.

There is, however, one area where there is a need to produce comparable regular information. That is the raising of capital in other countries where the need to restate information becomes a costly and regular annoyance. It is this area where the International Accounting Standards Committee can achieve most. Unlike the European legal process, the force for change exists at a commercial level, and on an international basis.

Summary

Different legal systems, capital raising mechanisms, and tax systems are among the explanations for European Union failure to harmonize the reporting of profits. Attempts like EU directives to narrow the differences have been frustrated by concepts which mean different things to different people, the need to

give concessions to countries to secure agreement, loss of meaning in translation, and national interpretation in response to national custom and practice. The use of hidden reserves, different approaches to depreciation and goodwill, and the timing of profit on long-term contracts are among the causes of bottom line variations.

Regulating the regulators

■ **Regulation of accounting practice is obviously desirable. But have regulators gone too far in devising conceptual frameworks and lost sight of their role of codifying best practice?**

by Paul Bircher

There is a line of argument that says that accounting standards are not necessary. Usually espoused by a certain strain of academic (so-called agency theorists), the argument runs that there exist sufficient incentives in an unfettered reporting environment for reporting managements to give clear and comprehensive information to their stakeholders. These incentives include such advantages to reporting managements as better career opportunities and rewards if they are seen to be frank reporters.

There is thus no need for costly regulators to exist, sticking their noses in to the smoothly running machine of corporate governance and accountability. These theories, however, are usually seen as elaborate rationalizations to support a laissez-faire regulatory culture.

Outside academic circles they are rarely taken seriously and, in all advanced countries with an established pattern of financial reporting from managements to shareholders and capital markets, this reporting process is regulated by the use of accounting standards.

'Agency theory' critique

However, although regulators may regard standards as necessary and even desirable, there are some perspectives of the agency theorists (and other more traditional critics of accounting standards) that are worth trying to remember as we move into an era of increasingly complex regulations.

Perhaps the first point to remember is that the job of regulators is to regulate. The reward structures surrounding a regulatory body are such that it gets little notice or reward for regulating smoothly but a lot of criticism for failing to regulate or regulating inadequately. There is thus an inbuilt tendency for it to produce more rules.

All observers will have their own view as to what constitutes the optimum level of regulations. However, in the UK, even the Accounting Standards Board (ASB) itself describes the phase it is moving into now as a secondary phase, having dealt with perceived abuses in its first seven standards.

Second, there are problems arising from the regulators' own needs to establish legitimacy and respect. Thus, the standards that they issue have to be seen as good. And in this respect a legitimizing theoretical foundation for their pronouncements is helpful. The major regulatory organizations have thus all developed a conceptual framework.

The identikit conceptual framework almost universally adopted is a variant of a theory of economic income. A reporting enterprise will have a certain fund of net assets recorded in its balance sheet at the start of a period (after adjusting for funds input or withdrawn). As a result, regulators feel that if they are able to define assets and liabilities in such a way as to be able to quantify the opening and closing wealth, then the income for the period can be identified as a residual.

Elegant though this is (and securely rooted in an economic tradition) this net assets (i.e. balance sheet) approach does not work very well for accounting. Balance sheets do not in fact record a company's opening and closing wealth and arguably never can. Not all the things a company owns are recorded in them and they are not drawn up in terms of the worth of things to it and even if they were the total would certainly not add up to the value of the company.

Furthermore, some of the items in balance sheets are not really even proper assets or liabilities, as the conceptual framework would describe them. Rather they are the result of accountants' traditional attempts to get a statement of the income for the period by looking at transactions in the period, rather than by considering movements between opening and closing funds.

The traditional approach attempts to get the income for the period right by looking at performance in the period and matching revenues and costs, using the balance sheet as a residual statement. The approach dictated by the conceptual frameworks being adopted by regulators is very different.

An example of this is deferred tax. As an investment incentive the tax man may give 100 per cent allowances – i.e. all of the cost of the asset can be deducted in one year for tax. This may mean that when you look at the accounts of a profitable company it may currently pay no tax. As a result, it appears super-profitable.

But accountants say that this is misleading – although it may be paying no tax now, it will have to pay a disproportionately high amount in future years (as the tax inspector will not even allow a deduction for depreciation, having already allowed the full asset cost as a deduction).

So it is considered right to make a provision for the higher tax that will be visited on the company in the future and to set it aside out of the profits for this year, which otherwise would be misleadingly high. However, it cannot really be said that this deferred tax balance is a liability (as usually defined in conceptual frameworks) as the 'creditor' for deferred tax is not really money that the company actually owes anyone, yet.

This, then, is an example of an accounting practice that is good but which is not consistent with the idea of the balance sheet being a record of the company's 'true' assets and liabilities.

In the drive to arrive at conceptually pure balance sheets, such things must be expunged. As a consequence of their legitimizing framework, therefore, accounting regulators find themselves (if they take their framework seriously, which some do not) having to overturn accepted practices just because they do not fit with the framework.

The final point to make about regulations is that a growing mass of regulatory pronouncements changes reporting culture.

Reporting effectively becomes a branch of the law, and reporting managements approach their task as a compliance exercise. Although there is still a legal requirement for financial statements to present a true and fair view, this develops, in a regulated environment, into a requirement to comply with extant regulations.

Although the law does say that the requirement to report in true and fair terms overrides any specific requirements, in practice compliance with regulations becomes a substitute for the exercise of judgment. Regulations are a double-edged sword. It is possible to hide behind the strict letter of regulation.

Thus, both because of a tendency to over-regulate and for reasons founded on the regulators' own needs to establish legitimacy, reporting managements can find themselves complying with more and more regulations which themselves tend to become more and more outlandish.

The push to regulation

However, although some of these points might be accepted, even by regulators themselves, accounting regulations did not just spring up out of nowhere. The original impetus in the different jurisdictions where they developed was usually failure by reporting managements to provide information that shareholders were entitled to expect.

In the UK in one important case, that of the Royal Mail Steam Packet Company, the judge commented that directors were not to regard shareholders as sheep who might look up if they were not fed.

Although non-accountants often think that the preparation of a set of accounts is a mechanical exercise, this is not the case. There is a lot of estimation and choice inherent in the process, and accounts can be 'flexed' within quite wide parameters. Although there is a literature that asserts that users of accounts can see through any manipulations, this is simply not true in anything other than trivial cases.

There has thus always been a divide between those reporting companies that use this to their advantage and companies that give full disclosure of the basis of preparation of their accounts and which resist the temptation to choose accounting policies to their advantage.

In a culture where the dissemination of information about corporate performance is deemed important, there has thus been a desire for the treatments and disclosure of these companies to be followed by all. This is the origins of accounting regulation – the codification of best practice. Codification of best practice is one thing, however. Regulation by framework is quite another. The loss of its original raison d'être is making accounting regulation the poorer. Regulators should resist the temptation to develop and implement frameworks, despite the legitimizing attractions of such. It is a task that they have been drawn into by their own needs rather than the needs of the community which they regulate.

Although regulators now feel divorced from their origins, they should try to recapture them – reporting companies should not be perceived as the enemy upon whom a regime of reporting practices has to be foisted.

The regulator's job should not be to devise new accounting practices from scratch, following the dictates of a conceptual model, but that of requiring all companies to follow the accounting practices and disclosures developed, tried and tested by the best companies. It is these companies that should constitute the origins of best practice and not the regulator, except in the most unusual circumstances. Regulators should thus consider rediscovering their old model of codification of best practice. Unfortunately, I am not optimistic that this is any longer possible.

Summary

The argument that accounting standards are not necessary is seldom taken seriously. But some criticisms can be considered. There is, for example, an inbuilt tendency for regulators to produce more rules. The conceptual frameworks they develop to establish legitimacy sometimes require that good, accepted practices are overturned. Compliance with regulations can too easily become a substitute for the exercise of judgment. The regulator's job should not be to devise new accounting practices from scratch but to require the adoption of those developed, tried and tested by the best companies.

Asset valuation: case studies from the oil and gas industry

■ **Mimi Alciatore explains what an asset is and, using the oil and gas industry as an example, explores some of the issues and problems in valuing and reporting assets.**

Assets are economic resources. When a company prepares its financial statements, it must determine whether a resource is an asset to be included in the balance sheet. For this purpose, a common definition of an asset is future economic benefits obtained by a company as a result of past transactions.

For some items, such as cash, it is usually straightforward to determine whether the item is an asset and how much it should be valued at on the balance sheet. But sometimes this assessment is not so obvious. For example, a primary resource of a consulting company is its consultants. Are these assets to be recorded on the balance sheet? Similarly, many companies have highly recognized brand names relating to their products. Are these assets and how should they be valued? The oil and gas industry provides rich illustrations of the problems encountered in determining whether a given item – such as unsuccessful exploration costs – is an asset, as well as determining how to value certain assets, such as oil and gas reserves in the ground.

These asset valuation issues are crucial as exploration costs and oil and gas reserves often constitute the majority of oil companies' total assets. How these assets are accounted for can dramatically affect the company's financial profile. This article describes the way in which the oil and gas industry has addressed the two fundamental accounting issues of asset identification and valuation. Although the illustration is from the oil and gas industry, the same problems of asset valuation and reporting must be addressed in all industries.

Unsuccessful exploration wells: to include as an expense or not?

The first major oil and gas asset valuation issue is accounting for the costs of unsuccessful exploration. An unsuccessful well, or 'dry hole', is one lacking economically producible oil and gas reserves.

The accounting options are to include dry hole costs as an expense in the profit and loss (P&L) statement or to record the costs as assets on the balance sheet, thereby 'capitalizing the costs'. Two different forms of 'oil and gas accounting methods' – full cost (FC) and successful efforts (SE) – have evolved.

Under SE, only those exploration costs that directly result in the discovery of reserves – successful wells – are recorded as assets. All exploration costs for dry holes are treated as expenses when the well is determined to be dry. The capitalized costs for the successful wells are amortized (depreciated) as the reserves relating to those wells (or 'properties') are produced.

For example, if a company produced 10 per cent of its reserves this year, it would amortize 10 per cent of the property's costs on the balance sheet and record it as an amortization expense on the P&L. By contrast, under FC all exploration costs are capitalized. Thus, exploration costs relating to both dry and successful wells are recorded on the company's balance sheet as assets and amortized as the company's reserves are produced.

The use of two vastly different methods has provoked much debate. Proponents of SE argue that dry hole costs should not be capitalized because they do not provide future benefits and therefore do not meet the definition of an asset. This argument is supported by research findings that investors value the capitalized costs for oil and gas properties (per barrel of reserves) of FC companies less than those of SE companies. They also appear to value FC earnings less than SE earnings.

Supporters of FC maintain that all exploration costs, dry and successful, are necessary costs for finding oil and gas. That is, it is the nature of the business that one will inevitably drill some dry wells in attempting to find reserves. Accordingly, the costs of the company's entire exploration program should be capitalized and then amortized against the revenue from the production of the reserves found. Some even claim that future benefit will be obtained from dry wells because they provide scientific data.

Financial implications

Using FC allows a company to delay recording (dry hole) expenses until later periods, making its current-period income look stronger than if it had used SE. However, in later years, the company will have higher amortization expenses (compared to SE) because it will amortize both dry and successful well costs. On the balance sheet, a company will also have a greater asset base if it uses FC versus SE, if there are unamortized dry hole costs on the books.

Nevertheless, under both SE and FC, all exploration costs will eventually be charged to the P&L, via dry hole and/or amortization expenses. The timing of the expenses affecting earnings will differ between the two methods but the total expenses over time will be equal. Such timing differences between accounting methods are common – as with capitalizing versus expensing research and development costs, such as for pharmaceutical companies.

Currently, both FC and SE are accepted oil and gas accounting methods in the UK, the US and Canada. Consequently, investors in oil companies must understand the differences between these two methods. It would be naive directly to compare a SE with a FC company without realizing that the financial numbers could differ partly because of the accounting

methods used rather than true economic differences.

The accounting method used can also affect many of the traditional ratios used in financial analysis. This point applies to analysing companies in general, not just oil companies. Analysts must identify accounting differences when comparing companies and consider the effects on the companies' financial statements and ratios. Finally, we find that companies that choose FC tend to be different (for example, younger) to SE companies. This finding also generalizes to all industries. It is not unusual to find that management's accounting method choices may be related to attributes of the company.

Oil and gas reserves

Intuitively, reserves seem to be assets, but are they reported in the financial records, and if so, where? And how can we value such assets, which cannot be directly observed?

Historical cost methods, such as SE and FC, are inherently limited in their ability to provide relevant information about the exploration and production (E&P) activities of oil companies.

First, the discovery of oil and gas is the most significant E&P event. However, this value-adding event is not recognized in earnings at the time of discovery but rather later when the reserves are produced.

Second, reserves are generally the most important asset for oil and gas producers but neither method provides information on the balance sheet about their value. Under both methods, the only measure on the balance sheet is the cost of the oil and gas properties and the exploration and development (E&D) costs.

However, there is no necessary relationship between E&D costs and the value of the reserves found. A company might spend a relatively small amount of money and make a major discovery or invest a large amount and find nothing.

To address this deficiency, reserve-based disclosures are now required in the UK and the US. In both countries, companies with E&P activities must report the estimated quantities of their proved reserves of crude oil and natural gas at the beginning and end of each year. The reserve quantity information is not reported in the financial statements but is supplementary information in the annual report.

All the same, the reserve quantity disclosures represent a dramatic departure from the tradition of historical cost accounting. These measures are based on management's estimates of future activity rather than on events that have already occurred.

The supplemental reserve disclosure requirements in the US go beyond reserve quantities. Companies must also report an estimate of the value of their proved reserves, called the 'standardized measure' (SM). The SM is defined as the present value of net revenues expected from future production of reserves.

Critics argue that such reserve value estimates are too unreliable to be publicly disclosed. This is due to: (1) the subjective nature of estimating reserve quantities and (2) the assumptions used in calculating the SM.

For example, all companies must use an arbitrary 10 per cent rate to calculate the present value of future revenues, which ignores differences in risk across companies. Further, year-end oil and gas prices must be used to estimate future net revenues; this assumes an unlikely scenario of prices holding steady over the life of the reserves.

Nevertheless, we have found that analysts do use the SM data and that the SM is correlated with oil companies' share prices and with the prices at which oil companies are acquired.

There are other issues relating to the reserves. Companies must decide if the properties have decreased in value, or become 'impaired'. For example, this might occur if wells drilled on neighbouring properties have been dry. Further, one should account for environmental liabilities relating to the properties. In the oil industry, these include not only environmental clean-up obligations but also the liabilities for dismantling the wells. Companies differ in the level of environmental liabilities

they account for and whether they address these obligations on or off the balance sheet, if at all.

Beyond the financial statements

In analysing a company, an investor must not only have a solid understanding of accounting principles but must also be knowledgeable in the economics and specific accounting procedures of the company's industry.

Reporting must go beyond the financial numbers if it is to provide relevant information for assessing a company's performance. For example, it is now generally accepted that oil companies report their reserve quantities in their annual reports.

This usefulness of non-financial information is evident in other industries. In the cellular phone industry, the population size of the subscription area is a key indicator of company value, overpowering more traditional financial measures. Financial statements can provide a useful starting point for learning about a company's value and performance, but it is just the beginning.

Summary

How assets are accounted for dramatically affects a company's financial profile. Oil and gas companies can either use the full cost (FC) or successful efforts (SE) forms for dry holes; under FC all costs are capitalised, under SE only costs that directly result in the discovery of reserves are recorded as assets. Historical cost methods such as FC and SE are limited in their ability to provide relevant information about exploration and production activities – reserve based disclosures such as their 'standardized measure' are therefore required in the UK and the US.

Suggested further reading

Alciatore, M. (1990) 'The reliability and relevance of reserve value accounting data', Journal of Accounting Literature.

Johnston, D., *Oil Company Financial Analysis in Non-Technical Language*, Pennwell Books, Tulsa, Oklahoma.

Accounting for takeovers

■ **Takeovers represent probably the most complex of accounting problems – not least because of differing approaches in different countries. Chris Higson offers some guidance.**

In terms of its ability to wreak accounting havoc, no corporate event can compare with the takeover of one company by another. Since takeovers are so prevalent and since the values involved are often very large, we need to understand the accounting treatment of takeovers if we are going to interpret financial reports. But the case of takeover accounting also demonstrates very clearly the difficulties in designing coherent and workable accounting rules.

The sources of difficulty should already be familiar to readers of the earlier articles on accounting in this module. Within one jurisdiction companies may account for takeovers in radically different ways; indeed acquisitive companies making several takeovers during the year have been known to use different methods of accounting within the same financial report. In addition there are significant differences in takeover accounting rules internationally.

Merger or acquisition?

Thus far we have talked generally about 'takeovers' and have avoided using the words 'merger' and 'acquisition'. While in everyday usage we tend to use these words loosely and interchangeably, in accounting they have specific applications and very different implications.

The question is what the new balance sheet and profit and loss account will look like after the takeover and in subsequent years. Accounting rules assume, unless there is evidence to the contrary, that the takeover is an *acquisition*. That is, though the transaction may have been friendly and agreed, rather than hostile and disputed, Company A clearly acquired Company B. Several things follow.

First, accounting rules see an acquisition as equivalent to the purchase of a bundle of assets. A has to bring B's assets into its balance sheet, not at the values at which they were carried in B's balance sheet, but at so-called 'fair values', or the prices A would have had to pay for them on the open market at the takeover date.

Second, A has to record the market value of any shares it issues as part of the consideration for B. If the consideration is greater than the fair value of the identifiable assets acquired, as is often the case, then it records the difference as the asset 'goodwill'.

However, sometimes it is unreasonable to talk in terms of a dominant party and of one company acquiring the other. So long as the takeover passes certain tests (these tests differ in their rigor from one country to another) then it can be accounted for as a *merger*.

In this case the assets of the two companies are added together at their existing book values – there is no 'acquired' company so it is not the case that one company's assets have to be revalued. Any shares that were issued are shown at their nominal, 'par value', and no goodwill is recognized.

There is another important difference between acquisition and merger accounting. After an acquisition the profit and loss account will only show the profit from the acquired company since it was acquired, whereas in a merger the full year's profit of both companies will be included. Suppose A has a profit of £10m in the year to 31 December 1995 and B has a profit of £6m and the two companies combine on July 1 to form AB. If A acquires B the reported profit for the year will be £13m; if it was a merger the reported profit would be £16m.

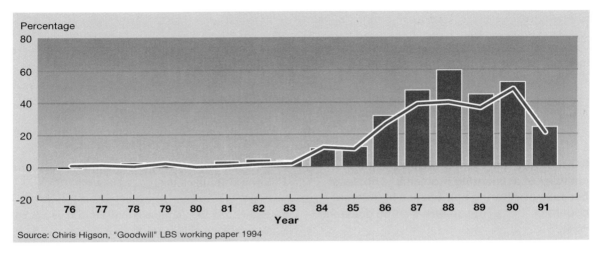

Percentage

Source: Chiris Higson, "Goodwill" LBS working paper 1994

Figure 1: Ratio of Goodwill to Bidder Net Worth

SmithKline Beecham, formed from the merger of the two drug companies, SmithKline Beckman of the US, and the UK's Beecham, provides a striking example of the different effects of merger and acquisition accounting.

The new group based its headquarters in Brentford in the UK and produced its first accounts in December 1989 under UK accounting rules. The transaction was accounted as a merger. This truly was a merger – the companies were of similar size, the group retained listings in both the UK and the US and management went to enormous lengths to ensure equality of treatment of the two workforces, with parity extending right up to the composition of the main board.

But because of the US listing, the SmithKline Beecham must also report under US accounting rules. Under the much more demanding US tests for merger the transaction was an acquisition of SmithKline by Beecham and so was 'purchase accounted' rather than 'pooled' in US parlance.

To see the effect of the accounting we will attempt to calculate return on equity using 1989 year-end figures. Return on equity is a much-used measure of profitability from the ordinary shareholders' perspective, which we will measure as the profit attributable to ordinary share-holders divided by the 'year-end book' or balance sheet measure of the shareholders' equity investment in the company. The relevant data

from the two versions of SmithKline Beecham's accounts are:

UK (MERGER)	US (ACQUISITION)

Profit attributable to ordinary shareholders
£130m.............................. £87m
Shareholders equity
–£297m........................... £3,545m

Whereas under acquisition accounting the return is a modest 2.5 per cent, under merger accounting it appears to be infinite, or rather it cannot sensibly be calculated since the equity investment in the business seems to be negative.

Clearly there are other sources of difference between the US and UK results, but in the SmithKline Beecham case the differences are predominantly caused by a shift from merger accounting to acquisition accounting. Book equity is almost £4bn higher in the US because the US balance sheet records nearly £4bn of goodwill and intangibles. Though there are other compensating items, the US profit figure is correspondingly reduced by £88m for having to amortize the goodwill and intangibles and by a further £144m, which was earned by SmithKline Beecham before the date of the merger and must therefore be excluded in acquisition accounting. The reader should perhaps be reminded that this is the identical company recorded under two different systems.

The UK has recently moved closer to US

practice in a new accounting standard, FRS6, which severely limits the use of merger accounting. However, there remain significant differences in practice internationally.

Goodwill

A second area of difficulty, which generates great controversy, is the treatment of goodwill in acquisition accounting. Goodwill is the difference between the price you pay for a company and the identifiable assets you receive.

As the SmithKline Beecham case shows, goodwill can be a very large number indeed. In most countries goodwill is carried in the balance sheet as a fixed asset and amortized against income over some period. However, this period varies widely across countries so that the same takeover will have a very different effect on earnings in different countries. For example in the US goodwill can be amortized over a maximum of 40 years, but in Belgium only 5 years. The International Accounting Standard recommends 5 years but will accept 20.

But UK companies have had an alternative; they can immediately net-off the goodwill against equity in the balance sheet and so avoid diluting reported earnings with goodwill amortization. Furthermore by taking 'merger relief', which became available under the 1981 Companies Act, acquirers were able to net goodwill against the share premium arising on the acquisition, giving a result which, save for the restatement of acquired assets at fair values, is substantially the same as merger accounting. UK companies clearly enjoy the 'netting' option since they have almost invariably chosen it in recent years.

However, the goodwill element in takeovers exploded in the mid-1980s. Figure 1 opposite plots the average goodwill in UK takeovers as a percentage of the acquirers' book equity. Whereas goodwill was negligible in the 1970s and early-1980s, and was negative in many takeovers, by 1987 it averaged over 60 per cent of the equity of the acquirer.

The rapid growth of the goodwill element in takeovers and the widespread netting of goodwill started to cause problems. Acquisitive UK companies were significantly depleting their book equity and some were seeking to restore it by capitalizing intangible assets, most controversially, brands. The growth in goodwill was not unique to the UK and at much the same time acquisitive US companies, which have to carry and amortize their goodwill, were complaining about earnings dilution and arguing that accounting rules gave UK acquirers an unfair advantage.

The simple and overwhelming reason for the growth in goodwill was the rise in stock market prices around the world relative to the book value of company assets.

In 1978 the average large UK company had a stock market value that was around £74 for each £100 of book equity. The acquirer who paid a (typical) 30 per cent premium to acquire control of a company was thus buying its assets at around book value. By 1988 the same company was trading at £168, so the acquirer would pay perhaps £210 for a company with book equity of £100. The shift in the market-to-book ratio was even more marked for small companies. Accounting has proved to be ill-equipped to deal with the large amounts of goodwill this generated.

In many countries, including the UK, goodwill amortization is not tax deductible. In this case, it is hard to see why it should really matter whether goodwill is carried and amortized or netted off against equity. The accounting is usually easy for analysts to unravel. But goodwill raises strong passions. Companies dislike diluting earnings with goodwill amortization because they believe markets value them on the basis of earnings in a rather uncritical way, but they also dislike the cumulative effects of netting goodwill off against equity.

In response the UK Accounting Standards Board (ASB) has brought forward a proposal that seems to offer the best of both worlds, whereby purchased goodwill is carried in the balance sheet unamortized so long as it passes an annual impairment test. It will be interesting to see how competitor nations react to this accounting innovation if it is implemented.

Summary

The words merger and acquisition have different implications in accounting. Unless there is contrary evidence the assumption is that a takeover is an acquisition – assets are then brought into the acquirer's balance sheet at 'fair values'. With a merger, assets of the two companies are added together at their existing book values. Other differences affect the profit and loss account.

In most countries goodwill is carried as a fixed asset in the balance sheet and amortized against income. UK companies, however, have been able to net it off against equity, so avoiding a dilution in reported earnings.

Finance

Contents

Tasks of the finance function 62
Harold Rose, London Business School
What exactly is the role of the financial function within a company?

The role of financial markets 64
Narayan Naik, London Business School
Banks, stock markets and derivatives markets play a vital economic and social role.

Assessing the rate of return 66
Elroy Dimson, London Business School
How companies can assess what return they require on capital investments.

Market efficiency 70
Ernst Maug, London Business School
Playing the market via financial transactions is no substitute for day-to-day operations as a way to add value.

Project approval: the key criteria 72
Adam Farkas, Budapest University of Economic Sciences visiting London Business School
The financial tools available to assess whether or not a company should undertake a planned project.

The capital asset pricing model 76
Elroy Dimson, London Business School
Investment requires a higher return for greater risk. But how do we know what the risk is? A simple model provides guidance.

Importance of capital structure 80
Michel Habib, London Business School
Capital structure – the balance between equity and debt financing – has major implications, as many real-life examples show.

The thinking behind dividends 82
Francesca Cornelli, London Business School
Dividend policy is a crucial area for management but the theory behind setting dividends is complex and controversial.

The changing world of finance 84
Harold Rose, London Business School
The main changes that have happened, are happening and will happen in the world of finance – and the factors driving them.

Introduction to options 87
Kjell Nyborg, London Business School
Options are superficially complex but fundamentally simple financial instruments that offer companies substantial advantages.

An introduction to futures markets: insurance, liquidity, immediacy 95
Mark Britten-Jones, London Business School
Futures markets have as much to do with the professional investment market as with the physical assets and commodities that underlie futures trading.

Living life on the hedge 98
Debra Perry, London Business School
Hedging is a way of covering a foreign exchange risk. But there are many complex considerations to take note of.

Warrants and convertibles 101
Anthony Neuberger, London Business School
Warrants and convertibles are a half-way house between debt and equity. But their true nature can be easily misrepresented and misunderstood.

The market for corporate control 103
Harold Rose, London Business School
Acquisitions make headlines but do they also make economic sense?

Buddy, can you swap a dime? 106
Ian Cooper, London Business School
Swaps are one of the more exotic financial instruments around yet in essence they are very simple.

The merits of project finance 109
Harold Rose, London Business School
Large-scale projects are sometimes not financed directly by the company or companies involved. Instead they turn to project finance, which is linked specifically to the risks and returns of a single project not to the performance of the company as a whole.

Are bosses worth the money? 111
Michael Brennan, London Business School
On the whole, seemingly excessive salaries have some justification but transparency and action on poor executive performance are necessary adjuncts.

Raising equity capital 116
Ivo Welch and Anthony Neuberger, UCLA and London Business School
Selling shares seems an excellent way for a company to raise money. But there can be considerable downsides for both investors and companies.

Several ways to go broke 119
Julian Franks, London Business School
The insolvency procedures in the US and the UK compared and contrasted.

Contributors

Harold Rose is Esmée Fairbairn Emeritus Professor of Finance at London Business School. He was previously first Director of LBS' Institute of Finance and was Group Economic Adviser at Barclays Bank.

Narayan Naik is Assistant Professor of Finance and Citibank Research Fellow at London Business School. His current areas of research interest include market microstructure, fund managers' contracts and herding in asset allocation.

Elroy Dimson is Professor of Finance and Prudential Research Fellow in Investment at London Business School. With Paul Marsh, he is editor of London Business School's Risk Measurement Service.

Dr Ernst Maug is Assistant Professor at Fuqua School of Business, Duke University. He previously taught at the London Business School and at the London School of Economics. His main research interests are corporate governance, managerial compensation contracts and institutional questions in financial markets.

Adam Farkas is Assistant Professor of Finance at Budapest University of Economic Sciences and is currently visiting London Business School. His current main research interest is option pricing in the valuation of real assets.

Michel Habib is Assistant Professor of Finance at London Business School. His fields of interest are corporate finance and financial intermediation.

Francesca Cornelli is an Assistant Professor of Finance at London Business School. Her research interests are contract theory, corporate finance and industrial organization.

Dr Kjell Nyborg is Assistant Professor of Finance at London Business School.

Mark Britten-Jones is Assistant Professor of Finance at London Business School. His research interests include derivatives, state prices and general equilibrium theory, and vector times series economics.

Debra Perry is Visiting Assistant Professor of Finance at London Business School. Previously, she has worked for British Petroleum where she was responsible for managing foreign exchange exposure.

Anthony Neuberger is Assistant Professor of Finance and Accounting at London Business School and S. G. Warburg Group Research Fellow, Institute of Finance and Accounting. His research interests include the structure of securities markets, option theory and corporate finance.

Ian Cooper is BZW Professor of Finance at London Business School. He researches, teaches and consults on derivative products, international and corporate finance.

Michael Brennan holds a joint position as Professor of Finance at London Business School and at the Anderson School of Management, UCLA, in the US. He is a past President of the American Finance Association and editor of the *Journal of Finance* and the *Review of Financial Studies* and has written extensively in the field of corporate finance.

Ivo Welch is Assistant Professor of Finance at UCLA in the US and EC post-doctoral Fellow at London Business School. His research interests include IPOs, corporate finance and the economics of conformity.

Julian Franks is Professor of Finance at London Business School. His research interests include takeovers, insolvency and corporate governance.

Introduction

Finance, it can be argued, is the very centre of business and therefore of management. It is certainly an area of which any general manager must have a very secure grasp. For that reason it is given considerable coverage in *Mastering Management*.

There are 19 separate articles within the Finance module and they cover: the role of the finance function within a company, financial markets and investment decisions, risk and return, market efficiency, project approval criteria, capital asset pricing, capital structure, dividend policy, changes in financial approaches, options, futures, hedging, warrants and convertibles, acquisitions, swaps, project finance, executive remuneration, equity finance and insolvency.

Related topics are covered in the International Financial Markets module (page 383).

Tasks of the finance function

■ **Finance is generally reckoned to be at the center of all managerial operations. But what exactly is the role of the financial function within a company?**

by Harold Rose

One way of depicting the management of a company is to divide its activities into three types: operations; strategy; and risk management.

These are not mutually exclusive, and indeed they overlap. But, in general, 'operations' refers to the daily management, in detail, of inputs and output; 'strategy' is the longer-term shaping of the company as a whole; and 'risk management' is a wide concept that embraces questions of operating risk, such as whether it is advantageous to use product range diversification to reduce risk or to change the structure of costs (heavy fixed costs cause profits to be volatile if sales revenue is unstable). It also covers financial risk, which is concerned with managing the risks arising from the choice of finance (debt financing can be like a fixed cost) and any risk arising from the foreign currency operations of the company.

The finance function of a company is involved in all three areas: in strategy via the setting of financial criteria for capital investment decisions; in risk management; and in operations by ensuring that sufficient funds, whether in the form of cash balances or lines of credit, are available to meet net cash deficits.

Using this framework, we can identify the three main finance functions of the company and their components (apart from the accounting and financial control functions) as follows:

Capital budgeting. Capital investment criteria. Financial valuation of capital projects. Cash flow budgeting.

Choice of capital structure. Debt:equity ratio. Choice of debt types. Dividend policy.

Liquidity management. Liquid asset/liability management. Cash flow monitoring.

At the risk of over-simplification, we can think of these three areas as following a logical order.

Decisions about capital investment, together with projections of cash flows arising from operations, determine the net amount of finance required over a planning period to meet planned cash deficits and to ensure a margin of flexibility.

This, in turn, gives rise to a need for decisions concerning the form financing should take, and to decisions about the dividend level. However, financing and dividend decisions have two dimensions. First, a company needs to decide its 'normal' ratio of debt to equity and its 'normal' ratio of dividend to equity earnings (its 'normal' dividend payout ratio). Secondly, it has to decide what departures to make from these 'normal' levels in a particular year.

Given its investment and financing policy, the job of liquidity management (the 'treasury' function) is to invest surplus cash balances to earn a satisfactory rate of return, subject to envisaged cash flow requirements, and to negotiate any short-term borrowing required. The liquidity management or treasury function also embraces policy decisions concerning the possible hedging of risks arising from unexpected movements in exchange rates, interest rates or commodity prices.

In all three areas of policy, the implications for corporate taxation may be important. It is part of the finance function to ensure that tax minimizing possibilities are given their due weight in the company's investment and financing decisions. The matter has to be put in this measured way because tax minimization may be available only at the expense of some disadvantage (for example, debt interest ranks as an expense for corporation tax purposes but heavy debt financing can endanger solvency).

Investment criteria and debt financing.

Perhaps the two crucial areas of financial policy in most companies are the setting of capital investment criteria in financial terms and the level of debt financing. As it is the special responsibility of the finance function to safeguard the interests of shareholders, the former will usually incorporate some minimum required rate of return, which logically should take into account both the prevailing level of interest rates and the riskiness of the 'project' concerned.

Other criteria may also be used, such as the 'payback period' which, however, gives little indication of profitability. In some industries, investment decisions may be taken on the basis of some operating criterion, such as the expected occupancy rate in hotels or sales or profit contribution per unit of area in the case of retail stores, as proxies for profitability.

The central tasks of the finance function are to safeguard the financial flexibility of the company and to ensure that capital project criteria are aimed at maximizing the wealth of the company's shareholders. This implies that project criteria should take into account the rate of return which shareholders could obtain on investments of a similar degree of risk outside the company.

Three issues nevertheless arise. The first concerns the possible contention that 'financial' criteria should be subordinated to 'strategic' aims. This is a false conflict. It is true that the financial consequences of many important business decisions, such as those concerning innovation, cannot be quantified. But a financial assessment may be helpful in identifying key elements in the assessment of 'strategic' projects, in identifying the minimum level of sales required to justify the venture concerned and in raising the question of alternatives.

For a 'strategic' project to benefit shareholders there must be at least the implicit assumption that, in its effect on the company, the rate of return will be at least commensurate with the risk being imposed on shareholders. It is perhaps up to the finance director, above all, to ask the awkward financial questions that are sometimes needed to keep the self-interested ambitions of other senior managers in check.

The second and related issue concerns the extent to which any financial criterion should dominate the general operations of the company. There is no single answer to this; for there are both successful companies where financial criteria are a close influence on the thinking of senior management and others where they appear to play a relatively remote part. Even in companies where financial criteria appear to play a definitely subordinate role, it remains the case that unless shareholders obtain an adequate rate of return their funds are being misused and that the consequent damage to the company's share price will ultimately provoke some reaction, in the form of a take-over bid, for example.

The final issue is whether the claims of shareholders, which it has been suggested are the special responsibility of the finance function, should take priority over other claimants on the resources of the company, such as those of customers, employees, suppliers and the local environment. Once again, there need be no conflict between these, to the extent that good relations with these claimants, by giving the company a good reputation, enhance the company's profitability in the long-run.

But some conflicts of interest may involve moral issues. It is the view of this writer that the responsibility of the finance function to seek to maximize the wealth of shareholders does not mean that managers are required to act in a manner which absolves them from the considerations of morality and simple decency which they would readily acknowledge in other walks of life.

Nevertheless, it has to be admitted that the possible conflicts of interest facing the finance function, which arise because of the many-sided nature of the responsibilities of managers in general in all types of organization, do not always have a ready solution.

Summary

Besides accounting, the main finance functions in a company are capital budgeting, choosing the most appropriate capital structure and managing liquidity. In all three areas minimizing corporate tax is likely to be an important consideration.

The financial consequences of some business decisions, such as innovation, cannot always be quantified but 'strategic' projects can still be usefully subjected to a financial assessment.

Suggested further reading

Brealey, Richard A. and Myers, Stewart C. (1996) *Principles of Corporate Finance*, McGraw-Hill.

Marsh, Paul R. and Wensley, Robin 'Must finance and strategy clash?', September/October 1989 *Harvard Business Review*.

The role of financial markets

■ **Financial markets play a vital economic and social role that has a profound influence on the quality of investment decisions and the well-being of the general economy, says** Narayan Naik

Historically, financial markets have consisted of two types of institution: stock markets (equity, bonds and other securities); and banks (or similar financial intermediaries). More recently, futures and options exchanges have grown and joined stock markets and banks as a third type of financial institution.

Financial markets play many important economic roles. They enable individuals to achieve a better balance between current and future consumption. For example, entrepreneurs with good investment projects may be in need of financing while individuals wanting to provide for their retirement may be looking for avenues in which to invest their savings. Financial markets bring the borrowers in contact with the lenders and in the process make both better off.

Financial markets also allow efficient risk sharing among investors. As we will see later, risks are of two types: diversifiable and non-diversifiable. Diversifiable risk can be eliminated by holding assets the returns of which are not perfectly correlated. Financial markets not only help investors in diversifying some of the risk, but also offer a wide array of financial instruments with very different risk-return relationships. This enables individuals to choose the risk profile of their investments according to their risk-tolerance levels. Investors who are extremely risk averse, for example, may choose to invest a large fraction of their wealth in risk-free securities (such as gilts), whereas more risk-tolerant investors may elect to invest in speculative stocks.

Furthermore, the presence of derivatives markets means that individuals can choose which non-diversifiable risks they want to bear and which they want to lay off via the futures or options markets. A non-diversifiable risk, by definition, cannot be eliminated through diversification. However, the presence of futures and options markets allows the transfer of risk from more risk-averse to less risk-averse individuals and from those who cannot manage risk to those who can. Thus, financial markets enable efficient risk sharing among investors.

Separating ownership and management

Financial markets also make possible the separation of ownership and management that is a practical necessity for running large organizations. Many corporations have hundreds of thousands of shareholders with very different tastes, wealth, risk tolerances and personal investment opportunities. Yet, as Irving Fisher showed in 1930, they can all agree on one thing – they should continue to invest in real assets as long as the marginal return on the investment equals the rate of return on similar investments in capital markets.

Since shareholders are unanimous about the investment criterion, they can delegate the operations of an enterprise to a professional management team. Managers do not need to know anything about the preferences of their shareholders; neither do they need to consult their own tastes. Managers need to follow only one objective: to invest in projects that yield a higher return compared with that offered by equivalent investments in capital markets (the opportunity cost of capital). Put another way, the manager's objective becomes that of investing in projects that in present value terms cost less than the benefits they bring in, i.e. investing in positive net present value projects. This objective maximizes the market value of each stock-holder's stake in the concern and therefore turns out to be in the best interest of all the share-holders.

The separation of ownership and management is a fundamental condition for the successful operation of a capitalist economy. It means that individuals can decide how much to consume now and how much to invest for the future. Once they have decided how much to invest, by using the wide array of financial instruments available in capital markets, they can choose the time pattern of consumption plan and the risk characteristic of the consumption plans that suit them.

The managers of large private corporations, on the other hand, can borrow money from capital markets to buy real assets. The real assets may be tangible, such as machinery, factories and offices, or they may be intangible, such as technical expertise, trademarks and patents. When the managers maximize net present value they make everyone better off. Thus, well functioning financial markets ensure that individual maximization leads to a socially optimal outcome.

Efficient allocation of resources

Financial markets lead to the efficient allocation of resources via information conveyed through market prices. Consider the case of a farmer who has land that can be used to grow wheat, corn or oatmeal. He is reasonably certain about how much it will cost him to grow any of these crops and how much output his land will yield. There is, though, considerable uncertainty about the price his crop will fetch after harvesting. This price uncertainty depends not only on factors such as weather conditions but also on the levels of demand and supply that may prevail in future.

However, the farmer can look at the futures prices of wheat, corn and oatmeal and, knowing his cost structure, decide which is the most profitable crop for him. He can also use the futures markets to assure a guaranteed price for the crop and then go ahead with planting the crop. In this way financial markets ensure that the land is put to its most efficient use.

The stock market aggregates diverse opinions of market participants and conveys how much the equity of a company is worth under current management. Suppose the shares of Company A are trading at a given price and suppose that another organization, Company B, can use the assets of Company A more efficiently. Then Company B may decide to acquire Company A. If it does so, the assets of Company A will be put to more efficient and productive use under the management of Company B.

If there were no stock market, then it might be difficult for Company B to notice that the assets of Company A were not being put to best use. Even if Company B noticed this, it might not be possible to acquire Company A and thereby transfer the assets. Thus, the presence of a well functioning stock market leads to the more efficient utilization of assets and enables poor management to be disciplined through a market for corporate control.

When a company announces a plan of future actions, such as starting a new project or the takeover of another company, the stock price may respond in a positive or a negative way. The management of the company can observe the stock price reaction and learn what the market participants collectively think of its proposed plan. If the stock price reaction is negative, the management may wish to re-examine its own calculations and reconsider its decision. Thus, the stock market helps management to get a second opinion about its investment decisions. Moreover, since stock prices reflect the value of the assets under current management, the market provides a measure of how well management is doing its job and therefore helps the process of evaluating managerial performance.

Banks play important economic roles as well. In addition to bringing borrowers and lenders together, banks also act as monitors of companies. If finance is provided entirely through the diverse ownership of shareholders, no one alone has an incentive to spend resources to monitor the management and ensure that it is acting in the best interest of those shareholders.

Monitoring is best carried out by only one party since duplication may not result in improved monitoring and would waste resources. But shareholders cannot combine to hire somebody to monitor because of a free rider problem; each would want others to bear the costs of monitoring the monitor. When a bank lends to a corporation, it has an incentive to be the single monitor.

To summarize, well functioning financial markets bring borrowers and lenders together, improve risk sharing, lead to the efficient allocation of resources, provide information to market participants, allow separation of ownership and management and help the monitoring of management. Together they improve the quality of investment decisions and the welfare of all market participants.

Summary

Financial markets serve a number of useful purposes. These include bringing borrowers and lenders together; sharing risk between investors; separating ownership and management; achieving a better balance for individuals between current and future consumption; efficiently allocating resources, effectively utilizing assets, and helping the process of evaluating managerial performance through the signals contained in market prices.

Suggested further reading

Franklin, Allen 'Stock markets and resource allocation', C. Mayer and X. Vives (eds) *Financial Intermediation in the Construction of Europe*, CEPR 1992.

Martin, Hellwig 'Banking, financial intermediation and corporate finance', A. Giovannini and C. Mayer (eds) in *European Financial Integration,* Cambridge University Press, 1990.

Assessing the rate of return

■ **The returns expected from risk-free and risky investments are obviously not the same. How can companies assess what return they require on capital investments? asks Elroy Dimson**

An investment that is risk-free offers a known pay-off over some period in the future. For example, it may offer £1,000 payable in the year 2010.

The best known risk-free investments are government bonds. The government can be expected to honour its promises, because it can always print sufficient money to meet its obligations (though there is always a risk of inflation, of course). In some countries, such as the UK (and, in the near future, the US), the government also issues index-linked bonds, which provide an income and capital repayment uplifted in line with inflation.

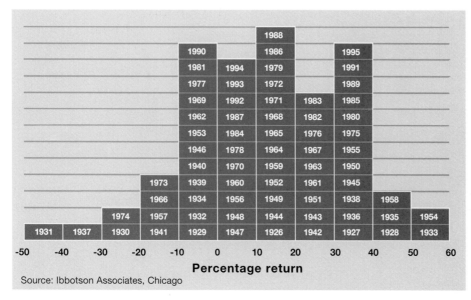

Figure 1: Histogram of returns on US equities 1926-1995

The chart shows years arranged in a histogram across the Percentage return axis (-50 to 60).

| -50 | -40 | -30 | -20 | -10 | 0 | 10 | 20 | 30 | 40 | 50 | 60 |

Source: Ibbotson Associates, Chicago

The promised return, or redemption yield, on government bonds is published daily in the *Financial Times*. These bonds provide a guaranteed return that is known today.

For example, at the time of writing one can earn a gross yield to redemption on conventional UK government bonds with a 5 to 15-year maturity of a little under 8 per cent. These gross yields equate to a yield after personal tax of some 6 per cent. These nominal yields vary over time and across currencies and issuers.

Similarly, index-linked government bonds provide a gross redemption yield of around 3.6 per cent for maturities running as far into the future as the year 2030. Net of personal income tax, their yield is around 3 per cent. This yield is measured in real terms, i.e. over and above the level of retail price inflation.

If a capital project is risk-free, it should be required to earn a rate of return that is at least equal to the risk-free rate of interest. If the project is located in the UK, and cash flows are projected in real (inflation-adjusted) terms, then the cash flows should be discounted at the risk-free real rate of interest. Following the discounted cash flow method (*see* the article by Adam Farkas on p. 72), the project should be accepted if its net present value (NPV) is positive.

Risky investments

But, sadly, capital investments are not usually risk-free. So what discount rate should we use if a project is risky?

If we want to know the wholesale price for copper, cocoa or crude oil, we look at the Commodities Prices section of the *Financial Times*. We can learn about the cost of these commodities by referring to prices on the London Metal Exchange or to the relevant commodity or petroleum exchange. By analogy, to learn about the wholesale price for capital, we must look at the market for risk capital, namely, the Stock Exchange.

What we would like to do is to take a project, such as building a new power station, and find its required rate of return by reference to a similar investment on the stock market. To do this we need to examine what risk means in that market.

Risk means that more things can happen than will happen. When we invest in shares, the returns may be higher or lower than we expect. Figure 1 shows the range of returns (capital gain or loss, plus reinvested dividends) on the US equity market since 1926. Similar data is also available for the UK and other countries. (Long-run rates of return on the major asset categories

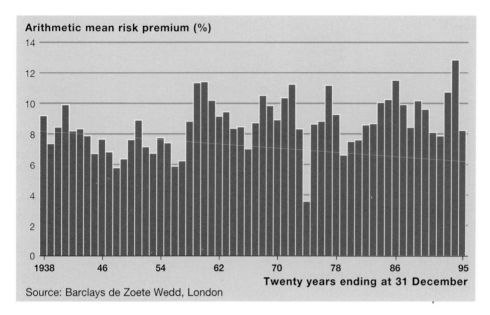

Arithmetic mean risk premium (%)

Source: Barclays de Zoete Wedd, London

Twenty years ending at 31 December

Figure 2: UK equity risk premia, 1938-1995

are summarized in the *Stocks, Bonds, Bills and Inflation 1996 Yearbook* published by Ibbotson Associates, and in the *BZW Equity-Gilt Study* published by Barclays de Zoete Wedd.)

Although returns of 10 to 20 per cent are the most frequent, the equity market has often given returns of 30 to 40 per cent, and has often given negative returns. Within the histogram, we identify the year(s) in which particular levels of return were achieved. The US equity market fell by more than 40 per cent in 1931, and rose by over 50 per cent in 1933 and 1954. These three extremes are shown in the left-hand and right-hand tails of the histogram.

Whereas equity investment is risky, treasury bills (essentially, government bonds with a maturity of under a year) are virtually risk-free. A histogram of the returns on treasury bills would show that in almost every year their return was between 0 and 10 per cent. The most extreme outliers were a few years at the beginning of the 1980s, when treasury bills gave a return of a little above 10 per cent. Because we know the return over the life of a treasury bill when we buy it, we sometimes refer to the return on bills as the risk-free rate of interest.

Investors do not like to be exposed to risk, unless they can expect to receive some

compensation for their exposure. An interesting comparison, then, is between the risky return on equities and the risk-free interest rate. The difference between these two rates of return is called the excess return. It measures the additional return received from investing in shares, rather than in treasury bills. If the excess return is, on average, positive, then investors are receiving a risk premium for exposure to equity market risk.

Figure 2 shows the arithmetic average risk premium for the UK, measured in real terms, and estimated over rolling 20-year periods ending in 1938, 1939, and so on to 1995. Over the entire period 1919 to 1995, the risk premium averaged between 8 and 9 percentage points per year. Over the period 1926-1995, Ibbotson Associates estimate that US equities provided an arithmetic average risk premium of between 8 and 9 percentage points. Similar figures are available for other countries. They suggest that the annual equity return can be expected to be some 8 to 9 percentage points higher than the riskless rate of interest.

Calculating the right rate

We now have two benchmarks. A company with a riskless investment opportunity ought to

■ Finance on the back of a postage stamp

The leading textbooks in finance are nearly 1,000 pages long. Many students learn by making notes on each topic. They then summarize their notes. Here is one student's summary of his Finance course: Time is money. . . Don't put all your eggs in one basket. . . You can't fool all of the people all of the time. . .

The idea that time is money refers to the fact that a sum of money received now is worth more than the same sum paid in the future. This gives rise to the principle that future cash flows should be discounted, in order to calculate their present value.

You can reduce the risk of an investment if you don't put all your eggs in one basket. In other words, a diversified portfolio of investments is less risky than putting all your money in a single asset. Risks that cannot be diversified away should be accepted only if they are offset by a higher expected return.

The idea that you can't fool all of the people all of the time refers to the efficiency of financial markets. An efficient market is one in which information is widely and cheaply available to everyone, and relevant information is therefore incorporated into security prices. Because new information is reflected in prices immediately, investors should expect to obtain only a normal rate of return. Possession of information about a company will not enable an investor to outperform. The only way to obtain a higher expected return is to be exposed to greater risk.

These three themes of discounted cash flow, risk and diversification, and market efficiency lie at the very heart of most introductory finance courses.

discount future cash flows at the risk-free rate of interest. Another company, facing an investment opportunity with similar risk to the equity market, ought to discount cash flows at a higher required rate of return.

The required rate of return on the equity market is equal to the risk-free interest rate plus the expected risk premium on the market. If we expect the risk premium in the future to be similar to its average value in the past, then the required rate of return would be equal to the risk-free rate plus the historical average risk premium. With a real risk-free rate of 3 per cent, this would imply a required rate of return of around 11 per cent in real terms.

We can also estimate the required rate of return for intermediate strategies. For example, an investment split equally between the riskless asset and the equity market would have a required rate of return of 3 per cent plus half the risk premium of 8 per cent, giving a required rate of return of 7 per cent in real terms.

If a company is to use these guidelines from the capital market, it needs to classify its capital projects according to their level of risk. Modern finance provides a number of ways of doing this. The article 'The capital asset pricing model' on p. 76 explains the intricacies of measuring the risks of individual companies, and how to translate their risk attributes into a required rate of return for appraising projects.

Summary

An important issue is what discount rate to apply on risky projects. Since the 1920s investors in the US and the UK have on average been receiving an excess return from investing in shares rather than treasury bills of around 8 to 9 percentage points. If we expect this 'risk premium' to be similar in future, then the required rate of return for an equity market investment would be equal to the real risk-free rate plus the historical average risk premium.

Suggested further reading

Stocks, Bonds and Inflation 1996 Yearbook, Ibbotson Associates, Chicago.

The BZW Equity-Gilt Study (1996) Barclays de Zoete Wedd, London.

Market efficiency

■ **Financial transactions often appear an excellent way for companies to add to their profits. But theory suggests that playing the market is no substitute for day-to-day operations as a way to add value.**

by Ernst Maug

One of the key concepts underlying modern corporate finance is the notion of *efficient markets*. From a practical point of view the concept is motivated by the question where analysts, fund managers and corporate treasurers can add value.

Should they wait with a new rights issue, borrow short term and bet on falling interest rates? Is it a good idea to acquire companies because they appear undervalued?

The criterion for real investments applies also to financial transactions: simply look at the net present value (NPV). The NPV of a bond issue is simply the proceeds of the issue minus the present value of all expected future repayments of principal and interest. The NPV of purchasing a share is the value of the share (the present value of future dividends) minus its price.

Markets are efficient if the NPVs of all these transactions are zero. If transaction costs are zero and all investors have access to the same information, then competition will eliminate opportunities for earning positive NPVs. All available information would be incorporated into prices.

Since these ideal conditions do not prevail, it is practical and customary to distinguish different *degrees* of market efficiency, depending on the amount of information reflected in prices. These are traditionally labeled as weak-form, semi-strong form and strong form market-efficiency.[1]

Weak-form efficient markets

A market is said to be *weak-form efficient* if current prices reflect all information contained in past prices. This form of efficiency is weak because it requires only a small amount of information to be incorporated into prices. Its implication is nonetheless very powerful. If markets are weak-form efficient, then past prices cannot predict price movements in the future, i.e. it rules out trends, cycles or any other predictable pattern of price movements.

It is instructive to understand why this is so. Assume, for example, that an agricultural stock moves in an annual cycle, booming in the autumn and declining in the spring. All investors expect that the regular drop in the spring will be reversed in the autumn, hence the stock becomes a one-way bet and everybody who knows the cyclical pattern will buy. Conversely, in the autumn, there will be strong sales pressure as all investors anticipate the seasonal decline.

However, such a situation in which everybody has an opportunity to make profitable transactions is not sustainable: the autumn sales will drive prices down, whereas the spring purchases of the stock will move prices up. As a result, the cycle will self-destruct.

A similar argument can be made for any regular pattern in prices: once many investors discover such a regular pattern, their trades will adjust prices and the pattern will disappear.

Hence, if markets are weak-form efficient there is no scope for profitable *technical trading rules*, since they are based on information that is already reflected in market prices. In fact, a very simple forecasting rule applies: the best predictor of tomorrow's stock price is today's price. More formally, this result is known as the '*random walk*' hypothesis. Tomorrow's price P_{t+1} can be expressed as today's price, P_t plus a random expectation error Σ_{t+1} which has an expected value of zero.

$$P_{t+1} = P_t + \Sigma_{t+1} \quad \mathrm{E}(\Sigma_{t+1}) = 0$$

This implication is empirically testable, and countless studies have been performed to show that financial markets are, indeed, weak-form efficient.

Semi-strong-form efficient

A market is said to be *semi-strong form efficient* if all publicly available information is reflected in market prices. This requires that no investor can consistently improve his or her forecast of future price movements simply by analysing macro-economic news, earnings statements, annual reports or other publicly available sources.

The empirically testable implication in this case is that financial markets react to relevant news fast and *on average* appropriately. This excludes systematic over- or under-reactions for the same reasons as stated before: if, for example, all investors knew that the market overreacts (or under-reacts) after the announcement of a dividend rise, then all investors who realize this would sell (buy) immediately after the announcement.

Numerous studies have been conducted to test stock price reactions after the announcements of news (dividend and earnings, stock splits, changes in accounting rules, macroeconomic indicators, rights issues, and others) and have generally confirmed that the markets incorporate public information efficiently and quickly. The implication of this finding is as powerful as the previous one. If stock markets are semi-strong-form efficient, then fundamental analysis cannot lead to profitable stock-picking.

There is one exception to the last conclusion: if a very smart analyst has a proprietary model for processing public information, which builds on relationships between variables nobody else has so far discovered, then he or she produces effectively original information in its own right. As long as the research results were not public, trading on this information might still be profitable in semi-strong-form efficient markets.

Strong-form efficient

A market is *strong-form efficient* if *all* relevant information (public or private) is reflected in market prices. This definition is the most stringent one, since it implies that nobody can ever profit from any information, not even inside information or the information produced by the highly original analyst mentioned above.

In a strong-form efficient market prices adjust instantaneously to orders based on private information. Studies have generally found that analysts and fund managers cannot consistently beat the market, whereas trades by corporate insiders are usually very profitable. Hence markets are generally not strong-form efficient.

More recently, studies more critical of stock market efficiency have documented 'anomalies' or effects which appear to be inconsistent with market efficiency.[2 and 3] Usually, these studies test a particular model of asset prices, so that a rejection of the test can indicate a failure of the particular pricing model as much as a failure of markets to be efficient. These studies cannot be discussed here. The book by Haugen referenced at the end of this article takes a critical view of the conventional wisdom on market efficiency.

The overall message of this discussion is fairly clear. In efficient markets there are no gains from trend spotting and 'timing the market' for rights issues, security repurchases or for speculating on interest rate movements when considering to borrow at long or short maturities.

Similarly, accounting changes are just as valueless as acquisitions of supposedly 'under-valued' companies. Corporations can add value through their operations. Financial transactions are usually zero-NPV activities, i.e. those that do not add value.

Summary

Markets are 'efficient' if the net present value (NPV) of financial transactions is zero. It is customary to distinguish different degrees of market efficiency, conventionally labeled 'weak', 'semi-strong' and 'strong'. Much empirical research seemed to converge to the conclusion that markets are semi-strong form efficient, but more recently some studies have been more critical. The concept is of fundamental importance for asset managers and corporate financing decisions.

Suggested further reading

Dimson, Elroy (1988) *Stock Market Anomalies*, Cambridge University Press, Cambridge.[2]

Fama, Eugene F. (1970) 'Efficient capital markets: a review of theory and empirical work', *Journal of Finance* 25, 383-417.[1]

Fama, Eugene F., (1991) 'Efficient capital markets: II', *Journal of Finance* 46, 1575-1617.[3]

Haugan, Robert A., (1975) *The New Finance: The Case Against Efficient Markets*, Prentice Hall.

Project approval: the key criteria

■ **The concept of net present value and discounted cash flow, as well as some more esoteric approaches, are detailed here.**

by Adam Farkas

Capital bugeting decisions

Corporate managers are continuously looking for tangible and intangible assets that can increase the value of their company and result in an increase of shareholders' wealth. Capital bugeting is concerned with identifying and valuing potential investment opportunities to enable the management to make sound investment decisions.

The concept of present value (PV) and net present value (NPV) form the basis for the valuation of real assets and investment decision-making. In this section, we have to develop these concepts into managerial decision-making tools that are widely used by corporations for the analysis of real assets with expected multi-period pay-off. Essentially, the method makes a comparison between the cost of an investment and the present value of uncertain future cash flows generated by the project. There are (at least) four major steps in a discounted cash flow analysis for a proposed project.

First, assuming that the project is all equity financed (i.e. all the necessary capital is provided by the shareholders), forecasts are needed as to what the expected incremental cash flows would be to the shareholders if the project was accepted. Second, an appropriate discount rate should be established that reflects the time value and risk of the project, and therefore can be used for the calculation of the present value of expected future cash flows. Third, based on the value additivity of present values, the NPV of the project is to be calculated. Finally, a decision needs to be made on whether to go ahead with the project or not.

Estimating incremental after-tax cash flows

Before starting to build the actual cash flow model of the project and doing the forecasting exercise, some significant technical decisions must be made. The analyst has to decide how to treat inflation. The cash flow model can be built in nominal terms or in real terms (i.e. net of inflation). Both approaches have advantages and disadvantages from practical aspects, but the important point is to be consistent throughout the model. Then, an appropriate forecasting time horizon needs to be selected. Occasionally this can be easy, because the economic life of assets under consideration is known, but at other times an arbitrary decision is necessary.

The incremental cash flows that companies forecast consist of four elements. The first is the cash flow from operations (i.e. the cash flow generated by sales less expenditures related to the operation of the project). The second is the cash flow from capital investments and disposal. The third results from the changes in working capital (net changes in short-term assets and liabilities). And last there are the additional corporate tax payments of the company resulting from the implementation of the project.

If the project is not expected to continue operations after the end of the forecasting horizon, the salvage value of assets need to be estimated. If management expects the project to last longer than the forecasting horizon, a continuation value for the project has to be established. The salvage or continuation value with its tax implications is then entered into the valuation model as the last expected cash inflow from the project.

Estimating the discount rate

The concept of present value includes the notion of the opportunity cost of capital. The appropriate discount rate, or the cost of capital, must first of all compensate shareholders for the foregone return they could achieve on the capital market by investing in some risk-free assets. It has also to compensate them for the risk they are undertaking by investing in this project rather than in a risk-free financial asset. Thus, the cost of capital is determined by the rate of return investors could expect from an alternative investment with a similar risk profile. Fortunately, the rich menu of traded financial assets provides managers with the opportunity to estimate the right rate.

Calculating net present value

Once the cash flow forecasts are finalised and the appropriate discount rate is established, the calculation of a project's NPV is a technical matter.

All future cash flows need to be discounted to arrive at their present values, and by adding them up, together with the present value of the necessary capital outlay, the NPV of the project is achieved.

By denoting the expected cash flow of the project in period t by C_t, and the present value of the necessary investment by C_o (which has a negative sign), and the discount rate as r, the NPV of the project is:

$$NPV = C_o + \frac{C_1}{(1+r)} + \frac{C_2}{(1+r)^2} + \ldots + \frac{C_n}{(1+r)^n} = \sum_{t=0}^{n} \frac{C_i}{(1+r)^n}$$

Note that this traditional NPV model framework assumes that all future cash flows can be discounted by the same discount rate, which for some projects might be too restrictive. However, the model can accommodate discount rates that vary from period to period as well as cash flow profiles with more than one change in the sign.

Decision criteria

Based on the DCF analysis of project proposals, the decision criterion that follows is relatively straightforward. Assuming that the company operates in a capital market environment where access to capital is not limited, the management should accept all projects with positive net present values and thereby maximize the company's value.

Project analysis

Project analysis tools are widely used methods developed to provide managers with a deeper insight and better understanding of the financial aspects of investment projects, as well as to shed some light on the assumptions behind expected cash flow forecasts. They can enhance the confidence of managers in the DCF analysis and point out major risk factors that can potentially jeopardize the expected outcome of the investment.

Sensitivity analysis

Sensitivity analysis is a very useful tool to identify key variables or value drivers of projects and focus managerial attention on the most important components of forecasts that are underlying the expected incremental project cash flows.

The analysis is carried out by measuring the change in the value of the project after shifting the value of one underlying variable up or down, corresponding to a more optimistic or pessimistic forecast. The magnitude of the change in the net present value shows the sensitivity of the project to that particular underlying variable.

If, for example, the NPV proves more sensitive to the market share of the company and to the amount of fixed costs than to the price of the product, then management should focus on the reliability of market share estimates and fixed cost forecasts, as well as concentrate efforts during the implementation to improve these factors.

Break-even analysis

Break-even analysis goes one step further. It points out the critical value of each underlying variable at which the project's NPV is zero. Referring back to the previous example, it would tell management that if the market share of the product drops below, or the amount of fixed costs exceed, a certain level, which are called the break-even market share or break-even fixed cost, the company starts losing money on the project. The concept of financial break-even for investment projects is therefore looking at where the project recovers its opportunity cost as opposed to accounting break-even analysis, which focuses on historical costs.

Scenario analysis

The previous two project analysis tools are concerned with only one underlying factor at a time, thereby treating them as non-interrelated. However, companies often find that certain market events would result in a change of several underlying variables at the same time. If, for example, there is a threat of a new competitor entering an existing market then the market share of the company as well as the product price is expected to drop. Scenario analysis allows management to investigate the effect of potential future scenarios of events, which are translated into the DCF valuation model as consistent changes of various combinations of the underlying variables.

Alternative decision criteria

Companies of all sizes and sectors have long been using a number of other decision criteria to evaluate their capital investment projects either as a supplement to, or worse, as a substitute for the NPV rule. Let us briefly summarize how some of these criteria work and compare them with NPV.

Payback and discounted payback

The simple payback period of a project is defined as the expected number of years it takes for the company to recover its initial investment outlay by implementing the project. The decision criterion is then given as a maximum number of years, or cut-off period, above which capital investment proposals should be rejected. This implies that the shorter the payback period, the better the project is.

However, there are two major shortcomings to this rule. First, it fails to recognize the time value of money. No investors would be satisfied by investing £100 today and receiving exactly the same amount a year from now and nothing afterwards, even though the investment has a one-year payback period. Second, the rule disregards expected cash flows from the project after the cut-off period. It prefers projects with large payoffs in the early years and perhaps nothing later to long-term projects with gradually increasing positive cash flows.

Companies often use the discounted payback rule to correct for disregarding the time value of money. This method involves the calculation of the payback period in terms of the present value of future cash flows generated by the project. However, the rule still does not give any weight to cash flows after the arbitrary cut-off date.

Therefore, its use should be restricted to comparing projects with very similar even cash flow profiles. One example could be parts of the property sector, where a number of investments are expected to produce long-term evenly distributed rental income.

Internal rate of return

The internal rate of return (IRR) of a project is defined as the discount rate that makes the project's $NPV = 0$, thus obtained by solving the following equation for r:

$$0 = C_0 + \frac{C_1}{(1+r)} + \frac{C_2}{(1+r)^2} + ... + \frac{C_n}{(1+r)^n}$$

For most projects the IRR rule gives an identical answer to the question whether it should be accepted or rejected. However, for some others, the use of IRR is not appropriate, or needs to be used with great care. These exemptions include projects where, instead of an initial investment, the cash flow of the project changes sign more than once over the forecasting period or when the company is ranking mutually exclusive projects either because of technical or capital constraints.

Profitability index

The profitability index (PI) of a project is defined as the ratio between the present value of future cash flows from the project and the initial investment (where C_0 is assumed to be negative):

$$PI = \frac{\sum_{i=1}^{n} \frac{C_1}{(1+r)^n}}{-C_0} = \frac{PV}{-C_0}$$

The rule says that all projects with a profitability index higher than 1 should be accepted, which is identical to the outcome of applying the NPV rule, since if $PI > 1$ it means that $PV > -C_0$, and thus $NPV > 0$. However, the profitability index is not useful when applied to ranking mutually exclusive projects since it captures the profitability, but not the scale, of projects.

Accounting measures

There are a number of accounting measures used in the process of investment decision making, such as the return on investment (ROI) or average book return on investment. The major problem with these measures in general is that they are based on book values that are often liable to arbitrary selection of accounting policies (for example on depreciation schedules).

In addition, book values and book income do not reflect the time value of money, therefore various adjustments are needed to arrive at meaningful results. This means the DCF analysis is clearly preferable to accounting measures in setting investment decision criteria.

Expanding the frontiers of capital budgeting criteria

As mentioned earlier, however, the assumptions underlying the DCF analysis represent a static approach to decision making, and can be very restrictive in some cases. The replacement of uncertain future cash flows by their expected value and the use of a single discount rate ignore the possibility of active managerial actions over the lifetime of the project.

For examples, managers take actions aimed at cutting the losses due to unfavorable market events and retaining or improving profits following favorable changes. This can change the risk profile of the project. Also, the standard DCF analysis works in terms of making a decision now or never. It ignores the opportunity managers may take to delay some strategic decisions pending the outcome of future events.

To overcome these drawbacks, various attempts have been made to develop more sophisticated decision criteria and investment analysis methods. These include decision tree analysis, the use of certainty equivalent cash flows and the application of option pricing theory in the valuation of real assets. The application of these methods have proved to be helpful complements to DCF analysis.

Summary

The basis for most investment decision making is present value (PV) and net present value (NPV). These are used to make a comparison between the cost of an investment and the present value of uncertain future cash flows generated by the project. At least four steps are involved: forecasting those incremental cash flows (which will require some technical decisions such as how to treat inflation); estimating the appropriate discount rate or cost of capital (determined by the rate of return investors could expect from another investment with a similar risk profile); using this information to calculate the net present value; and deciding whether the project should go ahead. Further illumination can be provided by sensitivity analysis (calculating the impact of changing one or more variables), break-even analysis (pointing out the critical value of each variable where the NPV is zero), and scenario analysis.

Other investment decision criteria include payback and discounted payback, the internal rate of return and the profitability index.

Suggested further reading

Brealey, Richard A. and Myers, Stewart C. (1988) *Principles of Corporate Finance*, 4th edn, McGraw-Hill, New York, Chapters 5-6, and 10-12.

Bierman, H. and Smidt, S. (1988) *The Capital Budgeting Decision*, 7th edn, The Macmillan Company, New York.

Copeland, T., Koller, T. and Murrin, J. (1991) *Valuation: Measuring and Managing the Value of Companies,* John Wiley & Sons, New York.

Kensinger, John W. 'Adding the value of active management into the capital budgeting equation', *Midland Corporate Finance Journal*, Spring 1987.

The capital asset pricing model

■ **Investment requires a higher return for greater risk. But how do we know what the risk is? A simple model provides guidance.**

by Elroy Dimson

In the article on assessing the rate of return (*see* p. 66) we noted that a capital investment project should be discounted at a required rate of return, or cost of capital, that is equal to the riskless rate of interest plus a risk premium. Historically, the average equity risk premium has been around eight percentage points. Projects that are riskless would have their cash flows discounted at the risk-free rate of interest; projects whose risk is the same as investing in the equity market would have their cash flows discounted at the risk-free rate plus, say, 8 per cent; and a project with intermediate risk would merit an intermediate discount rate.

To implement this idea, we need to agree on a method for estimating the riskiness of an investment. Until the 1960s, this would have been difficult. But in the early part of that decade there was an important breakthrough in the theory of finance.

Building on work by Harry Markowitz and James Tobin, Bill Sharpe formulated the capital asset pricing model (CAPM), a simple yet elegant model that relates the expected return on an asset to its risk, while giving a precise definition to what we mean by risk.

The key insight of the CAPM is that investors can expect a reward for an investment's contribution to the risk of a portfolio. There can be no expected reward for exposure to risks that can easily be diversified away. The required rate of return should be higher for investments that have a larger element of non-diversifiable risk.

Two types of risk

A portfolio invested in just one share is typically much more volatile than a diversified portfolio. By holding a large number of securities, investors can eliminate company-specific risk factors. However, there are limits to the power of diversification. Once the investor has holdings in every share in the market, the portfolio will still be quite risky. While diversification can eliminate company-specific risk, it cannot eliminate overall equity market risk.

Every share therefore fluctuates in value because of two elements of risk. The first is market risk, the tendency of the share to move with general stock market movements. The second element is specific risk, which encapsulates all events that are specific to individual companies while having nothing to do with general market-wide factors.

Investors do not like risk and need the prospect of higher expected returns before they will take it on. Since market risk cannot be avoided by diversification, investors require a

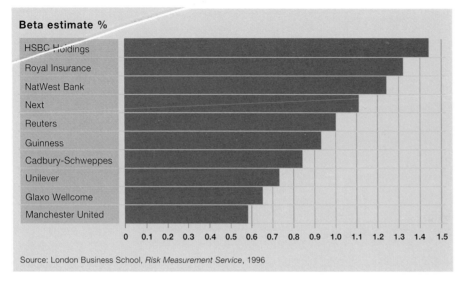

Beta estimate %

Source: London Business School, *Risk Measurement Service*, 1996

Figure 1: Recent estimates of Beta for some well-known companies

higher return for exposure to market risk. In the CAPM, market risk is measured by its beta. A stock with a beta of 1.0 tends to move broadly in line with the equity market; a share with a beta of 1.5 tends to move up or down by 1.5 per cent for each percentage point movement in the market.

The bar chart in Figure 1 lists recent estimates of beta for some well-known companies. Some companies have betas as high as 1.5 or even more and are an aggressive play on the equity market. If the market goes up, these shares can be expected to outperform others; in a bear market they can be expected to fall by more than average. Other shares have betas of 0.5 or less and these defensive companies are likely to do relatively well in a bear market while being left behind when share prices surge ahead. Most companies, however, have a beta that is close to the average of 1.0.

Required rates of return

To estimate the required rate of return for an investment, we therefore need to estimate the beta for a capital project. This is especially easy to do if the project essentially replicates, probably on a smaller scale, the existing business of the company. It is also easy if the project is typical of an industry sector for which betas are published.

A capital project with a beta of 0 would be riskless, and its cash flows should be discounted at the risk-free rate of interest. An investment in an equity index fund would have the same risk as the market, namely a beta of 1.0. This investment would have a required rate of return equal to the riskless rate of interest plus the expected equity market risk premium.

Suppose we are considering a project such as building a new power station, for which we have estimated a beta of 0.6. This is the same as the beta of a portfolio that is 40 per cent invested in treasury bills and 60 per cent invested in the equity market. The CAPM tells us that the required return should therefore be equal to the return on treasury bills plus 60 per cent of the expected market risk premium. In general, the CAPM tells us that the required rate of return on an investment is equal to the risk-free rate of interest plus a premium for risk. The premium for risk is equal to beta multiplied by the equity market risk premium.

The relationship between the required rate of return and beta is indicated in Figure 2 by the sloping line labeled 'risk-adjusted cost of capital'. The sloping line shows how the required rate of return increases as beta gets larger.

To use the CAPM to calculate the required rate of return, we need three items of data.

● The risk-free interest rate, which may be obtained from the Currencies and Money page of

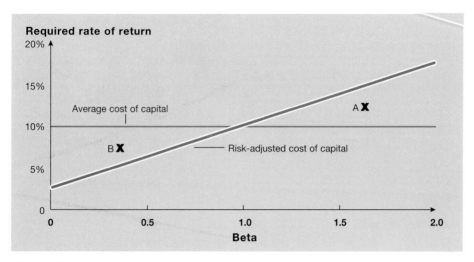

Figure 2

the *Financial Times*.
● The beta of the project, which may be estimated using the London Business School's *Risk Measurement Service*.
● The equity market risk premium has historically averaged around 8 per cent.

With a real interest rate of, say, 3 per cent, and an investment with a beta of 0.6, we would have a required rate of return which is equal to 7.8 per cent (i.e. $3 + 0.6 \times 8$ per cent). With a beta of 1.0, the required rate of return would be 11 per cent (i.e. $3 + 1.0 \times 8$ per cent).

Most projects have a risk level that is different from the beta of the company's shares. This is partly because many companies are financed partly with debt, which increases the riskiness of their shares. To estimate the riskiness of a capital investment project, we therefore need to remove the effect of borrowing from the beta of the company's shares.

The beta of the underlying business of the company is simply a weighted average of the beta of its equity and the beta of its debt. (The weights are the proportion of equity and the proportion of debt in the firm's capital structure.) If we make the simplifying assumption that the company's debt is so safe as to make its beta virtually zero, then the beta of the company's underlying business is equal to the beta of its shares multiplied by the proportion of equity in its capital structure.

For example, consider a company whose shares have a beta of 0.6. Assume the company is financed 83 per cent by equity and 17 per cent by debt. The beta of the underlying business would be equal to the beta of the shares multiplied by the proportion of equity. The company would have an 'asset beta' of 0.5 (i.e. 0.6×0.83).

To estimate the cost of equity capital for a company we should use the beta of its shares. But to estimate the cost of capital for the underlying business, we should use its asset beta.

Project risk
Some companies use only a single company-wide discount rate, even though they operate in businesses that embrace a wide range of risks. However, this can lead to inappropriate investment decisions.

Figure 2 shows why this is the case. The upward sloping risk-adjusted cost of capital line shows the required rate of return for projects with varying levels of beta. Projects with an expected return that plots above this line should be accepted, while those that plot beneath the sloping line should be rejected.

A high risk proposal, such as Project A, would be incorrectly accepted by a firm using a single, company-wide discount rate. On a risk-adjusted basis it should be rejected. A low risk proposal, such as Project B, would be incorrectly rejected

■ Alternative approaches

The cost of capital is an opportunity cost. It is the return which could be obtained in the stock market from an investment that is similar in risk and maturity to the capital tied up in the project. Financial economics offers four approaches to estimating the cost of capital:

● **The capital asset pricing model.** The CAPM is the standard approach to estimating the cost of capital.
● **Arbitrage pricing theory**, a competitor of the CAPM, developed in the mid- to late-1970s. APT can be seen as an extended version of CAPM, with multiple sources of risk and return.
● **Option pricing theory**, also developed in the 1970s. This is sometimes applied to valuing capital projects that have option-like characteristics.
● **The constant growth model**, originated in the 1930s and popularised in the 1950s. Its drawback is that it assumes a dividend growth rate that can be sustained indefinitely. It also ignores the riskiness of an investment.

Some companies use accounting-based approaches for estimating the cost of capital. These seriously flawed methods include:

● **The dividend yield.** This tends to understate the cost of capital because it ignores the capital gains anticipated by investors.
● **The p/e ratio** or its reciprocal, the earnings yield. This ignores the expected growth in company earnings.
● **Return on capital.** Some companies use RoC as a guideline, but it is absurd to estimate a low cost of capital just because a business earns a low accounting rate of return.
● **Return on marginal project.** Some companies rank projects from most to least attractive and accept those with the highest return. This is circular since projects cannot be ranked correctly unless one already knows the cost of capital.
● **Funding cost.** When projects are valued using the interest rate payable by the company, the discount rate fails to reflect the full riskiness of the investment.
● **Past return on the company's shares.** Use of the long-run return on a company's shares as a guide to the cost of capital implies that poorly performing companies have the lowest cost of capital. It is misleading.

Despite continued usage of inadequate methods for determining the cost of capital, more sophisticated businesses tend to use the CAPM. The APT tends to be used by utilities in the US, while option pricing theory is sometimes used for valuing natural resource investments such as mines.

when compared to the company's overall cost of capital. On a risk-adjusted basis it should be accepted. While there are other approaches to estimating the risk-adjusted cost of capital, the CAPM, as described here, is by far the most popular approach. It is widely used in the fields of company valuation, project appraisal and regulation.

required rate of return also requires the risk-free interest rate and the equity market risk premium. Most projects have a risk level that is different from the beta of their company's shares: using a single company wide discount rate can lead to inappropriate investment decisions.

Summary

The cost of capital can be estimated by arbitrage pricing theory, option pricing theory and the constant growth model. But the CAPM is the most popular approach. Here market risk is measured by the project's beta; calculating the

Suggested further reading

Dimson, Elroy and Marsh, Paul (eds) (1996) *Risk Measurement Service*, London Business School

Dimson, Elroy 'The discount rate for a power station', *Energy Economics*, Vol. 11, no.3, 1989

Brealey, R. and Myers, S. (1996) *Principles of Corporate Finance*, 5th edn, McGraw Hill

Importance of capital structure

■ **Academic theory suggests that the capital structure of a company has no effect on its value. But in practice capital structure has major implications, as many real-life examples show, says** Michel Habib

A central aspect of a company's financial policy is its choice of capital structure, particularly the extent of its relative reliance on debt and equity. The primary importance of this is well illustrated by the consequences of those choices that have gone wrong, of which the bankruptcy of Olympia & York, the heavily debt-burdened developers of Canary Wharf in London's docklands, is an example.

Does capital structure matter?

Yet in view of the importance of the choice of capital structure, it is perhaps surprising that the most famous result that pertains to this choice – the Modigliani and Miller propositions (*see* 'Suggested further reading') – is one that states that capital structure does not matter. The intuition behind this result is quite simple.

It is the cash flows that are expected to be generated by the assets of a company that determine its value. The manner in which these cash flows are divided between debt holders and equity holders, or, equivalently, the capital structure of the company, does not affect the cash flows themselves; it therefore does not affect the value of the company. To use an analogy first employed by Merton Miller, the manner in which a pizza is divided into slices does not affect the size of the pizza.

To illustrate the importance of the Modigliani and Miller result, consider the view that the cost of capital has been lower in Japan than in the UK and the US because of the greater reliance of Japanese companies on debt financing, which is cheaper than equity financing. The Modigliani

and Miller propositions suggest that the above view cannot be true as it stands. Since capital structure does not affect the total cash flows to the security-holders of a company, it does not affect the overall return they enjoy. It therefore does not affect the cost of capital of the company. The greater reliance on cheaper debt must therefore be offset by an increase in the cost of equity.

This is indeed the case, as the greater risk to which higher gearing subjects equity holders leads them to increase the compensation they require for providing equity financing. Thus, while Japanese companies did indeed have a greater reliance on cheaper debt, any advantage thus provided was offset by their higher cost of equity, with the possible exception of the 'bubble' years of the late-1980s.

Nonetheless, the idea that capital structure does not matter is clearly wrong. The importance of the Modigliani and Miller propositions resides in the fact that they serve to identify the sources of the importance of capital structure.

These can be found in the assumptions made by Modigliani and Miller in establishing their result. Among the assumptions they make are those of no taxes and no costs of bankruptcy; that the cash flows of a company are determined exclusively by the assets of the company; and that the value of both are known by all. The importance of capital structure is largely a consequence of the fact that these assumptions are not true.

Capital structure matters in the presence of taxes and bankruptcy costs. The fact that interest payments can be deducted from taxable income, whereas dividend payments cannot, imparts a preference for debt financing over equity financing. This preference is, however, offset by personal taxes, which have historically been lower on equity than on debt. It is also offset by bankruptcy costs, which clearly favour equity financing as bankruptcy is the consequence of a company's failure to meet its debt obligations.

Thus, a choice of capital structure based on taxes and bankruptcy considerations trades off the corporate tax advantages of debt with its personal tax and bankruptcy disadvantages. Changes in tax rates or bankruptcy procedures will alter the capital structures of corporations, as was the case, for example, following the introduction of Chapter 11 (part of US bank-ruptcy laws allowing a company to continue to operate under existing management while working with its creditors to reorganize the business) in the late-1970s. Chapter 11 lowered bankruptcy costs and was followed by an increase in the leverage of US corporations in the 1980s.

Efficient use of assets

Capital structure also matters when the cash flows of a company are determined not only by the assets of the company, but also by the manner in which these assets are used by its management. This is because, as first noted by Jensen and Meckling (see 'Suggested further reading'), the capital structure of a company affects the efficiency with which its assets are used.

To see this, consider for example an entre-preneur who wishes to raise funds in order to expand his business. Suppose the entrepreneur does so by raising equity. The entrepreneur now shares the profits of the company with the new shareholders of the company, and might reason-ably be presumed not to exert himself as much as he previously did, for his efforts will now benefit not only himself but also the new shareholders.

The same would be true, a fortiori, of a professional manager who owns a relatively small fraction of the equity of the company that employs him. Furthermore, the manager might be more reluctant to undertake profitable but risky ventures than would shareholders, for his investment in the company, primarily in the form of human capital, is likely to represent a much larger fraction of his total wealth than is the case for well-diversified shareholders.

The manager might engage in relatively unprofitable diversification for the purpose of decreasing the riskiness of the cash flows of the company, and might retain what is perhaps an excessive amount of liquid assets to guard against possible downturns, as was said to be true of the Chrysler Corporation by the buy-out group that tried to acquire it.

Debt financing rather than equity financing serves to avoid many of these problems. An entrepreneur who raises debt remains the unique shareholder of his company and is therefore unlikely to exert himself any less than he did prior to raising debt. Debt also makes it possible for the manager of a company to own a larger fraction of its equity, thus serving to align the interests of the manager with those of the other shareholders of the company, as has been observed in the case of leveraged buy-outs.

Debt may curb managers

Furthermore, interest payments on debt deny resources to managers in a manner that dividend payments, which are subject to the discretion of management, do not. As a result debt may serve to curb managers who might otherwise use these resources to engage in value-destroying diver-sification, or be tempted to retain more liquid assets than is strictly necessary to the conduct of the business.

Thus, the end of the Cold War, with the accompanying decrease in the number of profit-able projects available to defense companies, has seen a sizeable increase in the leverage of US defense companies, as documented by Goyal, Lehn and Racic (see 'Suggested further reading'). Also conversely more profitable corporations have lower gearing, because their managers must not be denied the resources necessary to the expansion of a profitable business. The lower gearing of more profitable corporations occurs, as noted by Brealey and Myers (see 'Suggested further reading'), in spite of the tax saving that higher gearing would provide. It is indicative of the greater importance of efficiency and risk-taking considerations.

Debt financing is not without its problems, however. An entrepreneur is more likely to take a reckless gamble with others' money than with his own, especially when he would obtain most of the gains should the gamble ultimately prove successful, as is the case with debt financing. Such gambles were the probable cause of the failure of many Savings and Loans associations in the US. A choice of capital structure therefore trades off efficiency and risk-taking considerations.

Finally, capital structure matters when the likely value of the cash flows and the assets of a company are known by the managers of the company but not by potential investors in the company. In such a case, more profitable companies will tend to raise a larger fraction of their external financing needs in the form of debt. More profitable companies are better able to service debt and can be recognized as such by investors, who will therefore pay more for their equity.

The choice of capital structure can thus be seen to be influenced by a wide variety of considerations: corporate and personal taxes, bankruptcy costs, efficiency, risk-taking and information. The relative importance of each will depend on the particular circumstances of the company, the industry, and the tax and legal systems.

Companies that have deviated from the capital structure that maximizes their value, such as those whose high gearing is the consequence of a series of losses, are unlikely to remain in such a state for long. They either go under or re-establish their optimal capital structure.

Summary

Debt is advantageous when it comes to limiting corporation tax, but there are disadvantages where personal tax and bankruptcy costs are concerned. The capital structure of a company is also important where its cash flow is determined not only by its assets but also by the manner in which management uses those assets. Debt, for example, helps curb managers tempted by value destroying diversification, or with a tendency to retain more liquid assets than strictly necessary.

Suggested further reading

Brealey, R. and Myers, S. (1991) *Principles of Corporate Finance*, McGraw-Hill.

Modigliani, F. and Miller, M. 'The cost of capital, corporation finance and the theory of investment', *American Economic Review* 49, 655-669, 1958.

Goyal, V., Lehn, K. and Racic, S. 'Investment opportunities, corporate finance and compensation policy' in the US defense industry, Working Paper, University of Pittsburgh, 1993.

Jensen, M. and Meckling, W. 'Theory of the firm, managerial behavior, agency costs and ownership structure', *Journal of Financial Economics* 3 305-360, 1976.

The thinking behind dividends

■ **Companies pay out large slices of their profits as dividends. Dividend policy is a crucial area for management, but the theory behind setting dividends is complex and controversial.**

by Francesca Cornelli

Corporations pay out a substantial portion of their after-tax profits as dividends. Between 1971 and 1992, US corporations paid out between 50 and 70 per cent of their earnings as dividends (Allen and Michaely, 1994 – see 'Suggested further reading'). Historically, dividends have been the predominant form of payout; share repurchases were relatively unimportant until the mid-1980s. Decisions on dividend policy are one of the most crucial for a company, yet dividend policy remains a controversial issue.

Miller and Modigliani, in 1961 (*see* 'Suggested further reading'), proved that in a world without taxes, transaction costs or other market imperfections, a company's dividend policy will not affect its value. The basic premise of their argument is that company value is determined by choosing optimal investments. Provided a company's investment program is held constant, a company's dividend policy, on these assumptions, affects only the amount of outside financing required to fund new investment. From the perspective of investors, dividend policy is then irrelevant because any desired stream of payments can be replicated by appropriate purchases and sales of equity. Thus, again on these assumptions, investors will not pay a premium for any particular dividend policy.

Dividend policy matters

Such a result is not consistent with the evidence, which is that corporations smooth dividends and that the market usually reacts positively to announcements of dividend increases and negatively to announcements of dividend decreases. However, Miller and Modigliani's analysis is based on restrictive assumptions. Therefore, dividend policy matters because one or more of the assumptions underlying the result is violated. A large part of the literature has focussed on the importance of taxes.

The usual argument is that since dividends are taxed as income, they have a tax disadvantage with respect to capital gains in a relatively light capital gains tax regime, especially for recipients in high tax brackets. Therefore, other things being equal, companies that pay out high dividends should be valued less than companies that pay out low dividends. In response to this argument, however, economists have argued that the increasing domination of the market by tax-exempt institutions, the reduction of personal marginal income tax rates, the moves in both the UK and US to tax dividends and capital gains at the same rate and the abundance of tax shelters have all combined largely to neutralize the potential tax disadvantage of dividend payments.

Another possibility is that capital markets are informationally imperfect. Investors have less information about a company's value than its managers, and therefore try to deduce information from the company's behavior. In particular, Miller and Modigliani suggested that dividends convey information about a company's prospects. The basic idea is that companies adjust dividends to signal their prospects. A rise in dividends typically signals that managers expect that the company will do better, and a decrease suggests that it will do worse. This is a costly way to convey information and therefore more credible than other forms of communication, such as words and forecasts, which are 'cheap'. These theories may explain why companies pay out so much of their earnings as dividends. Moreover, it is consistent with what we know about how companies set their dividend policy. Brealey and Myers (1991) (*see* 'Suggested further reading') summarize the research findings in four stylised facts.

First, companies have long-run target payout ratios. Second, managers focus more on dividend changes than on absolute levels. Third, managers smooth dividends. Fourth, they are reluctant to make dividend changes that might have to be reversed.

A survey by Edwards and Mayer (1986) (*see* 'Suggested further reading') has shown that in the UK a failure to sustain a steadily growing dividend stream was believed to have adverse effects on share-holders' perceptions and was regarded as being likely to lead to a share price fall. Moreover, companies indicated that only a drop in current earnings that was expected to persist for some time was likely to elicit a dividend reduction.

In the light of these theories, the market's response to the announcements of dividend changes does not imply that investors prefer dividends to capital gains. In fact, investors may be quite satisfied with receiving different levels of payout from different companies, even within the same industry. But when a company changes its dividend policy, investors will view it as conveying important information. The strong positive relationship between dividend announcements and security prices is thus really caused by the information about future earnings which the dividend announcement conveys.

Another assumption we can relax is that the parties involved have the possibility to write complete and fully enforceable contracts. Stockholders, bondholders and managers may have conflicts of interest. Jensen and Meckling (1976) (see Books panel) have argued that there are situations in which equity holders may try to expropriate wealth from debtholders, by distributing excessive (and unexpected) dividend payments. Both equity holders and bondholders may in effect agree to restrict dividends.

Indeed, most bond covenants contain constraints that limit both investment-financed dividends and debt-financed dividends. The other potential conflict of interest that may affect dividend policy is between management and shareholders. Managers of a publicly held company may allocate resources to activities that benefit them, but which are not in the shareholders' best interest. If equity holders can minimize the cash that management controls, it will make it much harder for management to go on (unmonitored) spending sprees. One way to remove unnecessary cash from the company is to increase the level of dividend payouts.

In conclusion, dividend policy seems to matter in the presence of market failure, such as imperfect information or agency costs. One question that has not been answered is why companies use dividends to solve these failures instead of other instruments for example, share repurchases, where they are allowed to signal information and debt to reduce agency costs.

Summary

Dividends have been the most important form of payment to shareholders yet dividend policy remains controversial. The thesis that it should not affect the company's value, for example, is inconsistent with market reaction to dividend announcements. One explanation is tax. Another is that managers adjust dividends to signal their view of longer term prospects. With payouts there may be conflicts of interest between equity holders and debt holders, and between managers and shareholders.

Suggested further reading

Allen, F. and Michaely, R. *Dividend Policy*, N. Holland Handbooks

Brealey, R. A. and Myers, S. C. *Principles of Corporate Finance*, (1991) McGraw Hill, fourth edition.

Edwards, J. and Mayer, C. 'An investigation into the dividend and the new equity issue practices of firms', IFS Paper, 1986.

Jensen, M. C. and Meckling, W. H. 'Theory of the firm: Managerial behavior, agency costs and ownership structure', *Journal of Financial Economics* 3, 1976.

The changing world of finance

■ **Finance is as subject to change as any other industry, perhaps more so. Harold Rose looks at the main changes that have happened, are happening and will happen – and at the factors driving them.**

Financial systems of free economies are subject to change just as non-financial sectors are, resulting in new opportunities and problems for both financial and non-financial companies, and for financial regulation.

Over the past 20 or 30 years, and even more so over the past 15, the main changes in financial systems, which are still continuing, have been the following.

The dissolution of boundaries between institutions

One obvious change has been the erosion of the boundary, in countries where it previously existed, between commercial and investment banking. For legal reasons, as in the US and

Japan, or for reasons of history, as in the UK, there was a distinction between investment banks and commercial banks.

Investment banks underwrite, issue and deal in corporate securities, and take (wholesale) deposits and lend to companies. Commercial banks take retail deposits from their network of branches and lend to a wider range of customers. Germany, with its 'universal banks' as well as commercial and savings banks, has long been the most important exception.

In the UK this separation ended in 1986, when the rules of the Stock Exchange were altered so as to permit the full ownership of securities houses by banks, foreign as well as British. This change was made mainly to permit securities houses to acquire the capital and contacts needed to compete more effectively in international markets. Commercial banks moved into investment banking in order to exploit the growth of securities markets and to protect their links with their corporate customers in the face of the latter's growing demand for new services involving securities, especially the newer financial instruments.

In other countries the division between the two forms of banking, a division supported by legislation, such as the Glass Steagall Act in the US, has been only partly dissolved; but competition from expanding securities markets will ensure that its days are numbered.

The dissolution of boundaries is to be seen in other aspects of the financial system. In the UK the legal barriers between commercial banks and building societies have been lowered, as have those between banks and the savings and loan associations in the US. The traditional markets of commercial banks have been invaded by non-financial companies.

For example, retail stores offer credit cards and, more recently, other financial services, as well as more traditional consumer loans. Multinational groups operate in wholesale money markets in a manner similar to that of banks. In several countries banks offer insurance services, and large insurance companies, especially in Germany, have entered into alliances with commercial banks in order to provide a fuller range of retail financial services.

The relative decline of commercial banking

The growing competition banks have been experiencing in their traditional business of lending and deposit-taking comes from deeper forces than the events specific to individual countries and markets. History shows that banks dominate the financial system of a developing country but eventually lose their share of financial transactions if we measure this by the proportion of the assets or liabilities of financial institutions accounted for by banks. Table 1 illustrates this decline in the UK.

Table 1: Percentage shares in total financial institutions' liabilities 1913-1994				
	Banks	Building Societies	Insurance Companies	Pension Funds
1913	64	4	32	-
1930	61	8	31	-
1939	55	12	32	na
1960	43	12	32	14
1970	32	17	27	16
1980	30	20	25	21
1990*	28	17	26	26
1994*	27	16	25	27

*Adjusted for Abbey National

Specific factors, such as the incidence of taxation or the demand for relatively illiquid forms of saving life insurance and pension funds as incomes grow have been part of the story. But more fundamental has been the inevitable loss of the advantages that banks used to have as 'financial intermediaries', which pass on net saving to net spenders, especially the business sector. These advantages lie in functions that people or companies cannot do for themselves (such as insurance against loan default) or do so at lower cost (for example, loan assessment and monitoring) or at lower risk (by the pooling of risks).

These intermediary functions of banking have weakened as banks' advantages have declined, with the result that there has been disintermediation in the form of security market financing or securitization, which has grown more rapidly than bank lending. Banks have lost their previous advantages of reputation and information-gathering, and transaction costs in securities markets have fallen. Many companies can raise finance in open markets on finer terms than banks, so that the margin between bank borrowing and lending rates has tended to decline, at least in the large corporate market.

However, it should be noted that banks have responded – to varying degrees in different countries – by expanding their fee-earning activities. In the US, at least, the share of banks in the total income, as distinct from the balance sheet totals of financial institutions, has not fallen over the past decade, So we may have to distinguish between what has happened to 'banking', as previously understood, from what has happened to 'banks'.

The spread of derivatives

Derivatives, such as, simple forward transactions, options, futures and currency and interest rate swaps are so-called because their value derives from that of other assets. In one form or another some derivatives (forward transactions and options) have been in existence for centuries, but the outstanding development over the past 20 years has been the development of traded markets for financial derivatives (commodity futures markets have existed since the later years of the last century).

The volume of transactions has grown many times over, especially in financial futures on organized futures exchanges, where transactions outnumber those in the underlying security, and in swaps, where there are no formal organized markets but where banks, in effect, act as market-makers through their large-scale 'over-the-counter' operations.

These developments have been fuelled by the increase in currency risk since the breakdown in 1971 of the former Bretton Woods system of relative exchange rate stability, and the interest rate shocks imparted by high and variable inflation, associated partly with the jump in oil prices in 1973 and again in 1979. Derivatives are used to hedge risks as well as to take speculative positions (unless there happens to be an equality between opposite hedgers, speculators are needed to fill the gap, as well as to set levels of prices generally).

Another stimulus has been the revolution in information technology, especially in the form of desktop computer networks, which facilitate the transfer of information on a global scale and make possible the computations and control mechanisms needed by companies involved in these markets on a large scale. The standardization of instruments has joined technology in helping to increase volumes and so bring down transaction costs to levels below those of transactions in the underlying securities themselves.

Modern financial institutions, especially banks, have therefore to be familiar with the potential use of derivatives, by their customers as well as for their own purposes. One implication of their use is that all types of organizations can decide more easily than before which risks to hedge when bearing them does not add value to the company and its shareholders. There are also implications for financial regulators, of a more problematical kind.

The crude charge that the growth of traded derivatives has made securities markets more volatile is not supported by the evidence. If anything, the volatility of equity markets has fallen in recent years in the US and perhaps in the UK, and following the sharp fall on Wall Street in October 1987 share prices in countries with futures markets fell by no more than in those without.

Increased freedom but increased regulation

The third main change has been the association of an increasing freedom of financial markets (in the form of the activities that financial institutions can carry out and in greater freedom of competitive pricing) with the greater regulation or supervision of financial institutions. Financial regulation has become a growth industry, perhaps inevitably; although the forms that regulation has taken are open to controversy.

The causes of change

The most pervasive cause of the changes outlined above has been the internationalization of finance, which stems from the relaxation and then the abolition of exchange controls on capital movements. Aspects of the internationalization of finance (euromarkets and international banking) are described in the International Financial Markets module on pages 386 and 388.

Internationalization has been both a cause and effect of international competition between different markets and institutions, and competition has promoted attempts at the international harmonization of regulation. The migration of institutions and markets across national boundaries has caused domestic markets and institutions to become more competitive. The customers of these have therefore gained.

The second most important cause of change has been the revolution in information technology already referred to. Technology has always left its mark on finance: branch banking in England was facilitated by the spread of railways from the middle of the 19th century, and international financial transactions in general multiplied after the laying of cables across the English Channel and then the Atlantic in the 1860s. Following the telephone, telex and then the computer network, the use of international fax and e-mail facilities is giving yet another stimulus to international transactions. The consequence is that money markets are already global and securities markets are in the process of becoming so.

Summary

Financial sector boundaries are disappearing. In the UK, for instance, the separation between investment and commercial banks ended in 1986, though such divisions have only been partly dissolved in other countries. The intermediary functions of banks have weakened but their fee earning activities have expanded. The volume of derivatives has been driven by currency instability and interest rate fluctuations. Information technology has been another stimulus.

Suggested further reading

O'Hara, M. 'Derivatives, what's needed to protect the financial markets', *Economic Affairs*, Spring 1995 ps 24-27, Institute of Economic Affairs, London.

Kaufman, G. G. and Mote, L. R. 'Is banking a declining industry? A historical perspective', *Economic Perspectives* May/June 1994 pps 2-21, Federal Reserve Bank of Chicago.

Rose, H. *The Changing World of Finance and Its Problems*, British-North American Research Association, London 1993.

Introduction to options

■ **Options are superficially complex but fundamentally simple financial instruments that offer companies substantial advantages.**

by Kjell Nyborg

Options have in recent years become fundamental to the workings of the world's capital markets but they have been in use for many centuries. The Romans and Phoenicians wrote options on cargoes transported by their ships.

During the tulip bulb mania in Holland in the 17th Century, there was an active options market, but many writers of put options refused to honour contracts when the tulip bulb bubble burst in the winter of 1637.

In the UK, options were declared illegal by Barnard's Act of 1733, which was not repealed until 1860. Options were temporarily banned again in the 1930s. In the past, and even in some quarters today, options have had a bad name, being associated with speculative activity and corrupt practices; a common ploy involved inducing brokers to recommend certain stocks by giving the brokers options on the same stocks.

It was not until the 1970s that options were transformed from relative obscurity into a staple of the financial markets. Perhaps the most important factor in this transformation was the publication in 1973 of the celebrated article by Black and Scholes in which the basic principles of option pricing and hedging were first explained.

Table 1: National amount of options worldwide as of end of fiscal years 1989-92 ($bn)				
Exchange-traded interest rate options	387	600	1,073	1,385
OTC interest rate options	450	561	577	634
Exchange-traded currency options	50	56	59	80
Exchange-traded equity index options	66	88	132	164
TOTAL OPTIONS	$953	$1,305	$1,841	$2,263

Source: GAO report on financial derivatives, options on individual equities and commodities are not included

The same year also saw the creation of the Chicago Board Options Exchange, the first registered securities exchange dedicated to options trading. Exchange traded options came to London in 1978, initially with call options on only ten stocks. LIFFE (the London International Financial Futures Exchange) now offers call and put contracts on around 70 UK equities. Table 1 gives an indication of worldwide options activity in recent years. As can be seen, options are traded on a variety of underlying assets both on exchanges and over the counter. The principles of option pricing and hedging, however, remain constant. This article will introduce the reader to these principles and to some of the terminology associated with options.

Definitions

There are two basic types of options.

A *call option* is a contract giving its owner the right to buy an asset at a fixed price (the strike, or exercise, price) on pre-specified dates. Notice that a call option gives the holder the right, but not the obligation, to buy a specific asset, for example, a given number of shares of Grand Metropolitan. The seller, or writer, of the option must deliver the asset if the option is exercised.

In return, the seller receives the strike price specified in the option contract. (In some cases the physical asset does not change hands when a call option is exercised. Instead, the holder of the call receives from the writer the difference between the value of the underlying asset and the exercise price – assuming this difference is positive.)

A *put option* is a contract giving its owner the right to sell an asset at a fixed price on pre-specified dates. As with call options, put options give the right, but not the obligation, to sell. When a put option is exercised, the holder sells the underlying asset to the writer at the pre-specified strike price.

The final date on which an option can be exercised is referred to as the expiry, expiration or maturity date of the option.

Options can be either European or American. A European option can be exercised only at the maturity date. An American option can be exercised at any date up to and including the maturity date. This classification, by the way, has nothing to do with the geographical origins of the contract. Most exchange traded options are American whereas non-traded (over-the-counter, or OTC) options are often European.

The price of an option is commonly referred to as the option premium.

Examples and payoff diagrams

Call options. Suppose you have bought a call option on one share of XYZ plc. The strike price is 100p. Suppose further that you have held the option until expiry. If XYZ plc stock trades at 110p at maturity, your call option is in the money and you should exercise. Excluding the premium you paid up front, the payoff from exercising is 10p. On the other hand, if the stock price at maturity is 90p, the option has finished out of the money and is worthless. Your payoff is 0. Figure 1 graphs the payoff at maturity as a function of the stock price of XYZ plc.

All call options held to maturity have the same general payoff diagram illustrated in Figure 1. The angle of the payoff line is 45 degrees (i.e. the line has a slope of one). Notice that the payoff to the call option can never be less than 0, regardless of how low the stock price

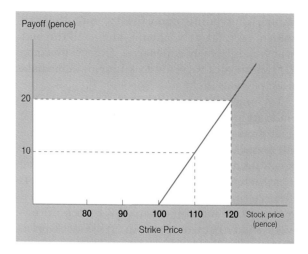

Figure 1: Payoff diagram buy call options

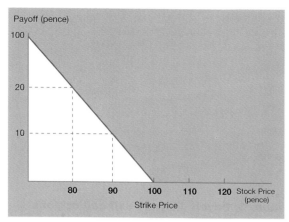

Figure 2: Payoff diagram buy put options

may be. As a result, the value of a call can never be less than 0.

Put options. Suppose now you have bought a put option on 1 share of XYZ plc with a strike price of 100p. Suppose further that you have held the option until expiry. If XYZ plc stock trades at 110p at maturity, your put option is worthless; the put option gives you the right to sell a share at 100p, but clearly it would be better to sell the share in the market at 110p. The put option would, therefore, expire worthless. On the other hand, if the stock price at maturity is 90p, your put option is in the money. By buying a share in the market at 90p and turning around and selling the same share through exercising your put option, you have made a payoff of 10p (excluding the premium paid up front). Figure 2 graphs the payoff at maturity as a function of the stock price of XYZ plc.

All put options held to maturity have the same general payoff diagram illustrated in Figure 2. The payoff line has a slope of -1. As seen in the figure, the payoff to the put option can never be less than 0. Hence, just like a call option, the value of a put option cannot be less than 0.

Comparing puts and calls

Comparing Figures 1 and 2, it is apparent that while the holder of a call option gains if the value of the underlying asset increases; the holder of a put option gains if the value of the underlying asset decreases. This makes sense since a call

option gives the right to buy the asset at a pre-specified price, while the put option gives the right to sell the asset.

Notice from Figure 2 that if XYZ stock is worthless at expiry of the put option, the payoff to the put option is 100p – the same as the exercise price. As is easily seen, this is also the maximum payoff of the put. Thus, unlike a call option, the payoff to a put option is bounded above. Finally, observe from Figures 1 and 2 that the value of an option at expiry is solely a function of the value of the underlying asset.

To complete our set of payoff diagrams, Figures 3 and 4 overleaf show the payoffs to a writer of a call and put, respectively. These are just the mirror images of Figures 1 and 2; every penny gained by the buyer of the option is a penny lost by the seller.

Put-call parity

This section will use the payoff diagrams in Figures 1 and 2 to show that there is a simple relation between the fair values of calls and puts. This relation is referred to as 'put-call parity' and is valid only for European options.

We will continue with the assumption in the examples that the underlying asset is a stock.

The values of a European call and a European put on the same non-dividend paying stock, with the same exercise price, and the same exercise date satisfy the following equation:

Call value – Put value = Stock price – Present value of strike price

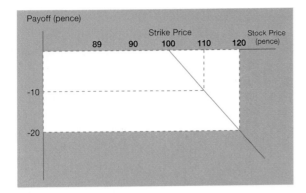

Figure 3: Payoff diagram sell call options

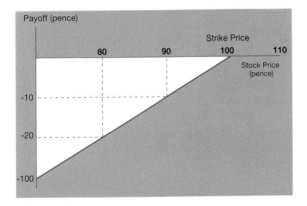

Figure 4: Payoff diagram sell put options

(Note that exchange traded options are typically not protected against loss of dividends. In these cases, if the underlying stock will pay dividends between the current time and maturity of the options put-call parity becomes:

Call value – Put value = Stock price – Present value of dividends – Present value of strike price.)

As an illustration, consider the call and put on XYZ described above. Suppose that the contracts are European and have one year to run. Suppose also that the current stock price of XYZ is 110p and that the one-year interest rate is 10 per cent. Using put-call parity, the difference between the value of the call and the value of the put is: Call value – Put value = 110p – 100p/1.1 = 19.09p. That is, the call is worth about 19p more than the put. If the call actually traded in the market for only 10p more than the put, we would have a

wonderful trading opportunity; buy the call (which is relatively cheap) and sell the put (which is relatively expensive). In fact, by doing the right trades we could lock into an immediate profit of about 9p.

To understand this, it is necessary to understand the arbitrage argument that lies behind put-call parity. Suppose you bought one call and sold one put (with terms as above). The payoff diagram for this portfolio can be constructed by combining Figures 1 and 4. Observe that the portfolio is completely exposed to the risk of movements in XYZ's stock price – every penny gained or lost in XYZ's stock price would be an equal gain or loss to your portfolio. Moreover, this is the only risk you face. (This ignores counterparty risk on the call. Exchange traded options have virtually no counterparty risk since all contracts are written with the exchange as the counterparty.) As a result, it is possible to create a perfect hedge by 'shorting' the stock. This observation forms the basis of put-call parity.

If you buy the call, sell the put, and short one share, you will have a portfolio that is worth –100p with certainty at maturity in one year. Thus, this is just a complicated way of borrowing the present value of the strike price. To avoid arbitrage, the initial cash flow from this complicated borrowing procedure must be equal to the initial cash flow from borrowing in the normal way. Hence: Call value – Put value – Stock price = Present value of strike price which is another way of expressing put-call parity.

Another way to see put-call parity is as follows. Borrow the present value of the strike price and buy one share of XYZ. In one year, you have an obligation to pay back 100p, but you also have the share which may be worth more or less than 100p. The payoff of this portfolio is illustrated in Figure 5. If the stock price in one year is 120p, then after repaying the loan, the portfolio is worth 20p. If the stock price is 80p, the portfolio is worth –20p. The alert reader will have noticed that Figure 5 is the same as Figures 1 and 4 combined. In other words, buying one call and selling one put gives the same payoff as buying one share and borrowing the present value of the strike price. To prevent arbitrage,

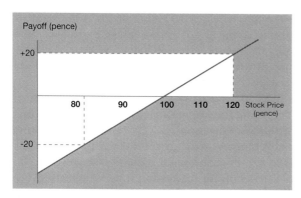

Figure 5: Payoff diagram buy stock and borrow PV (100)

these two strategies must have the same cashflow initially. But this is just put-call parity as given by the first equation above.

Let us return to our example where put-call parity was violated. To make the 9p risk-free arbitrage this is what you would do: (1) Buy the call and sell the put. This costs you 10p. (2) Short one share at the current price of 110p and lend the present value of 100p, for one year, giving a cash inflow of 19.09p. One year from now, the cash flows from (1) and (2) cancel each other. Thus, you would have made a profit of about 9p.

In the example, the second portfolio was constructed to be a perfect hedge for the first portfolio. Hence, you could take advantage of the relative mispricing between the call and the put without running any risk. Of course, in practice, traders will quickly take advantage of any deviation from put-call parity so that the condition is not likely to last long. Put-call parity is not valid for American options because of the possibility of early exercise. This is discussed next.

Early exercise of American options

Table 2 gives the costs and benefits of early exercise of American options. Although a call option gives the holder the right to buy the underlying asset, if this asset pays dividends the option holder is typically not entitled to the dividends. (Exchange traded options are typically not dividend protected, but some OTC options may be.) To receive the dividends, the call holder must exercise his option. There are

two drawbacks from exercising a call option early: (1) the option is lost, and (2) because of the time value of money, it is better to pay the strike price as late as possible. Thus for non-dividend paying assets it will never be optimal to exercise an American call option early. In such cases, the value of an American call will equal the value of a European call. If for some reason you no longer want a particular call option in your portfolio, you do not need to exercise it – you can sell it.

Since a holder of a put option receives the strike price when exercising the put, the time value of money gives an incentive to exercise puts early. Obviously, a counteracting force is that the option would be lost. Which of these effects is the stronger must be evaluated case by case. Unlike call options, we can therefore not say that it is never optimal to exercise put options on non-dividend paying assets early.

In fact, while dividends provide an incentive to exercise calls early, dividends are an additional reason not to exercise puts early. When you exercise a put early, you forego dividends. You can think of it this way: suppose that when you exercise a put, you sell an asset that you already own. If you did not exercise, you would receive the dividends that this asset would pay between now and the maturity of the put. However, if you exercise, those dividends will no longer accrue to you. (Even if you did not own the share, there would be a dividend cost from exercising a put early. It is an opportunity cost.) Since it may be optimal to exercise a put early,

Table 2: Costs and benefits of early exercise of American options		
	Benefits	**Costs**
Call	**Receive dividends**	**Lose option Pay strike price early**
Put	**Receive strike price early**	**Lose option Forego dividends**

put-call parity need not hold for American options. Hence, you should not be surprised if you observe deviations from put-call parity for exchange traded options.

Option pricing

Put-call parity only gives us a price differential. We will now look into the factors that determine the fair values of calls and puts. Table 3 provides an overview.

Table 3: Determinants of option value		
	Call	**Put**
Volatility	▲	▲
Strike Price	▼	▲
Time to Maturity	△	△
Current Asset Price	▲	▼
Interest Rate	▲	▼
Cash Dividends	▼	▲

▲ indicates that the option value increases when the fundamental variable is increasing

▼ indicates that the option value decreases when the fundamental variable is increasing

△ Increasing time to maturity has an ambiguous effect on the value of European puts. The value of European calls may also decrease as time to maturity increases if the underlying asset pays sufficiently large dividends.

Volatility. Volatility measures the variability, or dispersion, of future prices of the underlying asset. When volatility is high, extreme values are more likely, making options more valuable. This can be seen by reference to the call option payoff in Figure 1. Consider the following two alternatives of the stock price in one year: (1) the stock will be either 90 or 110 (low volatility), (2) the stock price will be either 80 or 120 (high volatility). Notice that the high volatility scenario gives a larger payoff on the upside. On the downside, however, the two scenarios give the same payoff of 0. As a result, the value of the option today in the high volatility scenario will be larger than in the low volatility scenario. A similar argument can be constructed for put options, by reference to Figure 2.

Current asset price. When the current price of the underlying asset is high, it is more likely that the asset price at maturity is high, which as we can see from Figure 1 has a positive effect on the value of the call. The opposite applies for put options.

Strike price. Since a call option gives the right to buy an asset at the strike price, it is clear that the call is more valuable when the strike price is low. Since a put option gives the right to sell an asset, the opposite applies.

Time to maturity. For American options, increasing time to maturity increases value since the effect is essentially to give the option holder a wider choice with respect to which date to exercise. For European options, we can identify two effects from increasing time to maturity: (1) the dispersion of the underlying asset value at maturity increases, (2) the present value of the exercise price falls. As discussed under the volatility heading, effect (1) tends to increase the value of both calls and puts. But notice that if the stock pays regular dividends, then increasing the time to maturity would increase the present value of dividends and, therefore, have a negative effect on European call values. Effect (2) tends to increase the value of call options, but decrease the value of put options.

Interest rates. When interest rates increase, this will tend to decrease the present value of the exercise price. As discussed above, this has a positive effect on call options, but a negative effect on put options.

Cash dividends. Since cash dividends cause the stock price to drop, an increase in cash dividends has a positive effect on put options and a negative effect on call options.

There might seem to be a serious omission from Table 3 – the expected return on the underlying asset. Intuition would suggest that when the expected return rises, call values should also rise and put values should fall. The reason why this is not so is essentially that the expected return of the stock price is already reflected in the current stock price. This leads to the remarkable conclusion that if we are in disagreement about the expected return of a particular asset, we should nevertheless be in agreement about the value of options written on that asset.

Although expected return is not important for the valuation of options, as we have seen, volatility is a key variable. Unlike the other variables listed above, with the exception of cash dividends, volatility is something which we do not know for certain. Although we could try to estimate a stock's past volatility, there is no guarantee that the stock will exhibit the same volatility in the future. Hence, different people may reach different conclusions about the value of an option because they have different opinions about volatility.

Because of this, options are often viewed as instruments for taking bets on volatility. Just as you may buy or sell stocks depending on your view of future stock prices, you may trade options depending on your view of volatility. If the market consensus is that the volatility of a specific asset is 30 per cent and you estimate volatility to be 20 per cent, your valuation of an option would be lower than the market price. If you stuck to your guns, you should then be writing options.

Of course, even if you are right about the volatility, you could end up losing money on your trades if the stock price changed sufficiently in your disfavour.

However, it is possible to construct an excellent hedge by taking positions in the underlying stock and a risk-free asset. In the case of writing calls your hedge portfolio would be long the underlying asset. However, unlike the hedge used to illustrate put-call parity, hedging an option requires a dynamic strategy with adjustments made over time, depending on changes in the market price of the underlying asset. Black and Scholes (1973) first demonstrated how to do this.

The fact that European options can be hedged (almost) perfectly, allows us to price them with great accuracy – assuming our estimate of volatility is correct.

The curved line in Figure 6 gives a graphical representation of the Black-Scholes call value as a function of current stock price. Notice that the call value is bounded below by the payoff diagram and bounded above by the stock price itself. The difference between the payoff line and the call value is called the time value of the option. The payoff line itself is often called the intrinsic value of the option. For the reader interested in pursuing option pricing in further detail, a few references are provided in the books panel.

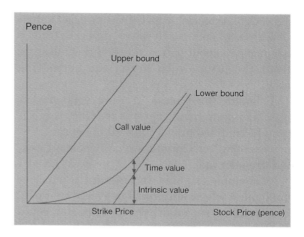

Figure 6: Call value as function of stock price

Real options. Option valuation can also be used in calculating the value of investment opportunities. Traditional discounted cash flow methods have shortcomings in valuing investments with significant operating or strategic options.

For example, a company may hold a lease on some land where it is considering building a plant. The company has the option to defer building, which it may do depending on market conditions. Because the time at which it would be optimal to start building, if at all, may vary, a straight DCF calculation would tend to undervalue the project – since the option would not be properly accounted for.

Other examples of real options include: the option to abandon a project, which is particularly important for capital-intensive projects; the option to alter the scale of production – relevant in cyclical industries and natural resource extraction; and the option to switch inputs or outputs. Most major and strategic projects usually involve some concealed real option.

Conclusion

We have seen that there is an important arbitrage relation between the prices of corresponding puts and calls. The basis for this put-call parity is the fact that a portfolio short a put and long a call can be replicated by buying the stock and borrowing. This basic principle of replication and arbitrage also underlies the

Black-Scholes model, which gives us exact values for European options. However, different traders can disagree about option values if they disagree about the future volatility of the underlying asset.

Although the phrase 'trading volatility' is often associated with options trading, there is more to trading options than taking speculative bets on volatility. Options are an important risk-management tool.

As a simple example, consider a US importer of Japanese electronics to be delivered and paid for in yen in six months. The importer could protect himself from a rise in the dollar cost of yen by buying call options on the yen denominated in dollars.

Many firms that have floating rate loans protect themselves against rises in interest rates by capping their borrowing rate. Caps are essentially call options on future spot rates. If rates rise above the cap rate the firms gain by borrowing below market levels. At the end of 1991, the worldwide total outstanding notional principal of caps was estimated to be around $300bn (£193.5bn).

Summary

It was not until the 1970s that options were transformed from relative obscurity into a staple of the financial markets. There are two basic types of option: call options and put options. A 'European' option can be exercised only at maturity; an 'American' option can be exercised at any date up to and including maturity.

For European options there is a simple relation between the fair values of calls and puts – referred to as put-call parity. The fact that these options can be hedged almost perfectly enables them to be priced accurately – disagreements usually arise over the volatility of the underlying asset. Other factors that determine the fair value include the current asset price, the strike price, time to maturity, interest rates and cash dividends.

Option valuation can be used in calculating the value of investment opportunities.

Suggested further reading

Black, Fischer and Scholes, Myron, 'The pricing of corporate liabilities'. *Journal of Political Economy* 81, 637-59, 1973

Cox, John C. and Rubinstein, Mark (1985) *Options Markets*, Prentice-Hall

Gastineau, Gary L. (1988) *The Options Manual*, 3rd edn, McGraw-Hill

Hull, John (1993) *Introduction to Futures and Options Markets*, 2nd edn, Prentice-Hall

Hull, John (1995) *Options, Futures, and other Derivative Securities*, 2nd edn, Prentice-Hall, 1995

Thrigeorgis, Lenos 'Real options and interactions with financial flexibility', *Financial Management* 22, 204-224, 1993

Global Derivatives Study Group, Washington DC, July 1993 'Derivatives: practices and principles', Report to Congressional Requesters, May 1994

'Financial derivatives: actions needed to protect the financial system', US General Accounting Office.

An introduction to futures markets: insurance, liquidity, immediacy

■ **Futures markets date back over 500 years but their real relevance is more recent and at least as much to do with the professional investment market as with the physical assets and commodities.**

by Mark Britten-Jones

From the simplest perspective, a futures contract is an agreement between two parties to make a particular exchange at a date in the future.

For example, a contract made on March 31 could call for the buyer to purchase one ounce of gold for $200 – the futures price – on June 30 from the seller of the futures contract. In this case gold is, as it is called, the physical or underlying on which the futures contract is based (usually a commodity or some form of asset). The spot price is the price that gold sells for in immediate exchange. Futures contracts differ from most commercial transactions in that the date of agreed exchange lags the agreement date by some significant period. The need for such arrangements is not new. In the 14th Century Italian merchants and textile manufacturers bought English wool for some years ahead so as to guarantee supply. In the 17th and 18th centuries the slow shipping times between the cotton-producing regions of the US and the Liverpool cotton market created a demand for cotton 'to arrive', that is for contracts on cotton that had not arrived in the market place yet.

It was from the cotton market in Liverpool and the commodity markets in Chicago that the modern form of futures markets developed. Presently there are futures exchanges operating in most developed countries. In the US the largest is the Chicago Board of Trade (CBOT). In Europe, the largest is the London International Financial Futures and Options Exchange (LIFFE), which specialises in futures on financial instruments. These exchanges are typically very active. For example, in 1994 LIFFE traded over 153 million contracts on a broad variety of financial instruments. Table 1 shows the futures contracts traded on LIFFE.

Table 1		
Money Market	**Bonds**	**Equity**
Eurolira	German Govt Bond	FT-SE 100 Index
Euromark	Italian Govt Bond	FT-SE Mid 250
3-months ECU	Long Gilt	Index
Euroswiss	Japanese Govt Bond	
Short Sterling		
Eurodollar		

Modern futures markets have several features that distinguish them from earlier forms and from other future-related contracts such as insurance:
- high level of contract retrading
- small amount of physical exchange
- very high degree of leverage
- low level of default.

These features derive from the institutional structure of the modern futures exchange.

Structure of the futures market

All modern futures exchanges have a clearing house separate from the futures exchange and its members. The clearing house guarantees the performance of every contract traded on the exchange, effectively becoming the counterparty in all trades. The London Clearing House (LCH) is the clearing house for LIFFE. In order to be able to offer this guarantee the clearing house administers a system of margins. Margins take two forms. An initial margin that is deposited with the clearing house when a position is opened; and a daily system of 'variation margins' that are collections or payments based on movements of the relevant futures price. The system of variation margins is also called marking to market as the variation margins are related to movements in the market-determined futures price.

The system of margins allows the clearing house to guarantee the performance of all contracts. Futures market participants thus need not be concerned with the identity and creditworthiness of their counterparty. The result is that futures exchanges can provide the rare combination of a very high level of leverage and a very low level of default risk.

Valuation

A useful way of thinking about the futures price is as a breakeven price for the underlying commodity. In our example, if at the delivery date June 30, the spot price for gold was $250, then the futures buyer can purchase an ounce of gold at $200, a price $50 below the current price. Profits of $50 are earned by immediately selling. On the other hand the seller of the contract loses $50. A spot price of $200 is the breakeven price as neither buyer nor seller profits at this price.

A futures price thus incorporates the market's beliefs about the likely course of the underlying price. This in turn will depend on the supply and demand conditions that are expected to prevail in the future. These expectations will typically change by the hour and by the minute. In some circumstances we can say more than this however.

Consider a commodity with a current spot price S and a futures price for delivery one year ahead F. We assume that borrowing and lending opportunities at an annual rate of r are readily available. Assuming the commodity is costless to store and ignoring real-world complications such as margins, we can state that the futures price is equal to the current spot price plus an additional component for interest: $F = S(1 + r)$. This pricing formula holds because any other futures price

results in arbitrage opportunities. Say the futures price was above this level: $F > S(1 + r)$, then an arbitrageur could:
- sell a futures contract *or*
- borrow S dollars in the money market and buy a unit of the commodity on the spot market for price S.

These transactions are offsetting with a total cost of zero. At expiration,
- the commodity is delivered at the agreed price *and*
- the principal and interest on the loan $S(1 + r)$ is paid.

The arbitrageur thus earns a risk-free profit of $F - S(1 + r)$. For risk-free profits not to be freely available the pricing formula must hold. Of course many commodities are impossible to store. In these cases the futures prices reflects forecasts of supply and demand conditions. Futures markets thus provide a valuable service to people who never trade futures by providing cheap, up-to-the minute forecasts for prices of a number of commodities and financial instruments.

Delivery

Only a very small percentage of contracts that are entered into actually result in the agreed exchange (called *delivery*) occurring. The majority of contracts are *closed out* by taking an offsetting position prior to the delivery date. For example, the buyer of a futures contract in our previous example could, at any time prior to the delivery date, sell a futures contract. He has thus offset his position in the physical by having contracts to buy and to sell one ounce of gold.

Of course the closing-out price will most likely differ from the price at which he or she bought and this difference results in a trading profit or loss.

The role of futures markets

Two basic approaches have been taken to explain trading in futures: the *insurance* approach and the *liquidity* approach. These roles are not separate but we shall examine them one at a time.

The insurance approach takes as a typical participant a producer or user of a commodity.

For example, a wheat farmer who is concerned about the risk of fluctuations in the price of wheat from now until his wheat is harvested may sell wheat futures contracts in order to lock in a price for wheat. By such an arrangement he can protect himself against falls in the wheat price that could result in bankruptcy, loan default and so on.

A more modern example might be that of a corporate treasurer who knows he or she will need to borrow money in six months time to finance a business expansion. By selling an interest rate futures contract he or she is able to hedge the company against rises in interest rates that may occur in the next six months.

This approach distinguishes two types of participants in the futures markets: *hedgers*, such as the farmer and corporate treasurer in the examples above, and *speculators*, who have no position in the underlying but are participating in the futures market in the hope of earning profits from their speculative activities.

The liquidity approach is perhaps a better explanation. It emphasizes the institutional features of futures markets that permit low transactions costs. The presence of contracts with well-defined terms, the performance guarantee of the clearing house and the book-entry accounting of open positions all reduce trading costs by centralizing search and credit activities.

This approach emphasizes *demand for immediacy*, which is the willingness to buy or sell now rather than wait. This demand depends on the volatility of the underlying price and the extent to which the underlying price affects the wealth of the buyer or seller.

Futures markets are a prime example of a market in which the demand for immediacy is high. Successful futures contracts usually have high underlying price volatility and a number of participants whose wealth is significantly exposed to the underlying price. Immediacy is of particular concern to intermediaries who may be protected once all the legs of a deal are in place but who are exposed when fewer legs are in place. Consider a bank's borrowing and lending activities.

When these are perfectly synchronized there is little risk because changes in market interest rates can be passed on in lending rates. But when there is a time gap between the borrowing and lending there can be a substantial risk of market rates moving from the rate at which the bank was able to borrow.

For many financial instruments the same sorts of risks are incurred by dealers who may have little risk when buying and selling orders are synchronized but who are exposed to big risks when only one leg of the deal is in place. In such cases a delay of even a few seconds can be important. The dealers' demand for immediacy is sustained by continual build-up and build-down of inventories in response to periodic Treasury auctions, stock and bond issuance, and portfolio restructuring by large institutional investors.

The role of a futures market is not just to provide hedging capability but to provide it extremely quickly. For these reasons futures markets have been very successful for hedging price risk on markets in which intermediaries hold significant inventories and for which price volatility is high. Viewed in this light the incredible growth in financial futures is not surprising.

Summary

Modern futures markets developed from the cotton market in Liverpool and the commodity markets in Chicago. They are distinguished from earlier forms by high levels of contract retrading, a small amount of physical exchange, high levels of leverage and low levels of default. All modern exchanges have clearing houses that guarantee contracts through taking margins.

A futures price incorporates the market's belief about the likely course of the asset's underlying price. Participants in a futures market include hedgers, such as farmers and corporate treasurers who adopt an 'insurance' approach, and speculators, who have no physical position but hope to earn profits from their activity. For them a futures market's liquidity – and immediacy – are particularly important.

Living life on the hedge

■ **Hedging is a way of covering a company's foreign exchange risk. But, says** Debra Perry, **there are many complex considerations to take note of.**

The recent spate of currency hedging disasters has brought into focus the whole issue of a company's hedging policies. Questions such as in what circumstances hedging is desirable, what hedging methods should be employed, and exactly what assets and liabilities of a company are exposed to foreign exchange risk are crucial to the exposure management process.

Currency hedging eliminates the risk of foreign exchange movements adversely affecting profits. The principal financial instruments currently used by companies for hedging are currency forwards, swaps and options.

A currency forward is simply an agreement to buy or sell foreign exchange at an agreed rate and at a certain time in the future. A currency swap can be seen as a series of forward contracts. Currency options, on the other hand, give a company the right, rather than the obligation, to buy or sell foreign exchange at a certain time in the future at an agreed price, thereby allowing the company to lock in a fixed amount of foreign currency to buy or sell, while allowing it to benefit from any favourable exchange rate movements.

Most companies tend to hedge their foreign exchange risk. However, it is not always clear that it is in the best interests of a company's shareholders for companies to do so. For example, if shareholders do not wish to bear exchange rate risk (which is not necessarily the case) they can always hedge for themselves. This can be accomplished either by constructing well diversified portfolios consisting of a multitude of currencies, so that the exchange rate gains and losses cancel each other out, or, alternatively, shareholders can engage in active hedging using the financial instruments mentioned above.

Is hedging really necessary?

Purchasing Power Parity (PPP) is another argument that disputes the need for hedging. PPP claims that exchange rate changes are offset by price level changes. As an example, PPP would state that if the inflation rate in the US is 10 per cent higher than in the UK, the US dollar should depreciate by 10 per cent, leaving relative prices unaltered.

Although empirical evidence suggests that these exchange rate changes take time to work themselves out, opponents of hedging argue that there is little exchange risk in the long run and hence hedging is redundant. Closely related to this is the argument that if foreign exchange exposure is left uncovered, the gains and losses tend to average out over longer periods and therefore it does not pay for a company to bear the cost of hedging.

Notwithstanding all these arguments, the most important case against hedging is the fact that it is costly, not only in terms of transaction costs, spreads and premia but also in terms of management time and effort. Highly trained personnel are required to ensure that hedging strategies are effective and calamities avoided.

Coupled with this is the problem that so-called hedging operations can become excessive and that it is often hard to draw the line between hedging and speculating. Corporate treasuries may easily be turned into profit centers with disastrous results.

Take for example, Shell's Japanese subsidiary, Shell Showa, which lost over $1bn (£0.6bn) in 1992 attempting to speculate on the yen/dollar rate in the forward market. Tight internal controls are needed to combat this problem, which further implies that top-level management should be able to understand fully any hedging strategies undertaken by the company. Sadly, this is often not the case.

But even when a company's management understands and agrees with all these arguments, it often still chooses to hedge. Why?

First, there is the conventional argument that a company is in business to provide a product or service, and since it presumably has no specific skill in predicting exchange rates it should hedge these risks so that it can concentrate its resources on what it does best.

However, there can be other reasons why it could be in a company's best interests to hedge. For example, even if exchange rate risk can be diversified away by the shareholder or is irrelevant in the longer term, there can still be substantial exchange rate risk in the short to medium term that can lead to a company suffering from 'financial distress' and, in the extreme, insolvency. This can be especially true if companies enter into fixed price contracts.

It goes without saying that insolvency is costly. It causes forced sales of assets, often at a knock-down price, as well as the loss of valuable debt tax shields. There are also legal and accounting costs, not to mention difficulties with suppliers and problems of retaining loyal customers and a committed management and staff as financial distress mounts. In fact, the risk of insolvency may be one of the most important reasons for some companies to hedge and this may be especially true of smaller and undiversified organizations.

In addition, there are certain other situations where a company with a variable income stream may suffer real losses. This will be the case if a company is operating in a country with a progressive taxation scheme as it pays proportionately more tax in high income years than in low income years; therefore it may pay to hedge.

Similarly, if there are asymmetric tax laws, this may lead to losses. As an example, consider a company that, through failure to hedge, loses its ability to utilize a tax credit and is unable to carry it forward to the next tax year. Yet another example is the case where a company has limited or costly access to additional capital and is unable to exploit a profitable investment opportunity because of exchange rate losses.

Finally, a strong incentive for companies to hedge is managerial risk aversion. Managers may not be rewarded sufficiently for large profits but are strongly penalized for large losses, including penalties in the form of the loss of power, prestige and, in the worst case, position. This is further enforced if a manager's remuneration package is tied to the profits of a company – most individuals prefer a more steady income stream to a highly volatile one.

What is at risk?

For companies that do engage in active currency hedging, one of the most crucial issues that the financial manager has to deal with is: what exactly is exposed to foreign exchange risk?

There are two main types of foreign exchange exposure.

The first, 'accounting' or 'translation' exposure, arises from the need to translate the balance sheet of a multinational's subsidiary into home currency terms. However, companies should be wary of hedging this type of exposure and should only consider doing so if it is associated with a real cash flow.

For example, consider a UK company that has a translation exposure in US dollars and therefore sells dollars forward. If the dollar subsequently rises and it never actually receives the dollars from the subsidiary, it is forced to buy expensive dollars in the spot market without an offsetting transaction. This could easily lead to insolvency or, at the very least, a cash flow problem. A common alternative is to finance foreign subsidiaries by borrowing in the foreign currency concerned, but it may not be desirable to let gearing policy be the servant of translation exposure.

The second type of currency exposure, 'economic exposure,' was developed as a more ongoing forward-looking approach to foreign exchange risk and is concerned with a company's future cash flows rather than merely its 'snapshot' accounting exposure.

Initially, it was defined only in terms of

transactions exposure, or the direct effects that arise when a company has an obligation to pay or receive a foreign currency at a future date.

More recently, however, companies have come to recognise a far more important source of foreign exchange exposure, one arising from the fact that currency fluctuations may cause changes in relative prices of goods across countries, which can affect a company's international competitiveness, altering its sales, profits and ultimately its value. Even companies that perceive themselves to be purely domestic can suffer from this type of foreign exchange exposure.

Consider the case of a German car manu-facturer. If its major competitors are Japanese, it may be highly exposed to the yen/DM rate even though it may believe it has no yen transactions on its books and therefore is not exposed in traditional terms. Hedging this type of exposure, if possible at all, has to be accomplished through alternative methods such as varying plant locations, altering the input mix or adopting various marketing strategies, which may be costly.

Nevertheless, purely financial hedging, although limited in the protection it provides, may help the company in that it buys more time to make these necessary 'real' adjustments. The main point is that it is important for a company to consider both types of economic exposure when designing its hedging strategy.

Conclusion

To conclude, it should be stressed that currency exposure should be hedged only if it could result in real economic losses for the company – such as possible insolvency, tax shield losses or missed investment opportunities. If a company does decide it is in its best interests to hedge, it is the task of the financial manager to decide exactly what is exposed and to choose the cheapest, most effective hedging method available to deal with this risk. Finally, but by no means least, one of the most difficult tasks a financial manager may face is to ensure that a hedge really remains a hedge.

Summary

Currency forward is an agreement to buy or sell foreign exchange at an agreed rate and at a certain time in the future. A currency swap is a series of forward contracts. Currency options give a company the right, rather than the obligation, to buy or sell foreign exchange at a future date.

Shareholders' ability to diversify their own portfolios, the purchasing power parity (PPP) theory, and the temptation to speculate are arguments against hedging. Justifications include the idea that companies should concentrate on what they know best, the reduction of short-term financial risk and managerial risk aversion.

It is important to distinguish between 'accounting' or translation exposure – which should only be done if it is associated with a real cash flow – and 'economic' exposure.

Suggested further reading

Dufey, Gunter and Srinivasulu, S. L. 'The case for corporate management of foreign exchange risk', *Financial Management* 12, No. 4, pp. 54-62, 1984.

Smith, C. and Stulz, R. 'The determinants of a company's hedging policies', *Journal of Financial and Quantitative Analysis*, Vol. 20, No. 4, December 1985.

Lessard, Donald R. and Flood Jr, Eugene 'On the measurement of operating exposure to exchange rates: a conceptual approach', *Financial Management*, Spring 1986.

Warrants and convertibles

■ **Warrants and convertibles are a halfway house between debt and equity. But, says** Anthony Neuberger, **their true nature can be easily misrepresented and misunderstood.**

Companies wanting to raise capital are often faced with an unappealing choice between issuing bonds with restrictive covenants and high coupons and issuing equity, which dilutes the interest of existing shareholders. One apparently attractive alternative is issuing convertible bonds. These are bonds that the investor can exchange for a fixed number of shares at some point in the future.

Investors like them because they have the security of a bond. They also allow the investor to share in the good fortune of the issuing company since they can swap the bonds for the shares if the shares do well. They appear attractive to issuers because they have a lower coupon than straight debt – investors accept the lower coupon in return for the conversion option.

If the debt is converted into equity – and this has tended to happen historically – the company will have ended up issuing equity but it will have sold the shares much more dearly than if it had issued straight equity originally.

Bonds with warrants are a variant on convertible bonds. The warrants entitle the investor to buy shares at a fixed cash price in future. Issues are frequently designed so that the cash that the company receives if the warrants are all exercised is equal to the face value of the bonds so the exercise of the warrants extinguishes the company's liability to the bondholders.

Cheaper than capital or debt?

Any argument that convertible bonds are generally a cheaper form of capital than either debt or equity must be fallacious. Miller and Modigliani showed that, under certain simplifying assumptions, a company's cost of capital could not be altered by splitting up its cash flows between securities in different ways. The implication is that a company can only increase its value by financing in one way rather than another if it can exploit some tax rule or some inefficiency in the capital markets or if it leads to the company's assets being more efficiently managed.

It is true that convertibles represent cheap debt when they are not converted and cheap equity if they are converted. But there is an offsetting disadvantage to the company issuing them. If the company does well the shares will be converted, so the convertible holders will dilute the equity when the existing shareholders least want to be diluted. If the company does badly it will be left with debt when it least wants to have issued debt. The argument for the cheapness of convertibles, though seductive, is flawed.

The very complexity of convertibles and warrants invites such illusions. Box 1 overleaf recounts the rise and fall of the Japanese equity warrant market. Bonds with warrants appeared to offer issuers a form of debt capital at negative rates of interest they would probably never have to repay.

Box 2 at the end of this article shows how the complexity was exploited by the advertising company Saatchi & Saatchi in 1988 to raise capital at a time when debt and equity looked hard to raise at any reasonable price. The cost of the convertible would not have been obvious to a casual observer but turned out to be sufficient to bring on a major financial crisis for the company.

Convertible bonds do not provide a golden road to a reduced cost of capital. But a company that wishes to raise capital may be unwilling to issue pure debt (because of strain on the balance sheet, cost of servicing in the short term and so on) or pure equity (unwilling to accept immediate dilution). Convertibles offer a middle way with intermediate advantages and disadvantages. In this respect a convertible bond may be an alternative to issuing a mix of debt and equity. But there are circumstances under which the convertible structure has particular attractions.

For example, consider a new venture that wishes to raise equity capital. There may be great advantages in leaving the original owners with full control so long as things go well. But outside investors may wish to take control of the assets if the company does badly. Convertible bonds offer a way of doing this.

If things go well they will initially be bonds with no control rights and then convert into a minority equity stake. If things go badly the company will be unable to service the bonds and the bondholders can take control of the business.

Another case where convertibles may be useful is where the total value of the assets of the company is clear but where the split of that value between shareholders and debtholders is not. If the company chooses to issue debt to finance expansion the market may deduce that management believes that debt is overpriced; they will therefore only buy the debt at a substantial discount.

Similarly if the company issues equity the market will only take it at a discount. If the company wants to avoid this discount it can issue convertible bonds because they are intermediate between debt and equity and their value is not so sensitive to information to which the company's management is privy.

Option pricing techniques

The valuation of convertibles has been revolutionised by advances in option pricing techniques. Previously, investors tended to value convertibles on the basis that they would be converted into equity, so they were valued like equity with a high yield.

Now it is accepted that the right way to look at convertibles is as straight bonds plus an option to buy the shares, where the price of exercising the shares is surrendering the straight bond.

Modern methods of option pricing normally used for valuing traded options can be used for valuing convertibles. There are a few specific issues – the dilution that accompanies the conversion option, the estimation of dividends and volatility in long maturity options, the risk of the company defaulting before the bond matures – but the same broad principles apply.

Convertibles have an important role to play in financing companies as a hybrid between debt and equity. But their complexity means that their true nature can be easily misrepresented and misunderstood.

■ The Rise and Fall of the Japanese Warrant Market

Many Japanese companies issued bonds with warrants in the 1980s. They appeared to offer cheap financing. Consider a good-name Japanese company that could issue straight debt in the Euromarkets paying 7 per cent in US dollars or 3 per cent in Yen.

Suppose instead that it issues $100m of seven-year debt with warrants attached. The warrants give the investor the right to buy shares at a 10 per cent premium to the current price. Obviously no one would want to exercise the warrants now. Because of the warrants the company might be able to issue the bonds in dollars with a coupon of 3 per cent rather than the 7 per cent they would have to pay if they did not issue them with warrants.

Given the 4 per cent interest differential between US and Japanese rates the company could swap the bond into Yen debt with an interest rate of minus 1 per cent. At worst the company would have succeeded in borrowing at negative interest rates. But things could turn out much better than that. Provided the share price appreciates by at least 10 per cent over the period the company would not repay the debt. The cash from exercising the warrants would repay the debt.

This is not cheap capital. In this example the company could have issued straight equity more cheaply. If the warrants are exercised the company will have raised $100m by selling shares that it could otherwise have sold for $90m now. But it is also committed to paying 3 per cent interest for seven years. The net discounted proceeds will be less than $84m.

So by issuing bonds with warrants the company is actually raising less money than it would by a straight equity issue. It also has the disadvantage that if the share price goes down the company is left with having to repay the debt.

■ The Saatchi Convertible

The complexity of convertibles provides much scope for disguising the nature of a company's liabilities. Saatchi & Saatchi, the advertising company, decided to raise new capital to finance its expansion plans in 1988. Its share price had fallen and it was unwilling to issue new equity. As a service company with few tangible assets and negative shareholders funds from a string of acquisitions, straight debt would have been costly and would have strained the balance sheet.

Instead the company decided to raise £ 175m through an issue of convertible preference shares. This counted as equity for accounting purposes. The preference shares would be redeemable at par in 2003. To reduce the coupon the company gave investors the right to put the shares back to the company at 120 per cent of their face value after five years.

This meant that investors were happy to accept a coupon of only 6.75 per cent against a yield on Treasury bonds of close to 10 per cent. They reasoned that if they put the bonds after five years they could get an all-in yield of 10 per cent; in addition they could benefit if the share price rose substantially.

The balance sheet showed that Saatchi's had issued preference shares that might have to be redeemed in 15 years for £175m. A naive reader of the accounts might have assumed they posed little danger to Saatchi's survival; as preference shares, Saatchi's could pass over the dividend. Problems could only occur in 15 years when the preference shares fell to be repaid, but by then they would probably have been converted into equity anyhow. Furthermore the fact that the coupon was only 6.75 per cent, and the conversion could only take place at a premium to the current share price, might be seen as evidence that Saatchi's had raised the capital very cheaply.

The reality was that Saatchi's had issued five-year deep-discounted debt with a yield of 10 per cent, together with an equity kicker. If presented in this way, the threat to Saatchi's survival some three years later would have come as no surprise. Because of a sharp deterioration in Saatchi's trading position it became clear that the company would not be able to honour the put. The terms had to be renegotiated with the convertible holders taking a massive slice of equity.

Although the information was all in the public domain, the convertible structure allowed the financing to be presented in a favourable light.

The market for corporate control

■ We all know that acquisitions make headlines, but do they also make economic sense? Harold Rose considers the evidence.

Acquisitions form an important part of corporate activity in the UK and the US. In the former, for example, at the height of the takeover wave at the beginning of the 1970s and that towards the end of the 1980s, up to 4 per cent of the country's total capital stock was acquired in a single year through acquisitions and mergers.

During the 1980s about one-quarter of takeover bids were contested, at least initially, by the incumbent management of the target company. Of such 'hostile' bids, about one-half were eventually successful.

To acquire control by inducing the equity shareholders of the target to accept its offer, the bidder usually has to pay a premium over the pre-bid price of up to 100 per cent of the latter, with a mean of about 25 per cent in the UK and some 15 per cent in the US. In some cases the premium may appear to be small but this may merely reflect the fact that the 'pre-bid' price had already incorporated the possibility of a bid. Bid premia tend to be higher in the case of contested bids, depending very much on whether another bidder is thought to be in the wings.

Effects on shareholders

Because of the bid premium, the shareholders of acquired companies obviously gain from the bid – on average about 30 per cent after one month from the initial bid in the UK and rather less in the US, adjusted for general market movements and the share betas of the companies concerned.

The effect on the shareholders of the bidding company is less clear. There tends to be on average a small (adjusted) rise in the bidder's share price over the month following the bid.

There is, therefore, a market expectation on average that acquisitions will benefit the bidder's shareholders; but the smallness of their gain over this period – only about 1 per cent in the UK according to some research – would imply that in a high proportion of cases bidder shareholders actually lose in the short-run, according to the measures used. Some, but not all, research concludes that the shareholders of bidder companies in the US actually lose on average around the bid period.

One problem with such negative findings is that they take as the measure of bidder shareholder gain the change in the bidder's share price after allowing for the change in the general market price level. Such a method implies that acquisitions and mergers have no effect on the market index itself. If, as some research concludes, acquisitions and mergers tend to raise the general level of share prices – through the expectation of widespread productivity or other gains – merely looking at a comparison between the change in the market and that in the bidder's share price will underestimate the gain to bidder shareholders.

It is true that, in accounting terms, there is some evidence, using data from the takeover boom in the UK in the 1960s, that the profitability of the bidder, relative to that of other firms, tended to fall in the years after the bid. However, the interpretation of this is uncertain for two reasons.

First, bids tend to be made when the reported profitability of the bidder is relatively high, so that a subsequent fall in profitability may be more a matter of timing than of acquisition performance. Second, if bidder shareholders are to gain, acquisitions ought be made if the *incremental* return to the bidder, i.e. as compared with not making the acquisition, is higher than the appropriate cost of capital involved. A time-series of relative profitability provides no information as to incremental return.

Although some acquisitions have no doubt been motivated by empire building on the part of the bidder's management (especially as managerial remuneration and prestige have until recently been more a reflection of company size than of profitability) and some are unsuccessful for other reasons, to infer that most acquisitions are commercially unjustified is to assume either that most bidder company managers are irrational or that they do not on average take the interests of their shareholders into account.

Both are extreme assumptions. Whatever the truth about past bids as a whole, the closer link between managerial remuneration and shareholder value being developed today can be expected to induce bidder firms to take the interests of their shareholders more fully into account.

Acquisitions as the removal of bad management

Acquisitions in the US and UK constitute a market in corporate control. 'Hostile' bids may be seen as one of the market's means of dismissing inadequate senior managers. Although there are undoubtedly instances of this, it does not appear to be the main explanation for hostile bids. Franks and Mayer (1994) find that in 80 contested bids in the UK in 1985 and 1986 there was no visible difference between the financial performance of contested target firms and that of non-contested target firms and non-merging firms in the six years prior to the acquisition.

Other economists, in the US, have found only a weak difference between the previous share price performance of target companies where there was a turnover of top managers in the target firm after the bid and those where there was not. Neither was there any difference in bid premia between 'disciplinary' and 'non-disciplinary' bids. Such findings appear to question the role attributed to acquisitions as a deliberate means of removing inadequate management even though Franks and Mayer have found that, in the UK, nearly 80 per cent of executive directors of target firms can expect to be dismissed or resign within two years of a successful contested bid.

What is clear is that, whether or not management is changed, contested acquisitions in the UK and US play an important part in industrial restructuring. Franks and Mayer find levels of asset disposals and other forms of restructuring to be particularly high in the case of contested bids, implying the enforcement of superior performance by the acquiring firm, even though hostile (like uncontested) bids result from the overall corporate strategy of the acquirer as often as from management failure on the part of the target firm.

The US and UK contrasted with other countries

Acquisitions in general, and contested bids in particular, common in the UK and the US, have been comparatively rare in countries such as Germany, France and Japan.

The underlying difference is to be found, first, in the relatively small size of the quoted company sector in France and Germany and, secondly, in the structure of share ownership and control.

In the US and UK share ownership is relatively diffused – among individual share-holders in the former and among institutions in the latter. In Germany, on the other hand, banks have a dominant position through their control of bearer share proxy votes and their chairmanship of supervisory boards; and companies can also frustrate hostile bids by placing limits on the voting rights of large shareholders.

In both France and Germany hostile bids are also made difficult by the existence of cross-company shareholdings; the same is true of Japan, where banks also play a central role in industrial groupings.

One (usually oversimplified) distinction is therefore sometimes made between the so-called 'bank-dominated' economies of Germany and Japan and the 'stock-market-dominated' systems of the UK and US.

A question that has engaged the attention – and prejudices – of economists and economic historians is whether one system or the other has been more encouraging to economic growth.

The question is too complex to be tackled here, but perhaps the essence of the matter is whether the stimulus to restructuring and the growth of new firms afforded by the role of the stock market in the UK and US has been more or less beneficial than the ability of management to take the long-term view that is claimed for bank-dominated systems by those who emphasize the long-term relationship between companies and their lead banks in Germany and Japan. This is a relationship which rests ultimately on the implicit promise by firms that they will not replace bank loans by new issue finance in good times or on the sheer absence of a well-functioning new issue market itself.

Whatever the true answer to this question, what is probable is that the widespread liberalization of capital markets that is taking place as a result of international competitive pressures (and, before long, may also result from the replacement of overburdened state pension schemes in some countries by private or corporate schemes) will increase the role of stock markets in so-called bank-dominated economies. If so, acquisitions in these countries will probably become more common.

Suggested further reading

Franks, J., and Mayer, C. 'Corporate ownership and corporate control: a study of France, Germany and the UK', *Economic Policy*, Vol.10, pp.191-231 (1994).

'Hostile takeovers and the correction of managerial failure', London Business School Discussion Paper No. 156.

Bittlingmayer, George 'The 1920s Boom, The Great Crash and After', Working Paper UCD.GSM.WP 13.93, revised April 1994, Graduate School of Management, University of California, Davis CA.

Meeks, G. (1977) *Disappointing Marriage: A Study of the Gains from Merger*, Cambridge

Buddy, can you swap a dime?

■ **Swaps are one of the more exotic financial instruments and they total twice the entire value of all the shares on the New York Stock Exchange. Yet in essence they are very simple says** Ian Cooper

What is a swap? A swap is an agreement between two parties to exchange amounts of money at various dates in the future. These amounts are set by a formula to be equal to the difference between the cash flows that will occur in two separate financial transactions. The swap thus effectively exchanges the cash flows that will occur in one financial transaction for those that will occur in another. Table 1 lists the most common types of swap.

Table 1: Types of swap

Types of cash flows exchanged	Name of swap
Fixed Interest Rate for Floating Interest Rate	Interest Rate
One Currency for another Currency	Currency
Equity Returns for Fixed Interest Rate	Equity
Commodity Flow for Bond	Commodity

Table 2: Value of swaps outstanding at year end

	$US	Y	DM	£	SwFr
Interest Rate: $8875 billion of which	37%	23%	10%	8%	2%
Currency: $915 billion of which	35%	19%	8%	5%	7%

Source: International Swap Dealers Association

The size of the swap market

The size of the interest rate and currency swap markets is shown in Table 2. Over the last ten years this market has grown from almost zero to nearly $10,000bn of face value of swaps currently outstanding. As a benchmark, the total value of all shares on the New York Stock Exchange is about half this. These swaps are heavily concentrated in the five major currencies, which account for almost 80 per cent of transactions.

The way a swap works

The mechanics of swaps are best illustrated by an example. Suppose that the entities participating in the swap (called counterparties) are a firm (F) and a bank (B). In this currency swap example F agrees to pay B an annual payment equal to 8 per cent of a sterling principal of £10m. The agreement lasts for three years, at the end of which the principal amount of £10m is also paid. In exchange, B agrees to pay F an annual payment of 6 per cent of a US dollar principal of $15m, with the principal payment also made at the end of three years. The contractual payments in the swap are shown in Table 3. One year from the initiation of the swap F will pay B an amount equal to £0.8m minus $0.9m. This payment will be made by calculating the value of this exchange at the current spot exchange rate on that date. The net amount owed will then be settled by a single payment. If, for example, the exchange rate is $1.7 per pound at that time, the net amount due from F to B will be: $(0.8 \times 1.7 - 0.9) = \$0.46m$. At subsequent payment dates a similar procedure will be followed. The net amount due in the swap at each payment date will be calculated using the current spot exchange rate. This amount will then be settled by a payment one way or the other between the counterparties. The amount to be paid at each payment date is thus uncertain at the date that the swap is initiated. It depends on the unknown value of the future exchange rate. The terms of swaps are always set in this way to include the possibility of payments being made both ways.

Table 3: Currency swap illustration

	year 1	year 2	year 3
Contact Cash Flow (from F to B)	£0.8-$0.9	£0.8-$0.9	£10.8-$15.9

The economics of swaps

Why would anyone wish to enter such a contract? We can use the above example to illustrate the economic structure of swaps. If we write the two components of the contractual cash flows from Table 3 on separate lines we get Table 4.

Table 4: Breakdown of the cashflows in a currency swap

	year 1	year 2	year 3
£	+0.8	+0.8	+10.8
$US	-0.9	-0.9	-15.9

From Table 4 it can be seen that the contractual cash flows in this swap are identical to the combination of owning a three-year 8 per cent fixed-interest rate £10m face value sterling loan and making the payments due on a three-year 6 per cent fixed-interest rate $15m face value loan. The swap thus achieves virtually the same economic consequences as buying a sterling debt and selling a $US debt. The differences between the swap and this combination of debt market transactions are:

● The swap avoids the purchase and sale of the debt instruments themselves and so may avoid such consequences as transaction costs, taxes and regulatory constraints.

● The payments in swaps are contracts for the net differences of two amounts so they have superior credit risk characteristics to the outright purchase and sale of two debt instruments.

For these reasons financial institutions, companies and investment funds frequently find it advantageous to use swaps instead of, or in combination with, other capital market transactions. Consequently swaps have played a significant role in the integration and globalization of capital markets.

The uses of swaps

Uses of swaps fall into three main types:
● Using a swap to transform an asset
● Using a swap to transform a liability
● Using a swap to trade a view.
Each of these is illustrated by an example below:
● Using a swap to transform an asset. Suppose

Table 5: Using a swap instead of trading securities

	year 1	year 2	year 3
Cash flow from owning $US bond	+$0.9	+$0.9	+$15.9
Swap cash flow	+£0.8-$0.9	+£0.8-$0.9	+£10.8-$15.9
Net cash flow from combination	+£0.8	+£0.8	+£10.8

that an investor is holding $15m of a 6 per cent three-year bond. He or she wishes to sell this and buy a sterling bond. Doing so, however, will precipitate a large capital gain and mean a large tax payment. As the taxable gain will be precipitated only if the investor sells the bond, virtually the same result could be obtained without the tax payment by continuing to hold the bond and entering the swap in Table 3. The effect of this is shown in Table 5. Adding the cash flow from the $US bond to the cash flow from the swap gives a net cash flow identical to that from holding a sterling bond. The investor is now effectively in the position of having sold the dollar bond and bought the sterling bond. This has been achieved via the swap transaction without precipitating the capital gain and the associated tax payment.

● Using a swap to transform a liability. Suppose a US company can borrow at a very favourable rate in sterling through a UK subsidiary because the interest rate is subsidised by a UK government agency. Suppose, however, that the company wishes to borrow in dollars rather than sterling because this better matches the preferred currency mix of its liabilities.
Without the possibility of a swap the company faces two choices, neither of which is optimal. It can borrow in pounds, the less preferred currency, and get the subsidy, or borrow in dollars, the preferred currency, and not get the subsidy. The solution is that the company borrows sterling and enters a swap. Suppose that the subsidised loan is a three-year 8 per cent sterling loan of £10m, then we can use the same swap example as before. This is shown in Table 6.

The effect of combining the sterling loan with the swap is that the company has a net liability in dollars, once the swap is added to the sterling loan. The terms on which the swap is made will reflect the fact that the sterling amounts the

Table 6: Liability swap

	year 1	year 2	year 3
Payment due on loan	-£0.8	-£0.8	-£10.8
Swap payment	+£0.8-$0.9	+£0.8-$0.9	+£10.8-$15.9
Net cash flow	-$0.9	-$0.9	-$15.9

company needs to receive in the swap are subsidised below current market interest rates. It will have to offer in the swap dollar amounts that are also below current dollar market interest rates. Its subsidised sterling borrowing will be transformed into subsidised dollar borrowing.

● Using a swap to trade a view. The swap shown in Table 3 will become more valuable if sterling rises against the dollar, sterling interest rates fall or dollar interest rates rise. Thus, in conjunction with other transactions, the swap can be used to speculate on any or all of these events.

Interest rate swaps

The basic ideas underlying interest rate swaps are identical to those of currency swaps. In an interest rate swap a stream of fixed-interest rate payments is exchanged for a stream of variable-interest rate payments. An example is given in Table 7. This shows a swap with a principal account of $10m. The payments in the swap are the difference between one year Libor (London Interbank Offered Rate) and a fixed rate of 6 per cent.

Table 7: Interest rate swap

	year 1	year 2	year 3
Cash Flow ($ millions)	$10\times(L_1\%-6\%)$	$10\times(L_2\%-6\%)$	$10\times(L_3\%-6\%)$

The actual level of one year Libor in the second and third years will be known only at the beginning of those years. In Table 7 these future values are denoted by L_2- and L_3- to symbolise that we do not yet know their values. Thus the future cash flows in the swap depend on the future outcomes of this interest rate, just as the future cash flows in the currency swap depend on the future exchange rate.

The uses of an interest rate swap correspond to those of currency swaps. The above swap could be used to transform an asset that pays a fixed interest rate into one that pays a variable rate. Alternatively, in combination with borrowing at a variable rate it could give effectively fixed-rate borrowing. Finally, it could be used to speculate that interest rates will rise. This would make the payments due in the swap shown in Table 7 rise, and hence make the swap more valuable.

This brief summary of swaps has covered only their most basic features. The size of the swap market means that other issues, such as the valuation of swaps, their credit risks, the management of bank swap portfolios, and the regulation of the swap market are of great current concern. Another area of interest is the development of new types of swap such as diff swaps, spread swaps, ratio swaps, spread locks and a host of other complex transactions.

Summary

A swap is an agreement that effectively exchanges the cash flows that will occur in one financial transaction for those that will occur in another. Swaps can avoid transaction costs, taxes and regulatory constraints; they can enjoy superior credit risk characteristics to the outright purchase and sale of two debt instruments. Swaps can be used to transform an asset, transform a liability and to speculate. A basic idea of an interest rate swap is the same as a currency swap. Swaps have played a significant role in the integration and globalisation of capital markets.

Suggested further reading

Das, Satyajit (1989) *Swap Financing*, IFR Books, London.

Overdahl, J. and Schachter, B. 'Derivatives regulation and financial management: lessons from Gibson Greetings', *Financial Management* (24.1, Spring 1995, pp 68-78).

Sorensen, Eric H. and Bollier, Thierry F. 'Pricing swap default risk', *Financial Analysts Journal* (May-June 1994, pp 23-33).

The merits of project finance

■ **Major projects are rarely financed directly by the companies involved. Instead they turn to project finance, linked to the risks and returns of a single project, not to the performance of the company as a whole, explains** Harold Rose

In the usual case lenders to a company have collectively a claim on its cash flows as a whole, except for lenders to a subsidiary where there is no explicit or implicit guarantee (in the form of a 'letter of comfort', for example) by the parent company. It is also from the company as a whole that the dividends are paid.

In the case of project finance, on the other hand, both lenders and equity investors look only to the cash flows of the project concerned (often a large-scale undertaking such as oil exploration or development or tunnel building) for their returns. This, too, differs from the case with a normal subsidiary, the operations of which are rarely confined to a single identifiable project. Where such a project is being initiated or spun off by a 'parent' company, the suppliers of finance to the project have no recourse, in the classic version of project financing, to the 'parent' company. Hence the American term 'non-recourse financing' for this situation. But hybrids have also been developed where the 'parent' company or sponsoring organization offers some form of minimum guarantee.

Why project financing?

There are several advantages of separate project financing to a sponsoring company, which will be an equity investor in the project. In the pure non-recourse case, the confinement of the debt liability to the project means that it falls outside the limit to debt set by the company's debt covenants. Insofar as debt financing provides benefits to the company's shareholders, in the

form of tax saving for example, this is a benefit to the company's shareholders they could not obtain if the company were already at its debt limit.

Moreover, if the cash flows of the project turn out to be insufficient to service the debt, the company is insulated against the 'financial distress' it might otherwise suffer. Because of this, and perhaps also because of a reduced fear on the part of the stock market that it was not being told the whole story, the failure of a separate project might have less effect on the sponsoring company's share price than in the case of an integrated company. (But separate project financing deprives the company of some of the advantages of pooling – the company has less protection against a fall in the profits of its 'own' operations.) Second, the performance of the managers of a project may be more visible and therefore more accurately assessable than that of those who are part of a diversified company. And if they are remunerated accordingly, their performance may be better than if the project were 'within' the company, to the benefit of both shareholders and lenders involved in the project.

The possible conflict of interest between shareholders and managers is further reduced where, as in the normal case, the final proceeds of the project are paid out to shareholders, say, of a joint venture, who then can decide as to their reinvestment.

Third, project financing is a particularly suitable vehicle for the financing of some forms of joint venture and of projects which are very large in relation to the size of the 'parent' company or where special operating skills are called for that are not fully available within the company.

Of course, the inability to draw upon the revenues of the 'parent' company is a disadvantage to lenders, and this will influence the terms on which they are prepared to lend. But lenders also gain, not only from the greater transparency of managerial performance and the likelihood of there being less 'managerial slack' but from the fact that surplus cash flows cannot be siphoned off to finance dividends or other activities in the 'parent' company. In this respect, too, the project's equity holders are shielded from conflicts of interest between themselves and possibly self-seeking managers more concerned with empire-building than with adding value for shareholders.

In short, project financing can make it easier for very large projects to be undertaken, enlarge debt capacity without increasing the risks to the company of insolvency or financial distress, ameliorate problems of 'agency costs' arising from the possible 'asymmetry of information' between the company and lenders and between shareholders and managers, and draw on outside specialist operating and managerial skills as well as outside finance.

There is also one further and more subtle possible advantage to both potential lenders and shareholders. Project financing enlarges the range of choice of both, by separating the cash flows and making it unnecessary for any particular set of investors to depend on all of them.

In technical terms, this is making markets more 'complete', which is usually to the advantage of society. Investors can still, if they wish, obtain the advantages of risk-spreading that a diversified company can provide by investing in a range of activities themselves; but unlike the case of investments in a diversified company, investors are given the choice.

Conditions for successful project financing

There are several requirements. First, the project must be operationally a stand-alone venture, usually with a definable termination date and with an agreed basis for returning both ongoing and final surplus cash flows to investors.

This requires there to be a separate legal entity for the project, with a finite life linked to the original purpose of the project. Costs and revenues of the project must depend on the project alone: there must be no interconnections with the costs or revenues of the 'parent' company. If the latter provides services to the project they must be clearly definable and priced in an agreed manner.

Second – and this is usually a condition needed to make the first apply – the success of the project depends on clearly understood factors, such as the market price of a mineral in a mining project.

Third, it must be possible for lenders and equity holders to understand the apportionment not only of the surplus cash flows from the project but also the risks arising from it.

Of course, it goes without saying that the parties to such a project are being unwise if they do not fully examine the risks they may be bearing, by subjecting their cash flow forecasts to a range of assumptions concerning pre-production delays, capital and operating costs, volumes and prices, by identifying the so-called critical variables involved and then by deciding how uncertainty as to their values might best be dealt with.

Project financing has taken many forms. There have been projects initiated by a single company, as in the case of BP's North Sea oil fields (involving a syndicate of 66 banks) and various mining projects, those organized by a non-operating sponsor or group of sponsors, joint ventures and forms of partnership. Privatization in some countries has been in project form.

The oldest examples of project financing go back to medieval times, when Italian bankers would finance mining and other ventures. The most common form of early project financing, however, was the overseas trading venture on a voyage basis, using the finite-life partnership as its legal form.

This was superseded by the joint stock form of continuing organization when the necessities of scale, complexity and continuity rendered the simple terminable partnership formed for a specific venture inadequate.

Over the past 20 years, however, there has been a revival of project financing in order to undertake very large projects (the Channel Tunnel is one example) and to finance other joint ventures and co-operative arrangements in which companies can pool resources and yet each make their distinctive contribution. Other examples include oil fields, pipeline projects, a variety of power generation projects in the US in particular, and joint research and development projects. In most such cases debt finance is provided by a group of banks. Size of project has been the common characteristic; but the case for modern project financing runs counter to yet another phenomenon, that of acquisitions and mergers. The balance of the argument for specialization, on the one hand, and that for diversification, on the other, has never remained constant. Project financing injects an element of flexibility into the choice.

Summary

Project finance, which goes back to medieval times, has seen a revival in the last 20 years. It can assist very large projects, enlarge debt capacity without adding to the company's insolvency risk, ameliorate problems of 'agency costs', and draw on outside operating skills as well as outside finance. To be successful the project must be stand-alone, factors such as market price must be clearly understood, and risks and rewards must be clearly apportioned. Project financing can be initiated by a single company, a variety of sponsors, joint ventures and forms of partnership.

Suggested further reading

Kensinger, J.W. and Martin, J.D. 'Project finance: raising money the old-fashioned way', *Midland Corporate Finance Journal*, Fall 1988.

Are bosses worth the money?

■ **Michael Brennan turns over the contentious issue of executive remuneration and finds that, on the whole, there are good economic reasons for high salaries.**

The issue of executive compensation continues to provoke lively, and sometimes acrimonious, debate on both sides of the Atlantic. In the US Congress has set a $1m ceiling on executive salaries; above this level they cannot be treated as tax-deductible expenses unless they are significantly performance related.

In the UK the Chancellor of the Exchequer has followed the recommendations of the Greenbury Report by removing the tax concessions on executive share options and public pressure has led to general abandonment of rolling multi-year contracts that compensate managers who are sacked for poor results.

What are the facts concerning executive pay in the UK? Why is executive compensation tending to rise so rapidly? Is the public concern justified? Should executive incomes be regulated? If so, how? If not, how should they be determined?

Below we briefly attempt to offer some answers to these questions.

Measured in 1993 pounds, the median level of salary plus bonus of the highest paid directors of the FT Top 100 companies rose from £135,000 in 1980 to £589,000 in 1993, a real increase of 336 per cent. At the same time there has been a growth in the use of share options, which, it is estimated, add another 10 per cent to the compensation of the typical boss.

Precise details of share option grants are not available for all companies but just considering base salary plus bonus, the pay of the typical highest-paid director in the UK rose from 10.6 times the pay of an average worker in 1980 to 22.2 times in 1990 and even more for executive directors of the largest firms. It should be noted, though, that this compares with a figure of about 50 for the US.

Upward pressure on executive compensation

To understand the tendency of executive compensation to rise, imagine yourself a non-executive director of a major company that is looking for a new CEO. A candidate has been found and a compensation consultant has provided the board with summary statistics on the compensation of CEOs of similar companies.

Should you offer your candidate a compensation package that would place him or her in the top quartile of similarly placed executives or should you offer something less? Well, presumably you wanted to get a top person for the job. Paying anything less than a top quartile package suggests that you have found a less than excellent candidate. Given that the decisions that the CEO will make may earn or cost the company millions or even tens of millions of pounds, it would be foolish to economize by saving a few hundred thousand pounds on a second rate CEO.

In other words, given the importance of the CEO position, companies will vie to hire the best or those that they think are the best for the position. This will tend to exert continuous upward pressure on compensation levels over a very wide range. A CEO who has a 10 per cent better chance than his or her peers of making the right decision about a strategic partnership that would require a £100m investment will be worth a good deal more to his company than the average CEO.

Thus, in an active managerial labour market such as one is likely to find during a period of rapid industrial change we should expect to find continuous upward pressure on compensation. Sophisticated shareholders are unlikely to be too concerned with the level of executive compensation although they may be concerned about the structure of the compensation package because of the nature of the incentives it creates.

A second factor tending to increase reported executive compensation in the 1980s was the reduction in marginal tax rates brought about under Reagan and Thatcher. This tended to change the composition of the compensation package, substituting taxable and measurable benefits for hidden fringe benefits.

Factors of even greater importance are increasing competition and a more rapid rate of change in the economy. Both tend to increase the rewards to good management and increase the costs of bad management, making companies more willing to pay for the right manager.

Related to this appears to be a shift in the relative importance of human capital relative to financial capital in fields as diverse as computer software (and hardware), entertainment, investment banking, investment management and advertising.

Examples abound. A striking one was the creation of the DreamWorks film production company by Steven Spielberg and partners. The company was valued at $2.5bn before any capital was supplied simply on the strength of the names of the founders. Edgar Bronfman was unable to entice Michael Ovitz to run MCA despite the offer of a package reputedly worth $200m. IBM thought that it was worth paying up to $8.5m over three years, in addition to a $5m signing bonus and 500,000 options on IBM's stock, in order to attract Lou Gerstner, who it believed would turn around that beleaguered company.

One of the highest paid executives in a UK company is undoubtedly J.G. Fifield of EMI, who received £7.5m in 1995 and over £8m in the previous year.

Is such compensation excessive? Is it more than he is worth to the company? It might seem so to an outsider. Mr Fifield runs the US-based EMI Music arm of EMI and apparently Chairman Sir Colin Southgate, who earns only about one tenth as much, thinks that Fifield is worth it. The figures appear to support him.

EMI Music earned 64 per cent of EMI's operating profits in the latest fiscal year and had an astounding 74 per cent pre-tax return on assets. It is clear that the profits of EMI Music are due not to the capital contributed by shareholders or to unique patents or production economies but to the talents of individuals who have an ear for popular music and are able to deal effectively with those who produce it.

Naturally, a good share of the profits then accrues to the individuals who generate them. If shareholders try too aggressively to capture a greater share of these profits, they are liable to find that they lose the services of those who generate them, as shareholders of Cordiant (formerly Saatchi & Saatchi) and Salomon Brothers have found.

Few people begrudge Bill Gates his billions because he happens to own a substantial piece of his company. Would IBM not have been better off if it had been able to entice him to run its software division and paid him a share of the profits – say $100m a year? It would be hard to argue that this would have been excessive compensation for a Gates. It was a similar share-of-profits contract that took Michael Milken's income to $500m a year before he became the target of Federal investigators.

A third element in the behavior of executive compensation is the globalization of industry. The expansion of product markets increases the scope of a CEO's decisions while also exposing them to more intense competitive threats. This has the effect of magnifying the economic consequences of managerial decisions.

Economist Alfred Marshall noted this phenomenon as early as the 1890s. In his 'Principles' he writes, in what could be a contemporary passage, that 'The relative fall in incomes to be earned by moderate ability. . . is accentuated by the rise in those that are obtained by many men of extraordinary ability. . . the operations, in which a man exceptionally favoured by genius and good luck can take part, are so extensive as to enable him to amass a large fortune with a rapidity hitherto unknown. The causes of this change are two. . . the general growth in wealth. . . and the development of new. . . communication by which men. . . are enabled to apply their. . . genius to undertakings vaster. . . than ever before'.

A final factor is the tendency towards internationalization of the executive labour market. It is perhaps no accident that Richard Giordano, the chairman of British Gas, the company that more than any other has brought the issue of executive pay to public attention, was originally brought from the US to run British Oxygen for a compensation package that was extremely generous by UK standards of the time and which also attracted complaints.

Although few executives actually change countries, those that do tend to introduce new norms into the local labor market – and the determination of executive compensation is strongly driven by norms and comparisons.

Is there a cause for public concern?

The media has tended to decry increases in the level of executive compensation. The implicit assumption underlying most of the media comment is that 'the bosses' set their own compensation and set it too high.

Yet we have seen that there may be good economic reasons for pay packages that seem high to the layman.

Nevertheless, it is important that conflicts of interest be avoided. The Cadbury Committee recommended that boards establish remuneration committees consisting mainly of non-executive directors and chaired by a non-executive and that executive directors should play no part in setting their own remuneration. It appears that most UK companies have responded to these recommendations.

Nevertheless, there are concerns that even non-executive directors may not be sufficiently independent.

Suspicions of self-dealing are compounded by an element of secrecy that still surrounds executive compensation in the UK – only about one half of the FTSE-100 companies now disclose details of individual directors' pay. Full disclosure of the complete compensation packages of all directors should be mandatory and included in statements sent to shareholders, option grants should be valued using the Black-Scholes model and the expense of granting options should be fully recognized in financial statements.

A more radical proposal would allow shareholders to vote on the level of executive compensation. While shareholders could not, and ought not, to be involved in the details of setting the pay and conditions of directors, they could be allowed to express a general level of approval by being allowed to vote to approve the current arrangements or to impose an across-the-board cut of, say, 10 per cent. While largely symbolic, the outcomes of such votes would focus attention on boards where abuse is occurring.

Public concern about executive compensation is based on notions of social equity. Some incomes seem to be just too high.

Plato said that no one in a community should earn more than five times the pay of the lowest paid worker. While few today would subscribe to such a rule, there is undoubtedly discomfort at the elephantine incomes available to the fortunate few. Huge disparities of income are undoubtedly bad for society for they tend to destroy belief in the fairness of the system and may lead to undue political influence.

If it is accepted that the disparities are too great, the question is whether this is best dealt with by controls and regulation or by the tax system. Most economists would suggest that if some individuals are able to earn rents by virtue of their position and talents, the most efficient way to limit these rents would be by taxation rather than by control and regulation. And it must be noted that the very high executive incomes that give rise to concern in some quarters were not an issue at the time of the dramatic cuts in maximum marginal tax rates that were made in the early 1980s.

However, the ability of individual countries to redistribute income by the tax system is now severely circumscribed by international labor mobility.

In some respects public concern clearly seems misplaced and its effects on policy unfortunate. Thus the Greenbury Committee accepted the arguments against rolling multi-year contracts. Yet such contracts may provide executives with the minimum financial security they require if they are to take decisions that offer high prospective returns but considerable risk, not only to the company but to the careers of the executives themselves.

Shareholders generally have better diversified positions than managers and are therefore more tolerant of risk in investment projects than managers. It would be unfortunate if the well-meaning reform of multi-year contracts were to lead to an increase in corporate conservatism.

Rather than being concerned about pay-offs to executives who are sacked, the Committee would have been better employed investigating whether executives who turn in poor performance are indeed sacked. The costs of retaining the wrong person in the CEO's position will generally exceed by far the cost of any termination payment. Well-paid but insecure managers are to be preferred to poorly paid but entrenched ones.

The Greenbury Committee also decried the granting of share options with exercise prices below the prevailing market price since such options are profitable even if the share price does not rise. But options are often criticized as a one-way bet for management. To the extent that the options are 'in the money' when granted, they penalize the manager for reductions in the share price as well as rewarding him or her for increases in the price and this helps to improve the alignment of management interests with those of stockholders.

Of course, the value of the options granted should be taken into account in considering the value of the total compensation package.

Incentive alignment

If shareholders are not too concerned with the level of executive compensation, they should be extremely concerned with the form that the compensation takes. If CEOs and other managers are to keep the interests of shareholders in mind and refrain from value-destroying exercises in diversification and acquisition, it is important that their compensation package gives them the right incentives.

Academic studies in both the US and the UK have found very little relation between changes in executive salaries and bonuses from year to year and the stock market performance of the company. The reasons for this are not clear.

To some degree it is a matter of timing; share prices react to changes in expected performance whereas bonuses are intended to reward achieved performance. A recent US study finds that the cumulative response of compensation to performance is over ten times that of the contemporaneous response.

It probably also reflects the natural unwillingness of boards to discipline managers for poor performance. It should be noted that a significant advantage of share options is that they penalize (or at least fail to reward) poor performance automatically, without the need for unpleasantness.

The ideal package will generally consist of some combination of salary, bonus and options or stock-related compensation. The bonus should be related to the economic value created by the manager and not to some inadequate proxy such as earnings per share, which is easily manipulated by leverage and accounting changes. For similar reasons the bonus should be based on sustained performance and not simply on the results of a single year.

One consultant advises his clients to set up a bonus 'bank' into which annual bonuses are 'deposited'; the bonus formula is geared so that there are penalties for poor performance in the form of withdrawals from the bank. The manager is then allowed to withdraw a fraction, say one-third, of the bank balance each year. In this way, the manager is given an incentive to maximize the long-run value of the company rather than to pursue myopic strategies and is also made sensitive to losses as well as profits.

Share options or other stock-related compensation have the advantage that they reward the manager precisely according to how well the shareholders do. Simple share options have the disadvantage that the manager benefits or suffers from movements in the share price that are caused by factors beyond his control such as general movements in the level of share prices. This defect can be corrected by tying the exercise price of the options to the general level of share prices or to the share prices of firms within the same industry.

Summary

Upward pressure on executive compensation can be expected during a period of rapid industrial change. In such conditions the managerial labor market becomes more active. Other factors which explain boardroom pay rises of the last 10 to 15 years are the substitution of taxable and measurable benefits for hidden fringe benefits (encouraged by cuts in marginal income tax rates), the growing importance of human capital relative to financial capital in many sectors, the globalization of industry (which has magnified the economic consequences of managerial decisions), and the internationalization of the market for top executives. An element of secrecy still surrounds the issue of compensation in the UK. This could be dealt with by more disclosure. More difficult is the public concern based on notions of social equity.

The issue here is whether excessive disparities should be dealt with by controls and regulation, or the tax system. The ability of countries to redistribute income via the tax system is now heavily circumscribed, but some of the flawed ideas of the Greenbury committee in the UK demonstrate the difficulty of trying to impose controls. Shareholders should be more concerned with the form than with the level of executive compensation.

Suggested further reading

Conyon, M., Gregg, P. and Machin, S. 'Taking care of business: executive compensation in the UK', *The Economic Journal*, May 1995, 704-714.

Jensen, M.C. and Murphy, K. 'Performance pay and top management incentives', *Journal of Political Economy*, April 1990, 225-264.

Conyon, M. and Leech, D. 'Top pay, company performance and corporate governance', *Oxford Bulletin of Economics and Statistics*, August 1994, 229-247.

Raising equity capital

■ **Selling shares seems an excellent way for a company to raise money. But there can be considerable downsides both for investors who take up the offering and the companies themselves.**

by Ivo Welch and Anthony Neuberger

Companies need capital for investment and expansion. One way of raising capital from investors is to sell equity – ownership rights in the company that entitle the investor to a share of the company's profits and a say in the way the company is run. Issuing equity looks like an easy way for management to raise capital. Unlike debt, the company takes on no obligations to repay the capital nor does it undertake to pay any particular income stream to the new investors. The only financial commitment is to treat new shareholders the same way as old shareholders when it chooses to pay dividends and make other distributions.

Yet companies appear reluctant to raise capital in this way. For example, in the UK between 1962 and 1975, companies raised cash by equity issues at an average rate of only once every 20 years. In the US since 1980 net new issues of stock have actually been negative in nine years out of 15; new issues have been more than offset by share repurchases and cash takeovers.

Issuing equity dilutes the ownership interest of the original shareholders while at the same time increasing the value of assets owned by the company. The fact of the new issue, the amount raised and the way the shares are issued will affect the way the market receives the new issue and the price of the company's shares.

In looking further at this question it is useful to distinguish two types of equity issue: the initial public offering (IPO), where a company sells its shares on the market for the first time; and seasoned issues, where a company that already has publicly traded equity decides to issue more. Among IPOs it is also worth distinguishing between primary offerings where the shares being sold are new shares and secondary offerings where the sale is of shares held by the company's current owners.

IPOs

IPOs commonly take place by first advertising to the public the pending sale of shares at a preset price. Subscriptions are then solicited and on the day of the offering the shares are sold to investors. If demand exceeds supply, the offering is oversubscribed and shares are allocated either according to the discretion of the underwriter, as happens in the US, or according to a rationing formula based on how many shares each investor asked for, as commonly happens in the UK. Occasionally, IPOs are heavily oversubscribed. Witness, for example, the NetScape IPO on Nasdaq (the National Association of Securities Dealers Automated Quotation system, a computerized system for providing price quotes for securities in the US) this August.

The company was selling no product (it produces an Internet Web Browser that is freely distributed), had revenues of only $17m and had never produced a profit. The IPO share price was $28 and 5m shares were for sale (about 14 per cent of the outstanding equity).

On the first day of trading, underwriters had received requests for more than 100m shares and within one minute, the after-market price shot to $71. At this price, NetScape had a market value of about $2.7bn and investors who received shares in the IPO reaped a windfall of $215m. This pattern, where IPOs in certain industries are 'hot' at a particular time is very common, especially in the US where venture capitalists hold portfolios of companies in various growth industries (such as biotech, networking companies, oil exploration and so on), and are waiting for the appropriate time to bring them to the market. Similarly, IPOs of REITs (real-estate investment trusts), closed-end funds and reverse leveraged buy-outs have come in clusters.

There are two principal flavors of IPO. In the case of placements (the equivalent of 'best-effort' IPOs in the US), underwriters act only as the issuer's agent. In offers for sale (the equivalent of 'firm-commitment' IPOs in the US) underwriters purchase all shares from the issuer and sell them as principal at a fixed price. Virtually all large IPOs by reputable underwriters are sold as firm offers for sale. There are two main empirical regularities in the IPO market, which have been documented both in the UK and in the US. First, IPOs appreciate on average by about 5 to 15 per cent on the first day of trading. The benefit of this underpricing is received only by those investors who actually buy their shares from the underwriter and sell them immediately in the aftermarket. Notice also that there is a very large variation in the first day returns – IPOs are by nature very risky investments. In general, the smaller the IPO, the riskier it is, and the greater the likely initial return.

Long-term underperformance

The second empirical regularity has been a slow but steady long-term underperformance relative to equivalent companies. In the US during the period 1975 to 1984 this has amounted to a 5 to 7 per cent a year lower average return over the three to five years after the issue. The equivalent underperformance in the UK during the period 1981 to 1988 has averaged between 2 and 7 per cent a year.

While these empirical regularities may not persist in the future, a casual view of the empirical evidence suggests that the smart investor would want to obtain shares in the offering and sell them immediately on the first few days of trading. However, it is not clear whether even this strategy is wise. For many years financial economists (including ourselves) have been trying to figure out why on the first

day of trading companies would leave so much money on the table for investors. One explanation centers on the winner's curse, which, in bald terms, says that the underwriter is likely to give you relatively more shares in the bad offerings. For example, suppose that half of all IPOs are undersubscribed and that investors in these IPOs incur an initial loss of 20 per cent. Furthermore, suppose that applications for the remaining IPOs amount to four times the number of shares on offer and that these IPOs provide an initial gain of 50 per cent. The average reported IPO underpricing is therefore 0.5 (50-20) = 15 per cent.

Now, if you asked your underwriter for £100 worth of shares, on average, half the time you would get all the shares you asked for and lose £20. The other half of the time, the offer would be oversubscribed and you would get only £25 worth on average and make a profit of 50 per cent of £25 or £12.50. So, net, you would end up losing £7.50 ÷ 2 = £3.75 per IPO, even though the IPO shares were indeed on average underpriced. The rationing 'against you' not only wiped out your profit, it actually caused you to make a loss.

However, there are other explanations, in which companies could quite rationally allow investors to reap a windfall profit. First, companies are often known to come back to the market for subsequent equity offerings, and may just want to be 'nice' to investors to 'leave a good taste in their mouths'. Actually, this is what most underwriters publicly claim to be the primary reason for IPO underpricing, although academics are still debating whether it is the case. (The empirical evidence is not too favorable.)

Second, institutional investors are known either to come in as a herd or to stay away altogether. In this case overpricing by even one penny could have drastic consequences, causing a complete offering failure. To 'play it safe' companies may be better off underpricing the IPO, just to make sure they do not suffer from such a 'negative' cascade of deserting investors.

Third, companies may need to underprice in order to get the appropriate level of co-operation and interest from underwriters and investors.

Fourth, in the US, companies whose stock

price subsequently falls below the issue price are often sued, and this prospect may induce companies to underprice. The consensus among researchers and practitioners is that each of these explanations is partly true at least part of the time. Because the shares of IPOs are tradeable immediately after the issue, the long-run underperformance of IPOs presents first and foremost a challenge to proponents of efficient market and specific equilibrium pricing models. Convincing explanations for this under-performance have yet to be found. One clue to the explanation may lie in the fact that the poor performance is concentrated primarily among younger and smaller IPO companies. Many of these smaller IPO companies are highly illiquid and this makes it more difficult for sophisticated arbitrageurs to short the stock and in the process to eliminate the underperformance.

Seasoned

When a company that already has shares in issue decides to issue additional shares it can do so either by selling shares on the open market at close to the market price, or it can offer the shares to its existing shareholders at a substantial discount. The former is known as a general cash offer while the latter is known as a rights issue.

The relative merits of the two alternatives have been much disputed. In a general cash offer, it is important to existing shareholders that any new shares are sold at or close to their fair price, for otherwise they are selling a stake in assets they own to third parties at below their true worth. In a rights issue existing shareholders get the right to buy the new shares at a heavily discounted price. The rights themselves are tradeable securities, so if shareholders do not want to take up their rights themselves they can sell the rights to other investors. The greater the discount the more valuable the rights.

This should make existing shareholders substantially indifferent to the size of the discount – the higher the discount the lower the value of the shares after the rights issue but the higher the value of the rights.

Companies often argue that general cash offers provide a more flexible means of raising capital because of the time required for a rights issue and the costs of creating and trading rights. Defenders of the rights issue point to the way the mechanism protects the interests of existing shareholders by giving them pre-emptive rights over new shares.

In most European countries companies are required by law or investor pressure to use the rights issue method. By contrast in Japan and the US, where both methods are allowed, the trend has been away from rights issues, and cash offers are the normal mode of issue.

Rights issues are often underwritten. If the rights are not taken up by the shareholders (normally because the share price has fallen below the subscription price) the underwriters step in and buy the issue. In this way the company can ensure that it will raise the capital it is seeking. Companies can avoid the need for underwriting by setting the subscription price sufficiently low, and indeed in Japan rights issues have traditionally not been underwritten.

Studies of seasoned equity issues in the US have shown that they are normally accompanied by a fall in the share price in the region of 2 to 3 per cent. While this does not sound large, the fall in market value may be as much as 30 per cent of the amount raised. The evidence from outside the US is less clearcut.

There are many explanations for this share price fall. Some argue that the increase in the supply of shares is bound to be accompanied by a fall in the price by the laws of supply and demand. But the argument is unconvincing. One share is a pretty good substitute for another, and it is hard to believe that the capital market's appetite for a particular kind of risk is so easily satiated. Furthermore, if the explanation is correct, one would expect the price fall to be largest for large issues, but the evidence on this is at best mixed. More plausible explanations for the fall include the suggestion that the announcement of the share issue itself conveys information to the market. The need for additional cash may tell the market that internal sources of cash are more limited than had been thought.

Another explanation is that managers are

better informed about the company's prospects than is the market; they will tend to raise equity when they believe their shares are relatively overpriced and will tend to avoid equity issues when they believe the shares are underpriced. The decision to issue new shares may therefore be seen by the market as a recognition by managers that there is bad news to come and the market reacts accordingly.

Explaining the price fall observed in the US is more than a matter of intellectual curiosity. If it reflects the impact of information that would ultimately affect the share price even in the absence of a new issue, then the issue merely accelerates the reaction. But if the fall is due to the new share issue itself then the declines would increase very substantially the cost of raising capital in this way.

Summary

There is a distinction between IPOs, where companies sell their shares on the market for the first time, and seasoned issues, where a company with publicly traded equity decides to sell more. In the case of placements (or 'best effort' IPOs) underwriters act only as the issuer's agent. In offers for sale underwriters purchase all shares for the issuer and sell them as principal at a fixed price. Research shows that IPOs appreciate by an average of 10-15 per cent on the first day of dealing, but under-perform equivalent companies thereafter. One reason for leaving money on the table is the winner's curse (the likelihood of investors getting more shares in bad offerings). Alternatively, companies may wish to keep investors 'sweet' pending subsequent offerings, they may not wish to risk a 'negative' cascade of deserting institutions or they may (in the US) fear legal action.

The relative merits of general cash offers (when shares are sold on the open market) and rights issues (when shares are sold to existing shareholders) is much discussed. Studies of seasoned equity issues in the US show that they are followed by a share price fall.

Several ways to go broke

■ **Julian Franks compares and contrasts the insolvency procedures in the US and the UK.**

In recent years, there have been serious criticisms of the bankruptcy codes in the UK and other countries. In the UK the government has published a consultation paper on proposed changes while in the US and Germany legislation has already been passed making important changes to the existing codes.

What has caused such unease? In the US there has been a strong feeling that Chapter 11 of the US code (under which a company continues to operate under existing management while working with its creditors to reorganize the business) is lengthy, expensive and too debtor-oriented. The result is that companies are often kept as going concerns under the existing management when they would be worth more to creditors if the company were auctioned or the assets liquidated.

In contrast, in the UK there is a strong sense that the UK code gives too much power to secured creditors and as a result, companies are too often liquidated when they would be better kept as going concerns.

Why do we need an insolvency code?

An insolvency code is required in order to stop the 'race to the courthouse', that is, when creditors smell trouble they each go to court to grab the unencumbered assets of the company. The result is that the company is prevented from using those assets and this threatens the continued operation of the company.

For example, in the case of the US company Wickes, when the company found itself in difficulties many of its 250,000 creditors applied to the court to grab assets such as stock, receivables and so on and the company quickly found itself unable to operate and sought the protection of the courts while it worked out a plan of reorganization.

In addition, an insolvency code may provide time and a process of resolving conflicts during the period when a company is to be sold as a going concern or liquidated and sold piecemeal. This may be of value not only to creditors and equity holders but also to other stakeholders such as employees, suppliers and customers.

How does the insolvency process operate?

The UK code. In the UK, if a company is insolvent the directors or creditors can make use of a number of procedures including liquidation, receivership and administration. The most widely used is liquidation – there were 15,051 in 1990. In the same year there were 4,318 receiverships and 211 administrations.

Liquidation is relatively straightforward. An insolvency practitioner is appointed to sell off the company either in whole or in part, usually in a matter of weeks. Speed not only reduces costs but also limits the loss of goodwill. Once a company is in the insolvency process customers will stop buying for fear that warranties will not be honoured and suppliers will no longer sell on credit to the company for fear they will not be repaid.

When a company goes into receivership its share of the market can fall precipitously. Receivership is more complex. A receiver can only be appointed if there is a particular kind of secured creditor, one with a fixed or a floating charge over the company's assets. In the event of

default, the particular creditor appoints an insolvency practitioner to act as receiver and represent his or her interests.

In the case of a fixed charge, the receiver can take possession or sell the particular assets the loan is charged on. In the case of a floating charge, the receiver takes control of the company and sells all or part of the company's assets until the creditor is repaid.

One important constraint is that the receiver cannot sell assets that are secured on the loans of other creditors. In addition, a creditor with a fixed charge may prevent the receiver from using those assets.

It is easy to see how conflicts of interest may arise between creditors and how some creditors may use their bargaining power to increase their payout at the expense of other creditors, especially unsecured ones. Loan contracts with banks frequently provide the bank with a floating charge and therefore banks often appoint the receiver.

The third procedure is called administration and was introduced in 1986. Unlike liquidation and receivership, the appointment of the administrator requires the court's agreement. In this event, the administrator must work out a plan of reorganization within three months and put the plan to all creditors for their approval. An important part of the process is the moratorium on creditors' claims during the three month period. Such a moratorium is not part of the receivership process.

A second difference is that the administrator works on behalf of all the creditors whereas the receiver works for the creditor that appointed him. The potential conflicts of interest created by receivership encourage unsecured creditors to favour the appointment of the administrator over the receiver. Despite these advantages only a small number of appointments have been made. One explanation is that if a creditor has the power to appoint a receiver, such an appointment effectively blocks the appointment of an administrator. In other words, creditors with a floating charge have an effective veto over the appointment. Some practitioners would favour abolishing the right of secured creditors to block administration.

The US code. Whereas the UK procedure is highly creditor-oriented, that is, the creditors take control of the company, the US procedures can be highly debtor-oriented. In Chapter 11, the management of the company can ask the court for protection from creditors. This permits the company to suspend most interest and principal repayments on its debts while the management puts forward a plan of reorganization to creditors for their approval. In about one half of cases, the existing management remains in control of the company throughout the period of reorganization.

However, the court closely supervises the reorganization process and management will continually have to seek the court's agreement to important expenditure decisions. The court-administered process also allows the company to raise new financing that is senior to pre-reorganization debt; this is called debtor-in-possession financing. New financing is especially important in Chapter 11 because of the length of time companies can remain in a court-administered reorganization.

Companies entering Chapter 11 remain there on average for more than two years and the costs of reorganization can be very high. In the Wickes case referred to above, the costs were between $75m and $120m and constituted between 16 and 26 per cent of the value of the reorganized company.

There are other procedures in the US code, most important of which is Chapter 7, the liquidation code. In this case, as in the UK, an insolvency practitioner is appointed to sell the assets of the company. This almost always involves its closure prior to sale. In 1993 in the Central District of the California Bankruptcy Court there were 57,752 Chapter 7 cases pending compared with 6,739 in Chapter 11.

Informal reorganizations

It should not be a surprise that the high costs of Chapter 11 have encouraged companies to work out their problems with creditors privately, that is, outside the formal bankruptcy process.

A relatively new procedure called pre-packaged Chapter 11s involves the company and its large creditors agreeing a plan of reorganization privately and then entering Chapter 11 to seek court approval. The latter is important because court approval effectively prevents creditors challenging the legality of the reorganization plan.

In addition, plans may be passed in Chapter 11 without all creditors agreeing; only a majority by number and two thirds by value are required, whereas workouts (see below) require the agreement of all parties. Pre-packs accounted for 43 per cent of filings for Chapter 11s in 1993. There are other forms of reorganization called workouts that do not involve court approval. These usually involve equity for debt swaps. Informal reorganizations are greatly helped by workout specialists and by 'vulture funds', which have been specifically set up to buy the debt of distressed companies and assist in their financial reorganization.

The UK market in informal reorganizations is less active than in the US. However, for large companies in distress, such as the Heron Corporation, informal reorganizations have proved feasible. If the company is important the Bank of England may become involved and encourage lenders to co-ordinate and act in a way that is consistent with the 'London Rules', which were developed to assist financially distressed companies.

Criteria for judging the efficiency of a code

There are four main criteria for judging the efficiency of a code:
- It should preserve promising enterprises while liquidating uneconomic ones
- It should minimize the direct costs of insolvency
- It should minimize the costs borne by other corporate stakeholders
- It should encourage adherence to debt contracts. It is worth considering how the UK and US codes stack up against these four criteria.

There is a strong view among some practitioners and some theoretical work that suggests the US code preserves uneconomic enterprises while the UK code liquidates economic ones.

In the latter case, the lack of an automatic stay of creditor claims while the company is being sold in receivership must bias the process in favour of liquidation. In addition, the fact that one creditor is in charge must also produce conflicts of interest that may not be easily resolved. Some of these obstacles are overcome by administration, but it is currently very easy for one creditor to block this procedure. The direct costs of the UK process appear much lower than in the US. The courts generally do not interfere in the process; in contrast the US courts are intimately involved in the process and this adds substantially to costs. The US code appears to score highly on protecting other stakeholder interests because it favours keeping companies alive, at least in Chapter 11. In contrast, the UK process takes little account of other stakeholders by leaving creditors very much in charge.

Finally, the high costs of the US code encourage companies to reorganize outside Chapter 11. This encourages senior creditors to offer equity holders and junior creditors more than they are entitled to according to the debt contact; these are referred to as deviations from absolute priority.

Recent studies of US reorganization plans show that deviations from absolute priority are more than three times larger in workouts than in Chapter 11, most of which is paid for by senior creditors. This shows that senior creditors are willing to pay large amounts to other claimholders to avoid the formal bankruptcy process. Such deviations appear smaller in the UK because the code is more creditor-oriented and the costs of the formal process are smaller.

Summary

Bankruptcy codes have been the subject of recent criticism. Chapter 11 in the US, it is said, keeps some companies as going concerns when they might be worth more to creditors if auctioned off; in the UK there is a sense that the code gives too much power to secured creditors. There are three main UK procedures: liquidation; receivership; and administration. US procedures can be highly debtor orientated, with companies often in court-administered reorganization for more than two years and costs very high. This has increasingly encouraged companies to reorganize outside the formal bankruptcy process.

Suggested further reading

Franks, J. R. and Torous, Walter, 'How shareholders and creditors fare in workouts and Chapter 11 reorganizations', *Journal of Financial Economics,* May 1994.

Franks, J. R., Nyborg, Kjell, and Torous, Walter, 'A comparison of US, UK, and German insolvency codes', London Business School working paper (1995).

Applied Statistics and Decision Support

Contents

Understanding data 126
Ann van Ackere, London Business School
The main methods of presenting statistical data.

Probability and distributions 131
Ann van Ackere, London Business School
Probability and distribution are at the heart of statistical analysis.

Taking samples 135
Ann van Ackere, London Business School
Behind the simple idea of sampling lies some complex mathematics.

Taking the risk out of uncertainty 142
Kiriakos Vlahos, London Business School
Risk and uncertainty are constant ingredients of business. But there are statistical ways to try to ascertain and overcome them.

Systems thinking and the art of modeling 147
John Morecroft and Ann van Ackere, London Business School
Thinking of business issues as a series of systems, each of which contains numerous feedback loops, is the basis of modeling and scenario planning.

Getting the combination right 156
Kiriakos Vlahos, London Business School
How can managers make sure they are making the right mix of products to gain maximum profits? The answer is 'optimization'.

Contributors

Ann van Ackere is Associate Professor of Decision Sciences at London Business School. Dr van Ackere's research interests include management of congestion in manufacturing and service operations, incentive theory, microeconomic modeling, systems thinking and computer simulation.

Dr John Morecroft is Associate Professor of Strategic Management at London Business School. His research interests include scenario modeling, feedback systems thinking, the dynamics of strategy, system dynamics and computer simulation.

Kiriakos Vlahos is Assistant Professor of Decision Sciences, London Business School. His research interests include energy-economy-environment interactions, mathematical modeling and optimization of production systems.

Introduction

Modern management is a numerically based art. Even so-called 'soft' areas – marketing, for example – are often heavily based on data. There are therefore no apologies for introducing the subject of statistics.

The Statistics module consists of six individual sections. Topics covered are the way data are presented and the effects this can have on interpretation, probability and distribution, statistical sampling, risk analysis, systems thinking and strategic modeling, and optimization.

Understanding data

■ **The presentation of statistics can lead to distortion. What are the main methods of presenting data, when is a method appropriate, and when are methods being used to manipulate the results?** Ann van Ackere **explains.**

This is the first in a series of simple notes on the use of data and quantitative analysis for business problems. Its focus is on the transformation of data into information.

Data refers to the numbers in the form they are being collected. For example, Table 1 shows (hypothetical) data on train delays for 120 journeys on a specific route. As such, this data provides little information. A glance at the table shows that some trains arrive on time and a few suffer long delays.

Table 2 (column frequency) presents the same data in the form of a frequency table: how frequently did each delay occur? This way of presenting data yields more relevant information: a quick glance indicates that 24 trains were on time, about 60 (24+15+12+10) arrived within three minutes of the scheduled time, and only four were more than two hours late.

The meaning of a statement such as '24 trains were on time' depends on how many trains were considered, in this example 120. It is often useful to generalize by restating frequencies as 'relative frequencies', i.e. as a percentage of the total. This is done in the last column of Table 2, which

Table 2: Train delays

Delay in minutes	Frequency	Relative frequency
0	24	20.00
1	15	12.50
2	12	10.00
3	10	8.33
4	9	7.50
5	6	5.00
6	4	3.33
7	3	2.50
8	2	1.67
9	1	0.83
10	1	0.83
11	2	1.67
12	2	1.67
15	1	0.83
17	1	0.83
22	1	0.83
23	1	0.83
24	2	1.67
26	1	0.83
27	1	0.83
28	2	1.67
30	1	0.83
32	2	1.67
34	1	0.83
37	2	1.67
39	1	0.83
46	1	0.83
48	1	0.83
51	1	0.83
63	1	0.83
72	1	0.83
85	1	0.83
94	1	0.83
118	1	0.83
132	1	0.83
163	1	0.83
352	1	0.83
486	1	0.83

Table 1: Train delays (in minutes) for 120 journeys; raw data

8	0	132	4	0	39	5	1	51	3	0	1	2	30	4
0	6	4	0	12	3	37	2	0	352	3	2	5	7	0
1	7	0	46	3	0	4	27	3	2	486	0	118	1	2
7	11	0	85	5	17	3	6	32	5	48	1	2	4	0
0	1	4	1	24	2	3	34	0	24	2	32	1	3	0
1	0	4	28	4	6	4	2	0	1	22	1	0	6	163
1	94	0	5	10	2	26	3	23	0	28	15	3	12	0
72	0	2	5	1	0	2	11	1	37	8	63	1	0	9

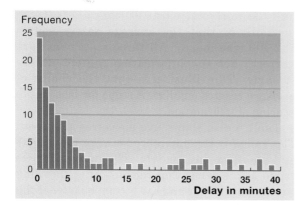

Figure 1: Frequencies (up to 40 minutes delay)

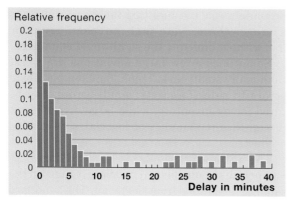

Figure 2: Relative frequencies (up to 40 minutes delay)

indicates that 20 per cent of the trains were on time, 50 per cent were at most three minutes late, and less than 4 per cent were more than two hours late.

The data of Table 2 is shown graphically in Figures 1 and 2 for trains up to 40 minutes late. Such figures are known as histograms. As most of the data points are concentrated on a small part of the full range of values, representing all the data on one graph would result in a large blur on the left, and the odd data point in the remainder of the graph.

So far the data has been analysed at its most detailed level. Often, a more aggregate representation may be adequate. Table 3 shows the 'grouped frequencies': for small delays we consider five-minute intervals, while for longer delays we consider intervals of 20 minutes or one hour.

Table 3: Grouped frequencies	
Delay in minutes	**Frequency**
0-4	70
5-9	16
10-14	5
15-19	2
20-24	4
25-29	4
30-34	4
35-39	3
40-59	3
60-119	5
120-179	2
>180	2

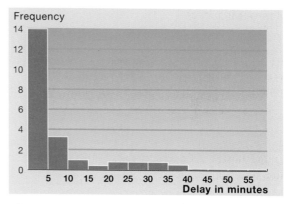

Figure 3: Histogram for grouped data (up to 60 minutes delay)

Figure 3 shows a histogram of the grouped frequencies. Note that the area of each rectangle is proportional to the corresponding frequencies: the first rectangle has a width of 5, and a height of 14, yielding an area of 70. Similarly, the rectangle 40-59 has a width of 20 and a height of 0.15 yielding an area of 3.

So far, the focus has been on showing all the data in an understandable format. Often it is useful to describe the data by a few summary measures that capture most of the information and enable easy comparison with other data-sets (for example, the corresponding 120 journeys of the previous year).

Location and spread

The most commonly used measures fall into two categories: 'measures of location', which provide information about what happens on average, and 'measures of spread', which describe the amount of variation across data points.

There are three commonly used measures of

location: the 'mean' (or arithmetic average), the 'median' and the 'mode'.

The mean is the most used, and is simply the average of all the data points. The median is the middle value: to arrive at it, rank the data points from smallest to largest and pick the middle one. The mode is the value that occurs most often. The value of these measures for the train-delay example is given in the column 'All data' of Table 4: trains are on average 20.4 minutes late; half the trains are at most 3 minutes late (the median): and the most frequently observed delay is zero (the mode).

Table 4: Measures of location and spread		
	All data	No outliers
Mean	20.4	13.6
Median	3	3
Mode	0	0
Range	486	163
Inter-quartile range	11	10
Mean absolute deviation	26.7	16.6
Variance	3466.6	710.4
Standard deviation	58.9	26.7

The railway management may argue that using all the data is unfair, as the calculations are heavily influenced by two 'outliers' (352 and 486 minutes) that distort the picture. The column 'no outliers' shows the measures excluding these two values. The median and mode are unchanged, but the mean is considerably smaller. This is a general observation: the median and mode are barely influenced by extreme values, while even a single outlier can have a strong impact on the mean.

There are no clear rules on whether the mean, median or mode is the most appropriate measure in any one situation. As illustrated above, the median and mode are less sensitive to the presence of outliers. The mode has the advantage of referring to a possible outcome; for example, the typical family has two children (the mode) while the average number of children per family is 2.2 (the mean).

The choice of measure depends on the information one wants to convey. Consider a personnel department providing information about salaries. They could state that the typical worker earns £14,000 a year (the mode); that half the workforce earns at least £17,000 (the median): or that the average salary equals £32,000 (the mean). All three statements are 'correct', but the information content differs strongly. This illustrates that the choice of measure creates significant scope for bias in the sharing of information.

Table 4 also shows five measures of spread. The 'range' is the difference between the largest and smallest data points. The 'inter-quartile range' is the range that remains after throwing out the top quarter and the bottom quarter of the data. The 'mean absolute deviation' (often referred to as the MAD) looks at the difference between each data point and the mean, in absolute terms (i.e. omitting the + or − sign), and averages these. Note that the mean deviation (i.e. without omitting the sign) would equal zero!

Sometimes a few large deviations are worse than many small ones. Think, for example, about errors in sales forecasts: small errors may be cared for by inventory, while large errors result in significant amounts of lost sales or spoiled products.

The 'variance' is similar in spirit to the MAD, but penalises outliers: it is the average of the squared deviations from the mean. The 'standard deviation' is the square root of the variance. It is the most commonly used measure of spread in statistics. Except for the inter-quartile range, all are heavily influenced by the presence of outliers.

An appropriately selected subset of these measures provides a good picture of the data.

For example, knowing the mean, median, range and inter-quartile range (plus our knowledge that delays are non-negative!) would enable us to provide a reasonably accurate sketch of the data.

So far the focus has been on a single data-set: delays. It is often useful to find out if there is a relationship between two (or more) data-sets. For example, the railway management may wonder if delays coincide with journeys where the train is particularly crowded. In this case, the data would consist of 120 pairs of numbers (delay, number of passengers).

Correlation

One useful measure in this context is the

coefficient of correlation. This is a number between -1 and +1 which measures the strength of the (linear) relationship between two variables (for example, delays and passengers). A coefficient of zero indicates that there is no linear relationship. A positive coefficient indicates that large values of one variable are associated with large values of the other. The closer the correlation coefficient is to 1, the stronger the relationship. A negative coefficient indicates that large values of one variable are associated with small values of the other.

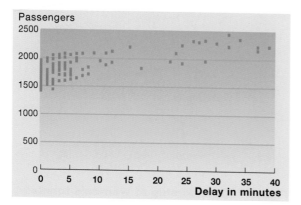

Figure 4: Delays and passengers

Figure 4 shows delays on the horizontal axis and number of passengers on the vertical axis. The correlation coefficient equals 0.71: longer delays tend to be associated with larger numbers of passengers.

The correlation coefficient plays a key role in portfolio analysis. To diversify risk, investors seek stocks whose returns exhibit a low degree of correlation.

Correlation does not imply causality. A correlation coefficient close to +1 or -1 can occur by chance (the population of India and the number of cars in the US, for example, exhibit a positive correlation). This is known as 'spurious correlation'. Two variables may also be highly correlated because both are driven by the same factors. For example, it is well known that in the UK there is a high degree of correlation between the number of betting shops and the number of churches in a town.

So far, the focus has been solely on the data-

points, without paying any attention to the time-dimension. When time does matter, we are dealing with 'time-series' data. For example, a company may consider the evolution of profits over time. Most macro-economic indicators are examples of time series (inflation, unemployment, interest rate, and so on.).

When considering time-series data, it is useful to distinguish between growth in absolute terms and the rate of growth.

Consider the three profit time-series of Figure 5. The top company exhibits a constant growth

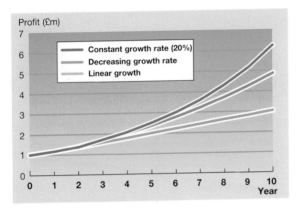

Figure 5: Growth of profits

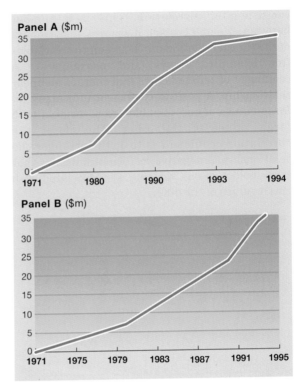

Figure 7: Sponsorship of women's tennis

rate: each year, profits are 20 per cent higher than in the previous year. The bottom company shows constant absolute growth (or linear growth): each year profits increase by £200,000. In the first year this represents a 20 per cent growth rate, but by year 10 this is only a 7 per cent growth rate. The remaining company seems to be doing fine, but in fact has a decreasing growth rate, from 20 per cent in year one, down to only 14 per cent by year 10, i.e. profits are increasing, but at a decreasing rate.

Graphs

Graphs are wonderful communications tools if used correctly. It is amazingly easy to make data tell the story you want by carefully selecting what you show and how you show it.

Consider Figure 6. Panel A shows a graph appearing in the 'Chairman's Statement' on the

first page of an annual report, indicating a healthy growth in profits. The company looks less attractive after reading the footnote on P.54 (Panel B). The graph of Panel A suffers from 'selection-bias'.

A graph similar to Panel A of Figure 7 appeared in a European newspaper to illustrate that the women's tennis game is in trouble. The figure seems to indicate a curb in the growth of sponsorship from 1990 onwards, and almost stagnation in 1994. A close look at the horizontal axis shows that time has not been drawn to scale. The correct graph is shown in Panel B. The situation does not seem to be too dramatic.

Summary

Data is of little use unless displayed in an understandable format. There are three commonly used measures of location: the 'mean', or arithmetic average; the 'median'; and the 'mode'. Which one you use depends on what you want to convey. The 'range', 'interquartile range', 'mean absolute deviation', 'variance' and 'standard

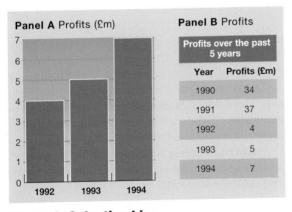

Figure 6: Selection bias

deviation' are all measures of spread. The relationship between two (or more) data-sets is often measured by the 'coefficient of correlation', though beware of spurious correlation.

Suggested further reading

Most elementary statistics textbooks include a chapter on data-presentation. Other useful references include:

Kaplan, P. D. 'Reaching for the perfect portfolio-asset allocation models using the Markowitz approach', *OR/MS Today*, 18 April 1993, 18-22.

Beattie, V., Jones, M. J. 'The use and abuse of graphs in annual reports: theoretical framework and empirical study', *Accounting And Business Research* Vol 22, No 88, 291-303, 1992.

Sugden, A. Public relations: 'the conflict with "true and fair"', *Accountancy*, September 1989, 102-105.

Ehrenberg, A. S. C. 'The problem of numeracy', ADMAP February, 1992, 37-40.

Probability and distributions

■ **From tossing a coin to opinion polls, probability and distributions are at the heart of statistical analysis, says** Ann van Ackere

The concept of probability is used to quantify uncertainty. Something can be uncertain because the true value is unknown (for example, the outcome of a toss of a coin, or the sterling/ dollar exchange-rate a year from now) or because it is unknown to you (for example, your competitor's marketing budget for next year).

These uncertain events are generally referred to as 'random variables', and are characterized by a 'distribution'. Consider, for example, tossing a coin. The outcome is a random variable that can take on two values: heads (H) or tails (T). Each outcome has a 'probability' associated with it. A probability is a number between zero and one, expressing how likely an outcome is. Here, H and T each have a probability of 0.5, which add up to 1. There are no other possible outcomes.

Figure 1 shows this distribution graphically. This is an example of a 'uniform distribution': all outcomes are equally likely. Note that the total area is equal to 1.

In the coin-toss example, the distribution is

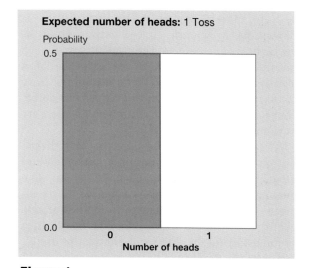

Figure 1

derived in an objective way. If the coin is fair, anyone would agree that the probabilities equal 0.5. In other instances, probabilities are subjective. Consider sketching a distribution for the sterling/ dollar exchange rate a year from now. You may consider the most likely value to be 1.5 (a 'point-estimate'), and be fairly confident that the actual value is somewhere between 1.4 and 1.65.

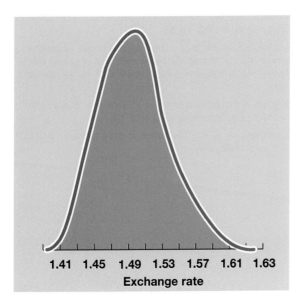

Figure 2

This would yield a sketch as shown in Figure 2. Another person would most likely come up with a different distribution.

Note that in Figure 2 the distribution is drawn as a smooth curve, rather than as rectangles representing the probability of each possible outcome. This is an example of a 'continuous distribution' (the exchange rate could take on any value in the range considered, there is not a specific number of discrete outcomes).

The coin toss example is a 'discrete distribution': one can list all possible outcomes and attach a probability to each of them. The outcome of a single toss is referred to as an event. One could be interested in more than one event, for example the number of heads in a sequence of tosses. Figure 3 shows the distribution of the number of heads in two tosses, and in four tosses. These are examples of the 'binomial distribution', which gives the distribution of the number of 'successes' (in our example, heads) out of a number of independent 'trials' (tosses), where each trial has two possible outcomes (H or T) with probabilities p and $(1-p)$. The binomial distribution occurs commonly in quality testing (how many defective units in a sample of 20?) and opinion polls (how many people out of 1,100 support a specific proposition?).

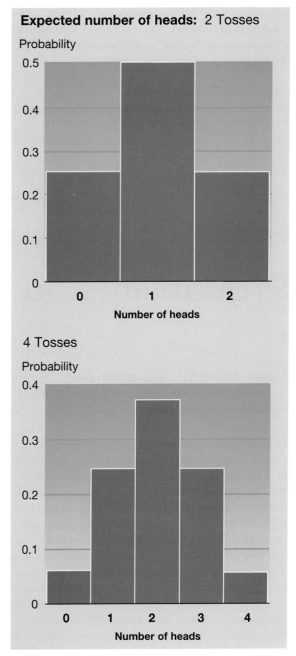

Figure 3

Normal distribution

As mentioned before, some variables have a continuous distribution, i.e., they can take on any value within a given range. Consider, for example, ordering a pint of beer. When pouring your glass, the barman (you hope) intends to

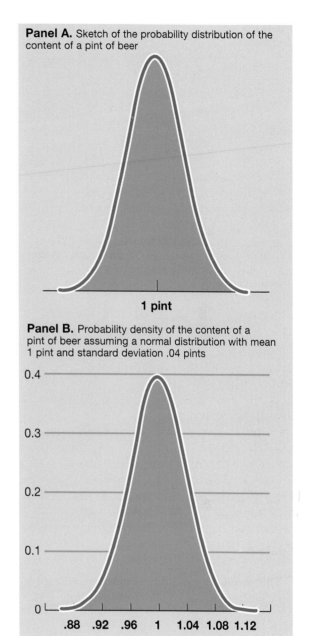

Panel A. Sketch of the probability distribution of the content of a pint of beer

1 pint

Panel B. Probability density of the content of a pint of beer assuming a normal distribution with mean 1 pint and standard deviation .04 pints

Figure 4

pour exactly one pint in your glass. If you were to measure the actual content, you would expect to find a quantity close to one pint. The difference between the actual value, and the target value of one pint, can be thought of as an error.

If one repeated this experiment many times, the data could be used to sketch the distribution of the content of a pint of beer. You would expect that 'on average' a pint contains exactly one pint, and that most of the errors are small, with possibly a few larger ones. You might also expect that you are equally likely to get 5 per cent of a pint too much or too little. This would result in a distribution as sketched in Panel A of Figure 4.

This is the shape of a 'normal distribution', also referred to as a 'bell-shaped curve'. It is characterized by a mean and a standard deviation. Panel B of Figure 4 shows the distribution of the content of a pint of beer, assuming a normal distribution with mean 1 pint and standard deviation .04 pints (and assuming that the glass can contain 1.12 pints!).

Assuming a normal distribution imposes some very specific assumptions on the probabilities of the possible outcomes. Specifically, there is approximately a 66 per cent probability of being within one standard deviation of the mean, a 95

per cent probability of being within two standard deviation of the mean, and a close to 99 per cent probability of being within three standard deviations of the mean. As for discrete distributions, the total area under the curve is equal to 1. A normal distribution with mean 0 and standard deviation 1 is referred to as the standard normal distribution.

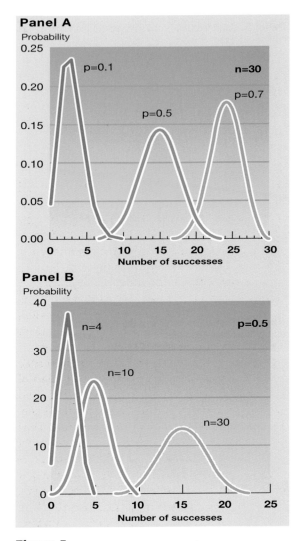

Panel A

Panel B

Figure 5

The normal distribution is more convenient to work with than the binomial distribution, which becomes cumbersome when the number of trials (n) is large. Fortunately, under some conditions, the binomial distribution is sufficiently similar in shape to the normal that it can be approximated by a normal distribution.

Panel A of Figure 5 sketches the shape of the binomial distribution for $n = 30$ and $p = 0.1$, 0.5 and 0.7 respectively, while Panel B sketches this distribution for $p = 0.5$ and $n = 4$, 10 and 30. Intuitively, when the number of events n is large and the probability p is close to 0.5, the binomial distribution approaches the bell-shape of the normal distribution.

This approximation is especially useful when dealing with opinion polls, where the sample size n typically exceeds 1,000, making the binomial distribution very much untractable.

Summary

Uncertain events, or random variables, are characterized by a distribution. A uniform distribution is where all outcomes are equally likely. A 'continuous distribution' is when variables can take on any value within a given range. A discrete distribution allows you to list all possible outcomes and attach a probability to them. The binomial distribution gives the distribution of the number of 'successes' from a number of independent trials. The normal distribution is sometimes referred to as a 'bell-shaped curve'.

Suggested further reading

Most introductory statistics texts include a chapter on binomial and normal distributions. A very legible text is *Coping with Numbers* by D. Targett. A more advanced text is *Complete Business Statistics* by A D Aczel.

Taking samples

■ **Sampling is at the heart of applied statistics; we only have to look at the opinion polls. But behind the simple idea lies some complex mathematics.**

by Ann van Ackere

This article focuses on the use of samples of data to infer information about the population from which they are taken. The most commonly encountered form of sample data in the press is opinion-polling: interviewers poll a sample of about a thousand people and make inferences about what the target population thinks about a specific issue.

This article addresses four issues: (i) why sample; (ii) how to take a sample; (iii) how to make inferences from a sample without prior knowledge about the population (confidence intervals); and (iv) how to use a sample to support or reject a hypothesis about the population (hypothesis testing).

The first question is: why sample? Why not use the whole population? When thinking about opinion polls the answer is obvious: time and cost. This also applies to manufacturing environments: testing every unit that comes off the production line is a lengthy and expensive process. In some cases, using the whole population is simply not an option because of destructive testing. On the other hand, sampling can be very accurate. In many instances there is no need to consider the whole population, as an appropriately selected and analysed sample can provide us with the desired degree of accuracy.

The term target population refers to the group of people or objects from which the sample should be taken. The sample is actually taken from what is known as the sampling frame; i.e. the 'list' of people or objects assumed to match the population. For example, consider sampling the workforce of a multinational company. The target population consists of the actual workforce. The sampling frame (for example, the list of names you receive from head-office) may differ from this, as people who recently left may still appear on the list, while new ones have not yet been added. This is one source of bias in sampling: if the sampling frame is very different from the target population, the sample is unlikely to be representative of the population. Of course some names could have been intentionally omitted, but that is another story. . .

An accurate sampling-frame is no guarantee of a representative sample. Two main causes of bias are non-response (in opinion-polls and surveys) and inappropriate sampling methods. Non-response is a problem to the extent that people who elect to respond to a survey may differ from those who do not. For example, a survey on customer satisfaction may yield a higher response rate from dissatisfied customers, causing a bias in the reported results. The resulting distortions can be quite dramatic, especially as response rates of 20 per cent or lower are not uncommon for such surveys.

To enable statistical analysis, a sample should be taken randomly; i.e. each element of the sampling frame must have the same probability of being selected or, if for some reason the probabilities do differ, this must be taken into account in the analysis.

Random sampling

The simplest sampling method is random sampling. With this method, each element of the sampling frame is assigned a number. Then a series of random numbers is generated, using either a computer or a table of random numbers. The sample consists of those elements whose number appears on the list of random numbers.

Table 1: Random numbers				
91	01	78	50	50
70	37	55	94	53
11	06	17	48	24
60	37	89	98	61
37	41	11	09	04

Table 1 shows an example of a random numbers table. Each digit is equally likely to be followed by any one digit. Consider having to select a random sample of five people out of 60 individuals. First, assign a two-digit number to each individual, for example, number them from 00 to 59. Then randomly pick a starting point in the table, for example the seventh digit of the second row, a 9. Next, look at the first pair of numbers: 94. (If there were 200 elements numbered 000 to 199, we would consider the first triplet of digits, 945.) There is no element in our population with this number, so skip it. The next pair is 53. The first element of our sample is the individual who was assigned number 53. The second element of the sample will be the individual numbered 11, and so on.

When information about different subgroups of the population is available, the use of stratified sampling can improve the quality of the sample. Intuitively, one wants to sample more from the larger subgroups and from those subgroups that exhibit more variation among the elements of the subgroup.

Consider polling customers of a supermarket chain. The population in the catchment area of a store located near a medium-sized village may be quite similar in terms of socioeconomic background. Therefore a small sample may be sufficient to get a reasonably accurate picture of this population. On the other hand, a store located in a city center may face a mix of local people, commuters and tourists, resulting in a much more varied population. A larger sample will be required to ensure that these different customer types are represented.

Stratified sampling will ensure that (i) the sample includes customers from all types of stores (the different strata) and (ii) the more heterogeneous populations are sampled more extensively. The analysis will take into account that these groups are over-represented in the sample by applying appropriate correction factors.

Cluster sampling is used to reduce costs when the population is spread over a large geographical area. Consider again the supermarket chain. If this chain has 500 stores across the UK and requires a sample of 2,000 customers, sending interviewers to each store to interview four people is not efficient. It may be more appropriate to randomly select, say, 20 stores (possibly using stratified sampling to ensure that all types of stores are represented) and interview 100 customers at each of these stores.

In this example, each store represents a cluster of the population. The company randomly selects a number of clusters and then interviews customers from these selected clusters.

There are circumstances where random sampling is inappropriate, either because it is too expensive, or simply impossible (for example, because of confidential or unobtainable data). For opinion polls, quota sampling is the most commonly used method. Interviewers are given specific instructions on the composition of the sample they must select. For example, Table 2 shows how an interviewer could be asked to select 200 people for a poll on traffic congestion. The aim is to avoid interviewer bias (an interviewer might be inclined to mainly select people from the same age-group) and location bias (picking people near a tube station might result in an over-representation of people commuting by public transport). Setting up a sampling frame of the UK population and selecting a random sample would be vastly more expensive.

Table 2: Quota sampling				
Gender:	Male		Female	
Commute by:	Car	Public transport	Car	Public transport
Age: 18-25	5	15	5	15
26-40	10	20	10	20
41-65	20	30	20	30

Convenience sampling

Convenience sampling describes the situation where one uses whatever sample happens to be available, either to cut costs or because no other data can be collected. The large number of behavioral studies using undergraduate students as sample is a classical example. This does raise the issue of 'generalizability' of the results.

Confidence intervals

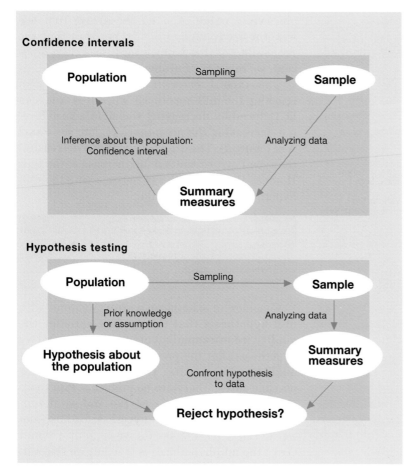

Hypothesis testing

Figure 1

How accurate is this estimate; i.e. how confident are we that the true value is close to the estimate $\hat{p} = 65$ per cent? As $\hat{p}$ follows approximately a normal distribution when the sample is sufficiently large, it is possible to write down a 95 per cent confidence interval [62 per cent, 68 per cent]. (*See* the technical section for details.) This means that if we were to take many such samples, we would expect the observed proportion $\hat{p}$ to lie between 62 per cent and 68 per cent for 95 per cent of these samples.

Obtaining a higher confidence level, say 99 per cent, comes at the expense of a larger confidence interval. In this example, we would expect 99 per cent of observed sample proportions $\hat{p}$ to lie between 61 per cent and 69 per cent. On the other hand, increasing the sample size results in a smaller confidence interval, i.e. a more accurate estimate. If 2,600 people out of 4,000 favour Eurostar, the point estimate $\hat{p} = 2,600/4,000 = 65$ per cent is unchanged, but the 95 per cent confidence interval equals [63.5 per cent, 66.5 per cent]. Note that multiplying the sample size by four only results in halving the confidence interval.

Once a sample has been selected, we can move on to the analysis stage. As mentioned in the introduction, two cases occur: (i) no prior information about the population is available and the sample is used to provide estimates about the population and (ii) the sample is used to test a hypothesis about the population. Figure 1 sketches these two scenarios.

Consider an opinion-poll aimed at estimating what percentage of people would favour travelling to the continent by Eurostar rather than by plane if both offered the same price. Assume that out of the 1,000 people interviewed, 650 express a preference for Eurostar. Based on this data, our best guess (or point-estimate) of the percentage of people who prefer Eurostar is $\hat{p} = 650/1,000 = 65$ per cent. The ^ above the p indicates that this number is an estimate of the

Hypothesis testing

Next, let us consider hypothesis testing. The Eurostar management may be convinced that, at equal price, half the travellers prefer Eurostar while the other half prefer flying. Denoting the proportion of travellers who favour Eurostar by $\hat{p}$, this results in the following null-hypothesis: $p = 50$ per cent, the alternative hypothesis being $p \neq 50$ per cent.

Assume we take a sample of 1,000 people. If the null-hypothesis is true, the observed

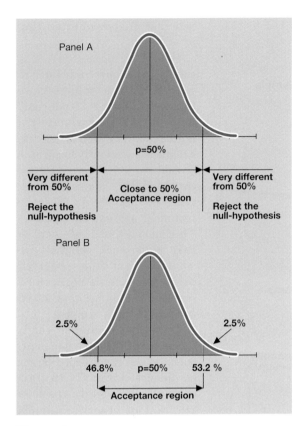

Figure 2

proportion of people who prefer Eurostar, $\hat{p}$, should be close to 50 per cent. If $\hat{p}$ is very different from 50 per cent we would reject the null-hypothesis in favour of the alternative $p \neq 50$ per cent. Thus, we need to define what we mean by 'very different'. Relying once more on the normal approximation, we obtain a picture as shown in Panel A of Figure 2. Whatever the limits we choose, there is always some probability that we observe a value of $\hat{p}$ outside these limits, although the null-hypothesis is true. This probability is known as the significance level or type I error. It is the probability of rejecting the null-hypothesis when the null-hypothesis is true.

Consider a 5 per cent significance level, as illustrated in Panel B of Figure 2. This implies that whenever we observe a value $\hat{p}$ outside the interval 46.8 per cent, 53.2 per cent, we reject the null-hypothesis. (*See* the technical section for mathematical details). In other words, if we observe a value of $\hat{p}$ so far away from the hypothesised value of $p = 50$ per cent that the probability of this happening is less than 5 per cent, we reject the null-hypothesis.

The type I error (i.e. the probability of rejecting the null-hypothesis when it is true) can be reduced by decreasing the significance level (i.e. increasing the acceptance region, see Panel A of Figure 2). The drawback is that a decrease of the type I error results in an increase of the type II error: the probability of not rejecting the null hypothesis when we should.

Table 3: Hypothesis testing		
	Do not reject the null-hypothesis	Reject the null-hypothesis
Null-hypothesis true	(a) OK	(b) Type I error
Null-hypothesis false	(c) Type II error	(d) OK

Consider an example of warranty claims, with null-hypothesis that the product satisfies the quality requirements versus the alternative hypothesis that the product does not satisfy the quality requirements. Table 3 shows the four possible cases. There are no problems with cases (a) (the null-hypothesis is true and we do not reject it) and (d) (the null-hypothesis is false and we do reject it). In case (b) we commit a type I error: the null-hypothesis is true but we reject it. In this example, this amounts to accepting a warranty claim, or scrapping a batch of goods, when the product satisfies the quality requirements. In case (c) we commit a type II error: the null-hypothesis is false, but we fail to reject it. This amounts to refusing a warranty claim when the product is defective.

The trade-off between type I and type II errors is therefore a trade-off between accepting unjustified warranty claims and rejecting justified claims. The choice of an appropriate significance level then rests on trading off the costs to the company of the two types of error: paying out unnecessary warranties versus unhappy customers. The only way to reduce both types of error simultaneously is to increase the sample size. But this is expensive in its own right.

Hypothesis testing plays a crucial role in quality control, and lies at the basis of the 6-sigma-chart. Consider a production process that consists of pouring an amount of liquid m in each can. If the process is under control, the actual amounts poured will be clustered closely around the target value of m. The null-hypothesis is thus that the average content per can equals m. If we take a sample of cans and observe an average content $\bar{x}$ very different from m we should conclude that the process is out of control and intervene. In this context, a type I error means intervening when the process is in control, i.e. an unnecessary interruption of production, while a type II error means not intervening when the process is out of control.

Consider filling cans of soft drink, with a target level of 33cl per can, i.e, the null-hypothesis is that $m = 33$. Assume that the filling process has a standard deviation of 1.2cl, and that we consider samples of 36 cans. In this case, the standard deviation of the sample mean equals 0.2cl (*see* the technical section for details). The 6-sigma-chart would look as shown in Figure 3. The bold horizontal line in the middle indicates the target $m = 33$. The four dotted lines are respectively one and two standard deviations above or below the mean.

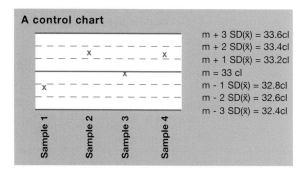

A control chart

Figure 3

The bold lines at the top and bottom are three standard deviations away from the mean. As production goes on, samples are taken at regular intervals and the observed sample means are indicated on the chart (the crosses). This provides an easy visual way of spotting if something is wrong. For example, the chart in Panel A of Figure 4 indicates the process is out of

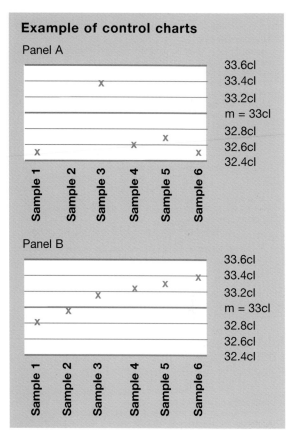

Example of control charts

Panel A

Panel B

Figure 4

control: several sample means are more than two standard deviations away from the mean. This is a very unlikely occurrence if the process is under control. The chart in Panel B also shows something is wrong. Although the sample means are within two standard deviations of the mean, there is a clear trend showing the production process is gradually getting out of control.

Suggested further reading

Most introductory textbooks contain several sections on the topics discussed in this article. More specific references include:

Price, F. Right First Time, Using Quality Control for Profit (1986), The Tools of Quality, Parts I-VII, Quality Progress, June 1990-December 1990

Deming, W.E. *Sample Design in Business Research*, 1960

Stratified Sampling

When it is known that the population consists of different subgroups (strata), each with its own characteristics, this information can be used to improve the quality of the sampling process. Information can relate to the size of the subgroups, the variance of the relevant variable within each subgroup, and the cost of sampling from each subgroup. Assume there are k subgroups. Let N_i, σ_i and c_i respectively denote the size, standard deviation and per unit sampling cost for subgroup i, $i=1, 2, \cdots, k$. Let $N=\sum_{i=1}^{k} N_i$ denote the total population size. How should we determine the number of elements to be sampled from subgroup i (n_j) to achieve the desired total sample size n?

If we only have information about the size of the subgroups, it is logical to sample proportionally to the group-sizes:

$$n_j = \frac{N_j}{N} n, \quad j=1, \cdots k.$$

Knowledge of the standard deviation of each subgroup enables us to sample proportionally more from those subgroups which exhibit more variability:

$$n_j = \frac{N_j \sigma_j}{\sum_{i=1}^{k} N_i \sigma_i} n, \quad j=1, \cdots k.$$

If cost information is available as well, this can be taken into account to sample proportionally more from the least expensive subgroups:

$$n_j = \frac{N_j \sigma_j / \sqrt{c_j}}{\sum_{i=1}^{k} N_i \sigma_i / \sqrt{c_i}} n, \quad j=1, \cdots k.$$

Sometimes, rather than having a given total sample size, we are limited by a budget constraint C. In this case, the budget can be allocated to the various subgroups as follows:

$$n_j c_j = \frac{N_j \sigma_j \sqrt{c_j}}{\sum_{i=1}^{k} N_i \sigma_i \sqrt{c_i}} C, \quad j=1, \cdots k.$$

yielding the following sample sizes:

$$n_j = \frac{N_j \sigma_j / \sqrt{c_j}}{\sum_{i=1}^{k} N_i \sigma_i \sqrt{c_i}} C, \quad j=1, \cdots k.$$

The first expression indicates that, other things being equal, a larger share of the budget goes to the more expensive subgroups, while the second expression shows that the resulting sample size is smaller for the more expensive subgroups.

Confidence Intervals for Proportions

An opinion poll indicates that 650 people out of 1,000 favour Eurostar over the plane. The resulting point-estimate for the proportion of people who favour Eurostar thus equals $\hat{p}$ = 650/1,000 = 0.65. Using the normal approximation, the standard deviation of this estimate equals $SD(\hat{p}) = \sqrt{\hat{p}(1-\hat{p})/n} = 0.015$. This yields a 95% confidence interval equal to

$$[\hat{p}-1.96 * SD(\hat{p}), \hat{p} + 1.96 * SD(\hat{p})] = [0.62, 0.68],$$

while a 99% confidence interval equals

$$[\hat{p}-2.58 * SD(\hat{p}), \hat{p} + 2.58 * SD(\hat{p})] = [0.61, 0.69].$$

The numbers 1.96 and 2.58 follow from the assumption of a normal distribution. It is common practice to round 1.96 to 2.

If we observe a point-estimate $\hat{p}$ = 0.65 in a sample of 4,000, the resulting standard deviation equals $SD(\hat{p}) = \sqrt{\hat{p}(1-\hat{p})/n} = 0.0075$, half the value obtained for a sample size of 1,000. This yields a 95% confidence interval equal to

$$[\hat{p}-1.96 * SD(\hat{p}), \hat{p} + 1.96 * SD(\hat{p})] = [0.635, 0.665];$$ multiplying the sample size by four enables us to half the size of the confidence interval.

Hypothesis testing for Proportions

Eurostar management's hypothesis that at equal fares, half the travellers favour Eurostar can be formalized as follows:

Null hypothesis: $p = 0.50$
Alternative hypothesis: $p \neq 0.50$

where p denotes the proportion of travellers who favour Eurostar. For a sample of 1,000, the standard deviation of $\hat{p}$ equals $SD(\hat{p}) = \sqrt{p(1-p)/n} = .016$. Note the use of the hypothesized value p to compute this standard deviation: this is the standard deviation of $\hat{p}$, under the assumption that the null-hypothesis is correct. This implies that if we were to take many samples of 1,000 people and if the null-hypothesis were true, then in 95% of these samples, the observed value of $\hat{p}$ would lie in the interval $[p -2 * SD(\hat{p}), p+2 * SD(\hat{p})] = [0.468, 0.532]$, and in the remaining 5%, $\hat{p}$ would lie outside this interval.

Referring to Panel **B** of figure **2**, this interval is the acceptance region for the hypothesis test, assuming a 5% significance level (i.e. a 5% probability that $\hat{p}$ falls outside this interval, resulting in the null-hypothesis being incorrectly rejected).

If the observed value equals $\hat{p}$ = 0.46, we have sufficient evidence to reject the null-hypothesis p = 0.50 in favour of the alternative $p \neq 0.50$. If the observed value equals $\hat{p}$ = 0.51, we conclude that we have insufficient evidence to reject the null-hypothesis. Note that we do not accept the null-hypothesis, we simply fail to reject it.

An alternative approach to defining the acceptance region is to ask the question: how unlikely is it to observe a value $\hat{p}$ that different from the hypothesized value p? Assume the observed value equals $\hat{p}$=0.46. If the null-hypothesis is true, $\hat{p}$ follows a normal distribution with mean p = 0.50 and standard deviation $SD(\hat{p})$ = 0.016. Thus, the observed value is $(p - \hat{p})/SD(\hat{p})$ = (0.50-0.46)/0.016 = 2.5 standard deviations away from the mean (see figure T1). This number is known as the z-score. We need to calculate the probability of observing a value from a normal distribution which is more than 2.5 standard deviations away from its mean. Using a table of the standard normal distribution (or a computer!) yields an answer of 1.24%. This means that the probability of observing a value of $\hat{p}$ that far away from the hypothesized proportion is 1.24%. In statistical terms, we say that the observed value is significant at the 1.24% significance level. It is then up to the analysts to judge whether or not this is sufficient evidence to reject the null-hypothesis.

Distribution of the Sample Mean

Consider the issue of testing whether the content of a can of coke equals 33cl. Figure T2 describes three relevant distributions: the distribution of the population (all the cans of coke produced by this factory), the distribution of the sample (the 36 cans of coke in the sample) and the distribution of the sample mean (if we took many samples of 36 cans, and computed the average content in the cans for each of these samples, what would the distribution of these averages look like?).

Figure T2 states that the sample mean $\bar{x}$ will be normally distributed, whatever the distribution of the population. This result, an application of the Central Limit Theorem, holds as long as the sample is sufficiently large. In practice, a sample size of 30 is sufficient. To illustrate this result, consider the distribution of the average number of heads per toss (the sample mean) in a sequence of n tosses (the sample size). Figure T3 shows this distribution for n = 1, 2, 4, 8 and 16 tosses. Observe how the distribution evolves from a Uniform distribution (all outcomes equally likely) to the bell-shape of the Normal distribution. This is a consequence of the averaging which goes on as the sample size increases. For n = 16, the average number of heads will only equal the extreme values of 0 or 1 if all 16 tosses yield tails or all 16 yield heads, two very low probability events. For n = 1, these probabilities equal 0.5 each. Thus, as sample size increases, extreme values become less likely, leading to the bell-shaped distribution. Consequently, the larger the sample size, the smaller the standard deviation of the distribution of the sample mean $\bar{x}$. Specifically, $SD(\bar{x}) = \sigma / \sqrt{n}$, where σ is the standard deviation of the population.

Two problems can occur with this approach: σ may be unknown, or the sample size may be too small. If σ is unknown, it can be replaced by its estimate $s = \sqrt{\sum (x_i - \bar{x})^2 / (n-1)}$, and the same procedure applies.

If we have a small sample ($n < 30$), we require the assumption that the population follows a Normal distribution. If σ is known, we can proceed as before. If σ is unknown, we can again substitute the estimate s for σ, but in this case the resulting distribution of the sample mean will no longer be Normal. Instead, it will be a t-distribution. The method remains the same, but instead of relying on the Normal distribution to calculate confidence intervals, acceptance regions and z-scores we must use the t-distribution. This distribution differs from the Normal distribution in that it has somewhat fatter tails, ie. the probability of extreme values is slightly higher but, as we reach a sample size of 30, the normal distribution is a good enough approximation.

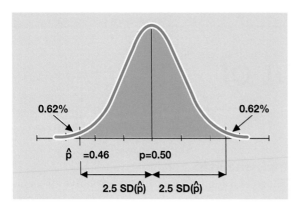

Figure T1

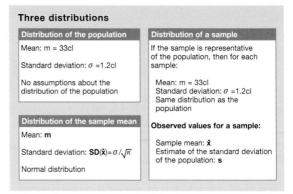

Three distributions

Distribution of the population	Distribution of a sample
Mean: m = 33cl	If the sample is representative of the population, then for each sample:
Standard deviation: σ =1.2cl	
No assumptions about the distribution of the population	Mean: m = 33cl Standard deviation: σ =1.2cl Same distribution as the population

Distribution of the sample mean	**Observed values for a sample:**
Mean: **m**	Sample mean: $\bar{x}$
Standard deviation: $\mathbf{SD}(\bar{x}) = \sigma / \sqrt{n}$	Estimate of the standard deviation of the population: **s**
Normal distribution	

Figure T2

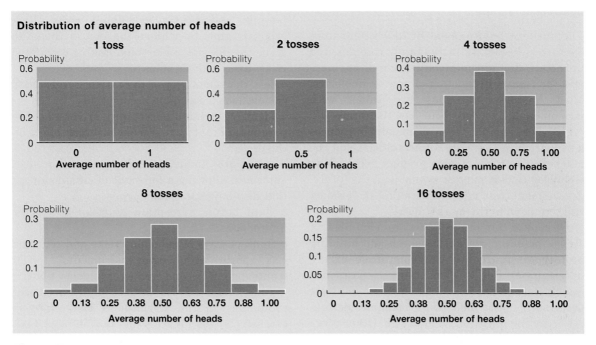

Distribution of average number of heads

Figure T3

Taking the risk out of uncertainty

■ **Risk and uncertainty are constant ingredients of business. But there are statistical ways to try to ascertain, and hence overcome, them.**

by Kiriakos Vlahos

The business environment in which companies operate is becoming increasingly complex and uncertain due to the globalization of business and the rapid introduction of new technologies. Most business decisions are taken with incomplete knowledge about how the future will evolve. For example, when a company introduces a new product, there are uncertainties about the market potential of the product, competing technologies that may be available in the future, development costs and the price that the product will command in the marketplace.

Of course companies can take a number of steps, including market research and building prototypes, to reduce the magnitude of the uncertainties. But decisions cannot be postponed indefinitely (what is often known as 'analysis paralysis'), and at some point companies need to act accepting a certain level of risk. Other types of business decisions with highly uncertain returns include:

● entering a new market, for example, Russia, where currency and political risks are very large
● investment in a new plant
● choosing between R&D projects
● oil explorations
● engaging in lawsuits.

Most personal decisions also involve risk. For example, if you are considering taking an MBA, you will be faced with uncertainty about the market for MBAs a year or two down the road, the incremental benefits to your career prospects, and your ability to finance the costs.

Risk analysis

There is a big difference between naive decision making under uncertainty, that ignores uncertainties and is based on a single view of the future, educated guesses that are based on gut feeling, and taking calculated risks. Risk analysis aims to achieve the last of these: to guide the decision makers into taking calculated risks. Risk analysis helps to:

● test the sensitivity of the rate-of-return/NPV calculations to the main assumptions
● identify the main uncertainty drivers, i.e. the parameters that have a make-or-break effect on the project
● calculate bounds to the possible project outcomes, allowing a foresight of circumstances that may have catastrophic consequences
● gain better perception of risks and their interactions
● think of ways of managing risks and reducing risk exposure with hedging instruments
● anticipate risks and create contingency plans.

Merck, one of the largest pharmaceutical companies in the world uses risk analysis extensively (see Figure 4 and box on page 146). Judy Lewent, CFO of Merck in an interview with *Harvard Business Review*, aptly summarized the benefits of risk analysis: 'What is the payoff of all this sophistication? In short, better decisions.'

Techniques

Today, managers have access to a range of techniques and tools for carrying out uncertainty and risk analysis. The main ones are briefly described below:

● Sensitivity analysis is the starting point for any type of uncertainty analysis. In its simplest form it involves asking 'what-if' questions. For example, what if interest rates increase to 10 per cent? Or what if the market share drops to 5 per

		Hours flown			
		800	900	1000	1100	1200
	50%	16	23	30	37	44
	55%	30	39	48	57	65
	60%	45	55	66	76	87
Capacity utilization	65%	59	71	84	96	109
	70%	73	88	102	116	131
	75%	88	104	120	136	152
	80%	102	120	138	156	174

Figure 1

cent? Spreadsheets make it particularly easy to explore this type of question. In addition, they provide a facility for semi-automated sensitivity analysis, calculating important outputs (profit, rate-of-return, and so on) for a range of values of input parameters.

This facility is called what-if tables and depending on the number of inputs you may have one-way, two-way and three-way what-if tables. As an example, in Figure 1, a small airline examines the sensitivity of profits to the capacity utilization of aircraft and hours flown. More exotic ways of presenting sensitivity analysis results have been developed, including tornado diagrams and spider plots. Figure 2 shows an example of a tornado diagram. The aim of sensitivity is to understand and challenge the assumptions.

● Scenario analysis is used in different contexts with different meanings. Michael Porter in his book *Competitive Strategy* defines scenarios as 'discrete, internally consistent views of how the world will look in the future, which can be selected to bound the possible range of outcomes that might occur'. Although there are more profound uses of scenario analysis, in the context of risk analysis managers may try to develop a pessimistic and an optimistic view of the future and test the business project against each. This will provide a range of possible outcomes as well an opportunity to think about strategies for dealing with downturns.

● Decision analysis. Both sensitivity analysis and scenario analysis, in the form described above, take no account of the relative likelihood of different events. For example, a simplistic scenario analysis may provide a range of possible outcomes for profit, but it tells you nothing about how likely are particular values in that range. Decision analysis and Monte Carlo simulation (Figure 3) assign probabilities to the various possibilities. Decision analysis involves the graphical representation of business problems using decision trees and influence diagrams. It is particularly suited to multi-stage problems in which different decisions are taken at different times as the various uncertainties get resolved.

Monte Carlo simulation

This technique is named after the roulette wheels in Monte Carlo, viewed as devices for generating random numbers. It has been used in other scientific fields for a long time, but it was David Hertz of consultants McKinsey & Co who suggested the use of Monte Carlo simulation for the evaluation of capital investments in an article published by the *Harvard Business Review* in 1979.

At that time, building a simulation model was a very laborious exercise involving low-level computer programming. Today, many packages

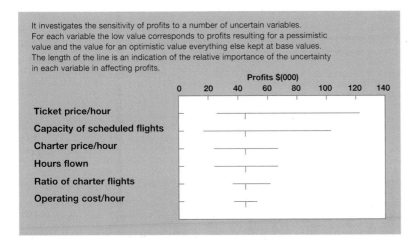

It investigates the sensitivity of profits to a number of uncertain variables. For each variable the low value corresponds to profits resulting for a pessimistic value and the value for an optimistic value everything else kept at base values. The length of the line is an indication of the relative importance of the uncertainty in each variable in affecting profits.

Figure 2: Tornado diagram

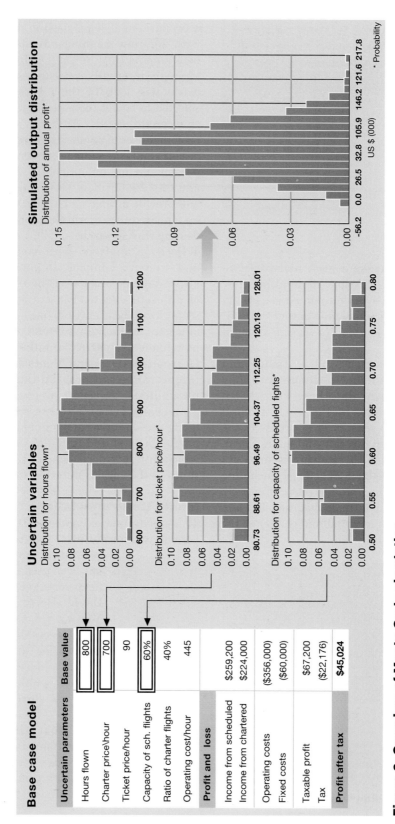

Figure 3: Overview of Monte Carlo simulation

are available that allow powerful risk analyses to be carried out with minimal effort using widely available spreadsheet technology, and this has made the technique very popular. One such package is @RISK, published by Palisade.

The basic steps required for carrying out risk analysis are illustrated in Figure 3 and explained below:

● *Step 1*: Build a base case cash-flow model for the investment you are evaluating, usually in a spreadsheet. The main inputs of such a model are costs, sales and price projections, interest rates and so on. The main outputs are the revenues, the year-by-year cash flow, rate of return, and net present value of the investment.

● *Step 2*: Model the uncertainty about the main inputs of the model using probability distributions. This can be done simply by typing appropriate formulae in the cells containing the inputs. For example, a formula such as UNIFORM(800,1100) specifies that the value of the cell is drawn from a uniform distribution between 800 and 1,100.

But where do these distributions come from? In some cases, for example in oil exploration, they may come from the analysis of historic or experimental data. In others they could reflect managerial judgments (for example, about sales of a new product) or expert opinion (about interest rates).

● *Step 3*: Specify the relationships between input variables. In many cases uncertain variables are not independent. For example, different fuel prices are known to be correlated. Also, market price and size should be related. These relationships require careful thought. Try to model them by including the correlation coefficient in the specification of the model. Most risk analysis packages provide facilities for the specification of the correlation matrix between the uncertain variables.

● *Step 4*: Run the simulation. What happens during the simulation is the following. The software package repetitively draws samples of all input parameters specified as probability distributions in a way that reflects the likelihood of each value being selected. For each set of sampled inputs it then calculates the outputs. At the end of the simulation the calculated outputs

are analysed and presented in a probabilistic form. For example, in Figure 3 you can see the resulting distribution of annual profit values. This distribution is taking into account the uncertainty in all input parameters as well as their interdependence.

The Monte Carlo approach to risk analysis is based on brute force. The same calculation is repeated a number of times for different values of the uncertain inputs. Like most other sampling techniques the results depend on the specific values that happen to be selected. To reduce the impact of chance on the results, a 'sufficient' number of iterations need to be carried out. Although it is difficult to predetermine what a sufficient number of iterations will be, there are some practical guidelines that help address this problem.

For example, start with a relatively small number of iterations, say 100, and then double them and observe the impact on the results. Repeat that process until there is little change in the shape and values of the output distributions. Some software packages automate this process by monitoring the convergence of simulation results.

Evaluating the simulation results

How do we use the results of a simulation exercise? Traditional cash flow models come up with a single number (NPV) that tells us whether or not we should proceed with a certain project. It is certainly more difficult to interpret a probability distribution about NPV or the rate of return. How do we use the information that the expected rate of return is 20 per cent but there is 10 per cent chance that it will be below 5 per cent?

The information generated by risk analysis is much richer than that generated by static cash flow models, but it takes some understanding of probabilities and a lot of common sense to make good use of it. And in any case the results of a static cash flow model are likely to be misleading. Here is a list of questions you should ask yourself that will help you to evaluate properly the results of a risk analysis exercise:

● what is the range of possible values for the main outputs?

■ Risk analysis at Merck

Merck & Co Inc. invests about $2bn in R&D and capital expenditure annually. Most of this investment goes into long-term, risky projects that are impossible to evaluate using traditional cash flow analysis.

The reason is that the uncertainties are so wide as to make single-point estimates of the various uncertain parameters nonsensical.

Instead Merck developed sophisticated risk analysis models based on Monte Carlo simulation. These models assign probability distributions to the various input parameters and produce a ranges of possible outcomes in a probabilistic form.

The Research Planning Model. Bringing new drugs to the market is a very long-term and unpredictable process. Only 1 in 10,000 explored chemicals becomes a prescription drug. Development of the Research Planning Model started in 1983 and by 1989 it was used to evaluate all significant research and development projects over a 20-year horizon.

Figure 4 provides a diagrammatic explanation of the model's operation. The major inputs to the model are probability distributions of R&D, manufacturing and marketing variables. The model takes into account a number of medical and technological constraints as well as macroeconomic assumptions. It then uses simulation to compute probability distributions of the cash flow and the return on investment from specific projects.

The Revenue Hedging Model. This model helps develop hedging strategies by simulating Merck's net position and US dollar cash flows. It takes into account expenditure, local currency revenue and exchange rate projections over a five-year planning horizon.

All these inputs are expressed as probability distributions. The model then evaluates the impact of different hedging strategies and provides assessments of the currency risks that the company faces. The model is now used continually in order to fine tune the hedging program in response to changing market conditions.

But how comfortable is senior management with the use of these and other sophisticated decision-support models? According to Judy Lewent, CFO of Merck, these models do not make decisions. Instead, they provide management with assessments of risk and return based on their (the managers') own judgments of the future developments in the market.

'Quantitative approaches do not daunt our CEO, Roy Vagelos, or other senior managers here. They don't view our models as some black box that completely ignores the great wisdom of management and tries to mechanize the decision making of the business. They understand both the potential and their limitations.'

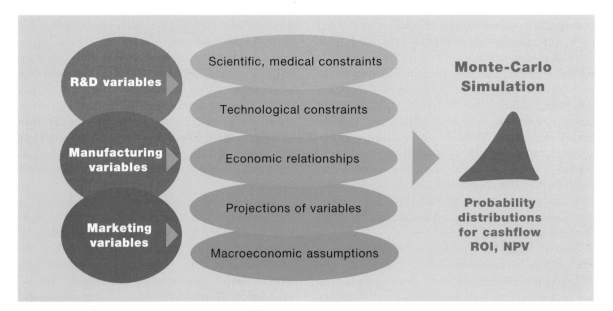

Figure 4: Merck's Market Research Model

- what is the expected rate of return? (It may well be different from the one you get from cash flow modeling using expected values of the input parameters)
- what is the downside of this investment?
- how could I cope with the downside?
- is there any combination of uncertainties that result in catastrophic consequences?
- which are the main uncertainty drivers causing the variation in profits?
- what can I do to reduce these uncertainties?
- how does the risk-return profile of this project compares to other alternatives?

Risk analysis does not provide simple answers. Instead it provides a means of exploring the trade off between risk and return. It is also an iterative process. Once you have identified the main uncertainty drivers you need to think about ways to reduce these uncertainties by taking advantage of various hedging opportunities or using better forecasting techniques, market research, and so on. But risk analysis is certainly a valuable tool for coping with a world in which just about everything is uncertain.

Summary

Most business decisions, such as launching a new product, are taken with incomplete knowledge about how the future will evolve. There is a big difference between naive decision making, educated guesses and calculated risks. Risk analysis aims to achieve the last of these. The main tools are sensitivity analysis (what if questions, what if tables), scenario analysis, decision analysis and Monte Carlo simulation. Some understanding of probabilities and a lot of common sense is required to make good use of a simulation exercise.

Suggested further reading

Clemen, R. (1990) *Making Hard Decisions*, Duxbury Press.

Bunn, D. (1984) *Applied Decision Analysis*, McGraw-Hill.

Hertz, D. 'Risk analysis in capital investment', *Harvard Business Review*, September-October, 1979.

Hertz, David and Thomas, H. (1984) *Practical Risk Analysis – An Approach through Case Histories*, John Wiley and Sons.

Nickols, N. 'Scientific management at Merck: an interview with CFO Judy Lewent', *Harvard Business Review*, January-February, 1994.

Palisade Corporation @RISK Risk analysis for spreadsheets, 1994.

Systems thinking and the art of modeling

■ **Thinking of business issues as a series of systems, each of which contains numerous feedback loops, is the basis of modeling and scenario planning.**

by John Morecroft and Ann van Ackere

The aim of this article of the Applied Statistics and Decision Support module is to introduce the systems thinking approach to modeling. It first discusses the feedback perspective that lies at the heart of the systemic view. It then introduces causal loop diagrams as a visual language to identify and represent feedback structures. Finally, it applies the systems thinking approach to a practical example to illustrate its usefulness.

Figure 1 illustrates the concept of a system. The individual in Panel A feels squeezed between two stones. A natural reaction is to give

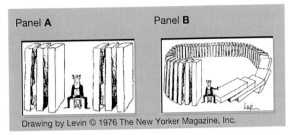

Drawing by Levin © 1976 The New Yorker Magazine, Inc.

Figure 1: A simple feedback system

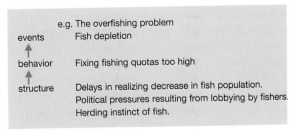

Figure 2: Structure drives behavior and events

one of these a little push. In the short run, this does indeed improve the situation, but Panel B indicates that he is in for a surprise . . . we live and work in systems of circular causality, but feedback paths and consequences are rarely as clear and direct as in Figure 1. Rather, they tend to be hidden and far from obvious. Two examples that are often in the news illustrate this: building motorways to relieve traffic congestion and intensifying fishing to compensate for reduced catches.

New motorways do indeed result in less traffic congestion in the short run, but as potential motorists notice this reduced congestion, they increase their usage thus creating more traffic and increased congestion. Similarly, as catches are reduced due to dwindling fish stocks, fishermen tend to spend an increased number of days at sea. This leads to further reductions in fish stock and even lower catches.

Taking a systems perspective helps in understanding behavior and events by focusing on the underlying structure of the system, thereby avoiding misperceptions that result from focussing on the immediate consequences of actions. The feedback structure consists of all the factors that affect behavior. These include physical processes such as accumulation of materials, people or equipment, obsolescence and ageing, as well as policies and decision-making processes.

The latter include factors such as information channels, reward systems, personal values, traditions, expectations and time delays, which together determine what decision makers pay attention to, how they react and how fast they react. All these elements together form the structure of a system. As illustrated in Figure 2, it is this underlying structure that drives

people's behavior, which in turn results in the events we observe. For example, one structural problem in the fishing industry is the difficulty that fishermen and fisheries biologists have in assessing the depletion of fish stocks. Because schools of fish such as cod or haddock huddle together in small but known areas, it is easy to form the false impression that there are lots of fish while in fact the surrounding ocean is dangerously depleted. In this example, the fishermen's traditions (where they fish) and the herding instinct of the fish are part of the system structure. This causes a specific behavior (high fishing quotas) and results in an event (fish depletion).

Causal loops

Describing the structure of a system can be a cumbersome task. Causal loop diagrams offer an accessible visual language to describe systems.

Panel A of Figure 3 shows a simple causal loop relating 'Hunger' to 'Amount eaten.' The arrow from 'Hunger' to 'Amount eaten' indicates a

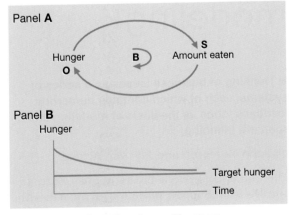

Figure 3: Balancing loop: Hunger

causal relationship between these two concepts: a change in 'Hunger' causes a change in 'Amount eaten'. The 'S' on the arrow indicates that both concepts move in the same direction: as hunger increases so does the amount eaten. The 'O' on the link from 'Amount eaten' to 'Hunger' indicates that for this causal link, the concepts move in opposite directions: as 'Amount eaten' goes up, 'Hunger' goes down. Going around the loop indicates that an increase in 'Hunger' leads to an increase in 'Amount eaten', which in turn yields a decrease in 'Hunger', thereby off-setting the initial increase. This loop is therefore referred to as a 'Balancing Loop' (as indicated by the 'B' in the center of the loop). The resulting level of 'Hunger' over time is as sketched in Panel B of Figure 3, where the horizontal line indicates the desired level of hunger. The balancing loop exhibits a goal-seeking behavior. Causal loops are either balancing (as in Figure 3) or reinforcing, as illustrated in Panel A of Figure 4.

Consider an increase in sales force. This leads to an increase in revenue, which results in a larger budget to marketing and thus a further increase in sales force. If no other factors affect this system, the resulting behavior over time would be as sketched in Panel B of Figure 4: unlimited exponential growth. In reality there are, of course, limits to market growth. The 'Model Boundary' insert outlines the approach to properly representing these limits.

The complexity of many systems results from the delay between when an action is taken, and

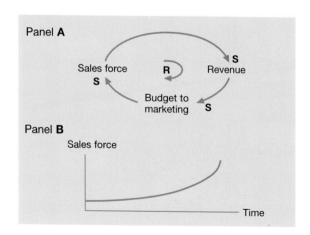

Figure 4: Reinforcing loop: Sales loop

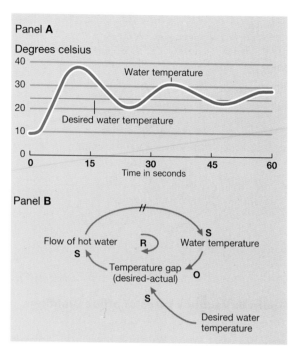

Figure 5: Taking a shower

when the consequences are observed. Imagine you are standing in the shower, and the water is ice cold. Your reaction is to increase the flow of hot water. It takes some time for the hot water to arrive, so you keep turning the tap until the water temperature is as desired. By then there is a large amount of hot water on its way to the shower, resulting in the temperature becoming too high. So you reduce the flow of hot water. This cycle is repeated until you (hopefully!) reach the desired temperature.

The resulting evolution of the temperature over time is sketched in Panel A of Figure 5. It is the delay in the arrival of hot water to the tap that prevents you from homing in smoothly on the desired temperature. Panel B shows the causal loop diagram for this shower. The 'Temperature gap' is the difference between the 'Desired water temperature' and the 'Water temperature.' An increase in this gap will cause you to increase the 'Flow of hot water' (S). This will, after some delay, result in an increase in the 'Water temperature' (S) and thus a reduction in the 'Temperature gap', yielding a balancing loop. The two lines crossing the arrow linking 'Flow of hot water' to 'Water temperature' (//) indicate the

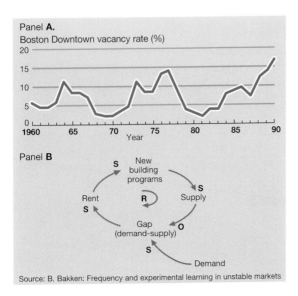

Panel **A.**
Boston Downtown vacancy rate (%)

Source: B. Bakken: Frequency and experimental learning in unstable markets

Figure 6: Vacancy rates of office buildings

presence of a delay. We thus have a balancing loop with delay.

Office over-supply

Let us switch to a more realistic example: demand and supply of office buildings. Panel A of Figure 6 shows the vacancy rate of office buildings in downtown Boston. Panel B shows the underlying structure. An increase in demand leads to a discrepancy between supply and demand, a 'gap'. This gap leads to higher rents and provides an incentive to start building programs. After a delay of several years, these result in increased supply. The delay between the action (start building programs) and the outcome (increased supply) leads to oversupply: the gap and resulting high rents continue to exist after sufficient building programs have started to close the gap. By the time all building programs are completed, there is ample over-supply.

When analysing the structure of a larger system, the causal loop diagram consists of a combination of balancing and reinforcing loops. Figure 7 shows a simplified version of such a model developed for a restaurant chain, which is part of a large conglomerate. The model consists of five main loops, three reinforcing ones (labelled R1, R2 and R3), and two balancing ones (labelled B1 and B2). The loop R1 is a classical example of how success breeds success: larger revenues allow for more spending on quality and thus higher quality. This results in higher perceived quality (it takes some time for customers to realize a change in quality and customer behavior is guided by how they perceive the quality of the restaurant rather than by the actual quality), higher value for

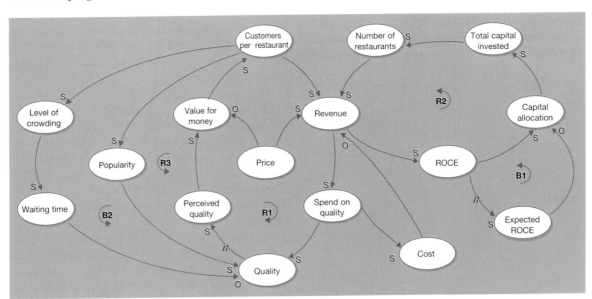

Figure 7: Modeling a restaurant chain

■ Model boundary

The market growth model of Figure 4, further described in the 'Stocks and Flows' insert, consists of one reinforcing loop. As pointed out, exponential growth cannot continue forever; there are limits to growth. When modeling such a structure, whether by building a causal loop diagram or a stock and flow model, the system thinker looks at the structure of the system to discover growth-limiting processes, as well as other reinforcing processes. Deciding which of these processes should be included in the model; i.e., defining the boundary of the model, is a crucial aspect of model building. Boundary definition is a matter of agreeing which aspects (or sectors) of the business system need to be included to properly portray the dynamic behavior that is being studied – in this case growth followed by saturation. Defining the boundary too narrowly may result in key aspects of the structure being overlooked, in which case the resulting model will be unable to reproduce the observed behavior. On the other hand, too broad a definition leads to large, unwieldy models, which are of little use in sharpening one's understanding of the structure being studied. Depending on the business setting (for example, consumer goods, novelty products, industrial goods) there are several options for sectors that might belong within the model boundary. For example, a model of the growth of a novelty consumer product such as

Rubik's cube would need to include a sector representing the pool of potential buyers (a stock) and the feedback process that limits sales growth as the pool is depleted – a balancing loop. Such a market sector would also include a reinforcing feedback loop to represent word-of-mouth sales – the more owners, the more opportunity to show off the product to friends and neighbours and so the more sales. A model of the growth of an industrial product such as ball-bearings or loudspeakers for hi-fi systems might need a more subtle approach to boundary definition, with a sector to represent capacity expansion of the loudspeaker manufacturer and another sector to represent how an industrial buyer (such as Sony or Philips) reacts to changes in the delivery time of the product. These new sectors, when linked to the original reinforcing sales loop, will create a more complex web of interlocking balancing and reinforcing loops capable of generating growth, stagnation or even sales decline, depending on the co-ordination achieved between the sales organization and the factory. The decision as to which sectors to include depends on why the model is being built; i.e., what specific dynamic behavior does it attempt to explain? The systems thinker should aim for the simplest possible model that is able to reproduce the desired behavior. Any unnecessary detail should be omitted.

money, more customers per restaurant and thus more revenues. The loops R2 and B1 relate to capital allocation. Diversified companies often face strong internal competition for resources and one of the main functions of the corporate headquarters is to allocate capital among these competing divisions. In this model, the amount of capital allocated to a division depends on the performance of that division in the previous year and on expectations of future growth.

There are two criteria for allocation of capital: absolute performance (i.e., return on capital employed, ROCE) and relative performance (i.e., actual performance versus expectations). The loop R2 indicates that higher revenues yield a higher ROCE. This provides the parent company with an incentive to allocate larger amounts of capital, resulting in a higher capital investment,

more restaurants and thus increased revenues. However, the expected ROCE depends on how well the division has performed in the past. As the division improves its ROCE, the headquarters' expectations creep up. Thus a ROCE that was considered satisfactory three years ago, may now be below expectations. In many diversified companies this is one of the critical expectations that deserves careful management. How does one keep presenting better and better results, without creating unrealistic expectations?

Loop B1 shows that an increase in ROCE leads to a higher expected ROCE and thus a lower capital allocation for a similar performance. This results in less capital investment, fewer restaurants and thus lower revenues. The remaining two loops (R3 and B2) deal with the overlapping effects of popularity and crowding. Would you enter a restaurant you do not know, if it is empty at 8pm? Or alternatively, wait a couple of hours for a table? Both these effects must be captured in the model: low levels of utilisation and overcrowding both decrease the attractiveness of a restaurant. When a restaurant is empty it is perceived to be unpopular, so an increase in the number of customers makes the restaurant look more attractive and the resulting loop R3 is reinforcing. However, if the level of crowding exceeds the target level, in other words the restaurant is packed, a further increase of crowding leads to longer waiting times and a decrease in quality. This yields the balancing loop B2.

A visual representation as in Figure 7 is useful in understanding the structure of the system and realizing the long-term consequences of various actions. The problem is that while the human mind is perfectly able to work through one loop, mentally evaluating the outcome of a change in one element of a multi-loop map such as Figure 7 is much more difficult. It is therefore important to take this type of analysis a step further and build a simulation model that enables one to use a computer to determine how the system of relationships evolves over time. There exists a variety of software, both on the Macintosh and Windows platforms, which allow this to be done. The 'Stocks and Flows' section describes such a model for the sales force example of Figure 4.

The use of simulation models enables one to ask 'what if' questions. For example, in the shower model we could look at the impact of either halving or doubling the time it takes for hot water to reach the shower. In the sales force example, we could look at the impact of a ten per cent increase in prices. In a model such as Figure 7, we could investigate the impact of delaying maintenance or increasing prices in an attempt to improve ROCE both in the short term and in the longer term. Systems thinking and strategic modeling are now widely used to deal with practical problems of business management and planning in a wide variety of companies and industries.

Companies using the approach include AT&T, BBC, BT, Exxon, Ford, IBM, Royal Dutch/Shell and SmithKline Beecham. Applications span scenario generation and regulatory change at the industry level as well as policy design, process re-engineering and what if scenarios at the business level. The box on 'The Process of Model Building with Management Teams' on page 154 describes one such application.

Suggested further reading

Forrester, J.W. 'The CEO as Designer', *McKinsey Quarterly*, 1992, number 2, pages 3-30.

Morecroft, J.D.W, and Sterman, J.D (eds) (1994), *Modeling for Learning Organizations*, Producing Press, Portland, Oregan.

Senge, P.M. *The Fifth Discipline*, Century Business, London, 1992.

De Geus, A. Modeling to Predict or to Learn, foreword to *Modeling for Learning Organizations*, edited by Morecroft J.D.W. and Sterman J.D., Productivity Press, Portland, Oregan, 1994.

Bunn, D.W., Larsen, E.R., and Vlahos K. Complementary modeling approaches for analysing several effects of privatization on electricity investment, *Journal of the OR Society*, vol. 44 number 10, pages 957-97, 1994.

Larsen, E.R., van Ackere, A. and Warren, K.D. The Growth of Service and the Service of Growth: Forthcoming in Decision Support Systems. Working Paper W-95-6, System Dynamics Group, London Business School (provides details about the model discussed in Figure 7).

'Building Resources for Competitive Advantage', pp 591 Module 18, Strategic Management and Implementation, *Mastering Management*, Pitman Publishing, 1997.

■ Stocks and Flows

Figure S1 shows a 'Stock and Flow' model for the sales force example presented in Figure 4. The rectangle represents the accumulation or 'stock' of sales people. Changes to this stock occur by the 'flow' of sales people labeled 'Hire or Fire'. The dotted line traces the reinforcing loop sketched in Figure 4. Note how formalizing a causal loop diagram to obtain a simulateable model requires one to make the links more explicit, thereby showing the decision-making process, as well as the elements influencing this process. To simulate the model, it is necessary to define exactly how each element depends on the other elements of the model. For example, Revenue is the product of Salesforce, Sales per Salesperson and Price, while the Discrepancy is the difference between the Allowed Salesforce and the Salesforce. For the interested reader, the equations are summarized in

Figure S2. Figure S3 shows an example of a simulation run. Initially, the salesforce is steady at 100 people. After 10 weeks, the price per unit is raised by 10 per cent from £1,000 to £1,100. This increases revenue, the sales budget and the allowable salesforce, creating a discrepancy between allowable salesforce and salesforce and resulting in a hiring decision. This increases the salesforce, revenues and, moving around the loop, leads to a further increase in salesforce. In this simple model the salesforce keeps growing. In reality, there are outside forces that will impose a limit on this growth. For example, the number of customers may be limited, resulting in less sales per salesperson as the number of salespeople increases. But these forces are outside the boundary of this simple model.

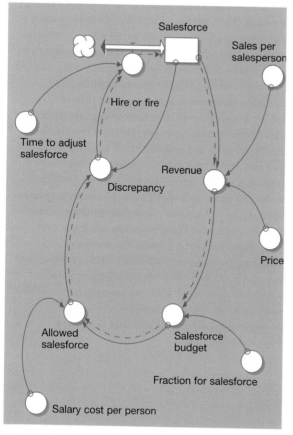

Figure S1

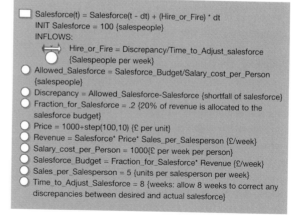

Salesforce(t) = Salesforce(t - dt) + (Hire_or_Fire) * dt
INIT Salesforce = 100 {salespeople}
INFLOWS:
   Hire_or_Fire = Discrepancy/Time_to_Adjust_salesforce {Salespeople per week}
Allowed_Salesforce = Salesforce_Budget/Salary_cost_per_Person {salespeople}
Discrepancy = Allowed_Salesforce-Salesforce {shortfall of salesforce}
Fraction_for_Salesforce = .2 {20% of revenue is allocated to the salesforce budget}
Price = 1000+step(100,10) {£ per unit}
Revenue = Salesforce* Price* Sales_per_Salesperson {£/week}
Salary_cost_per_Person = 1000{£ per week per person}
Salesforce_Budget = Fraction_for_Salesforce* Revenue {£/week}
Sales_per_Salesperson = 5 {units per salesperson per week}
Time_to_Adjust_Salesforce = 8 {weeks: allow 8 weeks to correct any discrepancies between desired and actual salesforce}

Figure S2: Equations

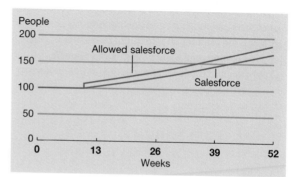

Figure S3

■ The Process of Model Buildings with Management Teams

Modeling the Upstream Oil Industry. In the past, business models were built by modeling experts with little or no input from management. Today, however, many organizations have come to realize that the process of model building provides a vital learning opportunity for an organization. A well-designed modeling project brings together an experienced management team in a rich interchange of ideas: to debate the key issues, to map the major interdependencies in the business, to develop shared understanding, to exchange mental models and to visualize alternative futures through simulation. A good illustration comes from a project with executives in the oil industry described in *Modeling for Learning Organizations* (Productivity Press, 1994).

The Oil Producers' Project – Outline of the Process. A group of senior managers and planners from a major oil company convened a project with the purpose of improving their understanding of oil market dynamics for use in global scenarios. The project team comprized ten people in all. The team attended three meetings lasting three hours each, facilitated by an experienced modeler. The facilitator used flip charts and whiteboards to collect information from the group discussion. One example of an output from the meetings is the overview of global oil producers shown in Figure P1, which provides a glimpse of the team's shared mental model of the industry. In their minds the complex world of oil producers can be usefully categorized into three sectors on the left representing Opec and two sectors on the right representing independent (non-Opec) producers and the market. From this broad conceptual framework flowed a fascinating discussion in which the team probed the intentions, motivations and plans of the major producers: the political and socioeconomic pressures shaping the production and quota decisions of Opec, and the commercial pressures guiding capacity expansion and production decisions of independent

producers. At the end of three meetings (nine hours of dialogue in all) emerged all the information necessary to create a systems view of global oil markets. Using this information a sub-group of the project team (four people) developed a simulation model in separate working sessions. The final model revealed a complex web of interlocking balancing and reinforcing loops that together maintain the balance of supply and demand that we take for granted in our day-to-day use of oil and petrol. These feedback loops interlink almost 100 concepts taken directly from the project team's conversations, including tangible factors such as market oil price, Opec quota, development cost, non-Opec capacity and reserves, as well as intangibles such as investment optimism, quota negotiating power, quota bias and punitive production.

Uses of the Model – Scenarios and Training. Figure P2 shows a simulation of the model representing a sustained Opec supply squeeze. Oil price rises steadily to a peak of $35 per barrel as Opec withholds supply. Meanwhile, high prices create an attractive investment climate for non-Opec producers, whose capacity grows to more than 30 million barrels per day. The simulation ends with a period of price instability as Opec's discipline and power evaporates in the face of declining market share. Needless to say, the supply squeeze simulation is not intended as a prediction of oil supply, price and demand. It is a scenario, an internally consistent story, intended to stimulate thinking about oil market dynamics. The simulation model can generate a wide range of industry scenarios including an Asian Boom, Green World, Opec supply glut and quota busting. Simulations like these, and many more, were incorporated into company scenarios. Subsequently the model was developed into a microworld – a gaming simulator with an attractive graphical interface – that allows teams to generate their own scenarios. The microworld is now used in management development and MBA programs.

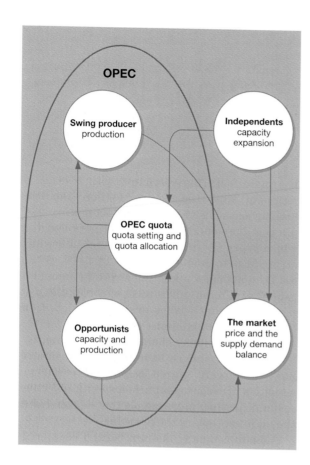

Figure P1: Oil producers and the market – boundary definition and components of a conceptual model

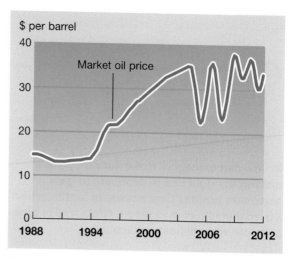

Figure P2: Sustained OPEC supply squeeze

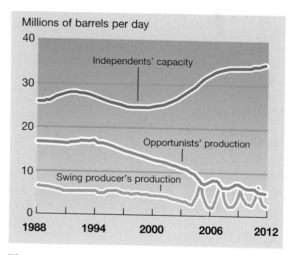

Figure P3

Getting the combination right

■ **How can managers make sure they are making the right mix of products to gain maximum profits? One answer is 'optimization' – a mathematical modeling system that is now a simple spreadsheet application.**

by Kiriakos Vlahos

Management often faces situations in which a limited amount of resources of various types, such as capital, labor, machine time and raw materials, need to be allocated to a number of different uses or activities (production, R&D, training, marketing and so on) so as to promote the company's objectives (profit, market share, employee satisfaction).

Most managers try to tackle these problems with 'what-if?' types of analysis in which the impact of alternative courses of action is invest-igated. But in decisions involving allocation of scarce resources, it is often desirable to ask normative 'what's best?' questions, for example 'what is the best production mix?' or 'how much should I be spending on marketing?'

The term 'optimization' describes a set of techniques that allow us to ask this type of question. More specifically, 'mathematical pro-gramming' helps us solve optimization problems when the relationships between the different factors can be expressed as mathematical equations.

When the mathematical relationships are linear the solution technique is known as 'linear programming'. It should be pointed out that in this context, programming does not refer to computer programming but rather to scheduling, i.e. what activities will be performed and at what level.

Here are some examples of business problems that can be addressed using optimization techniques:

● a manufacturing company, with a range of products and limited production facilities making decisions about the product mix.
● a company operating an oil refinery deciding which types of crude oil to purchase and which oil products to produce.
● a fund manager allocating a certain amount of capital to different investment opportunities.
● a retailer that wishes to supply outlets from central depots to minimize costs.
● an airline company allocating crews to flights.

All these problems have the same structure: how to allocate scarce resources to various activities in order to optimize a specific objective. A simple product mix example that demonstrates the main concepts is the following.

A small company manufactures TVs, stereos and speakers using a common parts inventory of power supplies, speaker cones and so on. The contribution of each product is $75, $50 and $35 respectively. It is the company's policy to produce at least 50 units of each product. The company would like to determine the most profitable mix of products to build for the next month given that parts are in limited supply. It is fairly easy to set up a spreadsheet that models the above problem

			TV set	Stereo	Speaker
	Number to build->		100	100	100
Part name	Inventory	no. used			
Chassis	450	200	1	1	0
Picture	250	100	1	0	0
Speaker cone	800	500	2	2	1
Power supply	450	200	1	1	0
Electronics	600	400	2	1	1
Profit contribution:			75	50	35
Profit:	By product		$7,500	$5,000	$3,500
		Total	$16,000		

Table 1: A product mix example

and calculates total profit as a function of the production levels for the three products. The layout of such a model is given in Table 1. You can see that for production levels of 100 for all products the total contribution to profit is $16,000. You can improve this contribution by trying different combinations of production levels but it is quite difficult to find the most profitable production mix while making sure that the various constraints are satisfied. Fortunately, modern spreadsheets have built-in optimization capabilities. The methodology for solving such a problem is as follows:

Step 1. Specify the objective function. You need to decide what you are aiming to achieve in a given business situation. In this case you are trying to maximize the total contribution to profit. One thing you need to remember when you specify the objective function is that costs you have already paid for or you cannot avoid are sunk costs and irrelevant in the context of this decision.

Step 2. Specify the decision variables. The decision variables are the levers under the control of management that can influence profit. In this case the management can influence profit by changing the production levels for TVs, stereos and speakers.

Step 3. Specify the constraints. In most business situations there are a number of internal or external factors that limit our choice of action. In this example you need to make sure that you use no more parts than you have available and that production quantities are greater than 50 units. In addition, you need to specify that the production quantities are positive, i.e. greater than zero. These last constraints are called non-negativity constraints. In this example these constraints are superfluous, given the previous constraints.

Step 4. Solve the optimization problem and find the optimal solution. For this step you can rely on one of the many optimization packages that are available. In most cases standard spreadsheet solvers will be sufficient. In Figure 1 you can see how steps 1-3 are carried out using the Excel spreadsheet solver. 'Profit', 'NoUsed', 'Inventory' and 'Production' are named cell ranges. Instead of typing these names you can

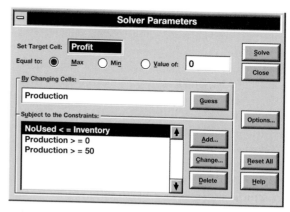

Figure 1: The Excel Solver Parameters dialogue box for the product mix example

just point to the appropriate parts of the spreadsheet using the mouse. Solving the optimization problem is just a matter of pressing the 'Solve' button. The optimal solution to this problem is to produce 175 TVs, 200 stereos and 50 speakers, resulting in a total contribution to profit of $24,875.

The same problem can be expressed algebraically as follows:

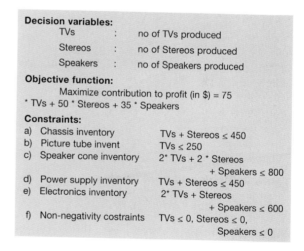

As you can see, all of the mathematical expressions used to define the objective function and the constraints are linear functions of the decision variables, so this is an example of a linear programming problem.

When we deal with complex real-world problems a single numerical answer is of limited value. We usually aim to develop a better understanding of the problem and the relationships between the problem parameters – often approximately known – our decisions and the outcomes. The sensitivity of the outcomes to parameter changes is of paramount importance. Often in this process, we discover unknown relationships and hidden links that lead to the creation of new decision alternatives.

Fortunately, the solution of an optimization problem is accompanied by useful information that helps us understand the problem better and grasp the sensitivities in an efficient way. Two concepts that are useful in analysing the results of an optimization problem are the 'slack' of the constraints and the 'shadow prices'.

Slack

Slack is the surplus amount of a limited resource (or the amount by which we exceed a minimum requirement) at the optimum. It is reported in the output of an optimization problem (see Table 2). Constraints with zero slack are said to be binding. These are the 'important' constraints that influence the optimal solution. Removing non-binding constraints from the problem formulation would not change the solution.

Name	Final value	Shadow price	Constraint limit	Slack
Chassis no. used	375	0	450	75
Picture tube no. used	175	0	250	75
Speaker cone no. used	800	12	800	0
Power supply no. used	375	0	450	75
Electronics no. used	600	25	600	0

Table 2: Slack and dual prices

Shadow prices

At the optimum, associated with each constraint is a quantity known as shadow price (also called dual price). This is the amount by which the objective value will improve if we relax the constraint by one unit, i.e. if we had an additional unit of a limited resource available. In economic terms, it is the most we would be willing to pay to obtain an additional unit of that resource.

If a constraint is not binding at the optimum (i.e., there is some slack), then the shadow price is always zero. This is logical because if not all of the available quantity of a resource is used, there is no incentive to obtain more of it. Conversely, we can deduce that if the dual price is non-zero, there is no slack in the constraint.

In Table 2, for example, we can see that the binding constraints (zero slack) are the speaker cones and the electronics inventory constraints. The shadow prices for these constraints show us that we could increase the profit contribution if we had an additional speaker cone or electronics unit by $12 and $25 respectively.

This is very useful information. For example, if we could purchase additional speaker cones for less than $12 we should certainly investigate that possibility further.

There is still a question about how many additional speaker cones we should buy if the price is less than $12; the optimization results can provide us with an answer, but this is beyond the scope of this article. It should be noted, though, how the first iteration of solving this problem has already helped us identify new courses of action that may have escaped us initially, namely the possibility of purchasing additional quantities of the different parts. This could lead to a new formulation of the problem and a further improvement of the profit contribution.

There are many applications of optimization to financial problems. One of the best known problems is that of portfolio optimization.

Given a set of assets with specified returns, standard deviations and correlations of returns, find the portfolio that minimizes risk (i.e. variance of returns) for a certain level of return. This is the well-known Markowitz Mean/Variance portfolio model. A simple example with three assets, A, B and C, is in Table 3. The problem of minimizing risk for a given level of return is a non-linear optimization problem because the variance of the total returns is a quadratic function of the variables denoting the fraction of the investment that goes into each of the assets. In our simple example the optimal portfolio that gives at least 13 per cent return consists of 80 per cent asset B and 20 per cent

Optimization in American Airlines

American Airlines is the world's largest airline in revenue terms, with more than 500 aircrafts that fly over 2,400 daily flight segments and provide transportation to over 160 cities worldwide. The importance of operations research and business optimization within American Airlines is reflected by the growth American Airlines Decision Technologies (AADT), the company's operations research department. The staff of this department has increased from 12 to 325 professionals since 1982. In 1988 AADT became a separate division with roughly 35% of its business coming from external customers. Robert Crandall, CEO and chairman of American Airlines credits a range of optimization-based decision support systems as the key reason for the success of the company in the extremely competitive airline industry. These decision support systems include:

- **TRIP (Trip Allocation and Improvement program)**
  This is a crew pairing optimization system that helps American Airlines manage its 8,300 pilots and 16,200 flight attendants. Its introduction led to annual savings of $20 million according to Crandall.

- **Yield Management**
  A sophisticated set of techniques developed to finetune overbooking practices and seat allocation among the different market segments is estimated to have boosted annual revenues by 5% or about $500 million.

- **Flight Scheduling**
  A set of optimization models were developed to tackle the complex problem of producing flight schedules that maximize the potential of the company's fleet and human resources.

- **Arrival Slot Allocation**
  This is another decision support system that reduces annual costs by $5.6 million. It allocates and re-allocates arrival slots optimally when flights are delayed or cancelled.

Adapted from an article in *OR/MS Today* published in August 1991.

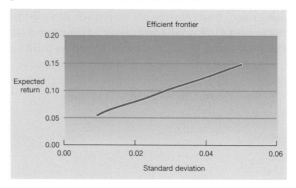

Assets	A	B	C	Correlation	
Return	8%	15%	5%	A,B	0.5
Standard deviations	0.04	0.05	0.01	A,C	0.2
				B,C	-0.1

Table 3: A simple portfolio optimization problem

asset C. By repetitively solving this problem for different levels of return we can construct the efficient frontier.

Figure 2 gives you the efficient frontier for the example problem, calculated using Excel. Fund managers often solve portfolio optimization problems with hundreds of assets.

Figure 2: The efficient frontier for the portfolio problem of Table 3

Many industries have a strong tradition in using optimization techniques with great success. Airline companies use large-scale optimization to schedule flights and crews and manage ground operations. Oil companies use optimization to control the blending of inputs in refineries and reduce the distribution costs of oil products. Electricity companies rely on optimization-based decision-support systems for short-term operational and long-term investment planning.

In the past optimization was a tool for specialists with access to vast amounts of computing power. Now it is accessible to any manager with a PC and a spreadsheet. In many situations involving allocation of scarce resources, the power of optimization can improve results dramatically. So, it is worth developing the habit of asking 'what's best?' questions in addition to 'what if?' ones

Summary

Many business problems involve the allocation of scarce resources to activities in order to optimize an objective. These can be addressed using optimization techniques – 'what's best' rather than 'what if?'.

Modern spreadsheets have built in optimization capabilities typically requiring the user to specify the objective, any decision variables and constraints.

Two concepts are useful in analysing the results of an optimization exercise. The 'slack' is the surplus amount of a limited resource at the optimum (constraints with zero slack are said to be 'binding'). The 'shadow price', also known as the dual price, is the most one would be willing to pay to obtain an additional unit of a limited resource. It opens up the possibility of purchasing additional quantities of parts to improve the profit contribution. Airlines (for flight and crew schedules), oil companies (to control the blending of inputs into refineries) and electricity companies (for operational and investment planning) have an optimization tradition. But the technique is available to any manager with a PC and a spreadsheet.

Suggested further reading

Dantzig, George B. (1963) *Linear Programming and Extensions*, Princeton University Press.

Eppen, G. D., Gould, F. J. and Schmidt, C. P. (1993) *Introductory Management Science*, 4th edn, Prentice Hall International.

Hillier, F. S. and Lieberman, Gerald J. (1986) *Introduction to Operations Research*, 4th Edn, Holden-Day.

Marketing

Contents

Why marketing still matters 165
Kamran Kashani, IMD
Contrary to some opinions, marketing is not going to disappear.

A new future for brands 171
Kamran Kashani, IMD
A new approach to brand building is needed.

Building brand relationships 175
Tim Ambler, London Business School
The brand as a 'personality' and marketing as a way of managing a brand's 'relationships' with consumers – relationship marketing – has emerged as a key way of understanding the whole subject of marketing.

Customers as strategic assets 183
David Schmittlein, Wharton
New technology and new approaches to marketing are allowing companies to collect, analyse and use information about their customers.

In praise of revitalization 193
Thomas S. Robertson, London Business School
Re-engineering is not everything. Companies also have to rediscover growth. Four classic routes to new markets.

Getting close to the customer 198
Jacques Horovitz and Nirmalya Kumar, IMD
One way to get close to customers is to identify the benefits each segment of the customers base responds to – and then provide it.

How to learn about markets 205
George Day, Wharton
A company's ability to learn may be its only sustainable advantage. But learning must be for a purpose.

Big questions for the 21st century 209
Jerry Wind, Wharton
Many of the requirements for marketing success in the next century are already apparent and being practised. Twelve factors that together will be critical.

Contributors

Kamran Kashani is a Professor of Marketing at IMD and Director of its MBA programme. His research interests are global marketing and business strategies.

Jacques Horovitz is Professor of Service Management at IMD. His research interests include the core competencies of the service corporation, designing and nurturing a service culture, and customer bonding.

Tim Ambler is Grand Metropolitan Senior Fellow at London Business School. Previously he was joint Managing Director of International Distillers and Vintners, where he had held various marketing positions. His research interests focus on the relational paradigm of marketing, especially international marketing, branding and advertising.

Nirmalya Kumar is Professor of Marketing at IMD. His research interests include distribution channels, marketing strategy, relationship marketing and retailing.

David Schmittlein is Professor of Marketing at the Wharton School of the University of Pennsylvania. His research interests include the development of probability-based models that describe social processes and improve managerial decision making, new product development, product management and the design and analysis of effective market research studies.

George Day is the Geoffrey T. Boisi Professor, Professor of Marketing, and Director of the Huntsman Center for Global Competition and Innovation at the Wharton School of the University of Pennsylvania. He has written ten books in the areas of marketing and strategic management and more than 100 articles for leading marketing and management journals.

Thomas S. Robertson is Sainsbury Professor of Marketing at London Business School. His research interests include market signalling, technology and innovation, new product diffusion and market defence.

Jerry Wind is the Lauder Professor and Professor of Marketing at the Wharton School of the University of Pennsylvania. He is the founding director of the SEI Center for Advanced Studies in Management and is the initiator and editor of the Wharton Executive Library.

Introduction

Marketing is often seen as among the more 'glamorous' elements of management. It is, however, a demanding and increasingly scientific subject that draws heavily on data collection and analysis. It is far removed from the glossy worlds of advertising and public relations with which it is often confused (though these are closely involved with marketing).

Marketing is a major contributing factor in the profitability of companies and managers must be able to co-ordinate the marketing effort with all other aspects of a business to achieve success.

The Marketing module begins with an article that responds to some recent criticism of marketing. Is marketing really about to disappear as a separate function? The article concludes that marketing will remain a necessary part of modern business but predicts some substantial changes.

The module continues with coverage of brands and brand building, the vital concept of relationship marketing, new uses of technology to predict and influence consumer behaviour, product innovation, market segmentation, marketing and strategy, and marketing in the 21st century.

Why marketing still matters

■ **A survey of managers confirms the enormous market changes that face organizations. One of the greatest rethinks is taking place in the marketing function but marketing is not going to disappear, says** Kamran Kashani

Is there still a place for marketing in the organization of the 21st century? Consider the following current trends pointing to the contrary:

● Mega brands are not what they used to be. Built on years of high and persistent advertising expenditures, they have come under increasing pressure from their low-branded, but low-priced, rivals. Some major brands have retrenched; others are undertaking a long-overdue soul-searching on what went wrong.

● Staff marketing departments, once fashionable, have all but vanished in many industrial organizations. They have fallen victim to management efforts to downsize and re-engineer. In these more streamlined structures, more focussed functions with clear line responsibility have replaced traditional staff marketing.

● Some specialist marketing skills are no longer in much demand. For example, at a time when progress in information technology has made it possible for middle-and senior-level managers directly to access front-line market data, many traditional marketing tasks that involved collection and analysis of such data for reporting to the rest of the organization have simply lost their raison d'être.

The above evidence may suggest that the days of marketing are numbered, that it has reached the end of its usefulness as a management discipline.

Yet an international survey of more than 220 managers carried out at IMD suggests otherwise. In fact, this broad-based survey suggests marketing is alive and well though it is living under a different guise. The data is compelling: more than 90 per cent of all respondents from a wide spectrum of countries and business sectors reported that although marketing has undergone major changes in their companies, it has come out stronger in stature and with more influence on strategic decisions.

Why the apparent contradiction? An in-depth look at the survey findings clearly shows that the marketing task has experienced a metamorphosis so that it can more effectively serve companies in increasingly shifting and competitive markets. To understand marketing's changing contribution better, in this section we will first highlight the survey's findings on the changes that are transforming competitive environments of companies. (A complete report of the survey findings can be found in the journal *Long Range Planning*.)

This section will show in some detail the forces that have made markets far more competitive and examine the evolving management challenges of operating in these contested markets. The survey results in respect of key management challenges will be reviewed and we will highlight how marketing has survived the market upheavals. The focus will be on the changes that have combined to redefine the role of marketing and enhance its contribution in today's business organization. We will conclude with a look at the 'new face' of marketing or why and how marketing still matters and the needed competencies of the next generation of marketers.

Market changes

If a single word can capture the essence of what the craft of management is expected to come to terms with today, that word is change. We asked the surveyed managers to identify the current

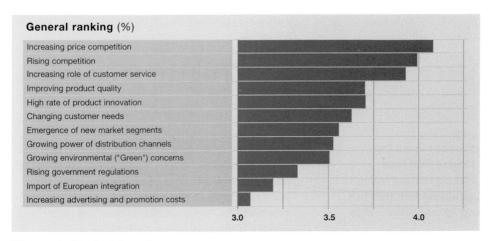

General ranking (%)

Increasing price competition	
Rising competition	
Increasing role of customer service	
Improving product quality	
High rate of product innovation	
Changing customer needs	
Emergence of new market segments	
Growing power of distribution channels	
Growing environmental ("Green") concerns	
Rising government regulations	
Import of European integration	
Increasing advertising and promotion costs	

3.0   3.5   4.0

Figure 1: Market trends

changes that promise to have long-term impact on their industries and, as such, are of high concern to management.

For the cross-section of industries represented in the sample, the managers identified three trends as being of utmost concern:

● Increasing price competition
● Rising level of (general) competition
● Increasing role of customer service.

(*See* Figure 1 above for a general ranking of the market trends of concern identified by the survey.)

A closer examination of the top-ranking trends suggests that, generally, companies are increasingly being affected by rising competition and growing pressure on prices itself probably a direct result of declining product differentiation and that management is looking for new sources of competitive advantage, including innovations in customer service.

A more sector-specific analysis of survey data shows that the race towards new sources of competitive advantage is particularly evident among high-technology companies, where products have traditionally been the main and often the only source of differentiation. In this sector, the issue of increasing price competition, increasing role of customer service, and rising (general) competition rank among the respondents' top concerns.

In fact, the preoccupation with rising price competition carries more weight among the high-technology companies than for the rest of the

sample. For these groups, the above three issues are topped by only, and not unexpectedly, the high rate of product innovation as the number-one concern. In the absence of a continuous stream of innovative and unique products, the managers from high-technology sectors suggest, the company has to live with the consequences of short product life-cycles, fast commoditization of once-differentiated products and the corresponding rise in price competition.

The growing power of distribution channels is an issue of high general concern to the consumer goods companies. Similarly, rising government regulations are a source of continuing apprehension in the pharmaceutical industry and ranked at the top of the list by drug manufacturers. In services, the emergence of new market segments and changing customer needs ranked along with the increasing role of customer service and rising (general) competition as the issues of utmost concern.

By contrast, while increasing price competition was highly rated in most sectors, it was ranked relatively low in services. The data suggests that, compared with the manufacturing sectors, rivalry in the services tends to focus less on price and more on service-related dimensions.

The key challenges

Besides current market trends with long-term impact, the surveyed managers also identified the specific challenges that they face in their own companies. While in the first instance the

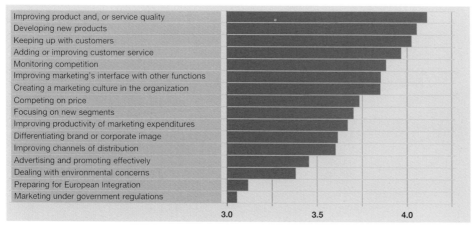

Figure 2: Management challenges

current external issues affecting the respondents' industries were highlighted, in the second exercise they ranked the degree to which diverse internal tasks were of importance to the conduct of their businesses.

The survey identifies four management tasks at the top of the important internal challenges:
● Improving product and/or service quality
● Developing new products
● Keeping up with customers
● Adding or improving customer service.

(*See* Figure 2 above for a general ranking of management challenges.)

A clearer picture of what management is up against emerges when top internal challenges are considered together with the major market trends highlighted earlier.

Across a wide spectrum of industries, management is striving to meet growing competitive pressures and the resulting price/margin erosions (already highlighted under external issues) with new and improved products or services aimed at ever-changing, and seemingly more demanding, customers including members of the distribution channel. In their written comments, the respondents highlighted the importance of achieving 'customer satisfaction' and establishing more effective ways of 'measuring and enhancing' it. Here again, the focus was on building and sustaining a differentiated position vis-à-vis customers in increasingly hostile market environments.

While the above list of top challenges was cited by most sectors, there were some exceptions. For example, the pressure on improving product and/or service quality is more evident among industrial goods companies than for others, especially the consumer-product makers.

On the other end of the scale, competing on price received its lowest ratings from the pharmaceutical sector, where prices in many countries tend to be government regulated. For that reason as well as others, the challenge of marketing under government regulations is felt appreciably the most by drug manufacturers. Also in this sector, which has for some time been characterized by consolidation among competitors, the task of monitoring competition ranked higher than in other sectors.

The future of markets
Besides examining the present state of affairs, the survey asked the managers to peer into the future and indicate how the market environment of their business was likely to change. More specifically, respondents were asked to rate the degree to which a diverse set of developments would affect their industries for the rest of the 1990s.

So, what does the rest of this decade hold for world markets? According to the general survey, three developments stand out as the most unsettling:
● Consolidation of competition: fewer and larger players

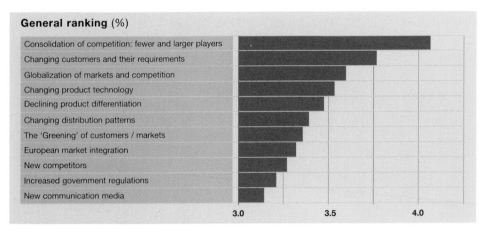

General ranking (%)

Consolidation of competition: fewer and larger players	
Changing customers and their requirements	
Globalization of markets and competition	
Changing product technology	
Declining product differentiation	
Changing distribution patterns	
The 'Greening' of customers / markets	
European market integration	
New competitors	
Increased government regulations	
New communication media	

3.0   3.5   4.0

Figure 3: Future developments

- Changing customers and their requirements
- Globalization of markets and competition.

(*See* Figure 3 above for a list of future developments and their ranking.)

Significantly, fewer but larger competitors appears at the top of everyone's list. The survey shows that, for a wide cross-section of industries, no other development comes even close in terms of its relative importance. This development is followed by the other two as those with the most potential have an impact on the future market environment of industries.

While consolidation of competition remains a top development of general concern, others tend to be more sector specific. For the industrial product category as a whole, changing customers and their requirements and changing product technology were ranked among the developments with the most potential impact.

In the consumer goods category, changing distribution patterns ranked along with changing customers and their requirements as the top developments to affect these markets in the future. In services, changing customers and their requirements and globalization of markets and competition were identified as developments with the most expected impact. Across the board, there is thus a certain commonality of likely developments in the marketplace: fewer and stronger competitors, ever-changing customers; and persistent pressure from changing technology and globalization of markets.

Marketing's new place

At a time of increasing competition, industry consolidation and fast-changing customer requirements all of which has brought about massive changes in the fortunes of companies is there still a place for marketing?

Our survey offers a positive answer. Among the surveyed managers there is a surprising degree of uniformity internationally and across a wide spectrum of sectors, from upstream raw materials to downstream consumer and industrial goods, and from high-technology products to low-technology services: marketing has evolved to take on a far greater role than previously.

There is catch here, however. Today's marketing is not what it used to be. The marketing function or, more accurately, the marketing process has undergone major changes in companies facing shifting and highly competitive markets. It has metamorphosed to serve better its top management clientele. Today's bolstered marketing reflects the following changes in its focus and impact:

- **From staff to line**. Marketing has disappeared as a separate function from many organization charts. Staff marketing has been replaced by more line functions such as segment or product management, where the focus is on customer segments or certain products and technologies. This shift, in line with a more streamlined organization, is to ensure that marketing thinking and action are better

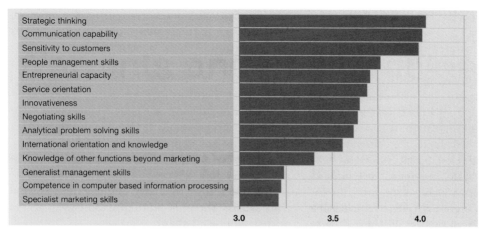

Strategic thinking			
Communication capability			
Sensitivity to customers			
People management skills			
Entrepreneurial capacity			
Service orientation			
Innovativeness			
Negotiating skills			
Analytical problem solving skills			
International orientation and knowledge			
Knowledge of other functions beyond marketing			
Generalist management skills			
Competence in computer based information processing			
Specialist marketing skills			

3.0   3.5   4.0

Figure 4: Managerial competencies

integrated in the day-to-day decisions of managers running important pieces of the business. In this respect, the marketing job has come closer to the front line.

● **From specialist to strategic**. With its more result-oriented scope, marketing has evolved beyond its traditional specialist focus. Tasks once exclusively associated with marketing, such as market and competitive assessment or end-user communication, are now only a part of a far more integrated marketing process that may include other functions such as upstream product development or downstream management of distribution. In its broader scope, today's marketing is far more strategic than in its previous role as a specialist function and with far more impact on results.

● **From isolated to widespread**. As marketing has broadened its scope, it has also become more diffused within the organization. That means marketing (or, more precisely, marketing orientation) is no longer an isolated concern of a few but has now become everyone's business and for good reasons. Companies are inculcating their managers in various 'back office' functions with market and customer mindedness the very attributes that were the exclusive domain of marketing people. A widespread appreciation of market forces and customer needs and how parts of an organization may contribute to creating a superior customer value is a necessity if the entire organization is to become market responsive. In a fast-changing market environ-

ment such an appreciation can make the difference between success and failure.

In short, marketing in its previous form has disappeared, only to return transformed, and commanding a greater share of top management's attention. In its new phase, marketing, though probably no longer a box in the organization chart, is potentially far more relevant to the management challenges, as highlighted earlier, than any other management process. It encompasses many of the qualities today's business organizations need to survive and prosper in their hostile markets.

A new set of competencies

What are the requirements for success in the new marketing job which, as we have seen, may not even carry the marketing title? Our survey attempted to identify the managerial skills and competencies the new generation of marketers (whatever their designation) will need to meet the challenges of their redefined job in the face of an increasingly difficult market environment.

From a long list of possibilities, and with a great deal of consistency among the diverse sectors represented in the sample, the surveyed managers identified three individual competencies that are by far the most relevant to the future performance of marketers. The top competencies are:

● Strategic thinking
● Communication capability
● Sensitivity to customers.

(*See* Figure 4 for a general ranking of managerial competencies.)

In their written comments, the respondents provided other managerial dimensions of high relevance to success in marketing, including leadership skills, profit orientation and in-depth understanding of the front line. It is important to note that the top-ranking capabilities are all of a generalist nature. In fact, the respondents ranked specialist marketing skills at the very bottom of the list, i.e. as least relevant to marketing performance.

The surveyed managers are clearly suggesting that the growing complexity of their future market environments, the various dimensions of which were highlighted earlier, requires a broader pallet of core capabilities that go beyond narrow and specialised skills. They are also indicating at a more specific level that there is a premium for managers who possess a longer-term strategic perspective of their markets and who are, in addition, highly receptive to cues from customers and other interlocutors inside and outside the organization i.e. the essence of effective communication.

Conclusion

Marketing is here to stay and that is not just wishful thinking. While the needs for many of its traditional activities have changed or simply disappeared, marketing's broadened contribution to today's business organization will ensure its survival as a management discipline well into the next century.

The reasons why marketing still matters have to do with what our survey has identified as the growing management challenges of operating in highly competitive market environments.

In its more front-line, result-oriented and strategic scope, marketing promises market-responsive management across the entire organization. When translated into concrete results, market responsiveness would mean a stream of new products that consistently offer customers a differentiated value, a customer-service performance that surpasses the customers' own expectations and competitive moves that set new standards of innovation for the industry and pre-empt market opportunities for rivals.

Such market-responsive management is what success in the fast-changing markets of the future will be all about.

Summary

The marketing function in companies may appear to be under threat from 'own label' products, re-engineering, and advances in information technology. But it is alive and well and has undergone important shifts in recent years so as to provide a better service for top management. It has frequently become more of a line than a staff responsibility, it has developed a strategic bias, and it has become diffused throughout the organization.

Increasing price competition, more (general) competition and the growing role of customer service are among the most important changes facing marketeers generally, according to a recent study. Four key management tasks stand out: improving product quality, developing new products, keeping up with customers and improving customer service. The three most relevant competences for marketeers are: strategic thinking, communication capability and sensitivity to customers. Specialist marketing skills appear to be among the least important.

A new future for brands

■ **Main brands are under pressure from own-brand competition and some poor management. If they are to survive, a new approach to brand building is needed, writes**
Kamran Kashani

Major brands have not been doing so well lately. Under unrelenting attack from low-priced alternatives, including retailers' own private labels, the makers of megabrands have blinked; they have began to retrench. This phenomenon can be witnessed across a broad range of product categories from personal computers to personal care and from foods to cigarettes. Consider the following evidence:

● IBM has seen its dominance of the personal computer industry eroded by the lower-priced clones that did not enjoy Big Blue's worldwide name recognition or reputation. In 1994, the company that had set the standard for the industry was finally displaced as the world's largest PC maker by Compaq, until recently a little known clone maker.

● Major consumer brands have been losing market share to private labels at an alarming rate. Currently, market shares of private labels in grocery products have grown to 18 per cent in the US and 15 per cent in Europe. All of this gain has come at the expense of manufacturer brands. Moreover, many manufacturers are even supplying their private label competitors to help make up for income shortfalls due to loss of market shares and pressures on margins.

● The growth of private labels has been even more dramatic in some markets. In the UK it stands at 30 per cent, in Germany and Switzerland at 23 per cent, and in France and Sweden at 20 per cent. Even in countries such as Portugal, Norway, Italy and Spain, where private label penetrations are below 10 per cent, private labels are on the rise.

● Procter & Gamble, one of the world's foremost brand marketers, has been forced to revise its premium-pricing policy to combat private labels and erosion in its market share. The new policy of 'Everyday Low Prices' means P&G will try to win back lost consumers with lower retail prices on many of its brands.

● Within a few weeks of 'Marlboro Friday', when Philip Morris discounted the price of its best-selling cigarette by a surprising 19 per cent, the combined stock market value of companies known for their strong brands fell some $47bn. (£30bn). The message: good brands are over-valued.

If all this bad news makes you believe that brands are dying and brand building is dead, think again.

Not just a name

Thinking again should begin with examining some of the fundamentals of brands and brand building. First, there is a good deal more to branding than just putting a name on a package. Branding is about creating and maintaining perceived consumer value. If that sounds too academic, think of consumer value as a better-made product, more convenient packaging or a more accessible and responsive after-sales service. Through effective branding, the manufacturer promises and delivers to the consumer a superior value found nowhere else.

Second, branding is also about deliberate management action to combat a natural market tendency towards commoditization i.e. where consumers do not see a difference among competing products. In the absence of effective brand building, consumers are likely to perceive all competing offerings as look-alikes and do-alikes. In such a commodity market, the lowest price, often accompanied by the lowest margin, wins the day.

Third, consumer value is not just in the eye of the beholder. Most of the time it is created through a superior product or service a fact sometimes ignored by brand marketers. Nescafe, easily the world's best-known brand of instant coffee, has reached the summit of its category through continuous product improvement. Since 1938, when the brand was born, it has undergone no fewer than seven metamorphoses, each time improving its taste and aroma, and thereby delivering a superior product to consumers. Similarly, Sony has succeeded in becoming the world's best-known brand in consumer and professional electronics thanks to a long history of innovative products far superior to anything else available on the market.

Finally, the payoffs of effective brand building are many. Brands that promise and deliver a differentiated consumer value tend to be better remembered, have a larger following of faithful consumers, be better protected from competition and enhance the manufacturer's bargaining power vis-à-vis trade channels. All these can bestow a better bottom line on the marketer.

Makers of Mercedes-Benz, Perrier, Kodak, Nike and IBM to name but a few household names in different product categories have in the past enjoyed all these benefits and more. But they no longer do, or not to the degree they once did.

Under fire

Beyond the fundamentals, every brand mentioned so far, and a long list of others, are under fire from low-priced rivals including private labels. Two sets of factors explain this turnaround in the fortunes of megabrands: market change and poor brand management.

Market change

Different consumers. Today's consumers are more educated and better informed; and they tend to be more sceptical of promotional claims not backed up by actual delivered values. For example, more and more buyers of up-market brands of passenger cars make their choice after consulting road test results published in car magazines. Consumers are also more eclectic. Their behavior does not quite fit into the old and convenient socio-economic segmentation schemes. It is known today that a growing proportion of the consumers of private labels are upper-class – the traditional buyers of premium-priced branded products.

Faster competition. Competitive behavior is swifter today. One feature of this change is the speed with which innovations are imitated by rivals. In the PC market, as elsewhere, the accelerating arrival of lower-priced 'me-too' products often within a matter of months has shortened the phase in which a unique concept could expect to reap premium prices and high margins.

Better retailers. With the arrival of point-of-sale information technology, today's retailers know more about the performance of the brands they sell than do the actual manufacturers. They are also managing their own private labels with greater professionalism. Gone are the days when private labels meant poor product quality, narrow variety or inferior packaging. Nowadays, in addition to relatively low prices, retailers' own brands enjoy features comparable to those of branded products.

The above developments among consumers, competitors and retailers have put great strain on all brands, weak and strong. Ironically, these changes mean that only brands with a well-established consumer franchise can hope to survive; others will fall victim to lower-priced private labels and copycats.

Poor brand management

Low investment. Under pressure for short-term results, many managers have deprived their brand of investment in long-term product development and consumer communications. Priority is often given to those developments with quick payback. Only a fraction of the 11,000-odd food products in the US in 1992 could be categorized as truly innovative; the others were just cosmetically different 'new and improved' versions of old merchandise.

Not surprisingly, there is evidence that private-label competition is strongest where innovations in branded products have been slow in coming. A recent study by McKinsey, the worldwide consultancy firm, shows that food categories with the highest rates of new product introductions are also those that stand up best against competition from private labels.

Excessive prices. A declining record of product innovation and superior value creation has been exacerbated by excessive pricing among traditional brand leaders. Procter & Gamble's Pampers, once unique in the baby diaper category, has been fighting copycats for years. Yet until recently, the company was charging premium prices approaching 35 per cent above its competition with the resulting steady decline in the Pampers market share. Similarly, IBM was pricing its PC's at 130 per cent above the clone makers, including its closest rival Compaq. Ironically, due to high cost structures not all such price premiums translate into high margins for the manufacturers. But confronted with comparable offerings, consumers have increasingly and quite naturally opted for what they perceived as better value for money.

A recent study in European markets shows that the greater the price differentials between branded goods and the retailers' own products, the better private labels perform. Where price differences are particularly significant, such as in the UK and Switzerland, private labels penetration is at its highest; the opposite is true in countries such as Norway or Italy.

Management complacency. Brand management in large corporations has fallen victim to its own success. Aimed at maintaining a comfortable status quo, short-termism, risk aversion and bureaucracy seemed to have displaced long-term vision, innovative thinking and a killer instinct the very ingredients responsible for the rise to success of the megabrands. 'Brand management by calculator' is how one disenchanted manager of an international food company describes the problem.

Another observer estimates that today's brand managers spend only about 20 per cent of their time actually dealing with brand management issues; the rest is taken up with administrative chores. Worse still, according to this same estimate, only 3 per cent of a typical brand manager's time is spent on face-to-face interaction with consumers.

Build strong brands: the new basics

Brands have declined not because consumers have stopped shopping for superior value, but because companies have failed to deliver it in a changed market environment. The lessons to be learned from the fall of major brands, and the rise of others, are many. They constitute the new basics of brand building:

Get lean. Past success is no excuse for getting fat and bloated, yet this is what many companies have done. Protected by well established brands and premium prices, brand builders have become sloppy with their costs and thus vulnerable to the more efficient low-price competitors. The first step, therefore, is to clean up a brand's backyard by improving its cost structure.

That often means pruning back the weak brands and allocating the released resources to fewer products with a stronger consumer franchise. Johnson Wax was able to generate large savings by reducing the company's multitudes of brands and product variety in Europe. Some of these savings were passed on to consumers in the form of lower prices for the remaining brands, thus making them more competitive.

Invest. Innovation is by far the most potent weapon against a brand's commoditization. Continuous investment in product and service innovation, and consumer value creation, keeps copycats at bay. But such investments can prove expensive.

Gillette spent $200m in bringing Sensor, its high-tech shaving system, to market. The costly technology involved in producing this advanced product, including 15 microscopic spot weldings on each of Sensor's twin blades, has kept competition to a minimum. Thanks to uninterrupted investment in new products, Gillette faces no private label competition and enjoys the lion's share of the world market for shaving products.

Listen. It is high time for brand managers to put the consumer where he and she belongs at the heart of their brand's value-creation strategies. First they must listen to what consumers have to say. And that will not be easy in corporate environments where elaborate market research, often done by outside agencies, has become a substitute for first-hand observations and insight into consumer behavior. Libby's highly successful Um Bongo fruit drink was developed by managers who listened carefully to how mothers and their children defined their ideal drink. By combining 'health for moms and fun for kids', this highly innovative entry in beverages is succeeding across a growing number of European markets.

Be bold. Textbook recipes will not save brands from decline in the face of their more aggressive competitors. What is needed is an attitude of creative brand building, charting new paths, setting new market and performance standards so as to retain existing consumers and attract new ones. That means taking risks. That also requires managers who are comfortable with unconventional decisions that go against the grain of their conventional organizations. Swatch's creation is one such example.

The brainchild of a few unorthodox thinkers in one of the world's most conservative sectors, the Swiss watch industry, Swatch was developed to fight low-cost Far Eastern watches. But the concept of a low-priced plastic watch as a fashion accessory did not initially have any following among the Swiss watchmakers. With more than 100m watches sold, that bold concept has more than proven itself and established Swatch as one of the world's most enduring global brands.

Think global. Converging consumer behavior now allows many single-market innovations to spread with unprecedented speed and become global success stories. This phenomenon also permits brand builders to achieve greater returns on their upstream investments in product development and manufacturing.

P&G is among a growing number of companies that have focussed on creating world brands. The company's Vidal Sassoon Wash & Go, an innovative European product concept combining shampoo and conditioner, has become,

in less than three years, one of the world's largest-selling brands in hair care. The success of the brand, available in more than 50 countries, is a testimony to brand building on a global scale.

In conclusion, let us return to the original question: do major brands have a future? The answer lies in the extent to which brand management meets the challenges of the new basics of brand building – the practices that aim to outperform competing offerings by giving the consumer a better deal, a superior value at a competitive price. Failing that, the future will belong to the more efficient price discounters and no-frills marketers.

Summary

Brands have been under unrelenting attack from low-priced alternatives as companies from IBM in personal computers to Procter & Gamble in personal care products will readily testify. This turnaround in brand fortunes can be explained by market changes such as more educated and better informed consumers, the speedy response of product imitators, and improved retailing skills.

Poor brand management (the art of creating and maintaining perceived consumer value) is also responsible: insufficient investment as managers strive for short-term results; excessive price differentials between branded goods and retailers' own products; and an absence of vision and innovative thinking.

Brand building is not dead but brand managers must concentrate on a new set of basics. They must improve their cost structures, often pruning back weak brands; they must invest (as Gillette did with its Sensor shaving system); and they must listen to consumers, embrace unorthodox solutions (like Swatch) and think global.

Building brand relationships

■ **The brand as a 'personality' and marketing as a way of managing a brand's 'relationships' with consumers – relationship marketing – has emerged as a way of understanding this vital function.**

by Tim Ambler

Relationship marketing has emerged in a number of guises. It is not just another form of marketing to put alongside services, retail, business-to-business and all the other special interests. Rather it is a way of understanding marketing itself.

The perception of marketing as managing a network of relationships between the brand and its various customers is fundamental and should be ranked alongside the traditional and strategic paradigms. We will briefly review all three. But first, what do we mean by 'products', 'brands' and 'brand equity' – the building blocks of marketing?

The first two are the means to satisfy, even delight, customers; brand equity is the asset that the marketer builds to ensure continuity of satisfaction for the customer and profit for the supplier.

This article reviews recent changes in the way the marketplace is perceived and the shift from a short-term, transactional, orientation to the perception that marketing is the management of long-term brand relationships. These and other trends are brought together formally as the 'relational paradigm'.

Building brand relationships is the key marketing function and 'brand equity' is the state of those relationships at any one time.

Measuring them, however, is not easy. Measuring customer behavior, i.e. whether they buy or not, is robust but indirect. Behavior is the consequence of the state of relationships, not a prior indication of what action the marketer needs to take. By the time the consumer has left the brand, it may be too late.

The marketer would like to know what customers think and feel about the brand. Brand equity is in the minds of customers yet the most popular measures of brand equity are behavioral, namely market share and relative price. We review whether these are enough and conclude with consequential advice for practitioners.

Products, brands and brand equity

Formal 'product', 'brand', 'brand family' and 'brand equity' definitions are not universally agreed by practitioners and academics but there is some consensus around:

● A product is any physical good and/or service that may be sold to a customer. Burger King supplies fast food but also fast service. Few products are not branded in some way. While oranges sold in a market, generally, are not, Outspan oranges are. Products branded with the retailer's name are known as 'own label' or 'own brand' in the UK and 'private label' in the US. Truly unbranded products are known as 'commodities'.

● A brand is a product plus added values, Tide laundry detergent, for example. A brand is a bundle of functional, economic and psychological benefits for the end user, more simply known as quality, price and image.

This 'holistic' (product plus) definition is more European than American. Some see the brand as just the added values applied to the product, i.e. the image, not including the product itself. In this alternative view, brand management and marketing are by no means the same. This 'added values' definition can be shown to be unsatisfactory but that should not detain us here.

A brand, in our sense, may primarily be a physical good, such as Texaco petrol, or a service, such as Visa. Usually there are some elements of service with goods and vice versa. Self-service petrol stations vary in their facilities and helpfulness. Visa supply a plastic card. The brand may be aimed at the consumer, such as Coca Cola, or business, such as Hewlett Packard. It may be complex with many products, such as Pillsbury, or have just one format, such as Baileys Irish Cream.

A company may have many brands, such as Unilever, or the company and its products may share the brand name, as is the case with Mobil. Retailers, such as Safeway, may sell manufacturer brands alongside their own brand, or just their own, such as Ikea, the Swedish furniture store group. Brands may be professional companies, such as Andersen Consulting, or not-for-profit organizations, such as Greenpeace and the Catholic Church. In short, anyone with a reputation to manage has a brand to manage.

In the simple case, the terms brand and product are interchangeable from the consumer's viewpoint. He or she buys a Hoover or a bottle of Bacardi. There is no need to pause to consider whether a Hoover is a vacuum cleaner or Bacardi is a white rum.

Over time, brands have been extended to cover other products. The consumer does need to distinguish between Virgin music, cola, airline tickets and vodka. They may be all designed to produce 'highs' but not of the same kind. Brand families are often complex connections between brand names and products. Special K is a sub-brand of Kellogg's and both names appear on the same pack. Kit-Kat chocolate bars now carry the Nestle name. Shell petrol is sold to consumers; Shell the corporation has relationships with shareholders and the community.

Of these various types, we are concerned with a single brand name applied to one or more products. This is the entity the marketer manages. The multiple branded situation, as in Nestle, is for another day.

Brand equity is such a rich concept that it is worth examining the components of this asset in detail:

● **Customers attitudes to the brand and purchasing behavior:** A brand's equity relates to the totality of all the stored beliefs, likes/dislikes and behaviors of those involved with the brand, i.e. their habits – both of thought and action. For example, awareness is a key measure of brand equity.

● **Not just consumer driven:** Depending on the marketing situation, the ultimate consumer, or end user, may be more or less important than the immediate customer. Likewise, the relative importance of influence agents, such as specialist journalists or professional advisers, outside the distribution channels will be determined by circumstances.

● **Information systems are included:** The customer's habits of thought may well be programed into their computers. For example, when a purchasing clerk at a supermarket requests vodka, which the computer translates to an order for Smirnoff, that programming is part of Smirnoff's brand equity.

● **Brand availability/distribution:** The space habitually provided to the brand at all levels of the distribution channels has been acquired over time with much effort and expense. It is a valuable part of the asset.

● **Long-term relationships:** Brand equity is the result of long-term relationships between those involved in the marketing (branding) process rather than one-off transactions. Continuity is key. Taking these components together, brand equity can be defined as: the aggregation of all accumulated attitudes in the extended minds of consumers, distribution channels and influence agents, which will enhance future profits and long-term cash flow. Or more succinctly: the sum of brand relationships with those in the market, weighted by their importance, which will enhance future profits and cash flow.

Thus, if one defines 'brand' broadly enough, building brand equity is the key role of the marketing manager. Of course, short-term profits are important for all the company's managers, but concern for the brand is the very special responsibility of the marketer. A brand's equity should not be confused with its valuation. 'Brand equity' is the intangible asset itself and valuation is the financial worth of that asset if it were bought and sold. A house, similarly, is an asset. Valuations for probate, for insurance, for sale and for purchase may all be correct and all be different. A house may also be measured in many non-financial ways: space, numbers of rooms, period of construction, overall dimensions. Critics of the brand equity concept suggest that the variation in valuations and measurements shows that brand equity does not exist. If one was only shown the valuations and measurements, and not the full picture, one might similarly conclude that the house did not exist.

Brand equity exists because those companies that own it make more money than those who do not. One could give the concept many other labels, such as goodwill or reputation, but its existence lies in the achievement of profits in a later period as a result of investment and activities in earlier periods. In this it is little different from inventory: a firm produces goods in one period and earns the profits when they are sold later. Brand equity can be seen as the store of the brand's future profits. In this section we have:

● Defined brands as goods and/or services (products) plus added values that provide functional, economic and psychological benefits for end users.

● Defined 'brands' to include their products. More complex 'brand families', which associate different brand names are not considered further.

● Defined 'brand equity' as the intangible asset associated with the brand and responsible for future profit flows.

● Distinguished between the brand, brand equity and 'brand valuation', which is the financial worth of the brand's equity.

● Defined brand equity in terms of the brand's relationships with customers at all levels of the distribution chain from immediate customer to end user (consumer). Relationships with other influence agents, e.g. journalists, may be important too. Using both a broad definition of customers, and extending their minds to include their computers, we can say that brand equity lies in the minds of customers.

Marketing as managing brand relationships

An advertisement for a whisky brand before the Second World War would include a fine picture of the bottle, a reason to buy ('Scotland's finest'), maybe a couple of glasses and the price.

They were trying to sell you a bottle of the stuff. Today, there may be no picture of the bottle, no overt reason to buy and certainly no price. They would like you to feel good about the brand, to believe that the lifestyle the brand seems to carry would mesh beneficially with your own lifestyle. Japanese domestic advertising carries this concept much further. Westerners may find it difficult to make any direct connection between the brand and the content of its Japanese TV commercial. However, the marketing intention is the same: if the consumer enjoys the sensations of the advertisement, then his relationship with the brand that paid for those sensations will be improved. These two examples from the consumer goods business are just the tip of a major sea-change that has swept across all varieties of marketing.

Ted Levitt, marketing specialist, observed in 1983: 'In a great and increasing proportion of transactions, the relationship actually intensifies subsequent to the sale.' In other words, the end of the process is not the transaction. The sale marks the beginning of the brand's relationship with its user. The thread is consistent. The brand is a personality. Just like us, it is not that easy to determine exactly how personal contact can be established in the first instance. The world provides more potential relationships than we can handle. Once contact has been established, however, managing the relationship lies very much in how we behave. So it is with the brand and its relationship with its customers. This first became obvious in industrial marketing. The small number of potential customers, in many cases, makes it critical to keep every one. Firms recognized that new customers are harder, and more expensive, to find than existing ones are to retain. One should consider the lifetime profitability of a customer, not the profit on any particular transaction. This thinking permeated to retail marketing.

A popular, and perhaps apocryphal, example is Nordstrom, the US premium department store group that originated in the north west. Complete life-time customer satisfaction is its creed. One customer returned a car tyre purchased some years previously with a complaint. Despite the time lag, he was refunded in full and without question. What was so unusual? Nordstrom had never sold car tyres. Industrial marketers seek to be so close to their main customers that the join is invisible. Just-in-time supply treats the customer's workshop as if it was the supplier's. Efficient Consumer Response (ECR) does the same for packaged goods. One time adversarial supplier/customer relationships have been replaced by maximum co-operation. Co-operation can be more profitable for both sides than conflict.

In order to realize the benefits of such arrangements, all parties need to co-operate, e.g. setting bar-code standards. Relationship marketing is not appropriate for all situations. It began with complex relationships where switching costs are commensurately high. In these circumstances, one purchase from a competitor may mean the customer is lost for good. Low-cost transactions, in a supermarket for example, may well not justify the relationship effort. Nevertheless, the feasibility threshold is being constantly lowered by technology. Today even supermarkets have loyalty cards. Databases hold more and more information about us all. Direct mail has evolved from junk to highly targeted missives of interest only to the recipient, or so they say. Maybe that will happen one day. Maybe also, the Internet and other network suppliers and interactive TV will provide all our marketing contact and shopping needs.

Meanwhile, the telephone is increasingly the carrier of relationship activity in all marketing sectors from industrial to grocery products. 'Customer care' telephone lines are now a major marketing activity. In the US, Pillsbury and a few other leading fast moving brand companies developed streamlined complaints procedures into powerful two-way consumer communications. Consumers are unwilling to write and, for food products, the rare production failures need to be discovered at once. If food is contaminated, urgent recall is needed. Packaging now includes a toll-free 800 number for consumers to call with any problems. Actual complaints dropped from 100 per cent towards 20 per cent of the calls as people became accustomed to the facility. They phoned for advice on product use, to make suggestions, to say thank you or just for a chat. Marketers recognized that rather than wait for cumbersome market research or consumer information so consolidated it had lost all value, there was a rich bank of consumer data phoning itself in daily. Relationships could be assessed and nourished right on line. Independent research has since confirmed that information obtained from those consumers who trouble to phone is representative of the brand's consumers as a whole. When Sony launched its 'PlayStation' computer games machine in 1995, it developed care lines to handle queries. The machine cost about £300 plus CD software, but declining service at retail level meant that customers needed new facilities for resolving problems.

Direct contact was necessary to maintain customer relationships. Manufacturers of personal computers do the same. For Sony, the UK phones were actually answered by the 'Decisions Group' company, which specialize in call center services. The staff, already trained on care usage, experienced PlayStations for themselves and, with online information available on their screens, were able to deal with queries of all types. The customers believed they were talking to Sony and that goodwill added to the Sony-customer relationship.

This article has ranged across current manifestations of relationship marketing in the consumer sector. We have seen that marketers are now less concerned with making the individual sales than with maintaining long-term customer contact. Managing these relationships has become the business of marketers.

The relational paradigm

To recap more formally, the recognition that the market should be seen as a network of commercial relationships came together in the 1980s from a variety of sources. Industrial purchasing behavior was shown by Scandinavian writers to be networks of long-term relationships. In the US, marketing academics increasingly recognized that the transactional view of marketing, based on micro-economics and now dubbed 'neo-classical', was not enough.

Marketers of services increasingly understood that it is cheaper and easier to retain an existing customer than find a new one. The vast majority of the business of large professional firms, such as accountants Coopers and Lybrand, comes from their existing clients. Emphasis switched from getting new clients to keeping existing clients for life. Firms of accountants started inviting their alumni to drinks parties. One was reminded of Woody Allen's quip in the taxi that his escort was so good looking that he couldn't keep his eyes on the meter. Study of distribution channels illustrated the importance of co-operative over hostile seller/buyer relationships.

Economists sought to explain why firms did not use the supposed efficiency of free markets but traded regularly with the same partners, even at higher prices. Sometimes firms vertically integrated and functions were 'internalized'. It has been shown that the 'transaction costs' of dealing ad hoc were greater than the efficiencies that could be had from regular dealings between the same people. If these transaction costs were added to market prices, the apparently higher prices of relational dealings became justified. These theories have since been manifested in the US with ECR (efficient consumer response) under which firms seek to co-operate through linked distribution, ordering and computer systems to smooth the flow of goods to the consumer and reduce inventory. The original report showed a potential saving in the US grocery business of $30bn.

Database marketing identified consumer and brand common interests on a segmented, if not individual, basis. General Motors introduced credit cards as much to gain access to details of their (potential) customers as to provide credit. Ford has launched *Ford Magazine* with an initial circulation of 650,000. Both intend to build brand relationships with existing and potential car owners.

The Chinese, both at home and overseas, have always traded on relationships. The word *guanxi* (business connections) has only been in use for the last few years but the idea that business should grow from friendship is far older. In the West, we do business first and make friends, perhaps, second. Thus whereas Westerners may be rather uncomfortable when giving business preference to friends, their Chinese equivalents are uncomfortable when they are not.

These strands were brought together to form what is widely known as 'relationship marketing'. The terminology is pervasive. The clerk who looks after your account at the bank or the telephone utility is now likely to be called your 'relationship manager'. Universalization may trivialize the concept. That would be a pity; it is a revolution in marketing thinking.

The term 'relational paradigm' is more precise and emphasizes just how fundamental is this view of marketing, or of business. The traditional micro-economic paradigm is no more 'wrong' than early astronomers were 'wrong'. Paradigms are just different ways of understanding. The challenge of the reformers is that it is too mechanistic, too transactional, too internally focussed on the company's actions, too rational and too financially oriented:

● **Too mechanistic** because sales are usually seen as a function of the marketing mix. Mathematically expressed:

$$y_t = f(p_t, a_{nt}, x_{nt})$$

or

$$y_t = f(y_{t-1}, p_t, a_{nt}, x_{nt})$$

where y_t represents sales for the period t, p_t is the price of the product x_{nt} is advertising, or promotional, element n for time t, and a_{nt} is the weighting factor of that element of the mix.

Traditional marketing thinking is more sophisticated than this but the equations above illustrate the type of thinking that is implicit.

● **Too transactional** because the focus is on the sales, or other results, from the period under examination rather than the accumulation of effects over the long term.

● **Too internally focussed** because of its concentration on the alternative marketing mix levers, i.e. what the company will do, rather than competitor actions. Outcomes may well be expressed in relative terms such as market share or share of voice, but planned actions tend not to be influenced greatly by competitive advantage.

● **Too rational** because, like the economics on which it is based, the underlying assumption is that people make rational choices based on analysed information. In practice the marketer has to address the emotional and experiential components of decision making and these are not separable.

● **Too financially oriented** because money is *assumed* to be the scarce resource, whereas often, managerial time is.

Recognition of these weaknesses led, in the 1970s, to the emergence of marketing *strategy* and 'sustainable competitive advantage'. This generated the second marketing paradigm, which may be termed 'conflict'. The dominant concept here is of competition. Market share is the key indicator of success. By comparison, the central concepts of the relational paradigm are:

● marketing is rooted in exchanges from which both parties benefit as a result of co-operation, not competition. This is not the zero sum game which the conflict paradigm implies for the marketers, e.g. total market share always equals 100 per cent.

● competition is thus important but secondary. It is, of course, essential to ensure choice, fairness and innovation.

● the market is a network of 'value laden relationships' connecting the brand, customers at all levels in the distribution channels, including end consumers, and other influence groups such as advertising agencies. Some systems include networks internal to the marketing organization.

● long-term relationships reduce risk as well as transaction costs and are thus beneficial for both sides.

● money is a key variable but so is managerial time. Relationships depend not so much on what is spent on them, though it helps, as the care and attention (both time issues) that they receive.

The marketing process is therefore the managerial activity to improve the relationships in the network from the perspective of the brand in order to improve brand equity, some of which may be distributed as short-term profits. This concept of marketing inputs in the form of human and financial resources and previous brand equity, being subjected to marketing process and resulting in profits, waste and brand equity to be carried forward is shown as Figure 1. Brand equity can therefore be defined as a vector of measures equal to

$$f(W_x R_{xb})$$

where x is each customer or significant influence agent, b is the brand, R_{xb} is the relationship x has with the brand and W_x is the importance weighting of that group of customers or influence agents. For example, a company whose brand strength depends solely on its immediate customers would have $W_{customer} = 1$; all other $W_x = 0$. In this paradigm, market orientation can be seen as the mirror image of brand equity using the same notation $f(W_x R_{xb})$. In other words, market orientation is the regard that the 'brand', i.e. the brand's managers, have for the other players in the network.

Market orientation, and its effect on profitability, is not the subject of this article but it is worth remarking that the reciprocal effect of relationships, i.e. an improvement of relationships in one direction, is most likely to stimulate an improvement in the reverse direction, gives credibility to these reciprocal definitions of brand equity and market orientation.

In this article, we reviewed the origins of the relational perspective, namely that the market should be seen as a network of long-term, value-added, co-operative relationships. We contrasted that with the traditional, neo-classical paradigm, largely based on micro-economics, and the conflict paradigm, which describes the market in terms of competition. None of these paradigms is wrong; they supplement each other. Finally we defined brand equity, and market orientation, in relational terms.

Measurement issues

Thus, in this perspective, building brand equity is the same as growing the relationships between the brand and its customers and significant influence agents. The marketer needs to measure progress by measuring the state of those relationships. Those with a financial orientation would wish to see all measurements expressed in financial terms, viz:

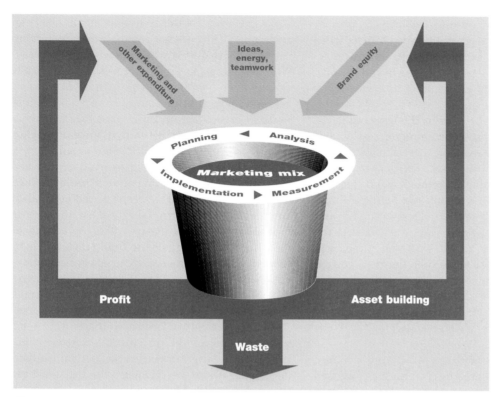

Figure 1

$$f(P_t, a_{nt}, x_{nt}) + BE_{t-1}$$

where BE_t and P_t represent Brand Equity and Profit at the end of period t, respectively, P_t is the price of the product x_{nt} is advertising, or promotional element n for time t, and a_{nt} is the weighting factor of that element of the mix.

Results from the marketing effort would be the profit plus increase in brand equity. Attractive as this is, the flaws are two-fold: no valuation methodology is yet satisfactory for this purpose and the focus is still on financial levers, not on relationships which cannot satisfactorily be explained by how much is spent on them. There are two approaches to measuring the relationships themselves, direct and indirect:

● **Directly** seeking to measure the state of relationships requires the marketer to establish what is in the minds of customers. The main variables are awareness and, depending on the category, attitudes such as perceived quality, perceived value, saliency (relevance), differentiation, esteem, familiarity, liking and fashionability. Some of these overlap.

● **Indirectly**, customers' behavior, whether they buy or not and under what circumstances, indicates the state of their brand relationships. Consumer behavioral variables include market share, relative price (share by value divided by share by volume), penetration (the per cent of the target market that has bought the brand in the last year), and loyalty (there are four ways of measuring this variable including share of category requirements). Retailer behavioral variables include availability or distribution, share of and position on shelf, and pipeline (number of days inventory). Neither approach is ideal and most businesses that seek to measure brand equity use some combination. The main problems with the indirect approach are:

No indication of what is in store. Market share and relative price are key indirect indicators but neither necessarily reflect the current status. They may reflect what has just been taken out of the brand, rather than what has been put in. For example, market share may be increased by bringing future sales into the current period. Loading the pipeline is common practice for sales forces bonused on volume sales. In this example, market share goes up when brand equity actually goes down, i.e. the indicator moves the wrong way.

Market share is subjective in the sense that the category chosen as the denominator is arbitrary. A vodka brand, for example, can be portrayed as a dominant force in the vodka category or a weak force in the white spirits sector. It can be gaining market share in one sector and losing market share in another. Since we have defined brand equity as an asset, a definition that leads to the conclusion that the asset is getting bigger and more valuable at the same time that it is getting smaller and less valuable is not very helpful.

Behavioral measures look back. The marketer wants to know what customers think now because that is a better guide to what now needs to be fixed.

The main problems with the direct approach are: *Cognitive bias.* Human decision making is based on a complex web of emotional, experiential and cognitive (rational thought) processes that cannot be separated. A consumer reaches out for one brand or another as the trolley passes through the aisle with barely a thought. When confronted by a surveyor with a clip board, the consumer feels impelled to make sense of this jumble to explain behavior in terms of awareness and attitudes. This rationalizing, and thereby inaccurate, process is known as 'cognitive bias'.

Variation by occasion. A brand suitable for one occasion will not be chosen for another. In human terms one might have immense respect for one's boss but not seek his or her company at weekends.

Family. 'Consumers' do not always buy for their own use. In some ways this is akin to business-to-business marketing where the buyer meets the organization's specifications rather than his or her own. The consumer is buying for the family, including household pets. What the family member buying cat food thinks may not be important; the cat will express its own opinion and that tends to be definitive.

Hypothetical questions. Consumers are reliable respondents for factual and behavioral questions,

e.g. what price did they pay – so long as they can remember. They are not reliable when it shifts to the hypothetical, e.g. what price would they pay. 'Would you pay £3 for this product?' tends to get the answer 'yes' even when, in reality, they refuse to pay anything more than £2.50. While neither direct nor indirect measures provide certain information on the dynamics of market change – i.e. what attitudinal shifts lead to what changes in market share – perceived quality has been shown to give some indication of future profitability, and thus current brand equity. As such, it may prove the single most important measure of brand equity. The selection of measures is less important than tracking them consistently over time. Many measures correlate, e.g. market share and brand loyalty, so that the direction of change over time is more significant than instantaneous variation between measures.

In this article we first abandoned financial valuations as invalid and failing to account for time or the way in which relationships are developed. We need to measure the relationships themselves. We considered direct measures of what customers think, feel and experience about the brand – i.e. the state of their brand relationships – and indirect measures based on purchase behavior. Both approaches have problems and, in practice, firms track a selection of both types of measure. Perceived quality is a key indicator.

Conclusions

Brand equity and relationship marketing, in various forms, have emerged from the 1980s as key concepts, fundamental to all forms of marketing. The two are linked in that both shift attention from short-term transactions and immediate profits toward a process of creating value through building and managing a network of value-added, long-term relationships. In this perception, marketing is the function of building brand relationships. This network can also be seen as the store of future profits. If brand equity and the existing state of relationships are the same thing, measuring one is also measuring the other. In the previous section, some of the difficulties of measuring brand equity were rehearsed.

Following this paradigm, practitioners are advised to identify the network of their brand's relationships. Resources (money, energies and time) should be focussed on those relationships that are more important and/or more capable of beneficial change. The impact of these activities on relationships should then be tracked, directly and indirectly, in a consistent fashion over time. The traditional advice to farmers applies equally to brand managers: live as if you will die tomorrow but farm as if you will tend that land for ever.

Summary

Relationship marketing – managing a network of relationships between a brand and its various customers – is a way of understanding marketing itself. Brand equity is the intangible asset associated with the brand and responsible for future cash flows. Brand valuation is the financial worth of the brand's equity.

Marketers are now less concerned with making individual sales than with maintaining long-term customer contact. The new network of co-operative relationships is in contrast with the traditional, neo-classical paradigm and the conflict paradigm. None of these is wrong: they supplement each other.

The 'network' argument came together in the 1980s. Marketers of services increasingly understood that it is cheaper and easier to retain an existing customer than find a new one. Study of distribution channels illustrated the importance of co-operative over hostile buyer/seller relationships. 'Relational' dealings were manifested in the US with efficient consumer response under which companies seek to co-operate through linked distribution, ordering and computer systems to smooth the flow of goods to the consumer and reduce inventory. The marketer needs to measure progress by measuring the state of relationships between the brand and its customers and significant 'influence agents'.

Financial valuations are invalid. In practice companies use a combination of direct measures (what customers think, feel and experience about the brand), and indirect measures based on purchase behavior.

Suggested further reading

Aaker, David A. (1991) *Managing Brand Equity*, The Free Press, New York.

Christopher, M., Payne, A. and Ballantyne, D. (1991) *Relationship Marketing*, Butterworth Heinemann, Oxford.

Customers as strategic assets

■ **New technology and new approaches to marketing are allowing companies to collect, analyse and use information about their customers.** David Schmittlein **describes the techniques, the advantages and some of the problems.**

Leading-edge companies have long recognized that their important assets go well beyond the usual balance sheet items to include knowledgeable and motivated employees, information and learning systems, technological expertise, supply and distribution contracts, and the like. Increasingly, these companies are placing their customers themselves – the 'installed base' of active consumers of the company's products or services – at the top of this asset list.

Of course, the importance of winning and satisfying customers is as old as the concept of marketing itself. What is new, however, is the active management of the company's current customer base as a key strategic asset. Indeed, many disparate marketing activities that are growing in popularity can be seen as reflections of this more basic shift in perspective. Such activities include loyalty and relationship marketing programs, integrated marketing communications and direct marketing, interactive marketing and electronic commerce, database marketing and mass customization.

Interest in these initiatives has increased greatly over the past decade. More importantly, the last couple of years have seen a 'breakout' in their use beyond a few specialized industries (for example, catalogue companies, credit/financial services) to include a spectrum of business-to-business marketers and the sellers of consumer durables, non-durables and services.

For many companies, the benefits of managing customers as strategic assets (MCSA) have been great. They include more loyal customers, who are less inclined to shop around or buy on price, more efficient, effective and highly targeted communications programs, reactivation of very profitable 'lost' customers at low cost, and more focussed and successful development of new products.

It is also, for many managers, a change in the way of doing business that causes substantial anxiety and frustration. MCSA requires a substantial financial investment in many cases, and often success relies on redesigned planning processes and multifunctional co-operation. Since specific customer asset management programs can bring such large financial returns, their details are also typically highly proprietary, and companies can find themselves benchmarking more against rumour and anecdote that against actual 'best practices'.

This article will examine in some detail the leading practices in MCSA and also the keys to its successful implementation in organizations. But before discussing how such a process can be managed effectively, it may be helpful to describe in more detail what strategic customer asset management means to leading practitioners and

why it represents such a major change in perspective on marketing activities.

The customer as an asset

Consumers who have chosen a company's products or services tend to develop a set of characteristics that are important and advantageous to the company. These include awareness of the breadth of its products, familiarity with their specific performance characteristics, and accommodation of them into a lifestyle or self-image or (for business customers) into established operating procedures.

In a heterogeneous marketplace, these are individuals who have revealed that they prefer the company's goods (at least some of the time). Given the inertia in repeat-purchase decisions they are unlikely to rethink that preference deeply or often.

Finally, the simple fact that the individual voluntarily elected to purchase the company's offering sets up a psychological pressure for this customer to feel good about that decision: that is, customers want to believe that they made the 'right' choice as a 'smart' consumer. In this respect they tend to seek out evidence (often provided by the company) that they have indeed been smart buyers. Certainly, current customers are important for all these reasons. But do they really qualify as 'assets' of the company, and if so how does this perspective change marketing practice? The case for managing customers as strategic assets rests on four conditions, only some of which may be met in some industries at present.

1. *Current customers are an unusually stable, predictable source of future sales.* Consider a particular manufacturer of various office products (both durables and non-durables), usually sold to small and medium-sized business customers. For each customer, this company knows what orders were placed, when and with which manufacturer's representative. One set of the company's customers placed the following number of office product orders during subsequent quarters of a recent year: April–June 1,793, July–September 1,700, October–December 1,670, January–March 1,617.

Understandably, expected future sales from

the current customer base often form the starting point for a plan to meet sales targets, with customer acquisition efforts established to close the gap between the two.

2. *Individual customers can be segmented very effectively in terms of future sales potential (i.e., their 'asset value') based on their history to date.* For the office products company above, the top 20 per cent of customers by geographic region (i.e., the top ten US states) are almost twice as active as the bottom 20 per cent. Similarly, when customers of the company are segmented by the nature of their business (i.e., by the US four-digit standard industrial classification code), the top 20 per cent of kinds of business customers are over three times better than the bottom 20 per cent.

To be sure, however, other characteristics also account for the behavior of individual customers and in fact both these 'geo-demographic' factors together explain only 3 per cent to 4 per cent of the variation in sales from customer to customer. In short, these usual segmentation criteria can create customer groups with different overall sales profiles but much of the variation in customer-by-customer sales inclinations is left unexplained. In contrast, using a standard set of measures from each customer's transaction history with the company (for example, number of orders placed, monetary value of the orders, how recently the account was active) it was possible to explain 40 per cent of the variation in sales from customer to customer. That is, the customer's sales history was ten times as effective in segmenting customers as were the geodemographics. Further, it was so effective at anticipating future sales potential that it left little to chance in targeting promotional programs.

This kind of experience has been repeated in many companies and accounts for the intensive efforts to create marketing-oriented customer databases that capture the customer's transaction history. With knowledge of customer history, the ability to anticipate their future makes it natural to view each such individual as an 'asset' of the corporation.

3. *Customers are subject to depreciation.* Just as with other assets, customer 'breakdown' or 'wearout' is an empirical fact of life. Notice how the number of orders placed by the static set of office products customers above declines quarter by quarter. Upon further investigation this was clearly the result of customer attrition – i.e., some customers were leaving the company to take their business elsewhere. More importantly, this attrition is often predictable, especially with the knowledge of a transaction history.

As an example, the Internet provider America Online has observed that new subscribers stay with their service an average of three years, generating on average $500 in revenue during that period. Other companies, including the telecommunications provider GTE, have investigated the factors that affect customer retention/attrition patterns. And still others have been using customer attrition patterns inferred from transaction histories alone, i.e., in industries where a customer's 'departure' for another company's products is not directly observable, as is the case for consumer non-durables. As an example, the market research company A.C. Nielsen uses attrition patterns to define competitive market boundaries for consumer products in France.

These customer asset/depreciation perspectives have become so widely accepted that they are now acceptable as accounting practice in the US, following a 1993 ruling of the Supreme Court. That is, companies can depreciate the value of a customer base acquired when the sales decline from that customer base can be predicted reliably through time (for example, based on past experience of tracking customers).

4. *Customers can be bought and sold.* An explicit valuation of future sales potential from specific customer groups is increasingly an important component of merger and acquisition decisions. For example, the recent merger of two large New York banks (Chase and Chemical) represents the combination of customer bases whose sales potential is to be realized with a smaller and more efficient corporate infrastructure.

Numerous examples of this customer-asset perspective also arise in the area of licensing and distribution. For example, a manufacturer's representative who builds a customer base in one

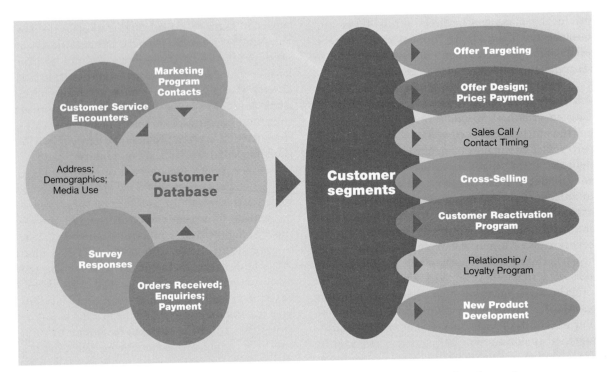

Figure 1: Managing customers as strategic assets: inference and action based on customer histories

territory has sometimes been ruled legally to 'own' those customers. And if the manufacturer wishes to replace the representative (for example, with a direct salesforce) the rep may have to be compensated for the future (depreciating) value of those customers. Similar evaluation of customer assets can be required in terminating licensing agreements. This was the situation faced by the Coca-Cola Co in France in 1988, where Pernod held the licence to market Coke. To compensate Pernod for its investment in developing this customer base, in terminating the license Coca-Cola reportedly had to pay Pernod approximately $200m.

In summary, customers often have an asset value that can be evaluated reliably, especially with the availability of detailed transaction history information. Next, some of the ways that such a perspective is proving useful to marketers.

The move from tactics to strategy

Tactical initiatives focussed on the company's customer base have an extended history, ranging from coupons and free product samples to purchase reminders sent via direct mail. Increasingly, the assets represented by a customer base play a role in long-run strategic actions of the company. Their role in merger and acquisition decisions was briefly touched on above. They are also key drivers of new product development programs, customer retention, loyalty and relationship programs, and cross-selling initiatives.

The major elements in the strategic use of customer assets are illustrated in Figure 1. It begins with the assembly of a marketing-oriented customer database including marketing program contacts with the customer, a transaction history (inquiries, orders, payment), merged with any customer service information, available geodemographic descriptions, media habits and any responses to surveys that may be relevant. From this information, segmentation of the customer base is a critical step, assembling groups of customers most appropriate for highly customized marketing programs that may include cross-selling, new product development (including mass customization in some cases), design and timing of customized communication programs, and (in the case of apparently lapsed customers) reactivation programs.

A managerial perspective

Current customers can be especially reliable sources of future revenue and can reliably be differentiated from each other based on their behavior to date. This is not to suggest customers can be taken for granted or that future sales are automatic. Rather, management of customers as strategic assets considers the need actively to manage customer groups just as other organizational assets require management.

Specifically, the customer's future revenue stream will stem from the mix of marketing programs offered to that individual. As a result, although assessments of 'Customer Lifetime Value' (LTV) have become common, increasingly the goal is not to calculate a single number for each customer representing summed discounted future cash flows, but instead to view LTV as an explicit function of communication, new product offering and cross-selling programs envisioned by the company.

Some of the most prevalent manifestations of MCSA that are being adopted by marketers are considered next.

Database marketing: to capture the customer, follow its tracks

The importance of observed customer histories for MCSA, and for many companies assembling a marketing-oriented customer database such as the one described in the figure is the starting point for managing customers in this way.

In some cases complete customer transaction records are maintained by the company as a matter of course, for example in many business-to-business markets and consumer services. In these areas, companies including IBM, American Express and Citicorp have spent millions of dollars building and maintaining such databases and using them to develop marketing programs.

In other sectors (for example, retailing where consumers use a store's credit card) transaction records are typically available to the company and are currently used for billing purposes. But (all too often) the information is not maintained past the billing cycle for assembly into meaningful and useful customer summaries. This is changing, with increased sophistication among retailers and with the entry into retailing of some companies that have traditionally been direct marketers and therefore have seen the benefits of customer database management.

In the consumer durables area, some products lend themselves to the easy capture of relevant customer information. For example, in automobiles Porsche has been known for its extensive database management initiatives among both prospects and current customers. On the other hand, for durables sold through retail channels companies such as Polaroid (cameras) and Braun (personal care products and household appliances) face a greater challenge in creating incentives (at either the retail or ultimate consumer level) to provide the needed customer transaction information.

Manufacturers of mass-marketed consumer non-durables are often seen as least able to assemble a useful customer database. But even here the situation is changing rapidly. Opportunities for partnerships with retailers (for example, grocery chains) that are creating individual customer purchase databases (based on frequent-shopper cards used during checkout) are being explored.

The changing economics of constructing and managing customer databases and the benefits that can accrue have even led such manufacturers to experiment with setting up such a database themselves. For example, Procter & Gamble has sent questionnaires regarding brand preferences and product usage for several product categories to a set of US households.

What distinguishes this initiative from other consumer surveys is that responses were explicitly not anonymous – the return envelope contained the customer's name and address. Therefore, the results can be used not just to project population characteristics such as overall brand preference levels but also to assemble a customer base from which these individual households can be contacted with customized initiatives (for example, new product free samples, coupons to induce certain households to switch brands and so on.)

Obviously assembling (and maintaining) such a database that would cover a significant fraction of US households would cost tens of millions of dollars. But the benefits can also be great. For a company such as Procter & Gamble that spends approximately $2bn a year on advertising (worldwide), such a customer base investment that would enable customization and micro-targeting of communication messages can potentially make economic sense.

Interactive marketing and mass customization

A variety of activities have become popular under the heading of interactive marketing, including customer toll-free telephone complaint/question/request lines, direct mail, inbound telemarketing (i.e., providing a telephone number for ordering) and integrated customer service/selling centers.

Although these programs are often viewed, along with mass customization efforts, as efficient and persuasive selling initiatives, they are equally important as methods for assembling detailed information on customer preferences and perceptions that provide the company with a substantial edge for the 'next' sales opportunity. As an illustration of this role for mass customization, a Japanese bicycle manufacturer offers at retail sites a fitting for a custom-made bicycle tailored to the customer's exact measurements. This information is relayed to the factory and within days the product is available for delivery. (Actually, the company has had to delay the shipping dates by a couple weeks. With the shorter turnaround time some customers refused to believe that a bicycle delivered this quickly could possibly have been customized.) Of course, having customer measurements (as well as the name and address) provides a major advantage for the company in inducing a replacement purchase at a later date. Levi's has offered a similar option in marketing jeans to women in the US. Individual measurements can be taken at a retail store and the company not only wins some positive customer perceptions regarding the quality of the product's fit, but also acquires a customer (name, address, measurements) for future marketing efforts.

Electronic commerce and the development of customer assets

Electronic commerce, including sales via the Internet, is another area that may appear to be primarily a new arena for persuasive one-shot selling but in fact is one where the greater challenge and opportunity involves building a loyal customer base through constructing a detailed marketing-oriented customer database.

Sales via the Internet are obviously an example of direct marketing, with customer transaction information captured by the company. But further, customer prospects (who have not yet bought) can be segmented by the type of information they have elected to collect (for example, from World Wide Web pages) or by their stated preferences if they respond to an invitation to provide such information.

As in earlier cases, the key to long-run marketing success is effective new product development or mass customization of offerings for such segments, and/or detailed customization of communication messages from the company to the customer/prospect.

Customizing communications

Strategic management of customer assets leads companies to collect detailed and useful information for each individual customer. Probably the single most popular use of that information is in targeted/customized communications. Implementation via direct mail or telemarketing programs is well-known. Equally important is its use in personal selling. At the brokerage company A. G. Edwards, brokers can call up a list of clients who have money coming due from maturing investments and contact them for reinvestment decisions. At the telecommunications company Bell South, representatives visiting a prospect for the first time receive a customized set of selling suggestions, via their personal computer, based on the prospect's known behavioral history. At Goodyear Tire, sales reps can tell each 'customer' (i.e., tyre retailer) how much product they can expect to use in the next month, how much inventory they have on hand and exactly what they should order.

Customer retention

Aside from the efforts at incremental/increased sales discussed thus far, preservation of the company's current customer asset base has finally begun to attract the attention it deserves.

The consulting company Bain & Co. has developed and popularized approaches for implementing 'zero customer defections'. As mentioned earlier, GTE has made a concerted effort to understand the leading indicators of imminent customer attrition and used that knowledge to segment customers based on this risk for particular marketing programs. In most businesses since customers do not explicitly announce a decision to take their business elsewhere developing such indicators of a customer's future is critical.

Taking a cue from the experience of direct marketing companies, certain indicators of the 'recency' of a customer's activity are often seen as important danger signals for attrition. As an illustration, Merrill Lynch has focussed many of its retail brokerage efforts on what it terms 'prime customers'. In one empirical study, the probability that various customer groups, based on their past history, would be prime customers this year was examined. When customers were grouped based on their prime status over the past two years, the results were:

PROBABILITY OF BEING PRIME THIS YEAR

Prime each of the past two years	0.63
Prime last year, but not year before	0.46
Not prime last year, but prime year before	0.14
Not prime either of the past two years	0.06

Notice the clear role played by both frequency (i.e., how many years of the past two the customer was prime) and by recency (i.e., among those prime one of the last two years, those prime most recently are over three times as likely – 0.46 versus 0.14 – to be prime this year). Companies are finding that customers at risk of departure can be dissuaded, often at reasonable cost. Indeed it has been suggested in some quarters that it is seven times as expensive to get additional sales from new customers as it is

to enhance sales from existing customers. Evidently this ratio will vary from company to company, but the key observation is that customer retention efforts can work. The greatest challenge to their implementation is often the sifting through customer records required to identify those truly at risk.

Integrated marketing communications

Integrated marketing communications (IMC) refers to the co-ordination of all elements of the communication program to provide synergies in persuasive impact and cost efficiencies – delivering the right message to the right customer decision maker at the right time. The various activities include direct marketing, personal selling, public relations, media advertising and promotions to draw the potential customer through the various decision stages that may precede purchase.

In the consumer sector the 'integration' component of IMC often requires the capture of customer information to serve as the basis for the next, targeted, customized communication element. Johnson & Johnson used this approach in introducing its Acuvue disposable contact lenses in the US.

An initial advertisement solicited a direct response inquiry from prospective customers. At the same time, a direct mail kit was sent to eyecare professionals who would also need to play a role in the ultimate sale. On receipt of the customer inquiry, Johnson & Johnson relayed that interest to a relevant eyecare professional, who was invited to solicit an appointment with the customer prospect. When such an appointment was made, the professional notified Johnson & Johnson, which in turn sent the consumer a discount coupon good for an initial order.

This program provides incentives for the eyecare professional to keep the manufacturer 'in the loop' as the consumer moves from prospect to customer. At the end of a successful sale, the manufacturer has a complete record containing both the customer's information and the identity of his/her eyecare professional. Future initiatives can be targeted towards either (or both).

This outcome would, of course, not be possible

via one-shot advertising advising the prospective customer simply to 'call your doctor'. Upjohn has used a similar integrated communication program to market its hair enhancement/ growth product sold under the brand name Rogaine. An image-oriented television commercial contained a toll-free number for initial inquiry. Those expressing interest to Upjohn received a 20-minute videocassette discussing the general problem and its resolution. (Males were sent a version organized around weekend whitewater rafting; the female version included a talk show with women discussing types and degrees of success).

Prospects were also sent the names of three local dermatologists or physicians whom they could contact. They were also sent one of 35 versions of an offer letter and a $10 voucher good for a visit to the doctor. To use the voucher, the prospect was required to obtain the doctor's signature and identification and return it to Upjohn. Again, the company both encouraged the prospect to move ahead in the decision sequence and via the same initiative acquired a complete customer record indicating the name/address of both the customer and of his/her doctor.

IMC is also growing in popularity among business-to-business marketers. Hewlett-Packard has been deeply committed to inte-grating its direct mail, telemarketing and face-to-face selling activities for business customers and prospects. Its investment in customer tracking and segmentation has allowed it to cut its average mailing size from 70,000 pieces to 10,000 with better lead generation and sales results.

Further, its closed-loop lead management process encourages the marketing and sales groups to co-ordinate activities in a systematic fashion based on the important characteristics of leads being pursued. It also encourages the assessment of profitability of the various components of the marketing communication program in moving the prospect toward a sale.

Developing new products

Management of customers as strategic assets leads a company ultimately to organize all its activities, including the development of new products, around particular customer groups whose perceptions, preferences and purchase behaviors are tracked through time. Certainly many companies have developed new products for particular customer groups based on specific observed behavioral histories. But the comprehensive organization of new product initiatives around such customer groups remains more a stated goal or ideal than actual practice.

As exceptions, it may be argued that such a perspective is reflected in the new products assembled for customer groups by Johnson & Johnson's baby care division and by financial service providers such as USAA. The latter company was created to offer insurance at reasonable cost to US military officers. It has retained that closed customer group (including immediate family members) as its focus since the Second World War and has expanded its set of financial service offerings, each tailored to the needs of this group of customers.

The company does not do outbound tele-marketing but has a world-class customer service group that handles inbound customer service calls using a rich query-based customer information system. This system is oriented during the service encounter toward identifying potential additional services in which the customer may have a current interest. The company has been able to translate this strategy into a status as the largest US direct mail firm, which also handles over 250,000 phone calls daily, managing a base of over 2m active customers that provide over $2bn in annual revenue.

Putting MCSA to work

Companies implementing MCSA have en-countered two major challenges.

First, assembling the information needed to describe, track and capture the customer as part of a defined asset base can be difficult and/or expensive. Further, the benefits offered may not seem to be available until that long costly process is completed.

Second, the active management of customer assets typically requires a degree of co-ordination across marketing (and non-marketing) functions that can be new (and painful) to the company and its employees.

The first challenge is being overcome by a combination of changing cost economics for data acquisition and management, by the development of better query-oriented software designed specifically for managing marketing-oriented customer databases, the opportunities to partner with other companies (including those downstream in the channel of distribution) to share information of mutual benefit, and the creativity of managers inventing incentives for consumers to wish to facilitate the collection of this information.

An example of the latter is the multimillion-person database on cigarette smokers and their brand preferences maintained by the largest tobacco companies. The customer incentive for providing that information is a free information/entertainment magazine targeted to smokers, the availability of which is dependent on providing the requested customer information. The second challenge, related to co-ordination of the company's information systems and its marketing programs, is being aided by an array of initiatives increasing cross-functional interaction in companies, including the shrinking layers of management, cross-functional new product development teams, and pushing responsibility for customer orientation beyond the marketing function to include manufacturing and R&D.

In the meantime, companies seem to have found the greatest success when initially implementing customer asset management on a project basis for a well-defined set of customers with a specific set of marketing initiatives (for example, cross-selling or customer retention) in mind. The asset management perspective itself will tend to drive the project to attain concrete, measurable (and measured) results. These results become the best incentive possible for investing further in customer information systems that enable the asset management process to develop further.

The future

Collectively, the elements of MCSA described above are clearly in their early growth phase of development. In many companies they are just beginning to represent a greater share of the overall marketing activities. Further, several are beginning to emerge from their previous restriction to a specific industry or sector.

The broadening interest and activity is being driven by both cost declines and observed success to date. In turn, growth is being fuelled by increased infrastructure in the form of customer information bases (whether created in house or available for sale, lease or co-marketing activities) and also in the form of management systems and experience in using such a perspective to develop and co-ordinate marketing programs. As with other assets, their possession can initially provide a strategic advantage for a company. Maintaining that advantage of course requires re-investment and enhancement of the asset itself. But unlike most other organizational assets, customer groups – if managed and maintained – cannot be easily 'copied' by the competition. In other words, part of the interest in managing customers as strategic assets is the sense that this is one of the few 'sustainable' competitive advantages open to the company.

This article has given at least brief mention to some of the leading industry practitioners of this perspective on marketing. It should also acknowledge those who have helped develop the concepts and practices being adopted and who have also helped describe these developments for a wider audience. Both David Shepard (of David Shepard Associates) and Robert Kestnbaum (of Kestnbaum & Co) are widely seen as innovators in developing ideas and experience from direct marketing that are important for managing customer assets.

Professor Robert Blattberg of Northwestern University's Kellogg Graduate School of Management has also been a leader in this area and has emphasized the assessment of a company's 'customer equity', i.e., the nature and degree of commitment to the company by these individuals. Finally, Professor Rashi Glazer of Berkeley's Haas School of Business has helped categorize and develop the kind of information-intensive strategies being used by companies for managing customer assets.

The coming years will see more growth for some of the activities above than others, and this pattern will differ from industry to industry as a function of the degree and nature of customer differences and the ability (and cost) to capture the required information by companies. New manifestations of customer asset management are also likely to arise. Therefore, managers need to assess the benefits of these various activities for their own company and industry. In this respect, it is helpful to consider the ways that the array of marketing innovations discussed above are different methods for implementation of a single basic perspective: the increased opportunity, and competitive necessity actively to manage the customer base as a key strategic asset of the company.

Summary

More companies are actively managing customers as strategic assets (MCSA), through loyalty and relationship marketing, electronic commerce and other initiatives. The case for doing so rests on customers being unusually stable, 'segmentable' on the strength of their sales history, subject to reliable measures of depreciation, and capable of being bought and sold.

The starting point for MCSA is assembling a customer database. Even manufacturers of mass-marketed consumer non-durables are exploring the possibilities, sometimes with retailing partners. Interactive marketing activities and sales via the Internet should be seen as opportunities to add to the database. Besides incremental sales, companies must also be alert to signs of customer defections – 'frequency' and 'recency' are useful indicators in this regard.

Integrated marketing communications (IMC) refers to the co-ordination of all elements of a communication program. In the consumer sector the capture of customer information often serves as the basis for the next targeted, customized communication. IMC, though, is also growing in popularity among business-to-business marketers.

The organization of new products around particular customer groups remains more a stated goal than actual practice. Under MCSA, companies have found information can be difficult and/or expensive to assemble, and the necessary degree of cross functional co-ordination outside their previous experience. Both challenges can be overcome.

Part of the interest in managing customers as strategic assets is the sense that it is a rare example of a 'sustainable' advantage.

Suggested further reading

Blattberg, R.C. and Deighton, J. (1991) 'Interactive marketing: exploiting the age of addressability', *Sloan Management Review*, vol. 33, 1, pp. 5–14.

Pine, B.J. II, Peppers, D. and Rogers, M. (1995). 'Do you want to keep your customers forever?' *Havard Business Review*, March/April vol. 73, 2, pp. 103–108.

Schmittlein, D.C. and Peterson, R.A. (1994), 'Customer base analysis: an industrial purchase process application', *Marketing Science*, vol. 13, 1, pp. 41–67.

Shepard, D. (1995) *The New Direct Marketing: How to Implement a Profit-Driven Database Marketing Strategy*, 2nd edn, Irwin Professional Publishing, Chicago.

In praise of revitalization

■ **Re-engineering is not everything. Companies also have to rediscover growth.** Tom Robertson **looks at the risks and rewards of four classic routes.**

The dominant strategic modality of business practice in the first half of the 1990s has been corporate re-engineering. Businesses have been downsized and rightsized and new processes have been designed to enhance productivity. Portfolios have been rationalized with a renewed emphasis on core businesses, such as General Motors' spinoff of its EDS subsidiary or SAS's exit from Intercontinental Hotels.

Perhaps the ultimate example of this philosophy was Al Dunlap of Scott Paper in the US who downsized the company, sold-off non-core business units and then sold the remainder of the company to Kimberly-Clark – all to the considerable benefit of Scott Paper shareholders and to Al Dunlap himself.

Yet, for many companies that are re-engineering, their sales are falling faster than their cost structures. So too is their ability to stay at the leading edge of innovation. The danger is that even if re-engineering has short-term cost benefits, it does not necessarily provide a vision for the future. Nor does it necessarily deliver the highest long-run benefit to shareholders. Neither does enhancing short-run shareholder value necessarily correspond with the long-run welfare of employees (who have been made redundant) or the welfare of the communities in which the company operates.

As the re-engineering movement dissipates in the latter half of the 1990s, increasingly the focus is on revitalization. More particularly, the need is for innovation and growth. BET, a specialist industrial supplier in distribution, security services and textile services, would seem to represent this new stage. Under CEO John Clark, costs have been reduced and the business has been rationalized with the sale of non-related business units. But now the time has come to deliver sales growth if shareholders are to see long-term rewards.

Similarly, while Lou Gerstner has stopped the haemorrhaging of cash and people at IBM, sales are flat and analysts question whether IBM can be a growth company again. The Lotus acquisition is an attempt to find a growth path. Nevertheless, Microsoft with almost $6bn in sales versus IBM's approximately $65bn has almost the same market value, largely because it is seen as a growth company of the future, whereas IBM is seen (perhaps incorrectly) as a company of the past.

Pathways to revitalization

Managers charged with putting a company on a growth trajectory have a portfolio of options. A classic approach to thinking about these options is the product/market matrix proposed by Igor Ansoff (*see* Figure 1 overleaf). The firm can pursue its existing markets (customer sets) or enter new markets and can emphasize its existing products or develop new products.

This provides four growth alternatives and the key question is the appropriate balance within the portfolio. What proportion of effort and resources should be devoted to each option? Each has different levels of risk and reward and short-run versus long-run benefits.

Market penetration. Here the objective is to generate additional turnover from existing markets. This is likely to be the most profitable alternative – in the short to medium term. If additional business can be gained from existing accounts, this is usually highly cost effective. Research by Heskett, Sasser & Hart is consistent with this by demonstrating the value of maintaining existing accounts versus the cost of

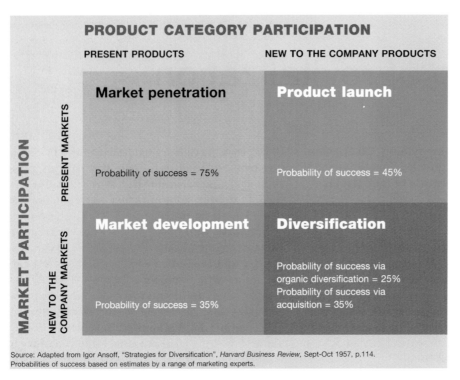

PRODUCT CATEGORY PARTICIPATION

	PRESENT PRODUCTS	NEW TO THE COMPANY PRODUCTS
	Market penetration Probability of success = 75%	**Product launch** Probability of success = 45%
	Market development Probability of success = 35%	**Diversification** Probability of success via organic diversification = 25% Probability of success via acquisition = 35%

MARKET PARTICIPATION — PRESENT MARKETS / NEW TO THE COMPANY MARKETS

Source: Adapted from Igor Ansoff, "Strategies for Diversification", *Harvard Business Review*, Sept-Oct 1957, p.114.
Probabilities of success based on estimates by a range of marketing experts.

Figure 1: Pathways to growth: the product/market matrix

continually developing new accounts. Generally, the firm loses money in the first year of bringing an account on board but the cumulative net present value builds substantially over time.

Nevertheless, market penetration is not a static strategy. Customer needs evolve and innovation is required. Such innovation is best characterized as incremental or continuous innovation and involves a constant enhancement of product benefits and positioning. We can see this in the stream of constant enhancements that Unilever introduces in fmcg (fast-moving consumer goods) categories, but we also see this in technology categories such as Boeing's sequence of enhancements of its 737 aircraft from the 100 series to the 800 series, now in the design phase.

Continuous innovation is driven by the duality of escalating consumer needs and competitive imitation. If a company rests on its laurels for long, it loses its edge in the marketplace. The escalation of consumer needs is shown by Sony's Walkman. This was deemed by consumers to be a breakthrough innovation

but within months their demands increased – more comfortable headsets, lighter weight, jogging capability and so on. In parallel, competitors such as Matsushita imitated quickly and offered product enhancements. Sony's leadership in the product category was sustainable only by enhancing the original product very rapidly in order to stay ahead of the curve of consumer benefit escalation and competitive imitation.

The pursuit of market penetration may also suggest process innovation. If the basic technology is deemed to have an adequately long potential life cycle, the firm may find it advantageous to invest in R&D or advanced manufacturing processes with the objective of reducing costs and heightening profits. Such innovation may be focussed on more cost-effective designs and manufacturing processes.

We see this today in the European battle for hygiene products, such as nappies and feminine hygiene, being waged by Molnlycke, Procter & Gamble and Kimberly Clark. Ongoing product enhancement is being combined with advanced manufacturing equipment that lowers per unit costs.

The probability of success when pursuing market penetration strategies is quite high. (see Figure 1). In a survey of marketing experts conducted by the author, the odds of success were 75 per cent, which is considerably higher than any other alternative in the growth portfolio. Nevertheless, we recognize that markets change, technologies evolve and that market penetration cannot be carried too far. It may be based on the firm's competencies of the moment and these competencies should be leveraged – to a point. But competencies may become rigidities and the firm must constantly scan the environment for new opportunities.

Market development. The pursuit of market development is a second growth alternative. The objective is to take existing products into new markets – perhaps via geographic expansion or via expansion to new market segments. Much of the growth at McDonald's in the 1990s, for example, is by selling its basic hamburger product line into new markets (such as China and Russia) as well as into new segments (such as airports and in-company). Most of Virgin Atlantic's recent growth is due to expansion into new routes, such as Hong Kong or San Francisco.

Market development is generally thought of as organic: that is, generated internally by the company. Growth may also be gained, however, by the acquisition of new customer bases or segments – 'bolt-on acquisition'.

For example, Hilton Hotels has achieved growth by the acquisition of compatible properties in markets previously under-represented. British Airways equity positions in US Air, Qantas and Deutsche BA provide avenues for market development in order to overcome regulatory hurdles in the US, Australia and Germany. Rentokil has achieved impressive organic growth but historically has also used a large number of small-sized bolt-on acquisitions to achieve its ambitious growth objectives.

The probability of success while pursuing a market development strategy is estimated by marketing executives at 35 per cent. The variance around this average is quite high,

however. Even the same company may have different levels of success in different markets, as exemplified by Marks and Spencer's varying pattern of success in Europe and its lack of success in North America. Body Shop has also seen a mixed pattern so far as it has expanded aggressively in North America in order to maintain 'first-mover' advantage over the host of imitators now appearing in the US market.

Product launch. Product development and launch are the lifeblood of the company of the future. Successful companies are increasingly demanding greater innovation, shorter product development cycles and more rapid new product penetration cycles. 3M, for example, has recently raised the ante by committing to 30 per cent of sales to be generated from new products developed within the past four years.

As a strategy for growth, the odds of success when a new product is launched are estimated at 45 per cent. Of course, most new products fail at some earlier point in the product development sequence – at idea generation, concept testing, prototype testing or test marketing. There is also tremendous variability in the new product launch success rate, depending particularly on the position on the innovation continuum (see Figure 2 overleaf).

As a generalization the odds of success are higher for continuous innovations, which involve minor changes in established patterns of consumption. This is the realm of brand or product line extensions – new models, features, flavours, and so on, which we have already discussed under market penetration as a strategy. By contrast the odds of success are much lower for radical or discontinuous innovations, which create new patterns of consumption – inventions such as digital video discs or personal data assistants, which still have to prove their value to consumers.

The odds of success may be one factor. But revenue potential is the other. Although incremental innovations have higher odds of success, they correspondingly have much lower revenue potential. A debate in the fmcg area today is why there has been such a lack of discontinuous innovation or why the focus has been so overwhelmingly on line extensions.

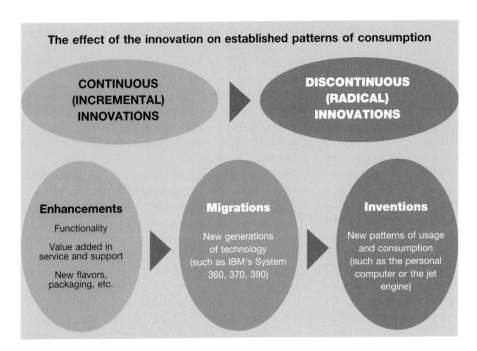

Figure 2: The innovation continuum

Although these can occasionally yield high incremental turnover, such as Frito Lay's $150m (£95m) extension into Cool Ranch Doritos (a flavour extension), the usual experience is a marginal increase in turnover, which is consistent with the limited growth seen in many fmcg product categories, especially when price increases are eliminated.

By contrast, discontinuous innovations are highly risky endeavours with huge potential payoffs. So many fail in their first incarnation. Time to takeoff is so often longer than anticipated or desired. The eventual design and applications for the product may be quite different than visualized at market introduction. One recent review of major technologies by Marketing Science Institute found that there was a long lead time to commercial success – generally five to 20 years. Furthermore, the company that invents the technology may not be the one that successfully commercializes it.

Examples abound. Matsushita, the worldwide market leader in VCRs, did not invent the technology. Fax and ATM (automatic teller machines) technologies took well over a decade to begin gaining market penetration. The original applications for VCRs (recording and time

shifting) were not the eventual dominant applications (pre-recorded programs) nor for microwaves (primary cooking versus reheating).

Yet, despite the risks, failure to endorse and embrace new technologies may be an even more problematic position for a company to take. Indeed, the real risk is that a new technology may be competence-destroying and render the skills and talents of existing competitors obsolete. This, for example, is the ultimate risk of biotechnology.

Although pharmaceutical companies have been slow to develop their own biotech competencies, they have protected themselves by taking equity positions in biotech firms or entering into alliances to serve as the manufacturing, marketing and regulatory affairs partners. Obsolescence of competencies is also the risk to traditional chemical film producers, such as Kodak. Under new CEO George Fisher, management now recognises that the company's future depends on embracing digital imaging technology and developing leading-edge core competencies in this area.

Increasingly, companies are exploring alternative routes to product development. In particular, although internal R&D may still be dominant, they are pursuing a range of alliances and outsourcing to develop and launch new products expeditiously. This may involve R&D alliances, components alliances, joint ventures, or licensing of technologies. Recent data collected by *Financial Times* writer Vanessa Houlder suggest that external R&D budgets will account for 35 per cent of US R&D budgets by 1996 and 60 per cent of Japanese R&D budgets. This trend to outsourcing R&D is driven by cost factors, an emphasis on pursuing only the organization's own core competencies and the more transparent global market that has emerged in technology transfer. Technology alliances and licensing may also be a necessary means of building new product success. This is particularly the case if the new product cannot succeed without the availability of complementary products and software or programs.

For example, the potential success of the new digital video disc developed by Hitachi, Philips, Sony and other partners depends critically on whether the studios will provide programs and movies on digital video disc (as a replacement for analogue tape VCRs). Relatedly, the success of a new product may be a function of what economists refer to as 'network externalities'. The notion is that a telephone is only of value if other people have telephones. In a sense, a VCR is only of value if other people have VCRs because only then will programs be made available.

Matsushita's success with VHS technology over Sony's Beta technology was a function of the alliance and licensing strategy which Matsushita pursued to make VHS the dominant standard while Sony went it alone. The question of whether Sony's Beta was a better technology was lost some place along the way.

Diversification. The final route to revitalization and growth is diversification. This is by far the riskiest strategy. Nevertheless, for certain companies at particular moments, this may be a necessary and logical strategy. If IBM, for example, had remained in its initial business – scales for weighing meat – it would not be one of the world's largest corporations today. Similarly, if IBM had not moved beyond mainframes for large corporate customers, it would be in rapid decline rather than stalled at its present turnover level.

Diversification, by which we mean entering new markets with new products, may occur based on acquisition or extension of the firm's existing resources and capabilities. The odds of success are 35 per cent if acquisition is pursued and 25 per cent if the firm extends on its own. In a 1987 study of acquisitions, Michael Porter (*see* 'Suggested further reading') found that firms subsequently divested over 50 per cent of their acquisitions in new industries and over 60 per cent in new fields.

Again it is the case that the range of success varies considerably. Although it is agreed that most acquisitions fail to meet expectations, the odds of success decline precipitously the further the firm strays from existing competencies. Kodak's foray into health care via its acquisition of Sterling Drug was far removed from its core business. By contrast, its move into digital imaging (while risky) may be a logical business decision, building on its commitment to picture-taking via whatever technology.

Acquisition has been criticised as sometimes stifling innovation. A company deploys its resources to take over an existing business rather than to pursue innovation. Yet, if driven by a vision of diversification, acquisition can be an innovative impetus for that company in pursuing new opportunities and moving in directions that might otherwise be blocked and which might have greater incremental potential than its existing business opportunities.

The way ahead

The restructuring and re-engineering movement of the past decade shows signs of abating. This phase in business history may have been necessary in rationalizing many major corp-orations that had grown bloated, especially at headquarters, and which had become overly rigid in their structures. Nevertheless, the gains in reducing costs, while important, do not provide a blueprint for the future.

The re-engineering concept must exist in tandem with revitalization and must show the means of growth and future opportunity. The growth portfolio that has been elaborated provides a way of considering growth options. The challenge is to pursue the right balance of objectives within the portfolio depending on market opportunities and challenges faced by each business unit and each product and brand, while considering the short-run and long-run advantages of pursuing today's customers with today's products versus tomorrow's customers with tomorrow's products.

An interesting question with which to confront managers is how to allocate the firm's resources to the four quadrants of growth. If we are looking at a 1996 resource commitment, what percentage should be devoted to each growth alternative? By making this decision process explicit, together with an assessment of the odds of success, an intriguing sense of the company's ambitions can be obtained.

Summary

Re-engineering must exist in tandem with revitalization if shareholders are to reap long-term rewards. The challenge, though, is to achieve the right balance of objectives. Ansoff's classic product/market matrix provides four options, each of which has a different probability of success. The four are market penetration (generating more turnover from existing markets, a strategy which is not static); market development (taking existing products into new markets, sometimes through 'bolt on' acquisitions); product launch (here the odds on success are higher for continuous innovations than for discontinuous ones, with alliances and research and development outsourcing also significant trends); and diversification (by far the riskiest strategy).

Managers have to decide how to allocate their company's resources to these four quadrants. They must consider the short-run and long-run advantages of pursuing today's customers with today's products against tomorrow's customers with tomorrow's products.

Suggested further reading

Adams, M. and La Cugna, J. 'And Now for Something Completely Different: – Really New Products'. Marketing Science Institute Cambridge: MA, Report Number 94-124, December 1994.

Houlder, V. 'Revolution in Outsourcing', the *Financial Times*, January 6, 1995, p.7.

Porter, Michael E. 'From competitive advantage to corporate strategy', *Harvard Business Review*, May-June 1987.

Heskett, James L., W. Earl Sasser, Jr. and Christopher, W. L. Hart (1990) *Service Breakthroughs*, The Free Press, New York.

Robertson, Thomas S. 'How to reduce market penetration cycle times', *Sloan Management Review*, Vol 35, Fall, 1993, 87-96.

Doughery, D. and Bowman, Edward H. 'The effects of organizational downsizing on product innovation', *California Management Review*, Vol. 37, Summer, 1995, 28-44.

Getting close to the customer

■ **Personal service is not easy in the mass market. One way to get close to customers, explain Jacques Horovitz and Nirmalya Kumar, is by identifying the benefits to which each segment of the customer base responds.**

One of the key marketing challenges facing companies today is how to make customers feel that they are unique, that they are truly special. As the CEO of a European company remarked: 'In the 1980s we looked for the customer in each individual. In the 1990s we must look for the individual in each customer.'

While the strategy of personalizing the

service/product for each customer, variously referred to as 'mass customization', 'segments of one', or 'relationship marketing' is seductive from a competitive perspective, it must be balanced against the capabilities and costs of providing such customer intimacy.

Some companies have made great strides in being able to serve small segments or even segments of one. For example, MCI in the US uses over 2,000 variables to understand the needs of each customer and design effective product promotion strategies to serve them.

Many US retailers track the transaction histories of their best customers and provide customers with gift certificates and additional services based on specified percentages of their total annual spending at the store. For example, customers at the upscale department store Nieman Marcus who spend $75,000 (£48,700) receive first-class airfare and accommodation for two to a choice of several events, including the Masters golf tournament and the Super Bowl.

Unlike airline frequent flyer programs, the most successful of these initiatives do not inform their customers in advance of the benefits they would receive but instead surprise them with unexpected gifts. The objective of these strategies is to get closer to the customer and engender loyalty. Blockbuster, the video rental chain, is reportedly trying to use its database of 36m customers and 2m daily rentals to implement a computerized system that recommends a list of ten movie titles based on the individual customer's rental history.

Although such customer intimacy is ideal, not all marketers can provide a unique service or product to every customer. Most companies simply do not have the capabilities to do so in a cost efficient manner. Furthermore, in many countries marketers must confront sensitive privacy issues as well as legal limitations with respect to exploiting customer data or transaction histories.

Companies that cannot or do not want to personalize service to the degree described above sometimes instead choose to work the 'averages'. Average service for the typical customer needs and expectations usually resulting in mediocre customer satisfaction and loyalty.

Is there another approach to address customer needs and expectations in a more personalized manner without in-depth knowledge of individual customers? Can it be possible for a service provider to offer an economical common core base available to all target customers and still adapt its service in a meaningful manner to different subgroups?

The answer is yes – through creative service benefit segmentation strategies. Such strategies are relevant to both service and manufacturing companies. Because of the adoption of advanced quality management techniques, manufacturing and/or product quality is a given in an increasing number of industries. It is a cost of entry rather than a differentiating factor forcing even manufacturing companies to look to service and support as the key distinguishing factors.

Creative service benefit segmentation

Usually, businesses resort to segmentation when they want to adapt their offer without jeopardizing economies of scale. It enables categorization of customers into homogeneous groups to more precisely target marketing efforts.

Most of the existing customer segmentation schemes that we have observed in industry tend to be based on demographic or psychographic variables that identify who the consumers are. Examples of such identifier variables are sex, age of the customer or lifestyle in consumer markets and size of the customer or industry group in business markets.

As an example, in catering it is usual to classify the market into four segments: in-company restaurants, schools, health institutions and prisons. We will refer to such segmentation schemes as market segmentation strategies. These market segmentation schemes describe who the customers are in each segment in the hope or the belief that the resulting segments seek different benefits.

Unfortunately, our experience indicates poor correlation between these market segments and the service benefits consumers seek. Thus when it comes to operationally serving each customer such market segmentation schemes are not very helpful.

For example, take the case of customers of

airport restaurants and bars. In one customer satisfaction study, we asked the management to provide us with a possible segmentation to draw customers for interviews. They gave us four: businessmen, tourists, local airport employees and groups.

This segmentation made some sense from a marketing point of view. Business people want a different menu (product) than groups. Price should be lower for frequent customers such as airport employees or high-volume customers such as groups. Promotion to groups is via travel agents and tour operators, and tourists will usually come earlier to the airport if they have a good image of the place.

On completion of the study, however, we discovered that there was in fact a common core service required by everyone using a bar or restaurant in an airport: a moment or an instant of relaxation. Everyone wanted to use the bar and restaurant as a means to avoid the crowd, reduce stress from going away, waiting for someone or working. But there were two segments based on service benefits that cut across all four market segments: 'in a hurry' and 'not in a hurry'.

It led our client to focus more – for everyone – on relaxation, separate the places from the crowd, find a place to put the luggage, reduce noise level, have a better view of flight departures/arrivals and create an atmosphere that helped reduce stress.

Then in order to achieve greater customer intimacy, barmen and waiters were trained specifically on how to observe those in a hurry in the bars (for example, if you serve a coffee and the person immediately takes money out of the pocket he or she is likely to be in a hurry). Alternatively, for a more elaborate restaurant, an express menu was offered as part of the offer. Those in a hurry would choose the items on the express menu. This service benefit segmentation, different from the market segments, helped the company personalize its service in a cost-effective manner.

How is it possible to obtain useful service benefit segments? Service segmentation starts, of course, with the customer. The process, through insightful qualitative analysis of customer needs, expectations, or insights from contact people and/or careful cluster analysis of customer satisfaction surveys, ultimately asks the following questions:

● Do all my customers have the same service needs and expectations?
● If not, can I regroup them into a few manageable clusters?
● Does it leave me with enough communality that I will have a basic common offer – as in the airport example above – or are the service benefit segments so distinct in needs and expectations that I have to offer different services to each segment?

Let's take the example of Midas. Midas operates within the overall segment of 'the fast mechanical repair' in the auto business as opposed to the 'guaranteed repair' still held mostly by authorized dealers or 'speciality repair' (such as electrics) offered by independent workshops or 'do it yourself repair' for the automobile enthusiast or 'heavy duty accidental repair' of body shops.

Within that segment, Midas offers repairs on brakes, silencers and exhaust-pipes with no appointment. Its main market segments are derived from three criteria: age of the car (the older the more likely they get the customer), size of the car (the bigger, the more product value and margins) and driver (women offer more potential for 'oversell').

From a service benefit viewpoint, none of the above criteria were applicable when we examined customer service expectations and satisfaction. It appears, in fact, that beyond fast repair there are two segments: the car lover and the utilitarian. Both want fast, reliable, no surprise one-time repair.

But in order to satisfy fully the car lover a number of additional services must be delivered. Focus the discussion on talking about the car, offer to check on other items, show tangible evidence of the work done (wash wheels when brakes have been changed), offer opportunities to look at the repair while the customer waits, provide old parts with packaging off the new ones to show parts have really been changed, call every six months/year to inform the customer that it is time for a check up, and so on.

For the utilitarian all of the above would be considered annoying. Talk about their life, give them a newspaper or a game to play with while they wait, offer to call a taxi or, better still, provide a replacement car. At the end of the repair reassure them that the little noise is gone, that the bill conforms with the estimate (no surprises) and that they can 'utilize' their car for X miles without any problems.

What this example demonstrates is that what achieving customer intimacy through service benefit segmentation requires above all is a 'customer orientation,' the ability to put yourself in the shoes of the different customer types and not to be hamstrung by the existing company viewpoint.

Once the segments are derived a further question needs to be considered: 'Is it economical to serve both the utilitarian and the car lover?' A quantitative check of the economics in this particular case revealed that about 50 per cent of customers fell in each segment, making it viable to serve both.

More specifically, for creative service benefit segmentation to be effective one must address the following three issues:

● Identification or how can we ascertain whether our next customer is a car lover or a utilitarian?
● Responsiveness or how can we train our service/contact personnel to adapt their sales and service strategies appropriately for the different segments?
● Affordability or can we provide different segments the service benefits they seek and still make money?

Identifying who belongs to which segment

In contrast to market segmentation schemes that rely on demographic variables (for example, males versus females), it is relatively difficult to identify which customers belong to which service benefit segment. Three main techniques can help identify which segment a customer belongs to and, therefore, the appropriate service level that customer should receive.

The most systematic, fool-proof system is to have customers self-select what level of service they want by having a very clear differentiated

offer. For example, Hear Music, a record and CD music chain in California, does just that. In a study of this industry we noticed that there were four service segments.

1. The 'passive consumer' interested only in quickly finding the top hits.
2. The 'eclectic' who has wide tastes – a little bit of jazz and classical, some house or hard rock to show the children he or she is not too old. Because eclectics do not specialize they need advice to help make their selections.
3. 'The specialist', on the other hand, knows more than the sales people about their selections.
4. And finally, 'the collector', who is looking for the masterpieces.

These four segments represent 30 per cent, 29 per cent, 25 per cent and 16 per cent respectively of the market.

Most music shops sell to everybody and it is often difficult to find your way through them. In fact, sales people, often recruited on the basis of their knowledge of music, spend their time either telling the customer where to find the latest hits or retreat into lengthy discussions with the specialist to share their common rave for the latest funk or rap release. In this maze, the 'eclectics' cannot find their way or advise easily.

Hear Music decided to cater solely to this segment. In a very elaborate wood decorated shop they have made a selection and in front of each selection they say what it is and why they chose it. You will neither find the top hits nor the funk. But the yuppie turned pappy (the wealthiest market!) can come out of the store content and with a full load of music he would never have dared to buy elsewhere.

Alternatively, if multiple service benefit segments (for example, the car lover and the utilitarian in the Midas case) are to be served in the same premises then it is sometimes possible to have customers self-select through innovative service design. For example, there are two kinds of customers who go to a toy store: those who have children and want to add to the collection and those who do not have children (at least of comparable age) but have been invited to a family with children and thought it would be wise to bring a present.

The biggest hurdle in a toy store for the

second group is sheer fright. So many toys. What am I going to choose? Where to go in the store? How do I know it is 'in'? Where is the boys section?

FAO Schwarts has smartly picked up this fright and transformed it into an opportunity. If you are just visiting friends who have children, as soon as you enter the store, there is a door on the left to a smaller, isolated area. There are about 20 toys – ten for girls and ten for boys, displayed on a shelf. You just have to point your finger and within 30 seconds the pre-wrapped present will be given to you. You pay to a cashier at a special counter right there and in less than two minutes you are out. Here the service provider has decided to cater to two segments with very different service needs under the same roof by merely separating the offer.

The second way, a little bit less systematic, involves asking questions. Let us take the example of insurance. A study has showed that people who bought insurance could fit into three categories: 'administrators,' 'pragmatics' and 'smoothes'. Administrators take their lawyers. Pragmatics want to hear the benefits, how much they need to pay and sign at the bottom of a prefilled document. The Smoothes will want to get a sense of what it would do for them and their family, discuss issues of who will get what and who needs to do what and possible consequences on the life of the beloved ones.

It is difficult to identify who is who without the insurance sales person asking a few questions in order to identify the service necessary to help the customer buy and sign a contract. In this case through probing and competent questioning, service providers will be able to personalize service and achieve customer intimacy.

At Club Med travel agencies a flyer called the 'keys to happiness' is given to all potential customers. By answering six questions on this flyer it can be determined what is the best type of vacation for them.

The third possibility consists of guestimating which segment a particular customer belongs to by observing behavior or through external 'clues'. If a customer drives into a garage with a very clean, orderly car, the chances are he is a car lover whereas if it is dirty or untidy he is probably a utilitarian.

In another example, there are two kinds of service benefit segments in the optical business. Those who wear glasses for the first time and those who need to change glasses because their sight has changed.

From a service viewpoint, their expectations are very different. The first timer is scared, does not know what to choose, feels he is sick and needs reassurance that he does not look ugly when wearing spectacles. On the other hand, repeaters are more at ease, know their requirements and so on. A customer who looks lost in an optical store in the face of all these choices and has no glasses on is probably a 'first timer'.

In summary, once service segments have been identified, the company must choose how it will classify a particular customer into the segments in order to adjust the service provided:

● Through systematic partition and signage so that the customer self-selects where he or she belongs.
● Through interactions with the contact person.
● Through observation of clues.

Of course, the more systematic the method, the better it is in terms of cost and fewer errors. However, the more complex and multi-dimensional segments are, the more it will require human intervention, which in turn leads us to the next aspect of service benefit segmentation: training service/contact people to respond appropriately.

Responding to segments through training of service personnel

Classical sales training teaches a good sales person to begin by asking questions to help uncover the needs of the customer and then construct a proposal to meet these expressed needs. However, consider the following service benefit segments often found in industry.

Buyers usually fall into three categories: 'order givers', 'delegators' and 'partners'. The order giver usually specifies what he or she wants, when they want it and asks for a price quotation and a delivery date. Any questioning by the salesman to 'uncover' needs will be merely considered a waste of time and energy – just tell me how much and by when.

On the other hand, the delegator has called you because he feels you are the specialist. If you can ask him what he wants, he will probably think you are incompetent.

The partner is the one who wants openly to discuss issues and bounce back ideas. He does not mind if the salesperson does not have preconceived ideas. On the contrary, he feels it helps. A major international insurance company has identified that selling insurance to corporations requires service benefit segmentation. Three service segments were identified.

1. The 'orderly' is very keen on having a full process before deciding on an insurance policy. He or she needs to see all contracts, take time before deciding and have several meetings to discuss issues. After sales service will include updates on where he stands.

2. The 'humanist' is more interested to know about what the insurance will do to people. He will want to involve employees in the decision making and have a clear picture of the advantage of that insurance on people and social policies.

3. The 'entrepreneur' wants fast decision making, time-saving devices such as pre-study done by the insurance company and papers already filled. He or she only wants to sign, he already knows his costs and risks.

This has led to an in-depth training of sales people to recognize through questions and observations who is who and to adapt their language, arguments, proposals and follow up to the different types of customers.

Affordability of serving different segments

The costs of serving different segments may vary considerably. It is necessary to examine whether the customers in a segment are bearing the costs of the services that they demand. If some service benefit segments cost more to serve than the price realized from them, then we may have either to persuade them to increase their revenue or, failing that, perhaps encourage them to leave.

Consider the supermarket industry. An industry study classified customers in terms of their average bill. The study found that the bottom 10 per cent of supermarket customers have an average bill of less than $10. Based on activity-based accounting it was discovered that supermarkets actually lose money on these customers.

In contrast, the top 10 per cent of customers have an average bill of around $50 and are very profitable for supermarkets. Unfortunately, through express checkout lanes most supermarkets give greater service (less waiting time) to the first group.

Realizing that the profitability of a transaction is closely related to the average bill, Food Lion, a supermarket chain in the US, has a program to encourage customers to increase their purchase per visit. Each week a set of items is put on sale and the percentage of discount that an individual customer receives on these items is based on the dollar value of their total purchases on that shopping trip.

A similar activity-based accounting study in the personal banking industry demonstrated that each time a customer comes in to see a bank teller, it costs the bank slightly more than $3 to serve the customer. In contrast, if the customer conducts their transaction through the ATM (automated teller machine) the cost is only about 25 cents. Well, the solution is then rather obvious. Customers with limited bank balances should be charged the difference ($3) for every transaction they conduct using bank tellers. This will encourage them either to use the ATMs or defect to competing banks who will then have to serve these unprofitable customers.

By the way, the people who pay more do not always need more service. In a study we did for Eurostar – the under-Channel train between London and Paris – we found three service segments: businessmen who just want to be left alone to work; families who want something for their children to do; and the 'travellers', people who want to visit France or the UK.

Those who need most interactions with the train personnel are the travellers – they want tips on where to stay, how to change trains and so on. Intuitively, we would put more personnel in first class, where businessmen are. But they do not need it – lots of newspapers and magazines are more appreciated. A good saving!

Conclusion

When personalization of service is not possible, it is still possible to develop customer intimacy through creative service benefit segmentation strategies. Such a process starts by looking at what customers expect, hear and see, whether they have common needs as well as different ones. This is not necessarily the same as classical market segmentation but may be of greater operational assistance in adapting to customers.

Once it is done either the company decides to create different service concepts for each segment or to serve a common core service and only adapt mildly to cater for differences. If the latter strategy is used, we need to use either self-selection (let the customer choose the appropriate service level) or direct observation of his or her attitudes and behavior or active questioning to identify which segment the customer in front of us belongs to. In addition, the staff have to be trained to identify and then adapt their sales/service strategy. Finally, the costs of serving the different segments must be estimated to ensure that the differentiated strategy is affordable.

The pay-offs of such a strategy are clear: more customized benefits-oriented service at a reasonable cost. The pay-offs are often best seen at the sales level. Studies show that between 20 per cent and 40 per cent of customer dissatisfaction with service comes from the fact they were misled when buying. The other pay-off, of course, is better customer retention and positive word of mouth because every customer feels treated well.

This approach is very valid when the sheer mass of customers does not make it possible really to know every individual and/or where the sheer number of service points and staff involved – especially in services with high turnover – make it unrealistic to make every employee passionate for every customer.

Such well known companies as Disney, Peugeot, Club Med, Haagen Dazs, Sachs, Axa among others have developed this approach with success while selling their service, delivering it/or transforming angry customers into ambassadors. It simply requires a little bit of imagination and insight into customer needs and expectations.

Summary

Although 'customer intimacy' is the ideal, not all marketers can provide a unique service or product to every customer. One way in which companies can adapt their offering to different sub-groups is to adopt what is known as a creative service benefit segmentation strategy. This can be done without jeopardizing economies of scale. Three issues must be addressed: the identification of different types of customer, the training of service/contact personnel so they can respond to the different segments, and the financial benefits. Customer categories can be filled by self-selection (customers choosing themselves) and direct observation of attitudes and habits. Buyers usually fall into three types – order givers, delegators and partners – which require a different response. It is important to make sure that customers are bearing the costs of the services they demand – for example activity based accounting has shown that supermarket chains lose money on customers with small average bills and yet through express checkout lanes they often give greater service to this group.

How to learn about markets

■ **A company's ability to learn may be its only sustainable advantage. But learning must be used to a purpose, says George Day**

Why do firms lose touch with their markets? Why are they surprised by shifts in customer requirements, slow to react to emerging competitors or unprepared to use innovative market channels? Without an effective ability to anticipate market directions, some firms continually miss opportunities, and when they do respond, their reactions are likely to be slow and ill-advised, or counter-productive.

In contrast, market-driven firms stand out in their ability continuously to sense and act on events and trends in their markets. They are better equipped to anticipate how their markets will respond to actions designed to retain or attract customers, improve channel relations or thwart competitors.

How do these companies develop and maintain the ability to keep learning about markets?

Actually, market learning involves much more than simply taking in information. The learning process must give managers the ability to ask the right questions at the right time, absorb the answers into their mental model of how the market behaves, share the new understanding with others in the management team and then act decisively.

Effective learning about markets is a continuous process that pervades all decisions. It cannot be spasmodic – as a large telecommunications equipment company concluded when it reviewed the failure of a major development project.

In reviewing the project failure, the evaluators carefully mapped a sequence of activities and decisions that stretched over four years. There was collective surprise when they realized there had been only one formal market study. The study was done at an early stage in the project. Thereafter, the team had become enmeshed in technical development, prototype testing, and regulatory and budget approval activities.

As time passed and the product concept evolved, the conclusions of that early market study became out-dated, but the development team made no visits to customers and did not test their assumptions about customer needs and trade-offs. Competitive activity was monitored but only to check on technical performance.

Having lost touch with the market early in the project, it was no surprise the team did not anticipate the emerging networking requirements of customers, which their project could not satisfy.

Further learning occurs within companies when the outcomes of an action are systematically evaluated: errors are detected, judgments confirmed or challenged, and information gaps identified. These insights go to augment the organizational memory and trigger further inquiries. (*see* Figure 1)

Competitors of a market-driven company such as Frito-Lay can acquire the same scanner data, adopt the hand-held computers the salesforce uses to enter store data and create a network for distributing the data – but it will not be nearly so easy to duplicate the wealth of experience built into the design of the organization, the training of the people, and the innovative, user-friendly analysis tools that are used to extract and communicate the meaning in Frito-Lay's market data.

Effective market learning

Effective learning processes in market-driven firms are distinguished by several characteristics:

● *Open-minded inquiry* – based on a belief that

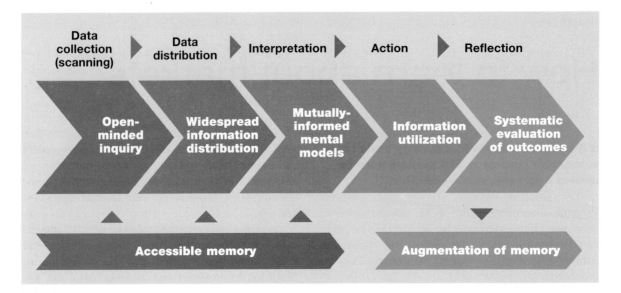

Figure 1: Market-driven processes for learning about markets

decisions are made from the market back to the company

● *Widespread information distribution* – to assure that relevant facts are available when needed

● *Mutually informed mental models* – that guide interpretation and ensure that everyone pays attention to the essence and potential of the information

● *An accessible organization memory* – to help the organization keep track of and build on what has been learned, so the knowledge can continue to be used.

Open-minded inquiry

Throughout a successful market learning organization, there is an openness to trends and events that present market opportunities.

Five basic elements combine to open the collective 'mind' to new information that can help anticipate emerging needs, and more accurately forecast how markets are responding, or may respond to changes in competitive strategy:

● Scanning with peripheral vision

● Buying 'decision insurance' (rather than conducting market research simply to confirm decisions or satisfy curiosity)

● Activating the sensors at the point of customer contact

● Learning from others (by benchmarking that goes beyond the obvious)

● Continuous learning.

It is particularly important to scan for developments that may be occurring outside the mainstream of market activity or in narrow niches that may erupt into dominant market applications in the future. This process needs directly and continuously to tap customers.

Continuous benchmarking that 'goes beyond the obvious' is the basis for the Japanese mastery of 'informed innovation'. It involves thoughtful examination and research probes to understand why a pioneer or competitor has succeeded and to identify deficiencies as a basis for introducing a superior product or developing a competitive edge in process or strategy.

This benchmarking should be internal as well as external. Companies such as Xerox often use the outcomes of benchmarking studies to shake-up complacent manufacturing and service groups with the news they are slipping behind.

Information distribution

Most organizations do not know what they know. They may have good systems for storing and locating 'hard' routine accounting and sales data but otherwise have problems finding where a certain piece of information is known within the organization or assembling all the needed pieces in one place.

The enemies of information distribution are the organizational chimneys or silos that constrain information flow vertically within functions. But transmitting and receiving information based on company-wide standards in systems, languages, protocols and file management procedures facilitate linkages and associations among different kinds of information, such as customer transaction records and production data, in the search for new insights.

When IBM recently suffered a serious constriction in the distribution of competitive information, it was able to utilize its own technology to unblock the flow.

At the peak of confusion there were 49 departments in 27 organizations each studying the same competitors. Literally hundreds of people were analysing the data but they seldom knew what others were doing or shared their conclusions with others. The impediments were local databases and files and locally restricted delivery vehicles and newsletters.

The information and interpretations could have been widely useful if they could have been found. Yet there were few incentives to surmount the systems barriers and integrate the knowledge. Excuses ranged from 'it's too secret to put in a database' to 'we don't have the time to be contacted by everyone in the corporation for the details' to 'my database is better and serves a different purpose.'

A top-down intervention was needed to create a common world-wide competitor analysis system of 'players' and 'searchers'.

The players compiled and entered the data into an integrated database containing full text or abstracts on more than 1.2m items from internal sources, vendors and publishers.

The searchers in marketing, development and research could access all this information through a network and database search engine that could easily extract data in response to specific inquiries.

The payoff from this system investment was considerable. First, the analysis of competitors was improved, with the ability to identify and cross-validate patterns of behavior across different countries and functions.

Second, the squeezing out of redundancy and duplicated effort meant more analyses could be undertaken with the same headcount. This was important for an organization trying to keep track of 5,000 competitors. Third, there were fewer surprises, since news of anticipated competitive moves was broadcast more widely and field people could be alerted more readily.

Keeping the information flow moving within the company is the key to keeping the ideas flowing. Companies with a superior kind of match between external collection and internal distribution of market information are better able to anticipate and respond to market trends. Decision makers are better informed. Innovations in products, processes and strategies are detected earlier; and the organization encounters fewer surprises in the competitive marketplace.

Mutually informed models

Before organizations can use the information they have collected, they must classify, sort and simplify it into coherent patterns. This is the role of mental models that affect both the information the organization seeks and selects during the inquiry stage, as well as the lessons they extract about appropriate actions.

These mental models help organizations in several ways. By imposing order on ambiguous, multidimensional and fine-grained market environments, they reduce uncertainty. They also help ensure that the organization pays attention to the essence and potential of the information rather than being deflected or inhibited by narrow assumptions of what is important or how the market should be defined.

Mental models of markets are pervasive and influential, but because they are often unexamined they can be misleading. The dangers of myopic interpretations became apparent during a recent planning session at Multiplex Corporation, a large global manufacturer of industrial material.

The main issue was a disturbing pattern of evolution of many of the markets it had pioneered.

Early in the life cycle of these markets, when

growth came by displacing other materials, the customers were relatively insensitive to premium prices. As the market matured, and competition intensified, large segments of the market were unwilling to pay a premium for the extra value Multiplex offered. This was a well-known and seemingly well-understood phenomenon, whose implications had painted Multiplex into a difficult corner.

The company's prevailing strategy was to hold price and retreat to the remaining segments of buyers still willing to pay a premium for superior value. Management recognised that this conceded an expanding territory to more recent commodity entrants who were able to parlay increased capacity utilization into ever lower costs.

Meanwhile, as the high end of the market continued to shrink, Multiplex faced sagging capacity utilization and rising unit costs, which further disadvantaged it in the growing commodity segments.

Because this strategic track was so unappealing, Multiplex management decided to challenge the premises they were following. After reflection, it appeared that the premises were derived from three mental models of the operation of markets. These models dealt with the attractiveness of the low end of their markets, the process of market saturation and the ways that customers exercised bargaining power.

Each of these mental models was well accepted in practice, widely communicated in planning documents and planning meetings, and potentially misleading.

In combination, they contributed to myopic decisions, sometimes triggered a self-fulfilling prophecy that accentuated the problem and foreclosed the consideration of other strategic options. Only when the functioning of these mental models was compared across several markets was their influence appreciated.

Organization memory

Market-driven inquiry and interpretation will be for naught if the lessons of experience do not lodge in the collective memory of the organization.

Organizations without practical mechanisms to 'remember' what worked and why have to repeat their failures and rediscover their success formulas over and over again.

Memory mechanisms are needed to ensure that useful lessons are captured, conserved and can be readily retrieved when needed.

The most familiar memory-repositories are institutional policies, procedures and rules. Companies are increasingly using information technology to create integrated databases with expert systems and decision calculus models embedded in them to enrich and maintain the collective memory. These technology fixes will only provide lasting aids to memory if supported by organizational processes that promote team learning and avoid the purging of memory through turnovers and transfers.

Ray Stata, chairman of Analog Devices, believes the ability of an organization to learn may be its only sustainable advantage.

The purpose of the learning is to help managers continuously anticipate market opportunities and respond before their competitors. It is not enough to be able to describe the current state of the market in exquisite detail and precisely calibrate a company's position relative to competitors.

Good managers must also use that knowledge to think through how the market will respond to actions designed to retain or capture customers and thwart competitors. Whether they succeed depends on the quality of the information uncovered during the inquiry state, the way their mental models color their thinking and the availability of market insights at the point of decision.

Big questions for the 21st century

■ **Many of the requirements for marketing success in the next century are already apparent and being practiced. Here Jerry Wind outlines 12 factors that together will be critical.**

Marketing, as a management function, appears to be in decline. Marketing as a management philosophy and orientation, espoused and practiced throughout the corporation, is however seen increasingly as critical to the success of any organization.

This is reflected in a heightened emphasis on being 'close to the customer', stressing customer satisfaction and customer relationship-building, understanding customer value and the enhanced product offering, and the brand equity represented in a loyal customer base.

Increasingly, these are the domains and responsibilities of employees throughout the organization, whether it is customer service, sales, manufacturing, R&D or top management, and not just of 'the marketing staff'.

This emphasis on marketing as a pan-organizational perspective, especially when combined with global organizations that are going through significant restructuring and are subject to the impact of rapidly expanding information technology, has critical implications for the organization's visions, objectives, strategies, the required organizational architecture and the competencies a company must seek in hiring and developing its employees.

The importance of marketing as a driving business philosophy has long been recognized by thoughtful business philosophers such as Peter Drucker. Yet it took the dramatic changes in the business environment that have led to the creation of new management paradigms and their associated corporate reinvention to focus the attention on marketing as a business philosophy and the need to rethink the role of the marketing function.

Some of the changes that are likely to be required in the marketing area by reinvented 21st century enterprises have already been initiated by some of the more progressive US companies. Yet, even these have still a long way to go in fully incorporating these changes.

In considering these required changes and their implications, management may want to consider 12 interrelated questions.

1. Is marketing and its focus on meeting and anticipating customer needs widely accepted as a key business philosophy?

This implies also a 'yes' to questions such as:
● Does your new product development process include joint development with customers?
● Do members of the organization view themselves either as 'internal customers' or as serving 'internal customers'?
● Do the business strategies focus on target segments and assure that the products and services are geared toward the satisfaction of the segment needs?

2. Are your business and corporate strategies focussed on creating value to all your stakeholders?

This is an expanded focus from the customer to all stakeholders including employees, suppliers, distributors, shareholders and others. It also stresses the importance of value creation as the driver of the marketing and marketing-driven business strategies of the organization.

3. Do your objectives include customer satisfaction and the creation of value?

This implies that the objective of the company should not be limited to profit, sales and market share but also include measures of the value the company creates for its customers – better informed customers, improved quality of life, earlier adoption of beneficial products and so on. This recognizes the importance of time as an objective that can stimulate strategies for shorter new product development cycles and faster market penetration.

4. Is the marketing function integrated with the other functions of the company as part of key value-creating processes?

This requires breaking the isolation of the marketing function and assuring its integration with the other key functions of the organization. A 'yes' answer also implies that the organization is cross-functional and organized around key processes.

5. Are the key marketing positions market segment (or key accounts) managers?

The shift is from product management to market or to product by market segment or to account management. This shift assures a market focus and the development of strategies for each market segment.

6. Are products viewed as part of an integrated product and service offering that delivers the desired benefit positioning for the target segment?

This shift, which is already accepted by many companies, is key in recognizing the importance of:
● an integrated product and service offering, not just the product.
● positioning based on benefits sought or problems solved, not feature positioning
● target market segments, not mass market

7. Is your marketing strategy global in its scope?

Given the increased globalization of consumer and resource markets, it is critical that a company develop global marketing strategies. This does not imply that the company has to export to all countries nor that it has a standardized global brand. Rather, it must consider the world as the arena of operations and develop a portfolio of products by market segments by countries by mode of entry – a portfolio that may include global as well as regional and local brands.

8. Are you utilizing market research and modeling for generating and evaluating your marketing and marketing driven business strategies?

And are you capitalizing on the opportunities offered by decision-support systems that incorporate database marketing and expert systems? This recognizes the enormous potential marketing science tools have for improved marketing and business decisions once taken beyond that current narrow focus on brand-level decisions.

Broad utilization of the advances in marketing sciences are also critical for the creation of a learning organization based on continuous measurement and forecast of market needs and market response to the activities of the company and its competitors.

9. Are you relying on information technology as an integral part of your marketing strategies?

The enormous advances in information technology offer unique opportunities to expand the scope of marketing strategies. Innovative approaches for capturing clients via information technology, such as those of American Hospital Supply and the many frequent flyer and frequent buyer programs as well as the electronic link between suppliers and retailers such as Procter & Gamble and Wal-Mart, are changing the nature of marketing strategies.

These changes, and the associated changes in database marketing and mass customization (as reflected in customized bicycles or jeans), allow an economical focus on segments of one.

10. Does a significant part of your marketing efforts constitute innovative practices not previously used by you and your competitors?

This focus on innovation in marketing practice is critical. Whereas an increasing number of companies stress the importance of product innovation (3M, for example, has an objective of at least 30 per cent of revenue from new products introduced in the last four years), it is increasingly important to focus on innovation in marketing practices.

This is specifically critical in the global information age when technology offers an increasing number of opportunities for innovation in distribution and marketing practices.

11. Are you forming strategic alliances for co-marketing activities and are you building your marketing strategies on the development of long-term relationships with your clients?

The increasingly complex world often requires critical success factors not possessed by a company. Strategic alliances offer options that enhance and leverage an organization's capabilities. It also recognises the shift from transaction-oriented client interface to a long-term relationship.

12. Are you focusing your attention and resources on message effectiveness (instead of media power) and value-based pricing (instead of discounting)?

This suggests a fundamental shift to playing smarter. It is not marketing muscle that is going to win but marketing sophistication – careful and creative targeting of messages and offerings to the needs of targeted customers.

To assure success in the 21st Century, it is not enough to answer yes to the 12 questions above. It is critical to assure the effective inter-relationship among the questions and that the corporate vision objectives and strategies reflect a marketing orientation.

Furthermore, the entire organizational architecture (culture, structure, processes, technology, resources, people, and performance measures and incentives) should be geared toward implementing the new marketing paradigm. A paradigm that while building on the historical foundations of marketing as the boundary role linking the organization to its environment is changing to focus on these 12 factors and their implications for marketing as:

● The leading business philosophy

● The knowledge and wisdom center of the company that provides all organizational members with concepts and findings about customers and tools for measuring and forecasting customer behavior and models and decision-support systems for improving the quality of marketing and business decisions

● The growth engine that through creative marketing strategies that utilize technology and mobilise the other business functions of the company stimulates the top-line growth of the company.

Summary

Marketing as a narrow management function may be in decline, but as a philosophy of the whole organization it is increasingly seen as critical to success. Among issues which need to be addressed are the importance of value creation for the customer, the integration of marketing with other functions of the organization, the division of marketing respon-sibilities, the challenge of globalization, the potential of new marketing science tools, the use of information technology, the need for innovative practices not tried by competitors, the opportunity of global alliances and long term client relationships, and the shift away from sheer media power as a winning strategy to message effectiveness.

Organizational Behavior

Contents

Deep roots and far from a 'soft' option 217
Jack Denfeld Wood, IMD
What makes organizational behaviour important?

What do new systems demand of employees? 224
Peter Cappelli and Nikolia Rogovsky, The Wharton School of the University of Pennsylvania
The impact of 'lean production' and other new systems of organizing work may be aimed at improving productivity – but what are the effects on employees?

The personality factor 229
Nigel Nicholson, London Business School
Personality is a key factor in work performance and one that science is now beginning to understand – and measure – more completely. The five main dimensions of personality and ways personality can be assessed.

Dealing with the attitude problem 235
Peter Cappelli, The Wharton School of the University of Pennsylvania
It has been argued that poor worker performance is based on poor educational achievement. But it may be even more a a result of poor attitudes to work.

Cultural diversity 240
Rob Goffee, London Business School
The growing diversity of our societies, the growth of cultural awareness among ethnic groups and the rise of the global corporation are making cultural diversity a hot issue.

Contributors

Jack Denfeld Wood is Professor of Organizational Behavior at IMD, Lausanne. His research interests are analytical psychology, leadership and teams, social structure and change, and culture and ideology.

Nigel Nicholson is Professor of Organizational Behavior at London Business School. His research interests include organizational change, and the role of culture, structure, strategy and values, personality and risk taking in business.

Nikolai Rogovsky is a PhD candidate at the Wharton School of the University of Pennsylvania.

Rob Goffee is Professor of Organizational Behavior at London Business School. His research interests include the dynamics of business start-up and growth, corporate culture and management development.

Peter Cappelli is Professor of Management at the Wharton School of the University of Pennsylvania, Chairman of the Management Department, Co-Director of Wharton's Center for Human Resources, and also Co-Director of the US Department of Education's National Center on the Educational Quality of the Workforce.

Introduction

Organizational Behavior is one of the most complex and perhaps least understood academic elements of modern general management, but since it concerns the behavior of people within organizations it is also one of the most central.

As an academic management discipline it is relatively new and draws heavily on theoretical models from a number of non-management areas, most notably sociology and psychology. As such, it is often regarded as one of the 'softer' areas of study. However, its concern with individual and group patterns of behaviour make it an essential element in dealing with the complex behavioral issues thrown up in the modern business world.

The module begins with an overview and introduction to the subject. Other subjects covered include organization–employee relations and stresses, personality, employee attitudes and cultural diversity.

Related topics are covered in a number of other modules: 6: Human Resource Management; 8: Managing People in Organizations; 11: Business Ethics; 13: Managing Across Cultures; and 16: Leadership Skills.

Deep roots and far from a 'soft' option

■ This área is something of an odd man out in business academia. But it can be argued that in its concern for the way people behave in an organizational context, it is key to the whole area of management, writes Jack Wood

Things used to be simpler. The teaching focus for schools of business administration was on the activities that any business organization had to do reasonably well to survive. The core curriculum at the earliest schools included required courses in marketing, production, finance, and accounting. Courses in 'organizational behavior' did not exist. In fact, organizational behavior did not exist. It had to be invented.

As the French would have it, organizational behavior is largely an Anglo-Saxon (read: Anglo-American) invention. Introductory organizational behavior textbooks give one the impression that organizational behavior is an academic discipline that has been around for a long time. This is not true. Organizational behavior (OB) is a relatively recent arrival; as an area of study, it was not born until the early 1960s. It has only in the last decade begun to make its way into the curricula of continental European universities via management education; yet organizational behavior is substantively different from other business school areas. It is not confined to the narrow bounds of any one business function.

The roots of organizational behavior reach deeply into the established academic disciplines, although it is not, strictly speaking, an academic discipline itself; it is a loosely related set of theories, methods and topics drawn from a wide variety of independent thought and research in the social and natural sciences, the humanities and the arts.

The areas of business activity covered by aspects of organizational behavior are broad, and range from discussing remuneration with an employee (understanding individual motivation), to running a meeting (understanding group dynamics), launching an international sales and marketing campaign (understanding cultural differences), or discussing a mutually beneficial joint-venture or merger (understanding the multi-dimensional nature of negotiation).

At its best, OB penetrates beneath the cultural myopia and conventional wisdom characteristic of our individual and collective behavior. At its worst, it simply apes the current management fad, or submissively serves as an apologist for entrenched social, political or economic interests.

Is the study of behavior in organizations important? I think it is vital. What the social sciences, humanities and the arts are to a university education, OB is to a business school education. The more technical a manager's training, the more important organizational behavior becomes. It is arguably the one area that can carry the burden of bringing the collective wisdom of human history into the decision-making calculus of developing managers. And this is no trivial task.

Historical perspective

The following is an introduction to the origins of OB, an outline of the breadth of its contemporary subject matter and the presentation of a framework that may be helpful in approaching the complex and confusing reality of human behavior within organizations. Where and how did organizational behavior as a discrete area of study originate? This is not a simple tale.

The late Harvard professor, Fritz Roethlisberger appears to have been the midwife of the term organizational behavior. After enduring some years of doctoral work in philosophy, and while informally counselling distressed undergraduates, Roethlisberger abandoned his thesis and began a chance collaboration with Professor Elton Mayo.

Mayo had arrived at Harvard on a Rockefeller grant and was reviewing some AT&T research that was already under way in its Western Electric division's manufacturing plant in Hawthorne, Illinois. The research had been rationally designed to explore issues such as worker productivity, but the findings were astonishingly inconsistent with the rational predictions; the workers did not behave as planned. These landmark 'Hawthorne' studies were among the first to identify the importance of informal social relations and apparently irrational behavior in organizations. Under Mayo's tutelage, Roethlisberger began to explore business organizations as 'social systems' by using the 'clinical' observations and the interview skills he had developed in his counselling days.

Business schools in the 1930s and early-1940s trained 'administrators'. The required courses reflected the significant business activities and included courses in production, marketing, finance, and control (accounting).

These were not drawn from any academic disciplines; they were primarily functional courses reflecting the functional realities faced by typical business organizations in day-to-day operation. The focus was pragmatic, and somewhat a-theoretical. The topic of human behavior, of course, arose during class discussions of finance, production and so on, but behavior was considered to be of secondary importance; it operated in the background, in the shadows, and was seldom very deeply understood or explored when it was addressed.

Following the Second World War, the intellectual climate at US universities was bubbling with innovation. Across the river from the business school at Harvard University, an interdisciplinary group of creative thinkers in social anthropology, sociology, and clinical and social psychology were forming the novel department of Social Relations. Roethlisberger felt strongly that a broader and more serious look at behavior was missing from the business curriculum, too, and in 1947 he helped introduce a new 'Administrative Practices' course – the first required 'people course' at the school.

The following year, discouraged by the political infighting between two faculty subgroups – those with a strong institutional business school loyalty and a generalist's inclination, and those with a strong disciplinary loyalty and a more rigorous scientific inclination, Roethlisberger withdrew from teaching in the Administrative Practices course and began a second-year elective titled Human Relations, where he had a freer hand to innovate.

He had by then assumed the informal leadership of the 'Mayo group' a small collection of business school faculty, mostly junior, who shared an interest in behavior. If Administrative Practices had been the 'grandfather' of the first organizational behavior course, then Human Relations was to be the father. But not without some pain.

'Touchy-feely' human relations

In the 1950s, 'human relations' was getting a bad name in the US, both within and outside academia. Critics in various quarters said human relations lacked rigour, was too soft and muddle-headed, was too trendy and was degenerating into what might be called a 'touchy-feely' California encounter-group ethos. Many of the critics were unfamiliar with human relations training as it was being developed at the National Training Laboratories (NTL) in the US and at the Tavistock Institute in London, but vociferous criticism has rarely been dependent on intimate knowledge or understanding of the matter at hand. This is particular true of behavioral topics.

Between 1956 and 1958, in an attempt to reduce the contentiousness surrounding the term human relations, Roethlisberger began informally using the phrase 'organizational behavior' in meetings and conversations. Organizational behavior began as a euphemism.

Politically, Roethlisberger hoped the term would be less inflammatory to non-behaviorally oriented colleagues and other 'tough-minded' critics. Substantively, he felt the term broad enough to include the study of people throughout an organizational system. Roethlisberger had become increasingly uneasy with the practice of looking at an organization only through the eyes of the managers, or even worse, only through the eyes of the chief executive officer. He believed that the term organizational behavior encompassed both a humanistic and a scientific orientation and direction. His faculty critics, predictably, tended to dismiss organizational behavior as merely old wine in new bottles. Nevertheless, in 1957, under Roethlisberger's guidance, OB earned an official, if grudging, existence among Harvard's business school faculty as one of the special fields in the new doctoral program. Subsequently, two reports published in 1959 by the Ford and Carnegie foundations criticized business schools for being too focussed on the traditional functional areas, and teaching too many courses, too narrowly and too superficially. Both reports recommended the introduction of required courses including organization and human relations. Due in part to pressure resulting from the reports, Harvard's business school faculty finally reorganized themselves in 1962 into the ten 'areas' already represented in the doctoral program; OB was one of these areas and Roethlisberger became the first area head and remained so until 1964.

The questions that had troubled Roethlisberger throughout his university tenure – questions about the scope of the 'knowledge and skills' needed to manage well, the definition of an academic field, the nature of the research endeavor and acceptable methods of inquiry – were not settled with the advent of OB as a faculty area at Harvard, its subsequent recognition as a distinct area of the American Academy of Management, or its inclusion as a department at European business schools.

Faculty in the OB field, unlike faculty operating within the traditional social science disciplines, have never had a consensus about such things as what constitutes acceptable research. Perhaps they never can develop such a consensus, because organizational behavior is in large part a non-business area among the business areas, and not one behavioral science discipline among other academic disciplines.

Organizational behavior today

Management textbooks frequently state as fact that organizational behavior is an inter-disciplinary field. It is not. It is in no way inter-disciplinary; multi-disciplinary perhaps, but not inter-disciplinary. OB is not a coherent field. It is a general area that encompasses thinking and research from numerous disciplines and sub-disciplines. It draws its material from psychology, sociology, anthropology, economics, the arts and humanities, law and medicine. Organizational behavior is in reality a hodge-podge of various subjects; a collection of loosely related or even unrelated streams of scholarly and not-so scholarly research. It is neither a discipline, nor is it a business function. And that makes it an anomalous area of management study.

Organizational behavior is not a business function like marketing, finance, accounting or production. The business function concerned with 'people' is personnel (or human resources management, HRM, if one prefers). Both OB and personnel/human resource management are concerned with 'people' but not in the same way. Personnel and HRM concern themselves with the design, implementation and administration of systems for the management and control of the people within an organization.

The occupation of the personnel or HRM specialist is with the functional aspects of employment, for example, hiring, firing, pay and benefits schemes, performance appraisal systems, promotions, training and development programs, transfers, retirement and so on. Most organizations have a person, group or department occupied with these issues; no organization, other than a university or business school, has an organizational behavior department.

This makes OB a slightly incongruous fit at business schools, yet it is the largest area of interest in the American Academy of Management, with 3,200 members, followed at a distant second by human resources management with 2,400 members. OB has something for nearly everyone, and that presents problems. One such problem is how to approach and comprehend the subject matter human behavior in a meaningful and practical way. How does one organize organizational behavior?

Macro and micro OB

Most faculty in organizational behavior have academic degrees in one of the social sciences or else they have degrees in general management or OB itself. They find themselves coming at research and teaching from a variety of directions. Perhaps the simplest way of reducing the complexity of organizational behavior is to divide the field into 'macro' and 'micro' elements; 'macro' OB focussing on the 'organizational' level of abstraction and taking a more sociological slant, and 'micro' focussing on the 'behavioral' level of abstraction and taking a more psychological slant.

To oversimplify a bit, a preoccupation with the *organization* in organizational behavior usually marks the teacher or researcher as 'macro-OB' with interests in formal organizational and structural questions. This comprises an array of students drawn mostly from management, sociology and economics who are interested in such topics as bureaucracy, 'socio-technical systems', complex organizations, technology, organizational change, corporate decision making, and even business policy and strategy. Macro-OB can trace its historical roots to such independent continental European thinkers as Max Weber and Karl Marx, to the mostly-British 'socio-technical school' associated with the Tavistock Institute, and to the mostly-American sociological and economics traditions of Robert Merton, Alvin Gouldner and James March and Herbert Simon, respectively.

A preoccupation with the *behavior* in organizational behavior, on the other hand, usually marks the teacher or researcher as 'micro-OB' with interests in informal organizational and individual and small group questions. This comprises an array of students of social psychology, sociology, anthropology and management who focus on topics such as motivation, communication, learning, perception, attribution, personality, attitudes and values,

individual and group decision making, leadership, group and inter-group dynamics, negotiation, job design, power, politics and conflict. Micro-OB can trace its historical roots to a variety of psychologists ranging from Abraham Maslow and Carl Rogers to Albert Bandura and B. F. Skinner.

The main difference between macro- and micro-OB is the level of abstraction and the selection by researchers of particular sets of explanatory factors for study. This 'level of abstraction' can be expanded beyond the two 'big' and 'little' categories characterized by the 'macro' and 'micro' partition. Most introductory OB textbooks differentiate the field of into three subsets, focussing on individual, group and organizational processes. One can continue in this vein and approach behavior with ever finer differentiation. Let me provide an example to illustrate the point.

Levels of analytical abstraction

I ran across the following incident in a daily paper several years ago and have, from time to time, used it in class to illustrate alternative ways of considering a behavioral event. The case is short: 'An elderly woman in a nursing home is found dead; she has apparently committed suicide.' That's it – the whole case. I then ask managers to write down as many alternative explanations of the tragic event as they can. After a few minutes, I ask them to share their hypotheses with the class and I write these hypotheses on the blackboard. The class generates dozens of alternative hypotheses. Whereas these explanations can fall into more than seven discernible categories, we seldom make it beyond two or three. Something gets in the way.

The first set of explanations typically generated concern the elderly woman herself: 'She was terminally ill and wanted to help the process along'; 'She was tired of living'; 'She was lonely'; 'She didn't kill herself, she died of natural causes' and so on. The underlying assumption is that her motivation and fate are an individual affair. This is the most frequent type of explanation for this or most other behavioral events. When making sense of the world, we often stop right there – at the individual level of analysis. Thus Adolph Hitler 'caused' the Second World War; he was responsible.

In a business context, an American board of directors hold the new CEO responsible for the increased quarterly profits of the company and reward him with a $6m bonus. Most of our institutions, for example our legal systems, reinforce this view. In a sense, they must, because it is virtually impossible for a legal system to hold larger social aggregates responsible, and if they do, these larger social aggregates, corporations for example, are simply handled legally as individuals. Assigning responsibility to individual entities makes things simple. But it seldom reflects the richness of reality. With a little probing: 'Why was the elderly woman lonely?', managers elaborate on their individual explanations with a second set of hypotheses.

This second set of hypotheses sketch aspects of a relationship between the elderly woman and another person: 'Her daughter wanted her money and murdered her'; 'The nurse was irritated with her and did it'; 'The woman in the bed next to her poisoned the elderly woman because she wanted to steal her jewellery'; 'Her husband quietly assisted her suicide to relieve her pain and suffering' and so on.

The underlying assumption is that no one is an island; to fully understand such an incident, one must consider relationships between individuals. This is the second most frequent set of hypotheses, and operates at the inter-personal level of analysis. Most of us, most of the time, use individual and inter-personal kinds of explanations to diagnose the causes of behavior. If we have married friends who are at the point of divorce, we typically blame one party or the other or attribute the break-up to irreconcilable (inter-personal) personality differences. Together, these two levels of analysis – *individual* and *inter-personal* – account for nearly all of the initial suggested hypotheses in our little case.

As they continue to generate explanations for the elderly woman's death, managers begin to run short of individual and inter-personal explanations, and so they offer ever more outlandish hypotheses. The more outlandish the hypothesis the better, actually, because the explanations cease representing events as artefacts of individual and inter-personal processes and begin to offer some surprisingly novel and interesting perspectives on processes operating on other levels of analysis – group, inter-group, organizational, inter-organizational and societal. The hypotheses at these higher levels of abstraction tend to include the patterns seen in the lower ones, for example, a triangular pattern of conflict.

The *group* level of analysis includes hypotheses such as: 'She was done in by her husband's jealous mistress' (love triangle); 'She was the despised parent, the father was the beloved parent – she the devil, he the angel – and the children were tired of paying the bills' (family group); and 'The other patients in her ward were tired of her complaining and made her the scapegoat for all the problems' (institutional group). The *inter-group* level of analysis includes hypotheses such as: 'Her ward and the other ward were competing for the best doctors, and the other ward won, throwing the woman's ward, and especially the woman herself, into a fatally deep depression'; 'Her daughter's family and her son's family were squabbling over her possessions, and she felt caught in the middle, so she killed herself'; 'The staff nurses and the staff doctors were at war, the nurses were demoralized and so care deteriorated causing many of the patients to despair'.

The *organizational* level of analysis might include hypotheses such as: 'The home's administration and physicians were determined to keep the nursing staff in a low-power position, so the nursing staff took it out on the orderlies and patient care suffered', or 'The nursing home was flat broke, and there was little to eat, so she was starving and desperate'. For the *inter-organizational* level of analysis, hypotheses include those such as: 'This nursing home lost accreditation with the social service agency responsible for funding because of poor management, and patient care suffered'; 'Her husband died, ending the provisions of his company's health care policy for his wife, and the social security administration refused to intervene, leaving her indigent and hopeless'.

At the societal level of analysis, we might find that: 'The health ministry was consolidating nursing home expenditures and was to eliminate this particular home, and move all the patients to an inner-city slum, causing panic in the patient population'; 'The lobby for retired people lost its bid to get money from the governmental ministry to ameliorate conditions at all nursing homes, so this one suffered considerably, particularly because it was in a labor district'; 'A referendum for supplementary funds to support hospitalized elderly patients was defeated by a coalition of upper and middle-class taxpayers and business interests, leading to big cuts in spending and under-nutrition of patients, which in turn led to . . '; or, finally, the plaintive refrain, 'What kind of society do we live in, anyway, where we shunt our elderly into nursing homes instead of caring for them at home?'

We could, of course, add higher levels of abstraction, such as the international and global levels, as well as complicate things by overlaying an historical approach in which we select and favor different levels of analysis for different periods.

Favorite levels of analysis

Although this little exercise in generating alternative hypotheses might seem like a parlor game, it is not a trivial way to approach behavioral events – it has real consequences. Journalists, historians, politicians and business leaders pick their favourite level of analysis to explain events all the time and then behave accordingly, often with untoward consequences. For example, let us take a current event.

We can attribute the death of a young Bosnian boy crossing the street to visit his grandmother in Sarajevo to various causes: a) the Serbian sniper; b) the carelessness of youth; c) the suffering and preoccupation of his one remaining parent; d) the Ottoman invasion; e) the assassination of Archduke Ferdinand in 1914 in Sarajevo; f) the Nazi sympathies of many Croatians during the Second World War; g) atrocities, real or imagined, committed hundreds of years ago – or hundreds of days ago; h) the

tragic after-effects of 50 years of communist totalitarian rule in the Balkans; i) the result of United Nations and Western incomprehension of, cynicism about, or fear and impotence in managing the bloody and melodramatic political theatre presented by Serbian leader Slobodan Milosevic, Bosnian Serb leader Radovan Karadic and Bosnian Serb General Ratko Mladic; j) EU and American fear of Muslim extremism, and so on.

Where we focus is where we find and assign responsibility, and this determines our subsequent actions. These actions, or inactions, frequently have unanticipated and disastrous consequences.

The world is a complex place and any social event is the result of many factors. If one systematically and carefully considers events with an approach such as alternative hypotheses generated from increasingly abstract levels of analysis – whether they be events in the Balkans war or problems in the executive committee – then one can develop a deeper understanding of the roots of behavior and one has the possibility of approaching, and using, some of the tools of organizational behavior.

So why study the subject?

Some years ago a young MBA student asked me with whom I preferred to work, 'MBA students or executives?' He had expected that I would say MBA students because they were generally presumed by the faculty, and by themselves, to be dynamic, aggressive, inquisitive and challenging. I said executives. 'Why?' he asked. 'Because the executives are experienced enough to take behavior seriously, including the non-rational and irrational aspects,' I responded.

Most of us begin our business careers largely with technical training and skills – we study commerce or engineering or computer science. Several years after taking our first job, however, someone asks us to manage a project team and none of the technical training we have had is sufficient to get a group together and get it to work; behavioral skills are necessary. Still later, when we reach the top levels of an organization, strategic skills have become much more important. But no matter how brilliant the abstract strategy, if we do not have the behavioral skills to formulate and implement the strategy effectively, it will fail.

OB takes the findings of the traditional academic disciplines and applies them to the practical world of business. It grounds the academic theories in concrete day-to-day reality. The current concerns of business leaders, whether at the strategic level of identifying the investment risks in Brazil or the operational level of implementing a joint-venture in Russia, tread the territory explored by organizational behavior.

Scarcely any important issue in business, external to the organization or internal, can escape having important behavioral implications. We have all found ourselves in organizations with no strategy, with no marketing plan or with no electronic data processing system. None of us has found ourselves in an organization without behavior. Markets are as much psychological mechanisms as they are economic ones. Family businesses may have other priorities than maximizing income.

The failure of organizations can not be laid at the feet of workers or shifting markets; organizational failure is a failure of management. Large organizations do not falter because they do not have the resources to succeed, they falter because they do not employ their resources wisely enough. It is not simply a question of knowledge, it is a question of wisdom. And where is this covered in business schools? In the 'hard data' quantitative courses?

Hard territory

The ground covered by OB is not 'soft' as sceptics prefer to believe, it is one of the hardest territories there is. Companies such as Thomson Electronics, Philips and IBM have had difficulties not because they did not have access to the highest technology or to adequate financial capital. They have had difficulties for organizational and behavioral reasons – they were not managing their people and technological resources as well as their competitors.

The US 'lost' the Vietnam war not because it had insufficient technology or capital. The failure was behavioral, a lack of understanding of the 'soft' issues – issues such as cultural differences, the critical influence of ideology, the sources of human motivation, dedication and sacrifice, the process of negotiation, the non-rational power of symbol and myth and their presentation in the visual arts, and, perhaps most poignantly for men like Robert McNamara, the US secretary of defence during much of the war, the unawareness of, or vain indifference to, the ancient Delphic admonition to 'know thyself'. McNamara's case is instructive.

In his mea culpa covering the American involvement in Vietnam, McNamara, former whiz kid and President of Ford Motor Company and former head of the World Bank, stands as a shining example of the limits of 'rational bottom-line' thinking. He was a quintessential manager and technocrat, and he tried to manage the Vietnam war with numbers and technology and calculations of bomb tonnage and body counts. McNamara was one of the principal architects of the disastrous policy from which the American people have yet to recover. He and his peers ignored the 'soft' stuff, and tiny North Vietnam 'won' where they were not looking.

Among business school areas, organizational behavior is almost the only unruly voice in a chorus of rationalists. OB repeatedly warns that people do not necessarily behave the way we wish them to; that no matter how well-intentioned, if we make decisions while ignoring the deeper social and psychological patterns within human nature, the final result will be exactly the opposite of what we intend, because we are dealing with a human world that follows its own imperatives – imperatives that do not comfortably fit into, and are not deeply explored by, other subject areas in business schools.

The benefits of taking OB seriously go beyond the narrow concerns of the external business environment. A working sensitivity to the rational, non-rational and irrational behavioral factors at play in organizations can help us be better managers, but perhaps more importantly, wiser individuals as well.

Summary
Organizational behavior – essentially an Anglo-American invention – at its best penetrates

beneath the cultural myopia and conventional wisdom of individual and collective behavior. Its origins as an academic subject can be traced to a chance collaboration between Fritz Roethlisberger, a Harvard professor, and Elton Mayo of 'Hawthorne' studies fame in the 1920s. It was not formally taught in business schools, however, until the 1960s.

OB is not a business function like marketing or finance (personnel being the function that deals with people). It is multi-disciplinary, a hodge podge of different subjects. 'Macro' OB is the preoccupation of those with interests in formal organizations and structural questions; 'Micro' OB is for those with an interest in informal organizations and individual and small group questions. Scarcely any important issue in business, external to the organization or internal, can escape having behavioral implications. OB repeatedly warns that people do not necessarily behave in the way they are expected to.

What do new systems demand of employees?

■ The impact of 'lean production' and other new systems of organizing work may be aimed at improving productivity but what are the effects on employees?

by Peter Cappelli and Nikolai Rogovsky

Efforts to reform the organization of work have traditionally started with the fact that mass production techniques associated with scientific management do not meet the psychological and social needs of workers.

The focus of these reform efforts is on the employee, employee behavior and the job, not the organization or production system. Job design and work organization are seen as the source of improvements in performance that are viewed as largely independent of the specific production system.

The key assumption implicit in this approach is that these work practices translate across organizations and contexts, improving the performance of individual workers by better meeting their needs and, in turn, improving organizations. There are many famous examples of work reform along these lines: the 'long-wall' mining experiments in the UK, the Topeka dog food plant in the US and, perhaps most prominently, the redesign of assembly line work at Volvo in Sweden, especially its Uddevalla plant, where autonomous teams of workers assembled entire cars on their own without an assembly line.

The current debate, especially in the US, takes much of the previous research as a given and focusses on the institutions of work organization such as employee participation and team work. One factor that distinguishes these from past efforts is the focus on production efficiency, as opposed to the needs of the employees. The common theme in all models of new work systems is that they represent a contrast to work systems associated with scientific management.

The contemporary debate in the US began by identifying 'high-performance' (HP) work systems in the context of new production systems. 'Lean' or high-performance production systems were identified and the work systems demanded by them were identified by definition as high-performance work. These production systems are most clearly seen with Japanese manufacturing and include techniques such as statistical process control, just-in-time inventory systems (JIT), continuous improvement, and total quality management.

Demanding more from employees

The models of lean production basically argue that increased quality, productivity, and flexibility can be obtained by making better use of employees. In particular, responsibility and decision making are transferred from administrative structures directly to employees or to their teams. These arrangements demand significantly more from employees than do work systems associated with scientific management, where tasks are narrowed and virtually all decision making is in the hands of management.

But it appears that they may demand less than the work systems associated with the behavioral models of work reform. Lean production work systems appear to demand more from workers in the way of stress and effort/work pace than do the behavioral models. They also offer workers substantially less autonomy. Employee decision making, when it occurs, happens in an aggregated, inter-team setting. The highly regimented tasks of lean production limit individual autonomy, and while they may offer more variety than do work systems governed by scientific management, it is substantially less than that associated with behaviorally based models.

On the other hand, these new production systems appear to be substantially more productive. The best evidence comes from the auto industry. The closing of Volvo's Uddevalla plant because of poor relative performance, despite being quite modern in terms of facilities, sent a powerful message to many about the future direction of work organization.

Although some have argued that the Uddevalla model could have succeeded with the right workers in the right context and higher standards from the suppliers, such arguments suffer when confronted with recent data from a study of auto assembly plants conducted by the Massachusetts Institute of Technology, which finds, for example, that the average Japanese plant is 119 per cent more efficient than the average European plant.

Lean production systems are associated with a series of work practices which are outlined below:

● Employee empowerment/participation in decision making: non-exempt employees take over some tasks previously performed by supervisors, engineers, and staff specialists.

● Teamwork: quality circles (focussing on quality and productivity issues), quality of worklife (QWL) programs, autonomous or semi-autonomous teams (taking over some direct supervision), all organize participation around groups. While participation means shifting some supervisory decisions to employees, teams go further and substitute for formal management structures.

● Job rotation/cross training: employees within teams swap tasks and become more inter-changeable. Employees learn a broader set of skills to make this possible.

● Supportive personnel practices: these include gainsharing, job security, pay-for-skill pro-grammes, training in basic communications/interpersonal skills and specific production knowledge, and socialization programs to develop high commitment. There are many different studies that examine the effects of work systems that feature these characteristics. Again, the MIT auto study suggests that high-performance production systems are as much as twice as productive as traditional systems.

Various studies of the effects of specific work practices have shown interesting results:

● Employee participation and team work provides (1) better quality decisions by involving more people who have better information (but often at the expense of speed); (2) higher commitment from participants; (3) a reduction in the number of supervisors and lower-level management required.

● Team work has the additional advantage of making the group responsible for production decisions. It generates peer pressure that helps enforce high levels of performance. There is substantial research showing positive effects of team-based work on reducing the need for management, increasing productivity and especially on achieving challenging goals that require creativity and problem-solving skills such as designing new products or developing new techniques.

● Job rotation and cross-training reduce fatigue, help produce greater job satisfaction, and reduce absenteeism/turnover problems (no need for specialized 'relief' workers or, worse, substitutes who cannot perform the job). The job design research shows substantial benefits to employee attitudes and behaviors (essentially turnover and absenteeism) associated with rotation or job variety.

● Supportive personnel policies. Gainsharing creates incentives to pursue the interests of the team or organization and participation makes it possible for workers to do so. Basic skills and production knowledge improve the participation process and the quality of employee decisions. High commitment systems help ensure that the greater autonomy workers have is used to benefit the organization.

Skill requirements

What skills do the new systems demand? The new production systems require more skills than scientific management systems, but less than behavioral experiments such as the one at Uddevalla.

The data in Table 1 examines changes in skill requirements using data obtained on 56,000 production workers over an eight-year period. The data suggests significant up-skilling for production jobs as measured by changes in Hay points, the job evaluation system introduced by Hay Associates to measure job requirements.

While there are no direct measures of the extent to which lean production techniques are driving these increases, the patterns are suggestive of that influence. Some of the up-skilling is due to the fact that tasks associated with quality control and 'housekeeping' have been pushed on to all the remaining jobs (the decline of employment in quality and house-keeping jobs is consistent with this interpretation). Not only has each job experienced up-skilling but the overall distribution of production

Table 1: Changes in the skill levels of production and clerical jobs 1978-86

Production jobs	Hay points 1978	Hay points 1986	Change in employment %
Assembly operations	104	108	0.598
Electrical work	245	250	-16.844
Housekeeping	103	102	-61.483
Inspection / quality control	115	128	-30.515
Machine repair and maintenance	213	226	12.162
Machine operations	143	147	2.496
Material handling	169	193	-12.230
Processing operations	129	135	-7.644
Stock-keeping	123	125	-8.226
Tool and die work	259	262	48.012
Clerical jobs			
Bank tellers	155	161	3.190
Clerks	125	131	-21.844
Typists	117	113	-56.098
Clerical support	172	176	-5.499
Computer support	166	157	-14.260
Customer service	141	159	129.412
Office equipment	111	90	-33.298
Telephone operations	108	95	9.126

jobs has shifted away from less-skilled and toward more-skilled positions.

Lean production essentially eliminates some jobs and pushes their tasks on to production workers. Some of those tasks, such as housekeeping, add little to the job. Other tasks, such as co-ordinating job design changes across teams, demand considerably higher skills, especially behavioral skills (communication, negotiation, and group dynamics skills). Adler notes that many of the tasks previously performed by industrial engineers, such as job analysis and redesign, are now being pushed down to the production teams.

This does not mean, however, that the workers in the teams need the skill set of an industrial engineer. The tasks transferred to the work teams are highly structured. The systems of performance measurement and control are already in place, as is the existing job design. The task facing the teams is to learn how to interpret information from the system in order to look for ways to improve it. They are not designing and setting up a new system.

Further, because these decisions are made in teams, it is not necessary for each worker to have all of the skills needed to handle every task, only that those skills be available somewhere in the work group. For example, not every worker in the group needs to understand how to use statistical process control techniques. If one person understands the notion of confidence limits, another can read the charts and a third knows their machine tools well enough to troubleshoot when the problems have been identified, they have a team that can make the technique work.

It is also important to remember that while these skill requirements are rising, they start at a low base. Data from Hay Associates suggests that a typical management job, for example, has skill levels about twice those represented by the production work here. Given the low base, it is certainly possible that workers already have the skills to meet the increasing skill demands represented by the data. Given the positive benefits of work practices associated with 'lean' production, why are they not used everywhere?

Different ways of implementation

Systems of work organization are in effect choice variables for employers. Research shows that the same technology, for example, can be implemented in very different ways with different effects on skill requirements and job design. Companies may make very different choices to solve the same problem of getting workers with adequate skills; some de-skill or make jobs simpler, some up-scale and introduce high-performance work systems, some recruit more intensively from outside and some retrain their workers. The anecdotal evidence from employers seems to indicate that having a model of high-performance work systems in the same industry may be one of the best predicters as to whether it will be adopted. There may be many reasons for this. Behavioral arguments suggest that various kinds of peer pressure and the search for legitimacy at the organizational level generate the need to copy practices of successful firms whether they are functional or not. Other arguments suggest that because the context in which practices function is so critical to their success, it makes sense only to pursue practices that can be shown to have succeeded in similar contexts.

A related issue is that the most important problem in introducing high-performance production techniques is not knowledge of the techniques but knowledge about the process of getting them accepted and implemented issues that may also be specific to the context. Studies suggest that lack of understanding about how to implement these systems is a much more important obstacle than is understanding the systems themselves. The fact that high-performance practices have spread most rapidly in manufacturing may be because the publicized model of Japanese manufacturing techniques made it easier for them to be adopted. There is no equivalent model for other sectors, however.

Another explanation, of course, could be that these techniques do not work as well elsewhere. By definition, the techniques of high-performance production systems are associated with production work, and not all of these techniques apply directly to other industries. Because one important attribute of these systems is the increased flexibility needed to handle variations in products, environments that do not demand – indeed may punish – change may not make great use of these techniques. There is relatively little use for high-performance production techniques in industries such as transportation, distribution or public utilities, perhaps because reliability and consistency are the prime considerations. Indeed, the work systems in these industries are often referred to as 'high reliability' systems. One of the more curious findings, however, is that there is little evidence of high-performance production systems even in organizations that have production-like aspects.

The processing of transactions in the back offices of financial services and related industries, for example, looks very much like an assembly line (more people are employed in these industries than in manufacturing). Yet there appears to be little – if any – evidence that high-performance production practices or even specific high-performance work practices are being used in these operations. Indeed, the effort in these facilities seems to be quite strongly in the opposite direction; to automate employees out of the process altogether. One explanation for the apparent absence of lean production practices or high-performance work systems in these industries might be that transactions processing is different from production work in at least one important way: there is little flexibility required in transactions processing because the product is so uniform. Processing cheques, for example, looks as much like the continuous production process of an oil refinery as even the assembly line of an auto plant. The work systems, therefore, may demand characteristics more like high-reliability than high-performance systems.

It is also possible, of course, that high-performance production or work systems might be successful here, albeit in a modified form, if they were given a chance. Perhaps no one is trying them because there is no model, no equivalent of the Japanese example in manu-facturing. The fact that even the work practices associated with high-performance work such as teams or job rotation, independent of high-performance production systems, are less common outside manufacturing may suggest that the problem has to do with the absence of models.

One issue that may affect the introduction of high-performance systems is the skill levels of the workforce. Both the production and work systems appear to demand higher levels of skill, and problems with the skills of the existing workforce are associated with difficulties in introducing some of the changes associated with high-performance work, as data from a recent survey by the National Association of Manu-facturers suggests.

Team working

Even where the production systems themselves are not spreading, many of the individual work practices noted above do seem to be taking root. Team work in particular seems to be behind much of the organizational restructuring in the US because it generates the immediate savings of eliminating management jobs.

A substantial proportion of the demand for new production systems is driven by the demand for flexibility itself driven by consumer tastes. The next wave of manufacturing so-called 'quick

response' production basically amounts to customized production, where output is essentially produced for specific orders rather than for inventory. Products and production runs under this system change constantly. And the pace of this change requires a different system of production.

The faster changes and smaller production runs these systems require mean that mass-production systems of work organization are too slow to change and too expensive per production run. A mass production assembly system breaks work down into very small tasks, with workers and machine tools dedicated to each part of the process. When products change, the line has to be shut down and 'retooled', changing the machine tools and the organization of tasks. Quick-response systems, in contrast, turn production over to a smaller team of workers with higher skills and flexible tools. The team may not be as efficient as the assembly line for a given product, but it can adjust to variations in products without substantial retooling. Its quick response to product changes allows producers to follow customer tastes more closely.

Because workers in this system perform more tasks, they need a wider variety of skills. Further, each worker has more autonomy because the work flow is not tightly governed by an assembly line. The Japanese companies that are the leaders in quick-response manufacturing actually see some production tasks shifting back from machines to workers as a result of quick-response systems. The long-term question, however, is whether improvements in the flexibility of automation will eventually catch up with quick-response systems. Put differently, quick response pushes more of the control of production on to individual workers because of limitations in the flexibility of current machine tools and production technology.

It is difficult to imagine that improvements in technology will not erode the advantage that skilled production workers have in flexibility over more automated approaches. Industries with longer production runs, such as the automobile industry, have already found it cost-effective to create machine tools and assembly line techniques that provide considerable improvements in the flexibility of production.

Finally, it is important to remember that changes in work practices invariably change products or services. Even minor changes in products can affect the way organizations compete. The decision to move from a low-skill work system to a high-skill, high-performance system, for example, is likely to mean that the output changes in ways that make it more competitive in some markets (for example, where quality and responsiveness matter) and less in others (for example, where price matters).

Wholesale changes in work practices may well create substantial changes in the way companies compete. In manufacturing, the changes appear to have had positive effects on corporate competitiveness. In other markets and business, the adjustment costs could be substantial. Efforts to introduce these work practices – especially to mandate them – need to weigh these costs and be certain that there is a market for the 'new' output that high-performance work practices create before they are introduced.

Summary

Efforts to reform the organization of work have traditionally been viewed as independent of specific production systems. A more recent focus, though, has been on production efficiency, notably through lean production models. These have been seen to benefit from empowerment, teamwork, job rotation and supportive personnel practices. More skills are required than under earlier scientific management systems, but less than under the behavioral approach.

Knowledge of how to get high performance production techniques accepted and implemented is more important than knowledge of the techniques themselves. In some industries there may be little use for them, but in others the reason for their absence may be the lack of an industry model. The skill level of the workforce may also be relevant.

A long-term question is whether improvements in the flexibility of automation will eventually catch up with quick-response systems.

The personality factor

■ **Personality is a key factor in work performance.** Nigel Nicholson **explains the five main dimensions of personality and looks at ways it can be assessed.**

What made Margaret Thatcher and Ronald Reagan so radically different in style yet so similarly successful as leaders? And what explains the close friendship that two such different people were able to forge? How much of the distinctive strong cultures of the two airlines British Airways and Virgin Atlantic was owed to the personality of their leaders, Lord King and Richard Branson? And did it also fuel the acrimonious conflict that flared so spectacularly between them?

There is an evident 'chemistry' that has something to do with character and style in the relationships leaders are able to develop with their followers or with each other. Each of us is familiar with this chemistry on a day-to-day level – gut feelings about people and situations, involuntary emotional reactions, sensations of immediate trust and empathy, or equally revulsion and discomfort.

Even among those to whom we are most closely bound – our children, parents or partners – we are aware of the importance of sharply defined similarities and differences of character between us. Indeed, as any parent will testify, it is amazing how early and uniquely striking differences appear in the temperament of our offspring. Some are active, others quiet; some are insatiably curious, others passive; some are highly strung, others placid and so on.

We also have a sense that these differences are important. They seem to prefigure in a general way what kinds of life and experiences each individual will have. In the adult world of work, we all around us see successes and failures in relation to tasks and relationships that seem to be directly traceable to the characters of the actors involved.

Our fascination with the rich array of human types that parade the world's stage has been evident for centuries, to be found in the speculations of philosophers and scholars and the inventions of story tellers. But it is in the last century, through the discipline of scientific psychology, that we have seriously begun to decode the complex and subtle chemistry of human personality and to identify its consequences.

In recent decades there has grown up a huge industry of personality measurement, bewildering in variety and usage, and increasingly applied in business. For the non-expert it is difficult to assess the legitimacy of claims for these methods and the limitations of their application. Moral and practical questions abound. We need to understand how and why we differ in personality, for what purposes can personality be measured and how can we use this knowledge in business?

The structure and origins of personality

Writers have offered various definitions of 'personality' – one of the broadest and most acceptable is 'those characteristics of the person that account for consistent patterns of behavior'

(Pervin, 1993, p.3, *see* 'Suggested further reading'). The key feature of this definition is that it seeks to identify those causes of behavior that stem from individual psychology rather than the force of circumstance. Clearly there are situations where individuals are constrained to behave alike, such as in mechanized environments and various formal social settings.

Personality reveals itself most when we are under minimal constraint, i.e., when we are free to choose how we act or react. Under conditions of constraint, such as when driving a car in heavy traffic or listening to a performance in a concert hall, the expression of personality is heavily muted, though not entirely silent, for it still colors our inward reactions to what is going on around us and, when constraint slackens, our outward actions.

This means that when we are constrained to behave in a similar way to others around us, personality shows through more in the style than the substance of what we do. For example, when chairing a formal meeting with a fixed agenda, personality factors influence what we notice and pay attention to, the feelings and intuitions we have, and how we choose our words. The sources of these differences between us are varied. Age, culture, gender, education, professional experience and social class all shape personality. But the raw material upon which these forces work already has the stamp of inborn individuality. The genetic basis of personality has been consistently indicated by twin studies: identical (monozygotic) twins, whether reared together or raised apart under quite different circumstances, exhibit remarkable similarities of personality not found in non-identical (dizygotic) twins.

Early childhood experience and the family milieu also exert a powerful formative influence, but as an overlay to the inherited matrix of temperament and character. By late adolescence personality has already achieved a complex form that persists, for most of us, with only moderate variation over the long span of adult years. There are exceptions – radical life changes, such as migration and major life crises, can produce marked shifts in some dimensions of personality. Otherwise, the maturing development of life-long learning only gradually raises and lowers the profiles of particular needs. It is much more our self-concept – how we think of ourselves – rather than our deeper rooted inclinations that changes over the adult life-span.

So what do we know about this deep structure? Decades of measurement and often fierce academic debate are beginning to resolve around a consensus – a five factor model, the so-called 'Big Five' dimensions found in repeated psychometric studies. Individual differences in personality can be seen as variations on these five themes – attributes that have evolved in the human species to fit us to the challenges of our existence.

Recently, scholars from the fast developing field of 'evolutionary psychology' have been fleshing out what this means. They point out that in evolutionary terms we retain the psychology of our ancestors – a species of tribal hunter-gatherers. Our environment might have changed a lot in the past half million years of homo sapiens existence but this is a too short space of evolutionary time to have let us shed the instincts of our direct ancestral forebears. The five factors that fit us for this existence are as follows:

Emotionality. Emotions are our radar in a world that is at one and the same time fraught with dangers and rich in opportunities for gratification. The biological basis of this radar is enshrined in the language we use to talk about it: 'gut' feelings, 'blood boiling', 'shivers up and down the spine', 'hair standing on end' and so on. These emotional responses are biologically 'hard wired' and much the same for all of us under extreme conditions of threat and satisfaction. But for a wide range of more normal conditions, we differ widely in how emotionally susceptible or reactive we are.

Some of us are extremely sensitive, not just to other people and situations but also to our own thoughts and reflections. Highly emotional people often suffer states of anxiety or melancholia, or are subject to mood swings and hot-blooded reactions. The opposite extreme finds people who are calm and unflappable, unselfconscious, resistant to stress and un-varying in mood. The latter might seem to be enviable to the former group, but it should be borne in mind that blunted sensitivity also has costs – OK for astronauts but a limitation for the functioning of some helping professionals.

Extroversion. As social animals we share a desire to be with each other, for survival, essential functions of bonding and breeding, and to accomplish complex and difficult tasks we could not attempt alone. There is safety as well as comfort in numbers. At the same time, unlike ants and bees whose individuality is inseparable from the group, we need to be able to function autonomously. This makes us all hosts to two contrary impulses – to join and to separate. We differ in the balance between these impulses. For some of us (extroverts), life's most significant and rewarding experiences are to be found in the outer world of action and extended social relationships. The preference of others of us (introverts) is for the inner world of reflection and autonomous experience and close circles of intimate social relations.

Openness. Curiosity is fundamental to our survival as creatures with weak bodies, large brains and enormously varying physical environments to inhabit. Put a young infant into a new room and before long it will start to explore and experiment in its new setting. Yet we also exhibit caution and a fondness for what is predictable and familiar. Differences in degree of preference for these two modes of adaptation are commonplace. Some of us are eager to try anything once, stimulated by creative impulses, and liberal in attitudes and tastes. Others of us like to keep our feet on the ground, stick with the tried and tested, and keep tuned into the native wisdom of conservative tastes and the legacy of tradition.

Agreeableness. Our social world poses us with another universal dilemma. On the one hand we need to establish bonds of warmth and trust with people beyond our immediate kith and kin in order to enjoy the fruits of social harmony. On the other hand, we recognize that we are necessarily in competition with others to secure advantage in resources, relationships and status. We differ greatly in our inner balance of these opposing tendencies. Some have a strong propensity to trust and seek empathy with others and to maintain a 'tender-minded' world view. Others are avowedly 'tough-minded', cynical, suspicious and ready to compete in an unpredictable world.

Conscientiousness. A fundamental burden of human existence is the need to work hard and achieve. This fits the inclinations of some of us more than others – the propensity to self-discipline, to prepare for future eventualities, to be orderly and organized, deliberate in decisions and able to drive ourselves forwards through uncongenial tasks. Yet many of us find a life of relaxed chaos more palatable, where we can feel free to follow whims and impulses. Across these contrasts – compulsive challenge vs careless ease – we find a different array of costs and benefits are visible.

One might ask what is the purpose of these variations in our dispositions? The answer is that the differences between us draw us in the direction of different tasks, relationships and environments, provide varied opportunities for productively combining interests and efforts, and lead us to create different microworlds in which we can feel effective and at home.

Our personality profiles incline us towards certain experiences and away from others. They make us feel comfortable in some settings and uncomfortable in others, and motivate us to stabilize or change our circumstances to create a good 'fit' with ourselves. On this reasoning it will be apparent that personality assessment can yield powerful insights and applications. In therapeutic or counselling relationships it can help us become clearer about our preferences and the themes underlying our customary choices and reactions, for example in helping us make career decisions and lifestyle adjustments.

However, although personality underlies and colors all behavior it does not always directly predict how we act. Standing between impulse and action are two major sets of buffers.

The first of these is *ability*. Strong social impulses do not guarantee the possession of social skills. A high desire to achieve is not a sufficient condition for competitive success. There is a correlation – for we do tend to practice the skills that our impulses and interests favor

and, as a consequence, we do often become proficient in them. Yet, independent of personality are a number of critical abilities, both inborn and learned: logical reasoning, language skills, physical strength, manual dexterity, musicality, numeracy, spatial awareness, and accumulated knowledge and expertise. We also possess personal attributes, such as age, ethnicity, gender and social class that influence the opportunities we have for certain kinds of experiences and how the world treats us.

The second set of buffers to the expression of personality are circumstantial: the *resources and opportunities* we have to act out our desires. When we take note of a particular piece of behavior by another person – for example, a negotiator angrily thumping the table – we may be inclined to reach for 'personality' as the most obvious explanation. To do so is to risk what psychologists call 'the fundamental attribution error' or the tendency to ascribe to personality what may be actually be caused by circumstance.

The negotiator's table-thumping may be well practiced and trained behavior, strategically staged to create a calculated effect, rather than an expression of underlying emotionality or tough-mindedness. Remembering the definition we offered at the outset, it is only when we see similar behaviors emerging across a range of circumstances – i.e., consistency – that we can point to personality as the cause. Does the negotiator also thump the dinner table at home?

How can we tell? This is what personality measurement seeks to achieve.

Personality measurement and its application

Since we cannot readily witness the range of a person's behaviors across time and situations we must rely on their self-report. Personality questionnaires do this by carefully constructing clusters of questions or 'items' that converge on the main dimensions of personality. This is achieved by two methods: convergent and discriminant validation.

Convergent validation involves gathering data for a large pool of items from a sizeable population and then using statistical criteria to

Figure 1: Major personality instruments in current use

Measure	Origins and use	Content
16 PF	One of the first instruments designed by factorial statistical methods by RB Cattell in the 1950s. Still widely used in business.	16 Factors, encompassing the main dimensions of personality.
MYERS-BRIGGS TYPE INDICATOR (MBTI)	Developed from a Jungian theoretical framework, it is unusual in placing respondents into an array of types rather than on continuous dimensions. Widely used in vocational applications.	16 types derived from 4 scales. Excludes "emotionality" but measures "Extraversion" and other factors.
EYSENCK PERSONALITY INVENTORY (EPI)	Pioneering measure with strong and varied research credentials. More used in clinical than occupational settings.	Three dimensions assessed: Neuroticism (emotionality), Extraversion and Psychoticism.
OCCUPATIONAL PERSONALITY QUESTIONNAIRE (OPQ)	UK commercially developed suite of measures, with extensive business database norms. Unusual for focus on work relevant factors.	Varying numbers of factors measured by different scoring methods. Encompasses the main dimensions of personality plus some occupational variants.
THE CALIFORNIA PERSONALITY INVENTORY (CPI)	A classic US originating measure. Used in various management studies, but relatively little applied in the UK.	18 scales covering the main dimensions of personality and some less commonly measured factors.
THE NEO-PI	One of the most recently developed instruments, comprehensive in design with strong theoretical base and extensive research support.	Designed to represent the "Big Five" structure, with 6 subscales for each dimension, yielding 30 in all.

weed out items that fail to converge on a given dimension. The surviving items constitute the measurement scales making up the instrument.

Discriminant validation involves applying the scales to demonstrate their ability to discriminate between samples known or predicted to differ in some observable behaviors or characteristics. By these means the best constructed measures have been able to identify such behaviors as people's proneness to neurotic illness and performance errors and to shed light on how individuals function in various occupations, such as sales, entrepreneurial and leadership roles.

However, as we have already noted, personality may often tell us much more about the unique style a person brings to a role rather than simply how well they perform it, for the latter will be heavily dependent upon their abilities (for which quite different measurement techniques exist). For this reason one can see how personality measures can be overused in business as simple selection tools, on the naive assumption that they directly predict performance. They are underused in other ways – as an aid to self-assessment and team-building.

One danger of naive usage can be to attempt to 'clone' populations of employees with similar profiles rather than consider what kinds of diversity might be optimal for organizational or group functioning. For example, how might it benefit an accounting firm to have individuals who deviate from the occupational norm? Or, conversely, how might I, as an individual, make a uniquely valuable contribution to a team in which my style and inclinations are different from others?

Another aspect of misuse is the use of poor-quality measures and untrained administrators. The field abounds with measures of many kinds, almost all of which are marketed commercially. Some of the most widely used and robust measures are described in Figure 1. These have all been carefully developed, though each has its own proponents and devotees. Professional advice should be sought on which is best suited to any application, though they contain many common elements and structural properties.

However, the field also contains measures that have not been developed to the same quality standards but which are marketed as scientific instrumentation. Non-verbal methods such as graphology (handwriting analysis), color preferences and projective tests (for example, the well-known 'ink blot test') all have adherents but negligible scientific credibility.

The British Psychological Society, the professional body for UK psychologists, maintains a watching brief over available measures and will advise on which meet acceptable standards. The BPS also maintains a register of chartered psychologists and their accredited competence to use tests of different kinds. Some test distributors also offer training courses and licensing schemes enabling non-psychologists to administer tests. Untrained administrators risk giving mistaken advice on the basis of test data and providing feedback to test-takers or client organizations in ways that can have materially damaging consequences.

A final major concern of test users is fake-ability. Since all personality measures depend upon honest introspection by the subject, there clearly exists the possibility of distortion, either by wilful desire to 'manage impressions' or by self-delusion. The bad news is that despite attempts by testers to incorporate 'lie scales' and other analytical methods to allow such motives to be identified and discounted there is in reality no ultimate guarantee. The good news is that well-made tests operate like a sophisticated interrogator, whose line of questioning and underlying model is difficult to discern and manipulate. For this reason, most people are unable to 'fake good'. However, the best protection is for testing to be administered where there is no motive to fake.

The potential for application of personality measurement goes far beyond simple prediction for selection and placement decisions. Now that we are reaching agreement about the core structure and functions of personality, new approaches to leadership, organizational culture, team behavior, entrepreneurship, stress, decision-making, risk-taking and many other vital business concerns are possible.

The effectiveness, climate and strategic development of a business depends upon the will, interests and style of its key actors and groups. Personality analysis can be a powerful tool to these ends – one whose potential is only just beginning to be realized – to help us understand and effectively manage the rich diversity of our organizational communities.

Summary

Personality theory and measurement through scientific psychology has been developing for the last century – in recent years it has increasingly been applied to business.

Personality can be defined as those characteristics that account for consistent patterns of behavior. It is shaped by age, culture, gender, education, professional experience and social class – but it has a crucial genetic base. Differences in personality can be seen as varieties of five themes: emotionality, extroversion, openness, agreeableness and conscientiousness. Although personality colors all behavior it does not always directly predict how we act – ability and circumstances are often influential.

Personality measures tend therefore to be over-used in business as a selection tool on the naive assumption that they predict performance; they are under-used as an aid to self assessment and team building. Some measures are simply poor quality and badly administered. Well made tests, though, are hard to 'fake' because of the line of questioning with the underlying model difficult to discern and manipulate.

Suggested further reading

Adler, S. and Weiss, H. 'Recent developments in the study of personality and organizational behavior' (1988) in Cary Cooper & Ivan Robertson (eds), *International Review of Industrial and Organizational Psychology*, Wiley, Chichester.

Furnham, A. (1992) *Personality at Work*, Routledge, London.

Hogan, R.T. 'Personality and personality measurement' (1990) in M.D. Dunnette (ed.) *Handbook of Industrial and Organizational Psychology*, 2nd edn, Consulting Psychologists Press, Palo Alto.

Pervin, L.A. (1993) *Personality: Theory and Research,* 6th edn, Wiley, New York.

Robertson, I.T. 'Personality and personnel selection' (1994) in C.L. Cooper & D.M. Rousseau (eds) *Trends in Organizational Behavior*, Volume 1, Wiley, Chichester.

Dealing with the attitude problem

■ **There have been many arguments that poor worker performance is based on poor educational achievement. But Peter Cappelli suggests that it may be even more a result of poor attitudes to work.**

The relationship between economic competitiveness and the quality of the workforce is a topic of heated debate in the US, much of which centers on whether high school graduates are adequately prepared for the work world. In the early 1970s there was a similar debate about the relationship between declining national productivity and the performance of the workforce. The general conclusion then was that the production workforce did not necessarily lack academic qualifications and that, indeed, many workers were overqualified for their jobs, which may have contributed to problems by creating unrealistic job expectations.

Workforce productivity problems seemed to lie within worker attitudes rather than with academic skills, especially in manufacturing. The efforts to address the problems of job satisfaction, commitment and citizenship focussed on redesigning jobs to help meet workers' psychological needs and improve work attitudes, and led to the 'quality of worklife' movement in the US.

By the mid-1980s, arguments about the relationship between the workforce and competitiveness suggested a new problem – workers entering the labor force were inadequately educated for the demands of the workplace.

The argument was not so much about a lack of vocational or occupational skills but about deficits in more basic educational skills. The high level of change experienced in many US organizations and the need for flexibility suggested that basic skills common to a range of jobs are important and that a solid grounding in reading, writing, arithmetic and communication skills would help graduates learn how to learn and how to adapt to changing demands in their jobs.

This position, which might be called the 'academic skills gap,' seems to have come less from direct evidence than from the logical combination of a series of related arguments.

Reports such as 'A nation at risk' (1983) warned about deteriorating student performance in secondary schools. 'Workforce 2000' (1988) argued that in the future the distribution of jobs would shift toward those positions that require higher levels of academic ability. Anecdotes about incredibly low levels of basic literacy among entry-level job applicants in urban areas helped to cement the conclusion that the 'supply' of skills among new entrants was eroding while 'demand' in the form of rising job requirements was increasing, forming a skills gap. More recent evidence suggests that some assumptions underlying the academic skills gap position are shaky. Evaluations of secondary school performance indicate that although there clearly are problems with student attainment, academic achievement overall appears to have rebounded from the lower levels of the late 1970s.

The fact that academic success in school has little impact on job performance makes it hard to argue that poor academic performance is the explanation for problems with job performance. Re-analysis of data used in 'Workforce 2000' suggests that the predicted sharp shift in employment toward higher-skilled jobs may not take place in the near future. The rate of the projected shift toward higher-skilled jobs in the economy actually appears to be slowing down compared to prior decades.

But the most telling evidence about the

deficits of high school graduates has been obtained by asking employers about the characteristics they believe entry-level candidates need in order to be successful and, more importantly, what current deficits they find among applicants and new workers. A number of surveys suggest that many employers think that the most significant deficit in new workforce entrants is the attitudes concerning work that they bring with them to their jobs. Many recent public policy recommendations have begun to include the development of employee attitudes as a crucial part of workplace skills. Although there is no easy way to know whether worker attitudes are more of a problem now than in the past, there is no doubt that the problem exists today and demands greater attention than it has been given.

Work attitudes and public policy

Despite the growing recognition that work attitudes are a fundamental component of a quality workforce, they have received virtually no detailed discussion in the public policy arena. Each report that mentions worker attitudes defines the relevant attitudes in different ways and the ways in which these attitudes might be developed is almost never discussed. The lack of clarity and information makes it difficult to find whether any consensus exists concerning problem areas and whether proposals for the development of work attitudes are reasonable.

The term 'work attitudes' describes an individual's evaluation and response to given situations. Someone with a negative attitude toward authority, for example, might interpret questions from a supervisor as interference and respond defensively. Someone with a more positive attitude might evaluate the same questions as interest on the part of the supervisor and respond as if being praised.

In most jobs, especially for those with complex tasks, employees have considerable autonomy in determining how they perform at least some aspects of their work. How workers perform their tasks, therefore, is strongly influenced by their attitudes – and the more autonomy jobs allow, the more important attitudes are for job performance. When workers lack appropriate work attitudes, employers have to provide costly substitutes or, where substitutes are not readily available, they must forgo technologies or markets entirely. For example, employers may introduce expensive monitoring systems in departments in which theft is a problem. High-performance work systems that rely on shifting responsibility to workers will fail when workers will not take responsibility. Customers and markets that demand high levels of personalized service will be lost if employees have poor attitudes towards other people.

Research has found that positive attitudes are related to higher levels of job performance. Proper work attitudes may be as necessary to organizational performance as adequate levels of educational skills. The question of whether public policy should be responsible, even in part, for developing work attitudes depends upon the means through which those attitudes are generated. The debate about work attitudes is the extent to which they are the product of innate dispositions or the result of the situation in which employees find themselves.

The closer one gets to an extreme position on either side of this debate, the less it becomes a public policy issue. For example, if attitudes are the result of genetically based predispositions, then the distribution of job attitudes is given and the selection of employees who have appropriate attitudes becomes the responsibility of the employer – there would be little role for public policy actions.

Similarly, if all attitudes are situational in their basis, the attitudes of a workforce would be completely specific to circumstances so each employer would be directly responsible for the attitudes held by their workforce and there would again be little role for public policy. The middle position offers the strongest arguments for public policy action. Clearly, there are situations that are thorough and intense enough to produce similar work attitudes in most participants. There is also persuasive evidence that work attitudes persist from childhood. The dual conclusions suggest room for a middle position and a public policy interest in workplace attitudes. Schools are the logical place to begin thinking about developing positive workplace attitudes, and virtually any program directed at youth before they enter the full-time workforce might also offer good opportunities.

Which attitudes are important for the workplace?

Many of the work attitudes that employers mention most frequently focus on basic dispositions that are closely associated with the concept of personality. Despite the fact that employers often list personality characteristics as central to work performance, a worker's personality is rarely a good predictor of actual job performance. The average relationship between measures of personality and job performance across studies is typically weak although a number of studies have found positive effects.

The most recent survey of research on personality and job performance by Barrick and Mount (1991) (*see* 'Suggested further reading') suggests that the relationship with performance is stronger than previously thought. Conscientiousness was the aspect of personality most consistently related to job performance. It was significantly related to all measures of job performance for all occupational groups – from success in training and job proficiency to productivity and promotion.

Motivation is sometimes described as the force that drives and directs behavior in a particular way. Many scholars believe not only that there are differences in motivational orientation between individuals, but that those differences take the form of dispositions that endure over time. Perhaps the most widely discussed attitude related to motivation is 'need for achievement' (nAch), which can be thought of as an aspect of personality that determines the desire for individual success.

McClelland and Boyatzis (*see* 'Suggested further reading') present evidence that nAch was especially important in predicting the success of lower-level managers and entrepreneurs. A recent survey of nAch research finds that it can be a very strong predictor of job performance when characteristics of the work situation are supportive.

McClelland argued that while nAch appears to be a part of personality, it could be developed in individuals through training programs. The more successful techniques for raising motivation include supervisor expectations, goal setting, expectancy and modeling. Understanding how people learn, especially the factors that determine the amount of effort they put into learning, is an issue closely related to motivation. Research suggests that individuals who believe that success in learning results from ability are much less likely to take on challenging learning situations for fear that the effort they are expending illustrates that they do not have the ability to succeed – they see effort as a proxy for failure.

In contrast, those who believe that success in learning is the result of effort are not discouraged from undertaking challenging tasks – they may see effort as a proxy for success. There can be little doubt that beliefs about whether learning success is primarily the result of ability or effort is something that can be shaped by one's environment and experiences. Initiative and self-determination are also characteristics closely associated with motivation. Initiative is important in part because it is a substitute for supervision. Research shows that management practices can raise levels of worker initiative by providing positive feedback, information and choices for workers to make. Previous research has shown that teachers can raise the level of initiative among their students in similar ways – by giving students some autonomy, acknowledging their perspectives and interests, and by providing feedback.

Persistence is an important work attitude that employers sometimes include under the general category of motivation. One can think of persistence as continuing effort made in the absence of positive feedback indicating success. While persistence can be a problem if one persists in irrational actions, it is generally thought to be an important and useful attribute. 'Prosocial' behavior is the range of actions in which members of organizations go beyond their prescribed roles for the good of the organization or others in it. One currently popular aspect of prosocial behavior is known as citizenship, which is described as altruistic efforts to help others in the organization. The key element of citizenship is that individuals do not believe that they will be rewarded or that the authority structure necessarily will even be aware of their actions.

Some aspects of citizenship include actions taken for the benefit of the organization per se, such as being punctual or voluntarily limiting time off from work. Much of the research on the causes of prosocial attitudes and behavior reflects the usual situational/dispositional debate. Evidence suggests that prosocial behavior is associated with reasonably stable dispositions. A good deal of the research that examines prosocial behavior is directed toward identifying situational factors that might explain it. Job satisfaction or sense of belonging to a group is associated with citizenship. A perception on the part of workers that the organization values them is associated with greater conscientiousness, and strong organizational cultures are also associated with higher levels of commitment.

Prosocial behavior can be taught on the job. Modeling and social learning from supervisors and reinforcement can also strengthen prosocial behaviors. The way workers are socialized into the organization shapes prosocial behavior, and one's early employment experiences are the most important for developing prosocial attitudes (for example, Bray et al, 'Suggested further reading').

Most important from the perspective of public policy is the conclusion that prosocial behavior is also developed as a result of experiences in early childhood. Researchers have found that interventions in the classroom lead to improvements in co-operation, helping behaviors and student discipline.

Should we teach work attitudes?
In 1976, 'Schooling in capitalist America' (*see* 'Suggested further reading'), an influential critique of US public education, argued that the US educational system primarily reflected the needs of the free enterprize system because it produced students who were socialized into the norms required in the work place. What readers found disturbing about the critique was that the values, norms and behaviors being inculcated into students through the schools appeared in conflict with values associated with personal growth and development. In particular, the value 'compliance with authority' was described as an attitude necessary to success on the job.

Given this indictment, it is ironic that employers in the 1990s complain that schools are not preparing students adequately for the work place, especially in terms of attitudes and behaviors. Part of the explanation is that what Bowles and Gintis argued in their book was required for work turned out in subsequent research not to be especially good predictors of job performance.

The current interest in teaching values in US public schools is high but seems focussed largely on attempts to halt destructive behavior outside school, especially in inner cities. There is, however, a clear overlap between these values and many work attitudes.

Two arguments in favour of trying to develop values that approximate some of the work-related attitudes seem especially compelling.

First, characteristics such as consistency or prosocial behavior would seem to be of benefit to individuals and society and go beyond aiding employers.

Second, and perhaps more important, experiences with the education system, with teachers and especially with peers, inevitably shape the attitudes of students. So why not be explicit about it?

How to change work attitudes
The 'Great Society' programs of the late 1960s spawned a reconsideration of the relationship between job skills and economic performance. Research designed to improve the labor market performance of the unemployed, especially the 'hard-core' unemployed, was based on the assumption that this group lacked values and work attitudes that were appropriate for the world of work.

But programs designed to change the work attitudes of the hard-core unemployed were often unsuccessful. One conclusion from the extensive research in this area is that once workers are in the labor force, it is very difficult and expensive to change their work attitudes. One survey found that family background, especially the extent of unemployment among adult males in the family, was a powerful predictor of hard-core unemployed status, suggesting that the pattern is set early in life and providing another reason for attempting to shape work attitudes and behaviors early. The field of developmental psychology examines the issue of how children develop attitudes and behaviors, and the study of moral development investigates how children develop values. Researchers have brought to popular attention the diversity of values in children and the complex process through which values are acquired.

The social learning perspective emphasizes that traditional learning approaches, such as role models and reinforcement, shape the values of children. The cognitive development view argues that children create their sense of values through an internal, cognitive process that follows predictable stages and that is largely independent of situations.

Cognitive development scholars also believe that interventions can help develop values in students and there have been efforts to introduce such programs into classrooms. While the social learning view is probably the dominant perspective, most scholars see room for a middle position that recognizes a role for both views. It is possible to identify the work-related attitudes and behaviors that are important in developing a quality workforce, and such values and behaviors may, in fact, support personal growth. Much of the research provides evidence for programs that have developed these character-istics in children and young adults, typically in schools.

Developing pedagogies encourage the belief that learning results from effort, that students can control their futures and that encouraging prosocial behaviors is a manageable goal, and many efforts are already under way to achieve that goal. School-based programs, often known as 'character development' or 'character education', are already in place in both private and public schools. The values and behaviors that these programs seek to develop – responsibility, self-discipline and adherence to rules – are certainly not at odds with those outlined above.

But the attitudes and behaviors needed for success in the workplace seem broader than those advocated by character development programs that focus on behaviors associated with control rather than attitudes. In addition, there is a disturbing possibility of conflict between programs to reform educational content and programs to develop behaviors and attitudes. Some of the new 'outcomes' based on curricula that emphasize mastery of real-world skills also make it more difficult to develop appropriate attitudes and skills.

For example, these programs may make it harder to recognize and reward student effort independent of results, which may be a key factor in developing student motivation. These arguments suggest that it is time to think about systematic attempts to include work attitudes and behaviors as part of the public policy agenda. In particular, the sooner a discussion of workplace attitudes and behaviors can be brought into the more general debate about education reform, the easier it will be to produce a system that aligns and reinforces the interests of schools and of the workplace.

Summary

It is hard to argue that poor academic achievement is the explanation for poor job performance. There is a growing recognition that work attitudes are a fundamental component of a quality workforce. An important question is whether such attitudes are the product of innate dispositions or the situation in which employees find themselves. A 'middle' answer will justify some public policy role. Conscientiousness has been the aspect of personality most consistently related to job performance. The most widely discussed motivational attitude is 'need for achievement' – this can be a strong predictor of performance when the work situation is supportive. Persistence is generally thought to be a useful attribute. 'Prosocial' attitudes are those actions in which members of an organization go beyond their prescribed roles for the good of the organization or of others in it. The social learning perspective emphasizes that traditional approaches (e.g. role models, reinforcement) shape the values of children. The cognitive development view argues that children develop their sense of values through an internal process.

Suggested further reading

Barrick, Mury and Mount, Michael K. 'The big five personality dimensions and job performance: a meta-analysis', *Personnel Psychology* 49(1): 1-26. (1991).

Bowles, S. and G., Herbert (1976) *Schooling in Capitalist America: Educational Reform and the Contradictions of Economic Life*, Basic Books, New York.

Bray, D. W., Campbell, R. J. and Grant, D. L. (1974) *The Formative Years in Business*, John Wiley and Sons, New York.

Commission on the Skills of the Workforce (1990) *America's Choice: High Wages or Low Skills*? Rochester, New York.

Committee for Economic Development, '*Investing in our Children*' (1984) National Center on Education and the Economy, Washington D.C.

An Assessment of American Education: Views of Employers, Higher Educators, the Public, Recent Students, and their Parents, (1991) Committee for Economic Development, Louis Harris Associates, New York.

Feldman, Roy E. (1980) *The Promotion of Moral Development in Prisons and Schools.*

Wilson Richard W. and Schochet, Gordon J. (eds) *Moral Development and Politics*, Praeger Publishers, New York, 286-328.

McClelland, David C. (1961) *The Achieving Society*, Van Nostrand Co, Princeton, New Jersey.

US Department of Health, Education, and Welfare, *Work in America*, Cambridge, MIT Press Massachusetts, for the 'Workforce 2000'.

Cultural diversity

■ **Cultural diversity is a hot issue. The main reasons are the growing diversity of societies, growth of cultural awareness among ethnic groups and the rise of the global corporation. Rob Goffee looks at some of the implications.**

The issue of 'cultural diversity' has attracted considerable attention over recent years. Although academic research remains predominantly North American, it is nevertheless true that the management of diversity has become an important social, economic and political issue within many industrialized economies in the 1990s. Several factors explain the recent interest:

● Labour market migration patterns have produced urban areas and regions that are increasingly heterogeneous in cultural terms. In

California, for example, a mixture of 'ethnic groups' constitutes in excess of 50 per cent of the population; in the city of Los Angeles itself there is no longer a majority population.

Similar patterns are evident in the urban areas of many large European cities; elsewhere the 'asianisation' of Australia has also produced a more culturally heterogeneous population.

Within some societies the emergence of 'domestic multiculturalism' has encouraged attempts to strengthen regulation of migration flows. Such controls are likely to increase, for example, around a unified Europe during the 1990s. At the same time, there are also policies to control discrimination and combat inequality – although the extent to which these are pursued is itself culturally variable.

In this respect, the 'management of diversity'

is a predominantly western phenomenon, unrecognized, for example, in some Asian societies.

● 'Multiculturalism' has been driven by different forces and produced different outcomes among the old socialist economies in Europe. There political regimes that held together diverse populations have been overthrown partially as the result of the powerful resurgence of regional, ethnic and religious differences.

This is producing a closer alignment between religious and ethnic groups and their representative political structures; the outcome, paradoxically, is less diversity within newly formed, smaller political states.

● Against this background there has been the emergence during the 1980s and 1990s of large global corporations that employ increasingly diverse labour forces. Restructuring processes among these so-called 'transnational' enterprises have tended to produce highly differentiated organizations that, in some respects, run the risk of disintegration.

As global businesses decentralize, delayer and devolve towards increasingly complex sets of differentiated centers – focussed upon distinct products, customers, regions and suppliers – they must also cope with a culturally diverse international labour force. The ability to manage this diversity is increasingly seen as an important executive attribute.

At the organizational level many global enterprises are seeking to develop strong yet flexible corporate cultures that can provide a sense of coherence and foster employee commitment among multicultural workforces.

What is cultural diversity?

An understanding of cultural diversity must begin with a definition of culture. These vary. Some writers refer to culture as 'historically created guides for living'; others to 'collective mental programing'.

A popular view is to see culture as deriving from a shared set of 'deep assumptions' that are not directly accessible but which may be indirectly reflected in the values, attitudes and behavior of individuals and groups. Such assumptions are 'cultural' because they are

learned (not innate), patterned, shared and passed down through generations. Cultural differences may be observed at many levels. A cultural group can be defined, for example, in national, regional, ethnic, religious, gender, generational or social class terms. But individuals are likely to be influenced by a complex interplay between several of these separate levels.

This fact alone should be sufficient to warn of the dangers inherent in excessive preoccupation with one cultural variable.

The fashionable obsession with national cultural differences, for example, can encourage unhelpful stereotyping: to describe someone as a 'typical' German, Japanese or American is effectively to write off other cultural influences that differentiate individual members of any nationality. This trap can be avoided by remembering that cultural characteristics refer – by definition – to shared rather than individual attributes.

What are the dimensions of cultural difference?

Cultural groups may share assumptions around a number of separable dimensions. Although these have been labeled in different ways by researchers, there appear to be some recurring dimensions that can effectively map cultural differences.

These include relationships with the physical environment (the extent to which it is taken as given or susceptible to human control); conceptions of space (how close is close? how is public differentiated from private?); conceptions of time (how the past, the present and the future are linked together, evaluated and understood); and understanding of the manner in which 'truth' is determined (through inductive or deductive reasoning, for example).

In addition, there are various dimensions around which differences in human relationships may be understood. These include such factors as orientation towards authority; acceptance of power inequalities; desire for orderliness and structure; the need to belong to a wider social group and so on. Around these dimensions researchers have demonstrated systematic

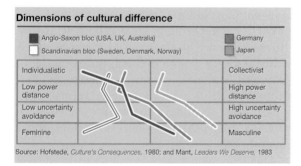

Dimensions of cultural difference

■ Anglo-Saxon bloc (USA, UK, Australia) ■ Germany
□ Scandinavian bloc (Sweden, Denmark, Norway) □ Japan

Individualistic		Collectivist
Low power distance		High power distance
Low uncertainty avoidance		High uncertainty avoidance
Feminine		Masculine

Source: Hofstede, *Culture's Consequences*, 1980; and Mant, *Leaders We Deserve*, 1983

Figure 1

differences between national, ethnic and religious groups. An influential model was developed by the Dutch academic, Geert Hofstede. His research is based upon a very large, worldwide survey of IBM employees matched for jobs. He identified four national cultural dimensions in work-related values that, together, explained more of the country differences in his sample than factors such as profession, age or gender. The four dimensions are:

● Power distance. The extent to which the less powerful expect and accept that power is distributed unequally (more authoritarian regimes tend to be associated with high power distance cultures; in such cultures, bosses have much more power than subordinates).

● Uncertainty avoidance. The extent to which uncertain or unknown situations are perceived as threatening (high uncertainty avoidance indicates a strong desire to structure and control the future).

● Individualism/collectivism. The extent to which individuals and families are expected to look after themselves (more collectivist societies are characterized by strong social ties that offer unconditional support and protection throughout life).

● Masculinity/femininity. The extent to which 'masculine' values – assertiveness, ambition, achievement – dominate as opposed to 'feminine' values – relationships, quality of life, service (gender roles are clearly differentiated in highly masculine societies; in more feminine societies gender roles overlap). When brought together these dimensions successfully differentiate clusters of national cultural groups. Figure 1

Value Dimensions and Management Dilemmas

1. Universalism vs. Particularism
When no code, rule, or law seems to quite cover an exceptional case; should the most relevant rule be imposed however imperfectly, on that case, or should the case be considered on its unique merits, regardless of the rule?

2. Analyzing vs. Integrating
Are we more effective as managers when we analyze phenomena into parts, i.e., facts, items, tasks, numbers, units, points, specifics, or when we integrate and configure such details into whole patterns, relationships, and wider contexts?

3. Individualism vs. Communitarianism
Is it more important to focus upon the enhancement of each individual, his or her rights, motivations, rewards, capacities, attitudes, or should more attention be paid to the advancement of the corporation as a community, which all its members are pledged to serve?

4. Inner-directed vs. Outer-directed Orientation
Which are the more important guides to action, our inner-directed judgements, decisions, and commitments, or the signals, demands, and trends in the outside world to which we must adjust?

5. Time as Sequence vs. Time as Synchronization
Is it more important to do things fast, in the shortest possible sequence of passnig time, or to synchonize efforts so that completion is coordinated?

6. Achieved Status vs. Ascribed Status
Should the status of employees depend on what they have achieved and how they have perfomed, or on some other characteristic important to the corporation, i.e., age, seniority, gender, education, potential, strategic role?

7. Equality vs. Hierarchy
Is it more important that we treat employees as equals so as to elicit from them the best they have to give, or to emphasize the judgement and authority of the hierarchy that is coaching and evaluating them?

Source: Hampden-Turner and Trompenaars *The Seven Cultures of Capitalism*, 1994

Figure 2

illustrates why, for example, Japanese management approaches might not transfer easily to UK, US or Scandinavian contexts. In more recent works Hofstede has added a fifth dimension – long-term orientation (personal thrift, perseverance, adoption of traditions to the modern context) – which appears to be a particularly distinctive feature of East Asian cultures.

A more recent model is provided by another Dutchman, Fons Trompenaars (*see* Figure 2). In a recent book with Charles Hampden-Turner he identifies seven managerial dilemmas that are linked to distinctive dimensions of cultural difference.

Evaluating the research

Cross-national research of the kind cited here has revealed remarkable differences in attitudes and values – often among managers.

One study, by Andre Laurent, revealed distinctive patterns for managers in various European countries, the US, Indonesia and Japan. For example, only 18 per cent of US managers agree that 'the main reason for a hierarchical structure is so that everybody knows who has authority over whom' compared to 50 per cent of Italians and 86 per cent of Indonesians.

Only 22 per cent of Swedes feel there is a problem with 'by-passing the hierarchical line in order to have efficient work relationships' compared to 46 per cent of Germans and 75 per cent of Italians.

Ten per cent of Swedes feel that a manager should 'have at hand precise answers to most of the questions that his subordinates may raise about their work' compared to 53 per cent of the French and 78 per cent of the Japanese managers. Responses such as these suggest important differences in conceptions of the managerial role and the organizational context within which it is embedded. But the link between expressed values and attitudes on the one hand and actual behavior on the other is problematic – as much social science research shows. Survey-based studies can quickly produce quantifiable results, but they reveal ideals and preferences. How these connect with day-to-day organizational behavior is under-researched.

Clearly, despite their widely varying attitudes, Swedes, Italians and Indonesians are able to work together within the structures of constraint and compromise that shape behavior within business corporations. How they do this is largely unknown. Even where research has focussed upon behavior, there are problems in translating findings into the work organization context. Laboratory studies of interpersonal communication, language use and group dynamics may produce fascinating evidence of differences in the minutiae of social mannerisms but their impact upon critical managerial actions and performance is often assumed rather than demonstrated.

If Italians use different facial gestures to the Germans, what is the significance? If Brazilians and Swedes have contrasting tonal patterns in speech, does this necessarily have any impact in their ability to develop successful work relations?

Finally, there is a limit in the extent to which contrived laboratory studies – often of inexperienced students – can shed light upon the behavior of employees in 'real' work organizations that have distinctive histories, politics and corporate cultures. All this is to argue that the manner in which cultural differences are actually worked out in business organizations is unlikely to be ascertained via surveys or laboratory experiments. Participant observation, longitudinal case studies and detailed ethnographies are more likely to yield insights. But these methods are slow, expensive and do not produce 'quick' publications.

The management challenge

Despite these reservations there is enough evidence – research-based and anecdotal – to suggest that the way in which cultural diversity is managed may be an important determinant of the effectiveness of large global corporations.

Research by John Hunt at London Business School, for example, consistently shows differences in the motivational profiles of managers. Some examples from Europe and the US are provided in Figure 3. Recognizing these differences often represents the first step in designing reward systems that are effective across culturally diverse groups.

Such differences are also important in understanding – and improving – the performance of culturally diverse work teams. Many managers are aware of the major determinants of effective team behavior: a clear set of interdependent tasks, role allocation guided by individual attributes, a concern to balance task achievement with group involvement.

But the form that these behaviors take is culturally variable. The balance between 'task' and more supportive 'group maintenance' activities is itself a cultural product. The proportion of effort devoted to maintenance activities is traditionally higher in more

Cross-cultural goal differences

N = 5500 Managers

	High mean ranking	Low mean ranking
Comfort Search for financial gain, avoidance of discomfort and stress.	1. Spain 2. UK/US 3. France	1. Belgium 2. Sweden 3. Netherlands
Structure Avoidance of risk; search for clarity, order and structure.	1. UK 2. France 3. Switzerland	1. Netherlands 2. US 3. Sweden
Relationships Avoidance of isolation; desire to belong to a team	1. Sweden 2. Netherlands 3. Germany/Spain	1. UK 2. US 3. Italy
Recognition Desire for achievements to be recognised.	1. Italy 2. US 3. UK	1. Sweden 2. Netherlands 3. Spain
Power Desire to manage and control others.	1. Germany 2. US 3. France	1. Spain 2. Sweden 3. Netherlands
Autonomy/creativity/growth Search for freedom, independence, novelty, challenge, development.	1. Sweden 2. US/UK 3. Netherlands	1. Spain 2. Italy 3. France

Source: Hunt *Managing People at Work*, 1992

Figure 3

relationship-oriented cultures such as Japan. By comparison, highly individualist societies such as the UK or the US may produce highly task-focussed teams. The meaning attributed to group behavior is also variable. 'Strong leadership' in one culture may be 'pig headedness' in another; mild humour for some may be heavy sarcasm for others; what one person sees as 'lively' contribution can be experienced by another as aggressive disruption.

These are precisely the kind of misunderstandings that can quickly block the effective functioning of work teams. Many appear unable to recover from these accident-prone beginnings. Although, then, culturally diverse teams appear to offer greater potential – particularly for innovative and creative work – they are typically more difficult and time consuming to establish successfully.

Recent work by Sue Canney Davison suggests factors in Figure 4 – 'Achieving high performance in international teams' – are critical in creating effectively functioning international teams.

Achieving High Performance in International Teams

Setting up the team

- Choose people with appropriate skills, knowledge and goals
- Assess costs - and then double them
- Remove organizational barriers and seek top management support
- Involve team members' managers in the process
- Share the rationale with the team
- Provide training and support
- Explain national cultural influences
- Clarify task, timescales, accountability.

Running the team

- Start slowly and end faster (rushing to complete the task typically produces poor group processes)
- Use help to facilitate group skills (eg feedback, surfacing differences etc)
- Encourage participation: summarize, check understanding, seek consensus, keep track of time
- Surface and address differences (rather than 'accommodate' them)
- Build in time to discuss and review team processes

Source: Sue Canney Davison 'Creating a High Performance International Team'. *Journal of Management Development,* 1991

Figure 4

The impact of corporate culture

Despite well-documented differences among diverse labour forces there are clearly variations in the extent to which these are acknowledged. In some corporations ethnic, gender and national differences are publicly recognized and reflected in carefully constructed human resource policies and personnel procedures. In the US, for example, some corporations now boast senior vice presidents 'for diversity'. But elsewhere diversity is barely on the agenda. Nancy Adler has differentiated distinctive cultural assumptions about diversity and their managerial implications. At one extreme there may be the assumption of 'homogeneity'. Dominant cultural groups within organizations may make the (implicit) claim that 'we're all the same here' – with the implication that everyone is 'like us'. This effectively makes the issue of diversity 'undiscussable'. There may be differences but they are publicly ignored.

Paradoxically, this pattern can be seen in organizations regarded as 'traditional' or 'conservative' and dominated by one – typically male – national group as well as in more contemporary and apparently 'progressive' organizations with more diverse senior management groups.

By contrast, ethnocentric assumptions recognize diversity but see it as a problem. The dominant view in such organizations is that 'ours is the best way', therefore differences are to be minimized. Many international businesses appear to be characterized by such assumptions.

As such, the task of management as the organization grows is to educate, socialize and ultimately convert 'locals' to the preferred norms, values and customs of the parent company.

Although it seems implausible – and, indeed undesirable – that many companies will ever lose touch with their cultural origins (Levis, Coke and McDonald's are intrinsically 'American' just as Volkswagen and Bosch are 'German'), it also appears unlikely that deep-rooted sources of local cultural diversity – stemming from family background, religion, ethnicity and so on – can be conveniently wished away. Synergistic assumptions are those that recognize that diversity brings both advantages and problems. The implication is that creative combinations of 'our way' and 'theirs' may be best.

This approach acknowledges diversity and seeks to manage it in ways that fully exploit available opportunities. This, in effect, is the ideology of those 'progressive' organizations that are now institutionalizing – through senior executive appointments – the new function of 'diversity'. It is still too early fully to assess the success of their efforts.

Management development issues

It is possible, however, to see the emerging ground rules that are likely to determine the ability of individuals to manage across cultures. These may be briefly summarized as follows:

● Recognize your own cultural 'biases'. Some discussions of the new international manager evoke an image of a slick, cosmopolitan who has completely lost contact with his or her cultural roots. Recent descriptions of the 'Euromanager' appear to fall into this trap. Yet it is clear that an appreciation of diversity inevitably starts with an acknowledgement of personal cultural origins. Respect for one's own culture is likely to increase respect for others.

More generally, it seems likely that leadership potential partially derives from these qualities. In effect, a sense of 'where you come from' can provide the platform upon which leadership qualities such as integrity, courage and honesty can rest.

● Assume others are different. Some differences are clearly visible and difficult to avoid. Physical attributes – for example, size, weight, height, skin color, hair length and so on – may fall into this category (although which physical attributes are noted and accorded significance is itself culturally determined). Other characteristics – such as individual values, attitudes and motives – are less visible and often more difficult to determine.

In the absence of reliable information there is a well-documented tendency for individuals to assume that others are 'like them'. In any setting this is likely to be an inappropriate assumption; for those who manage diverse workforces this tendency towards 'cultural assimilation' can prove particularly damaging.

● Assume differences are significant. Although we have earlier argued that some differences in attitude or behavior may have little or no consequence in the workplace, it is best to begin with the assumption that differences may be important. From this position, the manager can determine the impact of diversity on the basis of experience and careful observation. Assuming differences are insignificant is likely to damage relationships in such a way that recovery is impossible.

● Do not assume differences are always 'cultural'. There are several sources of difference. Some relate to factors such as personality, aptitude or competence. It is a mistake to assume that all perceived differences are cultural in origin. Too many managers tend to fall back on the easy 'explanation' that individual behavior or performance can be attributed to the fact that someone is 'Italian' or 'a Catholic' or 'a woman'. Such conclusions are more likely to reflect intellectually lazy rather than culturally sensitive managers.

● Use stereotypes carefully. It is difficult to avoid the use of stereotypes. Indeed, some would argue that (accurate) stereotypes carry useful information about the typical attitudes, norms and values of any particular cultural group. The mistake, of course, is to apply uncritically a research-based stereotype to any one individual. At the interpersonal level, cultural awareness is more likely to involve undermining rather than reproducing stereotypes.

Summary

Increasingly heterogeneous cities and regions, closer alignment between ethnic groups and the new political structures of eastern Europe, and the restructuring of transnational corporations help explain recent interest in cultural diversity. Cultural differences can be mapped around relationships with the physical environment, conceptions of space and time, expectations about the distribution of power, the extent to which the unknown is threatening, individualism/collectivism and masculinity/ femininity. In the workplace participant observation, longitudinal case studies and detailed ethnographies are more likely to yield insights into cultural difference than surveys or laboratory experiments.

At one extreme – homogeneity – diversity in organizations is undiscussable. Ethnocentric assumptions at least recognize diversity but see it as a problem (management's task being to convert 'locals' to the norms of the parent company). A synergistic approach acknowledges that it brings both advantages and problems.

Ground rules for managing across cultures include recognizing your own cultural bias, assuming others are different and that the differences are significant, not assuming that they are always 'cultural', and being careful about stereotypes.

Suggested further reading

Adler, N.J. *International Dimensions of Organizational Behavior,* 2nd edn, PWS-Kent, Boston.

Canney Davison, S. 'Creating a high performance international team', *Journal of Management Development*, Vol.13 No.2, pp. 81-90.

Hampden-Turner, C. and Trompenaars, F. *The Seven Cultures of Capitalism*, Piatkus, London.

Hofstede, G. *Cultures and Organizations*, McGraw Hill, London.

Hunt, J. *Managing People at Work*, McGraw Hill, London.

Laurent, A. 'The cultural diversity of western conceptions of management', *International Studies of Management and Organization,* Vol 13, pp. 75-96.

Mant, A. (1994) *Leaders We Deserve*, Blackwell, Oxford.

Human Resource Management

Contents

The art of managing people 251
Lynda Gratton, London Business School
Few companies succeed in linking the way they manage their human 'assets' with their overall business strategy.

Search for the virtual water cooler 258
Joseph W. Harder, The Wharton School of the University of Pennsylvania
The 'virtual office' has the potential for radical and positive redesign of work – but it may also pose some problems for people.

Key to competitive advantage 262
Peter Cappelli and Anne Crocker-Hefter, The Wharton School of the University of Pennsylvania
In theory, people management practices should reinforce business strategies. But in many companies distinctive human resource practices drive competitiveness.

Choices and the high-performance workplace 267
Larry W. Hunter, The Wharton School of the University of Pennsylvania
Human resource managers have come under increasing pressure from factors both outside and within organizations, not least the bundle of employee practices connected with the so-called 'high-performance workplace'.

Contributors

Dr Lynda Gratton is Assistant Professor of Organizational Behaviour at London Business School. She is also Director of the Leading Edge Research Consortium. The research on which this article is based is funded by the companies in that consortium.

Joseph W. Harder is Assistant Professor of Management at the Wharton School of the University of Pennsylvania. His research and teaching interests include leadership, teamwork, motivation, human resources management and organizational justice.

Peter Cappelli is Professor of Management at the Wharton School of the University of Philadelphia, and Chair of the Management Department. He is also co-director of Wharton's Center for Human Resources, and co-director of the US Department of Education's National Center on the Educational Quality of the Workforce.

Anne Crocker-Hefter is a consultant with Andersen Consulting Strategic Services and a MBA graduate from the Wharton School of the University of Pennsylvania, 1993.

Larry W. Hunter is Paul Yeakel Term Assistant Professor of Management at the Wharton School of the University of Pennsylvania. His research interests include the effects of companies' employment practices on both individuals and organizations, and the relationship of those practices to organizational strategy and to the broader environment.

Introduction

Like Organizational Behavior, Human Resource Management (HRM) is concerned with the individual or groups within the organization. However, as its name implies, HRM regards people as a 'resource' to be 'managed' rather than as a set of behaviors to be studied, though this should not be taken to imply a cold, mechanistic approach. The aim of human resource specialists is to maximize the potential of people and this usually means a co-operative approach.

Given the ubiquitous corporate cliché that 'people are our greatest asset' – which like most clichés contain a strong element of truth – the effective management of human resources is a major consideration for all general managers.

The HRM module begins with the presentation of recent new research into the way human resource management can be aligned with business strategy. It is followed by an examination of the implications of 'hot desking' and the 'virtual corporation', a further look at the relationship of human resources to business strategy and concludes with the development of the 'high performance' workplace.

Related topics are covered in other modules: 6: Organizational Behavior; 8: Managing People in Organizations; and 16: Leadership Skills.

The art of managing people

■ **Few companies succeed in linking the way they manage people with their overall business strategy. But, as research carried out at London Business School shows, this can be achieved with significant results, writes** Lynda Gratton

A key challenge facing organizations in the late 1990s is how they can continue to deliver sustained competitive advantage in the short-term while preparing for longer-term success.

The main sources of competitive advantage in the past decades may have been access to financial resources or the use of technology; these sources are now viewed as necessary but not sufficient. For many companies the sources of sustained competitive advantage rest not only with the access to finance or capital but within the organization, with people capable of delivering the 'customer delight' or rapid innovation that will place a company ahead of its competitors.

Even the most casual observation of life in many companies will pinpoint the crucial impact of lack of integration between the plans of the company and the human resource processes. How often do corporate plans and mission statements remain simply that senior executive rhetoric that has little meaning to those people with the task of delivering customer delight or bringing complex products rapidly to the market place?

Corporate mission statements extol customer satisfaction or product innovation. But when the communication fanfare is over and the customer-focus workshops have been completed, what is left? Groups of people trying to make sense of the paradoxes and mixed messages with which they are faced, who try to understand the underlying message of customer delight when no attempt is made to provide them with the skills necessary to deliver it, who are rewarded and promoted for delivering short-term financial targets and who see the people who try hardest to understand customers' needs penalized for the time they take to do so.

Faced with this plethora of contradictory messages, employees, in their quest for 'sense making', look at which behaviors are rewarded, what skills are promoted, who is developed. It is these messages, not the corporate rhetoric, that form the basis of the sense making process and which give the steer on how to behave. If these human resource processes and policies are misaligned, failing to reinforce the business strategy and corporate rhetoric, then performance will suffer.

Linking HR and strategy

Here, we examine how explicit links between individual performance, human resource processes and business strategy are created and sustained. These explicit links between HR policy and practices and overall organizational strategic aims are a central feature of strategic human resource management (SHRM). Some of the key contextual variables of strategic human resource management are shown in Figure 1.

There has been a great deal of debate about the nature of the relationship between these variables. Four questions appear to be especially significant:

● How does the linkage between business strategy and human resource strategy work?
● What are the key internal and external contextual variables that affect the design and implementation of human resource strategies?
● What are the key HR activities that link business strategy to performance?
● What role does line management play in influencing outcomes?

How does the linkage between business strategy and human resource strategy work?

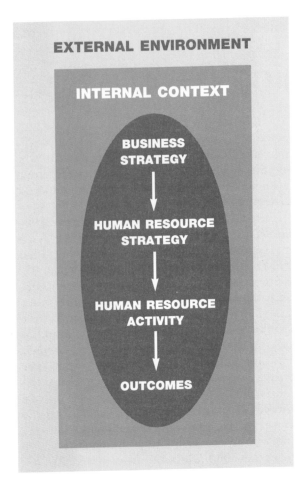

EXTERNAL ENVIRONMENT

INTERNAL CONTEXT

BUSINESS
STRATEGY

↓

HUMAN RESOURCE
STRATEGY

↓

HUMAN RESOURCE
ACTIVITY

↓

OUTCOMES

Figure 1

Much attention has been devoted to understanding how human resource management relates to business strategy. It has been argued that organizational effectiveness depends on a tight fit between business strategy and HRM. For example, Miles and Snow (*see* 'Suggested further reading') argue that 'the human resources management system must be tailored to the demands of business strategy'.

They categorize organizations into four types, depending on the particular strategy they are pursuing, as either Defenders, Prospectors, Analysers or Reactors, and advocate a particular set of HR practices designed to support each of these strategic types.

Others advocate a fit between HR strategy and stages in the organizational life-cycle or between a particular competitive strategy and

'needed role behaviors'. However, recently these 'fit' models have been criticized on a number of counts. The concept of fit can imply rigidity and inflexibility – it could be that lack of fit may be equally important for facilitating organizational change in response to an external crisis. In addition, the matching of HRM processes to business strategy implies a unitary business strategy, when in many organizations there are different strategies. The concept of 'fit' may also be overly rational – that what is planned is implemented.

But we know from Henry Mintzberg's work (*see* 'Suggested further reading') that strategy has two aspects – what is planned and what is achieved; thus, it can be either 'intended' or 'emergent'. In other words, there is the formal, planned (or intended) strategy and there is the strategy that comes about on an informal basis, which is 'emergent'. Similarly, human resource strategy is a pattern and can be either intended or emergent and is not necessarily the result of a formal planning process.

Both HRS and strategy can therefore be emergent and, if they are, this raises interesting questions concerning the nature of any 'fit' between the two. The acknowledgement of this dichotomy is critical for advancing our understanding of the process of strategic human resource management.

What are the key external and internal variables?

Considerable progress has been made recently in recognizing the importance of contextual variables, even though in some cases these have been highly complex. The contextual variables that have been identified fall into two main categories: external variables at the level of society, and internal, organizational variables.

External context. At the social level, demographic factors are changing the shape of the workforce, with a declining number of young people entering the job market. This clearly has a knock-on effect on human resource strategies in areas such as how to continue to attract young people to the organization, or how to attract people from alternative groups (for example, women returners), and how to design a rewards package to ensure that they remain with the organization.

Other changes at the social level include increased education in the workforce and the associated question of how to design challenging jobs, together with factors such as women's increased career aspirations and the associated pressures on organizations to increase provisions to enable women to pursue careers.

Technological changes are also highly significant for organizations and can give rise to alterations in the structuring of work. At the economic level changes in, for example, the balance between public and private sector, inflation or the shift from manufacturing to services can have big implications for the way in which people are managed.

New employment legislation, such as equal opportunities laws, can equally affect human resource strategies, and the way in which success is defined in society can be markedly influenced by political changes.

Internal context. At the broader, societal, level there are many factors that affect the way in which people are managed within organizations. It is through the mediation of the 'organizational environment', however, that these broader environmental changes are made meaningful to individuals. They include such elements as technology, culture, philosophy and management style, structure and the 'dominant coalition'. One of the most frequently referred to aspects of the internal environment is organizational culture. This involves a 'shared vision' and a common understanding of organizational goals and values and is historically founded. To quote from Adler and Jelinek (*see* 'Suggested further reading'): 'Culture, whether organizational or national, is frequently defined as a set of taken-for-granted assumptions, expectations or rules for being in the world. . . the culture concept emphasized the shared cognitive approaches to reality that distinguish a given group from others.'

Similarly, management philosophy in terms of the nature of the psychological contract with employees is an important intervening variable. The type of culture an organization has can exert a strong influence on the nature of its business strategy and also on its chosen human resource

strategy, as well as being influenced by them. One particularly important aspect of organizational culture is the nature and style of leadership.

The concept of organizational power has also been described as significant to understanding the SHRM process. One example is the 'dominant coalition', or the most powerful group, usually the management operating team. Their needs and expectations of the HR department will help to shape its activities. In addition to these, other internal stakeholders, such as employee groups, managers, employees and professional staff, who hold a stake in the way human resources are managed in the organization, also influence SHRM.

Organizational structure is another significant feature of an organization's 'inner context' that influences HRS, and the characteristics of the HR department itself for example, the way in which it acquires and uses knowledge of the rest of the organization, the level of HR expertise, the nature of the HR expertise, the nature of the HR information system, the ability to identify and plan for the future, and infrastructional linkages.

HR activities that link business strategy to performance

This question has been central to the work of the Leading Edge Research Team based at London Business School and the Judge Institute of Cambridge University. Since 1992 the research team has examined how eight large companies link business strategy to individual and team performance. The model showing the main areas of linkage is presented in Figure 2. It focusses on those necessary to deliver short-term business performance and prepare for longer-term business success.

We would argue that the closer or stronger the linkage between business strategy and human resource processes, the greater competitiveness and organizational effectiveness. In the following, the processes are described with reference to strong linkage to business strategy.

Delivering short-term goals

This model has as a core the cycle of activities

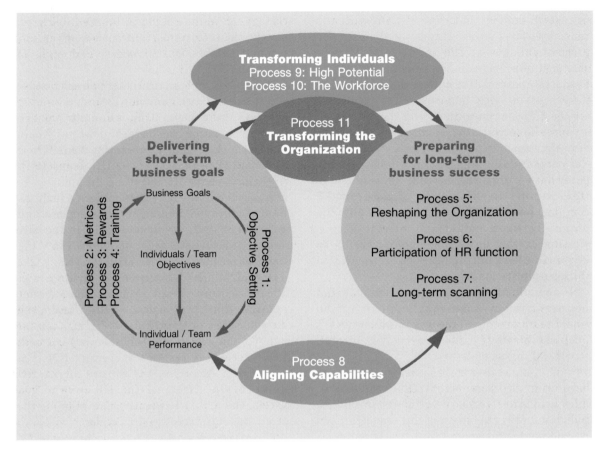

Figure 2: The People Process Framework

that link the annual business objectives to the performance of individuals via objective-setting, performance appraisal and measurement, rewarding, and targeted technical and managerial training.

Process 1: Individual and team objectives linked to business goals. An essential aspect of performance management are those processes that cascade business objectives into the objectives and responsibilities of individuals and teams. These processes are increasingly important as the trend towards decentralization gives managers and employees more authority and responsibility for the delivery of business objectives. At the strongest level of strategic integration it could be expected that the business objectives of the overall strategic plan are clearly articulated to the individual and are transformed into clear objectives that are discussed and agreed on an annual or bi-annual basis.

Process 2: Performance metrics and appraisal reflect business goals. Measurement and appraisal of performance becomes vital in that responsibility is placed on individuals and teams. This measurement serves as the basis of management control and the means by which the contribution of the business unit to the organization can be recognized. The emphasis on metrics has historically been on financial measures such as profitability or return on assets. However, for those companies striving to create strong linkage with business strategy, the emphasis has to be on metrics associated with all aspects of business strategy, not simply financial targets.

To achieve the strongest level of linkage, the processes have to be capable of measuring a wide range of outcomes, including those requiring 'softer' measures such as customer satisfaction or team-building competencies. This combination of the 'hard' and the 'soft' is a central aspect of those performance metrics and appraisal processes that are strongly linked to business strategy.

Process 3: Individuals and teams rewarded for business-focussed preference. Reward processes can be one of the greatest sources of leverage available to a company in its quest to increase organizational performance and effectiveness. Yet it remains one the most under-utilized and potentially complex tools for driving organizational performance. The importance and complexity of linking reward strategies to business goals in a systematic manner has been a recurrent theme in the research, as is the importance and difficulty of linking rewards to the longer-term view.

If reward processes are strongly linked to business strategy it could be expected that they would reinforce the behaviors crucial to those the business strategy emphasizes, (for example, long-term versus short-term, customer focus versus financial results). High enough to encourage effort, information concerning the allocation of rewards is communicated to the individual so that the reward system is accepted and performance measures are believed.

Process 4: Training reinforces and supports the business goals. A key aspect of the delivery of short-term business goals is the ability of the organization rapidly to develop the skills and competencies required. This can be crucial as technological changes demand a whole new set of skills. The emphasis is on understanding of the skills and competencies required, an analysis of individual and team training needs, and the design and delivery of this training.

Preparing for long-term success

The processes supporting the delivery of longer-term business success are divided into four clusters. The first cluster focusses on the processes and routines that ensure the people imperatives of the longer-term vision of the company are understood. The emphasis here is on 'emerging' strategies and aims to capture both the informal and formal processes that create iteration.

In the second cluster, the emphasis is on the role the human resource function plays in developing long-term strategy documents and emphasizes the formal process of involvement and documentation.

In the third cluster, the scanning processes are examined, particularly those processes associated with the capability to understand the longer-term people trends.

The fourth cluster concerns those processes that bridge from the needs of the future to the capabilities of the present.

Process 5: Reshaping the view of the organization. As far back as the 1960s it was well understood by organizations, such as the oil group Shell, that the ability to respond quickly to changing needs and build long-term organizational capability depended in part on the ability of managers to visualize and create mental pictures of the future. This allows managers to move from the fire-fighting mode to one where they have the potential to think in the longer term.

Yet while this concern with the longer term has been widely acknowledged to be a 'good thing', the actual processes that could support this perspective are less well understood. At the highest level of strategic integration it could be expected that cross-functional management teams work through a process in which they discuss the various potential scenarios of the future. These scenarios are described against a number of variables, some of which refer to people.

In particular there is debate about the potential structure of the company (key job roles, interfacing processes, networking mechanisms); the culture (norms, key behaviors); senior management (experiences, skill sets); people (skill sets, aspirations and motivations, age, experience) and supporting HR processes (selection, reward, development).

These discussions create an understanding of some of the main determinants for future success and how these can be measured and mapped against current capabilities.

Process 6: HR function fully participating. In the second cluster of processes, the focus is on the role that people issues have in the formal strategic planning process. It examines in detail the means by which people issues are formally integrated into strategic planning.

The level of integration between strategic plans and human resource plans and strategies is well understood. At the lowest level, people aspects are simply integrated into fully formed strategy documents. At the next level of strategic integration there is some interaction between the formulation of the strategic plans and the plans for human resources. At the highest level of strategic integration people are fully integrated into strategy formulation. At this level the interactions between the human resource representatives and other members of the strategy team are numerous and mutually interactive, occurring on both a formal and informal basis.

Process 7: Long-term scanning takes place. The reshaping processes described earlier are essentially a set of inward-focussed processes designed to understand the people implications of the long-term business strategies. However, processes and routines that increase awareness of the probable external context have a major role to play. The range of these scanning processes are well understood and include trend analysis and environmental scanning (for example, demographic, socio-cultural, political and legal). This scanning process allows the management group to 'identify the issues that rise to attention' and by doing so those issues are capable of being sources of 'pain' or 'gain'.

Process 8: Focus on the future. It is not sufficient for organizations to create leverage from the routines and processes that support the delivery of short-term business goals. For longer-term success the focus must also be on those processes and routines that create a vision of the future and begin to map out the key people implications of this vision.

Transformational processes

However, without a set of transformational processes the vision of the future remains simply that, a fantasy that will never achieve reality. The transformational processes are clustered at an individual and organizational level. At the individual level the first cluster is around those processes designed to identify and develop future

senior executives. The second focusses on the means by which the skills and abilities of key individuals are transformed in line with future needs. At the organizational level the emphasis is on those processes and competencies that support successful transformational change, which are at the very heart of the organization's ability to learn.

Process 9: Transforming high-potential individuals. This cluster describes those processes and routines capable of identifying those people with high potential and creating development tracks that take them through significant work experience and targeted development to entry to succession planning or 'back-stop' processes where their names appear on the company's succession lists.

The processes that support the development of high-potential cadres are well understood and have been documented across many companies. They cover a broad range of activities that include training, coaching, self-improvement and the provision of significant job experiences.

Process 10: Transforming the workforce. While much attention is paid to the high potential groups that will be the basis of the future senior management cadres, the long-term viability of the company also depends on key groups of people whose skills and knowledge may contribute to a core competence. These groups may include, for example, the customer-facing roles in retail banking or the central marketing roles in a manufacturing company.

While many of the individuals in these positions will not attain senior executive posts their continued performance, motivation and commitment to the company may be critical to the capability to deliver long-term business success.

The processes that transform the current skills of the workforce to meet future needs have two elements. The first is the forecasting of the future skill needs. The basis of this has been described in those processes concerned with preparing for long-term business success. It is acknowledged that this forecasting of future staffing needs can be difficult, particularly in times of rapid change. However, if strong linkage is to be established with long-term business strategy then this projection of future staffing requirements is critical.

The second element is those career planning processes that support the longer-term development of the workforce. While this commitment to the longer-term development and retention of people with important skills may be vital to a company, the policies and processes that support this commitment are fraught with difficulties.

No western company can now support a policy of life-time employment; to do so would run counter to the long-term flexibility and cost effectiveness that may be central to long-term success.

Companies face a real paradox here. Dismantling the processes associated with long-term careers creates flexibility but breaks the psychological contract that may be crucial to retaining key skills. However, those with the strongest linkage with business strategy will have created a portfolio of career development processes that provide broad support to the development of the workforce.

Process 11: Transforming the organization. The focus on individuals skills, motivation and commitment are central to the transformation of the organization. In widening the focus of attention we must understand those processes and routines that support the transformation of the organization at a macro level. These processes link the understanding of the longer term with current capabilities and include understanding the current state of the system, planning for change, transitional management and understanding the desired outcomes.

This requires a capacity to implement strategic plans, yet be adaptive and responsive in the face of unanticipated pressures at all levels of the organization. This capability must be supported by project management and change agent skills among a significant number of managers, models of change and an understanding of the patterns of change over time.

What role does line management play in influencing outcomes?

Developing and delivering a strategic approach to human resource management is complex and requires time and resources. We know that line managers have a a big role to play and those companies most able to integrate business strategy with people management do so in part through commitment from their line management.

In the final part of this article we consider, from the London Business School research, those factors that influence the capability of line managers to practice strategic human resource management. We identify the four factors that have an impact on line mangers in each of the organizations we considered. In those companies where line managers took an active and committed role in people management we found:

● *People management objectives set:* people management is an important aspect of the performance appraisal process and people management capability is assessed (through team feedback and completion of personal development plans) and seen as a key performance objective.

● *People management training in place:* those organizations with committed people managers emphasized the role of training in people management skills. However, across all the companies the emphasis on people management objective setting and training was in part undermined by two aspects of the external and internal context; the pressure for short-term results and the impact of organizational restructuring.

● *Short-termism:* in many organizations the key drivers are to maintain and increase share price through cost costing, emphasizing short-term income. This external pressure has two distinct effects on managers' capacity to manage people. First, managers understand both formally, through performance objectives, and informally, through the demands of their bosses, that the main priority is the 'hard stuff', 'the numbers', while the softer people management issues are of less significance. Second, managers have (as a result) little incentive to invest time in processes such as transforming individuals that do not have a short-term pay off.

● *Impact of organizational restructuring:* all of the organizations we studied had undergone a significant program of restructuring. The managers who remain are faced with a wider span of control and larger numbers of staff reporting to them. This places considerable pressure on the time available for people management activities, with the result they have less time to respond to day-to-day issues and are reluctant to invest time in mentoring and coaching younger staff because of the opportunity costs of foregoing other activities. What we begin to see are the hidden costs of delayering organizations. When organizations are 'flattened', the softer elements of managerial roles are among the first to be squeezed out of day-to-day activities.

Summary

Some academics argue that companies should adopt a particular set of HR practices depending on their strategic 'type' or stage in the organizational life cycle. Others say the concept of 'fit' can cause rigidity and inflexibility. HR strategy can either be planned or emergent. Its design and implementation can be affected by external variables such as the number of young people entering the job market, an increasing level of education, or new employment laws, and by internal variables such as corporate culture, leadership style, and the 'dominant coalition' (or most powerful group) phenomenon.

An important issue for companies is to identify HR activities which link business strategy to performance. Key processes highlighted in recent research on eight large companies include: reflecting business goals in individual and team objectives, and in performance measures; rewards; training; visualizing the future; and identifying and encouraging individual talent. The same research suggests that people management is an important part of the performance appraisal process.

Suggested further reading

Adler, N.J. and Jelinek, M. (1986) 'Is organization culture culture sound?' *Human Resource Management*, 25(1): 73-90.

Barney, J. (1991) 'Firm resources and sustained competitive advantage', *Journal of Management*, 17: 99-120.

Lundberg, C.C. (1985) 'Toward a contextual model of human resource strategy: lessons from the Reynolds Corporation', *Human Resource Management*, 24(1): 91-112.

Miles, R.E. and Snow, C.C. (1984) 'Designing strategic human resources systems', *Organizational Dynamics*, Summer: 36-52.

Mintzberg, H. (1978) 'Patterns in strategy formation', *Management Science*, 24(9): 934-48.

Schuler, R.S. and Jackson, S.E. (1987) 'Linking competitive strategies with human resource management practices', *Academy of Management Executive*, 1(3): 207-19.

Tichy, N.M., Fombrun, C.J. and Devanna, M.A. (1982) 'Strategic human resource management', *Sloan Management Review*, 23(2): 47-61.

Search for the virtual water cooler

■ **The 'virtual office' is held up as the way we will work in the future. But it may also pose some problems for people, says**
Joseph W. Harder

A building is, we hope, a fairly stable thing. Certain features, such as load-bearing walls, foundations and mechanical systems lend an air of permanence, and somewhat constrain changes that organizational designers might like to make. But at the same time, new ways of designing work are requiring flexibility of furnishings and adaptability of space.

As an example, whether it is referred to as hotelling, hot desking, just-in-time space or non-territorial offices, the idea that people no longer have their 'own' desk but must use whatever is available at the time means that furnishings and equipment must be suitable for several individuals of potentially different heights, sizes and weights.

This includes chairs that can be customized, articulated keyboard holders and adjustable lighting, so that each user can adjust the environment for his or her best usage. Flexible and easily assembled furniture systems are becoming more important, so that physical space can be adapted for either individual or team work.

One tension that is resulting is between control and empowerment. An effect of what are becoming known as 'virtual offices' is that individuals are largely removed from having supervisors directly overseeing their work. This means, of course, that self-motivation is increasingly important. It also makes it more difficult for managers to evaluate performance. This is especially true in cases where teams are used or where process and not just outcome is considered relevant, for example where ethical issues might arise.

For the increasing number of employees working away from the physical office, the autonomy or freedom to perform the job as desired is juxtaposed against the potential loss of visibility, a lack of access to the grapevine and a danger of being passed over for salary rises and promotions in favour of someone who has more 'face time'. For the manager, the traditional ideas of controlling and appraising performance become problematic with increased tele-commuting and the diffusion of individual responsibility through the use of team-based work.

Power vs performance and status vs functionality are also relevant trade-offs to consider in changing physical space.

Space = status

In research on perceptions of organizational justice around non-financial rewards, including offices and parking spaces, the rule for parking spaces perceived as most just was first-come, first-served, an equality of opportunity if you will. The sense of fairness for the reserved parking space, whether for high status or high performing individuals, was not as high. But for office space, status came out solidly on top, followed by performance, with equality a distant third.

Indeed, the typical large US organization has used office space as much for its symbolic value as a reward for loyalty and initiative as it has for its functionality. This begs the question of how the virtual office might arouse feelings of injustice, which can affect motivation, morale and job satisfaction.

At IBM's Cranford, New Jersey, location hotelling has allowed a decrease from 400,000 square feet to 100,000. But a by-product of this has been that hierarchical distinctions have completely vanished, at least as far as types of work spaces go. In Ernst and Young's attempts at hotelling, partners, managers and staff get different types of offices depending on rank. This is not to imply that one is a better approach than the other, just that one reinforces traditional notions of status and power and one subverts them.

Another example of performance and functionality vs power and status comes from a top business school's recent move to a new building. It was designed in a modified U shape so all faculty members had a windowed office. It provided limited access to students, since it was a separate building from the one housing the classrooms, had stairwells that were locked to the outside and students, of course, didn't have keys so elevators, which were slow and balky despite being new, were necessary to access faculty offices.

However, another design innovation showed how crucial it is to consider social, as well as technical, factors. The original plan called for a re-engineering of the administrative assistant function, with the best secretaries being promoted to 'cluster heads', supervising three or four other secretaries. The four faculty members whose offices were closest to each secretary were then to share that person's services.

So offices were assigned to faculty members based on a plan to divide the secretarial work equitably. For example, since finance professors typically require different types of assistance than management professors – more equations in research papers, fewer items of correspondence with colleagues and so on – each secretary was supposed to have a mix of types of professors. In addition, this plan was supposed to encourage cross-departmental thinking and inter-disciplinary research among faculty.

But what happened next was somewhat surprising, except perhaps to those of us who study organizational behavior. Faculty members began to trade, negotiate, barter and power play with each other for different offices. They did this for two broad reasons. One, some professors wanted to be closer to their faculty buddies, so deals were worked out. Most of these got people from the same departments closer together. Second, faculty members desired the services of some particularly competent secretaries more than others, and attempted to get offices within their cluster. So much for interdisciplinary thinking and workload equity. They should have known better than to try this with business school faculty.

The two briefcases approach

The concept of hotelling also raises issues of privacy vs publicness. Some studies have shown that employees have greater work satisfaction when they are able to add personal touches to their work environment. A picture of the family reminds them why they work so hard, perhaps, or an award on the wall is a reminder of prior success when the current going gets tough. According to one anonymous industrial designer, discussing Arthur Andersen's use of hotelling, staff typically 'live out of two briefcases – one containing work, the other containing things which personalize their desks'.

Earlier this year an article in the *New York Times* told the story of Peggy Roswell, an executive at Chiat Day advertising agency who is one of about 40 employees who lost their offices as part of a pilot program to create a 'virtual office'. The personal touches that used to adorn the walls of her office, such as pictures of her daughter and her softball team, now sit in a cardboard box in the back of her Nissan Pathfinder. Without an office, she says, she 'lost a sense of security of an office with my name on it'. She adds: 'But it's something we have to let go of.' While she seems understanding of the change, many others may not feel so charitable and may fear the upsetting of traditional ways.

Joan Hilliers, an office designer of 36 years, asserts that it is becoming increasingly important to design 'plonk' space. That, of course, is simply a place where workers can plonk down their stuff when they need some dedicated and perhaps secure space. The question becomes: how much do they really need to get by?

Beginning in the 1960s, especially in high-technology companies, it became fashionable to have open offices or cubicles rather than the closed private offices that had largely prevailed to that point. The aim was to encourage co-operation, decrease shirking or non-productive behavior, and reinforce an egalitarian organizational culture.

But there have been some unintended consequences of this office configuration, and it is important to consider these in light of the move to more team-oriented ways of working. Mary Jo Hatch, a professor of management at Copenhagen Business School, carried out a study in which managers kept logs of their workdays. One of her counterintuitive findings was that managers with private offices communicated with more people, and more openly, than did managers in open offices.

The open communication is perhaps not too surprising, given that closed doors often yield more honesty. But that managers in private offices had wider communication networks was interesting. On follow-up, it was found that managers in private offices made more effort to communicate with others, largely because they were not being seen widely. Managers in open offices had the perception that they were connected, but it was with a smaller set of people.

Apple Computer recently designed a new research and development complex and chose to go with private offices, clustered around team space, rather than cubicles. It seems that so many employees had home computers, modems and the like, that they were staying home to avoid the distractions of their open offices. Only by giving them some privacy could Apple encourage them actually to come to work, where many of the best new innovations come from people informally bouncing ideas off each other.

The move to the virtual office has its own holy grail – the search for the virtual water cooler, a place where employees can gather informally to exchange information, make informal plans, build esprit de corps and quench their thirsts in more ways than one.

Technology might yet provide the answer, but it is a sticky problem. Hewlett Packard just came out with a product called Omnishare, in which two people in different locations can have the same document on their screens simultaneously. If you scribble notes on your screen, your partner can see them and respond.

A related approach appeared in an experiment done at the Xerox Technology Research Park in Palo Alto in the late-1980s in which engineers were working on a common project in three different locations. The engineers each had a video camera trained on their room, with the picture from the other two locations beamed in. So each location had one camera and two screens.

After some initial awkwardness with the technology an amazing thing happened. One engineer got out of his seat and approached one of the video screens that was showing a technical drawing from another site and began drawing on the screen with a pen. His drawings in turn were broadcast to the other two sites on their screens and truly collaborative work occurred.

Some companies have local area networks that run company-specific newsgroups or bulletin boards, but since these have wide access, some self-censoring typically occurs. This leads into the next dimension, security vs access.

The information highway is providing unprecedented access to information, yet we have really only scratched the surface. A recent survey found that only 6 per cent of Americans go 'online', and only 5 per cent use the Internet. Also significant is that 30 per cent of Americans dislike or have mixed feelings about computers, and 34 per cent say that computers make no difference in their lives.

Access to information will likely only continue to increase. But with access goes a concern about security. An article in the *Wall Street Journal* stated that reported intrusions into computer networks in 1993 totalled more than 1,300, and many times that number went unreported.

Home vs office

Along with the benefits of the virtual office go some other concerns. As we have seen, opportunities for casual interactions are limited and creativity, innovation and perhaps even morale and a sense of group purpose can be adversely affected. Back to Ms. Roswell at Chiat Day, who says: 'I've been hesitant to set up an office in my home. I got into the agency business because I wanted to be part of an agency.'

The fact is, though, that the distinction between home and office is becoming blurred.

With this blurring comes the danger of overload and stress, as it becomes increasingly difficult to separate work demands from other responsibilities and desires, and achieve an appropriate balance in the two. As Ms. Roswell says: 'I have a feeling now that it is no longer my life fitting into my work, but my work fitting into my life.'

'It's an office, not the office,' said Michael Bell, the director of corporate real estate for Dun and Bradstreet, at a conference entitled 'Home, Sweet Office'. Similarly, Jay Chiat, principle of Chiat Day, says: 'Work is no longer a place but a process.'

Still, as Paul Saffo, of the Institute for the Future in Menlo Park, California, comments: 'Heaven is the anywhere, anytime office...Hell is the everywhere, every time office.'

What we are really talking about is revamping the way in which work gets done.

Hotelling (and telecommuting) have so far been a small firm phenomenon, with 44 per cent of employees in small firms involved compared to 10 per cent in larger firms.

The magazine *Architectural Record*, in an article on the impact of technology on the workplace, asserted that 'the typical post-war American office tower is becoming obsolete.

Historians credit a nascent service sector and the development of the elevator for making skyscrapers possible. But as computers become smaller, more powerful and more versatile, they become a physical leveller; electronic 'streets' have rendered the real street obsolete.'

Michael Brill, Professor of Architecture at Suny-Buffalo and the President of the Buffalo Organization for Social and Technological Innovation, talks about the decline of large urban office buildings: In the past, he says: 'We put all the information in file cabinets and buildings and then each day brought people in to work on it; that's what those (office buildings) are all about. And that's just profoundly different now, let alone 20 years from now.'

Summary
The idea that people no longer have their own desks – a phenomenon increasingly known as the 'virtual' office – is creating new tensions in the world of work. Self motivation is more important than before and what individuals gain with greater autonomy they risk losing in loss of visibility and access to the grapevine. Controlling and appraising performance becomes a problem for managers. Given traditional perceptions of office space as a reward for status and loyalty, moreover, will 'hotelling' arouse feelings of injustice? Another issue concerns the security and well being which come from the personal touches (family photos, etc.) in a traditional office. Designing this 'plonk' space in modern buildings has become more difficult. Research shows, moreover, that there have been some unintended consequences of new configurations, including the finding that managers in private offices communicate with more people, and more openly, than managers in open offices.

Key to competitive advantage

■ **In theory, people management should align and reinforce business strategies. But in many companies distinctive human resource practices drive competitiveness.**

by Peter Cappelli and Anne Crocker-Hefter

The 'best practice' bandwagon
Popular business literature frequently offers models of best techniques for managing employees. The current interest in identifying 'best practices' through benchmarking argues that best management practices are readily identifiable and can be transferred across organizations.

The notion that effective companies have 'core competencies' is perhaps the best-known of the resource arguments, but the search for unique competencies seems to contradict suggestions that companies should adopt similar practices or copy those of competitors.

Much of the interest in best practices is directed at the management of employees, but the notion of a single set of 'best' practices in this area may be overstated. The first difficulty is to explain why the variance in employment practices across, and even within, companies continues to be so large.

Is the variance simply an artefact? When we see companies that have not adopted best practice techniques, are we simply looking at those companies that will ultimately fail? There are examples in virtually every industry of successful companies with very distinct approaches to managing people, and we argue that these distinctive human resource practices help create unique competencies that differentiate products and services and drive the competitiveness of companies.

People management as the core competency

There may be no such thing as a 'best practice' for managing people. Companies in competition search for ways to differentiate their products and to find market niches where they are protected from competition. The argument that there should be a 'fit' between human resource practices and business strategies can be traced to manpower planning. It is not new in management circles, though it has been eclipsed by best practice and benchmarking arguments that take business strategy as a given and then suggest how human resource practices can reinforce strategy.

What is new here is the argument that people management practices are the beginning of efforts to create distinctive competencies and, in turn, business strategies. The most obvious way employee management practices create distinct competencies is through employee selection. Competencies are also created by employment practices such as training, rewards and work organization that develop skills and behaviors that help an organization create distinctive competencies.

It is worth examining some real-life examples.

Sales as the service: retailing

Sears and Nordstrom are legends in the retailing industry. Sears is one of the pioneering companies in the science of employee selection, relying on some of the most sophisticated selection tests in American industry.

Employees receive extensive training in company practices; management keeps track of employee attitudes and morale through frequent and rigorous employee surveys. Sales representatives, who work on salary rather than commission, are given intensive training in Sears products, the company's operating systems and sales techniques.

Nordstrom operates with virtually no formal personnel practices. Its hiring is decentralized, using no formal selection tests. Managers look for applicants with experience in customer contact but the main desirable qualities seem to be pleasant personalities and motivation. The company has only one rule in its personnel handbook: 'Use your best judgment at all times.' Individual sales clerks virtually run their areas as private stores.

Nordstrom maintains a continuous stream of programs to motivate employees to provide intensive service, but it offers very little of what could be thought of as training. Its commission-based pay system makes it possible for sales clerks to earn sizeable incomes. Nordstrom sales personnel are ranked within each department according to their monthly sales; the most successful are promoted (virtually all managers are promoted from within) and the least successful let go.

Information and advice as the 'product': professional service companies

Boston Consulting Group and McKinsey & Company are among the world's leading strategic consulting companies. Both have worldwide operations, and their reputations for thoughtful leadership and quality service are comparable. Both companies hire from the best undergraduate and MBA programs, competing for the top students. Both have rigorous selection procedures and exceptional compensation.

Yet the characteristics of the people the two companies hire and the way they are managed differ in important ways that relate to the ways the companies approach their markets. BCG tends to attract candidates with very broad perspectives on business. BCG alumni often leave to start their own companies, and BCG also maintains something of a 'revolving door' with academia, hiring business school professors as consultants and sometimes losing consultants to business schools. Once hired, consultants jump right into research, albeit closely supervised, and the formal training they receive is likely to be in the form of outside courses.

Many of BCG's projects start with a clean-sheet approach, so that what clients buy are original solutions and approaches to their problems from consultants whose varied backgrounds and entrepreneurial spirit help produce a unique product.

McKinsey, on the other hand, historically hires from on-campus recruiting and rarely from other employers. It prefers candidates with backgrounds in technical areas who have depth in some functional area of business. Their new entrants come in as 'blank slates' and McKinsey provides extensive training in the company's method of project execution and management, even though it is highly tailored to each client's situation.

The company expects the career path to the highest position – senior partner – to take approximately 12 years (versus six to eight at BCG), which gives the consultants a long period to learn to fit in. McKinsey products and techniques are regarded as proprietary and are not publicized, so McKinsey's core competency is the consistent products and techniques that constitute the 'McKinsey way'.

Going beyond services

The link between employees and product market strategy is sometimes less direct when one moves away from services because many factors in addition to employee behavior affect the company's 'product'. But there are still relationships between the way employees are managed, the competencies employees help produce and the way companies compete.

The shipping business

It is difficult to find two companies with people management systems that are more different than those at two top overnight courier services, Federal Express and UPS.

FedEx has no union, and its workforce is managed using most of the current 'hot' items in contemporary human resource management. The company has pay-for-suggestion systems, quality-of-worklife programs and a variety of other arrangements to 'empower' employees and increase their involvement.

FedEx employees have had an important role in helping to design the work organization and the way technology has been used, and their hustle and motivation helped make FedEx the dominant force in the overnight mail business.

UPS has none of these people management practices. Employees have no direct say over work organization matters. Their jobs are designed by industrial engineers according to time-and-motion studies, and the performance of each employee is measured and evaluated daily against company standards for each task. There are no efforts at employee involvement other than collective bargaining over contract terms.

UPS pays the highest wages and benefits in the industry, and offers employees 'gainsharing' and stock ownership plans. Virtually all promotions at UPS are filled from within, offering entry-level drivers excellent long-term prospects for advancement. As a result, UPS employees are also highly motivated and loyal to the company. The productivity of drivers at UPS, the most important workgroup in the delivery business, is about three times higher than at FedEx.

The scale and scope of UPS's business demands an extremely high level of co-ordination across its network of delivery hubs that may only be achievable through highly regimented and standardized job design. The procedures must be very similar, if not identical, across operations if the different delivery products are to move smoothly across a common network that links dozens of hubs.

Changes in practices and procedures essentially have to be system-wide to be effective. Such co-ordination is incompatible with significant levels of autonomy of the kind associated with shop-floor employee decision making. It is compatible with the system-wide process of collective bargaining, however. At FedEx there are fewer co-ordination problems, allowing considerable scope for autonomy and participation in shaping work decisions at the work-group level and more of a 'high commitment' approach.

Food and beverages: Coca-Cola and Pepsi

Few products appear to be more similar than soft drinks, yet 'the Cola Wars' that mark the competition between Coke and Pepsi show how even organizations with highly similar products can be differentiated by their business strategies.

Coke is the most recognized trademark in the world. First marketed some 70 years before Pepsi, Coke has been a part of American history and culture, and its business strategy centers on maintaining its position and building on its carefully groomed image. Compared to other companies its size, Coca Cola owns and operates few ventures besides Coke and has relatively few bottling franchises with which to deal.

Managing Coca Cola therefore requires a deep company-specific understanding and feel for the trademark that cannot be acquired outside the company or even quickly inside it. Coke creates an employment system that instills those skills and hangs on to them.

Coke typically hires college graduates with little or no corporate experience and provides them with intensive training. Jobs at Coke are secure — virtual lifetime employment for adequate performers. A system of promotion-from-within and seniority-based salary increases keeps employees from leaving. The people-management system ensures that only career Coke managers who have been thoroughly socialized into worrying about the company as a whole get to make decisions affecting the company.

Perhaps the main point in understanding Pepsi is simply that it is not Coke. From its early position as a price leader ('Twice as much for a nickel') to contemporary efforts to find a 'new generation' of consumers, Pepsi cleans up around the wake left by the Coke trademark. Pepsi has found new markets by becoming highly diversified and therefore faces a much more complicated set of management challenges. It needs innovative ideas to identify market niches and the ability to move fast to exploit those niches.

Its people-management system makes this possible. Pepsi hires employees with experience and advanced degrees and fosters individual competition and a fast-track approach for those who are successful in that competition. The company operates in a decentralized fashion with each division given considerable autonomy, and performance is evaluated at the operating

and individual levels. Pepsi employees have relatively less job security and perhaps less loyalty to the company than their counterparts at Coke. What Pepsi gets from this system is a continuous flow of new ideas, the ability to change quickly and the means for attacking many different markets in different ways.

Conclusions

The pattern of practices described above suggests a clear division between companies that develop employee competencies within the company (Coke, McKinsey) and those that assemble them ready-made from the outside market (Pepsi, BCG).

Companies that develop talent from within also tend to rely more on group and organizational efforts to achieve competencies, while the companies that hire it from the outside rely more on individualism and individual efforts.

The skills and behaviors needed for individual-based performance are readily available on the outside market because they can be produced and used in many settings. The skills that generate organization-based performance, in contrast, are likely to be specific to that organization and therefore are unlikely to be produced anywhere else. Developing employees from within also creates and passes on the kind of strong culture that reinforces group and organization performance.

Companies that secure skills and competencies in the outside market obviously face a dilemma: if these competencies are in fact available to everyone on the open market, how can they generate a unique competency and competitive advantage for any one company? One answer is that a company may be better at spotting talent on the open market or at managing that talent than are those competitors who are also trying to secure skills and competencies directly from the market.

Another important theme appears in the product market. There is a clear division between organizations that compete by moving quickly, adjusting to new opportunities, and companies that have developed a superior approach to a long-standing market.

The two themes relate to each other in an

extremely straightforward manner: organizations that compete through flexibility, moving quickly to seize new opportunities, do not develop employee competencies from within because it does not pay to do so. The opportunity is likely to be gone before the investment to develop competencies for addressing the opportunity can be recouped. Instead, these organizations rely on the outside market to take in new competencies, individualism to sustain performance and the outside market to get rid of old competencies.

Organizations that compete through established markets and relationships, on the other hand, rely on organization-specific skills developed internally and group-wide co-ordination.

There may well be a natural equilibrium in the marketplace between these two kinds of firms. Companies such as Pepsi exist in part because they have competitors such as Coke that do not, perhaps cannot, adapt quickly to new opportunities. Similarly, companies such as McKinsey succeed because their competitors lack the depth of competencies and long-term investments that they have established.

One factor that helps sustain this equilibrium is the difficulty in changing strategies. Historical investments in a particular approach create considerable inertia and reputations that affect employee selection long after those investments have been exhausted. Going from an 'inside' employment strategy to a market-based, or 'outside', approach can probably be done more easily than the reverse.

The increase in the need for flexibility driven by competition that virtually all companies feel may be exacting a toll on employers that develop their own competencies. Even companies such as Coca Cola and McKinsey are beginning to take in more talent from the outside. In the future, companies may reduce the extent to which they develop competencies inside, although the variance in these practices across companies may still be great. Several policy implications flow from these observations. One concerns training. In most industries, there are markets for organizations that move quickly, too quickly to merit making substantial investments in training and development. It is difficult to imagine any sensible public policy that could encourage these organizations to develop their talent themselves. Efforts to do so would change their core competencies and push them out of their current market niches.

The scope for autonomy/worker participation, teamwork and related issues that are sometimes labeled as 'high performance' work systems is at least in part driven by the choice of product market strategy. According to the extent to which individualism drives performance or co-ordination in turn shapes the scope for work organization, so efforts to change these dimensions will also change core competencies and business strategies. If, in fact, the need for flexibility in product markets continues to increase, the extent to which companies will invest in specific skills and competencies may erode. It is an important empirical question whether companies with highly skilled, broadly trained employees can be more flexible in their product markets than can companies that hire-and-fire to change their competencies.

The former may well be better at creating flexibility within their current product market but the latter may achieve more flexibility in moving across product markets. Certainly companies in the US appear to have decisively moved toward the latter position, which will reduce the extent to which distinctive competencies are created within companies. Whether this change will make the high-competence, specific-skill niches of companies too short-lived to be profitable or whether companies will find lower-cost ways of creating the necessary competencies is an open question. The fact that distinctive ways of competing appear to be driven by competencies and capabilities that are created by unique sets of employee management practices helps explain several interesting observations about the business world.

The first is the substantial variance in management practices across employers that persists despite the pressures to adopt practices that appear successful and 'legitimate'. The second, related observation is that many practices that have been demonstrated to be 'best' in some companies never seem to sweep over the business community, even after being promoted for years. Both observations are perfectly compatible with the notion that differences in business strategies are functional and are generated by differences in management practices.

None of this suggests that all practices are equally good. For practices that are not central to an organization's core competency, there may indeed be best practices that clearly cut across companies; for companies with similar strategies, hence similar core competencies, it may also be possible to identify management practices that dominate others – 'lean production' among automobile assemblers, for example.

To be a source of sustained competitive advantage, a practice must be something that does not easily transfer to competitors. Unlike technology or new designs, management practices can be extremely difficult to reproduce, and the fact that these practices are so difficult to change and transfer helps explain the basic notion that core competencies should drive business strategy and not visa versa. It may be easier to find a new business strategy to go with one's existing practices and competencies than to develop new practices and competencies to go with a new strategy.

Summary
People management should be the beginning of efforts to create distinctive competencies and, in turn, business strategies – but there may be no such thing as best practice in this area. Sears and Nordstrom are both highly successful retailers, yet they have widely different recruitment policies. Some companies develop competencies from the inside (organization specific skills); others, such as those that compete through flexibility and responding quickly to market opportunities, secure them in the outside market. Going from an inside to an outside approach is probably easier than the reverse.

If the need for flexibility in product markets continues to increase, the extent to which companies will invest in specific competencies may erode. Unlike technology or new designs, management practices can be extremely difficult to reproduce. It may therefore be easier to find a new strategy to go with existing skills and practices, rather than vice versa.

Choices and the high-performance workplace

■ **Human resource managers have come under increasing pressure from practices connected with the 'high-performance workplace'.**
Larry W. Hunter examines what is happening and suggests a way forward.

The management of people inside organizations is, clearly, a potential source of competitive advantage for companies. Core competencies often depend critically on the management of people, for effective human resource management contributes to the creation of skills, fosters consistent effort by employees, and reinforces cultures that foster productivity and quality.

This wisdom is now conventional, but its acceptance has been accompanied by a curious phenomenon. Simultaneously with the growing acknowledgement of the primacy of people in creating and maintaining an effective organization, human resource management (HRM) as both a term and as an organizational function has fallen into some disrepute. HRM has traditionally had two faces. On one side, it may be positively directed towards meeting workers' needs: bettering wages and opportunity, providing a voice for workers, perhaps even ownership in the organization.

Some are troubled by this face, having seen HRM as a pernicious substitute for more independent forms of employee representation such as trade unions. And indeed many organizations operate on the theory that effective management of people can forestall the formation of independent organizations. But today this aggressively positive role actually exists independent of the HR function itself, and is aimed not simply at forestalling unionization but at good management.

A generation of managers who have read Douglas McGregor and Abraham Maslow (or have, at the least, been taught by those who have read McGregor and Maslow), may not require a specialist function to tell them what workers want; they may even decide to give them some of it. Line managers see this face of HRM as innocuous, if a bit soft, and occasionally unconnected to business reality.

The other face of HRM is more troubling to both managers and workers. This is the face of bureaucratic compliance: with laws, with policies and procedures.

Today's human resource managers find themselves under criticism for doing what they have long been asked and expected to do. The elaborate systems they have set up to ensure that people are paid fairly, that relevant laws are followed, and organizational policies are enforced consistently and equitably throw bureaucratic obstacles into the paths of innovative managers and workers.

All the while the function expends scarce organizational resources on tasks that in themselves appear to create little value for the company: producing pay cheques, enforcing arcane selection criteria, or designing elaborate and rigid job evaluation schemes.

Streamlining HRM

The HR function is under increasing pressure to produce more with less, and is ripe for the application of 'business process re-engineering'. Consultants travel the globe offering to streamline human resource groups through work redesign, the more effective use of technology and outsourcing of much of the work to specialist companies. Indeed, Randal Schuler of New York University has argued that the HR function in American business must transform itself or face its own demise. One key to understanding the tumult in the HR profession is to cast it in a broader context. Human resource management happens inside companies, whether or not there is a strong and effective human resource function. Whether human resource managers are to add value to organizations (Schuler's 'transformation') or line managers are to incorporate HRM into their daily job description (the 'demise'), each must understand how the sets of policies and practices used to manage people can add value to or detract from organizational effectiveness.

That is to say, one must begin to understand contemporary HRM by seeing employment and labor relationships in their entirety, with the full range of workers and the wide variety of approaches to structuring work, labor and management practices in modern economies. One window into these relationships is to begin to understand human resource management as comprising the set of choices that organizations make about the way they will manage people. These choices might be organized and considered under a number of broad categories and I will focus on five here: staffing; training; work organization and job design; compensation; and employee voice and representation.

Organizations make choices in each of these areas, sometimes explicit, sometimes implicit. The choices are not unbounded, of course. Constraints in the broader environment – technology, the legal system or the state of the labor market – circumscribe HRM to some extent. But the range of choice is often wider than managers realize. Consider each of the areas in turn as encompassing a series of choices for the organization.

Staffing

Who will join the organization and what are the

criteria for selection? Should the company choose employees rather casually or, on the other hand, only after careful and costly searches? Should companies choose people for their ability to perform a specific range of tasks or because they seem to fit with a particular organizational culture? Promotion and career management also entail a series of organizational staffing choices. What are the criteria for promotion? Does the organization prefer to promote from within, rewarding service and loyalty, or hire from outside, seeking new ideas and skills?

Staffing also requires choices about the form that employment relationships will take. Should companies seek workers for long-term full-time relationships or, alternatively, establish any or many of a variety of forms of contingent employment, including part-time and temporary workers, outsourcing of particular tasks or functions, and the use of consultants and other externalized forms of technical expertise.

Employment security might be broadly guaranteed; on the other hand, such guarantees might be explicitly avoided or even broken (as in the current waves of downsizing).

Training

Human resource management implies choices about skill formation. Whose responsibility is skill development: the company's or the worker's? What level of investment in training is the organization prepared to make and for which workers? What sorts of skills are to be developed?

Will the company act proactively, training workers broadly to deal with a variety of potential situations or will training be more reactive, supplying workers with skills on an as-needed basis as technologies change or as staffing requirements demand it?

Work organization and job design

Will jobs be broadly or narrowly defined? Will workers be organized into teams or fill individual roles? If there are to be teams, will those teams comprise specialists or generalists? Are jobs to be enriched or enhanced, the source of opportunities to exercise skill and autonomy, or are they to be restricted and controlled, so that worker discretion and development are limited?

Compensation

Compensation clearly involves choices; though here constraints become most acute. In particular, labor markets and budgets may circumscribe the manoeuvring room available to companies in this area.

Still, companies might choose to offer relatively low or relatively high levels of compensation in comparison to competitors or reference groups. They also might choose different structures: backloading compensation so that the real payoff is on retirement or concentrating a large portion of pay in benefits, for example.

Another choice on top of level and pay structure reflects the company's decisions about the extent to which pay ought to be variable: over what time periods and for what reasons – the development of skills, the achievement of promotions or simply performance? And, if performance: individual performance, group performance, the performance of the entire organization? What share of the pay packet is to be placed at risk?

Employee voice and representation

Companies might choose to establish channels for monitoring employee concerns and providing employees with channels to communicate their views over the quality of working life, production issues or their rewards and treatment by supervisors.

These channels can be relatively passive (such as employee surveys) or more active (such as employee involvement committees). They may meet frequently, even daily, being built into the ebb and flow of daily work life (as with quality circles) or arise occasionally to address specific problems (as with increasingly popular focus groups). They may allow employees only to voice opinions or they may give real decision-making power to employees in any of a variety of areas.

Where workers are organized collectively, structures are more durable and likely to be more antagonistic, whether or not managers choose this route. Even then, managers make choices in dealing with unions. Do they avoid the union? Confront and challenge it? Seek to accommodate the union and to collaborate with it?

The high-performance workplace: where is it?

The challenge for contemporary human resource management is to see that as many of the choices as possible work in tandem to encourage and to enable the organization to achieve its goals and to create value.

Value creation has a systemic quality and human resource practices must be considered both as they relate to one another and as they relate to the broader environment.

In many industries, for example, an explosion of information and telecommunications technologies creates the potential for individual employees to achieve great increases in productivity at consistently high levels of quality and to provide more effective customer service.

A first step towards the realization of the potential unleashed by this technology might be built on broadened jobs and enhanced employee discretion or empowerment. But consider what must happen in other aspects of human resource management in order to support this change.

If no attention is paid to skill development, employees may either not understand how to use the technologies or use them improperly. The organization must reconsider its approach to staffing – effective recruiting and deployment of human resources – lest it discover that its selection criteria are choosing people who are unable or unwilling to use the new technologies to work effectively or advancing people who are uncomfortable with devolution of decision-making.

And a reward system must provide incentives rather than disincentives for the sorts of behaviors that the new work organization expects: problem-solving, teamwork, contribution to organizational performance. Today's notion of a 'high-performance workplace' comprises a set of practices similar to those just outlined. The high-performance workplace (HPW) features high employee involvement and lowered status differences between managers and workers; broader jobs and discretion for front-line employees, who are often embedded in a system of teamwork; a commitment by the employer to training; some component of performance-based pay; and careful selection of employees who are likely to fit into this system.

The specific details of the system may vary by context. Technology of production, for example, may circumscribe the latitude managers have to redesign jobs, so that teamwork looks like one thing in an auto plant and another in a retail bank. National institutions and cultural contexts also provide differences: Japanese high-performance workplaces feature a substantial biannual bonus for manual workers based on the performance of the company; US companies may award pay rises based on team achievement or measurable skill development, for example.

A number of careful empirical studies suggest that these systems really do work to improve performance in key areas such as productivity, quality and adaptability. Further, the effects appear to be strongest when the HPW practices are implemented as a system: there is a synergistic effect that cannot be produced through the implementation of a few individual practices.

No rush to adopt the practices

Yet, despite the evident allure of the system (and its clever name), we do not see companies rushing to adopt this model of HRM. Rather, innovations are often adopted piecemeal, if at all, and a substantial number of companies today seem to be more concerned about downsizing, cost-cutting and re-engineering than they do about implementing a high-performance workplace. Examining impediments to adoption sheds further light on how one might think about the role of HRM in today's organization. Why have companies not adopted the high-performance workplace?

As a first consideration, there is no reason to think that the sorts of capabilities fostered by the HPW are the only goals an organization might have. To take one obvious counter example, lowering costs is also desirable. While it is well and good to invest in human resources for the long run, some of this investment may require quite clear out-of-pocket expenditure and take time to produce results. The environment – for example, capital markets focussed on quarterly statements – may not permit such expenditure. Companies therefore may consciously choose alternate paths toward the creation of value.

Different paths may imply different approaches to the management of human resources. For example, a company may focus not on high quality, customization or adaptability but on predictably high levels of consistency – in the treatment of individual customers, for example, or the production of simple, basic products – at low cost.

It might therefore choose to limit employee discretion, to train only to produce these results and to pay the minimum necessary to retain workers able to carry out a limited range of tasks. And, of course, companies might especially seek to implement such an approach in regions or in countries with low wage rates; this may entail further disinvestment from alternate high-wage sites. What is more, the costs of HPWs are often more obvious, and easily measurable, than the benefits produced. Increases in training and changes in pay system require real expenditure. And many organizations have in place systems that distort the calculation. Focussing on numbers of employees rather than overall costs, for example, encourages the use of temporary workers who receive less training and have less alignment with the goals of the organization than do regular employees.

An organization may also consciously separate its approach to HRM for different segments of the workforce. A fast-food provider, for example, may embed its local management teams in something like an HPW, selecting them carefully, investing in their training and providing them with broad discretion and substantial pay incentives. Yet at the same time the same organization may choose practices for front-line employees that are designed first to control costs and second minimize discretion and maximize predictability. The above explanations seem reasonable and plausible (though, interestingly enough, they are only weakly supported by research evidence to date). They represent variations on the increasingly popular notion of 'strategic human resource management', which suggests that companies might rationally choose different bundles of HRM practices in the pursuit of different sorts of organizational goals.

More troubling, but equally plausible, are other explanations for the failure of HPWs to diffuse more widely. First, there are a variety of institutional obstacles to HPWs beyond the control of the organization. Regulation and legal requirements may serve as impediments to adoption of particular practices. Some of this regulation may be justifiable on social grounds, but often it has arisen in an earlier context, and fossilized without accommodating changes in technology or the labor market. Disconnects between national and regional approaches to skill development and the needs of both employers and workers may also slow adoption of the HPW.

Second, full implementation of the HPW is necessary in order to reap its benefits, but such implementation requires a redistribution of power within the organization. Those who believe they stand to lose by the redistribution may resist change; this in turn makes the adoption of the system even more expensive.

The HR function may be among the fiercest sources of resistance, posing obstacles to reform of compensation or hiring systems that would put more power in the hands of work teams, for example. Third, and related to the above point, is that there is a large grey area in which the costs and benefits of adoption are unclear. Here the norms and values of managers may act to encourage (or discourage adoption).

For example, Paul Osterman of MIT found, in a large survey of American establishments, that organizations with cultures unsupportive of what he called 'humanistic values' were much less likely than other organizations to adopt aspects of HPW other things being equal.

Finally, many companies appear to operate under the impression that they can achieve strategic advantages in all areas at the same time: that they can be at once the lowest-cost, fastest-growing, most adaptable company in their industries and markets – and maintain the highest levels of quality and customer service.

Or they hedge their bets, not knowing which of these attributes the market is likely to reward. This hedging may make sense from a market-based strategic perspective but attempts to be all things to all customers lead managers into incoherent bundles of practice.

They may, for example, introduce an empowerment movement in an environment in which training costs are being cut to nothing, which is later condemned as a foolish fad because it failed to produce results. Or a pay-for-performance program in which employees are not given enough discretion to be able to affect their actual performance in any significant way, so that they quickly become cynical about the whole initiative.

The role for HRM

Effective human resource management can no longer be concerned with simply executing a standard set of policies and procedures. Rather, it requires questioning and understanding the relationships between choices in managing people, the strategies and goals of the organization and the possibilities presented by the external environment.

HRM requires searching for sets of policies and practices that have a reasonable chance of producing capabilities that are valuable to the company. Whether or not it is explicit, these policies and practices are choices.

Where the organization has begun to choose policies characteristic of the high-performance workplace, this must be done with as clear an understanding as possible of the objectives of the organization, the costs of introducing the program, and the value of the new capabilities the program is expected to create.

Perhaps most crucially, HRM requires marrying the external and internal environments of the comp° Today's competitive environment features rapid technological change. Markets are increasingly global: product markets, capital markets, labor markets. Labor markets, particularly, as they are considered globally, feature an increasingly diverse work force, comprising not just men and women with different sorts of career objectives, but potential workers from diverse cultural and ethnic backgrounds. New technologies may require teamwork; diversity, on the other hand, may present challenges to teamwork unless it is managed properly. Today's HRM, then, requires that managers ask the following questions:

● What do we want our system of HRM to produce and reinforce, what skills, what behaviors? What strategic capabilities do we believe our choices of managing people will create? Do these capabilities have enough value in today's marketplace to make them worth the investment? What are the alternatives?

● To whom are we directing which kinds of HRM? For example, which groups of managers and workers should be matched with our lead strategy and who should be treated differently (and by what logic)? Should those we treat differently be in the company at all?

● Do we have a plan for getting there from here? Where immediate cost pressures may seem acute, will steps taken to address these problems (such as slashing payroll) destroy the organization's chance to survive in the long run? Or are they necessary if the company is to move into the future on a sound footing? If the answer is that drastic measures are necessary, is there a clear plan in place to use HRM to create competitive advantage once costs are reduced?

This question-raising path may be risky for individual managers to engage in but it is a prerequisite for organizations if they are to manage human resources effectively. The process may also be frustrating, for many answers will not be explicit: costs and benefits of particular approaches cannot be known with certainty.

It is possible that HR professionals in organizations can reposition themselves to play this role, even as they continue to strive to make their own staffs more efficient. Professionals familiar with these issues have begun to describe themselves as internal consultants, with line managers as their clients, or customers, for example.

But line managers may be equally interested in joining the fray, particularly where they see deficits in the approach of the organization to HRM: where job structures and work design seem inefficient, where skills are short or pay systems unsatisfactory for achieving desired goals.

In either case, the future of HRM does not lie in progressive initiatives unconnected to business goals or organizational and environmental realities. Neither does it lie in the production of standardized sets of best practices. Rather, it lies in ensuring that the choices made in managing people are made sensibly and with clear purposes in mind.

Summary

HRM has traditionally had two faces: meeting workers' needs and bureaucratic compliance. There are several areas where choices have to be made, and a clear purpose kept in mind. These include, staffing, training, work organization and job design, compensation, and employee representation. The High Performance Workplace is characterized by high employee involvement, low status differences, broader jobs, a commitment to training and some performance related pay – but many companies have either adopted these piecemeal or not at all.

One reason is that HR investment may conflict with other goals, e.g. cost cutting. The costs of an HPW are often more obvious than the benefits. And some firms consciously separate their approaches to HR for different segments of the workforce or to pursue different organizational goals.

Institutional obstacles, resistance to change, unsupportive cultures and incoherent strategies also explain why HPWs have not diffused more widely.

MODULE

8

Managing People in Organizations

Contents

Developing a work/life balance 278
Stewart D. Friedman, Perry Christensen, Jessica
DeGroot, The Wharton School of the University of
Pennsylvania
*New ways of working have brought work life and
everyday life into close proximity and potential
conflict.*

**Does empowerment deliver the
goods?** 283
Maury Peiperl, London Business School
*Latest fad or a real new way of achieving greater
levels of quality and service? The pros and cons of
empowerment.*

**The true worth of building high-
performance systems** 288
Michael Useem, The Wharton School of the
University of Pennsylvania
*The development of so-called high-performance
systems is emerging in the West, particularly the US,
as a distinct new approach to organizational design in
the face of ever-growing global competition.*

Contributors

Stewart D. Friedman joined the faculty
at the Wharton School of the University
of Pennsylvania in 1984. He is currently
Director of the Wharton Life Interests
Project the Wharton Leadership
Program.

Jessica DeGroot is an independent
consultant.

Perry Christensen works for Merck &
Co.

Maury Peiperl is Assistant Professor of
Organizational Behavior at London
Business School.

Michael Useem is Professor of
Management at the Wharton School of
the University of Pennsylvania and
Director of its Center for Leadership and
Change Management. His research
interests include corporate organization,
ownership and restructuring, and
leadership.

Introduction

The Managing People in Organizations module fills the gap between Organizational Behavior and Human Resource Management in that it looks at people both as a resource to be managed and administered and as human beings with human needs and talents to be developed.

This short module begins with a section looking at the demands that new styles of working are putting on employees. The following two sections examine 'empowerment' and the building of 'high performance' teams.

Developing a work/life balance

■ **New competitive strategies, the role of women and less stable family patterns have brought working life and home into potential conflict.**

by Stewart D. Friedman, Perry Christensen and Jessica DeGroot

The balance between work and life is an issue that companies can no longer afford to ignore. The costs are simply too great. The revolutionary changes that have taken place in the composition of the work force, the growth of non-traditional family structures, and shifts in values concerning the need for balance among roles, have focused heightened attention on the interrelationships between work and other life roles.

Consider these facts about US employment and family structure:
● Women now comprise 48 per cent of the work force.
● 60 per cent of married women workers have children under six years old.
● 40 per cent of all workers are members of dual-earner couples.
● 23 per cent of employees are single parents.
● A growing proportion of families have responsibility for the care of elders.
● Despite a small increase in men's participation in the home, women still bear the brunt of the responsibility for housework and child care.
● Today's downsized, delayered team-based organizations require greater involvement from all employers.
● nine- or ten-hour work days are the norm for business professionals.

These facts are part of a dynamic process of change in social forces that have sharply increased the complexity and magnitude of work/family concerns in organizations and society. Unlike the typical member of earlier generations of employees, a very large segment of today's work force – particularly its women – faces new and intense pressures to find ways of 'getting a life' while satisfying the needs of demanding careers.

In this article we will first describe the context and implications for business of changes in men's and women's roles and then consider the work/life balance issue as one of strategic business import. Finally, we will present what we have learned about developing the competencies that business professionals and managers of people need if they are to deal effectively with the question of balance, both for themselves and others in their organizations for whom they are responsible.

Changing roles for men and women

Work and family are the dominant life roles for most employed adults in contemporary society, and these two spheres of a person's life are closely intertwined. Until very recently, however, employers and management theorists paid little attention to the relationships between work and family. In the labor market for business professionals there was virtually no variation in lifestyle. Most were married men, with children, who pursued their careers with apparently little guilt or expressed conflict between their work and family roles. Marriage and the presence of children were generally regarded as desirable characteristics, indicative of an executive's personal stability and responsibility. In an era in which the model of a career was based on the assumption of a male bread-winner with a non-employed wife, with little variation in personal lifestyles, problems concerning work/family linkages were almost non-existent or ignored.

Two central tensions that business professionals now face in their lives are tensions between career and family and tensions caused by the differences between the experiences of men and women.

First, people seek to know how to find the time and energy to fulfil the various commitments we make to work, family and other people and groups. The time requirements of most business professional roles in today's competitive marketplace are such that less and less time is available for other activities. With parents working greater hours, then, what happens to the nurture of the next generation? And whither the cultivation of family and other pursuits outside of work that enhance the quality of life?

Second, numerous studies point to the conclusion that career and family experiences for men and women are different. However, few of these differences are benign; most are unduly constraining, and not only for women but for men too. The ability of men to give their individual attention, energy and time to their careers was made possible in the past through the full-time support of a partner who assumed almost total responsibility for home maintenance and child care. However, while the number of women in the workforce has grown, the resultant reduction in pressures on men to be sole bread-winners has not been accompanied by efforts on their part to increase their participation in the family domain.

These two tensions between career and family and between the experiences of men and women are deeply affected by recent changes in the definition of gender roles in our culture. The meanings of career and of family in the lives of men and women have changed, and with these changes many more questions are raised than reassuring answers provided about enacting central life roles. Behaviors learned through early lessons at home or school are, for many, no longer viable.

People now find themselves in an uncomfortable place, somewhere between the old world of traditional gender roles and a future in which new definitions of these roles offer greater flexibility and opportunity for fulfilment. Because the options available in life-choices about career and family are changing and increasingly diverse (with some growing, others shrinking), lifestyle decisions are more complicated than in the past.

Such choices are made especially complex because we are now in a period of transition that is forcing many men and women to navigate their way without the benefit of social and organizational road maps through a thicket of emergent roles at work and at home. A new kind of flexibility is required for individuals, organizations and society to make it possible for men and women to contribute meaningfully to society in a variety of roles. We are just starting, however, to grasp what it means to get to the point where such flexibility is the order of the day rather than the exception.

Towards work/life balance: a source of competitive advantage for business

Add to the challenges inherent in changing gender roles the pressures faced by most companies to do more and more with less and less in an increasingly turbulent economic environment, and you have the business problem that we seek to address: how to capitalize on these changes? Continuous improvement in work processes is critical for business success. And work must be accomplished in environments that are characterized by uncertainty and ambiguity in available resources and relationships. How can companies succeed in their primary financial objectives and, at the same time, take seriously the need to respect individual employees' lives outside work? Working smarter is an important part of the answer. But it's more than a re-engineering problem.

For organizations, the root of the issue is culture – big, deep, and powerful in its impact on the capacity of groups of people to get things done collectively. An organization's culture determines what behavior is acceptable for its members, and it is in cultural norms and beliefs where resistance to change in organizations most forcefully resides. Analogously, for individuals, at its root the issue is one of values similarly big, deep and powerful in its impact on the capacity of individual people to get things done in fruitful collaboration with others. One's values determine what behavior is acceptable for one-self, and it is in long-held values where resistance to change in individuals most forcefully resides.

So it is not surprising that among the managerial competencies we address, the primary one is 'strategic focus', or alignment of work/life balance issues with the central vision of a company. And among the individual competencies, the main one is 'values and volition', or knowing what counts and acting on it.

Companies that proactively address these issues will be at an advantage in generating the kind of employee commitment needed to compete effectively in the global marketplace. Work/life balance is a critical business issue today for two main reasons: productivity and labour market dynamics.

Productivity. It is generally asserted that the more work makes sense in the big picture of one's whole life, the greater the supply of energy and creativity one has available to apply to work. Furthermore, without balance, there are increased risks of stress-related medical problems, greater unwanted attrition and greater absenteeism. In other words, more balance means more productivity.

Labor market dynamics. The ties that once bound people to organizations are loosening; people in business today expect and demand from their organizations both greater autonomy on the one hand and greater concern for their individual interests on the other. Those companies that are able genuinely to create such work arrangements will be more likely to attract and retain the best and brightest in the labour market. For these are the very people women and men who will have the option to make employment decisions on the basis of the quality of life afforded by their employment.

In sum, effectively managing the work/life balance issue can yield competitive advantages to business. The challenges for business leaders are to know what skills are needed to do so and how to develop these skills.

Work/life balance competencies

In the Wharton-Merck Work/Life Roundtable we are concerned with the competencies needed by (a) business professionals to balance their lives and (b) managers of people to help others balance their lives.

Based on our work with our colleagues in the Roundtable a group of distinguished academic and business leaders we believe the critical skills are those listed below. It should be clear that these competencies are not specific to managing work/life balance issues; many are useful in dealing with other significant business issues, and so educational and other change initiatives that target these competencies can have benefits in other aspects of work.

Competencies for individual business professionals. There are three sets of competencies that individual business professionals need in order to balance their work with their other life interests. These competencies have to do with values and volition, roles and relationships, and performance and planning.

Values and volition: knowing what counts and acting on it
- clarifying life priorities, purposes and values
- elevating choice to a conscious level; being aware of trade-offs
- acting in a way that is consistent with values, including knowing when to get out of a bad situation.

Roles and relationships getting support from others to say 'no'
- clarifying boundaries among life roles; analysing areas of differentiation and integration
- proactively building relationships; networking; creating trust, goodwill and common ground
- taking risks by communicating needs and feelings; negotiating creatively to meet personal and company needs
- letting go of control, delegating, developing a comfort level with ambiguity.

Performance and planning: being reasonable about what you can do while thinking ahead
- accepting 'good enough'; giving less that 100 per cent at times; not demanding perfection of oneself
- anticipating demands and planning effectively in all life domains.

Being flexible, creative and spontaneous in work, family and other life roles. Competencies for managers of people. There are four sets of competencies that managers of people need to ensure that those for whom they are responsible in their organizations succeed in integrating their work and personal lives. These competencies have to do with strategic focus, support, skill-building and the structure of rewards and policy:

Strategic focus: aligning work/life balance issues with the central vision of a company
- communicating clear strategic goals and vision in both word and deed
- understanding how work/life issues can be used strategically for the business
- anticipating demands and planning effectively
- managing organization change without causing long-term adverse effects on employees' work/life integration.

Support: helping others to articulate their personal needs and interests
- understanding and assessing an employee's personal goals and abilities
- assuming an advocacy role to support employees
- listening, respecting, and responding to others' points of view.

Skill-building: developing employees' capacities for continuous learning and change
- encouraging employees to enhance their task and people skills
- modeling and encouraging thoughtful questioning of one's own or one's organization's tacit assumptions about work/life balance
- encouraging creative experimentation to allow employees to work smarter and with greater autonomy
- increasing organizational and employee flexibility through technology and other means.

Structure of rewards and policy: managing authority with fairness
- equitably rewarding commitment and productivity, not just time spent working
- negotiating equitable not necessarily equal solutions that integrate diverse employee and organization needs
- being aware of and equitably applying effective work/life policies and practices.

Changing individual behavior and corporate cultures

It is our belief that the skills listed above are the critical ones for individual business professionals and for managers of people seeking to be effective in achieving work/life balance for themselves and others. We suggest that, to the extent that people develop these skills, companies are more likely to achieve business success because of both productivity and labor market advantages that would occur as a result.

But teaching these skills – or, perhaps more accurately, providing opportunities for people to learn them – is a substantial challenge in its own right.

The challenge of developing work/life balance competencies

It has been observed that talking about work/life balance is not unlike talking about sex. It is personal, private and highly-charged emotionally because the subject evokes moral distinctions based on deeply held values and beliefs.

In the old world, business was business and personal was personal; the twain rarely met in the discourse of management. In today's world, however, the two domains have become inextricably linked. Thus the leadership challenge: how to address work/life balance issues in a manner that men and women in business see as legitimate and relevant to their professional goals.

What are the levers for changing individual behavior and corporate cultures so that individuals and organizations are better equipped to navigate the cross-currents of this brave new world in which the demands of work and other life roles converge in a myriad array of social and economic arrangements? How, in other words, are work/life balance competencies to be developed?

In our work in the Wharton-Merck Work/Life Roundtable, we are putting together ideas for action intended to affect change through educational means, as opposed to using policy initiatives or the manipulation of public cultural symbols, both of which are useful methods for business leaders and should complement educational efforts in a comprehensive change strategy. We are in the process of editing the *Wharton-Merck work/life balance resource guide*, a compendium of teaching and training methods aimed specifically at developing work/life balance skills for business professionals and for managers of people.

Each of the entries in the Guide is a learning activity that addresses one or more of the competencies described above. In addition to describing the principal design elements in how the competencies are taught, these entries contributed by an international group of academics, managers, trainers and consultants speak directly to the resistance one is likely to encounter in using the learning activity. The description addresses whether the audience (of business school students, executives, front-line supervisors, support staff, and so on) is likely to view the activity as relevant to business or their personal experience and whether the activity has some emotional risk; i.e. whether self-disclosure about personal issues is required.

Our goal is to present a variety of both traditional and innovative pedagogical tools that can be applied in a wide range of settings for the purpose of educating current and future business professionals and managers. Teaching methods in the Guide include case studies, analysis of organizational policies and practices, self-assessments, role plays, simulations and games, lectures, inter-group dialogues (among people in different demographic groups, for example), field projects (such as observing a day-in-the-life of a parent, or of a child in a two-earner family), interviews, and coaching or mentoring others.

Our emphasis so far in this effort is on teaching and training because it is through the educational system, both within business schools and within companies, that the attitudes and values that drive individual behaviors and corporate cultures can be addressed directly. Education is a critical piece of the change process; necessary, though not sufficient, we understand, without the support of useful, strong policy and consistent reinforcement through top management's symbolic action.

Summary

The old model of male bread winner/non-employed wife meant tensions between work and family were almost non-existent, or ignored. The problems today are finding time to pursue activities outside the job, and reconciling the different experiences of women and men.

Many people now find themselves in an uncomfortable place between the old world of traditional gender roles and a future in which fresh definitions of those roles will offer new flexibility and opportunities for fulfilment.

It is important to align the issue of balancing work and life with the central vision of a company those that do so successfully will reap the benefits of a more committed and productive work force. Individuals need to know what counts, and act on it, and to try to avoid always aiming for 100 per cent perfection. Managers need to help others articulate their personal needs and interests, to encourage others to learn and to change, and to provide fair rewards for employees.

Suggested further reading

Portions of this article are taken from a forthcoming book by Professor Friedman and Professors Jeffrey Greenhaus and Saroj Parasuraman, *Crossing great divides: business professionals' lifestyles in transition.*

Does empowerment deliver the goods?

■ Latest fad or a real new way of achieving greater levels of quality and service? Maury Peiperl examines the pros and cons of empowerment.

I recently telephoned a mail-order computer supply company to enquire about the price of some extra memory for my PC. I was extremely surprised when the saleswoman quoted me a price that was well below what I had expected. I asked if she was certain the price was correct.

There was a pause, presumably as she noticed that she had give me the wrong number. Then instead of correcting it, she amazed me by saying: 'You know what? You're right. That isn't the right price, but it's within my margin and I can give it to you at that price if you place your order now.' As I placed the order, I thought to myself, here is someone who is empowered to make decisions on behalf of her company, to respond immediately to unpredictable situations without checking with someone else.

If there is one concept from the domain of human resource management that has in recent years become popular with senior general managers in the US and Europe it is 'empowerment'.

This deceptively simple idea says that employees at all levels of an organization are responsible for their own actions and should therefore be given the authority to make decisions about their work. The basic idea is that if employees are given some degree of ownership over their jobs, they will be more likely to do those jobs well, to satisfy their customers and to participate fully in the life of the organization.

The ideas of personal responsibility and delegated authority are certainly not new. Participative management and self-management date back at least 20 years, particularly in the US. So how is empowerment different from these earlier concepts? And why are so many organizations now trying so hard to put it in place?

As is often the case, the difference lies mainly in the reasons behind the concepts rather than any major divergence in the concepts themselves. The need for empowerment does not come from management's desire to make employees more satisfied on the assumption that they would therefore be more productive. That was more the case in the 1960s, when Theory Y was popular and self-management first gained currency.

Today, the case for empowerment comes from business needs that are central to the success of a company: fast response to customers, strong cross-functional links at multiple levels, and the need to take opportunities that are too local, too fleeting or too many in number to permit a centralized decision-making process.

If empowerment means giving power to make decisions, then exactly what decisions should be taken by employees? There is no simple answer to this question, and it has been the fly in the ointment of many an empowerment program.

If decisions are held too close to the top, employees will be hampered in fulfilling their responsibilities and exercising their authority in a timely manner. On the other hand, if too many decisions are pushed too far down the organization, it runs the risk of being disjointed, with different parts of the whole coming into conflict.

At some fundamental level, the answer must be 'whatever decisions the employee thinks at the time it is appropriate for him or her to take'. Without this level of discretion, employees cannot be said to be truly 'empowered'. The point is, within broad limits, it must be up to the employee to decide what he/she can decide and what must be pushed up the ladder to higher management. There is a certain amount of risk attached to this, for both the employee and the manager. The employee is more exposed and the manager less in control. This is the nature of an empowered organization. It is in many ways the antithesis of the traditional management hierarchy.

The advantages of an empowered workforce

It is almost a given, particularly in service industries, that managers today will describe their primary source of competitive advantage as being their people. When value is delivered through information, personal interaction or group work, the human element is of paramount importance.

The only way to get real advantage in this kind of a business – where the main productive assets walk in and out the door each day – is to have everyone giving 100 per cent effort in the right direction all the time. This combination of effort and alignment rarely results from a top-down management model. Only a system of distributed decision making can provide the flexibility and motivation for people to maintain peak performance levels.

When an organization's overall direction is clear and its overall structure and resource base are adequate to its needs (all the job of top management), then an empowered workforce with responsibility and authority for most day-to-day decisions can have the following advantages:

Better customer service. Not only will employees in contact with customers be able to make decisions themselves and provide an appropriate response, they will also give the customers the (correct) impression that the customer is dealing with someone who has power and influence in the organization.

Flexibility. Empowered employees are ready to respond to changes and opportunities as they arise.

Speed. When employees know responsibility for outcomes rests with them, they can take action swiftly and locally to solve problems.

Formation of important cross-functional links. Without having to raise most operational issues up the hierarchy, employees are free to make the horizontal connections appropriate to their business. Cross-functional teams can form and re-form as necessary without the say-so of top management. Because these links are not officially resourced, they will tend to be efficient. Benefits come not from being on the team itself but from what the team contributes to the employee's regular work. If a link ceases to add value, the participants will drop it.

Morale. Many employees will feel better about their work if they know that they have more control over it. Individuals' high morale, if widely shared, can also give an organization a positive quality that is often visible to outsiders, such as customers, and is reciprocated by them, resulting in a feedback loop of increasing positive feeling.

Compensation for limited career paths. Many employees in organizations now face the prospect of limited advancement, given recent demographic trends and the tendency toward flatter hierarchies. If promotion is unavailable, companies need to find other ways of increasing employees' responsibilities and rewards. Broadening their responsibility and authority is one way to accomplish this. Empowered employees may find their jobs challenging and rewarding enough that promotion ceases to be their only criterion for remaining loyal to the organization.

What to look for

How can you tell if a workforce is empowered? Statements by top managers to that effect are rarely an adequate guide. The crucial indicators are the way employees interact with customers, managers and each other. Typical behaviors among employees that are evident within empowered workforces include the following (the list is largely based on Hackman, 1986, *see* 'Suggested further reading'):

1. They show an awareness of the goals and strategy of the organization. They take an interest beyond their functional speciality, paying attention to company publications, press reports, and financial and competitive data. They discuss their work in terms of how it fits in to the company's overall mission.

2. They take personal responsibility for the

outcomes of their work, showing by their behavior that they feel responsible for the results of what they do.

3. They continually monitor their own performance, looking for indications of quality and showing a concern for how they are doing on all performance dimensions. They correct and improve their performance without being asked to do so.

4. They seek additional resources when they do not have what they need to perform well.

5. They take initiatives to help people in other areas to improve their performance.

It seems an appealing list. But it is rarely seen in its entirety, at least not without some flaws. There are a number of problems embedded in the ideas behind empowerment that are important to consider.

The other side of the coin

Most of the potential difficulties associated with empowerment are the converse of its advantages:

Greater potential for chaos. The same local action that can lead to increased customer service can also lead to conflicting messages being given to customers and across departments. One employee may be willing to go further than the next in taking care of a particular need, leaving customers with different levels of service. Departments may evolve different policies on everything from office hours to the choice of word processors. Sometimes these conflicts will have to be resolved by statements of company policy. However, the more often this happens, the more the distribution of authority is undercut.

Lack of clarity. The flexibility and speed that result from distributed decision making are likely to lead to a lack of clarity about who is responsible for what. Job definitions become less useful and people often find themselves under more pressure because there are fewer limits to their responsibilities. A need for 'more breathing room' is a common complaint of employees in empowered organizations.

Breakdown of hierarchical control. The emergence of more cross-functional links often signals the breakdown of the formal hierarchy for the carrying out of many decisions. Control ends up being shared not only across hierarchical levels but across functional boundaries as well. Cross-functional teams may do an excellent job of problem solving (although this is by no means assured) but managers with ultimate responsibility for functional units are likely to feel a real loss of control, which they may reject as too risky.

Demoralization. Although empowerment seems attractive to many people, not every employee wants the responsibility that comes with it. Managers have a habit of assuming everyone is like them – desirous of more power and the concomitant rewards. This is only true for some people; others would prefer not to be burdened with additional authority and the decisions that come with it. These people may become seriously demoralized if they are forced to take a more active role in the management of their organizations.

How to support an empowered workforce

Typical elements of a system to ensure the success of an empowered workforce include the following:

Performance evaluations drawn from multiple sources. Decentralized decision making means employees will often be doing important work and making important choices away from their immediate manager's field of view. Thus in order to get a complete picture of their performance, they will need feedback from a variety of sources, not only their boss.

Cross-functional links and customer relations are also strengthened by the use of 360-degree feedback, in which an employee receives performance evaluations from a broad set of colleagues and, sometimes, customers. Also, in the case of empowered teams, it is important to let the team have some say in how its members are doing. Often these inputs are combined with the boss's own observations in a periodic evaluation meeting between the manager and the employee.

Variable rewards with some group component. Many if not most work organizations are set up as tournaments, in which members compete for promotions. In addition, many monetary reward systems are competitive in that salary increases and/or bonuses are generally rank-ordered, the highest awards being given to the highest individual performers. Although these systems can encourage individual striving for excellence, they work against co-operation at the margin – for example, helping out a colleague when it is not really necessary.

Because empowerment needs to be based on everyone pulling in the same direction, empowered organizations typically augment individual reward systems with some group-level rewards. These may take the form of profit sharing, awards for team achievement or an expanding bonus pool, in which the awards available to everyone individually depend upon the performance of the group as a whole. The presence of such reward systems ensures that empowerment does not cause excessive competition among members of the organization.

Error tolerance. Empowered organizations need to let employees learn from their mistakes and the mistakes of others. This means that where possible employees are not punished for honest mistakes but rather encouraged to make up for their errors and to do it better the next time. It does not mean that people do not have responsibility for their actions. With the power to decide comes ownership of the consequences of the decision, and this is evident in empowered organizations. If employees do not believe they can take risks, they will not innovate and will not learn. Therefore, unless an error is malicious or repeated, the empowered organization is typically tolerant.

Enhanced communication. Decision-making requires information, and an organization in which decision-making is widely distributed should likewise have widely distributed information. The presence of electronic mail, internal newsletters, well-stocked libraries, regular staff meetings and periodic cross-functional conferences signifies the organization's attempt to make information available. In addition, individuals in empowered organizations go out of their way to include all relevant persons in communications about decisions which affect them.

Generalist managers and employees. The highly structured organization with carefully defined positions in strong functional hierarchies needs functional specialists to fill those positions. It trains them in skills specific to its own complex workings, making them highly valuable to the company in their particular jobs. Crossing lines, however, or working on ad-hoc project teams, is more difficult for specialists, who may also have trouble placing customer problems in context.

The empowered organization tends to use more generalist employees – people who are trained in a variety of skills and who are expected (and expect) to move around the organization, filling in where needed and growing through 'horizontal promotions'. These people have a broad view of the organization and of their role in it. And although many organizations can no longer promise long-term job security, generalist employees may have an easier time than specialists finding other employment should it become necessary.

The empowerment paradox

One of the problems with moving toward an empowered workforce is that those companies most likely to be successful at empowerment are those that are part way there already and therefore in least need. Companies in which hierarchies are rigid and customer response quite slow invariably have more difficulty moving to an empowered model of work than those with less formal, flatter hierarchies and a reputation for quality service. Thus, the greater the need, the lower the likelihood of success.

A large manufacturing company I know has exactly this problem in two of its manufacturing sites. The Spanish operation is famous within the company for excellent industrial relations and high-quality manufacturing. Although not called by that name, empowerment is characteristic of the way the Spanish subsidiary works. People do what needs to be done, whether or not it is part of their official job description.

On the other hand, the company's German operation has a history of contentious labour relations and is badly in need of more flexibility and local initiative. Yet the mere idea of empowering workers has the management of this subsidiary up in arms. 'Empowerment is nonsense,' they seem to say, even as they face the possibility of a work stoppage. It is a case of the rich getting richer and the poor getting poorer.

So how do you do it?

Empowerment cannot be decreed by top managers and 'rolled out' to the workforce. It cannot be bought from or introduced by consultants, although there are many who would try to sell it. Like the mutual trust that supports it, by its very nature empowerment must develop over a period of time, through the beliefs and attitudes of the participants. And, unfortunately, it can be destroyed in moments when top managers, perhaps faced with a crisis, become uncomfortable with shared control and grab back the authority they had delegated.

It is in fact the changing role of the manager that best defines the empowered organization and points the way toward it: whereas the manager once acted as unilateral director of subordinates, in an empowered organization he or she acts more as a coach and facilitator, providing resources, guidance and support to help employees do their jobs well. This new role represents a major departure from traditional ways of doing business, and although most employees welcome the change, many managers are unable to undertake it.

Yet it is there that empowerment is born or dies, in the manager-subordinate relationship. If the firm's front-line managers are not confident in their people, the idea of empowerment is merely a dream. If they are confident, if that confidence is likewise reflected, and if individuals are willing to take some risks, new levels of quality and service are possible.

Summary

Empowerment says that employees at all levels of an organization are responsible for their awn actions and should be given authority to make decisions about their work. Its popularity has been driven by the need to respond quickly to customer needs, to develop cross functional links and to take advantage of opportunities that are too local or too fleeting to be determined centrally. Better morale and compensation for limited career paths are other advantages.

Potential difficulties include the scope for chaos and conflict, a lack of clarity about where responsibility lies, the breakdown of hierarchical control, and demoralization on the part of those who do not want additional authority.

Successful empowerment will typically require feedback on performance from a variety of sources, rewards with some group com-ponent, an environment which is tolerant of mistakes, widely distributed information, and generalist managers and employees.

The paradox is that the greater the need for empowerment in an organization the less likelihood of success. It has to be allowed to develop over time through the beliefs/attitudes of participants.

Suggested further reading

Hackman, J.R. (1986) *The psychology of self-management in organizations. Making hard decisions.*

Pallak, M. S. and Perloff, R. O. (eds) *Psychology and Work: Productivity, Change, and Employment*, American Psychological Association. Washington, D.C.

Rosenbaum, J. (1984) *Career Mobility in a Corporate Hierarchy*, Academic Press, New York.

Sonnenfeld, J.A. & Peiperl, M.A. 'Staffing policy as a strategic response: a typology of career systems', *Academy of Management Review*, 13 (1988).

The true worth of building high-performance systems

■ **The development of so-called high-performance systems is emerging in the West, particularly the US, as a distinct new approach to organizational design in the face of ever-growing global competition.**

by Michael Useem

Advocating performance in business is like advocating peace in wartime. We may be committed to the idea but the details can often elude us. Identifying the right particulars and making them work in an organization is the art of leadership. The productive practices need not be invented anew; they are often readily available from other sources. In an era of national economies, good performance meant having a better organization than competitors in the same industry in the same country. In a global economy, however, good performance means having an organization that competes worldwide. If not already on a par with the international leaders, an expeditious way to get there is to study and learn from the best. Japanese lean production systems are a good place to start. So, too, are emergent high-performance systems in the US. Both strive for the 'law of halves' or better – cutting quality defects, product costs and cycle times by 50 per cent or more.

Lean production systems

Japanese lean production, vividly portrayed by John Womack, Daniel Jones and Daniel Roos in their book *The machine that changed the world* (1990), is organized around five main principles: teamwork, quality control, customer focus, minimal buffers and continuous improvement. Womack and colleagues' detailed comparison of the Japanese automobile industry with traditional Western production revealed that Toyota's manufacturing methods slashed development time by half, factory space by half, work-time by half and defects by half. The book's subtitle, *How Japan's secret weapon in the global auto wars will revolutionize Western industry*, served as a warning. With globalization of the auto industry during the 1980s, car producers in Europe and the Americas could either revolutionize their organization and compete with the best worldwide or simply stop competing. The subtitle forecast the former, and the prediction was right.

According to studies by Wharton professor John Paul MacDuffie, many American and European auto plants have successfully adopted lean practices during the 1990s and greatly improved their quality and productivity, raising themselves on to a competitive plane with the best of Japan. A McKinsey analysis of productivity in the US, Japan and Germany shows why. This study focussed on nine industries, including food, computers and automobiles. It revealed that much of the national productivity differences in these industries is a result of national differences in company organization.

The study also revealed, however, that there is little exclusively national about the best designs. Japanese auto makers produce cars in the US with nearly the same quality and productivity standards pioneered in Japan. They proved that best practices can indeed be transferred across cultural chasms and national boundaries.

High-performance systems

As American companies have struggled against intensifying competition from abroad and more demanding investors at home, they have developed an alternative model to which the

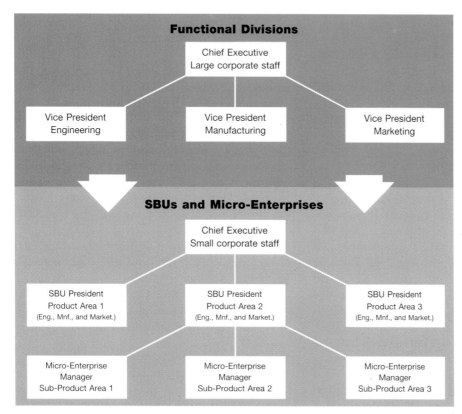

Figure 1: From functional divisions to strategic business units and micro-enterprises

rubric 'high-performance systems' is often applied. Though borrowing concepts from lean production, it is a distinct blend and one that seems to work well in economies where individualism is strong, lifetime employment is weak and shareholders are powerful.

Emergent organizational designs at such companies as AT&T, Du Pont, Ford, Hewlett-Packard, IBM, Kodak and Xerox reveal five main principles of high-performance systems: (1) customer-focussed operating units (2) devolved decision-making authority (3) streamlined management with tighter financial control (4) re-engineering of business process (5) the benchmarking of decisions against their contribution to shareholder value.

Customer-focussed operating units

Company managers sometimes allude to 'bringing the market into the firm'. This is not an effort to turn a company into a market or what are sometimes called 'networked' or 'virtual' organizations. It is, rather, an initiative to channel customer concerns directly to managers of operating units. Market surveys and focus groups are standard fare, but companies have also sought to insert customer concerns into a range of key decision points.

AT&T, for example, now requires its divisional managers to measure up on three criteria in their annual performance appraisal: EVA or economic value added (their contribution to company earnings); PVA or people value added (their effectiveness in managing and developing subordinates); and CVA or customer value added (their effectiveness in the eyes of major customers). Similarly, Southwest Airlines include frequent-flyer customers on some of its hiring committees. Such 'market-in' efforts are based on the organizational premise that routine management contact with customers, the creation of customer advocates inside the company and the insertion of customer criteria into decisions can help ensure company responsiveness to shifting market demands.

Taking this logic a step further, companies such as Xerox are also building their operating units around distinct products or services for internal or external customers. These output-focussed 'micro-enterprises' reduce hierarchy, stress teamwork, reward creativity and increase receptivity to the customer.

Devolved decision-making authority

Authority to succeed and fail is pushed lower in the organization, giving operating units greater autonomy. The traditional functional divisions cast around development, manufacturing and marketing are replaced with strategic business units focussed on broad classes of products or services (*see* Figure 1 above). These SBUs are given responsibility for setting strategy but are also held accountable for results. They in turn sub-divide themselves in similar fashion, with micro-enterprises their smallest operating units.

The number of SBUs varies greatly from company to company. Du Pont has grouped some 60 profit centers into a dozen business units. Xerox has created nine units. Their relationships to headquarters also varies, with some firms retaining more centralized functions than others. But they all share profit and loss responsibilities, giving them and those who lead them the feel of a quasi-independent business.

Strategic business units, micro-enterprises and intermediate operating levels incorporate as many company functions as possible, including planning, production and marketing. With relationships to customers more clearly established, managers and units acquire stronger incentives to respond. With responsibility for decisions more clearly delegated, they acquire greater power to act. And with accountability for results more clearly pinpointed, they acquire stronger reason to perform.

At the same time, cross-boundary management, which is the working relations among the now more autonomous units, is at a premium. In the wake of its restructuring in this direction, Hewlett-Packard managers have come of necessity to rely less on the authoritative power of office and more on the power of personal persuasion.

The skill sets required of those heading these more autonomous business units differ in other predictable ways from those who ran the traditional functional units. Managers who had risen to the top of the functional divisions were professional specialists who had mastered their technical terrain, be it engineering, manufacturing or marketing. Those who now sit atop the business units are management generalists who have working familiarity with engineering, manufacturing and marketing. These generalists, no longer the central office, carry most of the direct responsibility for meeting corporate objectives.

The same is true for those presiding over lower operating levels and micro-enterprises. Each has become a master of the house; all exercise leadership in their own way. In the words of one telecommunications executive, 'every manager must also be a leader'.

Streamlined management control; tighter financial control

Central offices, as a result, are scaled back, headquarters staffs are reduced and management layers are thinned. Operating units receive fewer policy directives from the corporate office but stronger financial directives.

During its 1993–95 restructuring, IBM reduced its corporate staff from 5,100 to 3,900 and subsequently put its headquarters up for sale. 'Our view of corporate headquarters,' offered its senior vice president for human resources and administration, 'is that there should be as little of it as possible.'

In thinning their management ranks, companies also expanded their spans of control. Seven layers in the pyramid and seven direct subordinates for each boss had been the historic norm for many large corporations. Now the thrust is to flatten layers, expand spans and transform the organizational pyramid from tall and narrow to short and wide.

Re-engineering of business process

Process restructuring, as championed by Michael Hammer and James Champny in their book *Reengineering the corporation: a manifesto for business revolution* (1993), entails streamlining

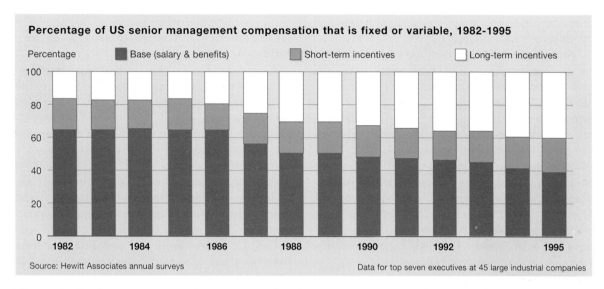

Percentage of US senior management compensation that is fixed or variable, 1982-1995

Percentage   ■ Base (salary & benefits)   ■ Short-term incentives   □ Long-term incentives

Source: Hewitt Associates annual surveys   Data for top seven executives at 45 large industrial companies

Figure 2: Senior management compensation becomes more contingent upon performance

processing and paperwork throughout the organization to increase quality, service and speed. Information systems are improved, job titles are expanded, employees are empowered, accountability is increased. Ford Motor Co reduced its accounts payable staff by three-quarters through installation of powerful data retrieval systems and elimination of most paperwork from the process of ordering and receiving products from suppliers. Through an extensive restructuring and re-engineering, Du Pont removed more than $1bn (£0.6bn) in fixed costs and nearly the same in capital expenditures and company debt. Though business process re-engineering often fails to produce anticipated gains, cost and time reductions of 50 per cent or more are often reported when it is effectively implemented.

Benchmarking for shareholder value

Finally, decisions and actions are more explicitly judged on the basis of the anticipated worth to stockholders. Employee promotion, compensation and dismissal are more contingent on performance measures better linked to share-holder value. Top management compensation has become increasingly tied to shareholder value in US firms through expanded use of share options. Between 1982 and 1995, the variable fraction of total compensation received by the top seven at

45 large companies rose from 37 per cent to 61 per cent. Virtually all of the drop in the fixed fraction has been filled by long-term incentive pay, up from 17 to 40 per cent of the compensation pie (*see* Figure 2). Since long-term incentive compensation is generally based on company share options, this has had the effect of focusing executive attention on shareholder value.

As a new chief executive assumed office at Eastman Kodak in 1993, for example, he received options to purchase more than 750,000 shares of Kodak stock, of little or no value unless the stock price increased substantially but potentially worth $13m to $17m if it did.

Detailed analysis of incentive packages for US chief executives in 1988, 1991 and 1992 reveals a sharp increase in the extent to which their compensation is linked, like that of Kodak's chief, to the production of greater investor wealth.

Global competition + shareholder pressure = high performance organizations

Together, these five principles are creating organizations that look and act differently. Hierarchies are flatter and spans broader; divisions are less functionally divided and more self-contained; authority is more decentralized and less authoritative; and accountability is more precise and less detached from owner interests.

Not surprisingly, employment systems are altered as well. Firms and employees display less commitment to one another. Internal labor markets are weakened as organizational capacities are strengthened, and temporary contracting, contingent workers and insecure careers have become more prominent. The results are uneven, with some companies displaying large improvements while others show little. Much of the difference depends on the exercise of leadership. Introducing high performance systems requires persistence in the face of resistance. But when successfully implemented, the record is compelling.

> **Research and experience with high performance work systems over two decades of experimentation in the U.S. reveals that they generally produce:**
> - Increased quality of products and services
> - Higher employee commitment and motivation
> - Lower employee turnover and absenteeism
> - Increased learning by individuals, teams, and work units
> - Enhanced ability to adapt to shifts in customer needs, production technologies, and enviromental conditions
> - Reduced costs, often by 40 to 50 percent

Figure 3: Impact of high performance systems

Global competition and shareholder pressures are sure to intensify during the years ahead. Foreign direct investment, foreign stock investment and cross-national joint ventures are ascendant during the 1990s. So too is the concentration of corporate ownership in the hands of institutional investors, giving them the muscle to demand more executive accountability.

Every company must develop its own organizational scheme for responding, but benchmarking and borrowing from the global best is one way to build the details that are the foundation of world-class high performance.

Summary

American companies have learnt many of the techniques of Japanese lean production, in the process developing their own 'high performance systems'. The model is a distinct blend and seems to work well in economies where individualism is strong, lifetime employment weak and shareholders powerful.

High performance systems operate according to five main principles: customer focussed operating units, whereby customer concerns are channelled directly to managers of operating units; devolved decision making authority (with strategic business units, sub-divided into micro-enterprises, given responsibility for setting strategy and held accountable for results); streamlined management with tighter financial control (scaled back head offices, thinned management ranks, wider spans of control); re-engineering of business process (with cost and time reductions of more than 50 per cent often reported); and the benchmarking of decisions against their anticipated worth to shareholders (with management remuneration tied more directly to shareholder value).

Production and Operations Management

Contents

Systems are never good enough 297
Thomas E. Vollmann, IMD
Any company that is content with its planning and control of manufacturing systems needs to ask itself questions.

Some measures of concern 302
Roger W. Schmenner, IMD
Traditional financial measurements are increasingly inappropriate for responding to the challenges that face manufacturing companies.

Ways to improve the company 307
Carlos Cordon, IMD
What are re-engineering, benchmarking and continuous improvement? And how and when can they be used to improve the way companies work?

Rigid flexibility and factory focus 311
Robert Collins, Roger Schmenner and
Carlos Cordon, IMD
Modern manufacturers must produce at low cost, deliver rapidly and frequently, and be responsive to customer demands – how?

Supply chain management 316
Thomas E. Vollmann, Carlos Cordon and
Hakon Raabe, IMD
By managing its supply chain as effectively as possible and matching its competencies with others, a company can attain a 'virtual integration' that can bring substantial competitive advantages.

Strategic management of the operations function 322
Terry Hill, Alastair Nicholson and Roy Westbrook,
London Business School
Can a company's manufacturing function support strategy? Not unless operations is involved from the beginning.

The 'greening' of industry – the hardest bit is still to come 327
Ulrich Steger, IMD
The environment is now an important – often vital – part of every manager's responsibility. But the real pressure on companies is yet to come.

Transformation: the difference between domination and death 330
Thomas E. Vollmann, IMD
Manufacturing companies face so many challenges that if they do not dominate their markets they must inevitably die. But domination requires change on a massive scale – so-called 'enterprise transformation' – that makes re-engineering look an easy operation.

Pan-regional manufacturing: the lessons from Europe 336
Robert Collins and Roger Schmenner, IMD
How are manufacturing companies in Europe managing the transition from a focus on nationally based to pan-regional manufacturing?

Thomas E. Vollmann is Professor of Manufacturing Management at IMD, Lausanne.

Terry Hill is Professor of Operations Management, Chair of the Operations Management faculty and Dean of the full-time MBA programme at London Business School.

Roger Schmenner is a Professor of Operations Management at the Indiana University School of Business, and a regular visiting professor at IMD.

Alastair Nicholson is Professor of Operations Management at London Business School.

Carlos Cordon is Professor of Manufacturing Management, IMD, Lausanne.

Roy Westbrook is associate Professor of Operations Management at London Business School.

Robert Collins is Professor of Business Administration at IMD, Lausanne. His research interests are in strategy formulation and implementation in the transformation of the manufacturing enterprise.

Ulrich Steger is Alcan Professor of Environmental Management at IMD. His research interests include environmental strategy and politics, innovation, globalization and organizational learning.

Hakon Raabe was a visiting researcher at IMD during 1995. He is currently a doctoral student at the Norwegian Institute of Technology. His research interests include manufacturing strategy and industrial networks.

Introduction

Production and Operations Management concerns the physical processes by which companies take in raw materials, convert them into products and then distribute them to customers (often business customers rather than the consumer end-user). It is therefore a vital part of the business process and ranks highly in the responsibilities of general management.

It is an area where – heavily influenced by Japanese manufacturing practices and such concepts as business process re-engineering – the rate of change in recent years has been very great.

The Production and Operations Management module is made up of nine separate articles that look at the way these changes are being implemented and their implications.

The topics covered include: the need to question existing production systems; how the improvements that such changes bring can be measured; the various 'improvement projects', such as re-engineering and benchmarking, that companies are using to streamline their production processes; a re-interpretation of the concept of 'factory focus'; supply chain management; strategic management of operations; 'green' issues in manufacturing; 'enterprise transformation'; and pan-regional manufacturing.

Systems are never good enough

■ There are always improvements to be made in the planning and control of manufacturing systems. Any company that is content with what it has needs to ask itself questions, says Thomas E. Vollmann

Manufacturing planning and control systems (MPCS) have always been an area for improvement in manufacturing companies. Organizations seem perpetually to wish they had better forecasts, more achievable scheduling systems, enhanced flexibility in responding to unforeseen customer requests, reduced inventory levels, higher customer order fill rates, shorter delivery times, greater capacity utilization, and a host of other desirables.

Moreover, there is no end to it. The appropriate answer to a question of a desired inventory turnover rate is always the same: twice what it is at the present time.

A key conclusion for this quest is the need never to be content with the present manufacturing planning and control system in a company. In fact, we often advise companies that if they have not had a hard look at these systems (as well as the related logistics systems) for several years, there is an excellent chance that significant payoffs can be achieved if they do.

But there is a natural progression in manufacturing planning and control systems that managers should think about in evaluating their own progress. Our experience indicates that one can find examples at almost any point along this progression.

Step 1: Informal systems

Informal systems for manufacturing planning and control are most obviously seen where there is a lack of computers, the throughput times for products are high, inventory accuracy is low, and the order of the day is expediting and panic. The same problems and conditions, it has to be said, are sometimes seen where there are indeed formal systems.

The key lesson is that one should never believe that 'what is purported to be the case is in reality the case.' No, it is always necessary for MPCS to pass the reality test of a visit to the factory to see that systems are in fact being used precisely as they are purported to be.

Informal systems are not prevalent today in larger manufacturing companies. Most of these firms have been so handicapped by such approaches that they are now out of business. An example is a large fork-lift truck company we examined several years ago. It had a good product, a great brand name, but all the classic problems of informal systems – the company no longer exists.

Step 2: Basic material requirements planning (MRP) systems

The first progression toward a modern MPCS environment is to implement a basic MRP system. This bases the need for all components on exploded information from bills of material. That is, for example, the exact number of rear left-hand green door panels in any particular time period is calculated directly from the schedule for how many four-door green cars are to be assembled in that time period. The need is not estimated, forecast or guessed: it is calculated exactly.

In order for this approach to work, several things are required. First, the bills of material must be accurate. Next, the assembly schedule must be met. Also, the detailed schedules for all the components must also be met in order to meet the assembly schedule. This is not as easy as it sounds, but the results are impressive.

The shift from informal systems to a working MRP system usually results in major benefits, such as inventory reductions of 40 per cent and similar improvements in lead times, meeting customer promises, and productivity improvements. Moreover, a working MRP system allows the company to know – not just guess – whether it can achieve particular objectives. For example, at a major producer of hospital beds, a very large unexpected order for their most expensive bed came in from Saudi Arabia. The MRP system allowed the company to see where it would run into problems with enough time to find solutions to them and to fulfill the order.

Step 3: Enhanced MRP systems

The first MRP system is rarely the last and if a company has had the same one for many years it needs to take a long hard look. MRP systems have been widely used for about 25 years. The early ones used home-grown software, but no one in their right mind would write their own software today unless it was a very special situation. One example would be an integrated circuits manufacturer that ended up with several quality grades of product coming from one batch; a customer order for a particular grade could be satisfied by substituting a superior grade.

In fact, many companies are now actively implementing new MRP-based systems based on packaged software. The intent is to use these systems to perform the basic manufacturing planning and control and to devote any special system design activities to practices that are unique to their particular company situation. This focus of resources is quite prevalent in attaining the benefits discussed under Steps 5 and 6 below.

More importantly, first MRP systems tend to use large periods – or 'buckets' – such as months. This leads to inherent extra costs and other problems. For example, a large food manufacturer traditionally gave its factories the schedule for month X on the 15th of month $X-1$. Meeting this schedule required the factories to carry extra inventories of almost everything, since it was not possible to get all their components from ground zero and still meet the monthly schedule.

Moreover, the schedule was 'met' if the products were finished on day 1 or day 31 of month X. This meant that sales needed to order one month ahead to be sure the goods would be available, which incurred the costs of both an extra month's worth of inventory and the larger forecast errors associated with an extended time horizon (and related panic costs of trying to meet unforecasted demands).

A related problem with monthly periods is what manufacturing people call the 'hockey stick' effect. A plot of output over the month starts low and increases sharply toward the end of the month rather than being constant. The end of the month panic conditions usually require overtime and other inefficiencies in order to meet the schedule. In addition, the panic conditions often also result in the organization falling back into the informal systems phase as heroic efforts are made to meet the schedule.

This problem is greatly magnified when the true monthly schedule is concerned with meeting shipments measured in financial terms. Then, a common practice is 'cherry picking' the next month's schedule in order to move large currency orders into the present month. Unfortunately moving the cherries from month $X+1$ into month X leaves month $X+1$ with the 'pits' i.e. this process guarantees that it will need to be continued. And almost always cherry picking is done outside the formal systems – demolishing their credibility.

All of this means that a fundamental enhancement to basic MRP systems is to work with smaller time periods. Many companies have moved first from monthly time buckets to weekly, then to daily and finally to essentially real-time or 'bucketless' systems. The move involves much more than running a computer more often. Work schedules and activities have to be synchronized with the new approach.

For example, in moving to weekly timing, companies typically run the system over the weekend, analyse the data on Monday/Tuesday, issue new orders on Wednesday, update data on Thursday/Friday, and re-run the system again over the weekend. Similar transformations in working approaches accompany daily and real-time systems.

There are other fundamental improvements that can and are being implemented in manu-

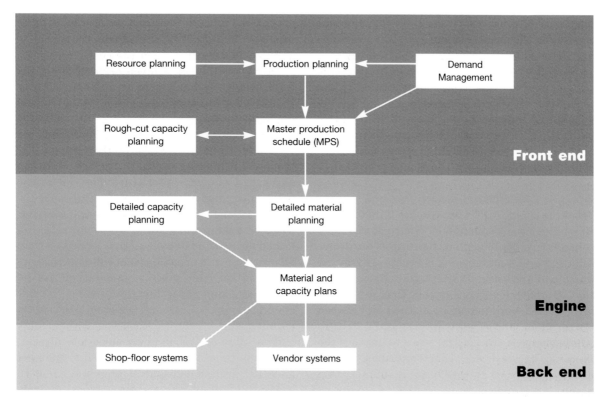

Figure 1

facturing companies. For example, one major food company is now exploring a new packaged MRP system that will give it a better integration between its various factories.

Step 4: Manufacturing resource planning

Basic MRP systems and their descendants are primarily focussed on the middle part or 'engine' of Figure 1. The emphasis is on lining up the schedules of component parts with those of the assembly of finished goods. But Figure 1 also shows a 'front end' that results in a master production schedule (MPS) and a 'back end' concerned with the detailed execution necessary on the shop floor in order to achieve the MPS. It is the entire MPCS shown in Figure 1 that truly determines the efficacy of a company's detailed planning. Enhancements thus come in all three areas of the figure, and companies need to work in all of them. Detailed improvements in all three areas are beyond our present scope, but a few examples of major improvement approaches

should provide a check-list for examining the performance of a company.

In the front end, demand management is an important area for improvement. Fundamentally, demand management recognizes that the forecast is only one input to the MPS and that order entry is a process by which forecasts are consumed. That means that order entry and the order backlog are very important in managing MPCS systems effectively.

Production planning is often a key area for enhancing MPCS performance. For many companies, it is only after achieving a good MPS system that they truly learn to understand the necessity of a monthly production planning cycle that drives the monthly financial meeting. That is, in well run companies the production plan becomes the driver and the financial results are the passengers.

Rough-cut capacity planning is an approach to test continually the MPS for feasibility – that is, can the plan be executed? Detailed capacity planning is performed at a much lower level of aggregation; it focuses on the same question but now using the entire database of shop schedules and detailed MRP records.

Shop-floor scheduling systems are at a base level concerned with continually lining up the priorities of orders to match the assembly schedules. Improvements are aimed at better utilization of capacity, attention devoted to bottlenecks, faster throughput times and closer coupling of schedules with customer priorities.

Step 5: Continuous improvement

All of the classic MPCS approaches tend to follow the 'mass production' model where centralized controls are implemented, tight procedures are followed and management is essentially of the 'command and control' variety. But at some point this approach is often rejected. Empowerment, self-directed work teams, no distinction between 'direct labor' and other workers, and a culture where everyone searches for ways to improve the processes by which work is accomplished leads to a very different approach to manufacturing planning and control.

Just-in-time (JIT) systems focus on speed as a key objective. They also are a part of reducing the 'hidden factory' of paper work and transactions. JIT systems try to minimize the number of discrete shop orders – instead basing manufacturing on simplified fast flows that are controlled only by the shop floor people.

An example is a car company that can be fairly sure that every car shipped will have one and only one radiator. If the supplier of radiators delivers several times each day there will be so few radiators in inventory that no one really cares, any bad ones can be sent back or tossed out, and the supplier can be paid on a daily basis by counting the cars completed, multiplying by the price per radiator and electronically transferring that amount into the supplier's bank account. All this is done with no paper: no invoices, no shipping papers, no bills of lading, no receiving papers, nothing.

JIT is supported by on-going process improvements, such as set-up time reduction, statistical process control, total preventative maintenance and a host of other activities that lead to 'lean manufacturing'. The focus is on

execution: routine foolproof execution with no problems and no need for systems constantly to check up on people.

One firm in the electronics industry coined the term 'coping mechanism' to describe any activity that was done to 'cope' with problems that should not exist in an ideal world. Thus inspection is there to cope with the fact that products may not be made right. The implication? Spend the money on making it right rather than on checking to be sure that it is right. There are many such coping mechanisms.

All cost money and they need to be rooted out. Further examples include cycle counting and locked storerooms to be sure that procedures are followed, most transactions associated with shop-floor control (the work should either not be started or completed so fast that there is no point keeping track of it) and most other control documents.

The 'M' in MRP has never stood for 'miracle'. Yet many times we have been asked to examine an MRP system because it does not seem to work. But in fact, the system is working quite well. It is the execution of the system commands that are at fault. When scrap is made instead of good product, there will almost always be a scheduling problem. Someone will have to scramble to make the schedule.

Thus we see that MPCS is not a stand-alone approach to improving manufacturing operations. But it is the backbone of improvement. If one cannot make schedules and hit them, then there will be little ability to achieve other objectives.

Supporting all of these initiatives is the fundamental shift in approach from command/control to teamwork and an empowered workforce. Indeed, the objective in such companies is to 'maximize the idle time' of all workers so that other work currently done by middle managers can be made a part of the basic manufacturing infrastructure and these people in turn made free to work more closely with customers to maximize customer perceived values.

A natural consequence of this form of thinking is a need for a change in performance measurements. But this is the source of another article in this subject.

Step 6: Supply chain integration

As stated at the outset, there is no real end to improvements that can be made to manufacturing planning and control systems. At some point one does run into definition problems, such as those noted above when the focus turns to techniques that allow for better execution of the MPCS. But that is not the issue. The goal is always to improve manufacturing; to make the routine things routinely; to reduce costs and improve customer perceived values – at the same time.

Supply chain management is another separate section in this series, but at this time, it is still instructive to understand how better relationships with customers and suppliers is a logical extension of MPCS, and why it makes sense for companies to look here for further benefits.

Everything we know about MPCS suggests that there are always two avenues to pursue for improvement. The first is to improve a particular situation in terms of its present problem definition. Thus one can do a better job of MRP, one can put in a new program, one can enhance the MPS, one can improve the shop-floor scheduling and so on. But another avenue is to redefine the problem in a broader context. The move from MRP to MRPII is a classic move in this direction, where a fundamentally larger problem is defined and solved – in an integrative fashion.

The boundaries depicted in Figure 1 certainly do not need to limit the search for operational excellence. Many firms have implemented logistics improvements where connections are built between well-functioning MPCS systems and the similar systems of their customers and suppliers. As noted above, this work is now often based on using packaged software to support the basic manufacturing activities. Doing so is largely a matter of redrawing the boundaries for the analysis. It is also a matter of overall optimization, based on some overall cost-objective function and the elimination of the 'zero-sum thinking' that pervades the thought process of far too many business people.

Conclusions

Manufacturing planning and control systems have a long history of improvement in manufacturing companies. This history has been continuous and it shows no signs of letting up. The managerial implications are that every manufacturing company should ask itself whether it has had a fundamental look at its MPCS approaches in recent times, what are the latest features of the best software packages and what might these do for the company, where is the company in terms of the continuum defined here for MPCS improvement, where should it benchmark its MPCS approaches, and how fast are improvements being implemented? Fundamentally, every manager owes this investigation to his company.

Summary

Companies should never be content with their manufacturing planning and control systems (MPCS). 'Informal' ones – typified by a lack of computers, high throughput times and low inventory accuracy – are no longer prevalent in large companies. Those that had them have mostly gone out of business.

The first step towards acquiring a modern MPCS is a basic material requirements planning (MRP) system. This allows a company to know whether it can achieve particular objectives. Early ones used home-grown software but many companies are now actively implementing them with packaged software. A fundamental enhancement to basic MRP systems is to work with smaller time periods – weekly, daily, or even real-time. The efficacy of a company's detailed planning, however, goes beyond lining up the schedules of component parts with those of the assembly of finished goods. Enhancements can also be made to the master production schedule at the 'front end' – in areas like demand management and production planning – and to detailed shop floor execution at the 'back end'.

Some measures of concern

■ **Traditional financial measurements are increasingly inappropriate for responding to the challenges that face manufacturing companies in today's competitive market, says** Roger W. Schmenner

If it is true that 'what gets measured gets managed', then what happens when the measures themselves are suspect? Many companies have spent considerable resources in pursuing advances in the wrong type of measures. There are two common errors of this kind:

● using the wrong measure to motivate managers so that they spend time improving something that has few positive (and perhaps many harmful) consequences for the organization; and

● failing to use the right measure, so that something that is important for the company is neglected. The first has been labeled a false alarm; the second, a gap.

The aim is to remove false alarms from the set of performance measurements to which managers should pay attention and to add performance measures that fill the gaps. The trick, of course, is to know which is which. Such false alarms and gaps, however, can be reliably identified using a relatively simple technique.

This technique asks managers to compare those items or areas where improvement is regarded as important for the long-run success of their companies with the performance measures linked to those areas. Ideally, heavy measurement emphasis should be placed on areas that managers think are critical for competitiveness. If great emphasis is placed on an area that many managers consider unimportant for the company's success, a false alarm is sounded. On the other hand, if there is little measurement on an area many consider critical to long-run success, then there is a gap.

Research has suggested that gaps are often associated with non-financial measures; false alarms with typical cost-based measurements. However, until an IMD study that forms the basis of this section, there has been no research on the universality of these findings across diverse industries, production types (for example, process versus assembly) or operating environments (for example, market leaders versus followers).

IMD questioned a group of 92 senior manufacturing executives around the world. They were all part participants of IMD's Managing Manufacturing program and were responsible for a diverse array of operations-related tasks in their companies. Of the 92, 72 were from, Europe, eight from Asia, five from South America, four from Africa and three from North America. The group was asked to consider the following areas where improvements are commonly sought:

● *Employee involvement* – the degree to which workers participate in decision making that affects their particular jobs.

● *Quality* – how well products manufactured conform to specifications and how well those specifications reflect what customers value.

● *Labor efficiency* – defined as standard hours/actual hours x 100 per cent. 'Standard hours' are usually defined by an engineering study of the job performed. A labor efficiency greater that 100 is considered good.

● *Machine efficiency* – a measure similar to labor efficiency but defined for a job done by a machine rather than a worker. If machine hours are less than standard hours then the machine efficiency is greater than 100 per cent.

● *Volume flexibility* – the need to vary quantities manufactured from one period to another by a considerable degree and to do so easily.

● *New product introduction* – the degree to which new products are easily and quickly developed, put into manufacturing and produced in appropriate quantities to meet initial market demand.

● *Process throughput times* – time in the factory from when raw materials are ready to be worked on until products are completely finished.

● *Integration with customers* – the extent to which a factory communicates and interacts with its customers.

● *Direct cost reduction* – reduction of costs that can be attributed directly to particular products: labor, materials and so on.

● *Overhead cost reduction* – reduction of support services costs of all types: administrative, equipment, maintenance, plant depreciation and so on.

● *Computer systems* – the benefits of all the services provided by computers: order entry, order tracking, scheduling, billing, payroll and so on.

Using these definitions as references, the respondents completed two seven-point scales for each of the 12 areas:

● a left-hand scale that assessed the 'extent to which long-run improvement is important'. This scale ranged from 'none' to 'great'

● a right-hand scale that assessed the 'effect of current performance measures on improvement'. This scale ranged from 'inhibit' to 'support'.

Respondents were also asked for further information such as their industry, company market share, percentages of the company's costs attributable to labor, materials and overheads; manufacturing throughput times, order lead-times, and an assessment of the company's capability versus others in the industry.

A gap exists when the left-hand scale's value tends towards 'great' but the right-hand scale tends towards 'inhibit'. Similarly, the left-hand tending towards 'none' and the right-hand towards 'support' signals a false alarm.

To identify the gaps and false alarms we subtracted the right-hand scale values from those of the left-hand scale for each of the 12 items and averaged the differences.

Sounding the false alarms and filling in the gaps

The general results Table 1 lists the mean scores for both the left-hand and right scales in order of descending perceived importance to the customer.

Table 1: Rank order of areas by extent of importance and by effect of current performance measures

Extent to which long-run improvement is important	
Customer satisfaction	6.609
Quality	6.098
Employee involvement	6.087
Overhead cost reduction	5.783
Integration with customers	5.587
New product introduction	5.576
Volume flexibility	5.402
Throughput times	5.141
Direct cost reduction	5.011
Labour efficiency	4.912
Computer systems	4.870
Machine efficiency	4.837
Effect of current performance measure of improvement	
Quality	5.451
Customer satisfaction	5.297
Direct cost reduction	5.165
Labour efficiency	4.878
Employee involvement	4.833
Machine efficiency	4.791
Overhead cost reduction	4.692
Throughput times	4.473
Integration with customers	4.407
Volume flexibility	4.374
Computer systems	4.286
New product introduction	4.146

Table 2 puts the importance of the area or item and the support for it from the performance measurement system together by looking explicitly at the gaps and false alarms. For example, in Table 1 quality is seen as both important and emphasized by existing measurement systems. Thus in Table 2 quality is neither a gap nor a false alarm; it is being measured correctly.

Employee involvement and customer satisfaction, though, are gaps. Table 1 shows customer satisfaction as the area needing the most long-run improvement. However, in the

Table 2		
	Performance measures	**Mean differences**
GAPS	New product introduction	1.483
	Customer satisfaction	1.308
	Employee involvement	1.256
THE MIDDLE HALF	Integration with customers	1.187
	Overhead cost reduction	1.077
	Volume flexibility	1.022
	Throughput times	0.670
	Quality	0.637
	Computer systems	0.593
FALSE ALARMS	Machine efficiency	0.044
	Labour efficiency	0.011
	Direct cost reduction	-0.165

The mean differences for each performance measure are not precisely the differences of the means shown in Table 1 because of missing data.
There is at least one but no more than 3 missing responses for each item.

lower half of Table 1 its 'effect' score (which is not shown) is significantly lower; hence the gap. Employee involvement is similar. The new product introduction gap is even more interesting. Though it scores in the middle of the range for 'importance for improvement', it ranks bottom on the scale measuring the effectiveness of current performance measures. Hence it, too, is a gap.

Table 2 isolates just three false alarms – direct cost reduction, labor efficiency and machine efficiency. There is a statistically significant difference in the figures between these three and the higher 'middle half'. However, there is no statistical difference between the three gaps – new product introduction, customer satisfaction and employee involvement and the upper entries of the 'middle half'. As a result, their designation is more arbitrary than those of the three false alarms.

The three false alarms highlighted by this study are consistent with earlier research. We and others have long decried the effectiveness of these financially driven, after-the-fact measures. They are among the usual suspects to be rounded up in any search for evidence of the waste that poorly conceived performance measures can bring to a factory.

● Direct costs are dwarfed by overhead costs. Trying to reduce them is harder to accomplish and worth less to the organization.

● Labor efficiency is susceptible to manipulation

to make an otherwise bad situation look acceptable. What is more, it does nothing to indicate how much waste is in the operation; one can be 'efficient' and still be wasteful. Labor efficiency measures do not show the worker how to do things better; they only tempt managers to push workers harder.

● Machine efficiency is similarly plagued with problems. Simply having machines producing many standard hours' worth of output is no guarantee that the factory is doing a productive job. As long as the factory has enough capacity for meeting the demands of the market, then one should not be concerned with machine efficiency. Only when one is concerned with buying machinery, or with divesting it, does machine efficiency become an input to the decision.

Though not so statistically significant, the three gaps – new product introduction, customer satisfaction and employee involvement – also make sense. They are all widely recognized as important and, at least in our survey sample, it is apparent that companies could become better at managing them and that they do not measure them effectively. The fact that any measurements used may well have to be non-financial and approximate should not deter us from using them. It is far better to measure the right thing inexactly and in timely fashion than the wrong thing with great precision and well after the fact. The clear indication is that time and resources should be devoted to developing measures of these items so that they can be better managed.

Some specific results

While the general results are illuminating, more detailed analysis is necessary to reach definitive implications concerning gaps and false alarms. What are gaps and false alarms for one industry may not be so for another. The response to the IMD survey can be broken down into five separate industries: food and tobacco, chemicals and metals, engineered products, electronics-related products, other.

Table 3 shows the results from these five industries. Some areas are common to all. Direct cost reduction, for example, is a false alarm for all five; machine efficiency for four of the five.

Table 3: Result for selected industry definitions

Category	Gaps	False alarms
FOOD AND TOBACCO	Customer satisfaction	Labour efficiency
	Integration with customers	Direct cost reduction
	Employee involvement	Throughput times
CHEMICALS AND METALS	New product introduction	Direct cost reduction
	Overhead cost reduction	Machine efficiency
	Customer satisfaction	Throughput times
ENGINEERED PRODUCTS	Employee involvement	Machine efficiency
	Volume flexibility	Labour efficiency
	New product introduction	Direct cost reduction
ELECTRONICS– RELATED PRODUCTS	Customer satisfaction	Computer systems
	New product introduction	Direct cost reduction
	Throughput times	Machine efficiency
OTHER	Integration with customers	Machine efficiency
	Customer satisfaction	Direct cost reduction
	Employee involvement	Volume flexibility

Customer satisfaction is a gap for four of the five and both new product innovation and employee involvement are gaps for three each.

There are also distinct differences and these provoke interesting analysis.

• Throughput time is a false alarm for both the food and tobacco and the chemicals and metals group, but a gap for electronics-related products. Many operations in the former two industries are continuous flow processes or can achieve considerable economies of scale. Reducing throughput times is not so important because throughput time is often considered a given because of process technology and machine design. This is not the case for an assembly intensive, high-technology and rapidly changing electronics-related industry.

• Integration with customers occurs as a gap for both the food and tobacco group and the 'other' category (which includes apparel). Both are influenced by powerful retail customers that underscore the importance of such integration.

• Overhead cost reduction is important for the chemicals and metals industries for reasons mentioned above in connection with process industries in general.

• Volume flexibility is a gap for engineered products, perhaps because it is often difficult in that environment to increase production quickly, particularly because it often involves changes for a substantial assortment of suppliers.

Results dependent on company performance

All respondents to the survey were asked to rate the manufacturing capabilities of their companies on a scale ranging from 'worst in industry' to 'best in industry', the extent of their market share compared to the industry leader and to rate the level of labor intensity in their company.

This produced some interesting differences. For example, companies with high manufacturing capability (as they perceive themselves) see gaps in two customer-oriented areas: integration with customers and new product introduction. The process industries, where investment is often very large, see volume flexibility as a gap whereas the more labor-intensive non-process industries see employee involvement as a gap.

There is much less volatility in terms of false alarms. The 'usual suspects' are out in force. The only exception, interestingly, is top capability companies in the process industry, who see quality as a false alarm, perhaps because these companies think it is a largely solved problem for them.

Companies with lower manufacturing capabilities, in both process and non-process industries, on the other hand, see customer satisfaction as a gap. Cost-related issues also intrude. In process industries, weaker performers cite overhead cost reduction as a gap; in non-process industries, throughput time. Market share and labor intensity as criteria produce little pattern, with marked differences across all categories and between process and non-process industries. There is much more consensus about false alarms again, the 'usual suspects'.

Conclusion

Through the use of a relatively simple technique, manufacturing managers have revealed the need for a careful assessment of performance measures. There is widespread agreement on false alarms: measures that should be abandoned because they encourage inappropriate managerial actions. Direct cost reduction, machine efficiency and labor efficiency are almost universally emphasized well beyond their importance. On the other hand, in somewhat less consistent findings, items such as new product introduction, customer satisfaction and employee involvement are frequently revealed to be gaps. In general, more emphasis could be placed on them. However, the results suggest that the specifics can vary greatly from situation to situation. Different performance measures apparently need to be added for different industries and for different levels of performance within those industries. In sum, the measures that should be discarded are relatively common and straightforward. The new measures that should be added are much more situation-dependent.

The overall conclusion is inescapable, however. All manufacturing companies need seriously to consider changing their performance measurements. The universality of the 'usual suspects' implies that if a company still utilizes the standard financial, after-the-fact measurements it is 'out of touch' and may well be employing measurements that impede the organization from making the improvements required to remain competitive in today's marketplace.

Summary

Many companies devote resources to measuring the wrong things, and those that utilize standard financial, after-the-fact measurements are probably out of touch.

'False alarms' describe those measures which motivate managers to improve areas where there are few benefits to the organization (and sometimes harmful effects); 'gaps' are when important areas are neglected. A recent IMD study of 92 senior manufacturing executives would suggest that the measurement of employee involvement, customer satisfaction and new product introduction are common gaps; measurement of the reduction of direct costs (which are typically swamped by overhead costs), of labor efficiency (susceptible to manipulation), and of machine efficiency were identified as three false alarms. What are gaps and false alarms for one industry, though, may not be common to all. Throughput time is a false alarm for the food and chemicals groups, for example, but a gap for electronic products. The results of the survey were also dependent on companies' perceptions of their own capabilities.

Suggested further reading

Dixon, J. R., A. J. Nanni, T. E. Vollmann (1990) *The New Performance Challenge: Measuring Operations for World-Class Competition*, Business One Irwin, II, US.

Ways to improve the company

■ **What are re-engineering, benchmarking and continuous improvement? And how can they improve the way companies work?**

by Carlos Cordon

Re-engineering, benchmarking practices and continuous improvement programs are methodologies that manufacturing (and service) companies are using to increase their competitive level. Many of these companies are achieving substantial improvements in quality, lead times, costs and service by using these methods. Typically, successful projects achieve performance increases from 30 per cent up to 400 per cent. Encouraged by this success, many other companies are embracing these methodologies.

Often, companies mix and use these methods without assessing their 'pros' and 'cons'. Moreover, some managers use these terms as if they meant the same. However, these methods have substantial differences and are not appropriate for all situations. Surveys show, for example, that more than 50 per cent of re-engineering projects fail.

These mixed results, spectacular successes together with high rates of failure, show the importance of understanding how these methods work, what results to expect and where it is appropriate to use them. Let's start by reviewing their characteristics.

Re-engineering

Re-engineering, according to Michael Hammer and James Champny, is 'the fundamental rethinking and radical redesign of business processes to achieve dramatic improvements in critical, contemporary measures of performance, such as cost, quality, service, and speed'.

In re-engineering, the project team starts with a clean sheet of paper, does not take anything for granted and questions all the aspects of the business. From this assumption the re-engineering project has the following main characteristics:

- It obtains these dramatic improvements by redesigning processes that cross functions and departments. These are the processes where the major opportunities for improvement exist.
- Top management should introduce and be responsible for the re-engineering initiative. Top management involvement is necessary for this radical and interfunctional approach to be accepted by the rest of the organization. For the same reason, the project team should include senior and experienced managers.
- It redesigns processes by minimizing the lead time needed for the entire process and by pushing decisions to the lower levels of the organization. For example, in re-engineering a billing process the main objective is to minimize the time from shipping to collecting the cash from the customer.
- Information technology (IT) usually plays a key role by making possible a radically faster and almost paperless process. However, it is important to remember that IT is only an enabling factor. Quite a few projects have failed because they were perceived as an IT project, not as undertaking a fundamental business process redesign.
- Often it requires the elimination of hierarchical levels, resulting in a flat and lean organization. The objective is that the lower levels of the organization, where the information and knowledge reside, are empowered to make the appropriate decisions.
- It aims to obtain dramatic improvements very fast. A well-known example is the accounts payable process at Ford. By re-engineering this process, Ford reduced the number of people needed from 500 to 125.

While re-engineering can provide high benefits in customer service, quality and costs, such projects have a relatively high risk. They tend to be quite disruptive to the organization and result in a high level of uncertainty about the future.

Candidates for re-engineering are processes that are facing a radical change in the industry, that have clear inefficiencies or that have not changed in the last, say, ten years. Further, companies in well-established and very competitive industries will find it difficult to improve their key processes radically. After adopting lean manufacturing, a company such as Ford would be unlikely to improve its production process by, say, 300 per cent. If that were the case, all other car manufacturers would disappear. But we might expect Ford to improve its accounts payable process by 400 per cent, because the company could afford to have a not very efficient process in that area.

However, in industries facing radical changes, re-engineering could make the difference between being the leader or disappearing from the marketplace. For example, electronics group Philips faced declining market share and profits at the end of the 1980s. At the beginning of the 1990s, top management launched the 'Centurion Program', a company-wide re-engineering project aimed at dramatically increasing speed and time to market. After losses in 1992, Philips was back to high levels of profitability in 1994.

Benchmarking practices

Benchmarking is a practice that rigorously examines and compares business practices with the 'best in the class', aimed at creating and sustaining excellence.

Companies have always benchmarked themselves with competitors and other companies in an informal way. However, as a formal and rigorous process benchmarking only started to be applied by companies in the last decade. It requires an open attitude and a high willingness to learn from others.

This benchmarking methodology consists of the following steps:
● The project begins by selecting a business process to improve. Typically, companies start

the benchmarking initiative with a pilot project to learn about the methodology and to overcome possible lack of credibility within the organisation. As with re-engineering, the bigger opportunities for improvement are in processes that cross functions and departments.

● A team is selected. Ideally, the leader of the benchmarking team should be the 'process owner'. That is, the person responsible for the process in the organization. Additionally, to ensure the success of this team, top management should actively and visibly support the initiative.

● The project team studies and documents in detail the company process. Often, on understanding the current process, the team improves it substantially by applying process analysis techniques.

● Simultaneously, the team develops a set of key process measures to compare with other companies' processes. These measures are not the main objective of benchmarking, but a way later on to identify best practices.

● Afterwards, the team looks for organizations to benchmark with. This search should include (if appropriate) other companies within the same corporation, competitors and the best companies in other industries. Often, managers are hesitant about the value of comparing themselves with companies outside their industry. For example, it could be argued that selling cars is different from selling fast-food. However, companies outside the industry are usually the best source for new processes and ideas. For example, the need for a consistent service quality and 'offer' from dealers or franchisees has striking similarities in the car and fast-food industries.

● Obtaining collaboration from the target companies to benchmark is not as difficult as some managers believe. Many companies are willing to be benchmarked provided that there is a *quid pro quo* and confidentiality issues are clearly spelled out. The benefit for the benchmarked company should be a discussion about the findings. In short, how the benchmarked company itself can improve.

● A visit to the benchmarked company is obviously essential. To make it efficient, the benchmarking company should send a well-prepared list of questions in advance. This should help identify areas of excellence for further detailed investigation.

● The investigation should result in revealing a set of gaps between the company's process and the best practices, and lead to a much better process. These differences in measures and processes should be made public within the organization to obtain a momentum for change.

● Subsequently the team develops an action plan to implement the new process. Having the process owner as the leader or a member of the project team proves to be a critical factor for implementation.

● Finally, the improvements obtained should be communicated to the benchmarking partners. That is, the benchmarked companies should learn from the benchmarking company's experience.

Benchmarking practices have the advantages of overcoming a natural disbelief in the feasibility of big improvements, of making sure that improvement targets are high enough, and of helping to create a learning and outward-looking culture in the company.

As with re-engineering, there are many success stories about benchmarking. At the beginning of the 1980s Xerox found that its Japanese competitors were selling photocopy machines for a price lower than Xerox's product cost. Through benchmarking, Xerox improved sharply its product development process and was able to beat back the Japanese competition.

While the risk involved in benchmarking projects is not high, the tendency to justify 'why our company is different' and the 'not invented here' syndrome can hamper the success of these projects. Also, a lack of focus and attention to the selection of the processes to benchmark can prove an obstacle. When, years ago, IBM executives tried to benchmark 300 processes they found it overwhelmingly difficult.

Candidates for benchmarking are those processes known to be inefficient or where there is some evidence that competitors or companies in other industries have better processes. Many companies have benchmarked critical processes, making important and, sometimes, big improvements.

Continuous improvement

A fundamental basis of Total Quality Management is a culture of continuous improvement. It is a culture rather than a project, because the aim is to improve continuously. It is an endless process. After one project, there is another project. This culture postulates that workers are the experts because they have the detailed knowledge of how the work is done. Thus, they are the best to improve the process. This view contrasts with the traditional Tayloristic approach in which the experts were the engineers and the operators just a pair of hands, who were asked to 'park their brains at the company's door'.

While top management should endorse and initiate the change, it is at the bottom of the organization that the responsibility for improving processes resides. Under this philosophy, work is done in teams. These teams are responsible for the individual operations they perform, for a proper co-ordination of these operations and for improving the process. The role of the supervisors and managers changes: they become team coaches, making sure that the teams have the resources needed to fulfill their missions.

To implement this cultural change a company should train its workers to equip them with tools for process improvement. Typically, this training includes techniques about:

● effective team working
● brainstorming
● problem identification and cause-effect diagrams
● problem solving process analysis
● project management
● statistical tools, etc.

Once trained in the use of these tools, the teams generate ideas for improvement and implement these ideas. With this spirit, mistakes are considered as opportunities for improvement. The objective is to obtain improvements in a continuous way. Teams analyse processes, document them and generate ideas for improvements. These are implemented following a 20-80 rule. That is, 20 per cent of the ideas generate 80 per cent of the gains.

The team is responsible for the implementation, being empowered to make experiments and changes. Once the implementation is finished, the gains obtained are publicized within the company and the continuous improvement process starts again. The advantages of continuous improvement are that it releases an enormous potential, motivates workers and that gains, while small in a short term basis, are very significant when accumulated over time. Many success stories exist about continuous improvement, the fantastic improvement in the quality of Japanese products over the last 40 years being the most prominent example.

However, implementing this change in culture requires years. It is difficult for supervisors and middle managers to change from being hierarchical bosses to become coaches. Typical mistakes include training workers too long before giving them the tools to use, saying they are empowered while continuing to act as a 'boss' and expecting very high gains in a short time.

Quite a few companies have dismantled their continuous improvement programs because of lack of impact on the profit line. That is, they expected profits fast while the reality is that a cultural change requires years. Another reason for this lack of financial results is that, if not properly managed, continuous improvement can lead to doing very efficiently the wrong things things that should not be done in the first place.

Also, the improvements obtained through this methodology tend to diminish over time. This is because at the start of the program, logically enough, the major opportunities are pursued. Thus, a big challenge for companies well into this cultural change is to maintain the momentum when gains diminish. Candidates for continuous improvement are those processes supporting the company's distinctive competencies. By constantly improving them, the company will remain competitive unless a revolutionary change happens in the industry.

Uses of each methodology

The above descriptions are 'stylized' to emphasize the differences between the methods rather than their commonalities.

But in fact these methods are usually mixed and customized by companies. Benchmarking is often part of a re-engineering project or a tool used for continuous improvement. While these adaptations can be appropriate, it has also happened that a re-engineering effort kills a continuous improvement program. The workers feel demotivated after having dedicated much effort to improving sub-processes that a re-engineering project simply eliminates.

These methodologies involve different risks, are aimed at different levels of improvements over time and involve a different attitude towards learning. Re-engineering has a relatively high risk because it aims at very high improvements in a short time. For a company with processes suspected to be far from efficient or in an industry facing big changes, re-engineering could be the required tool.

Benchmarking has a relatively low risk but requires an open mindset. For companies suspecting that other organizations have developed better practices or that face internal scepticism about the possibility of improvement, this methodology could be the most appropriate.

Finally, continuous improvement has a low risk but requires a major effort to change corporate culture. Companies must remain competitive. For that reason, it should be applied to their key processes. However, experience seems to indicate that it is better to start with re-engineering and benchmarking, if appropriate, and then later pursue the cultural change towards continuous improvement.

Summary

Re-engineering is intended to achieve big improvements in performance through the redesign of business processes. While re-engineering projects can be disruptive and create uncertainty, they can bring great benefits in customer service, quality and cost. Though high risk, they can mean the difference between being an industry leader and disappearing from the market place.

Benchmarking, which tends to be less risky, rigorously examines and compares business practices with the 'best in class' in other companies and other industries. It has the advantage of overcoming a natural disbelief in the feasibility of big improvements.

Continuous improvement is a culture rather than a project, because the aim is to improve continuously. One of its basic philosophies is that the experts are workers since they have the detailed knowledge of how work is done. Many success stories come from Japan, but continuous improvement takes time to make a bottom line impact and requires genuine empowerment of employees.

All three methods need top management support.

Rigid flexibility and factory focus

■ **Modern manufacturers must produce at low cost, deliver rapidly and frequently, and be responsive to customer demands – how?**

by Robert Collins, Roger Schmenner and Carlos Cordon

Consider the plight of consumer packaged goods producers. In recent years, consolidation in the retail trade has seen the emergence of hypermarkets and retail chains that dominate retail distribution in some countries. These companies and groups, often operating across country borders, wield a double-edged sword of power and influence. Their size, market shares and high volume/low price strategies put pressure on manufacturers to trim margins and lower costs.

With market intelligence from point of sale data systems, they can measure profitability per unit of shelf space and monitor stock levels in real time. This results in demands on manufacturers for rapid, frequent delivery of fast-moving items as well as extensive and ever-changing product diversity.

Producers are thus being squeezed as never before. How to secure low cost, quick and frequent delivery and flexibility in manufacturing all simultaneously? Can manufacturing be 'all things to all people?' The answer increasingly is yes, but it requires that factories follow the principle of what we term 'rigid flexibility'. The combination of these two words may jar, but they describe what has to be accomplished.

Manufacturing flexibility is not rooted in an 'anything goes' permissiveness in the factory or in the installation of complex hardware and systems. Rather, it is based on simplicity and discipline. Simplicity in such matters as product design and materials and information flows; discipline in quality improvement, the pursuit of standard procedures, training and so on.

It is simplicity and discipline that promote the flexibility, the constant adaptation and the learning of the 'world class' factory. Achieving rigid flexibility – attaining simplicity and discipline in an operation – is a considerable challenge. But here the familiar idea of 'factory focus' (developed by Wickham Skinner) can help.

Since the mid-1970s manufacturing managers throughout the world have reorganized their plants to create factory focus. Typically, factory focus means the isolation of distinct product lines within separate factories or 'plants-within-the-plant'. They have substantially improved performance in company after company. Factory focus works. But for the 1990s it works for very different reasons from those that led to its creation and popularity in the 1970s and 1980s. It works now because it helps promote simplicity and discipline, the pillars of rigid flexibility. To appreciate this, however, we must abandon some old ideas about manufacturing strategy.

Setting priorities

The original concept of factory focus was based on the observation that factories floundered when their product lines or production processes were so diverse that they called upon the factory to accomplish a set of vastly different manufacturing objectives or 'tasks'. Over time, the articulation of the 'manufacturing task' for a company has been translated as the establishment of a hierarchy of competitive priorities.

The usual priorities mentioned are four: product quality; product cost; delivery dependability; and flexibility, in terms of both product mix and volume.

The typical focussed factory exercise begins by trying to determine the rank ordering of these priorities for each product line of the factory with the intention of creating specific plants-within-the-plant for product lines whose rank orders of priorities are particularly at odds with one another.

Three critical characteristics are embedded in this traditional approach to factory focus:

1. It is essentially introspective because it tends to focus solely on the manufacturing function and decisions concerning such things as facilities, process technologies, workforce policies, and material planning and control systems.

2. It uses a vocabulary of cost, quality, delivery and flexibility.

3. It examines the trade-offs among these four competitive attributes. These attributes are viewed as mutually exclusive goals for the factory to pursue.

Factory focus stresses the importance of consistency of the manufacturing task with the needs of business strategy; consistency in the specification of process technology, workforce policies, factory systems and so on with the appropriate manufacturing task. The message has been that the resolution of trade-offs is inevitable and that manu-facturing cannot be 'all things to all people'.

We do not dispute the need for consistency in making manufacturing decisions. The effective implementation of the manufacturing task still requires consistent choices. However, world class competitors have demonstrated that establishing a hierarchical list of competitive priorities and focussing exclusively on the top of the list is shortsighted.

These competitors have mastered quality, delivery, cost and flexibility all at once. Indeed, for them this mastery is merely a necessary, although not a sufficient, condition for their competitiveness. Furthermore, researchers have shown that the best performing plants are not single purpose; they share a variety of competitive priorities.

Charged imperatives

This evidence about world-class operations provokes a re-examination of each of the three critical characteristics identified above. In our view the imperatives of factory focus have changed to:

1. An outward-looking orientation towards end-user markets and customer requirements that highlights the need for responsiveness.

2. A vocabulary framed by the recognition that responsiveness can only be met through the design and implementation of flexible, constantly adapting manufacturing processes and systems.

3. The abandonment of trade-offs (low cost or flexibility) in favour of complements (low cost and flexibility).

Operationally, how can manufacturing do all of this quick delivery of low-cost products that conform to all quality standards and provide, as well, enhanced product performance and features?

For years, technological solutions for the factory have been advocated. Proponents say factories can benefit from both economies of scale and scope. New, flexible equipment will keep cost down even as highly customized products are manufactured in small lots. The promise of this technology is beginning to be reaped, but it is not easy to do. As countless companies that have squandered their investment capital on promising technology that has underperformed can attest, the technology itself is not enough.

In our view, flexibility and constant

adaptation can only be achieved through the establishment of simple, foolproof operating environments in which operating procedures are carried out in a disciplined and dedicated fashion. A paradox of sorts exists. It is this: if the requirement is flexibility, then an atmosphere of permissiveness cannot be tolerated.

An analogy lies with the gymnast who has to maintain a strict regime of training in order to develop the strength and flexibility we so much admire. The factory is no different. When its 'training rules and routines' are bent or broken, then off-quality, extended throughput times, excessive complexity, rampant expediting and inventory write-offs can creep in to paralyze it. The antidotes are simplicity and discipline. They provide the framework for the rigidities that permit the factory to be flexible.

Consider again the consumer packaged goods producers. They have achieved low unit manufacturing costs through the establishment of standard product 'footprints' (can diameters, bottle heights, for example) that contribute to simplicity in factory operations but that permit great diversity in the look of the container and what gets put in it.

Such simplicity has been won through the discipline of design for manufacturability where systematic thinking and rules of thumb are rigorously applied to the design cycle.

The need for responsiveness comes in various guises: customization of products, the creation of additional product features, quick product development times, short lead times from order to delivery and frequent delivery of small quantities of product. If we examine the manufacturing initiatives that have been developed to meet these needs we can see that in each there is both simplicity and discipline, which support rigid flexibility in manufacturing. These developments are described below:

Supplier responsiveness. To achieve greater responsiveness from suppliers on price, quality, lot sizes, frequency of delivery and so on, manufacturers have rationalized their supplier networks. Simplification has been achieved though a shrinking of the supplier base and a concomitant reduction in 'transactions'. Materials handling has been reduced with an increase

in direct shipments to either distributor/ retailer locations or manufacturing lines. Manu-facturers have exacted greater continuous improvement 'discipline' not only from their supplier base but also from themselves. Suppliers are now on design teams, and company forecasts, production planning and order data are electronically shared with them.

Set-up time reduction. To achieve reductions in set-up time, manufacturers have committed themselves to a relentless 'search for waste' in existing set-up procedures. They have changed methods, reconfigured the workplace and re-engineered jigs and fixtures to simplify set-ups. They have also required the discipline of practice for those performing the set-up so that they can more easily adhere to the rigidly prescribed set-up methodology.

Throughput time reduction. Manufacturers have achieved impressive reductions in throughput times with the creation of manufacturing cells and their robotized equivalent, the flexible manufacturing system (FMS). The performance of cells is critically dependent on the identi-fication of the families of parts, components or products to be run through them a task that greatly simplifies their working. Such simplicity by itself, however, is not enough. The discipline of even-paced production planning, operator checking of quality and preventative main-tenance is also required for a cell to operate effectively.

Supply-demand management. Material require-ments planning (MRP) systems provide easy access to and visibility of information on the stocks and flows of material within the supply chain and the physical capacities of selected operations. Such a window of simplicity can only be achieved, however, if part numbers, bills of material, stocking procedures and engineering change notice updates are meticulously defined and data integrity scrupulously maintained.

Just-in-time manufacturing. A critical feature of just-in-time (JIT) manufacturing systems, in which cells are often included, are the simple, crystal-clear signals from downstream oper-ations to upstream operations about what to produce and when. JIT systems are disciplined ones, however, that include a constant devotion to problem solving and continuous improvement, the sharing of production planning and scheduling information, and 'good housekeeping'. However, some of the limitations of JIT systems are outlined in the accompanying box.

Right first time. If manufacturers are to achieve 'right first time' production and the kinds of improvements and commitment that can occur through employee empowerment, shopfloor workers need clear and simple definitions of what they are to do and how it fits with the objectives of the company. Otherwise they tend to feel lost rather than empowered. More than this, they also need the disciplined development of both operating and problem-solving skills through training.

■ Just in time but not for everyone

Since at least the mid-1980s the Japanese concept of just-in-time manufacturing has been enthusiastically embraced by many managers and academics in the rest of the world.

But now critics are questioning the effect JIT has on profitability. A recent study from Cambridge University, for example, concluded that a higher use of JIT was actually associated with lower operating profit margins in UK companies.

Should we infer that these techniques work in Japan but not in the UK (or other parts of the world)? Or is it unrealistic to expect profit margins to improve simply by applying a Japanese practice?

Research at IMD shows that the actual application of JIT varies very much from industry to industry. In the car industry almost all European and other manufacturers have adopted these techniques. But in the pharmaceutical sector, only a few companies are starting to use them.

It is probable that the lower profitability found in the Cambridge study has much to do with the industries in which companies compete rather than with the application of any particular technique.

While advocates of these techniques argue that the principles are universal, the reality is that JIT does not have a big impact on certain types of production process. For example, one of the objectives of JIT is to transform the factory so that a continuous flow of materials is achieved, resulting in lower work-in-process inventory levels and shorter production lead times.

Its application to many electronics manufacturers has resulted in significant benefits because these companies used to operate with high work-in-process inventory levels and long lead times. By comparison, many chemicals companies have always used continuous production processes and relatively low inventory levels because the high volumes they manufacture do not allow them to do otherwise. To expect improvements of similar proportions is therefore unrealistic.

At the opposite extreme of the manufacturing spectrum there are companies making non-repetitive products to customer specifications such as special machine tools or large electric motors. These companies usually apply JIT only in the most repetitive part of the factory where it is possible to achieve a continuous flow.

Here JIT will usually not significantly affect profitability because only a fraction of the operation changes. An unexpected consequence is often that some of these companies embrace JIT too enthusiastically and drop or out-source products or processes that do not fit into the new system. Products whose manufacturing processes fall outside this new quasi-continuous process are abandoned because they are no longer a 'core' product.

While these decisions may be sound in some cases, in others they could imply reduced volume and lower profitability. Even if JIT improves the factory operations, this practice implies a radical change in the 'factory culture'. Thus its implementation requires many resources and a high dedication from top management.

For example, if a company wants to become a JIT supplier it is likely that customers will demand that it has a quality certification so that products need not be tested for quality when received.

Some companies complain that they have been so busy obtaining the certification that they have not been able to dedicate any effort to improving quality. In some of these cases it is not clear whether the benefits outweigh the implementation and opportunity costs of management distraction.

Finally, to expect superior financial profits simply by applying JIT could in some cases simply be absurd. In an industry where all the competitors adopt JIT, it becomes a necessary, though not sufficient, condition for comparative advantage.

In other cases, companies facing serious problems have tried to apply JIT as a last resort. While in some cases this has saved a company, others have gone bankrupt and given birth to JIT horror stories.

JIT is neither a manufacturing panacea nor the manufacturing equivalent of alchemy. The profitability of a JIT application depends strongly on the company and the type of manufacturing process rather than on a particular national culture being different from the Japanese.

It is in creating simplicity and discipline that the benefits of factory focus spring up. Factory focus favours the rigid flexibility that can satisfy the marketplace's demands for responsiveness. When one embraces factory focus the wealth of initiatives sweeping manufacturing lean manufacturing, throughput time reduction, total quality management, benchmarking, delayering, employee involvement, multiskilling, even computer-integrated manufacturing (CIM) become even easier to implement. They are not disparate, faddish campaigns but tools that apply their own brands of simplicity and discipline to the creation of flexible manufacturing operations responsive to market needs. These tools have a place in the focussed factory. Indeed, they are more at home there than elsewhere. How is rigid flexibility achieved through factory focus?

1. Appreciation for an easily recognized and swift product flow. Focussed factories are easy ones to understand. The product flow is readily studied and improved. The benefits of a clean, swift product flow are clear to all and the feedback loops for quality control are short. There is simplicity and discipline inherent in the focussed factory. Because of this focussed factories adopt the JIT manufacturing philosophy easily.

2. A streamlined organization. Because of its simplicity the focussed factory does not need layers of overhead personnel. Line management and the workforce take on more for themselves. In addition, the discipline of employee involvement is easier to accomplish because all employees can more readily identify with the product and how it is made. We have seen focussed factories fend off huge increases in overhead hiring even as output demands soared and the direct labor ranks grew.

3. Better cost accounting and performance measurement. The most universal unanticipated benefit of factory focus is better knowledge of exactly how costs are built up in the product and also of how they could be reduced. In the focussed factory most sources of cost (overhead functions, equipment) are directly attached to a product line rather than allocated to it. With the simplicity and discipline of factory

focus in place they become direct costs and thus easier for management to see. Cost accounting no longer acts to impede visibility and thereby flexibility.

The factories of today must do everything well to be considered world class. The view that manufacturing is structurally unable to be 'all things to all people' is obsolete and should be abandoned. In its place comes a new view of all that manufacturing can accomplish, a view based on flexibility, constant adaptation and learning.

Such manufacturing competence is anchored in simplicity and discipline. These two traits provide the production process with what we call 'rigid flexibility'. Achieving rigid flexibility – applying simplicity and discipline to an operation – is a considerable challenge, but the concept of factory focus can be a great help. For the reasons cited above, focussed factories enjoy a natural simplicity and discipline. In such factories, attributes such as cost and flexibility can be treated as complements and not substitutes. This is the essence of manufacturing strategy in the 1990s.

Summary

Simplicity and discipline promote the flexibility, constant adaptation and learning which distinguishes the 'world class' factory.

Factory focus (typically the isolation of distinct product lines within separate factories) used to be introspective and based on trade-offs between cost, quality, delivery and flexibility. Now it has to be outward looking and such trade offs have to be abandoned.

New technology is not enough in itself. Manufacturing initiatives to improve responsiveness include the shrinking of the supplier base, simplified set-up procedures, the creation of manufacturing cells and just-in-time systems (though JIT does not necessarily work in all industries).

The goal of rigid flexibility can be achieved with factory focus because such factories are easy to understand, do not need layers of overhead personnel, and have better knowledge of their costs. The view that manufacturing is structurally unable to be 'all things to all people' is obsolete.

Suggested further reading

Wickham Skinner 'Focussed factory', *Harvard Business Review,* May/June 1974.

Hall, Robert W. (1987) *Attaining Manufacturing Excellence*, Dow Jones-Irwin.

Hall, R. W. and Nakane, J. 'Flexibility: manufacturing battlefield of the 90s', Association for Manufacturing Excellence, 1990.

Supply chain management

■ **By managing a business unit as effectively as possible and matching its competencies with others it can attain a 'virtual integration' that can bring big competitive advantages.**

by Tom Vollmann, Carlos Cordon and Hakon Raabe

Supply chain management (SCM) is a concept that extends the view of operations from a single business unit to the whole supply chain. Though increasingly a 'hot topic' and one beginning to be addressed by many companies, there is no common definition of SCM. The term is applied to a variety of business issues and practices.

Essentially SCM is a set of practices aimed at managing and co-ordinating the whole supply chain from raw material suppliers to the end consumer. The objective is to develop synergy along the whole supply chain rather than focussing on a particular business unit.

SCM is a progression on internal programs such as total quality management and lean production. These have often provided substantial improvements by breaking down barriers between departments and by efficiently managing the business processes. It is logical, therefore, to look at the improvement potential of cutting across companies and managing the whole supply chain. The assumption is that there are important synergies to be gained by managing the entire chain of supply and delivery.

The objective of developing synergy is obtained through reduction of costs and increasing the value provided. The most frequently cited benefit of SCM is cost reduction. A typical example is the reduction of inventory levels. Not so common is to find companies increasing the value provided through the chain. Some few companies are innovating by using new ways of 'bundling' products and services to increase the value for the end consumer.

A common way of visualizing the supply chain is to draw a streamlined pipeline that processes raw materials, transforms them into finished goods and delivers them to the end consumer. This may be an over-simplification. Relationships throughout a supply chain are in general many-to-many rather than one-to-one. A realistic picture is more complex, with a multitude of relationships between business units as in Figure 1. (We have, incidentally, taken the business unit, rather than the corporation, as the basis for our analysis. Business units are the building blocks of supply chains.)

Most companies have several suppliers and several customers. Often, business units compete for customers and have common suppliers. In this complex setting companies consider some relationships between customers and suppliers

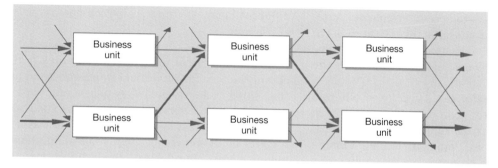

Figure 1: Complex setting

as more important than others in order to develop synergy. One of the first questions for a company to consider should be with which customers and suppliers it should develop new SCM practices.

There are many new ways of doing business associated with SCM. Some we consider best SCM practices are outlined below:

Reduction and consolidation of the supplier base. For example, Xerox has reduced its suppliers from 5,000 to 300 and selects and develops them. The automotive industry has 'tiered' suppliers. First-tier suppliers work closely with the assembler, operating as sub-assemblers; second-tier parts manufacturers supply the sub-assemblers.

● *Reduction and consolidation of the customer base.* Some companies are selecting the customers they want to develop. The objective is not to reduce sales but is more a question of how to serve different customers. A typical pattern is to ask small customers to buy through distributors, thereby reducing the number of direct customers and attached costs such as invoicing and debt collection. (Philips is a company that takes such a view.)

● *Co-ordination of price and inventory policies to reduce the amplification of demand variability – known as the 'Forester' effect.* For example, Procter & Gamble and Wal-Mart co-ordinate their inventory policies based on a system of every-day low price. The objective is to avoid the short-term demand increases – and the amplification of the supply chain – stemming from promotional campaigns and so on.

● *Sharing of information between business units to achieve the frequent, reliable deliveries*

necessary *for just-in-time manufacturing.* Sharing of information enables significant reduction in stock levels, stock-outs are more easily avoided as are stocks of obsolete products subject to mark down.

● *Linking computer systems to link processes.* With electronic data interchange, point-of-sale information from checkout scanners in stores is transferred directly and electronically to manufacturers' order entry systems. EDI enables cross-docking, by which products are shipped directly to the retail stores, bypassing warehouses. The consumer goods business is leading this practice, driven by powerful retail chains.

● *Early supplier involvement in product development.* Suppliers are involved early in the development stage of a new product to optimize the efficiency of the whole supply chain in making the new product. For example, when the US printer manufacturer Lexmark developed a new laser printer, its supplier of moulded plastic frames, Minco, was involved early in the process.

● *Design for supply chain.* Logistics is a central issue for SCM. Some companies are designing products to improve logistics throughout the supply chain. A good example is Hewlett Packard's DeskJet printer. It was designed so as to allow country- or market-specific attributes, such as power supply or user manual, to be added at distribution centers rather than at the central manufacturing facilities. The result was a restructuring of the distribution system and a substantial reduction of total stocks in the system.

● *Joint problem solving.* By working together, customers and suppliers may often achieve faster and better solutions to specific problems. Automobile component manufacturers often have resident engineers on customer promises to solve the technical problems that may appear in the assembly process.

● *In-plant representatives.* These exist where a customer in-house position is created for a person representing the supplier. This individual typically resides full time in the customer's purchasing office, operates on the customer's computer systems, uses the customer's purchase orders and places them with his own company, the supplier. In effect, the supplier representative is doing the customer's planning for the materials supplied, eliminating the need for the customer to plan.

Several strict criteria are used to select suppliers for this practice – long-lasting and trusted relationship; high supplier competitiveness; substantial volume; large number of transactions; low rate of technology change; no proprietary or core technology of the customer involved.

This system was pioneered by Bose Corp, a US manufacturer of home and auto sound systems in 1987.

● *Partnering with suppliers and customers.* The aim is to develop win-win situations where all parties benefit from the improvements. Close partnerships involving a range of business issues – and many of the practices already discussed – have been pioneered in the automotive industry. A prime example is Toyota and one of its major suppliers, Nippondenso.

● *In some cases, companies much bigger than their suppliers – and customers – may impose the co-ordination of the whole supply chain.* A comparison would be a conductor orchestrating a whole set of players. This level of co-ordination requires the 'conductor' to be a major force in the supply chain, implying an ability to control all the other players. Well-known cases are Benetton (sweaters/clothing) and IKEA (furniture/ interiors). The ability to co-ordinate the whole supply chain is not restricted to retail chains, but it is likely that such players in the supply chain are located quite near to the end customer.

To summarize, best SCM practices can be described as a set of linked processes . . . across different business units . . . which operate as a single unit.

This is 'virtual integration' as opposed to traditional vertical integration. The idea is to obtain the benefits of vertical integration and at the same time avoid the increasing costs associated with vertical integration, such as added management layers and reporting. Virtual integration, however, does imply questions about business unit boundaries, which are no longer well defined.

Given these best SCM practices, there are several reasons for business units to link processes in this way. What we consider the major driving forces can be classified in three dimensions along which synergy may be developed in a supply chain: cost reduction; value enhancement; network competition.

Cost reduction, by linking business processes across business units costs can be reduced, in a number of areas:

● Reduced transaction costs derived from a reduced number of suppliers. Fewer suppliers imply fewer relationships to be managed. This, combined with an improved flow of information, provides a reduction of costs for co-ordination, communication and decision making around transactions.

● Reduced demand variability due to improved information flow along the supply chain.

● Economies of scale achieved by a consolidation of customers and suppliers. Usually, consolidation provides increased volume per customer and suppliers and, therefore, economies of scale.

● Bureaucracy may be kept at a low level when integrating virtually. Vertical integration usually implies increasing bureaucracy and overhead costs.

● Improved time to market and cost-effective solutions in the design and development of new products through early supplier involvement.

● Reduced logistics costs such as costs of transportation, storage/warehousing and inventories.

This list of cost-saving areas does not pretend to be complete but indicates the substantial potential for savings inherent in SCM.

Value enhancement

Just as important as cost reduction, SCM

provides potential for increasing the value for the end customer. This notion is closely linked to the ability to customize products. The concept of mass customization tries to combine the best of two worlds – efficient mass production and customized products. However, practitioner experience suggests that this approach creates increasing complexity – in the form of product variance – with an increasing number of customers. In this respect, SCM provides easier achievement of mass customization in the sense of reduction/consolidation of the customer base and partnering with key customers. For example, some packaging companies are trying to team with food manufacturers and retailers to provide customized packaging for each retailer-food manufacturer combination.

Increased value may also be obtained by bundling products and services, providing an integrated solution for the customer. This seems to be achieved more easily if business units along the supply chain are linked together, with the focus jointly on the end customer. Again, new packaging solutions provide an example. Joint problem solving between packaging manufacturers, finished goods manufacturers, transporters and retailers may come up with integrated solutions offering transportation, damage reduction, storing and display in the same packaging product.

Network competition

Reducing costs and increasing value are both parts of gaining a competitive edge, and traditionally competition means business units competing for deliveries to the same customer. However, we have argued above that virtual integration may create questions about business unit boundaries. This in turn, combined with a consolidation of suppliers and customers, raises the question of what entities actually are competing against each other. Consider the following example:

An automotive sub-assembler is a sole source of a specific system to a specific car model of a car assembler. This partnership provides a major part of the supplier's sales, at least in a certain period of time. Thus, the supplier is relying totally on not only the success of his customer

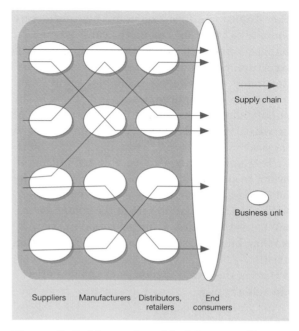

Suppliers   Manufacturers   Distributors, retailers   End consumers

Supply chain

Business unit

Figure 2: Spider webs of buisiness units

but also on the success of his customer's product. The significance of this is that competition takes place between supply chains as well as between 'classic' competitors.

In line with the complex network of supplier/customer relationships described initially, we prefer to describe the setting as spider webs of business units (*see* Figure 2). What these webs look like – and how they are changing – in terms of number of players and power structure has major implications for SCM applicability.

In consumer goods, where a limited number of retail chains are supplied by a limited number of major manufacturers, themselves having a limited number of major suppliers of, for example, packaging, SCM practices may be applied to the whole chain. If on the other hand, as seen in the nylon business, the raw material manufacturer has a large number of intermediate manufacturing customers – where no major players exist – this acts like a barrier to virtual integration throughout the supply chain.

In the consumer goods business, for example, a concentration at the retail end of the web (and the emergence of hypermarkets) enables domination of the total supply chain and thereby solid basis for SCM. The practice of moving tasks up the supply chain, as seen in the automotive industry's use of complete sub-assemblers, implies another change in the spider web power structure. Such a development increases mutual dependency between assembler and sub-assembler and requires close co-ordination of the supply chain. In this kind of spider web, SCM becomes not only applicable but almost a necessity.

To summarize again, we will argue that in order to understand network competition the following questions must be considered:

• Who are the major players in the spider web?
• What is the business unit's position in the web?
• What kinds of barriers to virtual integration exist?
• How is the power structure of the spider web changing?

Strategic response

The questions above are not just tactical but require managers to define a strategy for SCM. In the context of a spider web this implies more than defining a mix of products and market channels. SCM is about relationships between business units and the question of 'who to play with' is as important as 'what to play'.

To guide the election of partners, companies should look at the set of competencies of the business unit. In our view, competencies are constructs – of business processes, tangible and intangible assets, and skills, both individual and collective. By competencies we mean ways to synthesize what a business unit can do. Competencies may be classified in the following way:

Distinctive competencies. Competencies that provide the business unit with a unique competitive advantage. Examples may be a certain brand position, a specific manufacturing capability or a highly effective way of organizing its work.

Essential competencies. Competencies that are vital if the business unit is to perform in a certain business. These are the entry tickets for competing. In certain markets, for example the North Sea off-shore industry, it is almost a necessity for suppliers to be ISO9000 certified.

Plain competencies. These comprise tasks that need to be done but that do not have a direct effect on the product or service delivered. One example may be the payment of bills. For a car manufacturer, the process of paying bills, whether it is done extremely efficiently or not, will not have a significant effect on profits.

Although the above suggests three distinct classes of competencies, they should be thought of as spread out along a continuous scale. Neither is the picture static, as competencies tend to move along the continuum. As more and more suppliers to a given market obtain an ISO9000 certificate, this moves from being a distinctive competence to a necessity. In shipbuilding, CAD/CAM solutions once provided a unique competitive edge – now this competency is essential to compete.

Using this classification, a model for linking the business unit's competencies with those of both its suppliers and customers is shown in Figure 3.

Some suppliers deliver goods or services that have a direct impact on the unit's distinctive competencies. Others supply plain commodities or general services. In the same way, some customers are more likely to have an impact on the business unit's competitive edge than others. This is more a question of the customer's strategies and competencies than one of sheer size.

Suppliers that have the greatest impact on the distinctive competencies of the business unit should be linked with a closer degree of partnership than those supplying products and services of lesser impact on the performance of the business unit. Similarly, business units should partner and develop close relationships with customers according to the degree of fit between the respective competencies.

German car manufacturer Mercedes-Benz and its supplier Bosch provide a good example of competencies fitting each other. Both companies have a distinctive competency in supplying very reliable products. In other cases the distinctive competency of two partners may be more linked to the relationship itself, in effect a joint distinctive competency. The distinctive competency in the example of Procter & Gamble and Wal-Mart is inherent in the way these companies

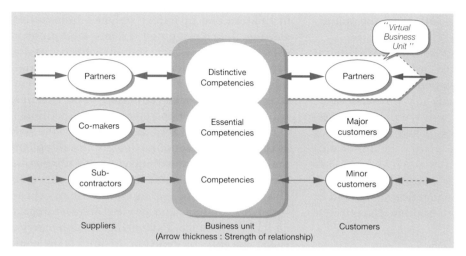

Figure 3

have linked themselves together with EDI and general information systems. For competitors, the total structure of this relationship is not easy to copy.

Companies should develop a portfolio view of customers and suppliers. The customer base may be categorized into partners, major customers and minor customers. Suppliers may be treated as partners, co-makers or sub-contractors. The partners, both suppliers and customers, linked to the distinctive competencies of the business unit make up what we call the 'virtual business unit'. Based on this portfolio thinking, a business unit could map its own spider web as shown in Figure 3.

This model proposes the alignment of business units' distinctive competencies – and the development of joint competencies – in order to provide a superior product, service or bundle of products and services to the end customer.

For example, a furniture manufacturer with a distinct competency in high-quality surface treatment of laminated wood should partner with the supplier of paint and with customers focussing on superior design and quality furniture. A low-cost manufacturer, however, whose distinctive competency is its manufacturing of inexpensive furniture should partner with discount chains and suppliers with similar competencies.

The process of partner selection is key to a business unit's performance and a vital factor is the alignment of the distinctive competencies,

strategies and change processes of the partnering units.

But while partnering can allow synergy, it can also involve risk. Despite mutual trust and long-term knowledge of each other, some important risks in partnering are:
● Long-term competitiveness of partners and evolving mutual dependencies.
● Possible loss of flexibility. If the area of partnership is subject to sudden and dramatic technological changes, a close relationship with a selected supplier or customer might restrict the business unit from access to new technology.
● Mutual bargaining positions. Although a customer would like to partner with one of its suppliers, this is not always feasible. A very big supplier to a small customer is a general example. The customer may want to see the supplier as a partner. But from the supplier's point of view he is a minor customer in a peripheral supply chain.

Virtual integration is not only a question of partnership. It also implies a game of power play. Partnering is about synergy – or what could be termed 'making bigger pies'. This includes increasing the value, or reducing the costs, by streamlining and simplifying processes. We believe this part of the relationship should be sharply separated from the power play occurring when 'the bigger pie is to be shared'. In this game, the business unit's share often depends on its bargaining power, derived from its competencies and its position in the supply chain.

The conflicts over pie-sharing may inhibit synergy. As disputes are to be expected in a partnership, as in all relationships, the issue is not to try to avoid them but how to resolve them. Conflicts are more easily resolved if general rules are defined in advance. Clear performance measures for the whole virtual business unit should be established and costs and benefits should be shared applying a total costs model. And clear channels of communication should be established and defined to facilitate the effective flow of information.

Summary

Supply chain management is a set of practices aimed at managing the chain from raw material suppliers to the end consumer. Business units rather than companies are the essential building blocks. Reduction and consolidation of supplier and customer bases, price co-

ordination and inventory policies, information sharing, linked computer systems, joint problem solving and customer in-house positions for suppliers are typical features. SCM is 'virtual integration', not traditional vertical integration. It is driven by cost reduction opportunities, value enhancement and 'network' competition.

In choosing partners, companies should look at the competencies of business units. Suppliers that have the greatest impact on the distinctive competencies of the unit should be linked with a closer degree of partnership than those supplying products and services of lesser impact on its performance. Partnering, though, carries risks, notably in relation to long-term competitiveness, the impact of rapidly changing technology, and mutual bargaining positions.

Suggested further reading

Axelsson, B. and Easton, G. (eds) (1992) *Industrial Networks: A New View of Reality*, Routledge.

Butler, C. and Bidault, F. Lexmark, B. 'Development gets under way', Lausanne, IMD. Case No. GM589 (1995).

Strategic management of the operations function

■ **Can a company's manufacturing function support strategy, particularly that of marketing? Not unless operations is involved from the beginning say** Terry Hill, Alastair Nicholson and Roy Westbrook

In many companies, corporate strategy is developed as a series of independent statements. Lacking essential integration, the result is a compilation of distinct, functional strategies that sit side by side, layer on layer, in the same corporate binder. Integration is not provided if, in fact, it was ever intended.

Functional dominance of the views of markets

and the failure to interface the perspectives, insights and capabilities of functions characterize this strategy development task. For example, in many companies major strategic decisions are made covering the markets and customers that are to be grown without any attempt to embrace the perspectives of operations as to its ability to support these requirements and to make anticipated profits. This failure is further compounded by the fact that operations investments are large (in terms of asset size) and fixed (in terms of the timescale to undertake change).

Given that the criteria by which many companies now win orders are provided by operations, knowing the timescales and investments involved for operations to give this support is a prerequisite in the strategy debate. However, this rarely happens. Instead, operations is placed in a reactive mode and very often finds itself unable to support customers and make money.

Functional strategies are concerned with prioritizing investments in line with support for markets. Understanding markets, therefore, is the common denominator for each function's strategic contribution.

But many organizations begin the process of strategy formulation on the incorrect premise that markets and marketing are synonymous. Marketing is a function; the market is the business. Though marketing will have an essential view of the market, the agreement must come on perspectives. Debating and agreeing markets is the very essence of strategy.

Operations (as with any other functional) strategy starts, therefore, with an agreement about markets – how a company competes in them, the operations tasks that follow, and the priority investments and developments that operations needs then to undertake. Without this clarity, functions are unable to link into their strategic role within a business. Doing the right things needs to replace the doing-things-right mentality of many operations executives. Thus, being effective rather than being efficient needs to drive the operations culture of the future.

How then is this change to be made? The key lies in understanding markets. Currently, the insights typically considered by a business are too broad to provide meaning. Companies are too often reviewed as wholes with corporate diversity overlaid by generality.

Customer voice and customer behavior

General descriptions of markets are appealing to chief executives faced with the task of developing strategies for businesses typified by difference rather than similarity. However, such similarity, though desirable, is inherently not available. Companies need to develop approaches to reviewing markets that deliver essential insights as to how they really work. While marketing's view of a market is necessary, it is not sufficient.

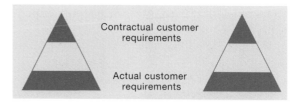

Figure 1: The level in an organization where actual as opposed to contractual requirements are made

Companies must supplement customer voice (the typical outcomes of marketing surveys and discussions with customers) with customer behavior (the reality of fulfilling orders and providing support for customer demands).

Customer voice is embodied in marketing reviews but customer behavior is found in the actual demands placed on the operations function of a supplier (*see* Figure 1). It is this latter insight that operations needs to provide within the strategy debate and that it alone understands and can explain through the data that it records in its order processing and managerial systems.

The debate about markets must provide better insights on which to build functional strategies. To do this there are three key issues.

First, avoid descriptions of markets expressed in general terms. The phrase 'customer service' is too general to provide key insights. The on-time and quick-response dimensions of delivery are crucial but invariably not provided. Is the term 'quality' referring to design or the need to provide a product/service to specification?

Given the essential nature of market understanding, companies cannot afford to lose these essential insights. However, they typically do. Not appreciating the inadequacy of their current market statements, companies fail to provide the level of understanding required more by default than design.

Second, as part of gaining a greater understanding of their markets, companies need to distinguish between qualifiers and order-winners. Qualifiers get and keep a supplier on a customer's short-list. Order-winners, on the other hand, are those criteria a supplier needs to provide at a level better than competitors who also qualify. However, that does not imply that

1) Corporate objectives

Growth
Survival
Profit
Return on investment
Other financial measures

2) Marketing strategy

Product markets and segments
Range
Mix
Volumes
Standardization versus
    customization
Level of innovation
Leader versus follower
    alternatives

3) How do products/ services win orders in the market place?

Price
Quality
Delivery: Speed
    Reliability
Demand increases
Color range
Product/service range
Design leadership
Technical support supplied

Productions / operations strategy

4) Process choice

Choice of various processes
Trade-offs embodied in the
    process choice
Process positioning
Capacity: Size
    Timing
    Location
Role of inventory in the
    process configuration

5) Infrastructure

Function support
Operations/planning and
    control systems
Quality assurance and control
Systems engineering
Clerical procedures
Payment systems
Work structuring
Organizational structure

Figure 2: Framework for developing an operations strategy

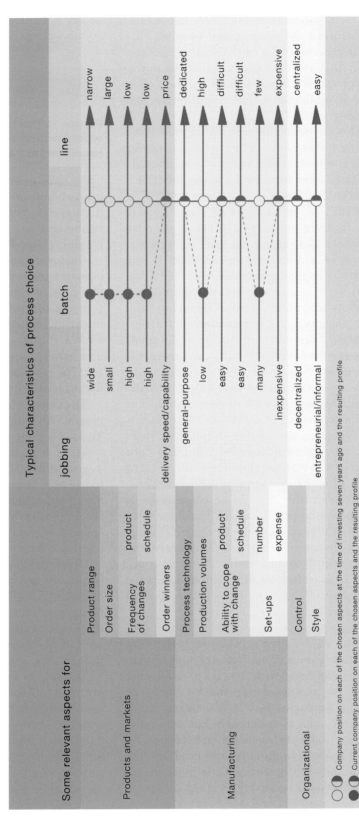

Figure 3: A product profile of a company's mainstream products to illustrate the impact of incremental marketing decison

⦵ Company position on each of the chosen aspects at the time of investing seven years ago and the resulting profile

⬤ Current company position on each of the chosen aspects and the resulting profile

The current year profile illustrates the dogleg shape, which reflects the inconsistencies between the high-volume batch processes and infrastructure invested in seven years ago, and the current market position.

qualifiers are less important than order-winners. Qualifiers have order-losing characteristics and thus play an essential role in the competitive stance of companies. But knowing what you need to do to qualify and what to win are key insights.

Finally, qualifiers and order-winners are time and market specific. They will be different from market to market and will change over time. Recognizing and providing these insights, therefore, is a far cry from the general statements of markets that typify most companies' strategic discussions. Difference, not similarity, is the hallmark of today's markets. Adequate insights are a prerequisite to developing functional support and developing strategic direction for the key functions within a firm. Figure 2 helps demonstrate this for the operations function.

Most firms start their debate about corporate strategy by listing the objectives they wish to achieve and then ask marketing to put forward a strategy for achieving them. This corporate marketing debate is at the front end of most companies' strategic process. However, the strategic debate typically stops here.

The assumption is that operations can support the marketing plans and achieve the projected level of profit and growth in agreed markets both today and in the future. Getting into the debate at the right time and the right level is an essential operations requirement in order to influence outcomes. The key to achieving this is through forcing detailed answers to the question: 'How do we win orders in our various markets?' Until this is understood, operations (as with other functions) is working in the dark in terms of its strategic role.

Operational vs strategic tasks

The overall task of all executives comprises operational and strategic elements. Managing and controlling the range of tasks for which they are responsible and undertaking these efficiently is a key role in operations. What this comprises and the approaches and concepts to adopt are dealt with elsewhere in this module. The essential recognition that both sets of tasks need to be undertaken is a key factor in creating competitive firms.

Markets vs operations

While markets are inherently dynamic (they will change whether you wish them to or not), operations is inherently fixed (operations will not change unless it is deliberately changed). Thus, the task to align and realign operations to the needs of agreed markets is a continuing requirement. A key element of this is to be able to test alignment or, ideally, highlight how the gap between market requirements and operational support will increase given projected strategies or actual/anticipated changes in the market. Figure 3 is an example of the approach to test alignment.

Here, a company in the late-1980s invested in processes designed to support the high-volume markets in which it competed. As competition increased and over-capacity prevailed, the company lost sales. In order to retain its revenue levels, marketing's strategy was to increase product range. As a result, customer order size reduced, the rate of new product introductions increased while marketing argued that price continued to be the important order-winner.

Over the following few years, this strategy prevailed and moved the company's position on these dimensions towards the left (*see* Figure 3). However, operations still had in place the processes in which it had invested in the late-1980s. Thus, operations was still attempting to support the current low-volume markets on its dedicated, less flexible processes and experiencing more set-ups, which were still long in duration and expensive in consequence.

What Figure 3 shows is that in the late-1980s operations was aligned with its markets but by the early-1990s the necessary alignment between markets and manufacturing no longer existed. The outcome was a rapid decline in profits and an increase in inventory resulting from manufacturing artificially inflating its volumes to go some way to compensating for the significant decline in customer order size.

The clear insight provided by product profiling enabled the company to identify the root cause of its decline and make adjustments to both the strategies pursued by marketing and manufacturing. Developments designed to move manufacturing to the left of its current position enabled the company to increase its alignment and gradually return to acceptable levels of profits.

Coping with difference

Driven by greater competition and customer expectation, markets are becoming increasingly different rather than similar. A key strategic task facing manufacturing, therefore, is how does it cope with difference. In the past, the approach adopted has been to seek a complex solution. However, this has singularly failed to provide the answer.

Recent developments in manufacturing have turned to a strategic alternative. As market difference signals different markets, then the alternative to supporting these with a single manufacturing function is to develop manufacturing strategies to support the different markets in which a company competes – the concept of focus.

Many companies are rearranging their manufacturing facilities based on a single provision supporting difference (the source of the complexity) by splitting their plant on the basis of the different markets in which their company competes and the different manufacturing task that follows – known as plant-within-a-plant focussed facilities.

Companies with several manufacturing plants, on the other hand, often choose to orientate one plant to support one set of market requirements and another to support a different set.

In either case, to retain focus companies then reposition products between the focussed units as the order-winners on which they compete change and the subsequent manufacturing task alters.

There are, however, constraints. Sometimes moving towards focussed plants requires duplicating existing processes and constrains its introduction. Sometimes, therefore, companies are able to focus some parts of their business while leaving the remainder unaltered. Where this is a more sensible development, companies are simply making sound choices between alternatives.

The important point is that approaches need to be based on what is best for the business as a whole and not based on competing dogmas.

Summary

Many organizations begin strategy formulation on the incorrect premise that markets and marketing are synonymous: marketing is a function, the market is the business. Companies must supplement customer 'voice' (the typical outcomes of marketing surveys and customer discussion) with customer behavior (found in the actual demands placed on the operations function of a supplier).

Better functional strategies come from avoiding descriptions of markets in general terms, by distinguishing between 'qualifiers' and 'order-winners', and by recognizing that difference, not similarity, is the hallmark of today's markets.

Markets will also change whether you wish them to or not, whereas operations are inherently fixed – thus the need to align the latter to the former is a continuing requirement. Many companies are rearranging their manufacturing facilities by splitting their plant on the basis of the different markets in which their company competes and the different manufacturing task that follows.

The 'greening' of industry – the hardest bit is still to come

■ **The environment is now an important part of every manager's responsibility. Ulrich Steger provides some points on how to handle environmental issues and also suggests that rapid industrialization poses some new challenges.**

Today there is a hardly a single corporation in any industry that is not under pressure to deal with environmental issues. Governmental regulation, competitive advances through innovation and increased consumer sensitivity have all helped to transform environmental issues from a political and moral subject into a fundamental business consideration.

The new regulations are often controversial but, in general, a company's environmental-management performance is seen as a useful indicator of its overall ability to deal with change, manage complexity and turn challenges into opportunities. In terms of competitiveness, the environment can no longer be regarded as a 'job-killer'. There is mounting evidence that the impact on employment varies considerably, depending on the establishment of clear priorities and time frames, and the mix of instruments employed.

Environmental risk exposure varies widely across different branches of industry but, today, even banks and insurance companies have to take account of environmental liability or environmental-impact assessments in project financing.

However, while the economic impact of environmental protection has not been as great as originally feared, progress is not as rapid as some had hoped. Sustainable development is not a revolution, it is part of structural change, moving ahead in steady slow motion rather than in leaps and bounds.

Areas of managerial action

Environmental management is not a separate activity to be left to a handful of experts on the corporate staff. It cuts across all functions of a company, from R&D to logistics, from finance to quality. Each of these departments has to carry out its conventional role as efficiently as possible but the decision-making criteria it employs now include environmental protection. Like quality, this cannot be 'inspected-in'; it has to be ingrained in the processes and routines of business. Here are some examples:

Production. Since the British Chlorine-Alkali Act of 1864, production has been the classical area of environmental regulation. Air emissions, polluted sewage or waste has to be treated, minimized or, best of all, avoided.

It is no longer adequate to deal with hazardous substances at the end of the process, at the point where they enter the waste stream. It is much more economical to prevent their occurrence in the first place. This may mean pressuring suppliers to alter the content of their materials or provide substitutes. Many hazardous solvents, such as metal-cleaning products, have been replaced by water-based variants or used in closed-loop systems. These developments were not driven by the economics of the process but energy-efficiency measures in this area often pay for themselves, as do the optimization of logistics or the on-site recycling of waste material.

Product development. In recent years, environmental attention has shifted from production processes to the product itself. Today, product R&D has to take into account not only a host of government regulations but also market requirements: these include the recycling and re-use of packaging, energy efficiency and emission standards in use, and take-back guarantees at the end of service life. The car may be the most visible example of this but is not by any means the only one. Products have to meet environmental requirements in addition to the normal standards of functionality, quality, and design, at a competitive price/performance ratio.

Mobilising employees' initiative and creativity. In product development, production, and marketing, environmental considerations cannot be met through a top-down process alone. Top-management commitment is essential but it is also necessary to raise employees' environmental awareness and foster their motivation.

Making environmental progress that is economically viable means paying attention to hundreds of details and taking many small steps to achieve continuous improvement. These are identified most effectively by those who work on the products and processes.

Rewarding proposals for increased environmental efficiency, training environment-conscious behavior, encouraging employees to be ambassadors for the environmental responsibility of the corporation are some proven techniques for motivating people to develop an environmental dimension to their work. There is only one essential precondition: the company's environmental statements must be matched by its actions.

Extended market relations. Many environmental problems cannot be solved effectively within the value chain of a single company. They require close co-operation with other organizations, such as suppliers, in the 'cradle-to-grave' chain.

A good example of this is to provide returnable containers or bottle systems in logistical or recycling loops. These are often economical, but the costs and benefits are spread unequally along the value chain. Through co-operation, corrective systems have to be developed and managed but, as with other strategic alliances, this requires striking a delicate balance between competition and co-operation (and possibly raising the suspicions of anti-trust-authorities). This kind of co-operation can only survive in the longer term if all partners, and the environment, benefit from it.

New services often spring up to provide the specific expertise to manage such complex systems; for example, designing, financing, washing, repairing and transporting standardized, returnable containers for fruits and meat. Other companies have developed markets for secondary raw material, which is often the element that prevents the achievement of higher recycling targets.

Internal and external communication. Since they have no proactive communication strategy, many corporations only reap half of the benefits of becoming 'green'. Some do not dare to talk about the environmental performance of their products because they are not sure that they are really 'clean'. Others exaggerate with heavily 'green' marketing, often promising more than the product can deliver. Both attitudes lower the credibility of business in environmental affairs.

The solution is to communicate 'greening' as a process of continuous improvement with a series of goals as intermediate steps towards sustainability and economic efficiency. This allows for a constructive dialogue with all stakeholders, including environmentalists. It can earn trust, which is necessary for co-operation with regulators and needs to be built up before critical situations arise. And it encourages employees to be part of the problem-solving process.

Transparency through responsible environmental reporting is one of the key requirements and, encouragingly, the possibilities of hiding environmental damage have diminished dramatically over the years through 'right to know' legislation enacted around the world. It should never be forgotten that scandal-seeking media feeds on unpublished information, not on the data from an official environmental report.

Tools for integration: environmetrics and eco-audits

Management is about action not intention. So the question is, how does a company move to integrate environmental criteria while preserving its economic viability? Two approaches should be mentioned: Environmetrics and the voluntary EU-Environmental Management and Auditing System (EMAS), based on a broad range of useful instruments that management science has developed in recent years.

Environmetrics is about transforming environmental issues into the universal corporate language – numbers. Only what can be measured gets done.

A lot of environment-inefficient decisions are based on the fact that, even today, most environmental costs are hidden in overheads and not allocated to products or processes. Activity-based accounting approaches in particular, but some much simpler calculations too, can create more transparency that will give clean technology a better chance than it has today – in investment decisions, for example. Environmental-performance indicators (EPI) enable companies to set clear targets and deadlines, to benchmark sites and compare management techniques against best practices inside and outside the corporation.

The EMAS, which is heavily influenced by BS 7750 and is a standard for ISO 14000, is basically a comprehensive management system rather than a technical measure for compliance. It stresses the need for integration through clear corporate goals, policy, programs and organization developed by the corporation. It defines reporting requirements and gives them credibility through an independent verification process.

It is hard to imagine that, in the years to come, corporations with high-risk exposure will not need this certification in order to preserve their operating license: customers, banks, insurers, shareholders – and maybe even the public – will demand this as a proof of 'due diligence'.

How clean is clean enough?

After 25 years of more or less exhaustive standard-setting in environmental regulation, much of industry is asking 'How much further should we go?'

Northern Europe has achieved a lot in trying to become clean, but has not yet really moved towards sustainability. The introduction of the catalytic converter is a good example: it made car exhaust a lot cleaner but, at today's energy consumption rates, the car is not a sustainable product.

The poorer 80 per cent of the world's population is rapidly catching up with the developed world's pattern of mobility and this is going to have an enormous impact on resource depletion and the environment, for example the greenhouse effect.

What has been achieved so far is the easy part – the environmental clean-up accomplished through technical means. Now comes the more difficult part – our basic patterns of production and consumption are being challenged as industrialization accelerates around the world.

This will require a fundamental change of attitude among consumers and managers, and also among regulators. To achieve sustainable development, the traditional command-and-control approach is as outdated as 'end-of-the-pipe' technology. Innovation is required at all levels and in all critical areas. This will accelerate the pace of structural change, creating new winners and losers. The most interesting phase of environmental management is yet to come.

Summary

Environmental management now cuts across all functions of a company, and has to be ingrained into processes and routines.

Production is the classical area of environmental regulation, with the emphasis moving from treatment/disposal of waste to prevention. Attention has also shifted to the product itself with a host of new requirements for those involved in R&D. Top management commitment may be essential but employee motivation needs to be fostered. Problems, moreover, are often best solved through close co-operation with suppliers and others in the 'cradle to grave' chain. Transparency through responsible environmental reporting is another key requirement.

Two ways of integrating environmental criteria into the company are through environmetrics (transforming environmental issues into numbers) and the EU's Environmental Management and Auditing System (Emas).

Northern Europe has achieved a lot in trying to become clean but it has not yet really moved towards sustainability.

Transformation: the difference between domination and death

■ **Manufacturing companies must dominate their markets or die. But domination requires change on a massive scale that makes re-engineering look an easy operation.**
Tom Vollmann explains how can companies manage it.

Many of today's leading enterprises and leading management thinkers agree that the stark choice facing companies in the light of massively changed environments and customer expectations is to 'dominate or die'.

Yet far too many businesses treat this warning somewhat dismissively and continue pursuing strategies aimed at improving 'the way we do business around here'. Domination of their industry or sector is rarely on their agenda.

Even so there seems to be a growing appreciation that the fundamental nature of change has altered the competitive environment to such an extent that what constituted a profile of a winning organization in the past does not necessarily apply any more. While around us we hear the thuds of dinosaur organizations hitting the deck (and even the Japanese giants show signs of wobbling), we need to be alert to a new species that has come into being. Their ways are catching hold and their performance is allowing them to seize the initiative.

Such new-species companies include Semco in Brazil, British Airways in the UK and Connecticut Mutual Life Insurance Company in the US.

The rules governing this type of 'third wave' company are fundamentally different from those governing their struggling predecessors. It is also clear that they did not arrive at their existing position through a process of slow evolutionary steps. At one time a transformative leap gave them a profile for dominance. This new profile will not only equip them to survive in the present environment, it will provide a platform for the next leap. And they will need to make that next leap – there is no room for complacency in the third industrial revolution.

Characteristics of dominance

When we use the term 'dominance' we are talking about those organizations that lead their industry, sector or niche by not only attaining but sustaining an influence in their area while remaining intensely customer focussed. The key words are 'sustaining an influence'. The ability to sustain in the face of intense competitive pressures will need to become the focus of management effort during the third industrial revolution.

People in Western companies in particular have a problem with notions about domination. They conjure up pictures of Big Brother or aggressive bullying nations with megalomaniacs for leaders. To dispel some of these notions it is important first to establish what we do not mean by the word 'dominance':

Being the biggest. General Motors may be the biggest automotive company but it does not dominate the industry. Companies such as Honda or Toyota, which are a lot smaller, seem to be the ones that are calling more of the shots.

Monopolistic competition. The dominant company does not need artificial barriers to entry to its business. It is periodically undergoing fundamental transformation as well as learning at such a rate that others will simply not be able to catch up.

The bottom line. Many firms make excellent financial returns yet cannot be considered as dominant – and vice versa. Financial returns are an obvious objective of dominance, but there are always time lags as well as confounding influences. Financial returns need to be seen as the 'passengers' with dominance as the 'driver'.

Dominance is not a singular steady state. A quick review of the companies cited in the book *In Search of Excellence* shows that many of them are now in trouble. Dominance is like a restaurant: only as good as the last meal. Influence can be seen or measured on any number of scales and depends on the way an enterprise measures success. Some may choose market share, others quality or innovation. It is whatever they feel allows them to exert an influence on the customer.

And these priorities change over time. In addition, the market is changing all the time. With the proliferation of products comes a proliferation of niches. The beer market, for example, contains the lager market, which in turn contains the imported brands of lager market, which in turn contains, say, German brands. Companies can be dominant on any of these levels.

Characteristics of death

When we talk about 'death' we mean those companies that do not exhibit any of the characteristics of dominance. A dying company does not lead, it follows. It is losing market share and capabilities. It has the wrong set of competencies. It is demoralized. Its activities and responses have little impact. In fact, what we observe around us are companies that are in a state worse than death – they have joined the living dead, aware (or not) that whatever they do makes little difference to their situation. Yet they feel compelled to keep on acting, producing, carrying on. And no one seems to care whether they survive or not.

Death is most often a long drawn-out affair. Even with inept management (or managers very capable at the wrong things) it still takes a long time to destroy a large company that had previously developed strong, if currently obsolete, capabilities.

The signals of death are evident long before the enterprise hits crisis mode: shrinking market share; reduced growth; unsatisfactory new product development; employee dissatisfaction; management shuffles; underestimation of competitors' capabilities; and so on. In too many cases the early signals are ignored. Even when

death symptoms start tickling the bottom line, excuses and palliatives rather than fundamental transformation are produced.

Dying may be slow and the dying enterprise may even be profitable in patches on the road to the graveyard. But there are unmistakable signs of impending doom – 'weak' signals at first, but which grow louder and louder until there is no ignoring them.

Some of the signals are:

Weak
- Loss of key marketable staff
- Underestimation of competition
- Loss of niche market
- Failures or delays in new product development
- Few people visiting customers

Clear
- Shrinking market share
- Reduced growth
- Little new product development
- Key customer exodus

Loud
- Employee dissatisfaction
- Staff turnover at all levels, especially management
- Serious bottom line problems
- Management rationalization
- Reactive knee-jerk responses

Crisis
- Major cutbacks
- Deep financial crisis
- Redundancies

What makes the difference? What is going on inside the death versus dominance companies? What are the differences in long-run strategic objectives and how are they being implemented in the organization in all of its functions? How do successful managers lead transformation? What are the distinctive competencies – those that will make a real marketplace difference? How are resources – throughout the enterprise – being deployed in the dominant companies and in the dying companies? What do the customers think?

Everyone is on the change bandwagon. Some are 'returning to core business'. Some are restructuring. Some are re-engineering. Few serious players doubt that the management of change has moved to the top of the corporate agenda. Change theories and tools proliferate. Change consultants criss-cross the globe spreading pearls of wisdom. Executives are bombarded with remedies that promise everything.

And yet companies that have been advised by the best and the greatest, which are into all the change tools on the planet, seem to be in the death spiral. Why? Once they dominated. Now they appear to be dying. From the executive office to the shop floor the question is how are companies to escape the death spiral? Clues that indicate an answer to this question seem to lie in the way companies view change and how they respond to it.

Below are the most commonly observed responses to faltering performance. They need to be considered alongside the characteristics of dominance – third wave companies – and those of death – companies stuck with old operational paradigms.

Some dying responses

Improvement programs. Improvement programs are part of every manufacturing company's daily life. Above the particular programs are the more general necessities such as speed, responsiveness, time-based competition, quality and flexibility. Clearly, all of these are important. The company that does not achieve them does so at its own peril. But these change programs and more general imperatives are necessary but not sufficient conditions for meeting the challenges facing manufacturing companies today.

Increasingly the capabilities generated by total quality management, just in time manufacturing and other 'world class' manufacturing techniques are only the ante to play in today's manufacturing competitive game. They are not winning cards. These improvement programs might have contributed to dominance in the past, when they were revolutionary. And even now some companies are achieving excellent paybacks from implementing these techniques. But they can no longer be the sole basis of

dominance. They are 'commodities of process' analogous to product commodities.

Financial restructuring. Financial restructuring is usually a response to crisis. The slide towards death has become bad enough to be seen repeatedly in the financial statements. When the excuses run out, the balloon goes up, top management issues a press release and 'financial restructuring' – too often a Band-Aid on a serious wound – begins.

Unfortunately, news of this kind of restructuring is usually welcomed by the financial community. The company's share price rises on the news and management is encouraged into dwelling in a fool's paradise.

The question rarely asked in these financial restructurings is: 'How are fewer hands to do the same jobs?' The result: burned-out employees with zero time to work on any type of proactive responses to the competitive marketplace. In fact, the organizational energy required to adapt to the reduction might have been expended on proactive improvement and redeployment of capabilities.

Downsizing is not always undesirable nor can it always be avoided. But companies often grossly underestimate its true cost. Conventional cost measurements and managerial ideologies encourage the delusion. It is comfortable and 'decisive' to get behind the 'concrete numbers' of x heads times y average salaries divided by one axe. It just takes more imagination and creativity to generate alternatives that redeploy human resources towards adding value to the business than to label them as waste and put them into the 'out' tray.

Management shuffles. Another misguided 'improvement' is the organizational reshuffle. Job titles are changed, job descriptions are rewritten, boxes are regrouped on the organization chart, there are winners and losers in the game of office politics, and life – or rather death – goes on. What is really important in the company has not changed – it is still business as usual.

If it has changed, few people know it, believe it and live it. As with the financial restructuring charade, cynicism can be a likely by-product, since people are not easily fooled. Without a well-developed and communicated new mission that clearly justifies a reorganization – and that focuses on capability development and increasing customer value – the result is far too often a major expenditure of resources inside the company instead of their deployment towards competitive dominance.

We can now compare these dying responses with some characteristics of a dominant response to change.

Some dominant responses

Paradigm shifting. A paradigm shift is necessary when the old set of operating assumptions is no longer valid. When a manufacturing enterprise adopts a philosophy of quality or time-based competition, a different set of operating practices needs to be implemented in the company. Old concepts have to be unlearned and new ones learned. New performance measures have to be adopted to guide actions and old ones discarded because behaviors must change profoundly.

Proactive transformation usually starts with a paradigm shift aimed at dominance rather than fine tuning. Concrete action plans, a well articulated process for implementation and periodic reviews of progress are also essential. But fundamentally the transformation needs to be integrated, consistent, feasible and desirable.

Proactive not reactive change. Change can be more or less proactive and will require organizations to dig very deep into their values, attitudes and beliefs in order to produce the appropriate response. Three levels of adaptation through transformation have been identified:

1. *Responsive/flexible.* Many companies are overhauling their manufacturing systems to cope with unexpected change, unpredictable demand, new customer preferences and other vagaries of the present marketplace. All this with minimum inventories. The intent is to transform their operations so that the company can respond like McDonald's: when two bus loads of boy scouts pull up unexpectedly, they all get a hamburger and no one waits in a queue for long.

2. *Anticipatory/forecasting.* Whenever possible it is better to anticipate required changes and shrink response time. Transformation based on closer linkages with customers and suppliers,

electronic data inter-change and strategic alliances based on infor-mation integration are some of the approaches being taken. Key Xerox suppliers, for example, have detailed knowledge of both the Xerox build schedules that they will support and the Xerox new product developments in which they are actively participating.

3. *Proactive/causing change.* Proactive responses on the part of leading-edge companies can dictate the terms of competition by changing the rules of the game. Creating new forms of physical distribution such as that put in place by Wal-Mart, bringing new products to the marketplace that people did not even know they needed, such as the Sony Walkman, seeing environmental issues as a way of defining the competitive agenda, creating a genuine learning organization, reskilling workers before they are obsolete, and cultivating a competitively superior culture are examples of proactive transformation.

Proactive transformation often begins with the definition of some desired 'scenario' or description of a competitive state. Thereafter the major changes required to achieve it are identified and put in place. Proactive transformation also implies a never-ending process of change not a one-time adjustment to solve some particular problem.

Enterprise transformation. As we embark on what people are calling the third industrial revolution the lessons of the past are so inadequate that what is mandated is fundamental transformation of the organization. The term transformation is not intended to create another synonym for restructuring or re-engineering. It is a process a company enters by one door and a different company exits at the other end.

Global recession has resulted in several corporate transformations – some proactive, others enforced by factors beyond management control. In the successful ones, the very shape and structure of enterprises have had to change, their competencies and capabilities have changed, their resources have changed, their outputs have changed, their attitude to customer service has changed and their fundamental raison d'être has shifted.

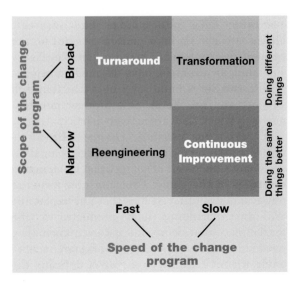

Figure 1

In the unsuccessful, their missions have reverted back to 'doing core business', crisis management has replaced strategy and 'passengers' (such as cost) replace 'drivers' (such as customer satisfaction). They certainly are not the companies they once were – they have indeed been transformed. But no one was steering the change towards dominance.

Crisis is a good launching point for transformation. The trouble is that while old ideas of what running a business is about hold sway, management reaction will too often gravitate towards fine tuning the old when instead they should react to a genuine opportunity to shape the new.

Transformation as an idea can also be seen in Figure 1. The two-by-two matrix has the scope of change on one axis and the speed of change on the other. For a relatively narrow scope of change where speed is fast, 're-engineering' comes to mind. Fast speed with broad scope may well be a turnaround situation requiring downsizing and tough decision making. For a relatively slow speed and narrow scope the classic Japanese kaizen approach of continuous improvement is descriptive. It is in the upper right-hand corner, where the scope of change is broad and the time frame for achieving that change is long, that the term 'transformation' seems most appropriate.

Restructuring, re-engineering and the like might well be effective in cutting out waste – human, material and time – but if by the end of the process of disruption the fundamental operational paradigm remains untouched, then it is unlikely that the changes will stand the test of time. In today's world, doing the same thing better is necessary but not sufficient. When the next crisis hits some other action might well be required to dig the company out of its hole. What needs to be taken on board is that the past description of what constitutes a winning formula has been rendered useless by the third industrial revolution. The past approaches to employees, suppliers and customers all need to be brought in line with third industrial revolution reality. In this reality, employees, suppliers and customers are different creatures capable of delivering different skills and demanding different products and services.

There will be few who disagree with these sentiments. Most companies more than ten years old are feeling the bite of intense forces and constraints. Even some newly established enterprises are struggling as their founding paradigms become obsolete. Those who have embraced today's paradigms are growing in leaps and bounds while others in their industries are retrenching. They are like children who have the latest electronic gadget up and running before their parents can even decipher the first page of the instruction manual.

Old established second-wave companies, particularly those that have managed to mass considerable assets and huge customer bases, might shrug at these ideas. They respond to problems by digging into the bag of tricks that produced a fix in the past. But at some point the best of tricks will not produce the goods. Vast sums will be spent, with little return. Ask all those 'excellent' companies that do not exist any longer.

Figure 2 plays a key role in understanding enterprise transformation. The difference between a company's costs and its prices is its profits. The difference between its prices and the value perceived by its customers for the overall set of goods and services provided is a set of 'extra benefits' or advantages that the company

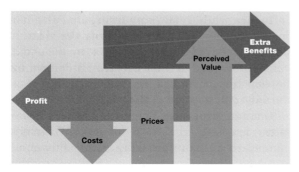

Figure 2

can exploit – either in the form of higher prices, greater customer loyalty, higher sales or perhaps improved market share. But in far too many transformation efforts the sole emphasis is on reducing costs. Most companies today would be better advised to focus their transformation efforts in increasing the perceived value in the marketplace. But, as previously noted, this is not an either/or trade-off. The objective is both lower costs and higher perceived value.

Higher perceived value has another crucial benefit. In many organizations the focus on cost cutting leads inevitably to head count reduction – often for those who have made the improvements. This game of 'you play ball with me and then I will hit you over the head with the bat' has dire consequences. Maintaining morale, nurturing a proactive change culture and other dimensions of good human resource management practices can be seriously set back, undermining key competencies and capabilities.

An example of playing the higher perceived value card is a packaging company that is developing a strategic alliance with a transportation company to provide a more interesting bundle of goods and services.

In essence, there is a set of customers who want to receive just-in-time deliveries from their suppliers but have to carry extra stocks to hedge against the arrival of damaged goods. But damage is a function of the package as well as the shipping methods. By designing packaging and shipping together the damage can be significantly reduced. Moreover, the shipping company can take back the packaging for recycling, solving another customer problem (disposing of the packaging) while bringing in

'raw material' for the packaging company.

A proactive attack on improving customer perceived values can provide the necessary 'growth' mentality to the transforming company. While obviously not a panacea, this mentality can provide a driving force for proactive change.

The four characteristics of strategic transformation

Finally, it is worth considering those criteria that make change truly transformative. Such change will need to be integrated and consistent across all organizational facets. It will also need to be feasible and desirable to stand any chance of success. If one of these four ingredients is missing it is likely to mean that the end of the process will be 'better sameness' with its beguiling short-term injection of adrenalin and hope.

Integration. Is the company's transformation plan integrated? Is there a clear linkage from what the marketplace dictates to the overall strategic intent down to the particular actions required and processes that need to be re-designed?

We call this linkage 'the golden cord'. It unites the key facets of the enterprise to one another, allowing them to be examined in order. But integration must be seen in a context. There is always a need to accelerate the change process. This must be driven from the top but supported throughout the enterprise, always searching for new triggering mechanisms followed by integrative actions.

Consistency. Do all of the various actions lead to the same place and are they mutually supportive? Does the management team have a clear sense of how things fit together? Do all the people in the company see the same picture on the top of the puzzle box?

Feasibility. Is the transformation plan capable of realization in the time allotted? Goals that stretch people are fine, but impossible objectives will surely lead to disillusion and cynicism. At the same time, there needs to be a perceived sense of urgency. Transformation requires unfreezing and fundamental change in the status quo.

Desirability. Is the overall transformation effort desirable both from the company's point of view and from that of the key players? At the company level, the strategic business unit level; and the individual level everyone must believe in the need for acceleration of change and be ready to buy into the resultant need for 'managed crisis'.

Of much more importance, however, is for companies in the West not to see dominance as just a better steady state than the one they now find themselves in. Dominance is the organizational state in which change is no longer a major upheaval but a way of life. The process for getting there does not just involve learning; more critical is the ability to unlearn. Compared to learning, unlearning is extremely difficult.

One executive on IMD's Manufacturing 2000 program (who came from a company that had undergone some big changes) said that he could now easily tell which employees would not be able to make it over the long run.

If anyone talked of things returning to normal or of some steady state where rampant change would not be part of daily life, then he or she clearly did not understand.

Summary

Dominant companies are those which sustain an influence while remaining intensely customer focussed. They are not necessarily the biggest, do not need artificial barriers to keep out competitors, and are not necessarily defined by bottom line performance. They are like restaurants: only as good as their last meal.

'Change' programs are no longer enough – many are only the ante to play in today's competititve manufacturing game. Financial restructurings often turn out to be merely the plaster on a serious wound, while management shuffles can conceal underlying problems.

'Dominant' responses require a paradigm shift with old concepts unlearned as well as new ones learned. They also involve companies in proactive change through which they become flexible enough to meet unpredictable customer demands, anticipating the market and dictating the terms of competition by changing the rules of the game. Enterprise transformation is not a synonym for re-engineering or restructuring – it effectively involves the birth of a different company.

Integration (the 'golden cord'), consistency, feasibility and desirability (getting the belief of the main players) are the main characteristics of strategic transformation.

Pan-regional manufacturing: the lessons from Europe

■ **How are companies in Europe managing the transition to pan-regional manufacturing? And how can those looking to enter other regions learn from their experience?**

by **Robert Collins and Roger Schmenner**

The arrival of the Single Market (however incomplete) and several years of difficult economic and competitive conditions have forced many manufacturers to rethink the way they operate in Europe.

IMD surveyed 93 manufacturing companies that operate in more than one European country to see how they were responding to the strategic challenges posed by the Single Market. The results, together with other research and analysis, point to some important lessons not only for companies operating in Europe but also for those looking for opportunities in other trade areas such as the Asia-Pacific region and the North American Free Trade Association.

The survey highlighted the difference between the traditional organization of manufacturing found in many long-established European companies and the pan-regional organization of more progressive European manufacturers and some US and Japanese companies in Europe.

One important difference is plant location. Many European manufacturers have located, or have inherited, plants that traditionally served their host countries and, perhaps, small neighbouring countries and former colonies. Typically each plant produces the entire range of output that the company's local sales force sells, or at least much of it.

Because some of the countries served have limited populations the plants themselves may be small compared to similar plants in major markets. The locations are typically dictated by historical accident or proximity to the company's major market. The plants are paired with their local sales companies and they run their operations independently of similar company operations in other European countries. Product characteristics and packaging are generally the province of the local sales companies. Above marketing and sales and production operations reigns a country managing director.

Pan-European manufacturing

The pan-European manufacturer is organized in dramatically different fashion, though it is a fashion that is familiar to many American or Japanese companies operating in Europe. Rather than a geographically based strategy, the pan-European producer follows a product-based strategy. Different products are made in different factories and are shipped over a broad geographic area.

A company switch to a pan-European orientation typically involves a narrowing of product line responsibilities for plants and an increase in the markets they serve. Importantly, such a switch in strategy frees management to concentrate on a limited product line in any one factory. Such a reorientation results in more attention being paid to product flows, redesign of plant layouts, better materials handling, new investments in equipment and different work-force practices. Critical mass can be achieved in staff areas such as new product development, purchasing and process engineering.

With a change to a pan-European strategy, the scale of operations is likely to increase. Thus, more specialization within manufacturing can be sought. Reorganization can concentrate manufacturing and design know-how, and state-of-the-art approaches can be more easily mastered. Overheads may decline, especially relative to the volumes produced. This is because the narrowed product line can facilitate a more 'visible' production process and less need for 'systems' to run the factory because teams can act to delayer the levels of military-style hierarchy that prevail in some European companies.

Company organization typically changes. Because the brand and product have become pan-European in character, it usually makes sense to centralise selected aspects of the marketing and sales functions. This is becoming a vital prerequisite if major customers are themselves organized as pan-European companies.

Centralization leaves the country manager with considerably less responsibility and power. Even more power is ceded if manufacturing is reorganized as well so that the country's plants produce less than a full line of products. Manufacturing management then becomes a co-ordinator of networks of plants, rather than autonomous units.

The results of such a switch in strategy can be dramatic, particularly with respect to the lowering of production costs.

Take Company A, a confectionery marker. As a result of aggressive merger and acquisition activity it had almost 20 plants scattered throughout Europe, each making an assortment of products for small, well-defined geographic areas. With the advent of pan-European thinking the company closed about half of them and recommissioned the others so that product lines are now made at separate locations in what are termed international manufacturing centers.

The national sales organizations and distribution channels are unchanged but are now fed by the product line-specific international manufacturing centers.

Company A has been able to reconfigure the layouts of its factories so that materials move from factories to markets much more economically. The increase in volume has justified more automation. There are fewer set-ups and the time lag in the feedback of information regarding quality and other operational issues is now much shorter than before. Not only has this re-organization increased productivity, but the simplification of the factories has also meant that products costs are now better known. This, in turn, has permitted manufacturing to resist marketing 'whimsy' more effectively than ever.

Pan-European manufacturers are rethinking their approach to plant scale. The choice of product line for each plant can be made with an eye to 'minimum efficient scale'. Furthermore, the capacity utilization of these plants can be more effectively managed. In moving to pan-European operations, the generous buffer capacity typically present in the independent, country-based plants are squeezed out of the reduced number of plants kept in operation.

Lean production
The shift to pan-European manufacturing offers more than cost and scale benefits. Our research shows that although many European manu-facturers are adopting at least some of the latest manufacturing initiatives – JIT, TQM, employee involvement and so on – pan-European manu-facturers are moving much more swiftly. They are far ahead of the competition in under-standing and implementing the key ideas of time-based competition and lean production.

Companies that have successfully introduced pan-regional manufacturing strategies in Europe have become experienced in managing oper-ations in a multicultural, multilingual environ-ment and in coping with differences in economic performance and national political agendas. American and Japanese multinationals in particular have been able to treat Europe as a greenfield site in terms of plant size and location. They tend to think of it in the same way as their home markets, where product-specific plants servicing geographical areas are the norm. Nevertheless, more progressive European com-panies, such as TetraPak, Schindler and Borealis have used the introduction of the Single Market to implement pan-regional manufacturing strategies.

Their European experience will be invaluable to many of these companies as they prepare for the major opportunities opening up in other areas of the world. For example, with high import tariffs and low labor market efficiency, Brazil today is in a situation similar to that of Spain and Portugal before they joined the European Union. Equally, the impressive eco-nomic growth rates and expanding markets of the Asia-Pacific region pose similar complex choices to those faced by American and Japanese companies when they entered Europe.

In looking at pan-regional strategies based on the European experience, companies need to consider the following:

1. Avoid manufacturing myopia. Companies moving into a new region for the first time have an excellent opportunity to adopt a pan-regional rather than a national perspective in defining markets and locating plants. This can help them avoid the problems of overcapacity, duplication and insufficient scale that often hamper traditional companies in Europe. For some companies it may mean overcoming the 'national market' mindset and opposition from internal 'country king' supporters.

For the pan-regional producer, costs are an increasingly important factor in choosing plant locations: particularly labor costs and the costs of access to suppliers and sister plants within the company. Other factors include government location incentives and local or national policies on such issues as building regulations, the environment and employment laws.

Companies may be influenced by pan-regional customers. To serve a demanding pan-European company, one supplier had to build several new plants using dramatically improved designs that facilitated teamwork, improved quality as well as speeding up materials handling.

The decision to open or close a plant is often highly political, particularly if opening a plant in a new region affects production 'at home'. To make the decision more objective, some companies use classical mathematical programming techniques. Based on the forecast level of demand for individual countries or submarkets in the region, these techniques can allocate output of particular products to specific plants and assess the total costs, including physical distribution, of various possible plant networks.

2. Build product-focussed plant networks. As we have seen from the experience of pan-European strategies, product-focussed operations concentrate experience in a few locations and these tend to increase in size to reach optimal efficiencies. Single-market plants may often be under-sized relative to the prevailing technology and therefore more costly. Just over half the plants in the IMD survey supplied domestic markets and, on average, were a quarter of the size of plants serving larger export markets. Even mass-market producers such as Renault, Volvo, Peugeot and Fiat are wondering whether they have sufficient scale. In the chemicals industry, where Europe has traditionally been a world player, concerns about scale and overcapacity have led to a number of asset swaps; for example, ICI and Du Pont in nylon, and ICI and BASF in polypropylene.

But 'optimal' plant size does not automatically mean very large. One electronics and electrical machinery company has recently concluded that sites employing 1,000 to 2,000 people are preferable to their existing manufacturing network, which has both small sites employing 100 to 200 people and very large ones employing 5,000 or more.

3. Build pan-regional organizational structures. Many European firms are organized into 'manufacturing companies' that distribute their products through 'sales companies' – often one in each of the major countries. These local companies are used to being largely independent in product formulation, pricing, packaging and sourcing policies. The result is more customization, more small-scale runs and more uncoordinated manufacturing activity than in equivalent operations in companies from other regions.

Moving to a pan-regional manufacturing strategy means reassessing the balance between centralized task-sharing and local autonomy. A pan-regional organization is not a confederation of national entities and, as we have seen, centralization leaves country managers (if any) with considerably less power and responsibility. Marketing and sales strategy becomes a headquarters role, although implementation remains with local management. This in turn means that production planning and logistics for the various manufacturing facilities need to be co-ordinated regionally.

Pan-regional strategies also affect the distribution system. Although the number of warehouses can be reduced as plants ship larger quantities directly to major customers, transportation costs may actually rise because the finished goods need to be shipped over a wider area. However, most pan-regional companies estimate that increases in transportation expenses will be offset by savings in the manufacturing process.

Not all companies will centralize their organizations to the same degree. One European food producer has centralized quality control, production engineering and financial control much more than marketing and production, believing taste differences between countries call for caution in introducing pan-regional manufacturing.

4. Adopt rigid flexibility. Research by IMD suggests that pan-regional manufacturers understand more clearly than nationally based manufacturers the need for flexibility in production. Flexibility is needed to customize products, to create additional product features, to shorten product development times or to ensure short lead times from order to delivery.

Flexibility is not achieved by having numerous plants produce a wide range of products for one country. It is achieved by redesigning the way a plant operates. It means combining simplicity with discipline – a combination we term 'rigid flexibility'. (The concept of rigid flexibility was dealt with in detail in an earlier article (see p. 311)).

Many packaged goods producers exemplify rigid flexibility. They have achieved low unit manufacturing costs by adopting standard product 'footprints', such as can diameters and bottle heights. These contribute to simplicity in operations such as filling, packaging and palletising, with fewer changeovers and greater operating speeds, yet permit great diversity in the look of the container and its contents. Such simplicity has been developed though the discipline of design for manufacturability, where systematic thinking and rule of thumb are rigorously applied to the design cycle.

5. Standardize systems and procedures. Efficient material flow and information exchange within a pan-regional strategy require standardized systems and procedures – quality, parts management, production control – as well as more standardized products and packages. Our survey showed that pan-European producers tend to be much more standardized in all categories than nationally based firms. For example, 86 per cent of pan-European companies had increased standardization in product formulations/engineering in the past five to ten years compared with 70 per cent of nationally based companies. Pan-European companies are also more likely to have standardized packaging, product numbering, component and part numbering, quality-assurance standards, and computer-based planning and control systems.

This suggests that standardization is not only a function of the size of a plant's market but also of how much product-line responsibilities are narrowed. It also suggests that pan-regional manufacturers are more likely to adopt 'rigid flexibility' in their approach to manufacturing. For example, a pan-European television manufacturer faced with the multiplicity of television 'standards' in Europe designed an electronics module that was standard for all its TV receivers of a certain size. The module could be easily customized on the assembly line to meet specific country requirements while all other assembly steps remained unchanged.

6. Identify obstacles to implementation. In Europe many manufacturing firms have found that progress towards a pan-regional strategy can be severely hampered by the constraints of external stakeholders such as national governments, international agencies and pressure groups. These constraints need to be recognized at an early stage.

Some of them are political, such as government regulations that affect pharmaceutical companies in the location of formulation plants or public-sector procurement policies that deny foreign telecommunications firms access to a number of national markets.

The level of environmental awareness and control can also be important. Chemicals companies operating in Europe are faced with significant capital investments to support health, safety and environmental initiatives. As a result, they tend to concentrate disparate process units in a small number of large, complex sites.

Other obstacles are far more subtle. Differences in culture, customs and cuisine across a region force manufacturers of consumer goods to decide whether individual country requirements can be satisfied through a number of plants in various markets or fewer plants dedicated to a sub-set of those markets. A lack of common standards and product harmonization in industries such as telecommunications and electronics can raise the same issues.

In conclusion, it is apparent that lower trading barriers, improved physical distribution and competitive cost pressures are all driving companies towards pan-regional, even global, manufacturing. Companies moving into new geographic regions have an opportunity to pursue pan-regional strategies from the outset. However, these strategies require new competencies, in particular a disciplined approach to standards and procedures. Without them, pan-regional manufacturing networks will steadily come to resemble the confederations of national entities that exist in many European companies in their home region today.

Summary

The single market has forced a rethink of many companies' European operations. Traditional plants typically produce an entire range of goods which are then sold by their local sales-force. Pan-European producers, by contrast, follow a product led strategy and tend to centralize marketing and sales.

Pan-regional manufacturing offers more than

cost and scale benefits – research shows that such companies are ahead in the adoption of the latest manufacturing initiatives, and have become experienced in cross cultural management.

Companies considering the pan-regional approach need to overcome 'national market' mindsets and opposition from 'country kings'; they may well be influenced by pan-regional customers. Optimal plant size does not necessarily mean very large. The exercise will involve reassessing the task sharing between centralized authority and local autonomy. Flexibility can be achieved by redesigning the way plants operate, while standardization in product formulations/engineering is likely to increase. Obstacles – political, cultural, etc – need to be identified at an early stage.

Information Management

Contents

Managing strategic intelligence 346
Donald A. Marchand, IMD
Strategic intelligence needs to be disseminated organization-wide and not confined to a specific function. New IT software is helping.

What is your company's information culture? 351
Donald A. Marchand, IMD
Aligning the way a company handles information – its 'information culture' – with its strategy is a key task for managers.

It's strategy that counts 357
Xavier Gilbert, IMD
Information technology cannot of itself deliver a competitive edge. It has to be used to support a competitive strategy.

The information infrastructure: promises and realities 360
Donald A. Marchand, IMD
Answers to ten key questions about the implications of the 'information superhighway' for the business world.

Contributors

Donald A. Marchand is Professor of Information Management and Strategy at IMD. His research interests include the strategic role of IT in enterprise transformation and business process redesign.

Xavier Gilbert is Professor of Business Administration at IMD.

Introduction

Information is increasingly the lifeblood of any organization and the management of information and the use of new information technologies such as management information systems is now an important part of any manager's job.

The Information Management module aims to give both an overview of the issues involved in this important subject and techniques for improving information flows and control.

The module begins with a section on the management of strategic intelligence using new technology and continues with coverage of corporate information cultures, information technology and strategy, and global information infrastructures.

Managing strategic intelligence

■ **What a company needs to know about its business environment to plan for the future needs to be disseminated organization-wide.**

by Donald A. Marchand

One of the basic challenges that faces a company's senior management is creating a new mindset about the future in order to anticipate trends. The challenge is that the existing mindset contains the company's knowledge about customers, competitors and industries and is usually the basis of the company's current success.

How does a company decide on a change of direction before it is too late to achieve it? How does a management team learn about the future and anticipate trends before a crisis looms, making it difficult for the company to respond? How do senior managers resist the temptation to assume that past explanations of success are still reliable indicators of the future? If a company operates on a global basis, how do its management teams make the continuous assessment of economic, social and political trends around the world that influence the company's views about future risk and success?

Managing change successfully begins with the *willingness* to anticipate the future – to develop foresight about future opportunities. This is often motivated by a need to learn but also by a fear of failure – a deep feeling that there is a continuous risk of misjudgment. Complacency bred of past successes leads to unexamined assumptions, blind spots and taboos that not only block the creation of new mandates among managers but make it very difficult to sense, communicate and use intelligence about future trends. It should not be surprising that managers wait for alarm bells to go off before they seriously consider alternative paths to the future.

What strategic intelligence is and is not

Companies have historically used several different approaches to develop foresight and intelligence about future trends. Some, such as oil company Shell, have relied on a strategic planning group to carry out research on future trends and have used their findings in developing scenarios tied to the corporate strategic plan. Others, notably consumer products companies, look to their marketing department for surveys on customer needs and market trends.

Many larger companies, pharmaceutical producers for example, entrust the monitoring of future trends to the corporate or R&D library, which collects and distributes published information such as new technology assessments. Still others call on specialist research companies or market forecasters on the assumption that these outsiders bring fresh information and form unbiassed views on product and market trends.

While many companies still use one, or a combination, of these functional approaches to learning about the future, it is clear that leading companies are now making a different set of assumptions about strategic intelligence. They no longer view it as a function at all but rather as a process for systematic learning – a continuous business activity concerned with shaping the future and providing a way consistently to challenge corporate blind spots, hidden assumptions and taboos.

And there is another difference. The traditional approach draws on the military model of operational intelligence built around a group of key specialists who prepare analyses as a basis for senior management decisions on major issues such as mergers and acquisitions. The new model, however, sees intelligence as a general-management responsibility that must become part of the learning culture and behavior of managers throughout the company.

Strategic intelligence can, therefore, be defined as follows: it is what a company needs to know about its business environment to enable it to anticipate change and design appropriate strategies that will create business value for customers and be profitable in new markets and industries in the future.

Strategic intelligence should not be equated with 'competitor' intelligence, which is focussed on a company's existing competition. Nor should it be confused with 'competitive intelligence', which is prepared by small groups of 'intelligence analysts' working for senior executives to help them make key decisions such as whether to enter a joint venture with a specific company.

The value of strategic intelligence comes from improving the capabilities of managers and workers in a company to learn about changes in the business or industry environment which will require rethinking business practices. They must then share their perceptions, new information and insights wherever in the company such information is needed. The challenge for strategic intelligence is to increase the 'intelligence quotient' of all managers and employees in a company rather than to assume that a monopoly of intelligence about competing in the future rests with a particular function or specific senior executives.

The 'process' vs the 'functional' view of strategic intelligence

If strategic intelligence is a business process rather than a function, what are the value-creating steps in that process? How are mental models and data converted into information and knowledge that managers can act upon?

In the functionally oriented company, there are many pools of external and internal intelligence that the functional departments already collect and sometimes use in making decisions. For example, the sales department collects information on customer contacts, transactions and services; the marketing department surveys market trends and customer satisfaction; the R&D group analyses technology developments and new product ideas; the manufacturing function focusses on process innovations and product engineering; the information technology unit monitors IT industry trends and technical developments; and the human resource department monitors workforce changes and recruitment.

Strategic intelligence in a functionally oriented company is often confined to these isolated pools of data to which specific groups apply their existing mindsets concerning the company's direction and strategies for success. There are three barriers to sharing and using strategic intelligence to shape the future.

First, the pools of data are shaped by the functional view of the company rather than a broader, general-management view. Second, interpretation of the data is affected by hidden assumptions, blind spots and taboos about the company's past successes, current directions and extrapolations about the future. Third, until recently there were no effective software and document-management tools such as Lotus Notes to facilitate the sharing of pools of intelligence among geographically dispersed managers.

The good news is that the power of Lotus Notes and similar software for the management of semi-structured, text-based information provides the opportunity for new approaches to collecting, sharing and using strategic intelligence laterally among groups of managers and employees. The bad news is that most companies that have purchased thousands of copies of Lotus Notes for their managers and employees have yet to use this functionality in the program, choosing instead to use it as a fancier form of e-mail and document-sharing facility. Planners, marketing staff, librarians or competitive intelligence specialists continue to act as the storekeepers and the gatekeepers of intelligence data.

It is not surprising that many managers in functionally oriented companies have either adopted a military model for intelligence gathering and handling, or that they perceive the value of strategic intelligence as limited to areas such as acquisitions, competitor assessments and new technology evaluations. In these companies

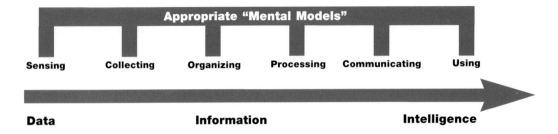

Figure 1

strategic intelligence has been largely confined to the top of the organization and rarely been used to meet the needs of other levels of managers.

In contrast, the 'process' view is based on a very different set of assumptions. First, not all knowledge or decision-making responsibility lies at the top of the company, and strategic intelligence should be organized to address the needs of business-unit and other general managers.

Second, sharing strategic intelligence rather than processing it centrally encourages a diversity of interpretations and views about the future. This is a critical assumption where changes in industries, markets and customers are occurring so rapidly that no single group of senior executives can cope with the diverse signals from the business environment nor properly factor them into new mindsets about future business strategies and opportunities.

Third, software such as Lotus Notes and global networks for managing and sharing documents make diverse sources of internal and external intelligence accessible to teams of managers acting on common problems and issues anywhere, anytime.

Fourth, the current challenge is not to confine strategic intelligence to the top of the company but to distribute it broadly, in line with the more lateral approaches to delegating responsibilities for action. In this context, strategic intelligence should be part of a company's fundamental culture rather than being grafted on as another function.

Creating value through the strategic intelligence process

The cross-functional view of the strategic intel-ligence process contains six major activities. Figure 1 shows how each of these activities helps to add value to intelligence and influences the creation of value in the subsequent activities.

- *Sensing* involves identifying appropriate external indicators of change.
- *Collecting* focusses on ways of gathering information that are relevant and potentially meaningful.
- *Organizing* helps structure the collected information in appropriate formats and media.
- *Processing* involves analysing the information with appropriate methods and tools.
- *Communicating* focusses on packaging and simplifying access to information for users.
- *Using* concentrates on applying information in decisions and actions.

Each stage can involve a mix of general managers, staff and functional specialists. As a result, the entire process is only as good as its weakest link and is strongly influenced by the mental models or mindsets that are shared by those involved. Asking the right questions from a decision-making point of view effectively determines the capacity of the rest of the process to generate useful intelligence. Moreover, looking at the six stages as a cross-functional process provides a basis for strategic benchmarking of best practices related to the process itself as well as to the outputs of the process in terms of information quality, speed of delivery, cost of production, and flexibility to accommodate continuous change.

Organizing the process

There is no one best way to organize the strategic intelligence process. In some companies, and for certain types of decision-making performed by

Figure 2: Competitive intelligence process: two approaches

Key dimensions	Centralized approach	Decentralized approach
1 Information Culture	Control	Sharing
2 Future Orientation	Intelligence for Key Decisions	Open to Learning & Unlearning
3 Structure	Vertical	Lateral
4 Process	Highly Focused	Highly Interactive
5 Scope	Oriented to Senior Management	Broad Management Learning
6 Time Horizon	Short - Medium Term	Medium - Long Term
7 IT Role	Operational	Strategic
8 Organizational Memory	Centralized; Narrow Band	Open; Broad Band

the chief executive, a centralized approach is appropriate. For other companies, a more distributed approach is preferable with processes being developed among communities of managers sharing business-unit, geographical or customer-oriented roles.

Perhaps it is simplest to think of these approaches as opposite sides of a continuum. There are likely to be many variations between individual companies as to the best method of centralizing or decentralizing their strategic intelligence process. These will be driven by their need to anticipate change and develop strategies fast enough to invent the new business before the inevitable decline of the current business. As shown in Figure 2, different assumptions about the value of strategic intelligence to the company create key differences between the more centralized approach and the more distributed approach:

- The information culture is control-oriented on a need-to-know basis, rather than one in which sensitive information is freely shared inside the company and perhaps with suppliers, customers and other stakeholders. How far do senior managers 'trust' their colleagues to use strategic intelligence appropriately?
- The future orientation tends to focus strategic intelligence on key decisions where specific trade-offs are being made, as opposed to developing a culture of enquiry, learning and anticipation of future changes in mindsets and critical trends. The traditional 'military' model tends to be linked to key competitive moves rather than to continuous sensing of the company's environment in situations of high uncertainty, complexity and risk.

- The structure of the strategic intelligence operation is more vertical with divisional groups feeding information to a corporate unit for review and interpretation. In the distributed approach, a more lateral organization enables information to be shared among managers in overlapping teams or groups with constantly shifting boundaries.
- Professionals are involved at every stage, whereas in the distributed approach high quality strategic intelligence results from interactivity among different but overlapping communities of managers and employees.
- The strategic intelligence organization is oriented almost exclusively to senior management needs rather than aiming at building management learning competence throughout the company.
- The approach to strategic intelligence is short- to medium-term, as opposed to medium- to long-term with managers seeing it as playing a part in shaping the company's future.
- The role of IT is more operational since fewer people are involved in the strategic intelligence process. In the distributed approach, the role of IT can be strategic as companies develop standardized network-oriented approaches to sharing information and as software is developed for sharing information among diverse communities of managers. It is interesting to see Unilever and other companies buy thousands of copies of Lotus Notes for their managers to foster cross-functional communication and intelligence sharing.
- The organizational memory is highly controlled and narrowly focussed. In the distributed model, organizational memory is preserved across the company and is wider in

coverage based on the needs of large numbers of managers acting in groups, task forces and teams. In addition, the software makes the updating and packaging of organizational memory much easier it is simply a keystroke and mouse function rather than a paper duplication and mailing operation.

Ultimately, a company's approach to organizing the strategic intelligence process will be strongly influenced by its view of process management, its organizing principles, its learning style and its values.

It will also be strongly shaped by the seemingly paradoxical view that a company anticipates the future best, not by controlling intelligence and creative thinking among managers, but by opening its intelligence processes to managers and employees, thereby encouraging diversity of assumptions and mindsets about the future. While this may fly in the face of those who think of intelligence processes as secretive, only available on a 'need to know' basis, it is more consistent with the view of the company as a continuous learning organization that has a robust culture for collecting, sharing and using diverse sources of strategic intelligence to shape its future.

Winning the future with strategic intelligence

The purpose of strategic intelligence is illustrated in the Sigmoid Curves in Figure 3. Sigmoid Curves have long been used to illustrate the product cycle of a company where a new product or service is launched, goes through a period of rapid growth until the market matures and the success of the company declines. Unless a company is able to develop another new product or service to reach new markets and customers to start another journey along the Sigmoid Curve its growth and profitability as well as its competitive position will suffer.

The main objective of strategic intelligence is to avoid the situation at Point C where a company may see the future clearly but cannot

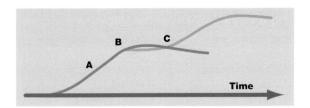

Figure 3: Using strategic intelligence to anticipate change

respond fast enough, or has to use repeated waves of restructuring and downsizing to bring its capabilities in line with the shift to new products and markets as represented by the second curve.

The intent is to use the time between A and B to create a strategic intelligence capability that can develop a range of inputs on the complex and dynamic changes that a company is experiencing, and to anticipate the next wave of change and market opportunities before the competition. The key to making the process successful is to develop a robust process where strategic intelligence is sensed, processed, communicated and used.

At the same time, it is essential to create a culture where a diversity of mindsets are explored, tested and selected so that the company is capable of rapid navigation in market conditions that are constantly shifting.

Summary
Many companies still use one or a combination of different functional approaches to monitor future trends. Leading businesses, though, increasingly see strategic intelligence (to be distinguished from 'competitor' intelligence and 'competitive' intelligence) as a process for systematic learning. The new model requires it to become part of the culture and behavior of managers throughout the organization. There are key differences between the 'distributed' approach and a more centralized approach to this issue.

What is your company's information culture?

■ **Aligning the way a company handles information with its strategy is a key task for managers.** Donald Marchand **explains the various types of information cultures and the strategies for which they are appropriate.**

This question in the headline may sound strange, but one of the critical elements in a company's efforts to manage change is its information culture. This can be defined as the values, attitudes and behavior that influence the way people sense, collect, organize, process, communicate and use information.

There are three principal reasons why the task of shaping the information culture should be on a manager's agenda today. First, it is no longer just part of the overall organizational culture. More and more companies recognize the need to transform themselves in their industries and markets. To shape the future involves understanding what the future is likely to look like, which in turn requires the assimilation of diverse sources of business, market, political, technological and social information.

Second, while information technology makes it easier for companies to network and share information among managers and employees, it is important to look at the way people actually use that information. Simply making work-stations, networks and multimedia capabilities available to thousands of managers and employees does not automatically increase intelligent use of information in an organization.

Third, information cultures can vary among functions, departments and teams with different impacts on how people sense, collect, organize, process, communicate and use information. As a result, many managers would agree that information cultures are important in shaping strategy and implementing change, but they are uncertain how to influence the way their employees use information to achieve results.

Metaphors for the corporation and hidden assumptions about information cultures

Metaphors to describe the company often contain hidden assumptions about what information cultures are acceptable. By encouraging the use of metaphors, managers communicate how information should and should not be used.

Four metaphors for the company are frequently used today. One of the most influential is military. Management language often describes the company as an army unit where better command, communication, control and intelligence about the competition can ensure success. A variation compares the chief executive to an American football quarterback who guides the team up the field with set plays and well-established roles. Another version is management writer Peter Drucker's view of the company as orchestra, all reading the same musical score under the guidance of the conductor. All three indicate an information culture strongly based on control and 'the need to know.'

Another powerful image is the corporation seen as a machine. Here, the focus is on problem solving as a key to acceptable organizational behavior. Company processes are often referred to as needing fine tuning or repair. This metaphor has produced the notion of 're-engineering', where a company's structure, methods and information flows are candidates for elimination, simplification, redesign or automation.

A third metaphor is an organism that responds and adapts to its environment. This biological view is powerful in describing team behavior where members search for, share and adapt to external and internal information to develop responses to change. It is best illustrated by situations in which the company must respond to an external crisis in a new way. Shell's change of position on sinking its North Sea oil platform in the Atlantic is a good example of adapting to outside signals and pressures.

Managers sometimes describe their company, department or team as a soaring eagle, a fleet-footed gazelle or a steely-eyed hawk. Each metaphor contains assumptions about how people will develop, use and act on the information needed to perform their tasks.

The fourth metaphor for the corporation is the brain. The company is viewed as a network of neurones capable of flexible, agile and innovative use of information and knowledge. The 'networked' organization anticipates and creates innovative paths to shape future success. This metaphor has gained support from managers who see the company as a 'learning organization' and implies an information culture focussed on developing new, innovative products or markets, or radically redesigning the terms of competition. A recent example is Microsoft's efforts to enter the online information service industry and the video industry simultaneously.

Four information cultures

Four common information cultures exist in companies today (see Figure 1). Each one influences the way people use information – their information behavior – and reflects the importance that company leaders attribute to the use of information in achieving success or avoiding failure.

First is the *functional* culture, where information is used as a way to exercise influence over others. This culture is most closely associated with companies that operate in a command and control hierarchy where the functional division of labour is reinforced by the 'need to know' approach to information sharing.

The information behavior associated with this culture is control. Here the term is not used as a negative but to describe a necessary part of any company's activities; many business processes are used for control in areas ranging from

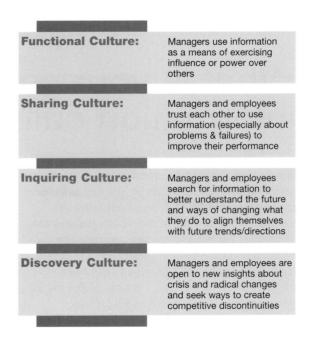

Functional Culture:	Managers use information as a means of exercising influence or power over others
Sharing Culture:	Managers and employees trust each other to use information (especially about problems & failures) to improve their performance
Inquiring Culture:	Managers and employees search for information to better understand the future and ways of changing what they do to align themselves with future trends/directions
Discovery Culture:	Managers and employees are open to new insights about crisis and radical changes and seek ways to create competitive discontinuities

Figure 1: Information cultures defined

accounting to procurement. The issue is whether control is a positive aspect of the company's culture or whether it breeds inflexibility and inward-looking behavior.

ABB, the Swiss-Swedish engineering firm, is well known for its corporate financial reporting system covering all its 1,600-plus business units worldwide. To operate a global company with so many business units and a relatively small corporate staff requires managers to appreciate the importance of supplying accurate and complete performance-related information. Without a positive view of the need for control, ABB would be unmanageable.

In a *sharing* culture, managers and employees trust each other enough to use information to adapt and improve processes and performance. The open sharing of information about actual or potential failures is necessary for problem solving and adapting to change. However, many companies have launched Total Quality Management or Business Process Redesign initiatives while at the same time informally penalizing managers and employees who expose failures and errors. On the other hand, some companies, such as Bose Corporation, view information about failures and defects as a precondition for successful change. They find that sharing information among teams and functions, and with customers and suppliers, helps to remove problems and achieve greater product and process improvement.

In the *inquiring* culture, managers and employees try to improve their understanding of future trends and determine how they can best change to meet the challenges ahead. The dominant information behavior is anticipation.

In many companies today, there are pockets of an inquiring culture in activities concerned with customer sensing, market research, competitive intelligence, technology assessment and R&D. However, in many industries, such as semi-conductors or software design, these are insufficient. Constant vigilance is needed from everyone in the company from the CEO down. Intel's CEO, Andrew Grove, says 'only the paranoid survive' because changes in product capabilities in the semiconductor industry are so rapid – less than 18 months – and production investment for a new chip-manufacturing site is so great: $1.5bn to $2bn.

Fourth is the *discovery* culture. Here, managers and employees are open to new ways of thinking about crisis and radical change. These companies deliberately shed old ways of doing business and seek new perspectives and ideas, aiming to create new products and services that redefine competitive opportunities for companies across markets and industries.

Microsoft is radically redefining the traditional view of a software company in order to compete simultaneously in online information services, entertainment production and video distribution. The company is not merely anticipating or adapting to change but rethinking and altering the basis on which it will compete in software and other industries. While many companies may have pockets of discovery culture focussed on competitive intelligence, new product design, creating business scenarios, partnering with customers and suppliers, or forming strategic alliances, only a few, like Microsoft, make it an integral part of their strategy.

Dysfunctional information behavior

The converse of the information behavior

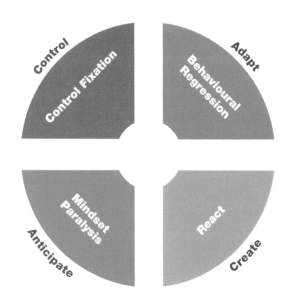

Figure 2: Dysfunctional Information Behaviors

mentioned above includes several kinds of dysfunctional information behavior. These can actively undermine a company's response to market and industry changes, or resist change-management initiatives.

Many companies have launched TQM (total quality management) programs with the intention of making continuous improvement an integral part of their business strategy, but have retained a control culture concerning information about defects and failures. TQM initiatives are often still-born because senior managers foster the wrong information behavior to support the idea or they encourage dysfunctional information behavior during the change process.

As Figure 2 indicates, there are four types of dysfunctional information behavior.

In companies with a *control fixation*, managers do not seek new information when new problems arise but employ more of the same control-oriented information they have always used. For example, in a declining market, a company's corporate leadership requests more detailed accounting and financial control-based information when the real issues of decline have to do with customer defections, mature products or potential new market entrants. At some point, almost all big companies develop control fixations that not only take up a great deal of senior management time but reinforce a defensive, wait-and-see attitude among employees.

Behavioral regression exists when managers facing new problems ask for even lower levels of information. Common examples include the senior manager who, experiencing a sudden downturn in company performance, announces that travel expenses will be submitted in more detail and reviewed by him. Or the CEO who becomes defensive and ignores customer input on product performance because these products were developed 'on his watch'.

Mindset Paralysis occurs when accepted ways of using information block a manager's ability to alter his approach to doing business or anticipating change. In a company that had experienced several years of downsizing and cost reduction, the CEO rejected a capability-building investment plan with strong long-term potential for growth. The mindset he had developed through several years of cost reduction was blinding him to new opportunities to invest.

In other cases, a long history of corporate success, such as General Motors and International Business Machines enjoyed in the 1970s and early-1980s, reinforces the existing company culture and blocks the perception of new products and competitors. Although senior executives in these companies were shown information that challenged their existing market strengths, their mindset did not let them view this information in a different context.

Companies in the *react* mode that are facing crises and radical industry threats tend to respond with 'Fire, Ready, Aim!' Managers immediately develop 'action plans' before they really know whether these actions will make matters worse or better.

Aligning information cultures to a change in strategy

I often ask two questions of participants in IMD executive development programs: 1) What are the dominant information cultures and types of behavior you encounter? 2) How well aligned are they with the business and change-management strategies in your company or business unit?

Invariably, these questions trigger intense debate, since the majority realize that their information cultures are often mis-aligned with their strategies and expectations. Many executives indicate that their companies are facing unprecedented changes in their markets and customer expectations, yet acknowledge that their dominant information behavior is control. Others have been promoting TQM programs in the business units, yet admit they are a long way from having a sharing culture among managers and employees in which errors and failures can be constructively addressed.

Still others have successfully implemented a sharing culture for continuous improvement, but recognize that for their company to survive over the next three to five years will require a more radical shift, towards anticipatory and creative information behavior.

In recent years, Nokia, the Finnish telecommunications group, has gone though a radical restructuring of its core business, selling off businesses that were mature and building new businesses in cellular phones, tele-communications services, and multimedia products. Today, Nokia must foster cultures of inquiry and discovery to compete successfully with larger firms such as Motorola and Ericsson, to invent new products as product cycles are radically shortened, and to stay ahead in R&D by focussing on new technologies with strong market potential.

The Nokia example illustrates three important indications of whether executives have the right information cultures, and whether their information behavior is aligned to their change strategies. First, a company must assess which types of information behavior it should promote in order to address different levels of uncertainty and complexity in its markets and industries (see Figure 3).

In mature and stable markets where uncertainty is low, and complexity of the products and processes is also low, *control* behavior is suitable for monitoring errors and problems.

When market uncertainty is low, but product and product complexity are high, a *sharing* behavior is required, aimed at continuously

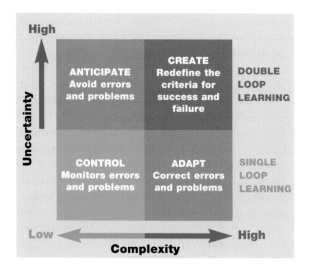

Figure 3: How uncertainty and complexity influence information behaviors

correcting errors and problems through TQM or related initiatives.

Where market and industry uncertainty are high, but product and process complexity are low, *inquiry* culture behavior can help avoid errors and problems in business or product strategies when competitors are changing and new entrants to the industry are threatening.

When both market uncertainty and product/process complexity are high, the company needs a *discovery* culture, redefining the terms of success and failure. Control, adaptive and anticipatory behavior will not succeed when the pace and scope of change are so dynamic.

Second, a company must evaluate its information behavior relative to the growth/maturity of its markets and products, shown by different positions along the S-curve (*see* Figure 4).

Entrepreneurial companies launching new ventures typically have a discovery information culture. After a few years, they generally develop an inquiry culture as they encounter larger or more established competitors. Then, as the company's new products or services succeed, a sharing culture allows continuous defect and problem correction. Finally, as the company's products mature, a control fixation leads to decline and the company starts to rethink its core businesses and competencies.

At this stage, the company must adopt a dual strategy: managing its day-to-day business while promoting a discovery culture that will develop new market opportunities and products. Nokia has done this over the last three years.

Third, a company must determine whether its information cultures and behavior are achieving appropriate results. In their early years, entrepreneurial companies can design organization and business processes aligned with their strategy, hire new managers and employees who fit the culture, and set up an IT (information technology) infrastructure that can foster the desired information behavior. In an established corporation it is more difficult.

Few large companies are so centralized that one dominant information culture operates consistently throughout. Much more typical are companies with a culture that varies between corporate headquarters and the business units,

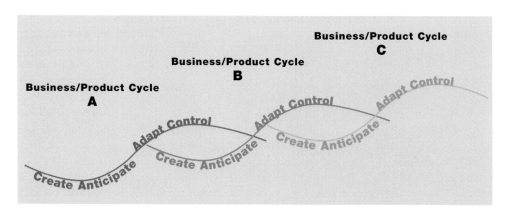

Figure 4: Aligning information behaviors to cycles of business growth/maturity

as well as between growth-oriented and mature units. The challenge is to achieve the right balance of information cultures to match the company's position in the market. Five years ago a well-known European electronics company had an information culture dominated by the manufacturing and product-design function. Control and adaptation were the dominant types of information behavior. Today, the company has moved to anticipation and creativity and become more market- and customer-oriented.

Managing information cultures

Managers face considerable challenges today in aligning information cultures and behavior with their business and change-management strategies. First, they must treat the information and knowledge flows of the company as 'visible' rather than invisible assets. Second, they must not assume that the IT infrastructure will resolve this problem operating within the existing information cultures and behavior. If anything, as computer and communications networks provide the tools for using information and knowledge for competitive advantage, how and why employees use that information will become more important. Third, knowledge workers will be more attuned to the managerial attitudes that influence the way information and knowledge is used. They will find it easier to recognise dysfunctional information behavior in managers or information behavior that is out of line with the company's professed cultural values or business goals. Fourth, companies that are the first in their industries to align their information cultures and behavior with their business and market strategies will derive a competitive advantage.

Managers have to treat the handling of information and knowledge as a distinct core competence in the company. They will need to answer several key questions:

● What are the sources of information and knowledge that provide a sustainable competitive advantage in their businesses?
● How do the company culture, organization and practices currently influence information cultures and behavior?
● Does the company have the right mix of information behavior and cultures to manage change successfully today and in the near future?
● What gaps in capabilities and competencies must managers address to align their information culture with their business and market strategies?

It is the unique responsibility of managers to address the critical issues that affect the present and future competitiveness of their business. In today's information-based companies, one of these critical issues is the alignment of information cultures and behavior with business and change-management strategies.

Summary

There are four common information cultures in companies today: functional, where information is used to exercise influence over others; sharing, in which managers and employees trust each other enough to use information to adapt and improve processes and performance; inquiring, where they try to improve their understanding of future trends; and discovery, which requires an openness to new thinking about crisis and radical change.

It's strategy that counts

■ **Information technology cannot of itself deliver a competitive edge. IT has to be used to support a competitive strategy, explains** Xavier Gilbert

Many companies find information technology (IT) is not delivering the promises made on its behalf. Although its capabilities have often been oversold, IT is not the culprit. Technology cannot rescue conventional strategies that attempt to adapt to change through a protracted sequence of moves. Successful strategies lead change – with speed as an essential instrument. Speed-based strategies fully leverage IT.

Speed as a strategic dimension

Many companies develop innovative products but fail to secure a sustained competitive advantage. They only have a product. Other elements of the competitive formula are missing. The distribution system is not adapted to the product or to the level of service required. The market has been insufficiently segmented and marketing lacks focus. Production systems are adapted from previous products although the competitive conditions may be different.

These missing elements will eventually appear, as the need for more value or lower cost is imposed by competition, and when the company's different functions get their act together. This generally happens by instalments: first the engineers, then the marketers and later the 'bean counters'. These 'piecemeal' strategies can barely respond to industry change. Clearly, they cannot lead change, which demands imposing a new competitive formula on competition, and turning a one-time head start based on innovation into durable competitive advantage.

Real innovation comes not from a new product alone, but from a competitive formula – product design, manufacturing approach, marketing focus, channels and service. The new formula imposes on the company's industry a more attractive balance between the perceived value and delivered cost of the offer. Such a formula must be implemented in one stroke, rapidly, for competitive advantage to accrue.

Value-based strategies and cost-based strategies are normally mutually exclusive. Speed, however, is a lever to increase perceived value without increasing delivered cost, or to reduce delivered cost without losing perceived value. Speed works on both sides of the perceived value/delivered cost competitive equation. Faster response to the market boosts perceived value. It also requires a more fluid organization with less red tape – a cheaper organization.

The new winners leverage their innovative competitive formulas with speed. They obtain market feedback continuously and rapidly. They rapidly adapt their competitive formula to such feedback. New products are developed rapidly. Manufacturing processes and channels are tuned to maximize throughput speed.

Examples of the effects of the 'virtuous circle' of speed abound. A widely publicized study by McKinsey & Co demonstrated that a new product reaching the market six months behind schedule has already lost 36 per cent of the total profit potential available over its life cycle. On the other hand, if the new product reaches the market on time but development costs were 50 per cent above budget, the total profits are reduced only by 3.5 per cent. Toyota, Nissan and Honda, can develop a model within 24 months, on average. It takes 36 to 48 months for GM, Ford and Chrysler. At the same time, development costs for a Japanese model are $1bn-$1.5bn, compared to $3.2bn-$4bn for a US model.

Speed of response is not possible with conventional organizational approaches where the different specialized functions can only intervene sequentially, in a form of 'buck-passing' exercise. Speed of response requires multidisciplinary teams, which use a common information base to trigger action rapidly, coherently and simultaneously in a whole range of different functional areas. IT can be a formidable ally in achieving this type of co-ordinated progress.

Operating information systems

Corporations often seem to hope that IT will transform their 'piecemeal' strategies into winning propositions. But since these strategies are built on a protracted sequence of conventional moves drawn from the standard repertoires of the separate, unco-ordinated functional areas, IT can only improve the effectiveness of the operating systems within each function.

Operating information systems help the various functions perform some of their specialized tasks. A cost accounting system helps accountants value inventory. A sales system records sales and prepares invoices. A production system schedules production. Even when the sales and production systems are connected, operating tasks are usually the focus. And even when an application is quite innovative, like airline reservation systems, it is still, conceptually, an operating system. Operating information systems are necessary, but they cannot be expected to do what they were not designed for. Because they focus on specialized tasks, they cannot help multidisciplinary teams share the same information, to recognize an opportunity and respond rapidly and coherently.

Competitive information systems, on the other hand, focus on information needed to build and sustain a competitive advantage. This information is multidisciplinary. It is the nervous system that co-ordinates the functions involved simultaneously in the implementation of a competitive advantage. Competitive information systems link several operating systems and 'polarize' them toward competitive advantage. Operating information systems help an organizational unit do its job right. Competitive information systems help several units do the right job implementing a competitive formula.

The conceptual distinction between competitive information systems and operating information systems is often missed, resulting in dis-illusionment with IT. But the real fault is insufficient thought given to developing a competitive advantage. Many try to apply IT without the strategic foundations needed to think in terms of competitive information systems.

The 'competitive' approach

Competitive information system implementation must start from the competitive formula. The competitive formula depends not on the exceptional strength of one function or another but on effective relationships between several functions. Without these relationships, the competitive formula falls apart. These relationships constitute the *key success factors* of the formula.

Ikea's competitive formula relies on a rapid adaptation of its product line to market demand. Fast and effective logistics are a key success factor. To respond to demand, furniture kit parts made by subcontractors must be ordered, shipped and regrouped in the right store at the right time. A lot of different functional operating information systems must be brought under the umbrella of a competitive information system that will focus them on a 'fast response, low inventory' formula.

Information clusters

Each key success factor is supported by an 'information cluster'. The cluster retrieves and processes the information on which a key success factor depends. For Ikea, sales information must be collected at the point of sale, compared to inventories, compared to the manufacturing plan, and fed to a warehouse or subcontractor for action. Because a competitive formula normally relies on several key success factors, it will also require several information clusters.

Information clusters consist of *databases* and *applications*. A database may reside within a computer, in paper files or in people's memories. A database includes the information needed to achieve a particular key success factor. This information should be systematically identified and related to the decision and action points associated with a key success factor.

Applications are the processes by which information is collected, processed and fed into the decision and action points associated with key success factors. Applications may be computerized, mentally performed by an 'expert' or calculated on the back of an envelope. Applications must also be identified systematically to construct an overview of the information cluster required by a particular key success factor.

Competitive information systems do not focus on IT but on the competitive formula, its key success factors, and the related information clusters. These topics require no understanding of IT. But they do demand an understanding of the competitive advantage pursued by the company. This understanding is the responsibility of operating management. Should there be a gap in this understanding, EDP (electronic data processing) cannot, and should not, fill it. In general, observations show it is not IT that is lacking, but strategic thinking.

Whose job is it?

Applying optimal IT to a well-understood competitive formula remains a difficult task, however. Selecting systems or designing applications is not really the problem, although this choice is complicated by rapidly changing technology and by 'expert' dogmatism, which is directly proportionate to uncertainty over the technology's future direction. The main impediments to the implementation of competitive information systems, however, come from three other sources.

First, when a competitive formula has been selected, the link to information clusters remains difficult to establish. As the fish is not aware of the water it swims in, the information user is often not aware of the information he actually uses. Establishing this link demands a complete grasp of the competitive formula and its key success factors. This overview of how the company competes and how IT can be applied to the competitive formula requires a high-level, general management perspective.

Second, competitive information systems are investments that cannot be justified using traditional criteria. They involve investment in a change process to train people within the organization to compete differently than they have in the past. Decisions on these information systems require more judgment and vision than pencil pushing. They must be made at a high level in the organization, with the full involvement or back-up of top management. This investment is an authentic strategic decision, not because of its cost, but because it is at the heart of the competitive formula. Hardware is a minor element of the total investment.

The third difficulty in getting competitive information systems implemented results from intra-organizational confrontation between two IT cultures. Decisions about competitive information systems do not rely much on 'understanding bits and bytes'. They can rarely be made by a company's EDP department, which frequently will have a bias resulting from past technology choices and applications. Designing competitive information systems requires a fresh mind and a willingness to question (naively) what is taken for granted – qualities rarely found among technology specialists.

The lead role in implementing competitive information systems requires:
- understanding the selected competitive formula and its information implications;
- an overview of new IT capabilities;
- an absence of inhibition or bias towards this area.

This role is increasingly played by the 'chief information officer', a new type of position, or by members of 'strategic development' units, another new organizational development. In both cases, these are fairly senior staff who have a thorough understanding of the competitive advantage pursued by the company, who are on the lookout for opportunities to reinforce it through IT, and who can make a synthesis between the two, not only conceptually, but also at the interpersonal level.

A competitive advantage?

IT alone is rarely sufficient to gain a durable competitive advantage. A high-quality fountain pen is insufficient to write a high-quality novel. Starting from technology and looking for places to apply it is likely to produce bad novels and bad corporate strategy. IT only helps the exploitation of opportunities generated by competitive formulas. Technology is widely available but creative competitive formulas using response speed to provide an innovative offer and catch competitors on the wrong foot are not.

Summary

Innovation allied with speed of response is the new competitive weapon. But rapid action requires multi-disciplinary teams with a common information base. Operating information systems are necessary but cannot do this. Competitive information systems focus not on IT but on the competitive formula, its key success factors, and related information clusters. Problems arise in linking these clusters if traditional criteria are used; and if a questioning mind is not applied to the decision.

The information infrastructure: promises and realities

■ **Donald Marchand answers ten key questions about the implications of the information superhighway for the business world.**

For many managers and executives today, it is difficult to make a realistic evaluation of the impact the global information infrastructure (GII) will have on their industry and company.

Navigating between the promises of business transformation and the realities of markets and customers leaves many frustrated and fearful of unexpected developments or competitors who may turn their industry upside down. On the other hand, many managers recognize the pace and scope of the GII's impact will vary in different parts of the world. So the perception of the future is heavily influenced by where it is made.

In discussions with hundreds of general managers who attend IMD executive development programs each year, I have developed a list of ten questions that they should ask themselves in thinking about the evolution and impact of the GII on their business and industry.

What is your working definition of the GII?

The global information infrastructure really involves pronounced shifts in national information infrastructures (NIIs). They will change from highly monopolistic and regulated operations to more competitive and privatized companies that can compete across borders and traditional definitions of the telecommunications industry. Today's marketplace is highly influenced by three key developments:

● The digitalization of data, voice, images and text has blurred the boundaries between the telecommunications, computer, media and consumer electronics sectors. The collapse of these traditional boundaries has caused a flurry of alliances, acquisitions and deals between companies trying to exploit potentially lucrative, yet risky, business opportunities in the redefined global information industry.

● Competition is increasing between different forms of infrastructure provided by cable, phone, wireless and satellite companies. This is due to deregulation in developed markets and to new 'green field' opportunities in emerging markets. For example, competition remains intense among Western European and North American telecommunications, computer and wireless companies for market share in countries such as the Czech Republic, Hungary, the Ukraine and Russia, with joint ventures being formed even among existing competitors.

● The GII is increasingly seen as a 'network of networks' where it is important to be able to operate seamlessly between networks and among diverse media such as digital voice, data, text, images and sound. This capability is critical in seeking industry standards for interconnection and the transfer of content over diverse networks.

Thus, the GII is broader in scope and impact than the Internet, although the latter is a powerful prototype for the GII and a driver of its popularity around the world. Indeed, the Internet and the World Wide Web with their millions of users have become the testbed networks for many new forms of interactive information services and transactions such as 'electronic cash' and electronic retailing.

Is the GII a global, regional or local development?

Despite its name, the focus of the GII is not exclusively global. It will emerge differently in various countries and regions of the world and will be strongly influenced by trading cultures and local opportunities for business and economic development. In this sense, the GII will evolve on a local and regional basis.

Variations in the pace of evolution of NIIs raise concerns in less-advanced countries. Since commercial investments in these countries are likely to be smaller and slower than NII investments in more developed countries, they fear they may be left out of the GII and lose its anticipated benefits.

While this is a serious issue for the poorest countries in Africa and parts of Asia, for many other developing countries such as China, India, Indonesia and Malaysia, the pace of information infrastructure growth is likely to accelerate. It will be driven by intense competition among global telecommunications, wireless, satellite and computer companies to invest in these emerging economies with currently low rates of technology use.

What 'content' will create new markets for interactive, digital services?

This is perhaps the most interesting and provocative question a manager can ask about the GII. To date, the evolution of the GII has been driven by supplier-push rather than demand-pull. There are four reasons for this:

● The deregulation and privatization of public telecommunications has been motivated by the desire to increase competition in services and stimulate demand for them. In the US, for example, the annual volume of local and long-distance calls since the break-up of the Bell System has more than doubled. A large part of this growth in traffic and revenue is due to lower prices for existing services and the offer of new services.

● Added value in the communications and computer industries has moved from hardware and network access to software, services and information content. Yet companies such as IBM, AT&T, British Telecom and others have often found difficulty in offering consumer information services that generate the same level of profits as their more mature businesses.

● While there has been a flurry of merger and acquisition activities among entertainment, media and consumer electronic companies, the markets for their products are not currently large enough to fill the gap between the available communications and technological capacity and the demand for new 'content' services.

● Even in industries such as banking and financial services, the demand for online banking and access to consumer account information has been weak or concentrated in specific niches such as computer-literate professionals in consumer markets.

For the next three to five years, new services offered by *suppliers* will continue to drive the development of consumer markets. This is in contrast to business markets, where *demand* for communication services with business-oriented content is growing rapidly.

How will intellectual property be protected and a 'fair return' on investments assured?

These issues represent two of the most important constraints on the evolution of 'content services' over the GII:

● National and cultural standards regarding intellectual property differ significantly around the world.

● The EU is currently exploring the co-ordination of copyright laws and policies among member states to avoid barriers to the flow of content across borders.

● The rules for intellectual property protection are neither uniform nor equally enforced, as illustrated by the dispute between the US and China over software and CD-Rom duplication.

● The tracking of online dissemination and use of intellectual property, as well as the capability to collect payment, is not well-developed in interactive networks. This is especially true of the Internet, which was never intended to be used for commercial purposes.

How will standards governing the communications, applications and services for the GII keep up with technological and commercial changes?

Many experts believe that standards for the GII can no longer be set by consensus or negotiation in international standards bodies since these procedures are too slow and inflexible.

On the other hand, the establishment of de facto industry standards by the key players is also unsatisfactory since these will tend to reflect and support some companies' dominant positions in the market, for example Microsoft's dominance of the PC market through its Windows operating system.

How will the security and confidentially of transactions and communications be provided?

The multimedia capabilities of the World Wide Web on the Internet have demonstrated the vulnerability of intellectual property and the lack of confidentiality on global networks. In addition, as competition intensifies among service providers in many countries, the security of financial transactions over online networks may be jeopardized by organized crime and by hackers.

The social and economic benefits of being able to transact business anytime, anywhere pose serious challenges to law-enforcement authorities when electronic commerce crosses legal and jurisdictional boundaries. Clearly, international agreements and organizations to protect electronic commerce will have to be put in place over the next five to ten years as more criminal elements learn to exploit the openness and instant availability of large commercial and consumer networks.

How 'universal' will interactive services be over the GII?

In many countries, PTT authorities have established standards for 'universal' services for voice communications. However, as more countries deregulate and privatize their telecommunications, the coverage and funding for universal services may decline.

In addition, the definition of what is covered by universal service may change as individuals demand not only basic phone services but also computer workstations, modems and software to access the Internet or public and private providers.

How will governments raise the revenue to subsidize universal service? Will the future definitions of universal service create groups which feel left out of the world of electronic commerce and communications?

What is an appropriate timetable for the evolution of the GII?

Many forms of broad-band multimedia services will not be available at an affordable price until well past 2000, although some of these services are already being used by certain classes of individuals and businesses. The timing of service availability will vary for several reasons:

● NIIs will not be deregulated or privatized at the same time in all countries, and modernization will take place at different speeds.

● In most of the less-developed countries, the

technologies to deploy inexpensive digital services will be installed over the next five to ten years.

● The necessary investments in telecommunications infrastructure will be very significant and must compete for funds with other infrastructure investments. The Asian Development Bank, for example, recently estimated that countries within its region will have to spend $150bn (£95bn) to upgrade their telecommunications infrastructures to developed-country levels, while, at the same time, they will need to invest almost $300bn on their transport, power and water systems.

● The evolution of standards for intellectual property protection, security and confidentiality will require serious efforts at multilateral cooperation among governments and industry groups before these standards are effectively employed.

Who will be the new winners and losers in the global information economy?

Many of today's mergers and acquisitions are based on assumptions that markets and revenues will grow to cover the cost of these deals and establish new sources of profitability.

However, although many of the large companies involved have deep pockets, it is clear that not all the mergers and acquisition ventures will be profitable. Repeated tests of interactive video services in the US have yet to achieve any profitability for companies, such as BellSouth, that have piloted them.

In addition, many companies will select technology options that may not succeed in local markets or may turn out to be uncompetitive. In Finland today, cellular phone services for businesses and consumers are rapidly replacing traditional copper wire services. On the other hand, new companies such as Netscape may succeed beyond their wildest dreams as their software products are incorporated into large, global and regional networks.

What is clear is that the factors that produce success and failure are rapidly changing, and forecasting which companies and joint ventures will succeed is a high-risk activity.

How will societies, cultures, and governments adapt to the emerging realities of the GII?

There is a strong tendency today to condemn any movement to control, slow or block the evolution of the GII as irrational, reactionary or repressive. But, clearly, local differences in cultures, government policies and religious or ethnic values will have a significant influence on access to the GII and on its content services.

For example, recent debates about pornography on the Internet and World Wide Web have raised important questions about the regulation of content on these networks. Not all cultural and social-value conflicts over the evolution of the GII will be irrational or driven by questionable political motives; some will reflect genuine concerns about the preservation of diverse values, attitudes and behaviors. These differences will also influence emerging business opportunities on the GII and directly affect markets and services.

The development of the GII is both revolutionary and evolutionary. Over the next five to ten years the global shift of the telecommunications infrastructure in developed and less-developed countries will cause revolutionary, long-term changes in commerce, social communication and governance. On the other hand, the GII will also evolve in many local contexts and offer new opportunities to reshape markets and services in industries and trading regions. The development of global and local information infrastructures has as much potential for good and for bad as the advent of the superhighway in the 1950s and 1960s.

Summary

The global information infrastructure (GII) is broader in scope and impact than the Internet. The GII will evolve on a local and regional basis – in many developing countries the pace of information infrastructure growth will be driven by global telecommunications and computer groups. New services offered by suppliers will continue to drive the development of consumer information markets; in business markets, by contrast, demand is growing rapidly. The rules for intellectual property

protection are neither uniform nor equally enforced. An important question is whether standards can in future be set by consensus or in international bodies. Organized crime and hackers pose a threat to the security of financial transactions over online networks.

The coverage and funding for universal services may decline, creating groups which feel left out. The timing of service availability will vary from country to country. Forecasting which companies/joint ventures will succeed is highly risky. Local differences in culture will have a significant influence on access to the GII.

Business Ethics

Contents

Marketing an ethical stance 368
Thomas W. Dunfee, The Wharton School of the
University of Pennsylvania
'Social cause marketing', in which companies identify
themselves and their products with a particular social
or ethical stance has proved a powerful tool. But is it
ethical?

Gifts, grease and graft 371
Jack Mahoney, London Business School
When is it ethically correct to accept a business gift
and what is the moral difference between offering a
bribe and bowing to extortion?

Buyer beware: are marketing and
advertising always ethical? 375
Jack Mahoney, London Business School
It may be legal and honest but is it decent, when the
odds seem to be stacked against the consumer?

Discrimination and privacy 379
Jack Mahoney, London Business School
Discrimination on grounds other than job-relatedness
is obviously wrong – but what actions to take to make
sure it doesn't happen?

Contributors

Thomas W Dunfee is Kolodny Professor
of Social Responsibility at the Wharton
School of the University of Pennsylvania.
His current research interests focus on
social contract theory and business
ethics and on developing ethical
standards for business transactions.

Jack Mahoney is Dixons Professor of
Business Ethics and Social
Responsibility at London Business
School. His books include *Teaching*
Business Ethics in the UK, Europe and
the USA (1990) Athlone, London, and he
is founding editor of the Blackwell's
quarterly *Business Ethics: a European*
Review.

Introduction

As one of the articles in this module spells out, the subject of business ethics is often the butt of weak jokes. Yet if the concept of studying this topic seems strange to some managers they need only remember the many examples of corporate scandals that have filled the business press in recent years.

Even if one ignores the ethical considerations involved and adopts a purely realpolitick approach, business ethics remain important because of their impact on business. Ethical investment trusts, employee issues such as discrimination and sexual harassment, and consumer response to environmental concerns all have a direct effect.

The four sections of the Business Ethics module cover all these issues – from social cause marketing, corruption, advertising and marketing to privacy and discrimination.

Marketing an ethical stance

■ **'Social cause marketing' has proved a powerful tool. But is it ethical? And what has business got to do with such social and moral issues anyway?**

by Thomas W Dunfee

Social cause marketing is riding high in the 1990s. Consumers support firms on the basis of their identification with preferred social causes. Organizations in the US such as Business for Social Responsibility and the Social Venture Network provide a forum for managers and owners who believe that acting ethically and being identified with certain social issues will yield long-term business success.

Yet in spite its of apparent successes, social cause marketing still faces critical, unresolved questions. How should corporate performance be judged? What constitutes 'ethical' practices? What are the limits? Is any cause that sells in the market place legitimate? Does social cause marketing 'politicize' business? And is it consistent with the basic role of business?

Critics argue that business ethics is too abstract and disconnected from business realities to be able to provide practical guidance in defining ethical practices. Others adopt the Milton Friedman position that social cause marketing can only be justified when it maximizes returns to shareholders.

From another tack, strident moralists who see ethical issues in striking black and white refuse to accept that managers are qualified to judge social causes. 'Everyone knows what is right and wrong,' they assert, labeling anyone who disagrees with their views as 'unethical'. They are highly suspicious of the ability of business managers to make judgments about social causes and they suspect their motives when they do.

Finally, there are those who view any

business interest in ethics as highly politicized; as a surreptitious method for advancing a nefarious political agenda.

In seeking to answer these charges and questions, it is first necessary to look more closely at the phenomenon of social cause marketing. It involves companies aligning themselves with popular social issues in order to induce customers to prefer them over their non-aligned, 'plain vanilla' competition.

Positive association

Companies such as international cosmetics chain Body Shop and ice cream producer Ben & Jerry's receive substantial free media publicity as a result of their identification with popular social issues. Consumers respond to the opportunity to purchase products or services consistent with their social preferences, even paying a premium over competing products. Identification with popular causes is also good for employee morale and recruitment. Employees who feel a positive association with their employer's publicized values are more likely to be loyal and happy.

The Body Shop is a prime example. It has aligned itself with the 'green' and animal rights movements, among others. Strategies include directly associating with organizations such as the Friends of the Earth and Greenpeace and prominently featuring displays and brochures supporting its preferred social causes in its outlets.

In addition, it has developed specific programs such as Trade-Not-Aid to implement developing-world sourcing of ingredients. Anita Roddick, its flamboyant founder, rejects Friedmanism by proclaiming: 'I don't have any duty to share-holders at all', while vaunting the organization's charitable contributions and social causes. The causes are presented as worthy and not merely as a merchandising strategy. Body Shop products are carefully positioned to be consistent with the company's social image its 'natural' products sold in reusable containers.

The success of this approach contributed handsomely to the rapid growth of the Body Shop during its early years. Free publicity stemming from media coverage of the social issues substituted for advertising, while the marketplace reaction validated academic claims of consumer preferences for companies clearly identified with popular social causes.

Recently, though, this engine of success has been threatened as the Body Shop, Ben & Jerry's and other companies practicing social cause marketing have come under attack in parts of the media for not living up to their own self-touted standards. Critics challenge claims that Body Shop products are genuinely 'natural' and allege that the Body Shop practices a double standard on its important issue of animal rights. Similar questions arise about the significance of developing-world sourcing for products and the levels of charitable contributions made by the company.

Ben & Jerry's is criticized for causing arterioscleroses in farm pigs (they provided waste ice cream products to local farmers to include in swill) and for not providing adequate benefits to indigenous peoples through their program for sourcing in rain forest regions.

Higher standards imposed?

The reactions to these charges among the supporters of the corporate social responsibility movement have been mixed. Some have argued that higher standards should be imposed on companies that engage in social cause marketing. Companies that promote themselves as particularly socially responsible should, in the eyes of this group, have impeccable records to support their claims.

Others are concerned about the tendency to single out for criticism organizations that, in their view, are at least trying to do the right thing. The criticisms often seem picky (certainly there is a lot of leeway in the definition of 'natural' products). Supporters of social cause marketing are afraid that if businesses

practicing it are automatically held up to a higher standard of scrutiny than is typically applied to marketing claims, it may discourage many from taking even minimal steps to be socially responsible. They fear that an intense 'hypocrisy inquisition' may have the perverse effect of driving out any semblance of the true social responsibility faith.

There is some merit to these concerns. One potential response to anticipated adverse publicity is for companies to become guarded about disclosing their efforts to implement ethics programs or support popular social causes. If organizations become secretive about their ethics programs out of fear of the hypocrisy watch, the programs themselves may suffer.

Is social cause marketing compatible with the basic role of business? Consistent with the anti-hero nature of the early-1990s, critics of the social responsibility movement may scoff 'at baby boomers who graduated from Beetles to BMWs and want to go out and buy Rainforest Crunch ice cream and think they've done their bit'. Although we have all met people who make this reaction understandable, marketplace sovereignty should extend to all types of consumer preferences. Individual consumers are fully entitled to select products and retailers on the basis of alignment with their personal social preferences.

They may, if they wish, pay more than the competitive price or accept inferior products because of social preferences. One might try to persuade social cause consumers that they are not acting 'rationally', but ultimately it is their choice. Social cause consumers may also choose to boycott a firm because of its record of harming the environment or because of its identification with a disfavoured social issue.

Such consumers may even boycott agnostic firms that fail to engage in social cause marketing. The fundamental rights of liberty possessed by all humans guarantee this broad range of choice. Social cause marketing only succeeds when sufficient numbers of consumers are willing to make market choices based upon their social preferences. So viewed, social cause marketing is essentially both democratic and strongly consistent with consumer sovereignty. More broadly, social cause marketing is an essential ingredient for a working market place of ethics in which individuals are enabled to act consistently with their ethical and social preferences. Consumers are free to refuse to do business with those companies they consider unethical and loyally to support those they view as moral exemplars. As a consequence, representations of companies' social positions and of the social characteristics of their products should be treated comparably to traditional marketing representations about products and characteristics. Whether or not products are natural or packaging is recyclable is important to a certain set of consumers. Misrepresentations of social characteristics mislead those consumers into acting inconsistently with important, even cherished, personal values, thereby causing consumer injury in the same manner as a car that fails to live up to what the manufacturer says about fuel consumption.

Social representations engendered by companies as part of their marketing strategy should be evaluated in the same manner as other 'seller representations'. When coarse misrepresentations are made, for example that containers are recyclable when in fact they are not under the most common usage of the term, then the actions are clearly unethical.

The fact that some actions can be defined as unethical does not immediately require, as some seem to believe, that there be an external enforcement mechanism to enforce morality. Instead, in a manner consistent with the European Union's eco-management and audit scheme, a better approach to the problem of deceptive social cause claims is to encourage and allow voluntary programs in which organizations may disclose information concerning social positions and practices through designated channels that can serve to enhance consumer confidence in the information. Trustworthy third-party certification schemes should be particularly effective in this domain.

The media plays a special role in social cause marketing. As mentioned earlier, an important advantage of such marketing is the ability of companies to ride free media publicity as a substitute for expensive advertising. Instead of formal advertising campaigns, companies that engage in ethical marketing attract publicity through press releases, highly visible speech making and the social activities of senior corporate executives.

As the conduit for this benefit, the media has a special obligation to ensure that claims are reasonably legitimate. Journalism that questions companies prominently engaged in social cause marketing is a healthy development. Informed consumers will provide adequate enforcement of morality in most instances.

Although much of the attention to social cause marketing has been in reference to businesses that identify themselves with liberal social causes, the phenomenon works in all directions. Some organizations identify themselves with conservative social causes, by sponsoring conservative talk shows or by identifying themselves with specific positions, such as those taken by the pro-life movement in the US. Both conservative and liberal think tanks push ethical agendas.

This is fully consistent with a marketplace of social preferences. Communities and members within communities have substantial moral free space in which to define for themselves the ethical norms they would like to see guide economic activities. The marketplace for social preferences empowers individuals to be able to act consistently with their social preferences. It allows for the establishment of collective community norms of preferred behavior through purchasing behavior. On the other hand, there are, and should be, clear limits as to the range of community norms that can be actualized through such a process. Limits may be found in what may be described as 'hyper-norms' – universal norms reflected in a global convergence of social, political, religious and philosophical thought. For example, anti-Semitism is not a legitimate basis for social cause marketing.

Social cause marketing is an important component of the marketplace for morality and allows individuals to express their moral preferences. Individuals must often confront the specific context of a decision before being able to formulate their ethical preferences.

Judgments pertaining to ethics are often bounded by informational and time constraints in the same manner as are economic judgments. Bounded moral rationality exists in the same manner as bounded economic rationality. Social cause marketing is a means by which individuals may act within the moral free space of their communities to generate social contracts of ethical norms.

So long as these norms are consistent with hyper-norms, this is a healthy and legitimate enterprise. Consumers should be free to boycott or prefer suppliers based upon identification with social causes.

Summary

Social cause marketing still faces unresolved questions. An important component of the market place, it provides a means for individuals to express their moral preferences. The free publicity which contributes to its success, has been overshadowed by a 'hypocrisy inquisition' with suggestions that companies do not live up to their standards. Trustworthy third-party certification schemes can be effective, and the media has a special responsibility to verify claims.

Gifts, grease and graft

■ **When is it ethically correct to accept a business gift and what is the moral difference between offering a bribe and bowing to extortion?** Jack Mahoney **tries to offer an answer.**

Like most human activities business often needs some form of social and human lubrication to make its machinery run smoothly. As that most sociable of people, Dr Johnson put it: 'A man should keep his friendship in constant repair.' And in business this can take the form of entertainment, gifts, mutual favours and other expressions of respect and friendship.

Handling gifts and entertainment
In themselves such actions can be quite innocent. On the other hand, they can also have an ulterior motive when their aim is to secure preferential treatment in business. Signals that this is happening can take various forms, including the scale of the gift or entertainment, which may on occasion be well beyond what the recipient is accustomed to and which he or she can find flattering to the ego.

Another signal that undue influence is being attempted can be the absence of any special reason for the gift or celebration, although paradoxically sometimes particular circumstances, such as Christmas time or a promotion or a family event, can also provide an occasion to look to one's ethical defenses. Sometimes, too, there can be a suggestion of shared secrecy or of a transaction that no one else need know about. And frequently danger bells can start ringing when the giving or entertaining is all one-way and there is no question of reciprocity or of returning hospitality or giving.

In handling entertainment and gifts two fundamental questions need to be near the front of one's mind, quite apart from the obvious ones about not infringing the law or stated company policy. First, try to be quite clear about the motive behind the offering, which may not be good for one's self-esteem. The second is a sober realization of how one's power or influence may be solicited or expected in return for favors received. In addition, experienced businesses and business people have also produced a number of rules of thumb for handling gifts and hospitality that can usefully be borne in mind. First comes strict respect for one's company policy, which might require outright refusal, declaring anything received or explicitly accepting it for charity, or which might stipulate accepting and giving presents of only nominal value. Companies that have a code of conduct for staff invariably give a prominent place to this 'conflict of interests'.

Account can also be taken of what is accepted practice or etiquette in a particular region, market or industry. In some cultures an exchange of small gifts is a normal and necessary prelude or accompaniment to conducting business; in others, as in the UK, some expressions of public corporate hospitality have become accepted practice and have the merit of transparency.

Not a few individuals, however, and even some companies, have misgivings about increasing lavishness in corporate hospitality and about the public and even shareholder image it can create. As a result – and not just because of the recession – they have begun to retrench or simplify in this area.

One pragmatic suggestion about accepting gifts is that they should be limited to what one can consume within 24 hours – although this may depend on one's capacity. Other lines of reaction include declining while trying gently to make clear the need to avoid even the appearance of conflicts of interest or even accepting (for once) while intimating that receipt will not influence one's independent judgment.

Other considerations could well include the need to set a good example to others, especially to junior or new colleagues, asking oneself what others would think if they knew or discovered what was happening, and the wisdom of seeking advice when in doubt.

Bribing for business

Adam Smith once wrote that when people in the same line of business get together conversation almost invariably turns to ways of conspiring against the public. That may be rather too sweeping a view to adopt, but what does appear generally true is that when business people get together with ethicists the conversation soon turns almost inevitably to the subject of bribery in business.

It was the Lockheed bribery scandals in the US that helped cause the rise of modern business ethics in that country as well as resulting in the Foreign Corrupt Practices Act (1977), which made bribery of major overseas officials by US citizens a criminal activity. In the 1970s the UK had its Poulson affair affecting local and even national government. The network of corruption which emerged led to a royal commission and the resulting requirement for MPs to list their business interests. Italy, Spain, France, Ireland, Germany, Japan, Russia, Belgium – the list of bribery scandals appears almost endless and causes major and mounting concern about the prevalence of the practice.

In these circumstances, trying to take an ethical attitude to bribery based on moral integrity, whether on the part of a company or of individuals within it, appears almost a lost cause. Much, indeed, is made of the pragmatic approach that bribery is unavoidable for successful business when everyone else engages in it and it is part of a local culture.

However, it is easy to state that bribery is universal (especially to explain failure) but perhaps less easy to establish. In any case its being a common practice in some area or region or industry does not justify it on ethical grounds, particularly if a government is opposed to it and trying to combat it. Even tacit official acquiescence – or collusion – in a practice on the part of government does not necessarily justify one ethically in following that practice. The comment has been well made that not only individuals but also particular societies can be 'ethically handicapped' in some respects. Slavery, apartheid, and racial and sexual discrimination are obvious evidence of the possibility.

A totally different approach to bribery is to be seen in those companies that simply refuse to have anything to do with paying bribes, although it may be salutary to recognize there can be a difference between sweeping policy statements at top level and actual practices on the ground. It might also be noted that refusal in principle to pay bribes is a policy that can be more easily pursued by large powerful companies, either because they can choose which markets to keep out of or leave or because they may have sufficient local clout to conduct their business without having to resort to paying for the privilege. The issue, however, becomes more acute ethically for smaller or less powerful companies and especially for local businesses that are strictly limited in the options open to them.

Facilitating payments

Is it possible ethically, then, to find a middle way between pragmatic moral fatalism and absolute refusal on principle? Can one identify a practical ethical approach to the subject that can take account of the circumstances and pressures in which companies can find themselves, especially in certain cultures?

Precisely because of the widespread concern and frequent moral discomfort that the subject arouses, the effort appears worth a try. In such an effort a useful beginning can be made by looking more closely at what the ethical issue actually involves.

We might define a business bribe as an inducement aimed at influencing an official to act improperly in the exercise of their duties, such as granting a contract unfairly, ignoring safety regulations, relaxing licensing or tax conditions, or otherwise giving preferential treatment for a consideration.

This, however, can prompt the reply that there are many so-called bribes that do not aim to influence officials to behave improperly or to do what they ought not to do. On the contrary, many bribes are aimed at inducing officials to do what they actually should be doing, whether it be issuing the correct documents in time, keeping goods moving, providing normal services or generally discharging the ordinary duties of their office. These are the payments that are variously, and accurately, described as 'facilitating' or 'commissions' or 'grease', for that is their purpose in some societies – to lubricate the business machine and keep its wheels turning.

Climates of extortion

Where such a practice and expectation is well-nigh endemic in a culture it prompts a further reflection: that what is involved is more accurately described as extortion rather than as bribery.

More than one Italian business leader, ranging from the automobile to the fashion industries, has claimed that regular payments over the years to local and national politicians were not a matter of bribery. It was a question of paying extortion as the only way to continue to conduct a legitimate business in Italian society. Obvious parallels can be drawn with paying 'protection money' in the US early this century or more recently in Northern Ireland and in parts of the former Soviet Union.

This enables one to recognize a broad difference between, on the one hand, tendering a bribe as an unforced offer of an inducement for unfair preferential treatment and, on the other hand, paying extortion simply as a condition for being permitted to conduct one's legitimate business in a particular society.

It is interesting to note that the International Chamber of Commerce observed in its 1977 report on the subject that 'the truth is that much bribery is in fact the response to extortion. Enterprises have too often had the experience, in many countries, of having to choose between giving in to extortion or not doing business'.

Working within such an analysis can enable us to identify conditions in which payment of bribes, such as forced personal or political contributions – which are really extortions – could on occasion be ethically justified. For one thing, they tend to apply across the board and may not therefore have the harmful consequences that bribes otherwise possess – that of buying preferential treatment not based on product quality and of thus undermining competition and market principles and expectations.

They do, however, have other wrongful features, such as violating the law and company policy (where these exist), creating extra costs for owners to which they might well object if they were aware, colluding in other people's dishonesty and profiting from it, and generally contributing further to the corruption of the society concerned and various of its members. For these reasons if extortion were acceded to, it seems it would have to be both unavoidable and reluctant.

It would have to be unavoidable in the sense that paying it really is the only way in which one can go about one's normal and legitimate business in that society. It would also have to be reluctant. This is not just in the obvious sense that one would rather not succumb to such blackmail or 'shakedown' but that it goes against the grain insofar as the business one is conducting is making a positive contribution to the local economy and society and is, one presumes, otherwise being conducted ethically.

It seems necessary to add, however, that reluctantly going along with extortion on these conditions would also imply a wish for conditions to be otherwise and would oblige a business to do what it could to bring that about by combating the practice. Otherwise it would be too easy to fall into the attitude of moral fatalism mentioned above. In other words, in such less than perfect situations doing the ethical thing may involve doing the best in the circumstances while also doing one's best to improve the circumstances.

Parallel problems

Interestingly, there are other problem situations in business similar to that raised by bribery and extortion that can confirm this ethical line of solution. Apartheid in South Africa was a case in point a decade ago. Today the violation of human rights or degrading local working conditions in various societies can raise ethical misgivings for companies wishing to do business in those societies.

These individual cases pose the general ethical question of whether one can ever be justified in doing business in or with a country that contains cultural features one considers ethically wrong. Some powerful business leaders and companies prefer not to be associated with such political or social conditions. Others may find it ethically acceptable to develop legitimate business interests there for good commercial and social reasons. These may include, for example, contributing to the local economy and opting for

a policy of steady influence and gradual economic, social and political improvement.

Such was the attitude of companies working in South Africa and applying the Sullivan Principles there to weaken apartheid from the inside, and such is the attitude adopted elsewhere by some members of the UK business branch of Amnesty International. The eventual bloodless dismantling of apartheid in South Africa may be an indication that work from within society is at least as necessary as pressures from outside to bring about major ethical improvements.

Reluctant compliance with local customs of bribery and extortion may be similar, provided attempts are genuinely made to combat them. Such attempts can include companies working either individually or in combination to mobilize business and public opinion to introduce bribery-free clauses and conventions, to encourage a free media, to press for bureaucratic reform of recruitment, salaries and procedures, and to campaign for local and international legislation and law enforcement.

If, in addition, such endeavours are made a condition of grants, loans and contracts, then much can be done to work towards a situation in which bribery and extortion become either unnecessary or impossible and business can flourish more freely.

Summary

When considering gifts or entertainment always consider two questions. What is the motive behind the offering, and how could your influence be solicited in return for favours? In some cultures an exchange of gifts is a necessary prelude to doing business, but there are also pragmatic ways of saying No (admittedly easier for big companies than for smaller ones).

The Lockheed scandal in the US and the Poulson affair in the UK shaped those countries' thinking on bribery. Just because the practice seems universal in certain countries, however, does not mean it can be justified on ethical grounds.

When bribery is a response to extortion – which it frequently is – there may be a stronger case for condoning it. However, instances would

have to be unavoidable and entered into with reluctance, resisting any hint of moral fatalism. The same goes for working with countries with cultural features one considers ethically wrong. Working from within society may be at least as necessary as working from outside to bring about improvements.

Suggested further reading

Extortion and Bribery in Business Transactions, International Chamber of Commerce, 1977.

M G Velasquez (1992) *Business Ethics: Concepts and Cases*, Prentice-Hall.

Buyer beware: are marketing and advertising always ethical?

■ **Marketing and advertising set out to inform. It may be legal and honest but is it decent, when the odds seem to be stacked against the consumer?** Jack Mahoney **looks at both sides of a complex issue.**

Marketing is fundamentally an ethically sound activity insofar as it aims to find and present ways of satisfying people's needs and wishes and thus of expanding their freedom and contributing to their personal and social fulfillment.

This centrality of the consumer, however, which gives a positive ethical tone to marketing as a function of business, also alerts us to his or her vulnerability in a relationship that is asymmetrical and unbalanced in favour of the supplier's information and other resources.

It was such considerations that led John F Kennedy in 1962 to propose the four 'consumer rights': to safety (security, including non-observable defects); to information (involving relevant knowledge and disclosure); to choose (amid the diversity available through competition); and to redress (or to be heard or compensated).

Production and pricing

The fundamental concern to respect individuals

and their interests generates ethical conclusions regarding the various aspects of marketing. Thus, market research should not only exemplify respect for honesty, accuracy and objectivity in dealing with people but should also have regard for their unique individuality, neither imposing on them nor invading their physical and psychic privacy.

Again, the process of acquiring corporate intelligence should desirably not have recourse to deceitful approaches or false interviews or to hiring away employees of other companies in order to gain access to their corporate secrets.

Product management should routinely take account of safety factors, including health warnings and tamper-proof and child-proof packaging. It should be careful to provide information about important product qualities, including their contents and ingredients, and to give due and timely notice of any replacements or improved products that are being planned.

Ethical respect for the recipients of business's attentions also affects product differentiation and innovation and will include not only the honesty and genuineness of differences being developed but also the deception involved in reducing the size of a product while keeping its price fixed and various features of packaging, including slack and wasteful packaging.

Environmental sensitivity 'from the cradle to the grave', involving raw materials, production processes and disposal and recycling of products, should mean more from the ethical point of view than sales gimmickry and should honestly reflect the increasing environmental sensitivities and expectations of customers and society at large. Companies wishing to present an ethical profile in their marketing will also take care to provide channels of customer reaction and redress, including prompt product alerts and recalls when necessary.

Many of these ethical conclusions are straight-forward enough. But probably one of the most difficult ethical issues in marketing affects the pricing of products and in settling on what should count as a 'fair' price or as a 'reasonable' return on costs.

If the word 'profiteering' has any meaning, it implies that there are ethical limits to what price one can set for a product. The ways in which various sales practices are described clearly presupposes the possibility of overcharging and thus of taking unethical advantage of customers and others.

Predatory pricing to ruin a competitor, collusion in price fixing by members of an industry, objections to price maintenance in such commodities as books and non-prescription medicines, price discrimination in different parts of the market, and price 'gouging' (i.e. exploiting people's needs) all imply by contrast that there is such a thing as a fair price. On the other hand, prestige pricing may be a matter of ethical indifference, when luxuries or an elite segment of the market are concerned and individuals may be thought quite capable of looking after themselves in their pursuit of non-necessities.

Perhaps this indicates that a crucial factor in considering the ethics of pricing non-luxuries lies in competition and the possibility of customer choice that it offers. In other words, to suggest that an ethical price for necessities is simply constituted by what people are prepared to pay must depend on what choice is available to them. This may be answered in terms of how great their need is for the product and of whether they have the opportunity to shop around and purchase it at a competitive price.

Making informed choices

Possibly the area of marketing that is most ethically sensitive in ordinary business activities, at least in the eyes of the public, is that of advertising. As we have already noted, this is fundamentally an ethically sound activity. It is a valuable feature of society and of business in drawing attention to goods and services that are available to satisfy people's needs, desires and wishes. It expands human freedom by increasing choices; it can inform, stimulate and entertain; and mostly it is 'legal, decent, honest and truthful', as the International Chamber of Commerce observes.

It also contains an ethical tension which is the basis of most of the moral issues that can arise in advertising. On the one hand the potential customer seeks information in order to make an informed choice. On the other the potential seller seeks to persuade in order to make a sale. The ethical trick may be how to combine sales influence with respect for the individual's freedom of choice and exercise of personal responsibility.

If respect and support for the individual in their freedom of choice is at the heart of ethical advertising, this involves two major conditions about his or her power to exercise choice: that it be adequately informed and that it be unforced and freely exercised.

First, to be 'informed' takes us into the area of knowledge and communication about various goods and services that are on offer. Here there can be no substitute for customer awareness of the true state of affairs about products and the options available. Obviously unethical behavior is found in inducing ignorance or error through lying, deliberate misrepresentation and serious omission.

However, there are also less obvious problem areas in the matter of providing appropriate information. What counts as 'appropriate'? Total disclosure about a product can raise costs and can also result in information overload that defeats its purpose. Yet concealment, omissions or the withholding of relevant information would materially affect the customer's purchasing decision. Presumably the acid test is whether the aim of an advert is to provide the most useful information to help the consumer make a reasoned choice.

This still begs a question about 'usefulness', of course, but it is a good question, and one to be kept continually in mind. For example, it can be used to apply particular ethical scrutiny to small print disclaimers, press 'advertorials', TV 'infomercials', exaggeration, puffery and generally inflated claims for goods or services as part of an enquiry about whether they help or hinder informed choice.

There is, of course, the old Latin maxim, *caveat emptor*, or 'let the buyer beware', to indicate that customers have their own responsibility to be adequately informed and to take obvious precautions, including seeking expert advice, and so on.

There is clearly much point to this observation, which bases ethical considerations on what is sometimes called the 'reasonable consumer'. Such a person might reasonably be considered able to read adverts with a wary eye, aware of possible conventions and harmless exaggeration. Alongside this, however, one has also to take into account the presence of what can be called 'market illiterates', particularly when the market in particular expensive commodities is increasingly complex, as it is in the case of computers and financial services.

In addition, there may be particular markets or segments, children, for example, which cannot be expected to be sufficiently intelligent to assess information or to have sufficient presence of mind to make sure they are adequately knowledgeable and therefore in a position to make a truly informed choice. This, of course, is why many people have serious ethical reservations about advertising aimed directly or obliquely at children.

Consumer freedom

Consumer choice that is fully human is the ideal towards which advertising should ethically aim. This means that such choice must be not only informed but also unforced, that is, free from 'undue pressure'. Again, there are areas where what counts as undue pressure is not always obvious.

One may be clear enough about physical coercion or about wearing customers down through sheer exhaustion, as has been alleged of some time-share sales agents. It is also interesting that widespread rejection of subliminal advertising arises from concern that influence is being exercised, literally, 'below the threshold' of people's consciousness, which is thus regarded as an invasion, not now of their physical, but of their psychic privacy.

The same may be said of manipulating people in the sense of getting them to do something without their being aware of it or of why they are doing it. For example, how ethical is it to encourage impulse buying?

Yet there must also be a place for due influence, as in any human interchange. There is thus ethical scope for exercising influence on other people on a rising scale, beginning with straight information and proceeding to suggestion, advocacy and persuasion, before reaching the unethical extreme of manipulation.

Playing on people's feelings and emotions to influence their decisions and choices and to secure their agreement and consent is a normal part of social interaction. After all, we are not computers, to the possible despair of economists, and our choices are not based simply on rational or logical grounds. They are also influenced by our feelings of being attracted or repelled by something on offer, or by a presentation, package or advert highlighting its power to satisfy our various needs.

This is the basis of contending that one is really selling satisfaction and states of mind rather than simply goods or services: well-being, and not just a package holiday or a designer suit; security, and not just insurance or a warranty; even beautiful feet or sexual confidence, and not just shoes or cosmetics.

Problems arise, however, if emotions are being exploited or if impressionable and vulnerable sectors of society are being targeted, such as immature children, despairing sick people and socially insecure ethnic or age groups. In such cases the ethical risk is that what is at work is manipulation rather than persuasion.

Perhaps a clue to this is an absence of the sales resistance and robust skepticism that might normally be expected of consumers. Some critics of advertising methods, however, would go further and fault the whole industry on the grounds that it is in the business of arousing dissatisfaction and of creating unnecessary or undesirable needs in people.

Yet this seems more an observation about culture than about advertising. For there is a place in human living not simply for satisfying inborn animal needs for food and protection but also for satisfying acquired human needs and tastes that are culture-inspired and part of socialization, including needs for a variety of goods and services of a pleasing kind, standard and promise.

A further defense of modern advertising presents it as an expression of art, operating according to recognised conventions of presentation, enjoyment and appreciation, and sometimes indulging itself and its viewers in harmless fun and entertainment.

The point is well made and yet it is also worth bearing in mind that humour has a powerfully disarming effect. Moreover, whatever else it sets out to do there is no doubt that in laying out its wares advertising ought to respect persons, personal priorities, preferences and ethical values. Possibly, too, individuals need to remind themselves regularly that not all our needs, wants, desires and wishes have to be satisfied. There is always room in life for what one American described as the tragedy of the excluded alternative. And certainly there is much scope in schools for critical consumer education.

On a wider canvas there is little doubt, also, that in the explicit and implicit values and views of life and relationships that are portrayed regularly in the fantasy world of advertising (the perfect kitchen, family, body and so on) there is a danger of sending misleading or highly selective signals to its recipients.

Part of the 'social responsibility' of business, then, must lie in the authenticity and fidelity with which in its advertising it portrays reality, as well as the respect which it and the rest of marketing show for individuals and their responsible autonomy.

Summary

The satisfaction of consumer needs provides a positive ethical tone to marketing – but the consumer is also vulnerable. A difficult issue is what constitutes a 'fair' price – predatory pricing, price discrimination and 'gouging' all imply that there is such a thing.

Advertising is also fundamentally sound from an ethical point of view, provided the consumer is adequately informed and free to choose. Problems arise if emotions are being exploited or if vulnerable sections of society, such as immature children, are being targeted. Corporate social responsibility is at stake.

Suggested further reading:

Laczniak, Gene R. and Murphy, Patrick E. (1993) *Ethical Marketing Decisions*, Allyn & Bacon.

International Chamber of Commerce *Marketing Codes, including International Code of Advertising Practices*, Paris 1987.

Discrimination and privacy

■ **Discrimination on grounds other than job-relatedness is obviously wrong – but what actions to take to make sure it does not happen?** Jack Mahoney **discusses some prickly issues.**

There is quite a lot of discussion in the UK and other countries these days about what business is for and whether its sole aim is long-term profitability or whether it also has responsibilities, perhaps sometimes overriding, towards its various stakeholders and to society at large.

One way to approach the question of what a business is for is to recognize that the answer depends on who is asking the question, whether it be the shareholders, management, customers, suppliers, workers or local communities. All, in fact, have different expectations of a business and see it performing different functions depending on their own interests and projects and involvement in it.

In particular, the men and women who are employed by a company will have their own expectations of it. These expectations obviously include the financial consideration of providing a living, but many individuals also look for some measure of personal fulfillment, job satisfaction and a pleasant work environment with congenial colleagues.

In fact, it can be argued that individuals who invest a large part or a major proportion of their lives in a particular company are morally entitled to have some expectations about how they are treated by, and in, that company.

Many conditions of employment are, of course, covered by legislation in such areas as health and safety, equality of opportunity and conditions of dismissal. Many other aspects of working life, however, even when not legislated for, are heavily dependent for their success and observance on the practical application of ethical values and norms.

Much of this ethical approach to people in their work environment comes down to a fundamental respect for individuals and to a regard for their basic human rights. This article highlights two issues and their ethical aspects that can arise within an organization: its attitude to discrimination in appointments and promotion, and its attitude to respecting the personal privacy of employees.

Discrimination

The topic affecting the human rights of individuals that is most prominent in the news at present involves discrimination in employment policy and the place of reverse discrimination, particularly in the light of the current backlash against it in the US and the continuing debate about it in Europe.

The latter half of this century has witnessed a growing sensitivity to the presence of racial and sexual discrimination in western society in general, and this applies also in business, not only in stereotypes in advertising and sales, but also in recruitment and promotion and, recently, in laying off employees.

The basic meaning of discrimination is to make a distinction. No one can take ethical exception to distinguishing or discriminating between people if it is done on the grounds of appropriate qualifications and criteria. Clearly there are working situations where such factors as abilities, qualifications, sex, race, age and so on are job-related and can justifiably be taken into account in making appointments.

On the other hand, such decisions become wrongful discrimination against someone if they are based on criteria that are non-job-related and on characteristics of color, sex, caste, nationality, religion, disability and age that are simply not relevant to the post to be filled.

Discrimination can take a variety of forms in any organization. At its simplest it is individual when it is practiced unchecked by prejudiced members of the organization.

However, it can also be structural as a result of conditions of appointment or promotion relating, for example, to educational successes or previous experience or other requirements. Sometimes such qualifications may actually be unnecessary for a particular job or type of job and then they can, either by accident or deliberately, screen out members of certain classes or groups that may not meet those over-demanding conditions of appointment.

Finally, discrimination can also be occupational when it reflects a common presumption that certain people or, more accurately, certain classes of people are capable of performing only certain tasks and not others, and of filling only certain jobs in society or in a company.

It is easier to marshal arguments against unfair discrimination than it is to identify what should or can be done about it. The unjustifiable economic and other harm inflicted by such behavior on individuals and their dependants, and even their descendants, are obvious enough. Less obvious perhaps, but no less real, can be the opportunity costs to business of limiting its pool of potentially valuable employees. And it is not necessary to spell out how deep-rooted practices and policies of unjust discrimination can have a serious impact on society in terms of alienation, resentment and sometimes violent reaction.

Other deeper ethical arguments against the practice arise from realising that stereotyping people according to one shared characteristic simply ignores their personal differences and their individuality and dignity, as well as denying their basic human equality and refusing to grant recognition to their freedom of access, opportunity and choice.

Possible remedies for the individual and collective ills created by discrimination in business can apply to the past, the present and the future. So far as concerns the past, the attempt to make amends in terms of compensatory justice, especially over the years or the generations, runs into insuperable difficulties. How to identify who are, or were, the actual victims of harm done and who are, or were, the perpetrators of that harm? How 'guilty' were they? And what form could compensation take and who is responsible for arranging or providing it?

Positive discrimination

Controversy surrounds one hitherto rather popular line of solution, described variously as positive or reverse discrimination. This involves deliberately redressing the balance in favour of groups currently suffering from present or past discrimination by appointing members of such groups, even though more qualified candidates are or may be available.

Reasons urged in favour of such policies include the ethical obligation to make restitution to those now suffering from past wrongs, to exact such recompense and punishment from those who are now unfairly profiting from such wrongs and eliminating future discrimination. Often an additional factor urged in support of positive discrimination is that other attempts to remedy the situation are inadequate or are simply not working, so that desperate measures are required and may perhaps need to be applied only for a period until a fair balance has been secured.

Yet such a sweeping remedy of now discriminating in favour of classes or groups that were previously discriminated against does not take into account the fact that not every member of such a group may have suffered, nor the fact that not every member of a group against which it is now proposed to discriminate has profited from such previous unfair preference.

In fact, a program of reverse discrimination is a blanket policy of applying criteria that are not job-related. As such it suffers from exactly the same ethical defect as the situation it is meant to remedy and only creates new victims in its attempt to recompense earlier ones.

Moreover, the 'tokenism', rather than merit, which is involved in such appointments carries with it a risk of low self-esteem and respect from others, endangers the morale of individuals and workforce and can produce general disillusion and resentment.

Affirmative action

A suggestion that often accompanies recourse to a policy of reverse discrimination is to set and aim at filling 'quotas' of hitherto unrepresented groups. This estimating of representative percentages and setting a figure to be achieved in a set time has been popular until recently in public policy in the US, although it is illegal in the UK.

It suffers from the basic discriminatory defect of not considering individuals in their own right and on their own merits for particular positions. Less potentially unjust, however, is the suggestion of setting less specific 'goals' to remedy a current inequitable situation. It is easily rejoined that since they involve only a vague promise to improve and set no firm target or quota at which to aim, such goals are in danger of being ignored. On the other side, however, if there is an accompanying deter-mination to monitor situations regularly, then the setting of anti-discriminatory goals can be one stage in a wider program of steps to be taken.

Sometimes such a proposal, which does not go as far as positive discrimination, is termed affirmative action. Confusingly, sometimes affirmative action is taken to mean the same thing as positive discrimination, but here it is understood as planning and executing deliberate, institutional and ethical steps to remove imbalances and discrimination from business once and for all.

So understood, a corporate program of affirmative action can include recruitment and promotion practices where only job-related criteria are applied. Recruitment advertising, for example, is not just non-discriminatory in content (a matter of legal compliance) but also in its placing. New avenues are actively explored for encouraging applications, especially to counter the unhappy past experiences of some groups in society or to remedy the tarnished reputation of companies.

Affirmative action policy can also take into account composing sensitive application forms that seek strictly job-related information (perhaps with a detachable section for monitoring purposes); sensitive interviewing

that may avoid single interviewers; and training programs for relevant individuals who are being considered for appointment or promotion in order to help them compete on equal terms and to win, when they do, solely on merit.

Finally, a new willingness to consider adaptability in working conditions can also be useful evidence of a genuine wish to remedy a company's history of discrimination and to adapt conditions to a wider spectrum of individuals' needs and assets.

As for the future and the encouragement of business practices and policies that respect people for the individuals they are and for the talents and qualities they possess, there is much to be said for the point that the basic underlying issue is one of deep-rooted social prejudice that involves, literally, pre-judging a situation.

If so, then the long-term aim must be to remove prejudices by all appropriate and available structures, including legislation to prevent individuals being unfairly treated, in society and at work; education by law and by good practice; and peer example and support through industry and business codes of conduct that address the issues and are strictly applied.

Aiming for the introduction of such attitudes in the business environment, quite apart from attempting to influence society at large, could very usefully be considered part of the 'social responsibility' of business.

Employee privacy

An interesting parallel to the basic criterion of job-relatedness in considering the ethics of appointments and promotions in business arises when one turns to other issues that can often cause concern in the working of an organization, those connected with individual privacy and confidentiality.

Part of modern human resources policy in-volves getting to know employees in order to take account of any particular circumstances affecting them and so to contribute to their enhanced performance in the workplace.

Such a self-interested policy, however, has to recognize that there are limits to the information a company is entitled to seek about its members in such areas as their personal life-style, sexual preferences, affiliations, use of alcohol, drugs and so on.

What is at stake here is the psychic as well as physical privacy of individuals and the respecting and safeguarding of their personal autonomy and freedom. This seems to imply that if a company wishes to acquire personal information about individual employees, then the burden of proof to justify such a wish is on the company.

However, the dividing line between one's private life and one's working life is not always an easy one to identify. For example, absenteeism or unsatisfactory work can call for an explanation and may indicate that some circumstances in a person's private life can overflow into their working life and may affect the quality of their work. In such circumstances the criterion that emerges to justify a firm's seeking information about its employees which might otherwise be considered purely private is that of performance-relatedness.

In some cases an individual may volunteer relevant personal information that they may consider they owe the company as an explanation of failure to perform. In such cases it should be accepted that a tacit condition of such disclosure is that it applies only to those who 'need-to-know'.

However, one may go further and conclude that when performance is adversely affected, then the company is ethically justified in enquiring into the reason for such behavior. In such a situation, not only should the company realize its obligation to restrict access to that information to those who share the same 'need-to-know'. It may also be in a position to bring corporate support procedures or programs into play to help the affected individual.

Summary

Everyone has different expectations of a company – particularly those who work for it. Many aspects of employment are covered by legislation, others depend on the observance of ethical values and norms.

Discrimination against someone is wrong where it is not job related – it is individual when practiced unchecked by prejudiced members of an organization, structural when it relates to job or promotion conditions, and occupational when it reflects a common presumption that certain classes of people are only capable of performing certain tasks.

Positive discrimination has been a popular remedy in the past. But the effect can be disproportionate and carries the risk of creating new victims, low self-esteem and workforce morale.

Affirmative action – planning and executing deliberate, institutional and ethical steps to remove imbalances – does not go so far and can involve actions in the recruitment, interviewing and training fields.

The dividing line between working life and private life is another delicate area. Information should be restricted to those who 'need-to-know' but a company is entitled to know the reason for adverse performance.

Suggested further reading

De George, Richard T, (1995) 4th edn *Business Ethics* Prentice Hall, Englewood Cliffs.

'Focus on women in business', *Business Ethics. A European Review*, vol 2, no 1 (January 1993), pp. 5-36.

International Financial Markets

Contents

Euromarkets: their uses and worth 386
Harold Rose, London Business School
Euromarkets continue to grow and to provide considerable benefits. An explanation of what they are and how they work.

International banking 388
Harold Rose, London Business School
International banking constitutes a web of cross-border transactions that account for a very large proportion of most banks' operations.

Cities of gold 391
Richard Brealey, London Business School
The factors that create financial powerhouses and the possible threats of competition they face.

Benefits and costs of international portfolio investments 394
Evi C. Kaplanis, London Business School
Investing in a portfolio of international investments helps spread risk. But investors rarely invest to the full extent possible.

The political economy of European economic and monetary union 398
Geoffrey Garrett, The Wharton School of the University of Pennsylvania
The transition to monetary union in Europe is fraught with difficulties. Geoffrey Garrett analyses the likely implications for EU member states.

Contributors

Harold Rose is Esmée Fairbairn Emeritus Professor of Finance at London Business School, London. He was previously first Director of London Business School's Institute of Finance and was Group Economic Adviser, Barclays Bank.

Evi C. Kaplanis is a visiting Senior Research Fellow at London Business School and formerly Associate Professor of finance at LBS. She is a consultant on international portfolio investment, derivatives products and portfolio investment, and developing markets.

Richard Brealey is Tokai Bank Professor of Finance at London Business School. His research interests include corporate finance and portfolio investment.

Geoffrey Garrett is Associate Professor of Management at the Wharton School of the University of Pennsylvania.

Introduction

Financial markets are now increasingly international. Technology allows information to be almost instantly available in all markets and allows the rapid transfer of huge amounts of finance.

The International Financial Markets module examines this subjects and presents a more rounded, global view than is possible in the Finance module alone.

It begins with an examination of two central components of the international financial world – euromarkets and international banking – and continues with an examination of international financial centres, international portfolio investment and the implications of monetary union in Europe.

Euromarkets: their uses and worth

■ **Though established to overcome restrictions in domestic markets that have largely been deregulated, euromarkets continue to grow and provide benefits.** Harold Rose **explains what they are and how they work.**

'Euromarkets' and 'eurocurrencies' refer to financial transactions denominated in currencies other than that of the country in which they take place. Thus a eurodollar loan or bank deposit is one denominated in dollars but made outside the US.

The prefix 'euro' derives from the fact that such transactions, which are sometimes also described as 'offshore' transactions, originated in Europe, with London as the main eurocurrency banking center. Today, however, nearly half of so-called eurocurrency transactions take place outside Europe, through regional centers such as Hong Kong, Singapore and some Caribbean countries and, to a lesser extent, in New York and Tokyo. The US dollar is the main euro-currency, followed by the yen and deutschemark, reflecting their role in international trade and finance.

Limited banking transactions in US dollars and sterling, the then dominant world currencies, were made in Germany during the hyper-inflation that followed the First World War. The modern, worldwide, network of eurocurrency transactions developed in the 1960s, following the relaxation of exchange controls carried out by western European countries in 1958. Nearly 80 per cent of international banking transactions are made in eurocurrencies; and, in addition, active markets have developed in eurocurrency security issues, especially in eurobonds and, if to a lesser extent, in euro-commercial paper and equities.

The advantages of eurocurrency transactions

The growth of euromarkets began mainly as a way of avoiding various restrictions and costs in domestic banking and securities markets. These included interest rate ceilings, restrictions on foreign investment imposed in the US and the prohibition, in 1957, on the use of sterling bank loans to finance trade between countries outside the UK.

Today only the imposition by central banks in some countries of non-interest-bearing reserve requirements on domestic bank deposits remains as a major domestic regulation favouring euro-currency banking transactions. Even so, euro-markets have continued to grow as a result of other advantages they possess.

These include: the convenience to a customer of transacting in a foreign currency with a local bank instead of one overseas; the ability to follow daylight hours across countries; the assembly of very large bank loans through syndication (95 per cent of syndicated international bank loans are in eurocurrencies); low taxes in some centers; and the ability to separate currency from political risk (the former Soviet Union preferred to hold its dollar deposits outside the US during the 1950s and 1960s).

Other factors in the growth of eurocurrencies

Special factors influence the pace of growth of eurocurrency banking transactions from time to time. The sharp rise in oil prices in 1973 and again in 1979-80 led oil-exporting countries to have large balance of payments surpluses, which they invested to a great extent in dollar bank deposits held partly outside the US. But this phase of expansion was brought to an end by the Mexican debt moratorium of 1982.

One possible explanation for the growth of banking euromarkets that was mooted 20 years ago now has little support. This is the view that eurobanking involves a significant credit multiplier process, by which a shift in deposits from domestic to euromarkets leads to a total increase in deposits that is a multiple of the original shift.

The modern view is that there is usually very little if any such multiplier effect. The existence of euromarkets does not undermine the ability of central banks to control money rates; but, as money supply targets or indicators are usually defined in terms of domestic deposits, the movement of eurocurrency deposits, which can be a substitute for the former, may complicate the interpretation of monetary conditions.

The eurocurrency transactions of individual banks are to a considerable extent portfolio adjustments made in response to perceived currency and interest rate risks. Interbank transactions play a larger part in these adjustments than they do in domestic banking, so that the volume of 'gross' eurocurrency transactions is perhaps three times that of 'net' transactions with non-bank customers.

The extent to which non-banks choose to hold deposits as eurocurrency rather than as domestic currency deposits depends on a comparison of relative returns and costs in the two types of market. High reserve requirements, for example, force banks to offer lower interest rates on domestic as opposed to eurocurrency deposits. The reduction in reserve requirements in several countries in recent years is one reason why the proportion of eurocurrency deposits in international banking markets has fallen from 90 per cent to just under 80 per cent over the past decade.

Eurobonds

About half of international borrowing is now in the form of bond issues, and about 80 per cent is in the form of eurobonds. (Euro-commercial paper programs and, even more, medium-term euronote programs have also grown substantially, the latter exceeding $200bn in 1994.)

Originally the term 'eurobond' was reserved for bonds denominated in a currency other than that of the location of issue, but nowadays it is also used to apply to issues by a foreign lender in the currency of the country where it is issued, as long as distribution is largely to international investors made through a syndicate of investment houses. Eurobonds are always unsecured and are mainly fixed-interest bonds. About four-fifths of eurobond issues are said to be swapped into another currency in some years.

Like that of eurocurrency banking the initial development of eurobond markets was a reaction to restrictions on, and the transaction costs of, foreign bond issues in the currency of domestic markets. As eurobonds are unregistered 'bearer' bonds, from which withholding tax is not usually deducted, they also offer tax benefits. But the disadvantages of domestic currency bonds have become relatively unimportant for one reason or another.

Despite this, and despite improvements in domestic bond markets, the share of eurobond issues in international borrowing has continued to grow, from 20 per cent in 1980 to over 40 per cent in 1993, at the expense of syndicated bank loans.

Eurobonds now account for three-quarters of the total stock of international bonds. This growth has been helped by the standardization of issue arrangements such as the form of the issue document and interest payment and clearing arrangements, which has kept issue costs down. The eurobond issue market is a flexible and competitive one, free from the high transaction costs typical of cartelized markets such as France, Germany and Switzerland and of highly regulated markets such as those of New York and Tokyo.

Figure 1: Borrowing on the International Capital Markets (1984-94)

Flows $bn	1984	1989	1992	1993	1994
Bonds	111.5	255.7	333.7	481.0	428.6
Other	85.8	210.8	276.0	337.6	539.0
TOTAL	**197.3**	**466.5**	**609.7**	**818.6**	**967.6**
of which:					
Eurobonds	na	na	276.1	394.6	368.4

Source: OECD Financial Market Trends

Eurobonds are usually listed on the London or Luxembourg stock exchanges. London is thought to have three-quarters of trading in the secondary market, which is usually an over-the-counter market, in which banks act as dealers. Small issues may have relatively low liquidity, but bid-offer spreads on high-quality bonds have fallen as improvements in the market have been made.

The benefits of euromarkets to business

The development of euromarkets has widened the access companies have to loan markets and has brought down borrowing costs relative to the underlying level of interest rates. Even relatively small companies can tap eurocurrency markets through their banks; and companies can borrow in whatever market is most advantageous to them and swap proceeds into the currency they need to spend.

Competition from euromarkets has helped to break up cartelized domestic markets and has played a large part in the liberalization of domestic markets, to the benefit of borrowers. By facilitating international financing and helping to reduce real interest rate differences between countries, euromarkets have played a part in creating a world capital market, to the benefit of world economic growth.

Summary
Euromarkets growth began as a way of avoiding domestic restrictions; now convenience, 24-hour trading, syndication, tax and political risk are among the drivers. The old credit multiplier argument – including the idea that euromarkets undermine the ability of central banks to control money rates – now has little support. The movement of eurocurrency deposits may nevertheless sometimes complicate the interpretation of monetary conditions. Euromarkets have created a global capital market.

Suggested further reading

Lewis, Mervyn K. and Davis, K. T. (1987) *Bank for International Settlements Annual Reports Domestic and international banking*, Philip Allan.

Rose, H., 'International banking developments and London's position as an international banking center', London Business School City Research Project, The Corporation of London 1994.

International banking

■ **International banking constitutes a web of cross-border transactions that account for a very large proportion of most banks' operations.**

by Harold Rose

International banking may be defined as all banking transactions with non-residents and those with residents but in a foreign currency. The former are also described as 'cross-border' or 'external' transactions and account for some 85 per cent of all 'international' banking transactions. International banking must be distinguished from 'overseas' banking, which consists of transactions of 'foreign' banks with the residents of the country in which they are located as well as with non-residents.

Interbank transactions

Interbank transactions create a web of international banking dealings and in recent years have constituted over 70 per cent of bank cross-border claims and about 50 per cent of bank domestic lending in foreign currency. These are higher figures than the proportion of interbank transactions in purely domestic transactions. In the UK, for example, sterling interbank deposits have accounted for about 30 per cent of all domestic sterling deposits in recent years.

Interbank transactions do three things. They enable banks individually to adjust their positions arising from deposit and loan mismatches in a different currency as well as mismatches between assets and liabilities with different maturities or other interest rate characteristics. Second, they form a link between international banking centers. Third, they provide a chain of credit risk transfer. Interbank transactions therefore create a worldwide network of liquidity and risk-spreading, a network that has grown with the help of technology, which has reduced transaction costs and has facilitated bank transactions in international money and foreign exchange markets, which are largely interbank markets. Some banks specialize in interbank transactions, and most engage in two-way business in order to avoid being branded as persistent borrowers, which somewhat inflates the volume of business.

Cross-border lending to non-banks (*see* Figure 1) shows that the stock of bank cross-border loans to non-banks has grown more rapidly than the level of world trade, but with some sign of deceleration since 1987. The growth of international banking has been helped by the abolition of exchange controls and other restrictions, and this was particularly true of the 1960s, which saw the creation of euromarkets. However, the period of fastest growth, relative to world trade, took place between 1973 and 1983, when the four-fold increase in oil prices led banks to act as intermediaries between OPEC surplus countries and countries with large payments deficits, especially the less developed countries, until the subsequent fall in oil prices and the Mexican debt moratorium in 1982 brought this phase to an end. Lending to OECD countries has since come to dominate bank cross-border lending.

More permanent factors accounting for the high ratio of lending to trade include, on the demand side, the international needs of both domestic and overseas customers, which form the main reason why banks set up overseas offices. Multinational industrial concerns have become more numerous since 1945 and operate on a large scale. On the supply side, the advance of technology has reduced transaction costs for international financial transactions and has facilitated the control of overseas operations, making possible the emergence of networks of overseas banking offices, with dramatic effects on global trading and position-taking.

Besides the growth in cross-border lending, another feature of the expansion of international banking transactions has been the increase since the early-1980s in the use of derivative instruments for financial risk control in international transactions, particularly in the form of currency and interest rate swaps, in which banks act, in effect, as market makers. As a result of the liberalization of markets, international banking markets have become increasingly integrated with domestic markets. Competition from foreign banks has played a part in reducing profit margins on domestic lending, especially in centers, like London, where obstacles facing the incursion of foreign banks are low.

Integration of domestic with international markets has also resulted in differences between domestic and international interest rates in a particular currency becoming small and usually stable. The development of international banking has been an indispensable element in the progress towards a world capital market in

End-year	1) Loans to Non-banks: Stocks ($bn)	2) World Imports ($bn)	1) as % of 2)
1963	18.7	147.7	13
1974	144.1	811.6	18
1984	768.1	1877.2	41
1987	1231.3	2422.1	51
1994	2322.6	4226.1	55

Figure 1: Bank cross-lending to non-banks and world trade (1963-94)

Source: IMF International Financing Statistics

which the flow of saving can be directed towards capital investment offering the highest risk-adjusted returns, with a benefit to the long-term rate of world economic growth.

Slowing international growth?

It is unlikely that, relative to world trade, international financing transactions in general and cross-border banking transactions in particular will go on expanding at their past rate. The stimuli of the 1960s and 1970s have disappeared and the regulatory advantages of international markets are weakening because domestic capital markets have become more liberalized.

Moreover, the share of banking in financial transactions in general is likely to continue to fall as banks lose part of their relative information and cost advantages as financial intermediaries to other types of institution. Transaction costs have fallen in securities markets; and issuing and dealing procedures have been improved, especially in the case of eurobonds, which compete with all but very short- term international bank lending.

Bank syndicated lending (of over one year) accounted for about half of recorded borrowing on capital markets before the jump in oil prices in 1973 and was still at this level in 1982-82, before the collapse of bank lending to the LDCs (less developed countries). Despite some recovery in recent years, the proportion of international lending taking the form of bank syndicated lending has fallen to about a quarter, having lost relative ground to eurobonds, commercial paper and medium-term note issues (in which, however, banks play a part as issue managers and distributors).

International banking centers

London is the largest international financial center and can claim to be the only true world center. Others, such as Hong Kong and Singapore, are mainly regional centers; and New York and Tokyo owe their importance chiefly to the size of their national economies. The size of London in both banking and securities trans-actions is out of all proportion to the size of the British economy. London also has the widest variety of international financial transactions.

London is host to the largest number of foreign banks – about 550 – but the influx has slowed in recent years. London's share of recorded bank cross-border claims remains the highest but has fallen from over 18 per cent of the world total in the mid-1980s to 14 per cent, despite an increase in the ratio of Britain's claims to exports, which have maintained their share of world trade in recent years. The main gainers have been the regional Asian centers, where economic growth has been strong, and France, where liberalization of international transactions has been the greatest influence.

A fall in London's share should not be regarded as a loss of competitiveness, and fast economic growth in Asia and elsewhere increases the volume of world banking transactions, raising the absolute level of banking transactions passing through London. Instead, the main threats to London's ability to compete are the liberalization of markets abroad and, perhaps, the tightening of supervision of banks in Britain. Such developments would weaken an advantage London has long possessed – its relative freedom from restrictive regulation.

Summary

Interbank transactions create a worldwide network of liquidity and risk spreading. Cross-border lending to non-banks has grown more quickly than the level of world trade, though there are indications that the rate of growth is slowing. London's loss of market share should not be regarded as a loss of competitiveness. Liberalization of markets abroad and any tightening of banking supervision in Britain, how-ever, would weaken its traditional advantage.

Suggested further reading

Lewis, Mervyn K. and Davis, K. T. (1987) *Bank for International Settlements Annual Reports Domestic and international banking*, Philip Allan.

Rose, H., 'International banking developments and London's position as an international banking center', London Business School City Research Project, The Corporation of London 1994.

Cities of gold

■ **London is part of the triumvirate of top financial centers – New York and Tokyo being the others.** Richard Brealey **discusses what creates such powerhouses and the possible threat of competition.**

In most countries wholesale financial services have concentrated in a single center and only in strong federal systems has this pressure to centralize been slower to prevail. Yet even in these cases a dominant city has generally emerged – Frankfurt in Germany, Zurich in Switzerland, Toronto in Canada and Sydney in Australia.

This concentration of domestic financial services is repeated in the international arena, where activity is highly concentrated in three centers – London, New York and Tokyo. Each is located so that the financial baton is passed from one to the other as the globe revolves. In the case of Asia, the highly regulated structure of Japanese financial services has left a partial vacuum that has allowed other centers such as Hong Kong and Singapore to establish important regional outposts.

London's changing role

A substantial proportion of financial business in both Tokyo and New York is domestic in origin. London, by contrast, is pre-eminently an international center. For example, London dominates the market for international bond and equity issues, and is by far the largest center for foreign exchange trading. It has the largest financial and commodities futures markets outside the US. It is the main center for FRA (forward rate agreement) business, and together with New York is the major swap market. It is second only to Tokyo in the value of funds under management and it is home to the world's largest markets for insurance and shipbroking.

But London's role as a financial center has changed substantially. During the 18th and 19th centuries London was principally a commercial center, which brought with it a need for markets in insurance, shipping and commodities. By the beginning of this century it had evolved into a world banking center. About half of world trade was settled in sterling in 1914, the transactions carried out by London banks with non-residents were also mainly in sterling and this, together with the convertibility of sterling into gold until 1914, made it essential for banks to hold balances in London. Because international banking transactions were confined to trade finance and foreign investment, a large international center could develop only in a country that was a consistent overseas lender, a condition that the UK met.

Today sterling is only a minor international medium of exchange and the UK has not been a consistent net overseas lender for 80 years. London's resurgence as a financial center followed the relaxation of exchange controls in 1958 and the development of the eurocurrency and eurobond markets in the 1960s. However, its role has changed from that of a net exporter of funds and an international banking reserve center to one of a financial entrepôt and a complex of international markets and supporting activities.

If London's commercial pre-eminence played a major role in the growth of its financial services, London's attractiveness has been greatly enhanced by its freedom from invasion and political strife. It has also benefitted from its openness to immigration and foreign business entry as well as a pragmatic legal, tax and regulatory system.

Developments in services

The location of financial activity and the

changing role of London have both been influenced by developments in the nature of financial services. Since the early-1960s there has been a very rapid rate of product innovation. The causes of this wave of innovation are varied. In part it has probably represented a catching up from the stagnant years of recession and war. But it has also been driven by technology, which has improved information flow and reduced dealing costs.

Developments in financial economics have been important for they have made it possible to value and hedge complex financial instruments. Undoubtedly also, governments have had a role to play. For example, the development of the euromarkets owed much to the interest rate ceilings on bank deposits in the US and on the interest equalization tax on US purchases of foreign securities.

Innovation in financial services proceeds by often wasteful experiment. But within this confused process we can distinguish four broad themes, each of which has important implications for the location of financial services.

Internationalization. Since 1950 the dollar value of world trade has grown by about ten per cent a year and there has been a simultaneous rapid growth in overseas expansion by large multi-nationals. These developments have provided a considerable impetus for banks to establish overseas branches to provide banking services to customers with business abroad.

While overseas branching before the 1950s was largely limited to banks of colonial powers, over the following decades there was a rapid increase in foreign banking. Worldwide foreign bank assets increased in real terms by 21 per cent a year between 1950 and 1980. In London, which is the largest beneficiary of this development, the number of foreign banks increased from 73 in 1960 to nearly 550 today.

But the internationalization of finance has involved much more than the development of worldwide networks of financial institutions. The development of the eurocurrency and eurobond markets has provided an international market-place for capital in which firms from different countries can market their securities to a wide clientele of international investors.

With the subsequent dismantling of exchange controls in most developed countries, the euromarkets and domestic capital markets have become linked so that there is effectively a single world marketplace for capital rather than a series of disconnected domestic markets. This consolidation of capital markets has been to the benefit of the principal financial centers.

Securitization. The second big trend has been the declining role of banks in analysing credit and linking borrowers and lenders. As in-formation and credit ratings have become more widely available and issue costs have fallen, corporations have increasingly by-passed the banking system and issued their securities directly to the market.

For example, in the US outstanding commercial paper has expanded over twelvefold in the past 20 years. The effect of this develo-pment has been to change financial centers from being primarily centers for bank lending to markets for issuing and dealing in securities.

Derivatives. The increased volatility of interest rates and exchange rates following the collapse of Bretton Woods in 1973 prompted a greater interest in risk management and provided a marketplace for a variety of risk management products. The launch of the first financial futures contract in the US in 1972 was the start of a development which 20 years later saw total open interest in futures, forwards, swaps and options of $17,000bn (£10,760bn) worldwide.

The concentration of financial services. As noted above, financial services are highly con-centrated in the major urban centers. There are several pervasive forces that affect location and lead to this concentration of activity.

● Financial centers require a supportive legal, tax and regulatory structure and a congenial environment for foreign institutions. These have been important preconditions for London's success. However, tax and regulation are easily copied by rival centers and are unlikely to form a source of long-term advantage.

● Financial services need to tap a large pool of highly specialized labor, much of which is developed by a process of apprenticeship. For example, in Greater London some 300,000 people are employed in financial institutions.

● Financial markets also rely heavily on supporting services such as telecommunications, legal and accounting services, business information services, and so on. In the UK, finance accounts for over 20 per cent of business's purchases of accounting, legal and computing services and over 30 per cent of telecommunications services. Thus financial centers act as a magnet for other business services.

● In traded markets, business gravitates to where the liquidity is. A market with a large share of the business offers both greater immediacy and depth and so creates a virtuous circle by attracting business from less active markets.

● Partly because the quality of financial products is not transparent, financial business relies heavily on trust and this in turn is reinforced by a network of personal relationships and by a center's reputation for fair dealing.

Of course these forces are not uniform in their effects. Trading and underwriting activities, for example, tend to be highly concentrated in major centers, while origination and bank lending are more easily dispersed.

The important feature of all these attributes is that they create what economists refer to as 'externalities'. By this they mean that each company derives extra benefit from the proximity of other companies. These externalities protect the incumbent producer, so that it is possible for no one city to have an inherent advantage over the other, but once financial services have concentrated in one center there is no incentive for an organization to quit.

It is frequently suggested that the benefits of proximity are likely to be weakened by improvements in telecommunications, since these are reducing the need for face-to-face contact. There are certainly ways in which this occurs. For example, it is no longer necessary for dealers to display their wares on an exchange floor or for investors to employ agents to walk the floor seeking the best prices. Prices of financial instruments can be widely disseminated and the costs of search have fallen dramatically.

Nevertheless, the principal effect of improved communications has persistently been to encourage centralization by allowing financial centers to access wider hinterlands. The development of the telex and long-distance telephone networks led to the demise of many regional stock exchanges in the first half of the century, while a parallel development today is resulting in international competition between exchanges. The principal threat to established centers is political. At the extreme, they are vulnerable to war and civil strife. But there is always a danger when governments have wider objectives that over-ride the interests of the financial center and lead to restrictive regulation or damaging changes in the tax rules.

Summary

International financial services are concentrated in London, New York and Tokyo. London is pre-eminently an international location – its role has changed from that of net exporter of funds and international banking reserve center to that of financial entrepôt and a complex of international markets and supporting activities. Internationalization, securitization and the development of derivatives markets have had important implications for the location of financial services.

Suggested further reading

This article draws on the *The Competitive Position of London's Financial Services*, the final Report of the City Research Project, March 1995, a project sponsored by the Corporation of London and managed by London Business School.

Benefits and costs of international portfolio investments

■ **Investing in a portfolio of international investments helps spread risk. But investors rarely invest to the full extent possible.**
Evi C. Kaplanis **considers why.**

The concept of international investment is as old as the financial markets themselves. There is significant evidence, going back to the 13th century, that investors were investing significant proportions of their wealth in foreign assets. For example, the Bardi and the Peruzzi of Florence helped finance the English in the 13th century; the Dutch invested heavily in British and French securities during the 18th century. During the later period the Amsterdam capital market was underwriting securities for a number of European countries and the US. Two world wars and a major depression have set back this trend for international investment. However, interest in foreign investment is gradually re-emerging.

The benefits of diversification in the context of a domestic equity portfolio are well known. Investors are able to reduce their risk substantially by holding a diversified portfolio rather than a single stock. This is possible because prices of different stocks do not move in exact lockstep and thus investors are able to reduce their risk by spreading their investment in a portfolio of stocks rather than a single security.

There are, however, a number of economic factors that affect all domestic securities, such as interest rates and government policies. Investors can potentially eliminate part of the risk associated with domestic economic factors by investing in foreign markets as well. International diversification works – that is, it reduces risk without sacrificing return – only if the different stock markets are not perfectly correlated. (The extent of co-movement of two securities or two markets is often measured by the correlation coefficient. A correlation coefficient of 1 implies that the returns in the two assets move in exact lockstep, while a correlation coefficient of –1 implies that the returns of the two assets move in exactly opposite directions.)

Correlation between the major stock markets

For international diversification to offer substantial risk reduction the different national stock markets should be imperfectly correlated. Table 1 shows the relative independence of the major stock markets for the period January 1990 to December 1994.

**Period January 1990-December 1994
FTA market indices**

	US	Ca	UK	FR	Ge	Nt	Sw	It	Jp	HK	Sn
Canada	.6										
UK	.7	.5									
France	.5	.4	.7								
Germany	.4	.4	.6	.7							
Netherlands	.6	.6	.8	.8	.7						
Switzerland	.6	.6	.8	.7	.6	.8					
Italy	.2	.4	.4	.5	.6	.5	.4				
Japan	.3	.4	.3	.4	.3	.3	.5	.4			
Hong Kong	.4	.5	.5	.5	.5	.6	.5	.4	.2		
Singapore	.5	.5	.6	.5	.7	.6	.6	.5	.5	.7	
Australia	.5	.6	.6	.5	.5	.7	.6	.3	.4	.5	.6

Table 1: Correlation between nominal equity returns expressed in their own currency

It is interesting to note that although all the correlation coefficients are positive they are significantly lower than one, providing scope for diversification. There are also some general patterns in the correlation matrix. For example, there appears to be a northern European block that includes the UK, Germany, France, the Netherlands and Switzerland. These countries are highly correlated due to the strong regional links and the common economic factors that affect and influence these economies. As a result, a German investor, for example, would be better off in terms of diversification investing in the US, Canada or Japan rather than neighbouring countries.

Casual empirical evidence suggests that there is an upward trend in the level of correlation over time. Figure 1 shows the average correlation between ten major stock markets from 1967 to 1994. This increase in correlations could be due to greater integration of the physical and financial markets as a result of deregulation, technological change and better information channels. Therefore, domestic companies are now providing better exposure to international factors as a result of improved trade and foreign direct investment and thus the benefits from international investment by portfolio managers are somewhat dissipated, although they still remain significant.

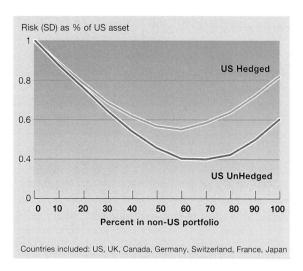

Countries included: US, UK, Canada, Germany, Switzerland, France, Japan

Figure 2: Variability of international equity portfolio for the US investor period: 1986-93

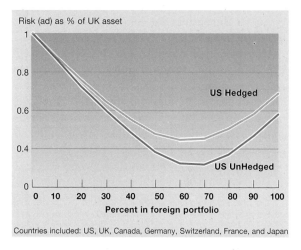

Countries included: US, UK, Canada, Germany, Switzerland, France, and Japan

Figure 3: Variability of international equity portfolio for the UK investor period: 1986-93

International diversification benefits

A number of empirical papers establish that international diversification pays (*see* Suggested further reading). Figures 2 and 3 illustrate the potential risk reduction US and UK investors could achieve through international investment.

These figures show the risk of international portfolios (measured by the standard deviation of the portfolio equity returns and expressed as a proportion of the risk of the domestic portfolio) as a function of the proportion invested in foreign assets. The foreign portfolio includes foreign

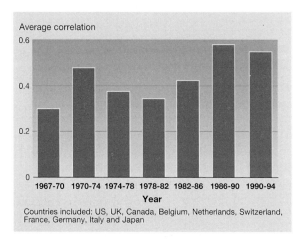

Countries included: US, UK, Canada, Belgium, Netherlands, Switzerland, France, Germany, Italy and Japan

Figure 1: Average international equity market correlations

holdings equally weighted. Results are given for two cases.

In the first case, the risk of exchange rate movements is not hedged and in the second the exchange risk is hedged away. The risk for a US investor who invests 50 per cent in the US and 50 per cent in foreign equities is 47 per cent of the risk of the domestic US market if exchange risk is completely hedged. The portfolio risk is higher (57 per cent of the risk of the domestic portfolio) if the currency exposure of the foreign investment is not hedged. Thus exchange risk dissipates some of the diversification benefits.

In theory, a perfect hedge of the foreign exchange exposure could be achieved through continuous hedging, and in practice investors can virtually eliminate their foreign exchange risk by following simple infrequent hedging strategies using forward exchange contracts. Figure 2 illustrates the diversification benefits for a UK investor.

(It is of course, possible that risk premia in the US and other foreign markets reflect the differences in variability in such a way that diversification brings no benefit. However, repeating the same exercise for all other countries results in similar risk-reduction patterns that demonstrate that there are potential diversification benefits.)

International diversification in equities pays because it potentially enables investors to spread risks specific to their own domestic economy without reducing expected return. Although these potential benefits have been reduced over the years as a result of greater integration of the physical and capital markets, there is still enough independence across the stock markets to justify international investments.

Home bias

In a domestic capital market investors would choose to hold the market portfolio of risky assets if they had the same expectations about returns. Similarly, one could argue that in a perfectly integrated world capital market, if investors agree on the prospects for investing in each country, they should hold the world market portfolio. The world capital market, however, is not fully integrated and investors are far from

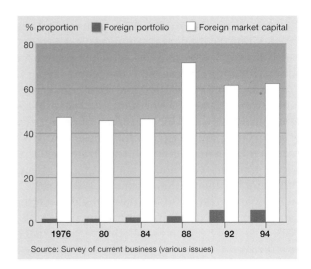

Figure 4: Foreign investment in equities by the US investor

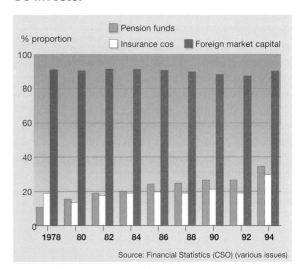

Figure 5: Foreign investment in equities by the UK pension funds and insurance companies

holding the world market portfolio.

Figures 4 and 5 show the domestic holdings of US and UK investors and their respective market capitalizations over the period 1975 to 1993. For example, in 1994, the typical US investor held 5.8 per cent of his equity portfolio in foreign markets and 94.2 per cent in the US market while if he was to hold the world market portfolio he would have to hold 62 per cent overseas and 38 per cent in the US.

In the early 1980s there was a noticeable

increase in foreign investment by UK institutional investors as a result of the abolition of the 'dollar premium' exchange controls system in 1979. Similarly in the 1970s and early 1980s a large number of financial institutions were prohibited from investing overseas because it was considered imprudent. As these restrictions were gradually removed foreign investment increased, though it is still very low compared with the market capitalization of these foreign stock markets.

The large home bias could potentially be explained by a number of barriers that investors face when investing overseas, such as foreign exchange risk, exchange controls, information gathering costs, withholding taxes or even some psychological barriers.

It is often argued that investors choose to hold mainly domestic assets in order to avoid foreign exchange exposure and to hedge themselves against inflation risk. Empirical evidence, however, is unable to support this argument. First, investors can eliminate foreign exchange exposure through simple hedging strategies. Second, empirical evidence suggests that domestic equities are not a very good hedge against inflation.

Barriers to foreign investment such as withholding taxes on dividends and safe custody fees can be taken at their face value. In addition, however, there are a number of barriers that are not easily quantifiable, such as information gathering costs, exchange controls and the risk of expropriation. Therefore, it is not possible to obtain an overall effective cost that would represent all the barriers to foreign investment.

An alternative way of looking at the problem is to estimate the implicit level of costs that would justify investors' behavior. In other words, how large should the barriers be in order to induce US investors to hold only 5.8 per cent of their equity investments in foreign stocks instead of 62 per cent (the foreign world market capitalization)?

Table 2 shows the average costs to foreign equity investment for investors from the major developed countries. For example, if the annual expected return for an investor on the foreign world market portfolio is 20 per cent, then the

Average deadweight cost	
Year	(% annually)
1982	4.98
1988	3.52
1993	2.70

Source: I.Cooper and E.Kaplanis (1986,1994,1995).

Table 2: Estimates of the average cost to foreign equity

implication is that he or she behaves as if the return from this foreign investment is 17.3 per cent, taking into account the 2.7 per cent cost to foreign investment in 1993.

The estimate of the level of the costs to foreign investment has been reduced significantly, reflecting the liberalization of the capital markets and the relaxation of exchange controls in a number of countries. But they still remain above observable costs such as withholding taxes.

Summary
International diversification works only if different stock markets are not perfectly correlated. Such diversification pays because it enables investors to spread risks specific to their own domestic economy without reducing the expected return, even if greater integration of the physical and capital markets has reduced some of the impact.
Despite the lifting of exchange controls foreign investment by UK institutions has remained relatively low. Foreign exchange risk is not an explanation, because of hedging strategies; nor can it be said that domestic equities are a good hedge against inflation. Other barriers, such as withholding taxes and safe custody fees, can be taken at face value though there are others that are not easily quantifiable. It is possible to estimate the implicit level of costs that would justify investors' 'stay-at-home' behavior.

Suggested further reading
Kindleberger, C.P. (1984) *A Financial History of Western Europe*, George Allen & Unwin.

Solnik, B. 'Why not diversify internationally', *Financial Analyst Journal,* August 1974.

Lessard, D. 'Principles of international portfolio selection', in *International Finance Handbook* (Giddy and George), Wiley & Sons,1983.

Speidell, L. and Sapenfield, R. 'Global diversification in a shrinking world', *Journal of Portfolio Management,* Fall 1992.

Kaplanis, E. and Schaefer, S. 'Exchange risk and international diversification in bond and equity portfolios', *Journal of Economics and Business,* 1991.

Cooper, I. and Kaplanis, E. 'Home bias in equity portfolios, inflation hedging and international capital market equilibrium', *The Review of Financial Studies,* Spring 1994.

The political economy of European economic and monetary union

■ **The transition to monetary union in Europe is fraught with difficulties.** Geoffrey Garrett **analyses the likely implications for EU member states.**

The central question about the future of Economic and Monetary Union (Emu) in the European Union (EU) is which countries will participate.

Looking at the Maastricht treaty's convergence criteria – particularly with respect to debt and deficits – Belgium, Greece, Italy and Sweden clearly will not make the grade by the end of the decade (*see* Table 1). But these are not hard-and-fast rules for admission.

Rather, admission decisions will be made by qualified majority on the basis of whether countries have made progress towards meeting the convergence criteria. Thus, countries with poor fiscal records might be voted into Emu for other reasons. Moreover, eligible countries may choose not to join Emu. Denmark and the UK secured optouts at Maastricht that allow them to decide whether to participate. The German constitutional court and the current Swedish government have claimed similar prerogatives. In this article I speculate about the transition to

Emu by analysing the likely macroeconomic effects of membership on member countries. It begins by assuming that the European System of Central Banks (ESCB) will operate as a textbook

Table 1: EMU Convergence Criteria, 1995 (Commission Forecasts)

	Inflation	Budget deficit	Public debt
MEET ALL CRITERIA			
Germany	2.2	2.4	59.4
Luxembourg	2.5	-1.6	9.8
FEASABLE TO MEET CRITERIA BY 1999			
Austria	2.5	4.9	65.0*
Denmark	2.1	3.0	78.0
Finland	2.2	5.0	70.0*
France	1.9	4.9	53.4
Ireland	2.7	2.0	83.7
Netherlands	2.4	3.5	78.8
Portugal	4.6	5.8	71.7
Spain	4.5	6.0	65.8
United Kingdom	2.9	4.6	52.4
MOST UNLIKELY TO MEET CRITERIA BY 1999			
Belgium	2.5	4.7	138.7
Greece	9.5	13.3	125.4
Italy	3.5	8.6	126.8
Sweden	3.5	9.6	78.9*
Convergence criterion	3.6**	3.0	60.0

Source: Antonio José Cabral, "Is Convergence Towards EMU making enough Progress", European Commission, Directorate General for Economic and Financial Affairs (DGII), March 17, 1995.
*accumulated public debt at the end of 1994.
**average of the three lowest inflation rates + 1.5 percentage points.

independent central bank – i.e. with price stability as its only objective.

Three factors will affect the likely domestic effects of joining such a monetary union:

● The larger the disparity between national monetary arrangements and those under Emu, the greater the domestic dislocations associated with the transition.

● The more encompassing are labor market institutions, the more effective will be the ESCB in containing inflationary pressures.

● The more countries trade with each other and the more symmetrical are the economic disturbances they encounter, the more likely that the benefits of giving up exchange rate autonomy will outweigh the costs.

The two countries that would clearly benefit from participation in the textbook Emu are Austria and Germany; to a lesser extent, Belgium, Denmark, Ireland and the Netherlands also belong in this category. The clearest loser would be the UK, but membership would also be costly for Finland, Greece, Italy, Portugal, Spain and Sweden. Finally, France sits in between these two groups.

But the ESCB, in practice, may not behave as a textbook independent central bank because decisions in the governing council of the ESCB will be taken by a simple majority of its members, many of whom will be central bank governors from countries with an interest in pursuing looser monetary policy.

Thus, whether price stability will be obtained under Emu depends largely on its size. The larger the monetary union, the greater the number of 'loose money' members. It is the specter of this outcome that motivates the Bundesbank's insistence on rigid adherence to the convergence criteria. It also helps explain the Emu enthusiasm of the Mediterranean countries – they believe they can gain the benefits of membership without having to pay the full price.

These economic battle lines are not the only issues that will affect the transition to monetary union. Nonetheless, one cannot analyse the broader geo-strategic considerations, influencing the behavior of the French and German governments in particular, without first understanding the political economy of Emu.

The dislocations of moving to monetary union

Economists believe that delegating monetary authority to a central bank that is politically independent lowers inflation without depressing growth or unemployment. Governments have electoral incentives to inflate the economy, but all economic actors know this and hence they anticipate expansionary macroeconomic policies. The only product of these policies will thus be inflation.

But even if making central banks independent would be helpful to all economies in the long run, there would nonetheless be significant short-term dislocations associated with such reforms. This is because economic actors are unlikely immediately to change their expectations to assume that tight monetary policies will always be pursued. This implies with respect to Emu that countries with less independent central banks when the Maastricht treaty was signed would suffer higher transition costs in joining the monetary union. Table 2 ranks EU members at the time of the Maastricht treaty and the ESCB on the two best indices of central bank independence. The ESCB would be marginally more independent than the Bundesbank. The Austrian, Danish and Dutch central banks are also quite independent. Central bank independence is lowest in Belgium and the

Table 2: The independence of Central Banks in the European Union		
Cukierman index[1]	**GMT index[2]**	**CBI rank**
European System of Central Banks[3]		
.68	13	1
Germany .66	13	2
Austria .58	9	3
Netherlands .42	10	4
Denmark .47	8	5
Ireland .39	7	6
Greece .51	4	7
France .28	7	8
United Kingdom .31	6	9
Belgium .19	7	10
Finland .27	–	11
Italy .22	5	12
Sweden .27	4	13
Spain .21	5	14
Portugal –	3	15

1. Cukierman's [1992: 381] legal independence measure for the 1980s.
2. The sum of Grilli, Masciandaro and Tabellini's [1991: 368-9] economic and political independence measures.
3. The ESCB value was calculated using Cukierman's and GMT's criteria.
Note: the data do not take into account central bank reforms undertaken after the signing of the Treaty of European Union in 1992.

Mediterranean and Nordic countries. These countries would bear the greatest transition costs in moving to Emu.

Labor market institutions and monetary arrangements

Encompassing labor market institutions that can co-ordinate the behavior of most of the workforce will internalize the externalities of wage militancy.

These institutions help ensure that wage increases do not erode the competitiveness of the exposed sector of the economy. This points to a free-rider problem regarding a central bank's threats to raise interest rates. Small groups of organized workers know that their wage militancy will have little impact on economy-wide inflation. Hence central bank threats to raise national interests in response to their wage militancy are not credible. This problem would be mitigated if all workers were co-ordinated by a powerful peak confederation of labor whose leaders care about nation-wide economic conditions.

In an open economy, employment and wages in the exposed sector are determined by their competitiveness in markets for which there is a world price. There is no world price for public sector services, where the government's willingness to prop up total employment will largely determine wages.

The tension between workers in the traded and public sectors would have damaging macro-economic consequences under an independent central bank. If the central bank reacted to public sector wage militancy by increasing interest rates, this would push up the exchange rate – with dire consequences for the traded sector.

This problem could only be eradicated by encompassing labor market institutions that ensure that wage growth in the public sector does not undermine the competitiveness of the traded sector.

This suggests that giving monetary policy authority to the ESCB will only help those countries with encompassing labor market institutions. Table 3 shows that conditions in northern Europe – and particularly Austria and

Table 3: Labor market institutions among EU members (1990)

	index of the concentration of trade union members	% of wage contracts covered by collective bargaining agreements	encompassment of labor market institutions (rank)[1]
Austria	1.00	98	1
Germany	.70	90	2
Belgium	.56[2]	90	3
Finland	.38	95	4
Sweden	.45	83	5
Denmark	.48	80[2]	6
Ireland	.47[2]	80[2]	7
Netherlands	.56	71	8
France	.22[3]	92	9
United Kingdom	.72	47	10
Portugal	.22[4]	79	11
Spain	.22[2]	68	12
Greece	.22[4]	68[4]	13
Italy	.37	47[2]	14

except where otherwise stated, data for trade union concentration from Golden and Wallerstein [1995].
1. sum or standardised scores for concentration index and bargaining coverage
2. derived from Cameron [1984]
3. author's estimates
4. data only available for 1985

Germany – are the most compatible with delegating authority to the ESCB.

Compare Belgium and Italy. Labor market institutions are quite encompassing in Belgium. A counterfactual estimate based on recent econometric work by myself and Christopher Way suggests that if Belgium joined Emu this would cut annual inflation by 4.4 percentage points and lower the unemployment rate by 0.6 points. In contrast, the move to Emu would hurt the Italian economy because its labor market institutions are much less encompassing. Its inflation rate would increase by 2.6 points and the unemployment rate would grow by 1 point.

Integration, shocks and monetary union

Let us now extend the Emu cost-benefit analysis to the utility for different countries of irrevocably fixing their exchange rates.

The EU Commission has highlighted the gains from Emu in terms of eliminating the costs of exchanging national currencies and stabilizing exchange rate expectations. But Barry Eichengreen, among others, has pointed out that these benefits are not large. Moreover, significant costs will be associated with giving up the exchange rate adjustment tool unless:
● the economic shocks a country experiences are similar to those in other members of the monetary union

- wages are highly flexible
- labor is highly mobile
- the fiscal system redistributes money from booming to recessionary economies.

None of the factors that might mitigate the costs of a monetary union is satisfied in Europe. Wages are less flexible and labor is less mobile in Europe than is the case in the US. And the EU's budget is tiny in comparative terms. It is inconceivable that these patterns will change dramatically with the move to Emu. Thus, the extent to which national economies are integrated to each other and face symmetrical economic disturbances is critical to the viability of their participation in Emu.

Table 4 describes trade relations in the EU. The first column reports the portion of a country's total trade that is done with other members. Intra-EU trade constitutes substantially more than half of all the trade done by member states. However, the second column shows that the importance of intra-EU trade to total economic activity varies widely.

Table 4: Patterns of trade in the European Union, 1992

	trade with EU		trade with Germany		trade integration rank
	%total trade	%gdp	%total trade	%gdp	
Germany	**54.1**	**34.9**	**-**	**-**	**-**
Belgium	74.8	106.7	23.4	33.4	1
Netherlands	75.4	84.3	26.3	29.4	2
Austria	66.1	52.5	41.5	33.0	3
Ireland	74.2	86.7	10.8	12.6	4
Portugal	80.9	65.6	16.4	86.7	5
Denmark	54.5	33.5	22.6	13.9	6
Greece	64.2	35.9	21.4	12.0	7
Sweden	55.8	35.6	16.6	10.6	8
France	63.0	18.2	18.2	9.0	9
UK	55.5	29.1	13.9	7.3	10
Finland	53.2	26.1	15.9	7.8	11
Italy	57.7	22.3	21.2	8.2	12
Spain	66.3	25.0	16.1	6.1	13

data from Eurostat and OECD, Statistics of Foreign Trade.
The trade integration ranks are based on the sum of standardised scores for EU trade/gdp and German trade/gdp.

Intra-EU trade is larger than Belgian GDP but constitutes less than one third of GDP for Finland, France, Italy, Spain and the UK. Thus, the internal EU market is not very important economically for three of the 'Big Four' countries in Europe.

The third and fourth columns show trading patterns with the key economy in Europe – Germany.

The major difference between these data and intra-EU trade as a whole is for Ireland and Portugal – for whom EU trade is substantial but not much is done with Germany. Nonetheless, the countries at the top of the trade-with-Germany league table are the same as those at the top of the intra-EU standings – Austria, Belgium and the Netherlands. So, too, are the five countries at the bottom of both lists. Combining these two measures, there are considerable variations among EU members in the potential benefits of participation in Emu.

The likely benefits are greatest for Austria and the Benelux countries. There is a considerable gap to the next tier of countries – the Scandinavian countries, Greece, Ireland and Portugal.

Finally, Finland, France, Italy, Spain and the UK stand at the bottom. Germany would belong in this last group since intra-EU is not particularly important to the national economy.

Table 5 presents a simple indicator of the co-ordination of business cycles over time correlations between national rates of GDP growth and the EU average and the German growth rate.

Table 5: The symmetry of Business Cycles in the European Union, 1965-92

correlation with annual national GDP growth rate

	EU average growth rate	German growth rate	symmetry rank
Germany	0.792	-	-
Netherlands	0.819	0.750	1
France	0.906	0.650	2
Belgium	0.861	0.671	3
Austria	0.767	0.663	4
Spain	0.800	0.559	5
Italy	0.807	0.543	6
Greece	0.665	0.592	7
Denmark	0.652	0.596	8
Portugal	0.721	0.483	9
United Kingdom	0.613	0.406	10
Sweden	0.625	0.359	11
Finland	0.647	0.322	12
Ireland	0.377	0.320	13

data are from OECD Economic Outlook - Historical Statistics

There are some strong similarities between the trade and business cycles data. Again, the costs of membership are likely to be quite low for Belgium, Austria and the Netherlands, whereas

Finland and the UK are peripheral to the European core on both dimensions. The rankings of other countries change considerably.

While European trade is vital to the Irish economy, its business cycle is clearly misaligned with its European partners. Conversely, even though intra-EU trade is relatively unimportant to the French economy, its business cycle has been closely correlated with that of the EU and with Germany's in particular. The mismatch between the French and German economies in the 1990s is thus aberrant from a historical perspective.

Assessing the economic consequences of Emu

Table 6 divides EU members into five groups based on the analyses in the preceding sections about the likely overall macroeconomic consequences of participation in the textbook Emu (that is, run by an independent ESCB pursuing price stability in a DM zone).

Table 6: Expected economic consequences of EMU participation

		implicit increase in central bank independence[1]	labour market institutions[2]	market integration[3]	symmetry of business cycles[4]
I	Austria	small	strong	high	high
	Germany	small	strong	high	high
II	Belgium	large	strong	high	high
	Denmark	small	strong	high	low
	Ireland	small	strong	high	low
	Netherlands	small	weak	high	high
III	France	small	weak	low	high
IV	Finland	large	strong	low	low
	Greece	small	weak	low	low
	Italy	large	weak	low	high
	Portugal	large	weak	high	low
	Spain	large	weak	low	high
	Sweden	large	strong	low	low
V	UK	large	weak	low	low

1. the seven countries with the smallest implicit increase in central bank independence were coded "small"; the others were coded "large".
2. the seven countries with the most encompassing labour market institutions were coded "strong"; the others were coded "weak".
3. the seven countries that are most integrated into EU markets were coded "high"; the others were coded "low".
4. the seven countries with the most symmetrical business cycles were coded "high"; the others were coded "low".

There are two countries for whom the decision to be a part of this Emu would be easy – Austria and Germany.

Both countries have independent national central banks, and hence the dislocations from the transition to monetary union would be small.

Labor market institutions are very encompassing in both countries, and thus they are likely to respond efficiently to delegating monetary authority to the ESCB.

Trade with the EU and with Germany in particular is vital to the Austrian economy, and its business cycle is quite symmetrical with others in Europe. Intra-EU trade is far less important to the German economy, and the German business cycle is less symmetrical with the rest of the EU. But German economic conditions would likely have a marked impact on ESCB policy.

As a result, participation in Emu would not harm the German economy and would help cement its gains from the internal market. The UK is at the other end of the spectrum. The Bank of England continues to be heavily influenced by the government. British labor market institutions have become very fragmented following the Thatcher decade. The British economy is not well integrated into Europe – in terms both of trade patterns and business cycles. Thus, in addition to concerns about sovereignty, there is an economic justification for the unpopularity of Emu in the UK. Two groups of countries lie between these extremes. One comprises countries for whom, on balance, Emu ought to be a good thing. Belgium is clearly part of the EU economic core and its labor market institutions are relatively encompassing. But the dependence of Belgium's national central bank means that significant dislocations would result from the transition to Emu.

The problem for Ireland (and to a lesser extent for Denmark) is that its business cycle is very poorly synchronized with others in Europe. Labor market institutions in the Netherlands are not sufficiently encompassing. For the countries in the fourth group, there are more negatives than positives associated with the textbook Emu. The Mediterranean countries have dependent central banks and decentralized labor market institutions and are somewhat peripheral in economic terms. Labor market institutions are still quite encompassing in the Nordic countries, but these countries have dependent central banks and their economies are not tightly integrated into the EU core.

Finally, France sits right in the middle of the EU. The French business cycle is highly symmetric with the rest of the EU and the Bank of France is relatively independent. However, French labor market institutions are weak, and intra-EU trade is not very important to the French economy.

Now compare Table 6 with the current fiscal performance of member states (*see* Table 1). The UK will likely meet the convergence criteria by the end of the decade – but on my arguments it should not join Emu. Conversely, Belgium is one of the countries that would do well in the textbook Emu but its public debt poses a considerable obstacle to its admission.

For the countries that might meet the convergence criteria, the incentives for Denmark, Ireland, the Netherlands (and perhaps France) to participate are greater than those for Finland, Portugal and Spain. The simple point of this comparison is that there is little correlation between the current fiscal predicaments of EU members and the likely macroeconomic consequences of their joining. On these grounds, the convergence criteria make little sense.

A politicized Emu?

The preceding analysis was based on two assumptions about Emu. First, the ESCB will operate as a classically independent central bank. Second, Emu monetary policy will be geared to economic conditions in the DM zone.

Let me now relax these assumptions. Many of the ESCB's institutions do suggest that it is a 'super-Bundesbank'. This is not to say that it is immune from political pressures to loosen monetary policy. This has not been a problem in Germany because of the societal consensus supporting price stability. But one should be more sceptical about the ESCB.

It will take decisions on a simple majority of its governing council. If all EU members participated in Emu, there would be 21 votes in the council – six from its executive board with each of the remaining votes given to central bank governors from members states.

The board can be expected to act as classically conservative central bankers, pursuing price stability come what may. The Maastricht treaty tries to reform national central banks to make their governors more conservative. Nonetheless, national governors will sometimes be put under heavy pressure to vote for loose monetary policy in the ESCB. Consider the following plausible scenario. National central bank governors from Austria and the Benelux vote with Germany to maintain price stability in the monetary union. But other members are in recession or have high rates of unemployment. Hence, there are powerful pressures on their central bank governors to vote in the ESCB to loosen monetary policy. In this scenario, price stability would win by the barest majority – 11 to 10. The accession of any country currently in the EU membership queue would likely tip the balance in favour of loose money.

More importantly, France might not be Germany's stable ally inside Emu. For over a decade, French governments have pursued the *franc fort* – despite the domestic political costs of this policy – in the name of deeper European integration. But the temptation must be great for President Chirac or his successors to try to loosen European monetary policy once Emu exists and a large step toward deepening the integration project has been completed. If this scenario materialized, there would be a deep schism at the heart of the monetary union, between a German tight money bloc and a loose money coalition headed by France. This fear is at the core of Bundesbank efforts to generate strict adherence to the convergence criteria for admission to Emu. They could be used to exclude at least three likely members of the loose money bloc (Greece, Italy and Sweden). But this might not give the Germans a justification for opposing more important members of this coalition such as Spain and France. Moreover, voting on Emu membership will be by qualified majority. Germany and its allies do not have the votes to block the admission of loose money countries. They would need Belgium in this coalition to sustain a veto. Of course, Belgium's support would only matter if it were in Emu – but this would entail Germany turning a blind eye to Belgium's massive public debt.

There is an even more severe problem lurking for Germany. Would the German government, let alone the Benelux countries, be prepared to vote against the participation of France? This is very difficult to envisage. Alternatively, consider what could transpire if the convergence criteria were upheld, only four countries did not meet them (Belgium, Greece, Italy and Sweden), and Denmark and the UK exercized their opt outs.

What would the German government do when confronted with the option of whether to participate in a monetary union with Ireland, Portugal and Spain? The domestic cries to keep the DM would be very loud. Would German political leaders be prepared to ignore this criticism in the name of deepening the EU? This would be the ultimate test of the German commitment to European integration.

Thus, the endgame over monetary union will come down to the political will of the French and German governments, as has so often been the case in the history of European integration.

There are few economic incentives for Germany to participate in Emu. But Chancellor Kohl manifestly wants to leave as his legacy something akin to a federation of Europe.

On the other hand, while economic costs of Emu for France are very high, French leaders have shown a remarkable determination to endure these costs in the name of security on the continent in the post Cold War world.

The future will show whether the opposition of the financial markets and the general public (a curious alliance to be sure) will be strong enough to resist the determination of political leaders in France and Germany to cement European integration through monetary union.

Summary

Which countries will participate in Emu? Three factors will influence the domestic effects of joining: the extent to which countries' central banks are independent, the extent to which their labor market institutions can co-ordinate the workforce and contain wage increases, and the extent to which countries trade with each other.

On this basis the decision to be part of Emu should be easy for Austria and Germany. The UK, with a still heavily influenced central bank, fragmented labor institutions, and poorly integrated economy as far as Europe is concerned, is at the other end of the spectrum. Between these there is a group (including Belgium and Ireland) for which Emu on balance ought to be a good thing and another group (including the Mediterraneans) for whom there are more negatives than positives. France is right in the middle.

At the moment there is little correlation between the fiscal predicaments of EU members – crucial to their meeting the convergence criteria – and the likely macro-economic consequences of joining. The endgame over monetary union will come down to the political will of the French and German governments.

Managing
Across Cultures

Contents

Becoming globally civilized 408
Howard V. Perlmutter, The Wharton School of the
University of Pennsylvania
*True global effectiveness involves a number of
positive actions if organizations are to gain leadership
in a truly global civilisation.*

Culture is not enough 414
Jack Denfeld Wood, IMD
*Managers are constantly told to be aware of and alert
to 'cultural differences'. But differences between
individuals from different cultures may be less than
those between individuals from the same one.*

The subtle art of negotiation 419
Jack Denfeld Wood and Thomas R. Colosi, IMD
*The first of a three-part 'mini series' on negotiation
examines the often wrong-headed way in which
westerners approach the whole idea of negotiation.*

It takes more than two to agree 426
Jack Denfeld Wood and Thomas R. Colosi, IMD
*Second of a three-part 'mini series' on negotiation.
Negotiation involves far more than just the people
'across the table'. Negotiators have to convince the
other party, their fellow negotiators, their bosses and
the outside world.*

Managing negotiations 432
Jack Denfeld Wood and Thomas R. Colosi, IMD
*The final part of a three-part 'mini series' explains
some of the techniques and issues involved in
bringing negotiations to a successful conclusion.*

Russia's different problems 442
David Chambers, London Business School
*Management education is a key factor in the reform of
the Russian economy. But the key lessons are not
always the same as those needed by managers in the
West.*

Contributors

Howard V. Perlmutter is Emeritus
Professor of Management and Social
Architecture at the Wharton School of the
University of Pennsylvania, and founder
of the Multinational Enterprise Unit and
the Worldwide Institutions Research
Center. He is currently directing The
Emerging Global Civilization Project at
the Wharton Shool.

Jack Denfeld Wood is Professor of
Organizational Behavior at IMD,
Lausanne. His research interests are
analytical psychology, leadership and
teams, social structure and change, and
culture and ideology.

Thomas R .Colosi is the American
Arbitration Association's Vice-President
for National Affairs and a third-party
practitioner and neutral. He has authored
numerous papers and articles on dispute
resolution training techniques and
negotiations.

David Chambers is visiting Professor of
Comparative Management at London
Business School and Director of the CIS-
Middle Europe Center at London
Business School. His research interests
include enterprise restructuring in East
Europe, performance assessment,
forward planning and company
restructuring, and policy implementation
in public enterprises.

Introduction

The ability to manage effectively in a global environment – to manage across cultures – is rated a key element in modern general management. The globalization of business and the increasing mobility of managers means that the majority will spend at least some of their time working in multicultural teams or negotiating with managers from a different culture.

The Managing Across Cultures module looks at the implications of this from a number of angles including what one writer describes as the need for companies to be 'globally civilized', a section that questions whether cultural differences among managers are really as great as is suggested and the management development problems facing Russia, a country that is going though enormous cultural change. The module also contains a major highly revealing three-part section on negotiation.

Related topics can be found in the Organizational Behavior, Business Ethics and Socio-political Context and Business Environment modules.

Becoming globally civilized

■ **True global effectiveness involves a number of positive actions if organizations are to gain leadership in a truly global civilization.**

by Howard V. Perlmutter

Managers around the planet know they face unprecedented times ahead. The conjuncture of pluralistic political trends, the emergence of a more open world economy, the globalization of consumer tastes, the unabated technological thrust towards a digital world and common concerns about ecological consequences are but the first steps on a rocky road to building a global civilization.

It is not a matter of whether we will have a global civilization but of what kind. At one extreme is the view that some sort of post-modern Disney world is in the offing; at the other is a world of unbridgeable cultural chasms in which many regions will be only marginally connected to a world community.

Our view is that what kind of civilization is emerging on the planet cannot be forecast but a working assumption is that there will be both a vast and sometimes turbulent mosaic of cultural differences and a great variety of global hybridizations.

I have taken the global civilization process seriously and have formulated three long-term 'rocky road' propositions to understand the chaotic character of global trends. This led to inferring what kind of global corporate leadership and what global corporate competencies will be necessary to survive and prosper. At this point, however, it is easier to describe what are the core incompetencies firms currently possess and what are some of the challenges faced by global corporate leaders as the emerging global civilization begins to take shape. The first proposition is that, on balance, the driving forces toward the emergence of a global civilization are greater than the restraining forces. These include a greater global openness and transparency of nations, a greater acceptance of ideas and products from other cultures, a greater willingness to engage in multilateral action, and a greater recognition that bonds of economic interdependence must become denser and less reversible and that agreement about some shared values is necessary.

The path is not smooth. The State of Maharashta, for example, may decide to scrap a $2.8bn foreign-led power project but the consequences for India's climate for foreign investment would have been very serious. Sri Lanka hopes that unrest will diminish and then foreign investment will increase. The general trend is that almost every country is seeking foreign investment.

The construction of global electronic highways is another manifestation of the move towards an interdependent world. Note that the shared values are not a list of universal human rights but those which relate to how one behaves and influences others in foreign cultures, the quality of products and what constitutes good service. A *second and derivative proposition* is that in the emerging global civilization there is an abundance of paradoxes. For example, in Asia, the Middle East, Africa and Latin America there is evidence both for the westernization of tastes and the assertion of ethnic, religious and cultural differences, though these differences do not constitute unbridgeable cultural chasms in all sectors of a society. Instead there are trends toward cultural syncretism, or the hybridization of ideas, as for example, in country-specific accommodations between Japan and western industrialism, between western industrialism and Islamic fundamentalism and Asian Confucianism. So while national, religious and ethnic groups assert their identity, sometimes violently, the political reality is that these expressions of autonomy must coexist with increasing global economic interdependence. This applies as much to the US and Europe as it does to Algeria, Myanmar (Burma), North Korea, Libya and Cuba, to name just a few cases. In the wider world there are few universal values.

Concepts of democracy, the free market, human rights, the American theory of liberal internationalism and individualism are not universal. But the willingness to engage in business dealings is becoming a global norm and a kind of global business civilization is the leading edge of global change. A *third proposition* is that the massive nature of these global societal changes requires a transformation process for most institutions, especially nations and companies. The transformation becomes evident in the premises that underlay the changes in the architecture of companies. This is currently described as a paradigm shift, with implications for changing visions, missions, systems of governance, strategy, organizational culture and design. One specific change is that companies must operate globally as well as aspire for an insider status in an extraordinarily wide variety of cultural and national settings.

Global shakeout and shakeup

The main expression of the turbulent character of the emerging global civilization is the constant restructuring of global business sectors. The global shakeout and shakeup process in all industries – manufacturing and service – from accounting to zippers is manifested in tens of thousands of small boutiques to a limited number of mega-firms from advanced and emerging markets that are engaged in selective global expansion.

To deal with the size of the global economy some companies are consolidating through mergers and acquisition to reach the scale considered necessary to compete in the global arena. At the same time there is a trend toward global rationalization, seeking world standards for efficiency and productivity. These changes are often coupled with selling off incompatible businesses and seeking global leadership in global segments and niches. A striking element

of the global shakeout and shakeup process, in the face of considerable uncertainty, is the need to reach global markets rapidly by engaging more frequently in global strategic alliances. Rationalization, consolidation through merger and acquisition, segmentation and alliances are often attributed to global overcapacity, which, in our surveys, extends to over 80 per cent of all industries. Since the global overcapacity can be as high as 30 to 40 per cent, the expectation is that cost cutting, downsizing and re-engineering will not decline. So the need to grow globally increases.

Cross-cultural incompetencies

The global market means several hundred countries and thousands of cultures to consider. To operate effectively in different countries requires recognition that there may be considerable differences in operating in different regions. Consider Northern Europe versus Latin Europe, and even in the Northwest or the South of the US, or Tokyo and Taiwan. At the stage of early internationalization, it is not unusual for Anglo-Saxon firms to experience what appear to be cultural chasms with their counterparts in Latin America and Asian countries, as well as in different regions of those countries. There are many examples where companies simply do not find their way into a market or where their performance is less than successful. Only a very small proportion of the failures or the major difficulties are made public. Eurodisney in France received considerable media attention, but any careful scrutiny of the performance of a company in different markets will show the number of disappointments in foreign markets exceeds the successes.

To be sure, there are many examples of mutual acculturation. And a kind of successful hybridization process can take place, in both alliances and affiliates. Among these are the joint plant of GM and Toyota called Nummi in California, Hewlett Packard and Canon, which jointly make printers, and General Electric aircraft engine division and Snecma, the French aircraft group. But companies are still struggling with what kind of dynamic hybridization they need in China and India, given that these two countries combined have over 40 per cent of the world's population. One way to look at the lack of success in such countries is as evidence of core incompetencies – the bundle of activities and managerial skills that are mismatched in a great variety of countries in which companies feel they must do business. All organizations face major challenges to some degree in dealing with international competition. These include rapid changes in technology, the opportunities and risks of emerging markets, global overcapacity, the volatility of currencies and rapid international capital movements. The point is that some companies lack the bundle of managerial capabilities and skills that are required to be successful in some countries.

Take the example of a Korean firm trying to enter the US market. It first sends Korean expatriates there. When this does not work, it puts an American in charge. When the American does not work out, the company returns to the policy of sending Koreans, albeit ones with more experience. So far none of these alternatives appears to be effective. This partially explains the increase in international alliances, which allow the use of local managers. But there are also companies that have a history of failures in strategic alliances in some countries.

Cross-border and cross-cultural incompetencies in the management of alliances are formidable barriers to global expansion. Compare those companies that gain or lose ground in seeking a global market share in some of the largest and most competitive countries of Europe, the US, Japan and the emerging markets of Asia, Latin America, Eastern Europe including Russia, and the Middle East and Africa. Obviously there are some factors that are external to the enterprise to account for the degree of success and failure in different countries. Political and bureaucratic obstacles may make operating in specific countries very difficult for most companies. Economic downturns and social instability could also influence success. But it is also typically the case in every country that some companies succeed and others do not. Under those conditions we raise the possibility that a significant group of cross-border failures are due to 'cross-border and cross-

cultural incompetence'. Cross-cultural incompetence refers to a persistent inability to make significant contributions to perceived customer value in different cultures and countries. Cross-border and cross-cultural incompetencies are not fatal diseases. They can be overcome and can be unlearned. But in my experience, they are more widespread than reported and perhaps are more frequent than cross-cultural competencies.

By way of illustration, consider the case of computer group Apple in Japan. Apple began in Japan in 1979 with a global vision of Japan as a key market. In Stage I, in 1980, Apple picked the wrong partner, Toray, a textile firm with no computer experience and no contacts with computer equipment and software markets. Other less-than-suitable partners followed. Other mistakes were made. The high-priced Apple product was soon 'cloned' by cheaper imitations and sometimes these even outdid Apple in quality. In any case the high price was unsuitable for the targeted teenage and hobby markets. Stage II, from 1984 to 1987, was another learning period. Apple computers were upgraded but the software releases imposed American-style marketing onto the Japanese markets by simply translating US advertising and promotion. The ethnocentric approach seemed to be saying 'we're American and everybody else in the world buys our products so you should buy them'. Apple went through four general managers in five years. This did not help its credibility. In Stage III Apple found the right positioning but still had an undeveloped distribution system and staff. This was the stage where Apple Japan 'became a Japanese company with an American flavour' and the distribution system was eventually built up. In Stage IV, Apple in Japan was transformed, developing high-quality products and it sought to diffuse this capability worldwide. There was extensive support by the CEO, John Scully, who visited Japan four to five times a year and helped to build the Apple brand equity, and a strong Japanese team led by a Japanese national as president. A landmark at this stage was listing the shares in Japan in September 1990. But Apple's attempt to penetrate the Japanese education market is illustrative of the difficulties multinational corporations face. The most recent stage for Apple is less clear. It hired a Japanese executive with extensive experience with American companies and the ability to function as an insider in Japan. The goal was to make Apple Japan a center of worldwide excellence, and not just an insider to be treated on an equal footing with Japanese firms. Apparently the latter is not easy since Japanese government procurement for the educational system still favours Japanese companies. But there is evidence that in the latest period, Apple is gaining some access to the education market in Japan.

While Apple can be called a success in Japan, it still needs to develop credibility with a wide variety of constituencies that include diverse communities and government procurement bureaucrats.

How do we describe the changes in competencies that were learned? Does difficulty with local authorities come from choosing executives who cannot convince the government of the desirability of opening markets or simply from government preferences? To what degree can this only be circumvented through inter-governmental trade and investment negotiations?

Areas of cross-border and cross-cultural incompetence

We have conducted research on what appear to be the cross-cultural incompetencies leading to failure in different countries. Examples include Swedish and German firms in the US, Korean firms in Mexico, Canadian firms in Venezuela, French firms in Korea and Japanese firms in the UK. Nine areas of cross-cultural incompetence were identified. The first three are interrelated and seem to apply to a failure to be market driven:

1. *Inability to find the right niches.* Picking the right areas in which to compete is fundamental. Attacking an entrenched insider is usually not the most attractive route.

2. *Unwillingness to update adaptively.* Competition is keen and adaptive updating is required. This requires a responsiveness to local changes.

3. *Not having unique products.* Products are not viewed as unique and of a sufficiently higher added-value by customers in local markets.

The next four apply to other management attitudes and capabilities:

4. *A vacillating commitment.* It takes time to learn how to function in countries such as Japan. Instant success is not likely and even five to 10 years may not be too long. Patience is required. A vacillating commitment is an obstacle to learning.

5. *Assigning the wrong people.* Picking the wrong people, or the wrong top team, in an affiliate is usually given as one reason. But determining in advance who is 'wrong' is not so easy. Picking someone from the home country who does not understand the host country and whose main merit is that they have the trust of corporate headquarters can mean an ethnocentric bias, especially when the person chosen has limited adaptive capacities. The wrong person can also be a local person who cannot win the confidence of the home country.

6. *Picking the wrong partners.* There is also a list of difficulties in building alliances. A main limitation is picking partners who do not have the right bundle of capabilities to help reach the local market. Partnering depends on finding reliable and qualified partners and developing relationships in which visions are shared and which build on each other's strengths in an atmosphere of mutual trust with mutual benefits. Repeated failures are symptoms of cross-border and cross-cultural incompetence.

7. *Inability to manage local stakeholders.* This includes an incompetence in developing a satisfactory partnership relationship with unions, governments, schools and a wide variety of other constituencies, such as green groups that may have an important influence on the performance of the affiliate.

Two other factors are related directly to headquarters performance.

8. *Developing mutual distrust and lack of respect between HQ and the affiliates at different levels of management.* Here the incompetence is related to chronic troubles in relation to corporate headquarters, which loses confidence in a succession of managers in affiliates.

9. Inability to leverage ideas developed in one country to other countries worldwide. Innovations developed in one country that stay locked in the country of origin may be a manifestation of corporate incompetence.

Becoming globally civilized: global visionary leadership

What we are calling an emerging global civilization is being facilitated by the convergence of long-distance telecoms and a big cut in electronic processing costs. When information from anywhere in the world moves to another at the speed of light, the paradigm for space and time is altered irreversibly.

It is increasingly a simultaneous, neighbouring, functionally interdependent world, one with both violent and benign cultural conflicts that are not easily resolved. The Internet is but one example. Japanese participants on the Internet cannot participate unless they speak English. In accordance with my 'rocky road' propositions cited above, corporate leaders, often unwittingly, find that they must increasingly become globally civilized. They must accept the dignity of all humans, regardless of passport and cultural background. This involves helping to transcend and even mitigate cultural conflicts by accepting individuals from a great variety of cultural, racial, ethnic and religious backgrounds and seeking how they might learn from each other. The difficulties should not be underestimated. This kind of leadership is evident in a typical global consortium that aspires to reach people from a hundred or more countries. Corporate leaders must communicate that they are open to people in every country, that they can successfully engage in multilateral alliances to commit their firms to long-term interdependent relations, and in the process find shared values with all the stakeholders.

The 21st century global visions of executives express their mission as finding a leadership position in all the main geographical areas of the Americas, Europe, Middle East, Africa and Australasia and optimizing what can be learned in each area for customers everywhere.

In order to pursue their global vision they know they need to understand in real time the political, economic, socio-cultural, technological and ecological forces in all these areas. Then they can begin to comprehend some aspects of the emerging global civilization, from the changing needs of customers and from the strategies of competitors everywhere in the world. Their customers are people around the world who demonstrate through their preferences how they want to live. That there is a proliferation of Avon Ladies in Brazil's Amazon and in China, where they number more than 600,000, that the travel industry is the world's largest, or the fact that a Sambhuru warrior in Northern Kenya can own a cellular telephone are but a few examples of this phenomenon. The growth of telecommunications and computer technologies not only make the world closer-connected, it also creates a witness to global value shifts.

Green considerations are no longer fads but are steps toward fundamental changes in the world view about development and the environment. The World Bank recently cancelled a loan for a Nepalese project to build a large dam due to protests from environmental protection groups. Australia's BHP minerals group requires its workers to attend workshops on the behavior of grizzly bears as preparation for building North America's first diamond mine in the tundra of Canada's Northwest Territories with its Canadian partner. This is part of a program to make sure the project is acceptable by a set of constituencies including governmental, local and aboriginal communities as well as environmental groups.

Global leaders become globally civilized to the degree they formulate a global vision that they can communicate to a wide range of audiences around the world and that can inspire and motivate employees and investors around the world. The global vision is also the basis for building an internationally competitive top team composed of people who have not only the combination of direct experience and cross-border and cross-cultural competencies to do business in all markets of the world, but who can facilitate the transfer of ideas everywhere in the world.

In summary, becoming globally civilized for

leadership has many meanings. They include building global brand equity through networks of global partners, decreasing time to global markets, permitting mass customization and facing the cross-cultural challenges involved in moving ideas from local to global. It means importing concepts from one culture to another, getting people around the world involved in contributing to quality, customer service and so on, building global centers of worldwide excellence and encouraging the growth of cross-cultural competencies in their organization and promoting a global partnership culture. Leadership in the emerging global civilization will involve developing three major management capabilities:

(a) a global civilization mindset: which involves understanding the major interacting and emerging global political, economic, social, cultural, demographic, scientific, technological, medical and ecological forces, civilizational collisions and accommodations.

(b) global business literacy: understanding the new options in an era of hyper cooperation, periodic global over capacity, consumer value changes including the slow emergence of a global business ethics, as well as the blurring of sectoral borders leading to new global business paradigms

(c) global cross-cultural competencies: forming new forms of alliances (including electronic) involving cultural hybridizations in global real time with vendors, distributors, competitors, customers, and third sector organization to meet needs everywhere in the world.

We do not know whether this first global civilisation will be the last. According to Toynbee, at least 21 previous civilizations have disappeared. Becoming globally civilized does not mean that the world will be borderless or transcultural. In a world of at least 200 countries and tens of thousands of cultural distinctions, enterprises can make cross-national and cross-cultural competencies the building block for a global civilization that has some prospects for durability.

Summary

It is not a matter of whether we will have a global civilization, but of what kind. Paradoxes abound. The westernization of taste and assertion of cultural differences may be running in parallel, for example, but the willingness to engage in business dealings is becoming a global norm. Any careful scrutiny of the performance of a company in different markets will show the number of disappointments exceeds the successes. Successful hybridization can take place in both alliances and affiliates but some businesses simply lack the bundle of managerial capabilities required for foreign excursions. The case of Apple in Japan is instructive in this respect. From research in different countries nine cross-cultural 'incompetences' have been identified, including inability to find the right niches, unwillingness to update, inadequate products, vacillating commitment, sending the wrong people, picking the wrong partners, and failure to manage stakeholders. Becoming globally civilized does not mean that the world will be borderless or transcultural.

Suggested further reading

Perlmutter, H. V. 'On the rocky road to the first global civilization', *Human Relations*, 44(9): 897-920, 1991.

Simon, B. 'A shining future under the tundra', *Financial Times*, August 9, 1995

Donaldson, T. 'Values in tension: ethics away from home', Harvard Business review, 1996.

Perlmutter, H. V. 'The transactional corporation without boundaries: global enterprise networks and labour in the context of an emering global civilization' in Campbell, D. (ed) *Is the Single Firm Vanishing? Inter-enterprise Networks, Labour and Labour Institutions*, International Institute for Labour Studies, Geneva.

Culture is not enough

■ **Managers are told to be alert to 'cultural differences'. But, as** Jack Denfeld Wood **explains, differences between individuals from different cultures may be less than those between individuals from the same one.**

You are unique. There has never been anyone on the face of the earth exactly like you and there never will be again. This means that you are different from anyone else. These differences frequently lead to disagreement and conflict; and if we are to manage the disagreement and conflict effectively, we must understand the sources of these differences.

We see and feel these differences everywhere in our lives, and this is nowhere more apparent than when working internationally.

People differ in all sorts of ways – in overt appearance and in covert abilities, in the way they understand the world and in the way they understand themselves, in the things they make and in the things they value. For centuries philosophers and historians – and for the last hundred years an assortment of social scientists (anthropologists, archaeologists, economists, political scientists, psychologists, and sociologists) have been occupied with understanding the behavior of different peoples. In a sense, each of these professions attends to different facets of 'culture'.

In the past two decades, the word 'culture' has found its way into the popular business press via discussions of both 'corporate' and 'national' culture. Numerous articles and books aim to enlighten the general and business reader about the vagaries of culture. We are admonished to remove our cultural blinkers and see things from the perspective of others. We read comparisons of the cultural differences apparent in American, European, and Japanese management practices. But what is culture?

Culture

Culture has scores of definitions. Anthropologists tell us that culture constitutes the part of an individual's behavior that is learned from a particular group and shared with others, or that cultures differ in the material things they use, how they handle time and space, in what they value and in how they derive meaning in their own, very particular, context.

Organizational theorists tell us that culture includes explicit artefacts, values and norms, and implicit basic assumptions, or that culture is the pattern of basic assumptions with which a group copes with external adaptation and internal integration, or that culture is a collective mental program, or that culture is simply a shared system of meaning.

If one accepts a definition of culture such as 'collective mental programming' or 'shared basic assumptions', then culture defines the essential non-biological differences among all human beings. For the social scientist, this is a convenient definition, since it makes cross-cultural research relatively accessible. Cultural differences, defined as mental programming, can be found with paper and pencil survey questionnaires. This is how most management academics do cross-cultural research.

National differences are quite easy to come by with such surveys, although one should address at least two curious implications. One implication relates to the meaning of any given questionnaire item (and is generic to survey research in general) and the other implication relates to the finer distinctions which such a broad definition of culture may obscure.

First, the question of meaning. If 50 per cent of a Japanese sample agree with the statement: 'Individual effort counts for getting ahead' and 65 per cent of a British sample agree, what do we know? We know that if the sample is large, it is 'statistically significant' and if it is random for a given population, it marks a systematic difference – but how is it meaningful?

Do we know what behavior is classified as 'individual effort' by all those in both samples? Do we know what 'getting ahead' is for all those in each sample? Do we allow for different meaning for 'getting ahead' within each country? Do we understand that if half of the Japanese agree, half also disagree – and do we know why? Do we understand why fully 85 per cent of the combined Japanese and British sample answer the question in the 'same way' – either agreeing or disagreeing – with only a 15 per cent difference showing presumed cultural variation? Given 'western' presumptions about Japanese culture, this could arguably represent as much a striking cultural similarity as a striking cultural difference.

Second, the question of the scope of this definition of culture. Might there be a dis-advantage to employing a definition of culture as broad as 'collective mental programming'? Culture so defined encompasses virtually *every* aspect of thought and behavior. This has at least one unfortunate consequence.

If we consider the differences among a group of international managers as a function of their national cultural difference, we are unlikely to see, much less explore, other sources of similarity and difference. We will overlook, for example, differences between individuals within the same country, as well as similarities among in-dividuals drawn from different countries.

International managers: similarities and differences

If one probes a bit more deeply, culture may not always be the most useful or most precise factor to consider in understanding differences in an international setting. Other sources of difference can be equally, or even more, important. Let me illustrate with a real example.

When I first arrived to teach in Europe nearly a decade ago, my colleagues told me that cultural differences were what mattered – they claimed that cultural differences defined what happened in the groups and classes we taught. This seemed plausible, so I filed their claim away, then watched what really happened in several hundred seminars. I looked for the determining influence of culture, and I found something else.

When a new executive program begins on Sunday evening, it typically starts with an opening cocktail and a dinner. Participants from different companies and different countries arrive individually and may at first find themselves congregating in subgroups defined by their nationality – groups of French, Italians, Swedes or British initially huddle together and swap introductions and personal background information.

Once the initial 'getting-to-know-you' period is over, usually after a day or so, the demands of the course come into play and the managers begin to affiliate not so much with those who share their nationality, as with those who share other factors.

In essence, the executives affiliate with those who look at the world the way they do, or who have a similar, shall we say, management style. In other words, these participants affiliate with others who have the same sets of beliefs as they do or who have a similar character. The con-figuration of individuals and subgroups within the seminars are not defined exclusively by – or even predominantly by – culture but by ideology and personality. It seems to me that ideology and personality run 'across' national culture and tend to form dimensions along which individuals from different cultural backgrounds coalesce. How does this happen in such groups?

Ideology

Groups are decision-making entities. When you consider making a decision in a group, whether the decision is a 'moral dilemma' or is a 'business issue', you approach that decision with your own beliefs, values and attitudes. By 'belief' I mean a seemingly rational conviction about what is 'true' and what is 'false'. By 'value' I mean more of an emotional conviction about what is 'good' and what is 'bad'. By 'attitude' I mean an inclination toward (approval of, or agreement with) or a disinclination away from (disapproval of, or disagreement with), some 'fact'.

When discussing an issue with other group members, it quickly becomes apparent which of the others share your beliefs and values and which do not. In our social interaction, we tend to agree with and affiliate with those who share our beliefs, and we tend to disagree with and avoid those who do not share our beliefs. These beliefs and values need not be bound by our national cultural background. They rarely exist in isolation and are usually woven into a systematic tapestry which defines an ideology.

By ideology I mean a 'systematic set of beliefs and values'. Ideology is a way of viewing the world. It provides a systematic framework of 'ends' and 'means'. It is therefore both utopian (concerned with ultimate ends) and prescriptive (concerned with the means to achieve these ends). The more explicitly the ends and means are defined, the more 'ideological' is a belief system; the more vague or diffuse the ends and means, the less 'ideological' is a belief system.

Communism and Christianity, by this definition, are both ideologies: the one is concerned with the end of history, the other with the everlasting kingdom; and both with prescribing behavior for achieving their own desired end.

The systematic nature of an ideology may be partly conscious, or entirely unconscious. It may be conterminous with national boundaries, or it may, as in the case of Christianity and Communism, run across national boundaries. The degree to which the Catholic Church is, well, catholic, is a measure of the relative influence of its ideology over that of a specifically national culture. Similarly, the degree to which Communist party members (or socialists, or Greens) share beliefs about ends and means is a measure of the relative influence of the ideology over the influence of national cultures.

I shall have more to say about the role of ideology on the business environment in a future article, but it is worth pondering at this point the degree to which the great conflicts of the last several centuries have had their roots in specifically national cultural differences and how much these conflicts have had their roots in profound ideological differences.

Personality

Systematic differences exist between cultures, of course, but they also exist within cultures. Even when working within a single country – within the UK, for example – we can see differences in sex, in social class, in education, in age, in religious background, in political persuasion, in ethnic background, in physical appearance and in natural talents. Individuals also differ in their personality; it is part of their uniqueness.

By personality I mean something like 'character'. Our personality is the result of both our innate predispositions and our experiences as we were growing up. It is embedded in both our physiological and psychological constitution and is shaped by our personal and collective history.

There is ample evidence that personality takes systematic forms. While we are each unique, we also share personality characteristics in common with a number of other individuals. Personality is an important factor determining the configuration of individuals and subgroups within a working group. We tend to associate with those with whom we share similar personality attributes and to feel less comfortable and disagree more often with those who have different personality attributes from us. What do I mean by personality attribute?

The pioneering work of Carl Jung identified three systematic personality dimensions along which individual 'psychological types' could be found. The most familiar dimension of Jungian typology is extroversion-introversion. It is an important dimension in virtually every accepted theory of personality.

In the context of a group of international executives working together, the two personality types defined by extroversion and introversion are readily apparent. In the evening, the extroverts can be seen aggregating in a group at the bar after having eaten together. The introverts are conspicuous by their inconspicuousness – they can be seen talking quietly with one or two others before retiring to their rooms for study or going for a walk alone along the lake.

Individuals have a personality, but so do groups, organizations and national cultures. Cultures themselves can be classified along a dimension ranging from extreme extroversion to extreme introversion.

Thus some national cultures appear more strongly extroverted, Brazilian and American culture come to mind, while others occupy an intermediate position, the British and the Dutch, for example, and still other national cultures appear more strongly introverted, such as the Finnish and Japanese.

There is substantial evidence that all cultures contain individuals who tend to be either extroverted or introverted. Thus while one could make the case that an introverted American is comparable to an extroverted Briton and in turn an introverted Briton comparable to an extroverted Japanese, each of these cultures, when considered separately may leave roughly similar percentages of extroverts and introverts. Extroversion and introversion would then be the behavioral manifestation of a biological predisposition.

With only a little training, the extroverted or introverted individual is readily recognized by others of his or her same culture, but not as easily recognized by individuals from another culture. In management seminars, non-Italian managers have repeatedly misdiagnosed introverted Italians as extroverts, even though the Italian himself, and any fellow countrymen in his group, correctly guess that he is, in fact, an introvert. The scale may shift, but it contains a similar distribution of extroverts and introverts in different countries.

A culture matrix

Figure 1 describes my 'culture matrix', which shows the hypothetical relationship among cultural, ideological and personality factors. Different national cultures are pictured as discrete entities arranged along a particular dimension. Thus the US, the UK, France, Germany and Japan can be, and usually are, compared in a relative manner.

Notice that ideology and personality 'cut across' the cultural dimension. One can consider the three dimensions as being somewhat independent. That is, an individual from one country may well regard himself to be more similar to an individual from another country if the two have similar ideologies or personalities, than either of them will consider himself similar

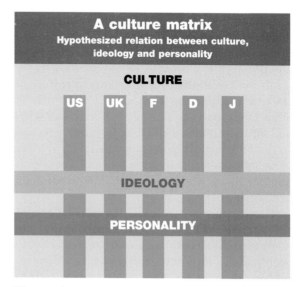

Figure 1

to someone from their own country who has a different ideology or personality.

For example, a British communist and an Italian communist, other things being equal, may well have more in common than either has with a free-market capitalist from their respective countries. Similarly, an extroverted and authoritarian French policeman and an extroverted and authoritarian German policeman will have more in common with one another than either will have with an introverted and gentle pacifist from their respective countries.

Even a pious and cosmopolitan Japanese Buddhist priest and a pious and cosmopolitan French Catholic priest will in many important respects have more in common than they do with atheist activists from their respective national Communist parties – the different cultures will inform aspects of the piety but the essential quality of piety is a human one, not a specifically Japanese or French one.

The intersection of culture, ideology, and personality

International management is one point of intersection for the dimensions of culture, ideology, and personality. If we are effectively to manage working with others in multinational groups it is helpful to recognize the influence of these three sources of differences.

I have found that even in groups with members from different countries, the horizontal dimensions of ideology and personality are usually better predictors of the structure of a small work group than is the national culture of the group members. Thus a Swiss manager is often more likely to find himself agreeing with and affiliating with a Swedish manager who has similar ideological beliefs or who has a similar personality to his, than he is likely to agree with another Swiss who is different in both ideology and personality.

Those who are similar in ideology and personality will tend to associate with one another and to avoid those who are perceived to be different. Two outgoing, conservative, right-of-center, free-market proponents or two 'tough-minded', decisive, take-charge, task-oriented managers will find themselves affiliating with one another, regardless of their nationalities or cultural backgrounds – as will two socialist, left-of-center, state-interventionist managers or two 'tender-minded' managers who are inclined to mediate disputes to maintain harmonious social relations within their team.

The contemporary culture literature has been invaluable in beginning to identify systematic differences between individuals with different national backgrounds. The problem is not so much that the contemporary culture literature is mistaken, as it is that most contemporary culture literature includes in the definition of culture all psychological 'programming' and may thus overlook the similarities among different national sub-cultures as well as the dissimilarities within any one culture.

The current focus on national cultural differences simply needs to take the 'collective mental programming' more seriously, and to continue the exploration of the dimensions along which differences exist within a culture as well as the similarity of particular dimensions across cultures. Otherwise, the management academics studying culture, who invariably come from different countries, will become captives of their own 'collective mental programming' – not their cultural programming, but their ideological programming – and they will be unable to recognize it.

Summary

National culture defines the essential non-biological differences among all human beings – but simply focussing on it may not be the most useful way of understanding differences in an international setting. Ideology and personality cut 'across' national cultures and tend to form important dimensions along which individuals from different cultural backgrounds coalesce. Ideology – a systematic set of beliefs and values – is a way of viewing the world. Personality is something like character – the result of both innate predispositions and experiences when growing up. The most familiar Jungian personality dimension is extroversion-introversion, and this can apply to groups, organizations and cultures as well as individuals. Extroverts and introverts are readily recognized by somebody from their own culture, but not as easily by someone from another culture.

The horizontal dimensions of ideology and personality are usually better predicters of the structure of a small work group than the national culture of group members.

The subtle art of negotiation

■ **In this first of three articles on negotiation,** Jack Denfeld Wood **and** Thomas R. Colosi **examine the problematic way in which westerners often approach the whole idea of negotiation.**

Negotiation as a topic of study is here to stay. Every month journal articles and books on negotiation appear. Most of these discuss techniques for influencing others. They tell us how to bargain better; they contain precepts, warnings, and lists of dos and don'ts. Some of them are good; some of them are not.

A few of them coach us on how to control our information, for example, when to make an offer. Some even tell us how to misrepresent our true interests. Others tell us how to make the quick killing – how to posture, wheedle, intimidate and bluff. Articles and books with a longer view tell us how to maintain a working relationship with the other party while we attend to our interests – assuming we have thought about, and understand, what our real interests are.

This and the following two articles on negotiation go several steps further. The first will sketch how we typically, and mistakenly, approach negotiation – some of the fundamental assumptions we hold as we approach the topic, and how these assumptions inadequately characterize the process of negotiation. The second article next week will sketch a multi-dimensional model of the negotiation process. Finally, in the third article we will explore in detail how one can intelligently use the multidimensional model to conceptualize and conduct an effective negotiation. Negotiation is visible everywhere – every day in newspapers and on the TV.

But negotiation is not just the province of international relations or international business.

We all negotiate. We negotiate at home, at work and in the market place. We negotiate with our family about the chores, with the boss about a rise and with the car dealer about the price of an automobile. When we add together the many millions of negotiations that take place daily at home, in commerce and in government we begin to look like a civilization of negotiators.

Negotiation is a central aspect of our collective decision-making processes. It is a very basic process but we do not sufficiently consider how it works. With few exceptions, students can still get their law, business or government degrees without ever running across a course in negotiation. This is a bit of a paradox – one of the things we do the most, we teach the least.

We use the wrong models

When one lives in a negotiating civilization and one is not trained to negotiate, it is difficult to negotiate well. Lacking training, we re-enact the models of behavior with which we are familiar in order to get what we want, and it frequently hurts us. Why? Because we are using the wrong models. People are different and these differences frequently lead to disagreement and conflict.

Over the centuries, cultures have established institutions to handle this conflict. Every culture has, for example, established norms and a moral code and procedures to enforce them. In highly complex civilizations this code is formalized into a legal system. The legal system clearly occupies a central place in western culture, and notably in Anglo-Saxon culture. Law provides an important cultural model of interaction for our citizens. It is two-party and adversarial.

Adjudication

A legal trial is a ritual with strict rules. The

basic players are three: the advocate for the plaintiff, the advocate for the defendant and a judge. This is what happens in court.

First, both sides present in opening statements their theory of the case; next, each side presents facts in support of that theory; they then present witnesses and exhibits as evidence in proof of the facts alleged; finally, each side closes with a summary argument of its position.

The judge is empowered by statute and common law to decide the case, and picks a winner and a loser. The loser has the right of appeal for review to a higher court. The appeal may or may not be heard. Legal training prepares one to go to court, but the job of being a lawyer requires other skills.

The percentage of cases filed for suit each year that are decided by adjudication is about 5 per cent. About 15 per cent of cases are dismissed, usually on procedural grounds, and about 80 per cent are never brought to trial because they are settled out of court, through negotiation.

Lawyers train to litigate in a courtroom setting but in practice negotiate outside it. We should understand a process as important as negotiation – but we do not.

Negotiation

Both a trial and a negotiation are decision-making processes but they do not function in the same way. If we get together to settle out of court we usually consider what we are doing as an extension of the larger adversarial legal process. And so we treat a negotiation as if it were a trial. But it is not a trial – it is a negotiation. And there are fundamental differences between the two.

Who decides? Who decides the outcome of a trial in a courtroom? The judge. Who decides the outcome in a bilateral negotiation? Both parties.

Who determines the facts? In the courtroom, the judge decides what facts are relevant and what facts are irrelevant. In a negotiation, the parties decide the facts, which are anything they agree them to be.

If one side marshals a thousand pages of computer printouts to support its position and the other side does not agree to accept the information, it is not a fact for the purposes of that negotiation, even if it were 'true' by some objective outside standard. Conversely, if one side makes an assertion based on an assumption and the statement is not questioned, then for the purposes of that negotiation it becomes a fact, even if it is 'false' by some objective standard.

Who wins and who loses? In a court of law, when a case is decided one side wins and one side loses. The process is designed that way. Negotiation is not designed for that.

In negotiation, if there is a chance for an agreement with joint gains and the parties do not come to such an agreement, both sides lose. If there is a chance for an agreement with joint gains and the parties come to such an agreement, both sides win.

How do we treat the other party? When two trial lawyers 'argue' a case in court, they often treat the other side, counsel and witnesses, roughly. But how do they treat the judge in the courtroom? With deference and respect because he has the power to determine the outcome of the entire process. It is unwise to irritate or insult the person who will decide your case.

But how do we habitually behave in our negotiations? We treat the process like a trial, or a game in which one side wins and the other side loses. We treat the other party like an adversary. We argue our side and try and convince them of the wisdom of our proposals. But for very practical reasons we should ask: 'Who will determine the facts and the outcome in this negotiation?'

We should treat the other party as someone who has the power to determine whether we get what we want or not – as we would treat the judge – with respect.

A trial is a decision-making ritual with formal and prescribed rules of behavior. Given that negotiation is also a decision-making process, what kinds of formal rules does it follow?

The first rule

The first rule of negotiation is this: *there are no rules for negotiation.* They exist nowhere. The other side takes positions based on their perceptions, assumptions and values. You take positions based on yours. Rules must first be negotiated and agreed upon among the negotiating parties.

'Pre-negotiation' agreements among parties

are needed on essential issues such as time, place, duration, participants and scope of the formal discussions as well as on seemingly trivial concerns such as the shape of the table.

In effect, such discussions are a negotiation about the *process* rules for the *substantive* negotiation to follow. But a discussion of process – for example, the seating arrangement – is just as substantive as is a discussion of, say, the price of a machine. Make no mistake about it: the negotiation of even seemingly trivial concerns is critical to the eventual outcome of any negotiation.

Preliminary discussions over the process rules are part of the negotiation. They count. During preliminary process negotiations, each side trains the other side on how it negotiates. If the other side demands a round table at the beginning of every meeting during the preliminary series of talks and we counter with a demand for a rectangular table, and after three weeks of getting pushed by them we say: 'OK, we'll take a round table', what have they learned about the way we negotiate? They have learned we do not last. Such discussions give information about each side's intentions.

The lessons learned carry over from negotiations over process issues to negotiations over substantive issues. This frequently leads to miscalculation, impasse and failed negotiation if we are resolute on a particular substantive issue but have waffled on process issues during the course of the negotiation. We are giving a double message, and the double message engenders confusion. We appear to be inconsistent, wishy-washy and unreliable to the other side. You should be consistent and treat substantive and process concerns as important. Any rules about the process or substance of the negotiation must be negotiated.

The essence of the process

The essence of courtroom litigation is ritualized verbal combat. There is little authentic exchange of information between adversarial parties within the context of a courtroom trial: there is the presentation of one's argument to the judge and a decision by the judge 'for' or 'against' one's side.

The essence of negotiation involves an authentic exchange, on the other hand, but an exchange of a particular kind. If we are negotiating a large automobile contract with our customer, say 100 automobiles for $1m, what are we really exchanging? Do we have the 100 automobiles outside in the parking lot and does our customer have a satchel full of banknotes? No. *The essence of negotiation is that it provides an opportunity, just an opportunity, for the parties to exchange promises and commitments through which they can resolve their differences and reach an agreement.*

Across the centuries we have placed many layers of 'sophistication' on top of the negotiation process but that does not change the essence of the process: it is based on the exchange of promises and commitments. The negotiation process is based on your word and on their word – on what you promise to do or recommend in exchange for what they will promise to do or recommend.

The importance of trust

Because the essence of the negotiation process is that it is an exchange of promises and commitments, we will not accept someone else's promise if we do not trust them and the people they represent. Similarly, the other party will not accept our promise if they do not trust us and the people we represent. That is why *any negotiation is essentially defined by the degree of trust in the relationship among the parties.*

The greater the risk in a negotiation, the greater the need for a trusting relationship because people do not take great risks with those they do not trust. The most effective negotiators are those who try to analyse the degree of trust in a given situation. An analysis of the trust in a relationship is a much better predictor of how well the negotiation will turn out than volumes of technical data supporting our position. We should spend time and resources analysing trust; and we should spend time and resources developing trust – it determines the success or failure of our negotiations.

By trust, we do not mean some fuzzy kind of feeling that leaves us vulnerable to the exploitation of others. We mean a solid kind of trust – being able to count on the other party and able to be counted on by them in turn.

Trust is an 'outcome' of a relationship and not an 'input'. It is developed and leads to credibility. One way to develop trust is to establish your reliability. You can even create a history of reliability. 'I'll call you at 12:37pm.' When do you call? 12:37pm. 'I'll fax our proposal to you at 9:00 tomorrow morning.' When is the proposal sent? At 9:00 in the morning. If you agree to the meeting at 10:30am, you are there, ready to begin, by 10:30am. If for some reason you are going to be there at 10:40, you call well before 10:30 to tell them you are going to be late.

Another way to build trust is to ensure that the other party is never surprised – that is key. You do not destabilize the people you are negotiating with by surprising them. For every move you make – even the smallest, most insignificant move or surprises you think will be pleasant for them – tip them off first.

If you agree to discuss certain agenda items, you arrive ready to discuss those items and you do not say 'I'm sorry, I'm not prepared to discuss that' or 'I have a few more items I'd like to put on today's agenda.' If you agree to bring Tom, Dick and Harry, you bring Tom, Dick, and Harry. Harry gets sick? You call them up well ahead of the meeting and tell them 'Harry is not going to be with us. I'm going to substitute Mary.'

It sounds simple, doesn't it? But so very many people disturb the trust and the relationship by simply not keeping their word on the smallest things and by surprising the other side.

But beware about letting them tell you how to be reliable. You pick the way that you are to be reliable and then demonstrate your reliability convincingly.

Importance of relationship

Negotiators should take a good hard look at why the relationship is important. If the relationship among parties to a negotiation is a positive one, you will have a relatively easy negotiation. If it is negative, you must expect a very, very difficult negotiation.

When we have a high degree of trust and confidence in our relationship, it is much easier to negotiate – much easier on us as negotiators to convince, to persuade and to educate each other. Many Westerners, but especially Northern Europeans and Americans, are problem-solvers. We are technicians. We focus on getting the job done – we focus on the task. We believe that after we have solved the problem then maybe we can take some time (if we have any) to get to know the people with whom we are dealing.

But the task is only half of the problem. The relationship with people is the other half, and those from other cultures place more importance on it. They may ask: 'What part of Europe are you from? Are you married? How many children do you have?' They want to understand the person with whom they are dealing. The 'problem' for the Westerner is technical. The 'problem' for non-Western cultures is often personal – the problem for them is the relationship. When the relationship is strong, any 'mere' technical difficulties can be easily overcome.

Other cultures place a higher value on harmonious relationships. Why? Part of the reason is that a harmonious relationship is generally more pleasant to have than a negative one. But there is a 'hard-headed' practical reason too. They want an easy negotiation – and not just today or this week. The relationship is the investment they are willing to make to ensure that things will run smoothly for a long time to come. Regardless of what technical problems come and go, the relationship will be the constant over time.

Non-Western cultures want to be able to depend on their Western counterparts. People from cultures where dependability is important do not like to take a risk with those whom they do not trust. One can always be deceived in a relationship. This is built into a process such as negotiation where each side hides information that might work to its disadvantage and to the advantage of the other party. The building of trust lessens the risk inherent in human relationships.

We are suggesting that attention to developing trust builds the relationship, which in turn lessens the risks to both parties inherent in a negotiation and provides the opportunity for the exchange of promises and commitments. Basic trust gives us the foundation we need effectively to educate the other side and to be educated by them.

The basic job

Negotiation is a decision-making process and as such requires the exploration of differences. Anytime a decision is to be made at least two different alternatives exist. In a typical bilateral negotiation, both sides approach each other with their own positions. These differences and subsequent disagreement are a necessary part of the process.

One can think of negotiation as an educational process in which one side attempts to educate the other side to see things as it does. Let us say we disagree about a particular point. You, as a negotiator, are after a behavioral change from me. Before I am going to change my behavior, you have to change my beliefs. And before I am going to change my beliefs, I have to doubt what it is that I believe. Conversely, I am not going to get a behavioral change out of you unless you first change the way you think about something. And you are not going to change the way you think until you first doubt what it is you believe. In short, if you do not agree with me about something, then my job is to create a doubt in your mind as to the viability of your position and vice versa. The basic job of a negotiator is to create doubts and uncertainties in the minds of others as to the viability of their position.

At this point you may be saying: 'Wait a minute, earlier you told us that we should "create trust", now you are saying that we should "create doubts", isn't that inconsistent?' Not necessarily. One can create doubts and influence others much more persuasively when one has their trust. That is one reason why we spend a lot of time on the relationship, building trust. Usually there are tough parts to a negotiation. If we get to the tough parts of a negotiation, to the parts where we do not agree and we do not trust each other, a deal is unlikely. But if we get to the tough parts, and trust is built into the relationship, we have a better chance of influencing the other side and coming to an agreement that benefits both parties.

If you want a hard time in a negotiation, do not spend any time preparing, do not spend time on the relationship, crank right into the business at hand, do not even see the other side as human beings, do not get in touch with the other person's perspective. But if you want an easier time, do just the opposite. Get to know them. Understand them. Build the trust and the relationship and then allow the educational process to unfold.

Managing expectations

We are often told by professional negotiators that we should raise and maintain our expectations in a negotiation. This is only half of the story. We spend entirely too much attention on what we expect, and not enough time on what they expect. It is much more important that you listen to them than that they listen to you.

We really do not spend enough time in any given negotiation, whether with our customers or our competitors, understanding what their expectations are. It is only after we understand their expectations that we can begin to manage their expectations. *The management of expectations, both lowering them and raising them when necessary, is critical for an effective negotiator.*

Very, very early in the negotiation, and throughout the process, it is necessary to manage the expectations of the other party about the eventual outcome and our ability to deliver. Why? Because we (a) want a better deal for ourselves and (b) want them to be satisfied. If they are not expecting much and they get 'something in the middle', they will be satisfied. If they expect a great deal and get 'something in the middle', they will be dissatisfied and poised to reject our offer. Lowering their expectations about the ultimate outcome of the negotiations will help.

Let us say we are beginning a commercial negotiation with another company. They think they can make $1 million on the deal. But by managing their expectations we convince them that they will be lucky if they can make $50,000. What happens? They will be delighted to get $100,000. And they will like us for it, rather than resent us. However, if we had asked them to settle for $100,000, but they had believed they could have gotten $1 million (because we had not effectively managed their expectations) the relationship may well have been spoiled and they may well have perceived that we had taken advantage of them.

Similarly, lowering their expectations about you will help too. Be modest. Play yourself down. If you try to impress them with your flash, your brilliance and your wealth, you are probably working against your own interests. They will tend to think of you as a tough opponent and will act defensively, close down their boundaries and prepare themselves for a battle. You will then have to work harder to lower the barriers that you really helped to erect.

If you behave in a low-key, relaxed, even dull manner, they will tend to think of you as conciliatory, perhaps even as an easy mark – and they may let their barriers down. We must manage their expectations by understanding them, and then create doubts in their minds when we need to change their expectations.

Positions, perceptions, assumptions and values

How do we manage expectations by creating those doubts?

First, we must educate ourselves about their positions. They will help us do it. They will be happy to. We must ask appropriate questions – and we must listen to their responses. They will even appreciate us for taking the time to do it. Second, we must look behind their positions, to understand their interests – their perceptions, assumptions and values. They will help us do that too. Third, and this is critical, we must look for and energize the seeds of doubt.

A position is only a position. Every position contains its own seed of doubt. In a negotiation, announcing an initial position is usually the first crude attempt to affect the expectations of the other side. No experienced negotiator comes to a negotiation believing that his or her initial position will be wholeheartedly accepted by the other party. The other side may come with the belief that theirs is a reasonable proposal, but they know that they need information to tell if this is so.

It is part of their job to get information from you. It is part of your job to get information from them – to educate yourself about their needs, to let them know what you need, to create doubts in their minds about their initial position and to lower their expectations about the ultimate outcome.

A perception is only a perception. Every perception contains its own seed of doubt. Their perception of the problem is an element with which you must work. But it is only a perception. Listen closely to learn how they perceive the problem in order to pick up where they doubt their own perception of the problem. Then energize their doubts about their perceptions until they change both the perception and then their position.

You will want to probe their perceptions for their underlying assumptions, which are generally difficult for them to articulate and are usually unconscious.

An assumption is only an assumption. Every assumption contains its own seed of doubt. Whether they know you personally or not, they carry assumptions about you because of the identity groups to which you belong – your nationality, your sex, your race, your profession and so on.

Listen carefully for these underlying assumptions. They contain seeds of doubt. For those assumptions that are negative, act in a way that is inconsistent with them if acting in such a way enhances your interests. For those assumptions that are positive and support your case, act in accord with them. Energize their doubts about their own assumptions. Their assumptions will also give you information about their values.

Values are fundamental to a person's identity. There are two problems with attempting to change another's values; one is ethical and the other is practical.

In the process of building a relationship and negotiating with others, you are going to learn a great deal about where people's values lie. Values are critical to who a person is and how each fits into his or her society. The ethical problem with attempting to change another's values is obvious.

We believe that the ethical targets for creating doubt are the positions, perceptions and assumptions that affect their expectations – that is an educational process. We do not believe it wise to target other's fundamental values for doubt creation.

The practical problem with changing another's values is that it is extremely difficult. The more central and culturally bound the values, the more difficult to change. Psychotherapists have difficulty helping people change their behavior and underlying values even when they want to change. You will be dealing with people who do not want to change. The probability of success in that instance is relatively small.

And even if you could change their values and they returned home to sell the deal to their higher-ups, if the higher-ups saw that their negotiators had turned their backs on their own values, the deal would be unacceptable. They would have begun to distrust their own team. You do not want to make the other party your clone, you just want them to agree with you and to have the credibility with the people who sent them to the negotiating table so that they will sell your ideas back in their home organization.

You might, however, be dealing with others who are quite interested in changing your values. You may want to keep in mind that your values were derived from the groups and culture to which you belong and if you are not clear about what values are central to you, or whom you represent, you leave yourself open to having them changed. Should others change your values significantly, you may be making future difficulties for yourself with those whom you represent.

Summary

Both a courtroom trial and a negotiation are decision-making processes, but contrary to frequent practice they do not function in the same way. The rules in any negotiation must themselves be negotiated at the outset. The process of a negotiation is based on the exchange of promises and commitments. It is defined by the degree of trust between the parties: building that trust (particularly important in non-Western cultures) lessens the risk inherent in human relationships. The basic job of a negotiator is to create doubts in the minds of others as to the viability of their position. Managing expectations is also critical. This should be done by finding out carefully about the other person's position and understanding their perceptions, assumptions and values. Perceptions and assumptions contain their own seeds of doubt. For ethical and practical reasons, though, it is unwise to target other people's fundamental values.

Suggested further reading

Fisher, R and Ury, W. (1981) *Getting to Yes, Negotiating Agreement Without Giving In*, Houghton Mifflin, Boston.

Bolton, R. (1979) *People Skills* Simon & Shuster, New York.

It takes more than two to agree

■ **In this second of three articles on negotiation,** Jack Denfeld Wood **and** Thomas R. Colosi **explain that negotiation involves far more than than just the people 'across the table'.**

In an earlier article on negotiation in this module we suggested that many Westerners do not understand the underlying process of negotiation. A person's view of negotiation derives from his or her cultural assumptions – assumptions that lead many westerners, notably those with an English-speaking background, to consider negotiation as an adversarial process.

But while differences, disagreement and conflict are aspects of the negotiation process, we have characterized the fundamental process of negotiation not as an adversarial one but as a joint decision-making one.

The essence of negotiation is broader than the resolution of conflict. It involves an exchange of promises and is a fundamental pattern of human interaction. When two parties sit at a table in a bilateral negotiation they manage the process together. The ultimate responsibility to decide the rules, facts and outcome of a negotiation resides solely with these two parties.

Since the essence of negotiation is the exchange of promises and commitments, there is an inherent risk to both sides that can only be lessened by the establishment of trust – in the sense of predictability, reliability and credibility. With increased trust, risk is lessened and mutual education becomes increasingly possible in the context of a working relationship.

The experienced negotiator manages the expectations of the other parties throughout the negotiation. Both parties are educated by the creation and maintenance of doubt. Each side attempts to create doubts in the other party's mind about their position, perceptions and assumptions.

The experienced negotiator looks behind these positions, perceptions and assumptions of the other side, energizes the seeds of doubt that are inevitably there and helps the other side to recognize its most basic interests and needs. This, in a general way, outlines the process of negotiation.

But to manage the process of negotiation effectively, we must understand the underlying structure of that process. The important components of the negotiation process that we have mentioned – the exchange of promises, the development of trust, the creation of doubt, managing expectations – all occur within the framework of a structure of relationships that themselves occur within organizational and societal frameworks. It is these relationships that form the structural dimensions of any negotiation.

The following model describes a four-dimensional structure. The dimensions define the core structural relationships among the basic elements in the negotiation process.

The structure of negotiation

When an arms control negotiation or a collective bargaining negotiation is reported, the press usually describes the negotiation as a meeting of two undifferentiated sides sitting across a table from each other. The report might say something like 'The Japanese and Americans sat down again today in Geneva' or 'The French government and the CGT have suspended their contract talks for an indefinite period as the union called a general strike'.

This description oversimplifies negotiation and portrays its structure in a one-dimensional way. Negotiation is said to be 'bilateral' when there are two parties engaged in discussions and is represented as a bargaining transaction between two elements (individuals, groups, companies or countries).

Even academic writing presents negotiation as a one-dimensional structure between two elements – two individuals such as a husband and wife, salesman and shopper, teacher and student, boss and subordinate or two groups such as arms-control delegations from Russia and Nato, parliamentary discussions between Social Democrats and Christian Democrats, commercial teams from Xerox and Fuji or collective bargaining teams from labor and management.

This portrayal of the process as a bilateral one overlooks the semi-private multi-dimensional structure of negotiation. Thus, while most negotiations are portrayed as two-party affairs, there are really four basic dimensions: (1) the horizontal negotiations between the two teams, (2) the internal negotiations within each team, (3) the vertical negotiations between each team and its organizational hierarchy, and (4) the external negotiations between each team and interested outside parties, such as the press, the public or the government. Successful negotiators have learned to manage the relationships along all four dimensions.

The horizontal dimension

The horizontal dimension is the one we read about in the newspapers. It is also the one we experience when we are negotiating with a salesman for a new car. It is the face-to-face interaction with the 'other side' and often takes place, literally or figuratively, across a table.

The horizontal dimension is the most visible stage on which the negotiation drama unfolds and it is often a quite formal and highly stylised affair. Misunderstanding the negotiation process begins with misunderstanding the horizontal dimension.

The H in Figure 1 overleaf stands for the horizontal dimension. The inexperienced negotiator or onlooker sees a lot of negotiating and bargaining occurring horizontally across the table. The experienced negotiator sees something else.

Most people think the 'real' substantive work of negotiation is done at the table. This is not true. If the negotiations have been handled well by both sides, the substantive work gets done behind the scenes, including discussions in the hallway with a representative from the other side, arguments back in the hotel within your own team and horse trading among departments within your own organizational hierarchy.

Those are the places where the key decisions are made about how many units – be they warheads, wages or widgets – can be 'delivered' to the other side at the table. The work that actually gets done at the table is largely concerned with setting the tone and agreeing on the process rules of that particular negotiation.

The horizontal dimension is an educational one. It offers a forum for educating the other side in obvious and not so obvious ways. Formally, you use this dimension to trot out your proposals, your computer printouts and your experts. So does the other side. Informally, both sides define the mutually acceptable rules of negotiation. You tip each other off as to how you do business. Are you trustworthy? Are you considerate? Are you dignified? Are you impatient? Can you be intimidated? Are you rigid and dogmatic or are you solid and reasonable?

The horizontal dimension provides a stage for both sides to perform. This permits the two sides to define the general tenor of the negotiations. If the relationship between parties is cordial, they use horizontal interaction to provide introductions, speeches and the tabling of well-prepared proposals.

If the relationship between parties is not particularly cordial, they use the horizontal interaction to stage angry accusations, insults and the tabling of non-negotiable demands.

The internal dimension

When we negotiate, the people sitting across the table from us are more than a group. They are a team. And their team comprises unique individuals. Their uniqueness gives an internal structure to their team. Experienced negotiators know that each team has both a formal and an informal internal structure and they strive to understand both. This team structure can be depicted as the internal dimension of a negotiation.

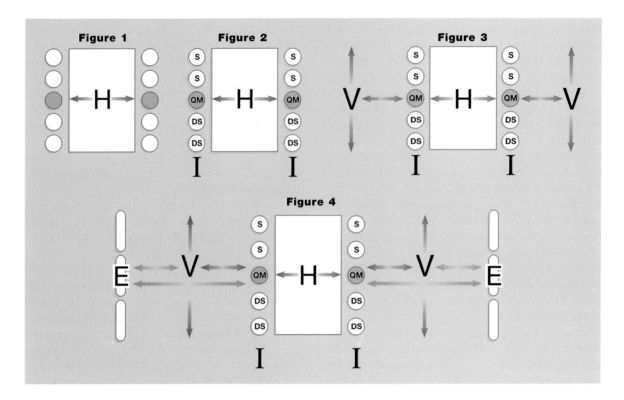

Figure 1

Figure 2

Figure 3

Figure 4

Members of groups quite naturally stereotype members of other groups. When we look at members of another group we tend to see an undifferentiated collection of people and assume they share uniform attributes. If we are labor representatives sitting across a negotiating table, we will tend to see the other team – management – as homogeneous and uniform. Conversely, if we are management representatives, we will tend to see the labor team in the same way.

This assumption of homogeneity is false and can lead us astray. No team is a monolith. Their team may look like a monolith, walk like a monolith and talk like a monolith – but that is because they dress alike and are well trained. The other side may consider your side to be a monolith but you know that your team is not because you have been fighting with them during the entire preparation phase of the negotiation. You found out at the first meeting of your team that there were fundamental differences among its members – in cultural background, basic values and personality. The differences among your team members represent the internal

dimension of the negotiation process and the differences tend to be systematic.

Usually the internal negotiations within a team are more contentious than the horizontal negotiations with the other team. There is more energy, emotion and considerably less diplomacy within your own team discussions than is true for discussions between your team and the team across the table.

The I in Figure 2 stands for the internal dimension of negotiation. The internal structure of each team includes three subsets of team members – the stabilizers (S), the destabilizers (DS) and the quasi-mediator(s) (QM).

During the preparatory discussions and the actual negotiations, the stabilizers, destabilizers and quasi-mediators become evident if we are attentive to what they say and how they behave non-verbally. This is true of understanding the internal structure of the other side as well.

Stabilizers. The stabilizers on your team are easy to recognise. Everyone has known and worked with stabilizers in school, at the office and in the shop. They are the nice guys on your team. The stabilizer sees negotiation as a way to avoid war, a court battle or a strike. They tend to be conflict-averse. They say things such as 'We're all just the same at heart' or 'Why can't we just be friends?' and 'Negotiation is a win-win process!'

Stabilizers demand little and offer much. They tend to have what Robert Bolton refers to as 'submissive' personalities and to be what Roger Fisher and William Ury call 'soft' negotiators (*see* 'Suggested further reading'). They allow people to push them around. They are soft on the people and soft on the issues.

If left alone, stabilizers can be taken to the cleaners by the other side. Stabilizers tend to trust others, even where that trust is not warranted. Stabilizers demonstrate their agreeable nature with their words and with their deeds. They also demonstrate their agreeable nature with their body language. They usually fall into line when authority is applied – your side's or the other's. They are easy for you to work with and they are easy for the other side to work with – and this is not necessarily an advantage for either side. Stabilizers must be managed.

Destabilizers. The destabilizers on your team are even easier to recognise than the stabilizers. To begin with, they are more verbal. You have been having trouble with them from day one. They do not like the negotiation process. They do not trust it. They think it is a waste of time. They do not like the other team. They do not trust them. They may not even like or trust you and their own team.

They think their own team should be back home doing something more constructive such as preparing for a strike or a war.

Destabilizers are generally not conflict averse. They even seek conflict. They say things such as 'It's a dog-eat-dog world' or 'Do unto others before they do unto you' and 'There are winners and losers in life – and in negotiation'.

Destabilizers drive hard bargains. They tend to have what Bolton calls 'aggressive' personalities or to be what Fisher and Ury call 'hard' negotiators. They tend to push other people around. They are hard on the people and hard on the issues. This is not necessarily a disadvantage for either side if the destabilizers

on your team and the other team can be managed.

Destabilizers tend to be autocratic and authoritarian. They normally resist any authority directly above them and are deferential to any authority exercized as they would exercise it – which is several layers above them.

If left alone, destabilizers can overpower, intimidate, create mistrust and ultimately sabotage the internal relationships on their own team, the horizontal relationships with the other team, the relationships among departments in their own organization and the entire negotiation process.

On a team where destabilizers want to fight and stabilizers want to make friends, someone is in charge. This is the formally designated head negotiator or team chief. If your team chief is a stabilizer, he or she may do everything possible to make a deal at any cost. So while you may get an agreement with the other team, you may never be able to sell it back home to your organization.

If your team chief is a destabilizer, he or she may do everything to sabotage a deal. So you may never get an acceptable agreement – by your team, by the other side or by your organization.

The quasi-mediator. Usually, if an organization is interested in coming to an agreement and understands the negotiation process, it sends a quasi-mediator to the table as head of the negotiating team.

He or she is usually the only one at the table who understands the process in full and is usually caught in the middle. Stabilizers tend to see the QM team chief as being a destabilizer and too hard on the other team, jeopardizing a possible deal. Destabilizers see the QM team chief as a stabilizer patsy who will unwittingly give away the store.

The quasi-mediator tends to have what Bolton refers to as an 'assertive' personality or to be what Fisher and Ury refer to as a 'principled' negotiator. The quasi-mediator is neither aggressive with others nor submissively permits himself or herself to be walked over. He or she is considerate with the people and firm on the issues.

The quasi-mediator is the one who orchestrates the negotiation process, if it can be orchestrated. As you sit in the seat of a team chief during countless negotiations, you gain experience and you realize that most of your time is spent mediating. You use the same skills heading a negotiating team that are used in a role as a professional mediator – convincing and persuading skills. A quasi-mediator is not, however, a neutral party. The quasi-mediator is, like any negotiator, an advocate for the interests of his or her side. But in that role as the head of a delegation, one finds oneself mediating between the other team, one's own team and one's own organization.

The vertical dimension

No matter how well you manage the other team and your own team, however, you must above all effectively manage the relationship with the organization that sent you to the table. The 'bottom line' of any negotiation is the line that is drawn by the people who sent you to the table to negotiate. This relationship is depicted by the vertical dimension of the core structural model of negotiation.

The vertical dimension of a negotiation marks the relationship between your team and your organizational hierarchy. The ultimate decision about whether or not your team can cut a deal with the other team lies with the people who sent you to the table. The two organizational hierarchies define the limits of any agreement that the two teams negotiate.

In Figure 3 (*see* p. 428) , the V stands for the vertical dimension of the negotiation process. They are also known as 'closers' or 'ratifiers' and they are the people with the authority and the power to approve, sign and ratify any agreement.

The real negotiation between your team and your organizational hierarchy typically starts out in a reactive way. Your team is becoming convinced and persuaded by some of the other team's arguments. You have discussed the issues horizontally with the other team and internally among yourselves and you begin to entertain the idea of modifying your position. Can you make a counter proposal? If the change in your position is significant, you must first check back home.

So you go to your organization and you say something like 'Vertical Hierarchy, the other side is making a lot of sense. We'd like you to change your policy so that we can change our position.' Your vertical hierarchy responds with something such as 'This is out of the question. Tell them NO!' So you go back to your team and your team goes back to the table and you tell the other team, 'no'.

Now the other team cranks up some more data, more computer printouts, more experts, some more 'facts' and begins to sound even more convincing and persuasive. So you again go back to your vertical hierarchy and say 'This is pretty good stuff. They have some very convincing material. You should really take a close look at this.'

About that time, your vertical hierarchy begins to question your loyalty and commitment to the organization. They say to themselves 'He's beginning to talk like the other side. Who's side is he on, anyway?' And so you begin to negotiate with your own organization – on behalf of the other team.

Consider this carefully: you are actually working for the other side. Why? Because you must, in a sense, become the instrument of the other team. Why? Because the other team does not have a chance of getting direct access to your organization. They know they must first go through you. They know they do not have a chance of getting what they want unless two conditions are met: (a) they must convince you of the reasonableness of their proposals and (b) you must effectively represent their interests to your organizational hierarchy, i.e. you must convince your organization of the reasonableness of the other side's proposals.

In short, you must be able to sell their point of view back to your organization. And they must be able to sell your point of view back to their organization.

You want their team to take your proposals back to their 'closers' and convince their organizational hierarchy about the reasonableness of your position. That is one reason why it is so important to have a good relationship with the other team. That is why you have not used tactics that surprise or destabilize the other team. That is why you have worked to become reliable and trustworthy to the other team. They are the means for your desired ends. They are your instruments for getting what you want.

The two teams at the table depend on each other to represent each other's interests.

If you have been as convincing as the other side has been, eventually your vertical hierarchy will ask you 'OK, how much of a change in our policy do you want?' You respond 'We want 100 per cent change, so we can go back and split the difference. It will give us more bargaining room'.

'How about a 10 per cent change?' 'How about 90 per cent change?' And so on, back and forth.

This bargaining with your organizational hierarchy is what happens as you try to move them off their bottom line. But too many times during a negotiation, this type of decision-making is crisis-driven – you run back to them with a hot potato, they jam around and cannot come to agreement and give it back to you and you go back to the table with their confusion to try to get an agreement. It will not work.

Your vertical hierarchy may not even know what position they want to take, so your first job is to help them understand what they want to do. Why not be proactive? Why not convince the folks back home when they first send you to the table to send you with clear orders? You will be more confident and they will get a better deal out of the other side.

The external dimension

The relationship that must be managed with interested outside parties defines the external dimension of the negotiation process. By 'outside parties' we mean those persons or groups without operational responsibility for the negotiated outcome, i.e. those other than (a) the negotiators themselves and (b) the people who retain the ultimate authority to accept or reject a negotiated agreement and who sent the negotiators to the table.

Depending upon the characteristics of a particular negotiation, outsiders might include the press, the government, the public, one's customers, one's competitors, shareholders or even other organizational members who might have an interest but no voice in the proceedings.

The E in Figure 4 (*see* p. 428) illustrates the external dimension of the negotiation process. Before one ever sits down at the negotiation table, one would do well carefully to consider the impli-cations of handling – or mishandling – the information of the negotiation process with those who operate outside it.

Outside parties are primarily interested in the substantive outcome of the negotiation, although they may pay particular attention to the subtle behavioral signals to gain access to that substantive information.

The process of negotiation is a private and delicate process, where mishandled information cannot merely put your side at a disadvantage but destroy the relationship of trust that has been painstakingly built among the parties.

Each team along the horizontal dimension must be able to meet alone and have the privacy to discuss alternative issues among themselves and with their own vertical organization without revealing to outsiders or to the other side their process of decision-making.

Additionally, for the process to work to the advantage of both sides it is necessary for the negotiation situation to provide a secure container for the exploration of alternative possibilities without publicly committing either of the negotiating parties to premature and possibly embarrassing situations.

Understandably, many negotiators, be they managers or diplomats, come to regard external parties, such as the press, as an inconvenient irritant or as an outright enemy. Negotiators may then attempt to hide information and avoid any contact with journalists.

This defensiveness frequently backfires and increases the interest of the outside media. External third parties will build their picture on innuendo and rumour if sufficient concrete information is unavailable – and sufficient concrete information is seldom available during negotiation because the negotiation process is a delicate developmental one and inappropriate sharing – or leaking – of information can have disastrous consequences.

Confidentiality is a professional precondition for an effective negotiation and must first be negotiated with one's own organization, with one's team, with the party across the table and finally with the external parties. The external relationship is best handled proactively and in concert with the other negotiating party. It should be approached with the same care and thoughtfulness as are the other dimensions.

In the final article on negotiation, we shall explore in more detail how to manage the structure and dynamics of the negotiation process.

Summary

The portrayal of negotiation as a bilateral process overlooks its semi-private, multidimensional nature. There are four basic dimensions to a negotiation. The 'horizontal' one is face to face interaction with the other side, often across a table. Little substantive work gets done but there is the opportunity for both sides to perform.

Differences among team members represent the 'internal' dimension of the process – often more contentious than the horizontal. Each negotiating team typically comprises stabilizers, destabilizers and quasi-mediators. The vertical dimension depicts the relationship between the negotiating team and the organization which sent it to the table. The external dimension is the relationship which must be managed with interested outside parties such as the press, government, shareholders and competitors. It is best handled proactively and in concert with the other negotiating party.

Suggested further reading

Fisher and Ury (1981) *Getting to Yes*, Houghton Mifflin, Boston.

Bolton, R. (1979), *People Skills,* Simon & Schuster, New York.

Managing negotiations

■ **In this final part of three articles on negotiations, Jack Denfeld Wood and Thomas R. Colosi explain some of the techniques and issues involved in bringing negotiations to a successful conclusion.**

In the two previous articles in this series on negotiation (*see* pp. 419 and 426) we discussed the inadequacy of our cultural assumptions about negotiation and explored several fundamental components of the negotiation process and how these components occur within a framework of relationships. This section looks at the actual management of the negotiation process.

Figure 1 shows the basic four-dimensional model of the negotiation process.

The 'H' stands for the horizontal dimension and is the one which is generally described in articles and books about negotiation.

The 'I' stands for the internal dimension – the negotiation which occurs among members of each negotiating team.

The 'V' stands for vertical hierarchy – the vertical relationship between your team and your organizational hierarchy.

The 'E' stands for the external dimension, or the relationship which must be managed with interested outside parties such as the public, the press and the government. (These dimensions were discussed in detail on pp. 426–32.)

The vertical dimension: managing your organizational hierarchy

The negotiation process, like chess, divides into

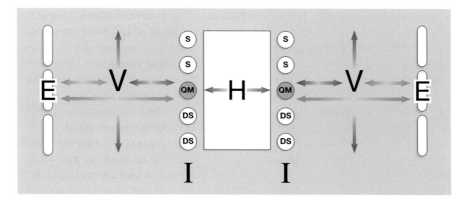

Figure 1

three sequential stages. The opening-game represents the pre-negotiation preparatory phase where the overall framework is articulated and the specific details put in place prior to commencing with formal meetings. The mid-game represents the initial face-to-face contact and the subsequent formal and informal meetings where behavior is more adversarial posturing than collaborative decision-making. Finally, the end-game represents the shortest, most intense meeting phase, where behavior is more accommodative and where proposals and counter-proposals are exchanged at an accelerated rate, leading in the end to an agreement.

While relationships along all of the four dimensions are important in all three stages of the negotiation process, probably the most important relationship to be managed during the preparatory stage is the vertical one with your organizational hierarchy. If the preparation phase of the negotiation has not been managed properly with your organization, it will be difficult, if not impossible, for you effectively to manage the process at the table.

In preparing for the negotiation with your organizational hierarchy, there is often considerable confusion about the goal, strategy, objectives and tactics to be employed. These terms are generally used interchangeably and it is helpful clearly to differentiate their meaning. (*see* Figure 2.)

The goal is simply the desired outcome. Once it is clearly articulated and agreed upon, an overarching strategy for reaching it can be put in place. Within the context of this overall strategy, specific objectives can be defined. Next, specific tactics can be identified and employed for use in achieving the objectives. Finally, the long-term implications of all of this must be considered – negotiating a multiyear natural gas supply contract is not the same as negotiating for a gold amulet at a middle-eastern bazaar while on vacation.

Nailing down the goal. Many negotiators have been sent to the table with sketchy instructions, have worked hard with other teams to hammer out common areas of interest and fashion a tentative agreement and then returned home

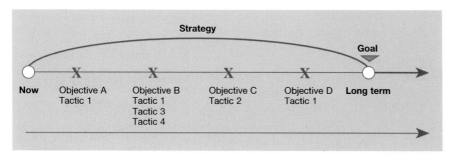

Figure 2

and attempted to 'sell' the agreements to their organizational hierarchy.

The vertical hierarchy is surprised and says 'no-way' and we lose credibility – both within our organization and with the other side because we must return to the table without approval of the tentative agreement. The subsequent table negotiation then becomes a form of damage control. The problems started right back in our organizations – when we were sent to the table with incomplete instructions.

Going into a negotiation without clear, explicit and comprehensive instructions is a prescription for disaster.

Defining the organizational strategy early. Typically, your own organization is not very clear why it wants to get involved in a negotiation in the first place. It is inevitable that any position you bring to the table will reflect a policy that is a patchwork quilt of many organizational threads. Your main job at the beginning will be to push your hierarchy specifically to define its positions and, more importantly, its underlying interests in the negotiation.

At the same time that you are getting clear instructions and a clearly defined position, you must also prepare an overall strategy and prepare your organization to alter its initial position later. You must challenge them to take into consideration what the likely reaction of the other side will be to their initial position. You and your organization are building a strategic negotiation framework and you are building some flexibility into that framework.

Relationships within organizations are complex. Individuals and even whole departments can appear to be overly accommodative, overly aggressive or relatively collaborative.

Because of this organizational complexity, you should work to understand the forces operating in your organization, which means having good answers to questions such as: How does it make decisions? Who are the key players? Who wants the negotiation to succeed? Who is indifferent? Who would like it to fail?

With knowledge of how your organization works you can begin to orchestrate it. You must force the fragmented parts of your organization to work together and give you guidance that is as clear, explicit and as comprehensive as possible.

When you have spent time with your own organizational hierarchy prior to going to the table, you set the stage for your successful return. It may not be easy to interact with the organizational hierarchy first, but you have to negotiate vertically before you can effectively negotiate horizontally, internally and externally.

Your relationship to your organizational hierarchy gives you tremendous leverage within your team and with the other team. When you have negotiated well vertically, that is when you can come home with agreements that you can be proud of.

Setting limits: tactical confidence and a short leash. It is ironic, but the less freedom to bargain you have at the negotiating table the more confident and secure you can be concerning your team's position during the negotiation.

Your tactical leverage as a negotiator at the table comes from that confidence you have when you know where you are going – that ability to be believed by the other side because you know what you can deliver. Your organizational hierarchy gives you that power and confidence. The more explicit they are about your restrictions, the more freedom you have from insecurity. The shorter the leash, the more freedom and confidence you will have.

Keeping them informed. Just as important as getting good negotiating instructions and having a short leash is keeping your organ-izational hierarchy informed of the progress of the talks. It gives you much more control over the process than you would otherwise have. A rule of thumb is to send them as much as they can take – then send them some more.

This helps them remain part of the process. It also protects you. It will keep you informed about what are acceptable and unacceptable agreements and about what the machinations back at headquarters portend for the negotiations.

The internal dimension: managing your team

The way to begin managing your own team is to have some say about its initial make-up as this will affect how the team will work together later. **Composition.** It is seldom possible to choose your own team. However, a rule of thumb is that you want a balanced mix of people – sufficiently similar for clear and effective communication and who speak the same language (figuratively as well as literally) but not gridlocked because of irresolvable social, cultural or ideological differences.

On the other hand, you do not want a team of clones; so you also need a team that includes individuals who are sufficiently different to permit a richness of perspectives.

The context and content of any negotiation, of course, should to some extent determine the composition of a team. If the negotiation is about designing a lunar lander, than you would want someone with technical engineering expertise and experience in designing lunar landers. But that is not enough.

Behavioral skills. If we analyse any negotiation and consider only the technical aspects under consideration, we will overlook the behavioral patterns and not understand what is going on between the different sides.

Some cultures, the Japanese for example, have a reputation for being very much concerned with the behavioral aspects of their customers and competitors.

Western negotiators have noted that on a typical Japanese negotiation team, individuals will be designated as behavioral process observers. They will have 'nothing' to do but watch the process of interaction, verbal and non-verbal, in order to understand better the negotiation. They try to understand the hidden meanings and messages within the negotiation – messages such as: are the words of the spokesmen congruent with their non-verbal behavior? Who are the informal leaders? Who is confident? Who is insecure? Who is trustworthy?

The important point to remember here is that we must not confuse technical expertise with process expertise. We must think through and address the process issues of a negotiation separately from the technical substantive issues. If we do not, the process aspect will inevitably be overlooked and we will severely handicap the negotiation – for both sides. Both sides have a responsibility to understand what is going on during the negotiation.

Establishing norms. Regardless of how a team is designed, you will likely end up with differences of opinion on your team. You will inevitably have both stabilizers and destabilizers, for example, and you will need to manage them. In the course of the negotiation, you will find it helpful to create norms of openness, discipline and privacy.

You need a team that is open, i.e. in which members are relatively open with each other. This requires leadership on your part to help set the tone for an atmosphere of safety (one can make mistakes...) and trust (...if they are honest ones).

Having an open team is helpful – but having a disciplined team is necessary. That means a group of individuals who are ready to work as a team. When time for discussion and debate is finished and a decision is to be made, a well-disciplined team will take responsibility for that decision, however it was made. There is an important difference between compliance and commitment, however, and the most effective discipline is not enforced by an authority from outside the individual but is generated from loyalty within each team member.

Your team should understand how it will be managed during the negotiation before it ever leaves the privacy of your office for the negotiation table.

Members need to know how the team will relate to the organizational hierarchy and what the procedures are for communication with the parties external to the formal negotiation.

And members need to know how the team is to relate horizontally with the other side, who will speak at the table or away from it, whether and when notes will be passed at the table. Well-trained teams, for example, never send a note on the subject under discussion. They think through the implications – 'What message are we giving by sending a note at this time? Is there a better time when we'll be giving another signal?' The conversations at the table are on the horizontal dimension; having conversations on the internal dimension at the table creates problems.

Caucus. The caucus is an adjournment of the direct discussions with the other side for the purpose of a private meeting of your team. The arrow in the figure points down toward a small triangle of Ss, DSs, and a QM. This depicts a negotiation team in caucus. Amateurish teams will conduct these internal negotiations in front of the other team or in public (at the table, in the hallway or at dinner) so the other team has no questions as to who is agreeing and disagreeing with whom.

More sophisticated teams will caucus in private, out of sight and earshot of the other team. And they will do this frequently. Effective use of the caucus is vital for you to negotiate effectively. If anything happens during a negotiation that you do not understand, that makes you feel uncomfortable, rushed, off balance, call a caucus. You cannot caucus too much. (*see* Figure 3.)

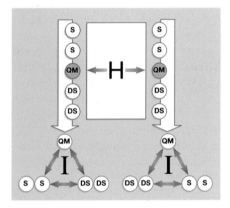

Figure 3

The general rules for caucusing need to be negotiated with the other team. Note well, however, that just as in passing notes, the context of when and how you call the break will be giving the other side information about you and how you operate.

Win-win sounds nice, but somebody usually loses. As an antidote to the win/lose adver-sarial mentality in which many negotiations take place, writers have begun to portray negotiation as a win-win opportunity. This reassuring talk about negotiation as win-win is not, strictly speaking, true. During a successful negotiation, there are usually losers as well as winners.

In complex negotiations, if a deal is struck, it is possible that the destabilizers on each team

'lost'. This is most obvious in an arms control negotiation, where the 'doves' and the QM may feel a fair deal has been consummated but where the 'hawks' may feel they have lost, and so may subsequently do everything in their power to destroy the implementation of the negotiated settlement.

No pious talk about 'win-win' solutions can hide this fact – at some point you will have to address the losers on your own team, and ensure that that dynamic does not destroy the agreement after-the-fact. Figure 4 shows the way the real win-lose pie is cut.

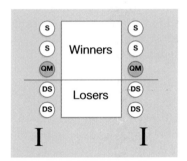

Figure 4

The horizontal dimension
If your organizational hierarchy and your team have been managed well, you still need to manage the negotiation with the other side along the horizontal dimension. You cannot come to any agreement without the other side, and managing the horizontal dimension is the heart of the process of negotiation.

Sitting at the negotiating table has sometimes been compared to sitting in a pressure cooker. The experienced negotiator has learned to manage them by identifying the sources of the pressure and, when necessary, lessening those pressures on his or her own team and on himself.

Some things you can do to reduce the horizontal pressure on your team are: (a) have an alternative to this negotiation; (b) realize that you have control of the process; (c) recognize that first impressions last; (d) practice; (e) give yourself time; (f) give yourself space; (g) avoid destabilizing the other team; (h) represent your true interests; and (i) notify the other team of your intentions.

- *Have an alternative.* Probably the best way to reduce the pressure on your team is to have a set of alternatives to the agreement that you are presently negotiating. The better the alternative, the less pressure on you at the table. Having a BATNA (Best Alternative To a Negotiated Agreement, Fisher and Ury, 1981) usually means, of course, that you have done some prior negotiation to develop an acceptable alternative.
- *Realize you have control of the process.* Remember the First Rule of Negotiation – that there are no rules for negotiation, they must first be negotiated. They cannot do anything without your assent.
- *First impressions last – putting the right foot forward.* Initial contacts set the stage for all subsequent meetings and mistakes can be lasting.
- *Practice makes perfect.* Many experienced negotiators prepare their teams for the table negotiations by practising among themselves. They take the negotiations seriously enough to scrimmage, i.e., to put themselves in the other team's place. Before trial, competent lawyers prepare two sides of the case, their own and the other's side.
- *Give yourself time.* An hour might be an unacceptably long period to wait in Germany or it might be an insignificantly short period in the Middle East or Far East. Other things being equal, if one party to a negotiation is looking at his watch, while the other party is looking at her calendar, the side looking at his watch is already at a disadvantage.

If we have a return flight on a specific date and the other side knows this, they may plan the negotiation to use time to their advantage. We have put ourselves in an increasingly disadvantageous position as we approach the deadline and we may be tempted to make unwise concessions in order to reach an agreement before we must leave.

Collective bargaining negotiations between labor and management almost always take place under a deadline imposed by the expiration of a contract and the threat of a strike. The parties often use the deadline to move the process forward. In a sense, they are like poker players upping the ante. This is a frequent tactic but it obviously has its drawbacks.

- *Give yourself space.* At some point in the negotiation, the other side will probe to discern the relationship between you, your team and the hierarchy that you represent. This can be either a legitimate search for information or a tactic to split your team and throw you off balance.

As a tactic to destabilize your side, the questions might be 'Do you have the authority to negotiate?' You do, of course, or you would not be there at the table. A more sophisticated destabilization tactic is: 'Do you have the power to close?' This is clearly intended to shake your confidence and self-assurance. An effective response to that question can be 'I believe that I have as much authority to close as you do'. Keep in mind before you get hooked by such questions, however, that you do not even want to have the authority to close. Very rarely will the 'closer' come to the table to negotiate – for some very good reasons.

Let us say you have negotiated a good price on a new car. The salesman excuses himself to check with his manager. He returns and says something like 'Though of course I can see the reasonableness of your proposal, my manager says we would be giving the car away at that price'. He has positioned himself between you and the 'real' decision maker.

By using his absent closer, the salesman has reduced his personal power yet in fact given himself more power in the negotiation.

We use the same tactic when we tell him 'I'll have to check with my spouse'. It may gratify your ego but if you tell him that you have the power to make the decision right then and there, you're bargaining at a disadvantage. Your apparent increase in personal power actually disempowers you to some extent. It is generally in your best interest to have your closer away from the table to protect you.

There may be times, however, when you want your closer(s) at the table. But this should only be done as part of a conscious strategy. In general, keep your closer away. It gives you more room to manoeuvre. And it makes it easier on your relationship with the other side.

- *Avoid destabilizing the other team.* The inexperienced negotiator often believes that if one wants an advantage in the negotiation, one should surprise the other side. This is a mistake. Surprises will destabilize and upset the other side. They will trust you less. In addition, you will be disadvantaged by their unpredictable response. You want to be able to manage the negotiation. If you destabilize the other side, you give up control of the process.

● *Represent your true interests.* Inexperienced negotiators sometimes think it advantageous to misrepresent their bottom line as much as possible. They make an unreasonable demand or take what looks to others as an unreasonably extreme position.

This is generally a mistake because it may look to others (such as the Japanese, who tend not to misrepresent their bottom line) as insincerity when you eventually shift your position and make large or frequent concessions. In addition, if you misrepresent your true interests, how can the other side satisfy them?

● *Notify the other team of your intentions.* Predictability is one of the reasons why it is so important to notify the other side of your intentions and your actions. Notification – tipping off the other side early about any irregularities – has several advantages: it increases the likelihood that they will trust you; it gives the relationship stability; it gives you credibility; it gives you an advanced warning of their probable reaction (and this is very useful information to have); and it gives you time to change your mind before you get publicly locked into a position.

There are several simple procedures that will be helpful for you in shaping the eventual outcome of a negotiation: (a) asking questions (b) paraphrasing their statements (c) taking better notes than they do (d) summarizing often and (e) closing on your own words.

● *Ask questions.* To convince you of anything, the negotiator must perform his or her basic job – to create doubts in the minds of the others as to the viability of their position. The way experienced negotiators educate one another – the way they manage information, persuade and create doubts – is not to make statements but rather to ask questions. Questions create doubts.

● *Paraphrase their statements.* Rephrasing their words into your own terms will go a long way towards giving you control over the substantive aspects of a negotiation. One of your jobs as a negotiator is to interpret to the other side what you heard them say. Getting the agreement of the other side on your paraphrasing will allow you to control the language of the negotiation. Do this often during the meeting, and you begin to define the course of the talks.

● *Take better notes than they do.* Taking notes of both meetings and phone calls with the other side has many advantages. It gives you material for the difficult analytical work that your team will be doing between meetings as you search for proposals that encompass your and the other side's interests. It gives you a record for your organizational hierarchy. And it gives you more control over the memory of the table process.

Go over your team's notes until everyone on your team agrees, then in the joint sessions compare your notes with the other side's. Yours will be better. Pretty soon they will be relying on your notes. Whoever controls the notes controls the memory of the negotiation. Whoever controls the memory controls the entire process.

● *Summarize often.* This will permit you to consolidate your control over the whole process. The summaries can be verbal at the meetings, but should continually be formally typed-up and agreed by the other side. You will probably find yourself negotiating over the wording of the summaries. Getting agreement on your summaries protects you from the other side trying to assert that you agreed on something that you haven't and thus keeps them from trying to wedge in any last minute concessions from you.

● *Close on your words.* If you have paraphrased their words into your own, taken good notes and made good summaries of the discussions, you help to put your side in a position to 'close' each session and the final agreement in your own words.

If you have ensured agreement on the small points covered along the way, whether they seemed important or not, you have done a lot to define the final agreement.

Shadow negotiations. Shadow negotiations are surreptitious conversations that take place away

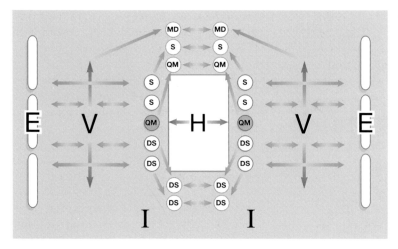

Figure 5

from the table. Although they might be an integral part of the strategic and tactical plan of a negotiation, shadow negotiations are usually impromptu or otherwise unauthorized private exchanges between individuals who are not on the same negotiation team but who share similar interests, such as ensuring the success or failure of the negotiation.

The principal shadow negotiations are pictured in Figure 5 as shaded arrows pointing away from the table, and implying that the conversations are indirect and often secret. Each of these shadow negotiations runs its own risks.

QM-QM shadow negotiations. As the nego-tiations progress and both sides become more comfortable with each other, you will begin to see changes in the tenor of the negotiations. As you build the relationship with the other team chief, you will begin to discover that you have the same job and the same problems. The person on the other side of the table – your opposite number – is struggling with exactly the same issues that you are.

The head of the two delegations may therefore find it helpful to speak alone from time to time.

When shadow negotiations occur more or less openly between the quasi-mediators they are often part of explicit team strategy. When initiated by the quasi-mediator without the knowledge of his or her team, the conversations usually concern how to handle members of his own team. One way you know the negotiation is

approaching closure, for example, is when you and the other quasi-mediator are relying on one another to take care of each other's problem team-members.

Two other reasons for quasi-mediators to get together alone are (1) to explore alternatives without affecting the expectations of those on one's own team (and thus the expectations of one's vertical hierarchy via the covert contacts of stabilizers or destabilizers) and (2) to defuse emotional situations.

To meet privately with the other team chief, you may need to cut out your team destabilizers and stabilizers – this is the 'walk in the woods' between the two chief negotiators. Such meetings can exacerbate suspicion on your team and make your internal negotiations more difficult unless you have discussed the strategic and tactical need for them and have established procedures for reporting back.

Stabilizer and destabilizer shadow negotiations. Shadow negotiations in which stabilizers or destabilizers are involved are either un-authorised contacts with members of the other team, secret contacts to allies back home in the vertical hierarchy or secret leaks to outside parties such as the press.

If the stabilizers get together, they may raise the expectations of the other side unrealistically. If the destabilizers get together, they may have enough power and enough muscle to tip over the whole deal. Unless you have a very good reason

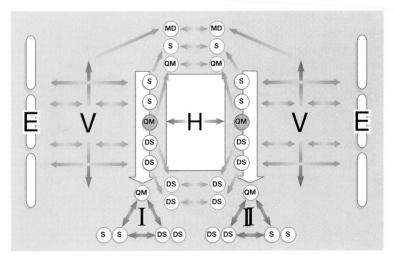

Figure 6

to the contrary, it is much wiser to limit the unplanned private exchanges to the team chiefs or to the whole group at 'planned' informal social gatherings.

If the stabilizers or destabilizers make unplanned and unreported contact with their allies in the organizational hierarchy, it is probably intended to influence the negotiation surreptitiously from that direction. They may be looking for support for their positions and trying to bring pressure to bear on the team chief to change his or her position on a particular issue.

If they are making secret contact with parties external to the negotiation, they can be attempting to create public pressure for their position and indirectly to put pressure on those in their organization and on their team who may disagree with them. These are all risky operations, from an individual standpoint, and can create irreparable damage to the success of a negotiation.

The external dimension: managing the outside parties

Virtually all of the real work in a negotiation is invisible to outside observers. Perhaps 90 per cent of what takes place occurs under the surface and is out of view.

One reason we know so little about the negotiating process is its inherent privacy. Basic to the process of negotiation is the discussion of tentative and exploratory proposals that necessitate privacy.

When exploratory proposals are leaked and made public, they typically become ammunition in the arsenals of one or another of the destabilizers. The leaks tend to derail the negotiation and serve to enhance the position of the destabilizers.

For these reasons, the 'private' negotiation table can be considered a semi-public platform. No matter how private and secret negotiation at the table appears, experienced negotiators assume that they can be exposed, intentionally or inadvertently. The substantive issues, especially the difficult ones, be they horizontal, internal or with the organizational hierarchy, are most effectively dealt with informally and in private among the appropriate representatives.

Part of any negotiation is a negotiation about the release of information concerning the progress of the discussions. From time to time one is expected, or required, to share information about the negotiation with interested outside parties. This is best planned for and negotiated in advance with one's vertical hierarchy and with the other negotiating team.

Conclusion

We have seen that a typical 'two-party' negotiation model reveals a multidimensional structure with negotiations along vertical, internal, horizontal and external dimensions. The complete multidimensional structure is illustrated in Figure 6.

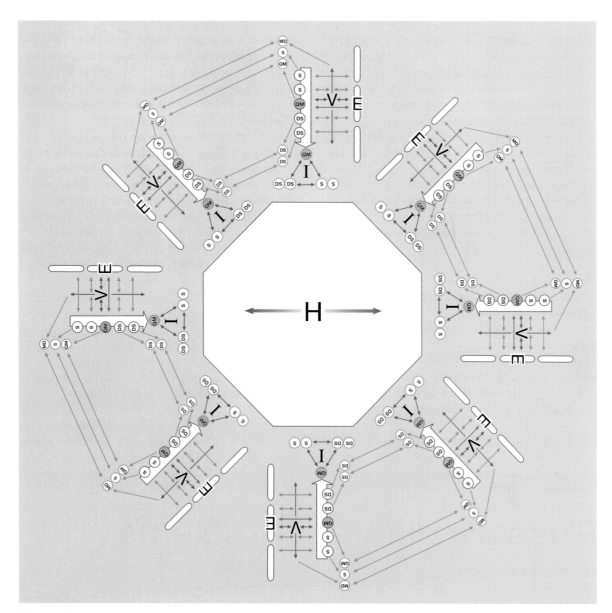

Figure 7

Many negotiations, however, are even more complex than bilateral ones. Figure 7 depicts the complexity of a multi-party negotiation such as at the U.N.

This is much more arduous to manage, principally because it is difficult to co-ordinate the different dimensions among all of the parties. Apart from the problem of complexity, however, the basic structural patterns of interaction and processes are the same in multilateral settings as are those we have sketched for bilateral negotiations. If you are aware of those patterns and understand them, you have a better chance of successfully managing the negotiation.

Remember, though, that a negotiated agreement is nothing but a promise on a piece of paper unless it is implemented. The best – and in the final analysis the only – guarantee of implementation depends on the trust that exists between the parties to a negotiation. The best way to ensure compliance is to keep a good relationship. Both sides should be willing to recognize the necessity for minor adjustments subsequent to the signing ceremony.

No list of insights or rules is by itself an adequate guide for successfully managing a negotiation. Negotiation is a behavioral event and 'knowledge' of how to do it will be of little help unless it is put into practice and the skills developed. Any application of these insights requires good judgment on how and when to employ them. That is where experience comes in. That is where you become the expert. 'What you do' is ultimately far less important than 'how you do it'.

Summary

In managing the vertical dimension (within your organizational hierarchy) it is important to nail down the goal of a negotiation, gain clear instructions, prepare a strategy, set limits to your freedom, and establish clear communications.

Where your own team is concerned (the internal dimension), consider its composition so as to get the balance right, include behavioral process observers, establish norms for openness, discipline and privacy, and make sure you caucus in private. Despite pious talk about 'win-win' you will have to address the losers on your own team.

Negotiating with the other side is the heart of the process. Ways in which you can reduce the pressure include: having a set of alternatives to an agreement, making a good first impression, preparing through practice, giving yourself time (deadlines have their pros and cons), having a 'closer' of the deal who is absent, not destablizing the other team, representing your true interests rather than taking an extreme position.

Suggested further reading

Colosi, T. 'The Iceberg Principle: Secrecy in Negotiation', in Bendahamane, D. and McDonald, J. Eds., *Perspectives on Negotiation,* US Government printing office, 1986.

Fischer, R. and Ury, W. (1981), *Getting to Yes, Negotiating Agreement Without Giving In*, Houghton, Boston.

Russia's different problems

■ **Management education is a key factor in the reform of the Russian economy. But** David Chambers **explains that the key lessons are not always the same as those needed by managers in the West.**

How well does management education travel across national frontiers? How readily does it transplant across the formidable border between the capitalist economies and the former command economies of what used to be the Soviet bloc?

The question is important because reform in the optimistically-named 'transitional' economies has cast management education in a major role. Business is seen as the engine of reform – in the political as well as the economic sphere. For business in the region to match the expectations placed on it, effective training of managers and of new recruits is an imperative.

The activity 'management training' features on the critical path. When London Business School ran its first courses for top managers from the then Soviet Union, in early 1989, there was some initial difficulty with the word 'manager'. The groups included 'general directors', and reporting to them 'senior specialists'. Their responsibilities were in some respects wider, in others narrower, than those of an equivalent Western manager.

Some appeared to occupy the position of feudal baron, covering not just the working life but also the health, housing and recreation of a one-company town. In contrast, many of the decisions that would rest with the chief executive and his or her board in a Western company were evidently being taken not in the enterprise but in the relevant ministry.

Again, decisions that in the West would be left to middle managers tended to be referred up to the general director. The label of senior specialist was accurate in most cases: an engineer or scientist who had risen to the top level in his or her enterprise without having had occasion to acquire general management skills.

These managers are now coping with uncertainties for which there is no close equivalent in the West. These include uncertainties over contractual rights and obligations, supplies, the taxation regime, payment arrears and law enforcement. In what ways can the repertoire of Western business education best be put to use in assisting them? Which topics from a comprehensive guide to management are going to play best in Penza and in St. Petersburg?

To answer these questions, London Business School has collected views from a carefully-selected sample of successful Russian top managers. The London Business School set out to identify businesses whose success had followed not just from trading but also from well-judged product-market positioning, operational improvements and re-investment in the company.

It then asked their chief executives to make short presentations to invited audiences of Russian and Western managers, outlining the main decisions they had taken, the obstacles they had overcome and the analysis and judgments underlying the decisions.

Four one-and-a-half-day seminars were held, starting in March 1994, in Moscow, Perm, Rybinsk and Ekaterinburg. Six or seven chief executives spoke at each seminar. They had been identified with the help of Western managers and journalists working in Russia, a trawl through Russian newspapers, discussion with Russian managers who had taken part in programs at the London Business School and through contacts with the local Chambers of Commerce.

The seminar series was entitled 'Learning from success' and it took place thanks to a generous grant from the Shell Company. Its purpose was both to draw attention to effective business practice which other Russian companies could emulate and to have these managers identify the topics for which training would be of most use to their companies.

The issues and priorities as perceived by these companies are representative of those occupying Russian enterprises today. Some were engaged in converting from military to civilian production, some were creating businesses in scientific institutes whose government funding had dried up. For others the priority was to set up new supply chains to replace those fractured by the breakup of the Soviet Union; yet more were changing their product lines in order to fill market gaps and shed unwanted products. A few were totally new businesses, responding to new business opportunities. Four examples from the seminar series illustrate noteworthy features of the companies now emerging in Russia.

Four Russian companies

Aviatika. The Aviatika Company is an example of military conversion. It leases part of a plant – in which MiG fighter aircraft were formerly built – for the manufacture of light aircraft used mainly for crop-spraying.

Most of its revenues, though, come from another of its businesses, as main dealer in Russia for the Chrysler Jeep. It won this agency because it was able to staff the maintenance and after-sales service units with highly trained technicians, trained in the aircraft industry. Aviatika's founder saw the opportunity to employ a resource severely undervalued in its existing use, namely the reserve of skilled labor capable of filling jobs ranging from product designer to automobile technician. Conversion in this case was a matter of converting people, not of converting machines.

MOST. The MOST Association has played an important part in creating or repairing supply chains. Originally formed to promote export of Soviet products and technologies to foreign markets, its structure turned out to be well suited to addressing a number of other problems faced by its member companies.

Industry's supply chains, back from the assembly of the final product through component manufacture to sourcing of raw material, tended to criss-cross the former Soviet Union with little regard to transport costs. With the demise of central planning, transport costs suddenly became important.

A second set of difficulties resulted from the political breakup of the Union. For example, one third of the carpets sold in Russia were made in Tadjikistan, but the raw materials came from Russia. Production stopped in the early 1990s due to a lack of raw materials. MOST was able to act as go-between in solving both types of problem: helping its members to find supplies from geographically convenient sources and setting up payment and credit arrangements so that cross-border transactions such as that with Tadjik carpet manufacturers could start again.

AvtoRes. The AvtoRes Group is an example of a company, which, freed to make its own decisions on what to produce, dropped a large number of uneconomic products and invested heavily to capture a newly opened market.

The group was formed in 1990 from departments in the Radar Ministry and is interesting partly because its internal structure recreates much of the organization of the former ministry, Gosplan, in miniature.

Decisions on what is to be produced or developed are made by the group's board of directors and passed down to managers of the enterprises. Materials procurement and the management of sales are undertaken centrally. Its main initiative has been to enter the market for refrigerated transport. With the disintegration of the Union, Russia was left without the relevant technology, most of which was located in the Baltic states and in Odessa.

In 1991 the group used 1bn roubles from accumulated reserves to build a competence in refrigeration in collaboration with Kamaz and Zil and with technology purchased in Korea and the US. Seventeen of the group's 52 factories now work in this program. Products include generators to allow storage and transportation of agricultural products, and drying, sublimation and forced-freezing equipment.

Dialog. The Dialog Group is an example of a wholly new organization, all of whose businesses operate in the service sector: a sector that was notoriously underdeveloped in the Soviet Union. Dialog was founded in 1988, initially as a joint venture, to sell and service personal computers.

In the following years it branched out into many other activities. By mid-1994 there were 78 subsidiaries and 3,500 full-time employees. The subsidiaries included a bank, a company providing medical services, a project-management company, an architectural company, a securities broker, a law company and a telecommunications company.

Dialog's managers explain that this proliferation of activities followed a simple logic. When the business was formed, most of its employees came from the Academy of Sciences, where they had been used to receiving good medical services from the Academy's Medical Institutes. Like other Russian enterprises at the time, Dialog needed to find alternative medical services for its staff.

Dialog was unusual, however, in organizing these services as a separate business, free to accept customers who were not its own employees. It followed a similar plan in setting up a company to provide legal services. Again, when the company wished to refurbish its own premises, organizations in the state sector showed little interest in taking on the work; therefore a company for the management of construction projects was formed.

In short, Dialog's requirements as a well-managed computer services company exposed a series of gaps in the support services available to businesses in Russia. In most cases some form of the service did exist but was of low quality, unreliable and slow. Dialog chose to treat these gaps as business opportunities, to which it responded through forming its own new service companies. These could trade not just with the parent company but also on the open market.

Transplants and rejects

It is easy to identify elements in any Western guide to management that will have little practical appeal to a Russian manager. Given the uncertainties of supply, the canny production manager has good reason to hold higher stocks of raw materials or components than would his or her Western counterpart. Analysis to help him decide how high these stocks should be and to eliminate obsolete stock is useful but concepts such as just-in-time and lean production evoke only hollow laughter.

To most Russian marketing managers, many of the choices presented in Western case studies (for example, between sales strategies, between distribution channels) presuppose an infra-structure of data collection and market intel-ligence that barely exists. Other choices are rendered empty by the lack of an established framework of commercial law. For example, pirating of software is endemic and because still there is no reliable legal protection of intellectual property rights, no company is going to make money from selling standard software on the Russian market.

Russian finance managers have been quick to recognize that they have much to learn from Western practice and they respond well to the intellectual puzzles offered in the behavior of Western financial markets. But in a situation where bank lending is seldom for more than six months and where there may not yet be a secondary market for the company's shares, discussion of optimal capital structure can be of little practical use.

These then are examples of topics and material that are of direct practical utility when taught to Western managers but of no more than intellectual interest to their counterparts in most Russian companies.

What then are the topics which the Russian managers identified, in the course of London Business School's four seminars on 'Learning from Success'?

● They want help in building systems of market intelligence and company information corres-ponding to those of the West. The MOST Association is an example of a company building such systems; virtually all of the speakers referred to the information vacuum left with the demise of central planning.

● They see that Western companies compete on many other dimensions than price: for example, in delivery lead times, reliability of supply, product variety, after-sales service. They want guidance in the skills, new to them, of designing the product-service package: determining the configuration of attributes the customer wants and tailoring the system of product design, manufacture, delivery and after-sales service to match this. Where, in this chain, is 'value' created? Aviatika, offering services as well as products, is an example of a company addressing these issues.

● They want tuition in the concepts of economic cost: the different 'costs' appropriate to different kinds of decision and their measurement in practice. They recognize that decisions on tender-ing for contracts, off-peak discounting, dumping, joint-product pricing, product-line rational-isation should not be made through mechanical application of accounting formulas. AvtoRes, with 52 factories in its group, is an example of an organization needing help of this kind.

● They all want help in preparing business plans for their enterprises. Some still saw this as a purely technical exercise. Their earlier training had been under the regime of Gosplan, and they envisaged a scaled-down Gosplan for the individual company. Others recognized that market estimates are a key component of the business plan, that allowing for the inherent uncertainty of these estimates is half the game and that they have much to learn from Western experience of planning at the company level.

● They recognise that the Western economies have provided live laboratories in which companies have experimented with different organizational forms: holding companies with small headquarters staff and relatively inde-pendent product divisions, highly centralized companies, companies whose divisions are defined sometimes in terms of product and sometimes of customer-group. These choices are topical in Russia, as the new financial-industrial groups manage diverse businesses and the new investment banks acquire controlling interests in newly privatized companies.

These are components of management education that leading Russian managers would wish to import from the West; they are the most favored topics from a longer list.

A Western management educator should perhaps end on a cautionary note. London Business School recently taught a course on business restructuring to a group of Russian top managers, all of whom had been exposed earlier to Western-taught programs in business finance.

One of the cases discussed in the restructuring course concerned a divisionalized company. A few quick calculations allowed the student-managers to spot that one of the divisions was losing money. The division in question manufactured and marketed contact lenses. To a man, the response of the Russian managers was: 'close it down'. This they believed to be the correct response a well-trained Western manager would give in a modern market economy. They were pleased to demonstrate that they had learned how to assess the financial performance of a division using Western-style analysis.

In fact, the trainer was able to show them some dozen actions the company could take in order to bring this division back to profit: a different selling strategy, segmentation of the market, a quick-order option and so on. The company in which the case had been written had indeed gone on to turn this division round. For the Russian student-managers, the salutary lesson was: do not let go of your common sense.

For the Western educator it is a blunter message: be sure at least that you are not making things worse!

Summary

Managers in the former Soviet Union had responsibilities that were in some respects wider, in other respects narrower, than their Western counterparts. Today's Russian companies, however, are coping with uncertainties for which there is no close equivalent in the West. Challenges and opportunities include converting from military to civilian markets, creating and repairing supply chains, the dropping of uneconomic products, and the filling of gaps in the support services available to Russian businesses.

Supply uncertainties, absence of data, and the lack of a framework of commercial law are among reasons why much Western management practice and experience is hard to transplant. Discussing optimal capital structures is also of little use. However, help in filling the information vacuum, guidance in designing a product-service package, and tuition in the concepts of economic cost and preparing business plans all invoke great interest in Russia. Different organizational forms for companies is a live issue there.

Applied Microeconomics and Industry Analysis

Contents

Keys to profit maximization 451
Kimya M. Kamshad, London Business School
An introduction to some of the basic concepts of microeconomics.

Making sure the price is right 455
Kathryn Graddy, London Business School
The workings of the law of demand, perfect competition and monopoly, the importance of incremental revenue and, not least, the value of a brilliant pricing coup.

Cartels and collusion 456
Kathryn Graddy, London Business School
Cartels are a fact of economic life – though they are not as easy to sustain as many might imagine.

A price for every customer 459
Kimya M. Kamshad, London Business School
How is a seller to set prices to maximise business? The answer is the complex world of price discrimination – making customers willing to pay high do so and offering lower prices to those less willing.

Natural monopolies regulation 462
Saul Estrin, London Business School
A free market requires no outside control. But so-called 'natural monopolies' need some supervision.

Keeping out the competition 464
Paul A. Geroski, London Business School
No one likes competition and companies with a leading position in a market will go to considerable lengths to keep out likely new opponents.

Meaning of market failure 468
Paul A. Geroski, London Business School
Transactions costs – the costs of purchasing above and beyond the market price – can lead to the economic concept of market failure.

Pros and cons of vertical integration 471
Kimya M. Kamshad, London Business School
When a company manufactures its own components or provides its own services rather than buying them in, that's vertical integration.

Competing in spite of the Law? 473
Ralf Boscheck, IMD
Anti-trust legislation and implementation is becoming tougher. But for companies faced with increasingly complex and international deals and negotiations, are these strict legal interpretations always fair or appropriate?

Contributors

 **Dr Kimya M. Kamshad** is Assistant Professor for Economics at London Business School and research fellow at the Center for Business Strategy.

 **Paul A Geroski** is professor of Economics at London Business School and Dean of the full-time MBA at LBS. His research interest include the dynamics of competitive processes, technological change and the evolution of markets, and the corporate growth process.

 **Kathryn Graddy** is Assistant Professor of Economics at London Business School.

 **Ralf Boscheck** is Professor of Economics and Strategy at IMD. His research interests include industrial and international economics; industry dynamics, public policy impact and antitrust analysis.

 **Saul Estrin** is Professor of Economics, Research Director CIS-Middle Europe Centre and Chair, Economics Faculty at London Business School.

Introduction

The Applied Microeconomics and Industry Analysis module is the main economics module of *Mastering Management*. Economics is the key science underlying most management theory and without a basic understanding of it few managers will be able to grapple with major business issues. The module is intended to be essentially practical rather than theoretical but even so it will cover most of the main elements of modern economic theory.

Topics covered include profits, costs, demand, pricing, price discrimination, cartels, natural monopolies, entry barriers, market failure, vertical integration and legal constraints on competition. Related topics can be found in the International Macroeconomy and Competitiveness, Finance, and Accounting modules.

Keys to profit maximization

■ **Kimya Kamshad provides an introduction to some of the basic concepts of microeconomics.**

Why did BMW purchase Rover and its four-wheel drive capabilities when BMW was already a well established player in the luxury car market? Why did Microsoft invest a fortune in the development of Windows 95 when its existing Windows software was already highly successful?

Why do Coca-Cola and McDonald's continue to spend huge amounts on advertising when both are already household names in most corners of the world? Why are pharmaceutical companies increasingly contracting-out much of their clinical testing activities when they used to perform all of them in house?

Most economists would argue (and the majority of businessmen would agree) that all of these business decisions have as their primary and fundamental motivation the quest for increasing financial reward.

Maximizing profits, or the excess of current revenues over costs, is the principal motivation for business activity and decision-taking in neo-classical economics. A further distinction is made between *accounting profits*, computed directly from the company's accounts, and economic profits, which take into account the *opportunity cost* of capital – i.e. the return from the next best alternative activity for which the company's capital could have been put to use.

Of course, decisions are not taken in a static time frame. Indeed, many business decisions will forgo current profits for future profits – the decision to invest in R&D in the hope of discovering patentable technologies that can be exploited in the future by means of new and improved products or cheaper and more efficient production technologies provides one ready example.

Thus in a dynamic context the *stream of future profits* (discounted to present value) is what most managers try to maximize when they make decisions and is the standard measure of the value of a company as a business entity.

High revenues, low costs

Maximizing profits involves simultaneously maximizing revenues while minimizing costs. Thus logically, any business decision that is able to lower costs without lowering revenues commensurately or increase revenues without increasing costs commensurately will improve profits.

Looking first at costs, a company's ability to control its costs varies depending on the length of time it has to react. Thus in a single instant in time virtually all costs are unalterable, or *fixed*, but as the amount of response time increases the proportion of costs that are *variable*, i.e. which can be altered, increases.

The distinction is important since in the *short run*, when some portion of the company's costs are unalterable, the company must still cover its fixed costs whether or not it produces any output. It should only then continue to produce output if it can sell that output at a price that covers the additional variable costs that it will incur for production.

In the *long run*, when all costs are variable, a company must only remain in business and produce if it can cover the entirety of its costs, including the opportunity cost of its capital. The company's scale of operations and investment decisions should be made in this context.

A simple example will help to illustrate. A printer operates two presses on one-year leases and employs one worker on a one-day contract. Each press costs £4,000 a year while the worker must be paid £40 per day. On any given day, all of the company's costs are fixed since the worker will have already been employed. For the following day, the cost of the presses remains fixed but the wage cost of the worker is variable, as his one-day contract can be allowed to lapse.

For the following year, all the company's costs are variable since the company has the option of not renewing the leases on the presses as well as not employing any workers. Now suppose the company receives an order for a printing job worth £50 to be performed tomorrow. This would be sufficient to cover the cost of the worker and contribute £10 to the fixed overhead, which must be paid anyway. The company should accept the job.

It should, however, turn down a day's worth of work that is worth less than £40, since it will be better off not hiring anyone to work and letting its presses lie idle. In the long run, or in this case in a year, all the printer's costs are variable so it should shut down unless it expects to cover the cost of the printing presses, the labor and the opportunity cost of the capital invested in the company.

Sunk costs

The decision to leave a business is often somewhat different from the decision to enter since entry usually involves a certain amount of one-off costs that are unrecoverable in the event of shut-down. For example, a new business must pay a fee to get its telephone lines connected; it must pay legal fees to set up contracts with its suppliers; it must purchase equipment that will be worth less if sold as second hand.

These types of non-recoverable costs, or *sunk costs*, affect an entrepreneur's decision to start a new business. But once in business they are no longer important to his or her decision to shut down. The reasoning is as follows:

Before these costs have been incurred, the entrepreneur will only embark upon a new venture if he or she expects to cover total costs, earn a return on capital equal to or greater than what could be earned in the next best activity, *and* cover any costs he or she must *sink* into the company. The sunk costs, once incurred, cease to be relevant since they are unrecoverable whether or not the company remains in business.

In the short run, a company can only produce more output by working its fixed factor harder. In the case of our printer, if he were to receive a huge order for the next day there would be insufficient time to increase the number of presses and he could only meet the new demand by increasing the number of workers. By increasing the number of workers from one to two the printer might be able to produce twice as much from the same two presses. By adding a further worker he may be able to produce more but probably not three times the original amount.

As more workers are added, each new worker's additional contribution to increasing output will be less than the contribution of the previous worker – a phenomenon known as the *law of diminishing marginal returns*. At some point congestion will become a problem and adding further workers will not help increase output and may ultimately even lead to reductions in output.

In the long run, of course, diminishing returns are not relevant since the company can alter both the level of its fixed factor and can also alter the type of technology it uses for production. Moves to new production technologies can have a huge impact on costs; consider, for example, the impact of assembly line production, introduced by Henry Ford, on the cost of automobile manufacturing.

More recently a number of software companies have taken to marketing their software via the Internet rather than building up a large network of retail outlets and a costly distribution system. While this new marketing approach has its limitations, its impact on costs, and in particular on fixed costs, is immense. Clearly these changes could have not been made instantaneously but the possibilities arose when a longer span of time was allowed for.

Technology determines costs

A company's choice of technology will determine the cost of production for different levels of output as it provides a mapping that transforms inputs (for example, steel, engines, tires) into a final output (automobiles). The choice of technology also determines which production costs are fixed in the short run (for example, factory equipment) and which are variable (for example, electricity).

For any level of output there exists an optimal technology for production that will yield the lowest-cost production for that particular level of output. Taking electricity generation as an example, low levels of output may be most 'costlessly' achieved by use of steam-powered generators but very high levels of output may be most costlessly achieved using nuclear technology.

Scale economies refer to the phenomenon of long-run unit costs that decline as output increases due to more cost-effective technologies becoming viable at higher levels of output. In industries such as electricity generation, industrial chemicals, machinery and so on it is almost always more cost-effective to produce at large scale than at small scale.

Usually there exists some level (or range of levels) of output and some associated technology at which scale economies are exhausted and the minimum unit cost of production is achieved. Broadly speaking, economists refer to this least unit cost range of production levels as *minimum efficient scale (MES)*. But in the long run a company will adapt its technology and its capacity in such a way as to be as close as possible to the long-run MES for that level of production, for example by building a factory or adding an extension to an existing factory.

Of course, aside from achieving the lowest unit cost for any given level of production, the other side to maximizing profits is to earn the highest possible revenues. The extent of revenues a company can achieve for its product depends on how much individual consumers are willing to pay for the product.

Consumers may differ in their willingness to pay for any good – this is apparent by the success of art auctions in locating the individual with the highest willingness to pay for the piece being sold. How much any consumer is willing to pay for a given product will depend on (1) his income, or wealth; (2) his tastes (for example, contemporary art versus classical); and (3) the prices of other goods that are related to this piece, either as substitutes (other works by the same artist) or complements (the cost of insuring the piece).

Reservation price

Economists refer to the *reservation price* as the maximum price an individual is willing to pay for one more unit of a particular good. Taken across a whole market, one could hypothetically rank all consumers in terms of their reservation prices for a particular product to measure the level of *demand* for different quantities of the product.

Then to sell, say, 10 units of output, a company must price in such a way so that the tenth ranked consumer just pays his reservation price for the product. So, for example, when a new technology emerges and production costs are still quite high (for example, the early days of computers) it is usually the adventurous and wealthier consumers at the upper end of the demand spectrum who tend to make the early purchases.

As the technology is refined and production volume increases, costs fall and prices can be lowered to allow the middle range of more cautious customers to purchase the good. This is typically when the market takes off and becomes a major market. Finally, when the technology and use of the good is so far advanced that it ceases to be a novelty or a luxury and rather becomes a necessity that is bulk-produced like a commodity, prices fall and the tail end of bargain-hunting consumers are lured in at the lowest prices.

The dilemma for companies is that at any given time, they can usually only charge a single price for the output they sell. Thus, in the above example, in order to capture the tenth customer in terms of demand ranking, they must sell to the first nine customers at a price *below* what they are actually willing to pay.

Thus if a company lowers its price to expand its market by one more person, it loses the value of the price reduction over all of the existing customers but gains the value of the revenue from the last customer. The sum of these two values is known as the *marginal revenue* and represents the change in total revenues due to one additional unit being sold.

Price elasticity of demand

Economists define the *price elasticity of demand* as the sensitivity of the level of output the company can sell to changes in the price it charges; i.e. the percentage change in quantity demanded divided by the percentage change in price charged.

In a market where consumers do not differ much in their willingness to pay for a particular good, say because they all have strong preferences for the good and there are no close substitutes for it (for example, a drug to cure AIDS), demand will be *inelastic*, or not very sensitive to changes in prices.

On the other hand in a market where abundant substitutes exist and consumers do not necessarily have strong preferences for a particular good, demand will be *elastic*, or highly responsive to changes in price.

Companies would ideally like to be in a position to face inelastic demand since this allows them more individual control over price and enables them to charge a higher price, all else being equal. Hence the vast sums of money spent on advertising consumer products are geared to strengthen consumer preferences towards a particular brand in such a way as to make demand less sensitive to changes in price.

Returning now to the original problem of maximizing profits, or the excess of revenues over costs, the company must choose a price-output combination that yields the highest revenue at the lowest cost.

Considering our spectrum of consumers, it can start with the first and consider how much that consumer is willing to pay and how much it would cost to serve that consumer. Then, moving on through the spectrum of consumers, each additional consumer added to the market will increase the company's revenues by the marginal revenue but will increase the company's costs by the *marginal cost* – the cost of making one additional unit of the product.

As long as the marginal revenue exceeds the marginal cost, adding that consumer increases overall profits. Once the two are equal, the last consumer makes no additional contribution to

profits and successive consumers beyond that point will actually add more to costs than they do to revenues and would therefore be unprofitable to serve.

Thus we arrive at the key profit maximization rule: companies must choose the price-output combination where *the marginal revenue from the last unit sold exactly equals the marginal cost of producing that unit.*

Exactly how companies interact in their pricing decisions under different types of market structure and how the pricing decision changes when companies charge different prices to different customers or groups of customers is covered in the next section of this module.

Summary

Maximizing profits involves simultaneously maximizing revenues while minimizing costs. In the long run a company can only remain in business if it can cover the entirety of its costs, including the opportunity cost of its capital. *Sunk costs* are non-recoverable in the event of a shut down. *Minimum efficient scale (MES)* is the level of output and associated technology at which economies of scale are exhausted and the minimum unit cost of production is achieved. The *reservation price* is the maximum price an individual is willing to pay for one more unit of a particular good. The *marginal revenue* represents the change in total revenue due to an additional unit being sold (including the impact of a lower price for all units). The price elasticity of demand is the sensitivity of the level of output the company can sell against changes in the price it charges. Under the key profit maximization rule companies must choose the price-output combination where the marginal revenue from the last unit sold exactly equals the marginal cost of producing that unit.

Suggested further reading

Begg, D., Fischer, S. and Dornbusch, R. (1994) *Economics* 4th edn, McGraw-Hill, London

Making sure the price is right

■ **How are prices set?** Kathryn Graddy **explains the workings of the law of demand, perfect competition and monopoly, the importance of incremental revenue and the value of a brilliant pricing coup.**

In 1931, the Pepsi-Cola Company was in bankruptcy for the second time in 12 years. The President of Pepsi, Charles G. Guth, even tried to sell the company to Coca-Cola, but Coke wanted no part of the deal.

In order to reduce costs, Guth purchased a large supply of recycled 12-ounce beer bottles. At that time, both Pepsi and Coke were sold in six-ounce bottles. Initially, Pepsi priced the bottles at 10 cents, twice the amount of the original six-ounce bottles, but with little success. Then, however, Guth had the brilliant idea of selling the 12-ounce bottles of Pepsi at the same price as the six-ounce bottles of Coke. Sales took off, and by 1934, Pepsi was out of bankruptcy and soon making a very nice profit.

Pepsi's pricing decision in 1931 was clearly crucial to the life of the firm. The primary background necessary for understanding the pricing decision is a good understanding of the law of demand – i.e. as price goes up, demand goes down – and some understanding of the amount by which a price increase effects a quantity decrease – i.e. the price elasticity of demand.

We will begin by examining the polar cases of pricing under perfect competition and pricing under monopoly, and then move on to examining Pepsi and Coke's situation.

Perfect competition

Alfred Marshall, a famous 19th century economist, used a fish market as an example of perfect competition. For the sake of argument, consider a fishmonger selling cod. How would he price his product?

First, he would look around and find out at what price his numerous competitors were selling cod. He certainly could not price above the competitors; since cod is pretty much identical, consumers should not care from whom they purchase. Furthermore, in fish markets, it is quite easy for consumers to compare prices. So, if he priced above his competitors, he would not sell any fish.

Suppose he decided to price below his competitors. All of the customers would certainly purchase from him. However, if he were still making a profit, the other competitors would also be making a profit at the lower price and would match the price cut in order to retain their customers. They may even consider lowering price more if they could still make a profit and capture further customers.

This reasoning, along with the ease of entry for new fish mongers if there is a profit to be made (which prevents collusion among fish mongers already in the market), ensures that the price being charged is equal to the cost of supplying an additional fish, or the marginal cost. A fish monger will be a price-taker, setting his price identically to his competitors' prices.

Monopoly

A firm is a monopoly if it has exclusive control over the supply of a product or service. Therefore, a monopolist, in his pricing decisions, cannot consider the pricing decision of rival firms. So, what does he consider?

The smart monopolist considers the *incremental* effect of his decision, i.e. what is the revenue to be received from selling one additional unit of a product and what are the costs of selling one additional unit of a product?

Certainly, if the costs of selling one additional unit of a product exceed the revenues, the monopolist would certainly not want to sell that additional product. The law of demand says that he could raise the price of his product and thus sell less. Alternatively, if the revenues of selling an additional unit of a product exceed the costs of selling that unit, the monopolist should want to sell more units. The law of demand says that he could sell more by lowering his price.

Thus, by setting the price correctly, the monopolist can sell the exact number of units such that the costs of selling one additional unit exactly equal the revenues of selling the additional unit, which, by the above reasoning, is the only optimal price. However, there is an additional complication: the costs of selling one additional unit do not include any part of the salary of the CEO or the rental costs of the plant, both which must be paid *whether or not the additional unit is sold*. Thus, in the long run, if a monopolist cannot cover his overhead by pricing in the optimal manner, he should shut down.

The situation in 1931 involving Pepsi and Coke clearly differs from either of the above scenarios, but what can we learn from the polar cases?

First, Pepsi clearly saw that Coke was pricing the six-ounce bottles at 5 cents. By pricing the 12-ounce bottles at 5 cents also, Pepsi made the bet that Coke would not cut its price. Coke did not see the need to cut price because its product was different from Pepsi's and it did not fear losing many of its customers. Whether the gain in revenues resulting from increased demand would offset the loss in revenue from the lower price depends on the price elasticity of demand.

The price elasticity of demand faced by Pepsi depends both on Coke's response to the price cut and the consumers' responses. As we saw above, Pepsi made the assumption that Coke would not cut price. In the Great Depression, Pepsi counted on a highly elastic consumer response, that is, the percentage change in quantity purchased by the consumer due to the lower price would be greater than the percentage change in price, and therefore profits would accrue to Pepsi.

What other concerns played a part in Pepsi's decision?

Pepsi may have considered an even lower price cut to generate more demand, if at 5 cents per bottle the incremental revenue from each bottle sold was greater than the incremental cost of producing the additional bottle. However, a lower price cut may have triggered a response from Coke. Finally, pricing a 12-ounce bottle at 5 cents, the identical price as the previous six-ounce bottles, was a brilliant ploy in that consumers were immediately able to grasp the significance of more cola at less price.

Suggested further reading
Besanko, D., Dranove, D. and Shanley, M. (1996) *The Economics of Strategy*, John Wiley & Sons, New York.

Cartels and collusion

■ **Cartels are a fact of economic life – though they are not as easy to sustain as many might imagine.** Kathryn Graddy **looks at some of the theory and philosophy behind collusion.**

Cartels are in trouble. The once mighty oil producers group Opec now cannot seem to get its act together. Co-operation between De Beers, leaders of the famous diamond cartel, and the Russian diamond industry is breaking down. Even the century-old price-fixing agreement among UK book publishers, the Net Book Agreement, has collapsed. But perhaps the surprising fact is not that these organizations have had trouble sustaining collusion, but that collusion succeeded at all.

The difficulty with sustaining collusion is often demonstrated by a classic strategic game known as the Prisoner's Dilemma. Two KGB officers spotted an orchestra conductor examining the score of Tchaikovsky's Violin Concerto. Thinking the notation was secret code, the officers arrested the conductor as a spy. On the second day of interrogation, a KGB officer walked in and smugly proclaimed, 'OK, you can start talking. We have caught Tchaikovsky.'

More seriously, suppose the KGB has actually arrested someone named Tchaikovsky and are interrogating Tchaikovsky and the conductor separately. If either the conductor or Tchaikovsky falsely confesses while the other does not, the confessor earns the gratitude of the KGB and only one year in prison, but the other receives 25 years in prison. If both confess each will be sentenced to ten years in prison; and if neither confesses each receives three years in prison. Now consider the outcome.

The conductor knows that if Tchaikovsky confesses, he gets either 25 years by holding out or ten years by confessing. If Tchaikovsky holds out, the conductor gets either three years by holding out or only one year by confessing. (Their jail sentences are demonstrated in Figure 1). Either way, it is better for the conductor to confess.

Tchaikovsky, in a separate cell, engages in the same sort of thinking and also decides to confess. The conductor and Tchaikovsky would have had three-year rather than 10-year jail sentences if they had not falsely confessed, but the scenario was such that, individually, false confession was rational. Pursuit of their own self-interests made each worse off.

This scenario is easily transferred to the pricing decision of a company. Consider two companies setting prices. If both companies would only keep prices high, both would gain. However, the first company to 'cheat' and lower price gains customers and it is thus in its interests to do so. Once one company has cheated and lowered price, the other company must follow suit. Both companies have lowered their profits by lowering price.

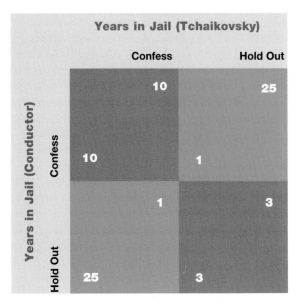

Figure 1

Grim trigger strategy

Clearly, companies repeatedly interact with one another, unlike Tchaikovsky and the conductor. With repeated interaction, collusion can be sustained. Suppose each company could communicate with the other that it would keep its price high as long as the other company also kept a high price. If, however, the other company lowered its price, it would lower its price also and keep a lower price for the foreseeable future. As long as the discounted present value of future profits when both companies have a high price exceeds the discounted present value of future profits when both companies have a low price *plus* the profits to be made from having a low price for one period while the other company has a high price, co-operation can be sustained.

This strategy is known as the 'grim trigger strategy'. The grim trigger strategy is clearly very costly: once one company has cheated once, both companies lose out forever. Given that a rival's pricing decision is not always observable, a mistake by one company (perhaps it loses a customer because of poor economic conditions but mistakenly assumes its rival has cut price) could be extremely costly for both companies.

'Tit-for-tat' strategy

Robert Axelrod, a well-known political scientist,

claims a 'tit-for-tat' strategy is the best way to achieve co-operation. A tit-for-tat strategy always co-operates in the first period and then mimics the strategy of its rival in each subsequent period.

Axelrod likes the tit-for-tat strategy because it is nice, retaliatory, forgiving and clear. It is nice, because it starts by co-operating, retaliatory because it promptly punishes a defection, forgiving because once the rival returns to co-operation it is willing to restore co-operation, and finally its rules are very clear: precisely, an eye for an eye.

A fascinating example of tit-for-tat in action occurred during the trench warfare of the First World War. Front-line soldiers in the trenches often refrained from shooting to kill, provided the opposing soldiers did likewise. This restraint was often in direct violation of high-command orders.

A famous economic example of co-operation occurred in the 1880s between railroads that controlled eastbound freight shipments from Chicago to the Atlantic seaboard of the US. These railroads formed a cartel known as the Joint Executive Committee. The cartel's existence was publicly acknowledged, as it was formed prior to US legislation prohibiting cartel agreements (primarily the Sherman Act (1890) and the Interstate Commerce Commission of 1887).

The cartel monitoring agreement took the form of market share allotments between companies. The difficulty in this situation was that the market share of an individual company depended not only on the rate it set but also on fluctuating demand conditions. Thus, if a company's market share increased, it could either be through a random increase in demand for its freight transportation relative to the demand for other railroads' freight transportation or because the non-conforming company lowered its rates.

In order to enforce the agreement, the railroads adopted a strategy that if they believed a company was cheating (cutting price in order to increase its own market share above the allotment) then all companies would lower price for a time and then revert back to co-operative behavior. It appears that non co-operative periods averaged about ten weeks in duration and primarily occurred in 1881, 1884 and 1885. Overall, the cartel was successful, lasting at least seven years.

Summary

Given the difficulty of sustaining collusion it is perhaps not surprising that cartels are breaking down. Repeated interaction between companies makes cartels possible, but the 'grim trigger' strategy runs the risk that once one partner has cheated both lose forever. A tit-for-tat strategy – co-operation in the first period, then mimicry of the rival's strategy in each subsequent period – is at the same time retaliatory and forgiving, as well as operating according to clear rules.

Suggested further reading

Axelrod, R. (1984) *The Evolution of Co-operation*, Basic Books, New York.

Dixit, Avinash K. and Nalebuff, B. (1993) *Thinking Strategically*, W. W. Norton & Company, New York.

Porter, Robert H. 'A study of cartel stability: the joint executive committee, 1880-1886', *The Bell Journal of Economics*, Vol. 14 (1983), pp. 301-314.

A price for every customer

■ Not every customer is willing to pay the same price for the same product. So how is a seller to set prices to maximize business? The answer, as Kimya Kamshad explains, is the complex world of price discrimination.

When Apple Computer priced its new Power Macintosh line of computers in 1994, it grossly underestimated the level of demand and was consequently unable to supply enough computers and parts.

Mercury One-2-One offered a promotion around the same time that entitled new buyers of mobile phones to free long-distance telephone calls on Christmas Day. The promotion backfired when the response was so large that many customers were unable to gain access to the network.

The question 'How should a product be priced?' is of enormous importance to businesses, and most companies allocate substantial budgets to market research both before launching a new product and, once launched, through the different stages of the product's life cycle.

Economists will argue that the level of demand for a product at any price is the sum of what all the individual consumers in the market would be willing to purchase. This demand, or willingness to pay, for any product will be affected by three key factors:
● individual consumers' preferences for the different characteristics of the product
● the price of close substitutes to the product and the price of goods that must be used in conjunction with it
● the level of each individual consumer's income.

This will apply to any product, be it cans of cola, automobiles or computers.

To forecast demand for, say, a new Apple Power-Mac, market researchers need to know the answer to questions such as: What portion of consumers want a new computer with the extra power and speed offered by the Power-Mac? How do consumers view the Apple Macintosh brand name relative to other brands such as IBM, Dell, Compaq, Hewlett-Packard and so on?

How will Apple's new computer compare in price to that of rival brands of equivalently powered computers and also to the price of computers that are slightly more or less powerful than the Power Mac?

Will there be a need for new software and/or peripheral equipment and if so what are the costs of purchasing these?

How well off are consumers (or companies) and will they be able to afford to purchase these new machines, either to meet expanding business requirements or to replace older machines and improve productivity?

First degree price determination

Even if sellers know the maximum amount that different customers are willing to pay, developing a pricing scheme that makes each customer pay that amount, a practice know as *first degree price discrimination*, can be difficult.

Under first degree price discrimination, the full benefit from the trade between buyer and seller accrues to the seller. At the same time, business is not lost by charging too high a price to customers who would not be willing to pay as much.

One strategy to achieve first degree price discrimination is to sell to the highest bidders through sealed bid auctions. The auction approach is best suited for situations where the volume of sales are low (usually due to scarcity of the product), where there are many potential buyers who are unable to co-operate among themselves and where buyers all have access to the same information about the product's characteristics.

The auction approach would enable the seller to identify those buyers with the highest willingness to pay and would yield the highest possible revenues for the same production costs. This is a common strategy for the sale of very special types of products such as art objects, antique furniture or the rights to the mining and exploration of plots of land. It is not suitable for most bulk-produced products such as cans of cola or computers.

Second degree price determination

Where the auction approach is not feasible, the company must do its best to approximate the first degree outcome using its pricing structure. There are two broad approaches to doing this.

The first is based on the notion that any individual consumer derives diminishing satisfaction from each successive unit of any product consumed. Thus a thirsty cola-loving consumer may get great satisfaction from the first can consumed and high satisfaction from the second.

But gradually the incremental value of each successive can will be lower and lower. Thus, this same consumer may be willing to pay a lot for the first can but not much for the sixth.

If the price per can is very high, the cola-loving consumer will only buy one can; other consumers may not buy any. So instead, the seller packs some of its cans into six-packs and sells them at a lower unit-price than the individual cans. But the consumer can only qualify for the lower price if she or he buys *all six cans*.

Thus the consumer who only wanted one can and gets a high satisfaction from that one can, will pay the higher price. At the same time, the business of the consumer who would have bought more at a lower price is not lost to the company either.

This form of price discrimination, which is based on the volume of consumer purchases, is very common and is known as *second degree price discrimination.*

Other forms of second degree price discrimination include *two-tier tariffs*, i.e. prices where the consumer must pay a flat fee for access and then a separate fee (which may be zero) for usage.

This is typical of many sports clubs, amusement parks and transport facilities offering monthly or annual access passes.

The idea in the case of a travel pass, for example, is that the traveller who travels infrequently pays on average a higher price per trip because the fixed access cost is spread over fewer trips. On the other hand, the high volume user spreads this fixed cost over so many trips that he or she may actually sit next to the infrequent traveller, consume the exact same services (meals, fuel and so on), but end up paying a lower average price for any given trip.

Third degree price discrimination

A second way sellers approximate first degree price discrimination is where, rather than pricing according to the *volume* of purchases, the company prices according to the characteristics of the *buyer.*

Pricing based on what type of consumer is doing the purchasing rather than the volume of purchase is an approach known as third degree price discrimination.

This is very common in the sales of air and rail travel, subscriptions to newspapers and magazines, theater tickets and other products where consumers can be segmented into different groups who are likely to differ greatly in their willingness to pay based on certain easily identifiable attributes.

Students are one of the main beneficiaries of third degree price discrimination schemes, since they are known as a group to be much more price sensitive than the population at large. Other often identified groups include pensioners and the young, both of whom also tend to be more price sensitive, and business purchasers, who are often less price sensitive and may be willing to pay a lot for small quality improvements.

Suppose, for example, there are only two types of travellers: students and businessmen. Students pay for their travel out of their own pockets, while businessmen charge their travel to their employers who in turn deduct these expenses from their taxable income.

Since a typical student is likely to be willing to pay less for a travel ticket, all else being equal, than a typical businessmen, it makes sense for the company selling travel services to price higher to the businessman and lower to the tourist to get the largest possible volume of business out of each customer group.

Pricing schemes can be quite complex and may combine elements of second and third degree price discrimination: for example, discounted travel passes for students and pensioners. In any case, the main danger to the seller is that customers have an incentive to get together and trade among themselves to benefit from existing price differentials.

Thus, a student may try to purchase a ticket she or he does not plan to use for the express purpose of selling it to a business traveller and sharing the difference between the prices. Or, a holder of a travel pass may offer the pass to a friend to use, enabling the friend to benefit from the high volume of the holder's travel. If this were allowed to happen, the seller would lose the business of the high-price paying customer and would be better off offering a single profit-maximizing price.

The seller engaging in price discrimination must therefore take measures such as passport checks at the departure gate and photos on rail passes to make sure consumers are not able to engage in *arbitrage*, i.e. profit from their access to a lower price by selling to someone to whom such access is precluded.

The other danger the price discriminating seller faces is that a rival firm may enter with a single price that undercuts the incumbent's higher price. Then the rival will draw away the most profitable market segments and the original company will only be left with the low-margin discount buyers.

That is why price discrimination is only possible in imperfectly competitive markets, where direct competition by rivals is made difficult by entry barriers such as established brand names (computers), differentiated products (magazines), scale economies in production (air and rail travel), technology patents (pharmaceuticals) or where access to a key input is limited (fine art).

Summary

Demand for any product at a given price will be affected by individual preferences for the product's characteristics, the price of substitutes, and the level of individual consumers' incomes. Developing a pricing scheme based on the maximum amount different customers are willing to pay – known as first degree price discrimination – is difficult. One way of doing this is by auction, but that is only suitable for special and low volume products like art objects or mining rights.

Price discrimination based on the volume of consumer purchases (such as a lower unit price for a six pack and for an individual tin) is known as second degree price discrimination. This approach is often practiced by sports clubs or transport providers who charge consumers a flat fee for access and a separate fee for usage. Pricing based on what type of consumer is doing the purchasing rather than the volume of purchasers is known as third degree price discrimination. Here customers can be segmented into different groups, e.g. students and businessmen, defined by their different willingness to pay. Sellers engaged in price discrimination must take steps to ensure that customers do not engage in arbitrage.

Natural monopolies regulation

■ A free market requires no outside control. But so-called 'natural monopolies' need some supervision. Saul Estrin outlines the economic case for this assertion and examines various techniques for regulation.

In the past 15 years, the role played by regulators in UK industry has increased enormously, largely as a consequence of the Conservative government's privatization strategy. Regulators' impact on industry is very much at the center of the policy debate. In this section, I will explain why some industries are regulated and others are not, what regulators try to achieve and the way that they carry out their role.

To understand the fundamental economic problem posed by the so-called 'natural monopolies', one needs first to grasp why economists place such faith in free markets.

In certain industries, two key conditions hold. First, economies of scale are modest. This means that *long-run average costs*, i.e. the unit costs of production allowing choice of technique to vary, begin to rise quite sharply as output increases while the company is still supplying a relatively small share of the market. There are many production processes of this form – much of food processing, textiles, garments, wood and furniture making – fall into this category.

Second, it is relatively easy to enter the market as a supplier – for example capital requirements are very low, as in window cleaning. More significantly, *sunk costs*, i.e. costs that can not be recouped if entry fails, are low. Many service industries, such as car hire companies fall into this category.

One of the most important results in economics is that, with just these two conditions, markets will offer consumers the maximum attainable satisfaction, i.e. the highest possible output at the lowest possible prices without companies making losses. The threat of entry ensures that prices never exceed long-run average cost (for example, marginal companies in the industry cannot persistently earn above average profits). Moreover, competition also ensures that *price equals long-run marginal cost*. Hence the price of a good accurately reflects the opportunity cost of manufacturing it.

Problems arise from leaving everything to the market, however, if these two pivotal assumptions are not satisfied.

Economies of scale

An important example of where the two assumptions do not hold is the case of *natural monopoly*, a market structure in which unit costs fall as production increases until it is economic for a single company to satisfy the entire market; in other words, one company can supply the whole market at a lower cost than two. In economists' jargon, there remain economies of scale to be exploited when one company meets market demand. There are typically also major barriers to entry in such industries.

Most public utilities – electricity generation, water supply, gas supply and perhaps national telecommunications systems – have technologies of this sort. There are several special problems for these industries.

First, their size and capital intensity often puts particular strain on private capital markets in satisfying their investment needs. In the UK in the 1960s and 1970s, the strain was felt instead on the public coffers, and this was a major factor behind privatization. Note also that these companies are usually in the non-traded sector. The problem for the domestic economy caused by rampant economies of scale is usually resolved in practice by trade, which acts to expand demand and therefore market size.

Hence, while for example automobile or chemicals manufacture are also characterized by huge scale economies, governments have rarely seen it as their role to regulate companies in these industries. Such companies may be very large players in their domestic markets because of scale economies but still face severe competition on global markets.

The question for policy makers is what to do about natural monopolies. Left to themselves, they will charge monopoly prices and restrict output. The absence of any competitive threat will also probably leave such organizations wasteful, inefficient and sluggish. Since all costs can be passed on to the consumers, there will be little incentive for managers to keep them under control. Experience from, for example, the coalmines or the railways suggests that it will not be long before workers realise that they, too, can share in the economic rents by raising wages, improving working conditions and reducing hours relative to the norm in the private sector. Perhaps most seriously, the absence of competitive pressures may damage the motives for innovation and change, so crucial in such capital-intensive sectors.

If this outcome is bad, many of the alternatives are worse. If the government decides to break the company up, but there really are significant scale economies, long-run average costs in two or more companies will be much higher than if the company runs as a monopoly. In this perverse world, consumers could end up paying higher prices for more competition.

If the government decides instead to nationalize the companies and run them as if they were in competitive markets, the outcome may be even worse. The appropriate role, we saw above, would be for the government to tell public sector managers to set output levels where price equals long-run marginal cost. This would avoid the problem of low output levels (and high prices) characteristic of monopoly.

However, *when average costs are falling, marginal costs lie below average costs*. This is because, when unit costs fall as production increases, it must be true that each increment to cost with rising output is successively less than the last. Hence 'marginal cost pricing', as such a rule is called, leads to loss-making because the price set must be less than average cost.

In following such a rule, the Exchequer must implicitly agree to bear the resulting losses. The incentive problem for managers who have in effect been ordered to make losses will exacerbate the natural tendencies to inefficiency in monopoly noted above.

If, though, fixed costs are high and sunk costs are low, one way out is for the government to franchise the natural monopoly. Operators bid a price to operate the monopoly for a fixed period. In this case, entry does not dissipate economies of scale because only one company ever supplies the market, but the threat of entry is meant to keep the monopolists honest in the interim.

Franchising and regulation

In the UK, franchising is used to regulate commercial television and is planned for railways. However, franchising creates serious incentive problems for investment by companies at the end of the franchise period as they may be unwilling to reinvest earnings if they are not certain that their franchise will be renewed.

The only other way is to nominate a regulator who must fix the natural monopolist's price. In the UK, privatization has been accompanied by the formation of a regulator's office for all markets where it is felt that competitive pressures alone would not be sufficient to prevent the natural monopolies from exploiting consumers. Hence there are regulators for telecommunications, gas, electricity and water, but not for coal, oil, or aero engines (where Rolls Royce is the only major manufacturer).

How should regulators fix prices? As we have seen recently, this is a very sensitive decision because it affects profits, investment and the value of the utility companies as well as consumer welfare.

The traditional approach in the US was to regulate in such a way as to give companies a pre-determined rate of return, i.e. *rate of return regulation*. The problem with this was that it gave the utilities an incentive to raise their capital base.

In the UK, there is a pioneering price cap

regulation using a rate known as RPI-X. This means that the regulator caps prices at a level equal to the retail price index minus some value to reflect the expected rate of fall of average costs. In effect, the regulator looks at the change in the average price charged by the monopoly, requiring it to fall in real terms by some pre-determined amount related to expectations about the rate of technical advance. But this is a very hard figure to determine.

So the UK's privatized utilities will probably always need regulators, at least until scale economies are exhausted in these sectors. But the current rules do not seem to be working quite right yet. More thought is needed better to balance the conflicting needs of current consumers, future consumers and shareholders.

Summary

It is fine to rely on free markets if economies of scale are modest and entry costs low. An important example of where this is not the case is the natural monopoly like most utilities. Left to itself it will charge monopoly prices and restrict output. The trouble is that the alternatives – break up or nationalization – can be worse.

Where fixed costs are high and sunk costs low one way out is franchising (e.g. television and railways in the UK), though this creates incentive problems at the end of the period. The only other way is to nominate a regulator, either to fix a pre-determined rate of return or apply a price cap.

Keeping out the competition

■ **No one likes competition and companies with a leading position in a market will go to considerable lengths to keep out likely new opponents.** Paul A. Geroski **explains how strategic entry deterrence works in practice.**

Although all companies strive to develop one form of competitive advantage or another, relatively few are persistently successful over long periods. Innovative activity is almost always followed by waves of imitation and relatively few first movers are able to maintain their initial market position.

Although Tagamet was both revolutionary and one of the best-selling drugs of all time, it was eclipsed by an imitator, Zantac, in an embarrassingly short time. Similarly, companies such as Thorn-EMI, which first developed the CAT scanner, and Xerox, whose Palo Alto research labs developed many of the innovations that created personal computers, failed to generate any lasting success from ideas that have created whole new industries. The simple truth is that most large-scale expenditures designed to create competitive advantage are unlikely to realize a return unless that advantage can be sustained.

Economists think about this problem as one of creating, or strategically exploiting, *barriers to entry or mobility barriers*.

Entry barriers are structural features of a market that enable incumbent companies to raise prices persistently above costs without attracting new entrants (and, therefore, losing market share). Entry barriers protect companies inside a market from imitators in other industries. Mobility barriers, on the other hand, protect incumbents who operate in one part of a market from other established companies who operate in other parts of the same market.

Entry barriers give rise to persistent differences in profits between industries; mobility barriers create persistent differences in profitability within the same market. Although different commentators produce different lists, almost all sources of entry or mobility barriers fall into one of the three following categories: *product differentiation advantages, absolute cost advantages, and scale-related advantages.*

Product differentiation arises when buyers distinguish the product of one company from that of another and are willing to pay a price premium to get the variant of their choice. Such differences become entry or mobility barriers whenever imitators, whether they be new entrants or companies operating in other niches of the same market, cannot realize the same prices for an otherwise identical product as the incumbent.

On the face of it, it is hard to understand how this might come about since consumers will (surely) always prefer the lower-priced variant of two otherwise identical products. However, if it is costly for consumers to change from purchasing one product to purchasing another, then prices for otherwise identical products can differ for long periods of time.

Switching costs

Economists call costs of this type *switching costs* and business strategy textbooks are full of suggestions about how companies might try to create switching costs by locking consumers into their product.

Habit formation is an obvious source of switching costs and many marketing campaigns are designed to reinforce the purchasing patterns of existing customers and raise their resistance to change.

Further, many consumers sink costs into gathering information about new products and, once they have made a choice that satisfies them, they are likely to resist making further investments.

Both sources of switching costs are often reinforced by the use of brand names to help consumers quickly find familiar products. The value of these labels depends, of course, on the size of the switching costs that they help to sustain.

Finally, switching costs also arise when consumption involves the purchase of highly specific complementary products that lock consumers into existing purchasing patterns. Buyers of IBM mainframes often found that the large costs of rewriting software and recording data dwarfed price or performance differences that might otherwise have induced them to switch to one of IBM's rivals.

The well known aphorism 'you'll never be fired for buying IBM' reinforced this conservative buying behavior, much to the advantage of IBM's shareholders and the disadvantage of several generations of entrants. Current users of personal computers sometimes worry that some operating systems unnecessarily restrict their choice of software or force them to pay above the odds for what they can buy.

Absolute cost advantages

Absolute cost advantages arise whenever the costs of incumbent companies are below those of new rivals and they enable incumbents to undercut the prices of rivals (by an amount equal to the cost disadvantage) without sacrificing profits.

There are many sources of absolute cost advantages. Investments in R&D and learning-by-doing in production can be important in many sectors and they can occasionally be protected by patents. Similarly, privileged access to scarce resources (such as deposits of high-quality crude oil, much sought after airport landing slots or the odd scientific genius) can open up substantial differences in costs between companies producing identical products.

Many companies vertically integrate upstream to ensure control over limited natural resources or downstream to ensure access to the most valuable distribution channels, actions that can make entry anywhere in the value chain difficult. Companies also persuade governments to create absolute cost barriers in the form of tariffs, subsidies, trade quotas or other regulations, a form of activity that often benefits lobbyists, the companies who employ them and, sometimes, legislators but rarely works to the advantage of consumers (as most consumers of EU meat and other farm produce know).

Scale-related advantages create the most subtle form of entry and mobility barriers. They arise whenever a company's costs per unit fall as the volume of production and sales increases. Economies of scale in production (created by set-up costs, an extensive division of labor, advantages in bulk buying and so on) are the most familiar source of scale advantages but economies can also arise in distribution.

One way or the other, the important implication of scale advantages is that they impede small-scale entry. If costs halve as production doubles, then a small entrant will have costs per unit twice as high as an incumbent twice its size. Since it is unlikely that such an entrant will be able to differentiate its product enough to justify a price difference of this size, it must either enter at a scale similar to that of the incumbent or not enter at all. Needless to say, this compounds its problems, since raising the finance to support a large-scale (and therefore much riskier) assault on a privileged market can be much more difficult than raising funds for a much more modest endeavour.

Very few markets naturally develop entry or mobility barriers and, even when they do, very few incumbent companies rely on structural features of markets alone to protect them. Whether it be creating or exploiting entry barriers, companies with profitable market positions to protect usually need to act strategically to deter entry. Although there are as many different examples of *strategic entry deterrence* as there are imaginative corporate strategists, there are at least three types of generic strategies that companies typically employ: *sunk costs, squeezing entrants* and *raising rivals' costs*.

Sunk costs. Displacing incumbents is possibly the most attractive strategy for an entrant to follow since, if successful, it enables the entrant both to enter a market and monopolize it. Somewhat more modestly, if an entrant can at least partially displace an incumbent, it will make more profit after entry than if it has to share the market on a less equal basis.

To deter entrants from following this strategy, an incumbent needs to lock itself into the market in a way that raises the cost to the entrant of displacing it. This usually requires the incumbent to make investments whose capital value is hard to recover in the event of exit. Sunk costs raise the costs of exit (and so make it that much harder for the entrant to force the incumbent out).

Some incumbents do this by investing in highly dedicated, large-scale plant and equipment since this also enables them to reap economies of scale in production. These activities also have the additional benefit of creating product differentiation or absolute cost advantages.

In the case of cross-Channel travel competition, for example, Eurotunnel has an enormous potential competitive advantage over the ferry companies it competes against since once built the tunnel can never be redeployed on another route. Whatever else they may do, it is certain that the ferry companies cannot launch a price war with a reasonable hope of driving the tunnel out of the market.

Squeezing entrants. It is usually all but impossible to deter very small-scale entry and frequently it is not worth the cost. However, capable entrants interested in establishing a major position in a market are a much more serious threat and many entry-deterring strategies work by forcing entrants to enter at large scale while at the same time making this too expensive.

Squeeze strategies usually build on scale economies that prevent small-scale entry by forcing entrants to incur even more fixed costs (say through escalating the costs of launching a new product by extensively advertising), which increases their minimum scale of entry. Further, if these fixed costs are also sunk then these activities also increase the risks associated with entry.

The squeeze comes through actions that limit their access to customers, making the larger scale of entry much more difficult and expensive to realize than a more modest market penetration strategy might have been. This is often done by filling the market with more and more variants of the generic product, developing fighting brands closely targeted on theentrant's product or limiting access to retail outlets.

A simple glance at the shelves of most supermarkets will reveal many instances where the multiple brands of a single company (or a small group of leading companies) completely fill all the available space, leaving little or no room for an entrant (examples might include laundry detergents, ready to eat breakfast cereals and supermarket own brands).

Raising rivals' costs. Even when an incumbent is sure that it cannot be displaced by an entrant and it has managed to squeeze the entrant into a tiny niche of an existing market, entry can sometimes be profitable when the market is growing. Indeed, market growth is an important stimulus to entry since it automatically creates room for the entrant without reducing the incumbent's revenues.

However, most entrants have only modest financial support and any strategy that raises costs in the short run and slows the growth of their revenues may make it difficult for them to survive long enough to penetrate the market and turn a profit.

One rather obvious strategy of this type is to escalate advertising and, indeed, this is a very frequent response to entry by incumbents. Advertising is a fixed cost (which, therefore, disadvantages small-scale entrants) and it is often the case that what matters is the relative amount of advertising a company does rather than the absolute amount.

An advertising war initiated by an incumbent that raises total market advertising but keeps the advertising shares of companies relatively constant will, therefore, raise the entrant's costs without raising its revenues.

The interesting feature of this strategy is that an advertising war will also raise the incumbent's costs. What is more, investments in advertising are often sunk, meaning that they are likely to raise the exit costs of the incumbent. The important point is that the incumbent is able to turn what, on the face of it, appears to be a disadvantage to its advantage because entrants are more adversely affected by an advertising war than the incumbent is.

That is, some investments that incumbents make seem irrational because they raise costs without generating much, if any, additional revenue. When successful, however, they are justified by the fact that they protect existing revenue streams from entrants. This points to one of the most characteristic features of investments in entry deterrence: they do not generate net revenue so much as they prevent it from being displaced.

A company that successfully deters entry will have lower profits than a company that did not face an entry threat but that is not an interesting observation. What matters is that a company that successfully deters entry will preserve its profits while a company that has not been able to deter entry will see its market position, and the profits that it generates, gradually disappear.

Summary

Entry barriers are structural features of a market that enable incumbent companies to raise prices persistently above costs without attracting new entrants. Mobility barriers protect companies which operate in one part of a market from established companies which operate in other parts of the same market. Almost all sorts of entry and mobility barriers fall into one of these categories: product differentiation advantages (including switching costs), absolute cost advantages, and scale-related advantages.

There are many examples of strategic entry deterrence but companies typically employ sunk costs (which raise the cost of exit), squeezing entrants (through filling available shelf space in a supermarket, for example), and raising rivals' costs (e.g. by increased advertising). Companies that successfully deter entry will preserve their profits; those that do not will see their market position and profits gradually disappear.

Suggested further reading

Kay, J. (1993) *Foundations of Corporate Success,* Oxford University Press.

Geroski, P. A. (1991) *Market Dynamics and Entry,* chapter 5 Basil Blackwell, Oxford.

Porter, M. (1980) *Competitive Strategy,* Free Press.

Oster, S. (1990) *Modern Competitive Analysis,* Oxford University Press.

Meaning of market failure

■ **Transactions costs can lead to the economic concept of market failure. As** Paul A. Geroski **explains, this is particularly true in the market for ideas, especially in research and development.**

Most people think that the cost of purchasing a particular good or service is just the price that a consumer has to pay to get the right to consume it. But a moment's reflection suggests that this cannot be true.

Although I pay only 45p for my daily newspaper, the fact is that I have to walk 20 minutes each way to the newsagent to get it. Similarly, the true cost to me of having an accountant do my taxes includes not only his annual charge but also the many hours spent trying to make a sensible choice of accountant, explaining my personal circumstances to him and generally keeping an eye on what he does.

Although some of the circumstances surrounding a transaction are enjoyable (I like walking), others are a burden that most people would just as soon do without (like having anything to do with the preparation of tax forms). And, if the burden becomes too large, buying that particular good or service will just not be worth the effort.

The costs of consumption over and above purchase price are often referred to by economists as *transactions costs* and they are an easy statistic to use to judge how efficiently markets operate. In particular, a market is deemed to be efficient if: the good or service is made available to all interested consumers at a price not far from the marginal cost of providing it; and consumers do not incur excessive transactions costs in making their purchases.

Market failure is the term economists reserve for situations where transactions costs become excessive. The result of market failure is that too few people participate in the market. At the extreme, when transactions costs become very large relative to the purchase price the market will cease to exist. In a sense, transactions costs are like a sales tax and they can stunt the growth and development of a market in exactly the same way as excessive taxation.

Although market failure seems like a rather drastic way to describe a long walk to the newsagent, the fact is that transactions costs seriously inhibit certain types of economic activity.

The kind of markets that often operate poorly (if they operate at all) are those concerned with the production and sale of information, and the consequence of market failure is that too little investment in the provision of information is likely to be made by transacting agents.

Uncertainty

One source of market failure is uncertainty. Risky undertakings impose an added burden on those who undertake them and, when they are risk averse, they often try to avoid (or at least scale back) such activities. In principle, what is needed is a market that will enable those who do not wish to bear much risk to pass it on to those who do. In practice, well-developed capital markets have evolved for this purpose.

However, there is a limit to how much risk can be transferred, and this limit arises from a problem known as *moral hazard*. The difficulty is that insurance against risk often dulls incentives to operate efficiently. If, for example, I insure my £100,000 house for £150,000 against the risk of fire, it is in my interest to light the match. Even if I insure it for only £100,000, I have little incentive to take adequate fire precautions.

Moral hazard creates a range of transactions

costs. Even if I am able to persuade someone to insure fully my house, the contract I sign is likely to be laden with all kinds of complicated clauses that limit the insurer's liability in the event that I set a fire. Most parties to such contracts will also wish to set up regular monitoring arrangements to insure that the insured are behaving reasonably.

Possibly the most well know example of moral hazard arises in the management of corporations. Very few owners of large companies are able to run their enterprises with vision and energy. They hire managers to do it for them.

However, few people will accept management positions if they involve enormous risk. As a consequence, the remuneration of most managers is usually dominated by a salary that they receive regardless of the performance of the company. This form of insurance can, however, have a deleterious effect on their incentives to run the company and a whole architecture of corporate governance practices has been erected to try to ameliorate this problem.

Investments in R&D are a classic example of another type of activity, which, many people believe, is inhibited by excessive market failure. The problem arises because information is a *public good*. In the language of economists, this means that information is both *non-rival* and *non-exclusive*.

A private good (like a banana) is one for which the act of consumption is destructive – so either I eat the banana or you eat it (i.e. we are rivals for the consumption of it). By contrast, a good idea can be used over and over again (as anyone reading this can attest) and any person who uses it can do so without interfering with the ability of anyone else to use it.

What is more, it is difficult for anyone to establish property rights over particular ideas and if property rights to an idea cannot be assigned to a buyer, then that idea cannot be sold.

Consider the problems involved in selling a new idea (such as an algorithm for managing a stock control system or a design for a new machine tool). The first problem is that buyers need to know what the idea is and how they can use it before they will be willing to pay for it.

However, once an idea has been revealed to a buyer, he or she no longer has any reason to pay for it. Although it is possible for sellers to keep control of an idea by forcing the buyer to sign some sort of pre-revelation contract, the need to do this adds enormously to the costs of the transaction and, therefore, reduces its profitability.

The second problem is that once the seller has sold the idea to a buyer, that buyer becomes a competitor. Since ideas can be used over and over again without depreciating once they have been mastered, the original seller of an idea has no obvious competitive advantages over a well-informed buyer in trying to sell it to any third party.

Both of these problems taken together mean that the seller of a good idea is unlikely to realize anything like its true value to buyers through a series of market transactions.

This is a story which is familiar to anyone who has ever heard of Silicon Valley. The transistor was first developed by William Shockley and two colleagues in the labs of AT&T. But competition swiftly appeared as understanding of the basic science involved spread (AT&T was, in any case, prevented from entering the market by an antitrust decree). Further diffusion of the basic ideas involved in semiconductor production occurred as the result of mobility of personnel.

Shockley left Bell labs in the mid-1950s to form Shockley Semiconductor. Several years later eight senior employees left Shockley to form Fairchild Semiconductor. Employees (and founders) of Fairchild went on to create Rheem Semiconductor in 1959, Amelco and Signetics in 1961, Molectro in 1962, General Microelectronics in 1963 and so on.

Footloose ideas and hypermobile scientists and engineers are also a feature of the personal computer industry. In this case, much of the initial research work was done in Xerox's Palo Alto research labs and while Xerox's shareholders saw very little return for their investment in Palo Alto almost everyone else operating in the industry has.

The bottom line is that returns on investments in R&D are likely to be difficult to realize since imitation is facilitated by spillovers of information between individuals and the companies that employ them. Most people believe that this is a serious problem and that as a consequence too little R&D is done. What is needed is some kind of policy that insures that innovators will see at least a reasonable return for their efforts. There are at least three ways in which this can be done.

Safeguarding returns

Perhaps the most obvious is to try to enforce property rights on new ideas. This is typically done through the *patent system* (trademarks and other devices are also used to help establish intellectual property rights). Patents are basically options. They establish claims to the returns associated with a particular idea but have to be enforced by the patentee. Although a few patents have proved to be fantastically lucrative, most are relatively worthless and many patentees never exercise their option to claim protection.

A second strategy that companies use to appropriate the benefits of their innovations involves the use of *complementary assets*. Most ideas generate returns only when they are embodied in particular goods and services. This means that the idea is combined with a range of other inputs to produce something of value to consumers.

Even if the basic idea underlying an innovation cannot be protected, it is possible that it will generate returns if some of these other, complementary, inputs can be monopolized. Hence, a valued brand name, a lock on particular distribution channels, privileged access to skilled labor or some natural resource can effectively monopolize the market that grows up around a new idea and ensure that innovators appropriate most of the benefits of their activity.

Finally, the simplest form of protection is to suppress the market for new ideas altogether. Many companies have done this by *vertical integration*, that is, they have brought their R&D

facilities in-house to insure that the new ideas their research activities generate remain proprietary. (*A broad explanation of vertical integration is contained in the following Applied Microeconomics article.*) Vertically integrating R&D labs with manufacturing operations eliminates all market transactions associated with information flows and that means that it reduces transactions costs. In a sense, this is truly a market failure.

Summary

The costs of consumption over and above purchase price are often referred to as transactions costs. Market failure is the term for situations where these are excessive. R&D investment is an activity widely thought to be inhibited by excessive market failure because information is a public good. Ways in which innovators can be given a reasonable return is through patents, complementary assets (e.g. a valued brand name or lock on particular distribution channels), or vertical integration (which by eliminating market transactions associated with information flows thereby reduces transactions costs).

Suggested further reading

Milgrom, P. and Roberts, J. (1992) *Economics, Organization and Management*, Prentice Hall, New Jersey.

Charkham, J. (1994) *Keeping Good Company*, Oxford University Press, Oxford.

Stoneman, P. (ed.) (1995) *Handbook of the Economics of Innovation and Technical Change*, Basil Blackwell, Oxford.

Mowery, D. and Rosenberg, N. (1989) *Technology and the Pursuit of Economic Growth*, Cambridge University Press, Cambridge.

Tilton, J. *International Diffusion: The Case of Semi-Conductors*, The Brookings Institution, Washington DC, 1971.

Saxenian, A. (1994) *Regional Advantage*, Harvard University Press, Boston.

Kay, J. (1993) *Foundations of Corporate Success*, Oxford University Press, Oxford.

Pros and cons of vertical integration

■ **Vertical integration is when a company manufactures its own components or provides its own services. But, says Kimya Kamshad, whether this is an economically justifiable option can depend on many factors.**

The decision whether to make or buy – or in the language of economists whether to *vertically integrate* or *contract out* – any link in the value chain leading to the final sale of a good will depend on a number of factors that affect the efficient functioning of markets.

Generally speaking, vertical integration is most attractive when different types of market failures exist that threaten profitability. Bringing production in-house allows a company to internalize and thereby overcome market failures. But the strategy is not without its own costs in terms of efficiency and price.

Vertical integration is often the best solution where the activity in question is complex and hard to define under conventional legal contracts. Thus there is a moral hazard problem involved with contracting out if the contracting company cannot be legally covered for all possible contingencies.

One reason many pharmaceutical companies do not contract out activities such as the development of a cure for a particular disease, say Aids, is that it is difficult to tell whether lack of success in finding a cure arises from insufficient effort on the part of the contractor or an unfruitful line of research.

And with complex transactions, it may be hard to specify quality standards in legal terms – so that to the extent that higher quality is associated with higher costs, suppliers will have an incentive to produce lower-quality goods. This is one often cited reason why many automobile companies manufacture many of their parts in-

house. Also, since the information uncovered through R&D is a public good, if it leaks out its value is greatly diminished. Leakages may be harder to control through legal contracts with an independent supplier than if the research is done in-house.

Similarly, vertical integration will be attractive where outside suppliers of the activity are few and are likely to behave opportunistically, i.e. if there are not many suppliers then those that do exist may be able to exercise market power and extract economic rents in supplying the service in question. Such rent extraction by suppliers can be avoided if a company produces the activity in-house.

For example, in California's electricity market in the early 1980s, the state-regulated public utility companies were charging a premium to industrial users for their electricity use that, for politically motivated reasons, was used to subsidize the residential market. As the divergence between the price charged and the actual cost of the electricity became increasingly large, it became cost-effective for many of California's big industrial users of electricity to look to harness the energy produced in their manufacturing processes and generate their own electricity, bypassing the public utilities altogether.

More generally, vertical integration into activities where market power exists among suppliers allows the user to avoid the problem of *double margins*, i.e. of paying a mark-up to the supplier and basing one's own production levels and price on the marked-up price of the input rather than its true marginal cost. In such cases vertical integration has the added advantages of: creating entry barriers if the integrated company benefits from lower costs than non-integrated rivals and providing security against being locked-out from a key input in case a rival vertically integrates with the main supplier.

Barriers to entry

In most countries it is illegal to use vertical integration to monopolize a market. In one recent example, a US federal court ruled against Eastman-Kodak for attempting to monopolize the service and parts market for its photocopiers and business machines by refusing to sell parts to independent service operators that were competing against Kodak's own network of service operators. In doing so, Kodak was raising entry barriers in the market for the supply of parts and servicing by vertically integrating into the provision of this service.

Vertical integration is also particularly attractive where the intermediate activity has large *economies of integration* with another stage of the value chain. Economies of integration, also known as *economies of scope* or *synergies*, occur when the cost of one company performing two distinct activities is less than the cost of two companies performing them separately.

Such economies may arise for a number of reasons such as shared overheads, similar expertise, shared learning, better scheduling and co-ordination of tasks, better market information, reduced information requirements and lower transactions costs.

For example, many UK tour operators have vertically integrated into the airline business, allowing them to co-ordinate the number of air travel seats available to them with the number of spaces they have reserved in resorts, and to share the fixed overheads of their sales and marketing systems. They have also vertically integrated into travel agencies, which provides them with early market information on popular holiday destinations and other passenger trends.

Similarly, pharmaceutical companies developing new drugs often find that by doing the research in-house they can also find ways to lower the final production cost of the finished drug. Or, when automobile manufacturers manufacture certain key parts in-house, they are able to respond to breakdowns in the final assembly much more quickly.

In-house production will be less attractive where scale economies in the intermediate activity are large and the volume of the intermediate input required by the company is small, leading to a cost disadvantage associated with in-house production.

This is especially true for activities requiring large investments in capital equipment that will not be used at full capacity by a company only producing for its own use. For example, the volume of tyres required by an automobile manufacturer may not be sufficiently large to allow for least-cost production of those tyres in-house.

The automobile company has the option of producing more than its own requirements in order to reach the minimum efficient scale of operations and then selling the excess production on the open market. However, this strategy may be unattractive in that it exposes the company to the risks of the tyre market where it may also face the prospects of trying to sell tyres to its own rivals in the automotive sector who for reasons of their own may prefer independent suppliers.

Problems of vertical integration

Other disadvantages of vertical integration include the costs associated with entering a new and possibly unfamiliar business. The corporate press is filled with failed examples of established companies in one sector trying to enter another – one recent example is provided by the case of AT&T's purchase of NCR, aimed at gaining a successful foothold in the computing market and combining the provision of information systems with computing hardware. The combination was so unsuccessful that AT&T has since announced plans to split itself up into three separate companies, one of which will be made up of the computing division.

Another disadvantage of vertical integration is that higher overheads are needed for the vertically integrated operation, which may lead to larger losses in economic downturns than would be incurred if the company was purchasing its supplies on the spot market. The case of the European automotive industry in the recent recession provides a clear example of this where the worst affected companies were often those who did the least contracting-out.

The vertically integrated company must also

lock into a particular in-house supplier's technology, which may be inferior to existing or emerging alternatives. Similarly, the incentives of the vertically integrated supplier to provide the best service at the least cost may be less than that of an independent supplier competing for the organization's business.

Mercedes-Benz, among other companies, has been in the financial news in recent years as it has announced moves to increase out-sourcing of components formerly produced in-house to save on costs. Indeed, in recent years many European companies have followed the Japanese method of out-sourcing many inputs but at the same time reducing the number of suppliers being dealt with, allowing them to build much closer relationships with the remaining suppliers.

The UK retail group Marks and Spencer has been extremely successful in developing its own network of independent suppliers with whom it has special long-term relationships. Some large supermarket retailers now share automated check-out information with suppliers and provide them with their own sales forecasts to ensure a steady inflow of new supplies.

Like pure vertical integration decisions, these long-term relationships are not without their own risks and costs. The cost-savings from locking into a single supplier in terms of better information and a higher level of service and/or quality must be balanced against the loss of freedom to deal with other suppliers that may offer more competitive prices and the risk that the supplier may switch to supply a rival and take all the company's confidential market data with it.

Summary

Bringing production in-house allows a company to overcome market failures – it avoids the problem of double margins and being locked out from a key input, as well as providing synergies. In-house production will be less attractive, though, where scale economies in the intermediate activity are large and volumes required by the company are small. Other disadvantages include the costs associated with entering a new and possibly unfamiliar business, higher overheads, dependence on a single technology, and lack of incentive. Locking into a long-term relationship with a supplier is another option, but this has its risks.

Competing in spite of the Law?

■ **Antitrust legislation and implementation is becoming tougher. But are these strict legal interpretations always fair or appropriate?** Ralf Boscheck **reviews the situation.**

Recent reviews of competition policy developments across OECD member countries registered a universal tightening of regulatory frameworks and an increased vigour in enforcing guidelines against horizontal and vertical restraints to competition.

In the US alone the number of possible monopolies scrutinized rose from three in 1992 to 22 in 1994; over the same period merger and restraints to trade investigations have risen by 30 per cent and 60 per cent respectively. The number of European cases involving charges of abuse of dominance and concerted agreements swelled by almost 40 per cent between 1993 and 1994. Recently introduced 'cartel-busting' measures are expected to increase this number significantly.

Similar developments are reported for Japan, which, both in response to international access demands and to safeguard its process of deregulation, set out to enhance the power and independence of its Fair Trade Commission and shorten the list of exemptions to the Anti-Monopoly Act.

In addition to the evident interest in strengthening the forces of competition within their domestic markets, most OECD governments seek to harmonize procedures and assessment practices. Combined with the increased enforcement vigour, efforts to establish a global competition policy standard trigger widespread regulatory reforms.

The immediate result of all of this has been a wave of changes in national legislation and judicial views, which in some instances has already altered the legality of strategies and contracts. The list of recently affected companies includes household names such as Bayer, Digital Equipment Corporation, Eastman Kodak, Microsoft, Sony and Toshiba. What is the broader logic behind these changes? How are companies affected? How are they to respond?

Although the business community has been relentlessly calling for a fundamental re-evaluation of the emerging standards in keeping with current market developments and changing operational requirements, there has not been any noticeable progress in this direction.

In fact, there seems to be a widening gap between what companies perceive to be strategic imperatives in meeting market requirements and what policy makers are willing to accept. And yet, for the purpose of legal certainty and prosecution avoidance, companies need to incorporate current policy perspectives into their strategy selection and daily operations. For some of them, recently initiated compliance procedures and training programs have already turned out to be a good investment. But this is at best a short-term solution.

Regulatory trends

Given different regulatory backgrounds and experiences, most OECD countries obviously differ with regard to the extent and type of legislative changes that have been and will be introduced. And yet, there are a few general attributes that describe broadly significant trends with regard to substantive issues of competition law, the process of case evaluation and law enforcement, and the overall assessment of proposed reforms:

Restrictive. Increased concerns for the potential abuse of market power by some eminent enterprises make it necessary precisely to stipulate benchmarks for defining the relevant product and geographic markets as well as the critical concentration levels within them.

In both respects the international trend is towards increasingly narrower market definitions and lower concentration thresholds. Similar to this increased restrictiveness in structural terms, non-standard company conduct – i.e. commercial arrangements, contractual restraints and pricing issues, especially to the extent that they may be believed to facilitate abusive or exclusionary market conduct – is apt to meet with negative prejudice. Finally, the ultimate deterrent effect of competition law, i.e. the levels of remedies sought and fines imposed, is generally being increased.

Automated. Current legislative changes are generally geared towards issuing clear-cut distinctions between permissible and non-permissible market behavior so as to provide companies with legal certainty and to improve the efficiency of law enforcement.

For these reasons, the scope of case-based *rule of reason* evaluations remains limited; per se prohibitions or block exemptions will continue to present the principal form of legal stipulation. Opposition procedures, to the extent that they are available, merely provide companies with a means for expressing disagreement but, lest regulatory workload explode, are not intended to broaden the scope of permissible undertakings. In the face of market complexities, such legal formalism cannot but trigger ambiguity.

Ambiguous. Reviews of recent court decisions and policy developments reveal that regulatory reforms are neither self-evidently correct nor are they smoothly progressing in the intended direction.

Compare the conflicting reasonings underlying highly publicized decisions, as in the cases of the blocked take-over of de Havilland by Aerospatiale and Alenia versus the permitted merger of Nestlé-Perrier.

Consider the European Commission's interpretation of abusive market behavior in the case of TetraPak versus the Canadian Competition Tribunal's more lenient view on this issue, as displayed in its NutraSweet decision.

Await the Commission's findings from its investigations of Digital Equipment Corporation's alleged pre-emption of maintenance markets for its hardware and software products or Bayer's purported restrictions of parallel imports of cardiovascular drugs.

Then compare these with the recent US decisions on Eastman Kodak's service contract for copiers or the European debate on block exemptions for selective distribution and servicing agreements in the car industry, respectively. Then give up on searching for a unifying economic logic.

All these cases highlight the difficulties in determining and interpreting a company's relevant market, the sources of its economic power and, lastly, the impact of its competitive behavior and contractual relations on economic welfare.

They also cast in doubt the merits of a simplified competition reference in assessing commercial relations, especially with regard to a range of vertical restraints, pricing strategies and types of 'non-standard' co-operative undertakings.

The quasi-automatic application of such competition view may cause business arrangements to be distorted to fit the straitjacket of legal rules. Doing so may improve the administrative efficiency of law enforcement yet most likely at the expense of commercial viability and economic efficiency. Do current regulatory reforms capture the emerging realities of market competition?

Competitive dynamics

The above problems will become more pronounced as current economic, technological and competitive forces cause an ever-increasing number of companies to shed their preconceived industry definitions and seek positions that profitably leverage their skills and assets across broader markets.

In the process, the traditional view of companies competing in clearly defined arenas will be replaced by a broader notion of vertically and horizontally related activities whose co-ordination involves a mix of competition and co-operation within and outside of traditional market relations.

Figure 1 (see overleaf) provides a schematic representation of this trend by linking phases of the product life cycle to a typical sequence of patterns in industrial organization and a company's corresponding competitive and co-operative options.

Introducing an entirely new product concept, involving unique inputs, processes and channels of distribution, may at the outset require broadly integrated operations simply because the needed 'ingredients' are not widely available or the initial volume does not justify any productive specialization other than through the innovator itself.

Hence, to the extent that the typical venture initially needs to take over all, or most, of the vertically related activities, it develops and nurtures those assets and skills required to operate the entire industry on a limited product and geographic scope (phase 1).

The situation changes once a growing market volume allows for some degree of specialization. Selective de-integration sets in and companies develop a more focussed skill-base in support of expanding technology applications, product-lines and geographic markets (phase 2).

As markets mature, the continuation of the selective de-integration requires companies to retain control over vital technologies, assets and skills that are being leveraged across broad geographic and product markets, product line extensions as well as emerging product areas (phase 3).

Although industries obviously differ with regard to the extent and timing of these organizational patterns, developments are generally accelerated once the required level of fixed cost of stipulating, monitoring and enforcing market contracts can be reduced.

The two key drivers of this industrial

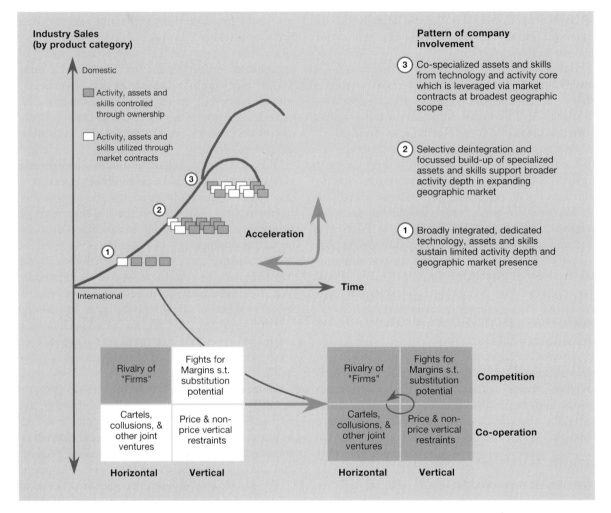

Figure 1

transformation are technological change and the extent of the market that can be reached. Yet, whether companies can attain the flexibility and efficiency advantages of such specialization and still safeguard their investments largely depends on the perspective of competition policy authorities vis-à-vis contractual and tacit commercial arrangements and the legitimacy of control within and across changing market boundaries.

Evidently, current market realities limit the regulator's ability to typecast any such competitive behavior for the purpose of rule making and law enforcement. Already troubled with the need to define the market boundaries and economic impact of competitive actions under conventional market conditions, authorities will find it even more difficult to create legal certainty for – rather than prohibiting – new forms of company organizations and industrial structures.

Obviously, contrary to the current legislative trend, not broad regulations but case-based evaluations of specific commercial relations and industrial structures would be required to assure legal justice and economic efficiency.

Hence, the basic adequacy of numerous competition rules and enforcement mechanisms – laying out the context in which companies are permitted to shape and adjust to their evolving competitive environments – needs to be reassessed. Should market rules or legal rules drive competition? What are the implications for companies today?

Corporate compliance: two steps

As national and international competition rules are becoming appreciably more stringent and abstract (that is, for the purpose of enforcement efficiency, removed from the case at hand), more and more companies are finding it necessary to re-evaluate the judicial underpinnings of even conventional market strategies.

Companies such as Allied Signal, Hewlett Packard or Caterpillar were among the first to employ corporate compliance programs and training schemes that essentially typecast business behavior in keeping with judicial references and thus ensured the continued legality of their daily operations.

Yet as the content of these programs meets market reality and companies need to determine their wider business direction, it becomes important to realize that effective corporate compliance programs are necessarily two-pronged. They involve routines to reduce the risk of infringement in the short-term and regular dialogue with regulatory authorities to maintain the long-term viability of commercial relations under changing market conditions.

Compliance routines

Under the impact of antitrust investigations and competitors' legal actions, most major US corporations have grown quite sophisticated in installing antitrust safeguards. Translating these into daily practice is far from trivial. Summarizing their experience, three major conclusions can be drawn. Compliance programs need to

● be rooted in a clear *credo of law* abidance endorsed by top management and supported by operating policies, criteria for performance evaluation and conditions for employment.

● involve *awareness*: a general enrolment, basic training course on competition issues to create a general frame of reference; *rules*: a comprehensive and explicit catalog of spelled-out 'do and do not' rules together with examples for illustrating dealings with competitors, buyers, suppliers, industry associations on issues of prices, discounts, payment terms, future production rates, market trends and so on; *procedures and routines*: an information gathering and sharing policy; a comprehensive record retention policy and disposal schedule; a policy regarding participation in industry association programs and events, such as trade fairs, statistical reporting programs or product quality programs.

● be *company and industry specific*: hence be formulated by the company's legal department, which is in any case the ultimate source of advice.

Dialogue with regulatory bodies

As current economic, technological and competitive forces cause an ever-increasing number of companies to re-evaluate their market position and conduct, two broad questions require answering:

1. *How will the relevant market be defined for the purpose of competition law enforcement?* At which level or levels of the value-added chain will this be – the level of the final product and geographic market or the level of a company's owned assets and skills on which its leverage and hence potential for abuse may rest?

To what extent will the broadening range of substitutes and international competitors at either level be incorporated into that definition? What kind of data will be used to describe competition and choice in markets for 'core competencies', key skills and assets as opposed to resulting products and services?

How will economic trade-offs be assessed when these sources of market power – as they frequently do – turn out to be intangibles? What is the appropriate time-frame for analysis? Is it the restrictive short-term perspective or are market forces allowed to replace the need for regulatory intervention in the medium and long-run?

2. *What are the permissible means and the legitimate span of control that any unit in the industrial value-adding chain may wield over the decisions taken by vertically related stages of production, distribution and consumption?* Which principle will ultimately replace the legal market/competition reference to accommodate

the need to sustain an efficient co-operation across markets by excluding competition? How will that principle be translated to guide the case assessment of current 'grey-area' business practices such as exclusive dealings, differential pricing, tied selling or various forms of horizontal co-operation?

Companies cannot afford to leave the answering of these questions in the hands of regulatory authorities.

Summary

Despite a variety of regulatory backgrounds, some broad OECD trends can be identified in competition law. Narrower market definitions and lower concentration thresholds are being set, higher penalties are being imposed. Legislative changes have tended towards legal formalism, but this has contributed to conflicting reasonings in some recent decisions.

The issue of whether regulatory reforms capture the emerging realities of market competition is likely to become more acute as the traditional view of companies operating in clearly defined arenas is replaced by a broader notion of vertically and horizontally related activities. The basic adequacy of numerous rules and enforcement mechanisms needs to be reassessed.

Effective corporate compliance programs require routines to reduce the risk of infringement in the short term – with an emphasis on rules and awareness training – as well as regular dialogue with regulators to ensure long-term commercial viability. How will markets be defined for the purposes of competition law? What principles can be used in grey areas like exclusive dealing and differential pricing to allow forms of horizontal co-operation?

Suggested further reading

EU Competition Policy Report, Brussels (1995).

OECD Competition Policy in OECD Countries, Paris (1995).

Hawk, B. (ed.) International Antitrust Law and Policy, Annual Proceedings of the Fordham Corporate Law Institute, Transnational Juris Publications, Inc., Irvington-on-Hudson, New York (1993, 1994, 1995 forthcoming).

Boscheck, R. 'Competitive advantage – superior offer or unfair dominance?', *California Management Review*, Vol. 37, Fall, pp. 132-151 (1994)

Boscheck, R. *Contract Logic and Efficiency Concerns*, IMD working paper (1996)

International Macroeconomy and Competitiveness

Contents

A tale of two economies 482
Stephane Garelli, IMD
Countries increasingly have two types of economies – one of 'proximity' that is largely concerned with the social provision and one of 'globality' concerned with maximizing the value chain.

The secrets that lay behind improved corporate performance 486
Marshall W. Meyer, The Wharton School of the University of Pennsylvania
Performance relies on measurement but apart from the standard financial ratios companies are not sure what they should measure or what the measurements mean.

Globalization and alliances in high technology industries 491
Bruce Kogut, The Wharton School of the University of Pennsylvania
What many take to be a modern-day growth in corporate alliances is not always a response to the need for economies of scale. Often it is a reaction to competition and new technological opportunities.

Managed trade and regional choice 494
Ralf Boscheck, IMD
The rapidly growing phenomenon of regional trade blocs. Are they, as many fear, barely disguised protectionism or a step towards global free trade?

Contributors

Stephane Garelli is a Professor at IMD in Lausanne and a professor at the University of Lausanne. He is also Director of the World Competitiveness Project at IMD.

Marshall W. Meyer is Professor of Management and Anheuser-Busch term Professor at the Wharton School of the University of Pennsylvania and Professor of Sociology at the University of Pennsylvania. He is president of Research Committee 17, Sociology of Organizations, of the International Sociological Association and is Associate Editor of *Administrative Science Quarterly*.

Bruce Kogut is Professor of Management at the Wharton School of the University of Pennsylvania and Director of the Wharton Emerging Economies Program. His research interests include international competition, foreign direct investment and international strategic alliances.

Ralf Boscheck is Professor of Economics and Strategy at IMD. His research interests include industrial and international economics; industry dynamics, public policy impact and antitrust analysis.

Introduction

The International Macroeconomy module deals with the role of companies within the global economy and is complementary to the Applied Microeconomics module.

The module begins with a section on 'market-driven' companies and goes on to cover the competitiveness of economies, the measurement of competitiveness, globalization and alliances in the high-technology industry and the implications of regional trading blocs.

A tale of two economies

■ **Countries increasingly have two types of economies – 'proximity' and 'globality'. The two can be in conflict but, says** Stephane Garelli, **the secret to a truly competitive society is bringing them into balance.**

Competitiveness is a hot issue these days. Companies have released massive gains in productivity by reducing head counts, flattening structures, re-engineering processes, saving space and 'reworking' work.

National and regional governments are also embarking on what appears to be a crusade for competitiveness. The US has created a Competitiveness Council and the European Union has a Competitiveness Advisory Group. Does everything, however, need to be sacrificed on the altar of competitiveness? How much change does a country (or a company) need to implement in order to survive in this new world of competitiveness? Is there a break-off point where the pursuit of efficiency threatens the very survival of countries and companies alike? The answer to these questions very much depends on the ability of a country to develop what could be called a *competitive society.*

A competitive society is a society that has found a dynamic equilibrium between wealth creation and social cohesion. It does not necessarily mean economic efficiency at all costs in all areas. As we shall see later, it may actually imply that people make a conscious decision to accept a certain level of economic inefficiency.

Obviously, a competitive society is one that identifies and actively manages all the facets of its competitiveness, from infrastructure to education (*see* box on p. 485). There is, however, an additional dimension: *it should also achieve a subtle balance between proximity and globality.*

One country, two economies

In any given country, two types of economy coexist: *an economy of proximity* that provides products and services close to the end-user; and *an economy of globality* that is characterized by a worldwide management of the value chain. These two types of economy perform different functions at a different cost. The debate surrounding the issue of competitiveness stems from the fact that it is not entirely clear any more which businesses or jobs belong to which type of economy.

During the past two decades, the revolution in world markets in technology and in management has generated big transfers of activities from one type of economy to the other (in general, from proximity to globality). As a result, many enterprises and people now operate within a new and very different frame of reference.

The economy of proximity

This is an economy that thrives on being close to the end-user. It comprises traditional activities, such as plumbers, butchers, bakers, construction companies or farmers, as well as newer types of businesses, such as companies providing the development and support of customized software. Finally, it includes activities with local social added-value, such as the health sector with such professions as medical doctors, dentists, pharmacists and so on.

Altogether, the economy of proximity generally accounts for the larger part of the gross domestic product. Countries, however, differ in their assessment of which industries should fall into this category. For example, railroads, post and telecommunications, airlines and so on as well as all sorts of 'strategically sensitive' industries might be included in certain countries. In others, such as the UK, they would be released through privatization. Such an economy of proximity displays its own particularities. It shows *very little mobility*. Craftsmen, public administrations, social services or utility providers do not thrive on physical mobility but rather on the multiplication of small entities close to the end-user. It is protected from foreign investors, who can be banned or strongly discouraged in certain sectors (such as tele-communications, water, energy, transport, construction and so on). Public procurements can also be closed or unduly restricted.

Finally, there can be substantial *interference with free-market mechanisms* such as market-sharing agreements, price-fixing, local preference schemes for public procurements (although, in theory, this type of practice should be banned by competition laws). The problem of this economy is that it is not always self-sufficient. Actually, it is generally considered to be relatively market-and cost-inefficient. On the other hand, it provides local employment (and votes).

The key issue, obviously, is *to what extent citizens are willing, or able, to subsidize* through their personal taxes or higher prices a system that is recognized and accepted as less efficient but which performs a social function. If citizens feel that they pay too much, then the question becomes *to what extent should the economy be opened to some free market mechanisms* (for example, in the health-care or education sectors) or to foreign competition?

Finally, the debate turns rapidly to tackling a fundamental dilemma – *what kind of social cost, such as unemployment, or eventually social destabilization*, are modern societies ready to pay as a counterpart for a potential increase in efficiency?

The economy of globality

Contrary to the economy of proximity, the economy of globality assumes that the factors of production need not necessarily be close to the end-user. It thrives by exploiting the different comparative advantages of nations worldwide and by integrating them into a global management of the value chain. It used to benefit only the very big companies – perhaps the 1,000 largest in the world. Nowadays, however, smaller companies also have access to the global economy through the opening of markets, the development of telecommunications, the pervasiveness of information technology and the

massive improvement in international logistics, especially in transportation. This economy is characterized by a relentless drive for performance. Because the value chain is managed globally, competition among countries (and indeed among units inside a company) is exacerbated. Cost-efficiency and value-added are the name of the game.

This often generates *structures that prioritize mobility and resilience*. The factors of production are very flexible and can be shifted easily from one place to another. Management follows the same principle. The consolidation of certain activities, including back-office functions, increases the performance pressure on geographical locations. It is a strategy that seeks to combine power and agility.

Finally, *ownership of the value chain is no longer a priority*. The cost of ownership is, today, under scrutiny. Outsourcing or alliances are emphasized at every point of the value chain. The objective is to control the value chain, not necessarily to own it.

What is the local value of an economy of globality?

The massive drive for cost-efficiency, mobility and global presence that prevail in an economy of globality raises fundamental questions that are on the leading edge of modern economic thinking:

The first one is *what is the real economic impact of global companies?* Mobility in procurement, manufacturing or distribution, outsourcing and alliances, induced employment rather than direct employment, make it very difficult to assess the magnitude of the added-value of global companies. The second question is *what is the contribution to the home economy?* 'Owning' blue-chip companies is prestigious but what advantages are there for the local economy? Modern headquarters comprise fewer people than ever. They centrally manage a network of geographically dispersed business processes. These activities are no longer necessarily located in the home country.

Finally, *who controls, if needed, the economy of globality?* For example, wide currency fluctuations can be a major threat to the economy. How can they be avoided? Is there a need for international investment codes, or international charters that set the ground rules for business ethics, and social and political practices? Such institutions as the G7, the OECD, or the World Trade Organization are currently investigating some of these issues.

Where the conflict between the two economies occurs

The fear of competitiveness arises in a country whenever the economy of proximity is threatened. Indeed, the economy of proximity is destabilized whenever the rules of competitiveness applying to the economy of globality start to invade its turf.

First, regional economic treaties and the GATT agreement force domestic markets to open up. In some sectors, such as telecoms or airlines, an anachronism is being corrected and such industries are being put back in the frame of reference where they belong. For other sectors, such as construction, agriculture or any activity traditionally protected in public procurements, the change is severe.

Second, many activities that traditionally fell into the economy of proximity are now falling into the category of globality. For example, hospitals used to be a local activity. Now, hospital groups have emerged and operate as private international companies. Food retailing is another example where the development of international supermarket chains is changing the life of local stores.

Sometimes, however, the two economies co-operate. Many enterprises now procure globally. The emergence of international networks, such as the Internet, accelerate this process. Electronic procurement and electronic sales will penetrate the world of industry as they have done the world of finance. Further pressure will be put on prices, but many new sales opportunities will also occur. Servicing of the product will probably continue to be sourced locally. The computer and the telecommunication industry provide numerous examples, and a similar phenomenon occurs when the butcher next door sells American beef or New Zealand lamb. In addition, outsourcing, which will continue to expand massively because of cost pressures,

should provide many more opportunities for co-operation with the economy of proximity.

It would be wrong to assume that globality is necessarily bigger than proximity, although at the enterprise level it is generally the case. Some US economists underline, rightly, that 90 per cent of what Americans consume is made in the US. Thus, they argue, the economy of globality is of little relevance (obviously the American automotive or consumer electronics industry would not agree). But for a large part of the US economy it is true. Wal Mart, the largest retailer chain in the world, reached that position with practically no sales outside the US.

Nevertheless, the US situation cannot be extrapolated to the rest of the world. The Netherlands depends on international activities for more than 50 per cent of its GDP (not to mention Hong Kong, Singapore, Malaysia or Ireland), and the European average is now running at close to 30 per cent. It is, therefore, correct to assume that most of the welfare creation in most countries is to be found in the economy of proximity. But, on the other hand, one cannot simply ignore that the economy of globality is rapidly becoming a fundamental part, both quantitatively and qualitatively, of the economic life of every country, even the larger ones.

Will the economy of proximity be globalized? This is probably the most common fear. It is unquestionable that the economy of globality has achieved considerable increases in productivity and added-value during the past decade. This is where the most significant revolution in competitiveness took place.

It does not mean, however, that an economy of proximity has no place in a modern and competitive economic society. For example, citizens are keen to retain the right to decide upon the level of environmental, social and medical protection they desire. They may also want to continue to subsidize certain sectors, such as culture in France, or agriculture in most countries. In other words, *they want to make, in certain cases, the political choice of a certain level of economic inefficiency.* This choice very much depends on the amount of economic resources that can be redirected, partly from the economy of globality, for that purpose. In simpler terms, are people willing (through taxes or higher prices) or able (through other revenues) to pay for it?

Unfortunately, in many countries, the question was not asked in these terms. Instead of increasing the revenues of a country (i.e. increasing its competitiveness) or raising its taxation level (i.e. redistributing wealth), governments have preferred to run massive public debt deficits to subsidize part of the economy of proximity. As a consequence, the net public debt, as a percentage of the GDP, of European countries and the US has doubled over the past 12 years.

Developing the competitiveness of a country is, therefore, a rather more subtle undertaking than just maximizing efficiency in every aspect. (Maximizing efficiency is comparable to concentrating on training an athlete's muscles only, without concern for his or her mental and spiritual development).

The value system of a country expresses itself essentially in its economy of proximity. This economy is thus, emotionally, very much linked to the people. The economy of globality, on the contrary, is often perceived to be more remote, impersonal, standardized and, finally, foreign to national concerns.

Each country's competitiveness will therefore depend upon its ability to manage a balance between the economy of globality, which mainly generates revenues and technology, and the economy of proximity, which mainly generates employment and social cohesion.

From competitive enterprises to competitive societies

During the past two decades, enterprises have moved from product-based competitiveness to process-based competitiveness, and now they are tackling structure-based competitiveness.

Today, enterprises seek to develop structures that are adaptive, resilient, cost-efficient, and which interface easily with the environment and the customer. The same applies for countries. The role of enterprises obviously remains central to a country's competitiveness. However, in addition, modern societies will have to manage

■ Ten Golden Rules of Competitive Societies

1. Create a stable and predictable legislative environment
2. Work on a flexible and resilient economic structure
3. Invest in traditional and technological infrastructure
4. Promote private saving and domestic investment
5. Develop aggressiveness on international markets (exports, etc.) as well as attractiveness for foreign value-added industries
6. Focus on quality and speed in the conduct of administration and reforms
7. Maintain a relationship between wage levels, productivity and taxation
8. Preserve the social fabric by reducing wage disparity and strengthening the middle class
9. Invest massively in education, especially at secondary level, and in the life-long training and improvement of the workforce.
10. Balance the economy of globality and the economy of proximity to ensure wealth creation, maintain social cohesion and preserve the value system citizens desire.

their structures efficiently – public administration, education, research, health and social security systems, and so on – while preserving the enthusiasm of citizens and the value system they care for. They will also have to master the capacity to reform themselves quickly.

Ultimately they should aim to become competitive societies, balancing globality and proximity, wealth creation and social cohesion, and managing change while preserving a stable value system. The constraints on competitiveness are very much to be found, not in enterprises, but in the capacity of a country to develop its own model of a competitive society. Such a model may be different in Britain, in Chile or in Malaysia. But everywhere it will define how much competitiveness a country can take. And everywhere it will determine how successful a country can be.

Summary

The economy of *proximity* thrives on being close to the end-user, and involves both traditional

and new businesses as well as activities with local social added-value. It shows little mobility, is protected from foreign investors and can be cost inefficient – but it expresses a country's value system. The economy of *globality* – to which smaller companies increasingly have access – thrives by exploiting the different comparative advantages of nations. It is where the most significant revolution in productivity has taken place. Competitiveness will continue to depend on a country's ability to manage the balance between the two.

The secrets that lay behind improved corporate performance

■ **Performance relies on measurement, but apart from the standard financial ratios companies are not sure what they should measure or what the measurements mean. Marshall Meyer outlines some pitfalls and solutions.**

One of the most profound changes in business is the new emphasis on performance. The cover of the January 3, 1994 Forbes magazine showed an executive with a cane around his neck, about to be pulled offstage. The headline read: 'Perform – or else'.

Urgency about financial performance is accompanied by heightened awareness that financial performance cannot be sustained unless the non-financial underpinnings of financial performance – innovation, productivity, product quality, customer service, customer satisfaction – are measured and improved.

This message is at the core of the quality movement and reverberates in countless articles and the nearly 400 books published each year on quality management. Corporate re-engineering efforts communicate a similar message: financial performance depends on inventing processes that are both more efficient and serve the customer better – which means that current processes must be understood, measured and improved.

Many businesses are grappling with the choice of non-financial measures to complement the financial measures they now have in place. Few, however, are comfortable with the choices they have made and some have given up. 'It's impossible,' more than one manager has told me. This brings to mind a quip made some years ago by the psychoanalyst Ralph Greenson: 'Not only is psychoanalysis impossible, but it is also very difficult.'

The difficulty in this instance is not measuring non-financial performance. Measuring is easy. Today, almost any aspect of non-financial performance can be measured and monitored inexpensively and, often, unobtrusively.

One pharmaceutical house tracks the activity of its computer support staff by counting e-mail messages between line businesses and the support staff. Customer satisfaction surveys are legion. The difficulty is not measuring but, rather, knowing what to measure and knowing what requires attention and what can be ignored – at least for the time being.

Since all aspects of non-financial performance potentially affect long-term financial performance, managers are tempted to measure everything about people, processes, products and customers that the quality gurus and re-engineering experts believe important. The temptation to measure is especially powerful when the competition is engaged in a frenzy of measurement – how can we forego the potential advantage of measuring and benchmarking our results against theirs?

This temptation can be overcome by remembering that to measure everything is ultimately to create confusion rather than information. Physicists have long understood that a quantum world does not permit both the position and momentum of a particle to be known. In his new book *Fire in the Mind*, George Johnson generalizes this quantum principle to information: 'If you know everything, you know nothing.'

Finding an informative and manageable set of financial and non-financial measures for an organization, then, is one of the principal challenges facing managers. My research suggests that some firms are able to do this, but only when they have understood the key differences between financial and non-financial measures, how their measures should be configured (I will explain this presently) and some of the organizational conditions contributing to effective measurement.

Differences between financial and non-financial measures

One difference between financial and non-financial measures is their sheer number and relatedness. There are many more non-financial than financial performance measures. There are relatively few financial measures because most of them, financial ratios especially, are governed by accounting conventions and are standardized.

Many financial measures, moreover, are closely related because they are subsets or supersets of other financial measures. EBITDA, for example, is earnings before interest, taxes, depreciation and amortization. Cash flow is EBITDA plus additions to working and fixed capital.

Innovative financial measures do appear from time to time, but whether they are truly new and different is debatable. A recent addition to the stock of financial measures is EVA, or economic value added, a trademark of Stern Stewart & Company. EVA is roughly the difference between a company's total returns to bondholders and shareholders and returns that could have been earned from investing in other companies at similar levels of risk. EVA, in other words, is returns less the economic cost of debt and equity capital – which means that a company can be profitable but under water by the EVA measure. More recently, Stern Stewart has marketed a measure called Market Value Added or MVA. MVA is the market's valuation of the firm less the historical cost of capital.

Non-financial measures, unlike financial measures, are not governed by accounting conventions and are rarely standardized – indeed, near anarchy prevails in the realm of non-financial measurement. Without standardization, non-financial measures have multiplied rapidly. The only measures gauging process and product quality 30 years ago were rejects and returns – remember the amount of rework once done in automobile manufacturing.

Today, there are many measures of process and product quality: speed, conformance to product specifications, conformance to fixed quality standards such as ISO 9000, meeting or exceeding competitors' process and product standards.

Thirty years ago, hardly anyone had heard of customer satisfaction. Companies looked to market size and market share statistics to gauge whether or not they had met customers' needs. Today, almost all large companies survey customer satisfaction, although the exact measures differ. And as the evidence showing a link between customer satisfaction and profitability mounts, companies are beginning to look to measures of competitive customer satisfaction – are our customers more or less satisfied than our competitors' customers?

Aside from their number, there is less relatedness among non-financial performance measures than among financial measures.

Conformance quality – conformance to specifications – is an attribute of products and services, whereas customer satisfaction is an attribute of customers. Conformance quality may contribute to customer satisfaction (other things being equal, people prefer products to meet specifications and hence their expectations) but it also may not (people do not appreciate the cost of over-engineered products). There is no necessary connection between the two.

Not only is the relatedness of non-financial measures weaker than the relatedness of financial measures, but the relatedness of a non-financial measure to financial performance can be determined only through statistical evidence that can take months or years to gather.

Product quality, speed and convenience, or satisfaction with the manner in which the transaction was conducted may affect customers' willingness to engage in further transactions and hence future financial performance depending on circumstances – which can be complicated.

Another key difference between financial and non-financial measures is the tendency of non-financial measures to run down with use, to lose variance and hence the capacity to discriminate good from bad performance. The classic case of running down is batting averages in major league baseball in the US.

Differences in batting averages between the best and the worst players have diminished substantially since baseball statistics were first kept in the 1870s. There are no more 400 hitters.

Several explanations for diminished variation in batting averages come to mind. Perhaps the most cogent is suggested by the palaeontologist Stephen J. Gould, who argues that improvements in player selection due to the creation of the minor league 'farm system' coupled with improved coaching and training of major league pitchers and batters have caused differences in batting averages to shrink.

I have found that many performance measures exhibit diminished variance over time, for example, occupancy and length-of-stay statistics for hospitals, safety statistics for nuclear power plant, yields of money market mutual funds and even customer satisfaction – several companies report that customer satisfaction now exceeds 90 per cent and is not expected to improve further.

I have also found that organizations seek new and somewhat different performance measures when existing measures lose variance. Batting averages hardly figure in baseball contract negotiations nowadays – slugging percentage, on-base percentage, run production and the like have taken the place of batting average.

Hospitals have moved away from functional performance measures such as occupancy to disease-specific morbidity and mortality rates. The Nuclear Regulatory Commission is continually searching for new safety measures. Money market mutual funds compete today on service as much as on yield. Some companies are introducing measures of customer loyalty to complement customer satisfaction.

Although diminished variance in measured performance often occurs due to improvement, perverse learning, or gaming, also causes variance to diminish. Teachers teach to test. Police investigators elicit multiple confessions from suspects to maintain clearance rates. Workers learn how to meet their 'bogeys' exactly, sometimes by hiding or suppressing output, sometimes by sharing output with less productive colleagues.

The problem for managers is knowing when diminished variance signals improvement and when it signals gaming or outright deception. Usually, managers do not even try to distinguish improvement from gaming and deception. Instead, they search for new measures where variation exists and cannot be gamed away immediately.

Given the differences between financial and non-financial measures, why bother to measure non-financial performance at all?

The answer is that financial measures summarize past performance well but predict future performance poorly – very poorly indeed. Consider the ultimate financial performance measure – share price.

Shares of companies singled out as poor performers by the Council of Institutional Investors from 1991 through 1993 have since outperformed the market by about 50 per cent. The 20 highest-performing mutual funds in each year from 1982 to 1992 ranked, on average, at about the middle of the pack in each subsequent year.

Outstanding financial performance, to be sure, confers some advantages on companies. Those with outstanding financial results enjoy better access to debt and equity markets and better reputations than their less outstanding counterparts. But as often as not, outstanding financial performance is followed by mediocre performance.

It is no wonder, then, that many managers regard financial measures as backward-looking, as rear view measures telling you how well they did but not how well they are likely to do, and seek non-financial measures capable of predicting financial performance.

How to configure measures

I have some rules of thumb for combining non-financial and financial performance measures. The rules are simple in principle, although somewhat more difficult to implement in practice.

- *The number of measures*: there should be more than one or two measures gauging progress toward strategic objectives (multiple constraints will help to keep gaming in check) but fewer than five or six (remember George Johnson's law: 'If you know everything, you know nothing').
- *The balance of financial and non-financial measures*: there should be some of both. Including non-financial measures is especially critical, since these are the leading indicators of performance.
- *The properties of non-financial measures*: non-financial measures must meet three requirements. There must be variance or room for improvement – measures that cannot be improved cannot contribute to financial performance. They must be under your control so that you can take actions to improve them. And there must be a clear path from non-financial performance to financial results so that improvement in the former produces improvement in the latter. The first two requirements for non-financial measures – improvable and controllable – are fairly easy to meet. But the third requirement – a clear path from non-financial to financial performance – is more difficult to satisfy because it takes considerable evidence to demonstrate that non-financial performance produces financial results.
- *The level of constraint among measures*: a moderate level of constraint is desirable. Measures should be sufficiently constrained so that gains in any one of them reflect true

performance gains. Constraints should not be so severe that gains in one measure can be achieved only at the expense of other measures. Nor should constraints be so relaxed that gains in any one measure automatically produce gains in the others.

- *The availability of alternative measures*: new measures should be available should existing measures run down.

These rules of thumb were used in configuring performance measures for the distribution organization of a global electronics manufacturer. The key financial measure for the larger organization was ROA, return on assets.

Since the distribution organization was a cost center rather than a profit center, its contribution to the numerator of ROA was measured by order fulfilment costs – the lower the order fulfilment costs, the better the returns. The distribution organization's contribution to the denominator of ROA was measured by the ratio of total revenues to inventory – the higher this ratio, the smaller the fraction of assets tied up in inventory.

Two non-financial measures were chosen as well: the time needed to fill orders and the proportion of orders filled directly from inventory – experience had taught this organization that delays caused customers to defect to other sources.

Altogether, then, the distribution organization used four performance measures, two financial measures (order fulfilment costs and the ratio of revenues to inventory) and two non-financial measures (time to order fulfilment and orders fulfilled from inventory). The non-financial measures were improvable, controllable and predictive of financial performance. Together, these measures constrained one another moderately.

To illustrate some of the constraints: time to order fulfilment could not be managed by increasing order fulfilment costs (for example, by using air rather than surface transportation). And the proportion of orders filled from inventory could not be managed by increasing inventories and hence the ratio of inventories to revenue. Better ways of improving performance were required and, in fact, were ultimately discovered.

Moreover, even as these performance measures were being put into place, their replacements were under active consideration by the distribution organization.

Organizational conditions contributing to effective performance measurement

Effective performance measurement requires centralized control of performance measures. Since the 1950s, most large corporations have operated on an extremely decentralized basis: financial objectives are set for business units and business unit managers are permitted to pursue these objectives as they see fit.

These practices may change as companies begin introducing non-financial measures alongside financial ones and thinking about their overall configuration of measures.

Greater centralization of companies, I believe, will occur. Centralization will be needed to standardize non-financial measures, to compare and reward both financial and non-financial results, and to review and replace performance measures.

The distribution organization of the global electronics manufacturer illustrates the trend toward centralization.

Its performance measures were decided by the head of organization and his controller, and the controller retains responsibility for reviewing measures. In another global manufacturing firm, one vice-president has responsibility for performance measures worldwide.

In a global financial services company that historically has operated on a highly decentralized basis, common measures for front-office processes will somewhat erode the autonomy of country-based business units.

These cases, I believe, are not idiosyncratic. They reflect a simple logic of measurement: so long as performance is gauged by a single measure that can be compared readily across businesses, little central control is needed. Once, however, multiple measures, financial and non-financial measures, and the properties of these measures as well as constraints among them must be considered, some centralization is inevitable.

Summary

There is a growing realization that financial performance cannot be sustained unless the non-financial underpinnings are measured as well. Financial measures may summarize past performance but they predict future performance poorly. The problem is not the measurement as such, rather knowing what to measure, what requires attention and what can be ignored. Occasionally new financial measures like EVA come along – but there are many more non-financial ones. There is less relatedness among them, conformance quality for example being an attribute of product and services, customer satisfaction an attribute of customers. The statistics on which they are based can take months or years to gather and they have a tendency to 'run down' with use. Organizations often seek new performance measures when the old ones lose variance. Progress towards strategic objectives should be gauged by more than one or two measures, but less than 5 or 6. Make sure some of them are non-financial, though there must be a clear path to financial performance. Effective performance measurement requires centralized control of the measures.

Globalization and alliances in high technology industries

■ **What many take to be a modern-day growth in corporate alliances is not always a response to the need for economies of scale. Often it is reaction to competition and new technology opportunities, says** Bruce Kogut

Many people believe that there is a growing number of alliances among companies today. The cause of this growth is often said to be the importance of scale in operation and, hence, the need to access global markets by which to amortize the high fixed investments in research and development or plant and equipment.

Usually, a number of joint ventures are given as examples, often involving agreements between companies to build new plants for the production of computer memory semiconductors or for the assembly of aircraft.

There is, no doubt, more than a grain of truth to these observations but how many grains is anybody's guess. Part of the problem is that the world is simply getting bigger and there is more of everything – more people, more cars, bigger GNPs and more alliances. Consider the demand for semiconductors today compared to ten years ago. Is the growth in this demand much different than the growth in the fixed costs of production? Cannot the size of the US market support many plants just serving the domestic market?

What is true is that competition is more global for many industries. And the internationalization of competition has made it attractive for competitors to co-operate on an international basis. Sometimes this co-operation is simply to gain market access; other times it is to share new technologies or to learn new production methods; and occasionally, it is to stabilize competition on a worldwide basis.

The confluence of alliances and globalization suggests a causality between the two. But even here there is reason to be cautious if the more fundamental factors are to be recognised. And nowhere is this danger of misinterpretation greater than in understanding co-operative behavior in high technology industries.

Alliances and structural breaks

Alliances are frequently the outcome of structural breaks in an industry. Globalization is one kind of shock. The spate of joint ventures in the 1980s between auto manufacturers was partly the response to the internationalization of this market and the growing penetration of companies into each others' home markets. As this process matured, the number of major joint ventures has also slowed.

Another kind of structural break is that of technological change. In high-technology industries, breakthroughs in basic science or the discovery of new innovations open vast new arenas. These arenas represent rich technological opportunities that attract new investments and the entry of established and new companies. In the rush to succeed, alliances are formed for the sharing of ideas, plants, and of marketing and distribution channels.

Consider, for example, the industries of biotechnology and semiconductors. In biotechnology, a new field was opened up with the discovery of new methods of bioengineering by Boyer and Cohen in the 1970s. In semiconductors, the discovery of logic and memory devices caused the rapid development of new applications to computers, telecommunications and other specialized markets. These technological developments acted as structural breaks in the pharmaceutical and semiconductor markets. New companies were started up, incumbent companies entered these new fields and, in some cases, were forced out. The competitive climate of

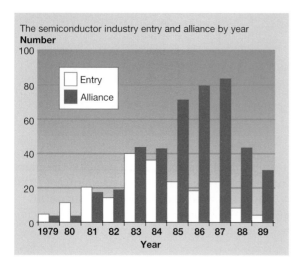

Figure 1

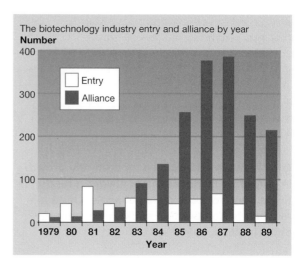

Figure 2

these industries changed radically over a few years. No wonder that alliances were a frequent event. To turn Clausewitz on his head, co-operation is competition by other means.

In Figures 1 and 2, the pattern of entry and alliance formation is given for the formative years of the 1980s. What is striking in both of these figures is that the wave of entrepreneurial activity is followed by a wave of alliance formation. Over time, both of these waves fell off towards the end of the 1980s. Alliances are, of course, still important, partly because technological change is still spawning new opportunities. Yet, the more fundamental point remains: it is simply not true that alliances increase at a steady rate with time.

Competition and entry induction

The similarity in the pattern of entry and alliances in biotechnology and semiconductors should not obscure the large differences between the two. Alliances in the former frequently involve the provision of licensing agreements by the start-up company for distribution access controlled by the larger company. Semiconductor alliances are substantially more oriented towards technology sharing, licensing or co-development. Because of the differences in market structure, the dynamics of competition and co-operation are very different. In biotechnology the nature of basic research

implies an uncertain process. The many start-up companies trade their technological promise for up-front capital and to avoid costly investments in sales forces. Alliances, especially foreign, are attracted to those start-ups that have had initial successes in the form of patents or completing clinical trials.

The semiconductor industry reveals a more complicated play between co-operation and competition because of the important role played by microprocessors. Microprocessors pose a problem of 'network externalities'. Some semiconductors need to be customized to the logic, or microprocessor, device. Moreover, software is also specialized to the microprocessor. As a result, software programers write to fit the specifications of the logic device.

In the 1980s, the fierce contest between Intel, National Semiconductor, Motorola and, secondarily, a few Japanese companies (for example NEC) led to a spate of co-operative agreements. Intel and its competitors welcomed entrants into the market who chose to align their technology to their standard. In effect, the promise of co-operation induced new companies to enter and to build upon the technology of the dominant semiconductor companies.

By the end of the 1980s, Intel had achieved a commanding lead in microprocessor sales due to the success of IBM-compatible personal computers, which used its standard. As the supplier to Apple Computer, Motorola was a distant second. National Semiconductor lost considerable market share and the logic devices of such Japanese companies as NEC were of importance only in Japan.

In 1985, about 3.5 per cent and 2.1 per cent of the semiconductor agreements included Intel and Motorola, respectively, as partners. Both companies licensed liberally to attract companies to their standards. By 1989, their share in alliances fell to 2.5 per cent and 1.65 per cent respectively, suggesting that the willingness to share technology eroded as their competitive strength increased to positions of dominance.

And yet National Semiconductor, which had become a second-tier player in the semiconductor market, moved from 1.6 per cent of the alliances in 1983 to 2.67 per cent in 1985 and to 3.2 per cent in 1989. (*These statistics are calculated from proprietary data shared by Dataquest with the author*).

Alliances in these high-technology industries are not simply the outcome of some trend to larger scale or the globalization of markets. They reflect very different dynamics of competition. To understand these alliances, it is necessary to understand their competitive context.

Death by acquisition

The uncertainty that characterizes new technologies provides an important motive for many of the alliances, especially those between large incumbents and new companies. An established company faces a difficult decision regarding the funding of research activities. An alternative to in-house research is to purchase equity in a joint venture or as a minority owner in a start-up company.

It is not surprising that joint ventures, because they are frequently motivated by uncertainty, do not have long life expectancies. For manufacturing ventures in the US, the half-life is about six years. Of the ones that die by outright liquidation, the ventures that represent a one-time transaction among partners face a higher risk of dissolution. Multiple ties between partners stabilises any one joint venture. It is striking, though, that most terminated ventures end by acquisition by one of the partners. In many cases, this buy-out reflects an explicit

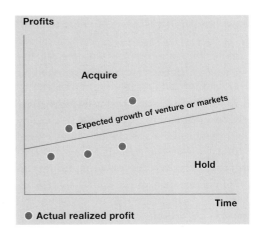

Figure 3: Timing of exercise to acquire joint venture

clause in the contract that gives one party the first option to buy the business.

The interesting dimension to this acquisition is that this option appears to be exercised at the point when the market is growing. In times of slow growth, the parties to the venture need not dissolve the business if the operating costs are not too high. The trouble starts when the market begins to grow. Suddenly, new capital must be committed and the venture is re-evaluated by the two parties. One party walks away with capital gains, the other with ownership of the venture.

In Figure 3, the option-like timing of an acquisition is illustrated. During the years in which the market is still nascent and profits are low, the parties to the venture wait and hold their positions. At the time the market takes off and profits are expected to grow, one party buys out the venture.

In high-technology industries, joint ventures are frequently the purchases of options on new technological opportunities.

It is when the technology is proven and the market turns up that one party exercises the option to buy it out. An important element to these alliances is who has the first right to buy and at what terms.

The third wave

The prevalence of termination by acquisition suggests a final wave to the pattern of alliances. The first wave is that of new entrants; the second of alliances; and the third that of their termin-ations.

As technological opportunities become market opportunities, alliances frequently convert to outright buy-outs.

There is no strong evidence to believe that alliances are increasing in relative frequency with the passing of each year. They were common features of the late-19th century in industrial countries as the second industrial revolution of chemicals and electricity opened up new vistas. They are currently in vogue in the revolutionary restructuring caused by new technologies in multimedia. They were popular in the 1980s due to the rapid globalization of markets and the expanding trajectory of new technologies. Their use will wane if and as these more fundamental forces themselves exhaust their territory of expansion.

Summary

The globalization of competition has certainly made it attractive for companies to co-operate more on an international basis.

The spate of joint ventures in the 1980s in the auto industry was partly a response to global-ization and the growing penetration by companies in each others' markets.

But the reason for alliances in high technology industries is more complicated, and there is no strong reason to believe that they are increasing in relative frequency each year. They are often the outcome of structural 'breaks', among which is the uncertainty that character-izes new technology. For this reason it is not surprising that joint ventures do not have long life expectancies. As technological opportunities become market opportunities, alliances convert to outright buy-outs.

Suggested further reading

Kogut, B., Walker, G. and Kim, D. J. (1995) *Co-operation and Entry Induction as an Extension of Technological Rivalry*, Research Policy.

Kogut, B. 'The stability of joint ventures, reciprocity and competitive rivalry', *Journal of Industrial Economics* December 1989.

Managed trade and regional choice

■ **Ralf Boscheck examines regional trade blocs, a rapidly growing phenomenon. Are they, as many fear, barely disguised protectionism or a step towards global free trade?**

Since 1992, the world's regional trade arrangements have nearly doubled to over 100. With the three largest groups – the European Union, the North America Free Trade Area and the Asia Pacific Economic Co-operation grouping

– already accounting for more than 45 per cent of global trade, it is not obvious whether this trend presents a stepping-stone towards, or a retreat from, free trade. Nor is it at all clear whether such managed economic interdependence will stifle or enhance the potential of associated companies, sectors and economies.

Yet, both corporate and public policy makers need to understand the impact of regionalization on insiders' competitiveness and outsiders' market chances. So far the Gatt has not challenged any of the agreements; yet tighter obligations emerging from the World Trade Organization and expected changes in the size and philosophy of these undertakings may trigger harsher reviews and retaliatory actions by non-members.

Obviously, whether any regional trade arrangement will ultimately want to contribute to or abstain from free trade depends on how its size and composition affect the welfare and competitiveness of its member countries. Although some structures seem intuitively more likely than others to prepare economies for external market challenge, there is little evidence to support such views.

Empirical studies, accounting for the costs and benefits of regional trade preference, have suffered from substantial difficulties in isolating clear-cut indicators and interpreting the politically contentious results. There is also no guidance in the ever-growing 'competitiveness' literature, which explores regional trade arrangements as just another 'weapon' in what it construes to be a global commercial 'battle'.

This section, therefore, returns to basic trade and alliance theories to illustrate potential developments in the competitiveness of associated trading partners and their internal and external bargaining about the allocation of adjustment costs over time. Applied to the cases of the EU, NAFTA and APEC, this reference sheds light on their respective options for enhancing regional competitiveness, as well as on their broader effects on global trade.

Trade, adjustment and regional preference

Most of economic theory not only cautions against government interference with trade but proposes a *unilateral* opening of borders to stimulate specialization in production in line with global productivity differences. The resulting exchange according to a country's 'revealed comparative advantage' increases its standard of living but requires a constant adjustment to international market conditions.

Conversely, meddling with free trade or factor mobility may support an otherwise unsustainable productive specialization but reduces

welfare, redistributes income from consumers to protected factor owners and in the long-run stifles an economy's facility to adjust.

Relative to these positions of 'openness to trade' and 'defensive protectionism', recent theories of international competition conclude that government involvement in global oligopolies may pay off, provided that it effectively blocks foreign entry into home or third markets, pre-empts competitor investments or otherwise broadly changes the rules of global competition.

The essential difference between these positions is one of attitude. The first perspective sees trade as a co-operative, positive-sum game in which competition enforces an efficient specialization of production for exchange.

The second position is frequently portrayed as a pessimistic, xenophobic and ultimately futile attempt to hide behind barricades lest the loss of competitiveness be exposed.

The third position looks at trade as head-on competition to enter new markets or upgrade otherwise non-competitive industries. Here, trade is at best a zero-sum if not a negative-sum game; competitiveness centers on the ability to shift adjustment costs.

Figure 1 illustrates the development of regional trade arrangements along two dimensions representing the induced transformation of the shared productive base and the conditions for co-ordinating needed adjustments.

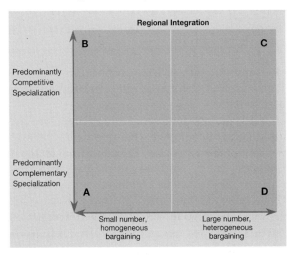

Figure 1

The vertical axis summarizes the economic effects observable within customs unions and free trade areas along a continuum ranging from competitive to complementary specialization.

In the case of *competitive specialization*, significant sectoral overlap and negligible market barriers inside the union fuel internal competition, induce and facilitate operation at competitive cost or, where economies of scale are insignificant, promote competitive, intra-industry specialization.

Either way, the union requires low levels of short-term protection and, in sectors where parity with outside supply can never be expected, avoids an inefficient allocation of resources by relying on international supplies.

Complementary specialization grows out of a limited degree of sectoral overlap, which is sheltered against viable external competition by means of substantial protection. Depending on the size of the internal market relative to cost-efficient output requirements, internal industries may never attain global productivity standards; low levels of internal competition and protection assure that there is also no incentive to do so.

The horizontal axis represents different bargaining conditions affecting the allocation of adjustment costs inside and outside the club. In dealing with the outside world, the group's cohesion is apt to improve members' international market access. The cohesion of the customs union depends on its ability to maintain devotion to the union and procedural consensus. This may initially require partners to be screened in terms of their contribution to overlapping industries, product and factor markets, and their attitude towards handling adjustment.

With increasing size and scope of the arrangement, however, the union's operations demand consensus and co-ordination of most economic and political decisions affecting structural adjustment. Achieving agreement on these issues seems easiest in times of economic growth and among a few fairly homogenous parties, who are able to maintain continuous communication and react quickly to economic disturbances.

With a growing complexity and volume of issues to be addressed, any international ad hoc co-ordination is likely to be replaced by some form of centralized decision making. This may involve a single, dominant country; a set of core countries able to accommodate the concerns of 'junior' partners at the price of allegiance; or some supra-national, independent institution.

Without such institutional arrangement and with an increased diversity in membership, disintegration is likely to occur.

Summing up these conditions, the horizontal axis represents the continuum of bargaining positions ranging from homogenous, small numbers to heterogeneous, large numbers.

In Figure 1, *Position A* represents a small sheltered club of complementary, largely import substituting producers; a similar group in *Position B* leverages substantial internal competition to participate efficiently in international trade.

Position C groups a large number of associated countries, whose competitive specialization and potential bargaining difficulties would ultimately make it preferable to co-ordinate directly through market forces – i.e. through free trade. *Position D* represents a large number of heterogeneous complementary producers, whose respective global competitive disadvantages affect one another, exacerbate intrinsic bargaining difficulties and make fundamental reforms unlikely.

How do the EU, NAFTA and APEC fit this picture? What are their current policy options and how do these affect the facility of associated economies to adjust to global market conditions?

The European Union
By the end of 1994, industrial production throughout the OECD was rising at the rate of 6 per cent, and the US rate of job creation exceeded the growth of its active population. At the same time, the EU's stagnating output coincided with 11.8 per cent of unemployment, i.e. 22 million people depending directly on unemployment benefits, mostly long-term.

Just over a year later, signs of cyclical improvement cannot mask the fact that the region is rapidly losing ground in its previous top-employment sectors and maintains its export position only in low-growth, low to medium-level technology products. Waning contributions from extra-EU trade are being compensated for by an increase in intra-Union and preferential trade; tariff and non-tariff instruments help to channel, moderate or block external competition on an industry basis.

Figure 2.1 (*see* overleaf) represents Europe's current 'crisis of competitiveness' as resulting from a history of enlargement, increased diversity but essentially complementary specialization across product and factor markets. The graph also tallies numerous frustrated attempts to install political co-ordination in support of the common market objective. In 1953, 1961, and again 1971, national parliaments rejected initiatives to transfer sovereign rights to a supranational body.

Lately, disunity has been sanctioned by the Maastricht Treaty itself, which, contrary to the supranational principals of the Single European Act, pushed the door open to increased inter-governmental haggling.

Moreover, although the disintegration of the European Monetary System had characterized the EC-12 as too diverse to be an 'optimum currency area' likely to co-ordinate a monetary union, the Union again broadened its membership or quasi-membership. Economic base and attitude towards adjustment had obviously not been the primary criteria for partnership selection; nor was this reflected in the distribution of representative power in institutions such as the EU Council. Current enlargement initiatives are bound to exacerbate the situation.

In view of the growing diversity and complementarity of EU producers and the likely dilution of core members' interest, it is not surprising that the traditionally pro-Union governments of France and Germany repeatedly called for a fundamental re-evaluation of the EU's founding contract.

Without some effective adjustment initiative, it was felt that a divisive but more realistic 'Community of Multiple Speeds' would reduce the level of economic and political inter-dependency currently stifling the potential of European companies, sectors and economies.

Relative to its current state, a 'New Founding Contract' in line with the original Franco-German view would group economies on the basis of similar sectoral interest, economic strength and philosophies. The resulting positions, represented in the left top quadrant of Figure 2.2 (overleaf), are characterized by enhanced administrative efficiency in dealing with increased competition and unconstrained ability to source from most efficient supplies.

Such opening up to free trade, presupposes market-creating initiatives that harmonize technical standards, liberalize public procurement, overcome fiscal barriers and dismantle state aid for adjustments. It would trigger exits from product areas in which factors are sub-optimally employed, expand market opportunities for trading partners and channel resources into segments with expected higher factor returns. With regard to the latter, the EU may still want initially to limit market access so as to attain competitive scale rather than concede to the efficiency advantages of pre-positioned international producers. Whether such infant-industry protection is wasteful depends on its net impact on sectoral competition.

Yet, even if one were to assume the required political resolve and consensus inside the Union, Europe's options are nevertheless conditioned by the market views of its trading partners. If regionalization is but an exercise to shift adjustment costs, the proposed New Founding Contract would reduce the EU's critical mass and hence lessen its position in trade disputes and market access talks.

What then are the respective options for NAFTA and APEC?

The North American Free Trade Agreement

NAFTA's two-year record today must list a mix of expected improvements, unplanned shocks, frustrated hopes and unwarranted fears. Its future will be determined by whether (and if so which) institutional adaptations are required to improve upon internal and external trading opportunities.

NAFTA's step-wise reduction of tariffs on

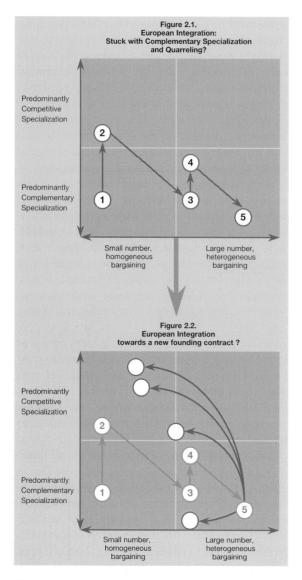

Figure 2.1.
European Integration:
Stuck with Complementary Specialization
and Quarreling?

Predominantly
Competitive
Specialization

Predominantly
Complementary
Specialization

Small number,
homogeneous
bargaining

Large number,
heterogeneous
bargaining

Figure 2.2.
European Integration
towards a new founding contract ?

Predominantly
Competitive
Specialization

Predominantly
Complementary
Specialization

Small number,
homogeneous
bargaining

Large number,
heterogeneous
bargaining

Figure 2

Commentary to Figure 2

Linked by the treaties of Paris and Rome, the heterogeneous post-war industrial structures and capabilities of the founding economies (1) fuelled intra-EC trade and soon began to develop larger areas of overlap.

Induced by subsidies originally under the European Agricultural Guidance and Guarantee Fund (1964) industrial Germany improved upon crop production; meanwhile France's industrial policies enhanced its manufacturing and technology base.

In parallel, substantial cuts in internal duties marked progress towards a common market.

The completion of the customs union, announced in July 1968, however, came with the 'realization' that non-tariff barriers to trade had been forgotten – internal competition in areas of overlap was hence limited (2).

The early 70s brought an opening of the Community towards African, Asian, Pacific and Caribbean economies under the first Lome agreement (1975), followed by preferential trade relationships with Israel as well as Magreb and Mashreq countries in 1976.

With Greece joining in 1981 and Spain and Portugal in 1986, the so-called Southern Enlargement resulted in additional diversity within the Community's industrial landscape (3).

The second half of the 80s saw especially Spain benefiting from regional development funds to enhance its industrial base.

Debates on positive adjustment strategies and rationalization culminated in the Cecchini report on the benefits of a completed internal market by 1992. While an overall improved economic climate significantly raised the level of trade, it was nevertheless below potential, as actual harmonization achievements were rather limited.

By the end of 1994, 231 out of 265 adopted Single Market measures still required transposition into national law (4).

The early 1990s brought Eastern European reforms followed by agreements with Poland, Hungary, the Czech Republic, Slovakia, Romania and Bulgaria as steps towards EU membership, including open free trade in industrial goods from 1995, steel in 1996 and textiles in 1997.

The Partnership and Co-operation Agreement with Russia of 1994 is to be expanded into a free trade area by 1998.

Aware of the potential but also massive costs of intra-industry specialization across broad areas of sectoral overlap, the EU shies away from free trade, as Eastern Europe's distorted input markets, especially in the area of energy and raw materials, are said to confer an unfair cost advantage over Western European suppliers. (5).

20,000 goods was ultimately to affect 365m consumers and an annual production volume of $US6.7bn. For all three partners the reasons for joining were largely economic although their dependence on the newly forged arrangement differed substantially. Eighty per cent of Canada's total exports earnings, representing about 23 per cent of its GNP, stem from the US. Seventy per cent of Mexican exports were sent to the US. But only 25 per cent of US exports went to Canada and only a fraction of this to Mexico.

NAFTA fitted Washington's long-term objective of linking North America in a stabilizing process of co-ordinated economic development. In addition, the US stood to gain from access to raw materials (for example Mexican crude oil), markets (electronics, printed media, cars) and low-cost labour to fuel competitiveness, demand and domestic job creation. In addition, NAFTA was seen as providing regional control over patent and intellectual property rights as well as a bargaining tool for dealing with other regionalization initiatives around the globe.

Canada's initial interest in NAFTA largely reflected its need to secure the benefits from the 1988 Free Trade Agreement with the US. Since then, Canada seems to have pushed aside purely defensive motives and has started to target Mexican export markets. It is currently spending CAN$27 million a year to attain a substantial foothold there.

As the world's fastest expanding export nation in 1990, Mexico sought NAFTA membership further to penetrate the North American market and safeguard against volatile US trade policies in the Americas. In addition, opening its economy through the liberalization of factor and product markets was to broaden the country's geographic base of foreign direct investments and facilitate the jump to large-scale industrial and export diversification.

For all three parties, NAFTA's immediate effects on trade, employment and investment were quite noticeable. Within the first six months alone, US exports to Mexico increased by 16.7 per cent and to Canada by 9.6 per cent. Imports from Mexico increased by 20.3 per cent and Canada's exports to the US increased by 10.2 per cent. According to estimates the US was able to offer 100,000 new jobs. In 1994, Mexico was able to attract direct investments of approximately US$9bn. Yet, turning these short-term benefits into a sustainable regional advantage called for an institutional design and leadership to manage the required change.

Mexican adjustment costs were most daunting. By mid-1994, the required liberalization had increased unemployment by 3.7 per cent. With inflation soaring up to 45 per cent from 7 per cent in 1994, interest on loans to Mexican industry more than tripled and purchasing power plummeted.

An international US$50bn injection was given under the provision that the country committed to a tighter money supply policy and placed its oil revenues as collateral. Concerned about its national sovereignty in the face of a seemingly daunting task of structural adjustments, the Mexican government invoked NAFTA emergency clauses to impose special duties on imports in threatened sectors. Criticized for thus delaying market adjustment, Mexico was however not alone in doing so.

The 53 per cent drop in the value of the peso had increased the volume of US-Mexican trade, but in the process had turned a $1.5bn US surplus during the first eight months of 1994, into a $10bn US trade deficit during the same period a year later. Whether changes in trade performance or basic rationalization had ultimately caused an additional 170,000 US jobs to be lost is subject to debate. A recent assessment by *Industry Week* concluded that although NAFTA has not triggered the feared 'mass migration of jobs to Mexico', it also has not proved to be the US job generator that its proponents had expected.

All three countries are involved in fierce disputes with one another on protective duties and subsidies in industries ranging from agricultural to car parts. In the absence of a supranational institution to supervize dispute settlement, NAFTA's Chapter 19 provides a private process involving a judicial review by a bi-national panel whose decisions are enforceable by domestic laws. Yet the panel's jurisdiction is limited to antidumping and countervailing duty proceedings.

Any complaint beyond these issues that is not dealt with by the Gatt falls under the provision of Chapter 20. This provides for a two-stage review whose recommendations are legally non-binding and hence frequently ignored. As a result, issues such as 'sufficient' safeguards for intellectual property rights and investments, 'appropriate' levels of environmental protection as well as 'acceptable' workers' rights invite unilateral interpretation and enforcement according to self-interest.

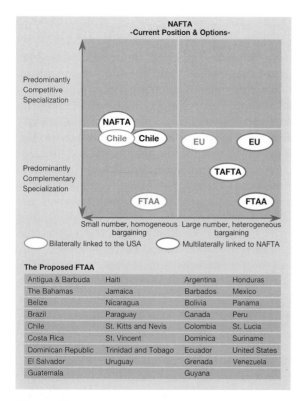

Figure 3

A potentially more equitable and transparent supranational dispute settlement system would limit national sovereignty and control. Such an instrument may nevertheless be needed in case the right to dispute the interpretation of the agreement will be extended to private parties, or NAFTA enlarges its scope and membership.

At this stage, however, Washington seems more interested in consolidating control over its existing set of trade arrangements than in enlarging it. For the time being, Chile's accession to NAFTA and the creation of a Free Trade Area of Americas (FTAA) seem to have been shelved. The US is reported to be in no rush to speed up talks about a Trans-Atlantic-Free-Trade-Area (TAFTA) with the EU or have its NAFTA partners join in talks with Brussels.

Concern about such controlling impact has led Canada and Mercosur to pursue independent talks with the EU. Meanwhile, Chile approached Canada for bilateral trade preferences. Given this, what are Washington's options in shaping NAFTA's external relations? Which strategy

would help NAFTA avoid Europe's sclerotic state of affairs?

Figure 3 puts NAFTA's current position and outlined options into perspective. At this stage, Washington's interest in consolidating NAFTA affairs while otherwise promoting multi-lateralism along the WTO outline is likely to provide the best external orientation for internal market adjustments. Any NAFTA-based arrangement with Chile, the FTAA, the TAFTA or the EU could prolong haggling over needed adjustments and hence dilute the competitiveness of the combined productive base. Any bilateral arrangement, although administratively more efficient than protracted multigroup bargaining, is second best to insisting on multilateralism.

In the absence of a unifying, institutional infrastructure, representing a NAFTA perspective to outside constituencies would require Canada, Mexico and the US to improve internal decision-making and adjustment management.

How does APEC address this issue?

Asia-Pacific Economic Co-operation

Whereas a tight control may help NAFTA to avoid the European fate of drifting towards protectionist and complementary specialization, APEC's diversity, size and 'cultural bias' made it opt for a more flexible approach to foster development and trade.

Asian-Pacific interdependence relies on the intra-regional transfer of industries from early starters to latecomers. This – within limits – has promoted regional trade, enhanced political stability but achieved little economic integration. Even institutional arrangements, such as the Association of South East Asian Nations, did not succeed in bridging the differences in economic philosophies between export-promoting Malaysia and Singapore and the poorer protectionist import-substituting countries around Indonesia. As a result internal tariff walls remained relatively high.

Furthermore, ASEAN did not provide a vehicle adequately to channel the regional investment interests of Australia, the US and Japan, or to link such booming subregions such as the Greater South China Economic Zone.

APEC was set up to address these needs and

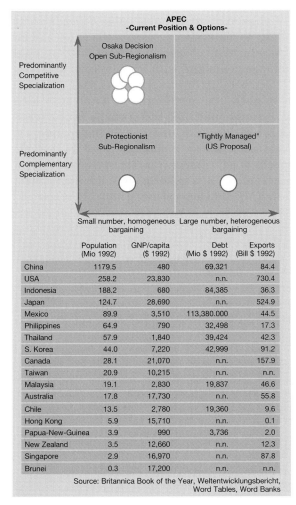

APEC
-Current Position & Options-

	Population (Mio 1992)	GNP/capita ($ 1992)	Debt (Mio $ 1992)	Exports (Bill $ 1992)
China	1179.5	480	69,321	84.4
USA	258.2	23,830	n.n.	730.4
Indonesia	188.2	680	84,385	36.3
Japan	124.7	28,690	n.n.	524.9
Mexico	89.9	3,510	113,380.000	44.5
Philippines	64.9	790	32,498	17.3
Thailand	57.9	1,840	39,424	42.3
S. Korea	44.0	7,220	42,999	91.2
Canada	28.1	21,070	n.n.	157.9
Taiwan	20.9	10,215	n.n.	n.n.
Malaysia	19.1	2,830	19,837	46.6
Australia	17.8	17,730	n.n.	55.8
Chile	13.5	2,780	19,360	9.6
Hong Kong	5.9	15,710	n.n.	0.1
Papua-New-Guinea	3.9	990	3,736	2.0
New Zealand	3.5	12,660	n.n.	12.3
Singapore	2.9	16,970	n.n.	87.8
Brunei	0.3	17,200	n.n.	n.n.

Source: Britannica Book of the Year, Weltentwicklungsbericht, Word Tables, Word Banks

Figure 4

create a regional platform in Canberra, Australia, in 1989. It brought together six ASEAN countries, Australia, Japan, Canada, the Republic of Korea, New Zealand, the US and the three Chinas – the PRC, Taiwan and Hong Kong.

Seven issue-oriented study groups were formed to develop regional agendas, which, at the 1994 Bogar (Indonesia) forum, were translated into a broad objective of a phased regional trade liberalization and development as a stepping stone for global, multilateral liberalization. But soon dissent emerged.

The US translation of development co-operation as trade facilitation and harmonization of technical, economic and social standards, triggered conflicts with China and Indonesia on issues of human rights and labor regulation. In response, Malaysia and other Asean countries promoted the East Asian Economic Caucus (EAEC) 'to preserve the Asian identity of the region'.

To contain potentially isolationist ambitions of the EAEC, APEC's eminent persons group called for 'open sub-regionalism' as a notion to allow for multiple speeds in accepting trade liberalization. That position came to be reflected in the Osaka Action Agenda, which resisted US demands for a stronger institutional framework and stuck to more consensus-based co-ordination.

To safeguard this position, Japan is likely to assume a more prominent role in APEC affairs, leading by example in pushing for domestic deregulation and international market access. In addition, Asean countries are courting the EU to have a European card in discussing with non-Asian APEC members. Figure 4 sketches the state of the debate around the evolution of APEC at the beginning of 1996.

At this stage, it is premature to speculate which direction the region will ultimately take. If one were to rely on the views of APEC's eminent persons group, the associated states, already accounting for about 56 per cent of world GDP, ought to impose trade and investment rules that are more liberal than those required by the Gatt. Rather than accepting the norm of competitive protectionism APEC would compete on liberalization.

Outlook

Regional trade preferences have become popular devices for managing trade and adjustment. By combining elements of free trade, protectionism, and (implicit) sectoral targeting, these arrangements could provide the means for restructuring global production in line with free trade, or, conversely, could stifle adjustment altogether and result in geographic market foreclosures.

Corporate and public policy makers ought to assess a region's market potential and attractiveness as production base with reference to the evolution of its underlying trading structure and the economic and political effects emanating from it.

Applied to the three major regional trade

arrangements, such an evaluation would present the EU as in need of a New Founding Contract that establishes economically efficient and politically viable sub-arrangements within which associated economies and sectors can be restructured at lower levels of political interdependency.

Apec seems to have learned from the European experience by accepting the need for multiple speeds of adjustment right from the start. However, whether its reliance on less formal consensus mechanisms and guidance will suffice in the long-run remains to be seen.

Washington's doubts may stem from its experience within NAFTA, whose enlargement it seeks to control lest the arrangement follows the fate of the EU.

Summary

Corporate and public policy makers need to understand the impact of regionalization on insiders' competitiveness and outsiders' market chances. Recent theories of international competition conclude that government involvement in global oligopolies may pay off, provided it effectively blocks foreign entry into home or third markets. In the case of competitive specialization significant sectoral overlap and negligible market barriers inside a customs union fuel internal competition: low levels of short-term protection are required. Complementary specialization grows out of a limited degree of sectoral overlap, which is sheltered against viable external competition by means of substantial protection.

Cohesion of the customs union depends on its ability to maintain devotion to the union and on procedural consensus. Without institutional arrangements and with an increased diversity in membership disintegration is likely. The EU is in need of a new Founding Contract which allows economies and sectors to be restructured at lower levels of political interdependency; Apec seems to have realized the need for multiple speeds of adjustment from the start; Washington seems more interested in consolidating control over NAFTA than in enlarging it.

Suggested further reading

Balassa, B. (1961) *The Theory of Economic Integration*, Richard D. Irwin Inc.

Grubel, H.G. and Lloyd, P.J. (1975) *Intra-Industry Trade*, Macmillan, London.

Hine, R.C. (1985) *The Political Economy of European Trade*, Wheatsheaf, Brighton.

El-Agraa, A.M. (1989) *The Theory and Measurement of International Economic Integration*, McMillan & St.Martins.

Thurow, L. C. (1992) *Head to Head: The Coming Battle among Japan, Europe, and America*, Morrow, New York.

Magaziner, I. and Reich, R. (1983) *Minding America's Business*, Vintage Books.

Luttwak, E.N. (1993) *The Endangered American Dream*, New York.

Prestowitz Jr., C. (1988) *Trading Places*, New York.

D'Andrea Tyson, L. (1992) *Who is Bashing Whom? Trade Conflict in High-Technology Industries*, Washington.

Helpman, E. and Krugman, P. (1989) *Trade Policy and Market Structure*, MIT Press, Cambridge, MA.

Krugman, P. and Smith, M.A. (eds.) (1993) *Empirical Studies of Strategic Trade Policy*, University of Chicago Press, Chicago.

Leadership Skills

Contents

What makes a leader? 506
Jack Denfeld Wood, IMD
*The first of two sections examining the nature of
leadership looks at some of the traits we traditionally
associate with great leaders.*

The two sides of leadership 511
Jack Denfeld Wood, IMD
*The second of two sections examining the nature of
leadership suggests that leadership is made up of a
task-oriented 'masculine' side and a relationship-
based 'feminine' side.*

**Business is changing fast and so is the
art of leading it** 516
Derek F. Abell. IMD
*The 'old' models of business leadership are not
sufficient for the new situations in which companies
find themselves – a redefinition of the competencies
that corporate leaders will need.*

Do leaders make a difference? 520
Michael Useem, The Wharton School of the
University of Pennsylvania
*In a huge global corporation can the leadership skills
of a single chief executive really have an impact? This
article argues that they can and suggests some skills
that all managers need to develop.*

Team building: the great outdoors 524
Jack Denfeld Wood, IMD
*Outdoor training has a mixed reputation. But, done
properly, it can be the most effective way to teach
leadership skills and teamwork.*

Contributors

Jack Denfeld Wood is Professor of
Organizational Behavior at IMD,
Lausanne. His research interests are
analytical psychology, leadership and
teams, social structure and change, and
culture and ideology.

Derek F. Abell is Professor of Strategy
and Marketing at IMD. He is currently
also on the faculty of the Swiss Federal
Institutes of Technology in Zurich and
Lausanne where he is directing a new
programme jointly developed with IMD on
leadership competencies.

Michael Useem is Professor of
Management in The Wharton School of
the University of Pennylvania and
Director of its Center for Leadership and
Change Management. His research
interests include corporate organization,
ownership and restructuring, and
leadership.

Introduction

Leadership is a personality trait but one that managers are increasingly required to demonstrate. The module on Leadership Skills begins with a two-part introduction to the nature of leadership and goes on to cover leadership competencies, the effects of corporate leadership, and leadership training and development.

What makes a leader?

■ **In the first of two articles (the second follows on p. 511) examining the nature of leadership, Jack Denfeld Wood looks at some of the traits we traditionally associate with great leaders.**

Leadership can mean many things to many people. It can evoke visions of a cavalry officer leading the Charge of the Light Brigade, or a conductor directing a symphony orchestra; it can evoke the stirring speech of a renowned politician or the rambling ravings of a marginal religious cult leader.

Leadership may be characterized one way by the journalist or the management professor dependent on the chief executive officer giving him access to his company or paying his consulting fee. Or it may be characterized in another way by the behavioral scientist who studies how formal and informal leadership actually operates in ad hoc groups or intact management teams. In any case, leadership is an inevitable and necessary aspect of human life – and it is not well understood.

The management literature on leadership is not very helpful. We are told that leaders have a set of innate traits or that there are authoritarian, laissez-faire and democratic leaders. We are told that leaders diagnose the situation and take the appropriate actions or that they can choose an appropriate 'style' for the circumstances.

We are told that leaders tend to be distant and work-oriented or sociable and interaction-oriented. We are told there is a difference between managers and leaders – that managers essentially address the mundane task of organizational maintenance whereas leaders initiate and promote an inspiring vision of change. We are told that there are transactional leaders who make only incremental changes and transformational leaders who make revolutionary ones.

The popular business press is not much help either. We are treated to the distinguished portraits of corporate visionaries on the covers of the glossy business magazines – 'CEO of the Year' – and we read laudatory articles about their clever deals and astronomical bonuses. Then five years later their companies have suffered a reversal of fortune, are in receivership and the leaders are nowhere to be found.

The management literature and the popular business press generally present leadership in a bright and sunny light; there is no darkness, there are no shadows. But that is not reality. Sometimes, the emperor has no clothes. Mercifully, when asked to describe leadership, managers demonstrate a more convincing and intuitive sense for it than do most of the management academics and business journalists who write about leadership. Below is what they have to say.

What managers think about leadership

I sometimes begin a discussion of leadership by asking the executives in a seminar: 'Without limiting yourself to any historical period, name individuals who you think have demonstrated exceptional leadership.'

I write the proposed names on the blackboard, and the list typically looks something like this: Hitler, Churchill, Stalin, Patton, De Gaulle, Napoleon, Genghis Khan, Alexander the Great, Hannibal, Lenin, Julius Caesar, John F. Kennedy, Eisenhower, Rommel, Mao Tse Tung, Mahatma Gandhi, Margaret Thatcher, Martin Luther King and a few more. Sometimes, someone will add names such as Jesus, Buddha, Mother Theresa or the Pope – but not often.

I then ask the executives to: 'Identify the characteristics which you think these leaders have in common.' They respond that the leaders: are military generals or politicians; are decisive; are credible; have strong personalities; demonstrate courage; have clear vision; have a simple message; are focussed; are good communicators; manifest charisma; mobilize followers; are in the right place at the right time; and are 'winners'. Sometimes, someone will point out that the list includes mostly individuals who: (a) eventually came to a bad end (b) are dead and (c) are male.

The exercise is instructive. The lists reflect the opinions of a cross-section of international managers – their shared conception of leadership drawn from a range of national cultures. There is surprising convergence in their conceptions of leadership; the attributes sketch a fundamental image.

When we think of leadership, we think of particular kinds of individuals with particular kinds of characteristics in particular kinds of situations. Taken together, the managers paint a clear but very narrow portrait of leadership and so, in class, we explore the traits in more depth.

Leaders are virtually all military generals or politicians. In a crisis, someone must take charge, and generals and politicians take command in times of national conflict and crisis. Most of the leaders identified above were called upon to manage crises that were threatening their people. A military or political context virtually guarantees the presence of conflict; those who assume leadership under such circumstances must expect conflict and most may secretly seek it.

While religious leaders such as Jesus or Buddha are seldom included, they do share many of the characteristics of the generals, dictators, presidents and prime ministers mentioned above. They also differ, however, suggesting a function of leadership that is generally over-looked. We shall come back to this point later.

Leaders are decisive. In an emergency, decisions must be made quickly and extra-ordinary measures quickly initiated. These leaders took action. They were not primarily thinkers; they were doers. And they became heroes to their followers because of that.

While they met crises head-on, they often did more than simply respond to crises in a decisive manner. A crisis may be difficult to control in any case, but it may be significantly easier if you have been the cause of it in the first place. Many of the leaders on the list had a hand in creating or otherwise magnifying the crises in which they found themselves.

More than a few leaders create a series of crises to allow themselves the freedom to control things in a more direct and autocratic manner. Most of us can recall supervisors who behaved in this way – and what is more, many of us have done this ourselves.

Leaders are credible. Those on the list were predictable and could be relied upon to do what they said they would do. Their actions may not always have been pretty but their behavior was demonstrably consistent with their announced aims and apparently congruent with their intentions.

Leaders have strong personalities. Strong leaders readily assume command and assert an authority over the situation and over other people. This kind of leadership is fairly indistinguishable from dominance, though leadership is not dominance. Dominance is invasive; it constrains, it immobilizes and it suffocates. Leadership draws others out. It liberates, it mobilises and it inspires. Men and boys have experience with this difference. And although it is virtually never articulated, domineering males frequently get the 'trap door' treatment from other males – they are tolerated for a short time and then subtly undermined and eventually unceremoniously disposed of.

And what of strong leaders? When does strength itself become a weakness? The 'iron lady' epithet earned by Margaret Thatcher suggests that strong leaders are made of iron. What are the characteristics of iron? Iron is a base metal and it is basic for survival. When forged, iron is hard and it is cold. It is able to be melted and shaped into instruments that do something to something or to someone else. It is the primary material for tools and it is the primary material for weapons. Iron is durable if cared for; it deteriorates if left unattended in the rain.

Might there be a fatal flaw to such strength,

like an invisible speck of rust within? When does having an iron disposition mean we have become too cold, too rigid, too brittle or too fixed to make finer differentiations in our environment or in ourselves? Hammers are made of iron, too, but you know the old saw: 'if the only tool you have is a hammer, then everything begins to look like a nail'.

Leaders demonstrate courage. Leaders who lead from the front demonstrate courage. They lead by example. They take personal risks. They are willing to stand out. This prominence makes them a lightening rod. Leaders draw energy from others – both positive and negative. Standing out is exciting. But standing out leaves one vulnerable, as the Japanese saying makes clear – the nail that sticks up gets hammered down. The wise leader is courageous; the foolish one is reckless. But who knows in advance which is which?

Leaders have clear vision. 'Vision' is one of those overworked buzz words that does not precisely capture what is intended. Vision is simply the faculty to see and it does not specify whether what is seen is close at hand or far away or is to be pursued or is to be avoided. The leader with vision is generally thought to see far into the future with remarkable clarity.

What is meant is that the leader provides a clear goal and a direction to which others can orient. The most powerful of the leaders listed above were those who articulated an ideology – a compelling utopian prescription of ends and means. In submitting to an ideology, both leaders and followers make themselves instruments in the service of something grander, often with disastrous consequences.

Leaders have a simple message. The 'something grander' concerns a fundamental change of the status quo, and while the implications can be distressing, the message itself is always simple. The leaders listed above did not convey complex concepts with complicated reasoning; the messages were simple and straightforward – and captivating. Their messages usually provided images, rarely with more than two or three facets.

Most of the messages operated simultaneously on multiple levels of meaning – on a conscious,

plausible and rational level and on an unconscious, mythic and irrational one. From Hitler's 'Thousand Year Reich' to Kennedy's 'New Frontier' their visions promoted a simple and bright message of change but drew on the darker power of unconscious symbolism. This is why people are willing to follow their leaders to the edge. And sometimes over the edge.

Leaders are focussed. The leaders above were committed to their vision and spent tremendous energy focussing on achieving their goal. The focus on a simple message helps draw energy from other areas of life and serves to attract, fuse and channel other concerns in the service of the one ultimate goal. Such leaders are unwavering in their singular focus and their dedication usually has a driven, obsessive and compulsive quality to it.

Leaders are good communicators. Good communication, of course, is a function of communicator, message and receiver. The leaders above are invariably characterized as good communicators, i.e. they were able to communicate their vision with a simple message in a focussed way and to attract a sizeable following. Their ultimate effectiveness as communicators was dependent on the readiness of the audience to hear, nevertheless, and many of the followers were only too ready to suspend their individual responsibility and merge into a collective fantasy. People at the end of their rope and seeking relief will grasp at any straw messiah, though it helps if the messiah is persuasive in his own right.

Leaders manifest charisma. A messiah may appear charismatic, but he may not possess charisma so much as be possessed by it. Charisma is a quality more easily observed on a stage or in a stadium than rationally explained in a newspaper or in a sitting room. There is a magical quality to charismatic leaders that may be due less to a personal trait than to the attribution of others – an aura whose source is perhaps more in the unconscious of the followers than in the person of the leader. Charisma is said to be a divine gift, a gift of grace, and thus charismatic leadership, and leadership in general for that matter, is in its deepest layers anything but a rational endeavour.

Leaders mobilize followers – towards the light, darkly. Charismatic leaders inspire – breathe life into – the deeper psychological layers of their followers. Truly charismatic leaders manifest an extraordinary power to mobilize others by touching an unconscious spiritual domain within them – a domain inhabited by larger-than-life images of gods and demons and situations that appear to have an archaic life of their own.

Recall Ayatollah Khomeini's description of America as 'The Great Satan' and Ronald Reagan's description of the Soviet Union as 'The Evil Empire'. These images operate in the darkness, beneath reason. According to a top US magazine, leaders do not come any better than Genghis Khan (1167–1227), who was voted Man of the Millenium. This should give one pause. In his *A History of Military Warfare* the distinguished British military historian, John Keegan, quotes Genghis Khan as saying that man's 'greatest good fortune is to chase and defeat his enemy, seize his total possessions, leave his married women weeping and wailing, ride his gelding and use the bodies of his women as a nightshirt and support.' Think about it. Man of the Millenium. Is this serious? We are like children playing with fire in an arms warehouse. Our comprehension of behavior is woefully superficial. To follow a charismatic leader in this way, people must be willing to give up a piece of themselves, to project their abilities and qualities, their profound capacity for good and evil on to the leader and to submit to a fate outside the narrow control of their own will.

One invests one's burden of petty responsibilities on to another and one gains freedom from those burdens and the promise of eternity. The extent to which followers become instruments of the collective is the extent to which they diminish themselves.

This connection between leader and follower is not simply the unconscious identification of the follower with the leader, his program or the larger collective, however. The follower is more akin to a conduit through which the collective unconscious archetypal images find expression in the form of a particular leader and group. The images become personified; it works from the inside out.

This is why both John Kennedy and Adolph Hitler are felt by people to have been remarkable leaders. They operated on the same psychological levels and tapped the same unconscious roots. Whether their respective exercise of leadership had a relatively benign or malign outcome is less the point than that the process of their leadership is the same in both cases.

For the follower, identification with the charismatic leader enlarges the self, filling the internal emptiness with eternal promise. The American 'political left' is still mooning around about the loss of 'Camelot' 32 years after Kennedy's assassination, but the loss was of their own innocence and their own mythical fantasies. Camelot and religious crusades are powerful, deeply compelling and lasting images, but they have a dark side. Once small and insignificant, I and the leader and the other chosen people are now larger than life. This is inflation and grandiosity – on a greater or lesser scale – and something eventually has to give.

Leaders are in the right place at the right time. The leaders on the list 'fit' the times. Perhaps they were simply 'lucky' to have found themselves in a timely confluence of events in a particular epoch; had Hitler been born at another time and in another place, he might well have ended up as a graphic artist, a crank or in an asylum. In an odd sense, the circumstances may determine the leader more than the leader determines the circumstances.

Leaders are winners. All of the leaders on the list can be considered 'winners' in some way. All of them, for example, have become immortal – or more precisely, their names and images have become immortal. Their success was not unconditional, however. Most did well for a time – and then came to a bad end down the road.

Leaders often come to a bad end. Many of the leaders listed were defeated militarily, were defeated electorally, were exiled or were killed.

The reasons for this fate are intimately bound up with the behavior that makes them such remarkable leaders in the first place. The same factors that serve them well at the beginning also do them in at the end. And despite wishful thinking to the contrary, these factors are not under rational control. There is a somewhat provocative school of thought that draws on psychoanalytic theory and which suggests that a group (or organization or country) under attack (or otherwise under stress) will select the individual who is the 'least well' (i.e. most anxious, least balanced, least stable, 'sickest' or otherwise most paranoid) as their leader.

This seems an extraordinary proposition, but it is not so fanciful a claim as it may at first appear. We can see this pattern nearly every day, at an individual personal level as well as at a national political level. At a personal level, one can see the pattern when a small group convenes for the first time, such as a small study group at a retreat or conference. It is usually one of the most anxious individuals who begins to organize and structure the proceedings by suggesting that everyone introduce themselves or that everyone share their expectations. They are simply assuming the early leadership of the group.

At a national level, one can see the pattern within the political arena. The rise and prominence of nationalist leaders such as Vladimir Zhirinovsky in Russia or Louis Farrakhan of the black Nation of Islam in the US is merely a more extreme manifestation of an otherwise 'normal' pattern of behavior.

The very anxiousness and instability of many leaders is a part of what is driving them to organize and structure their environment, assemble followers and march towards their goal. They are searching for relief from their interior specters, but since the specters are, at least in large part, internal, they can seldom be quieted by external changes.

If a crisis does not exist, or is insignificant, then one can easily be created or magnified to permit an heroic effort and the mobilization of one's followers in the service of an ideal. It is quite clear that many groups, organizations, and countries find an external threat useful in 'rationalizing' their interior fears and in mobilizing themselves. Paranoia is a poor basis for fashioning the social contract, however, and reality has a way of wearing down even the most durable collective delusions.

Leaders are dead. Neither the Third Reich nor the Iron Curtain could stand forever, or even for very long. And neither could the leaders

themselves. They are all dead. Mortality is good for one's leadership image; it enhances it. It is considerably easier to construct a flawless image of a leader long dead than it is to build the public image of a living person. For the deceased, the image or persona is all that is left, and we can easily reshape it and color it and inflate it to be larger than life.

For the living, on the other hand, there is a real person behind the mask, and this is inconvenient for nearly everyone concerned. Media consultants have made an industry out of image manipulation on behalf of their clients, but the clients have the disconcerting habit of upsetting this image by being themselves. As an actor, politician, religious leader, physician or chief executive officer, you may get the slavish deference of strangers on stage, at the podium, in the pulpit, at the hospital or in the subsidiaries – but back home your family and friends know who you really are and what you are really like. This may be one reason why so many leaders prefer to stay on the road.

Leaders are virtually all males. The list is almost exclusively male whether there are female executives in the class suggesting names or not. When asked why this is so, participants offer the explanation that we have been socialized to look at leadership as a male preserve and we tend to overlook women who are just as strong as male leaders because it upsets our stereotypes.

In other words, the argument goes, we are responding as we have been conditioned – to ignore strong women. But I think the explanation goes a bit deeper than that. When prodded for names of women who have been outstanding leaders, participants offer names such as Margaret Thatcher, Golda Meir, Joan of Arc, Cleopatra, Hillary Clinton, Catherine the Great, Eva Peron and so on.

These women are selected because they have the same leadership attributes as the males on the list, i.e. they exercise leadership in the same way that males supposedly do. 'Golda is the best man in my cabinet,' an Israeli prime minister allegedly quipped.

They also tend to personify the same narrow conception of leadership evinced by the male military generals and male political leaders. The problem is not that other women do not exercise leadership, it is that we do not consider their leadership behavior as 'leadership' because we tend to have a one-dimensional view of leadership.

It is not because women have not been taught to be leaders, it is because they have learned that truly effective leadership requires an additional set of skills and these skills lie along a dimension other than the one defining the traditional view of leadership. Heroic 'masculine' leadership does not exhaust the functions of leadership. The reason that Christ and Buddha and Mother Theresa and the Pope rarely make the 'short list' of leaders is the same reason that women in general rarely make the short list – they also attend to another facet of leadership. Stalin disdainfully asked 'how many divisions does the Pope have?' But the Soviet Union is dead and the Catholic Church is alive – and this is not accidental. Leadership includes the exercise of power in a different way from that associated with prominent heroic leadership.

In the second part of this article we will examine some of those different ways of exercising leadership.

Summary

Management literature and the popular business press tend to present leadership in a bright light; there is no darkness. But that is not the reality. Based on a cross-section of international managerial opinion in business school seminars, there is a surprising convergence in conceptions of leadership. The consensus tends to be clear but it is also narrow. The leaders cited are virtually all military generals, they are primarily doers rather than thinkers, they behave in a consistent fashion, and they have strong personalities which veer on the dominating. They lead by example and take personal risks, they provide a clear goal and direction for others, they have a simple, captivating and well communicated message, they are unwavering (often obsessive) in their focus, they are charismatic, they are generally shaped by their circumstances rather than the other way round, they are 'winners' who came to a bad end. Those women singled out tend to have the same attributes as males in the list which highlights our one dimensional view of leadership. Heroic 'masculine' leadership is only part of the story.

The two sides of leadership

■ **We think of leadership as getting the job done. But, argues** Jack Denfeld Wood, **in the second of two articles, leadership is made up of a task-oriented 'masculine' side and a relationship-based 'feminine' side.**

When considering leadership, many laymen and management academics take the broad historical view, much as we did in the first part of this article on p. 506. We employ the historical 'great man' approach: we read biographies of remarkable leaders, we identify key personality traits and we try to copy them.

If we need leaders for our organizations, we call in consultants to test our managers or we send applicants to assessment centers and we select those with the identified leadership traits. It costs a fortune – and none of it works very well. This is the traditional way to understand leadership, but it is not the only way.

Sociologists, such as Germany's Max Weber, had written about leadership as early as the

1920s. Weber's writing, which identified bureaucratic, patrimonial and charismatic leaders, was to influence later sociological thinking on leadership but rigorous scientific research had to wait until the Second World War made leadership a critical topic of investigation.

Leadership research got under way during the 1940s, in large part sponsored by the US military attempting to select officers. It was then that the young behavioral sciences first turned their attention to the question of leadership. The significant difference between the 'great man' and 'theoretical sociological' approaches – and the emerging 'behavioral' approach – was that in the latter case scientists began empirically to study what leaders actually did.

The two factor theory
In the 1950s the investigations blossomed from those just with military implications to include many different kinds of leaders in many different kinds of groups.

Through hundreds of studies ranging from boy scout camps and university experiments to factory floors and corporate boardrooms, groups were examined to identify the fundamental aspects of leadership.

Although each researcher tended to give the factors different names, two aspects of leadership consistently emerged – first, leaders focussed on accomplishing the immediate task of the group; and second, leaders focussed on maintaining the relationships among group members.

These two aspects – task and relationships – were found to be fundamental dimensions of leadership by scores of researchers. Thus the two factors have been labeled: autocratic and democratic leadership styles; production-oriented and employee-oriented behavior; directive and participative leader behavior; reflections of *Theory X* (negative and directive) and *Theory Y* (positive and facilitative) assumptions about the nature of human beings and appropriate leader behavior task behavior and socio-emotional support behavior, initiating structure and initiating consideration, and so on.

In short, for any group, the job needs to get done and the people involved need to be sustained in the process – and effective leadership attends to both aspects. Sounds simple. Is it true?

Are these two dimensions universal?
If these two behaviors – concern with task and concern with relationships – are fundamental leadership factors, then they should be evident in various groups in various cultures at various levels of complexity – from the small group to the larger social aggregates, from mixed-sex groups to same-sex groups.

Although there has been little rigorous cross-cultural research specifically addressing the 'universality' proposition, there is plausible support for it. Let's take the family as a basic example.

The family is the prototypical group. It is the first group into which we are born and it is the last group that bids us farewell. In virtually every family on earth, regardless of culture, the father and mother assume different roles. They exercise different aspects of leadership.

In most families, the male focus is on the narrower task behavior and the female focus is on the broader relationship behavior. Male leadership of a group tends to manifest more of an instrumental and exterior orientation; female leadership a more inter-personal and interior one. Both are equally necessary for success, but only the former is typically considered to be real leadership.

If our typical family is going on vacation, whether the family be North American, South American, European, African or Asian, it is usually the father who takes care of the mechanics of getting there and the mother who makes sure the family is intact and on speaking terms when they do arrive.

Father usually takes care of getting fuel for the car, changing the oil, having the snow tyres put on, picking the route and driving most of the way. Mother usually takes care of packing the lunch, bringing the bathing suits, packing the car toys, ensuring that baby's Number 25 Sunblock is remembered and refereeing the fights en route.

Part of the reason that managers – both male and female – select military men and politicians when asked to identify leaders is that leadership is considered to be synonymous with 'getting the job done' by both sexes – with accomplishing some objective task.

The way men typically approach their work is to make themselves instruments for the achievement of some impersonal task. Male leadership then focuses on accomplishing that impersonal task. Relationships are handled in an instrumental way in the service of the task. Any behavior that directly contributes to that task is considered to be leadership, the other things are considered to be merely support.

In an all-male or in an all-female group, both the task and the relationship aspects must still be addressed, of course. Both may be done by one individual or, as is more often the case, the two leadership roles are split among two or more individuals, as in a family.

In an all-male group, such as a military unit, both the task and the relationship aspects are addressed by different subsets of men. But if one adds a few women to the group, the women quickly assume, or are given, the relationship focus, i.e. it is quickly abandoned by the men or it is taken away from them by the women.

The same typically happens in an all-female group when one adds a few males. The men assume, or are given, the task focus as the women abandon it or it is taken from them by the men.

Male and female in larger groups

In larger social aggregates – in organizations and countries, for example – the same male and female split often holds, with the males most heavily represented in those functions concerned with 'task' and the females most heavily represented in those functions concerned with 'relationships'.

Within the private sector – in a large manufacturing enterprise, for example – the functions typically reflect this split by sex. The highest proportion of men are found in the 'line', especially in technical and engineering companies, whereas the highest percentage of women are found in the staff and support functions (administration, personnel and human resources, public relations).

Within the public sector, the story is somewhat different. A number of years ago I flew to Sweden, and was intrigued to see in the photo in the SAS in-flight magazine that the board of directors was entirely male. I asked a Swedish colleague when I landed why this was because I had been under the impression that women in Sweden were in very high leadership positions.

'Oh yes,' was his answer, 'but you see, they are most highly represented at the upper levels in the public sector. The large private business companies are still pretty much run by men.'

He was saying that the men were responsible for generating the wealth and the women were responsible for distributing it. The private sector creates the wealth and the public sector distributes it and makes sure that the linkages are healthy and relative stability is maintained among people – the infrastructure of roads, rail, phones, water, electric power, sewage, hospitals, schools and so on. The public sector is the 'relationship' sector and it is no accident that women are more highly represented there at a managerial level than in, say, the construction or aircraft manufacturing industries in the private sector.

Where the pattern is reversed – where women are highly represented in the private sector and men in the public sector – look carefully at the functions of the specific organizations within the larger social system and they will likely reflect the male-female differences. Women are relatively highly represented in the private sector in publishing houses, advertising and public relations agencies; men are relatively highly represented in the public sector in the military organizations.

In a family, an organization or a country, wealth must be created and wealth must be distributed for survival. In a family, these two aspects are reflected in the two functions of leadership typically adopted by fathers and mothers – concern with task and concern with relationships; in a manufacturing company, these two aspects are reflected in the production and administrative functions; in a society, these two aspects are reflected in the private and public sectors.

The one tendency may well represent a 'masculine leadership principle', can be viewed as 'progressive' and is occupied with destruction and 'change' of the material environment. The other tendency may well represent a 'feminine leadership principle', can be viewed as 'conservative' and is occupied with the preservation and stability of the social environment. The underlying conflict of interests between these two principles can be seen at various levels of social abstraction.

For society, the tension is between industry and government (the private and public sectors – in the US, the two principles even have their own capitals, New York and Washington, respectively). For the organization, the tension is between line functions and administrative staff functions ('overhead', as many line managers like to joke). For the family, the tension is between the male and female domains. And in the small group, the tension is between the relative priority given to the typically masculine orientation toward 'getting the job done' and the typically feminine orientation toward maintaining harmonious relationships.

Male, female and cultures

Different cultures have somewhat different priorities, and their leadership reflects their priorities. Several decades ago, I had the opportunity to interview a number of Japanese MBA students studying in the US. I asked them why their companies were paying the high tuition ($25,000 each year for two years) as well as their salaries, housing, family allowances and so on.

Were the companies hoping that the Japanese students learned Western management techniques, accounting and finance practices, and so on? I asked. 'Oh no,' they assured me, 'we are here to improve our English and to learn how Americans think.' 'What do you see as the biggest difference between the way Americans and Japanese do think?' I asked. One of the Japanese students strode to the blackboard and wrote the character Wa – harmony.

'This is the biggest difference we see,' they explained. 'You Americans and other Westerners are concerned with showing off, with standing out, with your individual prominence in a group. We Japanese learn early that harmony in a group is the most important thing. You can see it in our families, in our groups and in our organizations.'

This reflects patterns of socialization, of course, but it likely reflects innate biological differences and predispositions as well. Harmony is a central part of the relationship, or 'feminine', aspect of leadership, and individual decisiveness is a central part of the task, or 'masculine', aspect of leadership.

I wouldn't want to push this line of argument too far, but there is growing evidence that at a physiological level, males and females differ in ways that have broad behavioral implications. Thus females seem to be attuned to more diffuse internal sensory and external social stimuli – better hearing, better night and peripheral vision, more sensitive to changes in sound volume, touch, pain, others' distress, and others' body language – while males seem more attuned to and more focussed on external objective stimuli – higher metabolic rate, better daylight and perspective vision, faster reaction time to moving objects, better spatial, directional and mechanical ability, more assertive, aggressive and competitive.

The psychological correlates, presumably of the physiological differences, suggest that men and women may reason and make decisions in somewhat different ways. Men seem to be concerned more with abstract 'truth' and appear to process information and make decisions using objective reasoning, i.e. in a more logical, impersonal and detached way. Women, on the other hand, seem to be more concerned with interpersonal 'fairness' and appear to process information and make decisions using subjective reasoning, i.e. in a more empathic, personal and feeling way.

These two sets of attributes are complementary and, taken together, may have helped groups to survive over thousands of years. Perhaps they reflect two fundamental aspects of leadership. The masculine principle, in Western society at any rate, almost always garners more prestige than the feminine principle. This perhaps helps explain the selection of military and political leaders by both male and female managers. This reflects a bias toward one particular aspect of leadership, at the expense of the other.

At a social level, if either aspect becomes too important, then the system is thrown out of balance, will become pathological and will eventually collapse if corrective measures are not taken. Much of the ideological debate at a national political level may trace its roots to the more fundamental debate about the relative priority of the masculine principle (individual, competitive and capitalist?) and the feminine principle (community, harmonious and socialist?).

What does it mean for leaders?

Implications for leading in a group can, perhaps, be drawn from the patterns sketched above. At a personal level, it is helpful to be aware of one's own bias, whether this bias is primarily a function of genetic endowment or socialization – to develop the 'other' aspect in oneself and to revalue and make room for the 'other' aspect in the groups in which one exercises leadership.

For men, this typically means to round out their leadership skills by recognising and developing their relationship skills. For women, the opposite may be true, to round out their leadership skills by recognizing and developing their assertive and decisive task orientation.

Women, however, may face a more difficult challenge because there is tremendous social pressure on them to abandon the relationship principle altogether and become more like men. In this light, radical feminism is not so much an exaltation of the feminine domain and a denial of the masculine as it is nearly a complete absorption into the masculine domain – with the consequent disparagement of the traditional feminine relationship concerns, including family and children.

For both men and women, what is needed is to develop a deeper appreciation of the full range of skills at work in effective leadership.

Summary

Max Weber wrote about leadership in the 1920s – but it only became a serious topic for research in the 1940s and 1950s. Two aspects were consistently highlighted – the way leaders focus on accomplishing the immediate task of the group, and the way they maintain relationships among group members. In a family – and in other mixed-sex groups – the male focus tends to be on the former, the female on the latter.

Men are more typically found in 'line' jobs, especially in technical and engineering companies, women in staff and support functions. In the public sector – the relationship sector – it is the reverse. Women are more highly represented in public sector managerial positions than they are in, say, private sector aircraft or construction industries.

Harmony is a central part of the 'feminine' aspect of leadership, decisiveness an important feature of the 'masculine' side. There is growing evidence that at a physiological level males and females differ in ways that have broad behavioral implications, for example, men appear to be more concerned with abstract 'truth', women with interpersonal fairness. In Western society the masculine principle garners more prestige and helps explain why most managers, male or female, think of political and military figures when asked to identify leaders.

Business is changing fast and so is the art of leading it

■ **The 'old' models of business leadership are not sufficient for the new situations in which companies find themselves. Derek Abell offers a redefinition of the competencies that corporate leaders will need.**

Leadership has never been easy but the far-reaching changes taking place today in the business environment and within organizations are making it even harder. They are redefining all aspects of leadership:

- *Its substance* – what leaders have to do.
- *Its process* – how they accomplish it.
- *Its purpose* – the whys.
- What leaders will have to do.

Three phenomena are affecting the substance of what leaders do: new needs to manage change in parallel with running today's business; the growing influence of technology; and rising concern for sound management of processes and competencies.

Managing with dual strategies. The post-war strategic challenge for most leaders was to establish a 'success formula' for the business and implement it through well-harmonized policies for product development, manufacturing, marketing and finance.

The new challenge, by contrast, is a dual one. A leader has to continue *running* the business as effectively and efficiently as possible but at the same time has to *change* the business. This implies developing a vision and having a shrewd understanding of the internal and external forces (often technology forces) that are likely to create serious threats or offer new opportunities.

Change also implies mobilizing the entire organization to bring about change and building the new competencies and resources required for

the future. IBM's new leader Lou Gerstner must, for example, deliver improved customer benefits today while attempting a major transformation of the whole organization.

Capitalizing on technology. Technology's impact used to be limited mainly to product improvement and manufacturing-process improve-ment. It was concentrated in the high technology sectors of the economy. While leaders could not ignore technology, it seemed possible for them to manage it at arm's length through others with more technical competence. As a result, the route to the top in many companies was not through technology but via a financial, marketing or even a legal background.

Today, these traditional leadership career paths are in question. Technology is providing new ways to integrate supply, manufacturing and distribution, and is producing large gains in customer value at much lower cost (the basis of Benetton's success).

Technology is redrawing the boundaries between historically separate industries: for example, between computing, telecommunications and entertainment or between banking and other financial services, and (coming, I believe) between food and pharmaceuticals. Technology is redefining the management task itself, and in many companies is becoming the *critical agenda item for general management*.

Technology's role is not limited to high technology. It is becoming a decisive factor in many other sectors such as distribution, services, public administration and government. In all these fields, the leadership challenge is to build and use technology effectively and responsibly. Leaders therefore need to have a much firmer grasp of technology – and a greater ability to manage it – than in the past.

Refocussing on processes and competencies. The 'old' leadership role was to ensure that each function of the company performed in a way that was consistent with overall strategy. Both 'part-to-part' and 'part-to-whole' integration were critical.

The 'new' leader must continue to do this but with two distinctly new twists.

The first is effectively to manage the processes by which the various functions inter-relate. The large reductions in product development time claimed by such organizations as Sony, Philips, Hewlett-Packard and Renault (for the Twingo mini-car) all stem from improved inter-functional 'process re-engineering'. Similar gains are being made in order-to-delivery cycles. Process improvements will spread from operations to such activities as planning, strategy making and decision-making itself. Technology is frequently providing the means to this end.

The second new twist concerns competencies. Running each function effectively today is only part of the story; developing the competencies to run the business tomorrow is becoming the key competitive requirement. For example, at Sulzer, a Swiss-based machinery manufacturer, the company's leadership has identified four areas of competence as critical to the company's future: technology, marketing, finance and human resources. It is essential for the company's top management to take an active role in these areas whereas the 'old' view of Sulzer was that managing manufacturing was the critical functional task.

How leaders will have to work

Three main forces are affecting the process of leadership: the development of newer, flatter matrix forms of organization; the growing number of alliances and informal networks; and people's changing expectations and values.

Adapting to flatter matrix forms. Corporate diversity and complexity, together with the need to make quicker, more cost-effective decisions nearer to the customer, have largely disqualified hierarchical, command-type leadership. Increasingly, top management's job is to 'set the stage' for leadership to be exercized at lower levels in the organization.

But new dilemmas are emerging at those lower levels. There is a growing need to fragment the 'program' side of the organization to deal with increasing segmentation. Yet there is also a need to achieve economies of scale and scope in managing the company's key resources. The result is a wide variety of difficult-to-manage 'matrix' solutions, often featuring mid-level leadership roles where responsibility greatly exceeds direct authority.

These solutions are never as clear as top-down hierarchical leadership but they are more effective in today's complex, highly segmented markets. What is needed is a different type of consensus-building leadership involving multiple interests and parties.

Leading across organization boundaries. Leadership also needs to operate in the many new extended network and alliance structures. These have emerged in order to adopt new competitive approaches such as 'solutions selling' and because the technology requirements of many products and services exceed the competencies of any one organization.

The leadership challenge here is to find a common purpose, to derive common strategies and to engage in common action. This often means recognizing segments of customer opportunity and mobilizing the different players in a loose network of organizational alliances to seize that opportunity. The Canon-Olivetti link-up in copying machines is an example. Not only do Japanese and Italian cultures have to be reconciled but, more importantly perhaps, so do different *organizational* cultures and approaches.

Recognizing changing expectations and values. Reto Domeniconi, Nestle's Chief Financial Officer, is quoted as saying: 'To get excellence, the greatest source of untapped resources is from middle management down. But people play old games; knowledge is power and initiatives get blocked.' It is certainly true that when the whole organization can be mobilized to do a better job today and change for tomorrow, the results can be dramatic. The leadership question being asked is – how to accomplish this?

Experience teaches us several lessons. First, change is required from the top down. Decision-making and implementation authority has to be genuinely delegated; second, there has to be comprehension, commitment and the ability lower down to take on the new roles. One without the other spells catastrophe. Experience also shows that these new roles have to be learned – they cannot be acquired overnight.

As well as striking this balance, it is important to provide a frame of reference for managers at lower levels, giving them both strategic guidelines and a clear statement of the company's culture and values. Previously, companies generally relied on the 'integrity' of their top management. Now, with leadership much more widely distributed and with many people at lower levels confronting complex ethical questions, such a framework is becoming essential.

There is growing evidence that discussing precedent-setting examples may be more important than making policy statements. And that the leader's job is to foster this process rather than just proclaiming rules.

The new whys of leadership

During the post-war period of growth and development, the purpose of leadership generally centered on getting an operation up and running, achieving growth in output and sales, and producing reasonable financial returns.

Over the last decade or so, organizational purpose has given more weight to providing 'customer satisfaction'. In parallel, yesterday's concern for growth in volume has succumbed to pressure for bottom-line performance, even when this means shrinkage rather than growth. The expressions 'customer orientation', 'customer-focussed', 'market-driven' are all manifestations of the new 'whys'.

Two new 'why' are already on the horizon: the creation of meaningful employment and broader societal perspectives.

Creating meaningful employment. When Nissan decided to downsize one of its subsidiary operations in Spain, its sales also declined. Apparently, customers like to buy from successful companies as measured by growth not just by the bottom line.

This is understandable if one recognizes that customers buy into a relationship and do not just make an individual product transaction. Other companies are finding it harder to recruit first-class new candidates, who are attracted by career opportunities as much as by profitable operations.

There is a growing realization among senior management that employees, together with customers and equity holders, are important stakeholders, if not stockholders, in the organization of the future. They recognize that cost cutting has to be replaced by more new value-creation in the marketplace – the only sure way to create meaningful employment not only in quantitative but also in qualitative terms.

Taking a societal perspective. Society at large enters the picture at many important points.

First, there are growing concerns for sustainable development. The pendulum has swung from the belief that the environment is mainly a public policy matter to the view that the green movement offers profitable opportunities and that companies themselves will be the solution to our environmental problems. Both positions are somewhat extreme and the practical challenge is to find the mix of public policy and enterprise purpose that will produce the right results.

Second, there is a broader issue: quality of life versus quantity of consumption. So far, few leaders have felt it necessary to take a position on this issue, let alone include it in decisions about the future direction of their company.

Third, there is the even more fundamental issue of the underlying 'belief system' on which future business activity will have to be built, and the 'capitalism versus capitalism' debate is growing.

Can the Anglo-Saxon form adequately respond to the broader societal issues? Can the Rhinish (German) model do any better; and what about emerging Asian approaches? What role does economic competition play or are there areas where more co-operative behavior would be beneficial? Is competition based on narrow economic criteria the best way to achieve broader social and societal goals or do the performance criteria themselves have to be enlarged?

If so, what kind of measurement and incentive

systems would be needed to implement these new directions? The single biggest change in future leadership responsibilities is likely to revolve around these new 'why' questions.

What do these changes mean for managers?

For those in charge today:

● Make a real commitment to adapt to the new leadership task; not to resist it. Your company, and your own survival, may be at stake.

● Compensate for any gaps in your competence by having people in your team who have the skills and perspectives that you lack, for example technology-management abilities.

● Avoid 'reflex' management behavior; in the world that is unfolding past experience may not be the best teacher.

● Instead, take advantage of others who have relevant new experience from other sectors and other cultures.

● Use an experimental approach; learn as you go along.

● Make careful investments in preparing your successors.

For those preparing tomorrow's leaders:

● Recognize that the most difficult task will probably be to inculcate the new 'whys' and the new 'hows', at least as much as the new 'whats'.

● Understand that a new breed of leader will probably be needed in the 21st century. The case has never been stronger for comprehensive leadership built on sound technical foundations.

● Experiment with leadership assignments that quickly provide the new type of broader experience. Combine these with coaching by people who personally provide examples of new leadership approaches.

● Invest in the kind of management education and development experience for the next generation which reflects the new agenda.

Summary

Business leaders today need a dual strategy – they have to run their business as efficiently as possible, yet at the same time they have to change it. They need to have a much firmer grasp on technology, which is providing new ways to integrate supply, manufacturing and distribution and which is redrawing the boundaries between historically separate industries.

Three main forces are affecting the process of leadership: the development of newer, flatter matrix forms of organization; the growing number of alliances and informal networks; and people's changing expectations and values.

Leadership of late has become more focussed on customer satisfaction and the bottom line, but the pressure is increasingly to create more meaningful employment and to confront broader social and societal issues, such as the environment, quality of life and belief systems for a capitalist economy. The case has never been stronger for comprehensive leadership built on sound technical foundations.

Do leaders make a difference?

■ **In a huge global corporation can the leadership skills of a single chief executive really have an impact?** Michael Useem **argues that they can, and suggests some skills that all managers need to develop.**

We are the masters of our own fate but are we also the masters of our company's fate? Organizations, after all, are flywheels of stability. With the work of hundreds or even thousands of employees fine-tuned and orchestrated for common purpose, can I really expect to make a difference as a corporate leader?

One answer is to consider the fax that arrives as a pleasant shock. A head-hunter is asking if you would accept appointment as either athletic director of a professional football team or music director of the Opera metropolitan. While you may have never touched a football or appeared on the opera stage, the head-hunter's fax reassures you that both organizations want your management skills.

Inspired by a latent mid-life crisis, you impulsively say 'why not?' Since both organizations have already contracted their high-priced talent for next season, both have excellent back offices and both have pre-eminent reputations to ensure a steady box office, you feel confident about the 1997 season. In other words, your leadership in the short run cannot make much of a difference one way or the other. But you are sure it will in the longer run and you are wondering what it will take and how much of a difference you can really make.

How much leadership matters

One way to answer the question of the difference you make is to study what happens to the stock price of a company when a high-profile executive is either hired or fired. The rise and abrupt fall of a Chief Financial Officer at Eastman Kodak is illustrative of both.

Christopher J. Steffen had been hired by Kodak in January 1993 to help turn around a company whose earnings and stock price had been languishing. He was characterized as the 'white-knight Chief Financial Officer who could save stodgy Eastman Kodak' and investors applauded his publicized hiring.

The company's stock price soared in the days that followed his hiring, adding more than $3bn to the company's value. In an immediate dispute with the chief executive, however, the '$3bn man' resigned 90 days later. Investors dumped Kodak shares with vigor, driving the company's value down the next day by $1.7bn. It would seem that a single person can add – or subtract – billions to or from a company's value.

But this, you find, is an unsatisfactory way to gauge a leader's impact on an organization since it is so short-run and has more to do with expectations than actual performance.

So let us turn to a kind of thought experiment. Several studies have asked what happens to company performance over the several years after a chief executive has stepped down and a new CEO has taken office. Performance here is taken not to be investor forecasts but actual financial results – earnings per share, returns on assets. The extent to which a chief executive makes a difference should be evident in the upward or downward movement of the financial measures following the turnover at the top.

To make the most conservative test, we limit the analysis to large companies where a single individual can be expected to make least difference. We also take a confounding factor into account that could falsely inflate or deflate this CEO effect: if the economy is rising when the succession occurs, the successor could be falsely credited for an upturn in company earnings.

Conversely, if the economy is falling, the new chief executive could be unfairly blamed.

Using powerful statistical methods, the studies confirm two things. They show, first, that our inertial guidance systems are very strong. Some 90 per cent of the variability in company earnings is driven by the economy and the organization, regardless of who is in high office.

But the studies also confirm, second, that the person at the helm does make a significant difference. A successful new CEO can raise company performance by some ten per cent, an unsuccessful new CEO can drop it by ten per cent. Against a backdrop of an enterprise with thousands of employees, years of tradition and narrow profit margins, the fact that a new chief executive can move those margins up or down by ten points says that executive leadership does make a substantial difference.

When leadership matters most

When is your leadership most likely to make a difference? We remember wartime prime ministers and presidents better than peacetime leaders and the same is true for company executives. Organizational leadership matters most during a period of stress and uncertainty.

This conclusion emerges from study of 48 firms among the Fortune 500 largest US manufacturers. Researcher Robert House asked two direct subordinates of each of the companies' chief executives to assess the extent to which the CEO is:

- visionary
- showed strong confidence in self and others
- communicated high performance expectations and standards
- personally exemplified the firm's vision, values, and standards
- demonstrated personal sacrifice, determination, persistence, and courage

He also assessed the extent to which the companies face environments that are dynamic, risky and uncertain. Taking into account a company's size, sector and other factors, House found that these CEO leadership qualities identified a significant difference in a company's net profit margins when the company is facing a highly uncertain environment. When the firm is not so challenged, however, such leadership qualities make far less of a difference.

Several practical implications follow. Your own leadership matters most when it is least clear what course you should follow. The decisions and actions of those above, beside and below you also matter most when the organization is facing tough competition or needs strategic redirection.

Unfortunately these are the very moments when developing leadership is least practical. Periods of normality – when strategies are working and earnings are strong – are therefore the times when leadership is best developed even though the need is least evident. In short, build your organization's leadership now for later challenges before it is too late.

What qualities make a difference?

In developing your own leadership and those who work with you, what qualities should you cultivate? Every organization requires its own unique blend of leadership for the challenges it faces, and no single 'best practice' can be found. Leadership qualities are contingent on circumstance and you will have to fashion your own path.

Still, overlaying the unique are a set of more transcendent qualities that serve leadership well in many company settings. To identify these, it is useful to think of three sources of power that come with appointment to a new position, whether athletic director of a football team, music director of an opera company or managing director of a business corporations:

Powers of the office – acquired on taking the job

- Power to reward: hire, praise, promote and raise
- Power to punish: criticize, reassign, demote and fire
- Power of authority: approve, sign-off, disapprove

Powers of the person – brought to or developed on the job

- Power of expertise: knowledge, information, experience
- Power of character: integrity, charisma, expectations

Powers of the transformed organization – created on the job

- Power of empowerment: delegate, authorize, make accountable
- Power of reorganization: redesign, restructure, re-engineer

The powers of office constitute the organization's authority vested in you and their effective execution is the domain of good management. Building beyond the powers received on taking office is the terrain of good leadership. Leadership can be viewed as the exercise of power – the power to get things done – above and beyond the formal powers of your position.

Effective application of one's personal powers is akin to what we often think of as *individual leadership*. The rhetorical skills of Martin Luther King or John F. Kennedy come to mind. Effective changes in a company's operations might be thought of as *transformational leadership*. The administrative inventions of General Motors' Alfred P. Sloan or General Electric's Jack Welsh are called to mind here.

The powers of the person

What precisely are the personal skills that you should consider further cultivating to enhance your individual leadership?

Researchers have helped us identify those skills through several approaches. One is to ask you and your work colleagues each to identify a moment when you feel you did your very best.

After you and your colleagues have each picked your own moment, describe them to one another. Then, the crux of the exercise, identify the general elements that are shared in most or all of the personal experiences. If you would try this tomorrow with your work associates, I forecast that the transcendent elements will resemble those on a list that recurrently emerges when such exercises are conducted by leadership consultants James M. Kouzes and Barry Z. Posner:

Challenging the process
- Searching for opportunities
- Experimenting

Inspiring a shared vision
- Envisioning a future
- Enlisting others

Enabling others to act
- Strengthening others
- Fostering collaboration

Modeling the way
- Setting an example
- Planning small wins

Encouraging commitment
- Celebrating accomplishments
- Recognizing contributions

A second avenue for identifying the generic elements of effective personal leadership is to compare great leaders with the less great in similar circumstances. Set within organizations, we would contrast an exceptionally effective divisional executive or boss with a predecessor or successor who proved far less successful.

If you repeat this exercise across many such paired comparisons in your own organization, I predict that the elements will resemble those on another list developed by researchers David A. Nadler and Michael L. Tushman:

Envisioning
- Articulating a compelling vision
- Setting high expectations
- Modeling consistent behavior

Energizing
- Demonstrating personal excitement
- Expressing personal confidence
- Seeking, finding and using success

Enabling
- Expressing personal support
- Empathizing with others
- Expressing confidence in people

Powers of the transformed organization

Whatever the personal leadership abilities you bring to or develop in the office, you can also reorganize your operations to increase your effectiveness. What avenues of change best contribute to the development of this transformational leadership?

Again the answer is unique to each company and the challenges it faces. But during the early-1990s, a package of changes proved especially potent for many US companies such as Motorola, Xerox, Du Pont, and Ford.

The full package was discussed in 'The true

worth of building high-performance systems' in Module 8, p. 275 of *Mastering Management* but I single out one illustrative element here. As a competitive strategy, many firms have sought to become more product-flexible, more customer-focussed, more swift to market. This has required upgrading employee skills, expanding information technologies and forming cross-functional teams. But for these elements to constitute the high-octane fuel in-tended, a traditional decision-making structure of centralized command and control will not work.

The leadership challenge here is to transform the decision-making system into one of delegated responsibility and accountability. Research studies confirm that empowered subordinates are more likely to devolve authority, share information, train and mentor their own subordinates, and provide greater latitude and autonomy within their operations.

The delegation, of course, cannot be done willy-nilly for it must be accompanied by appropriate incentives and performance appraisals. But if instituted as a full package, it has the effect of giving you more power to get the job done. The seeming paradox is that by sharing power you at the same time become more powerful. Part of the leadership challenge, then, is to introduce the restructuring and re-engineering required to realize the full horse-power of your operating unit.

We have always known that history is made of leadership acts large and small by chiefs of state and untold heroes. We have also learned that companies are made of leadership moments large and small by chief executives and unsung workers. The art of management is preparing yourself and others to lead at those episodic but critical moments when the organization's fate is indeed in your hands.

Summary

Judging by the stock market's reaction to Kodak in early 1993 a single person can add or subtract billions of dollars to a company's value. Statistically powerful studies, indeed, have confirmed that a CEO can raise company performance by ten per cent more than it would have been without him or her, an unsuccessful one can drop it by ten per cent.

Organizational leadership matters most during a period of stress and uncertainty. The best times for developing leadership, though, are during periods of normality when the need is less evident.

No single 'best practice' is available but there is a set of transcendent qualities which serve well in many situations.

Three sources of power come with the appointment of a new position: the power of the office, the power of the person and the power of the transformed organization. Leadership can be viewed as the exercise of power above and beyond the powers of formal position.

Team building: the great outdoors

■ **Outdoor training has a mixed reputation. But Jack Denfeld Wood argues that, done properly, it is one of the most effective ways to systematically develop leadership skills and teamwork.**

'Leadership can't be taught,' executives often assert. 'One is either born a leader or one is not.'

And so we find ourselves facing a dilemma. How do you teach one of the most fundamental and important aspects of collective human life when it is so ill-defined? How do you teach people to be leaders when many of the attributes appear to be un-teachable? How do you teach, for example, charisma?

You can imagine yourself in Napoleon's shoes and picture yourself meeting the obstacles he met or failed to meet but will this help you to become a leader like Napoleon? Will reading a biography of an Olympic ski champion help you to become an Olympic ski champion?

I believe leadership is a complex of skills, that these leadership skills can be developed systematically and that most of us have the capacity to do so. But to develop leadership skills – or any skills for that matter – those skills must be clearly identified, understood and practiced. It is not enough to read about and accept traditional concepts of leadership, much less contemporary images of it.

Many companies put 'leadership sessions', 'group work' or 'team-building' activities in their management development programs. These activities frequently include 'experiential' exercises intended to immerse participants in action, after which they sometimes have the opportunity to review their behavior.

The considerations for using experiential group exercises for leadership training often include a somewhat vague sense that leadership is important, that it has something to do with

groups and that having groups running around will be fun and somehow good for the participants – and, incidentally, for the program's evaluation ratings as well.

These considerations are often accompanied by an unspoken belief that it is beneficial to change the pace of the training and give participants a break from sitting in a classroom and listening to technical lectures. Or even that it provides a diversion from the 'real work', i.e. the incessant problem-solving and action-planning centered around ordinary business concerns.

Taken together, these considerations suggest a rather unpromising approach to behavioral training in general and to leadership and team-building activities in particular.

Outdoor leisure activities included in management development programs for participants' amusement are of limited educational value. You might enjoy a brisk round of cross-country skiing or value the memory of pristine mountain scenery, but such activities by themselves are neither leadership training nor meaningful team-building. Even more rigorous activities (parasailing, exploring caves, white water rafting, rock climbing, hiking or floating down a river canyon) may or may not be leadership development and team-building depending upon how they are handled – or mishandled.

This article focuses specifically on outdoor leadership training and team-building activities. We shall not discuss either outdoor leisure activities or outdoor activities used for diversionary purposes or simply for participant enjoyment, regardless of how important that enjoyment might be for the participants, for the program ratings or for company morale. The focus is on serious behavioral learning.

In three decades of military, academic psychology and management education experience, I have found outdoor training – when it is done well – to be the best way of examining the fundamental structure and dynamics of leadership and one of the best ways of developing individual leadership skills and of successfully building team cohesiveness. When outdoor training is poorly conceived or poorly executed, however, it is at best a complete waste of time and at worst physically or psychologically harmful.

The value of outdoor experiential training depends on three principal factors: the individual participant; his or her organization, and the vendor responsible for supplying the training.

The participant's readiness and willingness to learn is essential. The client organization should have a clear purpose, well-defined objectives and realistic expectations for the training. And the people putting on the events need to know what they are doing – technically and psychologically. Aligning all three prerequisites is not an easy task.

The participant

'Why am I here?' is a good question for executives in outdoor experiential exercises to ask themselves. 'Because I've been told to be here' is the typical reply. Someone in the organization has heard about, read about or been on such a program and thinks it is a good idea for you to go on one too. Is it? That depends.

From time to time organizations send someone who is a 'problem case' on such a leadership program to get 'fixed'. I have worked with scores of managers who were sent by supervisors on extended leadership courses because those subordinates were thought to have had particularly glaring deficiencies in interpersonal skills.

But the learning process with individuals who are being forced to participate by their organizations takes considerable time and energy from all concerned and is promising only in the hands of the most highly skilled and sensitive facilitators.

Any ultimate success requires the eventual, if grudging, goodwill of the individual manager. As a participant, one can approach outdoor experiential events in several ways. One can say:

'This is nonsense, I'll never learn anything wearing a hard-hat and hiking boots and working with seven other managers outdoors in the snow.' Or one can say: 'I expect this kind of thing to be the most valuable training that I have ever had.' Or one can fall somewhere in between these two views and perhaps say: 'I'm sceptical but willing to keep an open mind and to participate actively.'

If one approaches the experience in the first way – that it is nonsense – it is unlikely that one will learn much of anything. But if one approaches the experience in either of the latter two ways then it is quite likely that one can learn a great deal – along a number of behavioral dimensions and at a number of psychological levels.

The client organization

Whereas one might argue that every organization can benefit both from executives with more highly developed leadership skills and from more cohesive teams, client organizations vary enormously in their knowledge about, and readiness for, outdoor leadership and team-building training. Outdoor training is challenging; it can be fun and it can be deeply rewarding but it is a quick fix neither for deep personal problems nor for deeper organizational ones.

If your company has 're-engineered' 50 per cent of your managerial staff out of work and is expected to lay off more personnel in the coming months and years, throwing a few days of outdoor exercises at the survivors is unlikely to have an especially positive effect.

With shrinking training and development budgets, companies are looking for shorter and shorter courses. It is not unusual for companies to demand a course of a day or two in leadership or team-building. Obliging vendors willing to sell their services for such short programs can always be found. But this is unlikely to promote serious learning. Serious behavioral work using outdoor training is most effective as an integral part of a larger training and development strategy.

Careful consideration must be given to company goals, training objectives and the selection of a competent supplier for such training.

The vendor organization

Client organizations, especially those in the UK and the US, are presented with a bewildering array of vendors with a variety of outdoor activities and programs. Outdoor activities are usually included in programs open for individual participants from different companies or as part of an 'in-company' course for one specific client organization.

The vendor organizations range from management training consultancies that have incorporated outdoor activities in their offerings to outdoor activity-based organizations that increasingly offer management and organizational development.

I believe that outdoor programs have been too eagerly 'sold' by vendors who have had a limited understanding of their own exercises and too eagerly 'bought' by clients with only a vague idea of what they wanted or needed.

It is the job of a competent vendor to explain its programs and to dissuade the client organization from embarking on a training program for which it is not adequately prepared.

Corporate clients are concerned with getting the most out of their training budgets, and rightly so. Two corporate concerns frequently voiced include the tailoring of the exercises to support company objectives and the applicability of the learning back home.

Suppliers generally offer to tailor their programs to individual client needs. And while this is a laudable attempt at customer focus, it is even less convincing for leadership and team-building exercises than it is for more typical management development activities.

Specific outdoor activities can be combined to address general learning objectives, of course, but some wariness is probably in order if vendors promise to design a unique outdoor program with unique exercises for your particular company. This is probably more salesmanship than it is responsible program delivery.

It is also somewhat unrealistic for client organizations to expect, or for vendors to promise, direct and immediate transfer of learning to the back-at-work situation. Transfer of learning depends mostly on the interest, receptivity and motivation of the individual participant and his or her organization.

The underlying pedagogy of most outdoor exercise suppliers may appear to be similar but this does not guarantee similarly effective results. The concepts in the promotional literature, for example, may identify that 'individual', 'team' and 'organizational' factors operate in human life but whether all three factors are adequately understood and explored in a particular program remains less certain.

Similarly, most suppliers claim that effective leadership behavior is 'situational' and that 'experiential learning' follows an action-feedback-action cycle. But this does not guarantee that these concepts are skillfully employed in the field, any more than using the same medical terminology and surgical equipment guarantees an equally effective triple-bypass heart operation. Success ultimately depends on the skills of the person with the scalpel.

The extent to which leadership is developed and teams are actually built is dependent in large part on the depth of facilitation provided. It is by no means evident that all facilitators actually understand how groups and teams work. Nor is it evident that all facilitators understand the system dynamics that occur between client and vendor and affect a program.

The facilitator

Many of the activities used in outdoor leadership training are so good that they can even be done badly by relatively inexperienced or marginally competent facilitators and the program participants can leave the seminar believing that they have learned a great deal. But the results achieved are a fraction of the learning that could have been attained if the exercises were well-designed, well-integrated and well-facilitated.

Thorough facilitation requires several encounters with each activity and takes place, for example, during the event, in the debriefing immediately following the event, in the group review of the videotaped event in the evening and in a group's presentation and dialogue with other groups the following day. But multiple encounters with an event are no guarantee of significant behavioral learning. Given a motivated participant, excellent facilitation is the critical criterion for an effective learning experience. Participant learning is not in the boards and pipes and ropes and oars; the learning is in the facilitation.

Facilitators must profoundly understand themselves and their own behavior before they can be competent at helping others understand theirs. This is not always the case, even with well-known suppliers. It is not unusual for there to be an unconscious collusion between participants and some facilitators that goes something like this: 'I'll say nice things about you and your program if you let me avoid learning about myself.' This kind of collusion can also operate between the client organization and the vendor organization, making serious behavioral learning difficult if not impossible.

Participant enjoyment may be a by-product of good facilitation but it is not the primary goal of this kind of training. It is the primary job of a facilitator to help a participant deepen his or her understanding of his own and others' behavior and to help him develop and refine more effective behavioral skills. For most of us, this is a somewhat uncomfortable process. It is a process that is immeasurably aided by a competent group facilitator.

Origins and content of outdoor leadership training

Outdoor training activities have been around for a long time. They have been with the military from time immemorial, with quasi-military groups, such as the Boy Scouts, for over a hundred years, and with the business world for half a century. Outdoor activities are often an amalgam of military and quasi-military training activities, human relations training, an assortment of recreational and mountaineering activities, and routine corporate training and development procedures.

Early programs focussed on personal development and physical challenges such as sailing, rock climbing, ropes courses, getting a team over a wall, foraging for food and spending days alone in a dingy or solo camp site.

It was – and in some programs still is – a sort of gentle basic military training. One is given a few new skills and is exposed to a series of novel situations where these are applied and one expands one's behavioral repertoire.

The emphasis in outdoor activities for the corporate market has generally shifted from the early focus on individual physical challenge and character-building in the 1950s to the 'human relations' focus on interpersonal skills (communication, listening, giving and receiving 'feedback') in the 1960s and 1970s to 'leadership and team-building' today.

For many people the original 'back to basics' thread has a deep appeal but it's not for everyone. Since the initial courses, outdoor activity program content has been expanded, softened and gradually made accessible to a wider range of the general population and corporate clientele. To some extent, this change reflects both increasing concerns about liability claims as well as contemporary politically correct sensibilities.

It is also, however, a change in packaging more than in content, of fashion more than of substance. The basic activities, if they are good ones, are timeless.

Leadership and problem-solving exercises

One of the most effective approaches to the identification and understanding of leadership rests on group problem-solving exercises first used by the German Wehrmacht between the two world wars.

The Germans originally used the exercises for officer selection. They apparently found it difficult to predict leadership ability from intelligence tests or physical fitness endurance scores or school transcripts. They did find, however, that they could predict leadership ability by observing individual behavior within small group problem-solving situations that typically involved getting an entire group of peers over, under, around or through an obstacle(s) from a point A to a point B using only the equipment provided and within a limited time.

The Americans, British and Dutch military picked up these problem-solving exercises following the war. The British and Dutch currently use such exercises for officer selection; the American Army, Marine Corps and Air Force use them for leadership training.

Let us take a closer look at what one can learn about leadership from such exercises.

Decision-making

In any small group, decision making is more efficient, i.e. quicker, with the investment of authority in one person. It is unlikely that this decision-making will be more effective, however, if it is one person who makes the decisions unilaterally. A small group with a formal leader does not guarantee, and frequently inhibits, group success. Informal influence is always at play under the surface, as coalitions form along non-rational lines. Also, the world is becoming a more complex place and the decisiveness of 'authority' in pluralistic liberal democracies is neither as convincing nor as effective as it once appeared to be.

Formal versus informal structure and leadership

Outdoor exercise groups typically include around a half-a-dozen peers. This arrangement permits the observation of the formation of the informal social structure that is always at work even in the most strictly defined hierarchies. It also reflects natural leadership rather than leadership that is imposed by a formal organizational hierarchy.

From time to time, in team-building for example, individuals from different hierarchical levels of a single organization are mixed within a group. This helps bring to light the functional and dysfunctional aspects occurring between the formal and informal structure. It is a more delicate situation to facilitate but it can also be one of the more powerful situations for individual and group learning.

The outdoors lessens the effects of formal systems of hierarchy and increases the relevance of informal, ie more natural and spontaneous, behaviors. The casual clothing worn outdoors – jeans and hiking boots – helps to play down formal organizational differences. It is not that everyone is made to be equal but that natural differences become clearer as formally ascribed status is minimized.

If everyone is wearing jeans and trying to get across a raging river, family background, a large bank account and an impressive title are less relevant. Outdoors, we have more difficulty hiding – behind our massive desks, within our corner offices and inside our pin-stripe suits.

The relation between formal and informal leadership can also be highlighted if the facilitator asks the group to select a formal briefing leader, who is given the instructions and must subsequently explain the exercise to the group. This allows the exploration of different assumptions about leadership during debriefing. It is not unusual, for example, for informal leadership to be exercized by an *eminence grise* – a dominant individual who suggests (appoints) someone else to the post of formal briefing leader only to undermine this person by marginalizing subsequent contributions.

Time limits

Exercises vary in their time limits and a thoughtful program design includes activities of different duration. Longer exercises – a half day or more – tend to introduce ambiguity into the situation, permit time for more thoughtful planning, allow energy to diffuse and leave a group much more responsible for its own motivation. Short exercises with fixed time limits tend to mobilize a group's energy; they create a crisis atmosphere.

In a crisis you can 'get away with' behavior that you cannot get away with if no crisis exists. In an emergency, anyone in a group can assume command but some individuals are more susceptible to do so than are others.

In outdoor exercises, short time limits tend to draw out 'decisive' behaviors from those more inclined to 'take charge' – be they the more energetic, the less cynical or simply the more anxious and controlling personalities. Frequently, the more overtly autocratic or dominant members of a group are mobilized first. For a facilitator, this permits the exploration of the difference between 'dominance' and 'leadership'.

Dominance versus leadership

The difference between dominance and leadership has become increasingly evident over the years.

During doctoral research, I once observed and videotaped 12 different groups of US Air Force officers doing an identical exercise, sequentially, in the course of a day. The rules permitted one team member to be placed on the other side of an obstacle, some 15 metres from the rest of the group. In one group, the dominant male assigned himself the lone role and then shouted orders back to the remainder of the group, which had the necessary pieces of equipment. The rest of the group appeared to become 'brain dead', became immobilized and the entire group failed. The attempt to dominate rather than lead led to the failure.

I have another very vivid memory of an exercise with a similar result. During outdoor exercises in Squadron Officer School, a gung-ho Air Force Academy graduate in the group was attempting to dominate the decision-making process. The other group members, without saying a word, essentially stepped back and let him, literally, tangle himself up with a 50-gallon drum in a barbed-wire fence three meters in the air. They let him hang himself.

These images have recurred to me several times in business or faculty meetings where the same dynamic is in play. The vocabulary and tools may be different but the behavior is exactly the same. Dominance is not leadership and contains seeds of its own destruction.

Leadership versus having a leader

One can make a helpful distinction between a group having 'leadership' and a group having 'a leader'.

All groups need leadership but they probably don't always need one leader. The conscious installation of a formal leader or the unconscious installation of a dominant individual tend to 'over-determine' and restrict the fluid leadership function of a small group. The ability to facilitate the group achieving its goal, not necessarily by taking direct command, but by contributing in a more subtle way when that is called for, is, I believe, the essence of effective leadership.

When groups are working well, I have found that leadership emerges and submerges from different individuals depending on circumstances. The group norm becomes something like: 'the individual who can best move things forward at any particular moment freely assumes, and is allowed to assume, the leadership'.

This implies that relinquishing leadership is as important as assuming it – a lesson most politicians have difficulty grasping.

Leading and following

Exceptionally well-executed leadership is, I believe, virtually indistinguishable from well-executed followership. As individuals develop their leadership skills, and as groups begin to function as teams, the difference between leading and following evaporates. It reminds me of dancing.

When we were adolescents many of us were introduced to the mixed delights of ballroom dancing class. The boys were told that they must learn how to lead and the girls were told that they must learn how to follow. It was a stiff and tense and altogether awkward affair for everyone concerned. We maintained a bodily distance of 10 to 30 centimetres apart and were painfully self-conscious as we wrestled uncomfortably with each other over who was leading and who was following.

Over the years, mercifully, things improved. The difference between leading and following began to narrow as the physical distance and the psychological difference between leading and following became virtually indistinguishable. For professional dancers 'who is leading' and 'who is following' is largely irrelevant.

Dancing is like leadership in one respect: control is necessary but it has severe limitations when it is solely invested in one individual. A team where one individual tries to control the group will remain relatively undifferentiated and thus relatively undeveloped.

Too technical, too physical and too difficult

In the process of figuring out how to operate as an effective group, participants sometimes complain that the problem-solving exercises are too technical, too physical or too difficult. On the surface these complaints sound plausible but on closer inspection they are not as convincing.

If it is assumed that the skills necessary for the resolution of outdoor problem-solving exercises are technical, groups will cast about for 'the expert' – the person who will be able to solve 'the problem' for the group. They frequently look for the 'engineer' to do all the thinking. This ploy appears to have a number of advantages.

Under the guise of a rational choice, it puts all the responsibility on one or two group members and hence relieves the others from completely engaging in the activity. For the expert it is flattering to have the recognition, although assumption of this role carries some risk. For the others, it is a relief to put the major responsibility on someone else's shoulders.

My experience has been that a musician or philosopher has an equally good chance of exercizing leadership in this type of exercise. Groups of engineers are no more successful with these exercises than are groups of managers with other backgrounds. The exercises draw on the intuitive capacity and facilitative abilities of the participants and not on any narrow technical experience.

Groups fail at these problem-solving exercises for the same reasons that companies fail in the marketplace, not for technical reasons but for behavioral ones. They fail not because they have not got sufficient resources – groups virtually always have more than enough ideas to succeed – but because they have not employed the resources they do have sufficiently well.

The complaint that such exercises require extraordinary physical strength is generally untrue. The complaint is based on a set of particularly individualistic assumptions. The degree of physical strength required depends on the extent to which the group approaches an event as an individual challenge or as a group event.

If participants assume that each group member has to 'do it himself', some of the exercises are indeed physically difficult if not impossible. If, on the other hand, participants assume that the group as a whole is the basic

element, the exercises change their character dramatically.

Managers sometimes ask why the exercises cannot be made easier so that groups can 'succeed' and feel good. Many participants, and not a few facilitators, misconstrue the meaning of success and failure within the context of outdoor exercises. Success is not getting the team from A to B within the allotted time and using only the material provided; success is learning about how you work in a group and how groups work.

Successful completion of an exercise almost always hinders subsequent individual and group learning. Failure at an exercise almost always facilitates learning. It is virtually always necessary for a group to fail at the problem-solving tasks for them to learn much about themselves. I have been led to the paradoxical conclusion that one should fail early and often to maximize one's learning and development.

The purpose of outdoor leadership and team exercises is to learn about what makes and breaks leaders and teams – not to give participants a cheap 'victory' and encourage them in the illusion that they have mastered the profound subtleties of leadership and small group behavior.

Risk and responsibility

Outdoor exercises are not risk free. The major responsibility for physical safety lies with the organization putting on the training. The major responsibility for psychological safety lies with a group's facilitator. The ultimate responsibility for managing personal limits lies with the individual participant and his or her group.

Risks appear particularly evident where excitement is triggered – in exercises involving water (white water rafting and scuba diving), closed spaces (canyoning and caving) and heights (bungee jumping and bridge jumping).

The skilled facilitator, like the skilled instructor pilot, must be able to sense where the real dangers lay – physical and psychological – for the individual, for the group and for himself. A rule of thumb is that the most profound learning results from moving toward the anxiety. Moving in that direction means that the

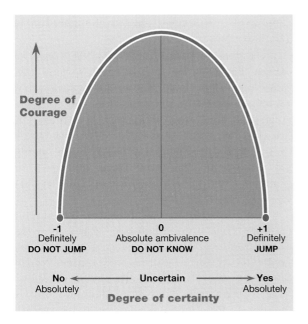

Figure 1

facilitator must operate in the zone where resistance has begun to surface and where the two most frequent mistakes include pushing participants too hard or letting them off too easily.

High-anxiety exercises are obviously not for every kind of management program, even though they can deeply enrich the individual and group experience, because they deal at the primary emotional level of fear and courage. I have come to understand courage in these events as a function of decisiveness and fear. This is illustrated in Figure 1.

Imagine a group presented with the opportunity to do a bungee jump. You may find an individual for whom this exercise presents no problem. He puts on the harness, steps over the railing and plunges ahead. Contrary to what one may assume, I do not believe that jumping in this case takes much courage.

You may, on the other hand, find an individual who refuses even to consider the possibility of jumping. Participants sometimes maintain that refusing to jump in this way requires a great deal of courage, principally because it goes against group pressure. I do not agree. Refusing at the outset to consider jumping does not take much courage either.

The greatest courage is demonstrated in a third possibility, where the individual is ambivalent and deeply uncertain about whether to jump or not. He or she feels the pull of the challenge but is afraid of jumping. I believe the greatest personal learning occurs at this point, where one engages the fear and goes as far as one can before one makes the decision to jump or not to jump. In the final analysis, it is not a question of jumping or not which defines courage, it is in how openly one explores the terrain of one's fear.

These kinds of exercises are both a personal and a team challenge and individual leadership in these circumstances means assuming individual responsibility to help others on the team explore their limits.

This is not an easy lesson to get across because other group members are often immobilized by such events. They are not sure where the boundary lies between supporting and encouraging another and being obtrusive and pushing him or her too hard. There are no easy answers to this dilemma. In fact, the learning is in the exploring dilemma. Leaving the others to their own fears is usually avoiding one's responsibility, just as offering quick reassurance is usually felt to be insincere.

Each group member has his own constellation of wishes and fears and it is precisely in exploring this terrain with one another that a participant learns to recognize and manage on a deeper emotional level.

But it's not the real world

'This isn't the real world' participants sometimes complain. 'We are just playing games, the situations are unrealistic and, in any case, we don't really behave this way back at work.'

This is an interesting perspective to consider. The behavior one observes during outdoor leadership activities is very real behavior. No one invents new behavior for a few days of outdoor training; we bring ourselves into the exercises. Our mothers would recognize us; so would our subordinates. So why the reluctance to see our behavior as real?

Simulations are a central part of most complex technical training. Many professions use simulations for training their members in technical skills. Surgeons practice on cadavers, lawyers practice in moot court, pilots learn their inflight procedures in make-believe cockpits, and management students engage in business simulations. Simulations are used because they are relatively inexpensive, compress time, allow errors and are relatively safe.

Well-run outdoor training can create a microcosm, a little laboratory that can replicate the essential pattern of group problem-solving – analysing the situation, identifying the problem(s), identifying the causes of the problem(s), generating solutions, selecting the most promising solutions and then developing, communicating, planning, implementing and modifying a workable strategy. All this in the course of an hour where the stakes are getting to the other side of a yellow line or finishing before the clock runs out, not in the course of a decade where the stakes are facing bankruptcy court or looking for other employment.

Claiming that behavior during outdoor exercises is not 'real' behavior often masks underlying concerns. The overt concerns may include physical safety or the usefulness of simulations in general but the covert concerns are usually related to psychological exposure – taking risks, being physically unfit, making mistakes, appearing foolish to oneself and to others, anxiety about unfamiliar situations, the need for maintaining control, dependency on formal organizational structure for security and so on.

The direct application of learning is an issue that is not specific to outdoor exercises but is general to any management development training. It may appear, because we normally work indoors with business attire, that a classroom session, such as a full day case discussion of business strategy, is a more relevant and a more applicable type of training. But I disagree.

Long after program participants have forgotten the case discussion and the numbers and the principles of the strategy, they will remember how it felt to take a risk and fail, to modify the plan and have another subgroup undermine it, and then to try again and go a little further. And that is a much more lasting image of how strategy is really enacted in life than are most case discussions.

The ancient Greeks believed that man draws upon three principal faculties – intellect, will and passion. Most of our training and most of our working life stress the exercise and development of our intellectual capabilities. We value – one might say overvalue – the intellect at the expense of our other faculties. Will and passion are relegated to the playing field and are tolerated in organizational life only if they serve narrow corporate interests.

Moving outdoors and allowing ourselves to engage in group problem-solving activities that have intellectual, physical and competitive components brings to light aspects of ourselves that normally operate only in the shadows. Much of the satisfaction from engaging in outdoor leadership exercises derives from successfully touching deeper psychological strata than the ones which we normally reveal.

Summary

The value of outdoor experiential training depends on aligning the attitudes of the individual participant, his or her organization, and the training vendor. Good facilitation is a pre-requisite for developing leadership and building teams – participant enjoyment is a by-product, not the primary goal.

Group problem-solving exercises first used by the German Wehrmacht provide one of the best approaches. Outdoor exercises groups typically comprise half a dozen peers, though different hierarchical levels can be usefully mixed.

All groups need leadership but they do not always need one leader – leadership in the best working groups often emerges and submerges from different individuals. Well-executed leadership is virtually indistinguishable from well-executed 'followership'. Failing early and often in outdoor exercises maximizes learning. Contrary to a common view the behavior one observes during outside leadership exercises is very real. In most training and working lifes the development of our intellectual capabilities is emphasized: moving outdoors gives us the chance to openly explore behavioral factors which otherwise operate only in the shadows.

Suggested further reading

Alderfer, C.P. (1984) 'An intergroup perspective on group dynamics' in *Handbook of Organizational Behaviour* (J. Lorsch ed.), Prentice-Hall, Englewood Cliffs, NJ.

Incomes Data Services August 1995 *Partial guide to outdoor training suppliers in the UK*, 193 St. John Street, London EC1V 4LS.

Ritchey, Col. Russell V. (1974) *Years of the Tiger*, Squadron Officer School, Air University, Maxwell Air Force Base, Alabama.

Managing Change

Contents

Choosing the right change path 538
Paul Strebel, IMD
*Change may be constant but it is not always the
same. Different types of change require different
responses. A model for analysing the path to take.*

Breakpoint: how to stay in the game 543
Paul Strebel, IMD
*An industry breakpoint occurs when the market is
presented by a new offering so superior that it
completely changes the rules of the competitive
game.*

Creating industry breakpoints 548
Paul Strebel, IMD
*If we can anticipate when a breakpoint is about to
arrive, can companies create their own breakpoints to
leap ahead of the competition?*

Management in the information era 552
Michael J. Earl, London Business School
*Information is the new resource and all companies
are information companies and all managers
information managers.*

Contributors

Paul Strebel is Professor of Strategy and
Change Management at IMD, Lausanne.
His research interests include change
management, turning points and
discontinuities.

Michael J Earl is Andersen Consulting
Professor of Information Management,
Deputy Principal (faculty and academic
planning) and Director of the Center for
Information Management at London
Business School.

Introduction

Change has become the one constant of modern management. The ability to respond to change and, indeed, to turn it to advantage is perhaps the top management skill required today. This response to and utilization of change is at the heart of managing change.

The Managing Change module covers all the most important aspects of change management and includes sections on how to choose the right change path, anticipating and creating the 'industry breakpoints' that lead to change, and the impact of information technology.

Choosing the right change path

■ **Change may be constant but it is not always the same. Different types of change require different responses.** Paul Strebel **presents a model for analysing the path to take.**

Those who pretend that the same kind of change medicine can be applied no matter what the context are either naive or charlatans.

Different situations demand different change paths. The kind of situation in which re-structuring makes sense is quite different from that in which experimentation might be appropriate. Thus, change leaders cannot afford the risk of blindly applying a standard change recipe and hoping that it will work. Successful change takes place on a path that is appropriate to the specific situation.

Where successful change paths are similar is in the three broad phases they go through: unfreezing the organization, that is, drawing people's attention to the need for change and identifying the value-creating idea; making change happen, that is, winning over people and dealing with resistance; and integrating the change, that is, following up the process and preparing for the next change.

The right approach to these steps, however, depends on the strength of the mainly external forces of change and the mainly internal forces of resistance.

For example, managing a crisis in the face of strong forces of change is completely different from trying to stimulate change when everything is still going well. Moreover, stimulating change in an organization with low resistance is not the same as trying to do so in the face of high resistance. Let us look at how the forces of change and resistance, in turn, shape the appropriate change path and use the framework to contrast different types of change.

Change forces

The strength of a change force, such as the emergence of a new technology, a shift in the behavior of competitors or a swing in the economic cycle, is determined by its impact on the business' performance (most frequently measured by market share, sales or profits).

A strong change force is one causing a substantial decline in the performance of a business under threat or promising a substantial improvement in the performance of a business.

It is useful to distinguish between the broad levels of change-force intensity: weak change forces whose nature and direction are difficult to discern; moderately strong forces whose direction can be seen but with only a minor impact on performance; and strong change forces with a substantial impact on performance.

Weak change forces imply proactive change. Proactive change occurs while the change force is still weak, before it can be identified clearly. The first big hurdle in proactive change is to get people's attention and establish the need for change.

Business performance, though no longer growing, is still strong. Thus, communication is unlikely to be effective; there is little to communicate, except the deep conviction that change is needed. This almost certainly will fall flat, given the mindset and cultural resistance to proactive change.

If the change leader has some idea what the change force is, he or she may be able to shock others into recognizing it too. More probably, he will not know what shock treatment to use because the change force is too vague. The effective way of getting attention is to challenge people to become change agents, to go out and expose themselves to the potential change forces and see what is involved. For this, the organization must be potentially open to change.

The second big hurdle is to identify the value-creating idea. In most proactive situations, a one-man-show or a single team effort is not enough to deal with the uncertainty about what should be done. On the other hand, change agents exploring the change forces can be asked, and will be eager, to come up with value-creating solutions.

Time is available. It should be used for experimentation. Experimentation by as many teams of change agents as the business and circumstances can support is the key to identifying a strong value-creating idea during the first phase of proactive change.

Moderate change forces require reactive change. Reactive change is called for when the forces of change have begun to affect performance but not so severely that survival, or the possibility of exploiting an opportunity, is threatened.

Getting people's attention is easier than in the case of proactive change because the change force can be identified by those willing to open their minds to the environment. Yet, in very closed organizations, shock treatment may still be necessary to open things up. Relying on communication alone may not be enough – people tend to nod their heads and continue as before. The most effective approach is still to expose people to the change force as directly as possible.

Once people's attention has been drawn to the need for change, value-creating ideas have to be developed. Since the change force is known, there is not the same need for exploration as in the case of proactive change. Nor is the same time available. Unleashing widespread bottom-up experimentation could be dangerous.

On the other hand, the company does not have to respond immediately, so there is room for creativity. A one-man show would miss the opportunity to get input from others and bring them on board. The most appropriate way of developing the value-creating idea is through multidisciplinary teams.

Strong change forces demand rapid change. Rapid crisis change is inevitable if managers wait until the business is on the edge of the performance precipice, where a threatening force confronts strong resistance. If nothing is done in time, the external stakeholders will force the business through a discontinuity that is out of management's control.

Unfortunately, this happens all too often, especially in industries in transition and in companies with strong power and role cultures that are blinded by political, structural and mindset problems. When the crisis takes hold, the threat to the survival of the business undermines the support of the stakeholders. They withdraw or hedge their commitment, and the political infighting over the remaining resources intensifies. The time for managed change shrinks rapidly.

One advantage of crisis change is that the change leader has the full attention of all the players. When the crisis hits, the shock opens up previously closed minds. People quickly become aware of the forces and need for change. They are waiting for the change leader to take charge.

Another advantage is that the direction of the change is clear. To save the business in the limited time available, only a few value-creating ideas are relevant: cut costs, regroup around the strong points, adapt the tactics of successful competitors. The more urgent the situation, the less the time for elaborate consultation or teamwork. It is important that the change objectives be put together quickly by one person with a small support group.

In the event of a strong positive force of change, such as a new product breakthrough, management also will want to capitalize on the opportunity as rapidly as possible. Getting people's attention should not be a problem if the opportunity is attractive enough. The value-creating idea is to commit the business to the new opportunity as quickly as possible. The best way of doing so will depend on whether the organization is open or closed to change.

Resistance to change

The strength of the resistance to a change force depends on what people have to gain and lose by changing, and on how the culture of the organization shapes the way they respond to change. An organization that is open to change, with a significant number of change agents and people who are willing to try new things, is said

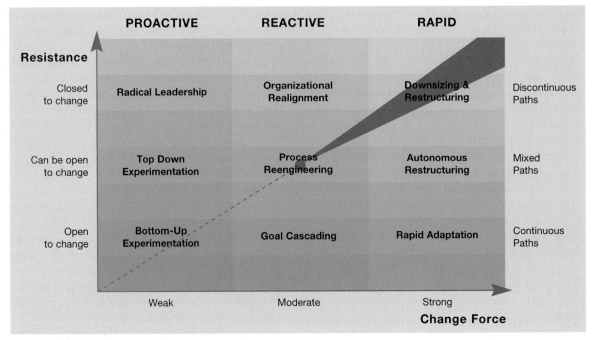

Figure 1: Contrasting change paths

to have low resistance; an organization that is partially open to change, with at least some change agents, is moderately resistant; while a closed organization, with very few change agents, has high resistance.

These levels of resistance can be combined with the levels of change force intensity to provide a simple way of contrasting change paths, making it easier to pick one appropriate to a particular context (*see* Figure 1).

We shall classify some of the more widely discussed change paths into three groups corresponding to the levels of resistance:

● discontinuous paths appropriate for closed organizations
● mixed paths appropriate for organizations that can be opened
● continuous paths appropriate for open organizations.

For each level of resistance to change, we start on the left of the exhibit and classify the change paths in order of increasing strength of the change force. Remember that as the pressure for change increases there is less and less time to get people's attention and experiment with the value-creating idea.

Discontinuous paths appropriate for closed organizations

In organizations that are closed to change, a radical approach is required to break the dominant culture of resistance and give the other players a more supportive environment in which to commit to the change effort.

This process should start with the resistors at the top. They have to be confronted with moments of truth: either they buy in or out. Once the resistors have been cleared out, the support group of change agents can be put together and others invited to join the effort. Such dis-continuous change can be very effective at changing mindsets and structure, but more follow-up time is required to change values, skills and behavior.

Radical leadership. Occasionally, headstrong leaders have a hunch that a closed organization must be shaken up, even though no identifiable change force is on the horizon.

For this to work, the hunch must turn out to be right and the leader must have enough power to drive the change through. Otherwise it is invariably a disastrous ego trip. It makes much more sense to try to open up the organization with limited experimentation or, alternatively, to wait until the forces of change emerge more clearly.

Organizational realignment. Some form of reorganization, either external via an acquisition or alliance, or internal in the form of a new structure, is employed to draw attention to the visible need for change, line people up in the direction of the identifiable change force, and confront resistors with a new reality.

Helmut Maucher of Nestle saw the emergence of global product lines in the food industry but was unable to get the regional Nestle organization to adopt the approach, until he had Nestle take over Rowntree with its global product lines. The acquisition quickly led to the formation of two global strategic product groups encompassing most of Nestle's potentially global product lines.

Downsizing and restructuring. When the change force reaches crisis proportions threatening the survival of the business, rapid radical restructuring is the only alternative for an organization closed to change. Operation Centurion at Philips exhibited all the typical characteristics of such a restructuring process.

One man, Jan Timmer, was at the center, focussing people's attention on Philips' financial crisis and working out the value-creating idea around lower operating costs and a ten per cent reduction in headcount. In one dramatic meeting, he confronted all the senior managers with the need for change. They had little choice other than to say how they could contribute to cutting operating costs in their business or plan their departure from the company.

Mixed paths appropriate for organizations that can be opened

Organizations that can be opened to change already contain pockets of change agents and team-oriented cultures. This makes it possible to initiate experimentation and get the change agents to convert others to the change effort. However, the influence of the change agents is limited by resistors.

Since it cannot be assumed that the change agents will be able to convert the resistors, management has to assist the change agents by dealing with the resistors directly. It can then accelerate the process by rolling out the change through the organization.

Top-down experimentation. In the absence of a clearly identifiable change force, the change leader must take advantage of the change agents that are present and the time available to initiate experimentation, while at the same time opening up the organization as much as possible. Once the new direction becomes clear, the rest of the organization can be asked to buy in.

At Sony, Akia Morita believed that there was a market for a small portable cassette player but only a few of his managers agreed with him. He set up task forces with these change agents to explore the possibilities of the concept. Their experimentation soon converged on a prototype. After the first mixed feedback from market tests, Morita decided to push the project through the organization to commercialization despite the misgivings of some of his senior managers. The resulting 'Walkman' turned out to be a run-away success that positioned Sony as leading player on the global scene.

Process re-engineering. Since both the reason for change and the value-creating idea can be more easily identified, there is less need for experimentation. The organization is open enough to permit the formation of a few multidisciplinary teams to work out the details of the idea and its implementation. Once the teams have fleshed out the new streamlined processes, the change can be implemented.

In a typical re-engineering program, for example, at the Banco d'America e d'Italia, teams of specialists from diverse functions redesigned the front-office procedures and back-office information systems and then used intensive communication and training to put the new processes in place in the branches.

Autonomous restructuring. This is restructuring led by change agents in middle management facing a strong change force. The pressure and required direction for change are so strong that before top management engages them in a dialogue, middle managers open to change begin to adapt spontaneously on their own.

If top management is alert, it can use the change introduced by these players as a model for driving rapid change through the rest of the organization.

Although not frequent, a number of examples have been documented. At Chrysler, when Bob Eaton took over, he soon recognised the pioneering re-engineering work being done by some middle managers and insisted that the rest of the organization follow in their footsteps. This has been so effective that Chrysler's new products have been used as models of economic design by its Japanese competitors.

Continuous paths appropriate for open organizations

In organizations that are open to change, the dominant change agents can be invited to do extensive frontline experimentation, as well as bring others on board.

There is usually little risk in leaving the resistors to last, because in an open organization, the change effort often builds up organically inside the existing organization, gradually invading it before taking it over entirely. The resistors are reduced to a shrinking group in the face of an accelerating change bandwagon. Although this may take longer to initiate than the top-down change appropriate in more closed organizations, the ownership of the change is more complete and the follow-up to the change effort much smoother.

Bottom-up experimentation. When the change force is unclear and the organization is open, the frontliners can be asked to do extensive experimentation, look for new value-creating ideas and implement them.

This was the approach adopted by Haruo Naito at Eisai, the Japanese pharmaceutical company. To test out his vision that the company could be redirected towards geriatric care, he invited his people to become innovation managers by exploring customer needs in the field and proposing new business projects to satisfy those needs. The Eisai organization was so open that within three years, some 20 per cent of the employees were working on integrated health care projects.

Goal cascading. When the forces of change are better known, there is not as much need to experiment. Rather the change leader can take advantage of the open organization by asking the people to work out the implementation of the value creating idea on their own level, in a cascading process of implementation from the top down through to the frontline.

When Seiko's planning department issued their report on market saturation and the increasing weakness in watch prices, Ichiro Hattori, the CEO, felt that the company should do something. After top management opted for diversification into electronic equipment, he cascaded the implementation down through the senior managers, junior managers and finally into a Total Quality Control program to 'ensure the highest level of corporate-wide implementation'.

Within four years Seiko had developed a new line of sophisticated graphics devices that accounted for 50 per cent of sales.

Rapid adaptation. Organizations that have been opened up by change provide fertile ground for nurturing on-going change. The ability to nurture on-going change is also a good test of whether the latest change effort has taken root. The need for this kind of follow-up is especially important after restructuring, which otherwise might remain quite superficial.

The two fundamental types of continuing change are continuous process improvement, or *kaizen*, and spontaneous managerial initiative, or 'intrapreneurship'. Unfortunately, in today's world, kaizen is often too inward-looking and not rapid enough to respond to strong forces of change. Intrapreneurship, on the other hand, involves bottom-up entrepreneurial activity in a direct response to market opportunities, which has been turned into a fine art by some American companies, among the most renowned being 3M and Hewlett Packard.

In choosing a change path, managers must remember that change is too uncertain to be predictable. Once an organization starts out on a path, the forces of change and resistance may respond in unexpected ways, making continual adaptation a necessity. Many change journeys involve more than one path. For example, downsizing, followed by re-engineering, and then implementation of rapid adaptation. By keeping an eye on the evolving interplay between the forces and altering the change path accordingly, change leaders can optimize their chances of success.

Summary

Different situations demand different change recipes. But all change paths go through three broad phases: unfreezing the organization, making change happen, and following up and preparing for the next one. It is useful to distinguish between the different levels of 'change-force' intensity. Weak change forces are difficult to discern and require skill in communications and in identifying the value creating idea – but there is time for experimentation. Moderate change forces are those which have started to affect performance but do not threaten survival: getting people's attention is easier and multi-disciplinary teams should be employed.

Those organizations with high resistance have very few 'change agents' and require a radical approach to break the dominant culture. The process should start with resistors at the top, can benefit from headstrong leadership (though can equally end in a disastrous ego trip), and requires some form of reorganization. In organizations that can be opened to change, management has to help the change agents, and top down experimentation is desirable. In organizations that are already open to change there is usually little risk in leaving the resistors until last. Bottom up experimentation and goal cascading should be possible.

Suggested further reading

Strebel, Paul (1992) *Breakpoints: How Managers Exploit Radical Business Change*, Part II, Harvard Business School Press.

Fry, N.J.N. and Killing, J. P. (1989) *Strategic Analysis and Action*, Prentice Hall.

Breakpoint: how to stay in the game

■ **An industry breakpoint occurs when the market is presented by a new offering so superior that it completely changes the rules of the competitive game.**

by Paul Strebel

No manager today can escape industry breakpoints. More and more frequently, industries are being shaken by dramatic shifts in competitive behavior that make current winning strategies obsolete. The best managers are left looking inept. Newcomers emerge out of nowhere to dislodge the established industry leaders. Companies and careers are being made and broken on the ability to adapt to, or exploit, the rapidly changing environment.

Understanding how industry breakpoints work and looking for signs of their arrival has become a must for the successful management of change.

What is a breakpoint?

An industry breakpoint is a new offering to the market that is so superior in terms of customer value and delivered cost that it disrupts the rules of the competitive game: a new business system is required to deliver it. The new offering typically causes a sharp shift in the industry's growth rate while the competitive response to the new business system results in a dramatic realignment of market shares.

Breakpoints can be illustrated with examples

from the personal computer industry. When Apple introduced its first machine, it offered individuals the possibility of decentralized computing power with a convenience and cost that was on a completely different level from that provided by centralized mainframes. The established computer companies, if they noticed Apple's innovation, certainly did not consider it a threat.

On the other hand, hundreds of small entrepreneurs saw the opportunities it opened up and the simplicity of Apple's first business system. They competed to define the form and content of a PC and this competition continued until their various machines began to resemble one another more and more closely.

IBM's arrival triggered a new industry breakpoint. It had the good fortune to enter the fray at a point when people could see what the optimal value and cost of a PC looked like. As a result, its offering created an industry standard. This gave it, and other companies, the chance to redesign and consolidate the business system in order to mass-produce PCs at low cost.

The existing entrepreneurs who were unable to match this shift in the competitive game and who were unprotected by niche segments, disappeared in the shake-out that followed. Indeed, to manage this breakpoint, Apple was forced to oust its founders and bring in a consumer marketing expert. Competition to expand the market and capture market share by lowering delivered costs continued until the players had more and more difficulty making money and began looking for a way out of price competition.

Apple's introduction of the Macintosh, with a completely new level of user-friendliness, marked the arrival of a new breakpoint. Competitors discovered that the market was ready for enhanced customer value in the form of hard discs, better graphics, greater speed and, especially, new operating software.

Ironically, Apple did not appreciate the significance of the shift in value it had created.

But Bill Gates did. He saw the opportunity opened up by graphics software and proceeded to develop the same for the IBM standard. The competitive emphasis on enhancing the value side of the offering continued until recession struck the US in the late-1980s.

The recession triggered another breakpoint. The PC business was now so large that it could not escape the impact of recession in its largest market. As the growth rate dropped, competitors were forced to emphasize cost reduction. To survive, the business system had to be streamlined. Market shares shifted to the low-cost clone manufacturers from the Far East and companies such as Compaq that were able to offer quality with portability at a very competitive price. Meanwhile, technology development continued with the arrival of new microprocessors and networking software.

As the recession lifted, the full extent of yet another breakpoint triggered by more powerful chips and software became apparent. The market growth had shifted towards laptops, work-stations and integrated networks – offerings that were quite different from the traditional PC.

The more important shift was in the distribution of power in the business systems needed to deliver the new offerings. Although the business systems differed from segment to segment, they were all now dominated by Intel for chips and Microsoft for software. Both IBM, universally admired for its management only a few years before, and Apple, the earlier star of the industry, were struggling to deal with the new situation, while most of the Far Eastern players were a shadow of their former selves.

Understanding breakpoint dynamics

The first framework that comes to mind for explaining breakpoints in the PC business is the industry life cycle driven by technology. Unfortunately, this classic concept is inadequate for two reasons.

First, breakpoints can be triggered by many other factors than technology, such as the economic cycle, government policy and shifting customer preferences. Even in the high technology PC industry, where technology could be expected to play a big role, the breakpoint was triggered by economic recession. The role of non-technological drivers can be much more important in services, for example.

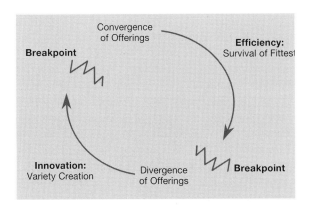

Figure 1: Evolutionary cycle of competitive behavior

Second, the smooth S-curve representation of an industry cycle is clearly misleading. The transitions between the phases of a life cycle marked by breakpoints are definitely not smooth but sharply discontinuous.

The best framework for understanding industry breakpoints is provided by the evolutionary cycle of competitive behavior (see Figure 1). When someone discovers a new business opportunity, whatever its source, there is a *divergence* in competitors' behavior as they rush in to explore the boundaries of the opportunity and innovate with new offerings.

This phase of divergent behavior corresponds to variety creation in the evolutionary cycle. The first Apple computer, the arrival of the Macintosh and, most recently, the new chips and software all triggered breakpoints. Divergent competitive behavior aimed at enhancing the value of the offering continues until it becomes impossible to differentiate offerings because value innovation has run its course and imitation of the competitors' best features has taken over. As the offerings converge and the returns to value innovation decline, someone sees the advantage of trying to reduce delivered cost. Competitors converge on total quality management, continual improvement, and re-engineering or restructuring of the business system in an attempt to cut costs and maintain market share.

Convergence leads to a shake-out of the less efficient. It corresponds to survival of the fittest in the evolutionary cycle. The IBM PC, the

recession and arrival of the clones marked convergent breakpoints. Cost cutting and consolidation continues until it becomes very difficult to squeeze further costs out of the business system. The returns from cost reduction decline, people see the advantage of looking for a new business opportunity and the cycle begins to repeat itself.

In brief, the competitive cycle suggests that there are two basic types of breakpoint:

● Divergent Breakpoints associated with sharply increasing variety in the competitive offerings, resulting in more value for the customer.

● Convergent Breakpoints associated with sharp improvements in the systems and processes used to deliver the offerings, resulting in lower delivered cost.

Every jump in customer value and reduction in delivered cost is relative to what went before. Whereas the competitive cycle tends to repeat itself, the industry continues to evolve. This can be diagrammed, as in Figure 2 (overleaf), which refers to the computer industry. The vertical axis represents increasing customer value and the horizontal axis indicates lower delivered cost.

Increases in customer value are depicted with vertical arrows, reduction of delivered cost with horizontal arrows and the intervening breakpoints with asterisks.

Although none of this is to scale, the diagram is a useful way of summarizing the evolution of the industry. Over time, in real terms, industries move up the diagonal with increasing customer value and lower delivered cost.

Some industries, such as those based on commodities, offer meagre opportunities for customer-value creation; they tend to evolve more in the direction of lower delivered cost resulting from breakpoints in extraction/production techniques and logistics. Other industries, such as clothing and fashion, offer fewer opportunities for cost reduction and evolve mainly in the direction of customer value.

Looking for breakpoints with leading indicators

Understanding the dynamics of breakpoints after they have occurred is of little use. What is

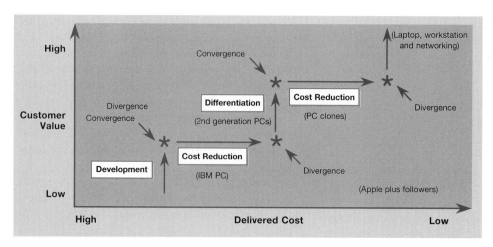

Figure 2: Breakpoint evolution of personal computer industry

needed for timely change management is a way of converting retrospective understanding into anticipation. But it is notoriously difficult to see breakpoints coming.

The experience of people in marketing, research, production and finance is made largely irrelevant by the new market, new business system and new economics. This is especially obvious with new product breakthroughs such as the first Apple computer. The established players had little chance of picking up this breakpoint in its early development. Their people had no reason to look in that direction. Similar blind spots can occur later in the industry's evolution if the business system is taken over by new entrants or by upstream players such as Intel or downstream players such as Microsoft.

Although some people in a company may see the breakpoint, a closed company culture may make it impossible for them to convince others. The concept of the PC was actually invented at Xerox but turned down as a project owing to its apparent irrelevance to copying systems. Steven Jobs and Steven Wosniak left Xerox to found Apple.

If Xerox's senior managers had seen the potential in the PC that the two pioneers saw, it is unlikely they would have let them go. The development of the copying and PC industries might have taken an entirely different path. Thus, companies need both a way of looking out for breakpoints and a culture that is sensitive

enough to recognize their significance when the signs are picked up.

The timing of breakpoints is impossible to predict because they might be triggered by many different factors and because they require both a latent market and a supplier with the right business system. However, with an understanding of an industry's evolution it is possible to look for patterns indicating that a breakpoint may be imminent. Specifically, the competitive cycle can be used to look for leading indicators of a potential breakpoint.

The tendency of the competitive cycle to oscillate between divergence (variety creation) on the one hand and convergence (survival of the fittest) provides the framework.

Convergence is usually easier to anticipate, because it is built on an offering that already exists. Typical indicators immediately prior to convergence are listed below. When several of these are in place, all that is needed is a player, or event, to trigger the breakpoint.

● *Competitors*: Convergence is visible in increasingly similar products, service and image.
● *Customers*: The differentiation between offerings looks increasingly artificial to customers and the segmentation in the market starts breaking down.
● *New entrants*: Very few on the horizon with the possible exception of players with new processes.
● *Distributors*: The bargaining power in the

industry often shifts downstream to distributors who play competitors off against one another.

- *Suppliers*: They cannot provide a source of competitive advantage because everyone knows how to use their inputs.

Divergence is more difficult to anticipate because it is based on a new offering that does not yet exist. However, if the following are in place, the industry is ready for a new offering that breaks with the past.

- *Customers*: An increasingly saturated market is accompanied by declining growth rates and restless customers.
- *New entrants*: Restless customers are attracting new entrants.
- *Competitors*: Declining returns may force them to experiment with new offerings or look elsewhere for profits.
- *Suppliers*: New resources and, especially, new technology are frequently the source of a divergent breakpoint.
- *Distributors*: They lag behind because they have to adapt to the new offering.

If a potential breakpoint is identified, a company needs the intelligence capability to recognize the implications. This intelligence capability requires an information system to combine and exchange individual information and to learn from others inside and outside the company. There is a role for both formal and informal systems, such as environmental scanning, benchmarking and interactive data banks. There are also multiple opportunities for cross-fertilization between functions, divisions and other sub-units of the organization.

Even more important are open attitudes throughout the company, especially on the part of leading executives, and a willingness to consider unusual, challenging scenarios.

Unfortunately, open attitudes are not natural. To develop them, managers have to become aware of their own mindset, the assumptions they have come to accept as facts. They must become students of their industry's evolution and, above all, of the players on its periphery. When it comes to anticipating breakpoints, in the words of Andy Grove, the CEO of Intel, 'only the paranoid survive.'

Summary

The personal computer industry provides a good illustration of 'breakpoints' – sharply discontinuous transitions between the phases of an industry life cycle. The best framework for understanding breakpoints is provided not by the economic cycle but by the evolutionary cycle of competitive behavior: the divergence which leads to a variety of new product offerings, the convergence which results in a shake out of less efficient players. It is notoriously difficult to see breakpoints coming; companies need an appropriate culture to spot the indicators.

Suggested further reading

Strebel, P. (1992) *Breakpoints: How Managers Exploit Radical Business Change*, Part I, Harvard Business School Press.

Creating industry breakpoints

■ **In the last article,** Paul Strebel **offered some insights into how to anticipate when a breakpoint is about to arrive. Here he provides guidelines on how companies can create their own breakpoints to leap ahead of the competition.**

How can a company create a breakpoint, or fundamental change, in its industry? Breakpoints are characterized by the arrival of a new offering with so much more customer value relative to delivered cost that it represents a quantum leap in the rules of the competitive game.

Most companies find themselves reacting to breakpoints created by others. Even if they anticipate the breakpoint, they cannot get their mainstream organization to adapt to the new rules of the game because it is so entrenched in the conditions that existed before.

Generating, rather than reacting to, a breakpoint requires a *three-part learning organization*:
● frontline managers who probe industry trends to discover new opportunities
● co-ordination managers who select and balance the development of opportunities with the needs of the mainstream organization
● top management that provides the strategic direction, nurtures an opportunity-oriented culture within the organization and from time to time commits major resources to the full-scale exploitation of opportunities with breakpoint potential.

Frontline managers must have a mandate to discover new opportunities

To look for breakpoint opportunities, some frontline managers have to be given a mandate to experiment. Others may be asked to implement change initiated by top management.

Giving people a mandate to experiment requires that top management let go. Experi-

mentation requires loose controls, toleration of failure and easy access to information and resources both financial and human. Top management has to show that it is willing to share the risk associated with frontline experimentation and change.

At least six different types of frontline change capability have been associated with the discovery of industry breakpoints. Three of these are customer value related and three delivered cost related:

Frontline change capabilities
Customer value related
● Directed innovation
● Spontaneous innovation
● Stakeholder networking
Delivered cost related
● Systematization
● Continuous improvement
● Process re-engineering

Directed innovation involves top-down innovation efforts. In established companies, senior managers form dedicated task forces to transform new ideas, often originating in the laboratory, into new market offerings. Examples include the task forces formed to develop the Sony Walkman, Canon Personal Copiers, and the IBM PC.

Spontaneous innovation starts from the bottom up. Stimulating this kind of innovation has been turned into a fine art by some US companies, among the most renowned being 3M and Hewlett Packard. Although an innovative market offering may draw on a new technology, the key is the entrepreneurial capability needed to transform the idea or technology into a business success.

Stakeholder networking involves the development of intense, value-creating relationships with key stakeholders. As networks evolve, they become the source of value-based innovation, as demonstrated by IKEA and Benetton.

Systematization is the capability required to standardize an offering and transform one-off operations into efficient volume production. This principally involves turning apparently unique activities into systematic routines and sequencing them most cost effectively.

Continuous improvement is *kaizen*, the bottom-up capability developed by Toyota, Canon and others that involves the entire workforce in improvement-oriented planning, execution and control. The central idea reflects the Japanese penchant for concentrating on people and processes rather than products and organization.

Process re-engineering involves reconfiguring the flow of business system activities, for example, to improve response to customers and the product development process, to target specific market segments and, in an advanced form, making the move to mass-customized products.

Putting any of these capabilities into place requires time, a focussed effort and a dedicated internal change program. Nurturing more than one is a major challenge for management, as the differences between the capabilities are significant.

Whereas the customer value capabilities require a loose approach to organization and control, the delivered cost capabilities require a tighter approach. Mastering all the capabilities may be impossible, especially for companies with a strong homogeneous culture. Some US companies, for example, have been very successful at creating customer value breakpoints through directed and spontaneous innovation. Yet, when it comes to delivered cost breakpoints, the highly individualistic culture of these companies results in a preference for re-engineering rather than continual improvement.

Global co-ordination can provide a way round this cultural constraint. Geographic regions encourage the development of different industries and organizational capabilities. Selective foreign investments allow a company to diversify its repertoire of breakpoint capabilities.

Hi-tech companies from around the world have capitalized on Silicon Valley's spontaneous-innovation culture to develop new offerings. Others are learning how to use Japanese acquisitions to strengthen their continual process-improvement techniques. Others have strengthened their capability for incremental engineering innovation by locating R&D close to German-speaking universities. And many will look to the US for the process re-engineering that leads to mass customization.

Co-ordination managers have to select and balance the development of opportunities with the needs of the mainstream business

Co-ordination managers act as gatekeepers deciding which opportunities discovered by the frontline deserve additional resources and attention. What guidelines should they use in selecting opportunities for further development?

The most valuable opportunities are those where leverage can be obtained by stretching and projecting existing competence into new areas. The pay-off to such linked development is typically higher because it builds on existing experience and resources. There are several types of competence leverage that can be used as the basis for constructing a portfolio of development opportunities.

Technological leverage, according to several studies, is key to the success of hi-tech companies. Some companies have been particularly adept at following a technology trail wherever the opportunities look most attractive and, in the process, occasionally triggering an industry breakpoint.

Yamaha started out in wood carpentry before moving into pianos in 1941. During the Second World War the company was asked to produce wooden propellers for aircraft. Wooden propellers led to steel propellers. After the war, the company applied its steel casting know-how to making motorcycle engines, for which there was a huge demand. In the mid-1950s there were so many Japanese motorcycle manufacturers that a shake-out occurred. After the shakeout in the early-1960s, only four remained: Yamaha, Honda, Kawasaki and Suzuki. When the price pressure continued, Honda moved into cars while Yamaha went into power boat motors where it captured 50 per cent of the market.

Business system leverage involves the stretching of functional competence in one or more of the activities in a business system to other markets and industries where the same activities are the key to success.

Bic, the French ballpoint pen manufacturer, leveraged its competencies in the low-cost manufacturing of plastics, advertising and mass merchandizing from the maturing pen market into disposable razors, disposable lighters, and wind surfboards. In all cases, it quickly created a high-volume, low-cost position by concentrating on the manufacturing, assembly and distribution activities and by buying-in non-plastic raw materials and components, such as the sails for the windsurfers.

Product market leverage involves the use of customer understanding to launch new products or product experience to penetrate new markets. Harley-Davidson's understanding of what customers were looking for was the key to its massive comeback in the heavy motorbike market. It led to the development of the Super-glide and other popular designs as well as the Harley Ownership Groups, clubs for owners, that shifted the rules of the industry game towards culture-specific dimensions where the Japanese competitors were at a disadvantage.

Using product related expertise to penetrate new markets is what Bill Gates of Microsoft is doing as he attempts to project his company's software expertise into the info-communication and entertainment industries.

Apart from selecting opportunities for development, co-ordination managers are responsible for managing the databank of learning experience – that is, preserving past experience, collecting intelligence from people in the field, sharing know-how between frontline managers and benchmarking against outsiders to bring best practice into the company. Few companies do all of this well. However, more and more are beginning to use interactive information technology to create databases of corporate experience and intelligence.

Co-ordination management's most delicate task is balancing opportunity development against the needs of the mainstream business. A

leading European medical equipment manufacturer found itself struggling to bring out a new generation of medical ventilators to protect itself from increasing competition in the low price end of the market.

So much effort was going into new product development, that if a consulting team had not pointed it out, they would have missed the possibility of simply stripping down and re-packaging an existing product to capture the growing medium-price market. Together with many other cases, this suggests that the task of developing opportunities should be managed separately from the mainstream business.

Top management has to time major resource commitments and mobilize the organization to exploit breakpoint potential

The art of timing the full-scale commitment of resources to an opportunity involves avoiding premature commitment on the one hand, and being too late on the other hand.

Sony committed itself prematurely to the Betamax videorecorder technology and to the introduction of digital audio tape. But its success with numerous other pioneering products such as the Walkman and the camcorder more than offset these lapses.

Philips had the reputation of not getting off the starting blocks. Its VCR 2000 technology was perfected to make it the best available but by the time it got to market the VCR race was half over. Yet, the joint launch of compact discs by Philips and Sony worked out extremely well, the combination of Sony's speed with Philip's perfectionism apparently providing the right timing. Since then, neither the separate launch of the minidisk by Sony nor the digital cassette by Philips has taken off. Co-operating again, this time on interactive video disc technology, Sony and Philips have found themselves recently up against a rival consortium.

In many cases the timing dilemma can only be solved, if at all, by the informed judgment of experts not only in the technology but also the readiness of the market. A breakthrough with a new value-cost offering cannot be made without regard to the cyclical evolution of competitive behavior (see 'Breakpoint: how to stay in the game' page 54).

After Ricoh developed an innovative desktop copier, it took advantage of the opportunity provided by alliances with cost-competitive suppliers of standard parts, assemblers and distribution channels to trigger a delivered cost breakpoint. With existing products looking more and more alike, and customers resisting price increases, the market seemed ready for a low-cost offering by Ricoh. Competitors without an efficient external network were unable to follow.

Once the decision has been made to go for full-scale commitment, the mainstream organization has to make a quantum change. For established companies, this is often the biggest obstacle to exploiting a breakpoint.

IBM's experience dramatically illustrates this. Highly successful in applying directed innovation to the creation of the IBM PC and in using that innovation to trigger a low-cost breakpoint, the corporation had enormous difficulty in lining up its mainstream organization with the resulting new rules of the computer industry game.

The most effective way to mobilize a mainstream organization depends on its corporate culture, especially on its openness to change. Organizations that are closed to change are typically tightly run. They require a sudden, radical move to break the resistance to change. In more open organizations an incremental approach that creates less organizational trauma and is therefore less costly can be used.

The two basic types of closed culture can be described as *role-based* and *power-based* (reflecting a classification developed by Roger Harrison). In both cases, change driven from the top is expected and therefore likely to be effective. A role-based culture can sometimes be mobilized by confrontation – through an alliance or acquisition – with another culture that is closer to the industry change force. For power-based cultures, however, this is often not enough. A sharper shock in the form of total re-structuring is typically needed to re-orient the organization.

Corporate cultures that are more open to change can be said to be *task-based* or *star-based*. Both of these kinds of organizations are driven primarily from the bottom. Once the potential to create an industry breakpoint has been identified, task-based organizations can be invited to implement it, often by cascading the implications of the opportunity down through the teams and task forces. In the looser, star-based, culture it is more natural to let the change percolate up through the organization from the front-line unit that identified the breakpoint potential. In these two cases, what looks like a quantum leap from the outside is, internally, a gradual process that results in significant change.

Creating breakpoints, to take the lead in an industry, requires the ability to orchestrate the three-part learning organization. Capable managers have to be identified, developed and put into place. This means making sure that frontline managers can innovate, network, systematize, improve and re-engineer. Those co-ordinating select and develop the opportunities created by the frontliners. Those at the top can commit the company to make the necessary quantum move when they sense that the timing is right. The top-flight companies of the future will be those that can create breakpoints whenever the industry environment provides the opportunity.

Summary

Generating, rather than reacting to, an industry breakpoint requires a three-point learning approach (see Figure 1). Frontline managers

Frontline managers	Middle managers	Top managers
■ Experimentation ■ Problem solving	Manage opportunity portfolio to provide: ■ Learning from own experience ■ Learning from others ■ Transfer of knowledge	■ Provide climate for frontliners and middle managers ■ Commit the company to exploit industry breakpoints from time to time
Discover new opportunities	**Select and develop new opportunities**	**Time full-scale exploitation of opportunities**

Figure 1 The three-part learning organization

must have a mandate to discover new opportunities through directed innovation, spontaneous innovation, stakeholder networking, systematization, continuous improvement (people and processes rather than products and organization) and process re-engineering. Putting any of these in place requires time, a focussed effort and a dedicated internal change program.

Global co-ordination can help here. Co-ordination managers act as gatekeepers deciding which opportunities discovered by the frontline deserve additional resources and attention. Competencies can be leveraged – the level of technology, business systems and product markets. Co-ordination managers are responsible for the databank of a company's learning experience: their most delicate task is balancing opportunity development against the mainstream needs of the business.

Top management has to mobilize the organization to exploit breakpoint potential as well as time the commitment of resources. The most effective manner will depend on a company's openness to change.

Management in the information era

■ **Our concept of management is going out of date. Information is the new resource and all companies are information companies and all managers information managers.**
Michael Earl **considers the implications.**

Our models of management originate from the industrial era. Today we are clearly well on our way towards the post-industrial or information era. Perhaps more than halfway through the transition from the old to the new economy, we can begin to see what the future looks like.

The fundamental difference is how we view business resources. Those of us brought up in the close of the industrial era were taught that resources of business comprised the 'four Ms' – men, machines, materials and money. Today we must add a fifth resource – information.

The way in which management in the future, therefore, has to change is that managers must understand information as a resource. We have to be able to manage information as an asset, both as a lever for business development and as a process for managing organizations. In short, every business becomes an information business and every manager becomes an information manager.

The information resource

As the key resource in the post-industrial era, information is the energy of enterprise, generating new products and services and enabling new ways of managing. But what is information? Defining and conceptualizing information has kept academics occupied for years and their conclusions are often conditioned by their base disciplines.

Scientists and technologists often see information as signals and are concerned with information as a matter of code, transmission and reception. Sociologists and psychologists frequently see information as communication and are concerned with cognition, interpretation and meaning.

Political scientists tend to connect information with power and are concerned with its distribution and manipulation. Information management academics seek distinctions between data, information and knowledge, often linking information value to decision-making.

Economists seemingly have most trouble dealing with information because, as a commodity, it differs from other resources. It is not necessarily scarce. Information exchange does not necessarily equate with traditional models of value exchange; if I pass on information to someone else, the receiver may gain value but I do not automatically lose value. And information can travel almost instantaneously and at trivial cost. Furthermore, the potential uses, and thus added value, of information are limitless.

These characteristics tend to torpedo traditional theories of the economics of trade and organization. Conversely, they pose both threats and opportunities for business; rules of competition and the market-place can be blown apart by creative use of information.

So if you are concerned about growing or preserving a business in the future, you have to see information as a resource and understand it as best you can. Implicitly or explicitly, you will need policies for acquisition, stewardship and use of information.

However, because information is intangible, this is easier said than done.

For example, since we cannot ever know the full scope of information that is available and since one person sees information in a piece of data or a message, which another does not, how can we be sure what information to collect and how? Then again, how is information stored? It is not just stored either on paper or electronically; it is stored in latent or actual form in our individual minds or collective memories. What, then, does stewardship of information mean?

And since use is unpredictable and can be 'good' or 'bad' depending upon the circumstances, what is the required balance between information freedom and information control?

These may seem arcane deliberations in a business context. However, when you realize that every business is an information business and every manager an information manager, they become ever more important issues for

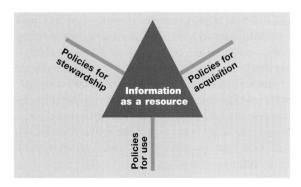

Figure 1: Information resource management

management in the future. We will need policies in the areas suggested in Figure 1.

Every business is an information business

In the last ten years or so, we have distinguished so-called information-intensive sectors from traditional ones. Financial services, airlines and retailers have been classic examples of the former.

We recognize that financial services businesses are factories of information transactions where new products are developed by mining databases of customer events and financial flows and trading is conducted through screen-based electronic markets.

We tire of hearing that competition in airlines is substantially based on commanding electronic channels of distribution via reservation systems and on aggressive sales and yield management by analysis of customer databases.

We see retailers investing in customer cards not just to offer frequent and volume purchasing discounts but to capture individual consumer behavior in order to customize offerings and develop newly targeted services.

So as computing, media and telecommunications converge, such businesses are building stepping stones to an information-driven market-place by creating home pages, shopping malls and information services over the Internet; by creating ventures with telecommunications companies and software houses, and by buying and appropriating information content.

The latest expression of this is the coming

together of media, entertainment and network companies to create the 'infotainment' sector. New sectors are emerging and conventional sector boundaries are being eroded. All these businesses are information businesses – they see information (broadly defined) as underpinning their business and information transmission or communication as their distribution channel. And the new businesses of tomorrow are being founded on information.

We see the entrepreneurs on our MBA programs building business plans for information-based businesses – multimedia forms of retailing, database analysis and marketing ventures, and electronic trading systems. The entrepreneurs and intrapreneurs of the industrial age are now being replaced by the 'infopreneurs' of the information age.

Strategic response

So what are the implications for today's and tomorrow's executives? Clearly they need an information strategy.

This includes, obviously, a technology platform strategy that ensures an appropriate infrastructure through which to do business in the information age. They need applications plans that guide investment decisions on the information systems required to support the business.

And they need the information policies described earlier to ensure that the key resource of tomorrow is not squandered by selling or losing information, by squabbling between divisions about who owns and has access to information, by building technology platforms that impede information flows, by developing managers and employees who do not have information skills, or by not thinking about information acquisition, stewardship and use in all the functional strategies that companies put together.

Tomorrow's information policy questions have to be addressed in strategy making for marketing, manufacturing, distribution, human resources, and research and development.

There is, however, a bigger strategic question. In the information age you cannot formulate business strategy as a whole without considering information as an asset. This is exemplified by the current wave of mergers and acquisitions around ownership of both information content and information distribution.

This is why today's information-intensive businesses have to consider threats such as new entrants coming from other sectors – insurers offering banking, retailers offering insurance, software companies offering money transmission and so on – and intermediaries being taken out by direct electronic traders.

Categorization by information intensity, however, is beginning to pose a problem. Conventional or traditional sectors that were not seen to be information-intensive are changing their spots. Who would have predicted that pharmaceuticals companies would buy health management and prescription-processing organizations for their information content or acquire informatics businesses in order to build technology-based health care services?

Could we have foreseen food companies buying up distributors in order to capture more direct information from the marketplace? Would we have imagined oil companies re-examining their retail and distribution strategies as they consider the second-order consequences of the information age? In short, every sector is an information-intensive sector and one vital implication follows.

In the past we have seen the need for information technology strategies to *support* business strategy. More recently, we have understood that IT creates opportunities to do business differently so that the linkage between information strategy and business strategy is *two-way*.

Now we see that, in the future, we cannot divide the two. The future has returned to business strategy making and in order to be positioned for the information age, the future cannot be conceived or planned for without information and technology being considered as strategic factors.

Thus IT strategy and business strategy become one. A business strategy is not complete if the information resource is ignored. Information and IT can *create* (or destroy) business. So the requirement of strategic management in

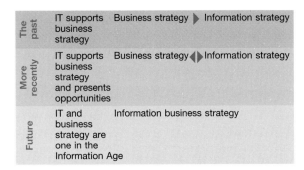

Figure 2: Linking IT and business strategy

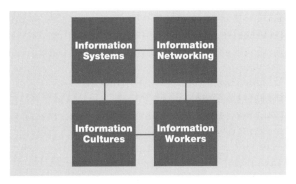

Figure 3: Organizational architecture of tomorrow

the future is to create an information business strategy. (*See* Figure 2)

Now let us consider what managers are doing in this environment. They have to think information in strategy making, they have to analyse and manipulate information in daily decision-making, and they have to manage information resources as IT becomes pervasive.

However, much of managerial work always has been seen to be concerned with information processing. And organization design has been seen as a matter of creating efficient and effective information and communication flows. Broadly defined, information processing occupies a substantial proportion of management and organizational time. So it is not surprising that delayering of organizations has been made possible by a mix of data processing, executive information systems and groupware.

Advanced forms of management information systems have made it possible to centralize and decentralize organizations. Telecommunications across enterprises, between enterprises and from enterprise to home have made virtual organizations a possibility.

One result of all these trends, together with the business changes described above, is that every manager becomes an information manager. Managers are not only expected to be skilled at using IT, they are expected to analyse, explore and play with information. They are expected to collect, add value to and share information. They will have to become as skilled at managing information resources as at managing conventional resources.

Tomorrow's manager probably will take this for granted. Today's managers are experiencing a

paradigm shift where the challenging questions are these. If my business is an information business, does it have a future and is it being mapped out? Since I am an information manager, do I have a future and am I reskilling myself to survive? The organizational architecture of tomorrow is being created today. (Figure 3). Information systems are required to support managers in creativity, decision-making and control. Information networks will exist to collect, share and disseminate information. All employees will be information workers who are skilled at IT use, information analysis and screen-based visualization.

Organizations will have to create cultures where it is easy and acceptable to share information and where meetings and management processes are about adding value to information more than disputing 'facts' and seeking data. Many of today's service and manufacturing sector companies are working through these challenges already and are demonstrating a third characteristic of the information age.

New models required for the information age

The new manager and the new business can be described by extrapolating today's trends. We in the business schools are doing this and can help prepare managers for the future. However our *theories* of management in the future are not robust.

Hitherto, we have seen much of management in the industrial age as being concerned with planning, organization and control. The scenarios of how these activities are practiced in the information age are likely to be very different from the past.

They include a shift from organizational hierarchies to multi-level networks, from bounded to virtual organizations, from decision-making by numbers and analysis to decision-making by exploration and creativity, from work based on physical action to time spent on intellectual reflection, from programed and orchestrated endeavours to business experiments and rapid change, from national and local context to global and cyberspace.

Our models of management are evolving but they cannot yet be robust. In fact, research and development on management in the information age is being done by bold executives in forward-thinking organizations.

Therefore to master management in the future, perhaps business schools and business need to work still more closely together to build the theories required for the information age – an age where it becomes more and more difficult to control information. If you want to, that is!

Summary

Information is now the energy of enterprise, generating new products and services and enabling new ways of managing. A technology platform strategy, applications plans and policies to ensure that information is not squandered are all necessary. In future the linkage between information strategy and business strategy will be more than just two-way – it will be indivisible.

Tomorrow's managers will have to become as skilled at managing information as at managing conventional resources.

Strategic Management and Implementation

Contents

Strategic investment decisions and emergent strategy 562
Patrick Barwise, London Business School
Strategy is rarely just the result of top-level analysis and planning. In practice most strategies emerge from a stream of decisions, especially strategic investment decisions, often initiated by mid-level managers.

Global strategies in the 1990s 572
Vijay K. Jolly, IMD
Global strategies do not mean huge companies operating in a single world market. They are much more complex than that.

The antitrust treatment of intellectual property 577
Dennis A. Yao and Tracy R. Lewis, The Wharton School of the University of Pennsylvania and University of Florida
Innovation often involves 'intellectual property' rather than tangible products and its strategic exploitation may involve licensing arrangements. Intellectual property is a special case that needs special antitrust handling.

Core competencies and service firms 583
Jacques Horovitz, IMD
The concept of core competencies was developed for manufacturing companies. But does it apply equally to organizations in the service sector?

Building resources for competitive advantage 591
Kim Warren, London Business School
Systems thinking and modeling show how companies can use a systematic approach to their resource base to develop meaningful strategic analysis.

Beyond product excellence 599
Dominique V. Turpin, IMD
The Japanese have shown the world how to excel at product quality. But they are changing the rules of the game again. Now the new competitive battleground is customer service.

Keeping ahead in the competitive game 602
George Day and David Reibstein, The Wharton School of the University of Pennsylvania
The essence of competitive strategy formulation is the ability to foresee the moves of competitors.

Alliances can bring hidden benefits 606
Francis Bidault and Thomas Cummings, IMD
Joint ventures and other co-operative dealings between companies can produce hidden benefits that come from the very process of partnership.

Environmental concerns: are they a threat or an opportunity? 609
Georges Haour, IMD
The environment is now firmly on the agenda as a business issue.

Contributors

Patrick Barwise is Professor of Management and Marketing and Director of the Center for Marketing at London Business School. He also heads tthe School's recently launched Future Media Research Programme. His book *Strategic Decisions: Context, Process and Outcomes*, co-edited with Vassilis Papadakis, will be published by Kluwer in 1997.

Dr. Vijay K. Jolly is Professor of Strategy and Technology at IMD, Lausanne.

Dennis A. Yao is Associate Professor of Public Policy and Management at the Wharton School of the University of Pennsylvania, and former Commissioner of the US Federal Trade Commission. Professor Yao's research interests are in the area of antitrust, intellectual property and procurement contracting.

Tracy R. Lewis holds the James Walter Eminent Scholar Chair in the Department of Economics at the University of Florida. He was former economic adviser to Dennis Yao at the Federal Trade Commission.

Jacques Horovitz is Professor of Service Management at IMD, Lausanne. He has also run his own service management consultancy for the last eight years and has written a number of books on the subject. His latest assignment has been with Eurodisney, co-ordinating management and quality development.

Kim Warren is Assistant Professor of Strategic Management at London Business School. His research interests include strategic modeling.

Dominique V. Turpin is Egon Zehnder Fellow of International Management at IMD, Lausanne. He has extensive experience of teaching and research in both Europe and Japan. His research interests include the strategies of Japanese companies inside and outside Japan.

George S. Day is the Geoffrey T. Boisi Professor, Professor of Marketing and Director of the Huntsman Center for Global Competition and Innovation at the Wharton School of the University of Pennsylvania. He has written ten books in the areas of marketing and strategic management and more than 100 articles for leading marketing and management journals.

David J. Reibstein is the William S. Woodside Professor and Professor of Marketing at the Wharton School of the University of Pennsylvania. His research interests include competitive marketing strategy, market segmentation, marketing models and understanding brand choice behavior.

Francis Bidault is a former professor at IMD. He is currently a Professor of Strategy and Innovation Management at Theseus Institute. His research interests include how companies develop and exploit their technology base through strategic alliance.

Contributors

 **Thomas Cummings** is a former research fellow at IMD, conducting research on various subjects, in particular strategic alliances. He is currently a consultant at Paras, a consulting company specializing in technology management, environmental management and business strategy.

 **Georges Haour** is Professor of Technology Management at IMD, Lausanne and former Director of the Managing the Industrial and Business Environment (MIBE) research project. His research interests include innovation management and the management of knowledge workers.

Introduction

Effective strategic management is the ultimate aim of all managers and of most management development programs. Creating and implementing strategy involves drawing together all of the many strands of general management and integrating them towards a common objective.

The Strategic Management and Implementation module of *Mastering Management* builds on all of the previous modules to develop a coherent sense of what evolving and implementing strategy entails.

It begins with an examination of strategic investment decisions and 'emergent' strategy. Further subject areas covered include: global competitive strategies in the 1990s, the role of intellectual property, core competencies for service companies, building resources for competitive advantage, product excellence, business and the environment, and strategic alliances.

Strategic investment decisions and emergent strategy

■ **Most strategies emerge from a stream of decisions, especially strategic investment decisions, often initiated by mid-level managers. As Patrick Barwise explains, this has important, and potentially beneficial, ramifications.**

'When I was younger I always conceived of a room where all these strategic concepts were worked out for the whole company. Later, I didn't find any such room. . . The strategy of the company may not even exist in the mind of one man. I certainly don't know where it is written down. It is simply transmitted in the series of decisions made.' (Interview by J. Brian Quinn 1978, *see* 'Suggested further reading'.)

The 20th century has seen a steady increase in the successful application of structured analysis techniques in business and management, from mass production starting in the 1900s through sophisticated database marketing in the 1990s. Analysis has been shown to outperform seat-of-the-pants management again and again – hence the growth of management consultants and business schools. Management consultancies are still growing fast, bidding up the starting salaries of MBAs from all the top business schools.

But while the mainstream of management thinking is still towards further development of this structured, analytical approach, we are also (in line with fashionable chaos theory) seeing some powerful counterflows. Many leading management thinkers are now arguing that analysis and, especially, planning have been overemphasized. These thinkers stress the need for insight, creativity, learning and innovation, and the 'people' skills.

Beyond top-down strategy

The strongest backlash against analysis and

planning has come in the area of business strategy. Business students still learn techniques of strategy analysis such as Porter's 'Five Forces' and the 'Boston Boxes' (*see* box on p. 563). But few today believe that these macro-analyses can really be used by a small group of people at the top of a large, complex corporation to develop detailed strategies and plans for everyone else to implement. Quite apart from all the people issues, the world is too complicated and unpredictable for strategy to be purely a top-down process, especially in dynamic markets such as high-technology and financial services.

Emergent strategy and investment decisions

In a fast-changing environment, successful strategies tend to emerge from a series of decisions, often initiated by mid-level managers close to markets and technologies. There may well be no detailed written strategy at all, as the introductory quotation illustrates.

The strategic decisions that form the building blocks of this kind of 'emergent' strategy usually involve resource allocation, often including substantial capital investment. Strategic investment decisions (SIDs) therefore have a central role in emergent strategy.

In the rest of this article, I describe emergent strategy, strategic investment decisions, the links between the two, and some implications for managers.

Analysis, planning, implementation and control

The top-down Analysis, Planning, Implementation and Control model still underlies much of what happens in firms, consultancies and business schools – *see* Figure 1 from Philip Kotler's top-selling *Marketing Management* text. But it is seen as a useful abstraction rather than

■ TECHNIQUES OF STRATEGY ANALYSIS

In business schools strategy analysis techniques are taught in courses on strategic management, business economics or marketing. Three widely taught techniques or frameworks are Porter's 'five forces', the 'Boston boxes' and the 'experience curve'.

● Porter's 'five forces'

Michael Porter of Harvard Business School developed a widely used framework that classifies the various forces of competition under five headings for each industry (see Figure A1). Direct competition is from rival companies in the same industry. Industry profitability is also affected by the competitive pressure or threat exerted by four forces external to the industry: suppliers of substitute products; potential new entrants; suppliers to the industry; and buyers. In analysing strategic and investment priorities, managers tend to look for opportunities in industries with weak competitive forces – few rivals, no close substitutes, high barriers to entry, suppliers and buyers with weak bargaining power. Porter's 1980 analysis (see Suggested further reading) explores each of these forces in detail.

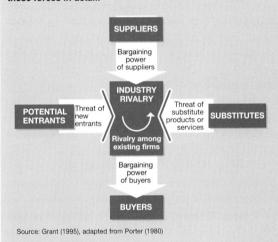

Source: Grant (1995), adapted from Porter (1980)

Figure A1: Porter's 'Five Forces'

● The 'Boston boxes'

The 'Boston boxes'-more formally the Boston Consulting Group's growth-share matrix – is a framework for 'portfolio planning' in a diversified company with many businesses. Each business is located on a two-dimensional grid. One dimension represents industry attractiveness, summarised by the real annual rate of market growth. The other dimension represents the business's competitive position, summarised by its market share relative to its largest competitor. (see Figure A2)

Portfolio planning models such as the 'Boston boxes' are deliberately oversimplified to reduce the amount of data and suggest priorities for further analysis. Their overall thrust, however, is towards investing in high-share businesses in high-growth markets ('stars') and divesting low-share businesses in low-growth markets ('dogs'). Most profit and cash is generated by 'cash cows' (high share, low growth). Much debate is about whether to continue investing in low-share businesses in high-growth markets ('question marks').

Annual real rate of market growth (%)

	High	Low
High	Star	Question Mark
Low	Cash Cow	Dog

High   Low
Relative market share

Figure A2: The 'Boston Boxes'

● The experience curve

Much strategy analysis, including Porter's 'five forces' and especially the 'Boston boxes', encourages companies to seek a dominant market position, reflected in a high relative market share.

Support for this idea comes from the Strategic Planning Institute's influential PIMS (profit impact of market strategy) studies in the 1970s, which found a positive correlation between business profitability and market share. This correlation is lower than many people suppose but, other things being equal, a high market share is associated with an increased return on investment through higher prices (based on product range/quality and bargaining power), lower costs and higher asset turnover.

The cost advantage of a company that dominates its market goes beyond static economies of scale (i.e. with a given technology, a large operation tends to have lower unit costs). The dominant company also has more scope to reduce costs over time by learning from experience.

This idea was studied, developed and disseminated by BCG from the late-1960s, summarised in the Law of Experience – 'The unit cost of value added to a standard product declines by a constant percentage (typically between 20 per cent and 30 per cent) each time cumulative output doubles'. Figure A3 shows a classic industry experience curve from this time.

Experience curves can also be found for individual companies over time and (less reliably) cross-sectionally between companies. Their importance is in focussing on the rate and sources of experience-based cost reduction.

Japanese time recorders 1962-72

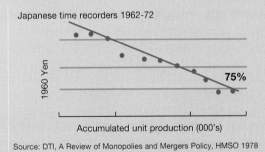

Source: DTI, A Review of Monopolies and Mergers Policy, HMSO 1978

Figure A3: The Experience Curve

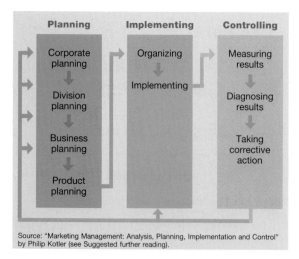

Planning	Implementing	Controlling
Corporate planning	Organizing	Measuring results
Division planning	Implementing	Diagnosing results
Business planning		Taking corrective action
Product planning		

Source: "Marketing Management: Analysis, Planning, Implementation and Control" by Philip Kotler (see Suggested further reading).

Figure 1: The strategic planning, implementation, and control process

an accurate description of what managers actually do.

What do managers do?

Researchers like Henry Mintzberg in North America and Rosemary Stewart in the UK have shown that the reality of management is quite different from the textbook model. Far from being reflective, systematic planners, 'managers work at an unrelenting pace. . . their activities are characterized by brevity, variety and discontinuity, and. . . they are strongly oriented to action and dislike reflective activities' in the words of Mintzberg (*see* 'Suggested further reading').

His research on chief executives also found that – rather than using aggregated information from a formal management information system, as implied by the top-down textbook model – they strongly preferred oral communication either by telephone or face-to-face. Moreover, 93 per cent of these oral contacts were arranged ad hoc.

This research stream spans at least 30 years and covers managers from foremen right up to chief executives, in several countries and many industries. There can be no serious doubt today that the way managers spend their time differs radically from the assumptions of the textbook model of top-down analysis, planning, implementation and control as clear separate activities.

What *should* managers do?

Thirty years ago it was reasonable to equate this chaotic reality with primitive unprofessional management. Managers and companies applying the textbook model would gradually out-perform those that did not, and management would evolve into a science and a profession. This has not happened. Despite the success of analytical techniques in many well-defined areas (such as mass production) the core processes of strategy and line management have not moved to the textbook pattern of Figure 1.

The big change in the last ten years or so is that we are increasingly forced to accept that, if what managers do differs from what the textbooks seem to say they should do, it is at least partly the textbooks, not the managers, that are wrong. We need to look closely at what successful (or effective) managers do if we are to understand where and why the textbook model is wrong.

The Honda story

A telling example of successful strategy is the story of how Honda took over the US motorcycle market in the 1960s – largely at the expense of British manufacturers.

In 1975, the UK government published a report prepared for it by the Boston Consulting Group (BCG) on strategy alternatives for the UK motorcycle industry. The report focussed on the economics of production (using such concepts as the experience curve) and on what BCG assumed was Honda's deliberate strategy for world market domination, described in the following extract:

'As recently as 1960, only four per cent of Japanese motorcycle production was exported. By this time, however, the Japanese had developed huge production volumes in small motorcycles in their domestic markets and volume-related cost reductions had followed. This resulted in a highly competitive cost position which the Japanese used as a springboard for penetration of world markets with small motorcycles in the early 1960s.'

According to this view, amplified in the rest of the report and later by strategy academics, Honda deliberately built a commanding cost advantage and then deliberately targeted the bottom end of the US market (notably with its lightweight 50cc Supercub) to exploit this advantage and outflank the established competition.

This version of the Honda story was a perfect example of the successful application of textbook deliberate top-down strategy using analytical techniques. But when Richard Pascale, a professor from Stanford, flew to Japan in 1982 to interview the six Japanese executives responsible for Honda's entry into the US market in 1959, they gave a quite different account of what actually happened.

According to Pascale (1984), these executives said that the low price of the Honda 50 in 1959 derived from the brilliant design of its powerful but lightweight 50cc engine, not from production economies of scale. In fact, at that stage Honda's production was quite inefficient. It had insufficient capacity to meet orders and had to subcontract much of the production. Faced with overwhelming demand, it did then invest in a large state-of-the-art plant, but this was in response to events rather than as part of a prior deliberate strategy.

The Honda executives' account of what happened when they went to the US in 1959 differs even more dramatically from the BCG version. Far from deliberately aiming to dominate the market by outflanking the competition with smaller machines, they set themselves a target of just 6,000 bikes per year after several years – the timescale was not specified – and actually downplayed their small bikes.

'With no compelling criteria for selection, we configured our startup inventory with 25 per cent of each of our four products – the 50cc Supercub and the 125cc, 250cc and 305cc machines. In dollar value terms, of course, the inventory was heavily weighted towards the larger bikes,' they told Pascale.

The dramatic success of the Honda 50 came about through accident, good luck and Honda US executives' willingness to respond to events and learn from the market. They did not even attempt to sell the small bikes until their larger ones started breaking down badly (serious oil leaks and clutch failures) as a result of being driven harder and longer than in Japan.

'Throughout our first eight months, following Mr Honda's and our own instincts we had not attempted to move the 50cc Supercubs. They seemed wholly unsuitable for the US market where everything was bigger and more luxurious.'

However, they added, 'we used the Honda 50s ourselves to ride around Los Angeles on errands. They attracted a lot of attention. One day we had a call from a Sears buyer. . . but we still hesitated to push the 50cc bikes out of fear they might harm our image in a heavier, macho market. But when the larger bikes started breaking, we had no choice. We let the 50cc bikes move. Surprisingly, the retailers who wanted to sell them were not motorcycle dealers, they were sporting goods stores.'

From this muddled start, Honda gradually and painfully moved towards the brilliant flanking strategy summarized by the slogan: 'You meet the nicest people on a Honda' – as opposed to the rather unpleasant people you were deemed likely to meet on any other motorcycle in the early-1960s.

Analytical concepts such as the experience curve undoubtedly help to explain how Honda was able to turn its initial design advantage in Japan and its unplanned success in the US into the world domination it still enjoys 30 years later. But the actual strategy process that led to this success was the very opposite of the textbook model.

Towards a new paradigm: emergent strategy

The Honda story is an extreme case but it illustrates the general principle that successful strategies need not be clearly formulated in advance.

As Mintzberg pointed out, although people normally equate the word strategy with planning – conscious prior intention – it can also mean other things. In particular, if we look at a company from the outside (the way BCG looked at Honda and the way we usually have to analyse competitors), we do not know its plans, if any. Instead, we here think of strategy as a

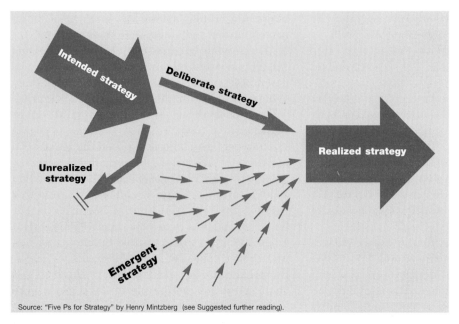

Source: "Five Ps for Strategy" by Henry Mintzberg (see Suggested further reading).

Figure 2: Deliberate and emergent strategies, from Mintzberg (1987)

pattern – consistency in a stream of actions over time. This pattern can only be seen after the event and may be either intended or unintended. Mintzberg's view is summarized in Figure 2 which shows how:

● Some intended (i.e. planned) strategy is not realized. The part that is realized is called *deliberate* strategy.

● Much realized strategy emerges from events that were not part of the intended strategy. This is called *emergent* strategy.

● Realized strategy is a varying combination of deliberate and emergent.

Strategic investment decisions

Mintzberg's concept of emergent strategy ties in with the increasing emphasis in business on adaptability, innovation and learning. As in the Honda story, it implies the need to learn from events and that strategy often develops one step at a time.

The technical buzzword for this is 'incrementalism'. Incrementalism can include large steps (for example, a major acquisition) as well as small. It is not the same as directionless 'muddling through': emergent strategy is a pattern, not a random walk. The individual steps may fit within an overall partly deliberate

strategy ('logical incrementalism') but the strategy must be adaptable.

As already noted, the steps of emergent/ incrementalist strategy usually involve a commitment of resources, including the development or acquisition of new resources. Formally, these steps usually surface within the organization as capital projects ('strategic investment decisions' or 'SIDs').

SIDs have always been seen as important and as one of the issues on which top management spends much time. But within the new paradigm of strategy and management, they can be seen as even more important.

First, most SIDs involve substantial capital expenditure. They therefore form a bridge between finance and strategy, the two very different main languages of top management. Moreover, modern financial analysis of capital projects uses net *incremental* cash flow, focussing on the difference in a company's net cash flow with, versus without, the project. SIDs are therefore well suited to encourage debate about the financial consequences of alternative strategic assumptions.

Second, SIDs involve complex management processes and are a powerful source of organizational learning. Much of the real-life

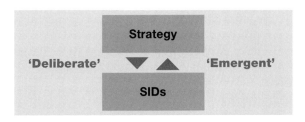

Figure 3: SIDs and strategy

strategy analysis in organizations occurs in the context of SIDs. This applies whether they are seen as the implementation of deliberate strategy or as the individual steps of emergent strategy (see Figure 3).

Must finance and strategy clash?

In principle, there should be no clash between finance and strategy: 'The financial criteria used to decide if a project will be profitable are entirely consistent with the tenets of competitive marketing analysis.' (Barwise et al, 1989, *see* 'Suggested further reading').

Guidelines for analysing SIDs tend to focus on project definition:

- Define the project boundaries (what gets included in the 'with' case)
- Use the right base case (what happens in the 'without' case)
- Choose an appropriate time horizon (long enough to match the period of value creation)
- Evaluate options (projects can both open and close later options)
- Unbundle the costs and benefits (these are often separable)

In addition, the projected cash flows should be discounted at the correct market-based cost of capital (Brealey and Myers 1996, *see* 'Suggested further reading' and *see* also *Mastering Management* Finance Module).

'Unfortunately, the financial analysis is all too often pinned on afterwards. An interactive process that relates the product-market specifics to the wider financial implications is not only a requirement for sound SIDs but also a powerful source of organizational learning.'

Managing SIDs as a process

Good project definition and analysis can help managers make better SIDs. But in large,

complex organizations SID-making also needs to be managed as a process. Typically, this matters more than the use of theoretically correct analytical techniques.

The SID process is usually bottom-up, triggered by divisional operating management. The main exceptions are major acquisitions and divestments. Interestingly, the evidence is that the opportunity is rarely new – usually, a company has explored it (or something very similar) once or twice before. This revisiting of opportunities affects organizational learning (discussed later).

Once the project is triggered, senior managers sponsor it and give it impetus. They also appoint a project team that typically comprizes divisional operating managers plus some support staff. Importantly, the main members of the project team and the project's proposers are likely to be directly involved in its implementation if it goes ahead.

There then follows a complex extended process with many stages and iterations. (This relates to a general feature of emergent strategy, that thinking and doing are not clearly separable). Much of the process consists of planning how the project will be implemented, often exploring minor tactical variations of a single major strategic option.

For example, if the project team becomes committed early on to a plant or warehouse of a particular size in a particular location, most of its energy will go into planning that option to be as efficient as possible and developing a strong case to persuade top management to invest in it.

In many cases top management intervenes before the project is proposed and suggests strategic alternatives, often requiring a radical redefinition of the project. This especially applies if the financial climate in the company becomes tighter, when management may be asked to scale down or postpone all new projects.

Finally, those projects that survive this process and are formally proposed to the board or investment committee are in most cases accepted. But the effective decision will usually have been made much earlier in the process. Indeed, top management must exercise its formal authority – the ability to say no – with care. If too many projects get turned down, a company can lose its best operating managers and discourage others from coming forward with new proposals.

This untidy process reflects the need to motivate operating managers but also the dramatic imbalance of knowledge and time between top management (which has the formal responsibility for allocating capital resources) and the operating managers (who develop and implement the strategic investment projects).

In one case we researched at London Business School, one main board member said to us: 'This project kept coming back – overall I would guess I spent a whole day on it'. In contrast, the project leader spent 140 days working full-time on the project. The project team's paper trail totalled 2,000 pages. This was reduced to two pages for the benefit of the board.

Formal planning and systems

In practice, formal strategic planning has only a minor role in SIDs. The role of group head office planners in divisional SIDs, for example, has been found to be largely administrative, mostly consisting of adding up financial numbers. Their influence on what gets proposed and implemented is minimal. Even within the business units, SIDs do not typically flow from an explicit prior strategy: the relationship between the explicit strategy and the individual strategic projects is complex, two-way and mostly implicit. At both levels – group and business unit – SIDs are dominated by line managers not by staff planners.

It is less clear whether capital budgeting systems have much influence on the process. Modern sophisticated companies have well-developed procedures using discounted cash flow. But – at least in our research – the procedure manuals were hard to locate and were certainly not used by line managers.

Rather, the impression was that junior staff within the business unit used the formal procedure to put the proposal into a form acceptable to head-office bureaucrats. There was no sense that the financial analysis might actually throw light on the strategic issues.

In practice the capital budgeting process leads to 'creeping commitments'. The procedure also uses other criteria in addition to NPV/DCF, especially payback and accounting ROI. These are unambiguously wrong according to modern finance theory. Often the procedure contains technical errors, for example, in the treatment of tax or inflation. (*See* the Finance module, p. 57, for a discussion of some of these issues.)

There are also often errors in the definition of the project. For example, most projects proposed do not have a clearly developed base case, ie what would happen without the investment? Cost and revenue forecasts are often incomplete and may include inconsistencies in the treatment of sunk costs and terminal values. (These issues have been covered in the Finance and Accounting modules.)

All this might sound as if formal capital budgeting systems are a waste of time. This is not so. 'While the formal systems are ritualistic, they are nevertheless necessary. . . They forced the players to be more specific about their key assumptions. . . (and options). . . set deadlines, facilitated the movement of information up, down, and sideways (and generated) commitment to the project.' (Marsh et al, 1988, *see* 'Suggested further reading'.)

The role of top management in SIDs

Top management is involved in SIDs both directly and indirectly. Although, as noted, there is a marked imbalance in time and knowledge between the project proposers and top management, the board will typically include some top managers with more detailed knowledge relevant to the particular project.

In some sectors, such as retailing, the business may be enormous – Wal-Mart is expected to be the biggest company in the world within five years – but because each store is a clone of a corporate formula, most of the board should have enough detailed knowledge to understand most proposals. Even in a diversified corporation, the process exploits the universal feature of management hierarchies that each manager wears 'two hats' as both the leader of one management group and a member of the next most senior group (*see* Figure 4).

This means that at each stage of the process

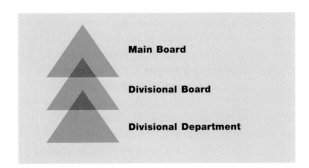

Figure 4: Senior Managers wear 'Two Hats'

one top manager, who typically has more detailed knowledge of the issues, is involved before the rest of his or her colleagues. As the process goes on, this manager may step in directly to suggest other options, question assumptions and test for commitment. Once satisfied, such managers inevitably become sponsors and advocates for the project, although this is rarely clearcut. On this basis, it would be quite wrong to think that top managers have no direct role in bottom-up SIDs. They intervene selectively but their influence can be strong.

In addition, top management influences SIDs indirectly both by managing the process of each major project – through the appointment of people into the project team and by setting limits, deadlines and project-specific criteria – and by controlling the broader organizational context. This context includes not only the reporting structure but also the performance measurement and reward systems and the style adopted by top managers in dealing with others.

The Honda story illustrates how Mr Honda himself gave the fledgling US team some initial advice (almost entirely wrong, in the event) but also the freedom and encouragement to adapt the strategy and turn what might have been a fiasco into one of the greatest business successes of the last 50 years.

Short-termism and politics
Top management also controls the capital budgeting criteria and these will have some influence on what gets proposed and implemented. In particular, if top management uses a DCF hurdle rate above the risk-adjusted cost of capital, or emphasizes payback or accounting ROI,

the firm will have a short-termist bias against investing in profitable long-term projects.

This bias is mitigated by the fact that project proposers to some extent adapt the numbers in their proposals to meet the company's criteria. They may do this partly by adjusting the cost and revenue assumptions, as cynics have long believed.

Our research suggests, however, that they mostly do something more subtle, choosing project definitions creatively in order to secure support for all projects they believe will increase the value of the business. So a project with strategic value, but which is hard to justify on the financial numbers, may be redefined by excluding overhead investment such as in IT or buildings so that the redefined project meets the required hurdles. Conversely, investment in infrastructure will tend to be bundled into other more demonstrably profitable projects.

This political behavior by project proposers does not mean that top management should necessarily try to control the process more closely. Effective product-market strategies grow from a detailed understanding of the market, the technology and the organization's competitive capabilities. Most of that knowledge is at an operating level. The proposers should know far more about the issues than top management and should also be able to run circles around any accountant sent from head office to 'police' project proposals.

The scarce resources are good projects and managers, not capital
More important, SIDs should not typically be seen as a process in which top management allocates a scarce resource – capital – to the most deserving supplicants. Capital is a commodity and should not normally be the scarce resource.

Most of the time, most large well-managed companies are not constrained by a lack of capital (exceptions include small businesses, companies in less-developed capital markets and companies in distress). Instead, the constraint on value creation is a lack of good projects and good managers (and others) to dream them up, develop and implement them.

Capital rationing may be used as a device to

encourage disciplined thinking. But if this device is used too heavily and capital is rationed excessively over long time periods, shareholder value is likely to be destroyed through underinvestment and failure to sustain the product and process innovation, the production capacity, the marketing and distribution, and the energy and enthusiasm needed for long-term market success.

One related implication of the emergent strategy perspective is a more positive view of middle management. Especially in the UK and US, we have often heard how middle managers act as a constraint on the successful implementation of strategy and a brake on corporate change and renewal. But in a world where much strategy is emergent, often through SIDs and other bottom-up developments, middle managers are a key resource.

'In the long run. . . a company's productivity depends to a great extent on how innovative its middle managers are' (Rosabeth Moss Kanter, 1982, *see* 'Suggested further reading'.)

SIDs as organizational learning

SIDs also play a major role in both organizational and individual learning.

Arie de Geus, former chief planner at Shell, gave a powerful and succinct definition of organizational learning in a Harvard Business Review article in 1988 (*see* 'Suggested further reading'): 'the process whereby management teams change their shared mental models of their company, their markets and their competitors.'

This definition emphasizes several key features of organizational learning. First, it is a process, not a type of analysis. Second, it is something done by managers, not by planners or any other support staff. Third, it is done by teams, not just individuals. Fourth, it involves change, which may be painful. This is unlikely to come from just following the formal procedure in a planning manual. Fifth, the thing which has to change to achieve organizational learning is managers' mental models, and preferably the mental models that are to some extent shared by different members of the management team.

Again, this is not achieved by writing numbers in boxes, the main activity involved in much so-called strategic planning. Finally, these mental models are about the company, its markets and its competitors, i.e. the elements of market-oriented competitive strategy.

The question de Geus sought to address was what induces such change. The answer that emerged was that organizational learning and change are induced by managers (and maybe others) working together on a problem that engages their energy.

The most energizing problem is a crisis. Many managers love crises and thrive on them. But crisis management involves high costs and risks. These may be unavoidable in cases where the company is unlikely to survive without drastic action. But for most companies most of the time the dominant challenge to management – bar none – is to induce value-creating organizational change without (or before) a crisis.

Routine planning systems are hopeless at this, especially if they are closely integrated with the budgeting system used for control. Budgeting is an inherently political process that most managers find mind-numbingly boring and which is mainly negotiation about targets and resources.

The annual planning/budgeting round is unlikely to involve managers 'working together on a problem that engages their energy' and is certainly ill-suited to the creative and open-minded exploration of strategic options. Managers often complain that the planning system has become an inflexible, costly, paper-shuffling exercise. Most major strategic decisions are made outside this framework of routine annual planning.

In contrast, SIDs are an excellent example of a process whereby management teams 'change their shared mental models of their company, their markets and their competitors'. That is, a SID has all the key features of organizational learning.

You can learn a lot from SIDs

A SID can also be a powerful source of individual learning by members of the project team. One notable feature of SIDs is that project team members become highly involved and committed to the project's success while also building new relationships inside and often outside the firm. SIDs also help these individuals develop beyond technical mastery of their previous specialisms towards a broader managerial view that includes a better understanding of other peoples' perspectives.

Top managers consciously use the appointment to such project teams as a way of developing high potential managers. Often, a project is the first opportunity for a particular young manager to be exposed to top management, and vice versa.

If your boss offers you the chance to work on a strategic investment project, jump at the opportunity. You will have to work long hours but the skills you will learn will be excellent preparation for managing in the 21st century.

Summary

Far from being reflective, systematic planners – as in the textbook model – managers in reality operate on a surprisingly ad hoc basis. The Honda story (as told to Richard Pascale) is a good example of how successful strategies need not be clearly formulated in advance. Realized strategy is a varying combination of deliberate and emergent (i.e. it emerges from events that were not part of the intended strategy). Such 'incrementalist' strategy ties in with the growing emphasis these days on adaptability, innovation and learning. In large complex organizations, strategic investment decision-making (SID) needs to be managed as a process, usually from the bottom up. Top managers intervene selectively, though their influence can be strong. Capital is not the scarce resource and should only be rationed to encourage disciplined thinking; good middle managers are the key ingredient.

Organizational learning and change are induced by managers (and maybe others) working together on a problem that engages their energy – SIDs are an excellent example of how this can be done. A SID can also be a powerful source of individual learning for members of the project team.

Suggested further reading

Barwise, P., Marsh, P and Wensley, R 'Must finance and strategy clash?' *Harvard Business Review,* September-October 1989.

Brealey, Richard A. and Myers, S C (1991) 5th edn *Principles of Corporate Finance* McGraw-Hill.

de Geus, A. 'Planning as learning', *Harvard Business Review*, March-April 1988.

Grant, R. M. (1995) 2nd edn *Contemporary Strategy Analysis* Blackwell.

Kanter, R. M. 'The middle manager as innovator' *Harvard Business Review* July-August 1982.

Kotler, P. (1994) 8th edn *Marketing Management: Analysis, Planning, Implementation, and Control,* Prentice-Hall.

Marsh, P., Barwise, P., Thomas K. and Wensley, R. (1988) *Managing Strategic Investment Decisions* Center for Business Strategy, London Business School.

Mintzberg, H. 'The manager's job: folklore and fact' *Harvard Business Review* July-August 1975.

Mintzberg, H. 'Five Ps for strategy' *California Management Review,* Fall 1987.

Papadakis, V. and Barwise, R. (eds) (1997) *Strategic Decisions: Context, Process and Outcomes* Kluwer.

Pascale, R. T. 'Perspectives on strategy: the real story behind Honda's success' *California Management Review* (Spring 1984).

Porter, M. E. (1980) *Competitive Strategy* Free Press.

Quinn, J. B. 'Strategic change: logical incrementation', *Sloan Management Review* Fall 1978.

Global strategies in the 1990s

■ **Global strategies do not mean huge companies operating in a single world market. They are, as Vijay Jolly explains, much more complex than that.**

Global competitive strategies are a bit like supernatural creatures – they can be imagined by each individual to suit his or her own reality while evoking a common concern. The best illustration are the slogans companies use to describe themselves. These range from 'Think Local Act Global' (Komatsu) all the way to its opposite 'Think Global Act Local (ABB) with everything in between.

Defining global strategies

Some 15 years have gone by since the term 'global strategy' entered our vocabulary, enough time to bring some clarity to its definition. We now know at least what it is and what it is not.

Consider first what it is not. Global strategies are not standard product-market strategies that assume the world to be a single, homogeneous, border-free marketplace. The Uruguay Round of trade and investment liberalization notwithstanding, the world is still a collection of different independent economies, each with its own market characteristics. Each, moreover, has its own societal aspirations that occasionally find expression in protectionist policies of one form or another.

Global strategies are also not about global presence or about large companies. A company can very well operate in all countries of the world. But if what it does in one country has no meaning for what it does in others, it is no different from the domestic companies it competes with everywhere.

To qualify as pursuing a global strategy, a company needs to be able to demonstrate two things:

● that it can contest any market it chooses to compete in
● that it can bring its entire worldwide resources to bear on any competitive situation it finds itself in, regardless of where that might be.

Selective contestability. Just as companies possessing a certain set of technologies and business competencies choose particular market segments to concentrate on, a global company can be selective about the countries in which it operates.

Many small, high-technology companies and luxury good manufacturers do just that. They compete where there is adequate demand to justify the investments needed to access the market; they focus their investments to achieve critical mass only in those markets they are interested in.

The important thing, however, is that they can and are prepared to contest any and all markets should circumstances warrant. They constantly scour the world for market openings, they process information on a global basis, and they constitute a 'potential' threat even in places where they have not yet entered.

Markets where such contestability exists, as a corollary, start to behave almost as if the company had already entered – provided, of course, the threat of entry is a credible one. This explains why telecom markets the world over are so fiercely competitive from the day they get liberalized – actually months and even years before the liberalizing rules come into force. The handful of international players in the equipment business are not only waiting in the wings but have products that conform to international standards and resources they can deploy for market access as soon as need arises.

Global resources for each Main Street. The corner shop that carries products by IBM,

Philips, Coca Cola or Du Pont knows from experience that there is something special about these products compared to those supplied by a small local company. In comparison, products from companies such as Nestle, Unilever or even Procter and Gamble did not seem so special – in the past at least. Their names, formulations and the way they were produced and marketed were not too different from domestic ones.

Just being present in several countries, in other words, does not constitute a global strategy. Globalism is an earned notion rather than being an entitlement created by the fact of operating in several countries.

A basic characteristic of a global company is that, regardless of the products it makes, it is able to bring its entire worldwide capabilities to bear on any transaction, anywhere. This underlies the importance of organizational integration in global strategies. Transporting capabilities across borders on an as-needed basis requires all local units to be connected and permeable, not isolated from one another.

This is also what allows global strategies to be 'within-border' strategies while, at the same time, being 'cross-border' ones. They are manifest on each Main Street, with local companies sensing they are dealing with a worldwide organization even while the latter employs a local competitive formula.

Main attributes of global strategy

This dual notion of market contestability and bringing global resources to bear on competition wherever a company is present is really what global strategies are about. Industries where such strategies are prevalent assume a character of their own, where no one can adopt strategies that are geared to one country alone. What companies do in one country has an inevitable consequence for what they do in others.

There is, of course, nothing absolute about global strategies. Being near-cousins of multi-domestic strategies, the best way to judge them is in terms of 'degrees of globalness'. At the risk of oversimplification, the more a company scores in each of the following five attributes, the more it can be considered a global competitor based on the definition just given:

- possessing a standard product (or core) that is marketed uniformly across the world
- sourcing all assets, not just production, on an optimal basis
- achieving market access in line with the break-even volume of the needed infrastructure
- the ability to contest assets as much as products when circumstances require
- providing all functions (or competencies) with a global orientation, even if they are primarily local in scope.

Standard products and marketing mix. While the advantages of having a standard product and marketing mix are obvious, this attribute involves several trade-offs in practice. Economies of scale in design, production and promotion need to be compared to the greater market acceptance that local adaptation often provides.

If a general conclusion can be drawn it would be the need at least to aim for a standard 'core' in the product and limiting marketing adaptations to those absolutely necessary. The more integrated countries become economically, the less latitude there is anyway for things such as price discrimination and channel selection. The same applies to situations where buyers themselves are global and expect similar products and terms on a worldwide basis.

Sourcing assets not just products. Sourcing products and components internationally based on comparative advantage and availability has long been a feature of international business. What is new is the possibility to source assets or capabilities related to any part of the company's value chain. Whether it is capital from Switzerland or national credit agencies, software skills from Silicon Valley or Bangalore, or electronic components from Taiwan, global companies now have a wider latitude in accessing resources from wherever they are available or cost-competitive.

The implication of this is that global strategies are as much about asset deployment for market access purposes as they are about asset accumulation abroad. The latter include local capital, technical skills, managerial talent, new product ideas as well as the host competencies that local partners and institutions can provide. Also, whereas previously assets accumulated locally were mainly to support a local business, it is increasingly possible – and desirable – to separate those needed for local market access from those intended to support the company's business elsewhere.

It is here that we associate partnerships and alliances with global strategy. They can supplement what a company already possesses by way of assets or complement what is missing, thereby speeding up the creation of the needed infrastructure as well as reducing costs and risks.

Market access in line with break-even. For a company to be a credible global competitor it does not need to be among the biggest in its industry. But it has to be big enough to generate the volume of sales the required infrastructure demands and to amortize up-front investments in R&D and promotion.

Today, it is the latter investments that count most. In the pharmaceutical industry, for example, it now costs around $400m to come up with a successful new drug. This puts a natural floor on the amount of sales to be generated over the life of the drug. The greater the presence of a company in all of the large markets, and the greater its ability to launch the drug simultaneously in them, the higher the likelihood of profiting from the investment made.

The same argument applies to other investments in intangibles such as brands. If we associate global competitiveness with size, it is chiefly on account of these types of investments. Unlike investments in plants and physical infrastructure, which can result in diminishing returns to scale, intangibles almost always translate into 'big is better'.

Contesting assets. Another distinguishing feature of a global company is its ability to neutralize the assets and competencies of its competitors. If a competitor switches its supply from a high-cost to a low-cost factory it too can do so; if a competitor gains access to a critical technology it can do the same; similarly, if a competitor is using one market to generate excess cash flow in order to 'invest' in another, it is able to neutralize this advantage by going to the relatively more profitable market itself.

Purely domestic companies and even those that are run on a multidomestic basis, lack such arbitrage possibilities. Just as in sourcing, to exploit these requires a global view of the business and the capacity to manage it in an integrated fashion.

All functions have a global orientation. As much of the foregoing suggests, global competition today is a lot more than about simple cross-border competition at the product or service level. It is equally about building and managing a multinational infrastructure. Frequently, the latter means internationalizing all of the competencies and functions of a company – its R&D, procurement, production, logistics, marketing as well as human resources and finance.

These functions are all geared to providing customers with superior products and services on a worldwide basis. The more they have a global orientation of their own the greater their contribution to the overall effort. Hence, even if their focus may be primarily national in scope, supporting a local business with no trade, for example, any contribution they can make to other units of the company helps.

All of these five attributes, taken together, operationalize a global strategy. The degrees of globalness in a strategy is the extent to which each is fulfilled in practice. The fact of not having a standard global product, for example, diminishes the scope of a global strategy but does not entirely destroy it, provided the company scores high on the other attributes. If anything, stressing one attribute to the exclusion of others can even be counter productive and unfeasible. What one needs is a good balance between all of them.

Local adaptation

Another important point to make about these attributes is that they do *not* assume a single, open global marketplace. Trade and investment liberalization coupled with improvements in transportation and communications are what have made global strategies possible. Trade protection, labor policies, investment incentives and a host of regulations continue to force a country-by-country adaptation of strategies.

It is also these realities, along with the

sociocultural differences between countries, that have caused many companies to stress the 'local' dimension in their business. And rightly so. If all companies confront the same set of market conditions, advantage goes to those who adapt their strategies best.

The best way to reconcile these local differences with the attributes required of a global strategy is to see them as constraints to global optimization. Localness, in other words, is another variable to incorporate in decision-making. Considering it as the basis for the strategy itself, however, is to deny all of the advantages a global company possesses. This is perhaps the biggest conundrum companies face today.

While adapting strategies to local conditions offers greater opportunities for revenue generation it has two main impacts:

● it causes over-investment in the infrastructure needed to serve markets

● it brings about a lack of consistency in whatever strategy is being pursued.

Neither is intrinsically bad. They can even contribute positively to the end result if approached correctly. All that is needed is to factor them in as variables to be considered, without losing sight of the overall objective of competing effectively both within and across borders. Consider the issue of over-investment, especially in capital intensive businesses such as semiconductors. While Intel has all its fabrication in the US, companies such as Texas Instruments, NEC and Mitsubishi Electric have consciously located abroad.

This not only permits them to benefit from generous investment incentives provided by local governments that want such facilities it also means they can mobilize local companies as co-investors to share the capital burden and help with market access.

More contentious is the issue of strategic focus. Should local subsidiaries be allowed to modify products and diversify into businesses that make sense for them only? Or should they be consistent with what the parent company focuses on? The answer to this depends on several things: a company's definition of its business scope and growth vectors; the sub-

sidiary's domain within the overall organization as well as the locus of its strategy making process.

Business scope and growth vectors pertain to a company's attitude to diversification generally. If its products and technologies provide adequate growth opportunities on a worldwide basis it is probably better off restricting each subsidiary to just those. If, on the other hand, growth is primarily driven through exploring and creating new market opportunities then local initiatives are usually welcome.

Logitech SA, a world leader in pointing devices for the personal computer industry, for example, permitted and even encouraged its Taiwanese company to develop special software products for the Chinese market because that would be an additional product to fuel its growth, reduce its dependence on the mouse and, incidentally, facilitate access to a new market. A company that comes up with a new cancer treatment, on the other hand, is likely to want to invest all its resources in commercializing that worldwide as quickly as possible.

The more a company's infrastructure and skills become dispersed and the more global responsibilities individual subsidiaries take on, the greater the need to see the initiation of strategies as a global process. What the parent knows and sees may not be the same as subsidiary management. Giving subsidiaries too narrow a mission based on a centralized notion of between-country competition not only constrains their potential for accumulating local resources but diminishes their potential for competing within their country as well.

Organizational implications

How companies ought to structure and manage their international operations has naturally been debated for as long as the debate on strategy itself. Because organizations need to reflect a wide range of company-specific characteristics – such as size, diversity, age, culture, technology – in addition to their global posture, it has proven hard to be normative. There are, however, certain key design considerations related to global posture that have dominated thinking and practice in recent years.

The most important consideration has to do with the greater need for organizational integration that global strategies require. Hence, when companies first tried to adapt their structures in the 1970s and early-1980s, most of them created elaborate matrix organizations giving equal status to products, geography and functions. While such organizations worked well for some companies, ABB being the leading example, they did not for others. ABB succeeded because of the nature of its business, its superior information system (called Abacus), its investment in developing a number of globally minded managers and a small but highly effective top management team. What ABB was able to do was to balance finely the need for local autonomy in decision-making with the strategic and organizational integration that managing the business on a global basis demanded.

Others that were not able to achieve this balance opted for tilting their matrix in favour of one or the other dimension. Most often, the dominant dimension became product groups or strategic business units, the assumption being that integrating each product's business system on a worldwide basis was the best way to optimize strategy and achieve coherence among different local units.

Where these 'product headquarters' were located mattered less and many companies consciously spread them around as a better way to integrate country organizations, give particular local managers a broader domain to look after and to exploit country-specific assets or competencies. Such dispersal had the attendant benefit of also reducing the role (and size) of corporate headquarters.

This fine tuning of structures continues today. To the extent one can discern a trend for the 1990s it would be one consisting of three things:
● reverting to a single locus of direction and control
● giving greater emphasis to functional strategies instead of business-by-business ones
● creating simple line organizations based on a more decentralized 'network' of local companies.

The move to a single locus is partly on account of the difficulty companies have experienced in managing dispersed product headquarters. The complex interactions between units they gave rise to, the lack of global reach on the part of some country organizations and the potential for confusion between corporate roles and business unit functions were apparently not compensated by whatever advantage they offered. But it is equally on account of the recognition of the importance of a coherent set of values, goals and identity, as well the need to avoid duplication of functions across the world.

Having functions as the primary dimension to co-ordinate global strategies also reflects the dual nature of the latter, combining asset deployment for market access reasons and asset accumulation for sourcing purposes. Another virtue of a functional orientation is that it is usually at this level that global alliances and asset accumulation takes place – the R&D function co-operating with other companies' R&D departments, procurement with suppliers, finance with local finance companies and so on.

While marketing can and should be managed nationally or regionally, R&D, finance and manufacturing lend themselves better to global co-ordination. Texas Instruments, for example, used to manage its business, including manufacturing, on a regional basis. Four years ago, it introduced the notion of the 'virtual fab', linking all its 17 manufacturing sites around the world into a single organization.

In addition to standardizing equipment and procedures across plants this allows the company to transfer expertise across units efficiently, allocate production optimally and interact with development on a global basis. Whereas, previously, the company had country-by-country sales forces it now has market-based teams with global responsibility for a product's success (*Business Week*, August 7, 1995, p. 46). The latter has proved particularly effective in serving the needs of global customers who expect similar conditions worldwide.

Whether to have a single set of global functions or to have them specialized by business unit depends on how diverse the latter are. The lesson companies have learned, however, is to avoid overly complex matrix structures and to allow local units sufficient autonomy at the business level.

The last point refers to the way individual units in a global company need to be treated. Based on the arguments made earlier, what one is seeing is an upgrading of their role, both as a locus for independent entrepreneurial effort as well as contributors to the business worldwide.

To perform this expanded role coherently they need greater empowerment coupled with all of the things that a network organization possesses – a commonly shared knowledge base, common values and goals, a common understanding of priorities and precommitments others have made, and a common set of measures to judge performance.

Shared values are known to replace the need for elaborate direction and control. Rather than planning for the synergies and interdependencies that are at the heart of a global strategy, effective networks create them voluntarily and in real-time. Global strategies in their present form have proved far too complex and demanding to be implemented in a centralized manner.

Summary

Companies with a genuinely global strategy can compete in any market they choose to enter, and can bring their entire worldwide capabilities to bear on any transaction, anywhere. Specific attributes include: possessing a standard product marketed uniformly across the world; sourcing all assets (e.g. capital and software skills as well as products and components) on an optimal basis; generating a volume of sales the local infrastructure demands; an ability to neutralize the assets and competencies of competitors when circumstances require; and internationalizing all functions such as R&D procurement, logistics and HR, even if they are primarily local in scope.

While adapting strategies to local conditions offers greater opportunities for revenue generation, it can cause over-investment in the infrastructure needed to serve markets and bring about a lack of strategic consistency. At an organizational level, the 1990s are seeing a move back to a single locus of direction and control (from dispersed product headquarters), a greater emphasis on functional strategies instead of business-by-business ones, and the creation of simple line organizations based on a more decentralized 'network' of local companies.

The antitrust treatment of intellectual property

■ 'Intellectual property', and its strategic exploitation may involve licensing arrangements. These can lead to antitrust actions, but argue Dennis Yao and Tracy Lewis, intellectual property needs special antitrust handling.

Antitrust policy towards intellectual property has traditionally focussed on defining the permissible restrictions that the property holder could initially impose on its licensees.

In recent US Federal Trade Commission cases, however, issues relating to 'downstream' renegotiation or reacquisition of licenses by the property holder have been important. In this section, we explore the policy issues raised by these downstream considerations and suggest a criterion for analysing their antitrust impli-

cations. Reacquisitions of licenses or renegotiations of license terms may become desirable
from a business perspective as new information
about technology and/or the market becomes
available.

New information may suggest that the initial
license agreement has deficiencies to be
remedied. While any inter-company relationship
has the potential to be improved through downstream renegotiation, arrangements involving
intellectual property are particularly ripe for
improvements.

This is because intellectual property licensing
generally involves new technology and markets
that are typically characterized by great uncertainty. These arrangements also often involve
entrepreneurs or companies venturing into
functions and markets that are new to them.
Also, such arrangements often require the
formation of untested partnerships that sometimes require adjustments over time.

What differentiates intellectual property from other forms of property?

Many argue that intellectual property should be
treated the same as other property and not be
given special status. For example, regulators
should allow any type of license or combination
with another company except when that
company is an actual or potential competitor.

However, identical treatment may only mean
that the framework for assessing agency action
should remain the same. It is possible that
intellectual property as a class will generally
present different issues and situations than
other types of property, and these differences, in
turn, will often lead to different antitrust
decisions.

Uncertainty. There are uncertainties regarding
the value of intellectual property and how it can
best be used and marketed. Furthermore, the
inventor is likely to know more about the
characteristics of intellectual property than
either potential licensees or the antitrust agency.
Uncertainty also exists because the novelty
normally associated with intellectual property
implies that the uses and future development
potential of the intellectual property are often
not well known.

In many cases a pure sale or simple transfer of
the license may be problematic because of the on-
going development of the intellectual property.
Innovations that are likely to be the base for
future patentable and unpatentable small and
large improvements pose additional problems for
potential licensing or venturing partners.

Intellectual property is often invented by
individuals or companies that are not best suited
to exploiting the property. This feature makes
some sort of sale, license or joint venture
appropriate both for private and social welfare
reasons. The need to find the optimal, or at least
an acceptable, partner exacerbates the problems
of uncertainty discussed above because sale or
contracts now must be negotiated by two or more
groups with potentially widely differing views
about the future.

While these uncertainties and information
asymmetries also exist for other inputs, they
exist to a greater degree with intellectual
property. Consequently, licensing contracts are
likely to be complicated and to contain special
features for dealing with information problems.

Differences between intellectual property and
ordinary property also exist regarding the need
to renegotiate contracts. When there is significant uncertainty about the value and use of
intellectual property, parties may renegotiate
contracts more often. Renegotiations may arise
because it is impossible to anticipate the types of
changes in conditions necessitating contract
adjustments in the future. Even where changes
in conditions can be predicted, such conditions
may be difficult to verify, thereby making
contingency provisions based on these conditions
ineffectual.

Public good. The public good characteristic of
intellectual property also distinguishes it from
other types of property. Unlike private property,
it is difficult to control the use and dissemination
of intellectual property once it is released. The
incentives to create intellectual property may be
diminished unless there are contractual provisions and restrictions on its use that preserve
the value of the property for the patent holder.

In the absence of these safeguards, innovators
are more likely to suppress the introduction of
intellectual property into the marketplace and to

reserve it exclusively for their own use. This suppression not only reduces the consumption value of the innovation but it also retards the rate at which subsequent spin-offs from the original innovation are developed.

In addition, a major concern of parties to an intellectual property contract is whether improvements or blocking patents might be developed by one of the parties to the detriment of the other. These efforts are also likely to be guided by marketplace demands and competition.

Antitrust and property rights: welfare and policy considerations

Public policy with respect to innovation involves a trade-off between inducing investment in innovation and trying to deliver the full benefits of innovation – once it has occurred – to consumers as quickly as possible. Here we look at three welfare considerations: the overall incentive to innovate; the incentive to license and develop the innovation; and the case-specific welfare effect.

Overall incentive to innovate. Many economists believe that innovation rather than competitive pricing is the source of the largest improvements in consumer welfare. In economics parlance, dynamic (innovative) efficiency is more important than static (price) efficiency.

A primary issue in inducing innovations is the problem associated with the appropriability of innovation rents and its effect on generating appropriate levels of investment in innovation. This problem can be greatly mitigated by an intellectual property policy such as patent protection.

Because a patent gives the holder exclusivity but not necessarily an economic monopoly, how the patent can be exploited in the marketplace will influence the expected rents to innovation and therefore the investment in innovation.

Therefore, one must design patent and antitrust policies to satisfy a participation constraint that the inventor must earn a sufficient return on his investment to induce the desired amount of innovative activity. Satisfying the participation constraint may necessitate some adjustments in the antitrust treatment of intellectual property.

Little empirical evidence exists on the influence of antitrust licensing restrictions on investment in innovation. Because use exclusivity is so closely related to market 'product' exclusivity, it seems nearly impossible to assess the impact of an intellectual property policy on incentives to invent without considering antitrust policy as well. Perhaps the point is best understood as referring to the effects of small changes in antitrust policy.

Also, antitrust treatment of intellectual property, when the value of the intellectual property is closely intertwined with intellectual property held by one's competitors, would appear closely to affect innovation investment.

Assuming that an antitrust agency's enforcement actions have a fairly significant impact on innovation incentives, the agency needs to assess whether existing intellectual property policies are over-encouraging or under-encouraging innovative activities before determining an appropriate antitrust policy. There appears to be little agreement on this question.

Thus, there is disagreement over whether minor changes in antitrust policy matter for inducing innovation and, if they do, there still remains the question of whether the joint effect of current patent and antitrust policies results in too little or too much innovation.

Incentives to license and develop the innovation. In designing antitrust policy one must respect the self-selection principle, which asserts that the inventor may always suppress the invention and reserve it for his or her (or its) exclusive use. The investor will only make the innovation available to others if he can arrange sufficiently profitable licensing agreements with other companies. The profitability of licensing is affected by antitrust treatment of intellectual property.

While consumers benefit from the existence of a monopoly-supplied innovation, they benefit more if the same innovation is supplied more competitively. In addition, the full value of the innovation will often not be reached without involving additional companies that can provide capabilities for further development, access to other complementary intellectual property, new applications, efficient and available manu-facturing, and effective marketing and dis-tribution.

Through its choice of how to exploit the property (for example, patent, license, joint development), the holder of the intellectual property determines the extent to which con-sumers will benefit from the property. When the holder of the intellectual property can contract in ways that will preserve a sufficient share of rents from the invention, other companies will often be enlisted to increase the total 'profit pie' that can be earned through taking the invention to market.

Anticipated antitrust restrictions on current and future use affect these choices and therefore affect the degree to which consumers will benefit from the innovation. Thus, antitrust policy may encourage or discourage various forms of licensing and co-operative arrangements. The extent of licensing may affect the incentives for future innovation as well. Several analyses show that licensing to a rival reduces the incentives for it to innovate. Over the long run this may reduce the rate at which new products are brought to market. On the other hand, prohibitions on wider licensing may stifle competition in the short run while increasing the future rate of innovation.

In designing policy for intellectual property, one must respect existing information con-straints. The inventor is likely to be privately informed about the value and novelty of his innovation.

Resolving problems associated with private information may necessitate complicated or unusual use restrictions in licensing agreements, which in turn may necessitate some adjustments to antitrust policies regarding intellectual property. The presence of asymmetric inform-ation (when one party has private information the other lacks) also increases the difficulty of regulating licensing arrangements and pre-venting anti-competitive behavior.

Case-specific welfare effects. Until now, we have been discussing how existing antitrust policy and law affect private choices about the development and use of intellectual property. When a particular case is presented, however, many will argue that the greatest weight should be placed on the impact of the decision on welfare relating directly to the product market under discussion.

This direct static welfare effect with respect to the particular piece of intellectual property in question involves conventional antitrust cost-benefit accounting oriented to determining if consumer welfare will increase or decrease as a result of the proposed transaction.

Downstream adjustments in contracting

How should an antitrust agency view proposed modifications to previously approved contracts and licenses between licensor, *Company A*, and licensee, *Company B*?

To think about this problem, consider the following hypothetical situation. *Company A* holds the patent to a new process. The antitrust laws encourage *A* to license the process to other competing companies because such licensing has the potential for decreasing price. Imagine that the antitrust law would permit *A* to license to a rival, *Company B*, with a bail-out clause that would permit *A* to revoke the license and to purchase the marketing assets of *B* at any time in the future.

Now suppose instead that *A* originally offers *B* a permanent license without provisions for repurchasing the license. At some later time *A* attempts to buy back the license from *B*. Should the acquisition be permitted?

We propose the following contracting criterion to aid one in thinking about this situation: approval of the acquisition should be conditioned on whether an initial long-term contingent license allowing *A* to repurchase (or adjust the terms of) the license would have been legal. We believe that evaluating cases using this criterion may allow one to draw some useful inferences about the behavior of *A* and *B*.

The argument for this criterion is that if the law were going to permit repurchasing of the license under an ex ante arrangement between *A* and *B*, it should not capriciously block the transaction later simply because it was not planned. Allowing more of these transactions would likely increase the amount of pro-competitive licensing that will occur and the use of more innovative forms of contracting and joint development of intellectual property. But one might ask why *A* did not write a complete contract with *B* allowing for these actions in the first place. Why should the antitrust authority need to solve problems between *A* and *B* that the parties should have anticipated and resolved initially?

This counter argument to the criterion overlooks the fact that there are several reasons why a complete contract specifying provisions for license termination or contract adjustment may not have been written.

It may have been too costly for *A* and *B* to specify all the possible future contingencies and actions appropriate for each contingency. Further, some contingent contractual provisions may not be enforceable if the court cannot verify ex post whether a particular contingency has actually occurred.

While we do not find the counter argument to be particularly persuasive, there is a related argument that is an important caveat to the use of the criterion. The type of contract that *A* signs with *B* may reveal information to the antitrust agency about the properties of the patented process *A* owns.

As noted above, it is costly to write and enforce complicated contingent contracts with bail-out clauses. If *A* insists on the contingent contract with the repurchase clause perhaps it indicates that the process is easily imitated and transferable to other applications. The self-selection principle suggests that to deny such a contract clause may cause *A* to suppress the introduction of the process. Thus, in this instance, the enforcement agency may be compelled to approve the contract.

On the other hand, suppose *A* sells a permanent license to *B* without any repurchase provisions. This may reveal that there is less need for *A* to protect the value of its patent against imitations and expropriations by other companies. Alternatively it may reveal that *B* has duly compensated *A* for the increased risk of expropriation in return for guaranteed access to *A*'s process.

Here, the argument for allowing repurchase of the license is somewhat less compelling. It is not necessary for ensuring that the innovation is disseminated in the market. The argument against repurchase is as follows. The fact that *A* did not initially contract for the termination of the license reveals that *A* did not believe that this provision was necessary to ensure the success of the licensing agreement. Consequently, there is no reason to allow the license to be terminated now since the parties did not feel it necessary to plan for the termination originally. We believe that there is a danger in carrying this line of reasoning too far, especially with respect to contract adjustments. An inference that unless a provision was included in the original licensing agreement it must not have been necessary to the success of the operation is not always valid. For example, it may be impractical to plan for all contingencies in the initial contract and, further, some provisions may be excluded because of disagreements over them that might have caused the negotiations to break down.

Would open-ended contract provisions, for example provisions that 'allowed' renegotiation but specify little else, circumvent the inability to plan for all contingencies problems? Such provisions might appear to solve the ex ante incentives problem posed were antitrust authorities only to use a case-specific welfare analysis. However, we do not think that the authorities would treat this provision as a 'get out of antitrust scrutiny free' card, so this solution seems unlikely to solve the un-predictable contingencies problem.

Fixed-term licenses present other related and interesting issues. When a license terminates (and we see no obvious reason why such provisions would be illegal under antitrust law), the licensor and former licensee may negotiate a new license.

Antitrust scrutiny would than be directed to the new license agreement in much the same way as antitrust scrutiny of renegotiation using the contracting criterion.

However, there is one significant difference: the information that should be used to assess the welfare effects in the renegotiation is what exists at the time of the renegotiation instead of what existed at the time of the initial license.

The contracting criterion is intended to help ensure that proper incentives for licensing and post-licensing actions are maintained in situations where uncertainty (especially concerning possibilities about which no one is aware), verification problems and differences of opinion prevent such incentives from being directly specified in the contract.

From the incentives point of view, using only information (and lack of information) available at the time of the original license agreement seems appropriate because the incentives for licensing and anticipated post-license actions depend on that information. This would not be the case in the new license setting. Indeed, from the antitrust evidence point of view, restricting one's analysis to using 'prior' information could allow some dubious agreements or activities to pass antitrust scrutiny because of lack of information rather than because of the substance of the information. In such cases, 'post' information would be useful.

Conclusion

Downstream adjustments to licenses or buy-backs of property rights present antitrust policy makers with interesting problems. One approach would be to consider only the case-specific effects on welfare, taking the existing situation as given.

For example, a producing licensor could not buy back its license from a licensee or re-negotiate the license unless consumer welfare is improved because the efficiencies that result (and are passed on to the consumer) outweigh the negative effects of reducing competition.

Such an approach is too narrow. Antitrust policy should also consider the indirect effects of the policy on incentives to license or otherwise exploit the intellectual property. While a case could also be made to consider the indirect effect of the policy on incentives to innovate, consideration of such an effect would require an assessment of the value of antitrust policy and intellectual property rights policy taken together. A more instructive approach for analysing downstream situations is to consider whether the same action as a contingent part of an original contract would have been acceptable to the antitrust agency. If so, then, permitting the downstream transaction should be seriously considered.

Summary

Intellectual property differs from other forms of property because of uncertainties regarding its value and how it can be used. There is also a public good issue – the likelihood that without safeguards innovators will suppress the introduction of an invention into the market place, thereby retarding the development of spin-offs. There is disagreement over whether minor changes in antitrust policy matter for inducing innovation.

In designing policy for intellectual property one must respect information constraints, and try to resolve problems associated with 'asymmetric' information (where one party to an agreement has more than the other). Downstream adjustments to licenses or buy-backs of property present antitrust policymakers with an interesting challenge. Looking at the case-specific effects on welfare is too narrow; considering whether the same action as a contingent part of an original contract would have been acceptable to the antitrust agency may be more instructive.

This article is an excerpt from *Antitrust Law Journal*, vol. 63, 1995, pp. 603-19.

Core competencies and service firms

■ **The concept of core competencies and the strategic advantages they can bring was developed for manufacturing companies. But does it apply equally to organizations in the service sector? Jacques Horovitz argues that it does.**

'Business development in the nineties will depend on a corporation's ability to identify, to cultivate and to use its core competencies'.

The concept of core competence first appeared in a now famous 1990 *Harvard Business Review* article by C.K. Prahalad and G. Hamel ('The Core Competence of the Corporation', *Harvard Business Review*, May-June 1990). Widely accepted today in strategy formulation, the concepts described in the article were all based on examples from industrial corporations.

The article described how GTE was left behind when NEC harmonized its computer and communication products and technologies by putting together its competencies in both fields to become a leader in telecommunications. It also showed how such companies as 3M, Canon, Honda, Sony and Casio developed core products, such as engines for desk-top laser printers, magnetic tapes, 'Post it' notes, motors, lenses and microchips, which in turn ended up in such products as cars, cameras, copiers, laser printers, personal stereos and microcomputers for diverse markets.

These transformations were possible because each company had technological core competencies: miniaturization for Sony, sticky tape for 3M, engines for Honda, microchips for Casio, optics and miniaturization for Canon. The article went on to describe how industrial companies work to develop manufacturing dominance in core products so as to be able to shape the evolution of end products. Thus Canon manufactures 84 per cent of all laser printer engines, even if its own share of the printer market is smaller.

What about services? Do they have core competencies at the heart of their offer? Where do they lie? How are these competencies identified and nurtured when they are not based on a tangible product or on a tangible technology but rather on a way to handle a customer?

Do you need to dominate your market in a core service competency if you do not sell it as a finished product? Is it also possible in the service industry to create new business opportunities by transferring competencies from one business to another as Canon did when, in 1976, it utilized the competencies in optics and imaging for the AE1 camera to introduce the first personal copier and surpass Xerox market share by 1983?

Today, services account for more than 70 per cent of employment and GNP. Many industrial corporations also owe their revenue and profitability to the peripheral services they add on to their products. This makes the issue both relevant and important. For example, what are the chances of IBM in succeeding in its move towards the service sector if the required core competencies differ from those in research or production or if they cannot be transferred? How does the service corporation choose to diversify in order to benefit from its know-how? Is the development of the service company into a new unrelated sector even possible?

In order to discover those competencies that can be used in business development for the service industry, let us consider the case of corporations that have never manufactured any products.

Générale des Eaux (GdE) – one of the biggest European players in water supply – participates today in a variety of businesses such as water, hospitals and security. The group recently purchased Elitair's catering division (serving airports and in-company cafeterias). Should this move be considered a diversification with no relation to GdE's existing businesses – with as few chances of success as any 'unrelated' diversification – or could it utilize its core competency in dealing with municipalities when negotiating a food service contract for a jail, school or hospital?

How could Accor be as successful in the hotel business as it is in the restaurant business? Are there common competencies? Does its recent investment in the tourism industry (the purchase of Wagons Lits Travel and the merger with Carlson, the US travel agency chain) call for the same competencies and know-how as with hotels and restaurants?

Why did Marriott recently separate itself from its real estate development efforts to concentrate on hotel management? Was it just a matter of finance or was it that the 'wheeler dealer' know-how of real estate has difficulty marrying with the daily management of the 101 details necessary in hotel management?

Why did Club Med fail in the airline business after purchasing Minerve – an air charter company? And why is Nouvelles Frontières – another European tour operator specializing in cheap travel for young adults – successful with the airline it has purchased?

Casino – one of the biggest foodstore chains in France – has recently divested from Hippopotamus, a theme steak house restaurant chain, which was taken over by Flo, a brasserie, restaurant group. Which organization stands a better chance of developing a chain of theme restaurants – the clean product, quality-oriented supermarket chain or the ambience-setting, convivial restaurant chain?

Bouygues, one of the world's leading construction companies, has invested heavily in television broadcasting with success (a 40 per cent market share in France). Is it completely foolish or can its know-how in human resources management and sense of purpose developed in the construction business be used in a completely different field such as the media?

Identifying core competencies

Another company, GPS, was started in 1981 by two entrepreneurs – a 'big six' accountant and the former president of Habitat. GPS was the first French company in the one-hour photographic film development retail business. People stop by to drop in their films, which are developed in an hour on machines that are on site in view of the customer (so-called 'minilabs').

Ten years later total revenues of the group had reached FF1bn, earned through Photoservice photo development retail shops, the distribution of photo and video products through 12 Photo Hall stores and optical distribution through 40 Grand Optical spectacles stores.

Grand Optical is a speciality store chain offering eye glasses in one hour, a big variety of choice via a previously unheard of store size (600 sq meters) and an efficient service.

GPS was successfully listed on the stock exchange in June 1994 with a share price of FF230. In September 1994, its share price was already 50 per cent up on the issue price with a price/earnings multiple of around 30.

Yet at first view, film developing and spectacles would seem to be very different businesses. The only points they have in common are that both belong to the retail sector and both offer 'one-stop shopping'. Were those GPS's only core competencies when it launched Grand Optical in 1989?

A more detailed examination reveals that GPS's core competencies are embedded in several ingredients: the one-stop shopping concept, customer service, excellent logistics and an 'open store' concept.

First, practically all the film developing stores were already installed in commercial centers where consumers typically spend about one hour doing their shopping. GPS also decided to create a 'store' concept for its photo business based on modern design and colors, open space to invite the customer to walk around the shop and making everything visible (including production) to the customer to show it is transparent and risk free.

Most opticians' stores are dark and you have to push a door to get in. There is a limited choice. So at Grand Optical, as in Photoservice, you can get in and out as you like and there are 4,500 models of glasses to choose from in a very bright, laboratory-like environment.

	Competencies developed with photo development retail shops	Competencies acquired through photo video retail stores	Competencies used by in One hour glasses
Business-specific competencies	One-hour photo development -->	Purchasing ----------------------> Novelty scanning ---------------->	One hour glasses Buying 4500 models Fashion buying
Generic competencies in retailing	Retail personnel mangement --> Selecting locations in commercial centers --------------------------> "One-stop shopping" --->	Logistics management ---------->	X X X X
Competencies related to strategic choices	"Open store" concept ---> Customer service --->	Complex product selling -------->	X X X

Figure 1: Applying GPS core competencies to photo development, photo video products and opticals

In addition, the customer service concept is reinforced by a welcoming and attentive staff offering coffee or water while you wait. There are special activities for children, a full guarantee (customers only pay for photos that come out right at Photoservice; glasses are replaced or repaired without questions for 12 months after purchase at Grand Optical). Other competencies came from Photo Hall, the photo and video product retailing activity. These included inventory management, customer advice on sophisticated items and novelty scanning in trade shows. The diversification from film developing in one hour to spectacles in one hour, which appear to be very different businesses, makes sense in light of the core competencies underlying both activities (*see* Figure 1).

Identifying those competencies is the first step towards business development. Do not focus so much on what is obvious at first glance but rather on a series of skills that can transfer across businesses. Failure properly to identify those skills can lead to risky and unprofitable development strategies or lost opportunities to diversify successfully. Most photo development retail chains have not entered other businesses and have stagnated. Most opticians too – in fact, most independent stores – are dying all over Europe and in the US.

The core competencies of service companies represent the essence of corporate know-how underlying each business. Precisely identifying them is a first step towards opening up to growth opportunities. Just because Club Med is in the travel business does not mean that the company has the appropriate know-how to manage aeroplanes, pilots, landing rights, leasing or maintenance.

Not understanding an activity in another sector means risking either too much laissez-faire in the unit's autonomy, particularly when times are hard. Alternatively, it can lead to inappropriate application of 'tried and true methods'.

When Club Med took over the ailing air-charter Minerve, management considered training flight crews in service quality. This was, perhaps, a nice idea, a natural reflex for a company so used to thinking in terms of human resources and talent development. It may not, however, have been enough, or a sufficient priority, to transform an ailing charter airline into a regular international airline participating in deregulation. There you talk about landing rights, usage rate of equipment and cost control.

It ended up as a big loss for Club Med. Considering Club Med's core competencies, other development opportunities naturally come to mind. The company has a unique way of creating a party atmosphere, of entertaining customers in wonderful locations, of making it easy to meet new people or take up new leisure-time activities. These are true customer benefits and a difficult combination to imitate. Such competencies could certainly be used for other present or future markets (from city or commercial center management to stadiums) but probably not in an aeroplane.

Cultivating core competencies

If a service company is to stay successful in its current business it needs to nurture its know-how. Otherwise, as with any resource, it depletes over time.

Cultivating core competencies implies a dual requirement for a service corporation. On the one hand, service design and development must constantly match global market needs and remain homogeneous from one service location to another (a hotel, a branch, a site, a region and so on) to support a brand. On the other hand, making this service available to customers requires a strong local commitment on the part of customer-contact employees. Successful corporations are those that are able both to centralize service design and decentralize service implementation.

This dual necessity often leads to a dual corporate structure. At headquarters, a 'product' structure determines standards and systems for each aspect of the customer value and designs training (sometimes also including recruitment and staff development). It performs long-term market analysis, introduces market data into the innovation process, designs the service product offer and disseminates its 'product' to the various units.

For example, Club Med's headquarters operations structure is made-up of directors in charge of meal services, tours, entertainment, sports and so on. They define the investment policy of all Club Med villages to maintain and develop the activities. They state the activities offered, the profile of 'GOs' (gentils organizateurs or activity leaders), their training and assignments. And, of course, for implementation, the Club Med unit is the resort village. The village chief's main objective is to satisfy the guests within the predetermined budget, staff allocation, activities and purchases.

A retail clothing store chain will similarly have a director for merchandising, another for development (responsible for store concepts and new openings), another for purchasing (who is in charge of finding the novelties that will appeal to the customer), one for styling – all responsible for designing parts of the service to customers. At store level, the manager's role is to motivate staff

to apply the predetermined purchase, merchandising, layout and even promotional policy. Thus, core competencies are centralized.

Indeed, some competencies are more likely to be even more centralized in the service sector than they are in industrial corporations, where R&D and manufacturing capabilities can be scattered throughout the world.

Franchise operations are probably the best example of how much centralization is required to be successful in service. A McDonald's or a Midas or a Haagen-Dazs centralizes its service concept, store design, selection and training of store managers, and design of training for store operators. In industrial companies, the R&D function provides the core products; in the service companies the output is quality standards, procedures and processes, and recruitment and training rather than prototypes or core products.

Service organizations that decentralize service design into the operating units encounter serious difficulties sustaining good performance. A good example is in the after-sale service offered by car manufacturers. This service is delegated to independent dealers. Research shows that approximately 50 per cent of consumers switch brands when they change cars because of bad after-sales service. That percentage falls to 25 per cent if the dealer offers good service.

Imagine a car manufacturer that could do a better job at designing and sustaining the competencies necessary to have an excellent after-sale service through its own service dealership – it could improve sales by 25 per cent.

Centralization of design does not, however, tell the whole story on how the core competencies find their way into the field. Efficient, customer-oriented implementation – especially in multi-location businesses such as retail, tourism, hotel and restaurant chains, transportation, car rentals and so on – requires granting local managers some autonomy. These managers must ensure that their customers, as well as their teams, are satisfied and that economic requirements are met.

For example, Quelle, a leading German mail order company, has decentralized its customer contacts (ordering, customer information, claims) to every major city in order to be closer to customers and their daily habits. But product relations, catalog production and direct marketing – three basic core competencies in the mail order business – are centralized. The local office promotes on a daily basis – within the boundaries of the product offer and customer stimulation policies – customer interactions that will make the buying a personalized experience.

Successful implementation

Successful implementation of a well thought-out service requires three ingredients: training, internal promotion and development, and rotating personnel.

Only people can share know-how. This implies a long process of training, internal career paths and job rotation. Only then – and with time – can everybody in the field acquire, understand, apply and defend the corporate service concept.

Those service corporations known for their excellence often use the ingredients above. Singapore Airlines trains stewards and stewardesses for 12 weeks (Air France for only three weeks). The first is rated as the number one airline on customer satisfaction. The other is number 11.

Most of the top management in Disney's theme parks are former 'cast members' who have gone through the ranks. Club Med's village chiefs and Accor's hotel managers are selected according to their team-leading skills. GPS has set up in-house training centers for photo development and opticals where trainees learn chemistry, preventive maintenance and photo finishing. The same is true for Hippopotamus, which created 'Hipposchool' for hostesses and 'grill chefs'. Such training is quite a heavy investment considering that personnel turnover can reach 200 per cent in the restaurant business. All Disneyland managers are first trained for coaching, so that they will transmit their know-how to new cast members. Another four-week training program will make them managers of autonomous units – called Small Worlds – while ensuring that they respect product design.

Mobility ensures that personnel acquire all of the corporation's know-how and that competencies are more rapidly widespread. Club Med is an extreme case, where 'nomad' GOs and village chiefs change sites every six months. Their know-how accrues with their years of training and experience across the globe and guarantees their high level of energy and homogeneous performance – they do not stay too long in the same place.

Exchange programs between Disneyland Paris and Disneyworld in Orlando have helped European employees embrace their corporate culture faster than any work manual could have. Rotating store managers or making front line workers multiskilled (by taking different jobs) is another example of such practices. Most successful service companies use internal promotion as a means to ensure that core competencies vibrate at every level of the company.

In contrast, the use of corporate know-how by people who may not stay with the company or who are managed by leaders who do not adhere to corporate culture will, little by little, lead to a loss of competitive advantage. Would Air France be where it is today if it had been consistently run by aviation 'pioneers'?

Disneyland Paris has understood this kind of necessity of culture and created 'show time' – one week a year people throughout the hierarchy return to their 'roots' in a Disney park working for the 'guests'. The same is true of Club Med, where all training managers return to the villages in the summer to get back to basics. Do banks without such systems have any competitive advantage other than price? (A notable exception is Japanese banks, where front and back office staff alternate every other week.)

Well performing large consulting firms have also understood that transferring know-how takes time and thus requires internal promotion. They recruit young people who start as junior consultants who will need 10 to 15 years of experience before they can become partners. On the other hand, consulting firms launched by experienced people who just share offices hardly ever develop. They lack core competencies beyond their individual personalities. As a result they stay small.

Redefining your competitive map

It is always difficult to see yourself bicycling when your are sitting on your bicycle. The same goes for competencies. How to identify which competencies are key? The process begins by carefully defining one's business in terms of customer benefits.

When asked what business they are in, most companies define it in terms of product: holidays, restaurants, airlines, leasing. When Danfoss Holland changed its business definition from selling air filters to selling clean air, it stopped selling products and started selling long-term air control service contracts that included filters, measurements, advice on dust prevention and so on.

When a sandwich shop decided to say it does not sell sandwiches but rather 'solutions to customer moods', it made a total change in its selling attitude as well as its product line. The success of the SAS airline in the 1980s was based on the famous slogan 'we are not in the aeroplane business but in the people business'. Ritz Carlton saying 'we are ladies and gentlemen serving ladies and gentlemen' tells a lot more about the atmosphere, types of contact and service attitudes than any training manual.

A broader definition helps look for new competencies outside one's own field. Take the example of the car dealer. In Europe car service shops typically open at 8:00am and close at 6:00pm (in Germany it is even 4:30pm). Customers beware! Wake up early to bring in your car and stop working early too. Successful service firms do not work that way.

Furthermore, when asked to take an imprint of your credit card so that you can pick your car up from the reception or sales people (who work until 7:30pm) after the workshop closes, the car dealer – at least one I know – will tell you it is impossible. Hotels, however, have done it for years without problems. It is called express check out. Benchmarking with other car dealers will not reveal such a practice. Only a broader view of the business will open eyes.

Travelling in Italy, a GPS manager saw in a Florence hotel bedroom that the maid had put a little note of the next day's weather forecast. This practice was immediately transferred to the windows of photo development stores to help customers choose their film sensitivity. By broadening the definition of one's business and looking at other fields, companies identify and enrich service competencies.

The rules of diversification

Whether the service corporation makes use exclusively of its own competencies in creating a new business or marries them to the competencies that exist in an acquired business, these capabilities must be the basis of any diversification strategy.

When Générale des Eaux purchased Orly Restauration (a chain of 400 company cafeterias), the corporate cafeteria market was saturated while business was growing for schools, hospitals and other institutions. GdE brought in its competence in dealing with community organizations such as cities, hospitals and jails to help Orly develop such contracts.

On the other hand, Orly Restauration had specific know-how in 'tailor-made solutions' acquired in serving the corporate market. GdE could then apply this approach to other activities, such as its building security business. This was undoubtedly advantageous as companies can benefit from one-stop shopping with contact people responsible for purchasing security as well as meal services.

In the same line of thinking, new businesses that could fit Disney competencies in customer reception, crowd management, theme development and children's imaginations could include movies, shows, shopping centers, stores and stadiums. Disney is in fact already or about to participate in all of these markets.

Redeploying competencies

When striving for success in a market, understanding which competencies customers require is vital to redefining the business. By explicitly identifying which core competencies are used to create value for the customers, it is possible to isolate and invest in those that are most significant.

For example, few insurance companies can claim that they offer specific customer benefits that cannot be found elsewhere. This is why many customers switch to a different insurance company when they notice the slightest price increase.

On average, an insurance company will lose 50 per cent of its customer base on a ten-year basis. Most insurance companies still accentuate a kind of know-how that does not serve customer needs – selling. While he or she may be treated like a VIP when signing the contract, once it is signed the customer quickly becomes anonymous – just a file. When damage occurs, the file becomes a 'hassle'.

In Germany, in the UK and more recently in France, new competitors have understood where customer value is in insurance. They have made most agents, brokers and salespeople obsolete and have made it possible to subscribe with a simple telephone call.

But they have also invested heavily in developing competencies in claim-processing services and in rapid customer service. For example, risk acceptance follows new procedures, damages assessment is simplified and payment accelerated, customer hotlines offer professional advice and so on.

Considering their growth rate, the redeployment strategy of these insurance companies is showing sure signs of success. They have understood where the important value is for the customers and redeployed their competencies from the seducing salesman to efficient, available, speedy claims management.

Nurturing competencies

It is the primary responsibility of top management to cultivate corporate know-how where core competencies are concerned. How? By creating the appropriate structure, by promoting internal career paths and job rotation, and by investing in competency training.

Here training does not mean offering such commonplace courses as foreign languages or computer literacy. Instead, it deals with investing heavily in learning that reinforces the core competencies of the corporation. If a core competency of Disney is crowd management or showmanship, that is where the major investments in training are made. If one Club Med

competency is celebration, every new GO should receive a course on how to celebrate.

The purpose of company education evolves from teaching to enhancing and disseminating the best corporate practices to all employees so that the whole organization can learn from them and grow. This is why in outstanding service companies, learning is done through meetings of peers, reunions, and the investigation and publication of best practices.

By nurturing this part of corporate culture, top management can build on much stronger assets than a mere collection of businesses. The core competencies involved become the very foundation of potential development as they are learned by all employees, who in turn can make the service happen on a daily basis with consistency and uniqueness.

How to use core competencies

We believe that the most difficult task for a corporation is properly to analyse its core competencies in order not to lose a competitive advantage. Are they unique? Are they hard to imitate? Do they bring about customer benefits? Can they help in entering other services or markets?

K-mart in the US has never succeeded in developing hypermarkets but it has been very successful in developing successful discount stores. On the other hand, Meyers has successfully developed a chain of hypermarkets. Why? Simply because Meyers' initial business was in groceries, food produce management and merchandising, which are the core competencies of a hypermarket. K-mart has constantly tried to develop hypermarkets by adding food to a non-food store and has failed.

The issue becomes even more difficult when a business has drifted away from its founder's purpose. The first generation of entrepreneurs tends to foster the climate of growth more than the subsequent management. What was originally accomplished was a matter of intuition, of will, of philosophy, of choice and, most importantly, of enthusiasm and employee mobilization through the founder's charisma and beliefs. This groundwork was the key to initial success and growth.

Later, as the organization grows, the extraordinary becomes ordinary, the explicit becomes implicit, determination is replaced by routine. This is where competency erosion starts threatening.

In 1993, Novotel – a three-star business hotel chain created in the 1950s – smelled danger and moved back to its roots, back to its original purpose. In a back-to-basics move, hotel managers were turned into hosts again and customers were reminded – through service and advertising – that Novotel stands for 'a light in the night'. Without these little 'extras', why should customers choose Novotel rather than any other hotel?

Do we pay enough attention to corporate legends from the past, to yesterday's heroes, to basic values to preserve, transmit and keep alive the core know-how of a company with its employees? Or do we allow ourselves to be tempted, as time passes, by cold-hearted calculations?

After 20 years of growing profits, Federal Express suffered a downturn in 1990. This was due to the purchase of the Flying Tigers, a specialist in large-size packages (which calls for a different kind of competence), and to heavy investment to develop business in Europe. In spite of this downturn, the on-going quality program (which cost $20m in 1991) was neither cancelled nor even reduced, though financially this would have been good for the bottom line.

However, quality at Federal Express is an internal part of the company culture and an ever-increasing obligation. It involves systems, aimed at constantly reducing the number of potential errors and constantly adding error prevention devices, as much as making people more and more proactive.

Are we always conscious of core competencies? What is their place in the corporate memory?

How are they transmitted? Whether this sharing of skills is ensured by seminar discussions (when corporate culture is based on oral tradition), by corporate 'bibles' or by intensive training, its mechanism is vital.

Unless competencies are preserved in corporate memory and personnel are constantly reminded of them, they tend to fade away – and so does the service company's competitive advantages.

Summary

The original concept of core competencies, as developed by Prahalad and Hamel, was based on examples from industrial corporations. But service companies, which account for more than 70 per cent of employment and GNP, respond to the same analysis. Identifying core competencies can be a first step towards opening up growth opportunities in such businesses – but they are not always obvious. Just because Club Med is in the travel business, for example, does not mean it can necessarily manage an air charter company successfully.

Successful companies are those which are able both to centralize service design and decentralize service implementation. This often involves a dual corporate structure.

Successful implementation requires three ingredients: training, internal promotion and development, and rotating personnel. A broader definition of competencies helps you look for new ones outside your own field. The issue is particularly important when a business has drifted away from its founder's purpose. Isolating competencies and investing in them can reinvigorate an enterprise. But they need to be preserved in the corporate memory and employees constantly reminded of them.

Building resources for competitive advantage

■ **Kim Warren builds on systems thinking and modeling to show how companies can use a systematic approach to their resource base to develop meaningful strategic analysis.**

Most managers know that building and conserving the resources of their business is critical to success. These resources may be tangible, for example cash, customers, products or staff, or intangible, such as product quality, staff morale or service standards.

These intangibles can be at least as hard to build and maintain as the tangible resources and can do extensive damage to a business if they are lost through mismanagement or misfortune.

Furthermore, resources are interdependent – good product quality is of little value if delivery performance damages market reputation; a highly motivated sales-force can do little with a poor range of products. 'Ranking' resources in order of importance is thus pointless – if any key resource is in bad shape the whole business is endangered.

Yet, in spite of the central importance of resources to a company's success, managers have been offered little to help them grasp the scale of resources or estimate the power of their resource base to deliver sustainable competitive advantage. Without such support, debate on strategy can easily degenerate into rhetoric about core competencies and the importance of 'vision'.

Alternatively, focus may turn to the strategy process, on the assumption that if we get this right, a powerful strategy will somehow materialize by itself. But those who have built and sustained strategically strong companies know that this rarely happens by accident or inspiration alone – it needs careful thought, constant analysis and deliberate action.

Resources and feedback

Resource levels. It is possible not just to specify tangible resources but to capture the intangibles too and the interdependencies between them. The starting point is to recognize that the management challenge is to build and maintain the level, or stock, of each resource.

We can think of any resource as being held in a 'tank' in which its stock or level is accumulated. Resources are built by boosting the flow of new resource into the tank and resource losses are flows out of the tank. We usually wish to raise the inflow to the stock and minimize the outflow. Increasing the level of a resource above certain limits is not always desirable, though, or may represent a waste – having more skilled staff than we need is costly and offering too wide a product range, for example, may be a disadvantage.

Let's try this stock-building idea with a resource that most of us will want to build and conserve – our customer base. This stock is raised by opening a 'tap' to let new customers enter. In the upper diagram of Figure 1, new customers may be won by marketing efforts, a strong sales-force, a competitive price or some combination of these. Customers are lost if a second 'tap' is opened, for example if our product

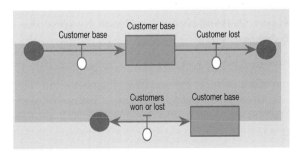

Figure 1: Building, and losing, the customer-base resource

quality is poor or deliveries are late. The shaded 'clouds' at the end of each 'pipe' indicate that we are not particularly concerned with where these customers come from, merely that they are won or lost from a large pool of potential customers. Some resource-flows may operate in either direction. A good reputation for after-sales support may attract new customers while a poor reputation may cause existing customers to be lost (lower diagram in Figure 1).

Now we can put some numbers on this idea. If we start with 1,000 customers and win 100 per month, the customer base grows in a straight line – after six months we have 1,600. That may not be good enough if our rivals take most of those away from us again, so perhaps we can do something to make this resource grow faster.

Reinforcing feedback to grow resources. A common system that generates growth is word-of-mouth – if we have an existing customer base and do a good job of serving them, they are likely to tell others. These new people join the customer base and create the possibility of a larger word-of-mouth effect (Figure 2). This system 'reinforces' its own growth, as indicated by the R in the middle. (This process was explained in detail by John Morecroft and Ann van Ackere in 'Systems thinking and the art of modeling' in module 4.)

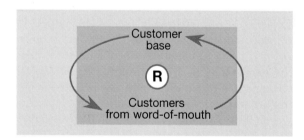

Figure 2: Reinforcing feedback to grow the customer base

Now we can estimate the scale of the resource-building effect by putting numbers on the resource and estimating the number of new customers that might be gained each month (Figure 3). The 'stock-and-flow' structure at the top captures the changing customer base, a device we need if we are to show that this change occurs through time.

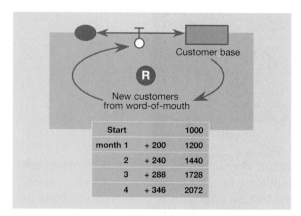

Start		1000
month 1	+ 200	1200
2	+ 240	1440
3	+ 288	1728
4	+ 346	2072

Figure 3: Quantifying self-reinforcing growth of the customer-base resource

This self-reinforcing mechanism alone will generate exponential growth, which clearly cannot continue for ever. Sooner or later, we will come up against some ceiling, either external (for example no more customers to win) or internal (for example no capacity to supply new customers). Note too, that the same reinforcing process can generate exponential decline. If reputation is poor, customers desert our business and tell others, so even more customers leave.

Balancing feedback that limits resource-building and decline. We also need to represent the kind of feedback that 'balances' the tendency for a resource to rise or fall. Service quality provides an example of this. Figure 4 shows a system where a limited service capacity allows us to deliver excellent service when customer numbers (our resource) are small but poor service if customer numbers are too large. This system, too, exhibits its behavior only through time – the quality of service determines the rate at which the customer-base grows or falls.

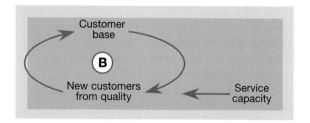

Figure 4: Balancing feedback limits customer numbers

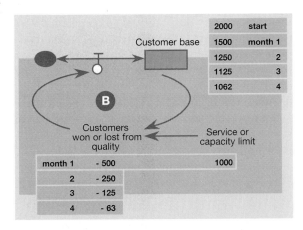

Figure 5: Quantifying balancing feedback that limits the customer-base resource

Figure 5 operationalizes and quantifies this concept using the 'resource' idea, by showing what happens if each month we lose 50 per cent of those customers who are above our capacity to cope.

Note that if the customer base starts below the 1,000 service capacity, this system shows the opposite tendency – to grow until such time as customer numbers again match this capacity limit. The numbers here are purely illustrative and to model any real situation we clearly need real data. This requires capturing managerial experience and judgment with questions such as: 'If you have 2,000 customers, but only enough staff to support 1,000, what fraction of your customers would you expect to lose each month?'

This might seem rather subjective but with thoughtful debate management teams can agree answers to such questions that produce a close match between the behavior of the model and of the real world. There are two further reasons for pushing these questions. First, managers *implicitly* make such judgments all the time – all we are doing is making them explicit and sharing them. Second, the very question itself proves to be a powerful means of helping managers understand the dynamics of their competitive situation.

The resource-system – an example in brewing

Now we have seen how to represent the building and depletion of just one resource-stock, we can look at the wider resource-system of a company, taking as an example the marketing of brands in the UK brewing industry.

The resources believed to drive market share and profitability in this industry include funds for advertising, the number of consumers interested in a supplier's brand and the number of retail outlets (mostly public houses, or 'pubs') stocking it.

Production capacity might seem an important resource but the industry is over-supplied and capacity is not in itself a source of advantage.

Retail outlets come in two forms: 'tied' pubs are owned by brewers while 'free' pubs are independently owned and operated. The tied pubs resource is more powerful than free pubs since the former are virtually guaranteed to stock the owning company's brand, whereas the latter have to be persuaded to do so and may switch between rival suppliers. In our resource-stock terminology, the tied pub resource is highly durable while the free pub resource is easily lost to rivals if, for example, a brand is unpopular with consumers or has too high a wholesale price.

Companies advertise their brands to create consumer interest then set wholesale prices and sell the brand into pubs to make it available. Sales revenue is a function of the number of pubs stocking the product, the average volume sold per pub and the price. A fraction of this revenue is reinvested in further advertising. This is a two-part reinforcing process, in which current revenues provide the advertising needed to drive future volumes and consumer awareness drives retail availability (Figure 6).

Intuition suggests that a company with more or bigger tied pubs should have an advantage in the race to exploit a new brand segment. For any initial level of advertising, it would expect to sell more than a rival with fewer or smaller tied pubs. This would fund higher advertising spending in future and hence create greater consumer awareness. The resource-rich company then gains further advantage because it can persuade more free pubs to stock its brand. But just looking at this picture, we can't know how large this advantage might be or how quickly it might grow.

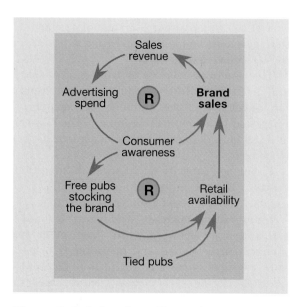

Figure 6: Reinforcing effect of pubs on brand-building

Operationalizing the brand-building model

To operationalize this conceptual model we must specify the key resources and the mechanisms by which they are accumulated and depleted. In contrast with the simpler example in Figure 2, it appears we now need three resource-levels, one for consumer awareness and one each for the numbers of free and tied pubs stocking the brand. The resource-building process now occurs between these complementary resources – we have moved to a simplified picture of the company's 'resource-system'.

Consumer awareness is stimulated by advertising levels and declines if such advertising is insufficient. The durability of consumer interest varies between different product types. Free pubs decide to stock a brand if there is sufficient consumer interest to support retail revenue and a sufficiently competitive wholesale price. They de-stock the brand at a rate that rises as these factors become less attractive. The key resource-stocks are given in Figure 7 and policy choices – price and advertising levels – are highlighted.

Although reinforcing feedback initially generates exponential growth, the model implicitly includes limits to that growth – the population of potential consumers is 'used up' and retail distribution becomes saturated.

This conceptual model portrays the dynamics for a single company and would adequately represent the exploitation of a single market segment by a monopoly supplier. To capture competitive dynamics, the model is copied to represent either individual rivals or groups of rivals. Consumer interest in each brand is 'pulled' between rivals according to the relative weight of advertising; the number of free pubs stocking rival brands depends on their relative consumer interest and the wholesale price of each.

We can now estimate the rate of change in the resource-system by adding illustrative numbers for the major brewers competing to exploit a large new product segment. Assume each of four companies owns roughly 4,000 tied pubs and there are around 35,000 free pubs, although each company's free pubs resource starts at zero. Take a market of 5 million potential consumers for a major brand segment, though again no brand has any consumers before the segment is developed.

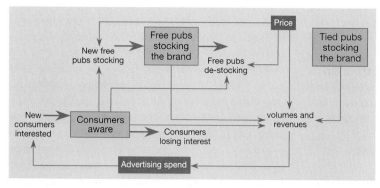

Figure 7: Dynamic resource model of brand-building

We need to add the sales volume that the average tied and free pub would sell and the price that would be charged.

We also need to estimate the critical rates in the system – how fast do consumers lose interest in a brand, how many newly interested consumers does a certain amount of advertising stimulate, how quickly do free pubs stock or destock a brand for any level of consumer interest and how do they balance this issue against the price being charged for the brand? As in our earlier example, these are complex and subtle questions about which managers in the companies concerned already make implicit judgments.

Simulating resource-building dynamics

Now it would be possible, if rather tedious, to do the necessary calculations by hand from period to period to see how fast a brand might develop or how brands might win or lose against each other. However, this manual process quickly becomes impractical for any but the simplest examples.

Fortunately, a new generation of simulation software is available to simplify the task. These products are highly intuitive, easy to use and can quickly create dynamic models of situations such as we are considering here.

The model described was built with companies divided into two groups of rivals. These groups can be set up with a wide range of different characteristics – large versus small, many tied pubs versus few, aggressive versus defensive pricing policies and so on. We will take here just three comparative tests.

A. Initial resource-advantage. The four major brewers do not have equal resource-strengths – some have larger tied pubs than others. Larger tied pubs sell more beer, generate more revenue to fund advertising and hence can drive greater take-up for a brand than in free pubs. Figure 8 shows the result for one of the four companies if its tied pubs are 30 per cent smaller (*line 1*), of equal size (*line 2*) or 30 per cent larger (*line 3*) than its three rivals.

Initial advertising of £2 million a year only builds consumer interest slowly. But as soon as any interest exists, sales volumes begin to rise

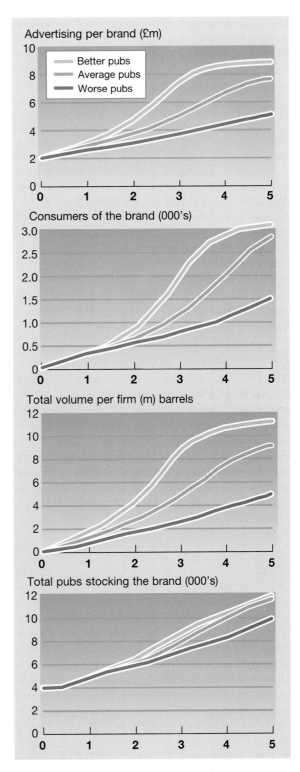

Figure 8: Impact of resource-advantage on brand-building success

because of the brand's presence in 4,000 tied pubs.

If those pubs are large (*line 3*) sales rise quite fast, generating enough extra revenue to fund a rapid increase in brand advertising. This, in turn, pushes up consumer interest, which is enough to persuade an increasing number of pubs to stock the brand.

If the company has smaller tied pubs than its rivals (*line 1*), those pubs provide too little revenue to put back into increased advertising and consumer interest is slow to develop.

Note that these results have given two specific types of information not normally available when assessing strategic advantage.

First, they tell us the scale of the advantage that has been created – we know how many consumers, how much advertising, how many retail outlets and how large the sales volume will be.

Second, the results tell us the speed with which the strategic advantage has developed – with a better resource the company has exploited its potential largely within three to four years; with an average resource, it has taken five years; while with a poor resource it is only half way there after five years.

B. Capability differences. If competitive advantage were only a matter of differences in the quantity and quality of resources held by rival companies, life would be simple if rather boring – the company with the initial advantage could be predictably forecast to win every time.

Yet new entrants and smaller companies in many industries overcome bigger rivals with such resource-advantages by having better organizational capabilities in key parts of their business. In our resource-building terms, 'capability' is the scale of the company's ability to build both individual resources and the resource system as a whole.

In our brand-building example, one company might produce better advertising and hence create more consumer awareness from the same expenditure as its rivals. It might have a more capable sales force, which can persuade more free pubs to stock its brand than the sales forces of its rivals.

Figure 9 shows the effect of these two

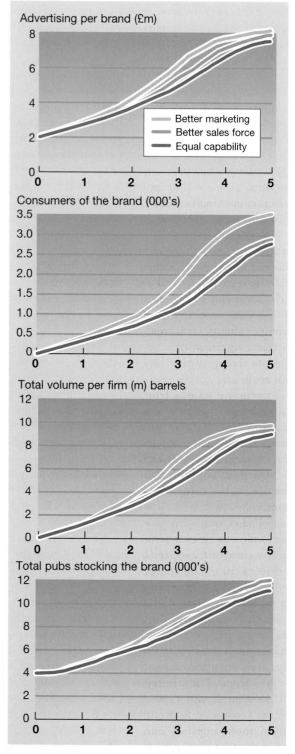

Figure 9: Effect of capability-differences on a firm's brand-building success

capability differences for a company with identical resources to its rivals. *Line 1* is the base case, in which the company is identical in all respects to its three rivals. *Line 2* shows what happens if the company has a 20 per cent stronger marketing capability than its rivals. ('Capability' here has a quite precise meaning – it is the number of consumers made interested in the brand by this company's advertising versus the number its rivals win with the same spend.) *Line 3* shows how the company does if its has a better sales force that can win 20 per cent more free pub customers than its rivals from identical levels of consumer interest.

The marketing capability advantage appears to be more powerful since it both raises consumer interest and increases the sales volumes in those pubs where the brand is stocked. A stronger sales force can win some increase in the number of free pubs stocking the brand but without any greater consumer interest – sales volumes do not increase significantly.

Note that we again have an indication of both the scale and speed of strategic advantage that the company enjoys from its relatively strong capabilities.

C. New entry. The last example concerns competitive entry to an established market. Understanding whether it is feasible to attack established suppliers in an industry is of considerable interest both to established companies and to would-be new entrants. To model this question, we need to allow some companies to build a strong initial position then trigger competitive entry by a potential entrant.

Figure 10 shows the prospects for a company trying to enter four years after three major rivals have already established a position in the market. The rivals have exactly the same resources and capabilities as in the earlier examples, and by year four have largely exploited the available market.

Two types of new entry are modeled in Figure 10. In *line 1*, the new entrant has the same initial resources and capabilities as the three established suppliers had when they launched, notably 4,000 tied pubs that immediately stock its new brand when it is launched in year four.

This initial jump in retail availability, with

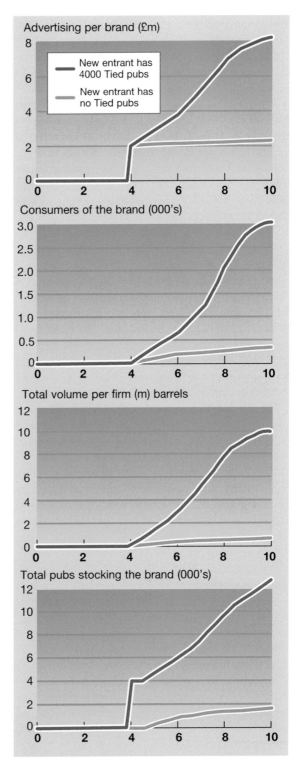

Figure 10: Potential for new entry by a firm with or without a key resource

the commitment of £2 million a year of base advertising, is sufficient to build the company's brand awareness among consumers, generating sales volumes to fund subsequent increases in advertising.

Line 2 shows a new company trying to enter without the resource of any tied pubs to stock its brand from launch. Its £2m of initial advertising builds some consumer interest, which in turn persuades some free pubs to take the brand but sales are so small that very little additional advertising resource is created and the brand stagnates at a low level.

Conclusions and further developments

The concept of strategic analysis has taken a beating in recent years, both from the demise of companies that once epitomized the 'planned' strategy approach and from commentators who have highlighted the failings of over-rigid planning systems.

However, it is arguable that competitive strategy has itself become more complex as companies have become more sophisticated in their strategic thinking and actions. Tools of strategic analysis that once provided a source of competitive advantage are now so commonplace that no-one benefits from their use.

Few new approaches have emerged to keep pace with this increased sophistication by practitioners, so strategic analysis has been stuck with a historic or static perspective when companies have moved to a forward-looking, dynamic view of industry and competitive conditions.

The systems perspective, developed here into a comprehensive, dynamic, resource-centerd model, goes a long way to filling the gap. Unfortunately, its application requires a detailed, thoughtful and team-based analysis that is both time-consuming and intellectually demanding. The reward for this effort is a far deeper understanding of a company's competitive options and likely outcomes than can be achieved by other means and greater confidence in strategic success.

This section has described only part of the journey in applying systems thinking to strategic analysis. It has sketched out two key steps: developing a conceptual model of the strategic issue (for example Figure 6) and operationalizing that picture in a simulation model.

But if the resulting insight is to be shared and used by a whole organization, we need a means to communicate these complex, dynamic ideas to all those in a company whose decisions and actions are central to the successful delivery of the resulting strategy. For that purpose, the types of model described here can be 'packaged' and equipped with a user-friendly computer interface that allows them to be used for management development.

Such 'management simulators' (also referred to as microworlds) are powerful and effective means for allowing large numbers of staff to experience and learn about the dynamics of their business and the strategic approach being adopted by their own company. Such devices are just now becoming feasible to produce and are in common use within leading business schools, and a handful of companies.

Summary

Strategic analysis has taken a beating from some commentators in recent years; some tools have become so commonplace that no one benefits from their use, and few new approaches have emerged to keep pace with the growing sophistication of practitioners. The systems perspective, which provides a much deeper understanding of a company's competitive options, goes a long way to filling the gap. Two key steps are the development of a conceptual model and the operationalizing of that picture in a simulation model.

Suggested further reading

Grant, R. M. (1991) *Competitive Strategy Analysis*, Blackwell (1991).

Dierickx, I. and Cool, K. 'Asset stock accumulation and sustainability of competitive advantage', *Management Science* No.35, 1989, pp. 1504-1511.

Morecroft, John D. W., and Sterman, John D. (1994) (eds.) *Modeling for Learning Organizations*, Productivity Press.

Beyond product excellence

■ The Japanese have shown the world how to excel at product quality. But, says Dominque Turpin, they are changing the rules of the game again. Now the new competitive battleground is customer service.

While Japan has been experiencing its most serious economic slowdown since the end of the Second World War, many Japanese companies have been rethinking their corporate priorities.

Many western corporations are gradually catching up on product quality but Japanese companies are again changing competition rules by adding extra value to their products and refocussing corporate efforts on customer service.

An executive from Matsushita Electric Industrial Co puts it this way: 'In the past, we were happy to provide the market with plenty of new products, matching any developments from our competitors in a matter of months. The focus was on having the flexibility to manufacture smaller quantities of many different products. Product quality is now taken for granted; now the name of the game is service excellence.'

During the 1980s, Japanese companies won major shares in international markets through product excellence, then a surrogate for customer satisfaction. While keeping up high product quality levels, they are now focussing as never before on meeting and exceeding customer expectations – selling 'packaged solutions' rather than simply finished products, improving delivery and installation times and offering application advice at no additional cost.

These are today's key success factors in world markets and we expect Japanese companies to be as intense on customer satisfaction as they have been about product quality.

Seven golden rules for improving customer service

Our recent research into Japanese companies has identified seven activities that are key to improving service quality. We recognize that many western companies are already engaged in some of these. However, this non-exhaustive list of current best practices in the service area may offer some fresh insights into maximizing customer satisfaction.

1. Define your corporate mission in terms of customer benefits. Many Japanese marketers believe that customer satisfaction is, quite simply, the primary goal of management. Major corporations often spell out this idea in their corporate mission statement.

For example, on the very first page of its annual report the leading Japanese manufacturer of household products and cosmetics states: 'Consumer trust is Kao's most valued asset. We believe that Kao is unique in that our primary emphasis is neither profit nor competitive positioning. Instead, our goal is to increase consumer satisfaction through useful, innovative products that meet real market needs. A commitment to consumers will continue to guide all our corporate decisions.'

2. Gain the commitment of senior management. Writing customer satisfaction into the corporate mission statement is not enough to turn a company into a customer-driven organization. Leading Japanese companies see the commitment of senior management as critical, just as it has been in quality management programs.

Yotaro Kobayashi believes in the importance of setting a personal example. As CEO of Fuji-Xerox, he spends half of his time on quality and customer issues. The Japanese executives we interviewed felt that management commitment is the major difference between the Japanese and western approaches to customer service.

A European executive who has worked for both a US and Japanese company comments: 'The first thing my boss from the US was interested in was the financial statement. The first thing my Japanese boss wants to see is a store, a retailer and a customer. Here, they do not simply talk about customer satisfaction, they do it.'

3. Select the right people. Japanese companies we visited seem to put greater effort than western ones into recruiting people with the right approach to the customer. Not only do leading Japanese companies recruit from the best universities, they pay particular attention to candidates' personalities. Through an extensive recruiting process they make sure that their future employees will have the required empathy for customers. As a result, the best companies have exceptionally competent, reliable and responsive employees.

4. Train and retrain. As with *kaizen* (continuous improvement), customer satisfaction in Japan is a spiral process that starts with training. Good training = positive service attitude = motivated employees = decreased staff turnover = improved service quality = satisfied customers.

Matsushita Electric states: 'We make people first, and in addition we make electrical products.' Every new employee goes through an intensive one-month training program that emphasizes the company's history, corporate philosophy and business etiquette.

New employees at Toshiba follow a similar program before being sent to work in a factory or to serve customers in a Toshiba store. Tokyo Gas, although it enjoys a monopoly in the Tokyo area, finds it important periodically to 're-educate' managers and employees by having them serve a few months in the customer departments of different branches. Even the Japanese post office occasionally uses leading Japanese department stores to retrain its employees in customer service.

5. Measure and communicate quality standards. In many businesses, the real action often takes place in the first 60 seconds of interaction with customers. Do employees make the right impression? Is the company perceived as being considerate and helpful? It is important for employees to know what role they are expected to play and be aware of what the customers expect.

Although many Japanese complain about the rough manners of their taxi drivers, westerners are often very impressed by their white gloves, the automatic passenger door and by receiving the exact change, sometimes with a free pack of tissue paper.

Doshin Kotsu, a taxi company in Tokyo, carefully explains its quality standards to all new drivers and to ensure that they are observed regularly conducts customer satisfaction surveys by means of questionnaires left in the taxis. Typical questions: Did the driver welcome you politely? Did he ask you which route you prefer? Did he remind you not to leave anything behind? Did he say good-bye?

Doshin Kotsu distributes the survey results throughout the company with details of customer perceptions, actions to be taken and awards made to the most customer-conscious employees.

6. Use technology to enhance customer satisfaction. Japanese companies are increasingly using technology in serving their customers. Kao has been a pioneer in customer communications since 1934 and its 'ECHO System' is the most advanced electronic consumer-consultation system in Japan.

The company receives 120-130 enquiry phone calls a day and wants its operators to be able to respond satisfactorily to everyone. A fast, user-friendly computer system gives each operator immediate access to 8,000 pages of information, including color pictures of any product with its packaging and the instructions printed on it. A detailed report of the customer's input is systematically entered into the system. This may include hand-written material, such as a diagram explaining a customer's problem, which is entered via an image scanner.

The system is linked to more than 100 terminals throughout the company, enabling people in R&D, production, planning, sales, marketing and other departments to retrieve calls and reflect on customers' experiences and suggestions.

7. Creatively exceed customer expectations. Giving customers more than they expect is the surest way to build and retain their loyalty. Delighted customers are more likely to come back and spread the word about how great your company is. (IDM Japan even found that customers who experience a problem and have it fixed quickly and politely are likely to have a higher level of satisfaction than customers who never experienced a problem!).

But you can only exceed customer expectations if you clearly understand them in the first place. Japanese car owners generally expect their dealers to fix problems free of charge until the warranty expires but now every manufacturer provides this service for the entire life of the vehicle.

Constant creative efforts are also made to enhance customer service in different ways. For example, Toyota is now working on delivering a car within one week of receiving the order, thereby exceeding most customers' expectations about how long they have to wait. While brand loyalty in Europe for local car manufacturers is less than 50 per cent, Toyota's brand loyalty rate in Japan is said to exceed 65 per cent.

Applying the golden rules

The Japan Management Association recently presented the results of a national survey on customer service. Surprisingly, it showed that the largest companies, ranked by sales volumes, are not necessarily the best in terms of customer satisfaction (and potential sales in the future).

Nissan, second to Toyota in sales volume, was ranked first because it involves potential customers in planning its new models. Yokohama Bank, 20th in total assets, was placed ahead of the larger banks because it responded fastest to clients at its teller windows.

All Nippon Airways, second to Japan Airlines in passenger volume, came top because customers rated its cabin service higher than JAL's. We can expect the leading Japanese companies to react vigorously and intensify their efforts to meet and exceed customer's expectations while still making a profit. It is the critical new area of competition.

A shift in the Japanese way to compete

For years many western companies decided to ignore their Japanese competitors. Today this is impossible. Japanese companies have achieved major competitive positions in an impressive number of industries.

But despite this history of success, some managers are tempted to believe that the slowdown in the Japanese economy means the end of strong Japanese competition. On the other hand, many western expatriates in Japan consider that leading Japanese companies will emerge from the recession stronger than ever. There is no doubt that their increased focus on the customer will help.

Matsushita Electric took a major step last year by mobilizing its whole organization to visit 10 million Japanese households. The objective? To discover what customers in the 1990s really need. One result of this massive effort is that the company has developed plans to manufacture more user-friendly products, deliver 95 per cent of parts within the indicated time, return at least 90 per cent of all repairs within 48 hours and reply to all customers' letters, requests for information and complaints on the day they arrive.

Conclusions

While many western corporations are gradually catching up on product quality, today the emphasis in Japanese companies is on achieving zero-defects in customer service.

Western companies are not necessarily at a disadvantage when competing with Japanese companies on this service dimension. In their search to give customers more value for money, we found that leading Japanese companies use simple and practical tools used by other excellent companies around the world. These include careful selection of employees, extensive training and far-reaching communications programs.

A major difference between Japanese companies and their western competitors may be a greater commitment from Japanese employees at all company levels to enhancing customer satisfaction in every conceivable way. As more and more companies apply the same marketing techniques, they are forced to look for new ways to differentiate themselves and attention to detail becomes an important source of competitive advantage.

Kao, for example, replies to a client's request

on the spot and Mazda takes care of a customer's insurance renewal. One western expatriate in Tokyo dismisses these initiatives as 'marginal managerial improvements' but in today's highly competitive environment, in which customers are becoming increasingly demanding and selective, such 'details' may very well make a critical difference in gaining and retaining them.

Keeping ahead in the competitive game

■ **The essence of competitive strategy formulation is the ability to foresee the moves of competitors, anticipate how they will react to our moves, and then take action with this in mind, say** George Day **and** David Reibstein

Competition is a game, as defined by game theorists, where success depends on both our actions and the reactions of competitors, customers, partners, and other stakeholders.

These 'games' are becoming more difficult to play – or to win – as competition intensifies. Globalization and technological change are spawning new sources of competition, deregulation is changing the rules of competition in many industries, markets are becoming more complex and unpredictable, and information flows in a tightly wired world permit companies to sense and react to competitors at a faster rate.

This accelerated competition means it is no longer possible to wait for a competitor to make a move before deciding how to react. The new watchwords are anticipation and preparation for every eventuality. Every move of a competitor is met with a rapid counter-move to ensure any advantage is temporary.

The most intense or hypercompetitive rivalries have spawned the cola wars where every move Coca-Cola makes is met by Pepsi Cola and every initiative by Pepsi is quickly countered by Coke. Today, every advertisement by MCI immediately stimulates a response by AT&T, and vice versa. The result is an advertising war in which collective annual spending has topped $1bn.

As soon as Kodak launches a new disposable camera, Fuji will have a similar model ready for the market. Even banks have launched credit card wars, where every offer of gifts or reduced charges is soon matched. No company can afford to let its rivals gain an obvious lead for long.

This is because customers make their choices based on what they perceive each company has to offer when compared to the other available choices. What constitutes a *powerful* computer or an *inexpensive* airfare depends on the power of the other computers that are available in the market and the fares of the other airlines on the route. In short, the deciding factor is not how good the product and/or service being offered is, but rather, how good a value it is relative to the competitors' offering.

Thus, one cannot afford to be complacent with a good new product, since some competitor's new offering will always be altering the perception of your product's quality.

Okidata's mistake. As a case in point, in the 1970s Okidata produced an excellent dot-matrix line printer and won a significant share of the printer market. However, it did not take long for Hewlett Packard to transform customers' perceptions of what a good printer was. First HP introduced an imported ink jet model that had some advantages over Okidata's line. And then it offered the Laserjets, a family of highly reliable printers based on a technological breakthrough that made them faster and quieter, that provided greater resolution, and even gave them substantial resale value.

Okidata complacently watched its share of the printer market rapidly erode while it continued to offer the customers the 'best damned (dot-matrix) printers on the market'. By stubbornly continuing to market a product that, compared with other available options, was no longer a wise investment for their customers, Okidata quickly lost its leadership position to Hewlett Packard. Soon the new HP printers proved their worth in the workplace, and Hewlett Packard captured the respect and loyalty of many of Okidata's former customers.

In mature markets breakthroughs that lead to sudden shifts in competitive position are rare. Here competition is at best a 'zero sum' game, where one company gains at the expense of the others. However, the more intense the rivalry, the more likely it is that it will deteriorate into a 'negative sum' game in which the process of competition imposes costs on all the players. An aggressive move to penetrate a market will backfire if the competitive response significantly raises the cost of doing business. For example, when a company greatly increases its advertising expenditures and competitors follow suit there will be no net gain for anyone, and costs will have increased.

Take the case example of the British bank which felt it could gain a competitive advantage over its competition by opening on Saturdays instead of just doing business in the normal Monday to Friday hours. Initially the move proved successful and the bank gained an influx of new customers. The customers were delighted that a bank had finally started to provide extended hours making it more convenient to do banking. It did not take long before most of the other banks were forced to respond in kind. While the banking customers were better off, the net effect for the industry was for all the banks to increase their cost of doing business without any appreciable increase in the level of banking. In short, the same level of banking was spread over six days instead of five.

Such mutually destructive behavior is especially damaging during the price wars that have so eroded profits in the airline, computer software, automobile tyre, and disposable nappy markets. After one company sets off the confrontation, by cutting its price, a series of retaliatory price reductions are quickly launched by its rivals, because no one wants to lose customers, volume, or share. Seldom does volume increase enough to offset the margin impact of the decline in average price level. The long-term danger is that once customers' expectations about the correct and reasonable price are driven to an unrealistically low level, the situation is difficult to reverse. Worse, as the rivals increasingly emphasize price, their customers become more and more price sensitive. When the price war ends, the customers' behavior may be drastically changed.

Managing competition

Competitive games are played in the fog. Because the true intentions, degree of resolve, and retaliatory reflexes of competitors are deeply and often deliberately obscured, their responses are likely to be misunderstood and under-estimated. There is a high price to be paid for such mis-steps, especially when mutually destructive behavior is triggered. There are other adverse consequence as well:

Ignoring a low-end competitor. Because the competitor was not seen as an immediate threat, it was able to gain enough of a toehold in the market to lure away customers in valuable adjacent segments.

Allowing a once durable advantage to vanish. The market leader was caught unprepared by unexpected competitive moves. Its surprised managers realised belatedly that, if they had had more foresight, the company could have easily thwarted the competitor.

Launching a new product without first assessing competitive responses. Before a new product could gain loyal customers, established competitors adapted their existing products to nullify the advantages of the new entry. In shortorder, unexpected rivals also appeared in the market.

During the post mortem debriefing it is

easiest for managers to blame their predicament on failures of analysis or managerial fortitude. Unfortunately, companies rarely see the issues so clearly during the critical strategy formulation stage. Beforehand we see numerous competitors striving for new edges in a market and looking for ways to outflank each other, without triggering retaliatory moves. They may send out signals to rivals to warn them not to try thwarting their initiatives. Often these signals are misinterpreted or ignored. And then, to complicate the situation further, unexpected developments in the market, economy, or regulatory areas that will further intensify rivalries may erupt at any time.

Nonetheless, some companies are better able to avoid self-inflicted wounds or the mutually destructive behavior that damages industry margins. What sets these companies apart is, first, an intense focus on competitors throughout the organization and a desire to learn as much as possible about their strategies, intentions, capabilities, and limitations. Second, they utilize these insights to anticipate the likely moves of the relevant competitors. Thus, they formulate strategies by devising creative alternatives that minimize or preclude or encourage co-operative competitive responses. They adroitly use many weapons other than price, including advertising, litigation, and product innovation. They play the competitive game as though it were chess, by envisioning the long run consequences of their moves. Their goal is long-term success, rather than settling for short-run gains, or avoiding immediate losses.

Our choice of topics to emphasize was strongly influenced by several premises drawn from our collective experience, the heuristics used by successful competitors, and a growing body of research on competitive processes.

First, we believe that companies pay more attention to what competitors have done instead of considering what they might do or will do. There is often an unstated and unrealistic assumption that the competitors will stand still rather than react or make their own moves to gain an advantage.

Second, managers' mental models strongly influence how they interpret competitive intelligence and formulate alternative competitive strategies. These mental models are necessary simplifications that managers use to make sense of complex and confusing competitive arenas.

Third, it is possible to avoid some of the destructive consequences of competition by properly specifying the game. For example, managers should consider ways of converting a market situation to a positive sum game rather than a negative sum game. They should then systematically use simulations or role playing the outcomes of different strategic moves.

Finally, successful companies view the cut and thrust of competition as opportunities to learn and systematically adapt to new situations. They routinely commit substantial resources to this learning process. Few investments have a higher pay off than this, if in the long run it helps secure the organization's market position and avoid corrosive price cutting.

Understanding the competitive arena

Many times companies waste precious resources responding to other companies in the same industry, but with whom they are not really competing. To be a true competitor, the company has to be selling to the same set of customers or market segment and serving some of the same functions. If the company is selling to a totally different segment, their actions may not affect one's sales, share, or profit.

The answer to whom to respond to must also be coupled with the question of whether it is necessary to respond at all. Some competitors' actions may not affect one's own market, even when they are selling into the same customer set. Further, some industries learn how to coexist 'peacefully'. This is generally neither black nor white, but lies along some continuum. Some industries will appear to be attractive, depending on the level of competitive intensity.

Whether to respond to competition depends on whether the competitive action has an impact in the marketplace affecting your performance, either short term or in the long run. Whether to initiate an action, and how, depends, in part, on your competitors' ability to respond by negating the impact of your actions. One clearly needs to assess one's competitive advantages and how sustainable they are before deciding how to respond. The next step is an assessment of the competitors' strategies and intentions. Can we learn from some of their actions or commitments (capacity, annual report proclamations, available resources, etc.) about their capabilities? One must also be cautious of who else might be entering the market, or the likelihood of new competitors. All of this is intended to give us a better ability to anticipate our competitors' actions or reactions.

Formulating your competitive strategy

The best strategy to choose is not independent of the strategy of one's competitors. Given an understanding of the competitors' strategies, the question then depends on how to select the best strategy. Game theory helps one decide whether it is best to compete directly, or whether it is more logical to try to co-operate with one's competitors. It might also help in deciding what is the easiest and fastest path to stabilising the market. Of course, one must also decide if it is best to be a leader or a follower. To lead, one has to have competitors that are willing to follow. Whether competitors are willing to follow depends on whether they are being led down a path which is also beneficial to them or are given no real alternative. Usually to a leader it is predictable and clear in which direction they are going. It is not always desirable for their strategy to be unknown or unpredictable to the competitor. Rather than to follow directly, the choice is always to respond to a competitor's actions by taking an action of one's own. The question is on what dimensions should one react?

If one understands how to make the decision on which dimensions to react, one should also be able to understand the dimensions on which one's competitors might be likely to react, and how quickly. Rather than either lead, with a desire to be followed, or follow someone else's lead, it is also possible that one may choose to preempt. This is to take an initiative which precludes the competition from taking a similar action. For example, building a large hotel in a community which more than provides ample required rooms might preclude any of the other hotel developers from building additional capacity themselves. This would serve as a relatively inflexible move which raises the question of whether flexibility is always desirable.

Evaluating the potential competitive strategies

Once the potential strategies have been conceptualized and generated, it is necessary to have some mechanism for evaluating what the potential consequences would be of each of these strategies.

Methods range from competitive strategy simulators to the simulation of customer tradeoffs as ways to evaluate the financial consequences of various sets of strategies. Any such evaluation must incorporate one's own strategy, as well as that of the competitors, in a dynamic assessment – that is, how each strategy might react to the moves of the other.

Summary

Accelerated competition means it is no longer possible to wait for a competitor to make a move before deciding how to react.

The new watchwords are preparation and anticipation. In mature markets competition is at best a 'zero sum' game; the more intense the rivalry the more likely it will be 'negative sum'.

What sets the best companies apart is an intense focus on competitors throughout the organization, and a fierce desire to learn about them. Such companies commit substantial resources to this process. They devise creative strategies using many weapons other than price, with long-term success rather than short-term advantage the goal.

Too many companies waste time by responding to the wrong rivals. Rather than either lead or follow, it is also possible to preempt, i.e. take an action which precludes the competition from taking a similar action.

Alliances can bring hidden benefits

■ The rationale for joint ventures and other co-operative dealings is usually clear-cut. But there are also hidden benefits that come from the very process of partnership itself, say Francis Bidault and Thomas Cummings.

In recent years, virtually every business leader has considered the possibility of forging an alliance of some kind. Every day brings announcements of more joint ventures, co-operative agreements or minority equity swaps between companies – even among some that were previously head-on competitors.

The obvious advantages to be gained from an alliance have been carefully examined and are quite well understood. But now senior executives are becoming increasingly aware of a possible bonus: the range of valuable, hidden benefits that an alliance can bring.

The obvious advantages

The specific advantages of an alliance vary enormously; no two alliances are designed to produce exactly the same benefits. The principal objective, however, is almost always to get access – to new technology, to manufacturing capacity, to markets and distribution, and to service capabilities.

Alliances can benefit the partners at various stages in the chain of business activities or, indeed, at several stages simultaneously. A good example is the formation of the Renault-Matra partnership to produce the Espace minivan. Renault benefitted from Matra's flair for product concepts, its design capabilities and its manufacturing competence. In exchange, Matra gained access to Renault's marketing, distribution and service resources. Most alliances are based on a similar intention to exchange resources and competencies between the partners.

Alliances are also widely recognized as a unique vehicle for learning from other organizations but this is also seen as a possible danger. Business academics Yves Doz, Gary Hamel and C. K. Prahalad make a convincing case that joint ventures between Western and Japanese companies are essentially learning races in which each partner tries to absorb more knowledge from the other in the shortest period of time.

The hidden benefits

In addition to the anticipated advantages of an alliance, a number of valuable extra benefits can arise from the act of implementing it. Most forms of alliance will require organizations to expose many of their manufacturing and management processes to their new partner and this, in itself, can generate valuable ideas for improvements in three ways:
● organizations are often required to prepare a detailed presentation of their expertise and this process can generate innovative ideas
● alliance partners place their expertise in a new context and this helps to highlight any weaknesses
● the new partner can be much more demanding than any customer as it comes to know its opposite number's operation intimately.

Alliances can thus shake up many parts of an organization by creating challenges and indicating possibilities for innovation and change.

An alliance is a source of innovation

Alliances generally require the partners to contribute some of their managerial or technical expertise to the partnership. This transfer of knowledge can be a valuable source of innovative ideas as it requires the partners to prepare a detailed explanation of operations they are very familiar with and probably have not examined objectively for some time. Ideas for improvement tend to be stifled by habits that no one questions.

Potain, one of the two world leaders in tower cranes, realised that if it wanted access to foreign markets it would have to join forces with local allies through licensing and joint ventures. One of its first partnerships was formed in Iran, where it had to help an Iranian partner set up the manufacturing facility. Several engineers and technicians were sent to the partner's site with all the available technical documentation.

This proved to be insufficient and Potain's engineering department, for the very first time, had to detail the entire process of crane construction. The experience produced a series of valuable suggestions for improving the technology. Similar important productivity gains have been achieved at many companies involved in technology transfers.

Even before the actual implementation of the partnership, preparing the presentation of your operating process can foster innovations. This is the first type of hidden benefit.

An alliance tests processes in a new context

Alliances typically involve applying knowledge under different conditions, such as a new geographical market, or with a new work force or a new material input. Knowledge is put to the test and this can generate valuable ideas.

The joint venture between Bekaert and Bridgestone in Japan offers an interesting example of how this process can work. Bekaert, a Belgian company, is a leading manufacturer of steel wires used as a reinforcing material in tyres. In the late-1960s Bekaert realized that it could not be successful in the fast-growing Japanese market without the help of a local partner. After considering different potential partners it chose Bridgestone, the largest Japanese tyre maker, and a joint venture was created to manufacture tyre cord to be supplied exclusively to Bridgestone.

Each partner had a clear objective. For Bridgestone, it was to gain access to the technology of a state-of-the-art supplier. For Bekaert, it was to gain access to a market that would generate income via royalties.

Bekaert's technology was successfully transferred and within five years the productivity and quality levels at the Japanese plant had reached those in Belgium. But the Japanese union was unhappy with the manufacturing process, which required heavy manual handling and involved a considerable waste of time.

They developed solutions for both problems and presented them to the joint-venture management. Their ideas were implemented and over the next five years productivity doubled. Bekaert later applied the same approach in Belgium with similar results.

Companies that transfer their technology sometimes find that their partners are outpacing them and they are being gradually abandoned. Bekaert's management avoided this problem by recognizing right from the start that they could learn something from a joint venture. They made a long-term commitment to continuous learning in which the partnership with Bridgestone was a major element. The company is now stronger than ever with an increased share of the world market.

The hidden benefits here arose by applying established expertise to a new situation and revealing a potential for improvement.

An alliance can improve management processes

Almost by definition, an alliance will bring the two partner organizations closer together as they come to understand each other's way of doing things, degree of freedom and room for manoeuvre. But one partner may also exert a pressure on the other that forces it to alter its operating procedures.

Such a process took place in the Matra-Renault partnership mentioned above. Matra-Automobile, a division of the French Matra group, was in a difficult situation. Its only model, a sports car, was not selling well and the company was losing money heavily. Peugeot was not interested in its new idea – the Espace, a minivan tailor-made for the European market. In 1983 it approached Renault, which agreed to back the project under one condition: that the design would be modified in such a way that the car could be changed into a commercial vehicle if it failed to appeal to the family market.

Matra-Automobile was very flexible in its approach and, recognizing that its survival was at stake, agreed to make the changes. Fortunately, after some initial hesitation the market warmed to the concept and the Espace became a far greater success than expected. By 1989 it was selling at the rate of more than 200 units per day whereas the original plans were for 50 units.

The scale of this success, however, created a serious challenge. Matra-Automobile, which built the body and assembled the car using Renault's engine and parts, was simply not accustomed to producing at such a volume. Quality problems began to arise. Renault was very concerned that its quality image would be damaged but had no solution to propose because its own production technologies were quite different. The alliance entered a phase of 'vigorous discussion' and Matra-Automobile recognized the urgent need to develop a special quality-management process that would work with its technologies and meet Renault's legitimate concerns.

It did this successfully and today the partnership has a very high share – around 45 per cent – of the 'monospace' segment in Europe, despite the fact that this booming market has attracted such competitors as Chrysler, Pontiac, Toyota, Nissan and Mitsubishi.

Matra benefitted by hearing and understanding what Renault was saying. It was particularly effective in mobilizing its energies to meet the challenge posed by its alliance partner.

A common benefit of all alliances: they expose more of an organization to the world

The experiences of these companies highlight a fourth hidden benefit that can arise from all well-managed alliances: they can provide companies with a mechanism to bring the challenge of competition to parts of their organization that are normally shielded from it.

Manufacturing and R&D, for example, are often only indirectly informed of what is happening in the market. They hear about competitors and their projects but the challenge is substantially dampened by the time it reaches them.

Alliance partners can introduce new threats as well as new opportunities. This can be a real benefit, if an organization responds positively, by helping to shake off bad habits, re-examine preconceived ideas and generate a desire to change and innovate.

Exploiting the hidden benefits of an alliance

The extra advantages of an alliance are not produced automatically. To ensure that they arise organizations must make appropriate choices about the way the alliance is managed.

1. Opt for joint operations wherever possible. An alliance does not necessarily require partners to manage their operations jointly: it is often possible to simply 'co-ordinate' actions with both partners continuing to work separately. But while this arrangement has significant advantages, particularly in preventing the leak of confidential information, it does not allow companies to benefit from testing their processes in a new context. Whenever the risk of leakage is limited, opt for joint operations. They lead to maximum exposure of each partner to the other's scrutiny.

2. Involve the best staff and management. Innovative opportunities always exist, but they are only recognized by people who are ready to see them. As Louis Pasteur said: 'Luck only smiles on the prepared mind.' Make sure the people designated to work on the alliance project have the right mindset to interact with the partner.

3. Rotate people. Since one of the hidden benefits of an alliance is to challenge an organization, the more people who hear about it the better. If a partner is presenting a clear and useful challenge, the management and staff involved in the alliance should be regularly rotated so that a maximum number of people are exposed to it.

4. Keep 'improvement' permanently on the agenda. Innovative ideas can only be developed through an alliance if the organizations are fully aware of the opportunities and ready to take them. When they explain the alliance internally top managers should make it clear that, in addition to the well-defined strategic advantages, one of the objectives is continuously to look for ways to improve their own organization's processes.

Implementing these suggestions is, no doubt, an extra burden for management but the rewards are well worth it. The benefits that arise from a well-planned alliance can make a real contribution to maintaining a healthy competitive organization. To put it another way, they are the best weapon an organization can have to combat one of the most common diseases that afflict successful companies – complacency.

Summary

Most alliances are based on a similar intention: to exchange resources and competencies between partners. Hidden benefits, though, can come in the form of innovations derived from detailed presentations of each side's expertise, the potential for improvement exposed in applying existing expertise to a new situation, and the pressure to perform from a demanding partner.

Environmental concerns: are they a threat or an opportunity?

■ The environment is now firmly on the agenda as a business issue. Georges Haour takes the retail business as an example to look at how industry is responding.

As compared to the first Environment Summit, in 1972 in Stockholm, many of today's ecological issues are increasingly planetary in their scope: ozone-depletion, the greenhouse effect, destruction of the rain forest, the Chernobyl accident and so on.

Lobbying public bodies to tackle ecological problems responsibly, environmentally conscious citizens have, at the same time, become more targeted, more visible and more pragmatic in their action. There is a realization that in order to have a chance of success the various stakeholders – people, public, private and non-governmental organizations – must respond to the challenge as partners. This is indeed not an easy partnership, as relationships between these stakeholders are tense and often antagonistic.

Citizen-customers from industrialized countries increasingly put pressure on politicians, communities and companies, particularly in areas such as plant safety and emissions (in a typical European chemical plant, 20 to 25 per cent of the overall investments aim at protecting the environment, compared to 5 per cent in many developing countries), public transport, re-use and recovery of materials in cars or packaging, as well as genetic engineering for agro-products and pharmaceuticals.

As with other constraints, such pressures may be perceived negatively, as an additional handicap, or positively, as an opportunity and stimulus to do things differently.

A good example of an industry squarely submitted to these pressures is retailing, which faces them in three main areas:
● 'green' products
● packaging
● logistics and stores.

'Green' products

What is a 'green' product? Here is a difficult notion. Between reason and emotion, bombarded with contradictory elements of information, changing with time, lobbied by their environmentally conscious children, influenced by the media, customers chaotically form their perception as to which products are *greener*.

Depending on the region, the culture and the time, criteria for *green-ness* indeed differ. They may include 'organically-grown' fruits and vegetables, no preservatives, low ecological impact in the use of materials or upon processing and usage (i.e. low energy consumption, no toxic substance used), long-life products, as well as returnable or minimum packaging.

Consider the example of the Canadian supermarket chain Loblaws. This company decided in 1989 to develop a line of green products. A team from the company was charged first to identify, among the products on the shelves, those which had a lower impact on the environment – such as phosphate-free detergents, energy-efficient light bulbs and so on.

In a second step, the team searched for more environmentally friendly replacements of existing products, such as unbleached coffee filters (without the residual chemicals left by the bleaching process). At that time, this particular item had to be imported from Sweden.

Loblaws also introduced products that displaced its own, for example re-usable cloth diapers (nappies), even though disposable diapers represented a relatively significant part of its sales volume.

Crucial here is the *credibility* towards customers. Nothing is more tempting than exaggerating one feature of a product in order to make it appear ecological. Sooner rather than later, customers notice and the exercise backfires badly.

An external watchdog to which the retailer may unload the responsibility for testing products and granting green labels, helping with communication with customers along the way, can be very useful here. Consumers' associations, independent organizations and consultants may play this role.

Straightforward and sustained communication must take place between retailers and customers if trust is to be maintained. Retailers need to explain candidly and plainly the rationale for the choices made.

This exercise in communication is a difficult one. For one thing, the information base keeps changing and new evidence may well pull the rug from under a product 'established' as being green – remember that the introduction of CFC carrier gases in aerosols was heralded as a very positive step, replacing dangerous, inflammable ammonia; years later, their impact on the ozone-layer made them an ecological pariah.

In the case of Loblaws, the 'green line' now counts well over 100 products, though many of them are more expensive than the alternative products, for example high-efficiency bulbs. These greener products sell well and contribute to a growing part of sales volume.

Packaging

The most ecological packaging is no packaging. This is, indeed, the solution requiring least materials and energy for conditioning and transport. Does this mean that we should go back to our grandparents' milk can? In most cases, the convenience and protection provided by modern packaging systems are too great to do without.

But, then, is a recycled glass bottle greener than a one-way plastic pouch or a plastic bottle? A full evaluation of materials and energy content, as well as transport, storage and preservation requirements, must be carried out for a complete 'life cycle analysis' (LCA) of the total product-package system.

Here again, analyses of the same system will yield different results depending on local conditions such as availability and price of materials, energy and transport. All these vary substantially from country to country.

Being a crucial interface with consumers, supermarkets are promptly stigmatized for what is perceived as wasteful packaging. They are also penalized by initiatives such as the German Dual system. Retailers must therefore either constantly come up with 'leaner' packaging systems in their own processing plants or demand such systems from their suppliers.

For example, the Migros chain in Switzerland has considerably simplified the packaging of yoghurts and of certain cosmetic products, explaining to its customers that the objective was to reduce the use of cardboard. The measure was well accepted by customers.

Refillable containers might have a renaissance in the future, à la Body Shop. Instead of having to take back, sort and store used packaging, supermarkets would much prefer to have customers bring reusable plastic containers to be filled at the store with bulk oil, butter, cream, cheese and so on so long as sanitary requirements are fulfilled.

In order to develop a satisfactory solution, a supermarket-chain might, in this case, find it beneficial to conclude an alliance with a manufacturer of refillable containers, such as 'Tupperware'.

Logistics and stores

Supermarket buildings are often seen as an eyesore in the suburban landscape. There is definitely room for improving on much of the utilitarian approach to supermarket architecture and the use of surrounding space. There must be a better, affordable, more imaginative way of designing facilities. There is no doubt that customers will increasingly reward retail-chains making efforts in this direction.

When it comes to the contents of the stores, how many brands of frozen peas does a supermarket need to carry in order to *satisfy* its clients? Maybe, in contrast with the US, European customers will increasingly accept a somewhat narrower choice of brands of a product in exchange for a saving in storage and display space as well as in refrigeration energy.

How far, though, can one streamline the product offering and who is actually educating the customer in a responsible way about this kind of trade off, when competitive pressures seem to push for a proliferation of the product offer?

Logistics are under increased scrutiny on the part of customers. Retail chains will be more and more under pressure to optimize trucking between warehouses and stores as road traffic reaches saturation in many areas of Europe and the trend to charge trucking with its full cost to the environment becomes irresistible. Certain retail chains are, for example, developing communication campaigns underlining how effectively they make use of rail transport to move their goods.

Telecommunications and computers offer radical alternatives in this area and are already central to the management of inventories and logistics. Innovation in this area is constant. For example, in one store of the Albert Heijn chain, customers scan the bar codes on products with a hand-held device, avoiding queues at the check out.

Information technology will probably offer the most revolutionary change since the deceptively simple innovation of self-service. Tele-shopping, now its infancy, presents the potential of turning the distribution industry inside out. Already with 'Minitel', millions of France Telecom subscribers have more than 3,000 services available at their fingertips, including distance-shopping and banking.

What will the Internet allow in the near future? Imagine a customer ordering his or her shopping list electronically: no need for super-markets any more, only warehouses. And instead of customers driving to the supermarket, small (electric?) trucks come around delivering the ordered goods to the home.

Furthermore, the customer not only orders from home but also pays by electronic bank transfer, at the time the order is made. The benefit of such a procedure will not escape the financial officers of the retail industry.

Conclusions

The green wave is here to stay. A chat with our own children will convince us of this.

The issue for business is to ride on this wave responsibly by integrating ecological concerns into every single management process, turning the demand for minimal environmental impact into business advantage.

Reconciling ecology with economy makes complete ethical and business sense. Indeed, ecological solutions favour optimal use of energy and materials, minimizing waste, transport and storage costs.

For a large part, it is simply plain good house-keeping and quality management. The chemical industry is practicing this by preventing the occurrence of waste, thus increasing yields and the energy efficiency of their processes.

The retail industry has a powerful influence as a role model promoting green practice in its own operations but also through its influence in demanding low environmental-impact solutions from its suppliers in the agricultural, packaging, equipment and transport sectors.

Finally, a vision: information technology is a powerful enabler of low environmental-impact solutions, through innovations such as tele-shopping. In the same way that video-conferencing, by cutting down on travelling, competes with air transport, IT could make it possible to break down the large supermarkets into several types of smaller units – convivial 'proximity stores' selling perishables – while the long shelf-life products (detergents, paper products and so on) are ordered electronically, billed and paid by electronic bank transfer and delivered directly from the warehouse.

In many ways, the concern for the environment is a source of renewal and competitiveness. It provides new reasons for listening to customers. Taken with the appropriate attitude, it is definitely an opportunity. The real threat is that your competitor may take advantage of that opportunity better than yourself.

Summary

Retailers face a number of environmental pressures. What constitutes a 'green' product, for example, is often difficult to define with customer perceptions often different according to region and culture. A relationship of trust, based on straightforward communication, needs to be developed.

Supermarkets are quickly stigmatized for wasteful packaging – refillable containers may make a comeback for bulky goods.

Logistics are also under increased scrutiny and IT and the Internet will allow new possibilities.

Socio-political Context and the Business Environment

Contents

The nature of ideology 616
Jack Denfeld Wood, IMD
Ideology has been and still is one of the greatest factors in human behavior. It also has enormous implications, both externally and internally, for business.

Globalization and multinationals 622
Stephen J. Kobrin, The Wharton School of the University of Pennsylvania
Globalization is talked of glibly, but if we are really entering a global economy, and not just a larger international market, then the implications for companies and managers are immense.

Contributors

Jack Denfeld Wood is Professor of Organizational Behavior at IMD, Lausanne. His research interests are analytical psychology, leadership and teams, social structure and change, and culture and ideology.

Stephen J. Kobrin is William H. Wurster Professor of Multinational Management at the Wharton School of the University of Pennsylvania and Director of the Joseph H. Lauder Institute of Management and International Studies at the University of Pennsylvania.

Introduction

The Socio-political Context and Business Environment module is a brief attempt to set business and the individual company within the context of the external environment.

The two-article module firstly examines the roots of ideology and goes on to a review of what globalization may really imply for business.

The nature of ideology

■ **Ideology has enormous implications, both externally and internally, for business.** Jack Denfeld Wood **examines what constitutes an ideology and what it means for managers.**

Ideology counts. Much of human history is the chronicle of human destruction at the hands of those with a different comprehensive and explicit ideological doctrine.

The great conflicts of the last several centuries have had their deepest roots in ideological differences. One can uncover the central role played by ideology as one reads historical accounts of the American, French or Bolshevik revolutions and observe the legacy of these ideological conflicts in contemporary political events and economic disagreement.

The power of ideology is equally evident today. In the 20th century, ideological conflict has been the major source of war and economic disruption as well as the central justification for large-scale regional and international violence.

Ideology is trans-cultural – it runs across national boundaries. The short flowering of international communism provides an example. Marx was a German academic who made his professional reputation while living in England and whose theories inspired the Russian, Chinese, and Cambodian revolutions. Even conflicts that appear to have their roots in national cultural differences are usually driven at a deeper level by ideology.

The 'iron curtain' may have fallen along the national boundaries between the liberal democracies and the former communist states but the boundary it marked was less a national or a cultural one than it was a psychological and an ideological one.

The German nation was cut in two and its cultural roots nearly severed by ideology. The painful process of German reunification today is a measure of the severity of that split – and the power of ideological influence against the cultural influences within a nation.

I believe that ideology is a powerful and not clearly understood psychological phenomenon with sociological and interpersonal, as well as political and international, implications.

One can observe the effects of ideology at a number of levels – in the belief system of an individual, in the structure and dynamics of a small group, in the investment decisions of a business, in the spending priorities of a national political party, in the negotiation of international trade agreements among sovereign states, and in terrorism and war.

The international landscape is littered with the victims of ideology. The rationale given for terrorist bombings might be based on historical political or economic grievances, real or imagined, but the violence is driven by deeply irrational psychological forces and justified through a collective ideological framework.

A definition of ideology

People look at the world in different ways. We have different beliefs about the nature of reality, we have different values about what makes life worth living, we have different attitudes concerning the desirability of certain events, and we are possessed and guided by radically different ideologies.

The words 'beliefs', 'values', 'attitudes' and 'ideologies' are frequently used interchangeably, as if they were synonyms. They are not. They have important, though subtle, distinctions.

By belief I mean a seemingly rational conviction about what is 'true' and what is 'false'. Belief is 'existential' in the sense that it concerns what is presumed to 'exist' as fact. A belief need not include a valuation.

By value I mean something more akin to a felt

emotional conviction about what is 'good' and what is 'bad'. True and false are not equivalent to good and bad. A value implies comparative worth. A belief can be more or less neutral but a value cannot. A value is always relative.

By attitude I mean approval of, or agreement with, or disapproval of, or disagreement with, some external object, fact or possibility. Thus I can believe the moon to be made of green cheese, I can value my family life and my attitude about an open immigration policy for Hong Kong Chinese can be positive or negative.

But none of these constitutes an ideology. An ideology is a comprehensive system that organizes and gives meaning to people. By ideology I mean: 'A systematic doctrine of human life; an ideology provides direction (an end state) and specifies appropriate behavior (means) for achieving this end.'

An ideology is not an assortment of opinions nor is it only a systematic framework of attitudes, beliefs or values. An ideology provides an organizing doctrine that gives direction, structure, and thus meaning, to life. An ideology can be infused with value and emotion but the appeal of an ideology is essentially spiritual and transcendental.

By providing direction (an end state) an ideology describes a goal, however improbable the goal's achievement may be. Thus an ideology describes an ultimate destiny, a final cessation of struggle, the end of history, an everlasting kingdom and so on. By specifying appropriate behavior (means) for achieving this end, an ideology provides its adherents with a practical day-to-day guide for action.

It is therefore both utopian (because it is concerned with ultimate ends) and prescriptive (because it is concerned with the means to achieve these ends). An ideology says: 'That is the goal and this is how to get there.'

An ideology inevitably reflects the perspective of a collective group experience and is often the major weapon used in a struggle for power. Ideology coalesces around a particular kind of life experience and becomes a systematization of that experience into a coherent doctrine. Thus an awareness of social class – of systematic differences in power – combined with a feeling of

envy relative to those in higher classes or of guilt relative to those in lower classes, helps determine the nature of the collective doctrine.

This is one reason why ideology is not bound by nationality – the experience of power or powerlessness is a universal one and not a peculiarly national one. Ideology is neither identical with, nor coterminous with, one's culture, race, sex or social class. Christianity and Marxism have found broad appeal.

Political and religious doctrines lie squarely at the heart of ideology. Such doctrines define a reality that can, and usually does, have rather far-reaching personal and social implications. Thus Marxist or Christian or Islamic doctrine and dogma, each bound into its own comprehensive utopian vision, have significantly more persuasive claim on the commitment and loyalty of their respective adherents than does, say, a humanistic or liberal-democratic ideology.

At a socio-political level, the more comprehensively and explicitly the 'ends' and 'means' are defined, the more doctrinaire, dogmatic and 'ideological' such a belief system appears to be. In contrast, the more vague or diffuse the ends and means, the less doctrinaire, dogmatic or ideological it appears.

The same can be said of an ideology's adherents, *mutatis mutandis*: the more strictly an individual follows the articulated (or unarticulated) doctrine, the more doctrinaire, dogmatic, and otherwise 'ideological' that individual appears to be.

Death, literal or figurative, has been the price one pays for crossing to the wrong side of an ideological divide. The Berlin Wall provided a graphic example. Ideologically speaking, heretics have always had a rough go of it from the orthodox – heretics have a different vision of the goal and how to reach it. At the ends of the ideological spectrum, the faithful reserve a special enmity for the apostate.

At a personal psychological level, an ideology operates at both conscious and unconscious levels. The closer an ideology touches the unconscious spiritual domain of a human being, the more profound it is felt to be. A substantial component of charismatic leadership involves the identification and articulation of a collective

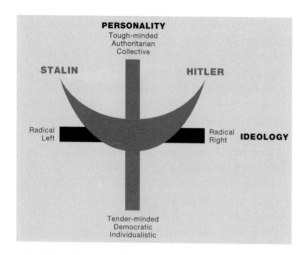

Figure 1: The intersection of personality and ideology dimensions

ideology – one that is easily grasped, explains a complex reality simply, taps profoundly irrational psychological strata and is willingly believed by its followers. An ideology provides a collective lens through which one perceives reality, but as a lens it must inevitably color and distort that reality.

Ideology and personality

There is, I suspect, an intimate relationship between ideology and personality, most noticeably at the radical extremities. Two individuals at opposite ends of an ideological spectrum may claim to represent radically different social programs, but both the programs and the sponsors show an uncanny similarity.

Joseph Stalin and Adolph Hitler were allies before they were enemies. They were at ideological extremes, the one on the left and the other on the right. But both men were the chief architects in the design and implementation of competing totalitarian systems. And both leaders had remarkably similar personality traits. This can be illustrated in Figure 1.

British social scientist Hans Eysenck has hypothesised a two-factor theory of ideology with both a political and a psychological dimension. People's personalities may be considered to array along a parabola defined as a function of these two factors. Thus, while one places Joseph Stalin and Adolph Hitler on opposite ends of an

ideological axis, they can comfortably occupy the same end of an intersecting axis defined by personality – both of them manifesting a similar 'tough-mindedness' (harder, collectivist, controlling and essentially authoritarian personalities) as opposed to a more tender-minded orientation of those found nearer the ideological center (softer, individualist, more permissive and essentially moderate personalities).

Those occupying radical extremes consistently misunderstand and misread those occupying the central and more moderate area. Radical leaders usually underestimate liberal-democratic political systems and leaders. Whereas most politically moderate individuals (and nations) appear to be 'softer' relative to such men as Hitler or Stalin (or Nazi Germany or Soviet Russia) they are by no means soft in any absolute sense.

Franklin Roosevelt and John Kennedy are good examples of individuals who were moderate along the intersecting dimensions of political ideology and personality and who were badly misjudged by their more extreme adversaries. When sufficiently provoked, moderate nations, political leaders and populations eventually mobilize to take a decisive stand against their more radical enemies. At least when they are forced, as in World War II, or the response carries little risk, as in the Gulf War.

Ideology and society

Whereas a literal death may come for those caught at the wrong end of the ideological dimension during revolutions and civil wars, a figurative death comes for those caught at the wrong end of the ideological dimension during daily organizational life in the liberal democracies. What may appear on the surface to be merely 'politics as usual' often has an underlying topography defined by profound ideological differences. The polarization in the American electorate is largely an ideological one defined by 'politically correct' thinking. The issues that periodically seize the popular imagination and hold the country in thrall are some combination of race, sex and violence. The O. J. Simpson murder trial and Clarence Thomas' Senate confirmation hearings for the US Supreme Court are two outstanding examples.

Clarence Thomas, the black appointee, found himself under attack for alleged sexual harassment by Anita Hill, a former colleague. The subsequent attack was an ideological one. Thomas found himself under vitriolic attack by a coalition of left-of-center groups of women and minorities not principally because he was male or black or because of alleged sexual harassment but because his ideology did not fit the 'politically correct' profile – a black American male was not supposed to think conservatively.

As a social phenomenon 'political correctness' is neither new nor peculiarly American – although Americans do, from time to time, demonstrate a remarkable enthusiasm for such things. Political correctness is simply the contemporary name given to an older and deeper ideological fissure that has marked the difference between left and right in virtually every large political system in the last century.

It marks the difference between the Social Democrats and Christian Democrats in continental Europe, between the Labour and Conservative parties in Britain, and between the Democrats and Republicans in the US.

One might reasonably argue that here the issue is relative power and that ideology is merely the rationalization used for the accretion, consolidation and exercise of power. The argument has some truth to it but it assumes ideology is a tool that is used rationally and cynically. I do not believe that ideology represents an exclusively – or even predominantly – rational phenomenon.

Ideology taps unconscious and irrational psychic levels. It is a fundamental organizing force which taps the spiritual need for meaning. It is the shared and basically non-rational belief in an ideology that possesses its followers and makes ideology a organizing force to be reckoned with. Whether ideological adherents are deluded or not in their collective beliefs is less significant than that a critical mass of them 'believe' and act accordingly.

An ideology is therefore not just a convenient delusion. It gives people a compass that keeps them oriented in the world. The deep human need for existential meaning assures that ideology will never wither away. Any particular ideology can weaken and decay and eventually collapse, of course, if it no longer adequately addresses reality. But it will quickly be supplanted by another ideology that more vigorously addresses exterior and interior reality.

I have suggested that there is an underlying and systematic pattern to contemporary political ideology – that an ideology is not merely a random assortment of beliefs, attitudes or values but rather a systematic doctrine of ends and means. On what is the underlying pattern of ends and means based?

Beneath the ideological rhetoric

In my doctoral research I set out in part to explore the underlying nature of ideology – to determine its foundations, at least in a liberal democracy. Participants in that research received a survey questionnaire comprising highly charged ideological items (for example, do you strongly agree or strongly disagree with such statements as: 'The death penalty is barbaric, and should be outlawed'; 'Overall, President Reagan is doing a good job'; 'Abortion is killing unborn human beings'; 'White males have too much power in America today'; 'If racial and gender differences in intelligence exist, there may be genetic grounds for those differences'; and so on).

An analysis of the survey results revealed a strikingly different pattern of responses depending on whether a respondent was at home on the political left or the political right. Thus when evaluating the ideological items, those on the left and those on the right not only took polar opposite positions on nearly all of those items, they also organized the items in two very different clusters.

The principal organizing factor that emerged for those on the left bundled together issues of equality and fairness. Those on the right bundled together issues of law and order.

That the left is concerned with equality and fairness and the right with law and order makes intuitive sense. For centuries the left has characterized itself as 'progressive' and has been concerned with changing the status quo and flattening society in order to re-distribute power, diffuse control and spread the wealth.

In contrast, the right has characterized itself as 'conservative' and has been concerned with maintaining social order, safeguarding institutions, and ensuring social and political stability.

Much political discourse is occupied with the tension between these two demands – the left trying to change things and the right trying to put a brake on that change. Both camps consider the other to be 'ideological'.

If one explores these two factors in more detail one discovers that they represent different aspects of justice. While a lengthy historical discussion of justice is beyond the scope of this article, I would submit that these two aspects of justice – lawfulness and fairness – appear again and again in both classic moral philosophy and in the give and take of everyday life and are the root of much ideological conflict.

Both Plato and Aristotle considered justice to be the fundamental virtue. Aristotle believed that justice comprised two distinct but inter-related elements: one of lawfulness and one of fairness – just the two factors that emerged in the survey research analysis of provocative ideological items.

In contemporary political philosophy, the two aspects are somewhat pedantically characterized as 'retributive' and 'distributive' justice.

Retribution is a disinterested application of justice. The laws and punishments for breaking the laws are spelled out. When someone breaks the law and is apprehended, he or she should be punished according to the law regardless of his or her background, former deprivations or privileges. This is 'conservative' ideological thinking to the core, and the argument has some pedigree.

On the philosophical left, the issue of equality has been thoughtfully argued by John Rawls. In his book, *A Theory of Justice*, Rawls draws on the influential social contract tradition in political theory of Hobbes, Locke and Rousseau. He develops his theory from a hypothetical situation of equality.

Van den Haag complains that 'Rawls does not dwell on retributive (penal), but mainly on distributive justice, which has indeed become fashionable among philosophers, whereas retributive justice is often regarded as old-fashioned'. One might well substitute 'progressive' for fashionable and 'conservative' for old-fashioned in this sentence to cast the debate in its proper ideological light. This is by no means an arcane philosophical debate on the abstract nature of justice; it encompasses the roots of todays ideological conflicts.

Distributive and retributive justice need not be mutually exclusive alternatives. However, in everyday discourse, and in today's political arena, concerns of 'equality and fairness' and 'law and order' are frequently dissociated and pitted against each other. The two orphaned aspects have long ago been adopted by the political right and the political left, respectively.

The debate routinely overlooks the inter-related legitimacy of both aspects of justice. As a civilization, we overlook the inter-relationship of the two aspects of justice at our peril. The split between law and order and equality and fairness will in all likelihood continue to be a major source of tension between 'haves' and 'have nots' – whether in the political arena of our own country, in the international arena among sovereign states, or in the writing relationship between labor and management – the 'haves' attempting to maintain stability and the status quo and the 'have-nots' attempting to initiate changes in the direction of greater equality. The underlying issue is one of control.

Ideology and business

The ideological tapestry in society provides the context for business. It makes a difference for business and society whether Russia or China fall back into a dictatorship or a civil war, whether the Islamic nations explode, implode or integrate smoothly into the world's evolving political and economic system and whether the World Trade Organization negotiations evolve smoothly or not.

The determination of all of these issues will in large part be based on ideological considerations. Ideological differences do not merely provide an external context for business, however. Ideological differences saturate the presumably rational organizational process of decision making.

Many managing directors and chief executive officers are vaguely aware that 'values' are important and that corporate 'vision' is necessary to move an organization forward. They are acknowledging, if only indirectly, the fundamental power of ideology. They frequently attempt to define and impose a corporate ideology (values and vision) on the organization, usually with mixed results.

One reason for the mixed results is that true ideology operates in the shadows, unconsciously and outside of awareness. Unconscious ideology is often behind conscious decisions about who gets the job and who gets the boot, who gets promoted and who gets passed over, and who gets the prison sentence and who gets off.

Ideology is based on differences, and these differences drive our social structures and our decision-making. Ideology is that basic. Understanding the effects of ideology makes a practical difference for the manager: it helps managers to be aware of the extent to which irrational factors operate in our groups and organizations – and in ourselves.

Managers in business are by no means exempt from ideological influence. On the contrary, they are as subject to its influence as is anyone else. Managers possess the same range of personality attributes and engage in the same pattern of decision-making as do others: the more extreme the personality, the more rigid the ideological framework; the more dogmatic and decisive the stance in decision making, the more uncompromising the subsequent action – whether the decision concerns corporate downsizing or ethnic cleansing.

There are doctrinaire socialists and there are doctrinaire capitalists. The measure of our dogmatism is a measure of our possession by the irrational aspects of a particular ideology.

Most of us work for private or public sector organizations – organizations that either produce or redistribute wealth. Both business and governmental organizations are driven by their own imperatives and both occasionally overlook the fact that there exist criteria in life other than microeconomic or electoral ones.

When one accepts as an article of faith that a free market economy (or a government-regulated one) necessarily makes things better, one is clearly in the clutches of an ideology. Neither a completely free market nor total government control can create and maintain a just society.

The conservative economic trickle-down theory has a habit of trickling capital into the portfolios of relatively wealthy investors, senior managers and large consulting firms; the socialist demand for radical equality has a habit of equalizing the poverty of the working and middle classes, killing initiative and centralizing power and control in the hands of a small governmental elite.

We do ourselves a disservice by not making our assumptions explicit and by remaining unaware of the full implications of our own ideology. We find significant tension and conflict between the claims of organizations in the different sectors – public and private – and we do not really understand why, and we do not really know what to do about it. We need to understand how we in business organizations are guided by ideology, or we will be its victims.

Summary

There are important but subtle differences between beliefs, values, attitudes and ideologies. Ideology is both utopian in that it is concerned with ultimate ends and prescriptive in that it is concerned with the means to achieved those ends. Its appeal is spiritual and transcendental. An ideology provides a meaning to life. There is an intimate relationship between personality and ideology which operates in organizations as well as in politics and religion – the more extreme the personality the more rigid the ideological framework. Decision-making is often complicated by ideology – at an overt level one sees differences of opinion about group direction, but covertly the polarization can often be characterized as differences among group members in deeply held, often unconscious, beliefs. Ideology and personality can be as influential as culture in predicting these patterns. The ideological tapestry in society provides the context for business – but understanding its effects inside the organization makes a practical difference for the working manager.

Suggested further reading

Wood, J.D. *A Theory of Small Group Structure*, Yale University, New Haven, (doctoral dissertation, 1987).

Eysenck, H.J. and Wilson, G.D. (1978) *The Psychological Basis of Ideology*, University Park Press, Baltimore.

Van den Haag E. (1975) *Punishing Criminals*, Basic Books, (1975).

Rawls, J. (1971) *A Theory of Justice*, Belknap Press, Cambridge, MA.

Globalization and multinationals

■ **Globalization is talked of glibly, but if we are really entering a global economy, and not just a larger international market, then the implications for companies and managers are immense.**

by Stephen J. Kobrin

As the 20th century draws to a close, the future of the international economy is difficult to predict.

On the one hand, trade and investment are growing more rapidly than world output and the international economy appears more deeply integrated than ever before. On the other hand, multilateralism is constantly threatened and regionalism – albeit in different forms and at different rates of progress – is stronger than ever before in the Americas, Europe and Asia.

Given the difficulties associated with the last GATT agreement and the birth of the World Trade Organization, an open, liberal international economy appears to be less than a certain bet at this point.

Where are we headed? Are we witnessing the emergence of a truly integrated 21st century world economy or the last gasps of a second 'global' economy about to crash on the shoals of regionalism and protectionism, as did the first during the great depression?

Late 19th and early 20th century flows of international trade and investment – both on an absolute and relative basis – were remarkable. Alan Blinder (ex vice-chairman of the US Federal Reserve) has argued recently that it took most of the post First World War era just to get back to the levels of international integration achieved during the first global economy.

The period from about 1870 to 1914 has been called the 'high water mark' and the 'golden age' of an open, integrated international economy. In fact, it is reasonable to ask whether the world economy of 1996 is really that different from that of 1896.

The international economy has changed substantially over the last century. It is broader in terms of the number of national markets included as constituent units and deeper in terms of the intensity of international economic transactions. More important, its dominant mode of organization is no longer trade and portfolio investment but the multinational corporation.

By the early-1990s, 37,000 transnational corporations with sales of about $5,500bn controlled about one-third of the world's private-sector assets.

Real meaning or jargon?

Yet, the question remains: does 'globalization' really have substantive meaning or is it simply jargon describing an economy that is a bit more international – a bit broader and deeper – than it was a century ago?

The answer is of practical importance. The first 'global' economy crashed in the 1930s with the formation of competitive and closed regional blocs. Is the second 'global' economy about to follow suit with the breakdown of multi-lateralism and the rise of the new regionalism?

I think not. Three interrelated phenomena sharply differentiate the emerging 21st century global economy from its predecessors.

First, dramatic increases in the scale of technology – its cost, risk and complexity – have rendered even the largest national markets too small to be meaningful economic units.

Second, the explosive growth of transnational strategic alliances signals a fundamental change in the mode of organization of international economic transactions – trade and the multi-national are being replaced by global networks of alliances.

Finally, the emerging global economy is integrated through information systems and information technology rather than organization hierarchies. The result is an electronically networked world economy where national markets are losing meaning as constituent units and geography is no longer the basis for the organization of economic activity.

In industries such as pharmaceuticals, semi-conductors and telecommunications, research and development costs are increasing rapidly while product life cycles are shrinking. In these and other high-technology sectors, even the largest national markets are too small to support competitive R&D efforts. Companies must expand internationally to support technological development.

Furthermore, in many of these industries, single company internationalization no longer suffices. Even the largest organizations can no longer 'bet the company' on the next generation of semiconductors or jumbo jets. Thus Boeing entered a joint development agreement with Airbus to explore development of a 'super-jumbo' and IBM, Siemens and Toshiba have formed an alliance to develop a 266 megabyte chip at a cost of $1bn.

As important as the cost and risk of tech-nology is its complexity – a broad range of rapidly developing technologies is needed to stay competitive in many fields. Cross-national and cross-original alliances have become mandatory as companies find that they must pool knowledge

to survive. Although comprehensive data on alliances is hard to come by, there is unanimous agreement that they have grown exponentially over the last decade.

The net result is that national technological independence is difficult, if not impossible, to achieve. In the emerging global economy, the scale and complexity of technology in many strategic sectors has fused markets trans-nationally and cross-border co-operation is no longer optional.

The multinational role

The rapid growth of international alliances represents a very significant change in the basic mode of organization of international economic activity. At the end of the 19th century, the vast majority of international economic transactions were organized through the market, through trade or portfolio investment. By the last quarter of the 20th century, multinational companies replaced the market as the primary mode of organization of the international economy.

Economic transactions were internalized as trade and investment were brought within the administrative or organizational hierarchy of the corporation. Direct investment and intra-company trade were the result.

Alliances represent yet another shift in the organization of international economic trans-actions – from organizational hierarchies to networks; from mass to flexible production; from large vertically integrated organizations to disintegration and horizontal networks of economic units; from 'Fordist' to 'post-Fordist' companies.

Networks are a very different form of economic organization from both markets and hierarchies. They are a social or relational form of economic interaction where reciprocity and trust are critical. Organizational concepts such as a definite center, unambiguous borders and a clear hierarchy lose meaning when networks become prevalent.

It is important to conceive of a networked world economy in terms of a complex web of relationships rather than a series of dyadic or triadic relationships. A large multinational may well be involved in hundreds of relationships linking parts of its organization – a manufacturing plant or a research lab – to parts of others. As Peter Dicken has noted, global networks are multilateral and polygamous.

The disintegration of vertically integrated hierarchies and their reintegration through networks is made possible by modern information technology. The various nodes in the network – manufacturing plants, research labs and other parts of organizations – are linked through computers and satellites. The emerging global economy is electronically networked.

One result is a developing asymmetry between international economics and international politics, an asymmetry resulting from a post-modern global economy situated in a modern political system.

It has two primary dimensions: the scope or extent of markets and the mode of organization. As noted above, in many of the industries now regarded as strategic, national markets are no longer large enough to support competitive R&D efforts. The minimally efficient market is larger than even the largest state. There is an asymmetry in the geographic scope of economic and political units.

Politics v. economics

Perhaps of more fundamental importance are asymmetries in the primary mode of organization. Politics is still organized geographically in terms of territory and borders while economic activity is increasingly organized in terms of electronic networks where geography and territory are irrelevant.

The result is a developing imbalance between a modern, territorially based and geographically organized international political system comprised of nation states and an emerging post-modern world economy where national markets and, indeed, the very concept of territoriality and geography are becoming less relevant.

This emerging asymmetry has critical implications for both states and companies. As Nicholas Negraponte observes, trade in atoms is being replaced by trade in bits.

The geographic organization of economic activity in terms of national markets with discrete and meaningful borders assumes that regardless of how international the world economy is, at the end of the day all economic transactions can be located precisely and unambiguously in (national) economic space. That assumption no longer holds.

The Indian software industry, which has emerged as a major exporter in recent years, provides an example. What is relevant here is a dramatic change in the mode of organization; 'body shopping' – the seconding of Indian programmers abroad – has been replaced by direct satellite linkages. An Indian programr can work directly on a computer located in the UK or the US.

That raises some interesting and important questions. The programming work done in India on British or American computeers is an economic transaction. Where is the economic value created? Who gets to control the transaction? To tax it? Do concepts relevant to geographic space apply to cyber space?

The existing international financial system may be a metaphor for the emerging networked global economy. Hundreds of thousands of computer screens linked via satellite creating an electronically defined market where geography loses meaning.

In a world economy comprised of networked alliances where organization centers, borders and hierarchies lose relevance, what determines the nationality of companies? Without the headquarters-subsidiary hierarchy, how do national governments exert control over 'their' multinationals? If the IBM-Toshiba-Siemens alliance is successful, is the technology American, Japanese or German? Who gets to control it and what are the control mechanisms?

If I am correct, managers of multinationals will have to deal with an economic and political environment of increasing ambiguity and uncertainty for some time to come. While political risk has always been of concern, typically it involved a single company and a single government. The 'new' political risk is likely to involve multiple companies and multiple governments – alliance partners with different strategic objectives caught between three, four or five governments with different policy objectives and economic philosophies.

While political risks in the past may have been tangential – a loss in a country representing only a small fraction of the world market – the 'new' political risks go right to the heart of a company's strategic competence and technological competitiveness.

Managers will find that they face an increasingly complex political-economic environment without the direct hierarchical control they had in the past. Complex, polygamous networks and relational control will be the norm. Managers of global companies will have to deal with very new problems in very new ways.

One can generalize and argue that we face a major systemic discontinuity. Nation states and national markets are but one of a number of historical modes of organizing political and economic authority and, in historical terms, relatively short-lived ones at that. Nation states arose from the decay of the feudal system in medieval Europe and became dominant only in the 16th century.

The modern international system of sovereign states was not formalized until the treaty of Westphalia in 1648. National markets are even more recent arrivals, created consciously by relatively mature political units in the 18th and 19th centuries.

It is not unreasonable to argue that the symmetry between states and markets in both geographic scope and mode of organization – which we tend to take as the natural order of things – is characteristic only of a very brief window of time: perhaps the 100 years spanning the late 19th to late 20th centuries.

The developing asymmetry between a global, post-modern world economy and a modern international political system comprised of territorially sovereign states may not be stable. The emerging electronically networked global economy may herald a systemic transformation comparable in scope and effect to the transition from the medieval to the modern political-economy in 16th and 17th century Europe.

Global managers will have to deal with a turbulent and unsettled world for some time to come.

Summary

The first 'global economy' crashed in the 1930s – is the second about to do the same with the breakdown of multilateralism and the rise of new regionalism? The scale of modern technology (which renders national markets too small), the extent of strategic alliances, and global integration through IT suggest not.

Our electronically networked world has produced assymmetries between territorially-based political systems and a post modern economy where geography is less relevant. 'New' political risk may involve multiple countries and multiple governments and go right to the heart of strategic competence and technological competitiveness.

Suggested further reading

Dickens, P. (1994) 'The Roeplie lecture on economic geography: global-local tensions: firms and states in the global space economy *Economic Geography* 70, pp. 101-120.

Gue henno, Jean-Marie, (1995) *The End of the Nation State*, University of Minnesota Press, Minneapolis.

Hirst, P. and Thompson, G. (1996) *Globalization in Question*, Polity Press, Cambridge.

The Future of General Management

Contents

The end of management? Classroom versus the boardroom 631
Rob Goffee and John W. Hunt, London Business School
Are managers an unnecessary part of business?

Managing in turbulent times 635
John M. Stopford, London Business School
The implications of turbulence for managers.

Toolboxes are out; thinking is in 639
Werner Ketelhöhn, IMD
Too often companies look for a 'toolbox' of supposed management solutions to help their managers react to complex problems when what they really need are managers able to think.

The new language lab 643
Johan Roos and Georg von Krogh, IMD
The ability to create and diffuse language will be the key to the future of management.

Redesigning for the 21st century 649
Bruce Kogut and Edward H. Bowman
It would be a serious mistake to believe that the current management thinking is simply a phase of eternal cycle between looking inward and outward.

Contributors

 **Rob Goffee** is Professor of Organizational Behavior and Chair of the Organizational Behavior faculty at London Business School. His research interests include the dynamics of business start-up and growth, changing characteristics of managerial careers and organizational change.

 **John W. Hunt** is Plowden Professor of Organizational Behavior at London Business School. His research interests include the successful integration of acquisitions, motivation, leadership and managerial competencies.

 **John M. Stopford** is Professor of International Business at London Business School. His current research interests include both the transformation of corporations to achieve radical performance improvements and the role of large-scale enterprise in the international political economy.

 **Werner Ketelhöhn** is Professor of Strategy at IMD in Lausanne. His research interests include corporate strategy, business strategy and network companies.

 **Johan Roos** is Professor of Strategy at IMD in Lausanne. His research interest lies in the intersection between managing knowledge development, co-operative strategies, and strategy processes.

 **Georg von Krogh** is Professor of Management at the Institute of Management, University of St Gallen in Switzerland. His research interests include strategic processes, corporate acquisitions and corporate knowledge resources.

 **Bruce Kogut** is Professor of Management at The Wharton School of the University of Pennsylvania and Co-Director of the Reginald H. Jones Center.

 **Edward H. Bowman** is Reginald H. Jones Professor of Corporate Management and Co-Director of the Reginald H. Jones Center, at The Wharton School of the University of Pennsylvania.

Introduction

The first module of *Mastering Management* is devoted to an analysis of the current standing of general management. This final module is forward-looking rather than retrospective and is given over to a series of visions of the future of management.

The end of management? Classroom versus the boardroom

■ **Rob Goffee and John Hunt dispute the idea that managers are an unnecessary part of business.**

We have convinced ourselves that the world is changing – and in a big way. Indeed, in business corporations we no longer talk modestly of 'change', preferring instead the dramatic language of 'transformation', 'turnaround', 'cultural renewal' and 're-engineering'.

The avowed ambition is to re-invent the modern work environment to produce 'learning organizations', 'networks', 'transnationals' and 'virtual corporations', all of which sound remarkably like the small free-form consulting companies owned by academics rather than like an airline, an hotel or a government department.

What is remarkable about the language of modern organizational analysis is the extent to which it describes a world that, literally, does not exist. According to those who have developed the term, there is no organization that displays all the characteristics of a 'full' transnational. The concept of a 'learning organization' is extremely complex; few would be confident in knowing when they have seen one. 'Network' structures dissolve the boundaries between one organization and another; with the 'virtual corporation' the disappearing act is complete.

There is a danger here that in our excited race to label the brave new world we may have forgotten the basics of human interaction at work. Most of the world's working population continue to be employed in small-or medium-sized (rather than 'global') businesses; they earn their living in an identifiable 'place'; they have familiar work routines; someone they recognize as a 'boss' and so on. It is easy – but misleading – to miss the fundamental continuities in working life.

One such continuity is the persisting need for management. Yet in contemporary efforts to rewrite the organizational landscape few seem to have found a legitimate place for managers. Indeed, from the 'Excellence' literature onwards there appears to have been a concerted effort to devalue their role, if not write them out of the script completely.

Many organizations have been following the script. Middle managers have been eliminated by 'delayering', replaced by technology, excluded by 'top-down' change programs and undermined by 'bottom-up' empowerment. Those at the top have been encouraged to see themselves as 'leaders', 'visionaries', 'magicians' and 'myth-makers' – anything, it seems, but managers.

To 'help' managers adapt to this new world, those who survive are increasingly likely to have tough and new performance targets (to provide 'stretch'), to have their 'competencies' measured and assessed (to provide 'development') and to have their performance deficiencies regularly subjected to scrutiny from just about every direction (to provide '360 degree' feedback).

Is it any wonder that talented young people often see their futures in professional, consulting, expert and entrepreneurial roles – *anything* but managing.

Managers and management

The number, distribution, working patterns and careers of *managers* may be shifting but the fundamental requirement for *management* – for control, co-ordination, direction – remains.

Some universals need to be restated despite all the hype.

- Producing and delivering goods and/or services does require managing the allocation of scarce resources.
- Flatter hierarchies, devolved power and process centered work designs do not eliminate the need for management or managers.
- Even in autonomous work groups a hierarchy develops in which group members allow one or more of their peers to 'manage the task' and others to 'manage the relationships'. Non hierarchical organizations are impossible. However, they may be flatter, segmented, devolved, involving of employees. But the totally egalitarian organization does not exist. Any social structure has ranks and grades, even if only on abilities or height or body weight.

Although it is plausible to imagine organizations without people called managers, it is by definition impossible to think of them without management. Contemporary debates turn not on whether the functions of management are necessary but how they should be fulfilled.

And here there are differences. For example, the extent to which management is clearly differentiated as a distinctive function varies. Historically, the UK and the US have differentiated the role and made extensive efforts to distinguish necessary qualifications, skills, competencies and so on. One result is business schools.

Germany and Japan have integrated managerial and technical functions much more closely and have not, until recently, developed an infrastructure of 'management development' institutions external to the workplace.

Similar contrasts can be drawn between organizations. In the past, large-scale manufacturing organizations have typically distinguished a clear managerial stratum; but professional organizations have not. It is ironic that whereas the former are eliminating managerial layers, many of the latter are now seeking to differentiate, develop and reward the role.

Similarly, there are variations in the extent to which functions are performed by the individual or the team. Individualistic cultures – such as the US, Australia or the UK – appear more comfortable with direction (leadership) concentrated in one person. More collectivist societies –

such as Germany, Sweden or the Netherlands – are more able to dissolve or disperse managerial functions throughout the team and resist any would be leader's attempt to be really different.

Fifteen years ago one of the venture capital companies asked London Business School to conduct programs for its investment analysts. The program was designed to suggest that in addition to the all-important financial analyses conducted before lending money to small businesses perhaps analysts should examine the competence of the managers.

The program began with an exhortation from the CEO that the financial data were the dominant question in lending venture capital but there could be a case for assessing more rigorously a company's managerial talent. Today the competencies of the managers is the dominant question when any group of analysts assess a company. Investors will lend on very little financial information if the track record of the managers has been positive. It is only some academics who seem to think that the role of managers is redundant.

Back to basics

What, then, are the skills that are necessary for the effective management of resources? From early enquiries at the turn of the century to the current obsession with competencies there has been a massive search to establish the managerial skills that lead to superior performance.

Various models of managerial competencies (Boyatzis, Kotter, Schroder and Cockerill) have been suggested, all of which have a very similar ring to them. These researchers suggest that high performing managers need four skill sets:
- Cognitive/perceptual
- Interpersonal
- Presentational
- Motivational

In simple terms what do these skill sets mean?

Cognitive. Successful managers (people who run things) endlessly collect information. They observe, watch others, scan the press, look for patterns and recurring events. They 'see' things often before they occur. They are curious, voyeuristic (in a business sense), inquisitive.

They also display a capacity to reduce chunks of information into simple frameworks for others to follow. They reduce the complex to simpler models, frameworks, diagrams. If this does not lead to greater clarity or to task achievement then they will drop that model or strategy and devise another.

Interpersonal. In interpersonal terms, high-performing managers know intuitively that their achievements depend on others. They are only as good as their team. Hence finding and developing good people and building a team are recognized as activities that generate output. In this sense they are, like entrepreneurs, instrumental in their behavior.

Presentational. In presenting (both orally and in writing) the superior performers are confident, can argue their case and can present their story professionally. They typically spend up to 80 per cent of their time on communication with others.

Motivational. These managerial skills relate to setting stretching goals and focussing their team's effort on those goals. Better managers are proactive rather than reactive. They are primarily motivated by power – a strong desire to make things happen, to control resources – not as a end in itself but as a means of achieving results.

'Imperfection' and 'difference'

For the past six years, researchers at London Business School have been analysing these skills. There are some important findings.

First, even the best managers are not perfect – they will not be good at all the skills listed above. Second, they learn early in their careers to 'buy' the skills in which they do not excel. That is, they see managing as a team effort in which there will be people who will complement their skills rather than compete with them. Finally, they strive endlessly for improvement, to make their team and its achievements even better.

The acceptance of imperfection is important. Effective managers do not pretend to be perfect; they need the help of others. They admit their flaws and even use them to win support from their team members. This requires high levels of maturity, self-knowledge and confidence.

However, while successful managers admit their vulnerability they also differentiate themselves from the rest. They have personality characteristics, values, skills or ways of behaving that they deploy to distinguish themselves. These are the attributes which some see as the distinguishing characteristics of those who 'lead' as well as 'manage'.

In a survey of the past bosses, present peers and current subordinates of over 100 chief executives the most frequently cited 'differences' in the CEOs rated by their colleagues as most effective were:

- Force of personality – 33 per cent
- Competence in the job – 26 per cent
- Good with people – 22 per cent
- Flexibility – 10 per cent
- Ethical beliefs – 6 per cent.

The future of management

So where does this leave us? Despite our excited visions of the future, it seems likely that hierarchical structures will persist as one of the most effective ways to allocate resources.

Further, managers will continue to be employed to allocate resources and to create the conditions under which people are motivated to perform. However, large bureaucratic companies will continue to segment to create flatter structures. The economies of scale argument will be increasingly balanced by the diseconomies of scale argument of the social scientists. That is, there are quite clear disadvantages in collecting more than 500 people in one location.

Within this context; several changes in the selection, development and reward of managers can be expected:

- Increasingly, feedback assessments will put a price on effectiveness in the management of relationships as opposed to just the management of outputs. This may mean that the strongly task oriented but interpersonally incompetent may be less frequent at the top.
- Career managers will be selected for their managerial competencies not just their technical expertise. Tailor-made development programs designed exclusively to develop these competencies are already available.
- There will be far greater recognition that some competencies are genetic and are not easy to

develop. Managers without the 'right' genes will not be subjected to yet further training programmes in an attempt to induce these skills. Instead managers will be encouraged to promote their strengths as what differentiates them from their subordinates and their weaknesses as what humanizes them. That is, rather than pretending to be infallible they will concede their flaws and build teams to compensate for under-developed competencies.

- Coaching managers to be more effective is a growth business. In the same way as individuals have fitness coaches, so too will companies increasingly help managers through the personal attention of a consultant rather than yet another training program.
- As in the past, effective managers will be highly prized. Indeed, far greater mobility will mean an even more expensive labor market. However, the time scale in which managers must prove their effectiveness will shrink. Working 'the team' will be essential simply because the mobile manager will not have the time to understand the business fully before he/she is assessed.

The vital skills will be the capacity of the manager swiftly to embrace the role, to build the team, to establish difference and to win compensation and support for weaknesses. The time between being appointed and being assessed as a manager is shrinking dramatically. Whereas once we might have expected a new CEO to turn round a struggling business in five years we are now expecting that manager to do so in 12 months. No one can do this alone.

The effective manager of the future will be increasingly 'project oriented' – building focussed teams effectively, dismantling and re-forming them, moving flexibly and easily from one project to the next; an agent of managed change.

Summary

Many contemporary efforts to rewrite the organizational landscape seem to devalue the role of the manager. But the fundamental requirement for management remains: to allocate scarce resources, and to manage people and tasks. The important debate hinges not on whether the function is necessary but on how it is to be fulfilled. There are differences here between countries and types of company.

Researchers suggest that effective managers need four skill sets: an ability to reduce chunks of information into simple frameworks; a capacity to develop people and build teams; presentational and communication abilities; and motivation. Even the best are not good at all these and will acknowledge that they need the help of others. Yet successful managers differentiate themselves from the rest through (among other things) force of personality and competence in the job. In future the management of relationships is likely to become more important, career managers will be selected for their managerial competences not just their technical expertise, and coaching will become an even bigger growth business. The time available to deliver results is shrinking dramatically.

Suggested further reading

Hunt, J. W. (1993) *Managing People at Work*, McGraw Hill.

Goffee, R. and Scase, R. (1995) *Corporate Realities*, Routledge.

Managing in turbulent times

■ **Turbulence has been the underlying theme running throughout the *Mastering Management*. John Stopford looks at the causes and the implications for managers.**

Competitive turbulence has been a constant theme for many articles in *Mastering Management*. Does the old Chinese curse 'may you live in interesting times' catch the sense of the future of management? Gone, it would seem, are the cosy days, if they ever really existed, when market leaders could rest on their laurels secure in the belief that their superior scale and market power would protect them from attack.

AEG, Boeing, Degussa, Gulf Oil, Sears Roebuck and many other famous enterprises have seen their market shares seriously eroded. Pan Am and other erstwhile leaders have crashed like giant trees in the forest. Other former leaders have, like the Cheshire Cat, disappeared leaving only their names behind. Dunlop is now a Japanese brand and RCA a French one.

Technology is one of the potent forces upsetting established markets, sometimes sweeping away yesterday's leaders, sometimes creating a new generation of companies such as Microsoft. The emerging multimedia technologies, for example, are changing habits of readership and information-gathering.

Educational text book publishers are having to consider how multimedia affects education in the home. If much of the growth of educational materials might lie in the realm of interactive CD-Rom and TV delivery systems, can they develop the needed new capabilities fast enough to stay ahead?

How can they plan when and in what to invest, given the current uncertainties? There are few theories available to help answer such questions. Managerial judgment – that elusive elixir – is required.

Technology is not, however, the only disturbing force. Managerial imagination and strategic innovation can combine to extend the boundaries of existing markets. Companies as diverse as Benetton, CNN and Wal-Mart share the characteristics of high ambition and constant experimentation as they transform their industries.

Others have overcome even more daunting challenges to return from the grave of near bankruptcy to capture regional or global leadership. The recovery of BOC's Edwards vacuum equipment subsidiary shows how a minnow can be transformed by outstanding leadership into first the rule-breaker for its industry and then the rule-setter.

These contrasting stories of challenge and response are only part of the turbulence. Individual managers often feel that they are even more at risk than their companies, for the price of survival of many western companies is the removal of layers of managers. The same trend is now visible in Japan, so strong are the cost pressures of global competition. Even the hallowed tradition of life-time employment is being challenged in leading companies, such as Nippon Steel andNissan.

How can one see the wood for the trees? Turbulence has created a 'bonfire of the certainties' as one British MP remarked a few years ago about public policy. So too in management, where theory is being challenged at every turn. Never before, it would seem, has management skill mattered more to make the difference between success and failure.

Rethinking strategy

At the heart of management is the need to define the purpose of the enterprise and to turn ideas into action through the imagination and energy of people at all levels in the organization.

Purpose cannot be defined solely in terms of financial targets. Few employees rush into work each day eager to make money for remote shareholders.

The magazine *Management Today* published a list of the most profitable UK company in each year during the 1980s and showed that most of them had either failed or been taken over by 1990.

To be durable, purpose has to be made more immediate and more tangible to people's working reality. Thus, much strategic thinking is adding ideas from the 'soft' side of management to give dignity, meaning and excitement to the competitive struggles.

In the 1970s, the dominant models of strategy were based on industrial economics and emphasized the importance of industry structure and position within an industry. To oversimplify the theory, managers were exhorted to pick a favourable segment of an industry, master the economic conventions and watch the profits grow.

Today's turbulence has dented confidence in such analytical recipes. That management can make a difference is underscored by the dramatic rise of Circuit City, a US retailer of consumer electronics, one of the most intensively competitive markets with wafer-thin margins – the hallmark of an 'unattractive' industry. Nonetheless, Circuit City produced a total shareholder return of 16,410 per cent, among the highest in the US, during 1972-92.

Competition is becoming less a 'war of position' and more a 'war of movement' in which success depends on rapid responses to changes and a willingness to innovate. As well as a battle of resources – the notion of the strong and the weak all playing by the same set of Queensbury rules – competition has also become a battle among competing strategies.

David *can* conquer Goliath, sometimes with only modest expenditures. For David to prevail he must develop an organization capable of accumulating and combining all forms of resource in innovative ways. Among those resources are capabilities, both of individuals and small teams and of the system.

High-performing companies have developed specialized assets and unique skills that add value to customers and are hard for competitors to copy. The difficulty of imitation increases as the parent companies finds new ways to leverage those capabilities across a broad range of activities.

Honda is now famed for its core capability in engine technology; 3M for its range of technology applications such as adhesives.

Core capability is a relatively new addition to strategic thinking. It provides an alternative perspective on organizing resources compared with conventional structure of product divisions.

Honda caught Mercury by surprise when it entered the outboard marine business some years ago. Why should an outboard engine company monitor a motorcycle/automobile manufacturer? Now the answer is obvious but not then for Mercury's planners, who were focussed on other outboard producers. Moreover, it is less obvious before the event how new capabilities might change industry boundaries.

Innovative strategies based on capability depend greatly on the *mechanisms* of control and governance in companies. Experimentation demands that some projects will fail.

But how to make failure legitimate? How often can a manager run failing projects before she or he is deemed unfortunate, careless or downright incompetent? What non-financial information should be used for control in companies? Can the currently fashionable ideas of stakeholder management be made operational, both for society at large and for companies in particular?

Such questions demand better answers than are available in today's textbooks, for slavish adherence to conventional wisdom all too often can lead to failure relative to innovative opponents.

Internal mechanisms are becoming a crucial form of 'glue' connecting the internal organization to the market. Because competitive battles are being played out over long periods, far beyond the range of reasonable forecasting, managers face the challenge of building organizational capability consistently over time.

High-performing companies have adjusted

their thinking on strategy and risk taking to meet this challenge.

Instead of regarding the long term as a distant return, they develop a perspective on industry evolution and how to shape it by their own actions. Instead of regarding high ambition as high risk, they aspire to high goals yet retain the flexibility to adjust to opportunity.

Instead of measuring commitment to a particular path in terms of the amount of money invested, they show commitment by their consistency in building capabilities over the long term. For them, such human development is an investment, not a training expense readily forgotten after the end of the budget period.

Rethinking general management

To maintain consistency of purpose and retain flexibility, general managers have at least seven distinct but related roles and responsibilities. Maintaining adequate performance on them all is a challenge for the future.

First is *leadership* to establish direction and purpose. Thomas Watson Sr, the founder of IBM, once observed 'it is harder to keep a business great than it is to build it.'

General managers who think of their role as maintaining the status-quo – often in the name of gaining efficiencies – risk failure by stasis. Small wonder that the CEOs of many innovative companies now attract great publicity.

Percy Barnevik of ABB, Bill Gates of Microsoft, Jack Welch of GE, Akio Morita of Sony are familiar names. Their visibility within and outside the corporation suggests an augmented role at the top. Despite the obvious risks of dependence on one person's view and likely obsolescence, the question of style of leadership is now an important agenda, part of the wider debate about how enterprises create value.

Second is *choosing* feasible strategies. No company can do everything. Deciding where and when scale is important is one example of choice. David Simon chairman of BP said recently that scale has become less important in some sectors of the oil business and is adjusting strategy accordingly. Unconvinced competitors are investing in the opposite direction.

Equally contentious are the debates about the relative merits of diversification and focus and the shedding of non-core businesses. General mangers have to exercise careful judgments in these matters, for there is little solid theory that can be applied to their particular circumstances.

Third is *selecting* the focus for building and (sometimes) experimentation and allocating resources appropriately.

Building means creating new knowledge, as Nonaka and Takeuchi show for new product development in Japanese companies (*see* 'Suggested further reading'). Building requires managers to make careful, and difficult, trade-offs between the present and the future.

For example, only a few years ago US and UK companies were criticized for having an excessive regard to short-term pressures in their capital markets and so damaging their longer-term futures. German and Japanese companies were praised for taking long-term views and being more patient for profits. Today, the critics have retreated as Japan and Germany remain in recession while many US and UK companies have regained position.

Fourth is *building* multiple capabilities, for success seldom depends on leadership in a single dimension of the business.

This role is closely related to the fifth responsibility: *orchestrating* all available resources. Orchestration requires that resource building is balanced against the quest for efficiency. It is not a choice of building or efficiency; it is building and efficiency.

Though middle-level general managers play an important role in such orchestration – they are experienced and close to the markets – they have become an endangered species as organizations become flatter.

Delayering is supposed both to reduce costs and increase organizational effectiveness. As Jack Welch, the CEO of General Electric, has remarked 'layers of management mask mediocrity.' The process can, however, go too far and destroy the essential knowledge base of the enterprise. Initial gains of the leaner-and-fitter variety can soon give way to what some call 'corporate anorexia' or "dumb-sizing".

In striking a workable balance, middle-level managers have to develop a greater perspective on the enterprise as a whole. Traditionally, the managerial hierarchy has had the perverse effect of conditioning managers in the same way that huskies are conditioned by the harness of the sled – only the lead dog gets to see the scenery. In flatter structures, many more general and functional managers have to see the scenery to make the whole system work effectively.

Enabling such shifts is part of the sixth challenge, managing continuous renewal, or *rejuvenation*, in which organizational learning plays a role. The imperative is to ensure that the strategy remains vital.

To keep risk within manageable proportions, high-performing companies are learning that renewal can often be accomplished by adding new capabilities in small 'layers'. Strategy is seldom well defined or workable when regarded as the 'big hit' or the single idea that will transform the companies' fortunes.

The final challenge is *managing external relationships* and is of two kinds.

First is the selection of appropriate partners in the burgeoning arena of strategic alliances. One way to augment scarce resource and capability is to form a strategic alliance with someone else. Over a quarter of all new international ventures over the last decade have been in some form of alliance, such as the BT/MCI deal in telecommunications.

Even so, many regard alliances as inherently risky and point to such examples as the break-up of the Rover/Honda alliance for evidence. Learning how to manage alliances is a new frontier for most general managers.

Other external relationships are those with government and society generally. Consumers are changing the norms of acceptable corporate behavior. Shell's traumas over the Brent Spar and the tragic events in Nigeria illustrate the problem. The need to maintain clarity and a publicly articulated position is often confounded by the absence of commonly agreed yardsticks for judgment.

Similar dilemmas face multinational companies when they are caught between two countries with mutually inconsistent policies. These dilemmas must be managed, even

resolved, for private enterprise has to be socially legitimate if it is to survive profitably.

Fear or excitement?

What does all this mean for the future of management? Has it all become so complex, confusing and risky that the Chinese fear of uncertainty produces a real curse?

If individuals respond only with fear they are unlikely to prosper as managers. The future will belong to those who see opportunity for innovation and who overcome the fears of a failure of imagination to combat the turbulence.

The future also lies with the ambitious. For them, strategy is a process of stretching resources. They challenge the well-worn conventions of the SWOT approach that provides a careful analysis of strengths, weaknesses, opportunities and threats and allows strategy to be chosen so as to 'fit' the market.

Instead, like great entrepreneurs from Andrew Carnegie onwards, they do not base strategy on today's resources but on a belief that they can create new ones faster than competitors.

As Poras and Collins have suggested from their study of leading, long-lived US corporations, the future lies with those who master the *and*s and get away from the *or*s.

Combining seeming opposites is often a way forward: higher quality *and* higher productivity; wider product ranges *and* lower cost; greater discipline in the system *and* greater tolerance and support for individuals' experiments; the drive for cash and profits *and* balancing all stakeholder interests.

Scott Fitzgerald, in the *Great Gatsby*, defined a first-class intelligence as the ability to hold two opposing thoughts in the mind and retain the ability to function effectively. Management in the future requires this sort of capability. It should be exciting.

Summary

Technology is not the only disturbing force. Managerial imagination and strategic innovation can extend the boundaries of existing markets. Competition has become a battle of strategies as well as a battle of resources –

core capability is a relatively new ingredient and one in which high performing companies are willing to make a long-term investment. General managers have at least seven distinct, but related, roles: to establish purpose and direction through leadership; to choose the right strategy (including whether to diversify or increase the focus); to make trade offs between the present and the future (in resource allocation, for example); to build multiple capabilities; to orchestrate all re-sources (with regard to efficiency); to ensure continuous rejuvenation of the enterprise; and to manage external relationships both with alliance partners and stakeholders. Successful managers increasingly need to resolve many traditional dilemmas by learning how to combine seeming opposites.

Suggested further reading

Baden-Fuller, C. and Stopford, J. (1994) *Rejuvenating the Mature Business*, HBS Press and *International Thompson* (1995), 2nd edn.

Collins, J. and Poras, J. (1995) *Built to Last: Successful Habits of Visionary Companies*, Century.

Hamel, G. and Prahalad, C. K. (1994) *Competing for the Future*, HBS Press.

Ikujiro Nonaka and Hirotake Takeuchi, (1995) *Knowledge-Creating Company: How Japanese Companies Create the Dynamics of Competition*, Oxford University Press.

Toolboxes are out; thinking is in

■ **Too often companies look for a 'toolbox' of supposed management solutions to help their managers react to complex problems. But what they really need are managers able to think, says** Werner Ketelhöhn

'The way decisions are taken around here is unbelievable! The process seems to drag on for ever. And when we get a decision it is often too late and wrong.'

This outburst came from the chief executive of a Scandinavian corporation but it reflects the thinking of many senior managers around the world. And so does the solution he proposed: 'I need to put together a toolbox, a set of recipes, that will enable my people to make decisions faster and better.'

Diagnosis

He was reaching for the wrong medicine. The real problem lay with the company's learning processes, which included a management-development program. These would not be improved by introducing a toolbox.

On the contrary, the situation could get worse if inexperienced and unskilled managers started blindly using tools to reach decisions. The arrival of spreadsheets and microcomputers did not make financial analysis any easier – it just produced extremely fast number crunching.

Creating a toolbox implies that management consists of a series of tricks that anyone can perform after enough practice. But a manager who plays a memorized tape each time he or she encounters a problem is not going to solve that problem. A tool cannot replace thinking. And training to use tools cannot replace education.

The chief executive should have been looking at his company's learning processes. Many companies boast of being able to attract the best management talent on the market but then complain that these people are not taking decisions properly. At the same time, the world's top management consulting companies recruit people of equal ability and sell their services at premium prices. Why are companies willing to pay for the advice of people who are no more talented than their own managers?

Part of the answer lies in the education given at the work place to develop competencies. Education is about learning to think critically and top management consulting companies have put systems in place to develop this ability.

Another important aspect is specialization. Consultants tend to specialize in analysis and synthesis while most managers specialize in getting things done. Much of the dissatisfaction that chief executives have with the decision-making process starts here – by viewing these two activities as separate and distinct.

Companies have to create the support processes needed to develop managerial thinking. They can, for example, take managers regularly out of the office to address families of problems and opportunities. Managerial networks are created, common analytical frameworks are applied and managers get used to synthesizing knowledge from a mass of facts and information. Most importantly, a common language and a shared management perspective are used across corporate divisions and functions.

Toolboxes

Creating a management toolbox can be appealing. The feeling that subordinates are thus fully equipped for decision-making reduces uncertainty at the top of the company. And, the thinking goes, any tool that has been overlooked can always be added or new models used to replace old ones. Managers will waste much less time in meetings since they will be using new, practical, action-oriented tools.

If only it worked! Companies could install the tools in a few microcomputers, fire all middle-level managers and employ high-school graduates to solve the company's management problems. Internal communications would not be needed, group work would be eliminated and much less time would be wasted. In other words, we would no longer need to think through management problems and opportunities.

Now the idea does not sound so attractive. The fact is that management is not about fixing things; it is about creating the conditions in which people are able to accomplish their professional objectives effectively. It is about encouraging, guiding and coaching people and developing processes in which they learn from one another. There are no expert systems that can replace managers.

The assumption behind the toolbox idea is that it will allow managers to produce instant solutions to complex problems. But a tool only works if you know what it is designed to do.

A hammer is meant to be used on nails and a screwdriver used on screws. Understanding analysis and synthesis does not come from using tools, it comes from education. If managers have not grasped the causal relationships in a given situation they will not know how to use the tools properly. Just as they will damage the woodwork if they hammer in a screw, they may use the wrong managerial tool and take damaging decisions.

Formulae creep in everywhere. Remember Laffer's Curve? The Reagan administration stuck to 'supply-side economics', which was based on this simple diagram showing how you can raise more tax dollars with lower tax rates. The blind application of this tool increased the US budget deficit by more that $2,000bn in 12 years.

Relying on formulae is dangerous for any business. Since they help management to avoid thinking through a given situation they are barriers to building a learning organization. A formula is simply a poor substitute for thinking.

Learning from analysis

The general manager of a business unit of a major German corporation was attending a three-day workshop on redesigning management processes. Halfway through he said: 'OK, OK, enough changes have been proposed. Now let's all stop talking and get back to work' and he cancelled the rest of the workshop.

What did he mean by 'work'? Was he saying

that trying to understand how things function is not work? Or that directing a team of talented people in the right direction is not work? Does he believe that co-operation is bad or learning is something to avoid? Perhaps he is afraid of subordinates who think.

Such meetings should certainly not be a waste of time. Effective group work leads to sharing data, information, intelligence and knowledge about best management practices. Organizations learn if groups of people are able to learn together – this is how core competencies are acquired.

One particularly good example is Benetton, the Italian clothing company. Benetton's rags-to-riches story was based on its refusal to accept established knowledge as the ultimate truth. Instead, it searched for continuous improvements and made a simple assumption – the way we understand things today can be improved tomorrow.

The process starts with collecting opinions on a specific issue. These are then used to create a hypothesis about causal relationships. Next, to confirm or disprove the hypothesis, data is gathered. But facts do not speak for themselves. They have to be analyzed to make their meaning clear and this analysis provides information about a causal relationship.

The process is repeated several times, each time improving the quality of the hypothesis, data, analysis and synthesis until the hypothesis is finally accepted as meaningful information. As Benetton managers used this information to decide on a course of action, they were already thinking about how to learn from the results.

Action learning

The Benetton network was created by 'trial and error' – experimenting and retaining what had worked – at each stage of the company's development. For example, Luciano Benetton did not have much faith in conventional market research. He believed that opening a shop taught him more about the market than reading volumes of studies.

His management philosophy was founded on three clear principles: 'The real essentials are very few; it is important to be creative; and do not be afraid of making mistakes.' This is simple but powerful stuff.

Action learning processes, such as that used at Benetton, start by incorporating new information into an existing body of knowledge. This indicates a causal relationship and, based on this, decisions about the allocation of resources are made and implemented. Then the results are compared with the expectations and the reasons for any deviation are reviewed. The new insights this produces are used to update the existing body of knowledge.

But this does not mean there is no analysis before decision-making, quite the contrary. At Benetton, opinions were carefully separated from information and causal relationships were reviewed through both analysis and action learning. The two processes are repetitive and complementary.

Thinking versus doing

The most important element in managerial decision-making is balancing thinking and doing. If you exaggerate the thinking process you can lead your company into a spiral of 'paralysis by analysis'.

On the other hand, if you rush into action you may promote a shoot-from-the-hip, 'Rambo' culture in the organization.

In each situation you have to find the right balance between the two. But, inevitably, some people prefer to think more while others cannot wait to start doing. So what can be done to accelerate the slow thinkers and slow down the speedy doers?

One simple question can tell you when it is time to stop thinking and start doing – are you satisfied with the process used to state the hypothesis, obtain the data, analyze the data and synthesize the information? If the answer is yes, it is time to take the information it has produced and get on with it.

Of course it is always possible to improve the quality of the information with more repeats of the thinking process. You can keep improving it and never be completely satisfied. But if the process is satisfactory, you already know enough to act and then to learn from results.

It is rather like an experiment in which

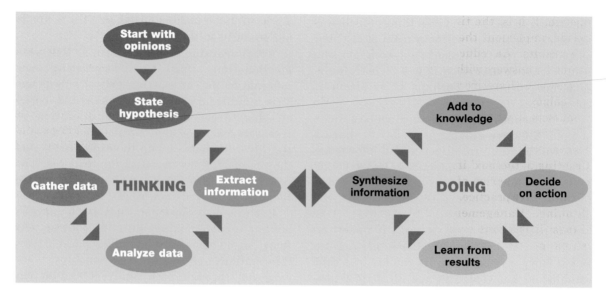

Figure 1

scientists learn from analysing the results obtained and feed this new information back into their thinking process. Managers should do the same – learn from their actions and feed the learning back into their knowledge base and their decision-making process. There is no reason to drag on decisions for ever. Educate your people to think critically.

If the answer to the question is no – if your managers are dissatisfied with the quality of their information – they should repeat the thinking process. And if the information is difficult to improve, thinking before doing becomes even more important.

Learning from analysis and learning from action are two complementary components of the learning process. This process can be illustrated by a continuous loop that winds around the two poles of thinking and doing (*see* Figure 1). There is not a thinking-doing dichotomy – no action is performed without some thinking and no thinking is performed without some doing. In other words, we cannot separate strategy formulation from implementation.

Consider some common management dilemmas. Who should decide on strategy – corporate or business unit management? Should we centralize or decentralize subsidiary management? Centralize or decentralize decision-

making? Shall we set objectives to stretch our managers or stick to those that are clearly achievable? Shall we make a specific business unit more specialized or keep its broad range of products? Should we emphasize short-term or long-term goals? Do we strengthen our product-development business system or our product-delivery business system?

These are not either/or issues with right and wrong answers. Thinking of them as such is what causes violent pendulum swings in corporate management approaches. Each situation needs to be carefully analyzed, then a decision has to be taken, put into practice and adjusted after observing the results.

Conclusion

When the decision-making process is not working well there is a temptation to search around for a theory of management (a toolbox) instead of thinking through each situation and learning from experience. But thinking and doing are not alternatives, they are inseparable; and problems arise when one is emphasized at the expense of the other.

Instead, managers need to be educated to think through a specific situation. They need to understand the process that has produced their information and judge whether or not it is good enough. If it is, the time has come for them to decide, implement the decision and learn from the results. An educated manager does not search for answers with universal validity but for an answer with specific validity in each situation.

Toolboxes are out; thinking is in. After all, what facts do we have about the future?

Summary

Creating a 'toolbox' implies that management consists of a series of tricks that anyone can perform after practice. But a tool cannot replace thinking. Management is not about fixing things; it is about creating the conditions in which people are able to accomplish their professional objectives effectively. There are no expert systems that can replace managers.

Organizations learn if groups of people are able to learn together – this is how core competencies are acquired. Benetton's rags-to-riches story was based on its refusal to accept established knowledge as the ultimate truth. The most important element in management decision-making is balancing thinking and doing: if the process used to state the hypothesis, obtain, analyse and synthesize the information is satisfactory you already know enough to act and then learn from the results. Thinking and doing are not alternatives, they are inseparable.

The new language lab – part 1

■ **In this and the following article** Johan Roos **and** Georg von Krogh **examine some of the latest thinking in management, in particular the application of epistemology.**

The urgent need to understand 'knowledge - workers' and to create 'learning organizations' is an important preoccupation for the current generation of managers. But the challenge is daunting due to the lack of clear and useful frameworks for how knowledge is created by individuals – and within groups – engaged in business enterprises.

Epistemology is the field of science that deals with the creation of knowledge and we have found that it contains numerous insights for management that will accelerate the pace with which companies can develop and make use of knowledge. Three of the most powerful concepts within the domain of corporate epistemology are:
● *Self-reference*: the observation that each of us carries our own unique frame of references, which is the source of both group creativity and group confusion. Because these frames are so individualized, you cannot 'force' self-reference to happen through the exercise of authority; it must be voluntary.
● *Languaging*: the process through which we both create new meaning and share meaning and frames of reference in language.
● *Self-similarity*: when the same basic patterns of interaction re-occur at different scales within the company – individual, group, strategic business unit and so on. This is one of the key features of the most powerful knowledge-development processes and management systems.

What you see depends on who you are

Traditionally in companies, directions have been decided on and resources allocated very much as a parent gives guidance and boundaries to a child. A hierarchy of authority underpins this process.

The company chief executive gains the backing of investors based on his or her understanding of the commercial environment, the corporation develops a strategy based on this understanding and gets it accepted throughout the organization by virtue of its authority over the various businesses. In like manner, managers impose this strategy on their subordinates by virtue of their authority and so on down the hierarchical line.

Underpinning this process is the assumption that when exposed to a new experience, we all see it as the same thing. In the authority-based company, it really does not matter who gathers the data, does the analysis and/or draws the conclusions. The higher up one is in the hierarchy, the more information/knowledge one is supposed to have. So, with a higher position in the hierarchy came the privilege of strategic thinking.

Of course this does not reflect the needs of a business environment in which technology is creating new industries requiring radically new knowledge and skills. Nor does it reflect the strategic priorities of empowerment, organizational learning and foresight. Nor does it reflect that authority in companies no longer rests on a profound knowledge base that has been rigorously tested and validated throughout a long corporate career.

Self-referencing refers to the commonsense, everyday observation that each of us has a unique set of experiences that makes us see and react to things differently. What you see depends on who you are. Through this continuous self-reference we develop new knowledge that will always be unique to each one of us. In turn, our private knowledge makes us see new things others do not.

This is why it matters who did the industry analysis, who made the claim about emerging technology or who did the market segmentation.

Although the differences between people's views eventually converge and become trivial on routine matters, they are the essential building blocks for the creation of new knowledge. This is also why every company always develops an ever-changing knowledge base.

While the exercise of command authority (where one individual tells another individual what to do) is sometimes necessary, excessive reliance on authority is an enormous barrier to the availability and creation of knowledge within a company. It prohibits individuals from successfully self-referencing.

Management also needs to understand norms, beliefs, values and world views of employees, groups, units and the whole company. All of those form the basis from which to see the future and to decide what new knowledge is legitimate and what is not.

This goes beyond alluding to vision/mission statements, job descriptions, organizational charts and other artefacts of the company. People participate in, and contribute their knowledge to, many organizations simultaneously, such as the company, the family and the basketball team. All of these experiences influence who they are and, therefore, what knowledge they develop and contribute to their companies.

Language as strategic resource

It is obvious that without language, knowledge could not flow from person to person within a company. It is equally obvious that if people speak different languages, then communication is stifled.

What is not always obvious is that due to self-referencing, people are constantly in the process of creating new language and new meanings, even if they share the same mother tongue. On the high value-added boundaries of knowledge creation, the ability to 'make' new language – and rapidly diffuse it through a company – is a strategic advantage.

The strategic significance of language is discussed in detail in the subsequent section.

Making management simple so that business can be complex

Businesses are turning Frederick Taylor's rules of management upside down. Work groups are autonomous and decide for themselves how and when to fulfill orders; employees are multifunctional so that they can participate in different teams and work units.

This is a traditional manager's nightmare. Policies that are productive in one setting may be disruptive in another. In the extreme case, specific policies and action plans might need to be different for each individual worker. To the traditional manager, this looks like anarchy, like chaos.

The new-style manager looks for a hidden order behind the throes of knowledge creation. He or she takes a clue from the repeating patterns observed in nearly all things in nature. When patterns or processes re-occur at different levels within a system they are said to be 'self-similar.' The notion has been popularized by colorful pictures of geometric shapes – so-called 'fractals' – and by books on chaos theory, ironically enough.

But the good news for managers is that self-similarity seems to be nature's way of reducing one form of complexity while giving other forms of complexity – including knowledge – the means to flourish.

People, groups and companies have the capacity to self-reference and 'language' the way we have described. For example, if a company can simplify its management systems so that essentially the same process is used to make individual, team, business unit and corporate management decisions, then the artificial limits to the size or shape of that company might be eliminated, i.e., it can become as large or as small as it needs to be.

At the same time it increases the number of different markets in which a company might be able to operate effectively – all without increasing the complexity of managing the company.

This is precisely how a manufacturing and financial services company in the US has set out to improve its strategic management capability. It defines management responsibilities in terms of a small number of key functions: to develop new knowledge in the form of new options; to decide on which options are relevant; and to implement these options.

The model is designed to be replicated at any level in the organization. Middle managers use it in their daily activities as do foremen in the manufacturing plant.

Conclusion

In a knowledge-driven society where more and more employees are seen as knowledge workers, management is not what it used to be. In this section we have offered some 'food for thought' for a different managerial frame in the guise of three new concepts: languaging, self-reference and self-similarity.

These are old concepts; they have been part of human culture for tens of thousands of years. Still, they are taking on a new life as strategic tools in the hands of managers in the knowledge age.

The meaning of these concepts in management is not only about reassessing how we collectively and individually use language and stimulate self-reference but rethinking how we view power, trust and co-operation as well as how we develop foresight and set directions. On a more profound level, however, it requires us to rethink what is knowledge, how we view work and what it means to be employed.

One thing is certain: managers who have ability, guts and the humility constantly to reassess and challenge their management thinking and practice will be more valuable to their employers than those who do not.

Summary

Three of the most important concepts within the domain of corporate epistemology are 'self-referencing', 'languaging' and 'self-similarity'. Self-referencing refers to the everyday observation that each of us has a unique set of experiences which is the source of both group creativity and confusion. Differences between people's views are essential building blocks for the creation of new knowledge – excessive reliance on authority in a company is an enormous barrier to this process. Languaging is the process through which we create and share meaning and frames of reference. The ability to 'make' new language (and rapidly diffuse it through an organization) is a strategic advantage. When patterns of processes re-occur at different levels within a system they are said to be 'self-similar'. This seems to be nature's way of reducing one form of complexity while giving other forms of complexity (including knowledge) the opportunity to flourish. Artificial limits to a company's size can thereby be eliminated, the number of markets in which a company can operate effectively can be increased.

The new language lab – part 2

■ **The ability to create and diffuse language will be the key to the future of management, say** Johan Roos **and** Georg von Krogh

Conversations are the backbone of business. Nothing gets done in a business without at least two people talking about it, and if they do not understand each other, things can go terribly wrong.

Every company has its own unique set of concepts and phrases – its own language – that cannot be easily translated or adopted by anyone else. Unless you are part of the conversations that made the language, and continually remake it, important meanings can be totally missed.

The success of a company in taking on a new product or market is directly related to its ability to create new language and rapidly diffuse it into operations. As Peter Drucker, management writer, has noted: 'Knowledge has become the key economic resource and the dominant, if not the only, source of comparative advantage.'

Since language is the currency of knowledge, it is the only means through which that advantage can be institutionalized and exploited.

Given the centrality of language to both the routine operation and the future success of business, it is ironic how few managers pay the slightest attention to it – or to the *conversations* that give rise to it. We have yet to see a strategic planning document with 'Manage the business conversations better' as a major bullet point, but the time has come to put it near the top of the list.

Strategic and operational conversations

There is a useful distinction to be made between the conversations that are primarily focussed on executing existing routines within a business and those trying to create a space for something new to take shape.

The former covers issues that have been talked about previously. Perhaps these issues were new to everyone at some time in the past and once required more extensive conversation but not any longer.

The latter calls for people to move into new and unfamiliar territory, perhaps talking about things that have never been talked about before.

Operational conversations are about exploiting the knowledge gained in the past and present. Strategic conversations are about creating the knowledge – and the language to diffuse it – that will be necessary for a successful future.

Managers instinctively seem to do a better job on the operational conversations than the strategic ones. Consider the following illustration: a general manager calls an afternoon meeting to discuss how to bring down the costs of maintenance on a production line. The discussion is lively and contentious but at the end a decision is hammered out and everyone leaves feeling like they accomplished something.

The following weekend the same group of managers gets together to talk about long-term strategy. The setting is a beautiful retreat center in the mountains; the company has spared no expense. There are long conversations about 'corporate culture', 'core competencies' and 'foresight' but the resulting statements feel fairly abstract and the managers' minds wander to a troubling employee or a contract that needs to be finalised. Most leave the meeting feeling that they wasted a lot of time and that nothing really will change.

This scene repeats itself with frustrating regularity. Managers who are proficient at talking about the day-to-day challenges in their businesses have trouble translating that success into their strategic conversations. 'Strategy sessions' end up focussing on day-to-day operational details or become over-structured, boring and political – a waste of time. The exceptions to this pattern are fondly remembered but remain exceptions.

In the days when a company's strategy took years to unfold and was tied to a fairly stable set of products, this limitation did not carry a great cost. Now they are under pressure to change directions in a matter of weeks or months. Like the obsolescence of computer equipment, a strategy has a very short shelf life. If managers are not proficient at talking about the future, their company will not have one.

One reason that managers have less success with strategic conversations is that they try to utilize the same rules and tools that they do in operational conversations. At first glance, one might think that the skills were transferable. A conversation is just a conversation, after all. Unfortunately, it does not work that way.

Managing strategic conversations

In most companies, operational and strategic conversations are two very different undertakings. Many common elements of operational conversations are in fact active barriers to successful strategic conversations. Managers need to abandon many of their well-worn habits and take a decidedly different course. This is not impossible but it takes discipline and attention to at least the following four basic rules:

Focus on building shared meaning, not on 'who's right'. In an operational conversation, a manager can request: 'Mary, make sure our new French client receives our standard marketing packet' without fear of being seriously misunderstood. This confidence is based on numerous conversations that have gone on before, both between the manager and Mary as well as a history of conversations among all the other workers before them.

Over time, the words and phrases develop widely shared meanings and a whole operational 'language' emerges that is as brief, clear and static as possible. There are clearly right and wrong interpretations of the language.

Newcomers are trained in the use and meaning of the language so that routines go smoothly. When people disagree, they strenuously advocate their own versions of 'the truth' to see whose version will prevail.

Strategic conversations have a decidedly different purpose. The future of the company does not yet exist; it must be created. The language surrounding the future of the company does not yet exist; it too must be created.

All of the conversations that will eventually give rise to operational routines have not yet taken place. There are no right or wrong answers yet. There is very little meaning that is shared. An executive may say: 'We must become a learning organization.' But everyone might understand the phrase in a different way.

If that fuzziness is allowed to persist, the routines that eventually result may not support each other and may even conflict. No one is right or wrong yet. Knowledge and perspectives must be shared before a powerful image of the future can be refined.

Strategic conversations must be a dialogue for understanding rather than advocacy for agreement. If an adversarial tone is allowed into strategic discussions then the creation of new knowledge and language will stop and the future shape of the company may turn out more like the present than it may need to be.

Leave authority at the door. Authority usually derives either from a manager's responsibility for a specific set of business operations (routines) or because an individual is known to possess a special knowledge to which others should defer. A general manager has the former, a technical expert has the latter, for example.

If a strategic conversation is sufficiently

future-oriented, then it is impossible to know just what knowledge will be most important or what operational routines will result. Authority will be created 'along with' the future of the company, not beforehand. Managers who jump the gun and try to 'take control' will greatly limit what the future of the company might be. So while one's current organizational authority is relevant to operational conversations, it is meaningless to strategic ones.

As a result, as soon as authority is used in a discussion, it ceases to be a strategic conversation and becomes operational.

More extreme uses of power, such as threats and intimidation, are even less compatible with strategic conversations and may even be disruptive to operational discussions.

Keep strategy conversations exclusively for strategy. The incompatibility between authority and strategy makes it extremely difficult to mix strategic and operational conversations.

For example, the management team of a major newspaper once decided to set aside three hours for a strategy meeting. They met at 11 a.m. in the boardroom of the company, a very prestigious and beautiful room. At 11:10, everybody had arrived – well almost everybody. The editor-in-chief was still missing. The managing director of the newspaper suggested the meeting should start but the others indicated they would prefer to wait.

More small talk. Even more coffee. Everybody looked at their watches. At 11:20 the editor-in-chief arrived, red-eyed, furious and with puffs of cigar smoke following in his wake. He slammed the day's newspaper on the table and exclaimed: 'Have you seen this?!? Page two and five are completely missing. Our best stories have vanished. Our best advertisers have had their expensive advertisements erased. Who is responsible?' As might be guessed, there was no conversation about strategy that day. Attention shifted immediately to operational concerns. The next time a strategy meeting was called, people winced and came prepared to talk about operations. It does not take such a radical departure from the agenda to undercut strategic conversations. We have seen situations where an innocuous discussion about choosing a secretary,

buying a new coffee machine or fixing a doorbell has had the same effect.

It is theoretically possible, of course, for an intensely knowledge-oriented company that is organized in a highly non-hierarchical manner to be able to blur the lines between strategic and operational conversations. But since most companies are still struggling with more rudimentary forms of decentralization, empowerment and shared decision-making, the exceptions to this rule are hardly worth noting.

Remove time pressure. Time is a scarce commodity in modern business and most managers typically seek a fast resolution to any discussion. Action is wanted, not words. If it were possible, some managers might prefer to eliminate conversation entirely, relying on the fewest possible words to communicate the desired results. Speed and efficiency are the watchwords of the operational environment and are in fact the goal of most operational conversations and language.

Strategy works to a different clock. Prematurely closing off strategic conversations only leads to poorer strategies and less successful operations. Ideally, strategic conversations have no 'beginning' or 'end'. The task of inventing the future of a company is on-going, and cannot be moulded to artificial deadlines. There is no simple rule to determine how much time is too much or too little.

The essential question, therefore, is how to use 'well' the time that is devoted to strategic conversations. The four rules above serve only as a starting point. Each company must invent its own best method of managing its strategic conversations.

The strategy of conversations

The development and diffusion of knowledge in a modern company are all about the development and diffusion of language. And the development and diffusion of language are all about the art of conversation. A word or phrase may embody a marvellous idea but it cannot really be called 'language' until it is successfully used in conversation with others.

The management of conversation needs to be a central concern of every manager who wishes to succeed in a knowledge-intensive age. The process through which we both create new meaning and share meaning and frames of reference in language is at the heart of knowledge development in organizations. It is a powerful concept within the domain of corporate epistemology. It is about the future of management.

Since the successful management of conversations still rests in the future for most companies, an interesting circularity arises: one of the first strategic conversations upon which a company must embark is how to engage in strategic conversations.

Without this knowledge and a language to diffuse it, there can be no progress. There is no logical way out of this loop, one must simply start talking about it – and talk about it as if the future depended on it. It does.

Summary

Language is the currency of knowledge and the time has come to put 'managing business conversations' near the top of the agenda. A distinction should be made between operating conversations (about exploiting knowledge gained in the past and present) and strategic conversations (creating new knowledge).

Managers are instinctively better at the former. At a time when strategic shelf lives are getting shorter, though, not to address the latter will be costly. There are four basic rules. Focus on building 'shared meaning', not on who is right (strategic conversations should be a dialogue for understanding). Do not try to take control – current organizational authority is not relevant. Do not mix the two types of conversation. Remove time pressures and remember that strategy works to a different clock than operational discussions.

All this mostly rests in the future so there is an important circularity for companies. One of the first strategic conversations they will need to have is how to engage in strategic conversations.

Suggested further reading

Roos, J. and von Krogh, G. (1995) *Organizational Epistemology*, Macmillan.

Roos, J. and von Krogh, G. (1996) *Managing Knowledge: Perspectives on Cooperation and Competition*, Sage.

Redesigning for the 21st century

■ **It would be a serious mistake to believe that the current management thinking is simply a phase of an eternal cycle between looking inward and outward, say** Bruce Kogut **and** Edward H. Bowman

We can understand the changes in corporations by peering at a mirror or through a window. The manager can ask what is it that we do well or should do better or what is happening in the market and how do I better position my product vis-à-vis my competitors.

There is the sense these days that more managers prefer the mirror over the window. It is tempting to say that these trends represent no more than the fads of managerial ideology. After a decade of looking outward to financial markets and to the conditions of industry competition, the market for this endeavour is saturated. So what we are witnessing is repackaging of the advice that consulting firms and business professors give companies.

We prefer the middle ground, where the question of how to vie in world markets is understood as a problem of the design of work and the choice of the markets in which to enter and compete. It is easy to dismiss the pre-occupation with the mirror of design as no more than a fad during troubled times. At the turn of the last century, the Italian economist and sociologist Vilfedo Pareto suggested that ideologies rise and fall along with the business cycle. The current discussion of the human-ization of the workplace is no more, by this view, than a reflection of the harder economic conditions of this decade.

But it would be a serious mistake to believe that the current public discourse is simply a phase of an eternal cycle between looking inward and outward. On the contrary, we are witnessing an historic structural break in the practice of organization and management. These changes are no less revolutionary than the wave of innovations associated with the names of Frederick Taylor and Henry Ford at the beginning of this century.

The most remarkable fact in the economic history of the 20th century has been the increasing concentration of production by the largest corporations in industrialized countries. It has been the sheer rapidity of this growth that has spelled the limits of its continuation. The labor forces of corporations today are vastly more productive than before. The rising productivity of labor has outpaced the growth of the value of output by big companies. By this statement alone, the implications are clear. Large corporations require increasingly smaller work forces to maintain the high levels of productivity and service.

There is, we suspect, a more fundamental change occurring than simply the outpacing of big company output by productivity growth. We are witnessing a major shift, in which the historical advantage of the large corporation is no longer assured. The uncertainty of markets, the importance of niches and innovations in

Table 1: Growth of large companies ($ billions)

	sales	assets	employees	inflation adjusted sales	inflation adjusted assets
FORTUNE 500 INDUSTRIALS					
1955	161	**122**	8605	**529**	461
1960	205	**176**	9179	**613**	544
1970	464	**432**	14608	**1180**	1078
1980	1650	**1175**	15909	**1875**	1370
1990	2304	**2416**	12429	**1933**	1966
FORTUNE 100 INDUSTRIALS					
1955	108	**83**	5460	**354**	313
1960	132	**117**	5632	**395**	361
1970	288	**279**	9110	**733**	696
1980	1115	**767**	8722	**1267**	894
1990	1645	**1820**	7888	**1380**	1481
GLOBAL 100 INDUSTRIALS					
1956	49	**32**	3917	**158**	117
1960	63	**60**	5738	**188**	186
1970	182	**196**	9029	**462**	488
1980	1037	**877**	9877	**1178**	1034
1990	2148	**2201**	10721	**1802**	1791
FORTUNE 100 AS PERCENT OF FORTUNE 500					
1955	67	**68**	63		
1960	64	**66**	61		
1970	62	**65**	62		
1980	68	**65**	55		
1990	71	**75**	63		
GLOBAL 100 AS PERCENT OF FORTUNE 100					
1960	48	**51**	102		
1970	63	**70**	99		
1980	96	**116**	113		
1990	131	**121**	136		

Source: *Fortune*, various issues.
Notes: Sales adjusted using US finished goods deflator (1982=100)
Assets adjusted using US capital equipment deflator (1982=100)

increasingly more wealthy societies, the creation of new flexible technologies and telecom-munication systems, and the growth of well-educated workers and managers have created a major break in the organization of work and its division among large and small companies.

Where are the sales?

These observations are visible in the very simple data in Table 1 regarding the relationship among the employees, assets, and sales of the largest US and global corporations. For the largest US corporations listed in *Fortune* magazine, there has been an absolute drop in the number of employees for the largest 100 and 500 com-panies. Moreover, the growth in sales (measured in constant dollars) has dramatically fallen over the last decade, even though the value of total assets continued to grow (especially for the largest 100 companies). In the US the sales of the largest corporations grew at a rate of only 80 per cent of the overall growth in manufacturing. No wonder that there has been such an increase in shareholder revolt over the past decade!

The stagnation in sales may be due to the overall loss of competitiveness of large US corporations. Indeed, during this period of time, the 100 greatest non-US companies experienced declining, but still formidable, sales and asset growth. We can compare their growth against the largest 100 US corporations. Note, first, that the American 100 has grown faster than the overall 500. Still, the global 100 has greatly outpaced the largest American corporations, to the point where they show, on average considerably larger assets, sales, and workforces.

We should not deduce, however, that the old trend towards large corporations is continuing in the rest of the world. Part of the non-US growth is due to overseas expansion during the 1980s. European and Japanese companies invested heavily in the US, and Japanese corporations also began to invest more aggressively in Europe.

Moreover, there are large country differences. Japanese companies are for example a lot smaller than their US counterparts. In 1990, General Motors had 616,000 employees compared to Toyota's 96,849; IBM, 373,816 to Hitachi's 290,811, etc.

Small is profitable?

The swollen global corporation is not a feature of Japanese capitalism. In certain countries, the trends show a diminution in the size of companies. In France – which has one of the best performing economies over the past decade – small and medium enterprises are growing at a faster rate than larger businesses. The most dynamic sectors in the Italian economy are dominated by smaller companies. And even among developing countries, the diversified and dynamic small companies sector of Taiwan looks more promising than the large Korean groups.

There are many ways to understand these changes. We accept the view that they indicate a revolutionary break with the design principles of mass production and economies of size. Competitive pressures are forcing large companies to redesign how work and management are organized in order to be more flexible, quicker, and market-oriented.

Of course the nature of product markets and competition is of fundamental importance. For example, IBM was caught in a difficult strategic position due to declining demand in its principal mainframe market and inroads made by ever-more powerful and smaller machines.

What compounds the difficulty of getting the strategy right, however, is that radical strategic change requires a design of the principles of organizing. But the new design is not clear. The wavering of IBM between spinning off affiliates but holding equity stakes or internally transforming the businesses is notable. Figuring out how to do new things is tremendously difficult in the absence of templates that can be borrowed from other corporate experiences. What a company wants to be capable of doing depends on how it does things. The 'how' and 'what' are linked. For many companies the capabilities which they desire consist of the ability to deliver high variety and quality products and services quickly and flexibly to the market. 'What' they desire to do forms the wish list of the capabilities to support their product and market strategies. However, the daunting question facing many companies is not what capabilities they should have, but how to acquire the organizing principles that generate these capabilities. Or, to use an old expression often used in connection with the transfer of US techniques to countries around the globe, the heart of the matter lies in developing the appropriate knowhow.

Table 2 matches a few fundamental organizing principles to the capabilities they generate. This list is hardly complete, but it provides insight into why we say that design is the terrain on which competition is fought. We believe that speed, cost competitiveness and quality are three of the most important capabilities for competing in markets today (see the referenced Bowman & Kogut book for further insights).

Table 2: Principles of design and capabilities	
Organizing principles	**Capabilities**
Just-in-time and Kanban	Speed
Multinational network	Operating flexibility
Multifunctional skills and autonomous teams	Quality

Consider, first, the organizing principles underlying the capability to be quick to the market. There is a fairly large consensus that in the case of manufacturing companies speed is generated by designing systems in which customer demand pulls the product by reverberating down the value chain of assembly to components. These systems, often called *kanban* after their Japanese origin, are usually coupled with just-in-time (JIT) deliveries and low inventories.

Flexibility is a capability that is particularly important when the prices of materials are unknown. How convenient it would be for a multinational company to respond to a sudden increase in the value of the yen by decreasing the amount of components sourced from Japan. To create this capability, however, means that the global company must be structured as a co-ordinated network of subsidiaries, that flexible transfer prices must be created, and that managers must be rewarded for taking advantage of unexpected changes in currency values.

Quality of product and service as a competitive objective has stumbled on the problem of complexity of delivery. To provide a menu of high-quality choices to the consumer has led to creating more autonomous teams of workers. Quality circles and team problem solving have been major workplace innovations oriented toward improving the variety and reliability of products and services.

Time to redesign the corporation?

These capabilities pose issues of design and of the leadership and motivation to implement corporate change. If board and shareholder meetings have become more confrontational it is because of the growing pressures to transform the corporation into a more competitive entity. The long-term decline in profits and market share for many corporations are bellwether signs that a radical redesign of the organization is required.

As surprising as it may seem, the linkage between what a company does and how it does it has been neglected by academic research and remains an open terrain of inquiry.

This neglect stems, no doubt, from the nature of how a school of business is itself organized. There is probably no organization more departmentalized and functionally organized than a university! The way knowledge is organized in the university and in the business school constrains what can be taught and researched. Over the past years, a revolution in the structure or, if you will, the organizing principles of business education has been under way.

Yet while changes in the curriculum have been made, or are in the process of being made, the thorniest problems are often posed by the implications for research. A great achievement of the modern university is the gains and knowledge made through research conducted by specialists.

At the same time, because of its role in training and educating the managerial workforce, the business school is caught between how to balance the virtues of specialization in research with the growing need to intermarry the functions.

What do these efforts to redesign the corporation mean for business schools? Imagine teaching a class of business students what French auto corporations should have done in 1980 to defend their home market against Toyota, Nissan, and Honda if Japanese car imports had not been limited by law to 3 per cent of the market. How easy it is to suggest that they should have produced better cars and designed them faster for the market. The more difficult challenge is knowing how to redesign the organization to do so.

Business schools were not at the cutting edge of these changes during the 1980s. The concepts of just-in-time inventory management, kanban systems, activity analysis and quality programmes were picked up more quickly by leaders in industry than by academic researchers. It was only after 1985 that JIT systems, widely held to be a major Japanese innovation in minimizing inventory levels, truly entered the curriculum in operations courses at Wharton. By this time, some US corporations had already invested considerable sums in recreating the supply networks in the US that they had observed, or had experienced through their affiliates in Japan.

Many say that the US business school is a contributor to the decline of the country's large corporations. The correlation looks damning; the country with the most developed system of business education in the world has slipped so rapidly from a position of economic leadership to a contender among many. There is no question that the US by almost any economic measure is no longer the single leading nation. And it has become common to place some of this blame on its business education institutions.

And why not? Almost one out of four students in US colleges and universities today majors in business. In 1957, one out of five US students matriculated in a business school. Since then, the number of business schools has grown five-fold.

The clever answer to these concerns has been that there is no problem. The correlation is easily dismissed as spurious. A class in statistics often begins with the story of how, in the 1800s, the peasants in Russia noted an association between cholera and the arrival of physicians, leading to their deep suspicion that modern medicine was responsible for the epidemics. Certainly, the business school bears no responsibility for the health of the American economy.

We are not so sure. Of course, the decline in the relative positioning of the US was almost foreordained, as its stature in the world economy after World War II was the result of the destruction of its major competitors. Yet, on the other hand, the US was a leader in national income, productivity, and export growth in the early part of this century. Its relative stature today is less than it was in the 1920s.

The early business schools in the US grew up teaching the practices that made US businesses the largest and most powerful in world history.

Functional lines evolved in almost all US business schools. Except for an occasional department of real estate, the emphasis has been to develop the functional and managerial skills of students without regard to specific industrial needs.

We should not underestimate the tremendous advancement in business education over this century. In the late 1950s, the Ford Foundation contacted two professors, Robert Gordon and James Howell, to survey the stature of business schools.

Cakes and ailing?

Their findings remain startling for anyone educated in a business school in recent years. Up to 1940 only 186 doctorates were given in business, the first Ph.D. being granted in 1927, only another 978 were given between 1947 and 1958. With one-fifth of all students majoring in business in the 1950s, it is not surprising that only 40 per cent of full-time teachers had doctorate degrees, 40 per cent of all teachers were part-time. Courses were highly applied, business schools provided frequently no more than a trade training. One 1959 study reported that 'an eight-course major at a large. . . university in baking science and management. . . includes courses in Principles of Baking; Bread and Rolls, Principles of Baking Cakes and Variety Products; Bread and Roll Production – Practical Shop Operation, and finally Cake and Sweet Baked products – Practical Shop operation'.

No wonder that the introduction of research findings in operation management courses were seen as representing, and in fact were, major improvements in teaching quality.

The claim that the problem of business schools lies in their emphasis on research strikes us as facetious. In the US and elsewhere, this view has a considerable history, even with respect to the natural sciences. A distinguished scientist visiting the University of Minnesota in 1908 remarked that 'the regents generally regarded research as a private fad of a professor, like collecting etchings or playing the piano, and they rarely interfered with it so long as (the professor). . . did not ask for money.'

The great advancement in the quality of teaching in business schools is linked to increased investment in research. Gordon and Howell (1959) openly despaired of the poor quality of research available to the practising manager in the 1950s. Since this report, research in business schools has moved substantially forward, to the point that fundamental innovations, such as the pricing of securities and options, can be traced to academic publications.

The dilemma facing business schools is that the categories of academic knowledge, as they were determined by the structure of business of the early part of this century, have become increasingly isolated from one another. The new curriculum changes are attempts to maintain functional training but within the context of greater experience in integrated and group problem-solving. New joint departmental committees to co-ordinate content and to reinforce commonalties across classes have supported these cross-functional efforts.

The current puzzle of research in business schools is that there is no clear idea of what should be the organization of academic efforts that would correspond to these new curricula. Specialization in research has driven the advancement of knowledge since the German university innovations of the 1800s. Must the business school give up this tradition to address the questions of importance to corporations and to its own academic community?

We do not propose the abolition of specialized research, not the least because it is unnecessary. Corporations continue to rely on specialists; cross-functional teams do not eliminate the functions.

The better answer lies in bringing the specialties together. An important side effect of transforming business school curricula is that the process brings into contact faculty from diverse backgrounds. The implications for research are many, but certainly include the promotion of more co-ordinated, cross-functional projects that are problem oriented and academically rigorous. The prospects for change in the area of research require the creation of institutional structures within the business school for long-term cross-functional co-operation.

Summary

Companies historically swing between peering into the mirror at themselves and looking out through the window at markets and competitors. At present they seem to be doing a bit of both, but they are witnessing a historic structural break in the practice of organization and management. Productivity growth is not only outpacing big company output; there is a more fundamental break in the organization of work and its division between large and small companies. These changes represent a break with the design principles of mass production and economies of size. Yet the new design is not clear. The daunting question facing many companies is not the capabilities they should have – speed, cost competitiveness and quality are three of the most important – but how to acquire the organizing principles that generate such capabilities.

Efforts to redesign the corporation have had implications for business schools. Recent curriculum changes have attempted to maintain functional training while bringing together previously isolated categories of academic knowledge. There are still outstanding organizational issues, though, for business school research.

Suggested further reading

Bowman, E. H. and Kogut, B. (eds) (1995) *Redesigning the Firm*, Oxford University Press.

Indexes

Subject index

A

absolute cost advantages 465-7
academic skills gap 235
accounting
    asset valuation 20, 33, 35-6, 50-2
    budgeting 23, 24-6, 62
    changing prices 20, 34-7
    control centers 21-4
    cost of capital estimates 79
    costing 29-31
    problems with 19-21
    quality costs 22, 26-9
    ROCE (return on capital employed)
        19, 32-4, 151-2
    standards
        international harmonization 41-7
        regulation 47-9
    for takeovers 53-6
acquisitions 46, 103-5, 185, 363
    accounting 53-5
    and innovation 197
ACSI (American Customer Satisfaction Index) 28-9
action learning 641
added value 361
adjudication 419-20
advertising 177, 467
    ethics 376-8
affirmative action 381
agreeableness 231-2
alliances 46, 109, 606-9, 638
    and globalization 413, 491-4, 623
allocation of resources 65-6
American Customer Satisfaction Index (ACSI) 28-9
antitrust policy on intellectual property 577-82
apartheid 374
applied statistics *see* statistics
approachability 8-9
arbitrage pricing theory 79
asset betas 78

assets
    complementary assets 470
    deployment and market access 573-4
    efficient use 81
    utilization costs 19
    valuation 20, 33, 35-6, 50-2
attitudes 235-9
    changing 238-9
    and public policy 236-7
    teaching 238
attrition patterns of customers 185
authoritarianism 10, 647-8
averages 128, 129

B

balance sheets 33, 35, 48, 50-2
bankruptcy 80-1, 119-22
banks
    commercial 85-6
    economic role 66
    eurocurrency transactions 387
    European System of Central Banks (ESCB)
        398-9, 403
    in Germany 45, 46, 85, 105
    international banking 388-90, 392
    investment 85
    syndicated lending 390
    in the United Kingdom 45
    valuing 38-40
behavior
    of consumers 172, 175, 323-5
    information behavior 353-4
    prosocial 237-8
    see also organizational behavior
benchmarking 206, 262, 291, 308-9, 310
betas 77-8
binomial distributions 132, 134
bonds 66-7, 101

eurobonds 387-8
Boston Boxes 562, 563
'bottom-up' budgeting 24-5
brands
    advertising 177
    brand equity 175-7
        measuring 180-3
    brewing industry marketing 593-8
    definition 175-6
    excessive pricing 173
    fundamentals 171-2
    loss of market share 165, 171
    and market change 172
    poor management 172-3
    relationship marketing 175-83
    value-creation strategies 173-4
    see also products
break-even analysis 74
breakpoints
    anticipating 543-7
    creating 548-52
brewing industry marketing 593-8
bribes 372-3
British Chlorine-Alkali Act (1864) 327
budgeting 23, 24-6, 62, 570
    capital budgeting 72, 568
building design 258-60
bureaucracies 11
business cycles 401-2
business ethics 368-71, 375-9
    discrimination and privacy 379-82
    gifts 371-4
    and marketing 368-71, 375-9
business process re-engineering 193-8, 268, 290-1,
    307-8, 541, 549
business schools 653-4
business system leverage 550

C

Cadbury Committee 113
call options 88, 89
capital
    allocation 65-6, 151-2
    budgeting 72, 568
    costs of 39, 73, 78, 79
    investment criteria 63
    raising equity capital 116-19
    rationing 569-70

    see also projects
capital asset pricing model (CAPM) 76-9
capital maintenance concept 36-7
capital structure 62, 80-2
capitalizing costs 50-1
careers 5, 284
    and family tensions 278-9
cartels 456-8
cash flow
    and bank valuation 38-9
    and capital structure 80
    discounted cash flow 67, 69, 72-3, 75
    models 72-3, 145
    monitoring 62
causal loops 148-50
CCA (current cost accounting) 35, 36
change
    breakpoints
        anticipating 543-7
        creating 548-52
    dominant responses 333
    forces for 538-9
    frontline change capabilities 548-9
    and leadership 519, 540-1
    proactive change 538-9
    rapid change 539
    reactive change 539
    resistance to 539-40
    selecting appropriate path 540-3
    in work practices 229
Chapter 7 insolvency procedure 121
Chapter 11 insolvency procedure 119, 121, 122
character development programs 239
charisma 508-9
chief executive officers (CEO) 6, 111-15, 520-1, 633
CIM (computer integrated manufacturing) 315
cluster sampling 136
cognitive skills 632-3
collusion on pricing 456-8
commercial banks 85-6
communications
    customizing 188-9
    language 644, 646
    and leadership 508
    and office design 260
    skills 8-9
    strategic conversations 646-9
companies see organizations
Companies Act (1981) 55

competencies *see* core competencies; skills

competition

    competitive societies 482-6

    evolutionary cycle 545

    and innovation 172, 636

    international 494-502

    and marketing strategy 180

    regulation 473-8

    and strategic management 347, 602-5

    strategic market entry deterrence 464-7

competitive advantage 251, 262-7

    and information technology 359-60

    and work/life balance 279-80

competitive dynamics 475-7

competitive intelligence 347

competitive societies 482-6

Competitiveness Advisory Group 482

complementary assets 470

computer integrated manufacturing (CIM) 315

confidence intervals 140

conflict resolution 10-11

conformance quality 487-8

conscientiousness 232, 237

constant growth model 79

consumer choice 377-8

consumers

    behavior 172, 175

    reservation prices 453

    social preferences 369-70

    see also customers

continuous distributions 132

continuous improvement 300, 309-10

contracting out 471

control centers 21-4

control charts 139

convenience sampling 136-7

conversations 646-9

convertibles 101-3

core capabilities 636

core competencies

    classifying 320

    cultivating 586-7

    diversification 588

    human resource management (HRM) 262-7

    identifying 584-5

    implementation 587

    leadership 516-19

    marketing 169-70

    nurturing 589

    redefining 588

    redeploying 588-9

    in service firms 583-90

    using 589-90

    in work/life balance 280-2

    see also skills

corporate compliance programs 477

corporate culture *see* organizational culture

correlation 128-9

    of major stock markets 394-5

costing process 29-31

costs

    absolute cost advantages 465-7

    of asset utilization 19

    of bankruptcy 80-1, 122

    and brand building 173

    of capital 39, 73, 78, 79

    capitalizing 50-1

    cost centers 22

    of foreign investment 397

    of insolvency 80-1, 122

    of products 29-30, 357

    and profit maximization 451-2

    of quality 22, 26-9

    of segmentation strategies 203-4

    sunk costs 452, 462, 466

    and supply chain integration (SCM) 318

    switching costs 465

    and technology 452-3

    transaction costs 468

CPP (current purchasing power accounting) 35, 36

creative accounting 19

creative service benefit segmentation 199-204

creativity 9, 10

cultural diversity 240-6

    definition 241

    dimensions of cultural difference 241-2

culture

    and change 551

    cross-cultural incompetencies 409-13

    cross-cultural research 414-15

    culture matrix 417

    definition 414

    and globalization 408-13

    ideology 415-16, 417-18, 616-21

    and leadership 412-13, 514-15, 517

    personality 416-17, 418

    see also organizational culture

currency

eurocurrency transactions 386-7
exchange rate risk 98-100
hedging 98-100
options 98
current cost accounting (CCA) 35, 36
current purchasing power (CPP)
accounting 35, 36
current value accounting 35-7
customer care lines 178
customer satisfaction 28-9, 167, 177-8, 303-4, 487, 599-602
customers
attrition patterns 185
behavior 323-5
and brands 176
building customer base 591-3
creative service benefit segmentation 199-204
LTV (customer lifetime value) 187
MCSA (managing customers as strategic assets) 184-92
personalizing services/products 198-9, 204
and product development 190
retention 185, 189
see also consumers; segmentation strategies

D

data
presentation 126-31
time series 129-30
database marketing 179, 187-8, 191, 358-9
debt finance 81-2
decision-making 143, 286, 290, 528
see also strategy
deferred tax 48
delayering 637-8
demographics 252
depreciation 30, 46
of value of customer base 185
derivatives 86, 392
swaps 106-8
see also futures; options
dimensions of cultural difference 241-2
direct costs 30, 304
direct marketing 188
discount rates 67, 73
discounted cash flow 67, 69, 72-3, 75
discounted payback periods 74
discrete distributions 132

discrimination 379-81, 379-82
disinvestment 33
distribution channels 166
distributions (statistical) 131-4
diversification 64, 76-7, 158-9
and corporate revitalization 197
international 394-8
dividend policy 82-4
dominance of markets 330-1, 333, 336, 563
downsizing 6, 332, 541

E

East Asian Economic Caucus (EAEC) 501
eco-audits 328-9
Economic and Monetary Union (EMU) 398-404
convergence criteria 398
economic consequences 402-3
integration shocks 400-2
and labor markets 400
economic value added (EVA) 487
economies
of globality 483
of integration 472
of proximity 482-3
of scale 453, 462-3
ECR (efficient consumer response) 178, 179
EDI (electronic data interchange) 317, 320
education 4, 10, 640
academic skills gap 235
business schools 653-4
and worker performance 235-6
effective market learning 205-8
efficient consumer response (ECR) 178, 179
efficient frontier 159
efficient markets 70-1
electronic commerce 188
electronic data interchange (EDI) 317, 320
EMAS (Environmental Management and Auditing System) 328-9
emotions 231
employees
effects of lean production on 225-6
involvement 303
privacy 381-2
profiling 233
representation 269
selection tests 263
skill requirements 226-7

staff selection 268-9

see also workforces

employment conditions 379

empowerment 225, 270, 283-7

EMU *see* Economic and Monetary Union (EMU)

entrepreneurs 7

entry barriers to markets 464-7, 472

environmental management 327-9, 376, 412, 609-12

Environmental Management and Auditing System (EMAS) 328-9

environmental-performance indicators (EPI) 329

environmetrics 328-9

EPI (environmental-performance indicators) 329

epistemology 643

equity markets

correlations 394-5

raising equity capital 116-19

returns 67-8

ESCB (European System of Central Banks) 398-9, 403

ethics *see* business ethics

eurobonds 387-8

eurocurrency transactions 386-7

euromarkets 386-8, 392

European Agricultural Guidance and Guarantee Fund 498

European System of Central Banks (ESCB) 398-9, 403

European Union 494, 496-7, 498

Competitiveness Advisory Group 482

Economic and Monetary Union (EMU) 398-404

harmonization of accounting standards 45-6

pan-regional manufacturing 336-41

EVA (economic value added) 487

exchange rate risk 98-100

see also currency

executive compensation 111-15

experience curves 563

exploration and development (E&D) costs 50-2

extortion 373-4

extroverts 231

F

factory focus 311-15

family structure 278

FCM (financial capital maintenance) 37

feedback 148, 591-3

finance function 6, 62-3

and change 84-7

financial capital maintenance (FCM) 37

financial markets

convertibles 101-3

derivatives 86, 392

swaps 106-8

see also futures; options

efficient markets 70-1

equity markets

correlations 394-5

raising capital 116-19

returns 67-8

euromarkets 386-8, 392

internationalization 86-7

regulation 86

role 64-6

warrants 101-3

financial performance measures 487, 488-9

financial reports *see* balance sheets; profit and loss statements

financial restructuring 332

financial services 391-3

five factor model of personality 231-2

fixed term licenses 581-2

flexible budgets 25-6

flexible manufacturing (FMS) 311, 313, 339-40, 652

forecasting 25

Foreign Corrupt Practices Act (1977) 372

'Forester' effect 317

franchises 586

franchising and regulation 463-4

free cash flow 38

Free Trade Area of Americas (FTAA) 500

free trade areas 494-502

frequency tables 126-7

full cost (FC) accounting 50-1

futures 65, 86, 95-7

delivery 96

role 96-7

structure 95-6

valuation 96

G

gainsharing 226

gas industry 50-2

general cash offers of shares 118-19

Germany

banks 45, 46, 85, 105

legal system 44
gifts 371-4
Glass Steagal Act 85
global information infrastructure (GII) 360-4
globalization
    and alliances 413, 491-4, 623
    competitive societies 482-6
    and culture 408-13
    and leadership 412-13
    local adaptation 574-5
    main attributes 573-4
    market contestability 572-2
    and multinationals 622-5
    and products 573-4
    strategies 572-7
goal cascading 542
goals 253-5
goodwill 46, 55
Gosplan 445
government bonds 66-7
graphs 130
Greater South China Economic Zone 500
'green' products 610
Greenbury Report 111, 114
grim trigger strategy 457
grouped frequencies 127
growth
    of large companies 650-1
    limits 151
    rates 129-30

H

harmonization of accounting standards 41-7
Hawthorne studies 218
hierarchical pyramid 4-5
high performance systems 224-5, 228, 288-92
high performance workplace (HPW) 270-3
histograms 127
historic cost accounting 20, 33, 34-5, 51
hotelling 259-61
human relations 218-19
human resource management (HRM)
    core competencies 262-7
    high performance workplace (HPW) 270-3
    and strategic aims 251-8, 263
    streamlining 268
hypothesis testing 135, 137-9, 140

I

ideology 415-18, 616-21
    and business 620-1
    definition 616-18
    and personality 618
    and political views 619-20
    and society 618-19
IMC (integrated marketing communications) 189-90
improvement programs 332
incrementalism 566
indirect costs 30
individualism/collectivism 242
informal production systems 297
information
    access 261
    behavior 353-4
    culture 351-6
    distribution 206-7
    global information infrastructure (GII) 360-4
    management 552-6
    and market failure 469-70
    software 347, 348
    strategic intelligence 346-50
    strategy 554-5
    systems 20-1
information technology 87, 349, 351, 359-60
    and competitive strategy 357-60
    and environmental impact solutions 611-12
initial public offerings (IPO) 116-18
initiative 237
innovation
    and acquisitions 197
    and alliances 606-7, 608-9
    and competition 172, 636
    competitive formula 357
    directed 548
    in financial services 392-3
    and patents 470, 579-80
    and products 166, 173, 193-7
    spontaneous 548
insolvency 80-1, 119-22
integrated marketing communications (IMC) 189-90
intellectual property 362, 363
    antitrust policy 577-82
interactive marketing 188
interbank transactions 389-90
interest rate swaps 108

internal rate of return (IRR) 74-5
international banking 388-90, 392
Internet 188, 261, 361, 362, 412, 611
interpersonal skills 633
inter-quartile range 128, 129
intrapreneurship 542
investment *see* strategic investment decisions
investment banks 85
investment centers 23
Iosco (International Organization of Securities
    Commissions) agreement 43
IPO (initial public offerings) 116-18
IRR (internal rate of return) 74-5
ISO9000 320, 487

J

job design 269
job rotation 225, 226
Joint Stock Act (1844) 45
joint ventures 46, 109, 606-9, 638
    and globalization 413, 491-4, 623
just-in-time production 300, 313-14, 315, 652

K

kaizen 542, 549
kanban 652

L

labor costs 30, 34
labor markets 280, 400
    and Economic and Monetary Union (EMU) 400,
      402
    managerial 112
language 644, 646
lapsing budgets 25
leadership
    authoritarianism 10
    and change 519, 540-1
    competencies 516-19
    and culture 412-13, 514-15, 517
    and dominance 529
    global visionary leadership 412-13
    importance 520-3
    male and female split 513-15
    outdoor training 524-33
    powers of the person 521-2

qualities 521-2
    relationship aspect 512-3
    task aspect 512-13
    traits of great leaders 506-11
    two factor theory 512
lean production 224-9, 288
    implementing 227-8
    and pan-regional manufacturing 338-40
    skill requirements 226-7
    work practices 225-6
learning 639-41
legal systems 44-5, 419
legislation and competition 473-8
licensing 579, 581-2
line-item budgets 25
liquidity management 62
location measures 127-8, 129
logistics 611
London 390, 391, 392, 393
Lotus Notes 347, 348
LTV (customer lifetime value) 187

M

Maastricht Treaty 497
MAD (mean absolute deviation) 128, 129
management
    challenges 167
    future 633-4
    power axis 5-6
    reshuffles 332
    rethinking 637-8
    and shareholders 64-5
managerial pyramid 4-5
managers
    approachability 8-9
    attributes 8, 12
    careers 5, 278-9, 284
    and change 12-13
    and cultural diversity 243-6
    generalizing specialists 7-8
    inflexibility 11
    necessity of 631-4
    Russian managers 442-6
    short-term performance measurement 11-12
    skills 4-5, 10-11, 632-3
    specializing generalists 6-7
    time management 11
    transforming 256

turnaround specialists 6-7
manufacturing
    flexibility 311, 339-40, 652
    pan-regional 336-41
manufacturing planning and control (MPCS) 297-301
manufacturing resource planning 299-300
marginal revenue 453, 454
market failure 468-70
market orientation 180
market share 180, 181-2
market value added (MVA) 487
marketing
    brewing industry 593-8
    and business ethics 368-71, 375-9
    competencies 169-70
    customer voice 323-4
    database marketing 179, 187-8, 191
    direct marketing 188
    future 168-9, 170, 209-11
    IMC (integrated marketing communications) 189-90
    interactive marketing 188
    relationship marketing 175-83
    social cause marketing 368-71
    strategy 180
markets
    changes 165-6
    development strategies 195
    dominance of 330-1, 333, 336, 563
    effective market learning 205-8
    entry barriers 464-7, 472
    future 167-8
    mental models 207-8
    penetration strategies 193-5
    product/market matrix 193-4
    and strategic management 322-6
    trends 166
    see also financial markets; labor markets
'Marlboro Friday' 171
masculinity/femininity 242
mass customization 188, 199
material requirements planning (MRP) 297-9, 313
MCSA (managing customers as strategic assets) 184-92
mean 128, 129
    distribution of sample mean 140-1
mean absolute deviation (MAD) 128, 129
median 128, 129

mergers see acquisitions
MES (minimum efficient scale) 453
metaphors 351-2
microworlds 598
mission statements 251, 599
mobility barriers in markets 464-7
mode 128, 129
modeling 147-55
monetary union see Economic and Monetary Union (EMU)
monetary working capital adjustment (MWCA) 36-7
monopolies 330, 455-6, 462-4, 473
Monte Carlo simulation 143-7
moral hazard 468-9
motivation 237, 633
    self-motivation 259
MPCS (manufacturing planning and control systems) 297-301
MRP (material requirements planning) 297-9, 313
multiculturalism 241
multimedia 635
multinationals 622-5
MWCA (monetary working capital adjustment) 36-7

N

nAch (need for achievement) 237
negotiation 416-42
    adjudication 419-20
    caucus 435-6
    creating doubts 422
    destabilizers 429, 439-40
    four dimensional structure 426-32
    goals 433-4
    managing expectations 423-4
    organizational hierarchy 432-4
    organizational strategy 434
    privacy 440
    process rules 421
    quasi-mediators 429-30
    reducing pressures 436-7
    relationship among parties 422-3
    shadow negotiations 438-40
    stabilizers 428-9, 439-40
    team management 434-6
    and trust 421-2
net present value (NPV) 70, 72, 73

normal distribution 132-4
NPV (net present value) 70, 72, 73

O

objectives 253-5
OCM (operating capital maintenance) 36-7
office design 260
office space 259-60
oil industry 50-2, 154-5
Omnishare 261
openness 231
operating capital maintenance (OCM) 36-7
operations and strategic management 322-6
opinion polls 135
'optimization' 156-60
options 87-94
    American 88, 91-2
    call options 88, 89
    currency options 98
    early exercise 91-2
    European 88, 94
    payoff diagrams 88-9
    pricing 92-3
        and capital investment 79, 93
        and convertibles 102
    put options 88, 89
    put-call parity 89-91, 94
    share option grants 111-12, 114, 115
    and volatility 92, 94
organization memory 208, 349-50
organizational behavior
    importance 218-24
    macro and micro 220
    origins 217-18
    see also behavior
organizational culture 244-5, 253
    information culture 351-6
    and work/life balance 279, 281
    see also culture
organizational learning 570
organizational realignment 541
organizational structure 253, 575-6
    and leadership 528
    pan-regional 339
organizations
    categorizing 252
    dying 331-3
    restructuring 257-8, 332, 541-2

    transforming 257, 333-6
outdoor training 524-33
overheads 30, 305

P

packaging 319, 610-11
patents 470, 579-80
pay *see* remuneration; reward strategies
payback periods 63, 74
performance evaluation 285
performance management 253-5
performance measurement 302-6, 486-90
period costs 29, 31
persistence 237
personality 229-34
    and culture 416-17, 418
    five factor model 231-2
    of great leaders 507-8
    and ideology 618
    and job performance 237
    measurement 232-4
    structure and origins 230-1
personalizing services/products 198-9, 204
plant networks 339
political correctness 619
political risk 624-5
political systems 624-5
Porter's 'five forces' 562, 563
portfolio optimization 158-9
positive discrimination 380
power distance 242
power-based culture 551
PPP (Purchasing Power Parity) 98
present value (PV) 72
presentational skills 633
price elasticity of demand 453-4, 456
pricing
    auction approach 459-60
    collusion 456-8
    competing on price 166, 167
    and consumer segmentation 460-1
    ethics 376
    excessive pricing of brands 173
    and monopolies 455-6
    price discrimination 459-61
    regulation 462-4
    reservation prices 453
    transfer pricing 23

under perfect competition 455
volume of purchases 460
privacy 379-82
privatization 41
proactive change 538-9
probabilities 131-4
production function 5-6
production systems
    computer integrated manufacturing (CIM) 315
    and environmental management 327
    factory focus 311-14
    flexible manufacturing (FMS) 313
    high performance systems 224-5, 228, 288-92
    informal 297
    just-in-time 300, 313-14, 315, 652
    kanban 652
    manufacturing planning and control systems
        (MPCS) 297-301
    manufacturing resource planning 299-300
    material requirements planning (MRP) 297-9,
        313
    supply chain integration (SCM) 301, 316-22
    Total Quality Management (TQM) 309, 352, 353
    see also lean production
productivity
    national differences 288
    problems 235
    and work/life balance 280
products
    costs 29-30, 357
    development 190, 195-7, 327-8, 357
    differentiation 465
    and the environment 327-8
    ethical considerations 375
    and globalization 573-4
    'green' products 610
    innovation 166, 173, 193-7
    launching 195-7, 603-4
    and market leverage 550
    product mix 156-60
    product/market matrix 193-4
    Sigmoid Curves 350
    see also brands
profit and loss statements 50, 53-4
profitability index 75
profits 29, 30-1, 35, 45-6
    centers 22-3
    maximization 451-4
projects

approval 72-6
capital investment criteria 63
finance 109-11
risk 78-9
strategic investment decisions 562-71
prosocial behavior 237-8
Purchasing Power Parity (PPP) 98
put options 88, 89
PV (present value) 72

Q

quality standards 487-8, 599, 600, 652
    costs 22, 26-9
    hypothesis testing 138-9
questionnaires 232-3
quota sampling 136

R

radical leadership 540-1
random sampling 135-6
range 128, 129
rapid change 539
rates of return 63, 66-9, 77-8
re-engineering 193-8, 268, 290-1, 307-8, 541, 549
reactive change 539
receivership 120
regulation
    of accounting standards 47-9
    and competition 473-8
    of financial markets 86
    and franchising 463-4
    of natural monopolies 462-4
    and pricing 462-4
relational paradigm 178-9
relationship marketing 175-83
relative frequencies 126-7
remuneration 104, 255, 269, 270, 285-6
    for executives 111-15
replacement cost accounting 20, 35-6
required rates of return 77-8
Research Planning Model 146
reservation prices 453
reserve disclosure requirements 51-2
resource management 591-8
restructuring 257-8, 541
    autonomous 541-2
    financial 332

retailers 172
retention of customers 185, 189
return on assets (ROA) 489
return on capital employed (ROCE) 19, 32-4, 151-2
return on equity (ROE) 54
return on investment (ROI) 23, 75
Revenue Hedging Model 146
revitalization 193-8
reward strategies 104, 255, 269, 270, 285-6
  for executives 111-15
rights issues 118-19
risk
  diversification 64, 76-7, 158-9
    international 394-8
  exchange rate risk 98-100
  and the finance function 62
  and market failure 468-70
  political risk 624-5
  portfolio optimization 158-9
  project risk 78-9
  and rates of return 67-9
  risk premiums 68-9
  statistical analysis 142-7
RISK software 145
ROA (return on assets) 489
ROCE (return on capital employed) 19, 32-4, 151-2
ROE (return on equity) 54
ROI (return on investment) 23, 75
role-based culture 551
Russia 442-6

S

sales and marketing mix 179
sampling 135-41
SBUs (strategic business units) 290
scale economies 453, 462-3
scenario analysis 74, 143
SCM (supply chain integration) 301, 316-22, 318
SE (successful efforts accounting) 50-2
segmentation strategies 185, 186, 199-204
  costs 203-4
  customer identification 201-2
  for markets 199-200
  training of service personnel 202-3
self-motivation 259
self-referencing 643, 644
sensitivity analysis 73-4, 142-3
service firms 583-90

set-up times 313
shadow negotiations 438-40
shadow prices 158
share option grants 111-12, 114, 115
shareholders
  effects of acquisitions on 104
  and the finance function 63
  and financial markets 64-5
Sherman Act (1890) 458
Sigmoid Curves 350
simulation models 143-7, 152
Single European Act 497
Single Market 336
6-sigma-charts 139
skills
  academic skills gap 235
  cognitive skills 632-3
  communication skills 8-9
  and competitive advantage 265
  development 4-5, 10-11, 281
  and effective resource management 632-3
  required of employees 226-7
  see also core competencies
slack 158
smaller companies 651-2
social cause marketing 368-71
software 143, 157, 347, 348
  Lotus Notes 347, 348
  RISK 145
spread measures 127-8, 129
spreadsheets 143, 157
staff selection 268-9
stakeholder networking 548-9
standard costs 31
standard deviation 128, 129
star-based culture 551
statistics
  correlation 128-9
  data presentation 126-31
  distributions 131-4
  graphs 130
  location measures 127-8, 129
  modeling 147-55
  probabilities 131-4
  and product mix 156-60
  risk analysis 142-7
  sampling 135-41
  spread measures 127-8, 129
stereotypes 245-6

stock exchanges 45, 65-6
   see also equity markets; financial markets
'Stock and Flow' model 153
strategic alliances 46, 109, 606-9, 638
   and globalization 413, 491-4, 623
strategic business units (SBUs) 290
strategic conversations 646-9
strategic intelligence 346-50
strategic investment decisions 562-71
strategic transformation 335-6
strategy
   and finance function 62, 567
   global 572-7
   information strategy 554-5
   models 636
   and operations function 322-6
   and resource management 591-8
   rethinking 635-7
   value-creation strategies 173-4, 270
stratified sampling 136, 140
successful efforts (SE) accounting 50-2
Sullivan Principles 374
sunk costs 452, 462, 466
supply chain integration (SCM) 301, 316-22, 318
supply-demand management 313
surveys 135
sustainable development 327
swaps 106-8
switching costs 465
syndicated lending 390
synergy 472
systems
   approach to modeling 147-55
   standardization 340
   see also production systems

T

takeovers *see* acquisitions
task-based culture 551
taxation 42, 45, 62, 80-1
   and currency hedging 99
   deferred tax 48
   and dividend policy 83
teams 225-6, 228-9
   and cultural diversity 243-4
   and model building 154
   and negotiations 434-6
   outdoor training 524-33

technology
   and costs 452-3
   and customer satisfaction 600
   and globalization 623
      of high technology industries 491-4
   and leadership 516
   multimedia 635
   technological leverage 549-50
   see also information technology
telecommuting 261
telephones 178
Theory X 512
Theory Y 283, 512
throughput times 305, 313
time pressures 11, 648
time series data 129-30
'tit-for-tat' pricing strategy 457-8
'toolboxes' 639-43
'top-down' budgeting 24
Total Quality Management (TQM) 309, 352, 353
trade blocs 494-502
trademarks 470
training 255, 266, 269, 600
   outdoor training 524-33
   of service personnel 202-3
transaction costs 468
transfer pricing 23
transformations 256-7, 333-6
treasury function 62

U

uncertainty *see* risk analysis
uncertainty avoidance index 242
unemployment 239
unit of constant purchasing power (UCPP) 37

V

valuation
   of assets 20, 33, 35-6, 50-2
   of banks 38-40
   of futures contracts 96
value-creation strategies 173-4, 270
variance 128, 129
vertical integration 318, 470, 471-3
virtual integration 318, 319, 321
'virtual offices' 258-62
vision 8, 13, 508

global visionary leadership 412-13

W

wages *see* remuneration; reward strategies
warrants 101-3
what-if tables 143, 152
work attitudes *see* attitudes
work organization 269
work reform 224, 229
work/life balance 278-82
    and privacy 382
Workforce 2000 235

workforces
    empowerment 225, 270, 283-7
    productivity problems 235
    transforming 256-7
    see also employees
working capital 36-7
working conditions 379
World Wide Web *see* Internet

Z

zero-based budgeting 25

Name index

A

Abell, Derek 504, 516
Adler, N.J. 244, 253
Alciatore, Mimi 17, 50
Allen, F. 82
Ambler, Tim 163, 175
Amdahl, Gene 7
Ansoff, Igor 193
Aristotle 620
Axelrod, Robert 457-8

B

Bandura, Albert 220
Barnes, Rosie 17, 34
Barnevik, Percy 7-8, 637
Barrick, Mury 237
Barwise, Patrick 559, 562, 567
Bell, Michael 261
Benetton, Luciano 641
Bidault, Francis 559, 606
Bircher, Paul 17, 47
Black, Fischer 88, 93
Blattberg, Robert 191
Blinder, Alan 622
Bolton, Robert 429
Boscheck, Ralf 449, 473, 480, 494
Bowles, Samuel 238
Bowman, Edward H. 629, 649, 651
Branson, Richard 229
Bray, D.W. 238
Brealey, Richard 81, 83, 384, 391, 567
Brennan, Michael 60, 111
Brill, Michael 262
Britten-Jones, Mark 60, 95
Bronfman, Edgar 112
Bush, George 8

C

Cappelli, Peter 215, 224, 235, 249, 262

Carnegie, Andrew 638
Carsburg, Sir Bryan 17, 41
Chambers, David 406, 442
Champny, James 290, 307
Chiat, Jay 261
Chirac, Jacques 403
Christensen, Perry 276, 278
Churchill, Winston 9
Clark, John 193
Collins, James 638
Collins, Robert 295, 311, 336
Colosi, Thomas R. 406, 426, 432
Cooper, Ian 60, 106
Cordon, Carlos 295, 307, 311, 316
Cornelli, Francesca 60, 82
Crandall, Robert 159
Cray, Seymour 7
Crocker-Hefter, Anne 249, 262
Cummings, Thomas 559, 606

D

Davison, Sue Canney 244
Day, George 163, 205, 559, 602
de Geus, Arie 570
DeGroot, Jessica 276, 278
Dicken, Peter 624
Dimson, Elroy 59, 66, 76
Domeniconi, Reto 517
Doz, Yves 606
Drucker, Peter 209, 351, 646
Dunfee, Thomas W. 366, 368
Dunlop, A. 193
Dunlop, A. 6-7

E

Earl, Michael 536, 552
Eaton, Bob 542
Edwards, J.S.S. 33, 83
Eichengreen, Barry 400

Eisenhower, Dwight 10
Estrin, Saul 449, 462
Eysenck, Hans 618

F

Farkas, Adam 59, 72
Farrakhan, Louis 510
Fifield, J.G. 112
Fisher, George 196
Fisher, Irving 65
Fisher, Roger 429
Ford, Henry 452
Franks, Julian 60, 104, 105, 119
Friedman, Milton 368
Friedman, Stewart D. 276, 278

G

Garelli, Stephane 480, 482
Garrett, Geoffrey 384, 398
Gates, Bill 113, 544, 550, 637
Geneen, Harold 9
Geroski, Paul A. 449, 464, 468
Gerstner, L. 7, 8, 112, 193, 516
Gilbert, Xavier 344, 357
Gintis, Herbert 238
Giordano, Richard 113
Glazer, Professor Rashi 191
Goffee, Rob 215, 240, 629, 631
Gordon, Robert 653
Gould, Stephen J. 488
Gouldner, Alvin 220
Goyal, Vidhan 81
Graddy, Kathryn 449, 455, 456
Gratton, Lynda 249, 251
Greenson, Ralph 486
Griffin, Paul 17, 38
Grove, Andrew 353, 547
Guth, Charles G. 455

H

Habib, Michel 59, 80
Hackman, J.R. 284
Hamel, Gary 583, 606
Hammer, Michael 290, 307
Hampden-Turner, Charles 242
Haour, Georges 560, 609

Harder, Joseph W. 249, 258
Harrison, Roger 551
Hatch, Mary Jo 260
Hattori, Ichiro 542
Hertz, David 143
Higson, Chris 17, 19, 32, 53
Hill, Anita 619
Hill, Terry 295, 322
Hilliers, Joan 260
Hitler, Adolph 509, 618
Hofstede, Geert 242
Horovitz, Jacques 163, 198, 560, 583
Houlder, Vanessa 197
House, Robert 521
Howell, James 653
Hunt, John 243
Hunter, Larry W. 249, 267

I

Ittner, Christopher D. 17, 26

J

Jelinek, M. 253
Jensen, Michael 81, 84
Jobs, Steven 546
Johnson, George 487
Johnson, Lyndon 9
Jolly, Vijay 559, 572
Jones, Daniel 288
Jones, Reginald 9
Jung, Carl 416

K

Kamshad, Kimya 449, 451, 459, 471
Kanter, Rosabeth Moss 570
Kaplanis, Evi C. 384, 394
Kashani, Kamran 163, 165, 171
Kay, J.A. 33
Keegan, John 509
Kennedy, John F. 375, 509, 618
Kestnbaum, Robert 191
Ketelhohn, Werner 629, 639
Khomeini, Ayatollah 509
King, Lord 229
Kobayashi, Yotaro 599
Kobrin, Stephen J. 614, 622

Kogut, Bruce 480, 491, 629, 649, 651
Kohl, Helmut 404
Kotler, Philip 562
Kouzes, James M. 522
Kumar, Nirmalyar 163, 198

L

Laurent, Andre 243
Lehn, Kenneth 81
Levitt, Ted 177
Lewent, Judy 142, 146
Lewis, Tracy 559, 577
Luttmer, Franz 13

M

McClelland, David C. 237
MacDuffie, John Paul 288
McGregor, Douglas 268
McNamara, Robert 223
Mahoney, Jack 366, 371, 375, 379
March, James 220
Marchand, Donald A. 344, 346, 351, 360
Markowitz, H. 76, 158
Marsh, Paul 568
Marshall, Alfred 113, 455
Marx, Karl 220, 616
Maslow, Abraham 220, 268
Maucher, Helmut 541
Maug, Ernst 59, 70
Mayer, C. 33, 83, 104, 105
Mayo, Elton 218
Meckling, William 81, 84
Merton, Robert 220
Meyer, Marshall 480, 486
Michaely, R. 82
Miles, R.E. 252
Milken, Michael 113
Miller, Merton 80, 83, 101
Mintzberg, Henry 252, 564, 565-6
Modigliani, Franco 80, 83, 101
Moldt, Edward 7
Morecroft, John 124, 147, 592
Morita, Akio 541, 637
Mount, Michael K. 237
Myers, Stewart C. 81, 83, 567

N

Naik, Narayan 59, 64
Naito, Haruo 542
Negraponte, Nicholas 624
Neuberger, Anthony 60, 101
Nicholson, Alastair 295, 322
Nicholson, Nigel 215, 229
Nyborg, Kjell 60, 87

O

Osterman, Paul 271
Ovitz, Michael 112

P

Pareto, Vilfedo 650
Pascale, Richard 565
Peiperi, Mayry 276, 283
Perlmutter, Howard V. 406, 408
Perry, Debra 60, 98
Pervin, L.A. 230
Plato 620
Poras, Jerry 638
Porter, Michael 143, 197, 562, 563
Posner, Barry Z. 522
Prahalad, C.K. 583, 606

Q

Quinn, J. Brian 562

R

Raabe, Hakon 295, 316
Racic, Stanko 81
Rawls, John 620
Reagan, Ronald 229, 509
Reibstein, David 559, 602
Robertson, Thomas S. 163, 193
Roddick, Anita 368
Roethlisberger, Fritz 217-19
Rogers, Carl 220
Rogovsky, Nikolai 215, 224
Roos, Daniel 288
Roos, Johan 629, 643, 646
Roosevelt, Franklin 618
Rose, Harold 59, 62, 84, 103, 109, 384, 386, 388
Roswell, Peggy 260, 261

S

Saffo, Paul 261
Schmenner, Roger W. 295, 302, 311, 336
Schmittlein, David 163, 183
Scholes, Myron 88, 93
Schuler, Randal 268
Scully, John 410
Sharpe, Bill 76
Shepard, David 191
Shockley, William 469
Simmonds, Andy 17, 44
Simon, David 637
Simon, Herbert 220
Skinner, B.F. 220
Skinner, Wickham 311
Sloan, Alfred P. 522
Smith, Adam 372
Snow, C.C. 252
Southgate, Sir Colin 112
Spielberg, Steven 112
Srebel, Paul 536, 538, 543, 548
Stalin, Joseph 618
Stata, Ray 208
Steffen, Christopher J. 520
Steger, Ulrich 295, 327
Stewart, Rosemary 564
Stopford, John 629, 635

T

Tagge, Gert 9
Taylor, Frederick 644
Thatcher, Margaret 229, 507
Thomas, Clarence 618-19
Timmer, Jan 541
Tobin, James 76
Toynbee, A. 413
Trompenaars, Fons 242

Turpin, Dominique 559, 599

U

Ury, William 429
Useem, Michael 276, 288, 504, 520

V

Vagelos, Roy 146
van Ackere, Ann 124, 126, 131, 135, 147, 592
van den Haag, E. 620
Vlahos, Kiriakos 124, 142, 156
Vollmann, Thomas E. 295, 297, 316, 330
von Krogh, Georg 629, 643, 646

Y

Yao, Dennis 559, 577

W

Warren, Kim 559, 591
Watson, Thomas 637
Webber, Ross A. 2, 4
Weber, Max 220, 511-12
Welch, Ivo 60, 116
Welch, Jack 11, 522, 637
Westbrook, Roy 295, 322
Wind, Jerry 163, 209
Womack, John 288
Wood, Jack Denfeld 215, 217, 406, 414, 419, 426, 432, 504, 506, 511, 524, 614, 616
Wosniak, Steven 546

Z

Zhirinovsky, Vladimir 510
Zimmermann, Jochen 17, 19, 21, 24, 29

Organization index

A

ABB 7-8, 352, 572, 576
A.C. Nielsen 185
Accor 584, 587
Accounting Standards Board (ASB) 47, 55
AEG 635
Aerospatiale 475
A.G. Edwards 188
Air France 587
Airbus 623
Albert Heijn 611
Alenia 475
Allied Signal 477
Amelco and Signetics 469
American Academy of Management 219
American Airlines 159
American Express 187
American Hospital Supply 210
Amnesty International 374
Analog Devices 208
Andersen Consulting 176
APEC (Asia Pacific Economic Co-operation) 494, 500-1
Apple Computer 260-1, 410, 459, 493, 544, 545
Arthur Andersen 260
ASB (Accounting Standards Board) 47, 55
ASEAN (Association of South East Asian Nations) 500
Asia Pacific Economic Co-operation (APEC) 494, 500-1
Asian Development Bank 363
Association of South East Asian Nations (ASEAN) 500
AT&T 152, 289, 361, 469, 472, 602
Aviatika Company 443, 445
Avon 412
AvtoRes Group 444, 445
Axa 204

B

Bacardi 176
Baileys Irish Cream 176
Bain & Co 189
Banco d'America e d'Italia 541
BASF 339
Bayer 474, 475
BBC 152
Bekaert 607
Bell South 188, 363
Ben & Jerry's 368, 369
Benetton 318, 549, 635, 641
BET 193
BHP 412
Bic 550
Blockbuster 199
BMW 451
Body Shop 195, 368-9
Boeing 194, 623, 635
Borealis 338
Bosch 245, 320
Bose Corporation 318, 352-3
Boston Consulting Group 263-4, 563, 564
Bouygues 584
BP (British Petroleum) 110
BPS (British Psychological Society) 234
Braun 187
Bridgestone 607
British Airways 195, 229, 330
British Gas 113
British Oxygen Company (BOC) 113, 635
British Petroleum (BP) 110
British Psychological Society (BPS) 234
BT (British Telecom) 152, 361, 638
Burger King 175
Business for Social Responsibility 368

C

Canon 409, 517, 548, 549, 583

Carlson 584
Casino 584
Casio 583
Caterpillar 477
Catholic Church 176
Chase Bank 185
Chemical Bank 185
Chiat Day 260
Chrysler Corporation 81, 357, 542
Circuit City 636
Citicorp 39-40, 187
Club Med 202, 204, 584, 585, 586, 587, 589
CNN 635
Coca-Cola 176, 186, 245, 264-5, 266, 451, 455, 456, 602
Commerzbank 45
Compaq 171, 173, 544
Competitiveness Advisory Group 482
Competitiveness Council 482
Connecticut Mutual Life Insurance Company 330
Control Data 7
Coopers and Lybrand 179
Cordiant 113

D

Daimler-Benz 41, 46
Danfoss Holland 588
David Shepard Associates 191
De Beers 456
de Havilland 475
Decisions Group 178
Degussa 635
Deutsche BA 195
Deutsche Bank 46
Dialog Group 444
Digital Equipment Corporation 474, 475
Disney 204, 587, 588, 589
Doshin Kotsu 600
DreamWorks 112
Du Pont 289, 290, 291, 339, 522
Dunlop 635

E

Eastman Kodak 172, 196, 197, 289, 291, 472, 474, 475, 520, 602
EDS 193
Eizai 542

Elitair 583-4
EMI 112-13, 464
Ericsson 354
Eurodisney 409
Eurostar 137, 203-4
Eurotunnel 466
Exxon 152

F

Fair Trade Commission 474
Fairchild Semiconductor 469
FAO Schwarts 202
Federal Express 264, 590
Fiat 339
Flo 584
Flying Tigers 590
Food Lion 203
Ford 6, 152, 179, 289, 291, 307-8, 357, 522
Ford Foundation 653
France Telecom 611
Frito Lay 196, 205
Fuji 602
Fuji-Xerox 599

G

GATT 41, 484, 494-5, 622
General Electric 9, 11, 409
General Microelectronics 469
General Motors 6, 179, 193, 330, 354, 357, 409, 651
Générale des Eaux (GdE) 583-4, 588
Gillette 173
Goodyear Tire 188-9
GPS 584, 587
Grand Optical 584, 585
Greenpeace 176
GTE 185, 189, 583
Gulf Oil 635

H

Haagen Dazs 204, 586
Harley-Davidson 550
Harvard University 218, 219
Hay Associates 226, 227
Hear Music 201
Heidemis NV 13
Heron Corporation 121

Hewlett Packard 176, 190, 261, 289, 290, 317, 409,
    477, 517, 542, 548, 602-3
Hilton Hotels 195
Hippopotamus 584, 587
Hitachi 197, 651
Honda 330, 357, 549, 564-5, 583, 636, 638
Hoover 176

I

IASC (International Accounting Standards
    Committee) 42-3, 46
Ibbotson Associates 68
IBM 152, 193, 197, 223, 242, 289, 361, 465, 583
    benchmarking 309
    chief executive's remuneration 112
    database marketing 187
    employee numbers 651
    erosion of market dominance 171, 172, 173, 354,
        544, 545, 551
    hotelling 259
    information distribution 207
    joint ventures 623
    restructuring 290
ICI 339
IDM Japan 601
Ikea 176, 318, 358, 549
IMD 165
Intel 353, 492-3, 544, 575
Intercontinental Hotels 193
International Accounting Standards Committee
    (IASC) 42-3, 46
Interstate Commerce Commission 458
ITT 9

J

Japan Airlines 601
Japan Management Association 601
Johnson & Johnson 12, 189, 190
Johnson Wax 173
Joint Executive Committee 458
Judge Institute 253

K

K-mart 589
Kamaz 444
Kao 599, 600, 601-2

Kawasaki 549
Kellogg's 176
Kestnbaum & Co 191
Kimberly Clark 6, 193, 194
Kodak 172, 196, 197, 289, 291, 472, 474, 475, 520,
    602
Komatsu 572

L

Leading Edge Research Team 253
Levi's 188, 245
Lexmark 317
Libby's 174
Loblaws 610
Lockheed 372
Logitech SA 575
Lotus 193

M

McDonald's 195, 245, 333, 451, 586
McKinsey & Co 143, 172, 263, 264, 266
Marketing Science Institute 196
Marks and Spencer 195, 473
Marriott 584
Massachusetts Institute of Technology 225
Matra 606, 607-8
Matsushita Electric 194, 196, 197, 599, 600, 601
MCA 112
MCI 199, 602, 638
Mercedes-Benz 172, 320, 473
Merck 142, 146
Mercury 636
Mercury One-2-One 459
Merrill Lynch 189
Meyers 589
Microsoft 193, 352, 353, 362, 451, 474, 544, 550
Midas 200, 586
Migros 611
Minerve 584, 585
MIT 270
Mitsubishi Electric 575
Mobil 176
Molectro 469
Molnlycke 194
MOST Association 444, 445
Motorola 354, 492, 493, 522
Multiplex Corporation 207-8

N

NAFTA (North American Free Trade Area) 494, 497-500
National Association of Manufacturers 228
National Semiconductor 492, 493
National Training Laboratories (NTL) 218
NCR 472
NEC 492, 493, 575, 583
Nestlé 172, 176, 475, 541
NetScape 116, 363
News Corporation 41-2
Nieman Marcus 199
Nike 172
Nippon Airways 601
Nippon Steel 635
Nippondenso 318
Nissan 357, 518, 601, 635
Nokia 354, 355
Nonaka 637
Nordstrom 177-8, 263
Norsk Hydro 41
North American Free Trade Area (NAFTA) 494, 497-500
Nouvelles Frontières 584
Novotel 590
NTL (National Training Laboratories) 218
Nummi 409

O

Okidata 602-3
Olivetti 517
Olympia & York 80
Opec 154, 456
Orly Restauration 588

P

Palizade 145
Pan Am 635
Pepsi 264-5, 266, 455, 456, 602
Pernod 186
Perrier 172, 475
Peugeot 204, 339, 607
Philip Morris 171
Philips 197, 223, 308, 317, 517, 541, 550
Pillsbury 176, 178
Polaroid 187
Porsche 187

Potain 607
Proctor & Gamble 171, 173, 174, 187, 188, 194, 210, 317, 320

Q

Qantas 195
Quelle 586-7

R

RCA 635
Renault 339, 517, 606, 607-8
Rentokil 195
Rheem Semiconductor 469
Ricoh 551
Ritz Carlton 588
Rover 451, 638
Rowntree 541
Royal Dutch *see* Shell
Royal Mail Steam Packet Company 49

S

Saatchi & Saatchi 101, 103
Sachs 204
Safeway 176
Saloman Brothers 113
SAS (Scandinavian Airline Services) 193, 588
Schindler 338
Scott Paper 6, 193
Sears Roebuck 263, 635
Seiko 542
Semco 330
Shell 98-9, 152, 176, 255, 346, 352, 638
Shockley Semiconductor 469
Siemens 9, 623
Singapore Airlines 587
SmithKline Beecham 54, 152
Snecma 409
Social Venture Network 368
Sony 172, 178, 194, 197, 333, 474, 517, 541, 548, 550, 583
Southwest Airlines 289
Sterling Drug 197
Stern Stewart & Company 487
Sulzer 517
SunBeam 7
Suzuki 549

Swatch 174

T

Takeuchi 637
Tavistock Institute 218, 220
TetraPak 338, 475
Texaco 175
Texas Istruments 575, 576
Thomson Electrics 223
Thorn-EMI 112-13, 464
3M 195, 210, 542, 548, 583, 636
Tokyo Gas 600
Toray 410-11
Toshiba 474, 600, 623
Touche Ross 45
Toyota 318, 330, 357, 409, 549, 601, 651

U

Unilever 194, 349
Upjohn 190
UPS 264
US Air 195
USAA 190

V

Virgin 176

Virgin Atlantic 195, 229
Visa 175, 176
Volkswagen 245
Volvo 224, 225, 339

W

Wagons Lits Travel 584
Wal-Mart 210, 317, 320, 333, 484, 568, 635
Wang Laboratories 7
Wharton School 5, 6, 7, 8
Wickes 120, 121
World Bank 412
World Trade Organization 41, 495, 622

X

Xerox 206, 261, 289, 290, 309, 317, 333, 464, 469, 522, 546

Y

Yamaha 549-50
Yokohoma Bank 601

Z

Zil 444

NOTES

NOTES

NOTES

NOTES

NOTES

NOTES

NOTES

NOTES

NOTES

NOTES

NOTES

NOTES

Have you Mastered Management?

We are sure that you have found this book useful. We want you to continue your pursuit of management excellence!

We will be developing a series of opportunities for executives to stay in touch with the latest management thinking. Among the upcoming series, we are planning to publish: *FT Mastering Enterprise*, *FT Mastering Finance* and *FT Mastering Marketing*.

If you would like to receive information on the *Mastering Series* as it becomes available, please fill in the application form below and return it to:

Financial Post DataGroup
Print Publications Division
333 King Street East,
Toronto, Ontario
M4A 4N2
Fax: (416) 350-6501

Mr/Mrs/Miss/Ms Initial _____ Last name _____

Department _____

Job title _____

Company _____

Address _____

_____

City: _____ Prov/State: _____ Postal Code: _____

Phone: _____ Fax: _____

Areas of special interest: _____

1 _____

2 _____

3 _____

4 _____

5 _____

Preferred newspaper _____

Preferred business magazine _____

Any comments on *Mastering Management* or future projects:

_____

_____